The New

Food Lover's Companion

FIFTH EDITION

Sharon Tyler Herbst
Ron Herbst

BARRON'S

All inquiries should be addressed to:
Barron's Educational Series, Inc.
250 Wireless Boulevard
Hauppauge, New York 11788
www.barronseduc.com

ISBN: 978-1-4380-0163-0

Library of Congress Control Number: 2013008951

Library of Congress Cataloging-in-Publication Data
Herbst, Sharon Tyler.
  The new food lover's companion : more than 7,200 A-to-Z entries
describe foods, cooking techniques, herbs, spices, desserts, wines,
and the ingredients for pleasurable dining / Sharon Tyler Herbst,
Ron Herbst.—Fifth edition.
        pages cm
  "Prior editions ... 1990 under the title Food lover's companion"—Title
page verso.
  Includes bibliographical references and index.
  ISBN 978-1-4380-0163-0 (alkaline paper)
1. Food—Dictionaries. 2. Cooking--Dictionaries. I. Herbst, Ron.
II. Herbst, Sharon Tyler. Food lover's companion. III. Title.
  TX349.H533 2013
  641.503—dc23   2013008951

PRINTED IN THE UNITED STATES OF AMERICA

9 8 7 6 5 4 3 2 1

CONTENTS

v

Dedication

Dedicated with love to Bonnie. Thank you for bearing
with me while I worked on this latest edition.
Ron

Acknowledgments

There are myriad people behind the scenes in a tome of this scope—some trying to make sure the book is as error-free as possible, others simply there because they love and support me. So here's a warm and affectionate thanks to all those special people, with apologies to anyone I may have inadvertently omitted.

To my wife, Bonnie, for her love, support and all the great dinners—and especially for the fabulous tomatoes from the garden. To Lew and Joyce Herbst (Ron's brother and sister-in-law), Kay Tyler (Sharon's mom) and Jim and Tia McCurdy (Sharon's brother-in-law and sister) for their lasting love and support.

For their special friendship throughout the years: Sue Bain, Sally Bernstein, Leslie and David Bloom, Walt and Carol Boice, Beth Casey, Bob and Jan Fisher, Lee and Susan Janvrin, Daniel Maye, Emma Swain and Wes Jones, and Glenn and Laura Miwa.

To those who have either been a major part of our support system over the years, or who contributed suggestions for additions to this fifth edition, including: Oscar Anderson, Gary Danko, Allen and Gayle Ferrell, Julie and Ron Goodlin, Charles Luna, Robert Lyle, Holly Hartley, Barry and Kathy Herbst, Brian and Gabe Herbst, Ruth and Phil Hicks, Talley Sue Hohlfeld, Benjamin Keaton, Eszter Kiss-Deák, Kristy Korb, Andrew and Jessica Leslie, Tyler and Andressa Leslie, John Levesque, John Maxwell, Brian Maynard, Tom McGillivary, Gregory Millo, Richard Mori, Cindy Pawlceyn, Norman Van Aken, and Juan Velez. Many thanks again to Glenn Miwa for his help with Japanese pronunciations. And a very special thanks to Ralph Ewton, former Associate Professor of Languages and Linguistics, University of Texas at El Paso, not only for his numerous suggestions for additions to the book but for his many recommendations regarding pronunciations throughout the book.

Also a special thanks to those who surrounded me with love and support these last few years as I went through some trying times, especially Ginny Bassi, Pete Beck, Lou Berl, Dan Callarman, Bonnie Castello, Rudy Duran, Floranne Fanti, Mo Ghausi, Linda Gomez, Ruth and Phil Hicks, Paul and Ellen Meuse, Gary Musco, Peggy Payne, Ruy Pereira, Shay and Alice Pickton, Greg Rockwell, Ron and Sara Ryba, Kevin and Tania Scheer, Karl Savatiel, Jim and Jackie Smith, Cathy Tennant and George and Susan Williamson.

And last, but certainly far from least, the incredibly hard-working crew at Barron's: Bruce B. Morris, managing editor; Kevin Ryan, editorial director; Chris Ciaschini, production director; Bill Kuchler, art director; and the myriad behind-the-scenes people involved in the artwork, layout, printing, and everything else it takes to bring a book of this magnitude together.

Thank you one and all!

Introduction

"People who are not interested in food always seem rather dry and unloving and don't have a real gusto for life."
—Julia Child

This is the fifth edition of a book Sharon Tyler Herbst began writing in 1987. It is extremely gratifying for a book to be welcomed by so many for so many years. The response from our readers has been overwhelmingly enthusiastic and warm, which tells me that you love this continually evolving culinary universe as much as I do.

I look back in wonder remembering how daunting a task it seemed to be as Sharon began writing the first *Food Lover's Companion*, a tome that took three years to complete. The 3,000 entries in the first edition grew through each new edition until now, in this fifth edition, there are over 7,200 entries. When I began *The New Wine Lover's Companion* in 1993 I really found out what a formidable task it was to put together a book of this scope. I had helped Sharon by doing research (while I worked my regular job) during the early editions of *Food Lover's Companion* but truly didn't realize the effort required until I worked on the wine book. But, as Sharon has said before it is really an enlightening educational adventure. When Sharon passed away the gauntlet passed to me for updating this fifth edition. Sharon loved and was dedicated to this book. I felt a great responsibility to keep the quality and workmanship at the high level Sharon did throughout the previous editions; hopefully I've done that.

You'll find this fifth edition of *Food Lover's Companion* markedly changed. Not only have many of the existing terms been appended or revised, but over 500 new listings have been added. Sprinkled throughout this book are thousands of informative tidbits ranging from facts on how to choose, store and use ingredients to the origins of various foods and dishes to historical lore on food and drink. There are also pronunciations for all but the most basic words.

In the end, this new *Food Lover's Companion* is bigger and better than ever, all for the love of food and drink. I trust you'll find it both enjoyable and informative. And, at the very least, I hope that you receive as much pleasure from reading this book as we did from writing it.

How to Use This Book

ENTRIES ARE ARRANGED alphabetically and cross-referenced. Alphabetization is by letter, rather than by word, so that multiple-word entries are treated as single words. For instance, **al dente** is handled as though it were spelled without spacing (*aldente*), and therefore follows **alcohol** and precedes **ale**.

Entries are in lowercase, unless capitals are required for the proper form of the word, as in the case of **Kahlúa** and **Nantua sauce**. All but the most basic words have pronunciations (see Pronunciation Guide, page x). A term with several meanings will list all its definitions in numerical order within the main listing.

Common-usage acronyms and abbreviations appear in their natural alphabetical order. For example, **MSG** follows **mozzarella cheese** and precedes **muddle**.

CROSS-REFERENCES are indicated by SMALL CAPITALS and may appear in the body of a definition, at the end of a definition or in lieu of a definition.

Cross-references are used within the body of a definition primarily when the term may not be familiar to the reader. For instance, the listing for **Rossini** states: "Dishes that include FOIE GRAS, TRUFFLES and a DEMI-GLACE. . . ." Therefore, though listings for most foods, cooking techniques, kitchen equipment, etc. will be found in *The New Food Lover's Companion,* common entries (such as **butter**, **lettuce** or **poach**) are not indicated in small capitals as cross-references in the body of a definition. A word that is cross-referenced will only be capitalized the first time it's used. Cross-references at the end of a definition refer to entries related to the word being defined.

When a word is fully defined elsewhere, a cross-reference rather than a definition is listed. In the world of food, many terms have more than one name, often depending on the region in which they're used. For example, **alligator pear** is cross-referenced to its more common name, **avocado**. Additionally, subtypes of a species or grouping, such as **alewife**, are cross-referenced to the main listing (in this case, **herring**). Different spellings of a term are also cross-referenced. **Akvavit**, for instance, refers the reader to the more common spelling of **aquavit**.

ITALICS are used in this book for several reasons. One is to point out that the term being defined also goes by another name. **Squid**, for example, is also called *calamari*. Additionally, italics are used to indicate foreign words and publication titles, and to highlight cross-references at the end of a listing (the end of the **giblets** entry states: *See also* VARIETY MEATS).

BOLDFACE PRINT is used not only for main entry headings, but for subentries within a definition as well. For example, the definition for **chocolate** uses boldface to highlight the headings of the various types of this food (**unsweetened chocolate**, **bittersweet chocolate**, **milk chocolate**, etc.), which are defined within the body of that entry.

BRACKETS surround an entry's pronunciation, which immediately follows the listing and precedes the definition. *See* Pronunciation Guide, next page, for complete information.

Pronunciation Guide

All but the most basic words are accompanied by pronunciations, which are enclosed in brackets [—]. I've always thought that the standard phonetic alphabet and diacritical marks such as a tilde (~), diaeresis (¨), breve (˘) and circumflex (^) slow the reader down because one must often look up the symbol in a chart at the front of a book to see how it affects a word's pronunciation. Ever the advocate of the most direct route, I've chosen to use the "sounding-out" phonetic method, with the accented syllable indicated by capital letters. On a word like **matsutake**, for example, the common dictionary-type of phonetic is *mät so˘o tä' ke˘*, which would force most readers to look up the sounds represented by the diacritics. In this book, however, the word is simply sounded out as *maht-soo-TAH-kee*.

Following is a list of the basic sounds (based on common American usage) employed in this book's pronunciations:

a	as in **can** or **add**	**j**	as in **gin** or **juicy**
ah	as in **father** or **balm**	**k**	as in **cool** or **crisp**
ay	as in **date** or **face**	**o**	as in **odd** or **bottle**
ch	as in **church** or **beach**	**oh**	as in **open** or **boat**
ee	as in **steam** or **beer**	**oo**	as in **food** or **boo**
eh	as in **set** or **check**	**ow**	as in **cow** or **flour**
g	as in **game** or **green**	**uh**	as in **love** or **cup**
i	as in **ice** or **pie**	**y**	as in **yellow** or **yes**
ih	as in **if** or **strip**	**zh**	as in **beige** or **vision**

Note: A single *i* is used for the long i sound, as in *pie*. The exception to the *single* i rule is when an *i* is followed by a consonant, in which case an *e* is appended. For example, **papaya** is phoneticized [puh-PI-yuh], whereas the word **Fahrenheit** (where the vowel sound is followed by a consonant) is phoneticized [FEHR-uhn-hite].

Foreign Sounds

eu A sound made with the lips rounded as if to say *oo* (as in *food*) while trying to say *a* (as in *able*).

euh An *e* in French (not *é* or *è*) is often pronounced with an *oo*, as in *book* or *wood*.

n An italicized *n* is used to indicate that the *n* itself is not pronounced, and that the preceding vowel has a nasal sound.

r An italicized *r* indicates that the *r* sound should be diminished, with a sound more like *w*.

rr The appearance of *rr* indicates the sound of a rolling *r*.

A

aamsul *see* KOKAM

abalone [a-buh-LOH-nee] A GASTROPOD MOLLUSK (*see both listings*) found along the coastlines of California, Mexico and Japan. The edible portion is the adductor muscle, a broad foot by which the abalone clings to rocks. As with any muscle, the meat is tough and must be pounded to tenderize it before cooking. Abalone, used widely in Chinese and Japanese cooking, can be purchased fresh, canned, dried or salted. Fresh abalone should smell sweet, not fishy. It should also be alive—the exposed muscle should move when touched. Choose those that are relatively small and refrigerate as soon as possible. Cook abalone within a day of purchase. Fresh abalone is best sautéed and should be cooked very briefly (20 to 30 seconds per side) or the meat will quickly toughen. Abalone is known as *ormer* in the English Channel, *awabi* in Japan, *muttonfish* in Australia and *paua* in New Zealand. Its iridescent shell is a source of mother-of-pearl. *See also* SHELLFISH.

abalone oyster mushroom An OYSTER MUSHROOM variety that resembles the large edible portion of an ABALONE. The mushroom is white with traces of gold scattered throughout. The flesh is meaty with a rich, earthy flavor. It shouldn't be eaten raw—always cooked. Abalone oyster mushrooms are native to China but cultivated in various locations around the world, including the West Coast of the United States. *See also* MUSHROOM.

abará *see* ACARAJÉ

abbacchio [ah-BAHK-ee-yoh] Italian for a very young lamb.

Abbaye de Belloc (Bellocq) [ah-bay-EE deuh behl-LAWK] Semihard sheep's-milk cheese that's been made for centuries by the Benedictine monks at the Abbey de Belloc in the Pays Basque area of southwestern France. The cheese is traditionally made with milk from Manech sheep, though milk from other breeds may be used. It comes in 8- to 11-pound wheels with a hard brownish rind and a pale ivory interior. Abbaye de Belloc has a rich buttery flavor with hints of nuts, fruit and caramel. Abbaye de Belloc undergoes RIPENING for 6 months and must have a minimum FAT CONTENT of 60 percent. *See also* CHEESE.

Abernathy biscuit A firm biscuit similar to HARDTACK with added sugar and CARAWAY SEEDS. It was created by Scottish doctor John Abernathy as a digestive aid and is still popular in Scotland.

abgoosht *see* ABGUSHT

abgusht [ab-GOOSHT] Persian stew usually made with lamb, CHICK-PEAS, beans, onions, potatoes, tomatoes and various herbs, but many variations exist. It's also spelled *abgoosht* and sometimes called *dizi*, which is the name of the pot in which it's served. It's common to separate the broth and serve it as soup, mashing the solids on a separate plate and serving them with FLATBREAD.

à blanc [ah BLAH/VK] A French term meaning "in white" and identifying foods, usually meats, that aren't browned during cooking.

Abondance; Tomme d'Abondance (AOC; PDO) [ah-bohn-DAHNC; tom dah-bohn-DAHNC] SEMIHARD cow's-milk cheese from the department of Savoie in eastern France. The name has two origins—Abondance cattle and the Abondance valley in the Haute-Savoie. This cheese dates back to the fifth-century monks of l'Abbaye de Saint d'Abondan and became renowned in 1381, when the abbey became the official supplier of Savoyard cheeses for the pope's election at the conclave of Avignon. It is RIPENED for a minimum of 90 days. Abondance comes in 15- to 20-pound wheels with dark yellowish brown rind and a pale golden interior. Its FAT CONTENT ranges from 40 to 49 percent. Its flavor is complex with fruity and nutty characteristics. Abondance is also called *Tomme d'Abondance. See also* CHEESE.

aboyeur [ah-bwah-YER] *see* BRIGADE SYSTEM

abricot [a-bree-COO] French for "apricot."

abruzzese [ah-broo-TZAY-zeh] An Italian descriptor for dishes (from pasta to veal) characterized by the liberal use of hot CHILES, in the style of Italy's Abruzzo region.

absinthe [AB-sinth] Reputed to be an aphrodisiac, absinthe is a potent, bitter LIQUEUR distilled from WORMWOOD and flavored with a variety of herbs. It has a distinct ANISE flavor and is 68 percent alcohol (136 PROOF). Absinthe is usually diluted with water, which changes the color of the liqueur from green to milky white. Because it's considered habit forming and hazardous to health, absinthe is prohibited in many countries and was banned in the United States in the early 1900s.

ABV; abv *see* ALCOHOL BY VOLUME

acaçá [uh-kah-SAH] Brazilian porridge of COCONUT MILK and rice flour that's steamed in banana leaves or cooked in a pot or pan, then cooled. When firm it's cut into slices or cubes and served with sauces and stews.

acacia *see* GUM ARABIC

A

açai; açai berry; acai [ah-SI-ee; ah-SAH-ee] Native to the tropical areas of Central and South America, the açai berry is being touted as the new superfood and is known by some as the "power berry." That's because it's exceedingly rich in nutrients including antioxidants, vitamins, minerals, oleic acid and potassium, to name a few. The dark purple grape-sized fruit grows on the açai palm, which is also called the cabbage palm because natives eat its young, tender leaf buds as one would cabbage. HEARTS OF PALM is another food source harvested from this tall palm. The açai berry contains only a small portion of pulp—about 90 percent of it is an inedible nut. The pulp, which has a flavor reminiscent of berries with a hint of chocolate, is quite delicate and deteriorates quickly. That's why consumers in North America only have access to açai in juice form (primarily as a concentrate), which can be found in the refrigerated or freezer section of natural food stores. It's also available as frozen pulp, or in a powdered form. Because of its ascribed health benefits, açai has become a favorite addition to SMOOTHIES.

acarajé [ah-kahr-ah-JEH] Brazilian FRITTER containing skinless BLACK-EYED PEAS combined with onion, dried shrimp and seasonings. The ingredients are formed into a ball and deep-fried in hot oil, usually dendê (*see* PALM OIL). The acarajé is then split and filled with a spicy mixture that includes hot pepper sauce, CARURU and VATAPÁ. In the **abará** version, the ball is wrapped in banana leaves and steamed. Acarajé is based on a similar dish called *akara* or *akkara* that slaves from West Africa brought to Brazil and parts of the Carribean.

Ac'cent *see* MONOSODIUM GLUTAMATE

aceite [ah-SAY-tay] Spanish for "oil."

aceituna [ah-say-TOO-nah] Spanish for "olive."

acerola [as-uh-ROH-luh] A tiny tree and the small, deep-red, cherry-like fruit that grows on it, found primarily in and around the West Indies. The fruit, which has a sweet flavor and one of the highest concentrations of vitamin C, is used in desserts and preserves. It's also called *Barbados cherry, Puerto Rican cherry* and *West Indies cherry*.

Acesulfame-K [ay-see-SUHL-faym-K] Formulated by the Germans in the late 1960s, this noncaloric ARTIFICIAL SWEETENER (also called *Ace-K* and *acesulfame potassium*) was approved in the United States by the Federal Drug Administration in 1988. It's 200 times sweeter than sugar and, unlike ASPARTAME, retains its sweetness when heated, making it suitable for cooking and baking. When used in large amounts, however, Ace-K has a bitter aftertaste, much like that of SACCHARIN. This sweetener is composed of carbon, nitrogen, oxygen, sulphur and potassium atoms. It's widely used in a broad range of commercial products including baked goods, candies and imitation dairy products. *See also* ALITAME; NEOTAME; SUCRALOSE.

acetic acid [a-SEE-tihk] Acetic acid is formed when common air-borne bacteria interact with the alcohol present in fermented solutions such as WINE, BEER or CIDER. Acetic acid is the constituent that makes vinegar sour. *See also* Food Additives Directory, page 900.

aceto [ah-CHAY-toh; ah-CHEH-toh] Italian for "vinegar."

aceto dolce [ah-CHAY-toh; ah-CHEH-toh DOHL-chay; DOHL-chee] Italian for "sweet vinegar." It refers to a sweet-and-sour combination of fruit and vegetables pickled with white wine vinegar, honey and mustard seeds. It also denotes the sweetened vinegar that results from the pickling process. The fruit and vegetables are usually served as an appetizer.

achar [ah-CHAHR] An East Indian word referring to pickled and salted relishes. They can be sweet or hot, depending on the seasoning added.

achee *see* ACKEE

achiote seed [ah-chee-OH-tay] The slightly musky-flavored seed of the annatto tree is available whole or ground in East Indian, Spanish and Latin American markets. Buy whole seeds when they're a rusty red color; brown seeds are old and flavorless. Achiote seed is also called ANNATTO which, in its paste and powder form, is used in the United States to color butter, margarine, cheese and smoked fish.

acid The word "acid" comes from the Latin *acidus,* meaning "sour." All acids are sour to some degree. Sourness (acidity) is found in many natural ingredients such as vinegar (ACETIC ACID), wine (TARTARIC ACID), lemon juice (CITRIC ACID), sour-milk products (LACTIC ACID), apples (MALIC ACID) and rhubarb leaves (toxic OXALIC ACID). When used in a marinade, acids—such as wine and lemon juice—are natural tenderizers because they break down connective tissue and cell walls.

acidophilous milk [as-ih-DAHF-uh-luhs] *see* MILK

acid orange *see* CALAMONDIN

acidulated water [a-SIHD-yoo-lay-ted] Water to which a small amount of vinegar, lemon or lime juice has been added. It's used as a soak to prevent discoloration of some fruits and vegetables (such as apples and artichokes) that darken quickly when their cut surfaces are exposed to air. It can also be used as a cooking medium.

acini di pepe *see* Pasta Glossary, page 883.

A

acitrón *pl.* **acitrónes** [ah-see-TRAW*N*] *see* NOPALES

ackee; akee; achee [ah-KEE] A bright red tropical fruit that, when ripe, bursts open to reveal three large black seeds and a soft, creamy white flesh. The scientific name, *blighia sapida,* comes from Captain Bligh, who brought the fruit from West Africa to Jamaica in 1793. It is extremely popular in one of Jamaica's national dishes, "saltfish and ackee." Because certain parts of the fruit are toxic when underripe, canned ackee is often subject to import restrictions. *See also* MAMONCILLO.

acorn Acorns are the fruit of the oak tree. Some varieties are edible and, like chestnuts, may be eaten raw, roasted or baked. They may also be ground and used as a coffee substitute.

acorn squash A somewhat oval-shaped winter squash with a ribbed, dark green skin and orange flesh. The most common method of preparation is to halve them, remove the seeds and bake. Acorn squash may then be eaten directly from the shell. *See also* SQUASH.

acqua [AH-kwah] Italian for water.

additives, food In the broadest of terms, food additives are substances intentionally added to food either directly or indirectly with one or more of the following purposes: 1. to maintain or improve nutritional quality; 2. to maintain product quality and freshness; 3. to aid in the processing or preparation of food; and 4. to make food more appealing. Some 2,800 substances are currently added to foods for one or more of these uses. During normal processing, packaging and storage, up to 10,000 other compounds can find their way into food. Today more than ever, additives are strictly regulated. Manufacturers must prove the additives they add to food are safe. This process can take several years and includes a battery of chemical studies as well as tests involving animals, the latter to determine whether the substances could have harmful effects such as cancer and birth defects. The results of these comprehensive studies must be presented to the Food and Drug Administration (FDA), which then determines how the additive can be used in food. There are two major categories of food that are exempt from this testing and approval process: 1. a group of 700 substances categorized as GRAS ("generally recognized as safe"), which are so classified because of extensive past use without harmful side effects; and 2. substances approved before 1958 either by the FDA or the USDA. An ongoing review of many of these substances is in effect, however, to make sure they're tested against the most current scientific standards. It's interesting to note that about 98 percent (by weight) of all food additives used in the United States are in the form of baking soda, citric acid, corn syrup, mustard, pepper, salt, sugar and

A

vegetable colorings. *For information on specific additives, see* Food Additives Directory, page 900.

ade [AYD] A drink, such as **lemonade** or **limeade**, made by combining water, sugar and citrus juice.

adjust, to In cooking, to "adjust flavoring" refers to tasting before serving, adding seasoning if necessary.

adobado *see* ADOBO

adobo; adobo sauce [ah-DOH-boh] 1. In Mexico, adobo is a dark-red, fairly piquant sauce (or paste) made from ground CHILES, herbs and vinegar. It's used as a marinade as well as for a cooking and serving sauce. CHIPOTLE CHILES are often marketed packed in adobo sauce. Adobo also describes a stewlike presentation of meat prepared in this sauce. The word *adobado* is used as an adjective for dishes that are prepared in this manner. 2. In the Philippines, adobo is a dish of meat (typically chicken, pork or beef) and occasionally fish that's been marinated in a mixture of palm vinegar, garlic, herbs, spices and sometimes coconut milk. The meat is browned before being simmered in a blend of the marinade and soy sauce. Coconut milk is sometimes added to the Filipino adobo, which is considered by many to be the country's national dish. *See also* SAUCE.

advieh [ad-vee-EH] Persian spice mixture usually containing cardamom, cinnamon, cumin seeds and rose petals, but variations may add black pepper, cloves, coriander, ginger and saffron. It's sometimes spelled *adwiya.*

advocaat [ad-voh-KAHT] A Dutch, brandy-based eggnog-flavored LIQUEUR. The full name is *advocaatenborrel,* Dutch for "advocate's (or lawyer's) drink."

adwiya *see* ADVIEH

adzuki bean *see* AZUKI BEAN

aebleskive; *pl.* **aebleskiver; æbleskive** [EH-bleh-skee-vor] Danish for "apple slice," aebleskive is a roundish Danish pancake about the size of a small orange with a texture like a fluffy buttermilk pancake. Traditionally aebleskiver were prepared with slices of apple inside, but modern versions have many variations both savory and sweet. They are made in a special **aebleskiver pan**, which contains indentations about half the size of the final roundish pancake. Halfway through, the aebleskiver are turned to finish cooking. Aebleskive is also sometimes spelled *ebleskive.*

aemono [ah-eh-MOH-noh] Japanese term meaning "dressed foods" and referring to saladlike dishes combined with a DRESSING complimentary to the ingredients. The composition of the dressings varies but is generally based on puréed TOFU. Aemono dishes are usually served chilled as appetizers, although Japanese diners sometimes eat them towards the end of a meal prior to the rice.

aerate [ER-ayt; AY-uh-rayt] A term used in cookery as a synonym for SIFT.

Affidelice [ah-fee-day-LEESS] *see* ÉPOISSES

affinage [ah-fee-NAHZH] The French term for the process of finishing (RIPENING) cheese to bring it to a perfect point of maturity. *See also* AFFINÉ.

affiné; *Fr.* **affineur;** *It.* **affinatore** [ah-fee-NAY; ah-fee-NYOUR; ah-fee-nah-TOH-ray] In the cheese world the term *affiné* most often refers to the process of RIPENING cheese—bringing it to peak maturity. In France an *affineur* is an expert in finishing (aging) cheese; in Italy this specialist is called an *affinatore*. Some cheesemakers turn their unripe cheese over to an *affineur*, who brings it to maturity. An *affineur's* duties may also include everything from packaging to marketing the cheese. Both words are from the French *affiner* ("to finish"). *See also* AFFINAGE.

affogato [ahf-foh-GAH-toh] A scoop of vanilla GELATO or ice cream topped with a shot of hot ESPRESSO. Though vanilla is traditional, chocolate gelato is sometimes used, in which case the dessert becomes *affogato mocha*. The word *affogato* comes from the Italian *affogare* ("drown").

affumicata; **affumicato** [ah-foo-me-KAH-tah; ah-foo-me-KAH-toh] Italian for "smoked," as in smoked meat or smoked cheese.

African horned cucumber *see* KIWANO

agar; **agar-agar** [AH-gahr; AY-gahr] Also called *kanten* and *Japanese gelatin*, this tasteless dried seaweed acts as a setting agent and is widely used in Asia. It is marketed in the form of blocks, powder or brittle strands and is available at Asian markets and natural food stores. Agar can be substituted for gelatin but has stronger setting properties (about 5 times greater) so less of it is required. Unlike gelatin, agar will set at room temperature.

agave [ah-GAH-vee; ah-GAH-vay] Also called *century plant*, this family of succulents grows in the southwestern United States, Mexico and Central America. Though poisonous when raw, agave has a sweet, mild flavor when baked or made into a syrup. Certain varieties are used in making the alcoholic beverages MESCAL, PULQUE and TEQUILA.

age; aged; aging To let food get older under controlled conditions in order to improve flavor or texture or both. 1. **Aged meat** has been stored 3 to 6 weeks at an optimal temperature of 34°F to 38°F and in low humidity. During this time it undergoes an enzymatic change that intensifies flavor, deepens color and tenderizes by softening some of the connective tissue. The longer meat is aged, the more quickly it will cook. The *cryovac* method of aging involves vacuum packing the meat with a vapor- and moistureproof film so the so-called aging takes place in transit from slaughterhouse to the consumer's home. 2. **Aging cheese** refers to storing it in a temperature-controlled area until it develops the desired texture and flavor. *See* RIPENING for more information. 3. **Aging spirits and wines** produces a smoother, more complex, and less harsh and tannic (*see* TANNIN) result. WHISKEYS, COGNACS, ARMAGNACS, as well as some better BRANDIES and RUMS, all benefit from aging, with many spirits governed by laws regarding minimum aging periods. Spirits that aren't aged include GIN, VODKA, NEUTRAL SPIRITS and certain brandies and rums. Aging is also beneficial to most fine red and white wines, whereas ROSÉ, light red wines and most whites are at their best soon after bottling and don't require further aging.

agedashi [ah-geh-DAH-shee] A Japanese dish of deep-fried TOFU served with DAIKON, KATSUOBUSHI (dried bonito tuna flakes), ginger and a dipping sauce made of SOY SAUCE and MIRIN.

aged meat *see* AGE

agekamaboko [ah-geh-kah-mah-BOH-koh] A special type of KAMABOKO (fish cake) that's deep-fried instead of steamed. It's also called *satsuaage* in some parts of Japan.

agemono [ah-geh-MOH-noh] A Japanese term referring to deep-frying (*see* DEEP-FRY) and the foods produced from this cooking method. TEMPURA is the most famous of the Japanese foods cooked in this manner. Deep-frying is done in a pan called an **agemono-nabe**, which is similar to a Chinese WOK.

aglio [AH-lyoh] Italian for "garlic."

aglio e olio [AH-lyoh ay AW-lyoh] Italian for "garlic and oil," referring to a dressing of garlic and hot olive oil used on PASTA.

agneau [an-YOH] French for "lamb."

agnello [ah-NYEH-loh] Italian for "lamb."

agnolotti *see* Pasta Glossary, page 883.

agraz [AH-grruhs] Sour, acidic SORBET made with almonds, sugar and VERJUICE that's popular in North Africa.

agresto [ah-GREH-stoh] Italian for "VERJUICE."

Agrocybe aegerita *see* PIOPPINI MUSHROOM

agrodolce [ah-groh-DOHL-cheh] The Italian term for a sweet-and-sour flavor (*dolce* means sweet, *agro* is sour); synonymous with the French AIGRE-DOUX.

agua; água [AH-gwah; AH-gwer] Spanish and Portuguese, respectively, for "water."

aguacate [ah-gwah-KAH-tay] The Spanish word for AVOCADO.

agua de Jamaica [AH-gwah day juh-MAY-kuh] *see* JAMAICA FLOWER

agua fresca [AH-gwah FREHS-kuh] Spanish for "fresh water," *agua fresca* is a refreshing drink popular throughout Mexico, Central America and the Caribbean; it's also found in many Mexican restaurants in the United States. The base for this beverage is sugar and water, which is flavored with various additions. Fruit versions include *agua de sandía* (made with watermelon) and *agua de melón* (cantaloupe or other melon). Other popular fruit additions include guava, mango, papaya and strawberries. Non-fruit renditions include *agua de horchata* (made with cinnamon, milk, rice and vanilla), *agua de jamaica* (flavored with dried hibiscus flowers), *agua de pepino* (cucumbers) and *agua de tamarindo* (made with TAMARIND seeds). Fruits and ingredients like cucumbers are puréed before being added to the sugar-water base. Agua fresca can be seen in Mexican restaurants in large, glass jars—it pairs particularly well with that spicy cuisine. In Mexico this cool, refreshing beverage is so popular that myriad street vendors sell it daily.

aguardente [er-gwer-DAYN-ter] Portuguese for "BRANDY," the broader meaning is for spirits distilled (*see* DISTILLATION) from fruit or vegetables.

aguardiente; aguardiente de caña [ah-gwahr-dee-EN-tay; ah-gwahr-dee-EN-tay day KAH-nyah] Spanish for "burned water" (akin to North America's FIRE WATER), *aguardiente* is a generic term for any of several potent, low quality SPIRITS. In Spain, the term refers to a BRANDY-based potable made from MARC. The South American *aguardiente de caña* is a coarse liquor based on sugar cane and sometimes flavored with anise seed. *See also* CACHAÇA.

ahi [AH-hee] The Hawaiian name for yellowfin, as well as bigeye TUNA.

aigre-doux [ay-greh-DOO] The French term for the combined flavors of sour (*aigre*) and sweet (*doux*). An *aigre-doux* sauce might contain both vinegar and sugar.

aïoli [ay-OH-lee; i-OH-lee] A strongly flavored garlic MAYONNAISE from the Provence region of southern France. It's a popular accompaniment for fish, meats and vegetables.

Airelle [ay-REHL] A cranberry-flavored EAU DE VIE.

Aisy Cendré [ay-ZEE sah*n*-DRUH] *see* ÉPOISSES DE BOURGOGNE

aiysh [i-yihsh] 1. Round, soft whole-wheat flatbread popular in the Middle East. It's thought to be a very ancient bread that originated in Egypt. 2. Boiled ball of dough made from millet, popular in countries in the Sahel region of north central Africa, including Algeria, Chad, Nigeria, Niger and Sudan. Also called *biya*.

ají [ah-HEE] Name used for chile peppers in the Caribbean and Central and South America, particularly in Peru. *See also* CHILE.

ají amarillo [ah-HEE ah-mah-REE-yoh] Translated as "yellow chile" and also known as *ají escabeche,* this CHILE is the most popular throughout Peru. Although many are yellow, they can turn a deep orange as they mature. This narrow chile grows from 3 to 7 inches long, has a full-flavored fruitiness and is hot, with a SCOVILLE SCALE rating of 30,000 to 50,000. Fresh ají amarillo chiles are available in South American and Mexican markets and can be found in these markets and on the Internet in canned, paste or dried form. The dried version is sometimes called *cusqueño*. *See also* CHILE.

ají escabeche *see* AJÍ AMARILLO

ají flor *see* BISHOP'S CROWN CHILE

ajijsuke-nori *see* NORI

aji-no-moto [ah-JEE-noh-MOH-toh] The Japanese name for MONOSODIUM GLUTAMATE (MSG).

ají panca [ah-HEE PAHN-ka] The *Panca chile* is 3 to 5 inches long, dark red to deep burgundy in color and sweet and fruity with a bit of smokiness. It's popular in South America, especially Peru, where it's one of the most commonly grown chiles. The ají panca is mild, with a SCOVILLE SCALE rating of 500 to 1,500. They are usually dried and can be found on the Internet whole or in powdered form. *See also* CHILE.

ajowan; ajwain [AHJ-uh-wahn] Though it's related to CARAWAY and CUMIN, ajowan tastes more like THYME with an astringent edge. This native

A

of southern India can be found in Indian markets in either ground or seed form. The light brown to purple-red seeds resemble celery seeds in size and shape. Ajowan is most commonly added to CHUTNEYS, curried dishes, breads and LEGUMES. It's also called *carom. See also* SPICES.

ajvar [EYE-vahr] A popular cooked relish in Yugoslavia and Greece made from roasted sweet red peppers, eggplant, garlic, olive oil, salt, pepper and, sometimes, PAPRIKA. Ajvar can be served as an appetizer or side dish.

akala [ah-KAH-lah] Hailing from Hawaii, this sweet, juicy berry resembles a very large raspberry. It can range in color from red to almost purple and is good eaten plain or in jams and pies.

akamiso *see* MISO

akara *see* ACARAJÉ

akee *see* ACKEE

akkara *see* ACARAJÉ

aku *see* TUNA

akudjura [ah-KOOT-joo-rah] *see* BUSH TOMATO

akule [ah-KOO-lay] This Hawaiian fish, also known as *bigeye scad,* is usually salted and dried. *See also* FISH.

akvavit *see* AQUAVIT

al [ahl] An Italian word meaning "at the," "to the" or "on the." For example, *al dente* means "to the tooth."

à la [ah lah] A French idiom meaning "in the manner (or style) of"; the full phrase is *à la mode de.* In cooking, this phrase designates the style of preparation or a particular garnish. *A la bourguignonne,* for example, would mean "as prepared in Burgundy."

à la carte [ah lah KAHRT] A menu term signifying that each item is priced separately. *See also* PRIX FIXE; TABLE D'HÔTE.

à la diable [ah lah dee-AH-bl (dee-AHB-lay)] *see* DIABLE SAUCE

à la king [ah lah KING] A dish of diced food (usually chicken or turkey) in a rich cream sauce containing mushrooms, pimientos, green peppers and sometimes SHERRY.

à la mode [ah lah MOHD] French for "in the manner (or mode) [of]," referring to the style in which a dish is prepared. The term has been Americanized to also mean pie topped with ice cream.

alaria [ah-LAHR-yah] A brown edible SEAWEED popular in some North Atlantic countries as well as Japan and other Asian countries. Alaria is used like a vegetable in soups and simmered dishes, as well as occasionally in salads. It's known as *badderlocks, dabberlocks* and *honeyware* in some North Atlantic countries. Alaria is available both in fresh and dried forms in Asian markets, specialty markets and natural food stores.

Alaska cod *see* SABLEFISH

Alaska king crab *see* CRAB

albacore [AL-bah-kohr] *see* TUNA

Albariño [ahl-bah-REE-nyoh] Low-yielding, high-quality white wine grape grown in Spain's Galicia region, as well as Portugal's Vinho Verde, where it's called *Alvarinho*. Although reasonably productive, these grapes are so thick-skinned that only a small amount of juice can be extracted from them. Albariño grapes can produce creamy, rich wines with complex flavors of apricots, peaches and citrus.

Albert sauce [AL-bert; al-BEHR] Usually served with beef, this is a rich horseradish sauce with a base of butter, flour and cream. *See also* SAUCE.

albóndiga; albóndigas [ahl-BON-dee-gah] The Spanish word for "meatball." *Albóndigas* is the name of a popular Mexican and Spanish dish of spicy meatballs, usually in a tomato sauce. **Sopade albóndigas** is a beef-broth soup with meatballs and chopped vegetables.

Albufera sauce; sauce Albuféra [al-BUH-fih-ra] A rich sauce named after one of Napoleon's famous generals, the Duke of Albuféra. The sauce is based on SUPREME SAUCE with GLACE DE VIANDE (meat glaze) and red pepper butter added to it. It's used mainly on SWEETBREADS and poultry dishes such as Poularde Albufera, a chicken dish also named after the duke.

albumen [al-BYOO-mehn] The old-fashioned word for egg white.

albumin [al-BYOO-mehn] The protein portion of the egg white, comprising about 70 percent of the whole. Albumin is also found in animal blood, milk, plants and seeds.

alcachofa [al-kah-CHOH-fah] Spanish for "artichoke."

alchermes [ahl-KEHR-mehs] Spicy Italian liqueur created by taking a neutral spirit and flavoring it with cinnamon, cloves, nutmeg, vanilla bean and herbs. It's not very popular because its bright-red color comes from a red dye obtained from the female kermes, a small parasite.

A

alcohol 1. The only alcohol suitable for drinking is ethyl alcohol, a liquid produced by distilling (*see* DISTILLATION) the fermented juice of fruits or grains. Pure ethyl alcohol is clear, flammable and caustic. Water is therefore added to reduce its potency. In the United States, the average amount of alcohol in distilled spirits is about 40 percent (80 PROOF). Pure alcohol boils at 173°F, water at 212°F. A mixture of the two will boil somewhere between these two temperatures. When cooking with alcohol, remember that the old saw claiming that it "completely evaporates when heated" has been proven invalid by a USDA study. In truth, cooked food can retain from 5 to 85 percent of the original alcohol, depending on various factors such as how and at what temperature the food was heated, the cooking time and the alcohol source. Even the smallest trace of alcohol may be a problem for alcoholics and those with alcohol-related illnesses. Because alcohol freezes at a much lower temperature than water, the amount of alcohol used in a frozen dessert (such as ice cream) must be carefully regulated or the dessert won't freeze. Calorie-wise, a one-and-a-half-ounce jigger of 80-proof liquor (such as Scotch or vodka) equals almost 100 calories, a four-ounce glass of DRY wine costs in the area of 85 to 90 calories and a twelve-ounce regular (not light) beer contributes about 150 calories. 2. A general term for any alcoholic liquor.

alcohol by volume (ABV; abv; alc/vol) The percentage of ALCOHOL content, which must be included on American alcoholic beverage labels. The term PROOF is sometimes used to refer to alcohol content; proof is exactly double the alcohol by volume percentage.

alc/vol *see* ALCOHOL BY VOLUME

al dente [al-DEN-tay] An Italian phrase meaning "to the tooth," used to describe pasta or other food that is cooked only until it offers a slight resistance when bitten into, but which is not soft or overdone.

ale [AYL] A category of alcoholic beverages brewed from a combination of HOPS and barley MALT where the yeast rises to the top of the FERMENTATION tank (rather than falling to the bottom, as with beer). Ale is typically stronger than beer and more bitter in flavor because of the hops. **Pale ale** (the name referring to its relatively pale to deep amber color as compared to dark ales like PORTER or STOUT) originated in England and has a flavor that's reasonably balanced between the hops and malted barley. **India pale ale**, originally produced in England for export to British soldiers stationed in India, is slightly more bitter than regular pale ale. **Brown ale** is lightly hopped, very full-bodied, slightly sweet and dark brown in color. The color and flavor are derived from caramelized malts. **Scotch ale** is amber to dark brown in color, full-bodied and has a strong malty flavor.

A

Although it originated in Scotland, it's now produced in other countries including Belgium and France. *See also* TRAPPIST BEER.

alecost *see* COSTMARY

à l'étouffée *see* ÉTOUFFÉE

alewife *see* HERRING

alfajores [ahl-fah-HOH-rehs] These cookies are a favorite in many South American countries such as Chile, Peru and Uruguay, and particularly in Argentina. Traditional versions consist of two cookies sandwiching a layer of the caramel-like mixture known as DULCE DE LECHE. The cookie can be made from WHEAT FLOUR, CORN FLOUR, CORNSTARCH or CHUÑO mixed with sugar, butter (or shortening) and a variety of other flavorings including peanuts, lemon ZEST and/or various nuts. Alfajores come plain or covered with a variety of coatings such as frosting, chocolate, powdered sugar or coconut. Besides *dulce de leche*, they may also be filled with fruit jams or pastes.

alfalfa [al-FAL-fuh] Though alfalfa is generally grown for fodder, the seeds are also sprouted for human consumption. Alfalfa sprouts are popular in salads and on sandwiches. *See also* SPROUTS.

Alfonso; Alphonso olive Large, oval-shaped South American olive that's cured in brine, wine or wine vingegar. It ranges from light to dark purple to purple-brown. Alfonsos have a soft, tender texture and a rich olive flavor that's slightly bitter. Also called *Maddelena olives*, they're found unpitted and pitted. *See also* OLIVE.

al forno (ahl FOHR-noh) Italian for "baked" or "roasted."

Alfredo sauce [al-FRAY-doh] An exceedingly rich sauce created in the early 1920s by Roman restaurateur Alfredo di Lello for his famous dish FETTUCCINE ALFREDO. Alfredo sauce is classically made with heavy cream, butter, grated PARMESAN, salt and pepper. Today's renditions can include additions such as egg yolks, flour and garlic. Although this sauce was created for pasta, it's now also used to dress everything from chicken to vegetables. *See also* SAUCE.

al fresco [ahl FREH-skoh (FRAY-skoh)] Italian for "fresh" or "cool," referring culinarily to dining outdoors, whether at a restaurant or a picnic.

alginic acid; algin [al-JIHN-ihk] A thick, jellylike substance obtained from SEAWEED. Alginic acid is used as a stabilizer and thickener in a wide variety of commercially processed foods such as ice creams, puddings, flavored milk drinks, pie fillings, soups and syrups. *See also* SODIUM ALGINATE.

A

alioli [ah-lee-YOH-lee] Spanish for "AÏOLI."

Alitame [AL-ih-taym] Although not sanctioned for use in the United States at this writing, Alitame is expected to soon become FDA approved. This supernova of ARTIFICIAL SWEETENERS is 2,000 times sweeter than sugar. It's a compound of two amino acids—alanine and aspartic acid. *See also* ACESULFAME-K; ASPARTAME; NEOTAME; SACCHARIN; SUCRALOSE.

Alizé de France [ah-lee-ZAY deuh FRAHNSS] A line of French COGNAC-based LIQUEURS using PASSION FRUIT and other fruit flavors. **Alizé Gold Passion** is golden-yellow and flavored only with passion fruit. The blue-colored **Alizé Bleu** adds VODKA plus cherry and ginger flavors to the passion fruit-Cognac base. **Alizé Red Passion** has a rich red color produced in part by the addition of cranberry juice. The pink **Alizé Rose** is enhanced with VODKA, and has added strawberry, LITCHI and rose petal flavors. **Alizé Wild Passion** is reddish orange and adds mango and pink grapefruit flavors.

Aliziergeist [ah-lih-TSEER-gighst] An Alsatian fruit brandy made from serviceberries, the brownish fruit of the Mediterranean service tree.

alkali [AL-kah-li] Alkalis counterbalance and neutralize ACIDS. In cooking, the most common alkali used is bicarbonate of soda, commonly known as BAKING SODA.

alkanet [AL-kuh-neht] A member of the BORAGE family, the alkanet plant has roots that yield a red dye, which is used to color various food products such as margarine.

alla [ah-lah] The Italian word meaning "as done by, in, for or with." Eggplant *alla parmigiana* refers to eggplant topped with tomato sauce, MOZZARELLA and PARMESAN.

allemande sauce [ah-leh-MAHND] A classic VELOUTÉ SAUCE thickened with egg yolks. Also called *Parisienne sauce*. *See also* SAUCE.

Aleppo pepper [ah-LEP-poh] Medium-hot chile pepper named after Syria's largest city, which is located in the north near the Turkish border. The color ranges from dark red to almost purple. It's sometimes compared to the better-known ANCHO CHILE although, with a SCOVILLE SCALE rating of about 10,000, the Aleppo has more heat. Very popular in Middle Eastern cooking, the rich, slightly fruit-flavored Aleppo only started to gain followers in the West in the 1990s. It can be found in dried form through the Internet.

Allasch Latvian in origin, this extremely sweet liqueur is flavored with almonds, anise seed and cumin. Its flavor is similar to (although not as complex as) that of KÜMMEL.

Allgäuer Bergkäse [AHL-gow-er BEHRK-kai-zer (-kah-zeh)] Hard cöw's-milk cheese from the Allgäu, an area that straddles the southern German states of Bavaria and Baden-Württemberg, bordering on Austria. *Bergkäse* means "mountain cheese" and refers to the Bavarian Alps that dominate this area. Allgäuer Bergkäse comes in large (up to 100-pound) wheels with yellow to brown rinds and pale yellow interiors containing a few small EYES. The flavor ranges from mellow with fruity and nutty traits for young versions to more complex, pungent flavors for aged cheeses. It has a minimum FAT CONTENT of 45 percent. *See also* CHEESE.

Allgäuer Emmenthaler [AHL-gow-er EM-men-tah-ler] *see* EMMENTAL

alligator This lizardlike reptile can grow up to 19 feet in length and is generally found in the swamplands of Louisiana and the Gulf States. Alligator meat is usually only available in its native regions. It comes in three basic types: the tender, white, veallike tail meat; the pinkish body meat, which has a stronger flavor and slightly tougher texture; and the dark tail meat, which is tough and only suitable for braising.

alligator pear *see* AVOCADO

alligator pepper *see* GRAINS OF PARADISE

allspice The pea-size berry of the evergreen pimiento tree, native to the West Indies and South America, though Jamaica provides most of the world's supply (allspice is also known as *Jamaica pepper*). The dried berries are dark brown and can be purchased whole or ground. The spice is so named because it tastes like a combination of cinnamon, nutmeg and cloves. Store in a cool, dark place for no more than 6 months. Allspice is used in both savory and sweet cooking. *See also* SPICES; Seasoning Suggestions, page 891.

allumette [al-yoo-MEHT] French for "match," referring culinarily to potatoes that have been cut into thin "matchsticks" and fried.

allumettes [al-yoo-MEHTS] Thin strips of PUFF PASTRY spread or filled with different savory mixtures (such as shrimp butter or grated cheese) and served as an HORS D'OEUVRE. A sweet filling turns this pastry into a dessert.

almendra [ahl-MEN-drah] Spanish for "almond."

almond The kernel of the almond-tree fruit, grown extensively in California, the Mediterranean, Australia and South Africa. There are two main types of almonds—sweet and bitter. The flavor of **sweet almonds** is delicate and slightly sweet. They're readily available in markets and, unless otherwise indicated, are the variety used in recipes. The more strongly flavored **bitter almonds** contain traces of lethal prussic acid when raw. Though the acid's toxicity is destroyed when the nuts are heated, the sale of bitter almonds is illegal in the United States. Processed bitter almonds are used to flavor extracts, LIQUEURS and ORGEAT SYRUP. The kernels of apricot and peach pits have a similar flavor and the same toxic effect (destroyed by heating) as bitter almonds. Almonds are available blanched or not, whole, sliced, chopped, candied, smoked, in paste form and in many flavors. Toasting almonds before using in recipes intensifies their flavor and adds crunch. Almonds are a nutritional powerhouse, packed with calcium, fiber, folic acid, magnesium, potassium, riboflavin and vitamin E. *See also* ALMOND EXTRACT; ALMOND OIL; ALMOND PASTE; JORDAN ALMOND; MARCONA ALMOND; NUTS.

almond cream A CRÈME PÂTISSIÈRE flavored with ground almonds and sometimes a spirit such as brandy, CRÈME DE NOYAUX or rum.

almond extract A flavoring produced by combining bitter-ALMOND oil with ethyl ALCOHOL. The flavor is very intense, so the extract should be used with care. *See also* EXTRACTS.

almond flour Blanched almonds ground into a fine powder used in cakes, cookies and other desserts. It's also called *almond meal*.

almond meal *see* ALMOND FLOUR

almond oil An oil obtained by pressing sweet almonds. French almond oil, *huile d'amande,* is very expensive and has the delicate flavor and aroma of lightly toasted almonds. The U.S. variety is much milder and doesn't compare either in flavor or in price. Almond oil can be found in specialty gourmet markets and many supermarkets.

almond paste A mixture of blanched ground almonds, sugar and GLYCERIN or other liquid. ALMOND EXTRACT is sometimes added to intensify the flavor. Almond paste is used in a variety of confections and is less sweet and slightly coarser than MARZIPAN. It should be firm but pliable before use in a recipe. If it becomes hard, it can be softened by heating for 2 or 3 seconds in a microwave oven. Once opened, it should be wrapped tightly and refrigerated. Almond paste is available in most supermarkets in cans and plastic packages. **Bitter-almond paste** is used to flavor the famous AMARETTI cookies.

al pastor [ahl pahs-TOHR] This Latino specialty is prepared much like the Greek GYRO but typically is formed of pork rather than lamb. Thin slices of marinated pork are stacked and molded onto a large spit, then topped with a large chunk of pineapple. As a vertical gas flame roasts the meat on the rotating spit, pineapple juice drips down the sides creating sweet, crispy edges. Slices of meat are shaved off the exterior as the spit turns. Numerous vendors in Mexico City sell **tacos al pastor**, tortillas topped with slices of this spit-grilled meat, pieces of the pineapple and other additions such as onions, cilantro and salsa. Such vendors are also found in U.S. cities with a large Mexican population. The term *al pastor* means "shepherd style" and it's thought that these tacos were adapted from similar lamb-based preparations (*see* SHAWARMA) brought to Mexico by Lebanese immigrants.

Alphonso olive *see* ALFONSO; ALPHONSO OLIVE

alsacienne, à l' [al-zah-SYEHN] A term referring to cooking "in the style of Alsace," a province in northeastern France whose French and German heritage is reflected in its famous cuisine. It usually refers to preparations of meat braised with sauerkraut, potatoes and sausage.

alum [AL-uhm] In cooking, these highly astringent crystals of potassium aluminum sulfate were once widely used as the crisping agent in canning pickles. Alum can cause digestive distress, however, and modern canning methods make its use unnecessary.

aluminum cookware [ah-LOO-mihn-uhm]; Br. **aluminium** [ahl-yoo-MIHN-ee-uhm] *see* COOKWARE AND BAKEWARE MATERIALS

aluminum foil Aluminum that has been rolled into a thin, pliable sheet. It's an excellent barrier to moisture, air and odors and can withstand flaming heat and freezing cold. It comes in regular weight (for wrapping food and covering containers) and heavy-duty weight (for freezer storage and lining pans and grills). Because the crinkling of foil creates tiny holes (increasing permeability), it should not be reused for freezer storage. Neither should it be used to wrap acidic foods (such as tomatoes and onions) because the natural acids in the food will eat through the foil. Although metal produces arcing (sparking) in microwave ovens, oddly enough, tiny amounts of aluminum foil can be used providing the foil doesn't touch the sides of the oven. For example, foil might be used in a microwave oven to shield the tips of chicken wings that might cook much faster than the rest of the wing.

Alvarinho *see* ALBARIÑO

amaebi *see* SUSHI

amakuchi [ah-MAH-koo-chee] *see* SAKE

amande [ah-MAHN] French for "almond."

amandine [AH-mahn-deen; a-mahn-DEEN] The French term meaning "garnished with almonds." It's often misspelled "almondine."

amaranth [AM-ah-ranth] Once considered a simple weed in the United States, this nutritious annual is finally being acknowledged as the nourishing high-protein food it is. Amaranth greens have a delicious, slightly sweet flavor and can be used both in cooking and for salads. The seeds are used as cereal or can be ground into flour for bread. Amaranth seeds and flour can be found in natural food stores, as well as in some Caribbean and Asian markets.

amardine [ah-mar-DEEN] Thin layer of lightly sweetened apricot purée that's dried in sheets (*see also* FRUIT LEATHER). Amardine is cut up and used to flavor drinks and desserts and is a popular flavoring ingredient in Middle Eastern cooking, especially lamb stews. Amardine is also called *qamar el deen* or *qamar el din*, which also refers to juice made by soaking the sheets in warm water.

amarelle [ah-mah-REHL] One of two groups of sour cherries, the amarelle has red-pigmented skin, but the flesh and juice are nearly colorless. Although some Europeans and Middle Easterners eat them raw, the amarelle is considered by many to be too sour for eating out of hand but perfect for cooking and flavoring LIQUEURS. The EARLY RICHMOND and the MONTMORENCY fall into this category of sour cherry.

amaretti [am-ah-REHT-tee] Intensely crisp, airy MACAROON cookies that are made either with bitter-ALMOND PASTE or its flavor counterpart, apricot-kernel paste. *Amarettini* are miniature versions of this cookie.

amaretto [am-ah-REHT-toh] A LIQUEUR with the flavor of almonds, though it's often made with the kernels of apricot pits. The original liqueur, *Amaretto di Saronno,* hails from Saronno, Italy. Many American distilleries now produce their own amaretto.

amaro [ah-MAH-roh] Italian for bitter or very DRY, used in relation to wine, as well as to describe the myriad bitter Italian LIQUEURS.

amasake; amazake [ah-mah-SAH-kee] A Japanese fermented drink made from KOJI and cooked rice. Amasake ranges in texture from relatively thin to as thick as a milkshake and can be served cold or hot. It's available in various flavors in natural food stores and Asian markets.

amazake *see* AMASAKE

amazu shoga [ah-MAH-zoo SHOH-gah] Thinly sliced or shredded fresh GINGER pickled in a sweet vinegar marinade. Amazu shoga is beige or pink in color, as compared to the bright red BENI SHOGA. It's used as a garnish for many Japanese dishes, particularly SUSHI. Amazu shoga can be found in Asian markets.

ambasha [ahm-BAH-shah] Ethiopian yeast bread that's shaped like a pizza. It's made with wheat flour and flavored with CARDAMOM, CORIANDER and FENUGREEK seeds, then topped with seasoning such as cayenne, cinnamon, cloves and ground ginger.

amberjack A lean, mild fish found along the South Atlantic coast. This member of the JACK family is hard to find in markets but, when available, is usually sold whole. Amberjack is best baked or sautéed. *See also* FISH.

ambrosia [am-BROH-zhah] 1. According to Greek mythology, ambrosia (meaning "immortality") was the food of the gods on Mt. Olympus. More recently, the word designates a dessert of chilled fruit (usually oranges and bananas) mixed with coconut. Ambrosia is also sometimes served as a salad. 2. A mixed drink made by shaking COGNAC, BRANDY (usually CALVADOS or APPLEJACK) and COINTREAU or raspberry syrup with crushed ice, then straining into a glass and topping off with cold CHAMPAGNE. It's said to have been created at New Orleans' famous Arnaud's restaurant shortly after Prohibition ended. 3. [ahm-BROH-zee-ah] A popular Brazilian dessert of Portuguese origin. It's an extremely rich egg CUSTARD flavored with cinnamon and cloves and served cold.

amchoor; amchor; amchur [AHM-choor] An East Indian seasoning made by pulverizing sun-dried, unripe (green) MANGO into a fine powder. Amchoor lends a tart, acidic, fruity character to many dishes including meats, vegetables and curried preparations. It's also used to tenderize poultry, meat and fish. Amchoor is sometimes called simply *mango powder;* it's also spelled *aamchur.*

amêndoa [ah-MEN-doo-ah] Portuguese for "almond."

américaine, à l' [a-may-ree-KEHN] A dish (often lobster) prepared with a spicy sauce of tomatoes, olive oil, onions and wine.

American cheese, processed *see* PROCESSED CHEESE

American gai lan *see* BROCCOLI RABE

American leg *see* LEG, LAMB

Americano [ah-meh-ree-KAH-noh] A bittersweet APÉRITIF made with sweet VERMOUTH, CAMPARI and sparkling water, served over ice in a HIGHBALL glass and garnished with a slice of lemon or orange. *See also* NEGRONI.

American Viticultural Area (AVA) An American system implemented in 1978 to identify U.S. wines in a fashion similar to the French APPELLATION system. Unlike the French regulations, however, the rules governing AVAs (under the jurisdiction of the Tax and Trade Bureau, previously BATF) are very lax. An American AVA is defined strictly by a geographic area, whereas in France the parameters are much more precise. A French appellation identifies the grape varieties that may be grown in a geographic area, the maximum production per acre, the minimum level of alcohol required for wines produced in the area and so forth. The only requirement for wine with an AVA designation is that 85 percent of the grapes must be grown in that viticultural area. Growers must petition the Tax and Trade Bureau to obtain an AVA designation for a region. The Bureau's decision is based on such characteristics as an area's topography, soil type, climate, elevation and, to some extent, historical precedent. AVAs range in size from several hundred acres to several million; some reside within other larger AVAs. For example, California's Napa Valley is an AVA that encompasses other AVAs including Howell Mountain, Stags Leap District and Rutherford Bench. The first AVA in the United States was the Augusta AVA in Missouri, established in 1980.

Amer Picon [ah-MEHR pee-KAWN] An extremely bitter (*amer* is French for bitter) French VERMOUTH-style APÉRITIF. It has a dark reddish-brown color and is flavored with gentian, orange, and cinchona bark, which yields QUININE—hence, the bitterness. Amer Picon is typically taken with SODA WATER, but is also used in various cocktails. Also known simply as *Picon*.

Amfissa; Amphissa olive (PDO) [AHM-fee-say] Named for the town of Amfissa in central Greece, this medium to large olive is sold both as a green olive and a mature, tree-ripened olive with dark-purple skin. The latter is sometimes called the *Greek black olive,* a somewhat generic term for several large, mature olives. The green variety is cured with salt brine and citric acid and has a firm, crisp texture and lemony-buttery flavor. The texture is softer with the mature version, and the flavor is rich and fruity with a slightly bitter edge. Amfissa olives enjoy PDO status. *See also* OLIVE.

ammonium bicarbonate [ah-MOH-nee-uhm by-KAR-boh-nayt] This LEAVENER is the precursor of today's baking powder and baking soda. It's still called for in some European baking recipes, mainly for cookies. It can be purchased in drugstores but must be ground to a powder before using. Also known as *hartshorn, carbonate of ammonia* and *powdered baking ammonia.*

amontillado [ah-mon-teh-LAH-doh] *see* SHERRY

amsul *see* KOKAM

amuse-bouche; amuse-gueule [ah-mewz-BOOSH (-GEURL)] French derivative for "appetizer," typically referring to a small one- or two-bite portion of something special or exotic to tickle the tastebuds. Such offerings are not on the menu and are presented to diners before the meal begins.

an *see* AZUKI-AN

anadama bread [a-nuh-DAM-uh] An early American yeast bread flavored with cornmeal and molasses. Legend says this bread was created by a New England farmer plagued by a lazy wife who served him the same cornmeal-molasses gruel every day. One morning, the disgusted farmer grabbed the bowl of gruel, tossed in some flour and yeast, and began stirring like crazy, all the while muttering angrily, "Anna, damn 'er!"

anago *see* SUSHI

Anaheim chile [AN-uh-hime] Named after the California city, the generally mild Anaheim is one of the most commonly available CHILES in the United States. It is usually medium green in color and has a long, narrow shape. The red strain is also called the *chile Colorado*. Anaheim chiles can be purchased fresh or canned and have a sweet, simple taste with just a hint of bite. Anaheims are frequently stuffed and commonly used in SALSAS. The dried red variety are those used for the decorative RISTRA, a long string (or wreath) of chiles. The Anaheim is a mild pepper with a SCOVILLE SCALE rating of 500 to 1,000.

analog cheese *see* SUBSTITUTE CHEESE

ananas [ah-nah-NAH] French for "pineapple."

anardana [ah-NAHR-dah-nah] Pomegranate seeds separated from the flesh and dried. Anardana has a slightly fruity, sweet-and-sour flavor. It's popular in India as a spice used in CHUTNEYS, in pastry and bread products and added to salads or vegetable dishes. Anardana can be found in Indian markets, either whole or ground.

anasazi bean [a-nuh-SAH-zee] A large, white dried bean with distinctive maroon markings. Anasazis (also called *Jacob's cattle beans*) have a fresh, sweet flavor and smooth texture. *See also* BEANS.

ancho chile [AHN-choh] This broad, dried CHILE is 3 to 4 inches long and a deep reddish brown; it ranges in flavor from mild to pungent. The rich, slightly fruit-flavored ancho is the sweetest of the dried chiles. In its fresh, green state, the ancho is called a POBLANO CHILE. It's a mild pepper with a SCOVILLE SCALE rating of 1,000 to 2,000.

anchoiade; anchoyade [ahn-show-YAHD] A paste made of ANCHOVIES, garlic and, sometimes, olive oil. It's generally used to spread on toast or bread.

anchovy [AN-choh-vee; an-CHOH-vee] Though there are many species of small, silvery fish that are known in their country of origin as "anchovies," the true anchovy comes only from the Mediterranean and southern European coastlines. These tiny fish are generally filleted, salt-cured and canned in oil (sold flat and rolled). Canned anchovies can be stored at room temperature for at least a year. Once opened, they can be refrigerated for at least 2 months if covered with oil and sealed airtight. To alleviate saltiness in anchovies, soak them in cool water for about 30 minutes, then drain and pat dry with paper towels. Because they're so salty, anchovies are used sparingly to flavor or garnish sauces and other preparations. *See also* FISH; ANCHOVY PASTE.

anchovy paste This combination of pounded anchovies, vinegar, spices and water comes in tubes and is convenient for many cooking purposes. It can also be used for CANAPÉS.

ancienne, à l' [ah lawn-SYAN] French for "in the old style," describing a traditional preparation method (usually for beef) of braising, then simmering.

andalouse, à l' [ahn-dah-LOOZ] A French term describing dishes using tomatoes, PIMIENTOS and sometimes rice PILAF or sausage. **Andalouse sauce** refers to mayonnaise mixed with tomato purée and pimiento. *See also* SAUCE.

andouille; andouillette [an-DOO-ee; ahn-DWEE; ahn-dwee-YET] A spicy, heavily smoked SAUSAGE made from pork CHITTERLINGS and TRIPE. French in origin, *andouille* is a specialty of CAJUN COOKING. It's traditionally used in specialties like JAMBALAYA and GUMBO, and makes a spicy addition to any dish that would use smoked sausage. Andouille is also good served cold as an HORS D'OEUVRE. **Andouillette**—a smaller version (1 inch or less in diameter) of ANDOUILLE—is a specialty of Normandy. It is sold cooked but not usually smoked. This SAUSAGE is traditionally slashed and grilled or fried.

anelli; anellini; anellone *see* Pasta Glossary, page 883

anesone [AN-uh-sohn; an-uh-SOH-nay] A clear anise-flavored LIQUEUR that is drier and of a higher proof than ANISETTE.

anethol; anthole [AN-eh-thohl] An essential oil found in plants like ANISE, ANISE MYRTLE, FENNEL and STAR ANISE that gives them their distinctive licorice flavor. Anethol is used to flavor liqueurs such as ABSINTHE, ANESONE, ANISETTE and OUZO.

angel food cake A light, airy sponge-type cake made with stiffly beaten egg whites but no yolks or other fats. It's traditionally baked in a TUBE PAN and is sometimes referred to simply as *angel cake*.

angel hair pasta *see* Pasta Glossary, page 883

angelica [an-JEHL-ih-kah] This sweet "herb of the angels" is a member of the parsley family. Grown extensively in Europe, its pale green, celery-like stalks are most often candied and used as decorations for cakes and other desserts. Angelica is also used to flavor LIQUEURS and sweet wines.

angelica powder; angelica seeds *see* GOLPAR

angels on horseback An HORS D'OEUVRE of bacon-wrapped, shucked oysters that are broiled, baked or grilled and served on buttered toast points. *See also* DEVILS ON HORSEBACK.

angel's share The amount of wine or spirit (such as bourbon) that vanishes during barrel AGING when a small portion of the liquid evaporates through the pores of the wood.

anglaise, à l' [ahn-GLEHZ] French for "in the English style," meaning food that is simply poached or boiled. The term can also be used for food that has been coated in breadcrumbs and fried.

angled luffa *see* ASIAN OKRA

angler fish The angler takes its name from the method by which it lures its prey: it lies partially buried on the sea floor and twitches a long filament that grows from its head. The filament resembles a worm and attracts smaller fish that are soon engulfed by the angler's huge mouth. Also known as *monkfish, lotte, bellyfish, frogfish, sea devil* and *goose-fish*, this large, extremely ugly fish is lowfat and firm-textured, and has a mild, sweet flavor that has been compared to lobster. Indeed, shellfish are an important part of the angler's diet. The only edible portions of this impressive fish are the tail, which is suitable for almost any method of cooking, and the liver (*see* ANKIMO). Unfortunately, the angler is being overfished and is now on a list of fishes to avoid. *See also* FISH.

angostura bitters [ang-uh-STOOR-ah] Formulated by German surgeon Johann Gottlieb Benjamin Siegert, who served under Marshall von Blücher at the battle of Waterloo, angostura bitters are the most widely known BITTERS today. Dr. Siegert created the bitter elixir (based on angostura bark, gentian root, rum and other ingredients) as a tonic to stimulate the troops' lagging appetites and improve their health. Although bitters are still taken as a DIGESTIF, angostura bitters are often used today as a flavoring in foods and drinks and are essential in many cocktails such as the MANHATTAN and OLD FASHIONED. At 90 PROOF, angostura bitters are the most potent among this genre.

anice [AH-nee-cheh] Italian for "ANISE."

animal fat Any fat (such as BUTTER, SUET or LARD) that comes from an animal. Because they are almost entirely saturated, animal fats are not recommended for people on lowfat or low-cholesterol diets. *See also* FATS AND OILS.

anise; anise seed; aniseed [AN-ihss] Known as far back as at least 1500 B.C., this small annual plant is a member of the parsley family. Both the leaves and seed have a distinctive, sweet licorice flavor. The greenish brown, oval **anise seed** perfumes and flavors a variety of confections as well as savory dishes. It's also used to flavor drinks such as PASTIS, ARRACK, ANISETTE and OUZO. Anise seeds have been used as a digestive for centuries, and in India they're chewed after a meal not only for digestion but to sweeten breath. Anise seed plays an important role in the cooking of Southeast Asia. Chinese cooks are more likely to use STAR ANISE than the seed. *See also* SPICES; Seasoning Suggestions, page 891.

anise hyssop [AN-ihss HIHS-up] A member of the Agastache genus of the mint family. Also known as *licorice hyssop* or *blue giant hyssop*, the plant produces tall, bluish flower-spikes in late spring and early summer. Anise hyssop's leaves are heart-shaped with serrated edges and have a grayish-green color often shaded with purple. The leaf's flavor is sweet and ANISE-like and the leaves are used to flavor teas and in MARINADES and salads, with vegetables and as a GARNISH. Although the anise hyssop is in the mint family, it's not closely related to HYSSOP; it is, however, closely related to KOREAN MINT.

anise myrtle; aniseed myrtle Australian rainforest tree that produces aromatic leaves containing ANETHOL, which is also found in ANISE and FENNEL and provides their licorice character. Anise myrtle is used as a spice and is cultivated for its oil, which is used as a flavoring agent.

anisette [AN-ih-seht; an-ih-SEHT] A clear, very sweet LIQUEUR made with anise seeds and tasting of licorice.

anitra [AH-nee-trah] Italian for "DUCK."

Anjou pear [AHN-zhoo] A large winter pear with firm flesh and a yellowish-green skin that is often blushed with red. It's sweet and succulent and is delicious both cooked and raw. The Anjou is available in most regions from the fall to the spring. *See also* PEAR.

ankimo [ahn-KEE-moh] The liver of a monkfish (see ANGLER FISH). A Japanese delicacy for centuries, it is becoming a favorite in upscale sushi restaurants. Traditionally ankimo is steamed and served with MOMIJI ORO-SHI, PONZU and scallions. Chefs are now using it in more creative ways, taking care not to overwhelm the delicate flavor. There's growing concern about ankimo's increasing popularity, as monkfish are overfished and have been placed on lists of fish to avoid.

Anna potatoes *see* POMMES ANNA

annatto [uh-NAH-toh] A derivative of ACHIOTE SEED, commercial annatto paste and powder is used to color butter, margarine, cheese and smoked fish. *See also* Food Additives Directory, page 900.

anolini *see* Pasta Glossary, page 883

antelope Currently, the only state that's farming antelopes for human consumption is Texas, where black buck and nilgai antelope are allowed to roam on huge preserves. Antelope meat is similar to that of deer, but leaner. As with other large game, antelope is sometimes sold in markets as venison. *See also* GAME ANIMALS.

antioxidants Substances that inhibit oxidation in plant and animal cells. Culinarily, antioxidants help prevent food from becoming rancid or discolored. In the body, many scientists believe that antioxidants may contribute to reducing cancer and heart disease. Ascorbic acid (vitamin C), which is easily obtained from citrus fruits, is a well known natural antioxidant, as is vitamin E, which is plentiful in seeds and nuts. Antioxidants are also abundant in CRUCIFEROUS VEGETABLES such as broccoli and Brussels sprouts.

antipasto [ahn-tee-PAHS-toh; an-tee-PAST-oh] Literally meaning "before the meal," this Italian term refers to hot or cold HORS D'OEUVRE. An assortment of *antipasti* could include appetizers such as cheese, cured meats, olives, smoked fish and marinated vegetables.

antojitos [ahn-toh-HEE-tohs] In Mexico, the word *antojitos* ("little whims") refers to what Americans call APPETIZERS.

Anzac; Anzac biscuit Hard, sweet biscuit from Australia made with baking soda, butter, coconut, flour, GOLDEN SYRUP, rolled oats and sugar. The name *Anzac* comes from the nickname given to World War I soldiers in the Australian and New Zealand Army Corps.

AOC *see* APPELLATION

ao nori; ao noriko [AH-oh NOH-ree; NOH-ree-koh] Green SEAWEED that's dried and used as seasoning; it's an abundant source of iron. *Ao* *nori* is the flaked version, whereas *ao noriko* is powdered. Both are available in small bottles in Asian markets.

AOP *see* PROTECTED DESIGNATION OF ORIGIN

Apalachicola oyster [ap-uh-lah-chee-KOH-luh] *see* ATLANTIC OYSTER

apee [AY-pee] Dating back to the 1800s, this soft, sour cream–based sugar cookie takes its name from the initials of its creator, Philadelphia cook Ann Page.

apéritif [ah-pehr-uh-TEEF; ay-pehr-ee-TEEF] A light alcoholic drink taken before lunch or dinner. Among the many popular apéritifs are AMER PICON, CHAMPAGNE, DUBONNET, KIR, LILLET and SHERRY.

aperitivo [ah-peh-ree-TEE-voh] Italian for "APÉRITIF."

Aperol [AHP-ehr-ol] A slightly sweet, slightly bitter, low-alcohol Italian APÉRITIF with a spicy orange-rhubarb flavor.

aphrodisiac [af-ruh-DEE-zee-ak] Named for Aphrodite, the Greek goddess of love, aphrodisiacs are substances (including food or drink) that are purported to arouse or increase sexual desire. Among the most widely touted aphrodisiacs are caviar, frog legs, oysters and truffles and, of course, one's imagination.

apio *see* ARRACACHA

à point [ah PWAH] 1. The French term used for food cooked just to the perfect point of doneness. 2. When referring to meat, *à point* means that a steak is cooked rare.

appaloosa bean [ap-pah-LOO-sah] A small, long and narrow dried bean that's white on one end and dark brown with tan streaks on the other. Its name comes from the Appaloosa horse—both horse and bean hail from the Palouse, an area that encompasses southeast Washington and northwest Idaho. *See also* BEANS.

appareil [ah-pah-RAY] In the culinary world, an *appareil* is a mixture (such as a marinade, sauce or frosting) that is prepared in advance and either used separately or as part of another preparation.

appellation [ap-puh-LAY-shuhn; *Fr.* ah-pel-lah-SYAWN] A term describing a designated area for grape-growing or food production, which is controlled by governmental (federal, local or both) rules and regulations regarding how wine or foodstuffs are produced. For wine, this includes such matters as which grape varieties do best in particular climates and soils, viticultural and winemaking practices, allowable yields per acre, alcohol content of the wine, and so on. For food products—cheese, for example—the regulations might dictate which breed of cattle the milk must come from, what type of feed the animals must eat and the minimum fat content for the cheese. Such rules vary from country to country but are analogous in their attempt to stimulate the production of quality wines and foods. Countries with their own appellation systems include France (Appellation d'origine Contrôlée—AOC), Italy (Denominazione di Origine Controllata—DOC), Portugal (Denominação de Origen—DO) and Spain (Denominación de Origen—DO). However, the appellation systems of individual countries are being replaced slowly by those of the European Union (EU). The two most widely used criteria are PROTECTED DESIGNATION OF ORIGIN and PROTECTED GEOGRAPHICAL INDICATION—sets of standards that apply to all EU-member countries. In the United States, foodstuffs are not yet regulated by such "protected name" regulations, but rather only by USDA rules and regulations that apply to how a product is produced. Wine regions in the United States are governed by AMERICAN VITICULTURAL AREA regulations, which are not as restrictive as those for most European appellations.

Appellation d'Origine Contrôlée *see* APPELLATION

Appenzeller [AP-pent-tsehl-ler] This whole-milk cow's CHEESE is named for an eastern Swiss canton (a state in the Swiss confederation). Of the more than 70 Swiss dairies that produce Appenzeller, only three make it with raw milk—the rest use PASTEURIZED. This cheese has a hard rind that ranges in color from pale yellow to golden brown. The interior is ivory to pale yellow with a scattering of irregularly sized EYES. Appenzeller's distinctively spicy, fruity and tangy aroma and flavor are in great part the result of *Sulz,* in which it's initially soaked and with which it receives regular brushings throughout RIPENING. Every cheesemaker has a different *Sulz* recipe (some with as many as 20 ingredients), which can include wine, cider, yeast, herbs, spices and salt. Appenzeller is marketed at three ripening levels: *Classic* (silver label)—3 to 4 months; *Surchoix* (gold label)—4 to 6 months; and *Extra* (black and gold label)—a minimum of 6 months. Appenzeller's FAT CONTENT is at least 48 percent. Reduced-fat versions have a minimum fat content of about 18 percent. They're called *Appenzeller* $1/4$-*Fat Mild* (silver and green label) and *Appenzeller* $1/4$-*Fat Mature* (silver and brown label), the latter being ripened for 6 to 8 months. *See also* CHEESE.

appetizer Any small, bite-size food served before a meal to whet and excite the palate. Used synonymously with the term HORS D'OEUVRE, though this term more aptly describes finger food, whereas **appetizer** can also apply to a first course served at table.

apple Grown in temperate zones throughout the world and cultivated for at least 3,000 years, apple varieties now number well into the thousands. Apples range in color from lemony yellow to bright yellow-green to crimson red. Their textures range from tender to crisp, their flavors from sweet to tart and from simple to complex. They're available year-round but are at their best in the autumn when newly harvested. Buy firm, well-colored apples with a fresh (never musty) fragrance. The skins should be smooth and free of bruises and gouges. SCALD (a dry, tan- or brown-colored area on the skin of an apple) doesn't usually affect its flavor. Apples come 2 to 4 per pound, depending on size. Store apples in a cool, dark place. They do well placed in a plastic bag and stored in the refrigerator. Choose apples by how you intend to use them—for eating raw or cooking. **All-purpose apples**, good for eating raw as well as for cooking include the following: BALDWIN, BRAEBURN, CORTLAND, CRITERION, ELSTAR, FUJI, GALA, GOLDEN DELICIOUS, GRANNY SMITH, GRAVENSTEIN, HONEYCRISP, IDA RED, JONAGOLD, JONATHAN, JUNAMI, LADY ALICE APPLE, LADY APPLE, MACOUN, MCINTOSH, NEWTOWN PIPPIN (also known simply as *pippin*), NORTHERN SPY, PINK LADY, RHODE ISLAND GREENING, STAYMAN WINESAP, WINESAP and YORK IMPERIAL. **For whole baked apples**, the apple of choice is ROME BEAUTY. Other good bakers are Braeburn, Gala, Gravenstein and York Imperial. Apples are a good source of fiber and vitamins A and C. They're also rich in the powerful flavonoid quercetin, which acts as an antioxidant and may prevent some cancers and protect the arteries and heart. Whole fruit is better than apple juice, which loses 80 percent of its quercetin during processing. *See also* CANDIED APPLE; CASHEW APPLE; CRABAPPLE; MAY APPLE; RED DELICIOUS.

apple brandy A generic name for any BRANDY distilled from apples. *See also* APPLEJACK; CALVADOS.

apple brown betty *see* BETTY

apple butter A thick, dark brown PRESERVE of slowly cooked apples, sugar, spices and cider. Used as a spread for breads.

apple cider *see* CIDER

apple corer *see* CORER

apple dumpling *see* DUMPLING

applejack A potent BRANDY made from apple cider and ranging in strength from 80 to 100 PROOF. France is famous for its apple brandy, CALVADOS. In the United States, applejack must spend a minimum of 2 years in wooden casks before being bottled.

apple pandowdy *see* PANDOWDY

apple pear *see* ASIAN PEAR

apple pepper *see* ROCOTO CHILE

applesauce A cooked purée (ranging in texture from smooth to chunky) of apples, sugar and, sometimes, spices.

apricot [AP-rih-kot; AYP-rih-kot] This fruit of ancient lineage has been grown in China for over 4,000 years. It now thrives in most temperate climates, with California producing about 90 percent of the American crop. A relative of the peach, the apricot is smaller and has a smooth, oval pit that falls out easily when the fruit is halved. Throughout the world there are many varieties of apricot, including Riland, Tilton, Blenheim, Royal and Chinese. In color, the skin can range anywhere from pale yellow to deep burnt orange; the flesh from a golden cream color to brilliant orange. Because they're highly perishable and seasonal, 90 percent of the fresh apricots are marketed in June and July. When buying apricots, select plump, reasonably firm fruit with a uniform color. Store in a plastic bag in the refrigerator for up to 3 to 5 days. Depending on size, there are 8 to 12 apricots per pound. **Dried apricots** are pitted, unpeeled apricot halves that have had a large percentage of the moisture removed. They're usually treated with sulfur dioxide to preserve their color. In addition to being rich in vitamin A, dried apricots are a valuable source of iron and calcium. The kernels of the apricot pits are used in confections and to flavor LIQUEURS. Like bitter almonds, apricot kernels are poisonous until roasted. *See also* PLUMCOT.

apricot brandy A generic term for any BRANDY distilled from apricots.

aprium *see* PLUMCOT

Apry [AP-ree] Another name for apricot BRANDY.

A.Q. A menu term meaning "as quoted," referring to generally high-priced dishes (such as lobster), the price of which may vary depending on the season. The server can quote the price of an A.Q. item.

aquaculture [AH-kwah-kuhl-tcher] The cultivation of fish, shellfish or aquatic plants (such as SEAWEED) in natural or controlled marine or freshwater environments. Though aquaculture began eons ago with the ancient Greeks, it wasn't until the 1980s that the practice began to expand rapidly. Aquaculture "farms" take on a variety of forms including huge tanks, freshwater ponds, and shallow- or deep-water marine environments. Today, the farming and harvesting of fish and shellfish is a multimillion-dollar business. Among the most popular denizens of the deep that are farmed are BIVALVES like OYSTERS, CLAMS and MUSSELS; CRUSTACEANS like CRAYFISH, LOBSTERS and SHRIMP; and FISH like CATFISH, SALMON, TROUT and TILAPIA. *See also* HYDROPONICS.

aquavit; akvavit [AHK-wuh-veet] A strong colorless Scandinavian LIQUOR distilled from grain or potatoes and flavored with caraway seed. It is served icy cold and drunk in a single gulp.

aqua vitae [AHK-wuh VEE-tee; AK-wuh VEE-tee] A clear distilled BRANDY; Latin for "water of life." *See also* EAU DE VIE.

aragosta [ah-rah-GOH-stah] Italian for "LOBSTER."

arak [AR-rahk; ah-RAK] 1. A name widely used in Asia and the Middle East for a fiery liquor made, depending on the country, from any of several ingredients including rice, sundry-palm sap and dates. Also spelled *arrack* and *arrak*. **arak; arrack; arrak** 2. A pungently aromatic yet light-bodied RUM from Java.

arame [ah-rah-may] A dried, Japanese SEAWEED that comes in narrow dark brown strands. Arame has a mild, slightly sweet flavor. It can be rehydrated and used in salads or sautéed with vegetables.

arachide [*Fr.* ar-ah-SHEED; *It.* ah-RAH-kee-dee] French and Italian for "peanut."

aram sandwich [A-ruhm; EHR-uhm] A sandwich formed by spreading a softened LAHVASH with cream cheese, then layering thin slices of sandwich fillings such as meat, cheese, lettuce, pickle and so on. This large flat round is then rolled jelly-roll style, wrapped tightly in plastic wrap and refrigerated for several hours. Before being served, the cylinder is cut into about 1-inch thick slices. The aram sandwich is also known as *levant*.

arancia [ah-RAHN-chah] Italian for an "orange."

arancine [ah-rahn-CHEE-neh] A Sicilian specialty of SAFFRON-flavored rice balls stuffed with varying ingredients that can include meat, meat sauce, vegetables (such as peas) and/or cheese. The rice balls are coated with breadcrumbs and usually fried, though they also can be baked. The word *arancine* means "little oranges" and refers to both the shape of the fruit and the orange color from the saffron. Arancine are a popular street food and often used as appetizers. The shape can be round or conical, depending on the region from which they hail. SUPPLI are very similar to arancine.

arapaima *see* PAICHE

Arbequina olive [AHR-beh-keen-nah] Small, round Spanish olive that's brine-cured and ranges from beige to taupe to greenish to dark brown. The Arbequina has a large pit with a modest amount of flesh, which is firm and tasty with a mild smokiness and nutty bitterness. It's named after the town of Arbeca in Catalonia, Spain, where much of the production takes place. These olives are also grown in other parts of Spain and in Australia, California and South America. *See also* SPANISH OLIVES; OLIVE.

Arborio rice [ar-BOH-ree-oh] The high-starch kernels of this Italian-grown grain are shorter and fatter than any other short-grain rice. Arborio is traditionally used for RISOTTO because its increased starch lends this classic dish its requisite creamy texture. *See also* RICE.

archiduc, à l' [ahr-shee-DOOK] A term referring to cooking "in the style of the Archduke." It usually refers to a dish or a garnish cooked with PAPRIKA and cream.

arctic bonito *see* TUNA

ardennaise, à l' [ahr-dehn-NAYZ] A term referring to cooking "in the style of Ardennes," a department in northeastern France. It usually refers to preparations using juniper berries, most often with small game birds or pork.

ardoria *see* SALMOREJO

arepa; arepas [uh-RAY-pah] Popular in Columbia, Venezuela and other Latin American countries, arepas are thick, round corn cakes, sized somewhat like hamburger buns or large ENGLISH MUFFINS. Pre-cooked white or yellow cornmeal is combined with water and salt and sometimes butter, grated cheese and/or egg yolks and then baked, grilled or fried. An arepa is often split in half (sometimes the soft center is pulled out and discarded) and filled with a variety of ingredients much like a sandwich. The fillings can include cheese, deli meats, eggs scrambled with various ingredients, chicken, beef, seafood or beans combined with items like cheese or meat. Sometimes arepas are simply split and spread with butter or cream cheese. They can also be left whole, topped with ingredients and eaten with a knife and fork. **Arepitas** are small versions that are served much like bread or biscuits to accompany meals.

arequipe [ah-ray-KEE-pay] *see* DULCE DE LECHE

Argenteuil, à l' [ar-zhawn-TEW-ee] A term describing a dish featuring asparagus, named after the French town that is world renowned for its asparagus.

arhat fruit *see* LUO HAN GUO

aril; arillus *see* POMEGRANATE

arlésienne, à l' [ahr-loo-ZHE-uhn] A term referring to cooking "in the style of Arles," a city in Provence. It usually refers to garnishes that contain tomatoes and often eggplant but also other ingredients such as olives, onions or chicory, depending on the dish.

Armagnac [ahr-mahn-YAK] One of the world's two great brandies (the other being COGNAC), Armagnac comes from Gascony, near Condom, a town southeast of Bordeaux. It's traditionally distilled once (as opposed to cognac's double distillation) at a relatively low temperature. This single DISTILLATION leaves more flavoring elements and produces a hearty, full-flavored spirit that's silky smooth. Armagnacs are AGED in black oak (for up to 40 years), which imparts more flavor and allows for faster aging than the Limousin used for Cognac. Despite the fact that Armagnac was first made at least 200 years before cognac, the latter outsells Armagnac today by almost seven to one.

arm chops *see* SHOULDER, LAMB

Armenian cracker bread *see* LAHVOSH

aroma In a general sense, aroma refers to a distinctive odor characteristic of a specific liquor, wine or food. In the world of wine, the word "aroma" traditionally refers to the simple fruity smell of the grape variety. In today's broader parlance, many use this term as a synonym for *bouquet,* the complex fragrance that a wine develops through FERMENTATION and AGING, specifically bottle aging. *See also* NOSE.

aromatic *n.* Any of various plants, herbs and spices (such as bay leaf, ginger or parsley) or liquids (such as wine or vinegar) that impart a lively fragrance and flavor to food and drink.

aromatic ginger Rhizome with reddish-brown skin and white flesh found in Indonesia, Malaysia and Thailand. As its scientific name, *Kaempferia galanga*, implies, aromatic ginger is part of the GALANGAL family. It's known by a variety of names in Southeast Asia and China including *cekur, cutchery, kencur, pro hom* and *resurrection lily*. It's very ginger-like with a hot, pungent, peppery quality. Aromatic ginger has limited availability but can be found in some Asian markets, often under the *kencur* name in dried form. This can be confusing since ZEDOARY and **lesser galangal** (SEE GALANGAL) are also sometimes referred to as *kencur*.

aromatic leaf garlic *see* JIMBU

aromatic rice A general term used for rices with a perfumy, nut-like flavor and aroma. Among the more popular aromatic rices are BASMATI (from India), JASMINE (from Thailand), TEXMATI (from Texas), WEHANI and WILD PECAN RICE (from Louisiana). *See also* RICE; RIZCOUS.

arrack; arrak *see* ARAK

arrabbiata [ah-rah-bee-AH-tah] Italian for "angry," referring culinarily to dishes with a spicy sauce of tomatoes, PANCETTA and CHILES.

arracacha [ayr-rah-KAH-chah] A tuber that's cultivated in South America, particularly Brazil. The roots, which look like large, squat carrots, have off-white skin but the dense flesh can be off-white, yellow or purple. They are cooked and eaten much like potatoes and sweet potatoes. The flavor can be compared to a mixture of cabbage, carrot, celery, chestnuts and parsnip. Flour similar to CASSAVA FLOUR is produced by pulverizing the roots. The arracacha is also known as *apio*, *celery potato*, *Peruvian carrot* or *white carrot*.

arrowhead A root vegetable with a crunchy texture and slightly bitter flavor. It's also known as *Chinese potato* and *swamp potato,* the latter name coming from the fact that it's grown under water. Choose roots that are firm and free of blemishes. Refrigerate in a plastic bag for up to 2 weeks; peel before using. Arrowhead is best cooked by braising, boiling or steaming and can also be added to soups.

arrowroot The starchy product of a tropical tuber of the same name. The rootstalks are dried and ground into a very fine powder. Arrowroot is used as a thickening agent for puddings, sauces and other cooked foods, and is more easily digested than wheat flour. Its thickening power is about twice that of wheat flour. Arrowroot is absolutely tasteless and becomes clear when cooked. Unlike cornstarch, it doesn't impart a chalky taste when undercooked. It should be mixed with a cold liquid before being heated or added to hot mixtures. Some British and early American cookie recipes call for *arrowroot flour*, which is the same product. Arrowroot can be found in supermarkets, natural food stores and Asian markets. **Fresh arrowroot**, also called *fung quat*, can sometimes be found in specialty produce markets. It's a misshapen vegetable that can range in size from 1 to 6 inches in diameter. When cooked, it has a nutty, slightly sweet flavor and soft mealy texture.

arroz [ah-ROHS] The Spanish word for "rice."

arroz con leche [ah-RROHS kon LEH-cheh] A Spanish pudding made from rice that's cooked in milk with various flavorings such as vanilla, lemon and cinnamon.

arroz con pollo [ah-ROHS kon POH-yoh] Literally "rice with chicken," this Spanish and Mexican dish is made with rice, chicken, tomatoes, green peppers, seasonings and, sometimes, saffron.

artichoke This edible thistle dates back eons and was prized by ancient Romans as food of the nobility. The word "artichoke" is shared by three unrelated plants: the globe artichoke, SUNCHOKE and CHINESE (or Japanese) ARTICHOKE. The globe artichoke (*Cynara scolymus*) is considered the *true artichoke,* and today, there are over 50 varieties of it grown around the world. In the United States, almost the entire crop is cultivated in California's midcoastal region. In Europe, France, Italy and Spain produce prodigious crops of this illustrious vegetable. The artichoke is actually the flower bud (its leaves tough and petal-shaped) of a large thistle-family plant. The buds grow on stalks, each of which has a primary bud at its tip and two or three smaller buds lower down. Below that are several very small buds, which are marketed as baby or cocktail artichokes, or sold for canning. **Fresh globe artichokes** are available year-round, with the peak season from March through May. They range in size from jumbo (great for stuffing) to baby (good whole for sautéing, frying, roasting or marinating to be used in salads). **Purchase artichokes** that have a tight leaf formation, a deep green color and that are heavy for their size. The leaves should squeak when pressed together. Avoid those that look dry or have split leaves or heavy browning. However, a slight discoloration on the leaf edges early in the season is generally frost damage (winter's kiss) and won't affect the vegetable's quality. In general, the smaller the artichoke the more tender it will be; the rounder it is, the larger its heart. Artichokes are best used the day of purchase but can be stored unwashed in a plastic bag in the refrigerator for up to 4 days; wash just before cooking. **Processed artichoke hearts and bottoms** are available canned (in brine or oil) as well as jars (in an oil marinade). Artichoke hearts are also available frozen. Labeling terms can be confusing—"artichoke crowns," for example, are actually artichoke bottoms, and the terms "hearts" and "bottoms" are sometimes used interchangeably. In actuality, the heart is a portion of the fleshy artichoke base including the attached tender pale leaves; the bottom is the entire base sans leaves. **To prepare whole artichokes for cooking**, slice off the stem to form a flat base. Snap off the tough outer leaves closest to the stem. Trim about 1/2 inch off the pointed top, then use scissors to snip off the prickly tips of the outer leaves. Rub all cut edges with lemon to prevent discoloration. It's easier to remove the fuzzy choke (use a teaspoon) after cooking, but it can also be done beforehand. Soaking artichokes in ACIDULATED WATER for an hour before cooking will improve their color and tenderness. **Cook artichokes** in stainless steel, glass or enamelware only (*see* COOKWARE AND BAKEWARE MATERIALS) to prevent discoloration and off-flavors. Artichokes are done when the bottoms can be pierced with a knife tip. Cooked artichokes may be covered and refrigerated for up to 3 days. **To eat a whole cooked artichoke**, break off the leaves one by one and draw the base of the leaf through your teeth to remove the soft portion, discarding the remainder of the leaf. The individual leaves may be dipped into melted butter or some other sauce. After the leaves have been removed, the inedible prickly choke is cut or scraped away and discarded so the tender base is accessible. Artichokes contain small amounts of potassium and vitamin A and absolutely no fat. *See also* POIVRADE.

artificial sweeteners This category of nonnutritive, high-intensity sugar substitutes includes ACESULFAME-K, ASPARTAME, NEOTAME, SACCHARIN and SUCRALOSE.

artisanal [ar-TIH-zen-ahl] This term implies that a food or beverage has been primarily handmade and produced in small batches by traditional, predominantly non-mechanical methods. Superior fresh, natural and local ingredients and attention to detail and excellence are all part of the artisan tradition. This results in products that resound of homemade goodness and quality. Among the many artisanal creations found in markets today are breads, cheeses, jams, oils, sausages and vinegars. *See also* FARMSTEAD.

arugula [ah-ROO-guh-lah] Also known as *Italian cress, rocket, roquette, rugula* and *rucola,* arugula is a bitterish, aromatic salad green with a peppery mustard flavor. Though it has long been extremely popular with Italians, American palates often find its flavor too assertive. Arugula (which resembles radish leaves) can be found in specialty produce markets and in most supermarkets. It's sold in small bunches with roots attached. The leaves should be bright green and fresh looking. Arugula is very perishable and should be tightly wrapped in a plastic bag and refrigerated for no more than 2 days. Its leaves hold a tremendous amount of grit and must be thoroughly washed just before using. Arugula makes a lively addition to salads, soups and sautéed vegetable dishes. It's a rich source of iron as well as vitamins A and C.

asadero [ah-sah-DEH-roh; ah-sah-THEH-roh] A white cow's-milk CHEESE of Mexican origin, made by the PASTA FILATA process and available in braids, balls or rounds. Asadero, which means "roaster" or "broiler," has good melting properties and becomes softly stringy when heated—very similar to an unaged MONTEREY JACK CHEESE. It's also sometimes referred to as *Oaxaca,* after the Mexican state where it originated.

asafetida; asafoetida [ah-sah-FEH-teh-dah] A flavoring obtained from a giant fennellike plant that grows mainly in Iran and India. It's used in many Indian dishes and can be found in powdered or lump form in Indian markets. Asafetida has a fetid, garlicky smell and should be used in very small quantities.

asam laksa *see* LAKSA

ascorbic acid [as-KOHR-bihk] The scientific name for vitamin C, ascorbic acid is sold for home use to prevent browning of vegetables and fruits. It's used in commercial preparations as an ANTIOXIDANT.

aseptic packaging [uh-SEHP-tihk; a-SEHP-tihk] A system of packaging food and drink products so the contents are exposed to a minimal amount of air; such products are typically vacuum-packed. Because oxygen is the major contributor to spoilage in most foods, aseptic packaging can retain a product's freshness for several months, even years. Milk, juices, chopped tomatoes and even inexpensive wines are packaged aseptically in plastic bags within cartons or boxes. The bags collapse as the contents are poured out, keeping the remaining food or drink relatively free of air contamination.

ash Cheesemakers have long used ash coatings to protect and dry a cheese's exterior, to promote RIPENING and sometimes simply as a stylish accent. Ash is used most often with cheeses made of goat's milk (see CHÈVRE). Though traditionally made from burned grapevines and roots, ash today is more commonly a powdered mix of charcoal and salt. Vegetable ash is made from dried vegetables reduced to ash.

ashak see AUSHAK

ash pumpkin; ash gourd see WINTER MELON

ashta [ahsh-TAH] Middle Eastern version of CLOTTED CREAM. Ashta is sometimes made with milk thickened with cornstarch and possibly breadcrumbs. Sweetened versions contain sugar and often ROSE WATER or ORANGE-FLOWER WATER.

ashure; ashura see ASURE

Asiago [ah-SYAH-goh] Hailing from Italy, Asiago has a rich flavor that can be pleasantly sharp in aged versions. It takes its name from *L'Altopiano di Asiago* ("the Asiago Plateau"), which is located in the foothills of Italy's Veneto region. It's made from whole or partially skimmed cow's milk, which may be PASTEURIZED or raw. Depending on the age of the cheese, the rind ranges from elastic and straw-colored to hard and brownish gray, and the interior from semisoft and ivory-colored to hard and deep gold. All Asiago has small to medium EYES. Other countries, including the United States, produce Asiago. American versions come in three styles: fresh (a soft whole-milk cheese aged for 2 to 4 months); medium (made with slightly skimmed milk and aged for at least 6 months); and aged (more heavily skimmed milk, ripened a minimum of 1 year). Young Asiago is used as a table cheese; aged over a year, it becomes hard and suitable for grating. *See also* CHEESE.

Asian basil *see* BASIL

Asian celery Said to have grown wild in Asia and the Middle East for centuries, this vegetable resembles an elongated bunch of common CELERY—but its stalks are slimmer, the leaves dark green and parsleylike. Asian celery can be found in some specialty produce markets. Choose firm stalks with no sign of browning. Store airtight in the refrigerator for up to 1 week. May be used fresh or cooked, the same as common celery.

Asian noodles Though some Asian-style NOODLES are wheat-based, many others are made from ingredients such as rice flour, potato flour, buckwheat flour, cornstarch and bean, yam or soybean starch. Among the more popular are China's CELLOPHANE NOODLES (made from mung-bean starch), egg noodles (usually wheat-based) and RICE NOODLES, and Japan's HARUSAME (made with soybean, rice or potato flour), RAMEN (wheat-based egg noodles) and SOBA (which contain buckwheat flour). Other Asian countries, including Korea, Indonesia, Thailand, Vietnam and the Philippines, have their own versions of the venerable noodle. Asian noodles can be purchased fresh and dried in Asian markets; some dried varieties can be found in supermarkets. Throughout Asian cultures noodles are eaten hot and cold. They can be cooked in a variety of ways including steaming, STIR-FRYING and deep-frying.

Asian okra Unrelated to common okra, this long, narrow vegetable has a tough, dark green skin with lengthwise ridges and a soft, off-white flesh with a mild flavor. Select Asian okra that is firm and unblemished. Refrigerate for up to 1 week; peel just before using in STIR-FRIES, soups or curry dishes. Asian okra is also known as *angled luffa, silk gourd* and *vegetable sponge*.

Asian pear There are over 100 varieties (most of them grown in Japan) of this firm, amazingly juicy pear whose season is late summer through early fall. In size and color, they range from huge and golden brown to tiny and yellow-green. In general, ripe Asian pears are quite firm to the touch, crunchy to the bite (unlike the European varieties we're used to), lightly sweet and drippingly juicy. The most common Asian pear in the United States is the Twentieth Century (also known as *nijis-seiki*), which is large, round and green to yellow in color. Ripe Asian pears should be stored in the refrigerator. Also called *apple pear*, *Chinese pear*, *Japanese pear* and *Nashi*. See also PEAR.

asopao [ah-soh-PAH-oh] Spanish for "soupy," *asopao* is the Puerto Rican version of PAELLA. This soupy stew is flavored with the Spanish staple SOFRITO and typically includes chicken, meat or seafood (or a combination of the three), rice and various vegetables, such as onions, bell peppers and tomatoes.

asparago [ah-SPAH-rah-goh] Italian for "ASPARAGUS."

asparagus This universally popular vegetable is one of the lily family's cultivated forms. The optimum season for fresh asparagus lasts from February through June, although it's available year-round in some regions. The earliest, most tender stalks are a beautiful apple green with purple-tinged tips. Europeans prefer white asparagus (particularly the famous French asparagus of Argenteuil), which is grown underground to prevent it from becoming green. White spears are usually thick and are smoother than the green variety. There's also a purple variety called *Viola*. When buying asparagus, choose firm, bright green (or pale ivory) stalks with tight tips. Asparagus plants live 8 to 10 years and the spear's size indicates the age of the plant from which it came—the more mature the plant, the thicker the asparagus. It's best cooked the same day it's purchased but will keep, tightly wrapped in a plastic bag, 3 to 4 days in the refrigerator. Or, store standing upright in about an inch of water, covering the container with a plastic bag. Asparagus is grown in sandy soil so thorough washing is necessary to ensure the tips are not gritty. If asparagus stems are tough, remove the outer layer with a vegetable peeler. Canned and frozen asparagus is also available. Asparagus contains a good amount of vitamin A and is a fair source of iron and vitamins B and C.

asparagus bean *see* YARD-LONG BEAN

asparges *see* RATTE

aspartame [ah-SPAHR-taym; AS-pahr-taym] An ARTIFICIAL SWEETENER that's 180–200 times sweeter than sugar. It's synthesized from two AMINO ACIDS (aspartic acid and phenylalanine), the building blocks of protein, and contains about 4 calories per gram. Regular aspartame breaks down and loses its sweetness when heated but is excellent for sweetening cold dishes. A new encapsulated (and therefore heat-stable) form of this sweetener has been developed especially for baking. At this writing, however, it's not available to consumers. *See also* ACESULFAME-K; ALITAME; NEOTAME; SACCHARIN; SUCRALOSE.

asperge [ah-SPEHRZH] French for "ASPARAGUS."

aspic [AS-pihk] A savory jelly, usually clear, made of CLARIFIED meat, fish or vegetable stock and GELATIN. Tomato aspic, made with tomato juice and gelatin, is opaque. Clear aspics may be used as a base for molded dishes, or as glazes for cold dishes of fish, poultry, meat and eggs. They may also be cubed and served as an accompaniment relish with cold meat, fish or fowl.

assaisonné [ah-say-zoh-NAY] French for "seasoned" or "seasoned with."

Assam tea [as-SAHM] Hailing from India's Assam district, this black tea produces a strong-flavored, full-bodied brew with a reddish tinge. *See also* TEA.

ASTA pungency units *see* GILLETT METHOD

Asti Spumante [AH-stee spoo-MAHN-teh] A sweet sparkling white wine generally served as a DESSERT WINE but sometimes as an APÉRITIF. Asti Spumante tastes decidedly of the MUSCAT GRAPE from which it's made. It hails from the area around the town of Asti in the Piedmont region of northern Italy.

asure; aşure [ah-SHOO-ray] Popular Turkish dessert made with a wide variety of ingredients such as barley, beans, chickpeas, fresh and dried fruits, nuts, rice, sugar and wheat—there are numerous variations. It's also spelled *ashure* and *ashura* and known as *Noah's pudding*. Turks prepare asure to commemorate the story of Noah and his ark, which is believed to have come to rest on Mount Ararat in Turkey as the great flood subsided. The interesting mix of ingredients represents the sparse food items that Noah had left at the end of his travail.

ataïf *see* ATAYEF

Atalanta; Atalanti olive (PDO) [aht-tah-LAN-duh] Named for the town of Atalanti in eastern Greece, this medium-large, round, green-ish-gray to purplish-brown olive has a soft fleshy texture. It's brine-cured and has a full earthy flavor that's slightly tart. Atalanta olives enjoy PDO status. *See also* OLIVE.

atayef [ah-TAY-if] Small Middle Eastern pancake that's filled with either sweet or savory ingredients. Only one side is cooked on a griddle, allowing the other side to remain porous. In one version the edges of the porous side are pressed together at one end, leaving an opening at the other end where a filling is inserted. Another version positions the filling on an open pancake, which is folded and completely sealed to form a half-round; it's then deep-fried. Sweet ingredients include sweetened walnuts or a clotted cream called *ashta*. A sweet atayef is usually served with syrup containing ROSE WATER or ORANGE-FLOWER WATER. Savory versions usually contain cheese. Atayef is also spelled *ataif*, *katayef* and *qatayef*.

atemoya [ah-teh-MOH-ee-yah] Though cultivated in Florida, this cross between CHERIMOYA and SWEETSOP is a native of South America and the West Indies. About the size of a large BELL PEPPER, the atemoya has a tough dusty green skin that has a rough petal configuration. The custard-like pulp is cream-colored and studded with a smattering of large black seeds. Its delicate, sweet flavor tastes like a blend of mango and vanilla. Atemoyas are in season from late summer through late fall. Though they often split slightly at their stem end when ripe, it's best to buy them when they're pale green and tender with unbroken skin. The fruit can continue to ripen at room temperature at home. Refrigerate ripe atemoyas 3 to 5 days. They're best served chilled. Simply halve the fruit, spoon out the pulp and enjoy. Atemoyas are high in potassium and vitamins C and K.

atkaru *see* PACIFIC THREADFIN

Atlantic croaker *see* DRUM

Atlantic oyster Also called *Eastern oyster,* this species has a thick, elongated shell that ranges from 2 to 5 inches across. It's found along the Atlantic seaboard and the Gulf of Mexico and is considered ideal for serving ON THE HALF SHELL. Atlantic oysters are sold under different names depending on where they're harvested. The most well known is the BLUEPOINT; others include **Apalachicola**, **Cape Cod**, **Chesapeake**, **Chincoteague**, **Indian River**, **Kent Island**, **Malpeque** and **Wellfleet**. *See also* OYSTER.

atole [ah-TOH-leh] Said to date back to pre-Columbian times, atole is a very thick beverage that's popular in Mexico and some parts of the American Southwest. It's a combination of MASA, water or milk, crushed fruit and sugar or honey. Latin markets sell instant atole, which can be mixed with milk or water. Atole can be served hot or at room temperature.

aubergine [oh-behr-ZHEEN] French for "eggplant."

au bleu [oh-BLEUH] The French term for the method of preparing fish the instant after it's killed. Used especially for trout, as in *truite au bleu,* where the freshly killed fish is plunged into a boiling COURT-BOUILLON, which turns the skin a metallic blue color.

au gratin [oh-GRAH-tn; oh-grah-TAN] *see* GRATIN.

au jus [oh-ZHOO] A French phrase describing meat served with its own natural juices, commonly used with beef. *See also* JUS.

au lait [oh-LAY] French for "with milk," referring to foods or beverages served or prepared with milk, as in CAFÉ AU LAIT.

au naturel [oh-nah-teur-EHL] The French term for food served in its natural state—not cooked or altered in any way.

aurore sauce [oh-ROHR] BÉCHAMEL SAUCE with just enough tomato purée added to tint it pink. *See also* SAUCE.

Aurum [OW-rum] A BRANDY-based, orange-flavored Italian LIQUEUR.

aushak [ah-SHAK] An Afghan dish, also spelled *ashak*, consisting of dumplings filled with chives, leeks and/or scallions topped with a meat and tomato sauce, yogurt and dried mint.

Auslese [OWS-lay-zuh] The German word for "selection," used in the wine trade to describe specially selected, perfectly ripened bunches of grapes that are hand-picked, then pressed separately from other grapes. The superior wine made from these grapes is sweet and expensive. *See also* BEERENAUSLESE; SPÄTLESE; TROCKENBEERENAUSLESE.

australus [aw-STRAY-lyus] *see* KANGAROO

Auvergne [oh-VEHRN] *see* BLEU D'AUVERGNE

aux champignon *see* CHAMPIGNON

avgolemono [ahv-goh-LEH-moh-noh] A Greek soup as well as a sauce, both of which are made from chicken broth, egg yolks and lemon juice. The main difference is that the soup has rice added to it. The sauce is thicker than the soup.

avocado [a-voh-KAH-doh] Native to the tropics and subtropics, this rich fruit is known for its lush, buttery texture and mild, faintly nutlike flavor. The fruit's name comes from *ahuacatl,* the Nahuatl word for "testicle," which is assumed to be a reference to the avocado's shape. Florida was the site of the first U.S. avocado trees in the 1830s but almost 80 percent of today's crop comes from California. Known early on as *alligator pear,* the many varieties of today's avocado can range from round to pear-shaped. The skin can be thick to thin, green to purplish black and smooth to corrugated. The flesh is generally a pale yellow-green and softly succulent. The two most widely marketed avocado varieties are the pebbly textured, almost black **Hass** and the green **Fuerte**, which has a thin, smooth skin. Depending on the variety, an avocado can weigh as little as 3 ounces and as much as 4 pounds. There are even tiny Fuerte **cocktail avocados** (also called AVOCADITOS) that are the size of a small GHERKIN and weigh about 1 ounce. Like many fruits, avocados ripen best off the tree. Ripe avocados yield to gentle palm pressure, but firm, unripe avocados are what are usually found in the market. Select those that are unblemished and heavy for their size. To speed the ripening process, place several avocados in a paper bag and set aside at room temperature for 2 to 4 days. Ripe avocados can be stored in the refrigerator several days. Once avocado flesh is cut and exposed to the air it tends to discolor rapidly. To minimize this effect it is always advisable to add cubed or sliced avocado to a dish at the last moment. When a dish containing mashed avocado, such as GUACAMOLE, is being prepared, the addition of lemon or lime juice helps to prevent discoloration. (It is not true that burying the avocado pit in the guacamole helps maintain good color.) Avocados are at their buttery best in raw preparations; cooking them longer than a few minutes diminishes their delicate flavor and can turn them bitter. Though avocados are high in unsaturated fat, the California Avocado Advisory Board states that half of an 8-ounce avocado contains only 138 calories. In addition, avocados contain a fair amount of vitamin C, thiamine and riboflavin.

avocadito [a-voh-kah-DEE-toh] Another name for the cocktail AVOCADO.

awabi [ah-WAH-bee] *see* ABALONE

Awamori *see* SHOCHU

ayam [ah-YAM] Indonesian for "chicken." SOTO ayam is a spicy chicken soup turned yellowish-orange from the infusion of TURMERIC and containing rice cakes or noodles. RENDANG ayam is a dish with chicken that's slowly cooked in coconut milk and various spices. LEMPER AYAM is an Indonesian snack food with chicken. AYAM PENYET is a fried chicken dish.

ayam penyet [ah-YAM pehn-yeht] Popular Indonesian dish of marinated chicken that's fried and then lightly smashed to loosen the meat from the bones. It is usually served with SAMBAL, TEMPEH and various vegetables.

ayran [AH-rahn] Hailing from Turkey, ayran is a refreshing, non-sweetened yogurt drink popular throughout the Middle Eastern world. It's typically a mixture of plain yogurt, water and salt. Some versions are flavored with garlic or mint. Ayran is called *abdug* in Iran and *than* in Armenia.

azeite [ah-ZAY-tee] Portuguese for "olive oil."

azeitona [ah-ZAY-toh-nah] Portuguese for "olive."

azúcar [ah-SOO-kar] Spanish for "sugar."

azufrado bean [ah-zoo-FRAH-doh] *see* PERUANO BEAN

azuki-an [ah-ZOO-kee-ahn] **An** is the generic term in Japan for sweet pastes made from a variety of legumes combined with sugar. Asuki-an, the most common sweet paste, is made from ASUKI BEANS and is used in a variety of Japanese sweets. There are two common types of azuki-an; **koshi-an**, which is a smooth paste, and **tsubu-an**, which has bits of bean in the paste.

azuki bean; adzuki bean [ah-ZOO-kee; AH-zoo-kee] A small, dried, russet-colored bean with a sweet flavor. Azuki beans can be purchased whole or powdered at Asian markets. They are particularly popular in Japanese cooking where they're used in confections such as the popular YOKAN, made with azuki-bean paste and AGAR. *See also* BEANS.

B & B A topaz-colored amalgam of BÉNÉDICTINE and BRANDY. This spicy, herbal LIQUEUR offers the best of both spirits in flavor and texture and is more like a flavored BRANDY because it's relatively DRY.

baba [BAH-bah] Also called *baba au rhum*, this rich, light currant- or raisin-studded yeast cake is soaked in a rum or KIRSCH syrup. It's said to have been invented in the 1600s by Polish King Lesczyinski, who soaked his stale KUGELHOPF in rum and named the dessert after the storybook hero Ali Baba. The classic baba is baked in a tall, cylindrical **baba mold** but the cake can be made in a variety of shapes, including small individual rounds. When the cake is baked in a large ring mold it's known as a SAVARIN.

babáco [buh-BAH-koh] Indiginous to Ecuador, this natural PAPAYA hybrid is torpedo shaped and has five flattened facets. When sliced cross-wise, the facets give this exotic fruit a pentagonal outline. Babácos range from 8 to 12 inches long and are about 4 inches in diameter. The edible skin turns from green to golden yellow as it ripens. The riper and softer the fruit, the more flavorful it is. The rich flavor of the extremely fragrant babáco is a cross between banana and pineapple, though not as sweet as either. The juicy, creamy white flesh has a texture similar to that of a CASABA MELON. The hard-to-find babáco is sometimes available in specialty produce markets. It will ripen quickly at room temperature, especially if placed in a brown paper bag. Refrigerate ripe fruit and use as soon as possible. Babáco is best eaten raw. It contains triple the amount of PAPAIN as the papaya and is a good source of vitamins A and C.

baba ghanoush; ghanouj [bah-bah gah-NOOSH] A Middle Eastern purée of eggplant, TAHINI, olive oil, lemon juice and garlic. It's garnished with pomegranate seeds, chopped mint or minced pistachios and used as a spread or dip for PITA or Middle Eastern FLATBREAD.

babka [BAHB-kah] A rum-scented, Polish sweet yeast bread studded with almonds, raisins and orange peel.

baby red hubbard squash *see* RED KURI

BAC; BAL *see* BLOOD ALCOHOL CONCENTRATION

bacalao [bah-kah-LAH-oh] The Spanish term for dried salt cod. *See also* SALTFISH.

Bacardi [bah-KAHR-dee] A variation of the daiquiri, the Bacardi is a classic cocktail that combines light rum, fresh lime juice and grenadine. A court ruling in 1936 declared that it was illegal to make this cocktail with any rum other than Bacardi, but who's going to tell?

baccalà [bah-kah-LAH] The Italian term for dried salt cod. *See also* SALTFISH.

back bacon *see* CANADIAN BACON

Bäckerei [BAY-kah-ri] German for "bakery."

Backpflaume [BAHK-pflow-meh] German for "prune."

back of the house In the restaurant business, this term refers to the kitchen area and staff and all the related goings-on (delivery and so on) that the public doesn't typically see. Conversely, the **front of the house** describes a restaurant's public areas, which would include dining room, bar and banquet room. *See also* BRIGADE SYSTEM.

bacon Side pork (the side of a pig) that has been CURED and smoked. Because fat gives bacon its sweet flavor and tender crispness, its proportion should ideally be ¹/₂ to ²/₃ of the total weight. **Sliced bacon** has been trimmed of rind, sliced and packaged. It comes in thin slices (about 35 strips per pound), regular slices (16 to 20 per pound) or thick slices (12 to 16 per pound). **Slab bacon** comes in one chunk that must be sliced and is somewhat cheaper than presliced bacon. It usually comes complete with rind, which should be removed before cutting. Bits of diced fried rind are called CRACKLINGS. **Bacon grease**, the fat rendered from cooked bacon, is highly prized—particularly in the southern United States—as a cooking fat. **Canned bacon** is precooked, needs no refrigeration and is popular with campers. **Bacon bits** are crisp pieces of bacon that are preserved and dried. They must be stored in the refrigerator. There are also VEGETABLE PROTEIN–based **imitation "bacon-flavored" bits**, which may be kept at room temperature. *See also* CANADIAN BACON; PANCETTA.

bacterial-ripened cheeses *see* SOFT-RIPENED CHEESES

badderlocks *see* ALARIA

bagatelle [bag-ah-tehl-AH] 1. French for "trifle," referring to a dessert resembling the English-originated TRIFLE. 2. A French sponge cake, also known as *fraisier* (meaning "strawberry"), incorporating CRÈME DIPLOMAT and strawberries sliced lengthwise, which are artfully arranged along the bottom edge with the cut side facing out.

bagel [BAY-guhl] A doughnut-shaped yeast roll with a dense, chewy texture and shiny crust. Bagels are boiled in water before they're baked. The water bath reduces starch and creates a chewy crust. The traditional **water bagel** is made without eggs and, because it doesn't contain fat, is chewier than an **egg bagel**. Bagels are the cornerstone of the popular Jewish snack of bagels, lox and cream cheese. Miniature cocktail-size bagels can be split, topped with a spread and served as an HORS D'OEUVRE.

bagna cauda (caôda) [BAHN-yah KOW-dah] This specialty of Piedmont, Italy, is a sauce made of olive oil, butter, garlic and anchovies. It's served warm as an appetizer with raw vegetables for dipping. The term comes from *bagno caldo,* Italian for "hot bath." *See also* SAUCE.

bagoong [bah-GOONG] A Philippine CONDIMENT that's popular in Hawaii and throughout the Pacific. Bagoong is made from shrimp or small fish that have been salted, cured and fermented for several weeks. The resulting salty liquid (called *patis*) is drawn off and used separately as a sauce or condiment. In addition to being served as a condiment, bagoong is used as a flavoring in many dishes. *See also* FISH SAUCE; SHRIMP SAUCE.

baguette; baguette pan [bag-EHT] A FRENCH BREAD that's been formed into a long, narrow cylindrical loaf. It usually has a crisp brown crust and light, chewy interior. A **baguette pan** is a long metal pan shaped like two half-cylinders joined along one long side. Each compartment is 2 to 3 inches wide and 15 to 17 inches long. This pan is used to bake French baguettes.

bahmi goreng [bah-MEE goh-REHNG] *see* NASI GORENG

bai horapa [BI hor-rah-pah] *see* BASIL

bainiku [BAH-nee-koo] *see* UMEBOSHI

bain-marie [bahn mah-REE] *see* WATER BATH

bai tong [BI tong] Thai for "BANANA LEAVES." Bai tong are used to wrap foods for steaming, roasting and boiling.

bake To cook food in an oven, thereby surrounding it with dry heat. It's imperative to know the accurate temperature of an oven. Because most of them bake either hotter or cooler than their gauges read, an OVEN THERMOMETER is vital for accurate temperature readings.

bake-apple berry *see* CLOUDBERRY

bake blind A term for baking a pastry shell before it is filled. The shell is usually pricked all over with a fork to prevent it from blistering and rising. Sometimes it's lined with foil or PARCHMENT PAPER, then filled with dried beans or rice, or metal or ceramic PIE WEIGHTS. The French sometimes fill the shell with clean round pebbles. The weights and foil or parchment paper should be removed a few minutes before the baking time is over to allow the crust to brown.

baked Alaska A dessert consisting of a layer of SPONGE CAKE topped by a thick slab of ice cream, all of which is blanketed with MERINGUE. This creation is then baked in a very hot oven for about 5 minutes, or until the surface is golden brown. The meringue layer insulates the ice cream and prevents it from melting.

baker's peel *see* PEEL

bakers' cheese Basically COTTAGE CHEESE with some of the moisture drained off. Bakers' cheese has a texture similar to that of fresh RICOTTA, but with a slightly tangier flavor. It typically isn't available to consumers—most of it is sold for commercial preparations such as blintzes, cheesecakes, pastries and pies. *See also* CHEESE.

bakeware *see* BABA; BAGUETTE; BAKING PANS; BAKING SHEET; BAKING STONE; BRIOCHE; BUNDT PAN; CAKE PANS; CATS' TONGUES PAN; CHARLOTTE; CORNSTICK PAN; CLOCHE; COOKWARE AND BAKEWARE MATERIALS; CRUMPET; FLAN; GEM PAN; JELLY ROLL PAN; KUGELHOPF; LADYFINGER; LOAF PAN; MADELEINE; MUFFIN PAN; PANETTONE; PEEL; PIE PANS; PIZZA PAN; PLETT PAN; POPOVER; PULLMAN PAN; QUICHE; RING MOLD; SPRING-FORM PAN; STEAMED PUDDING MOLD; TART PAN; TUBE PAN; Pan Substitution Chart, page 859. *See also* COOKWARE.

baking To cook food with dry heat, as in an oven. Baked foods include everything from bread to potatoes to meatloaf. The primary difference between baking and roasting is that the latter is typically done at higher heats, requires fat and isn't covered.

baking ammonia, powdered *see* AMMONIUM BICARBONATE

baking pans *see* BAKEWARE

baking powder A LEAVENER containing a combination of baking soda, an acid (such as CREAM OF TARTAR) and a moisture-absorber (such as cornstarch). When mixed with liquid, baking powder releases carbon dioxide gas bubbles that cause a bread or cake to rise. There are three basic kinds of baking powder. The most common is **double-acting**, which releases some gas when it becomes wet and the rest when exposed to oven heat. **Single-acting tartrate** and **phosphate baking powders** (hard to find in most American markets because of the popularity of double-acting baking powder) release their gases as soon as they're moistened. Because it's perishable, baking powder should be kept in a cool, dry place. Always check the date on the bottom of a baking-powder can before purchasing it. To test if a baking powder still packs a punch, combine 1 teaspoon of it with $\frac{1}{3}$ cup hot water. If it bubbles enthusiastically, it's fine.

baking sheet A flat, rigid sheet of metal on which cookies, breads, biscuits, etc. are baked. It usually has one or more turned-up sides for ease in handling. Shiny, heavy-gauge aluminum baking sheets are good heat conductors and will produce evenly baked and browned goods. Dark sheets absorb heat and should be used only for items on which a dark, crisp exterior is desired. **Insulated baking sheets** (two sheets of aluminum with an air space sealed between them) are good for soft cookies or bread crusts, but many baked goods will not get crisp on them. Cookies and breadstuffs may burn on lightweight baking sheets. To alleviate this problem, place one lightweight sheet on top of another for added insulation. For even heat circulation, baking sheets should be at least 2 inches smaller all around than the interior of the oven.

baking soda Also known as *bicarbonate of soda,* baking soda is an ALKALI used as a LEAVENER in baked goods. When combined with an acid ingredient such as buttermilk, yogurt or molasses, baking soda produces carbon dioxide gas bubbles, thereby causing a dough or batter to rise. It also neutralizes acidity and produces tender baked goods. Because it reacts immediately when moistened, it should always be mixed with the other dry ingredients before adding any liquid; the resulting batter should be placed in the oven immediately. At one time, baking soda was used in the cooking water of green vegetables to preserve their color. That practice was discontinued, however, when it was discovered that baking soda destroys the vitamin C content of vegetables.

baking stone A heavy, thick, flat round or rectangular plate of stone used to duplicate the baking qualities of the brick floors of some commercial bread and pizza ovens. A baking (or *pizza*) stone has a high heat retention and even heat distribution, and it absorbs moisture. Place it on the lowest oven shelf and preheat with the oven. The item to be baked is then placed directly on the stone in the oven. Dough-filled pans or baking sheets may be placed on the stone for a crisper, browner crust. When not in use, the stone can be left in the oven.

baklava [BAHK-lah-vah; bahk-lah-VAH] Popular in Greece and Turkey, this sweet dessert consists of many layers of butter-drenched PHYLLO pastry, spices and chopped nuts. A spiced honey-lemon syrup is poured over the warm pastry after it's baked and allowed to soak into the layers. Before serving, the dessert is cut into triangles and sometimes sprinkled with coarsely ground nuts.

balachan; blachan [BAHL-ah-shahn] A popular flavoring in the cuisines of Southeast Asian countries such as Malaysia, Burma and Indonesia. It is made from shrimp, sardines and other small salted fish that have been allowed to ferment in the sun until very pungent and odorous. It's then mashed and in some cases dried. Balachan is available in paste, powder or cake form in Asian markets.

baldino *see* CASTAGNACCIO

baldo rice [BAL-doh] A short-grain rice that's slightly smaller and a bit stickier than the more famous ARBORIO RICE but of similar high quality. Baldo rice is used to make creamy RISOTTO and has also become a favorite in Turkish cuisine. It's grown in the United States in small amounts and is available in Italian markets and through the Internet. *See also* RICE.

Baldwin apple A good all-purpose apple with red skin streaked with yellow. It has a fairly crisp texture and a flavor that's mildly sweet-tart with a slight spicy note. *See also* APPLE.

balloon chile *see* BISHOP'S CROWN CHILE

ballotine; ballottine [bal-loh-TEEN] Meat, fish or fowl that has been boned, stuffed, rolled and tied in the shape of a bundle. It is then braised or roasted and is normally served hot but can be served cold. Often confused with GALANTINE, which is poached and served cold.

balm *see* LEMON BALM; BEE BALM

baloney *see* BOLOGNA

balsamella [bal-sah-MEHL-ah] Italian for "BÉCHAMEL."

balsamic vinegar [bal-SAH-mihk] *see* VINEGAR

balsam pear *see* BITTER MELON

Balthazar [bal-THAY-zuhr] *see* WINE BOTTLES

bamboo shoot The tender-crisp, ivory-colored shoot of a particular edible species of bamboo plant. Bamboo shoots are cut as soon as they appear above ground while they're still young and tender. Fresh shoots are sometimes available in Asian markets and specialty produce markets and can be found at farmer's markets in the spring and summer. Canned shoots (sliced or whole) can be found in the Asian or gourmet section of most supermarkets.

banana Grown in the warm, humid tropics, bananas are picked and shipped green; contrary to nature's norm, they are one fruit that develops better flavor when ripened off the bush. Banana bushes mature in about 15 months and produce one 50-pound bunch of bananas apiece. Each bunch includes several "hands" of a dozen or so bananas (fingers). There are hundreds of banana species but the yellow, arched **Cavendish** (or *common*) banana is America's favorite. Choose plump, evenly colored yellow bananas flecked with tiny brown specks (a sign of ripeness). Avoid those with blemishes, which usually indicate bruising. Bananas that are still greenish at the tips and along the ridges will need further ripening at home. To ripen, keep uncovered at room temperature (about 70°F). For speedy ripening, enclose bananas in a perforated brown paper bag.

Ripe bananas can be stored in the refrigerator for several days. The peel will turn brown but the flesh will remain unchanged. Once exposed to air, a peeled banana will begin to darken. To avoid discoloration, brush with lemon juice or dip in ACIDULATED WATER. Now available in some markets are the squat, squarish 3- to 5-inch-long **Burro**, with its tangy lemon-banana flavor; the **Blue Java** (or **Ice Cream**) **banana**, which has a blotchy, silver-blue skin and tastes of ice cream; the **Guinea Verde**, which—like the plaintain—is more starchy than sweet; the chunky, 6-inch-long **red banana**, which turns bronzy brown when ripe; the **baby**, **dwarf** or **finger banana**, which is 3 to 4 inches long and sweeter than the Cavendish; the strawberry-apple-flavored **Manzano** (which turns black when ready to eat); the diminutive **Mysore** from India; and the **Orinoco** with its trace of strawberry flavor. The **plantain** (also called *plátano*), a very large, firm variety, is also referred to as a "cooking banana" and is extremely popular in Latin American countries as well as parts of Africa, Asia and India. Its skin ranges in color from green to yellow to brownish black, its flesh from cream to salmon-colored. Whereas the sweet banana is eaten ripe, the plantain is typically cooked when green. It has a mild, almost squashlike flavor and is used very much as a potato would be, in a vegetable side dish. If it's allowed to ripen, the plantain has a slightly sweet flavor and a soft, spongy texture when cooked. Bananas are high in carbohydrates and low in protein and fats; they're also rich in potassium and vitamin C. *See also* BANANA FLOUR; BANANA LEAVES.

banana chile *see* HUNGARIAN WAX CHILE

banana flour A nutritious and easily digestible powder made from specially selected bananas that have been dried and ground.

banana leaves The large, pliable leaves of the banana plant, used in the cooking of Mexico, Central and South America, the Caribbean and Southeast Asia to wrap food (rice, vegetables, meat or fish) to be baked or steamed. Banana leaves are available in Latin and Asian markets. Choose fresh looking leaves with no signs of browning. Refrigerate, tightly wrapped in a plastic bag, for up to 1 week; freeze for up to 6 months. Rinse the leaves well before using and cut out the leaf's spine. Soften by dipping into boiling water. The leaves may then be cut into appropriate-size portions before wrapping food.

banana pepper *see* SWEET PEPPERS

bananas Foster Created at New Orleans's Brennan's Restaurant in the 1950s, this dessert consists of lengthwise-sliced bananas quickly sautéed in a mixture of rum, brown sugar and banana LIQUEUR and served with vanilla ice cream. It was named for Richard Foster, a regular Brennan's customer.

banana split A dessert made of a banana cut in half lengthwise and placed in an individual-size bowl (preferably oblong). The banana is topped with three scoops of ice cream (traditionally chocolate, vanilla and strawberry), over which sweet syrups are poured (usually chocolate, butterscotch and marshmallow). The entire concoction is topped with rosettes of whipped cream and a MARASCHINO CHERRY.

banana squash A large oval-shaped winter squash with skin that ranges in color from pale tan to light red-orange and flesh that's orange to golden. It ranges from 2 to 3 feet long and is often cut and sold in pieces. It can be baked, steamed or simmered. Banana squash is available year round, although its peak season is from August to October.

bandaging; bandaged A technique that involves lining cheese molds or hoops with CHEESECLOTH or MUSLIN. Once the CURDS are added to the mold, the cloth is folded over the top of the cheese, which protects the cheese from drying out and helps retain its shape. It's not usually removed until the cheese has fully ripened (*see* RIPENING).

banger British slang for a number of sausages originally made of ground pork and breadcrumbs, though beef bangers are also now available.

banh hoi *see* RICE NOODLES

banh mi [bahn mee] Although *bahn mi* is the Vietnamese term for "bread," it usually has a more specific meaning, referring to a light, fluffy BAGUETTE and sometimes to the sandwiches made using it. This French-influenced baguette has a thin, crunchy crust that's a result of not only how it's baked but also the addition of RICE FLOUR, which supplements the wheat flour that has to be imported. Tangy banh mi sandwiches are gaining popularity throughout the United States. As with most sandwiches, there are myriad variations but the banh mi again shows the French influence by often using chicken liver or pork liver PÂTÉ spread on one side of the sandwich. The Southeast Asian influence is represented by the use of spicy sauces, chiles, herbs and seasonings and items like pickled DAIKON.

banneton [BAN-tahn] A French, cloth-lined woven basket in which bread is allowed to rise before being baked.

bannock [BAN-nuhk] Baked on a griddle, this traditional Scottish cake is usually made of BARLEY meal and oatmeal. Bannocks are sometimes flavored with almonds and orange peel and are particularly popular at breakfast or HIGH TEA. A version of bannock known as *Indian bread* or *frybread* is popular with American Indian tribes such as the First Nations people of Canada, the Inuit/Eskimo tribes of Alaska and Canada, and American Indian tribes in the United States. These versions are usually made with white or whole-wheat flour and are sometimes wrapped around a green stick and cooked over an open fire instead of a griddle.

Banon; Le Banon [ba-NON; bah-NAWN] A French cheese named after a town in northern Provence and traditionally produced with raw goat's milk, though PASTEURIZED versions are made with cow's, goat's or sheep's milk or blends of these milks. Banon is classically wrapped in chestnut leaves that have been soaked in MARC, white wine or vinegar water; the leaves are secured with raffia. Some versions are not wrapped in leaves but rather seasoned with herbs; others are coated with black pepper. Banon is sold in small rounds. The thin, off-white rind can develop light blue and gray mold as the cheese ripens; the interior is white. Banon cheeses are typically ripened for 2 to 3 weeks but sometimes for up to 2 months. They have a soft to semisoft texture and a mildly milky, lightly tangy flavor. The FAT CONTENT of Banon is about 45 percent. *See also* CHEESE.

ban pho [ban FOH] *see* RICE NOODLES

Banyuls vinegar [bah-NYUHLS] *see* VINEGAR

bap [bahp] 1. A soft yeast roll with a characteristic floury finish. Baps are popular in Scotland as hot breakfast rolls. 2. Commonly used in Korea to mean "cooked rice."

bar *see* BASS

barack Made of apricots, this Hungarian EAU DE VIE has a distinctive flavor somewhere between apricots and SLIVOVITZ.

barbacoa [bar-bah-KOH-ah] A traditional form of Mexican barbecue whereby meat is wrapped in fragrant leaves (such as maguey or banana) and cooked over hot coals in a covered pit in the ground. This slow cooking process both roasts and steams the meat while imparting a smoky quality. Pigs, goats and lambs are often cooked this way, and a specialty of northern Mexico called *barbacoca de cabeza* ("head") refers to a cow's head prepared in this manner.

Barbados cherry [bar-BAY-dohs] *see* ACEROLA

Barbados sugar *see* SUGAR

Barbaresco [bar-bah-RESS-koh] A premier Italian red wine from the Piedmont region. Barbaresco wines are made from NEBBIOLO grapes and must be aged a minimum of 2 years. They have rich, spicy flavors and are considered more elegant and refined than the more robust BAROLO wines, which are also from the Nebbiolo grapes.

barbecue; barbeque *n.* 1. Commonly referred to as a GRILL, a barbecue is generally a BRAZIER fitted with a grill and sometimes a spit.

The brazier can range anywhere from a simple firebowl, which uses hot coals as heat, to an elaborate electric barbecue. 2. Food (usually meat) that has been cooked using a barbecue method. 3. A term used in the United States for an informal style of outdoor entertaining where barbecued food is served. **barbecue** *v.* A method of cooking by which meat, poultry or fish (either whole or in pieces) or other food is covered and slowly cooked in a pit or on a spit, using hot coals or hardwood as a heat source. The food is basted, usually with a highly seasoned sauce, to keep it moist. North Carolina and Texas boast two of the most famous American regional barbecue styles.

barbecue sauce A sauce used to BASTE barbecued meat; also used as an accompaniment to the meat after it's cooked. It is traditionally made with tomatoes, onion, mustard, garlic, brown sugar and vinegar; beer and wine are also popular ingredients. *See also* SAUCE.

Barbera [bar-BEH-rah] Italian red wine grape that can produce excellent wine with a flavor redolent of ripe currants with a smoky nuance. Grapes from very hot growing areas have less flavor and produce wines with a higher alcohol content, which makes them better for blending with wines produced from other varieties. Noteworthy Barbera wines come from the Italian regions of Barbera d'Alba, Barbera d'Asti, Barbera del Monferrato, Colli Toronesi and Rubino di Cantavenna.

barberry Native throughout most of Europe and also grown in New England, the barberry has elongated bright red berries which, because of their high acidity, are seldom eaten raw. Some varieties produce white or yellow fruit. Ripe barberries are used in pies, preserves and syrups; they can also be candied. Green berries are sometimes pickled and used as a relish.

bar cookie A cookie made by spooning a batter or soft dough into a baking pan. The mixture is baked, cooled in the pan and then cut into bars, squares or diamonds. *See also* COOKIE.

bard To tie fat, such as bacon or fatback, around lean meats or fowl to prevent their drying out during roasting. Barding is necessary only when natural fat is absent. The barding fat bastes the meat while it cooks, thereby keeping it moist and adding flavor. The fat is removed a few minutes before the meat is done to allow the meat to brown.

barfi; burfi [BAHR-fee; BUR-fee] An Indian sweet made from milk, sugar and sometimes other flavoring ingredients such as nuts, fruit, seeds (cardamom, for example) and even vegetables like carrots. The milk mixture is cooked and condensed to the texture of creamy fudge. If cooked quickly the barfi will be white; cooked slowly, the sugars will caramelize, darkening the mixture to a golden brown.

barigoule; a la barigoule [bah-ree-GOOL] A traditional Provençal dish of artichokes braised with onions, garlic and carrots in a seasoned broth of wine and water. Originally the term *barigoule* referred to artichokes stuffed with barigoules, wild mushrooms also known as *saffron milk cap* or *Lactarius deliciosus*. Modern adaptations don't typically employ mushrooms, and the versions that do don't always include them as a filling. Then again, some "barigoule" preparations stuff the braised artichokes with other ingredients, such as spinach, carrots and cheese.

barista [bah-REES-tah] One who works at an ESPRESSO machine creating espresso-based drinks, such as CAPPUCCINOS and CAFFÈ LATTES. Many baristas undergo extensive training to earn a certificate in the art.

Bar-le-Duc [bar-luh-DOOK] A choice currant PRESERVE that originally came from the French town of Bar-le-Duc in Lorraine. The preserve was once made from white currants whose tiny seeds were removed manually. Today it's made with red and white currants as well as other berry fruits, and the seeds are not generally removed by hand.

barley This hardy grain dates back to the Stone Age and has been used throughout the eons in dishes ranging from cereals to breads to soups (such as the famous SCOTCH BROTH). Most of the barley grown in the Western world is used either for animal fodder or, when malted, to make beer and whiskey. **Hulled** (also called *whole-grain*) **barley** has only the outer husk removed and is the most nutritious form of the grain. **Scotch barley** is husked and coarsely ground. **Barley grits** are hulled barley grains that have been cracked into medium-coarse pieces. Hulled and Scotch barley and barley grits are generally found in natural food stores. **Pearl barley** has also had the bran removed and has been steamed and polished. It comes in three sizes—coarse, medium and fine—and is good in soups and stews. When combined with water and lemon, pearl barley is used to make **barley water**, an old-fashioned restorative for invalids. **Barley flour** or **barley meal** is ground from pearl barley and must be combined with a gluten-containing flour for use in yeast breads.

barm brack; barmbrack [BAHRM-brak] An Irish bread with raisins or currants and candied fruit peel. It's generally slathered with butter and served as a tea accompaniment. Literally translated it means "yeast bread," although it's not always made with yeast.

barnacles Marine CRUSTACEANS (not MOLLUSKS, as many think) of the subclass *Cirripedia* that form calcareous shells. Barnacles attach themselves to submerged surfaces such as rocks, ship bottoms, wharves, pilings and even whales and large fish. The most common of the barnacle species are the small **acorn barnacles**. They have whitish, cone-shaped shells with overlapping plates. Acorn barnacles are what one most often sees clinging to pilings and ships. More culinarily valued are the **gooseneck** (or *goose*) **barnacles**, which are known as *stalked barnacles*. The colorful "gooseneck" name purportedly comes from a medieval myth that said when barnacles grew to a certain size, they would fall off of the piling, pier or whatever object to which they were attached and into the water, at which point they would transform into geese. Gooseneck barnacles are particularly popular fare along the coasts of Morocco, Portugal and Spain, where they're quite plentiful. Because these barnacles attach themselves to ships, they have traveled to all parts of the world. The dark brown shell of the gooseneck is not hard like other species of barnacle, but rather more like a strong, leathery skin that surrounds a pinkish-white, fleshy tubelike neck (the edible portion). At the barnacle's apex is a cluster of white calcareous plates. Gooseneck barnacles are now being farmed in the state of Washington. They can be found in some specialty fish markets. Before cooking barnacles, thoroughly rinse them, rubbing gently to dislodge any sand. Most recipes call for quick cooking, either by boiling, steaming or grilling. Barnacles may be served hot, cold or at room temperature, usually with a simple embellishment of melted butter or any sauce commonly used for other crustaceans. To eat, peel off the outer skin, then bite off the neck. When removing the skin, a soupçon of orange (fabric-staining) liquid sometimes spurts out, so be cautious. The flavor of barnacles is compared variously to that of crab, lobster or shrimp.

Barolo [bah-ROH-loh] From the Piedmont region, this exceptional Italian red wine, made from Nebbiolo grapes, is known for its lush BOUQUET and robust BODY.

baron 1. In England, a large cut of beef (50 to 100 pounds, depending on the size of the animal) usually consisting of a double SIRLOIN. A baron of beef is generally roasted only for traditional or ceremonial occasions. 2. In France, a baron refers to the saddle and two legs of lamb or mutton.

Barossa Valley [bah-RAH-suh; bah-ROH-suh] This important Australian wine-producing region is located in the state of South Australia about 40 miles northeast of Adelaide. Vines were first planted in the Barossa in 1847, and over the years it's become one of Australia's best-known wine regions. Among the more successful white grapes in this region are CHARDONNAY, RIESLING and SÉMILLON. Shiraz (SYRAH)—with some vines dating back to the mid-1800s—is the most successful red grape, followed by CABERNET SAUVIGNON, GRENACHE and Mataro (MOURVÈDRE).

barquette [bahr-KEHT] A boat-shaped pastry shell that can contain a savory filling (when served as an appetizer) or a sweet filling (for a dessert).

barracuda [behr-ah-KOO-dah] The type most commonly found in American markets is the **Pacific barracuda** (also called **California barracuda**), which usually ranges from 4 to 8 pounds. It's a firm-textured fish with a moderate fat content and is best grilled or broiled. Barracuda can be substituted for WAHOO or MAHI MAHI. The **great barracuda**, whose flesh is often toxic, can weigh over 100 pounds and can exceed 6 feet in length. *See also* FISH.

Bartlett pear This large bell-shaped fruit has a smooth, yellow-green skin that is sometimes blushed with red. The Bartlett's flesh is sweet and juicy. It's generally available in the fall and winter and is delicious either cooked or raw. Developed in 18th-century England, it was introduced to America by Dorchester, Massachusetts, resident Enoch Bartlett. *See also* PEAR.

basil [BAY-zihl; BA-zihl] Called the "royal herb" by ancient Greeks, this annual is a member of the mint family. Fresh basil has a pungent flavor that some describe as a cross between licorice and cloves. It's a key herb in Mediterranean cooking, essential to the delicious Italian PESTO, and is becoming more and more popular in American cuisine. Most varieties of basil have green leaves, but one—**opal basil**—is a beautiful purple color. **Lemon basil**, **anise basil**, **clove basil** and **cinnamon basil** have green leaves but their perfumy fragrance and flavor matches their respective names. *Bai horapa* is the basil variety generally used in Southeast Asian cooking. It's commonly known in the West as *Thai basil* or *Asian basil* and differs from the basil variety used in Mediterranean cooking, which is often referred to as *common sweet basil*. Bai horapa has a more pronounced anise flavor, and the leaves are smaller, deep green and sit on purple-hued stems. Bai horapa is sometimes called *licorice basil* but this is actually a different variety. Basil is a summer herb but can be grown successfully inside during the winter in a sunny window. It's plentiful during summer months, and available year-round in many markets. Choose evenly colored leaves with no sign of wilting. Refrigerate basil, wrapped in barely damp paper towels and then in a plastic bag, for up to 4 days. Or store a bunch of basil, stems down, in a glass of water with a plastic bag over the leaves. Refrigerate in this manner for up to a week, changing the water every 2 days. To preserve fresh basil, wash and dry the leaves and place layers of leaves, then coarse salt, in a container that can be tightly sealed. Alternatively, finely chop the cleaned basil and combine it with a small amount of olive oil or water. Freeze in tiny portions to flavor sauces, salad dressings, etc. Dried basil, though it bears little resemblance in either flavor or aroma to the fresh herb, can be purchased in the spice section of most supermarkets. Store dried basil airtight in a cool, dark place for up to 6 months. *See also* HERBS; Seasoning Suggestions, page 891.

B

basilico [bah-SEE-lee-koh] Italian for "basil."

basil seeds [BAY-zihl; BA-zihl] Seeds of certain varieties of BASIL that, when soaked in water, swell and become gelatinous. Basil seeds are used in numerous Asian and Indian subcontinent drinks and desserts.

basket cheese Any of the various white, mild cheeses that are molded in a basket. These cheeses are generally SOFT to SEMISOFT and are marked with the imprint of the basket weave.

basmati rice [bahs-MAH-tee] Literally translated as "queen of fragrance," basmati has been grown in the foothills of the Himalayas for thousands of years. Its perfumy, nutlike flavor and aroma can be attributed to the fact that the grain is aged to decrease its moisture content. Basmati is a long-grained RICE with a fine texture. It can be found in Indian and Middle Eastern markets and some supermarkets. *See also* KAIJIRA RICE.

bass A general term for any of numerous (often unrelated) freshwater or saltwater fish, many of which are characterized by spiny fins. In fact, though many of these different species are often sold simply as bass, the only fish with the single name "bass" is a European species (unavailable in the United States), which in France is known as *bar* or *loup*. True basses include the GROUPERS, BLACK SEA BASS and STRIPED BASS. Among other fish that are commonly referred to as bass are the **largemouth**, **redeye**, **rock**, **smallmouth** and **spotted bass**, all of which are really members of the SUNFISH family. *See also* SEA BASS; FISH.

bastard saffron *see* SAFFLOWER OIL

baste To spoon or brush food as it cooks with melted butter or other fat, meat drippings or liquid such as stock. A BULB BASTER can also be used to drizzle the liquid over the food. In addition to adding flavor and color, basting keeps meats and other foods from drying out. Fatty roasts, when cooked fat side up, do not need basting.

bastela; bastila; bastilla *see* B'STEEYA

bâtarde [bah-TAHRD] Literally translated as "bastard," culinarily *batarde* refers to a traditional white loaf of bread that's slightly larger than a BAGUETTE.

batata [bah-TAH-tah] *see* BONIATO

Bath bun Said to have originated in the English town of Bath in the 18th century, this sugar-coated yeast bun is studded with candied fruit and currants or golden raisins.

B

Bath chaps This British specialty is the lower portion of a pig's cheeks, which are CURED somewhat like bacon. Chaps must come from a long-jawed pig rather than the flat-headed species. Though quite fatty, Bath chaps are served cold in the same way as ham, often with eggs. They can also be referred to simply as *chaps*. The name is assumed to have come from the original reputation of the chaps made in Bath, England. *See also* VARIETY MEATS.

batido [bah-TEE-doh] A Latin American drink made with water, fresh fruit pulp, a little milk, ice and, sometimes, sugar. A **merengada** is the same drink made with milk and no water; a **jugo** is the same but with water and no milk.

baton; batonnet [ba-TAWN; ba-tawn-NAY] 1. Culinarily, this French word describes a white loaf of bread that's somewhat smaller than a BAGUETTE. 2. The term can also refer to various small, stick (baton) shaped foods—such as vegetables or pastries—that may or may not have a filling.

batter An uncooked, semiliquid mixture (thick or thin) that can be spooned or poured, as for cakes, muffins, pancakes or waffles. Batters are usually mixtures based on flour, eggs and milk. They can also be used to coat food before frying, as in batter-fried chicken.

batter bread A yeast bread that is formed without KNEADING. It begins with a very thick batter that often requires extra yeast and, in order to stretch the GLUTEN so the bread will rise effectively, always demands vigorous beating (which can be accomplished with an electric mixer). The mixture should be stiff enough for a spoon to stand up in. A batter bread's texture won't be as refined as that of a bread that has been kneaded but the results are equally delicious.

batterie de cuisine [bat-TREE duh kwih-ZEEN] The French term for the cooking equipment and utensils necessary to equip a kitchen.

Bauerwurst [BOW-er-werst; BOW-er-versht] A coarse-textured German SAUSAGE that is smoked (*see* CURE) and highly seasoned. It's usually steamed or sautéed.

Baumkuchen [BOWM-koo-khehn] A German specialty dubbed the "king of cakes," Baumkuchen is particularly popular at Christmastime. This tall dessert is comprised of many thin cake layers that resemble a tree's growth rings. Baumkuchen translates as "tree (*baum*) cake (*kuchen*)." It takes a master baker to make this labor-intensive cake in the traditional way, which is to spoon a SPONGE CAKE batter over a revolving oven spit, one layer at a time, browning each layer before adding the next. Today, other pans are sometimes used; one method is to brush a thin layer of batter onto the bottom of a SPRINGFORM PAN, bake it for 2 to 3 minutes, then brush on another layer of batter and bake, and so on. Baumkuchen is traditionally enrobed in a thin chocolate glaze, though vanilla or other flavors may be used.

bavarese [ba-vah-REH-zeh] Italian for "BAVARIAN CREAM."

Bavarian cream A cold dessert composed of a rich CUSTARD, whipped cream, various flavorings (fruit purée, chocolate, LIQUEURS and so on) and GELATIN. The mixture may be spooned into stemmed glasses or into a decorative mold to be unmolded when set.

bavarois [bah-vah-*R*WAH] French for "BAVARIAN CREAM."

bavette d'aloyau *see* FLAP MEAT

bavettine *see* Pasta Glossary, page 883

bay leaf Also called *laurel leaf* or *bay laurel,* this aromatic herb comes from the evergreen bay laurel tree, native to the Mediterranean. Early Greeks and Romans attributed magical properties to the laurel leaf and it has long been a symbol of honor, celebration and triumph, as in "winning your laurels." The two main varieties of bay leaf are Turkish (which has 1- to 2-inch-long oval leaves) and Californian (with narrow, 2- to 3-inch-long leaves). The Turkish bay leaves have a more subtle flavor than do the California variety. Bay leaves are used to flavor soups, stews, vegetables and meats. They're generally removed before serving. Overuse of this herb can make a dish bitter. Fresh bay leaves are seldom available in markets. Dried bay leaves, which have a fraction of the flavor of fresh, can be found in supermarkets. Store dried bay leaves airtight in a cool, dark place for up to 6 months. *See also* HERBS; INDIAN BAY LEAF; INDONESIAN BAY LEAF; Seasoning Suggestions, page 891.

Bayonne ham [bay-YOHN] A mildly smoked ham that has been CURED in a wine mixture. It's produced in a small town near Bayonne, France. *See also* HAM.

bazina *see* KATSAMAKI

beach plum A wild, dark purple plum found growing in sandy soil along the Atlantic coast. Its flavor is reminiscent of a grape-plum cross but because it's quite tart and bitter, the beach plum is not good for out-of-hand eating. It makes superior jams and jellies, however, as well as a delicious condiment for meats. *See also* PLUM.

bêche-de-mer [behsh-duh-MEHR] *see* SEA CUCUMBER

beadlet *see* SEA ANEMONE

bean curd *see* TOFU

bean flakes Dried BEANS that have been steamed and flattened to hasten cooking time; available in natural food stores.

Beano *see* DIGESTIVE ENZYMES

bean paste *see* BEAN SAUCES; BEAN PASTES

beans These seeded pods of various LEGUMES are among the oldest foods known to humanity, dating back at least 4,000 years. They come in two broad categories—fresh and dried. Some beans, such as the BLACK-EYED PEA, LIMA BEAN and CRANBERRY BEAN, can be found in both fresh and dried forms. **Fresh beans** are commercially available in their fresh form and are generally sold in their pods. The three most commonly available fresh-bean varieties are the GREEN BEAN (eaten with its shell or pod), and the lima bean and FAVA (or broad) BEAN, both of which are eaten shelled. Store fresh beans in a tightly covered container in the refrigerator for up to 5 days; after that, both color and flavor begin to diminish. If cooked properly, fresh beans contain a fair amount of vitamins A and C; lima beans are also a good source of protein. **Dried beans** are available prepackaged or in bulk. Some of the more popular dried beans are the BLACK BEAN, CHICK-PEA, KIDNEY BEAN, PINK BEAN and PINTO BEAN. Dried beans must usually be soaked in water for several hours or overnight to rehydrate them before cooking. Beans labeled "quick-cooking" have been presoaked and redried before packaging; they require no presoaking and take considerably less time to prepare. The texture of these "quick" beans, however, is not as firm to the bite as regular dried beans. Store dried beans in an airtight container for up to a year. **Gas and beans:** The flatulence caused by dried beans is created by oligosaccharides, complex sugars that—because they're indigestible by normal stomach enzymes—proceed into the lower intestine where they're eaten (and fermented) by friendly bacteria, the result of which is gas (*see* DIGESTIVE ENZYMES). Dried beans are rich in protein, calcium, phosphorus and iron. Their high protein content, along with the fact that they're easily grown and stored, make them a staple throughout many parts of the world where animal protein is scarce or expensive. *See also* APPALOOSA BEAN; AZUKI BEAN; BEAN FLAKES; BEAN SAUCES; BEAN PASTES; BORLOTTI BEAN; CALYPSO BEAN; CANNELLINI BEAN; CHANNA DAL; CHRIST-MAS LIMA; COCO BLANC BEANS; DAL; FAGIOLINI; FERMENTED BLACK BEANS; FRENCH BEAN; FRENCH NAVY BEANS; GREAT NORTHERN BEAN; HARICOT BEANS; JACOB'S CATTLE BEAN; MARROW BEAN; MOTH BEAN; MUNG BEAN; NAVY BEAN; PEA BEAN; PERUANO BEAN;

PIGEON PEA; RATTLESNAKE BEAN; RED BEAN; RUNNER BEAN; SOYBEAN; SPROUTS; WHITE BEAN; WINGED BEAN; YARD-LONG BEAN.

bean sauces; bean pastes Seasonings made from fermented SOYBEANS and used in many Asian cuisines including Chinese, Korean and Vietnamese cookery. Bean sauces and pastes can range from thin to thick; some are smooth but others contain whole beans. These intensely flavored mixtures are used to enhance the flavor of many dishes. **Black bean sauce** is a thin, salty, full-flavored mixture made with mashed FERMENTED BLACK BEANS and flavored with garlic and, sometimes, STAR ANISE. **Hot black bean sauce** has a medium consistency and is a combination of black beans, CHILES, garlic, sesame oil and sugar. **Brown bean sauce** is thick and made with fermented yellow soybeans. **Sweet bean paste** is made with fermented soybeans and sugar, is quite thick, and has a sweet-salty flavor. Bean sauces and pastes can be found in Asian markets. They should be stored in a non-metallic, tightly sealed container in the refrigerator for up to a year. *See also* CHILE BEAN PASTE; HOISIN SAUCE; MISO.

bean sprouts *see* SPROUTS

bean threads *see* CELLOPHANE NOODLES

beard The common name for the *byssus*, or silky hairlike filaments that BIVALVES (such as OYSTERS and MUSSELS) use to attach themselves to rocks, piers, and so on.

béarnaise [behr-NAYZ] A classic French sauce made with a REDUCTION of vinegar, wine, tarragon and shallots and finished with egg yolks and butter. Béarnaise is served with meat, fish, eggs and vegetables. *See also* SAUCE.

beat To stir rapidly in a circular motion. Generally, 100 strokes by hand equals about 1 minute by electric mixer.

beaten biscuit A traditional Southern biscuit that dates back to the 1800s. Whereas most biscuits are soft and light, beaten biscuits are hard and crisp. The classic texture is obtained by beating the dough for 30 to 45 minutes until it becomes blistered, elastic and smooth. The beating may be done with a mallet, rolling pin, the flat side of a cleaver . . . any heavy object that will pound the dough into submission. One can also use an old-fashioned beaten-biscuit machine, a contraption with wooden or metal rollers reminiscent of an old-time clothes wringer. The dough is passed through the rollers, which are operated by a hand crank. This method takes no less time but saves on the wear and tear of the baker. After the dough is beaten, it is rolled out, cut into small circles and pricked with the tines of a fork before being baked.

Beaufort (AOC; PDO) [boh-FOR] hard cow's-milk cheese named after Beaufort, a small town in the department of Savoie in France's alpine region. The cheese, which may only be made in the Savoie and Haute-Savoie departments in the Rhône-Alpes region in eastern France, was well known in ancient Roman times and has continued to be popular over the centuries. Only Tarentaise cows' milk is used. Beaufort cheeses are soaked in brine for about a day and aged for a minimum of 4 months. The large 40- to 150-pound wheels develop thin, hard, golden-brown rinds and off-white to pale yellow interiors with small holes and cracks. Beaufort cheeses are firm and supple with mild, buttery, fruity and nutty flavors that become more complex as they age. There are two special versions: **Beaufort d'Été** ("from summer"), which is made from June to October, and **Beaufort d'Alpage** ("of mountain pasture"), made only in the summer in mountain chalets. Beaufort cheeses have a FAT CONTENT of approximately 48 percent. *See also* CHEESE.

Beaujolais [boh-zhuh-LAY] Light and dry, this fruity red wine comes from a hilly region in southern Burgundy. **Beaujolais Nouveau** is new wine, bottled right after fermentation without aging. It's very light and fruity and should be drunk within a few months.

bebida [bay-BEE-dhah] Spanish for "drink" or "beverage."

becadulce *see* PACIFIC THREADFIN

béchamel [bay-shah-MEHL; BEH-shah-mehl] Also called by its Italian name, *balsamella,* this basic French white sauce is made by stirring milk into a butter-flour ROUX. The thickness of the sauce depends on the proportion of flour and butter to milk. The proportions for a thin sauce would be 1 tablespoon each of butter and flour per 1 cup of milk; a medium sauce would use 2 tablespoons each of butter and flour; a thick sauce, 3 tablespoons each. Béchamel is one of the four original "mother sauces" (*see* SAUCE). The sauce is sometimes flavored with ONION PIQUÉ and a hint of NUTMEG. It was named after its inventor, Louis XIV's steward Louis de Béchamel. *See also* SAUCE.

bee balm Native to North America, this herb has spicy, citrus-like leaves, often used to make a tea called *Oswego tea*. In addition to *Oswego tea*, bee balm is also known as *bergamot* because of its aromatic similarity to the BERGAMOT orange. Fresh leaves and flowers are also used to flavor salads as well as meats and poultry. Bee balm falls under the genus *Monarda*, named after Spanish physician Nicolas Monardes, who wrote a book on New World plants in the 16th century. *Wild bee balm*, also called *horsemint*, is one of the species in the *Monarda* grouping. It doesn't have the delicate nature of the cultivated versions and is used mostly for medicinal purposes. *See also* LEMON BALM.

beech mushroom A very popular mushroom in Japan that is now cultivated in the United States. There are two versions, the white beech mushroom (also known as *bunapi-shimeji* and *white clamshell mushroom*) and the brown beech mushroom (also known as *buna-shimeji* and *brown clamshell mushroom*). Both are members of the scientific classification *Hypsizygus tessellatus.* Colors range from white to brown and stems range from 2 to 3 inches with small, thin caps on them. Beech mushrooms can be bitter in their raw state and blanching or cooking is recommended to draw out the flavor, which is sweet and mild and somewhat herbal and nutty. The name comes from wild versions found growing on beech trees. The beech mushroom, a member of the SHIMEJI family, was initially sold as HONSHIMEJI, but this turned out to be a different species. Look for solid examples, avoiding any with broken or shriveled caps. *See also* MUSHROOM.

beef Beef, the meat of an adult (over 1 year) bovine, wasn't always as popular as it is today. America has had cattle since the mid-1500s, but most immigrants preferred either pork or chicken. Shortages of those two meats during the Civil War, however, suddenly made beef attractive and very much in demand. Today's beef comes from cows (females that have borne at least one calf), steers (males castrated when very young), heifers (females that have never borne a calf) and bulls under 2 years old. **Baby beef** is the lean, tender but not too flavorful meat of a 7- to 10-month-old calf. Meat packers can request and pay for their meat to be graded by the U.S. Department of Agriculture (USDA). The grading is based on three factors: conformation (the proportion of meat to bone), finish (proportion of fat to lean) and overall quality. Beginning with the best quality, the eight USDA grades for beef are Prime, Choice, Select, Standard, Commercial, Utility, Cutter and Canner. The meat's grade is stamped within a purple shield (a harmless vegetable dye is used for the ink) at regular intervals on the outside of each carcass. USDA Prime and the last three grades are rarely seen in retail outlets. Prime is usually reserved for fine restaurants and specialty butcher shops; the lower-quality grades are generally only used for sausages and in cured and canned meats. Ideally, beef is at its best—both in flavor and texture—at 18 to 24 months. The meat at that age is an even rosy-red color. If the animal is over $2\frac{1}{2}$ years old it is usually classified as "well-matured beef" and, though more full-flavored, the meat begins to toughen and darken to a purplish red. Slow, moist-heat cooking, however, will make it perfectly delicious. *To store fresh beef:* If the meat will be cooked within 6 hours of purchase, it may be left in its plastic-wrapped package. Otherwise, remove the packaging and either store unwrapped in the refrigerator's meat compartment or wrap loosely with waxed paper and keep in the coldest part of the refrigerator for up to 2 days for GROUND BEEF, 3 days for other cuts. The object is to let the air circulate and keep the meat's surface somewhat dry, thereby inhibiting rapid bacterial growth. Cooked meat should be wrapped airtight and stored in the refrigerator. Ground beef can be frozen, wrapped airtight, for up to 3 months, solid cuts up to 6 months. *See also* BARON; BRAINS; BRISKET; CHUCK; CLUB STEAK; DELMONICO STEAK; ENTRECÔTE; FILET MIGNON; FLANKEN; FLANK STEAK; FLAP MEAT; HANGER STEAK; HEART; KIDNEY; KOBE BEEF; LIVER; LONDON BROIL; MINUTE STEAK; NEW YORK STEAK; NOISETTE; PORTERHOUSE STEAK; POT ROAST; PRIME RIB; RIB; RIB ROAST; RIB STEAK; ROUND; SHANK; SHELL STEAK; SHORT LOIN; SHORT RIBS; SIRLOIN; SKIRT STEAK; SWEETBREADS; T-BONE STEAK; TONGUE; TRIPE; VARIETY MEATS; VEAL; and Beef Chart, page 896.

beef à la mode [BEEF ah lah MOHD] A dish made by LARDING a piece of beef (such as a beef ROUND), marinating it for several hours in a red wine/brandy mixture before BRAISING it. The beef is sliced very thin and served with a sauce made from the MARINADE. The French name is *boeuf à la mode*.

beefalo [BEEF-ah-loh] A cross between the American bison (commonly called buffalo) and cattle, the beef strain being dominant. The dark red meat of beefalo is very lean and has a somewhat stronger flavor than beef. It may be cooked in any manner suitable for beef and is currently available only in specialty meat markets.

beefsteak plant *see* SHISO

beef tartare *see* TARTARE

beef Wellington A FILLET of beef that has been covered with pâté de FOIE GRAS or DUXELLES, wrapped in pastry and baked.

bee hoon *see* RICE NOODLES

beer A generic term for low-alcohol beverages brewed from a MASH of malted barley and other cereals (like corn, rye or wheat), flavored with HOPS and fermented with yeast. Technically, beers are only those beverages in which the yeast sinks to the bottom of the tank during FERMENTATION. Such bottom-fermented brews ferment at colder temperatures for longer periods of time, a process that produces a light, crisp tasting beverage. ALE—a generic category for top-fermented beers where the yeast rises to the top of the tank—is strong-flavored and high in alcohol. Beverages that fall into the bottom-fermented beer category include BOCK BEER, LAGER, MALT LIQUOR, PILSNER and VIENNA BEER. PORTER, STOUT and WHEAT BEER are all top-fermented and are, therefore, considered ales. To add to the confusion, some states don't allow the words "beer" or "lager" to be used on brews containing more than 5 percent alcohol, so the word "ale" is used to describe these beers. *Four ingredients play the primary roles in beer-making:* water, malt, hops and yeast. **Water** is critical because it comprises nine-tenths of a beer's volume. The quality and composition of the water from different beer-making regions contributes greatly to the character of the finished product. MALT, which is made from germinated grain (usually barley), provides beer with a slightly sweet character. How malt is treated—dried but not roasted, lightly roasted, heavily roasted, and so on—impacts a beer's flavor. **Hops** convey an agreeably bitter, dry flavor that balances the malt's sweetness. Yeast that's been specially cultivated (each brewer has their favorite strain) is used for brewing; different yeasts produce different results. LAMBIC BEER utilizes wild yeast for fermentation. **Beer's alcohol content** varies, with most beer in the United States ranging from 3.2 to 8 percent alcohol. Some European beers have less than 3 percent alcohol, while others range as high as 13 percent. In the United States, the term **light beer** refers to a brew with reduced calories and usually less alcohol. In Europe, this term distinguishes between pale and dark lagers. **Ice beer** (called *Eisbock* in Germany) is lagered at such cold temperatures (32°F—the freezing point of water) that ice crystals form. When this frozen water is extracted, the resulting beer has a much higher alcohol concentration, so some German ice beers reach 13 percent alcohol. **Nonalcoholic beer** (**brew**) has had the alcohol removed in one of two ways: by fully fermenting the product, then removing the alcohol, or by arresting the fermentation before it begins. As with alcohol-free WINE, nonalcoholic beer (also referred to simply as *NA*) contains a miniscule amount of alcohol (0.5 percent by volume). That's no more than many fruit juices, which, thanks to natural fermentation, can have an alcohol level ranging between 0.2 and 0.5 percent. Although such potables are commonly referred to as "beers," U.S. law requires they be labeled "brews." Because alcohol gives beer body and texture, nonalcoholic versions aren't as satisfying to those used to real beer. On the plus side is the reduced calorie count. Whereas an average 12-ounce beer contains around 150 calories (microbrews up to 200), a nonalcoholic brew weighs in somewhere between 60 and 90 calories—just about the midpoint between regular and diet sodas. The calories in beer come primarily from malt, which contains natural sugar in the form of dextrose. But we'll never see a calorie-free brew because malt also contributes a big part of beer's flavor. The price of nonalcoholic beer is certainly not as light as its flavor because such brews can be costly to produce. Still, they fill a niche and can be much more satisfying with a meal than a cloyingly sweet soft drink. **Storing and serving beer:** Beer, unlike most wines, should not be AGED but consumed as fresh as possible. Most lighter style beers (such as lager and Pilsner) should be served at about 45°F; colder temperatures cloud beer and diminish its flavor. Stronger ales should be served at about 55°F so their more complex flavors can be savored. *See also* BITTER; DORTMUNDER; FRUIT BEER; SAKE; TRAPPIST BEER.

beer cheese *see* BIERKÄSE

Beerenauslese [BAY-ruhn-OWS-lay-zuh] Any of several fine, sweet German wines made from superior, slightly overripe grapes that have been individually picked or cut from their bunches. Some Beerenausleses are made from grapes that have been infected with BOTRYTIS CINEREA (noble rot). Because of their special selection and picking, these wines are very choice and expensive. *See also* AUSLESE; SPÄTLESE; TROCKENBEERENAUSLESE.

Beerwurst *see* BIERWURST

beesting cake *see* BIENENSTICH KUCHEN

beestings *see* COLOSTRUM

beet Commonly known as the *garden beet,* this firm, round root vegetable has leafy green tops, which are also edible and highly nutritious. The most common color for beets (called "beetroots" in the British Isles) is a garnet red. However, they can range in color from deep red to white, the most intriguing being the **Chioggia** (also called "candy cane"), with its concentric rings of red and white. Beets are available year-round and should be chosen by their firmness and smooth skins. Small or medium beets are generally more tender than large ones. If the beet greens are attached they should be crisp and bright. Because they leach moisture from the bulb, greens should be removed as soon as you get them home. Leave about 1 inch of the stem attached to prevent loss of nutrients and color during cooking. Store beets in a plastic bag in the refrigerator for up to 3 weeks. Just before cooking, wash beets gently so as not to pierce the thin skin, which could cause nutrient and color loss. Peel beets after they've been cooked. In addition to the garden beet are the **spinach** or **leaf beet** (better known as Swiss chard), the **sugar beet** (a major source of sugar) and the **mangold** (used as fodder).

beggar's purse The name for an APPETIZER made popular by Barry and Susan Wine at their New York restaurant, the Quilted Giraffe. A beggar's purse consists of a mini CRÊPE topped by a teaspoon of the finest CAVIAR and then a dab of CRÈME FRAICHE. The edges of the crêpe are pulled up in pleats around the filling and securely tied with a CHIVE. The ruffle at the top makes this edible package look like a miniature purse. Beggar's purses are served at room temperature.

beignet [ben-YAY] A traditional New Orleans yeast pastry that is deep-fried and served hot with a generous dusting of powdered sugar. The name comes from the French word for "fritter." Savory beignets, such as herb or crab, are also very popular.

Beijing duck [BAY-jeeng] *see* PEKING DUCK

beijo de anjo [BAY-zhu DAHN-zhu] Portuguese for "angel's kiss," referring to a classic Brazilian dessert consisting of small cakes made of egg yolks and beaten egg whites that are baked and then poached in a vanilla-flavored syrup.

bejgli *see* MAKOWIEC

Bella di Cerignola olive [BEHL-luh dee chayr-uhn-YOH-luh] Large, oval-shaped Italian olive that's cured in a mild brine. They are green or black depending on ripeness. The firm-textured, meaty green version has a mild, almost sweet flavor. The black olive is softer and more flavorful. *See also* OLIVE.

belle Hélène [BEHL ay-LEHN] *see* POIRE HÉLÈNE

Bellelay [BEL-luh-lay] *see* TÊTE DE MOINE

Bellini [behl-LEE-nee] An APÉRITIF made with peach nectar and CHAMPAGNE. It was created in 1943 at Venice's renowned Harry's Bar in honor of the illustrious Venetian painter Giovanni Bellini. At Harry's Bar, it's customarily made with Prosecco, an Italian sparkling wine.

bell pepper *see* SWEET PEPPERS

bellyfish *see* ANGLER FISH

belly lox *see* SMOKED SALMON

belon oyster Though indigenous to France, this tender, sweet oyster is now being aquacultured in California, Maine and Washington. The belon is small, ranging from $1^{1}/_{2}$ to $3^{1}/_{2}$ inches across, and has a slightly metallic flavor. It's considered superior, especially for eating ON THE HALF SHELL. *See also* OYSTER.

Bel Paese [BELL pah-AY-zay] Translated as "beautiful country," Bel Paese is a popular semisoft Italian cheese with a mild, buttery flavor. The rind is thin, pale yellow and covered with wax; the pale yellow interior has small irregular EYES. Though originally and still made in a small town outside Milan, Bel Paese is now also produced in the United States. It can be served as a dessert cheese or for snacks and melts beautifully for use in casseroles or on pizza. Bel Paese has a FAT CONTENT of 45 to 50 percent. *See also* CHEESE.

beluga caviar [buh-LOO-guh] *see* CAVIAR

bench scraper *see* DOUGH SCRAPER

Bénédict, à la *see* EGGS BENEDICT

Bénédictine D.O.M.; benedictine [ben-eh-DIHK-teen] 1. A sweet LIQUEUR named after the Benedictine monks of the Abbey of Fecamp, Normandy, who first began making it in 1510. Though the recipe is a closely guarded secret, Bénédictine is COGNAC-based and flavored with various AROMATICS, fruit peels and herbs. The flavor is a delicate balance of honey, citrus and herbs. The D.O.M. on each bottle stands for *Deo Optimo Maximo,* the Bénédictine dedication "To God Most Good, Most Great." 2. A local specialty of Louisville, Kentucky, benedictine is a spread made with cream cheese, cucumbers and dill, all tinted brightly with green food coloring. It's named after its creator, caterer Jennie Benedict.

beni shoga [BEH-nee SHOH-gah] Gingerroot that's been pickled in sweet vinegar and colored bright red. Beni shoga is used as a garnish for many Japanese dishes, especially SUSHI, and is also eaten to refresh the palate. It's available in thin slices, shredded or in knobs and can be found in Asian markets. Beni shoga is also called *gari. See also* AMAZU SHOGA.

benne seed [BEHN-ee *see* SESAME SEED]

benne wafers [BEHN-ee] A traditional recipe from the Old South, benne wafers are thin, crisp cookies made with brown sugar, pecans and sesame seed.

bento; bento box [BEHN-toh] A thin metal or lacquered wooden box divided into compartments. The bento box is used in Japan for storing separate small dishes that comprise an individual meal (most often lunch). In Japan, the bento lunch, which is commonly available at train stations, represents fast food elevated to high culinary art and design. Each of the country's 5,000 stations sells a unique box lunch that reflects the cooking of the region. The beautifully designed bento boxes can take on myriad shapes including masks, tennis rackets, nuts, golf balls or other objects both traditional and whimsical. More than twelve million bento-box meals are sold to hungry travelers and commuters in Japan each day.

berbere [bahr-beh-REE] An Ethiopian spice blend containing garlic, red pepper, cardamom, coriander, fenugreek and various other spices. It's often used in stews and soups.

Bercy [behr-SEE; BUR-see] Bercy is a section of Paris after which two sauces are named. **Bercy butter** is a sauce made with a REDUCTION of white wine with shallots, butter, MARROW, lemon juice, parsley, salt and pepper. It's served with broiled or grilled meat or fish.

Bercy sauce is a fish stock–based VELOUTÉ with SHALLOTS—a reduction of white wine, fish stock and seasonings. It's served with fish. *See also* SAUCE.

bergamot [BER-gah-mot] A small acidic orange with a peel that yields an essential oil—called *essence of bergamot*—which is used for perfumes and confections. The peel is used in EARL GREY TEA. It's also candied and used in the same way as other candied fruit peels. *See also* BEE BALM.

Bergkäse [BEHRK-kai-zer (-kah-zeh)] *see* ALLGÄUER BERGKÄSE

Berkshire pork *see* HERITAGE PORK

Berlin doughnut *see* BISMARCK

berry *see* individual listings for AKALA; BARBERRY; BILBERRY; BLACKBERRY; BLUEBERRY; BOYSENBERRY; CAPE GOOSEBERRY; CLOUDBERRY; COWBERRY; CRANBERRY; DEWBERRY; ELDERBERRY; GOOSEBERRY; HUCKLEBERRY; JUNIPER BERRY; LINGONBERRY; LOGANBERRY; MULBERRY; OLALLIEBERRY; RASPBERRY; STRAWBERRY; THIMBLEBERRY; YOUNGBERRY

besan [BEH-sahn] Used in East Indian cooking, besan is a pale yellow flour made from ground, dried CHICKPEAS. This nutritious, high-protein flour is used for myriad preparations including doughs, dumplings, noodles, a thickener for sauces and in batter for deep-fried foods. Besan, also known as *gram flour*, can be found in Indian or Asian markets. Store, wrapped airtight, in the refrigerator for up to 6 months.

best if used by (before) date *see* PRODUCT DATING

beta carotene [BAY-tuh KEHR-uh-teen] One of the most important and abundant of the carotenes, a portion of which the liver converts to vitamin A. It should be noted, however, that while excess vitamin A can be toxic to the body, residual beta carotene is quickly eliminated. Scientists now believe that beta carotene is a powerful ANTIOXIDANT with properties that can contribute to reducing cancer and heart disease. It's found in vegetables like carrots, broccoli, squash, spinach and sweet potatoes. Beta carotene's orange-yellow pigment is also used as a coloring in foods like butter and margarine.

bêtise [beh-TEES] Bêtise, which translates to "foolishness," is a famous French hard mint candy that was born out of mistakes made by a candymaker's son, Afchain. It's said that he added too much mint flavoring and his handling introduced microscopic bubbles into the candy. The confectioner's customers loved the result, and the rest is history. The candy is associated with the town of Cambrai, where tons of Bêtises de Cambrai are produced each year.

betty Dating back to colonial America, betties are baked puddings made of layers of sugared and spiced fruit and buttered breadcrumbs. Though many fruits can be used, the most popular is **Apple Brown Betty**, made with sliced apples and brown sugar.

beugnon [bihn-YOHN] Sweet French FRITTER with a hole in the middle that is fried in hot oil, traditionally walnut oil.

beurre [burr] The French word for "butter."

beurre blanc [burr BLAHN; burr BLAHNGK] Meaning "white butter," this classic French sauce is composed of a wine, vinegar and SHALLOT REDUCTION into which chunks of cold butter are whisked until the sauce is thick and smooth. It's excellent with poultry, seafood, vegetables and eggs. *See also* SAUCE.

beurre composé [BURR com-poh-ZAY] The French term for "COMPOUND BUTTER."

beurre de Montpellier [burr deh mohn-peh-LYAY] A COMPOUND BUTTER made by mixing herbs such as CHERVIL, chives, parsley, spinach, tarragon and watercress with anchovy fillets, CAPERS, egg yolks, garlic, GHERKINS and shallots and working them into a paste that's then blended with butter and olive oil. Beurre de Montpellier is great as an accompaniment to hot and cold fish, poultry and meat. *See also* SAUCE.

beurre manié [burr mahn-YAY] French for "kneaded butter," beurre manié is a paste made of softened butter and flour (usually in equal parts) that is used to thicken sauces.

beurre monté; beurre monte [burr mawn-TAY (MAWNT)] Unflavored butter sauce made by whisking chunks of butter into a tiny amount of water over moderate heat to create an EMULSION. Beurre monté is used to poach meats, fish, shellfish and vegetables, infusing them with butter flavor as they cook. It's also the basis for various sauces created by adding flavors to the emulsion. Beurre monté translates to "mounted butter" and refers to the technique of whisking chunks of cold butter into a sauce (*see* MOUNT, TO). *See also* SAUCE.

beurre noir [burr NWAR] A French term meaning "black butter," referring to butter cooked over low heat until dark brown (not black). Beurre noir is sometimes flavored with vinegar or lemon juice, capers and parsley and served with eggs, fish, brains and some vegetables.

beurre noisette [burr nwah-ZEHT] The French term for "brown butter," referring to butter cooked to a light hazelnut (*noisette*) color, the stage before it becomes BEURRE NOIR.

bhuna [BOO-nah] Indian curry dish and cooking method in which spices such as CORIANDER, CUMIN, dried chiles, FENNEL, FENUGREEK and mustard seeds are dry roasted or gently cooked in a small amount of oil to bring out their flavor. The spices blend with the juices of the meat and vegetables with which they're cooked to create a thick, rich, flavorful curry.

Bhutanese red rice Short-grain rice grown in Bhutan and the main rice in the Bhutanese diet. Bhutan is located in the eastern Himalayas, and the rice is grown at the 8,000-foot level. It is reddish-brown to reddish-orange in color and turns pinkish when cooked. Bhutanese red rice has an earthy, nutty flavor. *See also* RICE.

Bhut Naga Jolokia pepper *see* SCOVILLE SCALE

bialy; *pl.* **bialys** [bee-AH-lee] Jewish-American in origin, this large very chewy yeast roll is round and flat with a depression in the center. The bialy is sprinkled with sautéed chopped onion before baking. The name comes from the Polish city of Bialystok.

Bibb lettuce *see* BUTTERHEAD LETTUCE

bibimbap; bibim bap [bee-BIHM-bahp; bee-BEEM-bahp] Korean for "mixed rice," bibimbap is an everyday dish commonly made to use left-overs. Rice is served with a variety of foods that can include just about any-thing—vegetables (such as cucumbers, DAIKON and SHIITAKE mushrooms), fried egg, KIMCHI, MUNG BEAN sprouts, sesame seed and oil, SEAWEED strands and *kochujang* (*see* CHILE BEAN PASTE). Though traditionally meatless, today's bibimbap will more often contain a small amount of meat (beef, pork, chicken or seafood). To serve this dish, the rice is placed in a large bowl and topped with the additions, most of which have been seasoned and sautéed. In the United States, bibimbap is becoming increasingly pop-ular as imaginative restaurant chefs stretch traditional limits by adding as many colors, flavors and textures as possible. *Dolsot bibimbap* (*dolsot* means "stone pot") is served in a stone bowl so hot that the layer of rice touching it turns crunchy and golden brown—indeed, anything touching the bowl will cook immediately. This dish is also called *pibimbap*.

bibim naengmyeon *see* NAENGMYEON

bible leaf *see* COSTMARY

bicarbonate of soda *see* BAKING SODA

biccari *see* CICCHETTI

Bienenstich Kuchen [BEE-nehn-stihsh (-stik) KOH-kehn] German yeast cake made with a custard filling and crowned with a crisp honey and almond topping. There are two theories about the name, which means "bee sting cake." According to one, the baker who invented the cake was stung by a bee attracted to the honey topping. The other indicates that bakers in the 15th century fought off a raid from a neighboring village by tossing beehives at them, and the cake was made in honor of the event.

Bierkäse; Bierkaese [BEER-kai-zer (-kah-zeh)] Though literally translated as "beer cheese," there is no beer in **Bierkäse**. The name comes from the German practice of dipping the cheese into beer as it's eaten. This cheese originated in Germany but is also popular in surrounding countries (such as Austria and the Czech Republic) and is a local favorite in Wisconsin, where it's also produced. **Bierkäse is made from** PASTEURIZED **cow's milk,** can be RIPENED for from 6 weeks to 3 to 4 months and, depending on its age, can range in texture from semisoft to semihard. Though there are regional differences, all Bierkäses are generally similar in style and comparable to LIMBURGER. The flavor can range from tangy and piquant when young to quite pungent with aging. This cheese is known by many names, the most common of which is simply *beer cheese. See also* CHEESE.

Bierwurst; Beerwurst [BEER-wurst; BEER-vursht] A German cooked sausage with a garlicky flavor and dark red color. It's usually sold as sandwich meat. *See also* SAUSAGE.

bigarade [bee-gah-RAHD] French for "bitter" orange.

bigarade sauce [bee-gah-RAHD] A classic French brown sauce flavored with oranges and served with duck. Bigarade sauce combines beef stock, duck drippings, orange and lemon juice, blanched orange peel, and if desired, CURAÇAO. The original French recipe used bitter Seville oranges (*bigarade* is French for "bitter orange"). Today's cooks should avoid using overly sweet citrus in this sauce. *See also* SAUCE.

bigaro *see* PERIWINKLE

bigeye scad *see* AKULE

bigos [BEE-gohs] A Polish dish consisting of layers of sauerkraut, onions and apples with cooked meats such as venison, chicken, duck, ham or sausages. The layers are buttered, stock is poured over all and the casserole is baked slowly to allow the flavors to mingle. Tradition says that *bigos* should be made several days in advance because it is best when reheated.

bihoon mai fun [bih-HOON mi fun] *see* RICE NOODLES

bilberry Also called *whortleberry,* this indigo-blue berry grows wild in Great Britain and other parts of Europe from July to September, depending on the area. Bilberries are smaller and tarter than their cousin the American BLUEBERRY, and make delicious jams, syrups and tarts.

billy bi; billi-bi [BILL-ee BEE] An elegant French soup made with mussels, onions, wine, cream and seasonings. The mussels are strained out of a classic billy bi, leaving a smooth and silky soup. However, today it is often served with the mussels. Though there are several stories of the soup's origin, the most popular is that Maxim's chef Louis Barthe named it after a regular patron who particularly loved the soup, American tin tycoon William B. (Billy B.) Leeds.

biltong [BILL-tong] Developed in South Africa and a staple in many African countries, biltong consists of strips of CURED, air-dried beef or game. Though its keeping properties are the same, it is a finer form of jerked meat than American JERKY. The best biltong has been compared to the PROSCIUTTO of Italy.

bind, to Culinarily, the term "to bind" can be used in two ways: 1. The process of making ingredients stick together in a mass by adding a binding ingredient, such as breadcrumbs or eggs. For example, MEATLOAF ingredients are bound together so they can be formed into the shape of a loaf. 2. To thicken a hot mixture by adding any of several ingredients such as butter, cream, eggs, flour, and so on.

binder In cooking, a *binder* is a thickening agent for soups, sauces and other mixtures. BEURRE MANIÉ, ROUX, egg yolks or starches such as FLOUR, CORNSTARCH and ARROWROOT are among those agents used for thickening. A binder is sometimes also referred to as a *liaison*.

Bing cherry A very large, delicious cherry that ranges in color from a deep garnet to almost black. The skin is smooth and glossy and the flesh firm and sweet. Bing cherries are good for cooking as well as out-of-hand eating. *See also* CHERRY.

biotechnology; bioengineered foods Very basically, food-related biotechnology is the process by which a specific gene or group of genes with desirable traits are removed from the DNA of one plant or animal cell and spliced into that of another. Such beneficial genes might come from animals, (friendly) bacteria, fish, insects, plants and even humans. In some instances, genes that create problems (such as the natural softening of a tomato) are simply removed and not replaced. Tomatoes, for example, are generally picked green and gas-ripened later because, during shipping, they would become soft, bruised and unmarketable. A bioengineered tomato, however, can be picked ripe and shipped without softening. The objective of food biotechnology is to develop insect- and disease-resistant, shipping- and shelf-stable foods with improved appearance, texture and flavor. Additionally, biotechnology advocates say that the process will produce plants that are resistant to adverse weather conditions such as drought and frost, thereby increasing food production in previously prohibitive climate and soil conditions. They also envision increasing nutrient levels and decreasing pesticide usage through biotechnology. On the other hand, critics argue that, because biotechnology is producing new foods not previously consumed by humans, the changes and potential risks relating to such things as toxins, allergens and reduced nutrients are unpredictable. They also worry that, because genetically altered foods are not required to be labeled, people with religious or lifestyle dietary restrictions might unintentionally consume prohibited foods. In answer to such concerns, the FDA has issued the following evaluation guidelines by which a bioengineered food will be judged for approval: 1. Has the concentration of a plant's naturally occurring toxicant increased? 2. Has an allergic element not commonly found in the plant been introduced? 3. Have the levels of important nutrients changed? 4. Have accepted, established scientific practices been followed? 5. What are the effects on the environment? *Frankenfood* is a term used to describe food that's been genetically altered.

birch beer Dating back to the late 1800s, this American carbonated drink (usually nonalcoholic) is flavored with an extract from birch bark. It's sweet and similar in flavor to root beer.

birch sugar *see* XYLITOL

bird *see* ROULADE

bird chile *see* THAI CHILE

bird's beak chile *see* CHILE DE ÁRBOL

bird's nest soup A classic Chinese specialty made from the nest of an Asian bird similar to the swift. These birds attach their nests to cavern walls in Southeast Asia by using a gelatinous spit. Because of their hazardous location, the nests are dangerous to collect and therefore very expensive. They are sometimes refered to as the "CAVIAR of the East." White nests and black nests are the two types used. The more desirable of the two are the white nests, composed mainly of the weblike strands of saliva and containing few foreign particles. Black nests contain feathers, twigs and insects and are labor intensive to clean. Both types must be cleaned and soaked overnight before using. They're available in Chinese markets.

birra [BEE-rah] Italian for "BEER."

birria [bih-RREE-ah] This rustic Mexican meat stew can be made with beef, goat, lamb, mutton, pork or veal, or some combination of these meats. Originally from Jalisco it's now found in other parts of Mexico and in Mexican restaurants in the United States. Birria uses less expensive cuts of meat, which are smothered with a spicy chili sauce and left to marinate for hours before the meat is slowly cooked until fork tender. The cooking juices are blended with a seasoned tomato sauce and served with the meat. Among the variations that have evolved are birrias that are akin to POT ROAST and others that are like SHORT RIBS. Restaurants that specialize in birria dishes are called *birrierías*.

biryani [beer-YAH-nee] A rice-based dish popular in India, Pakistan, Bangladesh and surrounding countries. Although there are many variations of this dish, biryani is basically a mixture of rice, herbs, spices and other flavoring ingredients, vegetables and/or meat or fish and yogurt. Biryani ingredients may be cooked together or in layers and each country has its own version. Malaysians, for example, add coconut milk to the mix. Although vegetarian biryanis are immensely popular, many renditions include meat, which is typically beef, chicken, goat, lamb or mutton. Exotic flavors come from a blend of herbs and spices such as bay leaves, cardamom, cinnamon, cloves, coriander, cumin, ginger, mint, saffron and turmeric. Packaged biryani masala (biryani spice blend) may be purchased in Indian markets, some supermarkets and on the Internet.

biscotte *see* RUSK

biscotto; *pl.* **biscotti** [bee-SKAWT-toh; bee-SKAWT-tee] A twice-baked Italian biscuit (cookie) that's made by first baking it in a loaf, then slicing the loaf and baking the slices. The result is an intensely crunchy cookie that is perfect for dipping into DESSERT WINE or coffee. Biscotti can be variously flavored; the most popular additions are anise seed, hazelnuts or almonds.

biscuit [BIHS-kiht] 1. In America, biscuits refer to small QUICK BREADS, which often use LEAVENERS like baking powder or baking soda. Biscuits are generally savory (but can be sweet), and the texture should be tender and light. 2. In the British Isles, the term "biscuit" usually refers to a flat, thin cookie or cracker. 3. The word biscuit comes from the French *bis cuit* ("twice cooked"), which is what the original sea biscuits aboard ship had to be in order to remain crisp.

biscuit cutter *see* COOKIE CUTTER

biscuit tortoni *see* TORTONI

bishop 1. The classic bishop, dating back to the 18th century, is a MULLED WINE (red) simmered with a roasted clove-studded orange and served hot. Conjecture suggests the name comes from the burgundy-color of a bishop's robes. 2. Today, the name bishop is also given to a COCKTAIL that combines red wine with lemon juice, orange juice, powdered sugar and cloves; it's served in a tall glass over ice and garnished with slices of orange and lemon.

bishop's crown chile; bishop's hat chile This CHILE's interesting three-sided shape inspired these names along with numerous others such as *balloon, Christmas bell, Nepalese bell* and *orchid.* The squat pepper is 2 to 3 inches wide and 1 to 2 inches tall, with three flaps that hang down over a small knob at the bottom. The chile turns from green to a deep reddish-orange as it matures. The three flaps of the chile, which are sweet and fruity tasting, are not that hot but the core of the plant contains a lot of spicy heat. Therefore, its SCOVILLE SCALE rating varies from 5,000 to 30,000. Other names for this pepper include *ají flor, campane, peri peri, pimenta Cambuci* and *Ubatatuba Cambuci.*

bismarck [BIHZ-mahrk] An elongated jelly-filled doughnut, also known as a *Long John* and *Berlin doughnut.* The bismarck can be baked or fried and sugar-coated or frosted.

Bismarck herring *see* HERRING

bisque [bihsk] A thick, rich soup usually consisting of puréed seafood (sometimes fowl or vegetables) and cream.

bistecca [bee-STAYK-kah] Italian for "beef steak."

bisteeya *see* B'STEEYA

bistro [BEES-troh; BIHS-troh] A small cafe, usually serving modest, down-to-earth food and wine. This word is also sometimes used to refer to a small nightclub (the French *bistrot* means "pub").

bitter A popular, golden brown English ALE, so named for its bitter essence, derived from HOPS. *See also* BEER.

bitter melon Also referred to as a *balsam pear,* this fruit resembles a cucumber with a bumpy skin and is used as a vegetable in Chinese cooking. When first picked, the bitter melon is yellow-green and has a delicate, sour flavor. As it ripens it turns yellow-orange and becomes bitter and acrid, which is how many people prefer it. **Chinese bitter melon** ranges from 6 to 10 inches long; **Indian bitter melon** is about half that size. Chinese bitter melon is available year-round in most Asian markets and some supermarkets. It can also be purchased canned or dried. The Indian variety can sometimes be found in Indian markets.

bitter orange *see* SEVILLE ORANGE

bitters Made from the DISTILLATION of aromatic herbs, barks, flowers, seeds, roots and plants, bitters are a liquid used to flavor cocktails, APÉRITIFS or foods. They are also used as a digestive aid and appetite stimulant. Bitters generally have a high alcohol content and are bitter or bittersweet to the taste. Bitters come in various flavors (including apricot, orange and peach) and have long been employed as DIGESTIFS, appetite stimulants and hangover cures. They're used in myriad mixed drinks, as well as many food preparations. The most popular bitters used for drinks today are AMER PICON, ANGOSTURA BITTERS, FERNET BRANCA, and **Peychaud's Bitters**. Among other well-known bitters around the world are **Abbott's Bitters** from the United States (Baltimore, Maryland); **Boonekamp bitters** from Holland; **Gammel Dansk** from Denmark; **orange bitters**, the most well-known (such as Holloway's) coming from England; **Stonsdorfer** and **Underberg bitters** from Germany; and **Unicum bitters** from Vienna.

bivalve Any soft-bodied MOLLUSK, such as a clam, scallop, oyster or mussel, that has two shells hinged together by a strong muscle.

biya *see* AIYSH

blachan *see* BALACHAN

black bean Also called *turtle bean,* this dried bean variety has long been popular in Mexico, Central and South America, the Caribbean and the southern United States. It has a black skin, cream-colored flesh and a sweet flavor, and forms the base for the famous black-bean soup. Black beans are commonly available in supermarkets. *See also* BEANS.

black beans, fermented *see* FERMENTED BLACK BEANS

black bean sauce *see* BEAN SAUCES; BEAN PASTES

blackberry Also called a *bramble* because it grows on thorny bushes (brambles), the blackberry is the largest of the wild berries. Purplish-black in color, it ranges from $1/2$ to 1 inch long when mature. Blackberries are widely cultivated in the United States and are available, depending on the region, from May through September. Imported berries fill the seasonal gap so blackberries are available in some areas year-round. Look for plump, deep-colored berries sans hull. If the hulls are still attached, the berries are immature and were picked too early; the flavor will be tart. Fresh blackberries are best used immediately but they may be refrigerated, lightly covered and preferably in a single layer, for 1 to 2 days. They are wonderful both for cooking and for out-of-hand eating. In Britain, blackberries and apples are a traditional duo for pies.

black bottom pie A rich pie with a layer of dark chocolate CUSTARD, topped with a layer of rum custard. The top is garnished with sweetened whipped cream and chocolate shavings.

black bread Almost black in color, this European peasant bread gets its hue from a variety of ingredients including dark rye flour, toasted dark breadcrumbs, molasses, cocoa powder, dark beer and coffee. It's a hearty, full-flavored loaf that, depending on the baker, can be lightly sweet.

black bun Not a bun in the sense of bread, the Scottish black bun is a spicy mixture of nuts with dried and candied fruit enclosed in a rich pastry crust. Traditionally, Scots serve it at Hogmanay (the New Year). It's best prepared several weeks in advance so the fruit mixture can ripen and develop flavor.

black butter *see* BEURRE NOIR

black cabbage *see* CAVOLO NERO

black calypso *see* CALYPSO BEAN

black cardamom [KAR-duh-muhm] A spice related to CARDAMOM with a slightly different character. Black cardamom, also known as *Greater Indian cardamom* or *Nepal cardamom*, does not have the spicy-sweet quality of true cardamom; instead it has more of a pungent camphor-like character with a smoky quality. Because of this, it's not used in sweet items like pastries, puddings or spiced cakes. And it's used differently than true cardamom in savory dishes, providing more body and flavor to MASALAS and to DAL and rice dishes. Black cardamom can be purchased either in the pod or ground. The latter, though more convenient, is not as full-flavored because cardamom seeds begin to lose their essential oils as soon as they're ground. *See also* SPICES; Seasoning Suggestions, page 891.

black chanterelle *see* TROMPETTE DE LA MORT

black cod *see* SABLEFISH

Black Corinth *see* CHAMPAGNE GRAPES

black cow A Midwestern U.S. name for a root beer FLOAT.

black cumin *see* KALA JEERA; NIGELLA SEED

blacken; blackened A cooking technique made famous by New Orleans chef Paul Prudhomme by which meat or fish is cooked in a cast-iron skillet that's been heated until almost red hot. Prudhomme's original specialty was blackened redfish. The food is customarily rubbed with a CAJUN spice mixture before being cooked. The extra-hot skillet combined with the seasoning rub gives food an extra-crispy crust.

black-eyed pea Originating in Asia, the black-eyed pea is thought to have been introduced to the United States through the African slave trade. This small beige bean has a black circular "eye" at its inner curve. It can be purchased fresh or dried. Though originally cultivated for animal fodder, black-eyed peas are now a popular LEGUME (particularly in the South) and are essential in the traditional dish HOPPIN' JOHN. Also called *cowpea* and, if the "eye" is yellow, *yellow-eyed pea.*

blackfish Also called *Chinese steelhead* and *black trout,* this lean Pacific fish is a favorite in Chinese communities. It has a delicious, delicate flavor but can be troublesome because of its network of tiny fine bones. It is suitable for most methods of cooking. *See also* FISH.

Black Forest torte Also known as *Schwarzwälder Kirschtorte,* this exquisite dessert hails from Swabia in Germany's Black Forest region. It's made by layering KIRSCH-scented chocolate cake, sour cherries and kirsch-laced whipped cream. Then it's coated generously with sweetened whipped cream and garnished with chocolate curls and cherries.

black fungus *see* WOOD EAR

black Indian salt *see* BLACK SALT

black kale *see* CAVOLO NERO

black mangosteen *see* KOKAM

black onion seeds *see* NIGELLA SEEDS

black pepper; black peppercorn *see* PEPPERCORN

black persimmon *see* BLACK SAPOTE

black poplar mushroom *see* PIOPPINI MUSHROOM

black pudding *see* BLOOD SAUSAGE

black radish Dating back to ancient Egypt, this large radish has a coarse, soot-black skin and a flesh that's white and crisp. The assertive flavor can be horseradish hot, the sting of which can be tamed with salt. Scrub and trim as you would regular radishes. Use in salads, soup, and STIR-FRY dishes.

Black Russian A COCKTAIL made with two parts vodka and one part coffee-flavored LIQUEUR served over ice. A FLOAT of $1/2$ ounce of cream makes it a **white Russian**.

black salt A special type of mineral salt used on the Indian subcontinent and in other parts of South Asia. Black salt is also known as *black Indian salt, kala loon, kala namak, rock salt, sanchal* and *sulemani namak*. It isn't actually black but ranges in color from pinkish-gray to dark reddish-purple. It has a smoky, sulfurous taste that some compare to cooked eggs. It's used as a seasoning in a variety of Indian and Pakistani foods and is a key ingredient in the spice blend CHAAT MASALA. Look for black salt or kala namak in Indian markets in either ground or lump form.

black sapote [sah-POH-tay] This exotic fruit (*Diospyros digyna*) is actually a member of the PERSIMMON family and unrelated to either the

MAMEY SAPOTE or the WHITE SAPOTE. It's grown in tropical regions including Eastern Mexico, Central America, Hawaii and southern Florida. Black sapote resemble green persimmons and range in size from 2 to 5 inches in diameter. As the fruit ripens, the skin turns from olive to deep yellow-green. Inside the inedible skin is a pulp that's brownish black, glossy and exceedingly soft; it may be seedless or contain up to 10 flat, brown seeds. The black sapote's texture and flavor have been compared to chocolate pudding (chocolate lovers might disagree), which is why this fruit is sometimes called the *chocolate pudding fruit.* It's also known as *sapote negro* and *zapote negro* and—in Hawaii—as a *black persimmon.* Black sapote are typically available from December to April and only in specialty produce markets (except in the regions in which it's grown). Choose firm, olive-green fruit free of bruises. Let ripen at room temperature until the fruit feels quite soft to palm pressure. Refrigerate ripe fruit in a plastic bag for up to 5 days.

black sea bass A true BASS, this Atlantic coast fish can be found from Cape Cod to Florida, though it's more abundant from New York to North Carolina. A best-selling fish, it can vary in color from brown to dark gray. It has a firm, moderately fat flesh that has a delicate flavor, due largely to its diet of crabs and shrimp. Black sea bass is sold whole, and in steaks and fillets. It's suitable for almost any method of preparation. *See also* SEA BASS; STRIPED BASS; FISH.

blackstrap *see* MOLASSES

black trout *see* BLACKFISH

black trumpet mushroom Distinctly trumpet-shaped, this mushroom ranges from 2 to 5 inches high. Its flesh is thin and brittle and can range in color from grayish brown to very dark brown or almost black. Black trumpets are distinctively aromatic and have an elegant buttery flavor. They're available midsummer through midfall in specialty produce markets. *See also* MUSHROOM.

black velvet A drink made with equal parts CHAMPAGNE and STOUT. A *brown velvet* substitutes PORT for stout.

black walnut This native American nut has an extraordinarily hard shell, which makes it extremely difficult to crack and therefore not as popular as the more widely known ENGLISH WALNUT. Its strong, slightly bitter flavor is highly valued by black-walnut devotees, but its high fat content makes it turn rancid quickly. *See also* NUTS; WALNUT.

blade pot roast *see* CHUCK

blade steak *see* TOP BLADE STEAK

blaff A classic poached fish dish of the French West Indies composed of a small whole RED SNAPPER that's been marinated in a mixture of lime juice, allspice berries, garlic and CHILES. The marinade is then combined with a large amount of water, sliced onion and a BOUQUET GARNI and brought to a boil. When the fish is plopped into the boiling cooking liquid, it makes a sound that resembles "blaff"; hence, the name. Blaff is traditionally accompanied by white rice.

blanc [BLAH/V] French for "white," as in BEURRE BLANC, which means "white butter."

blanc de blancs [BLAH/V duh BLAH/V; BLAHNGK duh BLAHNGK] French phrase meaning "white wine from white grapes." This term is used to describe CHAMPAGNES made exclusively from the white Chardonnay grape. It also refers to white wines made entirely from white grapes, rather than from a blend using some red grapes. *See also* BLANC DE NOIRS.

blanc de noirs [BLAH/V duh NWAHR; BLAHNGK duh NWAHR] The French term meaning "white wine from red grapes." This phrase is used for CHAMPAGNES and other sparkling wines that are made entirely from PINOT NOIR grapes. Occasionally the term *blanc de noirs* refers to still (nonsparkling) wines made from CABERNET SAUVIGNON, Pinot Noir or ZINFANDEL. The color of blanc de noirs wines varies in hue from pale pink to apricot to salmon. *See also* BLANC DE BLANCS.

blanch 1. To plunge food (usually vegetables and fruits) into boiling water briefly, then into cold water to stop the cooking process. Blanching is used to firm the flesh, to loosen skins (as with peaches and tomatoes) and to heighten and set color and flavor (as with vegetables before freezing). *See also* PARBOIL. 2. A horticultural technique whereby the leaves of plants are whitened or prevented from becoming green by growing them in complete darkness. It's this labor-intensive process that makes Belgian ENDIVE so expensive.

blancmange [bluh-MAH/VZH] A simple cooked pudding made of milk, cornstarch, sugar and vanilla. Gelatin may be substituted for the cornstarch. The hot mixture is poured into a mold, chilled, unmolded and served with a sweet sauce or fresh fruit. The original blancmange used pulverized almonds in lieu of cornstarch.

blanquette [blahn-KEHT] A rich, creamy stew made with veal, chicken or lamb, button mushrooms and small white onions. The name comes from the French word *blanc*, meaning "white."

BLBT *see* PINK SLIME

blend *n.* A mixture of two or more flavors combined to obtain a particular character and quality, as in wines, teas and blended whiskey. **blend** *v.* To mix two or more ingredients together with a spoon, beater or electric blender until combined.

blender A small electrical appliance that uses short rotating blades to chop, blend, purée and liquefy foods. Because blender containers are tall and narrow, air is not incorporated into the food so this appliance will not "whip" foods such as egg whites and cream. Blenders can be used for making soups, purées, sauces, milkshakes and other drinks, as well as for chopping small amounts of foods such as breadcrumbs and herbs. *See also* IMMERSION BLENDER.

blenny [BLEN-ee] A genus of small (4- to 6-inch-long) freshwater and saltwater fish characterized by its lack of scales; instead, its body is covered by a mucous membrane. The blenny has a mild, white, flavorful flesh and is best served fried. *See also* FISH.

bleu [BLEUH] 1. French for "blue," used in the cheese world to describe the myriad varieties of BLUE CHEESE. 2. A French term used for a steak cooked so rare that it is barely warmed through. À POINT is the next step, which means the steak is cooked rare.

bleu cheese *see* BLUE CHEESE

Bleu d'Auvergne [bleuh doh-VEHRN] Semihard cow's-milk BLUE CHEESE from southern France. To develop the blue veining, the milk used is inoculated with *Penicillium roqueforti*, the same mold used for producing ROQUEFORT, GORGONZOLA and STILTON. Once the cheese forms, thick needles are used to pierce it to allow air in and encourage mold growth. Small wheels of Bleu d'Auvergne are aged for at least 2 weeks, larger wheels for a minimum of 4 weeks. This cheese has a yellowish gold rind and an ivory interior with blue-green veins. The texture is moist, creamy and slightly crumbly; the flavor is buttery with a mild spiciness that develops with age. It has a FAT CONTENT of about 50 percent. *See also* CHEESE.

blewit mushroom The blewit's name comes from the contraction of "blue hat," an old English reference to the mushroom's wide (up to 6 inches or more), slightly tilted bluish-lavender cap. It's also known as *blue foot, blue leg* and *pied bleu*—names associated with its 1-inch stem, which is also a bluish-lavender color that fades as it matures. The flesh, which is a very pale blue, is firm, chewy and slightly slimy; the flavor is mild with an earthy and woody trait. Blewit mushrooms were quite popular in Europe before making their way to the United States. They are abundant in the wild, but the cultivated ones are preferred by many since the flavor of the wild versions varies dramatically. They're not good raw and should be used in cooked dishes only. *See also* MUSHROOMS.

blinchiki [bleen-CHEE-kee] Thin Russian pancake similar to a CRÊPE.

blind A term sometimes used for SWISS-STYLE CHEESES that have very few or no EYES.

blind baking *see* BAKE BLIND

blini [BLEE-nee] Hailing from Russia, blini (singular, blin) are small, yeast-raised pancakes that are classically served with sour cream and caviar or smoked salmon. Blini are traditionally made with buckwheat flour, although lighter versions combine buckwheat and wheat flours.

blintz [BLIHNTS] A tender, ultrathin pancake that can be made with any number of flours. The blintz is rolled to enclose a sweet or savory filling including cottage or ricotta cheese, fruit or meat mixtures. It's then sautéed until golden brown and served with sour cream.

bloaters *see* HERRING

blondie *see* BROWNIE

blood Over the centuries people like the Mongolian warriors used animal blood as a source of food, often ingesting it fresh. Today, some Masai of Tanzania still follow this practice, ingesting blood for nutrition as they travel with their herds. Elsewhere, blood (primarily from pigs, cows, chickens and geese) is still used as a thickening agent in some dishes, such as BLOOD SAUSAGE (also known as *black pudding* because of the dark color of cooked blood). Blood should never be boiled, or it will clot. A little vinegar keeps blood from clotting during storage. In winemaking, blood is used as a FINING agent to help clear suspended particles and clarify the wine. Blood is usually available by special order through some butcher shops.

blood alcohol concentration; blood alcohol content; BAC A term referring to a person's intoxication level, as determined by the weight of alcohol in a specific volume of blood. Factors computed to establish the blood alcohol concentration include the individual's weight and metabolism as well as the amount of alcohol ingested within a specific amount of time. Also called by the acronym *BAC* and *blood alcohol level*. *See also* Blood Alcohol Concentration Charts, page 903.

blood orange Grown primarily around the Mediterranean and now California, this sweet-tart orange has a bright red or red-streaked white flesh. Most blood oranges are best eaten fresh, but the more acidic varieties like the **Maltese** work well in cooked sauces like the HOLLANDAISE-based MALTAISE SAUCE. *See also* ORANGE.

blood pudding *see* BLOOD SAUSAGE

blood sausage Also known as *blood pudding* and in Ireland as *black pudding*, this large link SAUSAGE is made of pig's blood, suet, breadcrumbs and oatmeal. Almost black in color, blood sausage is generally sold pre-cooked. It's traditionally sautéed and served with mashed potatoes.

Bloody Mary A popular COCKTAIL made with tomato juice, vodka, Worcestershire sauce, Tabasco and other seasonings. It was created in 1921 by Pete Petiot, bartender at Harry's New York Bar in Paris. The Bloody Mary came to the United States in 1933, when Petiot joined the St. Regis Hotel as head barman of its King Cole Bar. It's said that the name "Bloody Mary" alluded to Mary Tudor, Queen of England and Ireland, for her bloody persecution of Protestants. Today, you'll find Bloody Marys made with everything from RUM to GIN to TEQUILA. Make it without liquor, and you have a **Virgin Mary**, also called a **Contrary Mary**.

bloom 1. Pale gray streaks and blotches that appear on the surface of chocolate. Bloom is a result of COCOA BUTTER forming crystals on the chocolate, usually caused by the chocolate being stored in too warm an environment. *See also* CHOCOLATE. 2. The pale gray film found on the skin of fruits such as grapes and plums. Fruit bloom is simply nature's water-proofing and completely harmless. 3. A natural, invisible, protective coating found on eggshells. This covering is washed off when USDA-graded eggs are sanitized; producers then replace it with a thin film of mineral oil. 4. To moisten GELATIN in a small amount of water before dissolving it in hot liquid.

bloomy-rind cheeses *see* SOFT-RIPENED CHEESES

blossom *see* ROUND WHITE POTATOES

blueberry Round and smooth-skinned, these blue-black berries are juicy and sweet. There are two main types of blueberries (often confused with HUCKLEBERRIES). The high-bush variety can grow up to 15 feet in height; the hardy low-bush blueberry plants are only about 1 foot high and thrive in Canada and the northern United States. Cultivated blueberries comprise the majority of those that reach the market and the season can span from the end of May to early October. Large New Zealand blueberries are in markets in the winter at a premium price. Choose blueberries that are firm, uniform in size and indigo blue with a silvery frost. Discard shriveled or moldy berries. Do not wash until ready to use, and store (preferably in a single layer) in a moistureproof container in the refrigerator for up to 5

days. Use blueberries in baked goods, jams, pies, pancakes, salads or, best of all, with a simple splash of sweet cream.

blue cheese; blue-veined cheese This genre of cheese has been treated with molds that form interior pockets and veins that can range in color from dark blue to blue-green to blue-black and everything in between. The mold used is PENICILLIUM—either *P. glaucum, P. gorgonzola* or *P. roqueforti*. Though the spores may be naturally airborne, most cheesemakers strive for consistency and add the blue-mold strain (either in a powder or in a liquid) to the milk or curds, or in some instances by spraying or inoculating the formed cheese. Because the cultures won't create bluing without air to feed the bacteria, the cheeses are pierced with metal skewers so that oxygen can reach the interior. Some of the more popular of the blues include GORGONZOLA, ROQUEFORT and STILTON. Blue cheeses tend to be strong in flavor and aroma, both of which intensify with aging. *See also* CHEESE.

bluefin *see* TUNA

bluefish Found along the Atlantic and Gulf coasts, the bluefish is nicknamed "bulldog of the ocean" because of its tenacity. It ranges from 3 to 10 pounds and has a fatty, fine-textured flesh that ranges in color from white to silver gray. Removing the dark, oily strip that runs down its center is important to prevent the flesh from absorbing a strong fishy flavor. Bluefish is best when baked or broiled. *See also* FISH.

blue foot mushroom *see* BLEWIT MUSHROOM

blue giant hyssop *see* ANISE HYSSOP

blue leg mushroom *see* BLEWIT MUSHROOM

blue licorice *see* KOREAN MINT

blue oyster mushroom One of the OYSTER MUSHROOM variants, the blue oyster mushroom has a blue-hued cap with a whitish stem. The flesh is smooth and firm. The flavor is mild but bigger than the lighter-colored oyster mushrooms; when sautéed it takes on a sweet, SCAMPI-like character. *See also* MUSHROOMS.

bluepoint oyster Though originally named for Blue Point, Long Island, where this oyster is said to have been first found, "bluepoint oyster" is now used as a general term referring to any of many small Atlantic oysters from 2 to 4 inches long. They are considered the best for eating ON THE HALF SHELL. *See also* OYSTER.

blue runner *see* JACK

blue-veined cheese *see* BLUE CHEESE

blush wines In the United States, the phrase "blush wine" has almost replaced that of *rosé,* which is considered somewhat passé. Initially, the term applied to very pale-colored ROSÉ WINES. Today, however, it's used to encompass a full spectrum of wines that, like rosés, are generally made with red grapes. The juice has had only brief (2 to 3 days') contact with the stems and skins—the reason for the wines' pale color. The term "blush," however, is broadly used to describe wines that can range in color from various shades of pink to pale orange to light red. Unlike the common rosé, blush wines can range from DRY to sweet and may be light- to medium-bodied. They should be served chilled—but not icy—and may accompany a variety of lightly flavored foods.

bobo nai cha; boba tea *see* BUBBLE TEA

bobotie [boh-BOH-tee] A popular South African dish made of minced lamb and/or beef mixed with bread, rice or mashed potatoes, onions, garlic and curry powder. The ingredients are blended with an egg-and-milk mixture before being baked. Partway through the baking process additional egg-milk mixture is poured over the top. Bobotie is served in squares or wedges.

bobwhite *see* QUAIL

bocaccio *see* ROCKFISH

bocconcini [bohk-kohn-CHEE-nee] 1. Small nuggets (about 1 inch in diameter) of fresh MOZZARELLA. Bocconcini are generally sold packed in WHEY or water. They can also be found marinated in olive oil, which may sometimes be flavored with herbs, garlic or red chile pepper flakes. 2. Italian for "mouthful," referring not to size, but to the appetizing appeal of dishes described in this manner. Therefore, in Italian cookery, the word *bocconcini* may be attributed to many dishes. For example, *bocconcini di vitello alla crema* is a rich preparation of veal chunks cooked with wine, butter, egg yolks and whipping cream. A less rich, but equally tempting, dish is *bocconcini Fiorentina*—pieces of veal or beef sautéed with garlic, onions and herbs, sometimes with the addition of tomatoes.

bock beer A full-bodied, slightly sweet, usually dark-colored German BEER with a malty (*see* MALT) flavor strongly evocative of HOPS. American bock beers are generally less bitter and lighter in both color and body. Originally, bock beer was brewed in the fall, aged through the winter and celebrated in the spring at traditional Bavarian bock beer festivals. There's no longer any seasonal connection to bock beer. **Eisbock** is a strong German "ice beer" that's lagered at such cold temperatures (32°F) that some of the water freezes. After the ice crystals are removed, the beer's alcohol concentration is high—about 13 percent.

Bockwurst [BAHK-wurst; BAHK-vursht] Delicately flavored with chopped parsley and chives, this ground-veal SAUSAGE is of German origin. It's generally sold raw and must be well cooked before serving. Bockwurst is traditionally served with BOCK BEER, particularly during springtime.

body A word used with food and drink to describe a full, rich flavor and texture. For instance, a full-bodied wine, beer or coffee has a complex, well-rounded flavor that lingers in the mouth.

Boeren Leidse met sleutels *see* LEYDEN

boeuf [beuf] The French word for "beef."

boeuf à la mode [beuf ah lah MOHD] *see* BEEF À LA MODE

boeuf bourguignon [BEUF boor-gee-NYO*N*] *see* BOURGUIGNONNE

boil "Bring to a boil" refers to heating a liquid until bubbles break the surface (212°F for water at sea level). The term also means to cook food in a boiling liquid. A "full rolling boil" is one that cannot be dissipated by stirring. *See also* HIGH-ALTITUDE COOKING AND BAKING.

boiled dinner *see* NEW ENGLAND BOILED DINNER

boiled icing A fluffy cake FROSTING made by gradually pouring a hot SUGAR SYRUP over stiffly beaten egg whites, beating constantly until the mixture is smooth and satiny. An Italian MERINGUE is made in the same manner.

boilermaker A shot of whiskey followed by a CHASER of beer.

boiling firepot *see* MONGOLIAN HOT POT

boiling potatoes *see* ROUND WHITE POTATOES

boiling-water bath *see* CAN, TO

boisson [bwah-SAW*N*] French for "drink" or "beverage."

bok choy [bahk CHOY] Also called *Chinese white cabbage, pak choy, pak choi* and *white mustard cabbage,* bok choy is a mild, versatile vegetable with crunchy white stalks and tender, dark green leaves. It resembles a bunch of wide-stalked celery with long, full leaves. Choose bunches with firm, white stalks topped with crisp, green leaves. Bok choy is available year-round in most supermarkets and should be refrigerated airtight for no more than 3 to 4 days. It can be used raw in salads, in a STIR-FRY or as a cooked vegetable. Bok choy is related to but not the same as CHINESE CABBAGE.

bok l'hong *see* SOM TAM

bolete; boletes [BOH-leet; boh-LEE-tuhs] *see* PORCINI

bolillo [boh-LEE-yoh] Shaped like a football and about 6 inches long, a bolillo is a Mexican roll made from dough similar to that for a French BAGUETTE. Bolillos have crisp brown crusts and light, chewy interiors and are most often used to make TORTAS—Mexican sandwiches. A **telera** is very similar but SCORED to divide it into three sections.

Bolivian rainbow chile The plant the Bolivian rainbow chile grows on is gorgeous, with leaves that vary from green to purple and purple blossoms. And then there are the beautiful CHILES, which look like erect, one-inch tall Christmas tree lights, displaying a plethora of colors all at once. They start out lavender and go to purple, yellow, orange and finally to red. The chiles themselves are hot, with a SCOVILLE SCALE rating of 10,000 to 30,000.

bollito [boh-LEE-toh] Italian for "boiled."

bollito misto [boh-LEE-toh MEES-toh] This classic Italian dish of mixed boiled meats is particulary popular in the Emilia, Lombardy and Piedmont regions. The meats, which include veal, chicken and COTECHINO sausage, are accompanied by a rich meat broth and a piquant green sauce.

bologna; baloney [bah-LOH-nyah; bah-LOH-nee] Precooked and highly seasoned, this popular SAUSAGE is usually sliced and served as a sandwich meat or cold cut. The word comes from Italy's city of Bologna, though true Italian bologna sausage is called *mortadella*.

Bolognese, alla; Bolognese meat sauce *see* RAGÙ

Bomba rice [BOHM-bah] Spanish rice said to be perfect for making PAELLA because it can soak up as much as three times its volume in liquid while remaining firm, making it more flavorful than other types of rice. Bomba is grown around the town of Calasparra in southeast Spain's Murcia province, where the CALASPARRA variety is also grown. Bomba is considered the superior of the two rice types, but it's hard to grow and takes a long time to mature. It becomes dehydrated during its slow maturation process, which accounts for its absorption abilities. Although growing difficulties have brought it close to extinction in the past, chefs and other food lovers kept up the demand for bomba, ensuring its survival. It can be found on the Internet but it is more expensive than most rice. *See also* RICE.

Bombay duck Not a duck at all, this pungent, flavorful food is actually dried salted fish. It can be found in East Indian markets and some specialty markets. Bombay duck is most often used to flavor curried dishes. It's also cooked until crisp and eaten as a snack.

bombe; bombe glacée [BAHM; bahm glah-SAY] A frozen dessert consisting of layers of ice cream or sherbet. The ice cream is softened

and spread, one layer at a time, in a mold. Each layer is hardened before the next one is added. The center of a bombe is often custard laced with fruit. After it's frozen solid, the bombe is unmolded and often served with a dessert sauce. The original bombe molds were spherical; however, any shape mold may be used today.

bon appétit [boh nah-pay-TEE] A French phrase with any of various meanings related to having a good (*bon*) appetite (*appétit*) such as "have a good meal," (I wish you a) "hearty appetite" or "enjoy your meal." *Bon appétit* was for a long time Julia Child's television sign-off.

Bonbel [bahn-BEHL] The brand name of a popular semisoft cheese sold in small paraffin-coated rounds. It's pale cream in color and has a mild flavor and smooth, buttery texture that's perfect with fruit; it's also used in sandwiches and salads. *See also* CHEESE.

bonbon [BAHN-bahn] A piece of chocolate-dipped candy, usually with a center of FONDANT that is sometimes mixed with fruits or nuts.

bone To remove the bones from meat, fish or fowl.

boneless lean beef trimmings *see* PINK SLIME

boniato [boh-NYAH-toh] A cultivar of the SWEET POTATO, the boniato has a skin that ranges in color from red to brown and a flesh that's creamy white. It's yam-shaped and can reach up to 12 inches long. Choose those that are unblemished and without sprouts; store in a cool, dark, well-ventilated place for up to a month. The boniato is popular in Caribbean cuisine and can be cooked in any way suitable for potatoes or yams. It's also known as *batata, camote* and *kamote*.

bonito *see* TUNA

bonne-bouche [bahn-BOOSH] French for "tasty little bite," referring to any of various small enticements such as a snack, tidbit or HORS D'OEUVRE.

bonne femme, à la [bohn FEHM; bohn FAM] Literally translated as "good wife," the term *bonne femme* describes food prepared in an uncomplicated, homey manner. Sole *bonne femme* is a simply poached fish served with a sauce of white wine and lemon juice, and often garnished with small onions and mushrooms.

booze *n.* Slang for alcoholic beverages. A **boozer** is one who tipples excessively—or *boozes it up,* or gets *boozed-up.* **booze** *v.* Slang for drinking in excess.

bo pho *see* PHO

boqueróne; boquerone [boh-kay-ROHN] Though the word is Spanish for "whitebait," in culinary circles *boquerónes* are fresh FILLETED anchovies (sometimes other small fish are used) that have been soaked in white wine vinegar for a period of several hours to several days, a process that bleaches them white. The fish are then drained and sometimes lightly rinsed. Boquerónes are usually served as TAPAS, napped generously in olive oil and sprinkled with chopped garlic and parsley and sometimes other ingredients such as onions and roasted red peppers.

borage [BOHR-ihj; BAHR-ihj] Bright flowers and hairy leaves distinguish this European herb whose flavor is reminiscent of cucumber. Both the flowers and leaves are used in salads, but the leaves must be chopped finely so their hirsute texture isn't offputting. The leaves are also used to flavor teas and vegetables.

Bordeaux [bohr-DOH] An area in southwest France considered by most wine enthusiasts to be the world's greatest wine-producing region, not only because of the superiority of the wines, but also because of the large annual production (500 to 750 million bottles). The wide popularity of Bordeaux wines in the United Kingdom (where they're called CLARETS) can be traced back to the period from 1152 to 1453 when the English owned this region—acquired through a royal marriage then lost in the 100 Years' War. The most celebrated of the Bordeaux wines are the reds, which make up more than 75 percent of the production. Nevertheless, the region's rich, sweet white wines from SAUTERNES are world-renowned, and its DRY white wines from Graves have a serious following. The five main Bordeaux districts with individual APPELLATIONS are Pomerol, Saint-Emilion, Graves, Sauternes and the Médoc (which has many individual appellations including Margaux, Pauillac, Saint-Estephe and Saint-Julien). The primary red grape varieties used in Bordeaux are CABERNET SAUVIGNON, CABERNET FRANC, MERLOT (with almost twice as much acreage as Cabernet Sauvignon), and occasionally Malbec and Petit Verdot. The primary white grapes are SAUVIGNON BLANC, SÉMILLON and Muscadelle. Bordeaux winemakers typically blend grape varieties for their wines, as opposed to the prevailing practice in the United States of producing VARIETAL WINES. It should be noted, however, that American vintners are now making more blended wines, which are called MERITAGE wines when approved Bordeaux grape varieties are used. In general, the vineyards of Saint-Emilion and Pomerol are planted more heavily in Merlot and thus produce softer, more supple wines. On the other hand, the vineyards of Médoc and Graves favor Cabernet varieties, which create more intense, tannic (*see* TANNIN) and long-lived wines. Some of the more famous châteaux in Bordeaux are Haut-Brion, Lafite-Rothschild, Latour, Margaux, Mouton Rothschild and Petrus.

bordelaise, à la [bohr-dl-AYZ; bohr-dl-EHZ] A French term meaning "of or from Bordeaux" and referring to dishes served with BORDELAISE SAUCE.

bordelaise sauce [bohr-dl-AYZ; bohr-dl-EHZ] A French sauce made with red or white wine, BROWN STOCK, bone MARROW, shallots, parsley and herbs. It's usually served with broiled meats. *See also* SAUCE.

börek; bourek; burek [BOOR-ehk] Though thought of as Turkish, these thin packets of pastry (ranging from PHYLLO to PUFF PASTRY) are found throughout the Middle East. They can contain a variety of fillings, including cheese, spinach or ground meat, and may be baked or fried. Borek are served hot as an HORS D'OEUVRE or with a salad as a main course.

borlotti bean [bor-LOH-tee] The Italian name for CRANBERRY BEAN.

borrachos *see* FRIJOLES CHARROS

Borrettana onion *see* CIPOLLINI

borscht; borsch [BOHR-sht; BOHR-sh] Originally from Russia and Poland, borscht is a soup made with fresh beets. It can be prepared using an assortment of vegetables, or with meat and meat stock, or with a combination of both. Borscht can be served hot or cold; it should always be garnished with a dollop of sour cream.

Bosc pear [BAWSK] A large winter pear with a slender neck and a russeted yellow skin, the Bosc is available from October through April. It has an agreeably sweet-tart flavor and is delicious fresh or cooked. The Bosc holds its shape well when baked or poached. *See also* PEAR.

Boston baked beans A melange of NAVY BEANS or PEA BEANS (the latter a favorite with New Englanders), SALT PORK, molasses and brown sugar, baked in a casserole for hours until tender. The dish is so named because it was made by Puritan Bostonian women on Saturday, to be served for dinner that night. Because cooking was forbidden on the Sabbath, leftover beans were served with BOSTON BROWN BREAD for Sunday breakfast . . . and, ofttimes, lunch.

Boston brown bread Rye and wheat flour, cornmeal and molasses flavor this dark, sweet STEAMED BREAD. It often contains raisins and is the traditional accompaniment for BOSTON BAKED BEANS.

Boston cream pie Not a pie at all, this dessert consists of two layers of SPONGE CAKE with a thick custard filling, topped either by a dusting of powdered sugar or chocolate glaze.

Boston lettuce *see* BUTTERHEAD LETTUCE

botarga *see* BOTTARGA

botrytis cinerea [boh-TRI-tihs sihn-EHR-ee-uh] Also called *noble rot*, this beneficial mold develops on grapes under certain environmental conditions. The mold causes the grape to shrivel, concentrating and intensifying both sugar and flavor. Most winemakers are exhilarated when noble rot descends on their grapes because it gives them fruit from which to make very elegant, intensely flavored DESSERT WINES. In California these wines are usually referred to as LATE HARVEST wines and in France, where noble rot is called *pourriture noble*, they're known as SAUTERNES. In Germany noble rot is called *Edelfaule*, and German winemakers are experts at producing a large variety of elegant botrytis-infected wines such as TROCKENBEERENAUSLESE and some BEERENAUSLESES.

bottarga; botarga [boh-TAHR-gah] An Italian term for cured ROE from gray or silver MULLET or TUNA that's used throughout the Mediterranean region. It's also known as *Mediterranean caviar* and, in France, *boutargue*. The roe sacs are salted, massaged to eliminate air pockets, pressed and formed and then sun-dried for several weeks. Bottarga is sometimes coated in beeswax to preserve it. The resulting dry block is grated, ground or sliced and used as a seasoning on pasta and other dishes. Bottarga is also served with olive oil and lemon or lime juice as an appetizer. In Sicily the version made from tuna roe is called *uovo di tonno*. The Japanese *karasumi,* made with mullet roe, is similar to bottarga.

Bottled-in-Bond A phrase sometimes used on labels of whiskey (and other distilled spirits) referring to the Bottled in Bond Act of 1894, which allows producers to bottle and store their DISTILLED SPIRITS in Treasury Department-bonded warehouses without paying excise taxes on them until they're shipped to the retailer. The conditions necessary for such a designation include: The whiskey must be produced at one plant during a single distilling season, be 100 PROOF (50 percent alcohol) and AGED for at least 4 years. Contrary to some beliefs, such labeling does not insure a high degree of quality.

bottle gourd *see* CUCUZZA

bottle sizes *see* Wine and Spirit Bottle Sizes, page 870

bouchée [boo-SHAY] The French word for "mouthful," a *bouchée* is a small PUFF PASTRY shell filled with various savory preparations such as creamed seafood. *See also* AMUSE-BOUCHE.

boucher [boo-SHAY] French for "butcher."

boudin blanc [boo-DAHN BLAH*N;* boo-DAHN BLAH*N*GK] 1. A delicate SAUSAGE, similar to a QUENELLE in texture, made with pork, chicken, fat, eggs, cream, breadcrumbs and seasonings. It is most often gently sautéed and served hot. The term is French for "white pudding." 2. In Louisiana, *boudin blanc* is a sturdier sausage made with pork, rice and onions.

boudin noir [boo-DAHN NWAHR] The French term for "black pudding" (*see* BLOOD SAUSAGE).

bouillabaisse [BOOL-yuh-BAYZ; BOOL-yuh-BEHZ] A celebrated seafood stew from Provence, made with an assortment of fish and shellfish, onions, tomatoes, white wine, olive oil, garlic, saffron and herbs. The stew is ladled over thick slices of French bread.

bouillon [BOOL-yahn] Any broth made by cooking vegetables, poultry, meat or fish in water. The liquid that is strained off after cooking is the bouillon, which can form the base for soups and sauces.

bouillon cube A compressed, flavor-concentrated cube of dehydrated beef, chicken or vegetable stock. **Bouillon granules** are the granular form of the dehydrated concentrate. Both the cubes and granules must be dissolved in a hot liquid before using.

boulanger;   boulangerie [boo-lahn-ZHAY;   boo-lahn-ZHREE] French for "baker" and "bakery," respectively.

boule [BOOL] French for "ball," referring culinarily to a round loaf of white bread. Also called *miche*.

Boule de Lille *see* MIMOLETTE

bou na pana *see* PACIFIC THREADFIN

bounce A popular beverage in Colonial days, bounce is made by combining rum or brandy with fruit, sugar and spices and allowing the mixture to ferment for 1 to 3 weeks.

bounceberry Another name for CRANBERRY.

bound *see* BIND

bouquet [boo-KAY] A term referring to the complex fragrance that develops in a wine through barrel or bottle AGING, particularly the latter. *See also* AROMA; NOSE.

bouquet garni [boo-KAY gahr-NEE] A bunch of herbs (the classic trio being parsley, thyme and bay leaf) that are either tied together or wrapped in CHEESECLOTH and used to flavor soups, stews and broths. Tying or bagging the herbs allows for their easy removal before the dish is served.

bourbon An American corn-based WHISKEY whose name comes from Bourbon County, Kentucky. Bourbon can be made legally in any part of the United States, though most of it still comes from Kentucky. All bourbon is based on one of two types of MASH (grain that's ground or crushed before being steeped in hot water and fermented): **sweet mash**, which uses fresh yeast to start the fermentation process from scratch; and **sour mash**, which combines a new batch of sweet mash with a portion of the residue from the previous fermentation, a technique similar to that used in making sourdough bread. The resulting liquor is often labeled **sour mash bourbon**. **Straight bourbon** is distilled from a mash of at least 51 percent but not more than 79 percent corn. If there's more than 80 percent corn, it must be labeled **corn whiskey**. Straight bourbon must also be AGED in new, charred oak barrels for a minimum of 2 years (although most bourbons are aged for 4 years or more), must not be over 160 PROOF (80 percent alcohol) and can only use water to reduce the alcohol level. **Single-barrel bourbon** comes from a single barrel; the number of the barrel is typically printed on the label. **Small-batch bourbon** generally refers to a high-quality bourbon blended from selected barrels. *See also* TENNESSEE WHISKEY.

bourguignonne, à la [boor-gee-NYO*N*] The French term for "as prepared in Burgundy," one of France's most famous gastronomic regions. Meat (usually beef, as in *boeuf bourguignonne*) is braised in red wine and usually garnished with small mushrooms and white onions. *See* FONDUE *for information on fondue bourguignonne.*

bourride [boo-REED] Similar to BOUILLABAISSE, this Mediterranean fish soup is pungent with garlic, onions, orange peel and sometimes saffron. It's usually thickened with egg yolks and flavored with AÏOLI. Bourride is traditionally served EN CROÛTE.

Boursault [boor-SOH] A soft, snowy rind surrounds this rich triple-cream semisoft cheese from France. Boursault can be made with raw or PASTEURIZED COW's milk and is RIPENED for 2 to 8 weeks. It has a soft, moist texture and a creamy-sweet flavor with a nutty nuance. Boursault comes in small paper-wrapped cylinders; avoid any with discolored paper. *See also* CHEESE.

Boursin [boor-SAHN] Created in 1957 by Frenchman Frank Boursin, this TRIPLE-CREAM cheese is made with PASTEURIZED COW's milk. Boursin has a smooth, creamy texture and a base flavor that's mild and delicate. It comes in several styles, all flavored: garlic and herbs, black pepper, shallots and chives, and one with figs, raisins and nuts. The most recent addition to this line is a light Boursin (flavored with garlic and herbs), which has 78 percent less fat and 64 percent fewer calories. Needless to say, it's not a triple-cream cheese. *See also* CHEESE.

boutargue [boo-TAHRG] *see* BOTTARGA

bovine spongiform encephalopathy (BSE) [BOH-vine SPUHNJ-uh-fohrm en-sehf-ah-LOP-ah-thee] Also known as **mad cow disease**, BSE attacks the central nervous system of cattle. Cows with this degenerative disease lose coordination, abandon routine habits and display unpredictable behavior. BSE belongs to a group of diseases known as transmissible spongiform encephalopathies (TSEs). There appears to be a link between BSE and a rare brain disorder in humans called variant Creutzfeldt-Jakob disease. BSE is not contagious, so it's not spread from one cow to another; rather, it's thought to spread through feed that's contaminated with transmittable BSE agents. How is the food supply in the United States affected by BSE? The USDA's Food Safety and Inspection Service (FSIS) is "responsible for ensuring that the nation's commercial supply of meat, poultry, and egg products is safe, wholesome, and correctly labeled and packaged." As of 2004, FSIS will not mark cattle as "inspected and passed" until confirmation is received that the cattle have tested negative for BSE. It also indicates that "brains and various other parts of cattle 30 months of age or older are specified risk material that are prohibited in the human food supply." So, it appears that lovers of calf brains can still enjoy this product, because the illness, were it present, would not have time to incubate in younger animals. In addition, the FSIS has taken steps to eliminate potentially diseased by-products from entering the food chain from older animals.

bovine somatotropin [BOH-vine soh-mat-uh-TROH-pin] *see* BST

bovolo [BOH-voh-loh] Italian for "SNAIL."

boxty [BOX-tee] Said to have originated during the Irish famine, boxty is rather like a thick pancake composed of mashed and shredded potatoes, flour and baking soda or baking powder. Like a SCONE, the dough is shaped into a circle, cut into quarters and baked on a griddle. Boxty is usually served as a side dish with meat.

boysenberry Horticulturist Rudolph Boysen created this hybrid berry in 1923 by crossing a RASPBERRY, BLACKBERRY and LOGANBERRY. It's shaped like a large raspberry, has a purple-red hue and a rich sweet-tart flavor. Choose boysenberries that are firm and uniform in size. Discard shriveled or moldy berries. Do not wash until ready to use, and store (preferably in a single layer) in a moistureproof container in the refrigerator for 2 to 3 days.

Bra (DOC; PDO) [BRAH] Although mainly made from skim cow's milk (pasteurized or unpasteurized), Bra cheeses sometimes contain small amounts of sheep's or goat's milk. The cheese is named after the town south of Turin in the Cuneo province in northwestern Italy's Piedmont region. There are three kinds: **Bra Tenero**, the semisoft version, which is aged for up to 6 months; **Bra Duro**, a firmer version, which is aged for 1 to 2 years or longer; and **Bra d'Alpeggio**, made only from the milk of cows that graze in mountain pastures during the months of June to October. Bra d'Alpeggio can only be made in certain areas and is more of an ARTISANAL cheese than the others. Bra cheeses come in 13- to 18-pound wheels, which are off-white to brownish-beige and have off-white to dark-yellow-orange interiors. The flavor ranges from mild to full-flavored in the aged versions. The FAT CONTENT for Bra cheeses ranges from 39 to 49 percent. *See also* CHEESE.

braciola [brah-JYOH-lah] The Italian term for a meat chop (*braciolette*) or CUTLET (*bracioline*), which may be wrapped around a STUFFING. Filled meat rolls, particularly if braised, are the same as the Italian INVOLTINO or the French ROULADE.

Braeburn apple This all-purpose apple has a skin that's pale green with muted red stripes; late in the season it turns deep yellow, washed with pinkish-red striping. The crisp flesh is sweet and slightly tart. *See also* APPLE.

brains Beef, pork and lamb brains are available in many supermarkets and most specialty meat markets. Buy brains that are a bright pinkish-white color, plump and firm. They're very perishable and should be used the day of purchase. Brains must be well washed, then BLANCHED in ACIDULATED WATER. They can then be poached, fried, baked or broiled, and are particularly delicious when served with BEURRE NOIR. For concerns about **mad cow disease**, see BOVINE SPONGIFORM ENCEPHALOPATHY (BSE). *See also* VARIETY MEATS.

braise [BRAYZ] A cooking method by which food (usually meat or vegetables) is first browned in fat, then cooked, tightly covered, in a small amount of liquid at low heat for a lengthy period of time. The long, slow cooking develops flavor and tenderizes foods by gently breaking down their fibers. Braising can be done on top of the range or in the oven. A tight-fitting lid is very important to prevent the liquid from evaporating.

bramble *see* BLACKBERRY

bran The outer layer of grains (such as wheat or oats) that is removed during milling. Bran is a good source of carbohydrates, calcium, phosphorus and fiber. It's found in cereals and baked goods and can be purchased at natural food stores and most supermarkets.

branch water A term first used in the 1800s referring to pure, clean water from a tiny stream called a "branch." An order for "bourbon and branch" is a nostalgic request for bourbon and water.

brandade [brahn-DAHD] The famous *brandade de morue* of Provence is a pounded mixture of salt COD, olive oil, garlic, milk and cream. This flavorful purée is served with CROÛTES and often garnished with chopped black truffles. Other salted or smoked fish can also be used to make brandade.

brandy A liquor distilled from wine or other fermented (*see* FERMENTATION) fruit juice. The name "brandy" comes from the Dutch *brandewijn* ("burned (distilled) wine"), referring to the technique of heating the wine during DISTILLATION. A number of sub-categories fall under the broad definition of brandy including fruit brandy, GRAPPA, MARC, POMACE and EAU DE VIE (*eau de vie* is French for brandy). Brandies made from apples and grapes are generally AGED in wood, which contributes flavor and color. Those made from other fruits are less likely to be aged in this fashion and are typically colorless. The finest brandies traditionally come from COGNAC followed by those from ARMAGNAC—both in southwestern France. *See also* AGUARDENTE; APPLEJACK; APRICOT BRANDY; AQUA VITEA; CACHACA; CALVADOS; KIRSCH; METAXA; PISCO; RAKI; SLIVOVITZ.

brandy Alexander A sweet COCKTAIL that is usually served after dinner. It's made with brandy, chocolate LIQUEUR and cream.

branzino [brahn-ZEE-noh] A member of the SEA BASS family found around Italy and other parts of the Mediterranean. It's also known as *spigola.*

brasier [BRAY-zer] *see* BRAZIER

brasserie [brahs-uh-REE] An informal French café that serves beer, wine and simple, hearty food.

Bratwurst [BRAHT-wurst; BRAHT-vursht] A German SAUSAGE made of pork and veal seasoned with a variety of spices including ginger, nutmeg and coriander or caraway. Though it is now available precooked, bratwurst is generally found fresh and must be well grilled or sautéed before eating.

Braunschweiger [BROWN-shwi-ger; BROWN-shvi-ger] Named for the German town of Braunschweig, this smoked liver SAUSAGE enriched with eggs and milk is the most famous of the LIVERWURSTS. It's soft enough to be spreadable and is usually served at room temperature.

brawn *see* HEAD CHEESE

brazier [BRAY-zer] 1. Also called a *rondeau*, a brazier is a pan specifically designed for braising (*see* BRAISE) food. It's typically large (from 15 to 28 quarts) and round with two handles. Most braziers are made of heavyweight aluminum, though there are now some smaller ceramic versions. All have tight-fitting lids to keep in the moisture necessary for this style of cooking. 2. The term can also refer to a square or round, bowl-shaped metal container, often topped by a grill. Small versions are used for heating or cooking food, and the heat source may be charcoal or electricity. Large outdoor braziers are used both as a heat source and for cooking. The word *brazier* comes from the French *brasier*, from *braise* ("hot coals").

Brazil nut Actually the seed of a giant tree that grows in South America's Amazon jungle. These seeds come in clusters of 8 to 24 inside a hard, 4- to 6-inch globular pod that resembles a coconut. The extremely hard shell of each seed, or "nut," is dark brown and triangular in shape. The kernel is white, rich and high in fat. Brazil nuts are rich in selenium, a powerful ANTIOXIDANT. *See also* NUTS.

bread *v.* To coat food with bread, cracker or other crumbs. The item is usually first dipped into flour, then into a liquid (beaten eggs, milk, beer, etc.), then into the crumbs, which may be seasoned with salt, pepper and various herbs. Breading will stick better if the food is blotted dry with a paper towel and refrigerated for 30 to 60 minutes before it's coated. Breaded food is usually fried (although it may be baked), which gives it a crispy crust and helps retain its moisture. **bread** *n.* A staple since prehistoric times, bread is made from flour, water (or other liquid) and usually a LEAVENER. It can be baked (in an oven or, as with pancakes, on a griddle), fried or steamed. Yeast is the leavener in **yeast bread**, which requires KNEADING to stretch the flour's GLUTEN. A yeast **batter bread** uses strenuous beating instead of kneading to the same end. **Quick breads** are so called because they require no kneading and use baking soda, baking powder or eggs to leaven the bread. As the name implies, **unleavened bread** (such as MATZO) uses no leavening and therefore is quite flat. Grains, seeds, nuts and fruit are often added to bread for flavor and texture. *See also* ANA-DAMA; BABKA; BAGUETTE; BAKEWARE; BARM BRACK; BÂTARDE; BATON; BISCUIT; BLACK BREAD; BOSTON BROWN; BOULE; BREADCRUMBS; BREAD SAUCE; BRIOCHE; BRUSCHETTA; CHALLAH; CHAPATI; CORNBREAD; CORNELL; CORN PONE; CROSTINI; CRUMPET; FICELLE; FLATBREAD; FOCACCIA; FRENCH BREAD; FRY BREAD; GARLIC BREAD; GINGERBREAD; HARDTACK; HUSHPUPPY; IRISH SODA BREAD; ITALIAN BREAD; JOHNNYCAKE; KHACHAPURI; LAHVOSH; LIMPA BREAD; MANDELBROT; MONKEY BREAD; MUFFIN; NAAN; PANCAKE; PANETTONE; PANKO; PAPPADAM; PARATHA; PETIT PAIN; PITA; POORI; POPOVER; PUEBLO BREAD; PUMPERNICKEL; ROTI; SALLY LUNN; SALT-RISING BREAD; SCONE; SODA BREAD; SOURDOUGH; SPOON BREAD; STEAMED BREAD; STOLLEN; TORTILLA; WAFFLE; ZWIEBACK.

bread-and-butter pickles Sweet pickles made from thin slices of unpeeled cucumber; usually pickled with onion and sweet green bell pepper, and flavored with mustard and celery seeds, cloves and turmeric.

breadcrumbs; bread crumbs There are dry and fresh (or soft) breadcrumbs, and the two should not be used interchangeably. **Fresh crumbs** are made by placing bread slices (trimmed of crusts or not) in a food processor or blender and processing until the desired size of crumb is reached. They can be stored, tightly sealed, in the refrigerator for a week or frozen for at least 6 months. Fresh breadcrumbs give more texture to breaded dishes. **Dry crumbs**—either plain or flavored—can be purchased in any supermarket. Homemade dry crumbs are made by placing a single layer of bread slices on a baking sheet and baking at 300°F until completely dry and lightly browned. The slices are cooled before processing in a blender or food processor until the desired texture is achieved. *See also* PANKO.

breadfruit Native to the Pacific, breadfruit is large (8 to 10 inches in diameter), has a bumpy green skin and a rather bland-tasting cream-colored center. It is picked and eaten before it ripens and becomes too sweet. Like squash, breadfruit can be baked, grilled, fried or boiled and served as a sweet or savory dish. It's available fresh in some Latin and specialty produce markets and may also be purchased canned.

breading A coating of bread, cracker or other crumbs that has been applied to food. *See* BREAD, *verb tense.*

bread machines Computer-driven machines that mix, knead, rise, punch down, bake and sometimes cool bread. The ingredients are measured and added to a single, nonstick canister, which becomes mixing bowl, baking pan and oven. A motor-driven blade in the canister's base mixes and kneads the dough; a heating coil handles the baking. Bread machines come in many models, but there are three basic loaf shapes: vertical rectangle, horizontal rectangle and cylindrical. There are several capacities available, ranging from $1/2$-pound to 2-pound loaves. It's important to follow manufacturer's directions (which can vary) for adding and layering ingredients. Failing to do so could prevent the yeast from mixing with the liquid, which would result in a failed loaf of bread.

bread pudding A simple baked dessert made with cubes or slices of bread saturated with a mixture of milk, eggs, sugar, vanilla and spices. Chopped fruit or nuts also can be added. **Bread and butter pudding** is typically made by buttering the bread slices before adding the liquid mixture. Both may be served hot or cold with cream or a dessert sauce.

bread salad *see* PANZANELLA

bread sauce A British sauce made with breadcrumbs, milk, onions, cream and various seasonings, usually including cloves. This thick sauce is typically served with wild game birds and other poultry. *See also* SAUCE.

bread stick; breadstick A relatively thin length of yeast bread that's typically crisp, though some bread sticks are soft. The length can vary from short 3-inch cocktail sticks to those almost 12 inches long. The circumference of bread sticks generally ranges between $1/2$ and 1 inch.

breakfast tea *see* ENGLISH BREAKFAST TEA; IRISH BREAKFAST TEA

bream [BREEM] The name applied to any of several freshwater or saltwater fish such as the American *porgy,* the Japanese *sea bream* and the French *daurade*. In general, bream can be grilled, baked or fried. *See also* FISH; PORGY.

breast, lamb The breast of lamb runs along the chest and belly and contains many small ribs and other bones. This area provides *Denver ribs* or *lamb ribs, lamb spareribs* or *riblets* and various pieces turned into ground lamb.

brebis [breh-BEE] French for "ewe" (female sheep), which in the cheese world refers to sheep's-milk cheese.

brek; brik [BREHK] From Tunisia, this savory, deep-fried TURNOVER usually contains a spicy meat or fish filling and often an egg. Though the fillings may vary, brek is traditionally served with HARISSA.

bresaola [brehsh-ay-OH-lah] Originating in Lombardy, Italy, bresaola is air-dried salted beef FILLET that has been aged about 3 months. It's typically thinly sliced, drizzled with olive oil and lemon juice and served as an ANTIPASTO.

Breton Far *see* FAR BRETON

brick cheese The name of this all-American Wisconsin cheese is said to have come from the fact that bricks were once used to weight the CURD and press out the WHEY; it's also brick shaped. Made from PASTEURIZED cow's milk, brick cheese is pale yellow and semisoft and has a mild, earthy flavor when young. As it ripens, however, it becomes almost as strong as LIMBURGER. *See also* CHEESE.

brick dough *see* WARKA

Brie [BREE] Acclaimed as one of the world's great CHEESES, France's Brie is characterized by an edible, downy white rind and a cream-colored, buttery-soft interior that should "ooze" when at the peak of ripeness. Though several countries (including the United States) make this popular cheese, Brie from France is considered the best and French *Brie de Meaux* dates back to the 8th century. Bries can be made from either whole, skimmed or partially skimmed cow's milk, which may be raw or PASTEURIZED. Total RIPENING time can range from 3 to 10 weeks. The flavor of ARTISAN versions can range from rich, sweet and nutty to more pungent and savory. Mass-produced renditions are typically milder, not as rich or complex and remain firm at room temperature. Because Brie must be perfectly ripe for the best flavor, select one that is plump and resilient to the touch; the rind might show patches of beige. The FAT CONTENT of Brie ranges from 45 to 60 percent. *See also* CHEESE.

brigade system An organizational system for professional kitchens instituted by Georges Auguste Escoffier toward the end of the 19th century. Escoffier established separate kitchen stations, each responsible for a certain part of the menu. This system proved so effective that a semblance of it is still in place in many of today's professional kitchens. The brigade system was modeled after French military organization, with the **chef de cuisine** (also called *executive chef*) acting as the "general." This system extended from the kitchen into the FRONT OF THE HOUSE, and in some restaurant hierarchies, the chef de cuisine has authority over areas like the dining room and bar. The **sous chef** (which means "under chef") is the second-in-command. This person fills in for the chef de cuisine when necessary and may have other full-time duties such as scheduling or overseeing food preparation. Beneath these positions are **chefs de partie**, also known as *station chefs* or *journeyman cooks*. Each one is responsible for a station that produces specific parts of the menu. Depending on the size of the kitchen these stations may include more than one chef or cook; in smaller kitchens responsibilities for multiple stations might be combined into one. An **aboyeur** is a *caller* or *expediter*—one who receives the orders from the wait staff, calls out and routes the orders to the correct stations and checks and assembles orders for delivery to the dining room. A **charcutière** is the chef or cook in charge of CHARCUTERIE items such as PÂTÉS, RILLETTES, GALANTINES, and CRÉPINETTES. The **entremetier** is the person or station in charge of not only vegetables but soups, pastas, egg dishes and other miscellaneous items. A **friturier** is the chef or station responsible for fried foods. The **garde manger** (or *chef garde manger)* is the person or station responsible for cold pantry items such as salads, PÂTÉS, CHAUD-FROIDS and other decorative dishes. The term *garde manger* also refers to the area in which such foods are prepared and stored. The **grillardin** is the person or station in charge of grilled foods. The **pâtissier** is in charge of baked goods, pastries and desserts; in large kitchens there may be a separate area with baking ovens, walk-in refrigerators and so on. The **poissonier** is responsible for fish dishes, the **rotisseur** is in charge of roasted items and associated sauces and the **saucier** handles SAUTÉED items and any related sauces. A **tournant** is an experienced chef that rotates from station to station to fill in wherever needed. In the front of the house, the **maître d'hôtel** (*maître d'*) is in charge of the dining room staff and is essentially the dining room manager. The **chef de sale**, or *headwaiter,* is responsible for service throughout the dining room, although this role is often filled by the maitre d' or dining room manager. A **chef de rang** is a dining room waiter, though one who's typically experienced and highly skilled in everything from proper table set-up and perfect delivery of food to dealing appropriately with the diner's needs. The **chef de vin** (also called *SOMMELIER*) is the wine steward with responsibility for acquiring, storing and serving wine.

brik *see* BREK

brik dough *see* WARKA

brill An excellent European saltwater FLATFISH closely related to the TURBOT. It has a delicate, light flesh that can be broiled, fried, baked, grilled or poached. *See also* FISH.

Brillat-Savarin [bree-YAH sah-vah-RAN] Semisoft, triple-cream (*see* DOUBLE-CREAM CHEESES) cow's-milk cheese created in honor of Jean Anthelme Brillat-Savarin, renowned eighteenth-century French gastronome and author of the famous *The Physiology of Taste.* French cheesemaker Henri Androuët introduced this cheese in the 1930s, just over 100 years after the gastronome's death. Cream is added to the milk to boost the FAT CONTENT. Brillat-Savarin comes in small 1-pound wheels and has a soft white rind and an off-white interior. The flavor is rich, buttery and sweet with a slight tang. *See also* CHEESE.

brine A strong solution of water and salt used for pickling, preserving and tenderizing foods. Herbs, spices or a sweetener such as sugar or molasses is sometimes added to flavor the brine. *See also* BRINING.

brining A technique whereby meat is soaked in BRINE (saltwater), which tenderizes, moisturizes and flavors it, as well as reduces the cooking time. Brining is an age-old process that has recently enjoyed a resurgence in popularity. The trick is the right balance of salt—too little and it won't do any good, too much and the food will taste salty. Other liquids (such as apple juice, beer or wine) can replace all or part of the water in the brining mixture. Use a non-corrosive container just large enough to contain the food and brine to cover. Over-brining can make the meat mushy and exceedingly salty. After brining is complete, remove the meat and discard the liquid—it's too salty to be used in cooking. This technique turns beef and pork gray, so brown meats well before continuing to cook.

brioche; brioche molds [BREE-ohsh; bree-AHSH] This French creation is a light yeast bread rich with butter and eggs. The classic shape, called *brioche à tête,* has a fluted base and a jaunty topknot. It also comes in the form of small buns or a large round loaf. Special fluted **brioche molds**, available in metal, glass or ceramic, are necessary for the *brioche à tête.* Brioche dough is also used to enclose foods such as sausage or cheese.

brisket [BRIHS-kiht] A cut of beef taken from the breast section under the first five ribs. Brisket is usually sold without the bone and is divided into two sections. The **flat cut** has minimal fat and is usually more expensive than the more flavorful **point cut**, which has more fat. Brisket requires long, slow cooking and is best when braised. Corned beef is made from brisket. *See also* BEEF.

brisling [BRIHZ-ling] *see* SPRAT

British terms *see* British and American Food and Cooking Terms Chart, page 888

broad bean *see* FAVA BEAN

broccoflower [BRAHK-uh-flow-er] Originating in Holland, this cross between broccoli and cauliflower looks like a light green cauliflower and has a milder flavor than either of its parents. The trademarked name *broccoflower* is owned by Tanimura and Antle, a California company. Choose a firm head with compact florets; the leaves should be crisp and green. Avoid any specimens with browning. Store unwashed tightly wrapped broccoflower in the refrigerator for up to 5 days. Wash thoroughly just before using. Broccoflower can be cooked in any way suitable for cauliflower. This vegetable is high in vitamin C, folic acid and copper.

broccoli The name comes from the Italian word for "cabbage sprout" and indeed, broccoli is a relative of cabbage, Brussels sprouts and cauliflower. This deep emerald-green vegetable (which sometimes has a purple tinge) comes in tight clusters of tiny buds that sit on stout, edible stems. It's available year-round, with a peak season from October through April. Look for broccoli with a deep, strong color—green, or green with purple; the buds should be tightly closed and the leaves crisp. Refrigerate unwashed, in an airtight bag, for up to 4 days. If the stalks are tough, peel before cooking. Broccoli, a member of the CRUCIFEROUS family, is an excellent source of vitamins A and C, as well as riboflavin, calcium and iron.

Broccolini The trademarked name for a cross between BROCCOLI and CHINESE KALE. This bright green vegetable has long, slender stalks topped with a bouquet of tiny buds reminiscent of miniature florettes. The flavor is sweet with a subtle, peppery edge; the texture is slightly crunchy. This veggie is also called *baby broccoli.* Broccolini is sold in small bunches and can be refrigerated for up to 10 days. This delicate vegetable is entirely edible and should be cooked briefly (for a crisp-tender texture) or served raw in a salad or as crudités.

broccoli rabe [RAHB] A vegetable related to both the cabbage and turnip family, the leafy green broccoli raab has 6- to 9-inch stalks and scattered clusters of tiny broccolilike buds. It's also called *American gai lan, brocoletti di rape, Italian broccoli, rabe, rape* and *rapini.* The greens have a pungent, bitter flavor that is not particularly popular in America where, more often than not, they're used as animal fodder. Italians are particularly fond of broccoli raab, however, and cook it in a variety of ways including frying, steaming and braising. It can also be used in soups or salads. Broccoli raab should be wrapped in a plastic bag and refrigerated for no more than 5 days.

broche, à la [ah lah BROHSH] French for "spit-roasted."

brochette [broh-SHEHT] The French word for "skewer." *En brochette* refers to food cooked on a skewer.

brocoletti di rape *see* BROCCOLI RABE

brodo [BROH-doh] The Italian word for "broth."

broil To cook food directly under or above the heat source. Food can be broiled in an oven, directly under the gas or electric heat source, or on a barbecue grill, directly over charcoal or other heat source.

broiler-fryer *see* CHICKEN

Brot [BROHT] German word for "bread."

broth A liquid resulting from cooking vegetables, meat or fish in water. The term is sometimes used synonymously with *bouillon.*

brown To cook quickly over high heat, causing the surface of the food to turn brown while the interior stays moist. This method not only gives food an appetizing color, but also a rich flavor. Browning is usually done on top of the stove, but may also be achieved under a broiling unit.

brown bean sauce *see* BEAN SAUCES; BEAN PASTES

brown betty *see* BETTY

brown butter Butter cooked until it's a pale brown color, akin to that of hazelnuts. The French term is *beurre noisette* ("hazelnut butter"). Brown butter is used to dress myriad foods including vegetables, fish, meat and pasta.

brownie A dense, chewy, cakelike cookie that is generally chocolate-flavored (hence the name), but can also be a variety of other flavors including butterscotch and vanilla (in which case it's called a *blondie*).

brown rice *see* RICE

brown sauce *see* ESPAGNOLE SAUCE

brown stock Any STOCK made from beef, veal or chicken bones (and sometimes meat) that have been browned before the liquid is added. Carmelizing the meat juices on the bottom of the pan, along with any vegetables (typically onions, carrots and celery), will enrich both color and flavor. *See also* SAUCE.

brown velvet *see* BLACK VELVET

bruise [BROOZ] In cooking, to partially crush an ingredient in order to release its flavor. Bruising a garlic clove with the flat side of a knife crushes without cutting it.

brûlé [broo-LAY] The French word for "burned," as in CRÈME BRÛLÉE.

brûlot *see* CAFÉ BRÛLOT.

brunch A combination of breakfast and lunch, usually eaten sometime between 11 A.M. and 3 P.M. Sunday brunch has become quite popular both for home entertaining and in restaurants. Though brunch is thought of as an American tradition, H. L. Mencken tells us that it was popular in England around 1900 . . . long before it reached the United States.

Brunello di Montalcino [broo-NELL-oh dee mawn-tahl-CHEE-noh] Regarded as some of Italy's best wines, Brunello di Montalcinos are made totally from a SANGIOVESE clone, Brunello ("little dark one"), so named for the brown hue of its skin. The wines are big, deep-colored and powerful and have enough TANNIN to be very long-lived. Brunello di Montalcino wines must be AGED for 4 years (5 for the RISERVA), $3^1/_2$ of which must be in wooden barrels.

brunoise [broo-NWAHZ] A mixture of vegetables that have been finely diced or shredded, then cooked slowly in butter. The brunoise is then used to flavor soups and sauces.

brunost [BROO-nohst] *see* GJETOST

Brunswick stew Brunswick County, Virginia, was the birthplace in 1828 of this hearty squirrel-meat and onion stew. Today, it is generally made with rabbit or chicken and often contains a variety of vegetables including okra, lima beans, tomatoes and corn.

bruschetta [broo-SKEH-tah; broo-SHEH-tah] From the Italian *bruscare* meaning "to roast over coals," this traditional garlic bread is made by rubbing slices of toasted bread with garlic cloves, then drizzling the bread with extra-virgin olive oil. The bread is salted and peppered, then heated and served warm.

brush To apply a liquid (such as melted butter or a glaze) with a pastry (or basting) brush to the surface of food such as meat or bread.

Brussels sprouts Said to have been cultivated in 16th-century Belgium, Brussels sprouts are a member of the cabbage family and, indeed, resemble tiny cabbage heads. Many rows of sprouts grow on a single long stalk. They range from $1/2$ to $1^1/2$ inches in diameter; the smaller sprouts are more tender. Brussels sprouts are available from late August through March. Buy small bright green sprouts with compact heads. Store unwashed sprouts in an airtight plastic bag in the refrigerator up to 3 days; longer than that and sprouts will develop a strong flavor. Brussels sprouts, a CRUCIFEROUS vegetable, are high in vitamins A and C, and are a fair source of iron.

brut [BROOT] A term applied to the driest (*see* DRY) CHAMPAGNE. Brut Champagnes are drier than those labeled "extra dry." The term *extra brut* denotes a wine that's extremely (sometimes totally) dry. Totally dry sparkling wines, which aren't slightly sweetened with a small amount of DOSAGE, are also sometimes called *brut nature* or *brut integral*.

Bryndza; Brinza [BRIHND-zah] A derivative of the Romanian word for cheese (*brânza˘*), Bryndza is a popular cheese that originated in Slovakia and is now produced throughout Eastern Europe. Though traditionally made from raw sheep's milk, it may also be produced from cow's and goat's milk and sometimes a mixture of milks. Bryndza is soft, stark white and comes in various sizes, from small tubs to molded blocks. It may be RIPENED for 2 to 4 weeks, and the flavor is generally fresh, rich, salty and tangy. The texture ranges from soft and spreadable to firm and crumbly, depending on the age. Some Bryndza is cut into chunks and preserved in BRINE, which produces a flavor and texture similar to that of FETA. Bryndza has a FAT CONTENT of about 45 percent. *See also* CHEESE.

bST The commonly used acronym for bovine somatotropin, a naturally occurring polypeptide hormone secreted by the anterior lobe of the pituitary gland. It promotes body growth, which is why it's also referred to as a *growth hormone.* bST influences the metabolism of proteins, carbohydrates and lipids. *See also* RBGH.

b'steeya [bs-TEE-yah] A Moroccan dish of PHYLLO dough (or MALSOUKA) surrounding a melange of shredded chicken, ground almonds and spices.

The "pie" is baked until a crisp golden brown, then sprinkled with powdered sugar and cinnamon. Also spelled *bastela, bastila, bastille, bisteeya* and *pastilla*.

Bual *see* MADEIRA

bubble and squeak A British dish of equal parts mashed potatoes and chopped cooked cabbage mixed together and fried until well browned. Originally, the dish included chopped boiled beef. The name is said to come from the sounds the potato-cabbage mixture makes as it cooks (some say it's from the sounds one's stomach makes after eating bubble and squeak).

bubble tea If you like something to chew on with your beverage, bubble tea's for you. Now popular around the world, bubble tea originated in Taiwan during the early 1980s. This unique concoction began as flavor-infused tea shaken with ice (which causes bubbles) and poured into a glass at the bottom of which were more "bubbles" in the form of tapioca pearls. Today the term *bubble tea* has evolved to mean almost any drink with tapioca pearls, always served with fat straws big enough to suck up the pearls along with the liquid. This isn't ordinary tapioca but rather big, black orbs twice the size of regular pearl tapioca. They have a soft, chewing gum/Jell-o consistency. And whereas regular tapioca is made from cassava root, most of the tapioca used for bubble tea is sweet-potato based and colored with caramel. During cooking, the light-brown pearls turn almost black, making for a showy presentation in drinks. Although some Asian markets carry jars of cooked tapioca pearls in syrup, they're hard to find. The large uncooked pearls (about $5/16$ inch in diameter and half again as large cooked) can be purchased online at bubbleteasupply.com, which sells everything necessary for bubble tea including the fat straws and myriad flavorings from honeydew to coconut to taro. Bubble tea goes by numerous names including *boba tea, bobo nai cha, momi, momi milk tea, pearl tea, tapioca ball drink, tapioca milk tea* and *zhen shou nai cha*.

bucatini; bucatoni *see* Pasta Glossary, page 883

bûche de Noël [BOOSH duh noh-EHL] Literally translated as "yule log," this traditional French Christmas cake is shaped and decorated to resemble a log. It's made of a sheet of GÉNOISE that is spread with mocha or chocolate BUTTERCREAM, rolled into a log shape and covered with more buttercream. The surface is ridged to resemble the bark of a log, and sometimes garnished with MERINGUE "mushrooms" and with "moss" made from chopped pistachio nuts.

bucherellatene [boo-KEHR-eh-lah-teh-neh] To prick something with the tines of a fork so air escapes during cooking. Bucherellatene is a technique often used in preparation of pie crust or puff pastry so the bottoms bake evenly and don't puff up. It is also used occasionally when preparing items such as potatoes or eggplant to be cooked in the microwave, ensuring that the air escapes and the vegetables don't explode.

Bûcheron [BOOSH-raw*n*] Hailing from France's Loire Valley, Bûcheron is a mass-produced RIPENED goat's-milk cheese. A white, bloomy rind (which is sometimes covered with ASH) covers a soft, spreadable PASTE that has a tangy yet mild flavor. Bûcheron comes in 11-ounce logs (*bûche* is French for "log") and is commonly available in supermarkets. *See also* CHEESE.

buck A drink made with gin, ginger ale and lemon juice. Dating back to the 1890's, a buck is essentially a RICKEY made with ginger ale. Although gin is traditional, almost any liquor may be used. The buck's distinguishing feature is that, after being squeezed to extract the juice, the citrus shell is traditionally put in the glass.

buckle Culinarily, buckle is an old American term for a simple, single-layer cake made with berries (such as a blueberry buckle) or other fruit. Sometimes the fruit is incorporated in the batter, while other times it's simply sprinkled on top of the batter before the cake is baked.

buckwheat A native of Russia, buckwheat is thought of as a cereal, but is actually an herb of the genus *Fagopyrum*. The triangular seeds of this plant are used to make **buckwheat flour**, which has an assertive flavor and is used for pancakes and as an addition to some baked goods. The famous Russian BLINI are made with buckwheat flour. **Buckwheat groats** are the hulled, crushed kernels, which are usually cooked in a manner similar to rice. Groats come in coarse, medium and fine grinds. **Kasha**, which is roasted buckwheat groats, has a toastier, more nutty flavor.

Buddha fruit *see* LUO HAN GUO

Buddha's hand *see* CITRON

buffalo The American buffalo, now being raised by approximately 2,000 producers in the United States, is really a bison—a shaggy, humped member of the cattle family. Buffalo meat is surprisingly tender and tastes somewhat like lean beef. It has no pronounced gamey flavor. Buffalo can be found on some restaurant menus and is available in some specialty meat markets. The cuts are similar to beef and can be substituted for beef in most recipes. However, because buffalo meat is so lean, it should be cooked slowly at a low heat. Buffalo is higher in iron than beef and lower in fat and cholesterol than most cuts of beef and chicken—as well as some fish.

buffalo fish Similar to CARP, this freshwater fish is a member of the sucker family. It has a coarse but sweet, lean flesh that can be baked, poached, sautéed or grilled. Buffalo fish can be purchased whole or in fillets or steaks. It's especially good in its smoked form. *See also* FISH.

Buffalo wings Buffalo, New York's, Anchor Bar originated this dish of deep-fried chicken wings served in a spicy hot sauce and accompanied by blue-cheese dressing.

buffet Culinarily, a buffet is a meal where guests serve themselves from a variety of dishes set out on a table or sideboard.

builders lime *see* PICKLING LIME

bulb baster *see* TURKEY BASTER

Bulgarian carrot pepper A narrow CHILE that is 3 to 4 inches long, has a bright orange color when mature and resembles a small carrot. Native to Bulgaria, where they are called *shipkas,* these peppers are known to produce a bit of heat along with their fruity flavor. The SCOVILLE SCALE rating ranges from 5,000 to 30,000.

bulgogi [BOOL-goh-gee] Also known as *Korean barbecued beef,* this dish consists of thin, tender strips of beef that have been marinated for several hours before being briefly grilled. Although *bulgogi* is Korean for "fire meat," this dish isn't particularly highly spiced. The MARINADE varies but is typically comprised of a combination of ingredients, which may include black pepper, garlic, onions, ginger, sesame oil, sesame seed, soy sauce, sugar and rice wine. Sometimes pear juice or pear PURÉE is used in place of or in addition to wine. The grilled meat is traditionally served with lettuce leaves, steamed white rice, *kochujang* (see CHILE BEAN PASTE) and sometimes KIMCHI. The rice and meat strips are placed in a lettuce leaf, topped with kimchi and kochujang and rolled up to be eaten by hand. *Daeji Bulgogi* is a similar dish made with strips of pork loin and a spicier marinade that includes red pepper flakes and red pepper sauce. Bulgogi is sometimes spelled *pulgogi.*

bulgur wheat; bulghur [BUHL-guhr] A nutritious staple in the Middle East, bulgur wheat consists of wheat kernels that have been steamed, dried and crushed. It is often confused with but is not exactly the same as cracked wheat. Bulgur, also called *burghul,* has a tender, chewy texture and comes in coarse, medium and fine grinds. It makes an excellent wheat PILAF and is delicious in salads (*see* TABBOULEH), and in meat or vegetable dishes, as with KIBBEH.

bullhead *see* CATFISH

bull's horn *see* SWEET PEPPERS

bullshot A drink composed of two parts beef bouillon and one part vodka, plus dashes of WORCESTERSHIRE SAUCE, BITTERS and TABASCO SAUCE.

bully beef A term used in Great Britain for CORNED BEEF, particularly canned versions.

bulochki s makom *see* MAKOWIEC

bun *see* RICE NOODLES

bunching onions *see* WELSH ONION

Bundnerfleisch [BOOND-ner-flysh] A Swiss salt-CURED, air-dried beef similar to (but considered superior to) Africa's BILTONG. It's available only in specialty gourmet markets.

Bundt pan [BUHNT] Originally the trademark name of a TUBE PAN with curved, fluted sides, "Bundt pan" is now the general name of any of that style of cake pan. Classic Bundt pans typically hold 12 cups of batter and are 10 inches in diameter by $3^1/_2$ inches tall. There are also mini-Bundt pans, with six 1-cup molds per pan. To prevent a cake from sticking to this pan, it's extremely important that all the creases of the fluted sides are well greased before pouring in a batter. Buying nonstick Bundt pans will save you the trouble. *See also* COOKWARE AND BAKEWARE MATERIALS.

buñuelo [boo-NWAY-loh] A thin, deep-fried Mexican pastry sprinkled with cinnamon-sugar.

bunya nuts [BUN-yuh] Actually the seed of the bunya pine (or bunya-bunya), an evergreen coniferous tree. Native to Australia's states of New South Wales and Queensland, bunya pines grow to 100 to 140 feet tall. The female trees produce football-size cones containing 50 or more seeds. The almond-shaped seed or "nut" is about 1 to $1^1/_2$ inches long and sheathed in a fibrous, tan shell. Bunya nuts have been an important Aboriginal food source for centuries. They have a starchy texture similar to a CHESTNUT and a flavor reminiscent of macadamias and pine nuts. They may be eaten raw or cooked (in soups, casseroles, pies and so on) or dried and ground into flour. Bunya nuts are available fresh from January through March and frozen during the rest of the year.

buon appetito [bwon ah-peh-TEE-toh] Italian for "good appetite," the French counterpart of which is BON APPÉTIT.

burbot [BER-buht] This freshwater COD has a fairly lean, white flesh with a delicate flavor. It can be poached, baked, broiled or sautéed. *See also* FISH.

burdock Known in Japan as *gobo,* burdock is a slender root vegetable with a rusty brown skin and grayish-white flesh. Cultivated primarily in Japan, it grows wild throughout much of Europe and the United States.

Burdock has a sweet, earthy flavor and tender-crisp texture. It's important to choose firm, young burdock, preferably no more than 1 inch in diameter; they will be about 18 inches long. Do not wash the earth-covered roots until ready to use. Store, tightly wrapped in a plastic bag, in the refrigerator for up to 4 days. Scrub before cooking; peeling isn't necessary. Burdock can be thinly sliced or shredded and used in soups as well as with vegetables and meats.

burfi [BER-fee] *see* BARFI

burghul *see* BULGUR WHEAT

burgoo [ber-GOO] Also called *Kentucky burgoo,* this thick stew is full of meats (usually pork, veal, beef, lamb and poultry) and vegetables (including potatoes, onions, cabbage, carrots, sweet green peppers, corn, okra, lima beans and celery). Early renditions were more often made with small game such as rabbit and squirrel. Burgoo is popular for large gatherings in America's southern states. Originally, the word "burgoo" was used to describe an oatmeal porridge served to English sailors as early as 1750.

Burgundy 1. One of the world's most famous wine growing areas, located in eastern France, southeast of Paris. The Burgundy region has established a reputation over centuries for fine wines, which vary considerably from region to region. Burgundy, known in France as *Bourgogne,* consists of five basic regions—Chablis, the Côte d'Or (divided into Côte de Beaune and Côte de Nuits), the Côte Chalonnaise, the Maconnais and Beaujolais. The focus in Burgundy is on three grape varieties—Pinot Noir and Gamay for red wines, Chardonnay for whites. Although wines made with Pinot Noir and Chardonnay get most of the attention, there are more Gamay-based wines produced (in Beaujolais) than in all of the remaining Burgundy region. Among the notable wines from this region are Chablis, Fleurie, Gevrey-Chambertin, Meursault, Montagny and Pouilly-Fuissé. 2. Burgundy is also a generic name used for ordinary, inexpensive red wine made outside of France in countries like Australia, South Africa and the United States. Although many of the bulk producers in these countries are starting to call these wines "red table wine," the word "Burgundy" still appears on some wine bottle labels.

buri [BOO-ree] *see* YELLOWTAIL

buridda [boo-REED-dah] An Italian fish stew, similar to the French BOURRIDE.

burielli *see* BURRINO

burnet [BER-niht] Native to Europe, burnet includes any of several herbs, the most common being **salad burnet**. Its leaves are used in salads and with vegetables. Like BORAGE, burnet leaves are also used to flavor drinks, such as tea. When crushed, they have a fragrance similar to cucumber. *See also* HERBS.

burnt cream The British version of the French CRÈME BRÛLÉE.

burnt sugar *see* CARAMELIZE

Burrata [boor-RAH-tah] According to some, this cow's-milk cheese was created as a means of using up scraps of mozzarella. It's an Italian creation made by the PASTA FILATA process, whereby the fresh CURD is dipped into hot WHEY, then stretched and kneaded to the desired pliability. To create Burrata, the cheesemaker uses the stretched curd to form a bag about $1/3$-inch thick, which is filled with bits of unspun mozzarella and cream. The top is twisted closed and the pouch is dipped in brine. The cream thickens inside the bag, which produces a soft, rich center with a fresh milky quality that oozes out when the cheese is cut. Burrata is often wrapped in asphodel leaves, which are similar to those of a leek. This fresh cheese usually can be found only in specialty cheese shops. Refrigerate immediately and consume within a few days. Most Burrata comes from Italy although it's also now being produced in the United States. *See also* CHEESE.

burrino; pl. **burrini** [boo-REE-noh; boo-REE-nee] A special PASTA FILATA-style cow's-milk cheese that hails from southern Italy (Apulia, Basilicata, Calabria, Campangna and Sicily). Burrino is made by hand-shaping the fresh cheese (such as MOZZARELLA or PROVOLONE) around a pat of very cold butter, then tying it at the top. Such cheeses may also sometimes be stuffed with other foods, such as a chunk of salami; some are smoked. Burrino, which can be fresh or RIPENED for a few weeks, is also called *burielli, butirro, manteca, piticelle* and *provole*, depending on where the cheese is made.

burrito [ber-EE-toh] A flour TORTILLA folded and rolled to completely enclose any of several savory fillings including shredded or chopped meat, REFRIED BEANS, grated cheese, sour cream, lettuce, etc.

burro [BOO-roh] Italian for "BUTTER."

bush tomato Native to the Australian outback, the bush tomato is part of the nightshade family and is related to the eggplant, potato and tomato. The ripe fruit looks like a yellowish cherry tomato. However, most are harvested after they become sun-dried and turn a reddish-brown color. This drying process intensifies the flavor, resulting in a taste similar to a regular sun-dried tomato with a slight bitterness and a hint of caramel. The bush tomato is often crushed; in its crushed form, it is commonly referred to as *akudjura*. Australia's Aboriginal people have used bush tomatoes for thousands of years as a staple of their diet. In recent years akudjura has been a rising star as a spice, added to everything from cheese to meat dishes, salads, soups and vegetables. There is limited availability in the United States, though some mail-order outlets offer akudjura through the Internet.

butcher's steak *see* HANGER STEAK

butcher's steel *see* SHARPENING STEEL

butirro *see* BURRINO

butter Made by churning cream until it reaches a semisolid state, butter must by U.S. law be at least 80 percent MILK FAT. The remaining 20 percent consists of water and milk solids. The U.S. Department of Agriculture (USDA) grades butter quality based on flavor, body, texture, color and salt. Butter packages bear a shield surrounding the letter grade (and occasionally the numerical score equivalent) indicating the quality of the contents. The grades, beginning with the finest, are AA (93 score), A (92 score), B (90 score) and C (89 score). AA and A grades are those most commonly found at the retail level. Butter may be artificially colored (with natural ANNATTO); it may also be salted or unsalted. **Unsalted butter** is usually labeled as such and contains absolutely no salt. It's sometimes erroneously referred to as "sweet" butter—a misnomer because any butter made with sweet instead of sour cream is sweet butter. Therefore, expect packages labeled "sweet cream butter" to contain salted butter. Unsalted butter is preferred by many for everyday eating and baking. Because it contains no salt (which acts as a preservative), it is more perishable than salted butter and therefore stored in the freezer section of some markets. **Whipped butter** has had air beaten into it, thereby increasing volume and creating a softer, more spreadable consistency when cold. It comes in salted and unsalted forms. **Light** or **reduced-calorie butter** has about half the fat of regular butter, possible through the addition of water, skim milk and gelatin. It shouldn't be substituted for regular butter or margarine in frying and baking. **Storing butter:** Because butter absorbs flavors like a sponge, it should be wrapped airtight for storage. Refrigerate regular butter for up to 1 month, unsalted butter for up to 2 weeks. Both can be frozen for up to 6 months. *See also* BERCY (butter); BEURRE BLANC; BEURRE MANIÉ; BEURRE NOIR; BEURRE NOISETTE; BROWN BUTTER; BUTTER SUBSTITUTES; CLARIFIED BUTTER; COMPOUND BUTTER; FATS AND OILS; GARLIC BUTTER; GHEE.

butterball steak *see* ROUND, BEEF

butter bean *see* LIMA BEAN

butter clam A small, sweet, hard-shell clam from Puget Sound. Butter clams can be cooked in a variety of ways, including steaming, stewing and frying. *See also* CLAM.

buttercream A light, creamy frosting made with softened butter, powdered sugar, egg yolks and milk or light cream. This uncooked frosting is beaten until light and creamy. It can be flavored in many ways and is used both as a filling and frosting for a variety of cakes and pastries.

buttercup squash A variety of TURBAN SQUASH that ranges from 4 to 8 inches in diameter and 2 to 3 inches high. It has a light blue-gray turban with a dark green shell flecked with gray. The flesh is orange and the flavor reminiscent of sweet potato. It can be baked, steamed or simmered. *See also* SQUASH.

butter curler A small (6- to 7-inch-long) utensil with a serrated hook at one end. The hook is drawn down the length of a stick of butter to make butter curls. The curls are then dropped into ice water to set their shape.

butterfat *see* MILK FAT

butterfish Found off the Atlantic and Gulf coasts, the small (average 8 ounces), high-fat butterfish has a tender texture and a rich, sweet flavor. It is usually sold whole and is sometimes smoked. Butterfish can be broiled, baked, grilled or sautéed. Depending on the region, they're also known as *dollarfish, Pacific pompano* and *pomfret. See also* FISH; SABLEFISH.

butterfly In cooking, to split a food (such as shrimp) down the center, cutting almost but not completely through. The two halves are then opened flat to resemble a butterfly shape.

butterhead lettuce One of two varieties of head lettuce (the other being CRISPHEAD). Butterhead lettuces have small, round, loosely formed heads with soft, buttery-textured leaves ranging from pale green on the outer leaves to pale yellow-green on the inner leaves. The flavor is sweet and succulent. Because the leaves are quite tender, they require gentle washing and handling. **Boston** and **Bibb** (also called **limestone**) lettuce are the two most well known of the butterhead family. The smaller Bibb is highly prized by gourmets. Both Boston and Bibb lettuce are sometimes referred to simply as "butterhead" or "butter" lettuce. *See also* LETTUCE.

buttermilk *see* MILK

buttermilk pie A favorite in the American South, this pie has a filling of buttermilk, butter, eggs, flour and sugar, plus flavorings like lemon juice, vanilla and nutmeg. It's similar to but tangier than CHESS PIE.

butter mold These decorative molds are used to form butter into fancy shapes. They come in ceramic, metal, wood and plastic; their sizes range from small, individual portions to large 8-ounce or more family-style molds. The molds are filled with softened butter and leveled off.

After chilling, the solidified butter is removed from the mold and refrigerated until ready to serve.

butter muslin British term for CHEESECLOTH.

butternut This native American nut grows in New England and is also known as the *white walnut*. It has a rich, oily meat which is generally used in candies and baked goods. Because of the high oil content, butternuts become rancid quickly. *See also* NUTS; WALNUT.

butternut squash This large, cylindrical winter squash looks rather like a pear-shaped bat. It's 8 to 12 inches long, 3 to 5 inches at its widest point and can weigh from 2 to 3 pounds. The color of the smooth shell ranges from yellow to camel; the flesh is sweet and orange. It can be baked, steamed or simmered. *See also* SQUASH.

butterscotch The flavor of butterscotch is a blend of butter and brown sugar. It is popular for cookies, ice-cream toppings, frostings and candies.

butter substitutes Found in powdered and granular forms, butter substitutes are made by a process that removes the fat and water from butter extract (a blend of modified butter oil and spray-dried butter). They contain no fat or cholesterol. What these "all natural" (according to the label) products do contain are such ingredients as maltodextrin (a carbohydrate derived from corn), corn syrup solids, salt, natural flavorings, buttermilk and cornstarch. As expected from the ingredients used, butter substitutes have an embarrassingly counterfeit flavor. They also have from about 8 to 12 calories per teaspoon, as opposed to butter or margarine's 33 calories per teaspoon. Butter substitutes may either be reconstituted by blending with a liquid, or sprinkled directly on to food. Because they're fat-free, they cannot be used for baking, frying or greasing pans. *See also* BUTTER.

butyric acid [byoo-TIHR-ihk] Found chiefly in butter, this natural acid not only produces butter's distinctive flavor but also causes the rancid smell in spoiled butter. Butyric acid, also called *butanoic acid,* is also found in some fruits and is produced synthetically to be used as a flavoring agent in various food products.

Byrrh [BIHR] A DRY, slightly bitter French APÉRITIF with a light orange flavor.

byssus [BIHS-suhs] *see* BEARD

caballo chile *see* ROCOTO CHILE

cabbage The word cabbage is a derivation of the French word *caboche,* a colloquial term for "head." The cabbage family—of which Brussels sprouts, broccoli, cauliflower and kale are all members—is wide and varied. Cabbage itself comes in many forms—the shapes can be flat, conical or round, the heads compact or loose, and the leaves curly or plain. In the United States, the most widely used cabbage comes in compact heads of waxy, tightly wrapped leaves that range in color from almost white to green to red. SAVOY CABBAGE and CHINESE CABBAGE are considered culinarily superior but are less readily available. Choose a cabbage with fresh, crisp-looking leaves that are firmly packed; the head should be heavy for its size. Cabbage may be refrigerated, tightly wrapped, for about a week. It can be cooked in a variety of ways or eaten raw, as in SLAW. Cabbage, a CRUCIFEROUS vegetable, contains a good amount of vitamin C and some vitamin A.

cabbage turnip *see* KOHLRABI

Cabernet Franc [KA-behr-nay FRAHN; FRANGK] Although similar in structure and flavor to CABERNET SAUVIGNON, this red wine grape is not quite as full-bodied, and has fewer TANNINS and less acid. It is, however, more aromatic and herbaceous. Unlike Cabernet Sauvignon, Cabernet Franc grows in cooler climates and ripens early. Therefore, it can be particularly important if weather conditions create a less-than-perfect Cabernet Sauvignon crop. Under such circumstances, the addition of Cabernet Franc might salvage the vintage.

Cabernet Sauvignon [ka-behr-NAY soh-vihn-YOHN; soh-vee-NYAWN] The most successful and popular of the top-quality red-wine grapes. Cabernet Sauvignon is the basis for most of California's superb red wines and the primary grape of most of the top vineyards in BORDEAUX'S Médoc and Graves districts. In Bordeaux, Cabernet Sauvignon is most often blended with one or more of the following grapes: Merlot, Cabernet Franc, Petit Verdot or Malbec. In California, wines are more often made with 100 percent Cabernet Sauvignon grapes, although some blending is now taking place. Cabernet Sauvignon grapes produce full-bodied, fruity wines that are rich, complex and intensely flavorful. There are a multitude of well-made Cabernet Sauvignon–based wines made throughout the world. Among the most notable are those from France's Château Lafite-Rothschild, Château Latour, Château Mouton-Rothschild and Château Margaux, and California's Beaulieu Vineyards, Caymus Vineyards, Heitz Wine Cellars and Robert Mondavi Winery.

cabinet pudding This classic English dessert is made with layers of bread, cake or LADYFINGERS (which may be soaked with LIQUEUR), dried fruit and custard. The pudding is baked, unmolded and usually served with CRÈME ANGLAISE. Another version of cabinet pudding uses gelatin and whipped cream; rather than being baked, it's simply chilled until set.

cabra [KAH-brah; KAY-bray] Spanish for "goat."

Cabrales [kah-BRAH-lays] A semisoft BLUE CHEESE from Spain named after a village in the Picos de Europa mountains. Although now primarily made with cow's milk, traditionally Cabrales was (and occasionally still is) made with a mixture of cow's, sheep's and goat's milk, though the mixed-milk version is rarely seen in the United States. Cabrales, which is considered one of the great blue cheeses, has a soft, creamy texture and a complex, zesty flavor. It's aged for $2^1/_2$ to 3 months, generally in natural caves. It has a FAT CONTENT of 45 percent. *See also* CHEESE.

cabrito [kay-BREE-toh] Spanish for "kid" (a young goat).

cacao [kah-KAY-oh; kah-KAH-oh] The tropical, evergreen cacao tree is cultivated for its seeds (also called beans), from which COCOA BUTTER, CHOCOLATE and COCOA POWDER are produced.

cacciatore; It. cacciatora [kah-chuh-TOH-ray; kah-chuh-TOH-rah] Italian for "hunter," this American-Italian term refers to food prepared "hunter-style," with mushrooms, onions, tomatoes, various herbs and sometimes wine. Chicken *cacciatore* is the most popular dish prepared in this style.

cacciuco [kah-CHEW-koh] A spicy Italian seafood stew similar to French BOUILLABAISSE made with assorted fish plus shellfish such as clams, mussels and/or shrimp in a tomato garlic broth. It's often seen on menus as *Cacciuco alla Livornese* because of its association with Livorno, Italy.

cachaça [kah-SHAH-sah] A Brazilian BRANDY made with sugar cane; also called *pinga* (PEEN-gah). The CAIPIRINHA is Brazil's most popular cachaça-based drink.

cachapa [kah-CHAH-pah] Thick corn pancakes popular in Venezuela, cachapas are made with a thick, lumpy batter (which sometimes includes fresh corn kernels) and baked on a griddle. They're topped simply with butter or cheese—or more exotically with spicy chicken, pork or beef—before being folded and grilled again.

cachito [kah-CHEE-toh] Popular throughout Argentina and Venezuela, a cachito is a CROISSANT or other savory PUFF PASTRY filled with chopped ham and cheese and heated until the cheese melts.

cachola *see* CAÇOILA

caciocavallo [kah-choh-kuh-VAH-loh] From southern Italy, *caciocavallo* ("cheese on horseback") is said to date back to the 14th century, and is believed by some to have originally been made from mare's milk. Today this cheese is made with cow's milk and has a mild, slightly salty flavor and firm, smooth texture when young (about 2 months). As it ages, the flavor becomes more pungent and the texture more granular, making it ideal for grating. Caciocavallo is one of the PASTA FILATA cheeses (like PROVOLONE and MOZZARELLA), which means it has been stretched and shaped by hand. It may be purchased plain or smoked (the latter referred to as *affumicato*) and typically comes in string-tied gourd or spindle shapes. *See also* CHEESE.

caciotta [kah-CHO-tah] A universal name for cow's- or sheep's-milk cheeses made throughout Italy. Caciotta are simple, soft and mild.

caçoila [CAH-sohy-lah] 1. Black clay pot used for cooking in Portugal. 2. Name given to a variety of stews made in such a pot. Caçoila is also spelled *cachola. See also* CHANFANA.

cactus *see* NOPALES; PRICKLY PEAR

cactus leaves (pads) *see* NOPALES

cactus pear Named for its pearlike shape and size, the cactus pear comes from any of several varieties of opuntia cactus. Its prickly skin can range in color from green to purplish red; its soft, porous flesh (scattered with black seeds) from light yellow-green to deep golden. Also called *prickly pear,* this fruit has a melonlike aroma and a sweet but rather bland flavor. It's extremely popular in Mexico, Central and South America, the Mediterranean countries and southern Africa, and is slowly gaining favor in the United States. Cactus pears are available in Latin markets and some specialty produce markets from fall through spring. Choose fruit that gives slightly to palm pressure. It should have a deep, even color. Ripen firm cactus pears at room temperature until soft. Store ripe fruit in the refrigerator for up to a week. Cactus pears are usually served cold, peeled and sectioned with the seeds removed.

Caerphilly [kar-FIHL-ee] This mild yet tangy cow's-milk CHEESE has a moist, semifirm texture and is generally sold in wheels or blocks. It's best eaten fresh (the English prefer it only a few weeks old), though some examples are ripened for 6 months. Though now produced primarily in England, Caerphilly originated in Wales and takes its name from the village in which it was first made; it was the traditional lunch of Welsh miners. This cheese has a FAT CONTENT of about 48 percent. *See also* CHEESE.

Caesar salad [SEE-zer] A salad consisting of greens (classically, ROMAINE LETTUCE) tossed with a garlic VINAIGRETTE dressing (made with WORCESTERSHIRE SAUCE and lemon juice), grated Parmesan cheese, croutons, a CODDLED egg and sometimes anchovies. It is said to have been created in 1924 by Italian chef Caesar Cardini, who owned a restaurant in Tijuana, Mexico.

cafe [ka-FAY] A small, unpretentious restaurant.

café [ka-FAY] French for "coffee."

café au lait [ka-fay oh-LAY] French for "coffee with milk." It usually consists of equal portions of scalded milk and coffee.

café brûlot [ka-fay broo-LOH] A traditional New Orleans flaming brew consisting of coffee blended with spices, orange and lemon peel and brandy. *Café brûlot* is generally made in a flameproof bowl and ladled into cups. In French, *brûlot* means "burnt brandy."

café con leche [ka-fay kon LAY-chay] Spanish for "coffee with milk."

café filtre [ka-fay FEEL-truh] French term meaning "filtered coffee" and referring to coffee made by pouring very hot water through a filter holding ground coffee. It's traditionally served black, in demitasse cups.

café mocha [ka-fay MOH-kah] ESPRESSO combined with chocolate syrup and a liberal amount of foamy steamed milk. A *café mocha* is usually served in a tall glass mug.

caffè [ka-FAY] Italian for "coffee."

caffè americano [ka-FAY ah-mer-ih-KAH-noh] Italian term for an ESPRESSO diluted with three parts water.

caffeine [ka-FEEN] An organic compound found in foods such as chocolate, coffee, cola nuts and tea. Scientific studies have shown that caffeine stimulates the nervous system, kidneys and heart, causes the release of insulin in the body and dilates the blood vessels.

caffè latte [ka-fay LAH-tay] ESPRESSO combined with a liberal amount of foamy steamed milk, usually served in a tall glass mug.

caffè macchiato [ka-fay mah-kee-YAH-toh] An ESPRESSO with a dollop of steamed-milk foam, served in an espresso cup.

cai cuc *see* CHRYSANTHEMUM LEAVES

Caipirinha [ki-pee-REEN-yah] Brazil's most popular spirited potable, the Caipirinha is made by muddling (*see* MUDDLE) lime wedges and sugar together in a tall glass, then adding crushed ice and the potent Brazilian sugar-cane brandy CACHAÇA. Substituting vodka makes it a *Caipiroska;* rum makes it a *Caipirissima.* The word *Caipirinha* is Brazilian for "drink of farmers."

cajeta *see* DULCE DE LECHE

Cajun cooking [KAY-juhn] Today's Cajuns are the descendants of 1,600 French Acadians whom the British forced from their Nova Scotian homeland in 1785. The local Indians transmuted the word *Acadians* to *Cagians* and, eventually, to *Cajuns.* Many confuse Cajun cooking with CREOLE COOKING but though there are many points of similarity, there are also distinct differences. Cajun cooking, a combination of French and Southern cuisines, is robust, country-style cookery that uses a dark ROUX and plenty of animal (usually pork) fat. Creole cooking places its emphasis on butter and cream. Some maintain that Creole cooking uses more tomatoes and the Cajuns more spices. Both cuisines make generous use of FILÉ POWDER and the culinary "holy trinity" of chopped green peppers, onions and celery. Two of the more traditional Cajun dishes include JAMBALAYA and coush-coush (a thick cornmeal breakfast dish).

Cajun popcorn A popular Louisiana snack and appetizer of crawfish (*see* CRAYFISH) tails that have been shelled, battered and deep-fried until extra crispy.

Cajun seasoning; Cajun spice seasoning There are many Cajun seasoning blends on the market today, all with their own distinct characteristics. Most are boldly flavored and sassy and representative of CAJUN COOKING. In general, a Cajun seasoning blend might include garlic, onion, CHILES, black pepper, mustard and celery. However, you can count on the fact that each Cajun seasoning blend on the market will be a little different from another.

cake A sweet, baked confection usually containing flour, sugar, flavoring ingredients and eggs or other LEAVENER such as baking powder or baking soda.

cake comb A flat, small (usually 5- by 5- by 4-inch), triangle-shape tool, generally made of stainless steel. Each of the three edges has serrated teeth of a different size. This tool, also called a *decorating comb,* is used to make decorative designs and swirls in the frosting on a cake.

cake of three milks *see* PASTEL DE TRES LECHES

cake pans Any of various size pans used for baking cakes. The shape can be round, square, rectangular or festive (hearts, shamrocks and so forth). TUBE PANS are used for ANGEL FOOD CAKE, RING MOLDS for SAVARINS and the like. Shiny pans are best for cakemaking because they reflect the heat and, thereby, produce cakes with tender crusts. When you're using glass cake pans, reduce the oven temperature by 25°F. *See also* BABA; BAKEWARE; COOKWARE AND BAKEWARE MATERIALS; LADYFINGER; MADELEINE; Pan Substitution Chart, page 859.

cala [kah-LAH] The word "cala" comes from an African word for "rice," and refers to a deep-fried pastry made with rice, yeast, sugar and spices. Calas resemble small, round doughnuts without a hole and are usually sprinkled with powdered sugar.

calabacita [KAHL-ah-bah-SEE-tah] Spanish for ZUCCHINI.

calabash *see* CUCUZZA

calabaza [kah-lah-BAH-sah] A pumpkinlike squash popular throughout the Caribbean as well as Central and South America. The calabaza, which is also called *West Indian pumpkin,* is round in shape and can range in size from as large as a watermelon to as small as a cantaloupe. Its skin can range in color from green to pale tan to light red-orange; its flesh is a brilliant orange. Calabaza has a sweet flavor akin to that of BUTTERNUT SQUASH; its texture is firm and succulent. It can be found in chunks throughout the year in Latin markets. Choose cut pieces with fresh, moist, tightly grained flesh with no signs of soft or wet spots. If you can find whole calabaza, look for those that are unblemished and heavy for their size; the stem should still be attached. Whole calabaza can be stored in a cool, dark place for up to 6 weeks. Cut calabaza should be wrapped tightly and refrigerated for no more than a week. Calabaza may be used in any way suitable for winter squashes like ACORN SQUASH and butternut.

calamansi; calamansi orange [kah-lah-MAHN-see] A small citrus fruit popular in the Philippines and other parts of Southeast Asia. The calamansi is also known as *acid orange, calamondin, Chinese orange, kalamansi, musk lime* and *Panama orange.* It's a hybrid whose parentage is unclear; some horticulturists theorize that the calamansi is the offspring of a KUMQUAT and MANDARIN ORANGE, while others speculate that it's a lime-mandarin cross. Calamansis look like round limes with thin green to greenish-yellow skins that turn orange as they mature. The orange pulp has relatively large seeds and is exceedingly sour, which is why this fruit is used as one would use lemons. Calamansis, which are high in calcium, potassium and vitamin C, are grown year-round in California and Florida but are more plentiful from November through May. They're not widely available but can be found in some Asian markets, produce stores and upscale supermarkets. Store calamansis in the refrigerator for up to 2 weeks.

calamari [kal-uh-MAHR-ee] *see* SQUID

calamata olive *see* KALAMATA OLIVE

calamondin; calamondin orange *see* CALAMANSI

Calasparra rice [kah-lah-SPAH*RR*-ah] Short-grain rice grown around the town of Calasparra in southeast Spain's Murcia province. Calasparra is the favorite rice for making PAELLA. BOMBA RICE, which is also grown around Calasparra, is considered to be superior but is more expensive. Calasparra rice matures slowly and is somewhat dehydrated when mature, allowing it to absorb liquids and flavors when cooked. *See also* RICE.

calcium A mineral essential in building and maintaining bones and teeth, as well as in providing efficient muscle contraction and blood clotting. Calcium is found in dairy products, leafy green vegetables (such as spinach, turnip greens and broccoli), sardines and canned salmon with bones and rhubarb.

calcium hydroxide *see* PICKLING LIME

caldeirada [kahl-DAY-ray-dah] Similar to a thick French BOUILLABAISSE, caldeirada is a seafood stew from Portugal made with an assortment of fish and shellfish, onions, tomatoes, white wine, olive oil, garlic and herbs. The stew is often ladled over thick slices of bread.

caldereta [kahl-DAY-ray-tah] A Spanish-influenced dish very popular in the Philippines. Caldereta is a stew originally made with goat meat but now often made with beef, chicken or fish. Other common ingredients include garlic, ground liver or liver spread, onions, peppers and tomato sauce or paste, but variations abound. The name comes from the Spanish *caldera*, a CAULDRON in which stews are made. Caldereta is also spelled *kaldereta*.

caldo [KAHL-doh] 1. Italian for "warm" or "hot." 2. The Spanish and Portuguese word meaning "broth" or "soup."

caldo verde [KAHL-doh VEHR-deh] *Caldo verde* ("green soup") is a Portuguese favorite that combines shredded KALE, sliced potatoes, LINGUIÇA sausage and olive oil for a deliciously satisfying soup.

caldron *see* CAULDRON

calf's foot jelly An ASPIC made by boiling calves' feet until the natural GELATIN is extracted. The liquid is strained, then combined with wine, lemon juice and spices and refrigerated until set. If sugar is added, it can be eaten as a dessert. Calf's-foot jelly was once thought to be a restorative for invalids.

calf's liver *see* LIVER

calico bean *see* LIMA BEAN

California corbina *see* DRUM

California Jack cheese *see* MONTEREY JACK CHEESE

California roll A type of SUSHI with a filling of crab or imitation crab (SURIMI), avocado and cucumber wrapped in a sheet of seaweed (NORI) and finished with an outer layer of rice (SUSHI MESHI). Sometimes this cylinder is rolled in toasted sesame seeds or TOBIKO. The exterior rice layer—not a traditional sushi approach—is the invention of Ichiro Mashita, the Los Angeles sushi chef who created the California roll in the 1970s to entice American palates that resisted the usual outer wrapping of nori.

calimocho *see* KALIMOTXO

callaloo [KAL-lah-loo] 1. The large, edible green leaves of the TARO ROOT, popular in the Caribbean islands, cooked as one would prepare turnip or COLLARD GREENS. 2. A Caribbean soup made with callaloo greens, coconut milk, okra, yams, CHILES, lime juice and any of various meats or fish, particularly crab, pork and BACALAO (salted fish).

calorie [KAL-uh-ree] A unit measuring the energy value of foods, calibrated by the quantity of heat required to raise the temperature of 1 gram of water by one degree CELSIUS at a pressure of one atmosphere. The four sources from which calories are obtained are ALCOHOL, CARBOHYDRATES, FATS and PROTEINS; however all these sources are not equal. For example, fat packs a hefty 9 calories per gram, over twice as much as the 4 calories per gram carried by both carbohydrates and proteins. Alcohol has 7 calories per gram, almost as many as fat. Clearly, fats and alcohol have a much higher caloric density than carbohydrates and proteins, so it's obvious that a 6-ounce serving of steak will be much more expensive calorically than 6 ounces of cauliflower.

calsone [kahl-SOH-nay] A filled egg pasta popular in Syria and other parts of the Middle East. Calsones are thought to have originated in Naples, where the filling was sausage, making them a relative of Italian CALZONES. When Jews were expelled from Italy in the 16th century by the Spanish rulers, they took calsones with them to Syria, where it became more popular to fill them with cheese. In addition to meat or cheese, other fillings such as spinach are sometimes used. Over time calsones or *kalsones* went from being fried to mostly steamed or boiled. A popular Syrian dish is *calsones b'rishta*, which combines cheese-filled calsones with noodles. The noodles, called *rishta* or *reshteh*, are made from leftover dough cut much like an Italian TAGLIATELLE.

Calvados [KAL-vah-dohs; kal-vah-DOHS] A dry apple BRANDY made in Calvados, in the Normandy region of northern France and considered one of the world's greatest. Calvados is double distilled in a pot still (*see* DISTILLATION), then aged in Limousin oak for a minimum of one year; some are aged for 40 years. The best Calvados comes from the *Pays d'Auge appellation contrôlée,* a designation that is noted on the label. Calvados is often used for cooking, particularly in chicken, pork and veal dishes. *See also* APPLEJACK.

calypso bean [kah-LIHP-soh] A medium-size, round dried bean that's part white (with a few black spots) and part black. This odd coloration is why the calypso is sometimes called *yin-yang;* other names for it are *black calypso* and *orca. See also* BEANS.

calzone [kahl-TSOH-nay; kahl-TSOH-neh] Originating in Naples, calzone is a half-moon shaped stuffed PIZZA. It is usually made as an individual serving. The fillings can be various meats, vegetables or cheese; mozzarella is the cheese used most frequently. Calzones can be deep-fried or brushed with olive oil and baked.

camarón; *pl.* **camarónes** [kah-mah-ROHN (ROH-nays)] Spanish for "shrimp."

Cambodian mint *see* VIETNAMESE MINT

Cambozola [kam-boh-ZOH-lah] Created in the 1970s by the well-known German cheese manufacturer Champignon Company, Cambozola is a soft-ripened cheese with a downy white rind and a creamy off-white interior streaked with blue veins. It's made from PASTEURIZED cow's milk and has a soft, creamy texture. The flavor is mild, buttery, slightly tangy and reminiscent of a cross between CAMEMBERT and GORGONZOLA.

cambric tea [KAYM-brihk] An American term used to describe a hot drink of milk, water, sugar and, if desired, a dash of tea. It was a favorite of children and the elderly in the late 19th and early 20th centuries. The name is taken from a fabric called cambric, which is white and thin . . . just like the "tea."

Cambridge sauce An older English mayonnaise-like sauce made from the yolks of hard-boiled eggs, oil and vinegar and seasoned with anchovies, CAPERS, BURNET, CHERVIL, chives, mustard, pepper, salt and tarragon, with a decorative touch of chopped parsley.

Camembert [KAM-uhm-behr] Legend has it that Napoleon christened this CHEESE "Camembert" after the Norman village where a farmer's wife first served it to him. Now world famous, this cow's-milk cheese is traditionally made from raw milk, though today PASTEURIZED versions abound. The original and classic French Camembert is *Camembert de Normandie*. However, today there are myriad versions produced in France, Italy, Switzerland, South America and the United States and many are factory made with pasteurized milk. Such versions lack the full flavor and soft, creamy texture of the original. Camembert has a white, downy rind and a smooth, creamy interior that, when perfectly ripe, should ooze thickly. When overripe, this cheese becomes runny, bitter and rank. Choose Camembert that is plump and soft to the touch. Avoid those with hardened edges, which may forecast overripeness. Camembert de Normandie has a FAT CONTENT of about 45 percent. *See also* CHEESE.

camomile *see* CHAMOMILE

camote [kah-MOH-tay] *see* BONIATO

camouflage melon Also known as *frog skin melon,* this fruit is named for the medium and dark green mottling on the skin. The sweet flesh ranges in color from off-white to celadon green. Choose a melon that's heavy for its size. Underripe melons will ripen at room temperature. Wrap ripe melons in a plastic bag and refrigerate up to 5 days. *See also* MELON.

campane chile *see* BISHOP'S CROWN CHILE

Campari [kahm-PAH-ree] A popular bitter, bright red Italian APÉRITIF, which is often mixed with soda. It's also consumed without a mixer and used in some COCKTAILS. Regular Campari has an astringent, bittersweet flavor; sweet Campari is also available.

can, to; canning A method of preserving food by hermetically sealing it in glass containers. The use of special canning jars and lids is essential for successful canning. The canning process involves quickly heating jars of food to high temperatures, thereby retaining maximum color, flavor and nutrients while destroying the microorganisms that cause spoilage. During processing, the food reaches temperatures of 212°F (with the boiling-water-bath method) to 240°F (using a pressure canner). Any air in the container is forced out between the jar and lid. A vacuum is created as the food cools and contracts, sucking the lid tightly to the jar. This airtight seal is vital to prevent invasion by microorganisms. Refer to a general cookbook for specific instructions on canning foods.

Canadian bacon Called *back bacon* in Canada, this lean smoked meat is a closer kin to HAM than it is to regular bacon. It's taken from the lean, tender eye of the LOIN, which is located in the middle of the back. Canadian bacon comes in cylindrical chunks that can be sliced or cut in any manner desired. It costs more than regular bacon, but it's leaner and precooked (meaning less shrinkage) and therefore provides more servings per pound. It can be fried, baked, barbecued or used cold as it comes from the package in sandwiches and salads.

Canadian whiskey Dropping the "*e*" from WHISKEY is traditionally British and is used in the spelling of Canadian whiskey. Made only in Canada, this distilled blend of rye, corn, wheat and barley is smoother and lighter than its cousins, RYE WHISKEY and BOURBON. It's wood-aged a minimum of 3 years with an average of 4 to 6 years. The casks used for aging can be new or previously used for bourbon, BRANDY or SHERRY, all of which lend their individual characteristics. Some producers create their blends before aging; others age the individual DISTILLATES first, then blend the whiskeys after aging.

canapé [KAN-uh-pay; KAN-uh-pee] A small, decorative piece of bread (toasted or untoasted) topped with a savory garnish such as anchovy, cheese or some type of spread. Crackers or pastry may also be used as a base. Canapés may be simple or elaborate, hot or cold. They're usually served as an appetizer with COCKTAILS. The word "canapé" is French for "couch." *See also* HORS D'OEUVRE.

canard [kah-NARD; kah-NAR] The French word for "duck."

canaria (canario) bean [kah-NAH-ree-ah (oh)] *see* PERUANO BEAN

cancellate *see* PIZZELLA

candied apple; candy apple An apple that's coated with a cinnamon-flavored red SUGAR SYRUP. This candy coating can either be crackly-hard or soft and gooey. A candied-apple clone is the **caramel apple**, which has a thick, soft caramel-flavored coating. Both versions are served on sticks for portable eating.

candied fruit and flowers Fruit or flowers that have been boiled or dipped in SUGAR SYRUP, then sometimes into granulated sugar after being dried. Candied fruits (also called *glacé fruits*) are generally used in cakes, breads and other sweets. Candied flowers are generally reserved for decorating desserts; candied fruits can also be used in this manner. The most common fruits that are candied are cherries, pineapple and citrus rinds. ANGELICA and GINGER are also candied favorites. Among the crystallized flowers, violets and miniature rosebuds and rose petals are the most common. Candied fruit and flowers can be found at gourmet markets and specialty shops. They should be stored airtight in a cool, dry place.

candlefish *see* SMELT

candlenut Used in Southeast Asian cookery, the tropical candlenut is hard and high in fat. The name comes from the fact that these nuts are also used in Indonesia and Malaysia to make candles. Whole or chopped roasted candlenuts are available in Indian and Asian markets. Candlenut is also known as *kukui nut*. *See also* NUTS.

candy *n.* Any of a number of various confections—soft and hard—composed mainly of sugar with the addition of flavoring ingredients and fillings such as chocolate, nuts, peanut butter, NOUGAT, fruits and so on. Sugar syrup is the foundation for most candies, the concentration of the mixture depending upon its temperature, which can either be checked by a CANDY THERMOMETER or by a series of cold-water tests. (*See* Candymaking Cold-Water Tests, page 866). Candy may come in tiny bits, small one- or two-bite pieces, or in the form of a candy "bar," containing several bites. Candy bars usually have a chocolate coating. So-called "nutritious" candy bars typically contain honey instead of sugar, and often substitute CAROB for chocolate. **candy** *v.* To sugar-coat various fruits, flowers and plants such as cherries, pineapple, citrus rinds, ANGELICA, GINGER, CHESTNUTS, violets, miniature rose petals and mint leaves. Candying food not only preserves it, but also retains its color, shape and flavor. The candying process usually includes dipping or cooking the food in several boiling SUGAR SYRUPS of increasing degrees of density. After the candied fruit air-dries, it is sometimes dipped in granulated sugar.

candy/fat thermometer A kitchen thermometer used for testing the temperature during the preparation of candy, syrups, jams, jellies and deep fat. It should register from 100° to 400°F. Choose a thermometer that is easy to handle in hot mixtures, such as one with a plastic handle. Many have adjustable hooks or clips so the thermometer can be attached to a pan. There are dual-purpose thermometers with readings both for candy and deep fat. *See also* Candymaking Cold-Water Tests, page 866; FREEZER/REFRIGERATOR THERMOMETER; MEAT THERMOMETER; OVEN THERMOMETER.

canestrini *see* Pasta Glossary, page 883

cane syrup Made from sugar cane, this thick, extremely sweet syrup is used in Caribbean and Creole cookery and is available in shops specializing in those cuisines.

caneton [kihn-toh*n*] French for "duckling."

canh chua [kahn TCHOO-ah] Vietnamese for "sour soup," referring to a favorite in southern Vietnam. The sourness comes from TAMARIND. Many variations exist, including *canh chua cá* (made with fish), *canh chua gá* (made with chicken), *canh chua tôm* (made with shrimp) and *canh chua chay* (a vegetarian version).

canja; canja de galinha [KAHN-zhah day gah-LEEN-yah] Portuguese for "chicken soup." Canja is a clear soup that usually includes chicken, rice or small ORZO-like pasta called *massa pevide* and various seasonings.

cannaroni *see* Pasta Glossary, page 883

canneberge [kayn-bayrahj] French for "cranberry."

cannella [kahn-NEHL-lah] Italian for "CINNAMON," translated as "little stalk."

cannellini bean [kan-eh-LEE-nee] A white Italian kidney bean, which is available both in dry and canned forms. Cannellini beans are particularly popular in salads and soups. *See also* BEANS.

cannelloni *see* Pasta Glossary, page 883

cannoli [kan-OH-lee]; *sing.* **cannolo** [kan-OH-loh] An Italian dessert consisting of tubular or horn-shaped pastry shells that have been deep-fried, then filled with a sweetened filling of whipped RICOTTA (and often whipped cream) mixed with bits of chocolate, candied citron and sometimes nuts.

canola oil [kan-OH-luh] The market name for RAPESEED OIL which, as might be assumed from the name, is expressed from rape seeds. For obvious reasons, the name was changed to canola by the Canadian seed-oil industry. Canola is, in fact, Canada's most widely used oil. It's commonly referred to there as *lear oil,* for "low erucic acid rapeseed" oil. The popularity of canola oil is rising fast in the United States, probably because it's been discovered to be lower in saturated fat (about 6 percent) than any other oil. This compares to the saturated fat content of peanut oil (about 18 percent) and palm oil (at an incredibly high 79 percent). Another canola oil selling point is that it contains more cholesterol-balancing monounsaturated fat than any oil except olive oil. It also has the distinction of containing Omega-3 fatty acids, the wonder polyunsaturated fat reputed to not only lower both cholesterol and triglycerides, but to contribute to brain growth and development as well. The bland-tasting canola oil is suitable both for cooking and for salad dressings. *See also* FATS AND OILS.

Cantal [kahn-TAHL] A semihard cow's-milk CHEESE from the department of Cantal in south-central France. One of France's oldest cheeses, Cantal can be made from raw or PASTEURIZED milk and can be aged from 30 days to 6 months or more. It has a thick, deep yellow rind with splotches of gray, red and orange. Depending on age, the interior color ranges from ivory to gold. When young, Cantal has a firm and elastic texture that becomes denser and harder with age. Flavorwise, young Cantal can be buttery and slightly tangy, with older versions becoming more piquant and taking on nutty characteristics. Cantal's minimum FAT CONTENT is 45 percent. *See also* CHEESE.

cantaloupe [KAN-teh-lohp] Named for a castle in Italy, the true cantaloupe is a European melon that is not exported. American "cantaloupes" are actually muskmelons (*see* MELON). When perfectly ripe, these cantaloupes have a raised netting on a smooth grayish-beige skin. The pale orange flesh is extremely juicy and sweet. Choose cantaloupes that are heavy for their size, have a sweet, fruity fragrance, a thick, well-raised netting and yield slightly to pressure at the blossom end. The stem end should be smooth and not jagged, the latter a sign that the fruit was underripe when picked. Avoid melons with soft spots or an overly strong odor. Store unripe cantaloupes at room temperature, ripe melons in the refrigerator. Cantaloupes easily absorb other food odors so if refrigerating for more than a day or two, wrap the melon in plastic wrap. Just before serving, cut melon in half and remove the seeds. Cantaloupe is an excellent source of vitamins A and C.

Cantonese cuisine [kan-tn-EEZ] *see* CHINESE CUISINE

Canton lemon *see* RANGPUR LIME

capacola; capacolo; capacollo [kah-pah-KOH-lah (KOHL-loh)] *see* CAPOCOLLO

capeado [kah-peh-AH-doh] Spanish term for foods covered in batter and fried. Sometimes used to describe the batter itself.

Cape Cod oyster *see* ATLANTIC OYSTER

cape gooseberry Though this intriguing berry grows wild in many locations throughout the continental United States, it's generally cultivated in tropical zones such as Hawaii, Australia, New Zealand, South Africa, India and China. At first glance the cape gooseberry (also called *golden berry, ground cherry, physalis* and *poha*), with its inflated, papery skin (calyx), looks somewhat like a Chinese lantern. The bittersweet, juicy berries that hide inside the calyx are opaque and golden in color. To use the berries, peel back the parchmentlike husk and rinse. Because of their piquant aftertaste, cape gooseberries go nicely with meats and other savory foods. They're wonderful in pies, jams and all by themselves. Gooseberries from Oregon are available in July and August; those imported from New Zealand can be found from October to January. Look for those with a bright golden color; green berries are not ripe. Cape gooseberries are high in vitamin C.

capelli d'angelo *see* Pasta Glossary, page 883

capellini *see* Pasta Glossary, page 883

caper [KAY-per] The flower bud of a bush native to the Mediterranean and parts of Asia, capers date back to 600 BC. The small buds are hand harvested, sun-dried and then typically pickled in a vinegar BRINE, though some are dry-salt cured. Capers range in size from the petite nonpareil variety from southern France (considered the finest), to those from Italy, which can be as large as the tip of your little finger. There are also the Spanish-imported stemmed caperberries that are about the size of a cocktail olive. Capers should be rinsed before using to remove excess salt. The pungent flavor of capers lends piquancy to many sauces and condiments; they're also used as a garnish for meat and vegetable dishes. Fried capers make a wonderfully crispy garnish and are easy to prepare. Heat about $1/2$ inch of olive oil in a saucepan and fry the capers (blotted dry) for 1 to 2 minutes, or until crisp. Drain on paper towels and use within 3 hours.

capicola, capicollo [kah-pih-KOH-lah (KOHL-loh)] *see* CAPOCOLLO

capocollo [kah-poh-KOHL-loh] An Italian meat product formed by seasoning the meat found between the hog's head (*capo*) and shoulder (*collo*) and letting it rest for about 10 days before stuffing it into a natural CASING and then aging it for at least 90 days. The flavor varies from region to region depending on the seasonings used; there are both hot (spicy) and sweet versions. *Capocollo di Calabria* has PROTECTED DESIGNATION OF ORIGIN status and can only be produced in Italy's Calabria region from locally raised pigs. Capocollo is most often served as part of an ANTIPASTO plate. It has several alternative spellings including *capacola, capacollo, capacolo, capicola, capicollo, capocolla* and *cappicola. See also* SALUMI.

capon [KAY-pahn] *see* CHICKEN

caponata [kap-oh-NAH-tah] A Sicilian dish that is generally served as a salad, side dish or relish. *Caponata* is composed of eggplant, onions, tomatoes, anchovies, olives, pine nuts, capers and vinegar, all cooked together in olive oil. It's most often served at room temperature.

cappa santa [KAH-pah SAHN-tah] Italian for "SCALLOP."

cappelletti *see* Pasta Glossary, page 883

capperi [KAH-per-ree] Italian for "CAPER."

cappicola [kahp-pih-KOH-lah] *see* CAPOCOLLO

cappuccino [kap-poo-CHEE-noh] An Italian coffee made by topping ESPRESSO with the creamy foam from steamed milk. Some of the steamed milk is also combined with the mix. The foam's surface may be dusted with sweetened cocoa powder or cinnamon.

capra [KAA-prah] Italian for "goat," *capra* appears on the labels of goat's-milk products, such as cheese.

caprese salad [kah-PRAY-say] A simple salad of fresh MOZZARELLA, tomatoes and BASIL, seasoned with salt, black pepper and extra virgin olive oil. It takes its name from southern Italy's island of Capri in the Gulf of Naples.

C

capsaicin [kap-SAY-ih-sihn] A potent compound that gives some CHILES their fiery nature. Most of the capsaicin (up to 80 percent) is found in the seeds and membranes of a chile. Since neither cooking nor freezing diminishes capsaicin's intensity, removing a chile's seeds and veins is the only way to reduce its heat. The caustic oils found in chiles cause an intense burning sensation, which can severely irritate skin and eyes. Capsaicin is known for its decongestant qualities. It also causes the brain to produce endorphins, which promote a sense of well-being.

capsicum [KAP-sih-kuhm] Any of hundreds of varieties of plant-bearing fruits called peppers, all of which belong to the nightshade family. Capsicums fall into two categories—CHILES and SWEET PEPPERS.

Capucello [kah-poo-CHEL-loh] A creamy Dutch liqueur with a nutty, coffeelike flavor, intended to be reminiscent of cappuccino.

Cara Cara orange *see* NAVEL ORANGE

carafe [kuh-RAF] A decorative beverage container, usually narrow-necked and fitted with a stopper. Carafes are generally made of glass and used for cold beverages.

carambola [kehr-ahm-BOH-lah] *see* STAR FRUIT

caramel [KEHR-ah-mehl; KAR-ah-mehl] A mixture produced when sugar has been cooked (caramelized) until it melts and becomes a thick, clear liquid that can range in color from golden to deep brown (from 320° to 350°F on a candy thermometer). Water can be added to thin the mixture. Caramel is used to flavor and color soups, stocks and sauces—sweet and savory. It's also used in desserts. When it cools and hardens, caramel cracks easily and is the base for nut brittles. Crushed caramel is used as a topping for ice cream and other desserts. A **soft caramel** is a candy made with caramelized sugar, butter and milk or cream, and sometimes corn syrup.

caramel apple *see* CANDIED APPLE

caramelize [KEHR-ah-meh-lyz; KAR-ah-meh-lyz] To heat sugar until it liquefies and becomes a clear syrup ranging in color from golden to dark brown (from 320° to 350°F on a candy thermometer). Granulated or brown sugar can also be sprinkled on top of food and placed under a heat source, such as a broiler, until the sugar melts and caramelizes. A popular custard dessert finished in this fashion is CRÈME BRÛLÉE. Caramelized sugar is also referred to as *burnt sugar*.

caraway seed [KEHR-uh-way] These aromatic seeds come from an herb in the parsley family. They have a nutty, delicate anise flavor and are widely used in German, Austrian and Hungarian cuisine. Caraway seeds flavor many foods including cheese, breads, cakes, stews, meats, vegetables and the liqueur KÜMMEL. They should be stored airtight in a cool, dark place for no more than 6 months. *See also* SPICES; Seasoning Suggestions, page 891.

carbohydrate A broad category of sugars, starches, fibers and starchy vegetables that the body eventually converts to glucose, the body's primary source of energy. There are two classes of carbohydrates—simple and complex. **Simple carbohydrates** are the sugars, which include GLUCOSE and FRUCTOSE from fruits and vegetables, SUCROSE from beet or cane sugar and LACTOSE from milk. Simple carbohydrates are absorbed by the body very quickly. **Complex carbohydrates** include starches and fiber and are most commonly found in whole grains and LEGUMES. Complex carbohydrates, which are generally large chains of glucose molecules, take longer to digest and provide more nutrients than simple carbohydrates.

carbonara, alla [kar-boh-NAH-rah] The Italian term describing a PASTA dish of spaghetti (or other noodles) with a sauce composed of cream, eggs, Parmesan cheese and bits of bacon. The sauce is heated only until it begins to thicken (2 to 3 minutes). It's important that the pasta be very hot so that when the sauce is poured over it, the eggs will briefly continue to cook. Fresh green peas are sometimes added for flavor and color.

carbonated water *see* SODA WATER

carbonate of ammonia *see* AMMONIUM BICARBONATE

carbonnade [kar-boh-NAHD] A French term for meat cooked over hot coals or directly over flames.

carbonnade à la flamande [kar-boh-NAHD ah-lah flah-MAHND] Beer, bacon, onions and brown sugar flavor this thick Belgian beef stew from Flanders. Also called *carbonnade of beef.*

carciofo; *pl.* **carciofi** [kahr-CHYOH-foh (-fee)] Italian for "ARTICHOKE."

cardamom [KAR-duh-muhm] A member of the GINGER family, this aromatic spice is native to India and grows in many other tropical areas including Asia, South America and the Pacific Islands. Cardamom seeds are encapsulated in small pods about the size of a cranberry. Each pod contains 17 to 20 tiny seeds. Cardamom has a pungent aroma and a warm, spicy-sweet flavor. It's widely used in Scandinavian and East Indian cooking. Cardamom can be purchased either in the pod or ground. The latter, though more convenient, is not as full-flavored because cardamom seeds begin to lose their essential oils as soon as they're ground. The seeds may be removed from the pods and ground, or the entire pod may be ground. A MORTAR AND PESTLE make quick work of the grinding. If using cardamom to flavor dishes such as stews and curries, lightly crush the shell of the pod and add the pod and seeds to the mixture. The shell will disintegrate while the dish cooks. Be frugal when using cardamom—a little goes a long way. Cardamom is also called *green cardamom* or *true cardamom* and it belongs to the genus *Elettaria*. It differs from the related BLACK CARDAMOM. *See also* SPICES; Seasoning Suggestions, page 891.

cardoni *see* CARDOON

cardoon [kahr-DOON] Tasting like a cross between artichoke, celery and SALSIFY, this delicious vegetable is very popular in France, Italy and Spain. The cardoon resembles a giant bunch of wide, flat celery. Cardoons can be found from midwinter to early spring. Look for stalks that are firm and have a silvery gray-green color. Refrigerate in a plastic bag up to 2 weeks. To prepare, remove tough outer ribs. Cut the inner ribs into the size indicated in the recipe and soak in ACIDULATED WATER to prevent browning. Cardoons can be boiled, braised or baked. Precooking about 30 minutes in boiling water is suggested in many recipes. Though high in sodium, cardoons are a good source of potassium, calcium and iron. Also called *cardoni*.

carenum *see* FRUIT MOLASSES

caribe chile [kuh-REE-bee] A yellow, intensely hot CHILE named for an Indian tribe who inhabited the Caribbean during the 15th century.

caribou [KEHR-uh-boo] *see* GAME ANIMALS

Carignan; Carignane [kah-ree-NYAHN] This red wine grape originated in northern Spain's Cariñena district. It was once widely grown in France's Languedoc-Roussillon region, California's San Joaquin Valley and countries ringing the Mediterranean including Italy, Spain, Algeria and Israel. However, Carignan acreage has diminished over the last several decades as it's been replaced by higher-quality grapes. The high-yield Carignan (often spelled *Carignane* in California) produces wines with deep purple color, high TANNINS and high alcohol. It's often blended with GRENACHE and CINSAUT.

carnaroli rice [kar-nah-ROH-lee] A short-grain rice that's viewed by many as better than the more famous ARBORIO RICE for making creamy RISOTTO. Some chefs believe that carnaroli holds its shape better and is more resistant to overcooking. It's more difficult to find than Arborio but is available in Italian markets and through the Internet. *See also* RICE.

carne [*Sp.* KAHR-nay; *It.* KAHR-neh] Spanish and Italian for "meat."

carne al pastor *see* AL PASTOR

carne asada [KAHR-nay ah-SAH-dah] Spanish for "roasted (or broiled) meat," carne asada is a popular Mexican specialty of thin strips of beef marinated in lime juice and other seasonings and quickly grilled. Traditionally TENDERLOIN or NEW YORK STEAK is used, though FLANK STEAK or SKIRT STEAK are often substituted. Carne asada can be eaten on its own with sides of rice and beans, or cut into smaller pieces and used in other Mexican specialties such as enchiladas, quesadillas or tacos.

carne de cerdo [KAHR-nay deh SAYR-doh] Spanish for "pork."

carnitas [kahr-NEE-tahz] Mexican for "little meats," this dish is simply small bits or shreds of well browned pork. It's made from an inexpensive cut of pork that's simmered in a small amount of water until tender, then finished by cooking the pieces in pork fat until nicely browned all over. Carnitas are usually eaten with SALSA and are sometimes used as the filling in TACOS and BURRITOS.

carnival squash Small to medium-size winter squash with a green, orange, yellow and white multicolored exterior and a pale orange to golden yellow interior. Carnival squash is a hybrid of SWEET DUMPLING and ACORN SQUASH. Its flavor is buttery, nutty and sweet. Cook the carnival squash as you would acorn squash. It's available year-round but is best in late summer to early fall. *See also* SQUASH.

carob [KEHR-uhb] The long, leathery pods from the tropical carob tree contain a sweet, edible pulp (which can be eaten fresh) and a few hard, inedible seeds. After drying, the pulp is roasted and ground into a powder. It is then used to flavor baked goods and candies. Both fresh and dried carob pods, as well as carob powder, may be found in natural food and specialty food stores. Because carob is sweet and tastes vaguely of chocolate, it's often used as a chocolate substitute. Carob is also known as *Saint John's bread* and *locust bean*.

Carolina rice This is the long-grain rice that is most popular in the United States. It was originally planted in North Carolina in the late 17th century from East African rice brought back by a sea captain. Carolina rice is now cultivated mainly in California, Texas, Louisiana and Arkansas. *See also* RICE.

carom [KAH-rom] *see* AJOWAN

carotene [KEHR-uh-teen] A fat-soluble pigment, ranging in color from yellow to orange, found in many fruits and vegetables (carrots, for one). It converts to vitamin A in the liver and is essential for normal human growth and eyesight.

carp The principal ingredient in the Jewish dish GEFILTE FISH, carp is a freshwater fish native to Asia but found throughout the world. It ranges in size from 2 to 7 pounds and favors muddy waters, which often give a mossy flavor to the lean, white flesh. This musky nuance is least evident from November to April. Carp is best baked, fried or poached. *See also* FISH.

carpaccio [kahr-PAH-chee-oh] Italian in origin, carpaccio consists of thin shavings of raw beef FILLET, which may be drizzled with olive oil and lemon juice or served with a mayonnaise or mustard sauce. The dish is often topped with capers and sometimes onions. It's generally served as an appetizer.

carpetbag steak Although claimed by many to be of Australian origin, an Australian cookbook, *The Captain Cook Book: Two Hundred Years of Australian Cooking,* declares that the carpetbag steak came from the United States. It is a thick-cut steak with a pocket cut into it. The pocket is stuffed with seasoned fresh oysters (sometimes with the addition of breadcrumbs), skewered shut, then the steak is grilled.

carrageen; carrageenan [KEHR-ah-geen; kehr-ah-GEE-nuhn] Also called *Irish moss*, carrageen is a stubby, purplish or reddish green seaweed found along the west coast of Ireland, as well as America's Atlantic coast. Dried carrageen is the source of **carrageenan**, which is used as a thickener, emulsifier and stabilizer in myriad food products (including ice creams, puddings and soups), cosmetics and medicines.

carrot This member of the parsley family has lacy green foliage and long, slender, edible orange roots. Carrots have been renowned for over 2,000 years for their health-giving properties and high vitamin A content. Their year-round availability makes them an immensely popular vegetable. If buying carrots with their greenery, make sure the leaves are moist and bright green; the carrots should be firm and smooth. Avoid those with cracks or any that have begun to soften and wither. The best carrots are young and slender. Tiny **baby carrots** are very tender but, because of their lack of maturity, not as flavorful as their full-grown siblings. Remove carrot greenery as soon as possible because it robs the roots of moisture and vitamins. Store carrots in a plastic bag in the refrigerator's vegetable bin. Avoid storing them near apples, which emit ethylene gas that can give carrots a bitter taste. A light rinsing is all that's necessary for young carrots and tiny baby carrots; older carrots should be peeled. If carrots have become limp, recrisp them in a bowl of ice water. The coarse core of older carrots should be removed. Carrots may be eaten raw or cooked in almost any manner imaginable.

carte [KAHRT] French for "menu"; *carte des vins* means "wine list." *See also* À LA CARTE.

caruru [KAH-ru-rru] A Brazilian stew made from okra, onion, palm oil, roasted nuts and shrimp. Caruru is often used as a condiment, especially as a filling for ACARAJÉ.

casaba melon [kah-SAH-bah] Though it was first cultivated in Persia thousands of years ago, the casaba melon wasn't introduced to the United States until the late 19th century when it was imported from Kasaba, Turkey. This large, round muskmelon (*see* MELON) has a thick yellow rind with deep, rough furrows. The creamy-colored flesh is extremely juicy and has a distinctive yet mild cucumberlike flavor. Casabas are now grown in California and are most readily available from May through September, though some can be found up until December. Choose a melon with an even-colored yellow rind with a slightly wrinkled appearance; it should give slightly when gently pressed at the blossom end. Avoid casabas with soft spots or mold. Store at room temperature until completely ripe, then refrigerate.

cascabel chile [KAS-kuh-behl] A dried, plum-shaped, dark blood-red colored CHILE that ranges in size from about 1 to 1½ inches in diameter. *Cascabel* means "little round bell" or "rattle" in Spanish, a name alluding to the rattling sound this chile makes when shaken. This chile, with its rich nutty flavor and medium heat, is excellent in sauces, soups and other cooked dishes. The cascabel chile is also known as *chile bola*. It's a mild pepper with a SCOVILLE SCALE rating of 1,000 to 3,000.

casein [KAY-seen; KAY-see-ihn] The principal protein in milk, which coagulates with the addition of rennin (*see* RENNET) and is the foundation for cheese. Casein is also used in the production of nonfood items such as adhesives, paints and plastics.

cashew apple Native to Brazil, India and the West Indies, this pear-shaped apple has a yellow-orange skin that is often blushed with touches of red. The flesh is tart and astringent and though not favored for out-of-hand eating, is used to make wine, LIQUEUR and vinegar. The cashew apple's biggest gift to the world is the CASHEW NUT, which grows on the outside of the apple at its base. Cashew apples are not imported to the United States.

cashew nut A kidney-shaped nut that grows out from the bottom of the cashew apple. The shell is highly toxic so great care is taken in shelling and cleaning the nut. Cashew nuts have a sweet, buttery flavor and contain about 48 percent fat. Because of their high fat content, they should be stored, tightly wrapped, in the refrigerator to retard rancidity. As with most nuts, roasting cashews brings out their nutty flavor. *See also* NUTS.

casing A thin, tubular intestinal membrane that has been cleaned and stuffed with processed meat, such as for salami and other sausages. The membrane may come from the intestines of sheep, hogs or cattle. Casings can be purchased—thoroughly cleaned and packed in salt—from specialty butchers. Today, most commercial sausages have casings of formed collagen.

cask 1. A large, strong, barrel-shaped, leak-proof container generally used for storing wines and other spirits. Most wine casks are made of oak. 2. The quantity such a container holds.

cassareep [KAS-sah-reep] Used primarily in West Indian cookery, cassareep is a bittersweet condiment made by cooking the juice of bitter YUCA with brown sugar and spices until it reduces to a syrup. Bottled cassareep can be found in Caribbean markets.

cassata; cassata gelata [kah-SAH-tah] A traditional Italian dessert served at celebrations such as weddings. The word *cassata* means "in a case (or chest)." One version of this dessert has a rich filling of RICOTTA, candied fruit and grated chocolate encased by thin slices of liqueur-sprinkled sponge cake. The cake and cheese mixture may also be layered. The dessert is chilled, then decorated with whipped cream, ricotta cheese or chocolate frosting. Another version, **cassata gelata**, is made by lining a mold with layers of ice cream of contrasting colors, then filling the center with a ricotta-whipped cream-candied fruit mixture. The mold is frozen completely before serving.

cassava [kuh-SAH-vuh] *see* YUCA

cassava flour *see* TAPIOCA

casserole This term refers to both a baking dish and the ingredients it contains. Casserole cookery is convenient because the ingredients are cooked and served in the same dish. A "casserole dish" usually refers to a deep, round, ovenproof container with handles and a tight-fitting lid. It can be glass, metal, ceramic or any other heatproof material. A casserole's ingredients can include meat, vegetables, beans, rice and anything else the cook desires. Often a topping such as cheese or breadcrumbs is added for texture and flavor.

cassia [KAH-see-uh; KASH-uh] *see* CINNAMON

cassia leaves *see* INDIAN BAY LEAF

cassis [kah-SEES] A European black currant used mainly to make CRÈME DE CASSIS liqueur and black currant syrup. *See also* LIQUEUR.

cassolette [kas-oh-LEHT] A small, individual-size cooking dish.

cassoulet [ka-soo-LAY] A classic dish from France's Languedoc region consisting of WHITE BEANS and various meats (such as sausages, pork and preserved duck or goose). The combination varies according to regional preference. A *cassoulet* is covered and cooked very slowly to harmonize the flavors.

castagna [kah-STAH-nyah] Italian for "CHESTNUT."

castagnaccio [kah-STAH-nyah-chee-o] Rustic cake based on chestnut flour, pine nuts and raisins. Because chestnut flour is sweet, sugar usually isn't added. Also, yeast or baking powder is missing, so the cake is flat and dense. Many variations exist, and ingredients such as other types of dried fruit, fennel seeds, orange rind, fresh rosemary or walnuts may be added. Catagnaccio is very popular in Tuscany, as well as the neighboring regions of Emilia-Romagna, Liguria and Piedmont. It also goes by the names *baldino, migliaccio* and *pattona*.

cast iron cookware *see* COOKWARE AND BAKEWARE MATERIALS

castor; caster sugar British equivalent of superfine granulated sugar.

Catawba grape [kuh-TAW-buh] Grown on the East Coast, this purplish-red grape is medium-size and oval in shape. It has seeds and an intense, sweet flavor. The Catawba is available from September to November but is mainly used commercially (for jams, jellies and white wines), and is rarely found in markets. *See also* GRAPE.

catchup *see* KETCHUP

catfish This fish gets its name from its long, whiskerlike barbels (feelers), which hang down from around the mouth. Most catfish are freshwater fish, though there is also a saltwater variety sometimes referred to as **hogfish**. The majority of the catfish in today's market are farmed. The **channel catfish**, weighing from 1 to 10 pounds, is considered the best eating. The **bullhead** is smaller and usually weighs no more than a pound. Catfish have a tough, inedible skin that must be removed before cooking. The flesh is firm, low in fat and mild in flavor. Catfish can be fried, poached, steamed, baked or grilled. They are also well suited to soups and stews. *See also* FISH.

cats' tongues Known as *langues-de-chat* in France and *lingue di gatto* in Italy, these long, thin cookies resemble their namesakes in shape. They are light, dry and slightly sweet. Cats' tongues may be flavored with citrus ZEST, chocolate or flavoring EXTRACTS. Two are sometimes sandwiched together with jam or another sweet filling; they may also be frosted. Cats' tongues are commonly made by pressing a thick batter through a pastry bag. A special **langues-de-chat pan** is also available in cookware shops. It has ten 3-inch long indentations with a slight hourglass curve in the middle.

catsup *see* KETCHUP

caudière; caudrée [koh-DYEHR; koh-DRAY] A French seafood stew or soup based on mussels and onions.

caudle [KAW-dl] A hot drink once popular in England and Scotland, especially with the elderly and infirm because of its purported restorative powers. Caudle was generally a blend of wine or ALE, GRUEL, eggs, sugar and spices.

caul; caulfat [KAWL] A thin, fatty membrane that lines the abdominal cavity, usually taken from pigs or sheep; pork caul is considered superior. Caul resembles a lacy net and is used to wrap and contain PÂTÉS, CRÉPINETTES, FORCEMEATS and the like. The fatty membrane melts during the baking or cooking process. Caul may be ordered through your local butcher. To prevent tearing, it may be necessary to soak the membrane in warm salted water to loosen the layers before using.

cauldron [CAHL-druhn] A large kettle or pot, often with handles. A cauldron is frequently used over an open fire for boiling water or cooking.

cauliflower [KAWL-ih-flow-uhr] In Mark Twain's words, "cauliflower is nothing but cabbage with a college education." The name of this elegant member of the cabbage family comes from the Latin *caulis* ("stalk") and *floris* ("flower"). Cauliflower comes in three basic colors: white (the most popular and readily available), green and purple (a vibrant violet that turns pale green when cooked). All cauliflower is composed of bunches of tiny florets on clusters of stalks. Some white varieties have a purple or greenish tinge. The entire floret portion (called the "curd") is edible. The green leaves at the base are also edible, but take longer to cook and have a stronger flavor than the curd. Choose a firm cauliflower with compact florets; the leaves should be crisp and green with no sign of yellowing. The size of the head doesn't affect the quality. Refrigerate raw cauliflower, tightly wrapped, for 3 to 5 days; cooked for 1 to 3 days. To use, separate cauliflower head into florets and wash. Cauliflower can be eaten raw or cooked in a number of ways including boiling, baking and sautéing. Whole cauliflower heads may also be cooked in one piece. Adding a tablespoon of lemon juice or one cup milk to the cooking water will prevent discoloration. Cauliflower, which is a CRUCIFEROUS vegetable, is high in vitamin C and is a fair source of iron. *See also* BROCCOFLOWER; ROMANESCA CAULIFLOWER.

Cava [KAH-vah] The official name for sparkling wine produced in various parts of northern Spain around Barcelona. The use of the word *cava* came about as a result of legal conflicts with France over the use of *champán*, Spain's word for CHAMPAGNE. The word *cava* (Catalan for "cellar") was chosen for Spain's sparkling wines because almost all such wines are made in the Catalan region. As with French Champagne, Cava wines must be made by the MÉTHODE CHAMPENOISE. The grapes used for most Cava wines are Macabeo, Parellada and Xarel-lo although CHARDONNAY is allowed and some producers use it extensively. Some *rosado* (ROSÉ) Cava is produced using Garnacha (GRENACHE), Monastrell (MOURVÈDRE) and PINOT NOIR. Cavas are typically earthier and less acidic than French Champagnes.

Cavaillon melon [kah-vi-yoo] A true European cantaloupe, which is not the same as the American cantaloupe that belongs to the muskmelon category (*see* MELON). The melon, also called *Melon de Cavaillon*, is named after Cavaillon, a town in France's Provence region. The Cavaillon melon is considered the same variety as the CHARENTAIS MELON. It has a thin, smooth to slightly netted skin that ranges in color from lime green to pale golden with darker green striping. The fine-textured flesh is orange, perfumy and very sweet with honey flavors. To be labeled a Melon de Cavaillon, the melons must pass inspection by the Cavaillon melon consortium for density, sugar content and appearance. Because only the best melons pass muster, few Cavaillon melons make it outside of France.

cavatappi *see* Pasta Glossary, page 883

cavatelli *see* Pasta Glossary, page 883

caviale [kah-vee-AH-leh] Italian for "CAVIAR."

caviar [KA-vee-ahr; KAH-vee-ahr] This elegant and expensive appetizer is simply sieved and lightly salted fish ROE (eggs). STURGEON roe is premium and considered the "true" caviar. The three main types of caviar are **beluga**, **osetra** (ossetra) and **sevruga**. The best (and costliest) is from the beluga sturgeon that swim in the Caspian Sea, which is bordered by Russia and Iran. Caviar production is a major industry for both countries. Beluga caviar is prized for its soft, extremely large (pea-size) eggs. It can range in color from pale silver-gray to black. Next in quality is the medium-size, gray to brownish gray osetra, and the smaller, gray sevruga caviar. The small, golden **sterlet** caviar is so rare that it was once reserved for Russian czars, Iranian shahs and Austrian emperors. Other popular (and much less expensive) types include **lumpfish caviar** (tiny, hard, black eggs), **whitefish caviar** (also called *American Golden*) with its small yellow-gold eggs and **salmon** or **red caviar** (medium-size, pale orange to deep red eggs). The word *malossol* on the label doesn't describe the type of caviar but rather the fact that the roe is preserved with a minimum amount of salt; *malossol* is Russian for "little salt." Caviar is extremely perishable and must be refrigerated from the moment it's taken from the fish to the time it's consumed. **Pasteurized caviar** is roe that has been partially cooked, thereby giving the eggs a slightly different texture. It's less perishable and may be stored at room temperature before opening. Once opened, refrigerate for no more than 3 days. **Pressed caviar** is composed of damaged or fragile eggs and can be a combination of several different roes. It's specially treated, salted and pressed, and can in no way be compared to fresh caviar. Be sure to read the label for information on how to handle the caviar you purchase. In general, store unopened fresh caviar in the refrigerator for up to a month; consume within 3 days of opening. Although only a spoonful of caviar supplies the adult daily requirement of vitamin B_{12}, it's also high in cholesterol and loaded with salt. Serve caviar very cold, preferably in a bowl surrounded by ice. Because silver and steel bowls may alter the flavor of caviar, it's classically served in containers made of mother-of-pearl, wood, horn or gold. Caviar should be presented simply, with toast points and lemon wedges. If desired, it may be accompanied by sour cream, minced onion and hard-cooked egg whites and yolks, garnishes purists deem unnecessary. Two classic caviar accompaniments are iced vodka and Champagne. Cooking greatly diminishes the flavor and texture of caviar, so add it to a hot dish just before serving, stirring gently to keep the eggs from breaking. Caviar has long been touted as a hangover cure due to its inherent acetylcholine content, which is linked to increased alcohol tolerance.

Caviar of the East *see* BIRD'S NEST SOUP; XO SAUCE

Caville Blanc d'Hiver apple A medium-large apple almost exclusively used as a cooking apple. Known as the classic dessert apple in France, the Caville Blanc d'Hiver apple has pronounced, uneven ribbing and is yellow with a rose blush and some tinges of green. The texture is dense and slightly crunchy. The flavor is sweetly tart with hints of banana and pear. *See also* APPLE.

cavolfiore [kah-vohl-FYOH-reh] Italian for "CAULIFLOWER."

cavolo [KAH-voh-loh] Italian for "CABBAGE."

cavolo nero [KAH-voh-loh NEH-roh] This member of the KALE family goes by myriad names including *Tuscan kale, Tuscan cabbage, dinosaur kale, palm tree cabbage, black cabbage, black kale* and *Lacinato*. Cavolo nero was developed in Tuscany during the 1700s and has become a staple in Tuscan cooking. It has very dark green (almost black), wrinkled leaves that are 10 to 12 inches long and very narrow. They are quite tender and have a mild flavor. Cavolo nero is prized in soups such as the traditional Tuscan RIBOLLITA. It's also good simply sautéed with olive oil and a little garlic. It's available during the fall and winter months. Choose heads with fresh-looking, dark green leaves with no sign of wilting. Refrigerate in a plastic bag for up to 5 days; wash just before using.

cayenne chile [KI-yehn] A bright red, extremely hot, pungent CHILE that ranges from 2 to 5 inches long and about $\frac{1}{2}$ inch in diameter. Cayennes are generally sold dried and used in soups and sauces. The majority of these chiles are used to make CAYENNE PEPPER. It has a SCOVILLE SCALE rating of 30,000 to 50,000.

cayenne pepper [KI-yehn] A hot, pungent powder made from several of various tropical CHILES that originated in French Guyana. Cayenne pepper is also called **red pepper**.

cazuela [kah-SWAY-lah; kah-THWAY-lah] 1. An earthenware CASSEROLE with a glazed interior used for centuries in Spanish cooking. 2. Thick soup or stew of beef, chicken, pork or fish and vegetables, beans, rice and almost anything else the cook desires. It's prepared in a cazuela casserole dish. 3. A punch (sometimes individual cocktail) made with TEQUILA, GRENADINE and lemon-lime soda. The punch is often served in a large cazuela casserole.

cece; *pl.* **ceci** [CHAY-chee] Italian for "CHICKPEA."

cekur *see* AROMATIC GINGER

celeriac [seh-LER-ee-ak] *see* CELERY ROOT

céleri bâtard *see* LOVAGE

celery Before the 16th century, celery was used exclusively as a medicinal herb. Now it's become one of the most popular vegetables of the Western world. Celery grows in bunches that consist of leaved ribs surrounding the tender, choice heart. There are two main varieties of celery grown today. The most common is the pale green **Pascal celery**. **Golden celery** is grown under a layer of soil or paper to prevent chlorophyll from developing and turning it green. Celery is available year-round. Choose firm bunches that are tightly formed; the leaves should be green and crisp. Store celery in a plastic bag in the refrigerator up to two weeks. Leave the ribs attached to the stalk until ready to use. Celery should be well washed and trimmed of leaves and at the base. Reserve the leaves for soups and salads. Celery is usually eaten raw, but is delicious cooked in soups, stews and casseroles. *See also* ASIAN CELERY.

celery cabbage *see* CHINESE CABBAGE

celery potato *see* ARRACACHA

celery root; celery knob This rather ugly, knobby, brown vegetable is actually the root of a special celery cultivated specifically for its root. It's also called *celeriac, celery knob, turnip rooted celery* and *knob celery*. Celery root tastes like a cross between a strong celery and parsley. It's available from October through April and can range anywhere from the size of an apple to that of a small cantaloupe. Choose a relatively small, firm celery root with a minimum of rootlets and knobs. Avoid those with soft spots, which signal decay. The green leaves are usually detached by the time you buy celery root. Refrigerate the root in a plastic bag for 7 to 10 days. This veggie can be eaten raw or cooked. Before using, peel and soak briefly in ACIDULATED WATER to prevent discoloration. To eat raw, grate or shred celery root and use in salads. Cooked, it's wonderful in soups, stews and purées. It can also be boiled, braised, sautéed and baked. Celery root contains small amounts of vitamin B, calcium and iron.

celery salt A blend of ground CELERY SEED and salt.

celery seed The seed of a wild celery called LOVAGE, most of which comes from India. Celery seed has a strong flavor and should therefore be used sparingly. It's used in pickling and to flavor soups, salads and various meat dishes. *See also* Seasoning Suggestions, page 891.

cellophane noodles [SEHL-uh-fayn] Also called *bean threads,* these gossamer, translucent threads are not really noodles in the traditional sense, but are made from the starch of green MUNG BEANS, white sweet potatoes or YUCA ROOT. Sold dried, cellophane noodles must be soaked briefly in hot water before using in most dishes. Presoaking isn't necessary when they're added to soups. They can also be deep-fried. Cellophane noodles can be found in the ethnic section of many supermarkets and in Asian grocery stores. Other names for cellophane noodles include *bean thread vermicelli* (or noodles), fensi, *Chinese vermicelli, dangmyeon, glass noodles, long rice, harusame, soun, sotanghon,* and *suun.*

Celsius [SEHL-see-uhs] A temperature scale (also called *centigrade*) in which 0° represents freezing and 100° represents the boiling point. The scale was devised by the Swedish astronomer Anders Celsius. To convert Celsius temperatures to FAHRENHEIT, multiply the Celsius figure by 9, divide by 5 and add 32. *See also* General Temperature Equivalents, page 862; Fahrenheit/Celsius Conversion Formulas, page 863.

cenci [chehn-chee] One of many names referring to thin, sweet pastry strips that are deep-fried and covered with powdered sugar or honey and possibly decorations. Cenci, which means "rags," also go by Italian names such as *chiacchiere, nastrini* ("ribbons") and *lattughe* ("lettuce leaves"). Because they are sometimes tied into a knot before frying, they've also been given names such as *angel wings, Italian* or *Polish bow tie cookies* and *Italian knot cookies.* Cenci are popular at holidays, especially during Italy's various carnivals.

centigrade [SIHN-tih-grayd] *see* CELSIUS

century egg *see* HUNDRED-YEAR EGG

century plant *see* AGAVE

cèpe [SEHP] *see* PORCINO

cephalopod [SEHF-uh-luh-pod] A class of MOLLUSK that includes the OCTOPUS, SQUID and CUTTLEFISH. It's the most biologically advanced of the mollusks. All cephalopods share two common characteristics—tentacles attached to the head, and ink sacs, which they use to evade their predators. Though cephalopods have never been broadly accepted in the United States, they're quite popular with many southern Europeans, Japanese and Chinese.

cera chile *see* ROCOTO CHILE

cerdo [SAYR-doh] Spanish for "pig." *Carne de cerdo* is "meat of pig" or "pork."

cereal [SEER-ee-uhl] Breakfast cereals are processed foods (usually ready-to-eat) made from cereal grains. W. H. Kellogg and C. W. Post were the first to begin mass-producing these foods, which have become a morning meal staple in the United States. *See also* CEREAL GRAINS.

cereal grains The word "cereal" comes from Ceres, a pre-Roman goddess of agriculture. Cereal includes any plant from the grass family that yields an edible grain (seed). The most popular grains are BARLEY, CORN, MILLET, OATS, QUINOA, RICE, RYE, SORGHUM, TRITICALE, WHEAT and WILD RICE. Because cereals are inexpensive, are a readily available source of protein and have more carbohydrates than any other food, they're a staple throughout the world. *See also* CHIA SEEDS; SPELT; TEFF.

Cerignola olive *see* BELLA DI CERIGNOLA OLIVE

ceriman [SEHR-uh-muhn] *see* MONSTERA

cerise [sehr-EEZ] French for "cherry."

cervelas *see* CERVELAT

cervelat [SER-vuh-lat] A style of SAUSAGE that combines chopped pork and/or beef with various mixtures of herbs, spices and other flavorings like garlic or mustard. Brains were once part of the recipe, but modern versions don't include them. Cervelats are uncooked but safe to eat as is because they've been preserved by curing, drying and smoking. They range from semidry to moist and soft. Cervelot is considered the national sausage in Switzerland, but many countries make cervelats; two of the more well known are Germany's THURINGER SAUSAGE and Italy's MORTADELLA. These sausages can be sliced and served with bread or cut into pieces and used in a variety of other dishes. Cervelat is also called *cervelas*, *servelat*, *zervelat* and SUMMER SAUSAGE.

ceviche *see* SEVICHE

Ceylon tea One of the world's most popular teas, Ceylon is a black PEKOE TEA whose leaves have been fermented before drying. A two-temperature drying process seals in essential oils that give this tea its special flavor. This superior tea originated in Ceylon (now Sri Lanka), but is now grown in other countries such as India and China. *See also* TEA.

cezve *see* TURKISH COFFEE

cha [CHAH] The word for "tea" in many Asian languages including Chinese, Japanese and Korean.

chaat [chaht] Snack food that originated in northern India and is sold at many outdoor venues (carts, food trucks, stalls, and so on). Chaat's popularity has spread throughout the Indian subcontinent and Southeast Asia and into the United States. It's also moved indoors into restaurants that specialize in chaat, especially roadside eateries frequented by travelers and truck drivers. Most chaat is made with dough, which can be prepared from a variety of flours such as BESAN, LENTIL and potato flour. The snacks are most often fried but occasionally baked or steamed. There are myriad forms of chaat with a broad range of different ingredients, but a common component is the spice mix CHAAT MASALA.

chaat masala; chat masala [CHAHT mah-SAH-lah] A blend of ground spices used in Indian cooking. There are many variations of chaat masala but the predominant flavors come from AMCHOOR, ASAFETIDA and BLACK SALT (kala namak). Chaat masala may be purchased in Indian markets. It's also easily prepared at home but should be made in small batches to retain its freshness. As with all spices, it should be stored in a cool, dry place for no more than 6 months. Chaat masala is used in cooked dishes and sprinkled on fresh fruit.

Chabichou du Poitou (AOC; PDO); Chabichou/Chabis

[SHAH-bee-shoo dew pwah-TOO; SHAH-bee] Mild, tangy, SEMISOFT goat's-milk cheese from France's Poitou-Charentes region. Cheeses come in 4$\frac{1}{4}$- to 6-ounce drum-shaped cylinders. They are RIPENED for a minimum of 10 days, though 3 weeks or more is not uncommon. Young cheeses are soft and moist, while older versions are firmer and become crumbly over time. Cheeses made from raw milk meet APPELLATION D'ORIGINE CONTRÔLÉE (AOC) regulations and may be labeled "Chabichou du Poitou." Those made from pasteurized milk to meet United States standards (see UNPASTEURIZED MILK/IMPORTED CHEESE DILEMMA) are not AOC-approved and are therefore simply labeled "chabichou" or "chabis." The FAT CONTENT for this cheese is about 45 percent.

Chablis [sha-BLEE; *pl.* sha-BLEEZ] Though the United States, Australia and South Africa all make a wine labeled *Chablis,* only France creates a *true* Chablis, made entirely from CHARDONNAY grapes. Considered one of the world's great white wines, French Chablis has a crisp, dry flavor with a decided flinty quality. It comes from a small area surrounding the town of Chablis, France. The very best French Chablis comes from one of seven *grand cru* ("great growth") vineyards that lie in a single block facing south and west toward the village. The term *grand cru* will appear on the labels of these special wines, followed by the name of the vineyard from which it came. Next in excellence are the Chablis labeled *premier cru* (meaning "first growth"). Others are considered "simple" Chablis or "petit Chablis."

chachouka; chackchouka [chahk-SHOO-kah] *see* SHAKSHUKA

chadec *see* POMELO

chafing dish [CHAYF-ing] Chafing dishes found in the ruins of Pompeii prove that this style of cookery is nothing new. Used to warm or cook food, a chafing dish consists of a container (today, usually metal) with a heat source directly beneath it. The heat can be provided by a candle, electricity or solid fuel (such as Sterno). There's often a larger dish that is used as a water basin (like the bottom of a double boiler) into which the dish containing the food is placed. This prevents food from burning.

chai [CHAI] 1. The word for "tea" in many parts of the world, especially northern India and surrounding areas. 2. An aromatic spiced tea (also called *masala chai*) favored for centuries in India, where chai stalls tended by vendors (*chaiwallahs*) have long been a popular gathering place. Masala chai is a blend of loose-leaf tea, milk and spices (*chai* *masala*), typically cardamom, cinnamon, cloves, ginger, freshly grated nutmeg and pepper. Masala chai can be found in natural food stores and specialty tea and coffee shops in a variety of forms, including liquid concentrates, powder and loose-leaf tea or whole spice packages. 3. **chai** [SHEH; SHAY] A French term usually referring to an above-ground building used for storing wine.

chakka [CHAH-kah] Yogurt thickened by wrapping it in a cloth and hanging it up for 12 to 18 hours so that some of the whey drain off. This technique is used in parts of India and Pakistan. SHRIKHAND is a popular Indian dessert made from chakka, which is similar to GREEK YOGURT.

chalazae [kuh-LAY-zee] Thick, cordlike strands of egg white that are attached to 2 sides of the yolk, thereby anchoring it in the center of the egg. The more prominent the chalazae, the fresher the egg. Chalazae don't affect the egg in any way, though some custard recipes call for straining to remove them for a smoother texture.

challah; hallah; challa [KHAH-lah; HAH-lah] Served on the Sabbath, holidays, other ceremonial occasions and for everyday consumption, challah is a traditional Jewish yeast bread. It's rich with eggs and has a light, airy texture. Though it can be formed into many shapes, braided challah is the most classic form.

chalupa [chah-LOO-pah] Spanish for "boat" or "launch," a chalupa is a corn tortilla dough formed into a small boat shape and fried until crisp. It's then usually filled with shredded beef, pork or chicken, vegetables, cheese or a combination of these, and served as an appetizer.

Chambord [sham-BORD] A French LIQUEUR with a rich garnet color and an intense black raspberry flavor.

chamomile; camomile [KAM-uh-meel; KAM-uh-myl] Though there are many varieties of chamomile, the one most commonly used is *Chamaemelum nobile*. For centuries the daisylike flowers of this perennial herb have been dried and used to make chamomile tea (TISANE), long valued for its soothing properties. The flowers are also used as a fragrance in shampoos and other hair preparations. The word "chamomile" comes from Greek for "ground (*chamos*) apple (*melos*)," in reference to the plant's low-growing profile and faintly apple-scented blossoms. In Latin cultures, chamomile is called *manzanilla* ("little apple"). *See also* TEA.

chamoy [CHAHM-ohee] Mexican fruit SALSA usually made with apricot, mango or plum plus CHILES, salt and citrus juice or vinegar. Chamoy, which is salty, spicy, sour and sweet, is used in savory and sweet dishes.

champ A traditional Irish dish made by combining mashed potatoes and green onions with plenty of butter.

Champagne; champagne [sham-PAYN] This most celebrated sparkling wine always seems to signal "special occasion." Though bubbling wines under various APPELLATIONS abound throughout the world, true Champagne comes only from the Champagne region in northeast France. Most countries bow to this tradition by calling their sparkling wines by other names such as *spumante* in Italy, *Sekt* in Germany and *vin mousseux* in other regions of France. Only in America do some wineries refer to their bubbling wine as "champagne." Dom Perignon, 17th-century cellarmaster of the Abbey of Hautvillers, is celebrated for developing the art of blending wines to create Champagnes with superior flavor. He's also credited for his work in preventing Champagne bottles and corks from exploding by using thicker bottles and tying the corks down with string. Even then, it's said that the venerable Dom Perignon lost half his Champagne through the bottles bursting. French Champagne is usually made from a blend of CHARDONNAY and PINOT NOIR or PINOT MEUNIER grapes. California "champagnes" generally use the same varieties, while those from New York more often are from the pressings of CATAWBA and DELAWARE GRAPES. Good Champagne is expensive not only because it's made with premium grapes, but because it's made by the *méthode champenoise*. This traditional method requires a second fermentation in the bottle as well as some 100 manual operations (some of which are mechanized today). Champagnes can range in color from pale gold to apricot blush. Their flavors can range from toasty to yeasty and from dry (no sugar added) to sweet. A sugar-wine mixture called a DOSAGE added just before final corking determines how sweet a Champagne will be. The label indicates the level of sweetness: **brut** (bone dry to almost dry—less than 1.5 percent sugar); **extra sec** or **extra dry** (slightly sweeter—1.2 to 2 percent sugar); **sec** (medium sweet—1.7 to 3.5 percent sugar); **demi-sec** (sweet—3.3 to 5 percent sugar); and **doux** (very sweet—over 5 percent sugar). The last two are considered DESSERT WINES.

champagne grapes Although known by the more glamorous name of "champagne grapes," this grape is actually the **Black Corinth** variety, sometimes also called the *Zante grape*. The seedless grape still flourishes in Greece, where it originated. It's names come from Zante, a small island off the Greek coast, and Corinth, an ancient Greek city. The grapes are extremely tiny (about $1/4$ inch in diameter), violet to purple in color and exceedingly sweet and juicy. In the United States, where California is the major grower, they're predominantly used to make the dried CURRANTS known as black currants or Zante currants. Champagne grapes are available in clusters in specialty produce markets from late summer to late fall. Refrigerate in a plastic bag for up to 1 week. These diminutive grapes are great with cheese and make a wonderful garnish for many dishes. *See also* GRAPE; RAISIN.

champignon [sham-pee-NYOHN] The French word for an edible "mushroom," generally the button variety. The term **aux champignons** refers to dishes garnished with mushrooms or served with a mushroom sauce.

chandon benit *see* SAW-LEAF HERB

chanfana [shahn-FAH-nah] Lamb or goat stew traditionally made in northwest Portugal. There, chanfana is cooked in a black clay pot called a *cachola* or *caçoila*. Recipes often call for the meat to marinate in red wine overnight. During cooking, ingredients such as bay leaves, garlic, lard, onions, paprika, parsley, red chile peppers and salt are added.

channa dal; chana dal [CHAH-nah dahl] Yellow split peas (*see* FIELD PEA).

chantaboon *see* RICE NOODLES

chanterelle [shan-tuh-REHL] A trumpet-shaped wild mushroom with a wonderfully nutty flavor and a color that ranges from bright yellow to orange. The chanterelle mushroom (known in France as *girolle* and in Germany as *Pfifferling*) has a delicate, nutty (sometimes fruity) flavor and a somewhat chewy texture. Chanterelles are usually imported from Europe and can be found dried or canned in many large supermarkets. Although they're not easily cultivated, chanterelles are found growing in parts of the Pacific Northwest and along the East Coast. They are occasionally found fresh in some markets during summer and winter months. Choose those that are plump and spongy; avoid ones with broken or shriveled caps. Chanterelles can be cooked as a separate side dish or as an addition to other foods. Because they tend to toughen when overcooked, it's best to add them to the dish toward the end of the cooking time. *See also* MUSHROOM.

chantilly [shan-TIHL-lee; shahn-tee-YEE] A French term referring to sweet or savory dishes that are prepared or served with whipped cream. **Crème chantilly** is lightly sweetened whipped cream—sometimes flavored with vanilla or LIQUEUR—used as a dessert topping.

Chaource [shah-OORS] A French cheese that takes its name from a town in France's Champagne region. Chaource can be made from raw or PASTEURIZED COW's milk and is produced in a manner similar to BRIE. It's RIPENED for a minimum of 2 weeks but usually for 4 weeks or more. Chaource has a white, downy rind with an ivory-colored center. Its fruity, rich flavor intensifies and becomes saltier as it RIPENS. The FAT CONTENT of Chaource is approximately 50 percent. *See also* CHEESE.

chap *see* BATH CHAPS

chapati; chapatti [chah-PAH-tee] An UNLEAVENED pancakelike bread from India, usually made from a simple mixture of whole-wheat flour and water. The dough is rolled into thin rounds and baked on a griddle. Pieces of chapati are torn off and used as a scoop or pusher for many East Indian dishes.

chapon [shah-POHN] A slice or cube of bread that has either been rubbed with garlic or dipped in garlic-flavored oil. The bread is then used to rub the inside of a salad bowl to impart the barest hint of garlic to the greens. The chapon may either be removed or—for a more intense garlic flavor—left in the bowl to toss with the salad.

chapuline [chah-poo-LEEN] Mexican snack of grasshoppers that are cleansed and then toasted or fried with a mixture of garlic, lime and salt, sometimes with AGAVE, chiles, EPAZOTE or onion added to the blend. Chapulines are especially popular in the Mexican state of Oaxaca.

char; charr A fish belonging to the genus *Salvelinus* and related to both the TROUT and SALMON. The *Dolly Varden trout* and the *Mackinaw trout* (or *lake trout*) are actually members of the char family. Char live in the icy waters (both fresh and marine) of North America and Europe. The *arctic char,* which has become more commercially available in recent years, is now raised on government-sponsored fish farms in Iceland. It has a pink flesh with a flavor and texture that's a cross between trout and salmon. Char can be baked, broiled, fried, grilled, poached or steamed. *See also* FISH.

character In the wine and spirit world, the word "character" describes a potable with distinctive, stylistic features.

charcuterie [shahr-KOO-tuhr-ee; shar-koo-tuhr-EE] Taken from the term *cuiseur de chair,* meaning "cooker of meat," charcuterie has been considered a French culinary art at least since the 15th century. It refers to the products, particularly (but not limited to) pork specialties such as PÂTÉS, RILLETTES, GALANTINES, CRÉPINETTES, etc., which are made and sold in a delicatessen-style shop, also called a *charcuterie.*

charcutière [shahr-KOO-tyayr] 1. *see* BRIGADE SYSTEM. 2. French brown sauce based on ROBERT SAUCE with julienned GHERKINS added. It is traditionally served with meats, especially pork chops.

chard Also referred to as *Swiss chard,* this member of the beet family is grown for its crinkly green leaves and silvery, celerylike stalks. The variety with dark green leaves and reddish stalks (sometimes referred to as *rhubarb chard*) has a stronger flavor than that with lighter leaves and stalks. There's also a *ruby chard,* which has a bright red stalk and deep red veins. *Rainbow chard* has stalks that come in a bevy of colors including pink, orange, red, purple, white with red stripes, ivory with pink stripes—the list is endless. Chard is available year-round but is best during the summer. Choose it for its tender greens and crisp stalks. Store, wrapped in a plastic bag, in the refrigerator for up to 3 days. The greens can be prepared like spinach, the stalks like asparagus. Chard, a CRUCIFEROUS vegetable, is a good source of vitamins A and C, as well as iron.

Chardonnay [shar-dn-AY; shar-doh-NAY] A top-rate, easy-to-grow, versatile white wine grape from which a broad spectrum of wines is produced. Chardonnay is one of the grapes used in making fine French CHAMPAGNE and white BURGUNDY. In California, the wine produced from this grape is referred to simply as "Chardonnay." These DRY, complex wines are variously described as buttery, creamy, nutty and smoky; their fruit descriptors include apple, lemon, melon and pineapple. There are hundreds of American wineries producing Chardonnay. Excellent wines also hail from Australia, as well as New Zealand, Italy and Spain. Chardonnay is also called *Beaunois, Gamay Blanc, Melon d'Arbois* and *Pinot Chardonnay*. It's sometimes mistakenly referred to as PINOT BLANC, a different variety.

Charentais melon [shar-en-TAY] A fruit of the European cantaloupe family (*see* MELON), the Charentais has a thin, smooth to slightly netted skin that ranges in color from dusty green to pale golden with darker green striping. The fine-textured flesh is orange, perfumy and very sweet with honey flavors. Charentais melons are typically available only at specialty produce markets and farmer's markets. Choose a melon that has a heady, sweet fragrance and is heavy for its size.

Charleston hot chile This relatively new variety of CAYENNE CHILE is touted to be up to twenty times hotter than the JALAPEÑO. Its SCOVILLE SCALE rating is 70,000 to 100,000. Ranging from 3- to 4-inches long, the Charleston hot changes color as it ripens, turning from yellow-green, to golden, to orange and finally to crimson red. It's generally available only at farmer's markets and specialty produce shops. *See also* CHILE.

charlotte; charlotte russe; apple charlotte [SHAR-luht] This classic molded dessert begins with a mold lined with SPONGE CAKE, LADYFINGERS or buttered bread. The traditional **charlotte mold** is pail-shaped, but almost any mold is acceptable. The lined mold is then filled with layers (or a mixture) of fruit and CUSTARD or whipped cream that has been fortified with gelatin. The dessert is chilled thoroughly and unmolded before serving. **Charlotte russe**, said to have been created for the Russian Czar Alexander, is a ladyfinger shell filled with the ethereal BAVARIAN CREAM, and decorated elaborately with whipped-cream rosettes. The classic **apple charlotte** is a buttered-bread shell filled with spiced, sautéed apples. Unlike other charlottes, this one is baked and served hot.

charmoula [chahr-MOO-lah] *see* CHERMOULA

Charolais (AOC) [shahr-oh-LAY] SOFT TO SEMISOFT goat's-milk cheese from the Charolais region in Burgundy, France. In order to receive AOC designation in 2010, the 252 communes in the area were required to use only goat's milk instead of adding some cow's milk, which was the usual practice. The cheeses, which have a minimum of 16 days of RIPENING, come in 2¾- to 3½-inch-tall rounds weighing from 9 to 11 ounces. The rind varies from ivory to beige with a bluish tint. The cheeses are fairly mild with a floral, grassy, tart character. The minimum FAT CONTENT of charolais is 45 percent.

charoli seed [CHAR-oh-lee] Small, dried, speckled seed from the *Buchanania lanzan* bush, which is cultivated across India but mainly in the northwest. The seed is surrounded by a hard shell that needs to be cracked open to reveal the flattened round, which is about the size of a large LENTIL. The seed, also called *chirongi,* is slightly soft, a bit oily and has a musky, nutty flavor with hints of almond, hazelnut and pistachio. In Indian cooking it's used to top various sweets such as HALVAS and SHRIKHAND and also ground to thicken sauces and stews. Charoli seeds are available in Indian and Middle Eastern markets. Store in an airtight container for up to 6 months. In hot climates they should be refrigerated because of their high oil content.

charoses; charoset *see* HAROSET

Chartreuse [shar-TROOZ] Originally made by the Carthusian monks in France's La Grande Chartreuse monastery, this aromatic LIQUEUR comes in green and yellow varieties. **Green** (*verte*) **Chartreuse** gets its pale yellow-green color from chlorophyll and has a minty, spicy flavor that's more intense and aromatic than its golden counterpart. **Yellow** (*jaune*) **Chartreuse** is lower in alcohol, lighter in body, sweeter (from honey) and has a pale yellow color attributed by SAFFRON. The term **Chartreuse V.E.P.** (*Vieillissement Exceptionnellement Prolongé*—"Exceptionally Prolonged Aging") describes limited lots of both green and yellow Chartreuse that have 12 years of oak-aging, a process that produces mellow, incredibly complex liqueurs with slightly lower alcohol levels.

chaser A beverage quaffed directly after drinking another (usually alcoholic) potable. For example, after a SHOT of whiskey, one might drink a beer "chaser" (a combination known as a BOILERMAKER).

chasoba [chah-SOH-bah] see SOBA

chasseur sauce [shah-SUR] 1. French for "hunter," chasseur sauce is a hunter-style brown sauce consisting of mushrooms, shallots and white wine (sometimes tomatoes and parsley). It's most often served with game and other meats. 2. Dishes prepared in a *chasseur style* are garnished with sautéed mushrooms and shallots. *See also* SAUCE.

château-bottled [sha-TOH] see WINE LABEL TERMS

Châteaubriand [sha-toh-bree-AHN] Contrary to popular belief, Châteaubriand is actually a recipe, not a cut of beef. This method of preparation is said to be named for the 19th-century French statesman and author, François Châteaubriand. It's a succulent, thick cut of beef (usually taken from the center of the tenderloin) that's large enough for two people. The Châteaubriand is usually grilled or broiled and served with BÉARNAISE and château potatoes (trimmed into olive shapes and sautéed in butter). *See also* SHORT LOIN.

Châteauneuf-du-Pape [sha-toh-nuhf doo PAHP] Literally translated as "new castle of the Pope," this famous wine comes from a village of the same name near Avignon, France. Each producer creates its own special blend from the classic 13 grape varieties permitted for this wine. Most Châteauneuf-du-Papes are dry, full-bodied red wines; a small number are white.

chatni *see* CHUTNEY

chaud-froid [shoh-FRWAH] *Chaud* (French for "hot") and *froid* (French for "cold") combine in this term to explain food (usually meat, poultry or game) that is first cooked, then chilled before serving. The distinguishing feature of a chaud-froid is that the food is glazed with an ASPIC, which is allowed to set before serving. Decorative vegetable cutouts are often set into the aspic for a colorful garnish.

chaurice [shoh-REEC] A Creole/Cajun pork SAUSAGE that's hot, spicy and full-flavored. Chaurice is used in Creole/Cajun cooking both as a main meat dish and in numerous dishes such as GUMBOS and JAMBALAYAS.

chawan mushi [chah-WAHN moo-SHEE] A savory egg-custard dish from Japan. The name translates to "teacup steaming" and refers to placing the egg mixture in a teacup and lightly steaming it. Chawan mushi is usually made with eggs seasoned with DASHI, MIRIN and soy sauce, plus small amounts of green onion, mushrooms and crab or shrimp, but ingredients may vary. The result is savory and creamy with a bit of UMAMI flavor.

chaya leaf [CHAY-yah] The leaf of a fast-growing shrub that's native to Mexico's Yucatán Peninsula. In Mexico and Central America it's prepared and eaten much like spinach is in the United States, which may be why it's sometimes referred to as *tree spinach*. Chaya leaf dates back to the Mayan culture, where it was valued for its health benefits. Studies show that it's actually richer in iron, calcium, potassium and other vitamins than spinach. The chaya leaf, like YUCA, is toxic unless cooked. In addition to its use as a vegetable, the leaves can be used to make tea.

chayote [chi-OH-tay] Once the principal food of the Aztecs and Mayas, this gourdlike fruit is about the size and shape of a very large pear. Beneath its furrowed, pale green skin is a white, rather bland-tasting flesh surrounding one soft seed. In the United States, chayote is grown in several states including California, Florida and Louisiana (where it's known as *mirliton*). Chayotes are widely available from September through May, but can be found throughout the year in Asian, Caribbean and Latin American markets as well as some produce markets. Look for those that are small, firm and unblemished. Refrigerate in a plastic bag up to a month. Chayotes can be prepared in any way suitable for summer squash. It can also be split, stuffed and baked like acorn squash, or used raw in salad. Because of its mild flavor it requires assertive seasoning. Chayote is known by many names around the world—*chocho* in Brazil, *chocho* and *choko* in the French Caribbean, *christophene* in France, *custard marrow* in Britain, *xuxu* in Vietnam and *vegetable pear* and *mango squash* in various English-speaking countries.

checkerberry *see* WINTERGREEN

cheddar; cheddaring [CHED-uhr] Cheddar takes its name from a village in southwest England's Somerset County, where production of this cheese began and can be traced to at least the end of the 16th century. Today there are a precious few British FARMSTEAD cheddar cheesemakers left and most of this cheese is factory produced in the U.K. and elsewhere. Unlike the names of many European cheeses, that of cheddar is not protected (*see* PROTECTED DESIGNATION OF ORIGIN). And the truth is, the word "cheddar" no longer refers to just the name of the English village, but rather to the PRESSING process by which the cheese is made. With this technique, known as **cheddaring**, slabs of partially drained CURD are stacked on top of each other and turned and restacked every 10 to 15 minutes for up to 1½ hours, which ensures that all slabs are evenly pressed. This produces a cheese with the characteristically smooth, tight texture of cheddar, CHESHIRE and LANCASHIRE. Cheddar is now the most widely made cheese in the world, with production in myriad countries including Australia, Canada, Ireland, New Zealand, Scotland, South Africa, Sweden and the United States. Though factory-produced cheddars abound, there has been a renaissance of traditional cheesemaking in the U.K., United States, Australia and elsewhere. Cheddar can be made from raw or PAS-TEURIZED cow's milk and can range in texture from semihard to hard. This cheese comes in a variety of sizes and shapes including rectangles and small wheels. Factory-produced cheddar is typically rindless and comes wrapped in plastic or covered with wax; the interior can range from off-white to orange. Farmstead cheeses have rinds that can range in color from golden brown to grayish brown; the PASTE varies from ivory to pale yellow. One signal of handmade cheddar is that it's wrapped in cloth. Another is that it isn't dyed orange with ANNATTO. Texture-wise, cheddar is smooth and tight. Factory-produced cheeses are typically slick and can be slightly gummy; those that are handmade are generally somewhat crumbly or flaky. The flavor of factory cheddars can range from bland to sharp, while farmstead versions are full and complex with notes of caramel, fruit, nuts and spice. On the whole, mass-produced cheddars are second-rate compared to traditional handmade versions. In general, cheddars are labeled with four RIPENING designations: mild (about 2 to 4 months), medium (4 to 8 months), sharp (9 to 12 months), and extra-sharp (aged over 1 year). That's a very broad spectrum, however, and aging times for cheddars can vary widely, depending on the producer, many of which openly indicate the length of time the cheese has been ripened. The FAT CONTENT of regular cheddar is 48 percent. There are also lowfat and nonfat cheddars, as well as some seasoned with ingredients such as garlic, basil, sage, horseradish, chili peppers and port. *See also* CHEESE.

cheeks *see* BATH CHAPS

cheese Author Clifton Fadiman said it best when he described cheese as "milk's leap toward immortality." Almost everyone loves one type of cheese or another, whether it's delectably mild, creamy and soft or pungent, hard and crumbly. To begin with, cheese can be broken down into two very broad categories—*fresh* and *ripened*. Within these basic categories, however, are a multitude of subdivisions, usually classified according to the texture of the cheese and how it was made. Naturally, many of these categories overlap because a cheese can have an entirely different character when young than it does when aged. Most cheese begins as milk (usually cow's, goat's or sheep's) that is allowed to thicken (sometimes with the addition of RENNIN or special bacteria) until it separates into a liquid (WHEY) and semisolids (CURD). The whey is drained off and the curds are either allowed to drain or pressed into different shapes, depending on the variety. At this stage it is called **fresh** (or **unripened**) **cheese**. Among the most popular fresh cheeses on the market today are

COTTAGE CHEESE, CREAM CHEESE, POT CHEESE and RICOTTA. In order to become a **ripened** (or **aged**) **cheese**, the drained curds are CURED by a variety of processes including being subjected to heat, bacteria, soaking and so on. The curds are also sometimes flavored with salt, spices or herbs and some, like many cheddars, are colored with a natural dye. After curing, natural cheese begins a ripening process during which it's stored, usually uncovered, at a controlled temperature and humidity until the desired texture and character is obtained. It can be covered with wax or other protective coating before or after this ripening process. Ripened cheeses are further classified according to texture. Ripened cheese has been linked with migraine headaches because it contains tyramine, a natural compound that can cause the dilation of the brain's blood vessels in tyramine-sensitive individuals. The longer cheese is aged (as with Camembert and Parmesan), the higher the tyramine levels. Soft cheeses, such as cottage cheese and cream cheese, have the lowest tyramine levels. If headaches hit after eating cheese, tyramine may be the culprit. **Hard cheeses** are cooked, pressed and aged for long periods (usually at least 2 years) until hard and dry, and are generally used for grating. Among the more well known of this genre are PARMESAN and PECORINO. **Semifirm cheeses** such as CHEDDAR, EDAM and JARLSBERG are firm but not usually crumbly. They have been cooked and pressed but not aged as long as those in the firm-cheese category. **Semisoft cheeses** are pressed but can be either cooked or uncooked. Their texture is sliceable but soft. Among the more popular semisoft cheeses are GOUDA, JACK and TILSIT. **Soft-ripened** (or **surface-ripened**) **cheeses** are neither cooked nor pressed. They are, however, subjected to various bacteria (either by spraying or dipping), which ripens the cheese from the outside in. Such cheeses develop a rind that is either powdery white (as in BRIE) or golden orange (like PONT L'ÉVÊQUE). The consistency of soft-ripened cheese can range from semisoft to creamy and spreadable. Some cheeses are further categorized by process. **Blue-veined cheeses**, for example, are inoculated or sprayed with spores of the molds *Penicillium roqueforti* or *penicillium glaucum*. Some of these cheeses are punctured with holes to ensure that the mold will penetrate during the aging period. The result of these painstaking efforts are cheeses with veins or pockets of flavorful blue or green mold. Another special-process category is **pasta filata** ("spun paste"), Italy's famous stretched-curd cheeses. They're made using a special technique whereby the curd is given a hot whey bath, then kneaded and stretched to the desired pliable consistency. Among the *pasta filata* cheeses are MOZZARELLA, PROVOLONE and CACIOCAVALLO. **Whey cheeses** are another special category. Instead of beginning with milk, they're made from the whey drained from the making of other cheeses. The whey is reheated (usually with rennin) until it coagulates. Probably the best known of this cheese type are GJETOST and Italian RICOTTA. There are a variety of **reduced-fat** and **fat-free cheeses** on the market today. They're commonly made either partially or completely with nonfat milk, and supplemented with various additives for texture and flavor. Unfortunately, the more the fat is reduced in cheese, the less flavor it has. Not only that, but the less fat there is, the worse cheese does when melted. The texture of such cheese turns rubbery when heated and, in fact, nonfat cheese never really seems to melt, but obstinately remains in its original form. For these reasons, low- and nonfat cheeses are best used in cold preparations like sandwiches. **Imitation cheese** is just that—a fusion that generally includes TOFU, calcium caseinate (a milk protein), rice starch, LECITHIN and various additives. It's a nondairy, nonfat, noncholesterol and nonflavor food that, for those who like cheese, is better left at the store. **Storing cheese:** *Firm, semifirm* and *semisoft cheese* should be wrapped airtight in a plastic bag and stored in a refrigerator's cheese compartment (or warmest location) for up to several weeks. Such cheeses can be frozen, but will likely undergo a textural change. *Fresh* and *soft-ripened cheeses* should be tightly wrapped and stored in the coldest part of the refrigerator, generally for no more than 2 weeks. If mold appears on firm, semifirm or semisoft cheese, simply cut away the offending portion (plus a little extra) and discard. Mold on fresh or soft-ripened cheese, however, signals that it should be thrown out. Firm and semifirm cheeses are easier to grate if they're cold. All cheese tastes better if brought to room temperature before serving. *See also* ABBAYE DE BELLOC; ALLGÄUER BERGKÄSE; APPENZELLER; ASADERO; ASIAGO; BAKERS'; BANON; BEL PAESE; BIERKÄSE; BLEU D'AUVERGNE; BLUE CHEESE; BOCCONCINI; BONBEL; BOURSAULT; BOURSIN; BREBIS; BRICK CHEESE; BRILLAT-SAVARIN; BRYNDZA; BÛCHERON; BURRATA; CABRALES; CAERPHILLY; CAMBOZOLA; CAMEMBERT; CANTAL; CASEIN; CHAOURCE; CHEESEMONGER; CHENNA; CHESHIRE; CHÈVRE; CHILE CON QUESO; COLBY; COLD PACK CHEESE; COMTÉ; CORNISH YARG; COTIJA; CREMA DANIA; CREOLE CREAM CHEESE; CRESCENZA; DANABLU; DANBO; DERBY; DOUBLE-CREAM CHEESE; EMMENTAL; ENCHILADO; ÉPOISSES DE BOURGOGNE; ESROM; EXPLORATEUR; EYES; FARMER CHEESE; FETA; FONDUE; FONDUTA; FONTINA; FRICO; FROMAGE BLANC; FROMAGER D'AFFINOIS; GIROLLE; GJETOST; GLOUCESTER; GORGONZOLA; GRANA; GRUYERE; HANDKÄSE; HAVARTI; HERVE; HOPFENKÄSE; IMITATION CHEESE; KAASDOOP; KASSERI; KOSHER CHEESE; KUMINOST; LANCASHIRE; LEICESTER; LEYDEN; LIEDER-KRANZ; LIMBURGER; LIPTAUER; LONGHORN; MANCHEGO; MASCARPONE; MIMOLETTE; MONTASIO; MONTRACHET, MUENSTER; NEUFCHÂTEL; NÖKKELOST; PANEER; PASTA FILATA; PETIT SUISSE; PORT-SALUT; PROCESSED CHEESE; PYRAMIDE; QUARK; QUESO AÑEJO; QUESO FRESCO; QUESO FUNDIDO; RACLETTE; REBLOCHON; ROBIOLA; ROMANO; ROQUEFORT; SAGA BLUE; SAGANAKI; SAMSOE; SAPSAGO; SBRINZ; SCAMORZE; SCHLOSS; SOY CHEESE; SQUEAKERS; STILTON; STRACCHINO; STRING CHEESE; SUBSTITUTE CHEESE; SWISS CHEESE; TALEGGIO; TELEME; TÊTE DE MOINE; TILLAMOOK; TOMME; TYBO; VACHERIN; VEGETARIAN CHEESE.

cheeseburger *see* HAMBURGER

cheesecake Though a cheesecake can be savory (and served with crackers as an appetizer), most of us think of the term as describing a luscious, rich dessert. The texture of any cheesecake can vary greatly—from light and airy to dense and rich to smooth and creamy. All cheesecakes begin with cheese—usually cream cheese, ricotta cheese, cottage cheese or sometimes Swiss or cheddar cheese. A cheesecake may or may not have a crust, which can be a light dusting of breadcrumbs, a cookie crust or a pastry crust. The filling is made by creaming the cheese and mixing it with eggs, sugar (for desserts) and other flavorings. The mixture is then poured into a special SPRINGFORM PAN and baked. After baking, the cheesecake is thoroughly chilled and generally topped by sour cream, whipped cream, fruit or some other embellishment.

cheesecloth Long a versatile kitchen helper, this lightweight natural cotton cloth won't fall apart when wet and will not flavor the food it touches. Cheesecloth has a multitude of culinary uses including straining liquids, forming a packet for herbs and spices (as with BOUQUET GARNI) that can be dropped into a soup or stock pot and lining molds (such as for COEUR À LA CRÈME). It comes in both fine and coarse weaves and is available in gourmet shops, supermarkets and the kitchen section of many department stores. In Britain it's sometimes called *butter muslin*.

cheese iron *see* IRONING CHEESE

cheesemonger A seller of cheeses—a "monger" is a dealer in a specific commodity, in this case cheese.

cheese steak Also called *Philadelphia cheese steak* after the illustrious city that's said to have originated this sandwich in the 1930s. It consists of an Italian or French roll topped by thin slices of beef, cheese (usually American) and sometimes sautéed onions.

cheese straws Strips of cheese pastry or plain pastry sprinkled with cheese, baked until crisp and golden brown. The pastry strips are sometimes twisted before baking. Cheese straws are served as an appetizer or an accompaniment to soups or salads.

cheese wire A long, thin wire with wooden handles at each end, used to cut large rounds or wedges of cheese.

chef de cuisine [shef de kwih-ZEEN] *see* BRIGADE SYSTEM

chef de partie [shef de pahr-TEE] *see* BRIGADE SYSTEM

chef de rang [shef de RAHN) *see* BRIGADE SYSTEM

chef de salle [shef de SAHL] *see* BRIGADE SYSTEM

chef de vin [shef de VAN] *see* BRIGADE SYSTEM

chef garde manger [shef gahrd mahn-ZHAY] *see* BRIGADE SYSTEM

chef's salad An entrée salad of tossed greens topped by cold JULI-ENNED cheeses and meats (such as chicken and ham), thinly sliced vegetables and slices of hard-cooked egg. The salad may be topped with any one of a variety of dressings.

chelo; chelow [CHEH-lo] In Persian cuisine, a long-grain rice such as BASMATI RICE that's cooked in boiling water until *al dente*. It's then drained and "steamed" with a little oil or butter in the bottom and along the sides of a pot until the rice is cooked and a crispy, golden crust (*see* TADIG; TAHDIG) forms. TURMERIC or SAFFRON is often added to chelo for additional flavor. Chelo is usually served with stews or KEBABS. *See also* POLO.

chemisé; en chemise [shuh-mee-ZAY; ahn shuh-MEEZ] The word *chemise* is French for "shirt" or "vest," and the term refers culinarily to a food that is wrapped or coated—such as wrapped in pastry, or coated with a sauce or aspic.

Chenango; Chenango strawberry apple A good medium-large, all-purpose apple with very pale yellow or green skin streaked in various shades of red. The flesh is white, juicy and tender and it's very flavorful with hints of strawberries. It's good for eating, applesauce and desserts. *See also* APPLE.

Chenin Blanc [SHEN-ihn BLAHN; SHEN-ihn BLAHNGK] Grown in California and France's Loire Valley, the Chenin Blanc grape makes intense, spicy, slightly sweet wine. Chenin Blancs have a strong acidity that modulates the sweetness and promotes good aging. This well-balanced grape is responsible for France's famed Vouvray, Côteaux du Layon and Saumur. It's also used to produce several of California's sparkling wines.

chenna [CHEHN-nah] A fresh, unripened CHEESE used throughout India, although it's most popular in the eastern part of the country. It is made from cow's or buffalo's milk and resembles a COTTAGE CHEESE that's been kneaded until it's closer to the consistency of a light CREAM CHEESE. Chenna, which is available in Indian markets, is used primarily in a variety of Bengali desserts. *See also* PANEER.

cherimoya [chehr-uh-MOY-ah] A tropical-American fruit belonging to the genus *Annona*, the cherimoya (*A. cherimola*) is one of several members of the Annona family, including SOURSOP and SWEETSOP. This large tropical fruit (called *custard apple* in Britain) tastes like a delicate combination of pineapple, papaya and banana. Irregularly oval in shape, the cherimoya has a leathery green skin that has a scaly pattern not unlike large, overlapping thumbprint indentations. The flesh, peppered with large, shiny black seeds, is cream-colored and the texture of firm custard.

Though Spain is the world's largest producer, cherimoyas are now grown in California and are available from November through May. Purchase fruit that's firm, heavy for its size and without skin blemishes; avoid those with brown splotches. Store at room temperature until ripe (they will give slightly with soft pressure), then refrigerate, well wrapped, up to 4 days. Serve cherimoyas well chilled. Simply halve, remove the seeds and scoop out the flesh with a spoon. Cherimoyas contain a fair amount of niacin, iron and vitamin C.

Chéri-Suisse A Swiss LIQUEUR with a cherry-chocolate flavor.

chermoula [chehr-MOO-lah] A thick North African sauce or paste used primarily as a marinade for fish or shellfish but also occasionally for meat and vegetables. Recipes vary, but chermoula typically consists of CILANTRO, garlic, lemon juice, olive oil, parsley, pepper and salt. Other flavoring variations include CAYENNE, cloves, CORIANDER SEEDS, CUMIN, onion, PAPRIKA, SAFFRON and vinegar. Chermoula is also spelled *charmoula*, *sharmoola* and *sharmoula*. *See also* SAUCE.

cherries jubilee A dessert of pitted BING or other dark red cherries, sugar and KIRSCH or BRANDY, which are combined, flambéed and spooned over vanilla ice cream. The cherries are usually prepared in a CHAFING DISH at the table and flamed with great flourish.

cherry Said to date as far back as 300 B.C., cherries were named after the Turkish town of Cerasus. Throughout the centuries, cherry trees have been lauded for their deliciously succulent fruit as well as for their beauty. Tourists flock to Washington, D.C., every year to see the cherry blossoms on the ornamental cherry trees that were originally presented to America's capital in 1912 by Tokyo's governor. There are two main groups of cherries—sweet and sour. The larger of the two are the firm, heart-shaped **sweet cherries**. They're delicious for eating out of hand and can also be cooked. The most popular varieties range from the dark red to purplish black BING, LAMBERT and TARTARIAN to the golden, red-blushed ROYAL ANN. MARASCHINO CHERRIES are usually made from Royal Ann cherries. **Sour cherries** are smaller, softer and more globular than the sweet varieties. Most are too tart to eat raw, but make excellent pies, preserves and the like. There are two groupings of sour cherries—AMARELLE, which have red-pigmented skin but clear flesh and juice, and MORELLO, which have red pigment in the skin and flesh. The best-selling amarelle cherries are the EARLY RICHMOND and the MONTMORENCY. In the past there have been numerous morello cultivars but today only the generic morello is easily found. Most fresh cherries are available from May (June for sour cherries) through August. Choose brightly colored, shiny, plump fruit. Sweet cherries should be quite firm, but not hard; sour varieties should be medium-firm. Stemmed cherries are a better buy, but those with stems last longer. Store unwashed cherries in a plastic bag in the refrigerator. **Dried cherries**—both sweet and sour—are available in many markets today. They can be eaten as a snack, or used in baked goods or desserts as one would use raisins. Cherries contain minor amounts of vitamins and minerals. *See also* CHOKECHERRY.

Cherry Heering *see* PETER HEERING

cherry pepper Also called *Hungarian cherry pepper,* this small (1 to 2 inches in diameter) pepper is round and bright red in color. It has a slightly sweet flavor and is mild with a SCOVILLE SCALE rating of 500 to 2,500. Cherry peppers can be found fresh and pickled in jars. *See also* CHILE.

cherry plum *see* MIRABELLE

cherrystone clam This East Coast medium-size clam (shell diameter of about 2½ inches) is of the hard-shell variety. Cherrystones are good both raw and cooked, steaming and baking being the most popular cooking methods. *See also* CLAM.

chervil [CHER-vuhl] A mild-flavored member of the parsley family, this aromatic herb has curly, dark green leaves with an elusive parsley-anise flavor and fragrance. Chervil is one of the main ingredients in FINES HERBES. Though most chervil is cultivated for its leaves alone, the root is edible and was, in fact, enjoyed by early Greeks and Romans. Today it's available dried but has the best flavor when fresh. Both forms can be found in most supermarkets. It can be used like parsley but its delicate flavor is diminished when boiled. Chervil is also called *cicely* and *sweet cicely. See also* HERBS; Seasoning Suggestions, page 891.

Chesapeake oyster *see* ATLANTIC OYSTER

Cheshire cheese [CHEH-sher] Hailing from the county of Cheshire, this rich, cow's-milk cheese comes in three varieties—white, red and blue—and has a reputation as one of England's most famous cheeses. The white (actually pale yellow) and red (apricot-colored) Cheshires are very similar, differing mainly in the fact that the red variety has been dyed with ANNATTO. They're young cheeses, having an average age of 8 weeks, with a semifirm texture and a mild, tangy, cheddarlike flavor. **Farmhouse Cheshire**, rarely exported, is usually aged about 9 months and has a richer, fuller flavor for the effort. **Blue Cheshire**, sometimes referred to as *Cheshire-Stilton*, is made like regular Cheshire except that *Penicillium roqueforti*-inoculated CURD is mixed with fresh curd to create the mold necessary for BLUE CHEESE. This version boasts a beautiful golden interior veined with blue and is just as rich as STILTON but milder in flavor. Cheshire cheese has long been a favorite for WELSH RABBIT. The FAT CONTENT of Cheshire is about 48 percent. *See also* CHEESE.

chess pie This is one of the South's favorite pies, with a simple filling of eggs, sugar, butter and a small amount of flour. Chess pie can be varied by adding flavorings such as lemon juice or vanilla, or substituting brown sugar for granulated sugar.

chestnut Mount Olympus, home of the gods, was said to have had an abundance of chestnut trees producing this sweet, edible nut. There are many varieties of chestnuts and the trees are common throughout Europe, Asia and the United States. Once peeled of their hard, dark brown outer shells and bitter inner skin, chestnuts can be enjoyed in a variety of ways including roasted, boiled, puréed, preserved and candied. They can be used in desserts or as a savory main-dish accompaniment. Fresh chestnuts, most of which are imported, are available from September through February. Choose firm, plump nuts without shell blemishes. Store unshelled nuts in a cool, dry place; refrigerate shelled nuts in a covered container. Chestnuts can also be found canned whole, in pieces or as a purée. They can be unsweetened, or sweetened as in MARRONS glacés. **Dried chestnuts**, as well as **chestnut flour** (dried nuts that have been ground to a powder), are often found in ethnic markets.

chèvre [SHEHV-*r*uh; SHEHV] French for "goat," chèvre is a pure white goat's-milk cheese with a distinctively tart flavor. Some of the better known chèvres include BANON, BÛCHERON and MONTRACHET. *"Pur chèvre"* on the label ensures that the cheese is made entirely from goat's milk; *mi-chèvre* means that it's comprised of at least 50 percent goat's milk, with the remainder typically cow's milk. The plural is *chèvres*, which originally referred to all French goat cheeses but is now widely used to refer to all goat cheeses, wherever their origin. *Chèvres* can range in texture from moist and creamy to dry and semifirm. They come in a variety of shapes including cylinders, discs, cones and pyramids, and are often coated in edible ASH or leaves, herbs or pepper. Store, tightly wrapped, in the refrigerator up to 2 weeks. Chèvre that is over the hill takes on a sour taste and should be discarded. *See also* CHEESE.

Chevreuil Sauce *see* POIVRADE

Chianti [kee-AHN-tee] 1. Named for the Chianti region in Tuscany, Italy, this sturdy, dry red wine was once instantly recognizable by its squat, straw-covered bottles (*fiaschi*). However, Chianti—particularly the better brands—is now more often found in the traditional Bordeaux-type bottle. Only a few vintners use the straw-based bottle, which today usually designates a cheaper (and often inferior) product. In Italy, Chianti has long been made from four or five grape varieties, including SANGIO-

VESE, Trebbiano and Malvasia. Today, however, the CABERNET SAUVIGNON grape is being added to some Chianti blends. The word *Riserva* on the label indicates that the wine is of superior quality and has been aged in oak for at least 3 years before being bottled. Labels indicating "Chianti Classico" refer to the central and original (dating back to the 14th century) growing area from which the grapes came. Chianti's bold flavor is particularly suited to highly seasoned foods. 2. A generic name used for rather ordinary, inexpensive red wine made outside of Italy in countries like Argentina and the United States. The grape varieties that go into such wines are varied and unregulated.

chia seed [CHEE-uh] Like FLAX SEED, chia seed is a rich source of omega-3 fatty acids (*see* FATS AND OILS), as well as the omega-6 fatty acid LA, protein and fiber. It also contains several essential nutrients, including calcium, phosphorus, magnesium, manganese, copper, niacin and zinc. Because of this, chia, formally known as *Salvia hispanica*, is fast becoming a favorite health food. It's a member of the mint family and was a significant component of the Aztec and Mayan diets. The seed has a nutlike flavor and is often used simply sprinkled over cereal, yogurt or salads, or eaten by itself as a snack. Chia seed can be ground and mixed with flour and used in baked goods. A drink popular in Mexico and Central America is **chia fresca**, made by mixing a couple of teaspoons of chia seeds with 8 to 10 ounces of water or fruit juice. Chia seed is naturally mucilaginous so the mixture will become a bit viscous. It's grown in Mexico, as well as some Central and South American countries, and can be found in natural food markets and some supermarkets. Chia seed, unlike flax seed, does not have a high fat content and can be stored for longer periods without going rancid.

Chiboust, crème; Chiboust [shee-BOO, krehm] *see* CRÈME CHIBOUST

chicharrón [chee-chah-RROHN] 1. This crispy rich snack is made from pork skin that has been deep-fried twice, once in 325°F oil, then again in 375°F oil, making it balloon into a honeycombed puff. It is available in Latin American markets. 2. In some parts of Central and South America, chicharrón refers to cooked pork that's finely ground along with onions, tomatoes and various seasonings. In El Salvador, it is often used as a filling in PUPUSAS.

chicken History tells us that today's chickens are descendants of wild fowl that roamed the dense jungles of primeval Asia. Thousands of years later, France's King Henry IV stated in his coronation speech that he hoped each peasant in his realm would have "a chicken in his pot every Sunday" (a quote later paraphrased by President Herbert Hoover).

It surprises many people that chicken wasn't always the reasonably priced meat it is today. Until after World War II, only the affluent (and chicken farmers) could manage even the proverbial Sunday chicken. Today, thanks to modern production methods, almost anyone can afford this versatile fowl, which provides not only meat and eggs but feathers as well. Chickens fall into several classifications. The **broiler-fryer** can weigh up to $3\frac{1}{2}$ pounds and is usually around $2\frac{1}{2}$ months old. These chickens, as the name implies, are best when broiled or fried. The more flavorful **roasters** have a higher fat content and therefore are perfect for roasting and rotisserie cooking. They usually range between $2\frac{1}{2}$ and 5 pounds and can be up to 8 months old. **Stewing chickens** (also called *hens, boiling fowl* and just plain *fowl*) usually range in age from 10 to 18 months and can weigh from 3 to 6 pounds. Their age makes them more flavorful but also less tender, so they're best cooked with moist heat, such as in stewing or braising. A **capon** is a rooster that is castrated when quite young (usually before 8 weeks), fed a fattening diet and brought to market before it's 10 months old. Ranging from 4 to 10 pounds, capons are full-breasted with tender, juicy, flavorful meat that is particularly suited to roasting. **Rock Cornish hen**, also called *Rock Cornish game hen,* is a hybrid of Cornish and White Rock chickens. These miniature chickens weigh up to $2\frac{1}{2}$ pounds and are 4 to 6 weeks old. Because of the relatively small amount of meat to bone, each hen is usually just enough for one serving. Rock Cornish hens are best broiled or roasted. **Squab Chicken** (*poussin* in French), different from the true SQUAB, is a very small, 4- to 6-week-old chicken that weighs no more than $1\frac{1}{2}$ pounds. These tiny birds are best broiled, grilled or roasted. The **cock** or **rooster** is an older bird and therefore rather tough. It's best used in soups or to make broths. **Free-range chickens** are the elite of the poultry world in that, in contrast to the mass-produced birds allotted 1 square foot of space, each range chicken has double that area indoors plus the freedom to roam outdoors. They're fed a special vegetarian diet free (according to most range chicken breeders) of antibiotics, animal byproducts, hormones and growth enhancers. The special diet and freedom of movement is thought by some to give this fowl a fuller, more "chickeny" flavor; the added amenities also make these birds much more expensive than mass-produced chickens. Free-range chickens average $4\frac{1}{2}$ pounds and are usually around 10 to 12 weeks old. **Chicken grades:** The government grades chicken quality with USDA classifications A, B and C. The highest grade is A, and is generally what is found in markets. Grade B chickens are less meaty and well finished; grade C is usually reserved for scrawny chickens. The grade stamp can be found within a shield on the package wrapping, or sometimes on a tag attached to the bird's wing. Chicken is available in markets throughout the year either fresh or frozen, and whole or cut into parts. The neck and GIBLETS (liver, gizzard and heart) are either packaged separately and placed in a whole bird's body cavity, or sold individually. Choose a meaty, full-breasted chicken with plump, short legs. The skin—which can range from cream-colored to yellow, depending on the breed and the chicken's diet—should be smooth and soft. Avoid chickens with an off odor, or with skin that's bruised or torn. Store chicken in the coldest part of the refrigerator. If packaged tightly in cellophane, loosen packaging or remove and loosely rewrap chicken in waxed paper. Remove any giblets from the body cavity and store separately. Refrigerate raw chicken up to 2 days, cooked chicken up to 3 days. For maximum flavor, freeze raw chicken no longer than 2 months, cooked chicken up to a month. Salmonella bacteria are present on most poultry (though only about 4 percent of salmonella poisonings are chicken-related). To avoid any chance of bacterial contamination, it's important to handle raw chicken with care. The first rule is never to eat chicken in its raw state. After cutting or working with raw chicken, thoroughly wash utensils, cutting tools, cutting board and your hands. Cook boneless chicken until the internal temperature is 179°F, bone-in chicken to 180°F. Don't let any raw juice come in contact with cooked chicken. The versatile chicken can be prepared in almost any way imaginable, including baking, broiling, boiling, roasting, frying, braising, barbecuing and stewing. Boning chicken will shorten any cooking time but will also slightly diminish the flavor. Chicken is an excellent source of protein, and a good to fair source of niacin and iron. White meat and chicken without skin have fewer calories.

chicken à la king *see* À LA KING

chicken cacciatore *see* CACCIATORE

chicken-fried steak Particularly popular in the South and Midwest, this dish is said to have been created to use inexpensive beef. It refers to a thin cut of steak that has been tenderized by pounding. It's dipped into a milk-egg mixture and seasoned flour, then fried like chicken until crisp and brown, and served with COUNTRY GRAVY.

chicken halibut *see* HALIBUT

chicken Kiev [kee-EHV] A boned chicken breast rolled around a chilled chunk of herbed butter, with the edges fastened so the butter won't escape during cooking. The breast is dipped in egg and then breadcrumbs and fried until crisp. When pierced with a fork or cut into, the chicken emits a jet of the fragrant melted butter.

chicken Marengo *see* MARENGO, À LA

chicken paprikash; paprikás *see* GOULASH

chicken Tetrazzini [teh-trah-ZEE-nee] Said to have been named for the opera singer Luisa Tetrazzini, this rich dish combines cooked spaghetti and strips of chicken with a sherry-Parmesan cheese cream sauce. Parmesan or breadcrumbs are sprinkled over the surface and the dish is baked until bubbly and golden brown. Turkey is sometimes substituted for chicken in this dish.

chickpea; chick-pea A round, irregular-shape, buff-colored LEGUME that's slightly larger than the average pea. Chickpeas (also called *garbanzo beans* and, in Italy, *ceci*) have a firm texture and mild, nut-like flavor. They're used extensively in the Mediterranean, India and the Middle East for dishes such as COUSCOUS and HUMMUS. They've also found their way into Spanish stews, Italian MINESTRONE and various Mexican dishes, and are popular in many parts of the Western and Southwestern United States. Chickpeas are available canned, dried and in some areas, fresh. They're most commonly used in salads, soups and stews. *See also* BEANS.

chicory [CHIHK-uh-ree] This ENDIVE relative has curly, bitter-tasting leaves that are often used as part of a salad or cooked as greens. In the United States, early endive is sometimes erroneously called chicory. Chicory is available year-round. Choose leaves that are brightly colored and crisp. Store unwashed greens in an airtight container in the refrigerator up to 3 days. Today's trendy RADICCHIO is a red-leafed Italian chicory. **Roasted chicory** (also called *succory*) comes from the roasted, ground roots of some varieties of chicory. It's used as a coffee substitute, and added to some coffees for body and aroma and as an "extender." This coffee-chicory blend is often referred to as "New Orleans" or "Creole" coffee and is a popular beverage in Louisiana.

chifferi *see* Pasta Glossary, page 883

chiffon [shih-FAHN] An airy, fluffy mixture, usually a filling for pie. The lightness is achieved with stiffly beaten egg whites and sometimes gelatin.

chiffonade [shihf-uh-NAHD; shihf-uh-NAYD] Literally translated, this French phrase means "made of rags." Culinarily, it refers to thin strips or shreds of vegetables (classically, sorrel and lettuce), either lightly sautéed or used raw to garnish soups, salads and other dishes.

chiffonade salad dressing A classic FRENCH DRESSING with the addition of finely chopped or shredded hard-cooked egg, green pepper, chives, parsley, beet and onion.

chiffon cake Said to have been created in the late 1940s by a professional baker, chiffon cake is distinguished from others of its genre by the fact that oil, rather than solid shortening, is used. It contains LEAVENING, such as baking powder, and stiffly beaten egg whites, which contribute to its rather spongecakelike texture.

chigae *see* JJIGAE

chihuacle negro [chee-WHAHK-l] Grown in Mexico's Oaxaca region, this dried CHILE ranges in color from chocolate brown to deep purple, and its shape resembles that of a small BELL PEPPER. It's mildly hot with a SCOVILLE SCALE rating of 1,000 to 2,000 and has a rich, fruity flavor.

Chihuahua cheese [chih-WAH-wah] *see* ASADERO

chikuwa [cheh-KOO-uh] *see* KAMABOKO

chilaca chile [chih-LAH-kuh] A mildly hot, rich-flavored CHILE that, when dried, is known as the PASILLA. The narrow chilaca can measure up to 9 inches long and often has a twisted shape. It turns from dark green to dark brown when fully mature. About the only place it can be found fresh in the United States is in farmer's markets. It has a SCOVILLE SCALE rating of 1,000 to 2,500.

chilaquiles [chee-lah-KEE-lehs] Because it was invented to use leftovers, this Mexican entree is sometimes called "poor man's dish." It consists of corn TORTILLA strips sautéed with other foods such as mild green CHILES, cheese, CHORIZO and shredded chicken or beef. The dish may also be layered like LASAGNA and baked.

chilcostle chile [cheel-KOHS-tl] A moderately hot dried CHILE with a unique spicy flavor. It's narrow and long (3 to 5 inches), with a deep paprika-colored skin mottled with streaks of dark orange. The chilcostle is grown in Oaxaca, Mexico.

chile; chili pepper; hot pepper; *Br.* **chilli** One of the wonders that Christopher Columbus brought back from the New World was a member of the *Capsicum* genus, the chile. Now this pungent pod plays an important role in the cuisines of many countries including Africa, China (Szechuan region), India, Mexico, South America, Spain and Thailand. There are more than 200 varieties of chiles, over 100 of which are indigenous to Mexico. They vary in length from a huge 12 inches to a $1/4$-inch peewee. Some are long, narrow and no thicker than a pencil while others are plump and globular. Their heat quotient varies from mildly warm to mouth-blistering hot. A chile's color can be anywhere from yellow to green to red to black. Dried chiles are available year-round. The availability of fresh chiles varies according to the variety and season. Choose those with deep, vivid colors; avoid chiles with any sign of shriveling or soft spots. Fresh chiles can be stored in the vegetable drawer of the refrigerator. As a general rule, the larger the chile the milder it is. Small chiles are much hotter because, proportionally, they contain more seeds and veins than larger specimens. Those seeds and membranes can contain up to 80 percent of a chile's CAPSAICIN, the potent compound that gives chiles their fiery nature. Since neither cooking nor freezing diminishes capsaicin's intensity, removing a chile's seeds and veins is the only way to reduce its heat. After working with chiles, it's extremely important to wash your hands thoroughly; failure to do so can result in painful burning of the eyes or skin (wearing rubber gloves will remedy this problem). Chiles are used to make a plethora of by-products including CHILI PASTE, TABASCO SAUCE, CAYENNE and the dried red pepper flakes commonly found in pizzerias. Chiles are cholesterol free and low in calories and sodium. They're a rich source of vitamins A and C, and a good source of folic acid, potassium and vitamin E. *See also* ANAHEIM; ANCHO; BIRD; CARIBE; CASCABEL; CAYENNE; CHARLESTON HOT; CHERRY PEPPER; CHIHUACLE NEGRO; CHILACA; CHILCOSTLE; CHIPOTLE; DORSET NAGA PEPPER; FRESNO; GILLETT METHOD; GUAJILLO; GÜERO; HABANERO; HUNGARIAN WAX; JALAPEÑO; JAMAICAN HOT; MULATO; NAGA JOLOKIA PEPPER; PASILLA; PEPPADEW; PEPPERONCINI; PEQUÍN; POBLANO; RED PEPPER; RED SAVINA; RISTRA; SANTA FE GRANDE; SCOTCH BONNET; SCOVILLE SCALE; SERRANO; SWEET PEPPERS; THAI CHILE; TOGARASHI.

Chilean sea bass Marketing name given to the PATAGONIAN TOOTHFISH and the Antarctic toothfish.

chile bean paste A paste or sauce made with fermented SOYBEANS, dried CHILES, garlic and other seasonings. This spicy, salty paste is popular in CHINESE CUISINE (Szechuan and Hunan) as well as in many Korean dishes. In Korea, chile bean paste is known as *kochujang* (or *kochu chang*) and *gochujang* (or *gochu jang*). *See also* BEAN SAUCES; BEAN PASTES.

chile bola *see* CASCABEL CHILE

chile con queso [CHIH-lee (*Sp.* CHEE-lay) kon KAY-soh] Spanish for "chiles with cheese," this warm melted cheese dip is flavored with CHILES (typically JALAPEÑOS) and more often than not chopped tomatoes, onion and garlic. The cheese base is usually CHEDDAR or JACK, though Tex-Mex versions traditionally use Velveeta, a processed cheese (*see* CHEESE). The classic accompaniment for this dip is TORTILLA chips.

chile de árbol [CHEE-lay day AHR-bohl] Translated as "tree chile" and also known as *bird's beak chile* and *rat's tail chile*, the chile de árbol is about $1/4$ to $1/2$ inch wide and 2 to 3 inches long with a slight curve. These Mexican chiles are bright red to reddish brown when mature, have a smoky, acidic flavor and are hot, with a SCOVILLE SCALE rating of 15,000 to 30,000. The chiles are sold fresh, whole dried and in powder form.

chile negro *see* PASILLA CHILE

chile pequeño *see* PEQUÍN CHILE

chile seco *see* SERRANO CHILE

chiles rellenos [CHEE-lehs rreh-YEH-nohs] Literally translated as "stuffed peppers," this Mexican specialty consists of cheese-stuffed mild green CHILES, cloaked with an egg batter and fried until the outside is crisp and the cheese inside is melted.

chili con carne [CHIHL-ee kon KAHR-nay; CHIHL-ee kon KAHR-nee] Spanish for "chili with meat," this dish is a melange of diced or ground beef and CHILES or CHILI POWDER (or both). It originated in the Lone Star State and Texans, who commonly refer to it as "a bowl of red," consider it a crime to add beans to the mixture. In many parts of the country, however, beans are requisite and the dish is called "chili con carne with beans."

chili oil Vegetable oil in which hot red CHILES have been steeped to release their heat and flavor. This spicy-hot oil is red-colored (from the chiles) and is a mainstay of Chinese cookery. It will keep 6 months at room temperature, but will retain its potency longer if refrigerated.

chili paste Widely used in Chinese cooking, this paste is made of fermented FAVA BEANS, flour, red CHILES and sometimes garlic. It's available in Chinese markets and many large supermarkets.

chili pepper *see* CHILE

chilipepper *see* ROCKFISH

chili powder A powdered seasoning mixture of dried CHILES, garlic, oregano, cumin, coriander and cloves. *See also* Seasoning Suggestions, page 891.

chili sauce A spicy blend of tomatoes, CHILES or CHILI POWDER, onions, green peppers, vinegar, sugar and spices. This ketchuplike sauce is used as a condiment. *See also* SAUCE.

chiltepín *see* PEQUÍN CHILE

chimichanga [chee-mee-CHAN-gah] This specialty of Sonora, Mexico, is actually a BURRITO that is fried or deep-fried. It can contain any number of fillings including shredded chicken, beef or pork, grated cheese, REFRIED BEANS and rice. To prevent the filling from spilling out during frying, the flour TORTILLA must be rolled around it, with the ends tucked in. Chimichangas are often garnished with SALSA, GUACAMOLE, sour cream and shredded cheese.

chimichurri This thick herb sauce is as common in Argentina as ketchup is in the United States. *Chimichurri* is a melange of olive oil, vinegar and finely chopped parsley, oregano, onion and garlic, all seasoned with salt, CAYENNE and black pepper. It's a must with grilled meat. *See also* SAUCE.

China-Martini [KEE-nah mahr-TEE-nee] A syrupy, bittersweet Italian LIQUEUR characterized by a decidedly herbal QUININE flavor.

chine *n.* This term refers to the backbone of an animal. It can also describe a cut of meat including the backbone with some adjoining flesh. **chine** *v.* A butchering term meaning to sever the backbone.

Chinese artichoke *see* CROSNES

Chinese black beans *see* FERMENTED BLACK BEANS

Chinese black mushroom *see* SHIITAKE

Chinese broccoli *see* CHINESE KALE

Chinese cabbage The heading "Chinese cabbage" is confusing, at best. This variety, *Brassica pekinensis,* is also called *napa cabbage, haku-sai, celery cabbage, wong bok* and *Peking cabbage,* just to name a few. Another *Brassica* subspecies—*chinensis*—is better known as BOK CHOY and is also called *Chinese white cabbage* and *white mustard cabbage.* It's clear that the confusion is warranted. The predominant variety of the *pekinensis* subspecies of Chinese cabbage has crinkly, thickly veined leaves that are cream-colored with celadon green tips. Unlike the strong-flavored waxy leaves on round heads of cabbage, these are thin, crisp and delicately mild. Chinese cabbage is generally available year-round. Choose firm, tightly packed heads with crisp, green-tipped leaves. Refrigerate, tightly wrapped, up to 3 days. Use raw, or sauté, bake or braise. It's a good source of vitamin A, folic acid and potassium.

Chinese chives *see* GARLIC CHIVES

Chinese cuisine The combined cuisines of China have often been compared to French cuisine as having made the greatest contribution to the world of food. Chinese cooking styles have been divided into five main regions: Southeastern (Canton), East Coast (Fukien), Northeastern (Peking-Shantung), Central (Honan) and Western (Szechuan-Hunan). **Cantonese** cuisine is famous for its meat roasting and grilling, fried rice, and BIRD'S NEST and SHARK'S FIN SOUP. The province of **Fukien** is noted for its multitudinous selection of soups and for its seafood dishes. The light, elegant **Peking-Shantung** style originated the famous PEKING DUCK, and is highly acclaimed for its subtle and artful use of seasonings. China's **Honan** province is the home of SWEET-AND-SOUR cooking, and the **Szechuan-Hunan** school is known for its hot, spicy dishes. **Mandarin** cooking and **Shanghai** cooking are not regional designations, but terms used to describe cooking styles. The word *mandarin* means "Chinese official," and mandarin cooking suggests an aristocratic cuisine that gleans the very finest elements from all the regions. *Shanghai* cooking refers to a cosmopolitan combination of many Chinese cooking styles.

Chinese date *see* JUJUBE

Chinese firepot *see* MONGOLIAN HOT POT

Chinese five-spice powder *see* FIVE-SPICE POWDER

Chinese flowering cabbage *see* CHOY SUM

Chinese ginger *see* FINGERROOT

Chinese gooseberry *see* KIWI

Chinese grapefruit *see* POMELO

Chinese jujube *see* CHINESE DATE

Chinese kale A vegetable with slender, bright green stalks ending in slightly darker leafy greens, which are sometimes accompanied by clusters of tiny white flower buds. Chinese kale has a flavor comparable to that of BROCCOLI RAAB and is used in Chinese cuisine, typically chopped in STIR-FRY dishes. It's available in Asian markets and some produce markets. Select firm stalks with crisp leaves. Refrigerate, tightly wrapped, for up to 1 week. Chinese kale is also known as *Chinese broccoli, kai lan* and *gai lan*.

Chinese keys *see* FINGERROOT

Chinese long bean *see* YARD-LONG BEAN

Chinese orange *see* CALAMONDIN

Chinese parsley *see* CORIANDER

Chinese pear *see* ASIAN PEAR

Chinese pepper *see* SZECHUAN PEPPER

Chinese pickle *see* TEA MELON

Chinese potato *see* ARROWHEAD

Chinese preserving melon *see* WINTER MELON

Chinese radish *see* LO BOK

Chinese rice wine *see* SHAOXING WINE

Chinese sausage Texturally similar to pepperoni, this dry, rather hard SAUSAGE is usually made from pork meat and a goodly amount of fat. It's smoked, slightly sweet and highly seasoned. Probably the most popular Chinese sausage in this country is **lop chong**. It and others like it are available in specialty meat shops and Chinese markets. Store up to 1 month in the refrigerator. Chinese sausage makes an excellent addition to STIR-FRY dishes.

Chinese snow pea *see* SNOW PEA

Chinese steelhead *see* BLACKFISH

Chinese vermicelli *see* CELLOPHANE NOODLES

Chinese white cabbage *see* BOK CHOY

chinois [sheen-WAH] A metal conical sieve with an *extremely* fine mesh, used for puréeing or straining. The mesh is so fine that a spoon or pestle must be used to press the food through it.

chinquapin [CHING-kuh-pihn] *see* CRAPPIE

chipolata [chee-poh-LAH-tah; chih-poh-LAH-tah] Sometimes called "little fingers," these tiny (2- to 3-inch-long), coarse-textured pork SAU-SAGES are highly spiced with thyme, chives, coriander, cloves and sometimes hot red-pepper flakes. The French term *à la chipolata* refers to a garnish of chipolata, chestnuts and glazed vegetables used to accompany roasts.

chipotle chile [chih-POHT-lay] This moderately hot CHILE with a SCOVILLE SCALE rating of 2,500 to 10,000 is actually a dried, smoked JALAPEÑO. It has a wrinkled, dark brown skin and a smoky, sweet, almost chocolaty flavor. Chipotles can be found dried, pickled and canned in ADOBO SAUCE. Chipotles are generally added to stews and sauces; the pickled variety are often eaten as appetizers.

chipped beef These wafer-thin slices of salted and smoked, dried beef are usually packed in small jars and were once an American staple. Chipped beef is also referred to simply as *dried beef*. "Shit on a shingle," known in polite society as *SOS,* is military slang used for creamed chipped beef served on toast.

chips The British word for what Americans call "FRENCH FRIES." Their potato chips are called "crisps."

chiqueter [shee-kuh-TAY] In French cooking, to FLUTE or CRIMP the edges of pies, tarts and other pastries.

chirashi [chee-RAH-shee] A term meaning "scattered sushi" and referring to a Japanese dish consisting of SUSHI MESHI (vinegared rice) served with various ingredients including chopped vegetables, SASHIMI, CURED fish, ROE, NORI and omelet slices. In Japanese homes, the ingredients are either scattered on top of or mixed throughout the rice. In sushi bars, chirashi is more formal—ingredients are separately arranged on top of the rice for a more elegant presentation.

chirinabe [chee-ree-NAH-beh] A Japanese one-pot dish consisting of chunks of a firm-fleshed fish (like COD or SEA BASS), TOFU and various vegetables. All ingredients are brought to the table raw along with a pot of simmering broth, which is placed on a heating element and kept simmering throughout the meal. Each diner adds their own ingredients, letting the food cook until tender before retrieving it from the communal pot. Chirinabe is served with various condiments, which usually include PONZU. *See also* MIZUTAKI; NABEMONO.

chitlins; chitlings [CHIHT-lihnz] *see* CHITTERLINGS

chitterlings [CHIHT-lihnz; CHIHT-lingz] Popular in American Southern cooking, chitterlings are the small intestines of freshly slaughtered pigs. The word itself comes from the Middle English *chiterling,* a derivative of the Old English *cieter* ("intestines"). And, although properly called "chitterlings," the more common usage is *chitlins,* the casual version of which is *chitts;* slang terms include *Kentucky oysters* and *wrinkled steak.* Chitlins must be thoroughly cleaned in order to remove all fecal matter and bacteria. This labor-intensive process, which requires turning the intestines inside out, can take hours. Once cleaned, chitterlings must be simmered until tender (2 to 3 hours), a process that emits a detestable stench. They can then be broiled, barbecued, added to soups, battered and fried or used as a sausage CASING. Chitlins have a chewy texture and an extremely high fat content (24 grams per 3-ounce serving). *See also* VARIETY MEATS.

chives Related to the onion and leek, this fragrant HERB has slender, vivid green, hollow stems. Chives have a mild onion flavor and are available fresh year-round. Look for those with a uniform green color and no signs of wilting or browning. Store in a plastic bag in the refrigerator up to a week. Fresh chives can be snipped with scissors to the desired length. They're delicious in many cooked dishes but should be added toward the end of the cooking time to retain their flavor. Both chives and their edible lavender flowers are a tasty and colorful addition to salads. Frozen and freeze-dried chives are also available in most supermarkets. Chives are a good source of vitamin A and also contain a fair amount of potassium and calcium.

chlodnik [CHLAHD-nihk] Of Polish origin, this BORSCHT-like soup is made of beets, onions, cucumbers, herbs and sometimes veal. It's served cold, garnished with sour cream.

chocho *see* CHAYOTE

chocolate The word "chocolate" comes from the Aztec *xocolatl,* meaning "bitter water." Indeed, the unsweetened drink the Aztecs made of pounded cocoa beans and spices was probably extremely bitter. Bitterness notwithstanding, the Aztec king Montezuma so believed that chocolate was an aphrodisiac that he purportedly drank 50 golden goblets of it each day. Chocolate comes from the tropical cocoa bean, *Theobroma* ("food of the gods") *cacao.* After the beans are removed from their pods they're fermented, dried, roasted and cracked, separating the nibs (which contain an average of 54 percent cocoa butter) from the shells. The nibs are ground to extract some of the COCOA BUTTER (a natural vegetable fat), leaving a thick, dark brown paste called chocolate liquor. Next, the chocolate liquor receives an initial refining. If additional cocoa butter is extracted from the chocolate liquor, the solid result is ground to produce unsweetened COCOA POWDER. If other ingredients are added (such as milk powder, sugar, etc.), the chocolate is refined again. The final step for most chocolate is conching, a process by which huge machines with rotating blades slowly blend the heated chocolate liquor, ridding it of residual moisture and volatile acids. The conching continues for 12 to 72 hours (depending on the type and quality of chocolate) while small amounts of cocoa butter and sometimes LECITHIN are added to give chocolate its voluptuously smooth texture. Unadulterated chocolate is marketed as **unsweetened chocolate**, also called **baking** or **bitter chocolate**. U.S. standards require that unsweetened chocolate contain between 50 and 58 percent cocoa butter. The addition of sugar, lecithin and vanilla (or vanillin) creates, depending on the amount of sugar added, **bittersweet**, **semisweet** or **sweet chocolate**. Bittersweet chocolate must contain at least 35 percent chocolate liquor; semisweet and sweet can contain from 15 to 35 percent. Adding dry milk to sweetened chocolate creates **milk chocolate**, which must contain at least 12 percent milk solids and 10 percent chocolate liquor. Though bittersweet, semisweet and sweet chocolate may often be used interchangeably in *some* recipes with little textural change, milk chocolate—because of the milk protein—cannot. **Dark chocolate** is a generic term used by some cooks for everything from bittersweet to sweet chocolate—as long as it's neither milk chocolate nor white chocolate. **Liquid chocolate**, developed especially for baking, is found on the supermarket shelf alongside other chocolates. It's unsweetened, comes in individual 1-ounce packages, and is convenient because it requires no melting. However, because it's made with vegetable oil rather than cocoa butter, it doesn't deliver either the same texture or flavor as regular unsweetened chocolate. **Couverture** is a term describing professional-quality coating chocolate that is extremely glossy. It usually contains a minimum of 32 percent cocoa butter, which enables it to form a much thinner shell than ordinary CONFECTIONERY COAT-ING. Couverture is usually only found in specialty candy-making shops. **White chocolate** is not true chocolate because it contains no chocolate liquor and, likewise, very little chocolate flavor. Instead, it's usually a mixture of sugar, cocoa butter, milk solids, lecithin and vanilla. Read the label: if cocoa butter isn't mentioned, the product is not white chocolate but CONFECTIONARY COATING (also called summer coating). Beware of products labeled **artificial chocolate** or *chocolate-flavored*. They are, just as the label states, not the real thing, a fact confirmed by both flavor and texture. Chocolate comes in many forms, from 1-ounce squares to $1/2$-inch chunks to chips ranging in size from $1/2$ to $1/8$ inch in diameter. Many chocolate chunks and chips come in flavors including milk, semisweet, mint-flavored and white chocolate. Chocolate should be stored, tightly wrapped, in a cool (60° to 70°F), dry place. If stored at warm temperatures, chocolate will develop a pale gray "bloom" (surface streaks and blotches), caused when the cocoa butter rises to the surface. In damp conditions, chocolate can form tiny gray sugar crystals on the surface. In either case, the chocolate can still be used, with flavor and texture affected only slightly. Under ideal conditions, dark chocolate can be stored 10 years. However, because of the milk solids in both milk chocolate and white chocolate, they shouldn't be stored for longer than 9 months. Because all chocolate scorches easily—which completely ruins the flavor—it should be melted slowly over low heat. One method is to place the chocolate in the top of a double boiler over simmering water. Remove the top of the pan from the heat when the chocolate is a little more than halfway melted and stir until completely smooth. Another method is to place the chocolate in a microwave-safe bowl and, in a 650- to 700-watt microwave oven, heat at 50 percent power. Four ounces of chocolate will take about 3 minutes, but the timing will vary depending on the oven and the type and amount of chocolate. Though chocolate can be melted *with* liquid (at least $1/4$ cup liquid per 6 ounces chocolate), a single drop of moisture in melted chocolate will cause it to SEIZE (clump and harden). This problem can sometimes be corrected if vegetable oil is immediately stirred into the chocolate at a ratio of about 1 tablespoon oil to 6 ounces chocolate. Slowly remelt the mixture and stir until once again smooth. *See also* CHOCOLATE SYRUP; COCOA NIBS; GIANDUJA CHOCOLATE; MEXICAN CHOCOLATE; TEMPERING.

chocolate-chip cookie *see* TOLL HOUSE COOKIE

chocolate fondue *see* FONDUE

chocolate pudding fruit *see* BLACK SAPOTE

chocolate syrup A ready-to-use syrup, usually a combination of unsweetened cocoa powder, sugar or corn syrup and various other flavorings. Chocolate syrup is usually quite sweet and is most often used to flavor milk or as a dessert sauce. It cannot be substituted for melted chocolate in recipes.

chokecherry Any of several varieties of wild cherries native to North America. These small cherries turn from red to almost black when mature. They're very astringent and, though not good for out-of-hand eating, make excellent jams and jellies. *Chokeberries* are the inedible fruit of an ornamental shrub. *See also* CHERRY.

cholent [CHAW-lent; CHUH-lent] Of Central European origin, cholent is a traditional Jewish food served on the Sabbath. It varies greatly from family to family, but generally consists of some kind of meat (such as BRISKET, SHORT RIBS or CHUCK), LIMA or NAVY BEANS, potatoes, BARLEY, onions, garlic and other seasonings. The ingredients are combined in one pot and simmered on stovetop or baked at a very low heat for many hours. Since cooking is forbidden on the Sabbath, many Jewish families prepare and combine the ingredients and place the cholent in a low oven at sundown on Friday, to be ready the following day, which is the Sabbath.

chongos [CHONG-ohs] Sweet, curdled-milk dessert that originated in the state of Michoacán in western Mexico. It has a texture similar to a moist cottage cheese and is traditionally flavored with cinnamon. Variations include the addition of vanilla or lemon flavoring. It is sometimes called *chongos zamoranos,* named after the Michoacán city of Zamora de Hidalgo.

chop *n.* A small cut of meat taken from the rib section and including part of the rib. Pork, veal and lamb chops are the most popular. **chop** *v.* Using quick, heavy blows of a knife or cleaver to cut food into bite-size (or smaller) pieces. A food processor may also be used to "chop" food. Chopped food is more coarsely cut than MINCED food.

chopsticks Thin, tapered eating utensils used throughout Asia. They normally range from 10 to 12 inches long (as short as 5 inches for children) and can be made from a variety of materials, including wood, bamboo and plastic. Chopsticks used for cooking or serving can be up to 20 inches long. Japanese chopsticks are pointed at the eating end, whereas Chinese chopsticks are blunt. To use chopsticks for eating, hold them about two-thirds of the distance from the pointed end, with the upper stick between your index finger and the tip of your thumb, much as you would a pencil. The bottom chopstick should remain stationary while the upper stick is moved in an up-and-down, pincerlike motion. Always keep the tips of the chopsticks even.

chop suey [chop SOO-ee] Dating back to at least the mid-19th century, this Chinese-American dish includes small pieces of meat (usually chicken) or shrimp, mushrooms, BEAN SPROUTS, WATER CHESTNUTS, BAMBOO SHOOTS and onions. These ingredients are cooked together and served over rice. Chop suey doesn't exist as a dish in China.

chop suey green *see* CHRYSANTHEMUM LEAVES

chorba [CHOR-bah] Though the word *chorba* is thought to be of Persian origin, this hearty soup is associated with the Turks, whose cuisine spread far and wide during the centuries of Ottoman Empire reign. During this time, chorba's popularity spread to North Africa, the Middle East and parts of Eastern Europe, each region personalizing the soup to taste. Most chorba soups include vermicelli or spaghetti noodles, potatoes, carrots, onions, tomatoes and garlic. One might compare it to an exotic minestrone (*see* MINESTRA). Some versions contain chicken or beef. In Turkey and Bulgaria tripe is a favorite addition, in which case the soup is called *schkembe chorba* or *shkembe chorba*. No matter the regional variations, chorba is not a delicate soup but rather big, bold and satisfying. Many countries (such as Tunisia) add plenty of extra garlic and hot chile peppers to ramp up the heat quotient. Chorba is also spelled *tchorba*.

choreg; chorek *see* TSOUREKI

chorizo [chor-EE-zoh; chor-EE-soh] A highly seasoned, coarsely ground pork SAUSAGE flavored with garlic, CHILI POWDER and other spices. It's widely used in both Mexican and Spanish cookery. Mexican chorizo is made with fresh pork, while the Spanish version uses smoked pork. The CASING should be removed before cooking. Chorizo makes a tasty addition to many dishes including casseroles, soups, stews and ENCHILADAS.

chorogi [CHAWR-oh-gee] *see* CROSNES

Choron sauce [show-RAWHN] Named for the French chef who created it, Choron sauce is a HOLLANDAISE or BÉARNAISE sauce that has been tinted pink with tomato purée. It can be served with poultry, meat or fish. *See also* SAUCE.

chou [shoo] French for "cabbage."

chouchouka [shoo-SHOO-kah] *see* SHAKSHUKA

choucroute [shoo-KROOT] This French word for "sauerkraut" describes it when cooked with goose fat, onions, juniper berries or caraway seeds and white wine. It can be served as a side or main dish. **Choucroute garnie** is sauerkraut garnished with potatoes and a variety of meats such as sausages, pork, ham or goose.

chou dofu; chou doufu *see* STINKY TOFU

chou fleur [shoo fleur] French for "cauliflower."

choux pastry [shoo] Also called *choux paste, pâte à choux* and *cream-puff pastry,* this special pastry is made by an entirely different method from other pastries. The dough, created by combining flour with boiling water and butter, then beating eggs into the mixture, is very sticky and pastelike. During baking, the eggs make the pastry puff into irregular domes (as with CREAM PUFFS). After baking, the puffs are split, hollowed out and filled with a custard, whipped cream or other filling. Besides cream puffs, *choux* pastry is used to make such specialties as ÉCLAIRS, GOUGÈRE and PROFITEROLES.

chow-chow; chowchow Thought to have been brought to America by the Chinese railroad laborers, chow-chow is a mustard-flavored mixed-vegetable-and-pickle relish. Originally, the term was used to describe a Chinese condiment of orange peel and ginger in a heavy syrup.

chowder A thick, chunky seafood soup, of which clam chowder is the most well known. The name comes from the French *chaudière*, a CAULDRON in which fishermen made their stews fresh from the sea. **New England-style chowder** is made with milk or cream, **Manhattan-style** with tomatoes. Chowder can contain any of several varieties of seafood and vegetables. The term is also used to describe any thick, rich soup containing chunks of food (for instance, corn chowder).

chowder clam The largest of the East Coast hard-shell clams, the chowder clam (also called *quahog* or *large clam*) has a shell diameter of at least 3 inches. As their name implies, these clams are often cut up to use in chowders. They're also excellent stuffed and as clam fritters. *See also* CLAM.

chow fun guo tiao *see* RICE NOODLES

chow mein [chow MAYN] A Chinese-American dish that consists of small pieces of meat (usually chicken) or shrimp and vegetables such as BEAN SPROUTS, WATER CHESTNUTS, BAMBOO SHOOTS, mushrooms and onions. The ingredients are usually fried separately, then combined at the last minute and served over crisp noodles.

choy sum Also called *flowering (white) cabbage* and *Chinese flowering cabbage,* this vegetable is, as one might guess, a member of the cabbage family. It has pale green stems and rounded, medium-green leaves. The leaves have a sweet, delicate flavor, and the crunchy stems have a pleasant bitter nuance. Sometimes the inner stems are tipped with tiny yellow flowers. Choy sum is available in Asian markets and some specialty produce markets. It should be refrigerated in a plastic bag for no more than 4 days. It can be used raw in salads or cooked in a STIR-FRY or as a vegetable. *See also* YU CHOY SUM.

Christmas bell chile *see* BISHOP'S CROWN CHILE

Christmas lima A large, flat dried bean with a white background and dark purplish markings. These beans (which are completely unrelated to the LIMA BEAN) have a sweet flavor similar to that of the CHESTNUT. *See also* BEANS.

Christmas melon *see* SANTA CLAUS MELON

christophene [KRIHS-tuh-feen] *see* CHAYOTE

chrysanthemum leaves Aromatic, moist, dark-green leaves from the *garland chrysanthemum*, also called *edible chrysanthemum,* are used in a number of Asian dishes. They are known as *shungiku* in Japan, *tangho* or *tongho* in China, *sukgat* in Korea and *tan o* or *cai cuc* in Vietnam and are sometimes called *chop suey greens*. The leaves are mildly bitter when young and become more bitter as they mature. Their taste is described as having various flavors such as carrot, celery, mint, JUNIPER, ROSEMARY and THYME. The leaves can be eaten raw or cooked, as you would leaf spinach. Choose young, fresh, green leaves that are free of yellowing.

chrysanthemum tea Popular beverage in East Asia made by steeping chrysanthemum flowers (either fresh or dried) in hot water, sometimes with the addition of ingredients such as GINGERROOT, honey, ROCK SUGAR and WOLFBERRIES. Proponents claim that it has a cooling effect on the body and numerous medicinal qualities, such as clearing head colds and alleviating influenza and sinusitis. Several varieties of chrysanthemum flowers are used, causing a variation in color from almost clear to bright yellow. Dried chrysanthemum flower tea is available over the Internet and at many Asian markets in bags and loose form. Cans of the beverage are sometimes available as well.

chuck An inexpensive beef cut taken from between the neck and shoulder blade. The most popular cuts of chuck are roasts and steaks. Chuck roasts usually include a portion of the blade bone, which is why they're sometimes referred to as *blade pot roasts*. For maximum tenderness, chuck cuts must be cooked slowly, as in stewing or braising. *See also* BEEF; Beef Chart, page 896.

chufa; chufa nuts [CHOO-fuh] Actually the tiny, tuberous roots of an African plant of the sedge family, chufa "nuts" are immensely popular in Spain and Mexico, primarily as a base for the refreshing drink, HORCHATA. They have a brown, bumpy skin and a sweet, chestnutlike flavor. Dried chufas are available in bags in many Latin markets and natural food stores. Store them, tightly wrapped, in a cool, dark place for up to a year. Besides their use in horchatas, chufas make an excellent snack. They're also known as *earth almonds, earthnuts* and *tiger nuts*.

chuño [CHOO-nyoh] A dehydrated potato product hailing from South America, particularly Bolivia and Peru. In the traditional method of producing chuño negro (black chuño), small, irregular potatoes are placed on a straw bed and left out overnight to freeze. After thawing the next day, the potatoes are gently stepped on to express moisture. This process is repeated, sometimes for weeks, until the potatoes are completely dry and look like small gray stones, at which point the skins are rubbed off. The white version—chuño blanco (also known as *tunta* or *moraya*)—is made from larger, rounder potatoes and prepared in a similar way, except that after being frozen they're placed in water (*tunta* in running water and *moraya* in still water) for two or more weeks before undergoing dehydration. Chuño can be stored for years and must be soaked in water before being cooked. It will absorb the flavor of the liquid in which it's cooked. Both black and white chuño can be found in cans (sometimes brined) in Latin markets. Harina de chuño is white chuño ground into flour, which is sold in sacks.

chupe [CHOO-pee] A hearty, creamy chowder popular in South America, especially Chile, Peru and other Pacific Rim countries. It can be made with quite a few variations—chicken, meat, offal, fish, shellfish, CHILES and a variety of vegetables may be used. *Chupe de camarones*, made with crayfish or shrimp, is extremely popular in Peru's coastal regions.

churn To agitate cream briskly so that the fat separates from the liquid, thereby forming a solid (butter). The old-fashioned butter churn consisted of a container fitted with wooden blades that, when a crank was rotated, would whirl the cream inside until it turned to butter. The modern household substitute for a butter churn is the food processor.

churrascaria; churrasqueria [*Pt.* shoor-RAHS-kah-ree-yah; *Es.* choo-RAHS-kah-ree-yah] Term for steakhouse in Brazil and Argentina.

churrasco [*Pt.* shoor-RAHS-koh; *Es.* choo-RAHS-koh] Used in Spain, Portugal, many Latin American countries and other Portuguese- or Spanish-speaking countries to refer to barbecued or charcoal-grilled meat. In some locales it also refers to the event of having a barbecue.

churro [CHOOR-roh] Similiar to a CRULLER, this Spanish and Mexican specialty consists of a sweet-dough spiral that is deep-fried and eaten like a doughnut. Churros are usually coated with a mixture of cinnamon and powdered (or granulated) sugar.

chutney [CHUHT-nee] From the East Indian word *chatni,* this spicy condiment contains fruit, vinegar, sugar and spices. It can range in texture from chunky to smooth and in degrees of spiciness from mild to hot. Chutney is a delicious accompaniment to curried dishes. The sweeter chutneys also make interesting bread spreads and are delicious served with cheese.

chymosin [KI-muh-sin] *see* RENNET

ciabatta [chah-BAH-tah] Italian for "slipper," describing a long, wide loaf of bread with a soft interior and a crisp, thin crust.

cicchetti [chee-KEHT-tee; chih-KEHT-tee] Popular in Venice's bars and pubs (called *biccari*), these small plates are the Italian counterpart to TAPAS. Cicchetti can include items such as deep-fried ARTICHOKE HEARTS, CALAMARI, MOZZARELLA or GORGONZOLA cheese, CROSTINI with toppings, PROSCIUTTO-wrapped melon, plates of olives, vegetables or marinated seafood, and small meat and fish dishes.

cicely [SIHS-uh-lee] *see* CHERVIL

cichetti *see* CICCHETTI

ciciones SEE Pasta Glossary, page 883

cider Apple cider was a highly popular early American beverage. Cider is made by pressing the juice from fruit (usually apples). It can be drunk straight or diluted with water. Before FERMENTATION, it's referred to as "sweet" cider. It becomes "hard" cider after fermentation, and can range widely in alcohol content. Apple cider is also used to make vinegar and brandy.

cider vinegar VINEGAR made from CIDER, usually apple.

cilantro [sih-LAHN-troh; see-LAHN-troh] The bright green leaves and stems of the CORIANDER plant. Cilantro (also called *Chinese parsley* and *coriander*) has a lively, pungent fragrance that some describe as "soapy." It is widely used in Asian, Caribbean and Latin American cooking and its distinctive flavor lends itself to highly spiced foods. Cilantro can be found year-round in most supermarkets and is generally sold in bunches. Choose leaves with a bright, even color and no sign of wilting. Cilantro may be stored for up to 1 week in a plastic bag in the refrigerator. Or place the bunch, stems down, in a glass of water and cover with a plastic bag, securing the bag to the glass with a rubber band. Refrigerate, changing water every 2 or 3 days. Just before using cilantro, wash and pat dry with paper towels. Both the leaves and relatively tender stems can be used in fresh or cooked dishes.

cinnamon [SIH-nuh-muhn] Once used in love potions and to perfume wealthy Romans, this age-old spice comes in two varieties— *Cinnamomum zeylanicum* (Ceylon cinnamon) and *Cinnamomum cassia* (cassia). Cinnamon is the inner bark of a tropical evergreen tree. The bark is harvested during the rainy season when it's more pliable. When dried, it curls into long quills, which are either cut into lengths and sold as cinnamon sticks, or ground into powder. **Ceylon** (or **tree**) **cinnamon** is buff-colored and mildly sweet in flavor; **cassia cinnamon** is a dark, reddish brown color and has a more pungent, slightly bittersweet flavor. Cassia cinnamon is used and sold simply as "cinnamon" in many countries (including the United States). Cinnamon is widely used in sweet dishes, but also makes an intriguing addition to savory dishes such as stews and curries. **Oil of cinnamon** comes from the pods of the cinnamon tree and is used as a flavoring, as well as a medicinal. *See also* SPICES; Seasoning Suggestions, page 891.

cinnamon cap mushroom *see* NAMEKO

cinnamon leaves *see* INDIAN BAY LEAF

Cinsaut; Cinsault [SAN-soh] A red-wine grape that is widely planted in France and particularly extensively grown throughout the Languedoc-Roussillon, where it contributes greatly to the area's huge volume of wine. In the southern RHÔNE where its yield is strictly controlled (a limited volume per acre), Cinsaut produces wines that are deeply colored, concentrated and flavorful. Here, Cinsaut is blended with many other grape varieties including GRENACHE, MOURVÈDRE and SYRAH. The South Africans have crossed Cinsaut with PINOT NOIR to create a grape variety they call Pinotage.

cioccolata [chyoh-koh-LAH-tah] Italian for "CHOCOLATE"; *cioccolata calda* is "hot chocolate."

cioppino [chuh-PEE-noh] San Francisco's Italian immigrants are credited with creating this delicious fish stew made with tomatoes and a variety of fish and shellfish.

cipolla [chee-POH-lah] Italian for "ONION."

cipollini; cipollini onions [chihp-oh-LEE-nee] 1. Bittersweet bulbs of the tassel hyacinth or grape hyacinth (*Leopoldia comosa* or *Muscari comosum*) that taste and look like small onions, which is why they're also called *wild onions*. They are popular in Apulia and other southern Italian regions, where they are sometimes called *lampasconi*.

Fresh cipollini are hard to find in the United States but do make an appearance in some Italian markets and farmer's markets during the fall. Jars of cipollini preserved in oil are also sometimes available. For peak flavor, fresh cipollini should be slowly simmered or braised. They can be served as an appetizer or vegetable. 2. Small (1 to 4 inches in diameter), sweet, flattened onions ranging in color from white to red with myriad variations in between. Cipollini onions (*Allium cepa*) have paper-thin skins that need to be removed before cooking. The name *Borrettana onion* is sometimes seen; it's a cipollini cultivar. They can be baked, braised, roasted and sautéed and may be added to a dish or served on their own. Buy firm, heavy, unbruised bulbs with dry, papery skins and no significant sprouting (this indicates an older bulb that may be sharp-tasting). They can be found in gourmet markets and are more widely available September through December. *See also* ONION.

cirhuleo chile *see* ROCOTO CHILE

ciruelo chile *see* ROCOTO CHILE

citric acid [SIHT-rihk] A white powder extracted from the juice of citrus and other acidic fruits (such as lemons, limes, pineapples and gooseberries). It's also produced by the FERMENTATION of glucose. Citric acid has a strong, tart taste and is used as a flavoring agent for foods and beverages. Small bottles of crystallized **sour salt** (also called *citric salt*) are often found in the kosher-foods section of supermarkets. Sour salt is used to impart a tart flavor to traditional dishes such as BORSCHT. *See also* SALT.

citric salt *see* CITRIC ACID

citron [SIHT-ron] 1. This semitropical citrus fruit looks like a huge (6 to 9 inches long), yellow-green, lumpy lemon. Citron pulp is very sour and not suitable for eating raw. This fruit is grown instead for its extremely thick, lemon-perfumed peel, which is candied and used in baking. The **fingered citron** (also called *Buddha's hand*), which looks like a yellow, multi-tentacled octopus, is also used as a flavoring rather than being eaten out-of-hand. Before being candied, the peel is processed in brine and pressed to extract citron oil, used to flavor LIQUEURS and to scent cosmetics. Candied citron can be purchased fresh in specialty markets, or with preservatives (necessary for the expected long shelf life) in supermarkets. Either should be stored in the freezer for maximum freshness. Candied citron halves are sometimes available, but it will more likely be found chopped or in strips. 2. Citron (pronounced see-TRAW*N*) is also the French word for "lemon"; *citron vert* (VEHR) is "lime."

citronella root [sih-truh-NEHL-uh] *see* LEMON GRASS

citrus fruits This large family of fruit includes among its members the CITRON, GRAPEFRUIT, KUMQUAT, LAVENDER GEM, LEMON, LIME, MANDARIN ORANGE, ORO BLANCO, POMELO, SHADDOCK, TANGELO, TANGERINE and UGLI FRUIT. Native to Asia, citrus fruits prefer tropical to temperate climates and thrive in many Central and South American countries, as well as the states of Arizona, California, Florida, Louisiana and Texas. All fresh citrus fruits share some degree of tartness and are rich in vitamin C.

citrus stripper A special tool with a stainless-steel notched edge that cuts ¼-inch-wide strips from the rind of citrus fruits as well as other fruits and vegetables. It's commonly used to make lemon or lime strips, which are used to flavor drinks or garnish dishes such as salads and desserts. The strips can be cut long or short, depending on whether the stripper is pulled from top to bottom (short strips) or in a long spiral around the fruit (long strips). A citrus stripper can also be used to cut decorative designs in vegetables such as cucumbers and zucchini.

citrus zester The stainless-steel cutting edge of this kitchen tool has five tiny cutting holes which, when the zester is pulled across the surface of a lemon or orange, create threadlike strips of peel. The zester removes only the colored outer portion (ZEST) of the peel, leaving the pale bitter pith. *See also* RASP GRATER.

civet [SIHV-iht; *Fr.* see-VAY; *It.* chee-VEHT] Culinarily, civet is a well-seasoned stew of furred game—usually rabbit—flavored with onions, mushrooms and red wine.

civet coffee *see* KOPI LUWAK

clabber *v.* To CURDLE milk. *n.* 1. Milk or cream that has curdled and thickened. 2. A popular dish of the Old South, clabber is naturally clabbered raw milk. Depending on its thickness, icy-cold clabbered milk was (and sometimes still is) enjoyed as a drink. It may also be eaten with fruit, or topped with black pepper and cream or simply sprinkled with sugar.

clafoutis; clafouti [kla-foo-TEE] Originally from the Limousin region, this country-French dessert is made by topping a layer of fresh fruit with batter. After baking it's served hot, sometimes with cream. Some styles have a cakelike topping while others are more like a pudding. Though cherries are traditional, any fruit such as plums, peaches or pears can be used.

clam American Indians used parts of the shell from these BIVALVE MOLLUSKS to make wampum—beads used for barter, ornamental, ceremonial and spiritual purposes. The two main varieties of clams are hard-shell and soft-shell. The HARD-SHELL CLAMS found on the East Coast (where they're also called by the Indian name, *quahog*) come in three sizes. The smallest are LITTLENECK CLAMS, which have a shell diameter less than 2 inches. Next comes the medium-size CHERRYSTONE CLAM, about 2½ inches across. The largest of this trio is the CHOWDER CLAM (also called simply "large" clam), with a shell diameter of at least 3 inches. Among the West Coast hard-shell varieties are the PACIFIC LITTLENECK CLAM, the PISMO and the small, sweet BUTTER CLAMS from Puget Sound. SOFT-SHELL CLAMS, also called *soft clams,* actually have thin, brittle shells. They can't completely close their shells because of a long, rubbery neck (or siphon) that extends beyond its edge. The most common East Coast soft-shell is the STEAMER CLAM. The most famous West Cost soft-shells are the RAZOR CLAM (so named because its shell resembles a folded, old-fashioned straight razor) and the GEO-DUCK CLAM (pronounced *goo-ee-duck*). The geoduck is a comical-looking, 6-inch-long clam with a neck that can reach up to about 1½ feet long. On the East Coast and in the Pacific Northwest, clams are available year-round. In California, the season is November through April. Clams are sold live in the shell, fresh or frozen shucked, and canned. When buying hard-shell clams in the shell, make sure the shells are tightly closed. If a shell is slightly open, tap it lightly. If it doesn't snap shut, the clam is dead and should be discarded. To test a soft-shell clam, lightly touch its neck; if it moves, it's alive. The guideline for buying shucked clams is plumpness and clear liquid. Store live clams up to 2 days in a 40°F refrigerator; refrigerate shucked clams up to 4 days. Clams can be cooked in a variety of ways, including steaming and baking. All clams should be cooked gently to prevent toughening. Clams are high in protein and contain fair amounts of calcium and iron. *See also* IPSWICH CLAM; SHELLFISH.

Clamart, à la [kla-MAH*R*] A French term referring to dishes garnished with peas. It can also refer to a garnish of potato balls.

clambake; clam bake An informal beachfront meal where clams, corn-on-the-cob and other foods including lobsters, mussels, potatoes and onions are cooked in a pit of hot rocks topped with SEAWEED, all of which is covered with wet canvas. Clambakes are sometimes replicated indoors by simply steaming all the ingredients in a large pot complete with seaweed.

clam chowder *see* CHOWDER

clam knife A small, sturdy, round-tipped knife used for opening live clams.

clamshell mushroom *see* BEECH MUSHROOM

claret [KLAR-eht] 1. A term used by the English when referring to the red wines from BORDEAUX. 2. Elsewhere, the word claret is sometimes used as a general reference to light red wines. Even though "claret" sometimes appears on labels it has no legal definition.

clarified butter [KLEHR-ih-fide] Also called *drawn butter,* this is unsalted butter that has been slowly melted, thereby evaporating most of the water and separating the milk solids (which sink to the bottom of the pan) from the golden liquid on the surface. After any foam is skimmed off the top, the clear (clarified) butter is poured or skimmed off the milky residue and used in cooking. Because the milk solids (which make butter burn when used for frying) have been removed, clarified butter has a higher SMOKE POINT than regular butter and therefore may be used to cook at higher temperatures. Additionally, the lack of milk solids prevents clarified butter from becoming rancid as quickly as regular butter. It also means that the butter won't have as rich a flavor. GHEE is an East Indian form of highly clarified butter.

clarify [KLEHR-ih-fi] To clear a cloudy liquid by removing the sediment. The most common method is to add egg whites and/or eggshells to a liquid (such as a stock) and simmer for 10 to 15 minutes. The egg whites attract any particles in the liquid like a magnet. After cooling for about an hour, the mixture is poured through a cloth-lined SIEVE to strain out all residue. Rendered fat can be clarified by adding hot water and boiling for about 15 minutes. The mixture is then strained through several layers of CHEESECLOTH and chilled. The resulting top layer of fat should be almost entirely clear of residue.

classico [KLA-sih-koh; KLAH-see-koh] Italian for "classic," used in the wine world to describe the wines from a wine-growing territory (usually the oldest in terms of grape cultivation and wine production) within a larger geographic region defined by the Italian classification system (*see* APPELLATION) known as DOC. One of the better known examples is *Chianti Classico.*

clay bakers *see* COOKWARE AND BAKEWARE MATERIALS

claytonia *see* MINERS' LETTUCE

clayudas [KLAY-oo-dahs] A thick, platter-sized corn TORTILLA that hails from Oaxaca in southern Mexico. Clayudas, sometimes spelled *tlayudas*, are baked until hard and crunchy and can be flat or folded over. They are typically topped or filled with ingredients like *aciento* (a grainy pork fat), REFRIED BEANS, meat, cheese, vegetables and SALSA.

cleaver Used mainly by butchers and Chinese cooks, a cleaver is an axlike cutting tool. Its flat sides can be used for pounding, as in tenderizing meat. Cleavers are usually heavy for their size, but evenly weighted. A good cleaver can cut through bone just as easily as it can chop vegetables.

The butt end can be used as a pestle (*see* MORTAR AND PESTLE) to pulverize seeds or other food items; the flat side is also great for crushing garlic.

clementine [KLEHM-uhn-tyn] *see* MANADARIN ORANGE

clingstone A term used to describe fruit that has a pit to which the flesh clings tenaciously, one of the most well known being the *cling* or *clingstone peach*. *See also* FREESTONE.

cloche [KLOHSH] French for a bell-shaped woman's hat, cloche refers culinarily to an unglazed stoneware, bell-shaped cover used in baking bread. This baking cloche is soaked in water, then placed over the bread dough prior to baking. When heated, the water-soaked clay produces steam, which coats the dough and gives the finished bread a crackling good crust. Cloches, which are about 10 inches tall, are available in gourmet shops. An unglazed earthenware casserole dish can be substituted. *See also* COOKWARE AND BAKEWARE MATERIALS.

closed (coded) date *see* PRODUCT DATING

clotted cream This specialty of Devonshire, England (which is why it's also known as *Devonshire* or *Devon cream*) is made by gently heating rich, raw milk until a semisolid layer of cream forms on the surface. After cooling, the thickened cream is removed. Clotted cream can be spread on bread or spooned atop fresh fruit or desserts. The traditional English "cream tea" consists of clotted cream and jam served with SCONES and tea. Clotted cream can be refrigerated, tightly covered, for up to 4 days.

cloudberry Found in northern climes such as New England, Canada and Scandinavia, the cloudberry looks like an amber-colored version of the raspberry, to which it's related. The berries are too tart for out-of-hand eating but make excellent jam. Cloudberries are usually wild and therefore hard to find in markets. Other names for this fruit include *bake-apple berry, yellow berry* and *mountain berry*.

cloud ear *see* WOOD EAR

clove 1. Considered one of the world's most important spices, cloves are the dried, unopened flower bud of the tropical evergreen clove tree. Reddish brown and nail-shaped, their name comes from *clavus,* the Latin word for nail. Cloves are sold whole or ground and can be used to flavor a multitude of dishes ranging from sweet to savory. *See also* SPICES; Seasoning Suggestions, page 891. 2. The term "clove" also refers to a segment of a bulb, such as in garlic clove.

club cheese *see* COLD PACK CHEESE

club sandwich; clubhouse sandwich A double-decker sandwich consisting of three slices of toast or bread between which are layers of chicken or turkey, bacon, lettuce, tomato and whatever else pleases the sandwich maker.

club soda *see* SODA WATER

club steak A tender, flavorful beef cut from the small end of the SHORT LOIN next to the rib. It has a bone along one side, but includes no portion of the tenderloin. *See also* BEEF; Beef Chart, page 896.

coagulate *see* CURDLE

coat, to In cooking, this term refers to covering food with an outer "coating." It can mean dipping or rolling food (such as chicken) in seasoned breadcrumbs or flour. The food can be dipped into beaten eggs before being coated with the dry mixture. Coating food in this manner usually precedes frying. A semiliquid, such as mayonnaise or sauce, can also be used to coat food.

coat a spoon A cooking technique used to test the doneness of cooked, egg-based custards and sauces. The mixture is done when it leaves an even film (thin to thick, depending on the recipe instructions) on the spoon. This film can be tested by drawing your finger across the coating on the spoon. If it doesn't run and leaves a clear path, it's ready.

cobbler 1. A baked, deep-dish fruit dessert topped with a thick biscuit crust sprinkled with sugar. 2. An old-fashioned punch made by mixing liquor (usually brandy, rum or whiskey) or wine with fruit juice and sugar. Cobblers are served over crushed ice, garnished with mint and slices of citrus.

cobb salad Hollywood's Brown Derby Restaurant made this salad famous in the 1920s, when restaurant manager Bob Cobb invented it as a way to use leftovers. It consists of finely chopped chicken or turkey, bacon, hard-cooked eggs, tomatoes, avocado, scallions, watercress, cheddar cheese and lettuce tossed with a VINAIGRETTE dressing and topped with an ample portion of crumbled Roquefort or other blue cheese.

cobnut *see* HAZELNUT

cochinita [koh-chih-NEE-tah] A classic Mexican dish from the Yucatán peninsula consisting of pork (traditionally baby pig) wrapped in banana leaves and slowly roasted. Prior to roasting, the meat is marinated in a mixture of ANNATTO or ACHIOTE paste, juice from SEVILLE ORANGES (or similar high-acid citrus) and other seasonings. The term *cochinita pibil* refers to the *pib*, a pit lined with stones and hot coals that was traditionally used on the Yucatán for cooking meats.

cock-a-leekie [KAHK-uh-LEE-kee] A Scottish soup made with chicken broth, chicken, leeks and, sometimes, oatmeal or cream.

cockle [KAHK-uhl] Any of various BIVALVES of the genus *Cardium* with a heart-shaped, radially ribbed "cockleshell." They have a tendency to be quite gritty and must be washed thoroughly to rid them of sand. Cockles, which have always been more popular in Europe than the United States, can be eaten raw or cooked, as with clams or oysters.

cocktail 1. A beverage that combines an alcohol (such as bourbon, gin, rum, scotch or vodka) with a mixer (such as fruit juice, soda or liqueur). Popular cocktails include MARTINI, OLD FASHIONED and TOM COLLINS. 2. This term also applies to an appetizer served before a meal such as a "seafood" or "fruit" cocktail, which would be a dish of mixed seafood or mixed fruit respectively.

cocktail frank *see* FRANKFURTER

cocktail sauce A combination of ketchup or CHILI SAUCE with prepared horseradish, lemon juice and TABASCO SAUCE or other hot red pepper seasoning. Cocktail sauce is used with seafood and as a condiment for HORS D'OEUVRES, etc.

cocoa butter [KOH-koh] The natural, cream-colored vegetable fat extracted from cocoa beans during the process of making CHOCOLATE and COCOA POWDER. It's used to add smoothness and flavor in some foods (including chocolate) and in making cosmetics and soaps.

cocoa mix [KOH-koh] Also called *instant cocoa,* this mixture of cocoa powder, dry milk and sugar is combined with cold or boiling water to make a cold or hot chocolate-flavored beverage.

cocoa nibs Roasted, husked cocoa beans broken into bits, cocoa nibs are used to add texture and a subtle chocolate flavor to baked goods like cakes and cookies, as well as to some savory dishes. These little chunks can be substituted for nuts or chocolate chips for crunch without sweetness.

cocoa powder [KOH-koh] Both CHOCOLATE and cocoa powder come from cocoa beans that grow in pods on the tropical *Theobroma cacao* tree, which is found in Southeast Asia, Africa, Hawaii, Brazil and other South American countries. Once cocoa beans are fermented, dried, roasted and cracked, the nibs are ground to extract about 75 percent of the cocoa butter, leaving a dark brown paste called chocolate liquor. After drying again, the hardened mass is ground into the powder known as unsweetened cocoa. The richer, darker **Dutch cocoa** has undergone a treatment (known as the Dutch process) whereby it's treated with an

ALKALI, which helps neutralize cocoa's natural acidity. Cocoa powder is sold plain or mixed with other ingredients such as milk powder and sugar, which creates an instant COCOA MIX. Cocoa mixes should not be substituted for cocoa powder in recipes. Store cocoa powder airtight in a cool, dark place for up to 2 years. *See also* COCOA NIBS.

coco blanc bean   *see* FRENCH NAVY BEAN

coconut   Malaysia is the motherland of the coconut palm, which now grows in parts of South America, India, Hawaii and throughout the Pacific Islands. This prolific tree yields thousands of coconuts over its approximately 70-year lifespan. Each coconut has several layers: a smooth, deep tan outer covering; a hard, dark brown, hairy husk with three indented "eyes" at one end; a thin brown skin; the creamy white coconut meat; and, at the center, a thin, opaque coconut juice. The smooth outer shell is usually removed before the coconut is exported. **Young coconuts** are those that are harvested early. Their meat is soft and chewy, and they still have their brown hairy husks. **White coconuts** are young coconuts with the husk removed, revealing the hard inner "white" shell. The coconut palm maximizes its potential by producing several products including food (coconut meat and buds) and drink (coconut juice, vinegar and toddy—the latter a potent fermented drink made from the tree's sap). Dried coconut meat, called *copra,* is pressed and used to make **coconut oil**, which is used in commercial frying and as a component in many packaged goods such as candies, margarines, soap and cosmetics. Coconut oil—one of the few nonanimal saturated fats—is used widely in the manufacture of baked goods such as commercial cookies. Certain major manufacturers have replaced it with the more expensive unsaturated fats with an eye toward cholesterol consciousness. The coconut palm's hard shells can be used for bowls, the fiber for ropes and nets, the wood for building, the roots for fuel and the leaves for baskets, hats, mats and thatching. The flesh of *unripe* coconut (usually not exported) has a jellylike consistency and can be eaten from the shell with a spoon. Upon ripening, the flesh becomes white and firm. **Fresh coconuts** are available year-round, with the peak season being October through December. Choose one that's heavy for its size and that sounds full of liquid when shaken; avoid those with damp "eyes." Whole, unopened coconuts can be stored at room temperature for up to 6 months, depending on the degree of ripeness. The liquid in a coconut (*see* COCONUT WATER) is drained by piercing two of the three eyes with an ice pick. This thin juice can be used as a beverage, though it shouldn't be confused with coconut "milk" (see below). Then the meat is removed and the inner skin scraped off. Chunks of coconut meat can be grated or chopped, either in the food processor or by hand. One medium coconut will yield 3 to 4 cups grated. Grated fresh coconut should be tightly covered and can be refrigerated up to 4 days, frozen up to 6 months. **Packaged coconut** is available in cans or plastic bags, sweetened or unsweetened, shredded or flaked, and dried, moist or frozen. It can sometimes also be found toasted. **Dessicated coconut** refers to coconut meat that's been shredded or flaked, then thoroughly dried (more than regular dried coconut). Unopened canned coconut can be stored at room temperature up to 18 months; coconut in plastic bags up to six months. Refrigerate both after opening. Coconut is high in saturated fat and is a good source of potassium.

coconut cream; coconut milk Coconut milk and coconut cream are sometimes called for in recipes such as curried dishes, drinks, salad dressings and so on. **Coconut milk** can be made by combining equal parts water and shredded fresh or desiccated coconut meat and simmering until foamy. The mixture is then strained through CHEESECLOTH, squeezing as much of the liquid as possible from the coconut meat. The coconut meat can be combined with water again for a second, diluted batch of coconut milk. **Coconut cream** can be prepared in the same manner, using 1 part water to 4 parts coconut. Milk can be substituted for water for an even richer result. Discard the coconut meat after making these mixtures. Canned coconut milk (regular and reduced-fat versions) and cream are available in Asian markets and most supermarkets. Do not confuse sweetened CREAM OF COCONUT—used mainly for desserts and mixed drinks—with unsweetened coconut milk or cream.

coconut oil *see* COCONUT

coconut water The clear liquid found in young, green COCONUTS. Coconut water is best extracted when the proportion of water to coconut meat is at its highest. As the coconut matures this liquid becomes milky, but it's not the same as COCONUT MILK. Coconut water is popular throughout tropical areas of the world where it can be obtained in bottles, cans and fresh green coconuts. It's become popular in the United States in recent years as a natural "sports drink." In addition to being a good hydrator, some promoters claim it has significant health benefits such as curing hangovers, cancer and kidney stones, reducing cholesterol, stopping aging and boosting immunity. Although coconut water is cholesterol- and fat-free, low in calories and contains electrolytes such as sodium, potassium, magnesium, calcium and phosphate, as well as small amounts of many essential amino acids, there are currently no studies involving humans to verify most of these health claims. It appears to be a good hydrator for use after exercising but may not be as good as manufactured sports drinks for heavy workouts. For example, it does not contain a lot of sodium, which can be easily lost during a heavy workout. Straight coconut water has a slightly bittersweet taste and is often augmented with tropical juices to create a taste more acceptable to the buying public.

cocotte [koh-KOT] This French word for "casserole" refers to a round or oval casserole with a tight-fitting lid. It can be either individual-size or large and is traditionally made of EARTHENWARE. The phrase *en cocotte* means "cooked in a casserole."

cod This popular saltwater fish can range from 1½ to 100 pounds and comes from the Pacific and North Atlantic Oceans. Cod's mild-flavored meat is white, lean and firm. It's available year-round and comes whole (the smaller specimens) or in large pieces. Cod can be baked, poached, braised, broiled and fried. Whole cod are often stuffed before baking. Cod can be preserved by smoking, salting or drying. **Salt cod**, an important staple in many tropical countries because of its storage properties, has been salted and dried. It's used to make the popular French dish BRANDADE. **Cod cheeks** and **tongues** are considered a delicacy. So are **scrod**, which are young cod (and haddock) weighing under 2½ pounds. HADDOCK, HAKE and POLLOCK are all close relatives of cod. *See also* FISH.

coddle A cooking method most often used with eggs, though other foods can be coddled as well. There are special containers with tight-fitting lids called "egg coddlers" made specifically for this purpose. Coddling is usually done by placing the food in an individual-size container that is covered, set in a larger pan of simmering water and placed either on stovetop or in the oven at very low heat. The gentle warmth of this WATER BATH slowly cooks the food. Coddling can also be done by gently lowering the food into water that's come to a boil and removed from the heat.

coded (closed) date *see* PRODUCT DATING

coeur à la crème [KEWR ah la KREHM] French for "heart with cream," this classic dessert is made in a special heart-shaped wicker basket or mold with holes in it. Cream cheese is mixed with sour cream or whipping cream (and sometimes sugar) and placed into the CHEESECLOTH-lined mold or basket. The dessert is then refrigerated overnight, during which time the WHEY (liquid) drains out through the basket or perforated mold. To serve, the dessert is unmolded and garnished with fresh berries or other fruit.

coffee Ethiopia is thought to be the motherland of the first coffee beans, which, throughout the ages, found their way to Brazil and Colombia—the two largest coffee producers today. Coffee plantations abound throughout other South and Central American countries, Cuba, Hawaii, Indonesia, Jamaica and many African nations. There are hundreds of different coffee species but the two most commercially viable are *coffea robusta* and *coffea arabica*. The sturdy, disease-resistant *coffea robusta*, which thrives at lower altitudes, produces beans with a harsher, more single-dimensional flavor than the more sensitive *coffea arabica*, which grows at high altitudes (3,000 to 6,500 feet) and produces beans with elegant, complex flavors. Some coffee companies are now identifying their beans as shade-grown coffee; this refers to a traditional, environmentally friendly method of growing coffee under tree canopies as opposed to the cultivation of coffee species that need ample sun, a method that requires deforestation. The coffee plant is actually a small tree that bears a fruit called the "coffee cherry." Growing and tending these coffee trees is a labor-intensive process because blossoms, unripe (green) and ripe red cherries can occupy a tree simultaneously, necessitating hand-picking the fruit. The coffee cherry's skin and pulp surround two beans enclosed in a parchmentlike covering. Once these layers are discarded, the beans are cleaned, dried, graded and hand-inspected for color and quality. The "green" beans (which can range in color from pale green to muddy yellow) are then exported, leaving the roasting, blending and grinding to be done at their destination. Coffee can be composed of a single type of coffee bean or a blend of several types. Blended coffee produces a richer, more complex flavor than single-bean coffees. The length of time coffee beans are roasted will affect the color and flavor of the brew. Among the most popular roasts are American, French, Italian, European and Viennese. **American roast** (also called **regular roast**) beans are medium-roasted, which results in a moderate brew—not too light or too heavy in flavor. The heavy-roasted beans are **French roast** and **dark French roast**, which are a deep chocolate brown and produce a stronger coffee, and the glossy, brown-black, strongly flavored **Italian roast**, used for espresso. **European roast** contains two-thirds heavy-roast beans blended with one-third regular-roast; **Viennese roast** reverses those proportions. Varietal coffee is coffee from a particular geographic region, such as Columbia, Costa Rica, Ethiopia, Kenya, New Guinea and Sumatra. Though the species of coffee clearly plays a role in determining its unique flavor characteristics, the growing environment also plays an important role. Estate coffee is even more specific and describes coffee from a single plantation. **Instant coffee powder** is a powdered coffee made by heat-drying freshly brewed coffee. **Freeze-dried coffee granules** (or **crystals**) are derived from brewed coffee that has been frozen into a slush before the water is evaporated. Freeze-dried coffee is slightly more expensive than regular instant coffee, but is also reputed to be superior in flavor. **Coffee concentrate** is a liquid EXTRACT of freshly brewed coffee that's diluted with water. It comes in many forms including regular, decaffeinated and flavored (vanilla, chocolate, and so forth) and can be found in most supermarkets. Coffee, tea and cocoa all contain **caffeine**, a stimulant that affects many parts of the body including the nervous system, kidneys, heart and gastric secretions. With the exception of the Madagascar coffee species—*Mascarocoffea vianneyi*—which actually *grows* beans that are decaffeinated, coffee beans must go through a process to produce **decaffeinated coffee**. The caffeine is removed by one of two methods, either of which is executed before the beans are roasted. In the first method, the caffeine is chemically extracted with the use of a solvent, which must be completely washed out before the beans are dried. The second method—called *Swiss water process*—first steams the beans, then scrapes away the caffeine-rich outer layers. Though there was once concern about the safety of solvent residues, research has found that the volatile solvents disappear entirely when the beans are roasted. Coffee, whether ground or whole-bean, loses its flavor quickly. To assure the freshest, most flavorful brew, buy fresh coffee beans and grind only as many as needed to brew each pot of coffee. Inexpensive grinders are available at most department and discount stores. Store whole roasted beans in an airtight container in a cool, dry place for up to 2 weeks. For longer storage, freeze whole beans, freezer-wrapped, up to 3 months. Since room-temperature ground coffee begins to go stale within a couple of days after it's ground, it should be refrigerated in an airtight container and can be stored up to 2 weeks. *See also* CAFÉ; CAFÉ AU LAIT; CAFÉ BRULOT; CAFÉ CON LECHE; CAFÉ FILTRE; CAFÉ MOCHA; CAFFÉ; CAFFÉ AMERICANO; CAFFÉ LATTE; CAFFÉ MACCHIATO; CAPPUCCINO; ESPRESSO; GREEK COFFEE; IRISH COFFEE; KOPI LUWAK; THAI COFFEE; TURKISH COFFEE; VIENNESE COFFEE.

coffee cake This rich, sweet, cakelike bread is usually eaten for breakfast or brunch. Coffee cakes can be made with yeast, but those using baking soda or baking powder take less time and are also delicious. Coffee cakes often contain fruit, nuts and sometimes a cream-cheese filling. They can be frosted or not and are usually best served slightly warm.

coffee grinder *see* GRINDER

cognac [KON-yak] Hailing from in and around the town of Cognac in western France, this potent potable is the finest of all BRANDIES. Cognac is double-distilled immediately after FERMENTATION. It then begins its minimum 3-year aging in Limousin oak. Stars on a cognac label denote the following oak-aging: 1 star—aged 3 years; 2 stars—aged at least 4 years; 3 stars—aged at least 5 years. Older cognacs are labeled *V.S.* (very superior), *V.S.O.P.* (very superior old pale) and *V.V.S.O.P.* (very, very, superior old pale). A cognac label can no longer legally claim over 7 years aging. It's been difficult for authorities to accurately keep track of Cognacs aged longer than this, so they've limited what producers may claim. Label terms *X.O., Extra* and *Reserve* usually indicate a Cognac is the oldest a producer distributes. *Fine Champagne* on the label indicates that 60 percent of the grapes came from a superior grape-growing section of Cognac called *Grande Champagne*. One designating *Grande Fine Champagne* proclaims that all the grapes for that cognac came from that eminent area.

Cointreau [KWAHN-troh; kwahn-TROH] The world's most distinguished orange-flavored LIQUEUR, made by France's Cointreau family since the mid-nineteenth century. Cointreau is clear and colorless with an intensely exotic, mildly bitter orange flavor—the result of a combination of the peel of sour oranges (from the Caribbean island of Curaçao) and sweet orange peel from Spain. *See also* CURAÇAO; TRIPLE SEC.

cola [KOH-lah] A sweet carbonated beverage containing COLA-NUT extract and other flavorings.

colander [KAWL-an-der; KUHL-an-der] Used for draining liquid from solids, the colander is a perforated, bowl-shaped container. It can be metal, plastic or ceramic.

cola nut; kola nut [KOH-lah] Caffeine and theobromine, used in the manufacture of some soft drinks, are derivatives of the cola nut, offspring of the cola tree that grows in Africa, South America and the West Indies. Chewing this nut (which is approximately the size of a walnut) is a favorite pastime of natives who claim it diminishes fatigue and thirst and (for some) has aphrodisiac properties.

Colbert sauce [kohl-BEHR; KOHL-behr] Named after the chief minister of King Louis XIV, this sauce combines meat glaze, butter, wine, shallots, tarragon and lemon juice. It's served with grilled meats and game. *See also* SAUCE.

Colby [KOHL-bee] Invented in 1885 by Joseph Steinwand in his father's cheese factory near Colby, Wisconsin, this cheese may be made with raw or PASTEURIZED cow's milk. It's similar to CHEDDAR but has a milder flavor and a softer, springier texture. These characteristics can be attributed to the fact that Colby is produced with a washed-CURD technique whereby the drained curds are stirred with water, a process that removes all traces of LACTOSE that natural bacteria might convert to acid. **Longhorn** is a Colby-style cheese that's sold in thick half-moon shapes. A popular hybrid is a mixture of Colby and JACK cheese, often called **Colby Jack** or **CoJack**. It's a blend of yellow-orange and ivory cheeses, the combination of which produces a marbled effect. All Colby cheeses have a minimum FAT CONTENT of 50 percent. *See also* CHEESE.

colcannon [kuhl-KAN-uhn] A delicious Irish peasant dish of milk- and butter-moistened mashed potatoes mixed with finely chopped cooked onions and kale or cabbage. *See also* CHAMP.

cold cuts Slices of cold meats like BOLOGNA, ham, LIVERWURST, roast beef, SALAMI, turkey and often various cheeses.

cold duck Originating in Germany, this pink sparkling wine is a mixture of CHAMPAGNE, sparkling BURGUNDY and sugar. Its origin is traced back to the Bavarian practice of mixing bottles of previously opened Champagne with cold sparkling Burgundy so the Champagne wouldn't be wasted. This mixture was called *kalte ende* ("cold end"); over the years, *ende* transliterated to *ente* ("duck"). The wines used to make cold duck are often of inferior quality. The resulting potation is quite sweet with few other distinguishable characteristics.

cold pack cheese A blend of shredded natural cheese (typically CHEDDAR) mixed with other ingredients (such as herbs, spices or wine flavoring), packed into molds and pressed. Cold pack cheese (also called *club cheese*) differs from PROCESSED CHEESE because it is produced without heat. The resulting cheese is firm yet creamy and spreadable at room temperature. *See also* IMITATION CHEESE; SUBSTITUTE CHEESE.

cold-pressed oils *see* FATS AND OILS

coleslaw From the Dutch *koolsla,* meaning "cabbage salad"—*kool* ("cabbage") plus *sla* ("salad"). Coleslaw is a salad of shredded red or white cabbage mixed with a MAYONNAISE, VINAIGRETTE or other type of dressing. Other ingredients such as chopped onion, celery, sweet green or red pepper, pickles, bacon or herbs may be added. There are probably as many variations of coleslaw as there are cooks.

collard; collard greens; collards [KAHL-uhrd] Long a staple of SOUL FOOD, collard (also called *collard greens* and just plain *collards*) is a variety of cabbage that doesn't form a head, but grows instead in a loose rosette at the top of a tall stem. It's often confused with its close relative KALE and, in fact, tastes like a cross between cabbage and kale. Collard's peak season is January through April, though it's available year-round in most markets. Look for crisp green leaves with no evidence of yellowing, wilting or insect damage. Refrigerate collard in a plastic bag 3 to 5 days. The Southern style of cooking the greens is to boil them with a chunk of bacon or salt pork. They can be prepared in any manner suitable for spinach or cabbage. Collard is an excellent source of vitamins A and C, calcium and iron.

Collins A tall, iced cocktail made with liquor (gin, rum, vodka, whiskey or brandy), lemon juice, sugar and soda water, and garnished with a lemon slice. The drink is served in a 10- to 12-ounce "Collins" glass. The most popular of this genre is the **Tom Collins**, which is made with gin and is said to have been named for its creator.

colostrum [kuh-LAWS-truhm] The foremilk (a thin, yellowish liquid) produced by cows (and other mammals) for the first five milkings after giving birth. Also known as *beestings,* colostrum is exceptionally rich in antibodies, minerals and vitamins. Bovine colostrum has been credited with health and healing benefits and is sometimes used as a dietary supplement.

comal [koh-MAHL] A round, flat griddle on which TORTILLAS are cooked. In Mexico, comals used over open fires are usually made of unglazed EARTHENWARE. Those intended for use with electric and gas heat are more often made of a light metal, such as tin. The earthenware and thin metal allow fast heat penetration, thereby cooking the tortillas quickly—important so they don't become dry and brittle.

comfort food The term "comfort food" is intensely personal and can mean ten different things to ten different people. Simply put, comfort food is anything that brings a feeling of cozy contentment—something that soothes and completely satisfies mind, body and spirit. In short, a culinary hug. For many, the term describes a favorite food from childhood, be it meatloaf or a peanut butter and jelly sandwich. Typically, comfort foods are homemade, hearty and rib-sticking, such as macaroni and cheese, fried chicken or mashed potatoes and gravy. But for some they can just as easily be storebought, such as potato chips or caramel corn. Whatever it is, comfort food should make you shut your eyes, rub your tummy and say *ahhhhh.*

Comice pear [kuh-MEES] This large, exquisite pear has a meltingly smooth, sweet flesh and fruit-filled fragrance. It ranges in color from greenish-yellow to yellow blushed with red. It's available from October to January and is best eaten raw. *See also* PEAR.

comino [koh-MEE-noh] Spanish for "CUMIN."

common brown mushroom *see* CREMINO

complete protein A *complete protein* food source is one that contains adequate amounts of the nine essential AMINO ACIDS. Most foods derived from animal sources are considered complete protein foods, whereas others such as fruits, vegetables and grains, which are generally lacking one or more of the essential amino acids, are called *incomplete protein* foods.

composed salad A salad in which the ingredients are artfully arranged, rather than tossed together. The dressing for a composed salad is usually drizzled over the top of the ingredients. In French the term is known as *salade composée.*

compote [KAHM-poht] 1. A chilled dish of fresh or dried fruit that has been slowly cooked in a SUGAR SYRUP (which may contain liquor or liqueur and sometimes spices). Slow cooking is important for the fruit to retain its shape. 2. Also called *compotier*, a deep, stemmed dish (usually of silver or glass) used to hold fruit, nuts or candy.

compound butter   Butter creamed with other ingredients such as herbs, garlic, wine, shallots and so on. The French term for compound butter is *beurre composé*.

Comté   [kawn-TAY]   France's most popular and widely produced cheese, Comté is made throughout five major regions of eastern France. Yet, even though production is massive, because **Comté** has APPELLATION status its quality is strictly controlled. Each cheese is rigorously graded on a 20-point system and those not attaining enough points are sold as GRU-YÈRE (French Gruyère isn't as esteemed as Swiss Gruyère). Comté is aged a minimum of 4 months, though 6 months or longer is more common. The texture is firm and supple, the flavor a complex yet savory mixture of butterscotch, nuts and fruit. The FAT CONTENT of Comté is about 45 percent. *See also* CHEESE.

concassé; concasser   [kawn-ka-SAY (SEHR)]   A mixture that is coarsely chopped or ground. The classic *concassé* is comprised of tomatoes that have been peeled, seeded, and chopped. *Concasser* is the verb form of the word.

conch   [KANGK; KAHNCH]   This GASTROPOD MOLLUSK (*see both listings*) is encased in a beautiful, brightly colored spiral shell. Conch is found in southern waters and is particularly popular with Floridians and Caribbeans. Summer is the peak season for fresh conch, which will most likely be available in Chinese or Italian markets or specialty fish stores. Store fresh conch, tightly wrapped, in the refrigerator up to 2 days. Conch can also be purchased canned or frozen. The footlike muscle can be eaten raw in salads, or tenderized by pounding, then quickly sautéed like ABA-LONE. It's also often chopped and used in chowders. Conch is sometimes erroneously referred to as *whelk,* which, though related, is a different species.

conchiglie; conchiglioni   *see* Pasta Glossary, page 883

conching   [KAHNCH-ing]   A manufacturing technique used to give chocolate a smooth texture. *See* CHOCOLATE for a more complete description of this process.

Concord grape   Grown mainly on the East Coast, the Concord is a beautiful blue-black grape that often appears to have been powdered with silver. This mild-flavored grape has seeds and a slip-off skin. It's available August to October and is used mainly for juice, jams and for out-of-hand eating. *See also* GRAPE.

condensed milk *see* SWEETENED CONDENSED MILK

condiment [KAHN-duh-ment] A savory, piquant, spicy or salty accompaniment to food, such as a relish, sauce, mixture of spices and so on. Ketchup and mustard are two of the most popular condiments.

confection [kuhn-FEHK-shuhn] A piece of candy or sweetmeat; also a sweet dish. A *confectionery* is a candy shop.

confectioners' sugar; powdered sugar [kuhn-FEHK-shuh-nehrs] *see* SUGAR

confectionery coating [kuhn-FEHK-shuh-nehr-ee] Used as a dip for candies, a confectionery or *summer coating* is a blend of sugar, milk powder, hardened vegetable fat and various flavorings. It comes in a variety of pastel colors. Some have lowfat cocoa powder added, but they do not contain cocoa butter.

conference pear A medium to large, long, slender pear with a russeted green skin. The conference pear has sweet, succulent flesh with a slight trace of pink when ripe. The name refers to an award it received in 1885 at the International Pear Conference.

confiserie; confiseur [kaw*n*-fee-ZREE; kawn-fee-ZEW*RR*] French for "candy store" and "confectioner" (candymaker), respectively.

confit [kawn-FEE; kohn-FEE] This specialty of Gascony, France, is derived from an ancient method of preserving meat (usually goose, duck or pork) whereby it is salted and slowly cooked in its own fat. The cooked meat is then packed into a crock or pot and covered with its cooking fat, which acts as a seal and preservative. *Confit* can be refrigerated up to 6 months. **Confit d'oie** and **confit de canard** are preserved goose and preserved duck, respectively.

confiture [kawn-fee-TYOOR] French for "jam" or "preserves."

congee [KAHN-jee] A gruel of boiled rice and water, which serves as a background for a host of other foods including fish, shrimp, chicken, peanuts, sesame seed and eggs. In China, where it's also known as *jook* or *juk,* congee is particularly popular for breakfast. Koreans also call it *juk* and in Thailand this dish is known as *khao tom gung*.

Congo bean *see* PIGEON PEA

conpoy *see* SCALLOPS, DRIED

con queso [kon KAY-soh] Spanish for "with cheese."

conserve [kuhn-SERV; KON-surv] A mixture of fruits, nuts and sugar, cooked together until thick, often used to spread on biscuits, crumpets and so on. *See also* JAM; JELLY; PRESERVE.

consommé [KON-suh-may; kon-suh-MAY] A clarified meat or fish broth. Consommé can be served hot or cold, and is variously used as a soup or sauce base. A **double consommé** has been reduced until it is half the volume (and has twice the flavor) of regular (or single) consommé. *See also* MADRILÈNE.

Conti, à la [KON-tee] A French term referring to dishes made or garnished with lentils (usually puréed) and sometimes bacon.

continental breakfast A light breakfast that usually consists of a breadstuff (such as toast, croissants, pastries, etc.) and coffee, tea or other liquid. The continental breakfast is the antithesis of the hearty ENGLISH BREAKFAST.

Contrary Mary *see* BLOODY MARY

convection oven A special gas or electric oven equipped with a fan that provides continuous circulation of hot air around the food, thereby cooking it not only more evenly, but also up to 25 percent faster. For most foods, the oven temperature can be reduced 25°F as well. Because convection ovens heat up so fast, there's usually no need for preheating. Convection ovens, unlike microwave ovens, do not require special cookware or major adjustments in cooking time or technique. There are also microwave-convection oven combinations, which combine the even cooking of convection with the speed of microwaving.

converted rice A term created by the brand name Uncle Ben's, used to describe parboiled rice. *See also* RICE.

cookie A cookie can be any of various hand-held, flour-based sweet cakes—either crisp or soft. The word *cookie* comes from the Dutch *koekje,* meaning "little cake." The earliest cookie-style cakes are thought to date back to 7th-century Persia, one of the first countries to cultivate sugar. There are six basic cookie styles, any of which can range from tender-crisp to soft. A **drop cookie** is made by dropping spoonfuls of dough onto a baking sheet. **Bar cookies** are created when a batter or soft dough is spooned into a shallow pan, then baked, cooled and cut into bars. **Hand-formed** (or **molded**) **cookies** are made by shaping dough by hand into small balls, logs, crescents and other shapes. **Pressed cookies** are formed by pressing dough through a COOKIE PRESS (or PASTRY BAG) to form fancy shapes and designs. **Refrigerator** (or **icebox**) **cookies** are made by shaping the dough into a log, which is refrigerated until firm, then sliced and baked. **Rolled cookies** begin by using a rolling pin to roll the dough out flat; then it is cut into decorative shapes with COOKIE CUTTERS or a pointed knife. Other cookies, such as the German SPRINGERLE, are formed by imprinting designs on the dough, either by rolling a special decoratively carved rolling pin over it or by pressing the dough into a carved COOKIE MOLD. In England, cookies are called *biscuits,* in Spain they're *galletas,* Germans call them *keks,* in Italy they're *biscotti* and so on.

cookie cutter A metal or plastic device, also called a *biscuit cutter,* used to cut decorative shapes out of dough that has been rolled flat. Cookie cutters are available singly or in sets. Dipping a cookie cutter into flour or granulated sugar will prevent it from sticking to soft doughs. A **rolling cookie cutter** has a wooden handle at the end of which is a metal or plastic cylinder marked with raised designs. When the cutter is rolled across the dough, it cuts a jigsaw-puzzle pattern of differently shaped cookies without any wasted dough.

cookie gun *see* COOKIE PRESS

cookie mold Most often made of wood, these decorative molds are used to create designs in some European cookies. The cookie dough is pressed into a floured mold, leveled off with a knife, then inverted onto a baking sheet. Cookie molds come in all sizes and shapes and are available at specialty kitchenware shops.

cookie press Also called a *cookie gun,* this tool consists of a hollow tube fitted at one end with a decorative template or nozzle, and at the other with a plunger. The tube is filled with a soft cookie dough that the plunger forces out through the decorative tip to form professional-looking pressed cookies. Cookie presses come with a selection of interchangeable templates and other tips. SPRITZ are one of the best-known cookies formed by this tool.

cookie stamp A small, decorative, round or square cookie imprinter, usually made of glass, ceramic or wood. When the stamp is pressed into a ball of cookie dough, it not only flattens it, but imprints a relief design on the surface. Cookie stamps come in many designs and are available at specialty kitchenware shops.

cooking cheese During the making of some cheeses, the CURDS are heated in WHEY while being stirred. This process tightens the curd's protein composition, compresses the texture and removes more whey. The higher the cooking temperature and the longer the time, the denser the resulting cheese. For example, for a very hard cheese like dry JACK, the curds are cooked at 131°F (55°C), whereas the curds for a softer cheese like HAVARTI are heated only to around 110°F (43°C). **Semicooked** cheeses are those heated at temperatures below 120°F.

cooking spray A nonstick blend that typically consists of vegetable oil and lecithin (or other emulsifier) packaged in an aerosol can. Such sprays prevent food from sticking to a pan, make cleanup easy and are a boon to health-conscious cooks who want to control fat. They come in several varieties, including canola oil, olive oil and butter-flavored oil. When spraying a pan, keep the surrounding area clean by doing so over the sink or open dishwasher door, both of which will be cleaned in the normal course of the day. Besides coating pans, use cooking sprays on any utensil or kitchen tool to keep foods from sticking—for example, a cheese grater, knife blade, kitchen shears, a food processor interior, cookie cutter, and so on. The only caveat is never to use the spray near an open flame, which will cause it to ignite and flare up. Also called *nonstick spray* and *vegetable cooking spray*.

cooking wine A wine labeled "cooking wine" is generally an inferior wine that would not be drunk on its own. It typically lacks distinction and flavor and is sometimes adulterated with salt. The rule of thumb when cooking with wine is only to use one you'd drink and to be sure the wine's flavor complements the food with which it's paired.

cookware *see* AGEMONO-NABE; BRAZIER; DOUBLE BOILER; FISH POACHER; FONDUE POT; FRYING PAN; GRIDDLE; GRILL; GRILL PAN; HIBACHI; LOAF PAN; OMELET PAN; PAELLA PAN; PIZZA PAN; SAUCEPAN; SAUTÉ PAN; STEAMED PUDDING MOLD; STEAMER; STOVETOP SMOKER. *See also* COOKWARE AND BAKEWARE MATERIALS.

cookware and bakeware materials The materials that comprise your cooking and baking equipment can make a huge difference in how the food turns out. A pan or baking sheet of inferior quality (which typically translates to one that's light and thin-gauged) can stew meat that you're trying to sauté, or can burn the cookies. Knowing the basics of materials used can help you choose equipment according to the task for which it's intended. To start with, let's discuss the term **nonreactive**, which refers to metals (such as stainless steel) that have no negative reaction to foods cooked in them. On the other hand, reactive metals like aluminum, copper and cast iron react detrimentally with certain foods, particularly those that are acidic, such as lemon juice, tomatoes and vinegar. The results include a metallic taste and discoloration of the food. In the case of copper, toxicity from verdigris can be a problem. Most copper and aluminum cookware (see following information) is lined with a nonreactive metal to make it usable with all foods. **Aluminum** is moderately priced, sturdy and a superior heat conductor. It comes in light and medium weights—the heavier the gauge, the more evenly the food will cook. *Anodized aluminum,* available in plain (matte or polished) or anodized (dark gray) finishes, is by far the preferred choice. It has undergone an electrochemical process that alters the metal's surface, to make it extremely hard, low-stick (though not nonstick) and *almost* nonreactive to acids (storing acidic foods in this cookware could cause a chemical reaction). These finishes are chip-, stain- and scratch-resistant but can spot and fade if cleaned in a dishwasher. Use a nylon pad (never steel wool) for cleaning; lighten oxidized surfaces by filling a pan with ACIDU-LATED WATER and boiling for 15 minutes. Don't buy *untreated aluminum cookware,* which can darken and pit when exposed to alkaline or mineral-rich foods, and when soaked excessively in soapy water. It can also discolor some foods containing eggs, wine or other acidic ingredients. Because aluminum may be reactive and easily scratched, it's often combined with other metals such as stainless steel. **Cast iron (ironware)** is fairly inexpensive and it absorbs, conducts and retains heat very efficiently. There are two basic styles—regular and enameled (see following section on Enamelware). Regular cast iron requires seasoning (*see* SEASON, TO), which gives it a natural nonstick finish, and creates a surface that doesn't react with or absorb the flavor of foods. Clean cast iron pans by first wiping them with a paper towel or soft cloth and, if necessary, gently scrubbing with a nylon pad. **Copper** is very expensive but is heavy duty and has superior heat conductivity, which makes it perfect for cream- and egg-based sauces. Copper is typically lined with tin or stainless steel to keep it from interacting with certain foods. The drawbacks to copper are that it isn't nonstick, requires polishing, and needs to be relined every 10 years or so (with average home usage). Still, it's the cookware of choice of many professionals. Never buy unlined copper pans, which can produce potentially toxic reactions with acidic ingredients like wine, lemon juice and tomatoes. Wash copper in hot, soapy water and dry immediately; brighten with copper polish. **Earthenware** isn't a good heat conductor but, because it retains heat well and releases it slowly, it's good for long-cooking dishes, such as baked beans and stews. It can be unglazed or glazed with a hard, non-porous coating. High-fired earthenware is hard and durable; low-fired versions are more fragile. Care must be taken to cool earthenware slowly and completely before washing in order to prevent the glazed earthenware from cracking. Most glazed earthenware can be washed in the dishwasher. *Unglazed earthenware* (also called **clay bakers**) are porous and must be thoroughly soaked in water before each use. **Enamelware** can be either cast iron or steel cookware that has been coated with thin layers of brightly colored porcelain enamel. *Enameled cast iron* is a good heat conductor, *enameled steel* is not. Enamelware is fairly easy to clean and doesn't interact with acidic ingredients. Light-colored enameled surfaces don't brown food as well as those that are dark and will also eventually discolor with use. Extreme overheating may cause the enamelware surface to crack. Because abrasives can scratch the enamel coating, use wooden or plastic utensils when stirring and a nylon pad when cleaning. **Glass**, **glass-ceramic**, and **porcelain** don't conduct heat well, but retain it efficiently, which means they're good for long-cooking dishes at medium heat. The combination glass-ceramic dishes can go from freezer to oven with no problem; whereas glass and porcelain dishes can break easily with sudden temperature changes. All three are nonreactive and easy to clean. **Nonstick** cookware and bakeware has a special coating fused to interior surfaces. This coating allows for fat-free cooking, prevents food from sticking and requires minimal cleanup. Some nonstick finishes are applied to the surface and can wear off over a period of time. Others are bonded right to the metal, making for a sturdier finish (and a higher cost). Most nonstick finishes are dishwasher safe but require the use of nonmetal utensils to prevent surface scratching. **Stainless steel** has poor heat conductivity, a problem somewhat reduced in well-made, heavy pans. But it also has many advantages: it doesn't react (as does some aluminum cookware) with acidic or alkaline foods; it is corrosion-resistant; it's strong and easy to clean; and it doesn't easily scratch, pit or dent. The best of all possible worlds is **clad metal** stainless cookware with a core of either aluminum or copper (both are excellent heat conductors) sandwiched between two thin sheets of stainless steel. **Stoneware** is strong, hard pottery that's usually fully glazed, then fired at very high temperatures (around 2,200°F). It's generally nonporous, chip-resistant and safe to use in both microwave and standard ovens. It's ideal for baking and slow cooking. *See also* BAKEWARE.

cooling rack   Used to cool baked goods such as cakes and breads, a cooling rack is made of a network of closely arranged wires, set on short legs to raise it above the level of the countertop. The raised surface provides air circulation so the baked goods won't get soggy on the bottom. It's important that the rack have thick, strong wires so it won't sag in the center. Cooling racks can be round, square or rectangular and can range from small to large.

copha   A highly saturated (*see* FATS AND OILS), solidified coconut oil (*see* COCONUT). Copha is extremely popular in Australia for everything from candy to pastries to toppings for cakes and cookies. It's typically melted with other ingredients (like chocolate), then drizzled over cake, or added to a candy mixture, and so on. LARD or SHORTENING can be substituted for copha in recipes but won't impart that subtle coconut flavor.

coppa; coppa ham   [KOHP-pah] 1. A cured meat taken primarily from the neck (and sometimes shoulder) portions of the hog. Coppa di Piacenza has PROTECTED DESIGNATION OF ORIGIN status—in fact, the entire area around Piacenza is devoted to coppa production. The meat must come from animals bred in Emilia and Lombardy. The trimmed flesh is massaged and flavored with a mixture of salt, pepper, sugar and various spices such as cloves, cinnamon and laurel seed. After a week's resting period, coppa is encased in a hog's diaphragm and aged for a minimum of 6 months. Coppa is most often served as part of an ANTIPASTO plate. *See also* SALUMI. 2. Italian for "cup."

copper cookware *see* COOKWARE AND BAKEWARE MATERIALS

copra [KOH-prah; KAH-prah] Dried coconut meat from which coconut oil is pressed (*see* COCONUT).

coq au vin [kohk-oh-VAHN; kohk-oh-VAH*N*] This classic French dish is composed of pieces of chicken, mushrooms, onions, bacon or salt pork and various herbs cooked together with red wine.

coquille [koh-KEEL; koh-KEE] 1. French for "shell." 2. A scallop shell or scallop-shaped dish in which various dishes (such as COQUILLES ST. JACQUES) can be served.

coquilles St. Jacques [koh-KEEL sah*n*-ZHAHK; koh-KEE sah*n*-ZHAK] Classically served in a SCALLOP shell, this special dish consists of scallops in a creamy wine sauce, topped with breadcrumbs or cheese and browned under a broiler.

coquito [koh-KEE-toh] This coconut-flavored eggnog is a Puerto Rican Christmas tradition and can be prepared both with or without rum. It's made with COCONUT MILK, SWEETENED CONDENSED MILK, whole milk, egg yolks, vanilla and cinnamon.

coquito(s); coquito nuts [koh-KEE-tohs] Hailing from South America, coquito nuts come from a feather-leaved palm tree native to Chile. They look like tiny ($1/2$ to $3/4$ inch in diameter) coconuts and have a brown exterior and white interior with a hollow center. They're crunchy and have a delicately sweet flavor reminiscent of coconut and almonds. Coquitos are sold shelled in packages and can be found in some natural food stores and specialty produce markets. Store in an airtight container in the refrigerator for up to 3 weeks. Eat whole as you would other nuts, or chop and add to salads and desserts, or grate as you would a whole nutmeg to garnish and flavor foods. Soften dehydrated nuts by pouring boiling water over them and allowing them to stand for 20 minutes.

Corail *see* PIÑATA; PIÑATA APPLE

coral Eaten plain or used in a sauce or COMPOUND BUTTER, coral is simply the ROE (eggs) of a CRUSTACEAN such as lobster or scallop. When cooked, it turns a beautiful coral-red color.

coralli *see* Pasta Glossary, page 883

corbina [kor-BEE-nuh] *see* WEAKFISH

cordial *see* LIQUEUR

cordon bleu [kor-dohn-BLUH] 1. A French term (literally translated as "blue ribbon") that referred originally to an award given to women chefs for culinary excellence. The term now can apply to any superior cook. 2. The term also refers to a dish—chicken (or veal) *cordon bleu*—in which a thin scallop of veal or chicken is topped with a thin slice each of prosciutto or other ham and Gruyère or other Swiss cheese, then another meat scallop. The stacked meats and cheese are then breaded and sautéed until golden.

core *n.* The center of a fruit such as an apple, pear or pineapple. Cores may contain small seeds, or they may be tough and woody, or both. **core** *v.* To remove the core from a fruit.

corek; çörek *see* TSOUREKI

corer A utensil designed to remove the core (or center) from fruit or vegetables. Corers are usually made of stainless steel and come in different shapes for different uses. An all-purpose corer, used for apples, pears and the like, has a medium-length shaft with a circular cutting ring at the end. The core can be cut and removed with this tool. Another kind of apple corer is shaped like a spoked wheel with handles and not only cores the apple, but cuts it into wedges as well. A **zucchini corer** has a long, pointed, trough-shaped blade that, when inserted at one end of the zucchini and rotated, will remove the center, leaving a hollow tube for stuffing. A **pineapple corer** is a tall, arch-handled utensil with two serrated, concentric cutting rings at the base. After the top and bottom of the pineapple are sliced off, the corer is inserted from the top and twisted downward. The tool not only removes the core, but also the outer shell, leaving pineapple rings.

coriander; coriander seed [KOR-ee-an-der] Native to the Mediterranean and the Orient, coriander is related to the parsley family. It's known for both its seeds (actually the dried, ripe fruit of the plant) and for its dark green, lacy leaves (CILANTRO). The flavors of the seeds and leaves bear absolutely no resemblance to each other. Mention of **coriander seeds** was found in early Sanskrit writings and the seeds themselves have been discovered in Egyptian tombs dating to 960 B.C. The tiny (1/8-inch), yellow-tan seeds are lightly ridged. They are mildly fragrant and have an aromatic flavor akin to a combination of lemon, sage and caraway. Whole coriander seeds are used in pickling and for special drinks, such as mulled wine. Ground seed is used in many baked goods (particularly

Scandinavian), curry blends, soups, etc. (*See* Seasoning Suggestions, page 891.) Both forms are commonly available in supermarkets. **Coriander leaves** are commonly known as *cilantro* and *Chinese parsley*. They have an extremely pungent (some say fetid) odor and flavor that lends itself well to highly seasoned food. Though it's purported to be the world's most widely used herb, many Americans and Europeans find that fresh coriander is definitely an acquired taste. Choose leaves with an even green color and no sign of wilting. Store a bunch of coriander, stems down, in a glass of water with a plastic bag over the leaves. Refrigerate in this manner for up to a week, changing the water every 2 days. Coriander leaves are used widely in the cuisines of India, Mexico, the Orient and the Caribbean.

corkage [KORK-ihj] A fee charged by some restaurants to open and serve a bottle of wine brought in by the patron. A quick call to the restaurant will confirm the amount of the corkage fee. Some restaurants charge a lower fee if the patron's wine is not on the restaurant's wine list, such as might be the case with an older wine or a particularly distinctive vintage.

corkscrew A tool used to withdraw corks from bottles. Typically, a corkscrew has a pointed metal spiral with a transverse handle at one end. There are many varieties of corkscrews, however, including one that holds the bottle while a crank handle drives the screw into the cork and then extracts it.

corn Throughout Europe, "corn" has always been the generic name for any of the cereal grains; Europeans call corn *maize,* a derivative of the early American Indian word *mahiz.* In fact, before settlers came to the New World Europeans had never seen this food—called *Indian corn* by colonists. What a wonderfully versatile and useful gift the Indians gave the world. Everything on the corn plant can be used: the husks for TAMALES, the silk for medicinal tea, the kernels for food and the stalks for fodder. Corn is not only a popular food, but the foundation of many by-products including BOURBON, CORN FLOUR, CORNMEAL, CORN OIL, CORNSTARCH, CORN SYRUP, CORN WHISKEY and laundry starch. The multicolored Indian corn—used today mainly for decoration—has red, blue, brown and purple kernels. Horticulturists developed the two most popular varieties today—white (**Country Gentleman**) and yellow (**Golden Bantam**) corn. **Yellow corn** has larger, fuller-flavored kernels; **white corn** kernels are smaller and sweeter. **Shoepeg corn** is a white corn variety with uneven rows of small kernels prized for their sweetness. The hybrid **butter and sugar corn** produces ears of yellow and white kernels. The peak season for fresh corn is May through September. The minute it's picked, the corn's sugar begins its gradual conversion to starch which, in turn, lessens the corn's natural sweetness. Therefore, it's important to buy corn as soon after it's picked as possible. Look for ears with bright green, snugly fitting husks and golden brown silk. The kernels should be plump and milky, and come all the way to the ear's tip; the rows should be tightly spaced. Fresh corn should be cooked and served the day it's purchased, but it can be refrigerated up to a day. Strip off the husks and silk just before cooking. Corn can also be purchased canned or frozen. Tiny **baby corn**, particularly popular with Thai and Chinese cooks, can be purchased in cans or jars. Unfortunately, its flavor bears little resemblance to the fresh (or even frozen) vegetable. HOMINY is specially processed kernels of corn. Corn is high in soluble fiber and is a good source of the B vitamin, folic acid and the antioxidant lutein. *See also* POPCORN.

cornbread An all-American QUICK BREAD that substitutes cornmeal for most (or sometimes all) of the flour. It can include various flavorings such as cheese, scallions, molasses and bacon. Cornbread can be thin and crisp or thick and light. It can be baked Southern style in a skillet or in a shallow square, round or rectangular baking pan. Some of the more popular cornbreads are HUSHPUPPIES, JOHNNYCAKES and SPOON BREAD.

corn dog Created in 1942 by Texan Neil Fletcher for the State Fair, a corn dog is a FRANKFURTER or other SAUSAGE dipped in a heavy cornbread batter and fried or baked. Corn dogs are often served on a stick for easy eating. *See also* HOT DOG; PIGS IN BLANKETS.

corned beef Beef (usually BRISKET, but also ROUND) CURED in a seasoned BRINE. Sometimes the brine is pumped through the arterial system. The term "corned" beef comes from the English use of the word "corn," meaning any small particle (such as a grain of salt). Two types of corned beef are available, depending on the butcher and the region. Old-fashioned corned beef is grayish-pink in color and very salty; the newer style has less salt and is a bright rosy red. Much corned beef is now being made without nitrites, which are reputed to be carcinogenic.

Cornell bread The Cornell formula to enrich bread was developed in the 1930s at New York's Cornell University. It consists of 1 tablespoon each soy flour and nonfat milk powder plus 1 teaspoon wheat germ for each cup of flour used in a bread recipe. These enrichments are placed in the bottom of the measuring cup before the flour is spooned in.

cornet [kor-NAY; kor-NEHT] French for "horn," a cornet can be any of several horn- or cone-shaped items including pastry (filled with whipped cream), a thin slice of ham (filled with cheese), or a paper cone (filled with candy or nuts).

corn flour Finely ground cornmeal, corn flour comes in yellow and white and is used for breading and in combination with other flours in baked goods. Corn flour is milled from the whole kernel, while CORN-STARCH is obtained from the endosperm portion of the kernel. In British recipes the term "cornflour" is used synonymously with the U.S. word cornstarch. MASA HARINA is a special corn flour that's the basic ingredient for corn tortillas.

corn husks These papery husks from corn are used primarily in making TAMALES, but they're also used to wrap other foods for steaming. Latin markets sell packaged corn husks, which must be softened before use. To do so, soak husks in very hot water for about 30 minutes, then drain, pat dry and use.

cornichon [KOR-nih-shoh*n*; kor-nee-SHOH*N*] French for "gherkin," cornichons are crisp, tart pickles made from tiny gherkin cucumbers. They're a traditional accompaniment to PÂTÉS as well as smoked meats and fish.

Cornish game hen *see* CHICKEN

Cornish pasty [PASS-tee] Named after Cornwall, United Kingdom, these savory TURNOVERS consist of a short-crust pastry enfolding a chopped meat-and-potato filling. Other vegetables and sometimes fish are also used. In the 18th and 19th centuries, pasties were the standard lunch of Cornwall's tin miners. It was common to place a savory mixture in one end and an apple mixture in the other so both meat and dessert could be enjoyed in the same pasty.

Cornish pepperleaf *see* MOUNTAIN PEPPER

Cornish Yarg Semihard FARMSTEAD cheese made in Cornwall, Britain, by Lynher Dairies Cheese Company. "Yarg" is not Cornish dialect but rather the backwards spelling of the last name of Alan and Jenny Gray, Welsh cheesemakers brought in to create the cheese. The Grays modified a 13th-century cheese recipe and used local nettle leaves to cover and protect the $2^1/_4$- to $6^1/_2$-pound wheels. The result is a rind with a grayish-green cast and an ivory interior. The texture is moist and crumbly, becoming creamier with age. A lemony tang adds to the mild, buttery character of the cheese. *Cornish Wild Garlic Yarg* is similar except it's covered with wild garlic leaves, which pass on an herbaceous flavor with light onion and garlic traits. *See also* CHEESE.

cornmeal Dried corn kernels that have been ground in one of three textures—fine, medium or coarse. There are two methods of grinding. The old-fashioned water-ground (also called stone-ground) method—so named because water power is used to turn the mill wheels—retains some of the hull and germ of the corn. Because of the fat in the germ, water-ground cornmeal is more nutritious, but won't keep as long and should be stored (up to 4 months) in the refrigerator. Water-ground cornmeal is available at natural food stores and some supermarkets. The newer style of milling is done by huge steel rollers that remove the husk and germ almost completely. The product can be stored almost indefinitely in an airtight container in a cool, dry place. Water-ground or stone-ground cornmeal is usually so labeled; steel-ground cornmeal rarely carries any designation on the package. Cornmeal is either yellow, white or blue, depending on the type of corn used. Yellow cornmeal has slightly more vitamin A than white. Blue cornmeal is available in specialty markets and some supermarkets. An increasing number of blue-corn products is also available, such as blue-cornmeal flakes (breakfast cereal) and chips. *See also* CORN FLOUR.

corn oil High in polyunsaturates, this odorless, almost tasteless oil is obtained from the endosperm of corn kernels. It has a high SMOKE POINT, and is therefore good for frying. It's also used in baking, for salad dressings and to make margarine. *See also* FATS AND OILS.

corn pone Extremely popular in the southern United States, corn pone is an eggless CORNBREAD that is shaped into small ovals and fried or baked.

corn salad Native to Europe, corn salad has nothing to do with corn . . . but it is used in salads. The narrow, dark green leaves of this plant are tender and have a tangy, nutlike flavor. In addition to being used as a salad green, corn salad can also be steamed and served as a vegetable. Though it's often found growing wild in American cornfields, it's considered a "gourmet" green and is therefore expensive and hard to find. It doesn't keep well and should be used within a day or two of purchase. Corn salad should be washed and drained completely of any excess moisture before being stored airtight in a plastic bag. It's also called *field salad, field lettuce, lamb's lettuce* and *mâche.*

corn smut *see* CUITLACOCHE

cornstarch A dense, powdery "flour" obtained from the endosperm portion of the corn kernel. Cornstarch is most commonly used as a thickening agent for puddings, sauces, soups, etc. Because it tends to form lumps, cornstarch is generally mixed with a small amount of cold liquid to form a thin paste before being stirred into a hot mixture. Mixing it with a granular solid like granulated sugar will also help it disperse into a liquid. Sauces thickened with cornstarch will be clear, rather than opaque, as with flour-based sauces. However, they will thin if cooked too long or stirred too vigorously. Cornstarch is also used in combination with flour in many European cake and cookie recipes; it produces a finer-textured, more compact product than flour alone. In British recipes, cornstarch is referred to as *cornflour*.

cornstick pan A rectangular cast iron baking pan with 6 to 8 molds shaped and imprinted like an ear of corn.

corn sugar *see* DEXTROSE

corn syrup A thick, sweet syrup created by processing cornstarch with acids or enzymes. Corn syrup comes in light or dark forms. **Light corn syrup** has been clarified to remove all color and cloudiness; **dark corn syrup**, which has caramel flavor and coloring added to it, has a deeper color and stronger flavor. Because it inhibits crystallization, corn syrup is particularly popular as an ingredient in frosting, candy, jams and jellies. It's also used as a pancake syrup, either maple-flavored or plain. Opened or unopened, corn syrup may be stored indefinitely at room temperature. It may also be refrigerated, though that will thicken the syrup. Over time, light corn syrup may begin to yellow, but that's not a detriment.

corn whiskey Still called *moonshine* and *white lightning* in some rural areas of the South, corn whiskey is distilled from a fermented mash of not less than 80 percent corn. It's distilled at less than 160 PROOF (80 percent alcohol). *See also* WHISKEY.

corossol [koh-rohs-SAHL] *see* SOURSOP

Cortland apple This all-purpose apple is a cross between the Ben Davis and the MCINTOSH and almost identically resembles the latter, though the Cortland is slightly larger and brighter in color. It's a vivid red with darker striping and the flavor is sweetly tart and perfumy. The flesh is juicy and crisp and doesn't brown when cut. *See also* APPLE.

corvina [kor-VEE-nuh] *see* WEAKFISH

corzetti *see* Pasta Glossary, page 883

cos lettuce [KOS] *see* ROMAINE LETTUCE

Cosmopolitan A COCKTAIL made by shaking together VODKA, COINTREAU, cranberry and lime juices and ice, then straining it into a cocktail glass, which may be rimmed with sugar.

costmary An herb belonging to the composite plant family, which includes daisies, dandelions, marigolds and sunflowers. The silvery, fragrant costmary leaves have a minty, lemony character. They're used in salads, and as a flavoring in soups, veal and chicken dishes and sausages. Costmary is also called *alecost* (because it was used in making ale), *Bible leaf* (because its long leafs were used as book markers) and *mint geranium*.

cotechino [koh-teh-KEE-noh] A specialty of several of Italy's Emilian provinces, this fresh pork SAUSAGE is quite large—usually about 3 inches in diameter and 8 to 9 inches long. It's made from pork rind and meat from the cheek, neck and shoulder, and is usually seasoned with nutmeg, cloves, salt and pepper. The best cotechino is delicately flavored and has a soft, almost creamy texture. It's a traditional ingredient in BOLLITO MISTO.

Côtes du Rhône [kot deuh ROHN] The generic APPELLATION given to red, white and rosé wines grown in an area covering 83,000 acres in France's Rhône Valley. The majority of RHÔNE WINES are red. Some of these are a deep ruby-black color, with full-bodied, concentrated flavors that benefit from at least 5 years' aging, while others are lighter and fruitier. The white Rhônes are fruity and dry and can be quite heady; the rosés can also be rather dry. Rhône wines are not made from one grape variety, but from a blend of from 2 to 13. The principal red grape is Grenache, but Carignan, Counoise, Mourvedre, Terret Noir and Syrah are also used. The white grapes used are Bourboulenc, Clairette, Marsanne, Muscardine, Picardan, Roussanne and Piquepoul (or Picpoule).

cotignac [koh-teen-YAK] *see* QUINCE

Cotija [koh-TEE-hah] A popular Mexican cheese named after Cotija de la Paz, a town in the state of Michoacán. It's made from either cow's or goat's milk and can be semisoft to very hard. Cotija, also called *Queso Añejo* or *Queso Añejado*, is very salty and is used mainly to season various Mexican-style dishes. It's now also being produced in the United States. *See also* CHEESE.

cotriade [koh-tree-AHD] From Brittany, France, *cotriade* is a fish soup made with potatoes and without shellfish. It's usually ladled over thick slices of bread.

Cotswald *see* GLOUCESTER

cottage cheese A fresh cheese made from whole, part-skimmed or skimmed PASTEURIZED cow's milk. "Sweet curd" cottage cheese—by far the most popular—has a rather mild (sometimes bland) flavor because the curds are washed to remove most of the cheese's natural acidity. The texture of cottage cheese is usually quite moist. If the curds are allowed to drain longer, pot cheese is formed; longer yet and the firm farmer's cheese is created. Cottage cheese comes in three forms: **small-curd**, **medium-curd** and **large-curd** (sometimes called "popcorn" cottage cheese). **Creamed cottage cheese** has had 4 to 8 percent cream added to it, **lowfat cottage cheese** has from 1 to 2 percent fat (check the label), and **nonfat cottage cheese** has, of course, zero fat. Cottage cheese is sold plain and flavored, the most popular additions being chives and pineapple (but not together).

Because it's more perishable than other cheeses, cartons of cottage cheese are stamped on the bottom with the date they should be pulled from the shelves. Store cottage cheese in the coldest part of the refrigerator for up to 10 days past the stamped date. *See also* CHEESE.

cottage fried potatoes *see* HOME-FRIED POTATOES

cottage pudding A dessert composed of a plain but rich cake smothered with a sweet sauce, such as lemon or chocolate.

cotton candy A fluffy, cottony confection made from long, thin SPUN SUGAR threads, which are wound onto a cardboard cone for easy eating. Cotton candy is often tinted with food coloring, most commonly pink, and is sometimes also flavored. It dates back to the early 1900s, and has been a favorite at amusement parks, county fairs and circuses ever since.

cottonseed oil A viscous oil obtained from the seed of the cotton plant. Most of the cottonseed oil produced is used in combination with other oils to create vegetable oil products. It's used in some margarines and salad dressings, and for many commercially fried products. *See also* FATS AND OILS.

cotto Italian for "cooked." *See also* SALAMI.

cou-cou *see* FUNCHE

coulibiac [koo-lee-BYAHK] This French adaptation of the Russian original (*kulebiaka*) consists of a creamy melange of fresh salmon, rice, hard-cooked eggs, mushrooms, shallots and dill enclosed in a hot pastry envelope. The pastry is usually made with BRIOCHE dough. Coulibiacs can be large or small but are classically oval in shape. They can be served as a first or main course.

coulis [koo-LEE] 1. A general term referring to a thick purée or sauce, such as a tomato *coulis.* 2. The word can also refer to thick, puréed shell-fish soups. 3. Originally, the term *coulis* was used to describe the juices from cooked meat.

country captain Now an American classic, country captain is said to have taken its name from a British army officer who brought the recipe back from his station in India. It consists of chicken, onion, tomatoes, green pepper, celery, currants, parsley, curry powder and other season-ings, all slowly cooked together over low heat in a covered skillet. The fin-ished dish is sprinkled with toasted almonds and usually served with rice.

country-cured ham Ham that has been dry-CURED in a mixture of salt, SODIUM NITRATE, sugar and other seasonings for a period of days (depending on the weight of the ham). The salt is then rinsed off and the ham is slowly smoked over hardwood fires before being aged 6 to 12 months. Most are sold uncooked, though fully cooked hams are now becoming more readily available. Country-cured ham is distinguished by its salty, well-seasoned, firm flesh. America's most famous country-cured hams come from Georgia, Kentucky, Tennessee and Virginia. *See also* HAM.

country gravy A gravy made from pan drippings, flour and milk. It can be thick to thin, depending on the amount of milk added. Country gravy is a popular accompaniment to CHICKEN-FRIED STEAK.

coupe [KOOP] Ice cream or sherbet with a topping of fruit, whipped cream and, traditionally, glazed chestnuts (MARRONS glacés). Classically, the dessert is served in a *coupe* dish, which is stemmed, and has a wide, deep bowl.

couronne de moine *see* DANDELION GREENS

court-bouillon [koor bwee-YAWN] Traditionally used for poaching fish, seafood or vegetables, a *court-bouillon* is a broth made by cooking various vegetables and herbs (usually an onion studded with a few whole cloves, celery, carrots and a BOUQUET GARNI) in water for about 30 minutes. Wine, lemon juice or vinegar may be added. The broth is allowed to cool before the vegetables are removed.

couscous; couscoussière [KOOS-koos; koos-koos-see-YEHR] A staple of North African cuisine, couscous is granular SEMOLINA. Cooked, it may be served with milk as porridge, with a dressing as a salad or sweetened and mixed with fruits for dessert. Packaged precooked couscous is available in Middle Eastern markets and large supermarkets. The name couscous also refers to the famous Maghreb dish in which semolina or cracked WHEAT is steamed in the perforated top part of a special pot called a *couscoussière,* while chunks of meat (usually lamb or chicken), various vegetables, chickpeas and raisins simmer in the bottom part. In lieu of a *couscoussière,* a colander set over a large pot will do. The cooked semolina is heaped onto a platter, with the meats and vegetables placed on top. All diners use chunks of bread to scoop the couscous from this central platter. Couscous varies from country to country—Moroccans include saffron, Algerians like to add tomatoes and Tunisians spice theirs up with the hot-pepper-based HARISSA.

coush-coush [koosh-koosh] Thick cereal-type dish that's a CAJUN breakfast specialty. It's made by stirring boiling water into a mixture of yellow cornmeal, baking powder, salt and pepper, then turning the mixture into a skillet containing preheated lard or bacon fat. During cooking, the pan becomes coated with a toasty brown crust, which is broken up and stirred into the cereal before serving. Coush-coush is served with plenty of butter, milk or cream and CANE SYRUP or sugar.

couverture [koo-vehr-TYOOR] *see* CHOCOLATE

cowberry Often found growing in pastures, the tart, red cowberry is a member of the cranberry family. It grows in northern Europe, Canada and Maine, and is used for sauces and jams. Also called *mountain cranberry*.

cowboy beans *see* FRIJOLES CHARROS

cowpea *see* BLACK-EYED PEA

cozonac *see* TSOUREKI

cozza; *pl.* **cozze** [KOHT-zah (*pl.* -zeh)] Italian for "MUSSEL."

crab Any of a large variety (over 4,000) of CRUSTACEANS with 10 legs, the front two of which have pincers, and sweet, succulent meat. There are fresh- and saltwater crabs, the latter being the most plentiful. The major catch on the Pacific coast is Dungeness crab, from the North Pacific come the king crab and snow crab, along the Atlantic and Gulf coasts it's blue crab and Florida waters give us the stone crab. **Dungeness crab**, the pride of the Pacific coast, can be found all the way from Alaska to Mexico. This large crab can range from 1 to almost 4 pounds; its pink flesh is succulent and sweet. **King crab** can measure up to 10 feet, claw to claw, and it isn't unusual for it to weigh 10 to 15 pounds. The delicately flavored meat is snowy white and edged with a beautiful bright red. It's found in the northern Pacific, and because it's most abundant around Alaska and Japan, it is also referred to as *Alaska king crab* and *Japanese king crab*. Because the species is rapidly dwindling, the king crab catch is rigidly quota-controlled. **Snow crab** is indigenous to the North Pacific and Canada's east coast and can measure up to 3 feet across. Its white flesh is tinged with pink and has a slightly salty flavor. **Blue crab** is so named because of its blue claws and dark blue-green, oval shell. It's found along the Gulf and Atlantic coasts and marketed in both its hard- and soft-shell stages. **Stone crabs** can be found along America's coast from North Carolina to Texas and is most prolific in Florida waters. Its name comes from its rocklike, oval-shape shell; only the claw meat is eaten. Because of that fact, fishermen usually simply twist off the claws and throw the crab back to grow new ones. This regeneration process can take up to 2 years of the stone crab's 10-year lifespan. Being clawless in no way inhibits the crab's feeding capabilities, because these crabs use their claws for defensive purposes only. Stone crabmeat has a firm texture and a sweet, succulent flavor. It's marketed precooked (usually frozen) because the meat has a tendency to adhere to the shell if frozen raw. **Rock crabs** and **Jonah crabs** both can be found on the northeast coast of the United States; rock crabs can also be found along the west coast. The flesh of both is white, firm, moist and sweet. **Golden crabs** are found in the south Atlantic and in the Gulf of

Mexico. They're so named because, when cooked, their shell turns a pale golden color. Their moist, delicate meat is white flecked with red. **Hardshell crabs** are available year-round in coastal areas. They're sold whole (cooked or live), and in the form of cooked lump meat (whole pieces of the white body meat) or flaked meat (small bits of light and dark meat from the body and claws). **Soft-shell crabs** are always sold whole and are in season from April to mid-September, with a peak in June and July. The term "soft-shell" describes a growth state of the crab, during which time it casts off its shell in order to grow one that's larger. Soon after the crab sheds its shell, its skin hardens into a new one. During those few days before the new shell hardens, these crustaceans are referred to as "soft-shell" crabs. In the United States, the **blue crab** is the species most commonly eaten in its soft-shell state. All live crabs should be used on the day they're purchased. Refrigerate them until just before cooking. Cook raw crabmeat within 24 hours after the crab dies. Crabmeat is also available frozen, canned or pasteurized (heated in cans at a temperature high enough to kill bacteria, but lower than that used in canning). Pasteurized crabmeat should be stored unopened in the refrigerator for up to 6 months and used within 4 days of opening. Whole crabs and crabmeat can be cooked in a variety of ways including frying, steaming, broiling or in soups, GUMBOS or CRAB CAKES. Crab ROE, available only in the spring, is a prized addition to the South Carolina specialty, SHE-CRAB SOUP. *See also* CRAB BOIL; CRAB IMPERIAL; CRAB LOUIS; OYSTER CRAB; SHELLFISH; SURIMI.

crabapple A small, rosy red apple with a rather hard, extremely tart flesh. Crabapples, available during the fall and early winter months, are too sour for out-of-hand eating but make outstanding jellies and jams. Spiced and canned whole, they're a delicious accompaniment for meats such as pork and poultry. *See also* APPLE.

crab boil Sold packaged in supermarkets and specialty markets, crab boil (also called *fish boil* and *shrimp boil*) is a mixture of herbs and spices added to water in which crab, shrimp or lobster is cooked. The blend can include mustard seeds, peppercorns, bay leaves, whole allspice and cloves, dried ginger pieces and red chiles.

crab cake A mixture of lump crabmeat, breadcrumbs, milk, egg, scallions and various seasonings, formed into small cakes and fried until crisp and golden brown.

crab imperial A classic American dish of crabmeat combined with mayonnaise or a sherried white sauce, spooned into blue-crab or scallop shells, sprinkled with Parmesan cheese or breadcrumbs and baked until golden brown.

crab Louis; crab Louie [LOO-ee] A cold dish in which lump crabmeat on a bed of shredded lettuce is topped with a dressing of mayonnaise, CHILI SAUCE, cream, scallions, green pepper, lemon juice and seasonings. The crab can be garnished with a quartered tomato and hard-cooked egg. Credit for the origin of crab Louis depends on to whom you talk. Some attribute this dish to the chef at Seattle's Olympic Club, while others say it was created in San Francisco—either by the chef at Solari's restaurant or the one at the St. Francis Hotel. Whatever the case, today there are about as many versions of this favorite as there are cooks.

cracked wheat *see* WHEAT

cracklings Delicious, crunchy pieces of either pork or poultry fat after it has been RENDERED, or the crisp, brown skin of fried or roasted pork. Cracklings are sold packaged in some supermarkets and specialty markets. "Cracklin' bread" is cornbread with bits of cracklings scattered throughout.

cranberry These shiny scarlet berries are grown in huge, sandy bogs on low, trailing vines. They're also called *bounceberries,* because ripe ones bounce, and *craneberries,* after the shape of the shrub's pale pink blossoms, which resemble the heads of the cranes often seen wading through the cranberry bogs. Cranberries grow wild in northern Europe and in the northern climes of North America, where they are also extensively cultivated—mainly in Massachusetts, Wisconsin, Washington and Oregon. Harvested between Labor Day and Halloween, the peak market period for cranberries is from October through December. They're usually packaged in 12-ounce plastic bags. Any cranberries that are discolored or shriveled should be discarded. Cranberries can be refrigerated, tightly wrapped, for at least 2 months or frozen up to a year. Besides the traditional cranberry sauce, this fruit also makes delicious CHUTNEYS, pies, COBBLERS and other desserts. Because of their extreme tartness, cranberries are best combined with other fruits, such as apples or dried apricots. Canned cranberry sauce—jelled and whole-berry—is available year-round, as are frozen cranberries in some markets. Sweetened dried cranberries, which can be used like raisins in baked goods or as snacks, are also available in most supermarkets. Fresh cranberries are very high in vitamin C.

cranberry bean Also called *shell bean* or *shellout,* and known as *borlotti bean* in Italy, the cranberry bean has a large, knobby beige pod splotched with red. The beans inside are cream-colored with red streaks and have a delicious nutlike flavor. Cranberry beans must be shelled before cooking. Heat diminishes their beautiful red color. They're available fresh in the summer and dried throughout the year. *See also* BEANS.

Cranshaw melon *see* CRENSHAW MELON

crappie Found mainly in the Great Lakes and Mississippi regions, crappies are large, freshwater sunfish that are about 12 inches long and range from 1 to 2 pounds. There are both black and white crappies; the latter is also called *chinquapin*. Crappies have lean flesh that is particularly suited to broiling or sautéing. *See also* FISH.

crawfish; crawdad *see* CRAYFISH

crayfish Any of various freshwater CRUSTACEANS that resemble tiny lobsters, complete with claws. Other coastal crustaceans (such as spiny or rock lobster) are sometimes mistakenly called *saltwater crayfish*. They are not, however, of the same species. Crayfish range from 3 to 6 inches long and weigh from 2 to 8 ounces. They're very popular in France (where they're called *écrevisses*), Australia (*yabbys* or *yabbies*), Scandinavia and parts of the United States—particularly Louisiana, where they're known as *crawfish* and *crawdads*. The great majority of the U.S. harvest comes from the waters of the Mississippi basin, and many Louisianans call their state the "crawfish capital of the world." Crayfish can be prepared in most manners appropriate for lobster and, like lobster, turn red when cooked. They're usually eaten with the fingers, and the sweet, succulent meat must be picked or sucked out of the tiny shells. *See also* SHELLFISH.

cream *n.* Upon standing, unhomogenized MILK naturally separates into two layers—a MILK FAT–rich cream on top, and almost fat-free (or skimmed) milk on the bottom. Commercially, the cream is separated from the milk by centrifugal force. Almost all cream that reaches the market today has been PASTEURIZED. There are many varieties of cream, all categorized according to the amount of milk fat in the mixture. **Light cream**, also called **coffee** or **table cream**, can contain anywhere from 18 to 30 percent fat, but commonly contains 20 percent. **Light whipping cream**, the form most commonly available, contains 30 to 36 percent milk fat and sometimes stabilizers and emulsifiers. **Heavy cream**, also called **heavy whipping cream**, is whipping cream with a milk fat content of between 36 and 40 percent. It's usually only available in specialty or gourmet markets. Whipping cream will double in volume when whipped. **Half-and-half** is a mixture of equal parts milk and cream, and is 10 to 12 percent milk fat. Neither half-and-half nor light cream can be whipped. **Nonfat half-and-half**, an oxymoronically named product that combines nonfat milk with corn syrup and thickeners, has half the calories and twice the sodium of real half-and-half. **Ultrapasteurized cream**, seen more and more in markets today, has been briefly heated at temperatures up to 300°F to kill microorganisms that cause milk products to sour. It has a longer shelf life than regular cream, but it doesn't whip as well and it has a slight "cooked" flavor. All other cream is highly perishable and should be kept in the coldest part of the refrigerator. **Pressurized whipped**

cream, contained in cans under pressure, is a mixture of cream, sugar, stabilizers, emulsifiers and gas, such as nitrous oxide. It's not really "whipped" but, more aptly, expanded by the gas into a puffy form. Aerosol "dessert toppings," which are usually made with hydrogenated vegetable oils, have absolutely no cream in them. . . and taste like it. Read the label—the fat content of real cream mixtures must be indicated on the product label. *See also* CLOTTED CREAM; CRÈME FRAÎCHE; SOUR CREAM. **cream** *v.* To beat an ingredient or combination of ingredients until the mixture is soft, smooth and "creamy." Often a recipe calls for creaming a fat, such as butter, or creaming a mixture of butter and sugar. When creaming two or more ingredients together, the result should be a smooth, homogeneous mixture that shows neither separation nor evidence of any particles (such as sugar). Electric mixers and food processors make quick work of what used to be a laborious, time-consuming process.

cream cheese Thanks to American ingenuity, cream cheese was developed in 1872 by William Lawrence, a Chester, New York, dairyman. The appellation comes from the smooth, creamy texture of this mildly tangy, spreadable cheese. The soft, unripened cheese is made from cow's milk and by law must contain at least 33 percent MILK FAT and not more than 55 percent moisture. For improved firmness and increased shelf life, most cream cheese has added stabilizers, usually a combination of ingredients such as CARRAGEENAN, GUAR GUM and XANTHAN GUM. American **neufchatel cheese** (not to be confused with the French NEUFCHÂTEL) is slightly lower in calories because of a lower milk fat content (about 23 percent). It also contains slightly more moisture. **Reduced fat cream cheese** has a milk fat content of between 16.5 and 20 percent, **light or lowfat cream cheese** can have no more than 16.5 percent milk fat and **nonfat cream cheese** has zero fat grams. The easily spreadable **whipped cream cheese** has been made soft and fluffy by air being whipped into it. It has fewer calories per serving than regular cream cheese only because there's less volume per serving. Cream cheese is sometimes sold mixed with other ingredients such as herbs, spices or fruit. Refrigerate cream cheese, tightly wrapped, and use within a week after opening. If any mold develops on the surface, discard the cream cheese. *See also* CHEESE; CREOLE CREAM CHEESE.

creamline milk *see* MILK

cream of coconut A thick, intensely sweet mixture of coconut paste, water and sugar, used in drinks like PIÑA COLADA and commonly available in supermarkets and liquor stores.

cream of tartar A fine white powder derived from a crystalline acid deposited on the inside of wine barrels. Cream of tartar is added to candy and frosting mixtures for a creamier consistency, and to egg whites before beating to improve stability and volume. It's also used as the acid ingredient in some baking powders.

cream puff A small, hollow puff made from CHOUX PASTRY (cream-puff pastry) filled with sweetened whipped cream or custard.

cream-puff paste; cream-puff pastry *see* CHOUX PASTRY

cream sauce A classic BÉCHAMEL made with milk and sometimes cream. The sauce's thickness depends on the proportion of flour to liquid. Cream sauces are used as a base for many dishes, such as chicken À LA KING. *See also* SAUCE.

cream tea Also called *Devonshire tea,* this British custom is an afternoon refresher of hot tea served with various accompaniments—almost always SCONES and CLOTTED CREAM and jam, and often other tidbits such as crustless cucumber or watercress sandwiches. *See also* HIGH TEA.

Crécy, à la [KREH-see; kray-SEE] A French term referring to dishes cooked or garnished with carrots. The name comes from Crécy, France, where the finest French carrots are cultivated.

crema [KREH-mah] 1. Italian for "CREAM." A dish served **"alla crema"** is with a cream sauce; **crema caramella** [kah-rah-MEH-lah] is a dessert (*see* CRÈME CARAMEL); **crema inglese** [een-GLEH-she] is a creamy dessert sauce (*see* CRÈME ANGLAISE); **crema pasticceria** [pah-stee-cheh-REE-ah] is pastry cream (*see* CRÈME PATISSIÈRE). 2. The word *crema* is also used to describe the creamy, buff-colored froth on the surface of an ESPRESSO. 3. In Mexican cookery, *crema* is akin to CRÈME FRAÎCHE, although somewhat thinner in consistency. It's typically used as a garnish drizzled over ENCHILADAS, BURRITOS and other such dishes.

crema caramella *see* CRÈME CARAMEL

Crema Dania; Crema Danica [KREHM-uh DAHN-yuh; DAHN-uh-kuh] Denmark gives us this exceedingly rich cheese in the form of small rectangles with a white downy rind and soft ivory interior. Crema Dania is a rich TRIPLE-CREAM CHEESE with 72 percent milk fat. *See also* CHEESE.

crema de membrillo [KREH-mah day mem-BREE-yoh] *see* QUINCE

crème [KREHM] The French word for "cream."

crème anglaise [krehm ahn-GLEHZ; krehm ahn-GLAYZ] The French term for a rich custard sauce that can be served hot or cold over cake, fruit or other dessert. *See also* SAUCE.

crème brûlée [krehm broo-LAY] The literal translation of this rich dessert is "burnt cream." It describes a chilled, stirred CUSTARD that, just before serving, is sprinkled with brown or granulated sugar. The sugar topping is quickly caramelized under a broiler or with a SALAMANDER. The caramelized topping becomes brittle, creating a delicious flavor and textural contrast to the smooth, creamy custard beneath.

crème caramel [krehm kehr-ah-MEHL; krem KAR-uh-mehl] Also known in France as *crème renversée,* crème caramel is a CUSTARD that has been baked in a CARAMEL-coated mold. When the chilled custard is turned out onto a serving plate it is automatically glazed and sauced with the caramel in the mold. In Italy it's known as *crema caramella,* and in Spain as *flan.*

crème chantilly *see* CHANTILLY

crème Chiboust [krehm shee-BOO] crème pâtissière lightened with ITALIAN MERINGUE. Crème Chiboust is most often flavored with vanilla, but other flavor variations can be used. It was created in the mid-1800s by a French pastry chef named Chiboust to fill his SAINT-HONORÉ and is also called *Crème Saint-Honoré* and simply *Chiboust.*

crème d'abricots [krehm dah-bree-KOH] A sweet apricot LIQUEUR.

crème d'amande [krehm dah-MAHND] A pink, almond-flavored LIQUEUR.

crème d'ananas [krehm dah-nah-NAHS] Pineapple-flavored LIQUEUR.

crème de [KREHM deuh] A French phrase meaning "cream of," and used to describe an intensely sweet LIQUEUR.

crème de banane [krehm deuh bah-NAHN] A sweet LIQUEUR with a full, ripe banana flavor.

crème de cacao [krehm deuh kah-KAH-oh] A dark, chocolate-flavored LIQUEUR with a hint of vanilla. White crème de cacao is a clear form of the same liqueur.

crème de cassis [krehm deuh kah-SEES] Black currant-flavored LIQUEUR; an integral ingredient in KIR.

crème de cerise [krehm deuh sehr-EEZ] A French cherry-flavored LIQUEUR.

crème de menthe [krehm deuh MENTH; MAHNT] Tasting of cool summer mint, this LIQUEUR comes clear (called white) or green-colored.

crème de noyaux [krehm deuh nwah-YOH] The word *noyaux* is French for "fruit pits," and this sweet pink LIQUEUR is flavored with the pits of various fruits. The resulting flavor is that of almonds.

crème de rose [krehm deuh ROSE] An exotically scented LIQUEUR flavored with rose petals, vanilla and various spices.

crème de violette [krehm deuh VEE-oh-leht; vyoh-LEHT] Dutch LIQUEUR, amethyst in color, perfumed and flavored with ESSENCE of violets.

crème diplomat [KREHM dih-ploh-MAH] CRÈME PÂTISSIÈRE with an equal amount of whipped cream folded into it. Crème diplomat, also called *diplomat cream*, is lighter in flavor and texture than crème pâtissière. It's used to fill various French pastries.

crème fraîche [krehm FRESH] This matured, thickened cream has a slightly tangy, nutty flavor and velvety rich texture. The thickness of crème fraîche can range from that of commercial sour cream to almost as solid as room-temperature margarine. In France, where crème fraîche is a specialty, the cream is unpasteurized and therefore contains the bacteria necessary to thicken it naturally. In America, where all commercial cream is PASTEURIZED, the fermenting agents necessary for crème fraîche can be obtained by adding buttermilk or sour cream. A very expensive American facsimile of crème fraîche is sold in some gourmet markets. The expense seems frivolous, however, when it's so easy to make an equally delicious version at home. To do so, combine 1 cup whipping cream and 2 tablespoons buttermilk in a glass container. Cover and let stand at room temperature (about 70°F) from 8 to 24 hours, or until very thick. Stir well before covering and refrigerate up to 10 days. Crème fraîche is the ideal addition for sauces or soups because it can be boiled without curdling. It's delicious spooned over fresh fruit or other desserts such as warm cobblers or puddings.

crème pâtissière [KREHM pah-tee-see-EHR] The French term for "pastry cream," a thick, flour-based egg CUSTARD used for tarts, cakes and to fill CREAM PUFFS, ÉCLAIRS and NAPOLEONS.

crème pralinée [KREHM prah-lee-NAY] CRÈME PÂTISSIÈRE flavored with PRALINE powder and used to fill various French pastries.

crème renversée [KREHM rahn-vehr-SAY] *see* CRÈME CARAMEL

crème Saint-Honoré *see* CRÈME CHIBOUST

cremino; *pl.* **cremini** [kray-MEE-noh; kray-MEE-nee] A dark-brown, slightly firmer variation of the everyday cultivated white mushroom. Cremini have a slightly fuller flavor than their paler relatives. They have a smooth, rounded cap that ranges in size from $1/2$ to 2 inches in diameter. The PORTOBELLO MUSHROOM is the fully matured form of this mushroom. The cremino is also referred to as *common brown mushroom* and *Roman mushroom*. *See also* MUSHROOM.

Crenshaw melon; Cranshaw melon Considered one of the most sweetly succulent members of the melon family, the Crenshaw is a hybrid of the CASABA and CANTALOUPE. It has a golden-green, smooth yet lightly ribbed rind and a beautiful salmon-orange flesh. The fragrance of a ripe Crenshaw melon is seductively spicy. These melons are large (5 to 9 pounds) with an oval shape that's rounded at the blossom end and slightly pointed at the stem end. They're available from July to October, with the peak season from August to mid-September. *See also* MELON.

Creole cooking [KREE-ohl] In the 18th century, the Spaniards governing New Orleans named all residents of European heritage *Criollo.* The name, which later became *Creole,* soon began to imply one of refined cultural background with an appreciation for an elegant lifestyle. Today, Creole cookery reflects the full-flavored combination of the best of French, Spanish and African cuisines. Its style, with an emphasis on butter and cream, is more sophisticated than CAJUN COOKING (which uses prodigious amounts of pork fat). Another difference between the two cuisines is that Creole uses more tomatoes and the Cajuns more spices. Both cuisines rely on the culinary "holy trinity" of chopped green peppers, onions and celery, and make generous use of FILÉ POWDER. Probably the most famous dish of Creole heritage is GUMBO.

Creole cream cheese [KREE-ohl] This southern Louisiana specialty has been produced since the 1800s. It's typically a mixture of PASTEURIZED (usually skimmed) cow's-milk CURDS and half & half cream. Depending on the producer, the texture of Creole cream cheese can vary from that of a very thick sour cream to whole soft curds nestled in sour cream. This specialty is used as a topping or, especially by southern Louisianans, eaten for breakfast with salt and pepper or sugar and fruit. Creole cream cheese may be carried in some gourmet markets but is generally available outside Louisiana only through the Internet or mail order.

Creole mustard [KREE-ohl] A specialty of Louisiana's German Creoles made from vinegar-marinated brown mustard seeds with a hint of horseradish. This hot, spicy mustard is available in gourmet markets or the gourmet section of some supermarkets.

crêpe [KRAYP; KREHP] The French word for "pancake," which is exactly what these light, paper-thin creations are. They can be made from plain or sweetened batters with various flours, and used for savory or dessert dishes. Dessert crêpes may be spread with a jam or fruit mixture, rolled or folded and sometimes flamed with brandy or liqueur. Savory crêpes are filled with various meat, cheese or vegetable mixtures—sometimes topped with a complementary sauce—and served as a first or main course.

crêpes suzette [KRAYPS (KREHPS) soo-ZEHT] Prepared in a CHAFING DISH, this illustrious dessert consists of an orange-butter sauce in which CRÊPES are warmed, then doused with GRAND MARNIER (or other orange LIQUEUR) and ignited to flaming glory.

crépinette [kray-pih-NEHT; kray-pee-NEHT] French in origin, this small, slightly flattened SAUSAGE is made of minced pork, lamb, veal or chicken and sometimes truffles. *Crépine* is French for "pig's caul," in which a crépinette is wrapped instead of a CASING. Crépinettes are usually cooked by coating them in melted butter and breadcrumbs before sautéing, grilling or broiling.

crescent cutter *see* MEZZALUNA

Crescenza [krih-SHEHN-zuh] A rich, creamy, fresh cheese, also known as *Crescenza Stracchino,* that's widely made in Italy's regions of Lombardy, Piedmont and Veneto. Its texture and flavor are similiar to that of a mild CREAM CHEESE, and it becomes very soft and spreadable at room temperature. Crescenza is made from uncooked cow's milk and is sometimes blended with herbs. It doesn't have a long shelf life and should be eaten within a few days. Crescenza can be found in some specialty cheese shops. It has a FAT CONTENT of approximately 50 percent. *See also* CHEESE.

crespelle [krehs-PEHL-leh] Thin Italian pancakes that are either stacked with different fillings between the layers or filled and rolled like CRÊPES.

cress There are many different varieties of this mustard-family plant, the most popular of which is WATERCRESS. Other types include **peppergrass** (also called *curly cress*), **broadleaf cress** (also called *cressida*) and **garden cress**. All cress varieties share a peppery tang. Choose cress with dark green leaves and no sign of yellowing. Refrigerate in a plastic bag (or stems-down in a glass of water covered with a plastic bag) for up to 5 days. Cress is used in salads, sandwiches, soups and as a garnish.

creste di galli *see* Pasta Glossary, page 883

crevette [kruh-VEHT] The French word for "shrimp."

crimp 1. To pinch or press two pastry edges together, thereby sealing the dough while forming a decorative edge with fingers, fork or other utensil. The pastry for a single-crust pie is crimped by turning it under to form a ridge, then shaping (or *fluting*) the raised edge into a fancy pattern. A raised crimped edge not only seals the pastry but acts like a dam to contain the filling during cooking. 2. To cut gashes at 1- or 2-inch intervals along both sides of a freshly caught fish. The fish is then soaked in ice water for up to an hour. Crimping a fish creates a firmer-textured flesh and skin that quickly becomes crisp when cooked.

crisp *v.* To refresh vegetables such as celery and carrots by soaking them in ice water until they once again become crisp. Other foods, such as crackers that have lost their snap, may be heated in a moderate oven until their crispness returns. **crisp** *n.* A dessert of fruit topped with a crumbly, sweet pastry mixture and baked until browned and crisp.

crisphead lettuce One of two varieties of head lettuce (the other being BUTTERHEAD). It's commonly known as **iceberg**, which, in truth, is a variety of crisphead. Other varieties include **Great Lakes**, **Imperial**, **Vanguard** and **Western**. Crisphead lettuce comes in large, round, tightly packed heads of pale green leaves. Though crisp, succulent and wilt-resistant, all crispheads have a rather neutral flavor. Choose those that are heavy for their size with no signs of browning at the edges. *See also* LETTUCE.

criterion apple An all-purpose apple with a bright yellow skin blushed with red and a shape similar to that of an elongated RED DELICIOUS APPLE. The moderately sweet flesh is crisp and resists browning. *See also* APPLE.

croaker *see* DRUM

crockpot *see* SLOW COOKER

croissant [kwah-SAHN; KWAH-sawn; kruh-SAHNT] The origin of this flaky, buttery-rich yeast roll dates back to 1686, when Austria was at war with Turkey. In the dead of night a group of bakers, hearing Turks tunneling under their kitchens, spread the alarm that subsequently led to the Turkish defeat. In turn, the vigilant bakers were awarded the privilege of creating a commemorative pastry in the shape of the crescent on the Turkish flag. *Croissant* is the French word for "crescent." Originally, the croissant was made from a rich bread dough. It wasn't until the early 1900s that a creative French baker had the inspiration to make it with a dough similar to puff pastry . . . and so a classic was born. Croissants can be made with buttered layers of yeast dough or puff pastry. They're sometimes stuffed (such as with a stick of chocolate or cheese) before being rolled into a crescent shape and baked. Croissants are generally thought of as breakfast pastries but can also be used for sandwiches and meal accompaniments.

crookneck squash Any of several varieties of summer squash with a long, curved neck that is slightly more slender than the base.

Crooknecks have a light to deep yellow skin that can range in texture from almost smooth when quite young to slightly bumpy as the squash matures. The creamy-yellow flesh has a mild, delicate flavor. Crooknecks average from 8 to 10 inches long, but are best when a youthful 6 inches. Choose firm squash with no sign of shriveling; the skin should be easily pierced with a fingernail. *See also* SQUASH.

croonack; crooner *see* GURNARD

croquant [kroh-KAW*N*] French for "crispy" or "crunchy."

croque madame [KROHK mah-DAHM] In France, this is a CROQUE MONSIEUR (toasted ham and cheese sandwich) with the addition of a fried egg. In Britain and America, a croque madame simply substitutes sliced chicken for the ham, with no sign of an egg.

croquembouche [kroh-kuhm-BOOSH] French for "crisp in mouth," this elaborate dessert is classically made with PROFITEROLES (tiny, custard-filled cream puffs), coated with CARAMEL and stacked into a tall pyramid shape. As the caramel hardens, it becomes crisp. For added glamour, the croquembouche can be wreathed or draped with SPUN SUGAR.

croque monsieur [KROHK muhs-YOOR] A French-style grilled ham and cheese sandwich that is dipped into beaten egg before being sautéed in butter. Croque monsieur is sometimes made in a special sandwich-grilling iron consisting of two hinged metal plates, each with two shell-shaped indentations. *See also* CROQUE MADAME.

croquette [kroh-KEHT] A mixture of minced meat or vegetables, a thick white sauce and seasonings that is formed into small cylinders, ovals or rounds, dipped in beaten egg and then breadcrumbs, and deep-fried until crisp and brown.

crosnes [krohn] Although this plant is native to China and Japan (which is why it's also called *Chinese artichoke* and *Japanese artichoke),* its name hails from Crosnes, France, where it was first cultivated after the French began importing it from China in the late 19th century. It's also known as *chorogi, Crosnes du Japon* and *knotroot.* Crosnes are small tubers that resemble ivory-colored caterpillars. They have a sweet, nutty flavor similar to that of a SUNCHOKE. Though rarely available in the United States, they can sometimes be found in specialty produce markets in the winter. Purchase those that are firm and light colored. Refrigerate in an open bowl for up to a week. Before using, scrub crosnes with a vegetable brush. They can be eaten raw, or boiled, baked or steamed. *See also* ARTI-CHOKE.

cross; crossing *n.* A fruit or vegetable created by breeding two varieties of the same plant family. For example, GOLDEN DELICIOUS and JONATHAN apples can be bred but tomatoes and watermelons cannot. Crosses are created in an effort to produce a plant with the best traits of its parents, such as better flavor or texture, high productivity, disease resistance or better adaptability to environmental conditions. **Cross** *v.* The act of creating or breeding a cross from members of the same species.

crostini [kroh-STEE-nee] 1. Meaning "little toasts" in Italian, crostini are small, thin slices of toasted bread, which are usually brushed with olive oil. 2. The word also describes CANAPÉS consisting of small slices of toast with a savory topping such as cheese, shrimp, pâté or anchovies. 3. Sometimes crostini refers to the equivalent of a CROUTON used for soups or salads.

croustade [kroo-STAHD] An edible container used to hold a thick stew, creamed meat, vegetable mixture and so on. A croustade can be made from pastry, a hollowed-out bread loaf or puréed potatoes or pasta that have been shaped to hold food. Before filling it with food, the container is deep-fried or toasted until golden-brown and crisp. Small filled croustades can be served as an appetizer or first course.

croûte [KROOT] French for "crust," *croûte* generally describes a thick, hollowed-out slice of bread (usually toasted) that is filled with food. It can also refer to a pastry case used for the same purpose. Additionally, the word *croûte* describes simply a slice of bread either toasted or fried. For example, *croûte landaise* is fried bread with FOIE GRAS topped with a cheese sauce. **En croûte** describes a food (usually partially cooked) that is wrapped in pastry and baked.

crouton [KROO-tawn] A small piece or cube of bread that has been browned, either by sautéing or baking. Croutons are used to garnish soups, salads and other dishes. They're available packaged either plain or seasoned with herbs, cheese, garlic and so on.

crown roast This special-occasion roast is formed from the rib section of lamb or pork LOIN by tying it into a circle, ribs up. After it's cooked, the tips of the bones are often decorated with paper FRILLS. The roast's hollow center section is usually filled with mixed vegetables or other stuffing.

cruciferous vegetables [krew-SIH-fer-uhs] The scientific name for a group of vegetables that research has proven may provide protection against certain cancers. Cruciferous vegetables contain ANTIOXIDANTS (BETA CAROTENE and the compound sulforaphane). These vegetables, which are all high in fiber, vitamins and minerals, are: broccoli, Brussels sprouts, cabbage, cauliflower, chard, kale, mustard greens, rutabagas and turnips.

crudités [kroo-dee-TAY] Often served as an appetizer, crudités are raw seasonal vegetables, frequently accompanied with a dipping sauce, such as BAGNA CAUDA.

crudo [KROO-doh] Italian for "uncooked," referring to raw food.

cruller [KRUHL-uhr] A doughnut-style dough (usually LEAVENED with baking powder) that's shaped into a long twist, fried and sprinkled with granulated sugar or brushed with a sweet glaze. The extremely light **French cruller** is made with CHOUX PASTRY (cream-puff dough). The word "cruller" comes from the Dutch *krulle,* meaning "twisted cake."

crumble *n.* A British dessert in which raw fruit is topped with a crumbly pastry mixture and baked. **crumble** *v.* To break food up (usually with the fingers) into small pieces, such as "crumbled" bacon.

crumpet [KRUHM-piht] Hailing from the British Isles, crumpets are small, yeast-raised breads about the size of an English muffin. They're made in **crumpet rings** (also called ENGLISH MUFFIN rings), which are 4 inches in diameter and about 1 inch deep. The rings are made of stainless steel and typically sold in packages of four at gourmet kitchenware shops. If you can't find them, substitute scrupulously clean 6¹/₈-ounce tuna cans with tops and bottoms removed. The unsweetened crumpet batter is poured into the crumpet rings (which have been arranged on a griddle), then "baked" on a stovetop. The finished crumpet has a smooth, brown bottom and a top riddled with tiny holes. Crumpets are toasted whole (unlike English muffins, which are split) and spread with butter or CLOTTED CREAM and jam, as desired.

crush To reduce a food to its finest form, such as crumbs, paste or powder. Crushing is often accomplished with a MORTAR AND PESTLE, or with a rolling pin.

crust This multipurpose word has many meanings, including the hardened outer layer of a cooked food such as bread; a thin layer of pastry covering or encasing a pie, pâté, etc.; and the sediment of organic salts deposited in a bottle of aged red wine.

crusta A COCKTAIL made with BRANDY (or other liquor), lemon juice, COINTREAU and MARASCHINO LIQUEUR. It was invented in the mid-1800s by the owner of Santina's Saloon in New Orleans. This drink's distinctive style comes from a sugar-rimmed glass and long citrus-peel spiral that drapes over the glass edge.

crustacean [kruh-STAY-shuhn] One of two main classifications of SHELLFISH (the other being MOLLUSK), crustaceans have elongated bodies and jointed, soft (crustlike) shells. The crustacean family includes BARNA-CLES, CRAB, CRAYFISH, LOBSTER, PRAWN and SHRIMP.

crystallized flowers; crystallized fruit *see* CANDIED FRUIT AND FLOWERS

csipetke *see* GOULASH

cuaje [KWAH-hee] *see* GUAJE

Cuarenta Y Tres [kwah-RAYN-tah ee TRAYSS] Spanish for "43," this LIQUEUR is so named because it's purportedly made from 43 different ingredients. It's bright yellow in color, extremely sweet and viscous and has a vanilla-citrus flavor. Also called *Licor 43*.

Cuba libre [KYOO-buh LEE-bruh; KYOO-buh LEE-bray] An iced COCK-TAIL made with rum, lime juice and cola.

Cubanelle *see* SWEET PEPPERS

cube 1. To cut food (such as meat or cheese) into $1/2$-inch cubes. Cubes of food are larger than diced or mirepoix. 2. A term also used to describe tenderizing meat with an instrument that leaves cube-shaped imprints on the surface (*see* CUBE STEAK).

cubeb [KYOO-behb] Historically, a cheaper alternative to black pepper (*see* PEPPERCORN). As the price of black pepper dropped, however, the use of cubeb diminished to the point that, until recently, it hadn't been seen much in the West. Cubebs, which are related to peppercorns, are the berries of a tropical vine found on various Indonesian islands, particularly Java—hence its alternate name, *Java pepper*. They're also called *tailed peppers* because the dark brown dried berries, which are slightly bigger than peppercorns, have a short tail—part of the vine that's left attached. Cubebs are still used in Indonesian cooking and some Middle Eastern spice mixtures, and they're starting to generate renewed curiosity in the West because of their flavor, which is somewhat hotter than standard black pepper and augmented with hints of allspice and cloves. They are available through Internet spice vendors. *See also* SPICES; Seasoning Suggestions, page 891.

cube steak A flavorful cut of beef taken from the top or bottom ROUND and tenderized (or cubed) by running it through a butcher's tenderizing machine once or twice. Cube steak would be too tough to eat without being tenderized.

cucumber Believed to have originated in either India or Thailand, the cucumber has been cultivated for thousands of years. This long, cylindrical, green-skinned fruit of the gourd family has edible seeds surrounded by a mild, crisp flesh. The thin skin, unless waxed, does not require peeling. Cucumbers are usually eaten raw, as in salads. The smaller cucumber varieties are used for pickles. As a cucumber matures, the seeds grow larger and more bitter. Therefore, the seeds of an older cucumber should be removed before it's used. The more expensive **English** (or **hothouse**) **cucumber** can grow up to 2 feet long and is virtually seedless and purportedly burpless. They're marketed shrink-wrapped in plastic. Cucumbers are available year-round, with the peak crop from May to August. Choose firm fruit with smooth, brightly colored skins; avoid those with shriveled or soft spots. Store whole cucumbers, unwashed, in a plastic bag in the refrigerator up to 10 days. Wash thoroughly just before using. Cut cucumbers can be refrigerated, tightly wrapped, for up to 5 days.

cucuzza; *pl.* **cucuzze** [KOO-koot-zah; *pl.* -zeh] 1. Vegetable that belongs to the gourd family but is often grown and harvested young so it's handled like summer squash (*see* SQUASH). If allowed to mature, it forms a hard exterior, is often referred to as *bottle gourd* and is used as a container and for other purposes, such as musical or percussion instruments. The skin of a young cucuzza is pale green and the flesh is white. It comes in many shapes and sizes, including some that grow to 3 feet or more. It can be prepared like zucchini, although the skin can be tough and should be peeled. It's grown in various parts of the world and goes by many names including *calabash*, *long melon*, *New Guinea bean*, *opo*, *Serpent of Sicily*, *suzza melon*, *Tasmania bean* and *zuzza*. The vegetable known as *snake gourd* is very similar but a different variety. 2. In some parts of Italy, cucuzza is a generic name for squash.

cueritos; cueritos en vinagre [KWEH-ree-tohs] Mexican name for pickled pork skin. There are two types: *cueritos grueso* ("thick") made from the ears, face and feet, and *cueritos delgado* ("thin") made from the main body.

cuisine [kwih-ZEEN; kwee-ZEEN] A French term pertaining to a specific style of cooking (as in Chinese cuisine), or a country's food in general. **Haute cuisine** refers to food prepared in a gourmet or elaborate manner.

cuisine, haute *see* HAUTE CUISINE

cuisine bourgeoise [kwih-ZEEN boor-ZHWAHZ] French for "middle-class cooking," referring to plain but good, down-to-earth cooking.

cuisine maigre [kwih-ZEEN may-GREH] French for "meatless, lean or lowfat cooking." Strict vegetarian cooking is referred to as *cuisine vegetarienne*.

cuisine minceur [kwee-ZEEN man-SEUR] Developed by French chef Michel Guérard in the 1970s, *cuisine minceur* is light-style, healthful cooking that avoids fat and cream.

cuitlacoche [wheet-lah-KOH-chay] Also called *corn smut, maize mushroom* and *huitlacoche,* this gourmet rage is actually a bulbous fungus (technically known as *Ustilago maydis*) that attacks ears of corn and makes the kernels swell to 10 times their normal size. The corn's color turns an ugly medium- to dark-gray verging on black. Although most U.S. farmers consider it a plague and destroy infected ears, the Aztecs are said to have prized cuitlacoche (in Nahuatl *cuitlatl* means "excrement," *cochi* means "black"). Enthusiasts say that cuitlacoche has a smoky-sweet flavor that's a cross between that of corn and mushroom. Cuitlacoche is currently being cultivated in limited quantities in California, Florida, Georgia and Virginia. It's sold canned and frozen in some gourmet markets. It can occasionally be found in specialty produce and farmer's markets (during corn season) and can also be purchased by mail order. Cuitlacoche is used in a variety of dishes including sautés, soups, casseroles—in general, any preparation where cooked mushrooms would be appropriate.

culantro *see* SAW-LEAF HERB

culatello [koo-lah-TEHL-oh] Hailing from Parma and made by the same masters that produce PROSCIUTTO di Parma, culatello is made from the hog's leg. It's salt-cured for 3 days, tenderized by massage and aged for at least 11 months. This distinctively pear-shaped ham is lean and rosy red and has a delicately sweet, clean flavor. Culatello di Zibello, which is traditionally produced in the territory adjacent to the River Po, is distinguished by a PROTECTED DESIGNATION OF ORIGIN designation. Culatello is often served as part of an ANTIPASTO platter. *See also* HAM.

Cumberland sauce A favorite with the English, this full-flavored sauce is a combination of red currant jelly, PORT, orange and lemon ZESTS, mustard and seasonings. It's excellent served with venison, duck and other game. *See also* SAUCE.

cumin [KUH-mihn; KYOO-mihn; KOO-mihn] Also called *comino,* this ancient spice dates back to the Old Testament. Shaped like a caraway seed, cumin is the dried fruit of a plant in the parsley family. Its aromatic, nutty-flavored seeds come in two colors, amber (the most widely available) and white. A spice known as *black cumin,* although related, is actually a different spice (*see* KALA JEERA). White cumin seed is interchangeable with amber. Cumin is available in seed and ground forms. As with all seeds, herbs and spices, it should be stored in a cool, dark place for no more than 6 months. Cumin is particularly popular in Middle Eastern, Asian and Mediterranean cooking. Among other things, it's used to make curries, chili powders and KÜMMEL LIQUEUR. *See also* SPICES; Seasoning Suggestions, page 891.

cup A PUNCH made as an individual drink, or for several servings, poured from a pitcher into wineglasses or punch cups.

cupcake A small, individual-size cake that's usually baked in a MUFFIN pan. Sometimes the cupcake mold is lined with a crimped paper or foil cup. After baking, the paper or foil is simply peeled off before the cupcake is eaten.

curaçao [KYOOR-uh-soh; KOO-rah-soh] A generic term for several orange-flavored LIQUEURS named for the dried peel of bitter curaçao oranges found on a Netherlands Antilles island in the Caribbean. Most curaçaos are amber in color, although a few are colorless and several are tinted blue. COINTREAU and TRIPLE SEC are the world's most popular curaçaos.

curado [koo-RAH-doh] *see* MANCHEGO CHEESE

curd 1. When it coagulates, milk separates into a semisolid portion (curd) and a watery liquid (WHEY). It's the addition of RENNET to the milk that makes the individual milk protein (CASEIN) cells clump together to form the curd mass, from which cheese is made. 2. A creamy mixture made from juice (usually lemon, lime or orange), sugar, butter and egg yolks. The ingredients are cooked together until the mixture becomes quite thick. When cool, the lemon (or lime or orange) curd becomes thick enough to spread and is used as a topping for breads and other baked goods. Various flavors of curd are available in gourmet markets and some supermarkets.

curdle To coagulate, or separate into curds and whey, as in cheese-making. Soured milk curdles, as do some egg- and milk-based sauces when exposed to prolonged or high heat. Acids such as lemon juice also cause curdling in some mixtures.

cure; curing To treat food (such as meat, cheese or fish) by one of several methods in order to preserve it. **Smoke-curing** is generally done in one of two ways. The cold-smoking method (which can take up to a month, depending on the food) smokes the food at between 70° to 90°F. Hot-smoking partially or totally cooks the food by treating it at temperatures ranging from 100° to 190°F. **Pickled foods** are soaked in variously flavored acid-based BRINES. **Corned products** (such as corned beef) have also been soaked in brine—usually one made with water, salt and various seasonings. **Salt-cured foods** have been dried and packed in salt preparations. Some of the more common cured foods are **smoked ham**, **pickled herring** and **salted fish**. *See also* PRESERVE; RIPENING; SODIUM NITRATE.

currant [KUR-uhnt] There are two distinctly different fruits called currant. 1. The first—resembling a tiny, dark raisin—is the seedless, dried Zante grape (*see* CHAMPAGNE GRAPES). Its name comes from its place of origin—the island of Zante, off the coast of Greece. In cooking, this type of currant (like raisins) is used mainly in baked goods. 2. The second type of currant is a tiny berry related to the gooseberry. There are black, red and white currants. The black ones are generally used for preserves, syrups and liqueurs (such as CASSIS), while the red and white berries are good for out-of-hand eating and such preparations as the famous French preserve BAR-LE-DUC and (using the red currants) CUMBERLAND SAUCE. Fresh currants are in season June through August. Choose those that are plump and without hulls. They can be refrigerated, tightly covered, up to 4 days. Currants are delicious in jams, jellies, sauces and simply served with sugar and cream.

curry From the southern Indian word *kari,* meaning "sauce," comes this catch-all term that is used to refer to any number of hot, spicy, gravy-based dishes of East Indian origin. CURRY POWDER is an integral ingredient in all curries.

curry laksa *see* LAKSA

curry leaf From a plant native to southern Asia, this fragrant herb looks like a small, shiny lemon leaf and has a pungent curry fragrance. Its flavor is essential in a substantial percentage of East Indian fare. Most Indian markets sell fresh curry leaves. Choose those that are bright green, with no sign of yellowing or wilting. They can be refrigerated in an airtight container up to 2 weeks. Packaged, dried curry leaves—also available in Indian markets—can be substituted for fresh but lack their snappy flavor. Also called *kari leaf.*

curry me *see* LAKSA

curry paste Available in East Indian and Asian markets and the gourmet section of some supermarkets, curry paste is a blend of GHEE (clarified butter), CURRY POWDER, vinegar and other seasonings. It's used in lieu of curry powder for many curried dishes.

curry powder Widely used in Indian cooking, authentic Indian curry powder is freshly ground each day and can vary dramatically depending on the region and the cook. Curry powder is actually a pulverized blend of up to 20 spices, herbs and seeds. Among those most commonly used are cardamom, chiles, cinnamon, cloves, coriander, cumin, fennel seed, fenugreek, mace, nutmeg, red and black pepper, poppy and sesame seeds, saffron, tamarind and turmeric (the latter is what gives curried dishes their characteristic yellow color). Commercial curry powder (which bears little resemblance to the freshly ground blends of southern India) comes in two basic styles—standard, and the hotter of the two, "Madras." Since curry powder quickly loses its pungency, it should be stored, airtight, no longer than 2 months. *For information on specific spices used in this blend, see individual listings. See also* Seasoning Suggestions, page 891.

curtido [koor-TEE-thoh; koor-TEE-doh] A type of slaw used in Mexican and Central American cuisine that's often compared to COLESLAW or SAUER-KRAUT. In El Salvador it's made with cabbage, onions, carrots, and oregano. Sometimes JALAPEÑO CHILES are added for a bit of spice. Traditional fermented versions allow the vegetables to sit out for several days until the slaw is lightly fermented and develops a tangy flavor. Pickled variations use vinegar or lemon juice and can be served sooner. In El Salvador, PUPU-SAS are usually served with curtido. The Mexican version is usually made from carrots, onions and jalapeños.

cush [KOOSH; KUHSH] 1. A sweetened, mushlike cornmeal mixture, fried in lard and served as a cereal with cream or CLABBER and sugar or cane syrup. 2. A Southern cornmeal pancake. 3. A Southern soup of cornmeal, milk, onion and seasonings.

cushaw [kuh-SHAW; KOO-shaw] Any of several types of CROOKNECK SQUASH, popular in CAJUN and CREOLE cooking. *See also* SQUASH.

cusk [KUHSK] Related to the cod, this large saltwater fish has a firm, lean flesh. It ranges from 1½ to 5 pounds and can be purchased whole or in fillets. Cusk can be prepared in a variety of ways including baking, broiling, poaching and sautéing. *See also* FISH.

cusqueño *see* AJÍ AMARILLO

custard A puddinglike dessert made with a sweetened mixture of milk and eggs that can either be baked or stirred on stovetop. Two of the most popular and well-known custards are CRÈME CARAMEL and FLAN. Custards require slow cooking and gentle heat in order to prevent separation (curdling). For this reason, stirred custards are generally made in a DOUBLE BOILER; baked custards in a WATER BATH. A safeguard when making custard is to remove it from the heat when it reaches 170° to 175°F on a CANDY THERMOMETER. Custards may be variously flavored with chocolate, vanilla, fruit, and so on. Stirred custards are softer than baked custards and are often used as a sauce or as an ice cream base.

custard apple *see* CHERIMOYA; WHITE SAPOTE

custard marrow *see* CHAYOTE

cutcherry *see* AROMATIC GINGER

cut in To mix a solid, cold fat (such as butter or shortening) with dry ingredients (such as a flour mixture) until the combination is in the form of small particles. This technique can be achieved by using a PASTRY BLENDER, two knives, a fork or fingers (which must be cool so as not to melt the fat). A FOOD PROCESSOR fitted with a metal blade does an excellent job of cutting fat into dry ingredients, providing the mixture is not overworked into a paste.

cutlet 1. A thin, tender slice of meat (usually from lamb, pork or veal) taken from the leg or rib section. Cutlets are best when quickly cooked, such as sautéed or grilled. 2. A mixture of finely chopped meat, fish or poultry that's bound with a sauce or egg mixture and formed into a cutlet shape. Such a formed cutlet is often dipped into beaten egg and then into breadcrumbs before being fried.

cuttlefish Sometimes referred to as the "chameleon of the sea" because it can quickly change its skin color and pattern, the cuttlefish, which resembles a rather large SQUID, has 10 appendages and can reach up to 16 inches in length. It can be prepared like its less tender relatives, the squid and octopus, but must still be tenderized before cooking in order not to be exceedingly chewy. Cuttlefish are most popular in Japan, India and many Mediterranean countries. Dried cuttlefish is available in some Asian markets. It should be reconstituted before cooking. **Sarume**, also available in ethnic markets, is cuttlefish that has been seasoned and roasted.

cuvée [koo-VAY] From the French *cuve* ("vat"), and referring to the "contents of a vat." In the CHAMPAGNE region of France, the word refers to a blended batch of wines. There, the large houses create their traditional house cuvées by blending several wines before the final sparkler is produced via MÉTHODE CHAMPENOISE. A deluxe version is often referred to as *cuvée speciale;* a *vin de cuvée* is the wine from the first pressing. Outside Champagne, the term cuvée is also used for still wines (*see* WINE), and may designate wines blended from different vineyards, or even different varieties.

Cynar [CHEE-nahr; chee-NAHR] A bitter Italian APÉRITIF made from artichokes and a medley of herbs and other flavorings. Cynar is served over ice, either plain or with a spritz of soda water.

dab Any of several varieties of FLOUNDER, the dab is a small FLATFISH with a sweet, lean, firm flesh. It can be prepared in any manner suitable for flounder. *See also* FISH; PLAICE.

dabberlocks *see* ALARIA

dacquoise [da-KWAHZ] A dessert of disc-shaped, nut-flavored MERINGUES stacked and filled with sweetened whipped cream or BUTTERCREAM. It's served chilled, often with fruit. *See also* MARJOLAINE.

daeji bulgogi *see* BULGOGI

daeji galbi *see* GALBI

dagi *see* PACIFIC THREADFIN

Dagwood sandwich Named after Dagwood Bumstead, a character in the "Blondie" comic strip, this extremely thick sandwich is piled high with a variety of meats, cheeses, condiments and lettuce.

daiginjo [di-JEEN-joh] *see* SAKE

daikon [DI-kuhn; DI-kon] From the Japanese words *dai* (large) and *kon* (root), this vegetable is in fact a large Asian radish with a sweet, fresh flavor. The daikon's flesh is crisp, juicy and white, while the skin can be either creamy white or black. Most range from 6 to 15 inches in length with an average diameter of 2 to 3 inches. Some exceptional daikon are fatter than a football and can weigh as much as 100 pounds. **Lo bok**, also called *Chinese radish,* is a variety of daikon common in China. Lo bok is large (about 5 pounds) and ovoid; its color is pale green on one end, fading into beige on the other. Its flesh is crisp with a distinctively sharp radish flavor. Choose daikon and lo bok that are firm and unwrinkled. Refrigerate, wrapped in a plastic bag, up to a week. These radishes are used raw in salads, shredded as a garnish or cooked in a variety of ways, such as in a STIR-FRY.

daiquiri [DAK-uh-ree] A cocktail made with rum, lime juice and sugar. Some daiquiris are made with fruit, the mixture being puréed in a blender. Frozen daiquiris are made either with crushed ice or frozen fruit chunks, all processed until smooth in a blender.

daizu [DI-zoo] Japanese term for "dried SOYBEANS."

dakgalbi [tahk-GAL-bee] A spicy STIR-FRIED chicken dish from Korea. Bite-sized chunks of chicken are cooked along with cabbage, SESAME LEAVES, leeks, sweet potatoes and rice cakes and flavored with spicy sauce called YANG NYUM JANG.

dal; dhal, dhall [DAHL] 1. The Hindi word for any of almost 60 varieties of dried PULSES, including PEAS, BEANS and LENTILS. 2. A pulse with the hull removed. 3. A dish made with lentils (or other pulses) that have been cooked in water, then seasoned variously with spices, tomatoes and onions. *Dals* may be spicy or mild—they're often puréed and typically served as a side dish. The most common *dals* found on menus are *channa dal* (a variety of small CHICKPEA that's split and without skin) and *massor dal* (orange lentils).

Danablu [DAN-uh-bloo] Also called *Danish Blue* and *Marmora,* this rich PASTEURIZED COW's-milk CHEESE was created by cheesemaker Marius Boel in the 1920s as Denmark's ROQUEFORT. It's milder and less complex than Roquefort, but has a zest all its own. Known as one of the world's best blues, the versatile, semisoft Danablu can be sliced, spread and crumbled with equal ease. There are two versions—*full fat* has a FAT CONTENT of 50 percent, while *extra full fat* contains about 60 percent. *See also* BLUE CHEESE; CHEESE.

Danbo [DAN-boh] This popular Danish semihard cheese is made from PASTEURIZED COW's-milk cheese. It has a yellow rind that may or may not be covered with wax or plastic. The smooth, supple interior has a scattering of EYES and a mild, buttery flavor. Some Danbo is flavored with caraway seed. Regular Danbo has about 45 percent milk fat; the lowfat variety contains only 20 percent fat. *See also* CHEESE.

dancy orange *see* MANDARIN ORANGE

dandelion greens [DAN-dl-i-uhn] The name dandelion comes from the French *dent de lion,* meaning "lion's tooth," a reference to the jagged-edged leaves of this noteworthy weed that grows both wild and cultivated. In France, this plant is also known as *pissenlit, couronne de moine* and *salade de taupe.* The bright green leaves have a slightly bitter, tangy flavor that adds interest to salads. They can also be cooked like spinach. The roots can be eaten as vegetables or roasted and ground to make root "coffee." Though they're available until winter in some states, the best, most tender dandelion greens are found in early spring, before the plant begins to flower. Look for bright-green, tender-crisp leaves; avoid those with yellowed or wilted tips. Refrigerate, tightly wrapped in a plastic bag, up to 5 days. Wash thoroughly before using. Dandelion greens have long been prized for their health benefits, such as being a mild diuretic and for lowering blood pressure. They are an excellent source of vitamin A, iron and calcium.

dangmyeon *see* CELLOPHANE NOODLES

dango [DAHN-goh] Japanese balls or round dumplings both sweet and savory. Buckwheat, millet, rice and wheat flours are all used to create a broad variety of dango. Other foods such as beef, chicken, fish and pork are often mixed with the flours—sardines are especially popular. Dangos may be cooked in a variety of ways such as boiled, steamed or deep-fried. *Kushi dango* usually refers to 3 or 4 dumplings that are steamed then skewered, grilled and served with a sweet sauce.

Danish blue cheese *see* DANABLU cheese

Danish lobster *see* PRAWN

Danish pastry This butter-rich pastry begins as a yeast dough that is rolled out, dotted with butter, then folded and rolled again several times, as for PUFF PASTRY. The dough may be lightly sweetened and is usually flavored with vanilla or cardamom. Baked Danish pastries (often referred to simply as "Danish") contain a variety of fillings including fruit, cream cheese, almond paste and spiced nuts.

Danziger Goldwasser *see* GOLDWASSER

dariole [DEHR-ee-ohl; dah-ree-OHL] A French term referring to a small, cylindrical mold, as well as to the dessert baked in it. Classically, the dessert is made by lining the mold with puff pastry, filling it with an almond cream and baking until golden brown. Today there are also savory darioles, usually made with vegetable custards.

Darjeeling tea [dahr-JEE-ling] This strong, full-bodied black tea comes from India's province of Darjeeling, in the foothills of the Himalayas. Darjeeling tea leaves are grown at about 7,000 feet and are considered one of India's finest. *See also* TEA.

dash A measuring term referring to a very small amount of seasoning added to food with a quick, downward stroke of the hand, such as "a dash of Tabasco." In general, a dash can be considered to be somewhere between $1/16$ and a scant $1/8$ teaspoon. *See also* PINCH.

dasheen [da-SHEEN] *see* TARO ROOT

dashi [DA-shee] Used extensively in Japanese cooking, dashi is a soup stock made with dried bonito tuna flakes (KATSUOBUSHI), KOMBU and water. **Dashi-no-moto** is this stock in instant form; it comes granulated, powdered and in a concentrate.

date With a history stretching back over 5,000 years, this venerable fruit grows in thick clusters on the giant date palm, native to the Middle East. The name is thought to come from the Greek *daktulos,* meaning "finger," after the shape of the fruit. Dates require a hot, dry climate and—besides Africa and the Middle East—flourish in California and Arizona. Most varieties range from 1 to 2 inches long and are oval in shape (though some are so chunky they're almost round). All dates have a single, long, narrow seed. The skin is thin and papery, the flesh cloyingly sweet. Dates are green when unripe and turn yellow, golden brown, black or mahogany red—depending on the variety—as they ripen. They're generally picked green and ripened off the tree before drying. When fresh, dates contain about 55 percent sugar, a percentage that increases dramatically as the date dries and the sugar becomes concentrated. Fresh dates are available in some specialty markets from late summer through midfall. Dried dates can be found year-round and are sold packaged—pitted and unpitted—and in bulk, unpitted. Chopped dried dates are also available in packages. Choose plump, soft dates with a smooth, shiny skin. Avoid very shriveled dates or those with mold or sugar crystals on the skin. Store fresh dates, wrapped in a plastic bag, in the refrigerator up to 2 weeks. Dried dates can be stored, airtight, at room temperature in a cool, dry place for up to 6 months or up to a year in the refrigerator. Dates are a good source of protein and iron.

daube [DOHB] A classic French dish made with beef, red wine, vegetables and seasonings, all slowly braised for several hours. Every region in France has its own version of daube, sometimes made in a special, very deep, covered pottery casserole called a *daubière*.

dau miu [dow MEW] Cantonese for "PEA SHOOTS."

daun keson *see* VIETNAMESE MINT

daun pandan [down pahn-DAHN] *see* SCREWPINE LEAVES

dauphine [doh-FEEN] 1. *Pommes dauphine* (dauphine potatoes) are CROQUETTES made by combining potato purée with CHOUX PASTRY (cream-puff pastry dough) and forming the mixture into balls, which are then rolled in breadcrumbs and deep-fried. 2. *Sole dauphine* is an elaborate preparation of deep-fried sole fillets garnished with mushrooms, crayfish, truffles and QUENELLES.

daurade [doh-RAHD] *see* BREAM

DC curing salt *see* SODIUM NITRATE

ddeock; ddeog *see* TTEOK

dduk *see* TTEOK

ddukbooki; ddukbookie *see* TTEOKBOKKI

debeard To remove the inedible hairlike strands from the shell of a MUSSEL.

decant To pour a liquid (typically wine) from its bottle to another container, usually a carafe or decanter. This is generally done to separate the wine from any sediment deposited in the bottom of the bottle during the aging process. Decanting is also done to allow a wine to "breathe," which thereby enhances its flavor.

decanter A narrow-necked, stoppered container—usually made of glass—used to hold wine, liqueur or other spirits.

decorating comb *see* CAKE COMB

decorating sugar *see* SUGAR

deep-dish A term for a sweet or savory pie made either in a deep pie dish or shallow casserole, and having only a top crust.

deep-fat thermometer *see* CANDY/FAT THERMOMETER

deep-fry To cook food in hot fat deep enough to completely cover the item being fried. The oil or fat used for deep-frying should have a high SMOKE POINT (the point to which it can be heated without smoking). For that reason, butter and margarine are not good candidates for frying; shortening, lard and most oils are. The temperature of the fat is all-important and can mean the difference between success and disaster. Fat at the right temperature will produce a crisp exterior and succulent interior. If it's not hot enough, food will absorb fat and be greasy; too hot, and it will burn. An average fat temperature for deep-frying is 375°F, but recipes differ according to the characteristics of each food. To avoid ruined food, a special deep-fat thermometer should be used. Most thermometers used for deep-fat are dual-purpose and also used as CANDY THERMOMETERS. Though special deep-fat fryers fitted with wire baskets are available, food can be deep-fried in any large, heavy pot spacious enough to fry it without crowding. To allow for bubbling up and splattering, the container should be filled no more than halfway full with oil. Fat or oil used for deep-frying may be reused. Let it cool, then strain it through CHEESECLOTH and funnel into a bottle or other tightly sealed container before refrigerating.

deer *see* GAME ANIMALS

defrutum *see* FRUIT MOLASSES

deglaze [dee-GLAYZ] After food (usually meat) has been sautéed and the food and excess fat removed from the pan, deglazing is done by heating a small amount of liquid in the pan and stirring to loosen browned bits of food on the bottom. The liquid used is most often wine or stock. The resultant mixture often becomes a base for a sauce to accompany the food cooked in the pan.

degrease [dee-GREES] Using a spoon to skim fat from the surface of a hot liquid, such as soup, stock or gravy. Another way to degrease is to chill the mixture until the fat becomes solid and can be easily lifted off the surface.

dehydrate [dee-HI-drayt] To remove the natural moisture from food by slowly drying it. Considered the original form of food preservation, dehydration prevents moisture spoilage such as mold or fermentation. Food can be dehydrated manually by placing thin slices on racks and allowing them to dry assisted only by sun or air. It can also be done with an *electric dehydrator,* which resembles a large three-sided toaster oven with anywhere from 5 to 10 wire-grid racks. The food placed on these racks dries with the aid of fan-circulated air. Dried foods are convenient to store and transport because of their greatly reduced volume and weight.

déjeuner [day-zhoo-NAY] The French word for "lunch."

dekopon [DEH-koh-pon] A very sweet, seedless citrus fruit with a distinctive protruding bump on top, much like a Minneola (see TANGELO). Dekopon, which is a hybrid developed in Japan in the early 1970s from other MANDARIN ORANGE hybrids, is large (about 10 ounces) with an easy-to-peel skin and superb flavor. Dekopon is a brand name that became genericized through common use as a descriptor for this fruit. It's also known by the name *shiranuhi* or *shiranui,* as *himepon* and *hiropon* in some parts of Japan and as *hallabong* in Korea. In the United States it has been introduced as *Sumo* by growers in California's Central Valley. Availability is still somewhat limited but it can be found in various supermarkets around the country.

Delaware grape Grown in the eastern United States, this small, pale red grape has a tender skin and juicy, sweet flesh. It's used as a table grape, as well as for some wines. *See also* GRAPE.

del giorno [dehl ZHOHR-noh] Italian for "of the day," referring culinarily to a menu item made especially for that day, as in "zuppa (soup) del giorno." The French counterpart is DU JOUR.

delicata squash [dehl-ih-KAH-tah] Also called *sweet potato squash,* the delicata has a pale yellow skin with medium green striations. Inside, the succulent yellow flesh tastes like a cross between sweet potatoes and butternut squash. The oblong delicata can range from 5 to 9 inches in length and $1\frac{1}{2}$ to 3 inches in diameter. Its peak season is from late summer through late fall. Choose squash that are heavy for their size; avoid those with soft spots. Delicata squash can be stored up to 3 weeks at an average room temperature. As with other winter squash, the delicata is best baked or steamed. It's a good source of potassium, iron and vitamins A and C. *See also* SQUASH.

Delicious apple *see* APPLE

della casa A term found on Italian menus meaning that a dish is in the style of the HOUSE (referring to the restaurant or TRATTORIA), such as "fettuccine della casa." *Vino della casa* would be the "house wine."

Delmonico potatoes [dehl-MAHN-ih-koh] Named after the 19th-century New York restaurant of the same name whose owner-chef created this dish. It consists of cooked and creamed diced (or mashed) potatoes topped with grated cheese and buttered breadcrumbs, then baked until golden brown.

Delmonico steak Another specialty made famous at Delmonico's (*see* DELMONICO POTATOES), the name stands for different cuts around the United States. In some parts of the country this tender, flavorful steak is a boneless beef cut from the SHORT LOIN. Depending on the region, butcher and so on, it's also referred to as a NEW YORK STEAK. In other sections of the United States the Delmonico steak is a boneless rib-eye steak (*see* RIB STEAK), also called a SPENCER STEAK. There's also a third description in some areas—a steak cut from the SIRLOIN, which is right next to the short loin. All Delmonico steaks can be broiled, grilled or fried.

demi-glace [DEHM-ee glahs] A rich ESPAGNOLE SAUCE, which is slowly cooked with beef stock and MADEIRA or SHERRY until it's reduced by half. The result is a thick glaze that coats a spoon. This intense mixture is used as a base for many other sauces. *See also* SAUCE.

demi-sec [DEHM-ee sehk] A French term meaning "half dry" used to describe wine that is sweet (up to 5 percent sugar). *See also* CHAMPAGNE.

demitasse [DEHM-ee-tahss; DEHM-ee-tass] Literally French for "half cup," the term "demitasse" can refer to either a tiny coffee cup or the very strong black coffee served in the cup.

dendê oil *see* PALM OIL

dengaku [deh-GAH-koo] Traditional Japanese preparation for foods such as eggplant and tofu, which are topped with a sweet MISO dressing, then skewered and grilled.

Denominação de Origen *see* APPELLATION

Denominación de Origen *see* APPELLATION

Denominazione di Origine Controllata *see* APPELLATION

Denver ribs *see* BREAST, LAMB

Denver sandwich; Denver omelet Also called a *Western sandwich*, this classic consists of an egg scrambled with chopped ham, onions and green peppers, sandwiched with two slices of bread and garnished with lettuce. A **Denver omelet** has a filling of ham, onions and green peppers.

Derby cheese; Derbyshire [DER-bee; DAHR-bee-sheer] This mild, semihard PASTEURIZED cow's-milk cheese has a natural rind that may or may not be waxed. The interior is yellow and the flavor is mild, buttery and slightly tangy. **Sage Derby** is generously flavored with the herb, which also lends color interest. Some versions are marbled green and white while others have a green-flecked center sandwiched with pale yellow cheese. The FAT CONTENT for Derby cheeses is around 45 to 48 percent. *See also* CHEESE.

dessert wine Any of a wide variety of sweet wines—sometimes fortified with BRANDY, all of which are compatible with dessert. Some of the more popular dessert wines are LATE HARVEST RIESLING, MADEIRA, PORT, SAUTERNES, SHERRY and some sparkling wines, such as ASTI SPUMANTE.

dessicated coconut *see* COCONUT

devein [dee-VAYN] To remove the gray-black vein from the back of a shrimp. This can be done with the tip of a sharp knife or a special tool called a deveiner. On small and medium shrimp, this technique need be done only for cosmetic purposes. However, because the intestinal vein of large shrimp contains grit, it should always be removed.

devil To combine a food with various hot or spicy seasonings such as red pepper, mustard or TABASCO SAUCE, thereby creating a "deviled" dish.

deviled egg *see* STUFFED EGG

devilfish *see* OCTOPUS

devil's food A dark, dense baked chocolate item (such as a cake or cookie). On the opposite end of the spectrum is the airy, white ANGEL FOOD CAKE.

devils on horseback 1. A "hot" version of ANGELS ON HORSEBACK (oysters wrapped in bacon strips), enlivened by the addition of red pepper or TABASCO SAUCE. 2. The British rendition of this appetizer consists of wine-poached prunes stuffed with a whole almond and mango chutney, then wrapped in bacon and broiled. Like the American version, these devils on horseback are also served on toast points.

Devon cream; Devonshire cream [DEHV-uhn (-sher)] *see* CLOTTED CREAM

Devonshire tea *see* CREAM TEA

dew beans *see* MOTH BEANS

dewberry [DOO-beh-ree] Any of several varieties of the trailing-vine form of the BLACKBERRY.

dextrose; dextroglucose [DEHK-strohs] Also called *corn sugar* and *grape sugar,* dextrose is a naturally occurring form of GLUCOSE.

dhal *see* DAL

D

dhansak [DAHN-sahk] Indian curry dish that is particularly popular with the Parsi community. Dhansak is traditionally made with goat meat but other ingredients such as beef, chicken, lamb or prawns are common today. It's a spicy, sweet-and-sour blend, with dried chiles or chile powder for heat, sugar or often pineapple for sweetness and lemon juice or TAMARIND adding the sour. There are myriad versions of the MASALA spice blend used to season dhansak. Lentils and other vegetables such as squash are also a part of this dish, which is usually served with rice.

diable sauce; à la diable [dee-AH-bl (dee-AHB-lay)] 1. A basic ESPAGNOLE SAUCE with the addition of wine, vinegar, shallots and red or black pepper. It's usually served with broiled meat or poultry. 2. *À la diable* refers to a French method of preparing poultry whereby the bird is split, sprinkled with breadcrumbs and broiled until brown, and served with diable sauce. *See also* SAUCE.

diavolini *see* Pasta Glossary, page 883

diavolo [DYAH-voh-loh] Italian for "devil." Culinarily, this term describes sauces (usually tomato based) that are moderately to liberally spiced with CHILES. Such dishes can also be referred to as **alla diavola** and **fra diavolo** ("brother devil").

dice To cut food into tiny (about $\frac{1}{8}$- to $\frac{1}{4}$-inch) cubes.

dietary fiber *see* FIBER, DIETARY

digestif [dee-zheh-STEEF] A French term for a spirited drink (such as BRANDY or COGNAC) taken after dining as an aid to digestion. The term *digestif* is now widely used in English parlance as well.

digestive enzymes Natural food enzymes that, when taken with gassy foods, help reduce flatulence—sometimes even stopping it before it begins. Gas-producing foods like beans, broccoli, cabbage, cauliflower, grains and onions cause trouble because they contain hard- or impossible-to-digest complex sugars (see CARBOHYDRATE) that ferment in the large intestine. Digestive enzymes help break down these complex sugars into simple sugars that are more easily digestible. They generally come in tablet form and are commonly available in natural food stores. Some, like the popular *Beano,* also come in a liquid form and can be found in supermarkets and drugstores.

digestivo [dee-jeh-STEE-voh] Italian for "DIGESTIF."

Dijon mustard [dee-ZHOHN] Hailing originally from Dijon, France, this pale, grayish-yellow mustard is known for its clean, sharp flavor, which can range from mild to hot. Dijon mustard is made from brown or black mustard seeds, white wine, unfermented grape juice (MUST) and various seasonings. The best-known maker of Dijon mustard is the house of Poupon, particularly famous in the United States for their Grey Poupon mustard. *See also* MUSTARD.

dill; dill weed; dill seed Thought by 1st-century Romans to be a good luck symbol, dill has been around for thousands of years and has a long history of culinary as well as medicinal uses. This annual herb grows up to a height of about 3 feet and has feathery green leaves called **dill weed**, marketed in both fresh and dried forms. The distinctive flavor of fresh dill weed in no way translates to its dried form. Fresh dill does, however, quickly lose its fragrance during heating, so should be added toward the end of the cooking time. Dill weed is used to flavor many dishes such as salads, vegetables, meats and sauces. The tan, flat **dill seed** is actually the dried fruit of the herb. Heating brings out the flavor of dill seed, which is stronger and more pungent than that of the leaves. It's most often used in the United States as part of the pickling mix in which dill pickles are cured. *See also* HERBS; Seasoning Suggestions, page 891.

dilute [dih-LOOT] To reduce a mixture's strength by adding liquid.

dim sum; dem sum [DIHM SUHM] Cantonese for "heart's delight," *dim sum* includes a variety of small, mouth-watering dishes such as steamed or fried dumplings, shrimp balls, STEAMED BUNS, POT STICKERS and Chinese pastries. *Dim sum*—standard fare in tea houses—can be enjoyed any time of the day. Unlike most dining establishments, servers in a dim sum eatery do not take orders, per se. Instead, they walk among the tables with carts or trays of kitchen-fresh food. Diners simply point to the item they want, which is served on small plates or in baskets. Each item usually has a set price. At the end of the meal, the check is tallied by counting the dishes on the table. Some dim sum restaurants add the price of each dish to a check that remains on the table, clearing dishes as they are emptied.

dinosaur kale *see* CAVOLO NERO

dioul *see* WARKA

diples [THEE-peuhls] A deep-fried, Greek pastry made from thin strips of sweet dough formed into bows or circles. Diples are usually coated with honey, cinnamon and nuts.

diplomat cream *see* CRÈME DIPLOMAT

diplomat pudding This cold, molded dessert consists of alternating layers of LIQUEUR-soaked ladyfingers (or sponge cake), jam, chopped candied fruit and custard (sometimes combined with whipped cream). Diplomat pudding is usually garnished with whipped-cream rosettes and candied fruit.

diplomat sauce A fish stock-based VELOUTÉ SAUCE enriched with cream, brandy, LOBSTER BUTTER and truffles. It's typically served with fish and shellfish. *See also* SAUCE.

dirty rice A Cajun specialty of cooked rice, ground chicken or turkey livers and gizzards, onions, chicken broth, bacon drippings, green pepper and garlic. The name comes from the fact that the ground giblets give the rice a "dirty" look . . . but delicious flavor.

disjoint To separate meat at the joint, such as cutting the chicken leg from the thigh.

dissolve To incorporate a dry ingredient (such as sugar, salt, yeast or gelatin) into a liquid so thoroughly that no grains of the dry ingredient are evident, either by touch or sight.

distillate [DIHS-tl-it; DIHS-tl-ate] *see* DISTILLATION *n*.

distillation *v*. The process of separating a liquid's components by heating it to the point of vaporization and collecting the cooled condensate (vapor that reverts to liquid through condensation) in order to obtain a purified and/or concentrated form. The apparatus that performs distillation is called a still, of which there are two types—pot still and continuous still. The **pot still** (which in France is called an **alembic**—sometimes spelled **alambic**) consists of a copper or copper-lined pot with a large rounded bottom and long tapering neck connected by a copper pipe to a condenser (a cooled spiral tube). As the fermented liquid (WINE for brandy, MASH for whiskey) in the pot comes to a boil, it vaporizes. The vapor rises up into the still's condenser, where it cools and returns to a liquid state. This condensation (condensate), which has a higher alcohol concentration than the original mixture, is collected in a receiving compartment. However, because alcohol boils at 173.3°F, water boils at 212°F, and a mixture of the two boils somewhere in between, the condensed liquid still contains some water. This means that redistilling (often several times) may be necessary to achieve the appropriate alcohol level—COGNAC and

SCOTCH WHISKY are distilled twice, for example, while IRISH WHISKEY undergoes 3 distillations. In this case, several pot stills may be lined up, distilling the condensate produced by the first pot still through the second pot still, and so on. The pot still, with its painstaking thoroughness, produces distillates that retain the CHARACTER and personality of their source ingredients. The **continuous still** was considered revolutionary when it was introduced in 1826. It's also known by several other names: *column still, patent still* and *Coffey still* (after a Scottish tax official, Aeneas Coffey, who made major improvements to it in the early 1830s). The continuous distillation process operates by repeatedly recycling a mixture of steam and alcohol until all the spirit is extracted. The continuous still consists of tall copper columns that continually receive cold mash that trickles down and over a series of steam-producing plates. As the alcohol vaporizes, it becomes part of the steam that, as it rises, goes through the liquid flowing down the plates. As the vapor interacts with this liquid, some of the alcohol in the liquid vaporizes and some of the steam converts back to liquid. The vapor is drawn into vents that then take it to a condenser and receiver. If the tower or column has enough plates, a very high level of alcohol concentration can be attained in this one continuous process. Sometimes, two or more towers or columns are used so that higher levels of alcohol or different levels of alcohol concentration can be produced. A single continuous still performs much like the redistilling process with multiple pot stills. The pot still, however, works in relatively small batches, and the continuous still has an uninterrupted flow of incoming material and outgoing product. The continuous still brought mass production to distillers and dramatically expanded Scotland's whisky industry in the 1800s. **distillation; distilled spirits; distillate** *n.* The end product of the distillation process. Distilled spirits include BRANDY, GIN, RUM, TEQUILA, VODKA and WHISK(E)Y. These liquors are based on cereal grains, fruit and sometimes vegetables, which are fermented (*see* FERMENTATION) before beginning the distillation process. After distillation, many are flavored in some way, either with added ingredients or by barrel AGING or both. In the United States, each type of distilled spirits must meet strict federal standards relating to the ingredients used (which must be FDA approved) as well as how it's made, labeled (to accurately reflect the contents), advertised and sold. *See also* ALCOHOL.

distilled water Water from which all minerals and other impurities have been removed by the process of DISTILLATION.

ditali; ditalini *see* Pasta Glossary, page 883

diver scallops *see* SCALLOP

divinity [dih-VIHN-ih-tee] A fluffy yet creamy candy made with granulated sugar, corn syrup and stiffly beaten egg whites. Nuts, chocolate, coconut or various other flavorings are often added to the basic mixture. When brown sugar is substituted for granulated sugar, the candy is called **seafoam**.

dizi *see* ABGUSHT

DO *see* APPELLATION

Dobos torte [DOH-bohs; DOH-bohsh] Created by Hungarian pastry chef József Dobos, this rich torte is made by stacking 9 extra-thin layers of GÉNOISE (or sponge cake) spread with chocolate buttercream. The top is covered with a hard caramel glaze.

DOC *see* APPELLATION

doce de leite [DOH-ser der LAY-ter] *see* DULCE DE LECHE

dock To pierce the top of a dough (as for bread and pizza crust) to keep it from rising erratically because of escaping steam. For the top of bread loaves, docking implements may include a knife, scissors or razor blade. For pizza doughs, crackers and the like, there's a special tool called a dough docker, which resembles a handle attached to a short rolling pin fitted with short, stubby spikes that pierce the dough. *See also* SORREL.

doenjang [DIHN-jahng] Korean fermented soybean paste. Doenjang, also spelled *dwenjang*, is somewhat like Japanese MISO. It's used as a condiment and as an addition to soups and stews.

doenjang jjigae [DIHN-jahng jee-GAY] Stew made with **doenjang** (Korean soybean paste) and a wide variety of other ingredients such as DUBU (tofu), onion, various vegetables, meat and seafood.

dogfish; spiny dogfish A name used for any of several smaller species of SHARK, although the reference isn't confined to one species. Dogfish genera include *Squalus acanthias* (known as **spur dog**), *Masterias* (**smooth hound**), *Mustelus canis* (**sand shark**) and *Scyliorhinus stellaris* (**nursehound**). The name refers to the small size and shape of the fish, the offspring of some of which are even referred to as "pups." Dogfish, which are found in the North and South Pacific, both sides of the Atlantic Ocean and the Mediterranean, have generally been considered TRASH FISH in the United States. That concept is gradually changing, however, and this moderately lean fish is gaining favor. The firm, fairly strong flavored flesh lends itself to full-flavored sauces. Dogfish is best baked or fried and is, in fact, the fish widely used in Great Britain for FISH AND CHIPS. *See also* FISH.

dolce; *pl.* **dolci** [DOHL-chay; DOHL-chee]. 1. Italian for "sweet," referring culinarily to desserts, candy or other sweets. 2. In Italy *dolce* is used to describe wines with a high degree of residual sugar.

Dolcelatte [dol-chay-LAHT-tay] Italian for "sweet milk," and a brand name for one GORGONZOLA *dolce*.

Dolcetto [dohl-CHEHT-oh; dohl-CHEHT-uh] Red-wine grape that's grown mainly in the southwest section of Italy's PIEDMONT region, where a number of DOCS are dedicated to the grape, including Dolcetto d'Alba, the best known. There are a couple of theories as to the name *dolcetto*, which means "little sweet one." It either refers to the sweetness of the grapes and the juice they produce or to the perception of sweetness in Dolcetto wines, even though they're usually made as DRY wines. Dolcetto wines have high acidity and are usually deep purple in color. They have perfumy BOUQUETS and rich, fruity, ripe-berry flavors, sometimes with a slightly bitter aftertaste.

dollarfish *see* BUTTERFISH

dollop [DOLL-uhp] A small glob of soft food, such as whipped cream or mashed potatoes. When referring to a liquid, dollop refers to a dash or "splash" of soda water, water and so on.

Dolly Varden *see* CHAR

dolma; *pl.* **dolmades** [DOHL-mah; dohl-MAH-dehs] From the Arabic word for "something stuffed," referring to grape leaves, vegetables or fruits stuffed with a savory, well-seasoned filling. Among the most popular dolmades are grape leaves stuffed with a filling of ground lamb, rice, onion, currants, pine nuts and various seasonings. Other foods used as casings include squash, eggplant, sweet peppers, cabbage leaves, quinces and apples. Dolmades are usually braised or baked. They may be eaten hot, cold or at room temperature, and served as an appetizer or entrée.

dolphin; dolphinfish [DAHL-fihn] *see* MAHI MAHI

donburi [dohn-boo-REE] 1. A Japanese dish of boiled riced topped with meat, fish, eggs and/or vegetables and broth. It can be served with spicy condiments. Sometimes this dish is called simply *don* or don may be added as a suffix to indicate a donburi dish. For example, *katsudon* is short for *tonkatsu donburi,* which is "pork cutlet on rice." Donburi is considered one of Japan's "fast foods" and there are chains of donburi restaurants specializing in quick meals. 2. The name of the large deep-footed bowl in which the previously mentioned dish is served.

doner kebab *see* SHAWARMA

dong qua *see* WINTER MELON

doo boo [doo-boo] Korean for "tofu." Also spelled *du bu*.

DOP *see* PROTECTED DESIGNATION OF ORIGIN

dopiaza; dupiaza [doh-PEE-ah-za] Classic Indian/Pakistani curry dish that dates back at least to the Moghul rulers of India (*see* MOGHUL CUISINE). Its name broadly translates to "two onions" or "double onions," referring to the process of adding onions at two different stages during cooking. Finely chopped onions are used to make the base curry sauce; larger pieces, fried golden brown, are added toward the end of cooking. Recipes call for many different versions of the spice blend and usually include meat such as beef, chicken, lamb or prawns, although there are some meatless variations.

dorado *see* MAHI MAHI

Dorrigo pepper *see* MOUNTAIN PEPPER

Dorset Naga pepper *see* SCOVILLE SCALE

Dortmunder [DORT-moont-er] Originating in Germany's largest brewing city, Dortmund, this gold-colored beer is darker and less bitter than PILSENER and stronger and paler than MÜNCHENER. It's also called simply "Dort." *See also* BEER.

dosa; dosai [DOH-sah] A thin pancake similar to a CRÊPE quite popular in southern India and nearby regions, as well as in some Southeast Asian countries. Dosas are usually made from wet rice and dal that's ground into a paste and allowed to ferment overnight, allowing natural yeasts to develop a flavor that's similar to buttermilk pancakes. There are myriad variations of the paste, lots of shapes the resulting pancakes can take and a diverse number of fillings and sauces that may be used. Some dosas are made from wheat instead of rice. One of the more popular variations is MASALA DOSA. Dosas are also known as *dosai* (sometimes used as the plural), *thosai* and *toshay*.

dosage [doh-SAHJ] A mixture of sugar and spirits (often brandy) that is added to CHAMPAGNE and other sparkling wine immediately prior to final bottling. The percentage of sugar in the syrup determines the degree of sweetness in the final wine.

dot To scatter small bits (dots) of an ingredient (usually butter) over another food or mixture. Distributing bits of butter over the fruit in an apple pie, for example, allows the butter to melt evenly over the pie as it bakes.

double boiler A double-pan arrangement whereby two pots are formed to fit together, with one sitting partway inside the other. A single lid fits both pans. The lower pot is used to hold simmering water, which gently heats the mixture in the upper pot. Double boilers are used to warm or cook heat-sensitive food such as custards, delicate sauces and chocolate.

double-cream (double crème) cheeses Any of various cow's-milk cheeses that have been enriched with cream so that they contain a minimum of 60 percent milk fat. **Triple-cream cheeses** must have at least 72 percent milk fat. Both double- and triple-creams can be fresh or ripened. They share the distinction of being seductively soft and creamy in texture with a mild, slightly sweet flavor. Because of their natural sweetness, these cheeses are perfect when served with fruit for dessert. *See also* CHEESE.

double Gloucester *see* GLOUCESTER

dòu fu [doh FOO] Chinese for "bean curd" (*see* TOFU).

dough [DOH] A mixture of flour, liquid and other ingredients (often including a leavening) that's stiff but pliable enough to work with the hands. Unlike a batter, dough is too stiff to pour.

doughnut; donut A small, typically ring-shaped pastry that is usually leavened with yeast or baking powder, and which can be baked but is generally fried. The traditional doughnut shape is formed by using a special doughnut cutter that cuts out the center hole in the dough. It can also be made with two biscuit cutters, large and small (for the hole). Fried doughnut holes are favorites with children. There are two main styles of doughnuts. **Raised doughnuts** are leavened with yeast and allowed to rise at least once before being fried. Besides the traditional ring-shape, raised doughnuts also come in squares and twists. Additionally, the dough is used to make oblong and round jelly-filled doughnuts—commonly called **jelly doughnuts**. **Cake doughnuts** receive their leavening power from baking powder and are chilled before frying to prevent the dough from absorbing too much oil in the process. The dough for cake doughnuts is often flavored with spices, orange or lemon zest or chocolate. **Crullers** are made from cake-doughnut dough. They're formed by twisting two (about 5-inch) strips of dough together before frying. Both types are usually either dusted with granulated sugar (cake doughnuts often with powdered sugar) or topped with a flavored glaze (such as chocolate or butterscotch). **French doughnuts**, though not as readily available as the other two types, are made with CHOUX PASTRY (cream-puff pastry dough). They're very tender and light.

dough scraper A rectangular tool, also called a *bench scraper* or *pastry scraper*, used to pick up dough, slice it into portions or to scrape residue from a work surface. It's made up of a flexible blade, usually stainless steel but it can be plastic, and a handle made of wood, plastic, or rolled up stainless steel.

doux [DOO] French for "sweet." On a CHAMPAGNE label, the term *doux* means the wine is very sweet—over 5 percent sugar.

DQ curing salt *see* SODIUM NITRATE

draft beer Beer served straight from the keg by means of a spigot. Unlike the bottled or canned varieties, draft beer hasn't been subjected to the PASTEURIZATION process. Also spelled *draught*.

dragées [dra-ZHAYZ] 1. Tiny, round, hard candies used for decorating cakes, cookies and other baked goods. Dragées come in a variety of sizes (from pinhead to $\frac{1}{4}$-inch) and colors, including silver. 2. Almonds with a hard sugar coating.

dragon fruit This member of the cactus family is native to Central and South America. The dragon fruit is shaped like a hand grenade and has a skin that ranges in color from yellow to shocking pink, depending on the variety. The tips of the pliable, downward-curving spines that cover the fruit are lime green. Pink dragon fruit have pink flesh and the yellow variety is off-white in color. The flesh of both is juicy and somewhat grainy, with myriad tiny edible seeds and a flavor reminiscent of kiwis and grapes. Dragon fruit (also called *pitaya* or *pithaya*) are available from August to December in specialty produce markets, some gourmet stores, and Latin markets (the latter also carry the fruit in cans and jars). Choose a fruit without blemishes that gives slightly to palm pressure. Refrigerate ripe dragon fruit in a plastic bag for up to 5 days. Halve, then cut away skin with a paring knife and use the fruit in desserts or salads. Dragon fruit may also be cut in half and the flesh scooped out with a spoon.

dragon's eye *see* LONGAN

drain To pour off a liquid or fat from food, often with the use of a COLANDER. "Drain" can also mean to blot greasy food (such as bacon) on paper towels.

Drambuie [dram-BOO-ee] A SCOTCH-based LIQUEUR sweetened with heather honey and flavored with herbs. It has a deep golden color and sweet-spicy, herbal-whiskey flavor with licorice overtones. The word *drambuie* is Gaelic for "the drink that satisfies."

draught beer [draft] *see* DRAFT BEER

draw 1. In cooking, to eviscerate; to remove the entrails, as from poultry or fish. 2. To CLARIFY a mixture, as in drawn butter.

drawn butter *see* CLARIFIED BUTTER

dredge [DREHJ] To lightly coat food to be fried, as with flour, cornmeal or breadcrumbs. This coating helps brown the food. Chicken, for example, might be dredged with flour before frying.

dress 1. To prepare game, fowl, fish and so forth for cooking by plucking, scaling, eviscerating, and so on. 2. To "dress a salad" simply means adding a DRESSING.

dressing 1. A sauce—usually cold—used to coat or top salads and some cold vegetable, fish and meat dishes. 2. Another name for STUFFING. *See also* SAUCE.

dried beef *see* CHIPPED BEEF

dried fruit Fruit from which the majority of the moisture has been dehydrated. The final moisture content of dried fruit usually ranges from 15 to 25 percent. Drying fruit greatly concentrates both sweetness and flavor, and the taste is much changed, as from grape to raisin or from plum to prune. Fruit can be dried in the sun or by machine. Machine-drying usually takes no more than 24 hours. Sun-drying can take three to four times as long, causing additional loss of nutrients through heat and time. Vitamins A and C are the most susceptible to depletion during the drying process, but a wealth of other vitamins and minerals remain in great force. Before drying, fruits are often sprayed with sulfur dioxide gas, which helps preserve the fruit's natural color and nutrients. Though decried by some, clinical research has shown no negative effects from sulfur intake. Imported dried fruit, however, is fumigated with chemical pesticides, which have been proven toxic to humans. Dried fruit is available year-round and comes in five basic designations: **extra fancy**, **fancy**, **extra choice**, **choice** and **standard**. These grades are based on size, color, condition and moisture content. Most dried fruit can be stored at room temperature, tightly wrapped in a plastic bag, for up to a year. Though dried fruits can be stored longer and take less space, they contain 4 to 5 times the calories by weight of fresh fruit. Dried fruit can be used as is or reconstituted in water. It may be eaten out of hand or put to a variety of uses such as in baked goods, fruit compotes, stuffings, conserves and so on. *See also* PRUNES; RAISINS.

dried limes *see* LIMES, DRIED, PERSIAN

dried plum *see* PRUNE

dried scallops *see* SCALLOPS, DRIED

dried shrimp *see* SHRIMP, DRIED

drippings The melted fat and juices that gather in the bottom of a pan in which meat or other food is cooked. Drippings are used as a base for gravies and sauces and in which to cook other foods (such as YORKSHIRE PUDDING).

drizzle To slowly pour a liquid mixture in a very fine stream over food (such as a sweet glaze over cake or bread, or melted butter over food before baking).

drop cookie A cookie made by dropping spoonfuls of dough onto a baking sheet. *See also* COOKIE.

drum Any of a large and diverse family of fish, so named for the odd drumming or deep croaking noise it makes, particularly during the mating season. Drum, also known as *croaker,* is a firm, lowfat fish found in temperate waters. **Croakers**, averaging 1 pound, are the small fry of the drum family and are usually sold whole. However, many drum can weigh up to 30 pounds and are generally sold in fillets and steaks. Drum can be baked, broiled or fried. Other members of the drum family include **Atlantic** and **black croaker**, **black drum**, **California corbina**, **hardhead**, **kingfish**, **redfish (red drum)**, **spot**, **weakfish** and **white seabass**. *See also* FISH.

drumette [druh-MEHT] The fleshy part of a chicken or turkey wing that goes from the shoulder joint to the elbow joint. Drumettes are typically fried, grilled or baked and usually served as an appetizer, often with a dip.

drunken beans *see* FRIJOLES CHARROS

drupe; drupe fruit [DROOP] Any thin-skinned fruit with a succulent, soft flesh and hard stone or seed in the middle. APRICOTS, CHERRIES, PEACHES and PLUMS are all classified as drupe fruits. Also called *stone fruit.*

dry *adj.* A term used to describe a wine or other beverage that isn't sweet. In wines, dry is also referred to as SEC (*see listing*). **dry** *v. see* DEHYDRATE

dry ice Dry ice is really crystallized carbon dioxide. It doesn't produce water when it melts and is generally used only for long-term refrigeration. Touching dry ice with bare hands can result in burns. **dry milk** Milk from which almost all the moisture has been removed. Dry (also called powdered) milk is less expensive and easier to store than fresh milk but has a disadvantage in that it never tastes quite like the real thing. It comes in three basic forms—whole milk, nonfat milk and buttermilk. Because of its milk fat content, **dry whole milk** must be refrigerated. **Nonfat dry**

milk is available in regular and instant forms; the former tastes slightly better, while the latter mixes more easily. **Powdered buttermilk** is simply desiccated buttermilk and is generally used for baking. Until opened, dry nonfat milk and buttermilk can be kept in a cool, dry place for up to 6 months. Refrigerating opened packages will help retain their freshness. A USDA "U.S. Extra Grade" shield on the label signifies that the product meets exacting government quality standards. Dry milks may or may not be fortified with vitamins A and D.

dry matter In the United States, a term referring to the non-liquid components of cheese (including FAT, LACTOSE, minerals and proteins). The liquid component varies from cheese to cheese and can range between 30 and 80 percent. The portion remaining is dry matter, also known as *solids*. The fat content of cheese is based solely on the solid materials and ignores the moisture content. On U.S. cheese labels the percentage of fat is indicated in one of several ways: "in dry matter" (or "IDM"), "fat on a dry basis" ("FDB") or "butterfat content." The synonymous term on French and other imported cheese labels is *matière grasse* or *m.g.*

dry rub *see* RUB

dtam mak huhng *see* SOM TAM

Dubarry, à la; du Barry [doo-BEHR-ee] Said to have been named after the Comtesse du Barry, mistress of Louis XV, this term denotes a dish using cauliflower—particularly cooked cauliflower served with cheese sauce. **Crème Dubarry** is a creamy cauliflower soup.

Dublin Bay prawn *see* PRAWN

Dubonnet [doo-boh-NAY] A bittersweet, fortified wine-based APÉRITIF flavored with herbs. Dubonnet comes in two styles: **Dubonnet rouge** (also called simply *red*), the richer of the two, is red-wine based and flavored with QUININE; **Dubonnet blanc** (also called *blond*) is a drier (*see* DRY), VERMOUTH-style apéritif. Dubonnet originated in France but is now also made in the United States.

dubu [doo-boo] Korean for "tofu." Also spelled *doo boo.*

dubu jjigae [DOO-boo jee-GAY] A popular Korean stew featuring TOFU.

duchess potatoes [DUCH-ihs] Cooked potatoes that are puréed with egg yolks and butter, then formed into small shapes or piped as a garnish and baked until golden brown. The term *à la duchesse* refers to dishes garnished with duchess potatoes.

duck; duckling　Any of many species of wild or domestic web-footed birds that live in or near water. As with so many things culinary, the Chinese are credited with being the first to raise ducks for food. Today's domestic ducks are all descendants of either of two species—the mallard or the muscovy duck. Comprising about half the domesticated ducks in the United States are the white-feathered, full-breasted **Long Island ducks**, known for their dark, succulent flesh. These direct descendents of the **Peking duck** (a variety of mallard) are all the progeny of three ducks and a drake brought from Peking on a clipper ship in 1873. Besides Long Island, the locations most widely known for the cultivation of superior ducks are Peking (now known as Beijing) and Rouen, France. Since most ducks are marketed while still quite young and tender, the words "duck" and "duckling" are interchangeable. **Broilers** and **fryers** are less than 8 weeks old, **roasters** no more than 16 weeks old. Domestic ducks can weigh between 3 and $5^{1}/_{2}$ pounds; the older ducks are generally larger. Fresh duck is available from late spring through early winter, but generally only in regions where ducks are raised. Almost 90 percent of ducks that reach market are frozen and available year-round. The government grades duck quality with USDA classifications A, B and C. The highest grade is A, and is usually what is found in markets. Grade B ducks are less meaty and well finished; grade C ducks are usually used for commercial purposes. The grade stamp can be found within a shield on the package wrapping or sometimes on a tag attached to the bird's wing. When buying fresh duck, choose one with a broad, fairly plump breast; the skin should be elastic, not saggy. For frozen birds, make sure the packaging is tight and unbroken. Fresh duck can be stored, loosely covered, in the coldest section of the refrigerator for 2 to 3 days. Remove any giblets from the body cavity and store separately. Frozen duck should be thawed in the refrigerator; it can take from 24 to 36 hours, depending on the size of the bird. Do not refreeze duck once it's been thawed. Duck can be prepared in a variety of manners including roasting, braising, broiling, and so on. Though higher in fat than other domestic birds, it is a good source of protein and iron. *For information about wild duck, see* GAME BIRDS.

duck press　A kitchen device used to extract the juices from a cooked duck carcass. This step is necessary for some gourmet duck recipes, specifically PRESSED DUCK.

duck sauce　*see* PLUM SAUCE

duff　A STEAMED (or boiled) PUDDING made with flour, eggs, dried fruit and spices, and once widely popular in England and Scotland. The name is a Scottish dialectal variation of the word dough, which was apparently pronounced as *rough*.

Dugléré [dewg-lay-ray] Dish created by chef Adolphe Dugléré consisting of poached sole served with a VELOUTÉ SAUCE augmented with white wine, shallots, tomatoes and parsley.

du jour [doo-ZHEU*R*] French for "of the day," referring culinarily to a menu item made especially for that day, as in "soup du jour." The Italian form is DEL GIORNO.

duk *see* TTEOK

dukka; dukkah [DOO-kah] An Egyptian spice blend comprising toasted nuts and seeds, the combination of which varies depending on the cook. Dukka usually has hazelnuts or chickpeas as a base, along with pepper as well as coriander, cumin and sesame seeds. The ingredients are ground together until the texture is that of a coarse powder. Dukka can be sprinkled over meats and vegetables, or used as a dip (preceded by olive oil) for breads, fresh vegetables and so on. It's available in Middle Eastern markets.

dulce [DOOL-say] *Dulce* is Spanish for "sweet."

dulce de leche [DOOL-say day LAY-chay] Dulce de leche is a CARA-MELlike mixture popular in Mexico, Central America and South America. Dulce de leche is known by various names such as *arequipe* in Columbia and Venezuela, *cajeta* in Mexico and *manjar* or *manjur* in Chile and Peru. The Portuguese version is *doce de leite*. In Spanish, *dulce de leche* literally translates to "sweet of milk," and more loosely as "milk candy." It's a simple preparation of sugar cooked with goat's and/or cow's milk for hours over low heat until the mixture becomes very thick and deep golden in color. Sometimes it's made by simply cooking SWEETENED CONDENSED MILK to that state. The consistency of this intensely sweet mixture can vary from easily spreadable, to that of a thick, dense frosting, to firm and candylike. In Argentina, where dulce de leche is extremely popular, it's used variously as a filling for cookies (such as for ALFAJORES) and pastries, as a cake frosting, as a dip for fruit, as a spread for toast or pancakes and as a flavoring or topping for ice cream and FLAN. Dulce de leche can be found in jars or tubs in Latin markets.

dulce de membrillo [DOOL-say day mem-BREE-yoh] *see* QUINCE

dulse [duhlss] Hailing from the British Isles, dulse is an edible, coarse-textured, red SEAWEED with a pungent, briny flavor. When dried, dulse remains supple though rubbery, which may be why some stalwart Irish use it like chewing tobacco. Dulse is primarily used in soups and condiments.

dumpling Savory dumplings are small or large mounds of dough that are usually dropped into a liquid mixture (such as soup or stew) and cooked until done. Some are stuffed with meat or cheese mixtures, others have small bits of ingredients interspersed in the dough. Dessert dumplings most often consist of a fruit mixture encased in a sweet pastry dough and baked. They're usually served with a sauce. Some sweet dumplings are poached in a sweet sauce and served with cream.

dumpster divers *see* FREEGAN

Dundee cake [duhn-DEE; DUHN-dee] A classic Scottish fruitcake made with candied citron, orange and lemon peels, almonds and various spices. The top of a Dundee cake is traditionally covered completely with blanched whole almonds.

Dungeness crab [DUHN-juh-nehs] *see* CRAB

dung gwa *see* WINTER MELON

durian [DOOR-ee-uhn] This larger-than-life fruit of the Malaysian tree can weigh up to 10 pounds, has a brownish-green, semihard shell covered with thick spikes, and is slightly larger than a football. To all but its Southeast Asian fans, the durian has a nauseating smell—a truth attested to by the fact that it's been outlawed by many airlines. The creamy, slightly sweet flesh, however, has an exquisitely rich, custardy texture. Asian markets sometimes carry fresh durian in the early summer months. Other forms available are frozen, canned and preserved dried durian.

Duroc pork *see* HERITAGE PORK

durum wheat [DOOR-uhm; DYOOR-uhm] *see* WHEAT

dust 1. In cooking, to dust a preparation (such as a cake or bread) involves lightly coating it with a powdery ingredient such as flour, powdered sugar or cocoa powder. The sugar, cocoa, etc. is typically placed in a fine sieve, then the strainer is tapped or shaken lightly to release a fine dusting of the ingredient. The dusting adds both flavor and visual effect. 2. The word "dust" is also used to describe inferior, coarsely crushed tea leaves.

Dutch oven A large pot or kettle, usually made of cast iron, with a tight-fitting lid so steam cannot readily escape. It's used for moist-cooking methods, such as braising and stewing. Dutch ovens are said to be of Pennsylvania Dutch heritage, dating back to the 1700s.

Dutch process *see* COCOA POWDER

duxelles [dook-SEHL; deu-SEHL] A mixture of finely chopped mushrooms, shallots and herbs slowly cooked in butter until it forms a thick paste. It's used to flavor sauces, soups and other mixtures, as well as for a garnish.

dwenjang *see* DOENJANG

eared pepper *see* PEPPER LEAF

Earl Grey tea This popular black tea was named for Charles Grey, the second earl in his line, who was also prime minister to King William IV in the early 19th century. An amalgamation of Indian and Sri Lankan teas, Earl Grey gets its elusive flavor from oil of BERGAMOT. The Earl is said to have been given the recipe by a Chinese mandarin with whom he was friends. *See also* TEA.

Early Richmond cherry So named because it's the first sour cherry available in the late spring, the bright red Early Richmond is excellent for cooking purposes. *See also* CHERRY.

earth almonds *see* CHUFA

earthenware *see* COOKWARE AND BAKEWARE MATERIALS

earthnut *see* PEANUT

earthnuts *see* CHUFA

Eastern oyster *see* ATLANTIC OYSTER

eau de vie [oh deuh VEE] French for "water of life," describing any colorless, potent BRANDY or other spirit distilled from fermented fruit juice. KIRSCH (made from cherries) and FRAMBOISE (raspberries) are two popular *eaux de vie*. *See also* AQUA VITAE; LIQUEUR.

ebi [eh-bee] Japanese for "shrimp" or "prawn."

ebleskive *see* AEBLESKIVE

Eccles cake [EHK-uhls] Named for the Lancashire, England, town of Eccles, this small domed confection has a filling of CURRANTS and other dried fruit mixed with sugar and butter and encased in a PUFF PASTRY shell.

éclair [ay-KLEHR] A small, oblong, cream-filled pastry made with CHOUX PASTRY (cream-puff pastry dough). Unlike CREAM PUFFS, éclairs are usually topped with a sweet icing.

écrevisse [ay-kreh-VEES] French for "CRAYFISH."

Edam [EE-duhm] Hailing from Holland, Edam is second only to GOUDA as Holland's most exported cheese. It's made from PASTEURIZED, partially skimmed milk and comes in spheres (with slightly flattened tops and bottoms) or loaves. Most mass-produced Edams are coated in red wax and are typically RIPENED for 6 to 8 weeks. A black wax coating typically denotes cheeses that have been ripened for a minimum of 17 weeks and sometimes up to 10 months. Edam has a pale yellow PASTE with a smooth, elastic texture and mellow, delicate flavor. Edam's FAT CONTENT ranges from

30 to 40 percent because it's made from skimmed (or partially skimmed) milk. *See also* CHEESE.

edamame [eh-dah-MAH-meh] The Japanese name for green SOYBEANS.

Edelfaule *see* BOTRYTIS CINEREA

edible chrysanthemum *see* CHRYSANTHEMUM LEAVES

EDTA Abbreviation for ethylenediaminetetraacetic acid, an ADDITIVE used in some processed foods to eliminate the possibility of rancidity caused by the transfer of trace metals during the manufacturing process. EDTA has a wide variety of nonculinary uses, including the treatment of lead poisoning.

eel The legends of eels have colored folklore throughout the ages. Some Philippine tribes say that eels are the souls of the dead, while in parts of Europe it's believed that rubbing the skin with eel oil will cause a person to see fairies. Whatever their origin or exterior application, eels are widely popular in Europe and Japan, where many consider their rich, sweet, firm meat a delicacy. This rather long, snakelike fish—of which there are both freshwater and saltwater varieties—has a smooth, scaleless skin. It spawns at sea and dies shortly thereafter. The European and American eel breed deep in Atlantic waters near Bermuda. The minuscule, transparent eel larvae drift on ocean currents for enormous distances—their journey to Europe taking about 3 years—until they reach coastal areas. There they transform into tiny, wormlike *elvers* (baby eel) and begin wriggling up inland waterways and crossing boggy grounds to reach small ponds and streams. After about 10 years of living in this freshwater habitat, the eel begins its migration back to Atlantic waters where it spawns and dies. The *conger eel,* a scaleless, saltwater "monster" fish that can reach up to 10 feet long and weigh over 170 pounds, is a relative of the common eel. Fresh eels, depending on the region, are available year-round, the fall being the peak season. Those under 2 pounds will be more tender. Before cooking, the thick, tough skin and outer layer of fat must be removed—a task usually handled by the fish dealer. Fresh eel should be refrigerated and used within a day or two. It's excellent baked, stewed or grilled. Because conger eel meat is very tough, it is most often used in soups and stews. Eel is also available jellied in cans or smoked. Though considered a fatty fish, the eel is high in vitamins A and D, as well as being a good source of protein. *See also* FISH.

egg *see* EGGS

egg cream This favorite New York City soda fountain drink has been popular since the 1930s. Egg creams don't contain a speck of egg but are so named because of the froth (resembling beaten egg whites) that crowns the drink. They're made with a mixture of milk and CHOCOLATE SYRUP into which SELTZER WATER is spritzed, causing the mixture to foam enthusiastically.

egg drop (egg flower) soup A Chinese soup consisting of chicken broth with shredded chicken or pork, BAMBOO SHOOTS, TOFU and dried SHIITAKE mushrooms. Before serving, beaten egg is swirled into the soup; therefore, the name.

egg foo yong [foo YUHNG] A Chinese-American dish made by combining eggs with various foods such as bean SPROUTS, WATER CHESTNUTS, scallions, ham, chicken or pork. Small, pancake-size portions are poured into a skillet and fried until golden brown. Egg foo yong can also be made in one large round. It is sometimes topped with a sauce of chicken broth, SOY SAUCE and various seasonings.

eggnog A homogeneous blend of milk or cream, beaten eggs, sugar, nutmeg and usually LIQUOR of some kind such as RUM, BRANDY or WHISKEY. Liquor-free eggnog has long been served to convalescents and growing children as a tonic. Some eggnogs are made by separating the eggs and stiffly beating the whites before adding them to the milk mixture, producing an airier brew. Commercial eggnog is sans liquor and is available in cartons beginning around mid-October. Canned eggnog can be found year-round in some locations.

egg piercer A kitchen tool with a sharp steel pin, usually spring-mounted, which pokes a tiny hole in the large end of an egg. This hole prevents the egg from cracking because the air inside (which expands during boiling) can gradually escape.

eggplant Because the eggplant is a member of the nightshade family, it's related to the potato and tomato. Though commonly thought of as a vegetable, eggplant is actually a fruit . . . specifically a berry. There are many varieties of this delicious food, ranging in color from rich purple to white, in length from 2 to 12 inches and in shape from oblong to round. In the United States, the most common eggplant is the large, cylindrical- or pear-shape variety with a smooth, glossy, dark purple skin. It's available year-round, with the peak season during August and September. Choose a firm, smooth-skinned eggplant heavy for its size; avoid those with soft or brown spots. Eggplants become bitter with age and are very perishable. They should be stored in a cool, dry place and used within a day or two of purchase. If longer storage is necessary, place the eggplant in the refrigerator vegetable drawer. When young, the skin of most eggplants is deliciously edible; older eggplants should be peeled. Since the flesh discolors rapidly, an eggplant should be cut just before using. Bitter, overripe fruit can benefit by the ancient method of salting both halves and weighting them for 20 minutes before rinsing; the salt helps eliminate some of the acrid taste. Eggplant can be prepared in a variety of ways including baking, broiling and frying. It does, however, have spongelike capacity to soak up oil so it should be well coated with a batter or crumb mixture to inhibit fat absorption. Many other varieties of this versatile fruit are now finding their way into some markets. The very narrow, straight **Japanese** or **Asian eggplant** ranges in color from solid purple to striated shades and has tender, slightly sweet flesh. The **Italian** or **baby eggplant** looks like a miniature version of the common large variety, but has a more delicate skin and flesh. The appearance of the egg-shaped **white eggplant** makes it clear how this fruit was named. It has a tougher skin, but firmer, smoother flesh. In general, these varieties can be cooked in many of the same methods as the large eggplant. They rarely require salting, however, and usually benefit from a short cooking time.

eggplant caviar A thick, puréed mixture of roasted eggplant, tomato, onion, olive oil and various seasonings. It's served cold or at room temperature as a dip or spread.

egg ring A round, bottomless, stainless steel ring, sometimes with a vertical handle, in which an egg can be poached or fried. The ring keeps the egg perfectly round during cooking. It's removed before the egg is served.

egg roll A small, stuffed Chinese pastry usually served as an appetizer. Paper-thin pastry wrappers are folded around a savory filling of minced or shredded vegetables and sometimes meat, then folded and rolled before being deep-fried or sometimes, steamed. Egg roll skins (the pastry wrappers) are available in the refrigerator section of Asian markets and most supermarkets. **Spring rolls**, so named because they're traditionally served on the first day of the Chinese New Year (in early spring), are smaller, more delicate versions of the egg roll.

egg roll skins (wrappers) Paper thin squares of dough made with flour, water and salt. They're larger than WON TON SKINS and are used to make EGG ROLLS and SPRING ROLLS. They can be purchased packaged in Asian markets and some supermarkets. Refrigerate for up to 2 months; freeze for up to 6 months.

eggs Legends about eggs have abounded throughout the eons. Early Phoenicians thought that a primeval egg split open to form heaven and earth; Egyptians believed that their god Ptah created the egg from the sun and the moon; and American Indians thought that the Great Spirit burst forth from a giant golden egg to create the world. In all of the early legends the chicken is never mentioned, making the answer to the question of which came first—the chicken or the egg—seem obvious. The most common egg used for food today is the hen's egg, though those from other fowl—including duck, goose and quail—are sold in many areas. Hens' eggs have long been bedeviled by their high cholesterol content (about 213 milligrams for a large egg), which is contained entirely in the yolk. Since the American Heart Association recommends that adults limit their cholesterol consumption to no more than 300 milligrams of cholesterol a day, strict cholesterol watchers generally either drastically reduce their egg consumption or eat the whites only. Most hens' eggs on the market today have been classified according to quality and size under USDA standards. In descending order, egg grades are AA, A and B, the classification being determined by both exterior and interior quality. The factors determining exterior quality include the soundness, cleanliness, shape and texture of the shell. Interior quality is judged by "candling," so named because in days gone by an egg was held up in front of a candle to see inside. Today, candling is more likely to be accomplished electrically, with the eggs moving and rotating on rollers over high-intensity lights. The interior quality is determined by the size of the air cell (the empty space between the white and shell at the large end of the egg—smaller in high-quality eggs), the proportion and density of the white, and whether or not the yolk is firm and free of defects. In high-quality eggs, both the white and yolk stand higher, and the white spreads less than in lower-grade eggs. Eggs come in the following sizes based on their minimum weight per dozen: jumbo (30 oz. per dozen), extra large (27 oz.), large (24 oz.), medium (21 oz.), small (18 oz.) and peewee (15 oz.). Large eggs are those on which most recipes are based. An eggshell's color—white or brown—is determined by the breed of hen that laid it and has nothing to do with either taste or nutritive value. The egg white is an excellent source of protein and riboflavin. Egg yolks contain all of the fat in an egg and are a good source of protein, iron, vitamins A and D, choline and phosphorus. The color of the yolk depends entirely on the hen's diet. Hens fed on alfalfa, grass and yellow corn lay eggs with lighter yolks than wheat-fed hens. CHALAZAE are the thick, cordlike strands of egg white attached to 2 sides of the yolk that serve to anchor it in the center of the egg. The more prominent the chalazae, the fresher the egg. Blood spots on egg yolks are the result of a natural occurrence, such as a blood vessel rupturing on the surface. They do not indicate that the egg is fertile, nor do they affect flavor. Contrary to popular belief, fertile eggs—expensive because of high production costs—are no more nutritious than nonfertile ones. They do contain a small amount of male hormone and do not keep as well as other eggs. **Storing eggs:** Eggs must always be refrigerated. When stored at room temperature, they lose more quality in 1 day than in a week in the refrigerator. Eggs should be stored in the carton in which they came; transferring them to the egg container in the refrigerator door exposes them to odors and damage. They should always be stored large-end-up and should never be placed near odoriferous foods (such as onions) because they easily absorb odors. The best flavor and cooking quality will be realized in eggs used within a week. They can, however, be refrigerated up to a month, providing the shells are intact. Leftover yolks can be covered with cold water and refrigerated, tightly covered, for up to 3 days. They can be frozen only with the addition of $\frac{1}{8}$ teaspoon salt or $1\frac{1}{2}$ teaspoons sugar or corn syrup per $\frac{1}{4}$ cup egg yolks. Tightly covered egg whites can be refrigerated up to 4 days. They can be frozen as is up to 6 months. An easy way to freeze whites is to place one in each section of an ice cube tray. Freeze, then pop the egg-white cubes out into a freezer-weight plastic bag. Both frozen egg yolks and whites should be thawed overnight in the refrigerator before being used. Hard-cooked eggs should be refrigerated no more than a week. Eggs are available in other forms including powdered and frozen (whole or separated). Commercially frozen egg products are generally PASTEURIZED and some contain stabilizing ingredients. Another egg product available to consumers is table-ready **pasteurized liquid eggs**, which can be found in a supermarket's refrigerated section. This product mixes the white and yolks, then pasteurizes them at a heat level that kills any bacteria without cooking the eggs. Pasteurized eggs are sold in 8- and 16-ounce cartons ($4\frac{1}{2}$ and 9 whole eggs respectively). They can be refrigerated unopened for up to 12 weeks from the pack date (*see* OPEN DATING). The multitalented egg is delicious not only as a food in its own right but has numerous other uses as a LEAVENER in cakes, breads and soufflés; a base for dressings such as mayonnaise; a thickener in sauces and custards; a clarifying agent for stocks; and a coating for breaded or battered foods. *See also* EGGNOG; EGG PIERCER; EGG RING; EGGS BENEDICT; EGG SCISSORS; EGG SEPARATOR; EGG SLICER; EGGS SARDOU; EGG SUBSTITUTES; EGG TIMER; EGG WASH; OEUF; OEUFS À LA NEIGE; OEUF EN GELÉE; STUFFED EGG.

eggs Benedict A breakfast or brunch specialty consisting of two toasted English muffin halves, each topped with a slice of ham or Canadian bacon, a poached egg and a dollop of HOLLANDAISE. The most popular legend of the dish's origin says that it originated at Manhattan's famous Delmonico's Restaurant when regular patrons, Mr. and Mrs. LeGrand Benedict, complained that there was nothing new on the lunch menu. Delmonico's maitre d' and Mrs. Benedict began discussing possibilities and eggs Benedict was the result.

egg scissors Used to remove the top of soft-cooked eggs, this circular gadget has a scissors-style handle. It's positioned over the top of the egg and, when the handle is operated, a ring of "teeth" or a ringed blade clips off the top third of the eggshell.

egg separator A device that resembles a small, handled saucer with a slot running around the center about $1\frac{1}{2}$ inches from the edge. Crack an egg into the separator and the yolk stays in the solid center portion, the white runs through the slot.

egg slicer A kitchen tool with a slatted, egg-shaped hollow on the bottom and a hinged top consisting of 10 fine steel wires. When the upper portion is brought down onto a hard-cooked egg sitting in the base, it cuts the egg into even slices.

eggs Sardou [sahr-DOO] Named for Victorien Sardou, a famous French dramatist, this specialty of Antoine's restaurant in New Orleans consists of poached eggs topped with artichoke hearts, ham, anchovies, truffles and HOLLANDAISE.

egg substitutes A liquid sold in cartons, this product is usually a blend of egg whites, food starch, corn oil, skim-milk powder, TOFU, artificial coloring and a plethora of additives. It contains no cholesterol but each serving is almost as high in sodium as a real egg. Egg substitutes can be scrambled and also used in many baking and cooking recipes calling for whole eggs.

egg timer A tiny "hourglass" that holds just enough sand to run from top to bottom in 3 minutes, the time it takes to soft-boil an egg.

egg wash Egg yolk or egg white mixed with a small amount of water or milk. It's brushed over breads, pastry and other baked goods before baking to give them color and gloss.

86 Restaurant slang for being out of a menu item, such as "86 the lamb chops."

einkorn [IN-korn] An ancient CEREAL GRAIN that belongs to the wheat family. Along with EMMER einkorn was one of the first wheat varieties to be cultivated; it grew wild until domesticated in southeast Turkey 7,000 to 9,000 years ago. Over time it was replaced by modern-day wheat varieties that were more productive. It's now regaining favor as a healthier alternative to today's wheat offerings. Einkorn is said to provide added levels of antioxidant vitamins, such as beta carotene, lutein, riboflavin and vitamin A. Its GLUTEN structure is also different and thought to be more suitable for those with gluten intolerance. Historically einkorn had a reputation for being difficult to use in baking, but today's methods produce satisfactory results that are welcomed since the grain retains more of its antioxidants during cooking and baking. Einkorn has limited availability; it can be found in natural food stores and through the Internet.

Eisbock [ICE-bahk] German for "ice beer." *See also* BEER; BOCK BEER.

Eiswein [ICE-vine] *see* ICE WINE

Elberta peach [ehl-BER-tuh] A large FREESTONE peach with a sweet, succulent flesh and red-blushed, yellow skin. It's good both for eating out of hand and for cooking. *See also* PEACH.

elbow pasta *see* Pasta Glossary, page 883

elderberry The purple-black, tart fruit of the elder tree. Elderberries can be eaten raw (though they're quite sour) but are better cooked for jams, pies and homemade wine. The creamy white **elderberry flowers** can be added to salads or batter-dipped and fried like fritters.

election cake This rich, yeast-raised cake is replete with nuts, candied fruit and sherry-soaked raisins. It was created in the 18th century to celebrate election day.

elephant ear *see* WOOD EAR

elephant garlic *see* GARLIC

elitses olive [AH-lee-tahs] Very small, brine-cured, oval-shaped olive from the Greek island of Crete. The elitses olive ranges from brownish-green to dark purple. It has more pit than meat, but the meat is fruity, nutty and sweet. Elitses olives are tiny—thus the name, which means "little olives." *See also* OLIVE.

elk *see* GAME ANIMALS

Elstar An all-purpose variety of apple developed in the Netherlands, a CROSS between a GOLDEN DELICIOUS and an Ingrid Marie variety. This medium-sized apple is marbled with a deep red overlaying a golden background. The texture is moderately crisp and the flavor sweet, with hints of nectarine and pear, but balanced with enough acidity to make it very flavorful. *See also* APPLE.

elver *see* EEL

embutido [em-boo-TEE-doh] 1. A popular Philippine MEATLOAF comprised of ground pork and/or chicken, various chopped vegetables and seasonings and almost always raisins and sweet pickles or pickle relish. Many recipes call for embutido to be topped with CHORIZO and hard boiled eggs. 2. In Spain and other Spanish-speaking cultures embutido refers to SAUSAGE, generally made of pork.

Emmental; Emmentaler; Emmenthal [EM-mawn-tahl] Produced since the 13th century, Emmental is Switzerland's oldest and most important cheese. It's named for that country's Emme Valley and is the SWISS CHEESE after which all others were patterned. The only true

Emmental is produced in Switzerland, but the name isn't protected so you'll also find "Emmentals" from other countries including Austria, France, Denmark, Finland, Germany and the United States. The majority of non-Swiss Emmentals are factory-produced with PASTEURIZED MILK. Swiss Emmental is made from raw milk from cows who've fed on grass and hay, but never silage. The giant 200-pound Emmental WHEELS are about 45 inches in diameter and up to 9 inches thick. The thin, hard rind ranges in color from pale yellow to yellow-brown and the ivory-yellow interior has a supple, smooth texture and a random scattering of cherry- to walnut-size EYES. Emmental has a buttery, delicately sweet, earthy, fruity flavor. Young examples have notes of hazelnut, aged versions become spicy. Authentic Emmentals will always have the words "Emmental" and "Switzerland" stamped on the rind. Minimum RIPENING time is 4 months, 8 months for "mature," and 12 months or more for "fully mature." **French Emmental** has been made for almost as long as the Swiss original and the recipes and production methods are primarily the same, though French versions are mostly factory-produced. Whereas regular French Emmental is based on pasteurized milk, those labeled *Emmental Grand Cru* are made with raw milk. Germany's **Allgäuer Emmenthaler** is typically made from pasteurized milk and is less flavorful than Swiss and French versions, in part because it's not aged as long. *See also* CHEESE.

emmer [EM-uhr] This ancient CEREAL GRAIN belongs to the wheat family and dates as far back as 20,000 years. Also known as *farro,* emmer was the primary grain cultivated by early Egyptians and became a staple of the Roman legions during their occupation of Egypt. Over time, emmer's popularity gave way to higher-yielding, easier-to-grow varieties of wheat grains. However, it began reemerging in Italy, where it's known as *farro,* and is now attracting attention from cooks around the world. Tuscany's Garfagnana area has been granted PROTECTED GEOGRAPHICAL INDICATION status for its *Farro della Garfagnana.* Though emmer is often confused with SPELT (which is sometimes also called *farro*), they are different grains. Emmer has a dense, chewy structure and a rich, nutty flavor. It can be used in pasta, bread and for RISOTTO-style dishes.

empanada [em-pah-NAH-dah; em-pah-NAH-thah] *Empanar* is Spanish for "to bake in pastry," and these Mexican and Spanish specialties are usually single-serving TURNOVERS with a pastry crust and savory meat-and-vegetable filling. They can also be filled with fruit and served as dessert. Empanadas range in size from the huge *empanada gallega,* large enough to feed an entire family, to *empanaditas*—tiny, ravioli-size pastries.

emperor grape In season from November to May, the large emperor grape comes from California and has an elongated oval shape. The thin, pale red to purple-red skin covers a mild-flavored flesh with scattered seeds. *See also* GRAPE.

Empire apple A medium-large, all-purpose apple that is a cross between MCINTOSH and RED DELICIOUS varieties. The Empire's skin is deep red with a light yellow-green background. It has fine-grained white flesh that's crisp and juicy and a good balance of sweet and tart, with a hint of berries and spice. *See also* APPLE.

emulsifier [eh-MUHL-suh-fi-er] Generally, any ingredient used to bind together normally noncombinative substances, such as oil and water. Egg yolks contain a natural emulsifier (LECITHIN) and are used to thicken and BIND sauces (such as HOLLANDAISE), as well as to bind ingredients in baking. XANTHAN GUM is a commercial emulsifier used in numerous foods like salad dressings and dairy products. Some commercial emulsifiers also inhibit baked goods from going stale.

emulsion [ih-MUHL-shuhn] A mixture of one liquid with another with which it cannot normally combine smoothly—oil and water being the classic example. Emulsifying is done by slowly (sometimes drop-by-drop) adding one ingredient to another while at the same time mixing rapidly. This disperses and suspends minute droplets of one liquid throughout the other. Emulsified mixtures are usually thick and satiny in texture. Mayonnaise (an uncooked combination of oil, egg yolks and vinegar or lemon juice) and HOLLANDAISE (a cooked mixture of butter, egg yolks and vinegar or lemon juice) are two of the best-known emulsions.

enamelware *see* COOKWARE AND BAKEWARE MATERIALS

enchilada [en-chuh-LAH-dah; en-chee-LAH-thah] This Mexican specialty is made by rolling a softened corn tortilla around a meat or cheese filling. It's served hot, usually topped with a tomato-based salsa and sprinkled with cheese.

Enchilado [en-chee-LAH-doh] Semihard to hard, cow's- or goat's-milk cheese that originated in Mexico. Enchilado is similar to COTIJA but slightly blander and differentiated by a red coating of mild chili powder or paprika. Younger versions are firm and crumbly with a salty, milky flavor that's slightly tangy and spicy. The more assertively flavored older renditions (called *Enchilado Añejo* or *Añejo Enchilado*) have a harder, drier texture that's good for grating. *See also* CHEESE.

en cocotte *see* COCOTTE

en croûte *see* CROÛTE

endigia [ahn-DEE-jee-yah] A cross between white ENDIVE and red-leafed Italian CHICORY, both of which are part of the botanical family

Cichorium. Endigia is proprietary, created by the French government during a decade-long propagation program. The magenta-colored leaves have a pearlescent white base and veins. The darker portions are slightly bitter while the lighter areas are somewhat sweet, the combination of which hints of nuttiness. Endigia is available year round, but typically only in specialty produce markets and through mail order. The small heads should have crisp, full-colored leaves with no sign of browning or wilting. Store in a plastic bag in the refrigerator for up to a week. Endigia has a crisp texture and may be used raw in salads or cooked by grilling, sautéing or baking.

endive [EN-dyv; AHN-deev; ahn-DEEV] Endive is closely related to and often confused with its cousin, CHICORY. They're both part of the same botanical family, *Cichorium*. There are three main varieties of endive: Belgian endive, curly endive and escarole. **Belgian endive**, also known as *French endive* and *witloof* (white leaf), is a small (about 6-inch-long), cigar-shaped head of cream-colored, tightly packed, slightly bitter leaves. It's grown in complete darkness to prevent it from turning green, using a labor-intensive growing technique known as BLANCHING. Belgian endive is available year-round with a peak season from November through April. Buy crisp, firmly packed heads with pale, yellow-green tips. Belgian endives become bitter when exposed to light. They should be refrigerated, wrapped in a paper towel inside a plastic bag, for no more than a day. They can be served cold as part of a salad, or cooked by braising or baking. **Curly endive**, often mistakenly called *chicory* in the United States, grows in loose heads of lacy, green-rimmed outer leaves that curl at the tips. The off-white center leaves form a compact heart. The leaves of the curly endive have a prickly texture and slightly bitter taste. **Escarole** has broad, slightly curved, pale green leaves with a milder flavor than either Belgian or curly endive. Both curly endive and escarole are available year-round, with the peak season from June through October. They should be selected for their fresh, crisp texture; avoid heads with discoloration or insect damage. Store curly endive and escarole, tightly wrapped, in the refrigerator for up to 3 days. They're both used mainly in salads, but can also be briefly cooked and eaten as a vegetable or in soups.

English breakfast A large, hearty breakfast that can include fruit or juice, eggs, ham or other meat, fish, cereal, baked goods, jam and tea. Compare to CONTINENTAL BREAKFAST.

English breakfast tea A hearty blend of several of various black teas (usually ASSAM and CEYLON). English breakfast tea is more full-flavored and full-bodied than a single black tea. *See also* TEA.

English Morello cherry *see* MORELLO CHERRY

English muffin This round, rather flat (3 to 4 inches in diameter by 1 inch high) "muffin" is made from a soft yeast dough that, after being formed into rounds (by hand or with CRUMPET RINGS), is baked on a griddle. It can be made at home but is readily available commercially in an assortment of flavors including sourdough, whole wheat, raisin, cinnamon and cornmeal. English muffins are halved before toasting. In order to produce a surface with the proper peaks and craters (which adds to their crunchy texture and provides plentiful pockets for butter and jam), English muffins must be fork-split and gently pulled apart. Using a knife to cut them in half will not produce the desired result.

English muffin ring *see* CRUMPET RING

English mustard An extremely hot powdered mustard containing ground mustard seeds (both black or brown and yellow-white), wheat flour and turmeric. The most well-known brand of powdered mustard today is Colman's, named for its 19th-century British developer, Jeremiah Colman. *See also* MUSTARD.

English pea The common *garden pea*, also known simply as *green pea*. But there's nothing common about its flavor, particularly during the peak months of March, April and May and again from August to November. The French are famous for their tiny, young green peas known as *petits pois*. Choose peas that have plump, unblemished, bright green pods; the peas inside should be glossy, crunchy and sweet. Because peas begin the sugar-to-starch conversion process the moment they're picked, it's important to buy them as fresh as possible. Refrigerate peas in their pods in a plastic bag for no more than 2 to 3 days. Shell just before using. Both English peas and the French petits pois are available frozen and canned. Peas are a fair source of vitamins A and C, as well as niacin and iron. *See also* PEA; LEGUME.

English sole Also called *lemon sole* in the United States, this species of FLOUNDER is low in fat and finely textured. It ranges from $1/4$ to 2 pounds and can be purchased whole or in fillets. It's often labeled simply as "fillet of SOLE." English sole can be prepared in a variety of ways including baking, broiling, poaching and sautéing. *See also* FISH.

English tomato *see* KIWANO

English walnut The United States (mainly California) is the world's leading producer of the English walnut (also called *Persian walnut*). It's grown in several other countries including China, France, India, Iran, Turkey and Yugoslavia. The English walnut has a wrinkled, tan-colored shell that encloses two large, double-lobed halves. Its sweet flavor makes it a delicious choice for out-of-hand eating, as well as a popular addition for all manner of foods sweet and savory. English walnuts are used to produce walnut oil; they also come in candied and pickled forms. They're available prepackaged or in bulk. English walnuts are a potent source of Omega-3 oils (*see* FATS AND OILS). *See also* NUTS; WALNUT.

enoki; enokitake; enokidake mushrooms [en-oh-kee] The cultivated variety of these crisply delicate mushrooms comes in clumps of long, spaghettilike stems topped with tiny, snowy white caps. (In contrast, the wild form has orangy-brown, very shiny caps.) Enoki mushrooms have an appealingly crunchy texture and mild—almost fruity—taste, unlike the bosky flavor of most mushrooms. They're available fresh year-round (depending on the region) in Asian markets and many supermarkets. They can also be purchased canned. Choose fresh mushrooms that are firm and white. Refrigerate, wrapped in paper towel then a plastic bag, up to 5 days. Before using, they should be cut away from the mass at the base of the stems. Enoki are particularly good raw in salads. They may also be used to garnish soups or other hot dishes. If used as part of a cooked dish, they should be added at the last minute, as heat tends to make them tough. These tiny mushrooms provide a good source of vitamin D, as well as small amounts of the B-complex vitamins. The enoki is also called *snow puff mushroom, golden mushroom* and *velvet stem*. *See also* MUSHROOMS.

enology [ee-NAHL-uh-jee] Also spelled *oenology,* this is the science or study of viniculture (making wines). One who studies the science is called an **enologist** (or **oenologist**). *See also* ENOPHILE.

enophile [EE-nuh-file] Someone who enjoys wine, usually referring to a connoisseur. Also spelled *oenophile*. *See also* ENOLOGY.

Enova oil *see* FAT SUBSTITUTES

en papillote *see* PAPILLOTE

enrich; enriched; enrichment 1. A term usually applied to flour that, after the milling has stripped it of the wheat germ and other nutritious elements, has niacin, riboflavin and thiamin added back into it. U.S. law requires that flours not containing wheat germ must have these nutrients replenished. *See also* Food Label Terms, page 876. 2. Enriching and thickening a sauce with the last-minute addition of an ingredient such as butter, cream or egg yolks.

ensalada [ahn-sah-LAH-dah] Spanish for "salad."

Entrammes *see* PORT-SALUT

entrecôte [ahn-treh-KOHT] Literally meaning "between the ribs," this French term refers to a steak cut from between the ninth and eleventh ribs of beef. It's a very tender cut and is usually cooked by quickly broiling or sautéing.

entrée [AHN-tray] 1. In America, the term "entrée" refers to the main course of a meal. 2. In parts of Europe, it refers to the dish served between the fish and meat courses during formal dinners. 3. In Australia, the entrée is the first course or appetizer.

entremesas [ehn-treh-MAY-sehs] Spanish for "APPETIZERS."

entremetier [ahn-truh-may-TYAY] *see* BRIGADE SYSTEM

entremets [AHN-truh-may] French for "between dishes," the word *entremets* on a menu refers to desserts. At one time, this word was used to describe small side dishes served between principal courses or with the main course.

epazote [eh-pah-ZOH-teh] A pungent, wild herb whose strong flavor is, like that of fresh coriander, an acquired taste. It has flat, pointed leaves and is available dried (and infrequently fresh)in Latin markets. Also called *Mexican tea* and *wormseed,* epazote is popular in many bean dishes because it's a carminative, which means it reduces gas. It's also used as a tea. *See also* HERBS.

épice [ay-PEES] French for "spice." *See also* QUATRE ÉPICES.

épices fines [ay-PEES feen] Literally meaning "fine spices," this complex blend of herbs and spices is usually marketed under the name SPICE PARISIENNE.

epicure [EHP-ih-kyoor] A person of refined taste, who cultivates the knowledge and appreciation of fine food and wine. *See also* GASTRONOME; GLUTTON; GOURMAND; GOURMET.

épinard [ay-pee-NAHR] French for "spinach."

Époisses de Bourgogne [ay-PWAHSS deuh boor-GO-nyuh] A washed rind cow's-milk cheese first created in the early 1500s by Cistercian monks in the Burgundian village of Époisses. It was a favorite of Napoleon and declared "King of Cheeses" by famous French gastronomic writer Brillant-Savarin in 1825. Its popularity dwindled in the 1900s, a victim of the two World Wars, and Époisses effectively disappeared until revived in the mid-1950s by Robert and Simone Berthaut. Since then it's gained a huge following of those who enjoy a strong-smelling, pungently flavored cheese. As it's ripening, Époisses is regularly brushed with a mixture of water and MARC. This process helps evenly spread desirable bacteria over the cheese's surface, producing a bright orange rind, a creamy texture and a savory, earthy flavor. The 7-ounce wheels are packaged in protective wooden boxes. Époisses has a minimum FAT CONTENT of 50 percent. The Berthauts also produce **Aisy Cendré**, a shorter-aged "young Époisses," and their **Affidelice**, which is washed with CHABLIS instead of marc. *See also* CHEESE.

equivalents *see* Ingredient Equivalents, page 842; U.S. Measurement Equivalents, page 869; and Approximate Metric Equivalents, page 871

erba (EHR-bah) Italian for "herb."

escabèche [es-keh-BEHSH] Of Spanish origin, escabèche is a dish of poached or fried fish, covered with a spicy MARINADE and refrigerated for at least 24 hours. It's a popular dish in Spain and the Provençal region of France, and is usually served cold as an appetizer. *Escovitch* is the Jamaican name for this dish.

escalope [eh-SKAL-ohp; eh-skah-LAWP] The French term for a very thin, usually flattened, slice of meat or fish. The tender escalope requires only a few seconds of sautéing on both sides. In the United States, this cut is known as "scallop."

escargot [ehs-kahr-GOH] French for "SNAIL."

escarole [EHS-kuh-rohl] *see* ENDIVE

escovitch [ess-koh-VEETCH] *see* ESCABÈCHE

espagnole, à l' [ah lehs-pahn-YOHL] A French term for foods prepared in the Spanish style, usually with tomatoes, onions, garlic and sweet peppers.

espagnole sauce [ehs-pah-NYOHL] A rich, reduced (*see* REDUCE) BROWN STOCK containing herbs, tomato purée or fresh tomatoes and a MIREPOIX of browned vegetables, all thickened by brown ROUX. Espagnole is one of the four original "mother sauces" (*see* SAUCE).

Espelette pepper *see* PIMENT D'ESPELETTE

espresso [ehs-PREHS-oh] A dark, strong coffee made by forcing steam (or hot water) through finely ground, Italian-roast coffee especially blended for making espresso. This form of brewing produces a thin layer of creamy, dark beige froth on the coffee's surface. Espresso is served in a tiny espresso (or DEMITASSE) cup. An *espresso doppio* [DOHP-pyoh] is simply a double espresso.

Esrom [EHS-rom] Hailing from Denmark, this semihard cow's-milk cheese comes in loaves of various sizes ranging from 2 to 5 pounds. Esrom has a thin rind that ranges in color from yellow-orange to yellow-brown. The supple, smooth interior is ivory to yellow and has irregularly shaped

EYES. Though Esrom has a distinctively smelly rind, its PASTE has a comparatively mild flavor that's buttery and spicy, becoming more robust with age. This cheese undergoes RIPENING for anywhere from 10 to 12 weeks. Esrom comes in two versions—*full-fat*, which has a minimum FAT CONTENT of 45 percent, and *extra full-fat* with at least 60 percent fat. *See also* CHEESE.

essences Concentrated, usually oily substances extracted from food such as fish, mint leaves, vegetables or flowers and used in small amounts to flavor various dishes. Like EXTRACTS, essences will keep indefinitely if stored in a cool dark place.

estate bottled *see* WINE LABEL TERMS

estouffade [ehs-too-FAHD] 1. A French stew whereby the meat is marinated in wine before being browned and slowly cooked in a tightly covered pan. 2. The term was also once commonly used to describe a rich, brown stock used for braising and to enhance other sauces.

ethyl alcohol *see* ALCOHOL

Eton mess English dessert consisting of pieces of meringue, whipped cream and fruit, usually strawberries but sometimes bananas or other fruit. It's traditionally served at Eton College, at one of the school's annual cricket matches.

étouffée; à l'étouffée [ay-too-FAY] A popular CAJUN dish of a thick, spicy stew of CRAYFISH and vegetables served over white rice. Its rich, deep color and flavor come from the dark brown ROUX on which it's based. The word *étouffée* comes from the French *étouffer,* "to smother" or "to suffocate." The term **à l'étouffée** refers to the method of cooking food in a minute amount of liquid, tightly covered and over very low heat. This method is also called *à l'étuvée.*

étuvée, à l' *see* ÉTOUFFÉE

eulachon *see* SMELT

evaporated milk This canned, unsweetened milk is fresh, homogenized milk from which 60 percent of the water has been removed. Vitamin D is added for extra nutritional value. It comes in whole, lowfat and skim forms; the whole-milk version must contain at least 7.9 percent milk fat, the lowfat has about half that and the skim version $1/2$ percent or less. As it comes from the can, evaporated milk is used to enrich custards or add a creamy texture to many dishes. When mixed with an equal amount of water, it can be substituted for fresh milk in recipes. Evaporated milk is less expensive than fresh milk and is therefore popular for many cooked dishes. It has a slightly caramelized, "canned" flavor that is not appreciated by all who taste it. Canned milk can be stored at room temperature until opened, after which it must be tightly covered and refrigerated for no more than a week. When slightly frozen, evaporated milk can be whipped and used as an inexpensive substitute for whipped cream.

eviscerate [eh-VIHS-uh-rayt] *see* DRAW

executive chef *see* BRIGADE SYSTEM

Explorateur [ehk-sploh-rah-TYOOR] This sensuously rich TRIPLE-CREAM CHEESE is made from cow's milk and contains 75 percent fat. It comes in chunky cylinders with white rinds. When ripe, the ivory interior has a sweet, buttery, slightly piquant flavor. Explorateur is RIPENED for 2 to 3 weeks and only pasteurized-milk versions can be imported into the United States. *See also* CHEESE.

extracts Concentrated flavorings derived from various foods or plants, usually through evaporation or DISTILLATION. Extracts can come in several forms including solid (as in a bouillon cube), liquid (such as vanilla extract) or jellylike (as with a DEMI-GLACE). They deliver a powerful flavor impact to foods without adding excess volume or changing the consistency. Liquid extracts will keep indefinitely if stored in a cool, dark place. *See also* ESSENCES.

extra brut *see* BRUT

extra dry *see* CHAMPAGNE

extra sec *see* CHAMPAGNE

eyes In the cheese world, the word *eyes* refers to the holes in cheese, a characteristic that makes Swiss cheeses *Swiss*. Eyes are formed by carbon dioxide gas (CO_2), which is produced by natural and harmless bacteria that's added during the initial stage of cheesemaking. Eyes (also simply called *holes*) can range in size from that of a pinhead to as large as a walnut.

faba bean *see* FAVA BEAN

fagara *see* SZECHUAN PEPPER

fagioli [fah-ZHOH-lee] Italian for "BEANS," typically referring to white KIDNEY BEANS.

fagiolini [fah-zhoh-LEE-nee] Italian for "little beans," referring to GREEN BEANS.

Fahrenheit [FEHR-uhn-hite] A temperature scale in which 32° represents freezing and 212° represents the steam point. The scale was devised by Gabriel Daniel Fahrenheit, an 18th-century German physicist. To convert Fahrenheit temperatures to CELSIUS, subtract 32 from the Fahrenheit reading, multiply by 5 and divide by 9. *See also* General Temperature Equivalents page 862; Fahrenheit/Celsius Conversion Formulas, page 863.

faisselle [fays-SEHL] 1. French for a perforated cheese MOLD, which comes in numerous sizes and shapes. Some European cheesemakers send fresh cheese (still exuding WHEY) in faisselle directly to market, where the purveyor turns out the cheese into a plastic bag and sends it home with the buyer. CHÈVRE is often formed in a faisselle. 2. Generic name for fresh cheeses shaped in such molds.

fajitas [fah-HEE-tuhs] SKIRT STEAK that has been marinated in a mixture of oil, lime juice, red pepper and garlic for at least 24 hours before being grilled. The cooked meat is cut into strips that are then usually wrapped (BURRITO-style) in warm TORTILLAS, accompanied by a variety of garnishes including grilled onions and sweet peppers, GUACAMOLE, REFRIED BEANS and SALSA.

falafel; felafel [feh-LAH-fehl] A Middle Eastern specialty consisting of small, deep-fried CROQUETTES or balls made of highly spiced, ground CHICKPEAS. They're generally tucked inside PITA bread, sandwich-style, but can also be served as appetizers. A yogurt- or TAHINI-based sauce is often served with falafel.

Falernum [fuh-LER-nuhm] A syrupy sweetener with a flavor reminiscent of lime, ginger and almonds. It's made in the West Indies, primarily used in mixed drinks and can be found in liquor stores.

falooda [fah-LOO-dah] Unique, sweet dessert beverage popular in India, Pakistan and surrounding countries. It's made with KULFI (ice cream), milk or water and is traditionally flavored with ROSE SYRUP—although chocolate, KESAR, mango, pistachio, strawberry and vanilla are also used—and mixed with BASIL SEEDS, FALOODA NOODLES and/or pearl TAPIOCA. Sometimes the falooda mixture is poured over scoops of ice cream, making it look somewhat like an ice cream soda. BUBBLE TEA with its use of pearl tapioca is another similar beverage. The basil seeds, falooda noodles and pearl tapioca all give the drink a chewy texture.

falooda noodles [fah-LOO-dah] Translucent threads, similar to CELLOPHANE NOODLES, usually made from arrowroot starch and sometimes cornstarch. The starch is cooked until it's thick; the mixture is then pressed through a SEV PRESS into a pot of ice water. The ice water helps the noodles form and keep their shape. In India and Pakistan, falooda noodles are flavored with ROSE SYRUP and used as a topping for KULFI (ice cream) or added to a FALOODA beverage.

Far Breton [BREH-tuhn; *Fr.* BRIHT-oh*n*] Originally a savory dish, the Far Breton became a sweet dessert around the 19th century. *Far* is from *farine*, the French word for "flour," and *Breton* refers to Brittany, a region in northwest France where the dish originated. It's traditionally made with prunes or raisins covered with a sweetened, flavored batter of eggs, milk and flour, then baked. It's similar to CLAFOUTIS, a French dessert from Limousin.

farce; farci [FAHRS; fahr-SEE] French for "stuffing." *Farci* means "stuffed."

farfalle; farfallini; farfallone *see* Pasta Glossary, page 883

farfel [FAHR-fuhl] 1. An egg-noodle dough that is grated or minced and used in soups. 2. In Jewish cookery, *farfel* refers to food—such as dried noodles—broken into small pieces.

Farga Aragon olive [fahr-GAH AYR-ah-gon; AYR-ah-gohn] Medium-size, oval Spanish olive that's brine-cured. The olives have deep-brown, dappled skins and tender, meaty flesh. The flavor is rich, nutty and complex. Despite the Aragon name, the Farga variety is also grown in neighboring provinces in eastern Spain. *See also* SPANISH OLIVES; OLIVE.

farik *see* FREEKEH

farina [fuh-REE-nuh] 1. Made from a CEREAL GRAIN, farina is a bland-tasting flour or meal that, when cooked in boiling water, makes a hot breakfast cereal. It's very easily digested and rich in protein. 2. Italian for "FLOUR."

farine [fuh-REEN] French for "flour."

farl; farle [FAHRL] 1. A thin Scottish griddle cake made of oatmeal or flour and cut into triangular wedges. Farls, which are similar to SCONES, take their name from the word *fardel* meaning "fourth part" and referring to a fourth part or quarter cut of a round cake. 2. The triangular wedge shape is also referred to as a "farl."

farmer('s) cheese This fresh cheese is a form of COTTAGE CHEESE from which most of the liquid has been pressed. The very dry farmer cheese is sold in solid loaves or log shapes and is sometimes available in dry curds (like cottage cheese without the liquid). This cheese has a mild, slightly tangy flavor and is firm enough to slice or crumble. It's sometimes flavored with a variety of seasonings including basil, caraway, dill, garlic and jalapeño. Farmer cheese is an all-purpose cheese that can be eaten as is or used in cooking. *See also* CHEESE.

farmstead; farmhouse A term used primarily in the world of cheese to describe cheeses that are produced on a single farm from milk that comes exclusively from that farmer's animals. The cheese is typically made in small batches by ARTISANAL methods with high-quality ingredients, which translates in the marketplace to better quality and higher cost. Artisinal cheese differs in the respect that the milk can come from the animals of other farms, though many artisan cheesemakers use their own animals for milk. Although the term *farmstead* is commonly used in the United States, in Europe the synonym is *farmhouse*.

farro [FAHR-oh] *see* EMMER

fasnacht; fastnacht [FAHS-nahkt] A yeast-raised potato pastry that's deep-fried like a doughnut. *Fasnachts* were originally made and served on Shrove Tuesday to use up the fat that was forbidden during Lent. They're diamond-shaped and often have a slit cut down the center before frying. They first appeared in Pennsylvania, though there is some argument whether the actual origin is German or Dutch.

fatback Often confused with SALT PORK (which comes from the sides and belly of a pig), fatback is the fresh (unsmoked and unsalted) layer of fat that runs along the animal's back. It is used to make LARD and CRACKLINGS and for cooking—especially in many Southern recipes. Salt-cured fatback is also sometimes available. All fatback should be refrigerated: fresh up to a week, cured up to a month.

fat content In the world of cheese, the word *fat* denotes the fat content of milk and, consequently, the cheese it produces. Also called *butterfat* or *milkfat*, this component greatly influences the flavor and aroma of cheese. Fat content varies from one animal type to another. For example, sheep's milk has proportionately the highest amount of fat and other non-liquid components (*see* DRY MATTER). Because of this, it takes less sheep's milk ($4\frac{1}{2}$ pounds) to make 1 pound of cheese than it does cow's milk (10 pounds). However, the type of milk (whole, nonfat, and so on) from which the cheese is made also affects the amount of fat. DOUBLE-CREAM and TRIPLE-CREAM CHEESES are made with extra cream that boosts the fat content. It would seem that rich, creamy cheeses are higher in fat than dense, hard cheeses. However, the final fat content listed on cheese labels is determined by measuring the fat in the total DRY MATTER of the finished cheese. This is because the moisture content may vary due to the fact that cheese continues to dry out during RIPENING while the solids stay constant. Since the percentage of fat in cheese is based solely on dry matter, a hard cheese such as PARMIGIANO-REGGIANO with a fat content of 32 percent could provide more fat per ounce than a soft cheese such as BRIE with a fat content of 45 percent.

fat mop *see* GREASE MOP

fats and oils There are myriad culinary uses for fats and oils including cooking, tenderizing baked goods and adding richness, texture and flavor to foods. Fat is one of the body's basic nutrients, providing energy by furnishing CALORIES. All forms of fat are made up of a combination of **fatty acids**, which are the building blocks of fats much as amino acids are the building blocks of PROTEINS. Fats and oils are either saturated or unsaturated, the latter classification being broken down into monounsaturated and polyunsaturated fats. To illustrate the difference between the terms saturated, monounsaturated and polyunsaturated, picture a fat molecule as a train of passenger cars (carbon atoms). If every seat on the train is filled by a "passenger" (hydrogen atom), then this is a *saturated fat* molecule. If there's one seat open in each car where a hydrogen-atom "passenger" can sit, the molecule is *monounsaturated;* if there are several seats available, it's *polyunsaturated*. In general, **saturated fats** come from animal sources and are solid enough to hold their shape at room temperature (about 70°F). Exceptions to this rule are tropical oils such as COCONUT oil and PALM oil, which, though of plant origin, are semisolid at room temperature and highly saturated. Saturated fats are the nutritional "bad guys" because they're known to be associated with some forms of cancer and to increase cholesterol levels, which can be a contributing factor to heart disease. In addition to the two aforementioned tropical oils, the most commonly commercially used saturated fats are BUTTER, LARD, SUET and hydrogenated vegetable oils such as MARGARINE and VEGETABLE SHORTENING. **Hydrogenated** (or **partially hydrogenated**) **oils** have been chemically transformed from their normal liquid state (at room temperature) into solids. During the hydrogenation procedure extra hydrogen atoms are pumped into unsaturated fat. This process creates TRANS FATTY ACIDS, converting the mixture into a saturated fat and obliterating any benefits it had as a polyunsaturate. Some researchers believe that hydrogenated oils may actually be more damaging than regular saturated fats for those limiting cholesterol in their diets. **Unsaturated fats** are derived primarily from plants and are liquid (in the form of an oil) at room temperature. Generally speaking, oils are composed (in varying percentages) of both monounsaturated and polyunsaturated fats. **Monounsaturated fats** are known to help reduce the levels of LDL (the bad) cholesterol. The three most widely used oils that are high in monounsaturates are OLIVE OIL, CANOLA OIL and PEANUT OIL. **Polyunsaturated fats** are also considered relatively healthy and include the following, ranked in order, most to least, of polyunsaturates: SAFFLOWER OIL, SOYBEAN OIL, CORN OIL and SESAME OIL. **Omega-3 oils** are a particular classification of fatty acids found in some plants (such as FLAX SEED) and in the tissues of all sea creatures. These special polyunsaturated oils have been found to be particularly beneficial to coronary health (purportedly lowering the bad LDL cholesterol and elevating the good HDL) as well as to brain growth and development. Among the popular fish that are particularly good sources of Omega-3 oil (in order of importance) are sardines, herring, mackerel, bluefish, tuna, salmon, pilchard, butterfish and pompano. High cooking temperatures can destroy almost half the Omega-3 in fish, whereas microwave cooking doesn't appear to have an adverse effect on it. Canned tuna packed in water is a quick and easy way for many people to get their Omega-3 oil, but it's worth noting that combining it with the fat in mayonnaise offsets any positive effects. Canned salmon and sardines are also excellent Omega-3 sources. **Storing fats and oils**. Saturated fats such as butter, margarine and lard should be tightly wrapped and refrigerated. They can usually be stored this way for up to 2 weeks. Hydrogenated vegetable shortening can be stored, tightly covered, at room temperature for up to 3 months. Refined oils, sealed airtight, can be stored on the kitchen shelf up to 2 months. Oils with a high proportion of monounsaturates—such as olive oil and peanut oil—are more perishable and should be refrigerated if kept longer than a month. *See also* ALMOND OIL; ANIMAL FAT; CHILI OIL; COCOA BUTTER; COTTONSEED OIL; FAT SUBSTITUTES; GRAPESEED OIL; GREASE; HAZELNUT OIL; MILK FAT; OILS; PUMPKIN SEED OIL; SUNFLOWER SEED OIL; TRANS FATTY ACIDS; WALNUT OIL; Frying Temperatures, page 867; Smoke Points of Popular Oils, page 867; Fatty Acid Profiles of Popular Oils, page 868.

fat substitutes; full-fat replacements

Synthesized substances created to replace fat in a variety of foods. Some products are made of fat-free ingredients, while others are fats that have been restructured so as to provide fewer calories per gram. The following are the products currently on the market. **Simplesse**, manufactured by NutraSweet, is composed of milk protein and egg whites. This all-natural fat substitute is very low in calories and cholesterol free. It's used in a variety of foods including frozen dairy products, yogurt, cheese spreads and salad dressings. **Leanesse**, a ConAgra product, is made from oat flour (Oatrim) through a heating-and-cooling process that produces a flavorless gel that imitates the texture of fat. It's used in foods such as frozen dinners and energy bars. Procter & Gamble's **Olestra** is a no-calorie, sucrose-polyester fat substitute composed of sugar and fatty acids and embodied in a molecule so large that it moves right through the human system without a trace. Olestra contributes the same cooking benefits (such as crispy FRENCH FRIES) and flavor as fat, but without the associated risks. It's typically used in shortening, oils and snacks. **Salatrim** is an acronym for "short- and long-chain triglyceride molecules," of which this full-fat replacement is comprised. In layman's terms these are processed vegetable oils that are more difficult for the human body to absorb. Sometimes referred to as a lowfat fat, Salatrim is classified as a saturated fat. However, compared to traditional fat's 9 calories per gram, it has 5 calories per fat gram (in the United States) or 6 calories per fat gram (per European regulations). It's used in baked goods, dairy products and confections but can't be used for frying. **Enova oil**, a trademark of ADM Kao LLC, is a combination of soy and canola oils that has been restructured through a patented process so less of it is stored as fat in the human body. Clinical studies in Japan and the United States have shown that using this converted oil may reduce fat mass and body weight. Per tablespoon, Enova oil is comprised of 8 grams of polyunsaturated fat, 5 grams of monounsaturated fat and only 0.5 gram saturated fat. It was introduced to the Japanese market in 1999 (as Econa Healthy Cooking Oil) and has been approved by the Japanese Ministry of Health, Labor and Welfare (similar to the United States' FDA). The FDA has acknowledged Enova oil's GRAS STATUS. *See also* FATS AND OILS.

fattoush salad; fattouche [fah-TOOSH; FAT-toosh] Middle Eastern salad of mixed greens, vegetables and chunks of crisp flatbread such as fried PITA tossed with a garlic, lemon juice, olive oil and SUMAC dressing. Fresh ingredients usually include cucumbers, lettuce, mint, onions, PURSLANE, radishes and tomatoes but a variety of other greens or vegetables may be used. The salad is sometimes spelled *fattush* or *fatush*.

fattush *see* FATTOUSH

fatty acids *see* FATS AND OILS; Fatty Acid Profiles of Popular Oils, page 868

fatush *see* FATTOUSH

fava bean [FAH-vuh] This tan, rather flat bean resembles a very large LIMA BEAN. It comes in a large pod that, unless *very* young, is inedible. Fava beans can be purchased dried, cooked in cans and, infrequently, fresh. If you find fresh fava beans, choose those with pods that aren't bulging with beans, which indicates age. Fava beans have a very tough skin, which should be removed by BLANCHING before cooking. **Habas** are dried favas with the skins removed. They're very popular in Mediterranean and Middle Eastern dishes, can be cooked in a variety of ways and are often used in soups. Also called *faba bean, broad bean* and *horse bean. See also* BEANS.

fedelini *see* Pasta Glossary, page 883

feijoa [fay-YOH-ah; fay-JOH-ah] This small, egg-shaped fruit is native to South America, though New Zealand is now a major exporter and California cultivates a small crop. It's also referred to as a *pineapple guava,* and is often mislabeled in produce sections as GUAVA. A thin, bright green skin surrounds the feijoa's exceedingly fragrant, cream-colored flesh that encases a jellylike center. The flavor is complex, with sweet notes of quince, pineapple and mint. New Zealand feijoas are available from spring to early summer; those from California reach the market in the fall. Choose fruit that has a rich, perfumy fragrance and gives slightly to the touch. Ripen by placing it in a paper bag with an apple for several days at room temperature. Ripe feijoas can be refrigerated 3 to 5 days. Before using, remove the slightly bitter peel. Feijoas are naturals in fruit salads, desserts and as garnishes. They contain a fair amount of vitamin C.

feijoada [fay-ZHWAH-duh] Brazil's most famous regional dish, feijoada is an assorted platter of thinly sliced meats (such as sausages, PIG'S FEET and ears, beef and smoked tongue) accompanied by side dishes of rice, BLACK BEANS, shredded KALE or COLLARD greens, HEARTS OF PALM, orange slices and hot peppers.

fell In the food world, "fell" refers to a thin parchmentlike membrane directly beneath an animal's hide. The fell is removed from many cuts of meat and left on some (such as a leg of lamb), where it can help retain the meat's juices.

fennel; fennel pollen; fennel seed [FEHN-uhl] There are two main types of this aromatic plant, both with pale green, celerylike stems and bright green, feathery foliage. **Florence fennel**, also called *finocchio,* is cultivated throughout the Mediterranean and in the United States. It has a broad, bulbous base that's treated like a vegetable. Both the base and stems can be eaten raw in salads or cooked in a variety of methods such as braising, sautéing or in soups. The fragrant, graceful greenery can be used as a garnish or snipped like dill and used for a last-minute flavor enhancer. This type of fennel is often mislabeled "sweet anise," causing those who don't like the flavor of licorice to avoid it. The flavor of fennel, however, is sweeter and more delicate than anise and, when cooked, becomes even lighter and more elusive than in its raw state. **Fennel pollen** is the golden yellowish powder taken from blooming fennel flowers. The flowers can be shaken to get fresh fennel pollen or dried, which allows the pollen to fall from the flower naturally. Fresh pollen is the best, but both fresh and dried provide an intense, sweet anise flavor. The popularity of fennel pollen has spread from Italy to the United States. It's used to flavor a broad spectrum of foods from olive oil, vegetables, fish and meat to salads and bread dough. Fennel pollen is expensive because, like SAFFRON, the production from each flower is minimal. On the West Coast of the United States, fennel grows wild and fennel pollen can be harvested by those willing to put a little effort into it. **Common fennel** is the variety from which the oval, greenish-brown **fennel seeds** come. The seeds are available whole and ground and are used in both sweet and savory foods, as well as to flavor many LIQUEURS. They should be stored in a cool, dark place for no more than 6 months. Though common fennel is bulbless, its stems and greenery are used in the same ways as those of Florence fennel. Fennel is available year-round—choose clean, crisp bulbs with no sign of browning. Any attached greenery should be a fresh green color. Refrigerate, tightly wrapped in a plastic bag, up to 5 days. Fennel is rich in vitamin A and contains a fair amount of calcium, phosphorus and potassium. *See also* HERBS; Seasoning Suggestions, page 891.

fen noodles *see* RICE NOODLES

fensi [fen SEU] *see* CELLOPHANE NOODLES

fenugreek [FEHN-yoo-greek] Native to Asia and southern Europe, this aromatic plant, also known as *methi* and *shambalileh* or *shanbalile,* is cultivated for its pleasantly bitter, slightly sweet seeds and for its small round leaves. Fenugreek seeds, which come whole and ground, are used to flavor many foods including curry powders, spice blends and teas. Fenugreek seeds should be stored in a cool, dark place for no more than 6 months. Fresh leaves are used in salads and cooked dishes; frozen leaves are an acceptable substitute for fresh ones in most cooked dishes. Dried fenugreek leaves are used in both Indian and Persian cuisines as an herb. Dried, frozen and occasionally fresh fenugreek leaves are available in Indian markets. Look for fresh fenugreek leaves that are crisp and bright green with no evidence of yellowing, wilting or insect damage. Fresh fenugreek leaves have a short shelf life and should be used immediately.

fermentation A process by which food or drink goes through a chemical change caused by enzymes produced from bacteria, microorganisms or yeasts. Fermentation alters the appearance and/or flavor of foods and beverages such as beer, buttermilk, cheese, vinegar, yogurt, liquor and wine. In WINE, for example, yeast enzymes convert grape-juice sugars into ALCOHOL, while in RUM, the enzymes convert sugar cane molasses into alcohol. With whiskeys, a MASH is made from cereal grains such as corn, rye or barley—diastase enzymes convert the grain's starches into sugar, which is subsequently converted by yeast to alcohol. And in cheesemaking, the fermentation of milk converts carbohydrates into acids, producing lactic acid from the lactose (milk sugar).

fermented black beans Also called *Chinese black beans* and *salty black beans,* this Chinese specialty consists of small black soybeans that have been preserved in salt before being packed into cans or plastic bags. They have an extremely pungent, salty flavor and must be soaked in warm water for about 30 minutes before using. Fermented black beans are usually finely chopped before being added to fish or meat dishes as a flavoring. They can be stored, tightly covered, in the refrigerator for up to a year. If the beans begin to dry out, a few drops of peanut oil will refresh them.

Fernet Branca [FAYR-nay BRAHN-kah] An extremely astringent, very brown Italian BITTERS. Long known as a DIGESTIF, Fernet Branca originated in Milan in the early 1800s. As with most such elixirs, Fernet Branca is made from a secret formula, but this one purportedly includes some 40 ingredients including rhubarb, chamomile and myrrh. Although many use this potable primarily as a hangover cure and stomach soother, Italians enjoy the 80 PROOF Fernet Branca as an APÉRITIF, either STRAIGHT or ON THE ROCKS.

ferratele *see* PIZZELLA

feta; Feta [FEHT-uh] One of the world's oldest cheeses, feta has been made in Greece and other Balkan countries for centuries. Today feta-style cheeses are made by numerous producers in countries around the world including Denmark, France, Germany, Israel and the United States. In October 2005, the European Union granted Greece PROTECTED DESIGNATION OF ORIGIN (PDO) status for its Feta, which meant that other European countries (which produce tons of feta-style cheese), had to rename their cheeses. Undoubtedly the European Union also will press the United States to discontinue using the name Feta. PDO-approved Feta must be produced by traditional methods, only in designated areas in Greece and primarily from sheep's milk, though up to 30 percent goat's milk may be added. Though traditionally made of sheep's or goat's milk, today large commercial producers often use cow's milk. Because it's cured and stored in BRINE, feta is often referred to as *pickled cheese*. White, crumbly and rindless, feta is usually pressed into square cakes. It has a rich, tangy flavor, contains from 45 to 60 percent milk fat and can range in texture from semisoft to semihard. *See also* CHEESE.

fettucce; fettuccelle *see* Pasta Glossary, page 883

fettuccine; fettuccini *see* Pasta Glossary, page 883

fettuccine Alfredo [feht-tuh-CHEE-nee al-FRAY-doh] Roman restaurateur Alfredo di Lello is credited with creating this dish in the 1920s. The FETTUCCINE is enrobed in a rich sauce of butter, grated PARMESAN CHEESE, heavy cream and plentiful grindings of black pepper. Other noodles may be substituted for the fettuccine.

feuilles de brick *see* WARKA

feuilletage [fuh-yuh-TAHZH] French for "flaky" or "puff pastry." Also called *pâté feuilletée*. *See also* PUFF PASTRY.

fiber, dietary Also referred to as *roughage,* dietary fiber is that portion of plant-related foods (such as fruits, legumes, vegetables and whole grains) that cannot be completely digested. Statistics maintain that high-fiber diets reduce cholesterol levels and cancer rates.

ficelle [fee-SEHL] French for "twine" or "string," referring culinarily to a long, very thin loaf of French bread, about half the size of a BAGUETTE.

fiddlehead fern A young, edible, tightly coiled fern frond that resembles the spiral end of a violin (fiddle). It is also referred to as *ostrich fern* and *pohole.* The shoots are in their coiled form for only about 2 weeks before they unfurl into graceful greenery. Fiddlehead ferns are a rich, deep green color and are about 2 inches long and $1\frac{1}{2}$ inches in diameter. They have a flavor akin to an asparagus-green bean-okra cross and a texture that's appealingly chewy. Fiddleheads can be found throughout the eastern half of the United States, ranging from as far south as Virginia north to Canada. They're available in specialty produce markets from April through July, depending on the region. Choose small, firm, brightly colored ferns with no sign of softness or yellowing. Refrigerate, tightly wrapped, for no more than 2 days. Fiddleheads should be washed and the ends trimmed before being briefly cooked by steaming, simmering or sautéing. They may be served cooked as a first course or side dish or used raw in salads. Fiddlehead ferns are a good source of vitamins A and C.

fidelini *see* Pasta Glossary, page 883

fideos *see* Pasta Glossary, page 883

field lettuce *see* CORN SALAD

field pea A variety of yellow or green pea grown specifically for drying. These peas are dried and usually split along a natural seam, in which case they're called *split peas*. Whole and split dried field peas are available packaged in supermarkets and in bulk in natural food stores. *See also* PEA; LEGUME.

field salad *see* CORN SALAD

fig Originally hailing from southern Europe, Asia and Africa, figs were thought to be sacred by the ancients; they were also an early symbol of peace and prosperity. Figs were brought to North America by the Spanish Franciscan missionaries who came to set up Catholic missions in southern California . . . hence the now-popular Mission fig. There are hundreds of varieties of figs, all having in common a soft flesh with a plenitude of tiny edible seeds. They range in color from purple-black to almost white and in shape from round to oval. The most well-known varieties today include the green-skinned, white-fleshed **Adriatic;** the pear-shaped, violet- to brown-skinned **Brown Turkey;** the large, squat white-fleshed, green-skinned **Calimyrna** (when grown in California) or **Smyrna** (when from Turkey); the **Celeste**, medium and pear-shaped, with a purple skin and pinkish pulp; the **Kadota**, a small, thick-skinned, yellow-green fruit; the **Magnolia** (also called *Brunswick*), large, with a pinkish-yellow flesh and amber skin; and the purple-black **Mission** (or *Black Mission*), with its extremely small seeds. Fresh figs are available from May through November, depending on the variety. They're extremely perishable and should be used soon after they're purchased. Figs may be stored in the refrigerator for 5 to 7 days. They're also sold candied, dried or canned in sugar syrup or water. **Fig concentrate** is a thick, syrupy, seedless purée of figs. It's used to flavor cakes and other desserts, as well as for a topping over ice cream, fruit, cake and so on. Fig concentrate can be found in natural food stores and some supermarkets. All figs are a good source of iron, calcium and phosphorus.

F

figaro sauce [FIHG-uh-roh] Tomato purée and minced parsley are added to HOLLANDAISE for this rich accompaniment to fish or poultry. *See also* SAUCE.

filbert *see* HAZELNUT

filé powder [FEE-lay; fih-LAY] Choctaw Indians from the Louisiana bayou country are said to have been the first users of this seasoning made from the ground, dried leaves of the sassafras tree. It's since become an integral part of CREOLE COOKING and is used to thicken and flavor GUMBOS and other Creole dishes. Filé has a woodsy flavor reminiscent of root beer. It must be stirred into a dish after it's removed from the heat because undue cooking makes filé tough and stringy. Filé powder is available in the spice or gourmet section of most large supermarkets. As with all spices, it should be stored in a cool, dark place for no more than 6 months.

filet *see* FILLET

filet mignon [fih-LAY mihn-YON] This expensive, boneless cut of beef comes from the small end of the tenderloin. The filet mignon is usually 1 to 2 inches thick and 1½ to 3 inches in diameter. It's extremely tender but lacks the flavor of beef with the bone attached. Cook filet mignon quickly by broiling, grilling or sautéing. *See also* BEEF; SHORT LOIN.

filetto [fee-LEH-toh] Italian for "FILLET."

fillet *n.* [fih-LAY; FILL-iht] 1. A boneless piece of meat or fish. *Filet* is the French spelling. 2. The breasts of poultry or GAME BIRDS are sometimes referred to as fillets. **fillet** *v.* To cut the bones from a piece of meat or fish, thereby creating a meat or fish fillet.

filo *see* PHYLLO

filter To strain through a paper filter or several layers of CHEESECLOTH.

filtered coffee *see* CAFÉ FILTRÉ

financière, à la [fee-nahn-SYEHR] French for "banker's style," alluding to the expensive ingredients in this French HAUTE CUISINE preparation. Such dishes (which can range from meat to poultry) are garnished with a mélange of TRUFFLES, QUENELLES, KIDNEYS, SWEETBREADS and MUSHROOMS and napped with a sauce flavored with truffles and MADEIRA. *Financière* preparations are often served in a VOL-AU-VENT.

fines herbes [FEEN erb; FEENZ ehrb] A mixture of very finely chopped herbs. The classic quartet is CHERVIL, CHIVES, PARSLEY and TARRAGON, though BURNET, MARJORAM, SAVORY or WATERCRESS are often used as part of the blend. Because they quickly lose their flavor, fines herbes should be added to a cooked mixture shortly before serving. Unlike BOUQUET GARNI, they're not removed from the dish before serving.

fingered citron *see* CITRON

finger lime; finger lime seeds Small, $1\frac{1}{2}$- to 3-inch-long citrus fruit that grows on small trees and shrubs in subtropical areas of Australia. The lime skins come in shades of yellow, green, orange, red, purple and almost black; the pulp varies in color as well. The limes can be used for a variety of purposes like other citrus, but it's the tiny juice sacs referred to as **finger lime seeds** that are causing a stir in the culinary world. The little tear-drop-shaped "seeds" are round and firm and hold their shape until squashed in the mouth, releasing a bright, tangy, slightly herbaceous, lemony lime flavor. They've been likened to caviar because of their ability to hold their shape when sprinkled on food and then deliver that burst of flavor. Orchards planted in California are now delivering finger limes to the U.S. market, although availability is still limited.

fingerling potatoes *see* POTATO

fingerroot Rhizome with a cluster of "fingers" growing from a central globular part, yellowish-brown skin and pale yellow flesh found in China and Southeast Asia. Fingerroot is also called *Chinese keys, Chinese ginger, gra-chai, krachai* and *temu kunci*. Although in the same general family, fingerroot is not **lesser galangal** (see GALANGAL), to which it's sometimes referred. Fingerroot has a lemony, gingery, somewhat medicinal flavor.

It's in Thailand that it finds most culinary use, appearing in curry pastes and soups and used to flavor other dishes. In other countries it's used mainly for medicinal purposes. Fingerroot can be found in both fresh and dried form in some Asian markets.

fining [FI-ning] The process of removing minute floating particles that prevent wines and beers from being clear (*see* CLARIFY). Besides egg whites and eggshells, other substances used to fine these liquids include GELATIN, ISINGLASS and diatomaceous earth.

finish The final impression of a potable's flavor and texture that remains in the mouth after swallowing.

finishing *see* RIPENING

finnan haddie; finnan haddock [FIHN-uhn HAD-ee] Named after Findon, Scotland, a fishing village near Aberdeen, finnan haddie is partially boned, lightly salted and smoked HADDOCK. It was originally smoked over peat fires, a rarity now in wide commercial production. In the British Isles, finnan haddie has long been a favorite breakfast dish. Though once exclusively from Scotland, it's now being produced in New England and other eastern coastal states. It's available whole or in fillets and can be refrigerated, tightly wrapped, for up to a month. Finnan haddie is best baked, broiled or poached. It's generally served with a cream sauce. *See also* FISH.

fino [FEE-noh] *see* SHERRY

finocchio [fee-NOHK-kee-oh] Italian for "FENNEL."

finocchiona [fee-NOHK-kee-oh-nah] Traditional Tuscan ground-pork SALAMI seasoned with FENNEL seeds that takes its name from the Italian word for fennel, *finocchio*. Finocchiona is aged for 5 months or more, resulting in a dry, firm salami. A variation of finocchiona made with a slightly coarser grind of meat and aged for only a few months is called *sbriciolona*. It's fresher, moister and somewhat crumbly.

Fiorentina, alla Italian for "in the style of Florence" (*see* FLORENTINE).

firepot; fire pot *see* MONGOLIAN HOT POT

firewater An American term coined in the 19th century referring to strong LIQUOR, usually WHISKEY. The word "firewater" is thought to be a translation from the Ojibwa word for "whiskey"—*ishkodewaaboo*.

firm-ball stage A test for SUGAR SYRUP describing the point at which a drop of boiling syrup immersed in cold water forms a firm but pliable ball. On a CANDY THERMOMETER, the firm-ball stage is between 244° and 248°F. *See* Candymaking Cold Water Tests, page 866.

fischietti *see* Pasta Glossary, page 883

fish All fish are broken down into two very broad categories—fish and shellfish. In the most basic terms, **fish** are equipped with fins, backbones and gills, while **shellfish** have shells of one form or another. (*For details on* SHELLFISH, *see that listing.*) Fish without shells are separated into two groups—freshwater fish and saltwater fish. Because salt water provides more buoyancy than fresh water, **saltwater fish**—such as COD, FLOUNDER and TUNA—can afford to have thicker bones. **Freshwater fish**—like CATFISH, PERCH and TROUT—can't be weighted with a heavy skeletal framework. Instead, their structure is based on hundreds of minuscule bones, a source of frustration to many diners. Additionally, fish are separated into two more categories: FLATFISH and roundfish. **Flatfish**, which swim horizontally along the bottom of the sea, are shaped like an oval platter, the top side being dark and the bottom white. Both eyes are on the side of the body facing upward. **Roundfish** have a rounder body, with eyes on both sides of the head. Further, fish are divided into three categories based on their fat content—lean, moderate-fat and high-fat. The oil in **lean fish** is concentrated in the liver, rather than being distributed through the flesh. Their fat content is less than $2^1/_2$ percent and the flesh is mild and lightly colored. Fish in the lean category include BLACK SEA BASS, brook trout, cod, DRUM flounder, HADDOCK, HAKE, HALIBUT, POLLACK, ocean perch, red SNAPPER, ROCKFISH and TILEFISH. **Moderate-fat fish** usually have less than 6 percent fat and include BARRACUDA, STRIPED BASS, SWORDFISH, bonito tuna and WHITING. The fat content of **high-fat fish** can reach as high as 30 percent (as with EEL), but the average is closer to 12 percent. Some of the more popular high-fat fish are Atlantic HERRING, BUTTERFISH, MACKEREL, SMELT, STURGEON and YELLOWTAIL. The wider distribution of fat in moderate- and high-fat fish gives their flesh a darker color, firmer texture and more distinctive flavor. When buying fresh, whole fish, look for the following characteristics: bright, clear, full eyes (cloudy or sunken eyes denote stale fish); shiny, brightly colored skin; a fresh, mild odor; firm flesh that clings tightly to the bones and springs back when pressed with your finger; and red to bright pink gills, free from any slime or residue. Whole fish comes either ungutted or DRAWN, meaning its entrails and sometimes its gills have been removed. A fish that has been DRESSED has, in addition to being drawn, had the scales removed. *Whole-dressed* usually refers to the whole fish; *pan-dressed* to a fish with head, tail and fins removed. **Fish fillets and steaks** should have a fresh odor, firm texture and moist appearance. Fillets are a boneless, lengthwise cut from the sides of a fish. They are usually single pieces, though *butterfly fillets* (both sides of the fish connected by the uncut strip of skin on the belly) are also available. Fish steaks are cross-sectional cuts from large, dressed fish. They're usually $^5/_8$ to 1 inch thick and contain a small section of the backbone. Fresh fish should immediately be refrigerated, tightly wrapped, and used within a day—2 days at most. Never store ungutted fish, as the entrails decay much more rapidly than the flesh. When purchasing **raw frozen fish**, make sure it's solidly frozen. It should be tightly wrapped in an undamaged, moisture- and vaporproof material and should have no odor. Any white, dark, icy or dry spots indicate damage through drying or deterioration. Avoid fish that is suspected of having been thawed and refrozen, a process that reduces the overall quality of both texture and flavor. Frozen fish should be stored in a moisture- and vaporproof wrapping in the freezer for up to 6 months. Thaw in the refrigerator 24 hours (for a 1-pound package) before cooking. Quick-thawing can be accomplished by placing the wrapped, frozen fish in cold water, allowing 1 hour to thaw a 1-pound package. Never refreeze fish. **Canned fish**, such as tuna, salmon and sardines, will generally keep for about a year stored at 65°F or less. However, since the consumer doesn't know under what conditions canned goods have been stored in warehouses, the best idea is to buy only what will be used within a few months. Fish are an excellent source of protein, B complex vitamins and minerals including calcium, iron, potassium and phosphorus. Both saltwater and freshwater fish are low in sodium content and, compared to meat, also low in calories. **Cooking fish:** Fish can be cooked in myriad ways including baking, broiling, frying, grilling and steaming. A general rule for cooking fish is to measure it at its thickest point, then cook 8 to 10 minutes per inch (4 to 5 minutes per half inch). To test fish for doneness, use a fork to prod it at its thickest point. The fish should be opaque, its juices milky white. Undercooked fish is transluscent, its juices clear and watery; overcooked fish is dry and falls apart easily. Another test is to insert an instant-read thermometer at the thickest point—fish that's done will register 145°F. *For further questions, call the free government-sponsored fish and shellfish hotline at 800-332-4010. See also* AKULE; AMBERJACK; ANCHOVY; ANGLER FISH; AQUACULTURE; BASS; BLACKFISH; BLENNY; BLUEFISH; BREAM; BRILL; BUFFALO FISH; BURBOT; BURI; CARP; CHAR; CRAPPIE; CUSK; DAB; DOGFISH; FLYING FISH; FUGU; GASPERGOO; GOATFISH; GREENLING; GROUPER; GRUNION; GRUNT; GURNARD; HAMACHI; JACK; JAPANESE AMBERJACK; JELLYFISH; JEWFISH; JOHN DORY; KINGFISH; LAMPREY; LINGCOD; MAHI MAHI; MULLET; OPAH; OPAKAPAKA; ORANGE ROUGHY; PETRALE SOLE; PIKE; PILCHARD; POMPANO; PORGY; RED MULLET; SABLEFISH; SALTFISH; SAND DAB; SARDINE; SEA BASS; SHARK; SKATE; SOLE; SPRAT; SUNFISH; SURIMI; TAMBAQUI; TILAPIA; TRASH FISH; TURBOT; WAHOO; WEAKFISH; WHITEFISH.

fish and chips A traditional British dish of deep-fried fish FILLETS and FRENCH FRIES, most often served with malt VINEGAR.

fish boil 1. An herb and spice mixture specifically created to complement fish and shellfish. The blend varies depending on the manufacturer, but typically includes allspice, bay leaves, cloves, ginger, mustard seeds, peppercorns and red chiles. Packages of fish boil (also called *crab* *boil* and *shrimp boil*) can be found in supermarkets. The contents are combined with the boiling water in which fish or shellfish are cooked. 2. An outdoor "picnic" in which fish, new potatoes and usually onions are cooked in huge pots of salted water over an intensely hot open fire.

fish gravy *see* FISH SAUCE

fishmonger The word *monger* is defined as a dealer in a specific commodity, so a fishmonger is one who sells fish and other seafood items. A woman who sells fish is often called a *fishwife*.

fish poacher A long (around 18 to 20 inches) oval pan specifically designed to poach whole filets, although individual pieces can also be cooked in it. A poacher is fitted with a steel rack (on which the fish sits above the poaching liquid), two handles and a tight-fitting lid.

fish sauce Popular throughout Southeast Asia, fish sauce can be any of various mixtures based on the liquid from salted, fermented fish. This extremely pungent, strong-flavored and salty liquid can range in color from ochre to deep brown. It's used as a condiment and flavoring, much as SOY SAUCE would be used. Fish sauces may be flavored variously—such as with chiles or sugar—depending on the use. Asian markets carry a wide variety of these pungent sauces including NAM PLA (Thai), *nuoc nam* (Vietnamese), PATIS (Philippines) and *shottsuru* (Japanese). Fish sauce is also referred to as *fish gravy*. *See also* GARUM;SAUCE; SHRIMP SAUCE.

fishwife *see* FISHMONGER

fitweed *see* SAW-LEAF HERB

five-spice powder Used extensively in CHINESE COOKING, this pungent mixture of five ground spices usually consists of equal parts of CINNAMON, CLOVES, FENNEL seed, STAR ANISE and SZECHUAN PEPPERCORNS. Prepackaged five-spice powder is available in Asian markets and most supermarkets.

fixed price A menu term referring to a complete meal for a preset price. The French term is PRIX FIXE; the Italian form is PREZZO FISSO.

fizz The name for this genre of drinks comes from an integral ingredient, "fizzy water" (CLUB SODA). Fizzes are made by shaking all the ingredients (typically liquor, lemon juice and sugar) together with ice, then straining the mixture into an ice-filled glass and topping off with soda. The most popular of this drink category is the GIN FIZZ, with all its permutations.

flageolet [fla-zhoh-LAY] A tiny, tender French KIDNEY BEAN that ranges in color from pale green to creamy white. Flageolets are rarely available fresh in the United States but can be purchased dried, canned and occasionally frozen. They're usually prepared simply, in order to showcase their delicate flavor, and are a classic accompaniment to lamb. *See also* BEANS.

flake, to To use a utensil (usually a fork) to break off small pieces or layers of food.

flaky *adj.* A term describing a food, such as pie crust, with a dry texture that easily breaks off into flat, flakelike pieces.

flamande, à la [flah-MAHND] *À la flamande* is French for "in the Flemish style," indicating a garnish of braised cabbage, carrots, turnips, potatoes and sometimes pork or sausages. It's a classic accompaniment to meat or poultry.

flambé [flahm-BAY] French for "flamed" or "flaming," this dramatic method of food presentation consists of sprinkling certain foods with liquor, which, after warming, is ignited just before serving.

flamed The American word for FLAMBÉ.

Flame Tokay grape *see* TOKAY GRAPE

flan; flan ring [FLAHN] 1. A famous Spanish baked custard coated with caramel. *See also* CRÈME CARAMEL. 2. A round pastry TART with a filling that's sweet (such as CUSTARD or fruit) or savory (vegetable, meat or savory custard). The pastry is usually formed and baked in a special **flan ring**, a bottomless metal ring with straight (about 1½-inch-high) sides. The flan ring is set on a baking sheet before the dough is baked.

flanken [FLAHNG-kuhn] 1. A strip of beef from the CHUCK end of the SHORT RIBS. 2. A Jewish dish using this cut of beef, which is boiled and usually served with HORSERADISH.

flank steak Long, thin and fibrous, this boneless cut of beef comes from the animal's lower hindquarters. It's usually tenderized by marinating, then broiled or grilled whole. In the case of *London broil,* the flank steak is cut and cooked in large pieces, then thinly sliced across the grain. *See also* BEEF; Beef Chart, page 896.

flapjack *see* PANCAKE

flap meat; flap steak A boneless cut of meat that's similar in texture and flavor to a FLANK STEAK, though slightly more tender. Whereas the flank steak is taken from the lower part of the animal, flap meat is taken from a section above the flank in the LOIN area. Flap meat, called *bavette d'aloyau* in France, benefits from being cooked quickly over high heat and not much past medium-rare. As with flank steak or SKIRT STEAK, it's important to cut flap steak across the grain for tenderness.

flat bone *see* SIRLOIN

flatbread; flat bread; flatbrod 1. A generic term for bread that is thin and flat, leavened or not. Breads like CHAPATI, FOCACCIA, FOUGASSE, LAVASH, NAAN, PITA and PIZZA are often referred to as flatbreads. 2. Thin, crackerlike traditional Scandinavian crisps are usually made with rye flour, though some are based on flour blends (wheat, barley or potato). Flat breads (*flatbrod* in Norwegian) are most often served with soups, salads or cheeses.

flatfish A species of fish (including FLOUNDER, HALIBUT and SOLE) characterized by a rather flat body, with both eyes located on the upper side. Flatfish swim on one side only; the side facing downwards is always very pale. *See also* BRILL; DAB; FISH; SAND DAB; TURBOT.

flat iron steak *see* TOP BLADE STEAK

flauta [FLAUW-tah] Meaning "flute," a flauta is a corn TORTILLA rolled around a savory (usually shredded meat or poultry) filling, then fried until crisp.

flavoring extracts *see* EXTRACTS

flax seed Though the most universal function of flax seed is to produce linseed oil (commonly used in paints, varnishes, linoleums and inks), this tiny seed contains several essential nutrients including calcium, iron, niacin, phosphorous and vitamin E. It's also a rich source of Omega-3 fatty acids (*see* FATS AND OILS). Flax seed can be found in natural food markets and some supermarkets. It has a mild nutty flavor and is often used simply sprinkled over hot dishes such as cooked cereal or stir-frys. The seed can also be sprouted and used in salads and sandwiches. Flax seed is naturally mucilaginous and, when ground into a flour and mixed with liquid, produces a blend with a texture akin to that of egg whites. This gelatinous mixture can be used in place of eggs to add body to baked goods—unlike eggs, however, it does not have a leavening effect. Because it has a high fat content, flax seed should be stored in the refrigerator or freezer, where it will keep for up to 6 months. Though it is considered a digestive aid, it should also be noted that, for some people, flax seed also has a laxative effect.

fleur de sel [fleur deuh SEHL] French for "flower of salt." Fleur de sel is an expensive sea salt gathered by labor-intensive hand-harvesting. *Paludiers,* the artisans who harvest the salt, use a series of dykes to evaporate the sea water and funnel it into small salt pans (areas of approximately 10 square yards) to complete the drying process and create the salt crystals. When the wind blows, a top crust may form; it is gently raked and harvested to procure the fleur de sel, a relatively white, delicately textured salt. This is done before the salt forms larger salt crystals that sink to the bottom of the salt pan. The larger crystals are harvested by gently pulling them into mounds at the side of the salt pan—this salt is called SEL GRIS. Fleur de sel has higher mineral and moisture content than regular salt and a more delicate, less salty flavor. Aficionados of this off-white sea salt say it should be used more as a condiment to be sprinkled on food rather than a seasoning agent like normal salt. Traditionally, fleur de sel is gathered from the clear waters off the coast of Brittany but other places along the west coast of France also harvest it. The Portuguese *flor de sal*, which also translates to "flower of salt," *Maldon salt* from the United Kingdom and *Trapani salt* from Sicily are examples of other sea salts harvested in a similar manner with comparable results.

fleuron [FLEUR-awn; FLOOR-ahn] A tiny, crescent-shaped piece of puff pastry used as a garnish, usually atop hot food.

flexitarian A person who primarily follows a VEGETARIAN regimen but occasionally eats meat or fish.

flip The original flip was made by plunging a hot fireplace poker ("flip iron" or "iron flip dog") into a concoction of rum, beer, sweetener and spices and stirring vigorously to heat and blend the drink. Adding beaten eggs to the poker-stirred potion changed the old-time flip to a *yard of flannel,* referring to the roughened surface caused by the cooked eggs. Today's flip always includes an egg and, depending on the version, may be served hot or cold.

float *n.* 1. A SOFT DRINK (such as root beer) with a scoop or two of ice cream floating in it. 2. A small amount of liquid (such as liqueur or cream) that sits atop another liquid without mixing in. **float** *v.* To slowly pour a liquid (such as LIQUEUR or cream) onto the top of another liquid so that it floats on top of the liquid below. In the case of a POUSSE-CAFÉ, several liquids are floated, one on top of the other, so as not to mix together.

floating islands 1. A light dessert of stiffly beaten, sweetened egg white mounds that have been POACHED in milk, then floated in a thin CUSTARD sauce. The dessert is also known as *oeufs à la neige,* "snow eggs." 2. In France, *île flottante* ("floating island") is LIQUEUR-sprinkled sponge cake spread with jam, sprinkled with nuts, topped with whipped cream and surrounded by a pool of custard.

flor de sal *see* FLEUR DE SEL

florentine [FLOHR-uhn-teen; FLAWR-uhn-teen] Though Austrian bakers are credited with inventing these cookies, their name implies an Italian heritage. They're a mixture of butter, sugar, cream, honey, candied fruit (and sometimes nuts) cooked in a saucepan before being dropped into mounds onto a cookie sheet and baked. The chewy, candylike florentines often have a chocolate coating on one side.

Florentine, à la French for "in the style of Florence (Italy)," and referring to dishes (usually of eggs or fish) that are presented on a bed of spinach and topped with MORNAY SAUCE. A "Florentine" dish is sometimes sprinkled with cheese and browned lightly in the oven. The Italian term is *alla Fiorentina*.

flounder Members of this large species of FLATFISH are prized for their fine texture and delicate flavor. Popular members of the flounder family include DAB, ENGLISH SOLE and PLAICE. In America, flounder is often mislabeled as *fillet of sole*— a misnomer because all of the fish called "sole" (except for imported European Dover Sole (*see* SOLE)) are actually varieties of flounder. Flounder is available whole or in fillets. It can be baked, broiled, poached, steamed or sautéed. *See also* FISH.

flour *n.* The finely ground and sifted meal of any of various edible grains. Giant steel or stone rollers are used to break and grind the grain. Most supermarkets carry **steel-ground flour**, meaning it's crushed with huge, high-speed steel rollers or hammers. The heat that is generated with these high-velocity machines strips away the WHEAT germ and destroys valuable vitamins and enzymes. The more naturally nutritious **stone-ground flour** is produced by grinding the grain between two slowly moving stones. This process crushes the grain without generating excess heat and separating the germ. Stone-ground flours must usually be purchased in natural food stores, though some large supermarkets also carry them. A flour can range in texture from coarse to extremely soft and powdery, depending on the degree of bolting (sifting) it receives at the mill. Wheat is the most common source of the multitude of flours used in cooking. It contains gluten, a protein that forms an elastic network that helps contain the gases that make mixtures (such as doughs and batters) rise as they bake. **All-purpose flour** is made from a blend of high-gluten hard wheat and low-gluten soft wheat. It's a fine-textured flour milled from the inner part of the wheat kernel and contains neither the **germ** (the sprouting part) nor the **bran** (the outer coating). U.S. law requires that all flours not containing wheat germ must have niacin, riboflavin, thiamin and iron added. (Individual millers sometimes also add vitamins A and D.) These flours are labeled "ENRICHED." All-purpose flour comes in two basic forms—**bleached** and **unbleached**—that can be used interchangeably. Flour can be bleached either naturally, as it ages, or chemically. Most flour on the market today is presifted, requiring only that it be stirred, then spooned into a measuring cup and leveled off. **Bread flour** is an unbleached, specially formulated, high-gluten blend of 99.8 percent hard-wheat flour, a small amount of malted barley flour (to improve yeast activity) and vitamin C or potassium bromate (to increase the gluten's elasticity and the dough's gas retention). It is ideally suited for YEAST BREADS. The fuller-flavored **whole-wheat flour** contains the wheat germ, which means that it also has a higher fiber, nutritional and fat content. Because of the latter, it should be stored in the refrigerator to prevent rancidity. **Cake or pastry flour** is a fine-textured, soft-wheat flour with a high starch content. It makes particularly tender cakes and pastries. **Self-rising flour** is an all-purpose flour to which baking powder and salt have been added. It can be substituted for all-purpose flour in yeast breads by omitting the salt and in QUICK BREADS by omitting both baking powder and salt. **Instant flour** is a granular flour especially formulated to dissolve quickly in hot or cold liquids. It's used mainly as a thickener in sauces, gravies and other cooked mixtures. **Gluten flour** is high-protein, hard-wheat flour treated to remove most of the starch (which leaves a high gluten content). It's used mainly as an additive to doughs made with low-gluten flour (such as RYE FLOUR), and to make low-calorie "gluten" breads. All flour should be stored in an airtight container. All-purpose and bread flour can be stored up to 6 months at room temperature (about 70°F). Temperatures higher than that invite bugs and mold. Flours containing part of the grain's germ (such as whole wheat) turn rancid quickly because of the oil in the germ. Refrigerate or freeze these flours tightly wrapped and use as soon as possible. Other grains—such as BARLEY, BUCK-WHEAT, CORN, OATS, RICE, rye and TRITICALE—are also milled into flours. **flour** *v.* To lightly coat a food, utensil or baking container with flour. Flouring food to be fried facilitates browning, and coating foods that tend to stick together (such as chopped dried apricots) helps separate the pieces. Flouring a pie, pastry or cookie dough will prevent it from sticking to a work surface; flouring your hands, rolling pin or work surface prevents dough from sticking. Dusting greased baking pans with flour provides for easy removal of cakes, breads and other baked goods.

flowering cabbage; flowering white cabbage *see* CHOY SUM

flowering kale Looking like a giant, multipetaled, ruffled flower, this vegetable comes in colors that range from white to pink to purple, all encircled by curly green leaves. Flowering kale (*Brassica oleracea*), which is the oldest member of the cabbage family, has a slightly bitter taste and semicrisp texture. It's available from September through December. Choose heads with fresh-looking, brightly colored leaves with no sign of wilting. Refrigerate in a plastic bag for up to 5 days. *See also* KALE.

flower pepper *see* SZECHUAN PEPPER

flowers, crystallized *see* CANDIED FRUIT AND FLOWERS

flowers, edible Flowers that are used as a garnish or as an integral part of a dish, such as a salad. Not all flowers are edible. Those that are must usually be purchased from specialty produce markets or supermarkets that carry gourmet produce. They can be stored, tightly wrapped, in the refrigerator up to a week. Flowers that have been sprayed with pesticides (such as those found at florists') should never be eaten. Some of the more popular edible flowers are: the peppery-flavored **nasturtiums; chive blossoms**, which taste like a mild, sweet onion; **pansies** and **violas**, both with a flavor reminiscent of grapes; and perfumy, sweet **roses**. Other edible flowers include: **almond, apple, borage, chamomile, lavender, lemon, lovage, mimosa, orange, peach, plum** and **squash blossoms, chrysanthemums, daisies, geraniums, jasmine, lilacs, marigolds** and **violets**. Edible flowers may be used culinarily in a variety of ways. They make colorful, striking garnishes for drinks as well as food—for everything from salads to soups to desserts. Some of the larger flowers such as squash blossoms can be stuffed and deep-fried.

Fluffernutter A sandwich created in 1961 by Durkee-Mower, Inc., the company responsible for the original Marshmallow Fluff (*see* MARSHMALLOW CRÈME). The sandwich has Marshmallow Fluff spread on one slice of bread, peanut butter on the other. Put them together and you have a Fluffernutter.

flummery [FLUHM-muh-ree] 1. A sweet soft pudding made of stewed fruit (usually berries) thickened with CORNSTARCH. 2. Old-time British flummeries were made by cooking oatmeal until smooth and gelatinous; sweetener and milk were sometimes added. In the 18th century, the dish became a gelatin-thickened, cream- or milk-based dessert, flavored generously with SHERRY or MADEIRA.

flute [FLOOT] 1. To press a decorative pattern into the raised edge of a pie crust (*see also* CRIMP). 2. To carve slashes, grooves and other decorative markings in vegetables (such as mushrooms) and fruits. 3. A thin, lightly sweet, flute-shaped cookie served with ice cream, pudding and so on. 4. A stemmed champagne glass with a tall, slender, cone-shaped bowl. 5. A thin, flute-shaped roll or loaf of bread.

flying fish; flyingfish Members of the family *Exocoetidae,* which are commonly found in tropical waters, especially throughout the Caribbean. The name of this fish comes from its ability to soar through the air for great distances, sometimes up to almost 350 yards. To manage this feat, the flying fish builds up speed in the water, then leaps into the air, extending its large, stiff pectoral fins, which act like wings. Flying fish have a firm texture and a pleasant, savory flavor. They're also prized for their ROE, known as TOBIKO. *See also* FISH.

foam In the food world, culinary foam consists of gelatin (or other gelling agent) mixed with a liquid (from cream to water to wine) and other flavorings, which may be herbs or spices or any of myriad puréed ingredients (such as berries, fish or potatoes). The savory or sweet blend is placed in a whipped cream dispenser fitted with a nitrous oxide (N_2O) cartridge, which forces the mixture out into a froth. Such foams are the inspiration of Ferran Adrià, innovative chef of El Bulli in Roses, Spain, one of the world's premier restaurants. Foams may be used as a base to a presentation or as a topping.

focaccia [foh-KAH-chyah] This Italian bread begins by being shaped into a large, flat round that is liberally brushed or drizzled with olive oil and sprinkled with salt. Slits cut into the dough's surface may be stuffed with fresh ROSEMARY before the bread is baked. Focaccia can be eaten as a snack, or served as an accompaniment to soups or salads.

foie gras [FWAH GRAH] Although the literal translation from French is "fat liver," *foie gras* is the term generally used for *goose liver*. This specialty of Alsace and Perigord, is in fact, the enlarged liver from a goose or duck that has been force-fed and fattened over a period of 4 to 5 months. These specially bred fowl are not permitted to exercise—which, combined with the overeating, creates a huge (up to 3 pounds), fatty liver. After the bird is killed, the liver is soaked overnight in milk, water or port. It's drained, then marinated in a mixture usually consisting of ARMAGNAC, PORT or MADEIRA and various seasonings. The livers are then cooked, usually by baking. The preparation, of course, depends on the cook. In general, goose liver is considered superior to duck liver; all foie gras is very expensive. At its best, it is a delicate rosy color with mottlings of beige. The flavor is extraordinarily rich and the texture silky smooth. **Foie gras au torchon** is a technique for preparing foie gras where it's wrapped in a clean cloth (*torchon* in French) and poached in a flavored liquid usually containing sweet white wine. Once poaching is finished, the foie gras is cooled and left to steep in the liquid for several days. **Pâté de foie gras** is puréed goose liver (by law, 80 percent) that usually contains other foods such as pork liver, TRUFFLES and eggs. **Mousse** or **purée de foie gras** must contain at least 55 percent goose liver. Foie gras should be served chilled with thin, buttered toast slices. A SAUTERNES is the perfect accompaniment.

fold, to A technique used to gently combine a light, airy mixture (such as beaten egg whites) with a heavier mixture (such as whipped cream or custard). The lighter mixture is placed on top of the heavier one in a large bowl. Starting at the back of the bowl, a rubber spatula is used to cut down vertically through the two mixtures, across the bottom of the bowl and up the nearest side. The bowl is rotated a quarter turn with each series of strokes. This down-across-up-and-over motion gently turns the mixtures over on top of each other, combining them in the process.

fond [FAWN] 1. A French term used in culinary parlance for "STOCK." There are three primary fonds in classic French cooking: **fond blanc** ("WHITE STOCK"), made from veal and poultry meat and bones and vegetables; **fond brun** ("BROWN STOCK"), made with browned beef, veal and poultry meat and bones and vegetables; and **fond de vegetal** ("vegetable stock"), made with butter-sautéed vegetables. *See also* FUMET. 2. The term *fond* also refers to the browned bits of food remaining in the pan after food has been sautéed or roasted. This fond is typically incorporated into a sauce by DEGLAZING—adding a small amount of liquid to the pan and stirring to loosen the bits of food.

fondant [FAHN-duhnt] A simple sugar-water-CREAM OF TARTAR mixture cooked to the SOFT-BALL STAGE. After cooling, the mixture is beaten and kneaded until extremely pliable. It can be formed into decorations or candy, which can be dipped in chocolate. Heating fondant makes it soft enough to be used as an icing to coat large and small cakes. FOOD COLORING and flavoring can be added for visual and taste appeal. Fondant can be refrigerated, tightly wrapped, for up to 3 months.

fondue; fondue pot [fahn-DOO] French for "melt," from *fondre*. The term "fondue" has several meanings—the first three definitions pertain to food cooked in a central pot at the table. 1. **Fondue au fromage** is a classic dish of Swiss heritage consisting of cheese (usually EMMENTAL and GRUYÈRE) melted and combined with white wine, KIRSCH and seasonings. Bite-size chunks of French bread are dipped into the hot, savory mixture. Such fondue is typically served (and sometimes prepared) in a **fondue pot**, which generally comes in a set with 6 to 8 long-handled fondue forks. The pot sits atop a stand fitted with a container for heat. *See also* FONDUTA; QUESO FUNDIDO. 2. **Fondue bourguignonne** is a variation whereby cubes of raw beef are cooked in a communal pot of hot oil, then dipped into various savory sauces. 3. Another version is **chocolate fondue**, a combination of melted chocolate, cream and sometimes LIQUEUR into which fruit or cake may be dipped. 4. In French cooking, the term "fondue" refers to finely chopped vegetables that have been reduced to a pulp by lengthy and slow cooking. This mixture is often used as a garnish, usually with meats or fish.

fonduta [fahn-DOO-tah] From *fondere* ("to melt"), this is Italy's version of FONDUE. It's a warm and silky mélange of FONTINA, cream, butter and egg yolks. Fonduta is used as a dip for bread chunks and also as a sauce for various foods including boiled potatoes, pasta, polenta and rice.

Fonduta Piemontese is this mixture blended with fresh white truffles. *See also* FONDUE; QUESO FUNDIDO.

fontina; Fontina Valle d'Aosta [fahn-TEE-nah VAHL-lay D'AOW-stah] Also called *Fontina Val d'Aosta* after the Italian valley from which it comes, this is one of Italy's great cheeses. While "fontina" cheeses are produced in Denmark, France, Sweden and the United States, the only genuine Fontina comes from this region. This cow's-milk cheese has a supple, smooth texture that can range from semisoft to semihard. The thin rind varies in color from yellow-gold to reddish brown and the interior from pale to dark yellow with a scattering of small EYES. Fontina's mild, buttery, slightly nutty flavor, and the fact that it melts easily and smoothly, make it perfect for almost any use. The majority of non-Italian fontinas, especially when young, tend to be blander and softer than the Italian original. Fontina Valle d'Aosta has a minimum FAT CONTENT of 45 percent. *See also* CHEESE.

food additives *see* ADDITIVES

food coloring Dyes of various colors (most commonly blue, green, red and yellow) used to tint foods such as frostings and candies. The most familiar form of food coloring is liquid, which comes in little bottles available at any supermarket. **Food coloring paste**, which comes in a wider variety of colors, can usually only be found in specialty stores such as cake-decorating shops. It's particularly suitable for mixtures that do not combine readily with liquid, such as WHITE CHOCOLATE. A little of any food coloring goes a long way, so it's best to begin with only a drop or two, blending it into the mixture being tinted before adding more.

food label terms *see* Food Label Terms, page 876

food mill A kitchen utensil that can be best described as a mechanical SIEVE. It has a hand-turned paddle that forces food through a strainer plate at the bottom, thereby removing skin, seeds and fiber. Some food mills come equipped with several interchangeable plates with small, medium and large holes.

food processor This kitchen appliance was brought to the United States from France in the 1970s and has since revolutionized a majority of home kitchens. It consists of a sturdy plastic work bowl that sits on a motorized drive shaft. The cover of the bowl has a feed tube through which foods can be added. An expanded feed tube—large enough for some whole items such as a tomato or onion—is available with some machines. The food processor is efficient and speedy and can easily chop, dice, slice, shred, grind and purée most food, as well as knead dough. Most processors come with a standard set of attachments including an

S-shaped chopping blade and several disks for slicing and shredding. There are special attachments including juicers and pasta makers, as well as accessories such as French-fry cutters, julienne disks and beaters. Food processors range from large to small in motor size and bowl capacity.

fool England is the home of this old-fashioned dessert made of cooked, puréed fruit that is strained, chilled and folded into whipped cream. The fruit mixture may be sweetened or not. Fool is traditionally made from gooseberries, though any fruit may be substituted.

foo yong *see* EGG FOO YONG

forcemeat A mixture of finely ground, raw or cooked meat, poultry, fish, vegetables or fruit mixed with breadcrumbs and various seasonings. The ingredients are usually ground several times to obtain a very smooth texture. A forcemeat can be used to stuff other foods or by itself, such as to make QUENELLES.

forestière, à la [ah lah foh-rehs-TYEHR] French term meaning "of the forest," referring to dishes (usually poultry, meat or game fowl) garnished with butter-sautéed potatoes or potato balls, bacon or SALT PORK and wild mushrooms such as CHANTERELLES, MORELS and PORCINI.

forest mushroom *see* SHIITAKE

formaggio [for-MAH-zhoh] Italian for "CHEESE."

Formosa Oolong tea Hailing from Taiwan (previously known as Formosa), this tea is considered one of the world's best, which also makes it quite expensive. It creates a pale yellow brew that has a flavor reminiscent of peaches. *See also* TEA.

forno, al [ahl FOHR-noh] *Forno* is Italian for "oven," and this term refers culinarily to dishes baked in the oven.

fortified wine *see* WINE

fortune cookie This Chinese-American invention consists of a plain, griddle-baked wafer cookie that, while warm, is folded around a small strip of paper with a fortune printed on it. The cooled cookie becomes crisp and must be broken in order to retrieve the fortune.

fouet [foo-AY] French for "WHISK."

fougasse [foo-GAHSS] A savory FLATBREAD usually linked with Provence—it's the French version of Italy's FOCACCIA. The dough is often formed into tree, leaf, wheat stalk or ladder shapes, with slits cut into the dough and slightly separated to produce the design. Before baking, fougasse is liberally brushed with olive oil and often sprinkled with various herbs. Some bakers knead other ingredients (such as roasted garlic or cheese bits) into the dough before baking.

Fourme d'Ambert; Fourme de Montbrison (AOC; PDO)

[FOORM dah*n*-BEHR; FOORM deuh maw*n*-bree-saw*n*] SEMIHARD, BLUE-VEINED cow's-milk cheese thought to have been produced in the Rhône-Alpes and Auvergne regions of central France for more than 2,000 years. It's made by small farms near the town of Ambert, on the western side of Mont du Forez. A nearly identical cheese, **Fourme de Montbrison**, is produced around the town of Montbrison, on the eastern side of the same mountain. The cheeses come in tall, slim drum-shaped wheels weighing 3½ to 5½ pounds, with splotchy gray and beige rinds and ivory-colored interiors containing blue veining. The texture is moist and creamy, and the slightly pungent flavor is mild and earthy with hints of fruit and nuts. The FAT CONTENT is approximately 50 percent.

fowl The term fowl is used generally to refer to any edible, mature, wild or domestic bird. Specifically, a fowl (also called *hen* or *stewing chicken*) is a female chicken over 10 months old and usually weighing 3 to 6 pounds. Because of its age, a fowl is best when cooked with moist heat, as in braising.

foyot sauce *see* VALOIS SAUCE

fra diavolo [frah DYAH-voh-loh] *see* DIAVOLO

fragola [FRAH-goh-lah] Italian for "STRAWBERRY."

frais [FRAY] French for "fresh," as in *fromage frais* ("fresh cheese").

fraise [FREHZ] French for "STRAWBERRY."

fraise des bois [frehz day BWAH] 1. An intensely sweet, tiny wild strawberry from France. 2. A colorless, strawberry-flavored EAU DE VIE.

fraisier *see* BAGATELLE

framboise [frahm-BWAHZ] 1. French for "raspberry." 2. A colorless, potent EAU DE VIE made from raspberries.

Frangelico [fran-JELL-ih-koh] A clear, golden-colored, hazelnut-flavored LIQUEUR enhanced with a secret formula of flower and berry essences.

frangipane [FRAN-juh-payn; *Fr.* FRAWN-zhee-pan] 1. A pastry made with egg yolks, flour, butter and milk that is very similar to CHOUX PASTRY. Baked frangipane puffs are often filled with FORCEMEAT. 2. A rich CRÈME PÂTISSIÈRE flavored with ground almonds and used as a filling or topping for pastries and cakes. Also called *frangipani*.

frankenfood *see* BIOTECHNOLOGY; BIOENGINEERED FOODS

frankfurter This smoked, seasoned, precooked SAUSAGE—also known as HOT DOG, *wiener* and *frank*—is America's favorite. Frankfurters can be made from beef, pork, veal, chicken or turkey. They may have casings or not and can contain up to 30 percent fat and 10 percent added water. They range in size from the tiny "cocktail frank" to the famous foot-long giants. The most common size is about 6 inches long. Frankfurters labeled **"beef"** or **"all-beef"** must, by law, contain only beef; fillers like soybean protein and dry milk solids are forbidden. **Kosher** frankfurters are all-beef sausages, usually liberally seasoned with garlic. Those labeled **"meat"** can't contain fillers either, but can be made with a combination of pork and beef, typically 40 percent pork and 60 percent beef. Sausages simply labeled **"frankfurters"** can contain up to $3^1/_2$ percent fillers and are usually made from a combination of meats. Almost all frankfurters contain SODIUM NITRATE and sodium nitrite, chemical salts that are reported to be carcinogenic. To store frankfurters, refrigerate in original package up until the manufacturer's pull date. Although precooked, frankfurters benefit from heating and may be prepared in a variety of ways including grilling, frying, steaming and braising. *See also* PIGS IN BLANKETS.

frappé [fra-PAY] 1. A mixture made of fruit juice or other flavored liquid that has been frozen to a slushy consistency. It can be sweet or savory and served as a drink, appetizer or dessert. 2. An after-dinner drink of LIQUEUR poured over shaved or crushed ice.

freddo [FREH-doh] Italian for "cold."

freegan; freeganism A person who collects food that's been discarded. The word was coined from the words "free" and "vegan," the second word referring to the fact that many of freeganism's early proponents hailed from the VEGETARIAN community. Today the definition has expanded to include others who collect and consume wasted food of any kind, and freeganism has grown into a political movement against waste in general. Most freegans collect food from surplus food sources such as supermarkets and bakeries that reject items that, though past their "use by" dates, are still safe to eat. Of course every movement has extremes, which in freeganism includes "plate scrappers" or "table divers"—those who search out leftovers from discarded restaurant meals. Another freegan-related term is "dumpster diver"—one who hunts through dumpsters and trash cans looking for discarded food, partially consumed or not.

freekeh [FREE-kah] Name given to a CEREAL GRAIN, usually wheat, that's harvested green, fire-roasted and then threshed and sun-dried. The process not only gives freekeh a smoky, nutty quality but delivers a higher concentration of vitamins and minerals than found in more mature grains.

It's a specialty of Arab countries such as Egypt, Lebanon, Jordan and Syria as well as the surrounding area, where it's eaten instead of rice. Freekeh is thought to have been discovered accidentally several thousand years ago in the Mideast when young, green wheat caught fire during an attack by an enemy force. When the scorched heads were rubbed, freekeh was discovered and found to be exceptionally good. Freekeh comes in either whole-grain or cracked form and can be found in natural food stores and Middle Eastern markets, through the Internet and even in some supermarkets. It's also spelled *frikeh* or *farik*.

free-range Poultry or animals allowed to roam and feed without confinement, as opposed to the majority of commercially bred animals, which are caged. *See also* CHICKEN.

freestone A term used to describe fruit that has a pit to which the flesh does not cling, as in a *freestone peach*. *See also* CLINGSTONE.

freeze-drying Also known as *lyophilization*, freeze-drying is a method of dehydrating a food (or any perishable item, such as blood plasma) by freezing it and subjecting it to a vacuum. This allows the ice to break free and form a vapor that's easily extracted. This instant ice crystal-to-vapor process is called sublimation. The dehydrated food is immediately packaged and sealed before moisture can be reabsorbed. Moisture contributes to decay and freeze-dried foods have almost none, which means they may be stored at room temperature for many years. They're also much lighter due to lack of water weight, particularly foods like fruit, which are 80 to 90 percent water. Foods that have been freeze-dried have microscopic pores where the ice crystals once were. When the substance is reconstituted with water, these areas are ready for quick absorption. Of all the techniques for drying food, freeze-drying has the least impact on flavor and texture. Such foods have proven invaluable for military and astronaut use, as well as for hikers.

freezer burn Frozen food that has been either improperly wrapped or frozen can suffer from freezer burn—a loss of moisture that affects both texture and flavor. Freezer burn is indicated by a dry surface, which may also have white or gray spots on it.

freezer/refrigerator thermometer A kitchen tool that registers temperatures from about −20° to 80°F. This thermometer is important because frozen food that's not maintained at 0°F or below will begin to deteriorate, thereby losing both quality and nutrients. Likewise, fresh food risks potential spoilage if refrigerated at a temperature higher than 40°F. A freezer/refrigerator thermometer should be positioned near the top and front of the freezer and left there for at least 6 hours (without opening the door) before the temperature is checked. If the thermometer's temperature doesn't read 0°F or below, adjust the freezer's temperature regulator and check in another 6 hours. Refrigerator temperature may be checked in the same way. *See also* CANDY THERMOMETER; MEAT THERMOMETER; OVEN THERMOMETER.

french, to 1. To cut a vegetable or meat lengthwise into very thin strips. Beans and potatoes are two vegetables that are commonly "frenched." 2. To cut the meat away from the end of a rib or chop, so that part of the bone is exposed.

French bean Any young, green string bean, all of which (including the pod) can be eaten. **Frenched** or **French green beans** are those that have been cut lengthwise into very thin strips. *See also* BEANS.

French bread A light, crusty, yeast-raised bread made with water instead of milk. The dark brown, intensely crisp crust is created by brushing or spraying the loaf's exterior with water during the baking process. French bread comes in many shapes, including the classic long, thin BAGUETTE, rounds and fat ovals.

French Colombard One of California's top two white-wine grapes, French Colombard is used extensively in blending as well as for a VARIETAL WINE. It produces a crisp, moderately dry, spicy wine that goes well with lightly seasoned dishes. It should be drunk young (under 4 years) and always served chilled.

French dressing 1. A simple oil-and-vinegar combination, usually seasoned with salt, pepper and various herbs. This classic dressing is also referred to as VINAIGRETTE. 2. A commercial American dressing that is creamy, tartly sweet and red-orange in color.

french fries Potatoes that have been cut into thick to thin strips, soaked in cold water, blotted dry, then DEEP-FRIED until crisp and golden brown. They are called *pommes frites* in France and *chips* in Britain. The name does not come from the fact that their origin is French, but because the potatoes are "frenched"—cut into lengthwise strips. Other versions of french-fried potatoes are *shoestring potatoes* (matchstick-wide) and *steak fries* (very thick strips).

french-fry *see* DEEP-FRY

French ice cream *see* ICE CREAM

French knife; French blade *see* KNIFE

French navy beans Not related to the common NAVY BEAN, these small dried beans are white with celadon shadings. Also called *coco blanc,* French navys have a rich bacony flavor and velvety texture. *See also* BEANS.

French 75 Named after the powerful French 75-millimeter howitzer cannon, this potent COCKTAIL is made by combining gin or brandy, lemon juice and cracked ice in a glass and filling it with CHAMPAGNE.

French spinach *see* ORACHE

French toast A breakfast dish made by dipping bread into a milk-egg mixture, then frying it until golden brown on both sides. It's usually served with syrup, jam or powdered sugar. In England, French toast is called "POOR KNIGHTS OF WINDSOR." The French call it *"pain perdu"* (lost bread) because it is a way of reviving French bread, which becomes dry after only a day or two.

fresco [FREH-skoh (FRAY-skoh)] *see* AL FRESCO

Fresno chile [FREHS-noh] Short and cone-shaped, the Fresno is as hot as the more well-known JALAPEÑO CHILE. Its SCOVILLE SCALE rating is 2,500 to 10,000. It ranges in color from light green to bright red when fully mature. Because of its heat, the Fresno is best used in small amounts as a seasoning. *See also* CHILE.

friandise; *pl.* **friandises** [free-yawn-DEEZ] A French term for confections—such as TRUFFLES, mints or PETITS FOURS—served after the dessert course.

Fribourgeois *see* VACHERIN

fricassea [free-kah-SAY-ah] Italian for "FRICASSEE."

fricassee [FRIHK-uh-see] *n.* A dish of meat (usually chicken) that has been sautéed in butter before being stewed with vegetables. The end result is a thick, chunky stew, often flavored with wine.

fricassee *v.* This word is also used as a verb, as in to "fricassee a chicken."

frico [FREE-koh] Italian for "little trifles," frico are lacy, crispy cheese wafers 3 to 4 inches in diameter. They're made by sprinkling spoonfuls of grated cheese (sometimes mixed with a soupçon of flour and herbs) onto a heated nonstick skillet and cooking until bubbly and golden. Frico may also be made on a lightly greased baking sheet in a moderate oven. In Italy, frico are classically made with MONTASIO, although other cheeses (such as ASIAGO, CHEDDAR and PARMESAN) can be used. After the crisps cool for a couple of minutes, a spatula is used to transfer them from the cooking surface to paper towels to cool completely. Frico can be eaten as appetizers or used to garnish soups, salads or other dishes.

fried rice An Asian dish of rice that has been cooked and refrigerated for a day before being fried with other ingredients, such as small pieces of meat and vegetables, and seasonings such as SOY SAUCE. An egg is also often added to the mix. The name of the rice depends on the main ingredient (besides rice), such as "chicken" fried rice, "shrimp" fried rice and so on.

fries 1. Also called *Mountain oysters, Rocky Mountain oysters* and *prairie oysters,* these are the testicles of an animal such as a calf, sheep or boar. Those from a younger animal are best. Fries can be special-ordered through most meat markets. They should be used as soon as possible, preferably within a day of purchase. Though they're not terribly popular in the United States, testicles are considered a delicacy in Italy and France. They can be sautéed, deep-fried, braised and poached. *See also* VARIETY MEATS. 2. Abbreviated term for FRENCH FRIES.

Friesengeist [FREET-zehn-gighst] A potent mint LIQUEUR from Germany.

frijoles [free-HOH-lehs] Spanish for "beans."

frijoles charros [free-HOH-lehs CHAH-rrohs] These "cowboy beans" take their name from *charros*, the traditional horsemen found in the Central West of Mexico, in and around the state of Jalisco. The basic recipe has garlic, onion and chiles such as SERRANOS or JALAPEÑOS, but most recipes add bacon or pork shoulder (*see* PICNIC HAM) for added flavor. Many variations abound, with the addition of various herbs (particularly CILANTRO), tomatoes and sometimes even a little beer (then they may be referred to as **borrachos** or "drunken beans").

frijoles de la olla; frijoles de olla [free-HOH-lehs deh lah OH-lyah] A staple of Mexican cooking, this "pot of beans" is simply made with beans, water, onions, a small amount of lard and a little salt. Of course there are myriad variations that might include garlic, bacon or some type of chile or herbs such as oregano, but the basic recipe is very simple. The beans are cooked until tender but whole and there's a rich, soupy broth left. A number of other frijole dishes use frijoles de la olla as a base.

frijoles refritos; refritos [free-HOH-lehs reh-FREE-tohs] A popular Mexican specialty consisting of cooked beans such as RED BEANS or PINTO BEANS that are mashed, then fried, often in melted lard. The term *frijoles refritos* translates as "refried beans." Although they are cooked twice, they are only fried once. Refried beans are sold canned in most supermarkets.

frikeh *see* FREEKEH

frill A decorative, fluted paper "sock" that is slipped over a protruding meat bone, such as in a CROWN ROAST.

frisée [free-ZAY] A member of the CHICORY family, *frisée* has delicately slender, curly leaves that range in color from yellow-white to yellow-green. This feathery vegetable has a mildly bitter flavor and is often used in the special salad mix, MESCLUN. Choose frisée with crisp leaves and no sign of wilting. Refrigerate in a plastic bag for up to 5 days. Wash just before using.

frita [FREE-tah] Spanish for "FRITTER."

frito [FREE-toh] Spanish for "fried."

frittata [frih-TAH-tuh] An Italian OMELET that usually has the ingredients mixed with the eggs rather than being folded inside, as with a French omelet. It can be flipped or the top can be finished under a broiling unit. An omelet is cooked quickly over moderately high heat and, after folding, has a flat-sided half-oval shape. A frittata is firmer because it's cooked very slowly over low heat, and round because it isn't folded.

frittelle [free-THE-leh] Italian for "FRITTER."

fritter A small, sweet or savory, deep-fried cake made either by combining chopped food with a thick batter or by dipping pieces of food into a similar batter. Some of the more popular foods used for fritters are apples, corn and crab.

fritto [FREE-toh] Italian for "fried."

fritto misto [FREE-toh MEES-toh] Italian for "mixed fried (food)" or "mixed fry," fritto misto is a selection of small, bite-size pieces of meat, fish or vegetables, dipped in a batter and deep-fried.

friturier [free-tew-RYAY] *see* BRIGADE SYSTEM

frizzante [freet-zahn-teh] An Italian term meaning "lightly sparkling," referring to wines with light effervescence. *See also* SPUMANTE.

frizzes [FRIHZ-ihs] A dry Italian pork or beef SALAMI flavored with garlic and anise. Its name comes from its squiggly, contorted shape. The hot style is corded with red string and the mild (or "sweet") is corded with blue string. Frizzes are most often used as a garnish, as on pizza or in pasta. *See also* SAUSAGE.

frizzle To fry thinly sliced meat (such as bacon) over high heat until crisp and slightly curly in shape.

frogfish *see* ANGLER

frog skin melon *see* CAMOUFLAGE MELON

frog's legs The only edible part of a frog is its hind legs. The delicate meat is tender and lightly sweet and can be most closely compared to the white meat of a very young chicken. Fresh frog's legs can be found from spring through summer in the fish section of many gourmet markets. They're usually sold in connected pairs ranging from 2 to 8 ounces. Look for those that are plump and slightly pink. Store, loosely wrapped, in the refrigerator for up to 2 days. Frozen frog's legs can usually be purchased year-round, though the flavor doesn't compare to fresh. Thaw in the refrigerator overnight before cooking. Because their flavor is so subtle, frog's legs should be cooked simply and briefly. A quick dusting of seasoned flour before sautéing in butter or olive oil will gild the lily perfectly. Overcooking frog's legs will cause them to toughen.

froid [FRWAH] French for "cold" or "chilled."

fromage; fromager [froh-MAHZH; froh-mah-ZHAY] *Fromage* is French for "cheese." A *fromager* is a cheesemaker, though the word is sometimes used to describe a cheese wholesaler or retailer.

fromage blanc [froh-MAHZH BLAH/V] Originating in France, where it's called *fromage fraise* ("fresh cheese"), this is a simple uncooked, unmolded, unripened cheese. Authentic fromage blanc is fat free but some cheesemakers increase the FAT CONTENT by adding cream. On French labels, the term *maigre* indicates a very low-fat cheese, and *allege* describes one that's very high in fat. Fromage blanc has a fresh, tangy flavor and a texture like thick sour cream. It's smooth and creamy and can be used in cooking, as a spread (sometimes with added herbs or other flavorings) or spooned over fruit. Fromage blanc is typically sold in 8-ounce tubs. *See also* CHEESE.

Fromage de Herve [froh-MAHZH deuh ehr-VAY] *see* HERVE

Fromage de Savoie *see* REBLOCHON

fromage de tête [froh-MAHZH duh TEHT] *see* HEAD CHEESE

fromage fort [froh-MAHZH FAWR] French for "strong cheese," *fromage fort* is a combination of leftover cheese scraps, wine, butter and sometimes seasonings such as herbs and garlic. Traditionally, the French would let this mélange ferment until good and stinky. Today, fromage fort is more likely to be blended together and either allowed to mellow in the refrigerator for a couple of days or served immediately as a spread for bread or crackers.

Fromager d'Affinois [froh-mah-ZHAY dah-fee-NWAH] This French treasure is made from pasteurized cow's milk. The downy-coated rind encloses a soft, smooth, ivory-colored paste, the flavor of which is delicate and creamy with hints of grass and mushrooms. Though Fomager d'Affinois has 60-percent FAT CONTENT, it tastes more like a TRIPLE-CREAM CHEESE because of a special process the milk undergoes. There is a sheep's-milk version of this cheese, which is labeled *Pavé d'Affinois Brebis*. Flavored versions include *Fromager d'Affinois Poivre* (black pepper) and *Fromager d'Affinois Ail et Fines Herbes* (garlic and herbs). *Fromager d'Affinois Léger* is a 25-percent reduced-fat version. *See also* CHEESE.

fromage fraise *see* FROMAGE BLANC

front of the house *see* BACK OF THE HOUSE; BRIGADE SYSTEM

frost, to 1. In cooking, "frost" means to cover and decorate a cake with a FROSTING or icing. 2. To chill a glass in the freezer until it's frosted with a thin coating of ice crystals.

frosting Also called *icing,* this sweet, sugar-based mixture is used to fill and coat cakes, pastries, cookies, etc. In addition to sugar, frosting can contain a combination of other ingredients including butter, milk, water, eggs and various flavorings. It can be cooked (as with BOILED ICING) or uncooked (as with BUTTERCREAM), and can range from thick to thin. Frosting must be thick enough to adhere to the item being coated, yet soft enough to spread easily.

frothy A descriptive cooking term referring to mixtures that are foamy, having a formation of tiny, light bubbles.

frozen custard *see* ICE CREAM

fructose [FRUHK-tohs; FROOK-tohs] Also called *fruit sugar* and *levulose,* this extremely sweet substance is a natural by-product of fruits and honey. It's more water-soluble than GLUCOSE and sweeter than SUCROSE (with fewer calories). Unlike glucose, it can be used by diabetics. Fructose comes in granulated and syrup forms. Except in the case of some liquids, such as a sauce or beverage, it should not be substituted for regular sugar (sucrose) unless a recipe gives specific substitution. When heated, fructose loses some of its sweetening power.

fruitarian [froo-TEH-ree-an] Although variations abound, the core definition of a fruitarian is one who eats raw fruits and seeds. Most nuts are generally included, as many are considered dried fruit (almonds, pecans and walnuts, for example) and others (like Brazil nuts) are actually seeds (*see* NUTS). Foods like cucumbers, olives and tomatoes that are fruits, but often not thought of as such, are definitely included. Some fruitarians also consume other foods, such as raw vegetables, though such individuals might be considered more of a raw-food vegan (see VEGETARIAN). Fruitarians live a lifestyle sans cooked foods not only because they believe raw foods are healthier, but because they feel the act of cooking foods contributes negatively to environmental changes. Critics of the fruitarian lifestyle point to the difficulty of sustaining it over the long term because of nutritional deficiencies that could eventually cause bodily harm.

fruit beer Mild ALES flavored with fruit concentrates. *See also* BEER.

fruit butter A sweet spread for bread made by stewing fresh fruit with sugar and spices until it becomes thick and smooth. *See* APPLE BUTTER.

fruitcake Traditional winter holiday cakes made with an assortment of CANDIED FRUIT and fruit rind, nuts, spices and usually liquor or BRANDY. Fruitcakes can have a moderate amount of cake surrounding the chunky ingredients, or only enough to hold the fruits and nuts together. **Dark fruitcakes** are generally made with molasses or brown sugar and dark liquor such as bourbon. Dark-colored fruits and nuts, such as prunes, dates, raisins and walnuts, may also contribute to the blend. **Light fruitcakes** are generally made with granulated sugar or light corn syrup and light ingredients such as almonds, dried apricots, golden raisins, etc. Fruitcakes are baked slowly and, after cooling, usually covered in CHEESECLOTH moistened with liquor or brandy and tightly wrapped in foil. Stored in this manner, they have tremendous staying power and, providing they are occasionally remoistened, can be kept for years.

fruit cocktail A mixture of various chopped fruits, served chilled as an appetizer. Any combination of fruit can be used, though a mixture of tart fruit (such as oranges and pineapples) and sweet fruit (peaches, melons or berries) is most appealing. The fruit may be spiced or drizzled with CHAMPAGNE or LIQUEUR for added flavor. Canned fruit cocktail is available, although the flavors of the individual fruits are barely discernible.

fruit molasses In Middle Eastern and Mediterranean areas when sugar was scarce, various fruits were boiled and reduced down to create molasses (syrups). These molasses were used as sweeteners in a variety of ways as a replacement for sugar. The tradition was carried on and molasses from carob pods, dates, figs, grapes, mulberries and pomegranates are still available in Middle Eastern and Mediterranean stores. In Turkey, fruit molasses is referred to as *pekmez* and is often mixed with TAHINI to make a breakfast spread. The practice of making fruit molasses goes back to at least ancient Rome, where different fruit juice or MUST reductions called *carenum, defrutum* and *sapa* were made.

fruit leather; fruit roll-up Puréed fruit that is spread in a thin layer and dried. The purée sometimes has sugar or honey added to it. After drying, the sheet of fruit is often cut into strips or rolled into cylinders for easy snacking. Rolls of fruit leather in a variety of flavors are available in natural food stores and most supermarkets. It can also be made at home.

fruits de mer [frwee duh MEHR] The French term translating as "fruits of the sea," referring to a combination of seafood.

fruit soup A Scandinavian specialty of cooked, puréed fruit combined with water, wine, milk or cream, spices and other flavorings. Danish apple soup is made, for example, with apples, cloves, lemon juice, wine, cream, sugar and curry powder. Though sugar is added to most fruit soups, they are not generally overly sweet. They may be served hot or cold.

fruit sugar *see* FRUCTOSE

frutta [FROO-tah] Italian for "fruit."

frutti di mare [FROO-tee dee MAH-reh] Italian for "fruit of the sea," referring to SEAFOOD.

fry *v.* To cook food in hot fat over moderate to high heat. DEEP-FRIED food is submerged in hot, liquid fat. Frying (also called *pan frying*) or SAUTÉING refers to cooking food in a lesser amount of fat, which doesn't cover the food. There is little difference in these two terms, though sautéing is often thought of as using less fat and being the faster of the two methods. **fry** *n.* 1. A special (usually outdoor) occasion at which fried foods are served, such as a *fish fry.* 2. The young of fish.

fry bread This specialty of many Southwest Indians (mainly Navajo and Hopi) is made of flour, water or milk and salt. It's formed into very thin rounds, deep-fried and served hot. It can be eaten with savory foods or drizzled with honey and enjoyed as a sweet. *See also* BANNOCK.

frying pan Also called a *skillet,* this long-handled, usually round pan has low, gently sloping sides so steam doesn't collect within the pan. It's used for frying foods over high heat, so it should be thick enough not to warp and should be able to conduct heat evenly. Frying pans come in various sizes, usually 8, 10 and 12 inches in diameter. **Electric frying pans** or **skillets** are often square or oblong in shape. Their heat is controlled by an adjustable thermostat unit that can be detached when the skillet is washed.

fu [FOO] A Japanese specialty made of dried wheat gluten made into a spongy dough. Fu is available fully cooked (roasted, deep-fried or baked), partially cooked and fresh or fresh-frozen. It's sometimes colored and comes in a variety of shapes including *namu fu* (fresh gluten cakes), *yaki fu* (cubes that have been roasted and dried) and *kohana fu* (little flower shapes that are cooked and dried and frequently used in instant noodle mixes). Fu is used in numerous Japanese dishes such as soups and other simmered dishes.

fudge A creamy, semisoft candy most often made with sugar, butter or cream, corn syrup and various flavorings. The most popular fudge flavor is chocolate, though maple (made with maple syrup), butterscotch (made with brown sugar or dark corn syrup) and vanilla are also favorites. Fudge can be plain and perfectly smooth or it may contain other ingredients such as nuts, chocolate chips, candied or dried fruit, etc. It may be cooked or uncooked, but both styles must be allowed to set before cutting.

fugu [FOO-goo] The Japanese name for certain species of puffer fish or blowfish, which, though considered delicacies, contain a poison so toxic it can kill. It's so imperative that fugu be cleaned and prepared properly that entire books have been written on the subject. In commercial Japanese kitchens, where this fish is used in both SASHIMI and NABEMONO preparations, only qualified cooks may deal with fugu. *See also* FISH.

Fuji apple A Japanese hybrid that's a cross between the once popular Ralls Janet and the RED DELICIOUS. This all-purpose apple is fragrantly sweet with an anise edge. The flesh is crisp and juicy, and the color is a soft green with pale red blushing. *See also* APPLE.

Fukien cuisine [FOO-kyen] *see* CHINESE CUISINE

fumé [fyoo-MAY] French for "smoked," referring culinarily to foods that are prepared in this manner.

Fumé Blanc [FOO-may BLAH*N* (BLAH*N*GK)] *see* SAUVIGNON BLANC

fumet [fyoo-MAY; foo-MAY] A concentrated STOCK, particularly one made from fish or mushrooms, used to add flavor to less intensely flavored stocks or sauces. *See also* FOND.

fumetto [foo-MEH-toh] Italian for "FUMET."

funche [FOON-chay] Puerto Rican cornmeal mush that's cooked like porridge and eaten for breakfast or as a snack, usually with milk and sugar added. In other parts of the Caribbean, similar dishes have names such as *cou-cou* (Barbados), *funchi* (Aruba), *fungi* (Virgin Islands), *funjie* (Antigua), *mayi moulin* (Haiti), *pastelle* (Trinidad), and *tun cornmeal* (Jamaica).

funchi *see* FUNCHE

fundido [fuhn-DEE-doh] Spanish for "melted." *See also* QUESO FUNDIDO.

funghi [FOON-gee] Italian for "mushrooms."

fungi *see* FUNCHE

funjie *see* FUNCHE

funnel cake This pastry is a Pennsylvania Dutch specialty made by pouring batter through a funnel into hot, deep fat and frying the resulting spirals until crisp and brown. Funnel cakes are served hot, often with sugar or maple syrup.

furikake [foo-ree-KAH-keh] Condiment usually containing toasted seaweed, sesame seeds, ground dried fish and salt. There are many variations, and other ingredients such as KIMCHI, MISO and SHISO are often included as well. Furikake was traditionally sprinkled on top of hot rice but today it's become a seasoning used on all types of food.

Furmint grape *see* TOKAY GRAPE

fusilli *see* Pasta Glossary, page 883

fusion food Cuisine created by combining ingredients and techniques from various cultures, the results of which are dishes that don't precisely fit into any of the originating cuisines. Most common today is a combination of Asian ingredients and techniques and Western ingredients and techniques. These might include ingredients commonly found in Chinese, Japanese, Thai or Vietnamese cuisines combined with French or Italian cooking techniques. The term *fusion cooking* was coined in 1988 by chef Norman Van Aken in a paper he wrote, but the practice of combining the cuisines of multiple cultures has existed for centuries. With today's air travel shrinking the world, not only can people experience a wider variety of cuisines (making "different" foods more acceptable), but fresh ingredients quickly can be shipped globally so these combinations are easy to achieve. **Pacific Rim Cuisine** is an example of fusion food and rather loosely defines dishes fused from the cuisines of countries in and around the Pacific Ocean.

futomaki [foo-toh-MAH-kee] *see* SUSHI

futsuu [FOO-tzoo] *see* SAKE

fuzzy melon Of Chinese origin, this cylindrical (6 to 10 inches long, 2 to 3 inches thick) gourd has a medium green skin covered with fine, hairlike fuzz, which it gradually loses as it ages. Its creamy-colored, medium-firm flesh is mildly flavored and has a tendency to take on the flavor of whatever food it's cooked with. Fuzzy melons—also called *hairy melons, hairy cucumber, mo gwa* and *fuzzy squash*—can be purchased in Asian markets and some specialty produce markets. Choose those that are fairly heavy for their size with wrinkle-free skins. Store ripe melons in a plastic bag in the refrigerator for up to 10 days. Fuzzy melons must be peeled before using. They're a popular addition to Chinese soups and STIR-FRY dishes.

fuzzy navel A cocktail made with orange juice and peach SCHNAPPS. The name is a conflation of peach "fuzz" and "navel" orange.

fuzzy squash *see* FUZZY MELON

G

gado gado; gado-gado [GAH-doh GAH-doh] This Indonesian favorite consists of a mixture of raw and slightly cooked vegetables served with a spicy peanut sauce made with hot chiles and COCONUT MILK. Sometimes the term "gado gado" refers only to the spicy sauce, which is used as a condiment with rice and various vegetable dishes.

Gaeta olive; Gyeta olive [gah-AY-tah] Small, blackish Italian olive that's either dry-cured, which produces dry, wrinkled, slightly brownish fruit, or cured in brine, which results in plumper fruit with a purplish cast. Gaeta olives are meaty and slightly tart to salty in flavor with hints of nuts. They are also grown in Morocco. *See also* OLIVE.

gai choy [guy CHOY] A deep green, broad-leafed cabbage with a pungent, mustardlike flavor. Gai choy is available in Asian markets and some specialty produce markets. Choose heads that are firm and blemish free. Refrigerate, tightly wrapped, for up to 1 week. Chop gai choy and use in soups or STIR-FRY dishes.

gai lan [guy LAHN] *see* CHINESE KALE

Gala apple A cross between Kidd's Orange Red and GOLDEN DELICIOUS, this all-purpose apple is red mottled with yellow. It has a perfumy flesh that's sweet, slightly spicy, crisp and juicy. *See also* APPLE.

galaktoboureko [gah-lahk-toh-BOO-ree-koh] A traditional Greek pastry prepared with a custard filling made with butter, eggs, milk, semolina and sugar—and possibly flavorings such as lemon, orange, ROSE WATER or vanilla—with a flaky PHYLLO dough on top and bottom. Galaktoboureko is served with a SUGAR SYRUP flavored with lemon, orange or ROSE WATER.

galangal; galanga root; galingale [guh-LANG-guhl] A rhizome with a hot, ginger-peppery flavor, galangal is used primarily as a seasoning. **Greater galangal**, also called *Laos ginger, Siamese ginger* and *Thai ginger,* is the best known and most widely available. It grows throughout Southeast Asia and is particularly popular in Thai cooking. This creamy white-fleshed rhizome is often used as a substitute for GINGER. *Laos* is the name given to the powdered form of greater galangal, which is slightly more intense than the fresh form. Greater galangel can be found in Asian markets. **Lesser galangal** has an orangish flesh and a much stronger, hotter flavor. It's not as well known and is seldom seen in the United States.

galantina [gah-lahn-TEE-nah] Italian for "GALANTINE."

galantine [GAL-uhn-teen; gal-ahn-TEEN] A classic French dish that resembles a meat-wrapped PÂTÉ. It's made from poultry, meat or fish that is boned and stuffed with a FORCEMEAT, which is often studded with flavor- and eye-enhancers such as pistachio nuts, olives and TRUFFLES. The stuffed meat roll is formed into a symmetrical loaf, wrapped in CHEESECLOTH and gently cooked in stock. It's then chilled, glazed with aspic made from its own jellied stock and garnished with items (such as pistachios, olives and truffles) that have been included in the filling. Galantines are normally served cold, cut in slices.

galbi [KAHL-bee] Also spelled *kalbi*, this Korean dish utilizes mari-nated beef or pork SHORT RIBS, usually FLANKEN, which are cooked on a grill. The ribs are cut crosswise so that each thin strip of meat contains several $1/2$-inch-long bones. The MARINADE varies but the mixture typically includes black pepper, garlic, onions, sesame oil, sesame seed, soy sauce, sugar and sometimes rice wine and/or pear juice or pear PURÉE. The pork version is called *daeji galbi*.

galbijjim *see* JJIM

galbitang [kahl-BEE-tahng] A Korean soup dish made primarily from beef short ribs. The rack of ribs is cut across the bone in thin slices, then simmered in water along with DAIKON radishes, garlic, onions and other seasoning for many hours. It's served with steamed rice or noodles that are added to the soup pot and cooked toward the end. The soup is also known as *garitang*, *galitang* and *kalbitang*.

galette [gah-LEHT] Hailing from France, a galette is a round, rather flat cake made of flaky-pastry dough, yeast dough or sometimes UNLEAVENED dough. The term also applies to a variety of tarts, both savory and sweet, and there are as many variations as there are French regions. They may be topped with fruit, jam, nuts, meat, cheese, etc. *Galette des Rois,* the tradi-tional cake served during Twelfth Night festivities, often contains a bean or other token, which is guaranteed to bring the recipient good luck.

Galia melon Hailing originally from Costa Rica, the Galia melon is now grown in many locales including Chile, Panama, Israel and the United States (California and most southern states). The rind of a Galia resem-bles a CANTALOUPE with a slightly more golden netting on a background of green. The flesh is pale green in color, very much like that of a HONEY-DEW MELON, and the flavor is very sweet. This melon is available from May through September and again in November and December. It's typically picked ripe and should be consumed shortly after purchase. Cut melon should be wrapped in plastic wrap and refrigerated for no more than 2 days. *See also* MELON.

galitang *see* GALBITANG

Galliano [gal-LYAH-noh] An Italian LIQUEUR with a brilliant saffron-yellow color, a thick, syrupy texture and an intriguing flavor that combines herbs flowers and spices. It gained notoriety in the United States when the HARVEY WALLBANGER was introduced in the late 1960s. Also called *Liquore Galliano.*

gallimaufry [gal-luh-MAW-free] Culinarily, any dish with a hodgepodge of ingredients, such as a STEW, RAGOÛT or HASH.

gamba [GAHM-bah] Spanish for "shrimp" or "prawn."

gambero [GAHM-beh-roh] Italian for "shrimp" or "prawn."

game animals A term applied to wild animals that are deemed suitable for human consumption. Some species are now domesticated and because their diets and activity levels are changed, their meat has a different flavor than that of field animals. Game animals are categorized as large game and small game. The most common large game meat is venison, which, though commonly thought of as deer, is a term that broadly includes the meat from elk, moose, reindeer, caribou and antelope. Other popular large game animals include BUFFALO, wild boar and, to a lesser degree, bear. Additionally, there are even rarer varieties eaten around the world such as camel, elephant, KANGAROO, zebra and wild sheep and goats. The most common small game animal is RABBIT. Squirrel is also quite popular, followed distantly by beaver, muskrat, opossum, raccoon, armadillo and even porcupine. Any game found in commercial markets is federally inspected. Whether purchased commercially or obtained directly from the hunter, the factors that determine the meat's quality include the age of the animal (younger animals are more tender), the animal's diet and the time of year the animal was killed (best is fall, after plentiful spring and summer feeding). Equally important is how the dead animal was handled in the field. The meat of many otherwise excellent animals is damaged (and sometimes ruined) because of the manner in which it is dressed and transported after the kill. The tenderness of a particular cut of meat from large game animals is similar to the corresponding cut of beef and pork. In general, wild game is less tender than meat from domestic animals because the wild animals get more exercise and are therefore leaner. What fat there is is generally rank-tasting and should be removed. For maximum tenderness, most game meat should be cooked slowly and not overdone. It can be cooked with moist heat by braising, or with dry heat by roasting (with an effort to ensure maximum moistness through BASTING, LARDING or BARDING).

game birds Any wild bird suitable for food, including the larger species (such as wild turkey and goose), medium-size birds (including PHEASANT and wild duck) and smaller game birds (such as the coot, dove, grouse, hazel hen, lark, mud hen, PARTRIDGE, pigeon, PLOVER, QUAIL, rail, snipe, thrush and WOODCOCK). Except for the few raised on game farms (which are usually expensive), game birds are not readily available. Those that are found in markets are usually of good quality. Most game birds are sold frozen; some of the smaller birds are canned. Factors affecting quality include the age of the bird and the manner in which it was treated after it was killed. Quality birds should have no off odor; the skin should be fresh-looking, not dull or dry. Young birds are best and can be identified by their pliable breastbone, feet and legs; their claws will be sharp. Wild birds are much leaner than the domesticated variety. Because of a lack of natural fat—particularly in younger birds—they must be BASTED, BARDED or LARDED before roasting. Older birds are best cooked with slow, moist heat such as braising, or used in soups or stews.

gammon [GAM-uhn] An English term that's taken from the Old Northern French word, *gambe*, which means "leg." Gammon refers to the upper portion of the pig's hind leg that's cured but not cooked and may or may not be smoked. In the United States this would be called HAM, but in England it must be cooked to be ham. Gammon is usually cut into steaks or into rashers that are much thicker than are common in American bacon.

ganache [gahn-AHSH] A rich icing/filling made of semisweet chocolate and whipping cream, heated and stirred together until the chocolate has melted. The mixture is cooled until lukewarm and poured over a cake or torte. **Ganache soufflé** is made from the same base but often includes a tablespoon or so of rum or cognac. When cooled to room temperature, the mixture is whipped to approximately twice its original volume. Whereas ganache is used to glaze cakes, pastries and tortes, ganache soufflé is generally used to fill them.

gandule *see* PIGEON PEA

garam masala [gah-RAHM mah-SAH-lah] *Garam* is Indian for "warm" or "hot," and this blend of dry-roasted, ground spices from the colder climes of northern India adds a sense of "warmth" to both palate and spirit. There are as many variations of garam masala (which may contain up to 12 spices) as there are Indian cooks. It can include BLACK PEPPER, CINNAMON, CLOVES, CORIANDER, CUMIN, CARDAMOM, DRIED CHILES, FENNEL, MACE, NUTMEG and other spices. Garam masala may be purchased in Indian markets and in most supermarkets. It's also easily prepared at home, but should be made in small batches to retain its freshness. As with all spices, it should be stored in a cool, dry place for no more than 6 months. Garam masala is usually either added to a dish toward the end of cooking or sprinkled over the surface just before serving.

garbanzo bean *see* CHICKPEA

garbure [gar-BOOR] A vegetable or meat soup so thick it could be considered a stew or casserole dish. Garbure has many variations, but most commonly contains cabbage, beans, potatoes and bits of pork, bacon or preserved goose. It's usually served with toasted or fried bread. Garbure is immensely popular with Basques and the most famous version comes from Béarn, France.

garde manger [gahrd mahn-ZHAY] *see* BRIGADE SYSTEM

garden orache *see* ORACHE

garden pea *see* ENGLISH PEA

garganelli *see* Pasta Glossary, page 883

gari [GAH-ree] *see* BENI SHOGA

garitang *see* GALBITANG

garland chrysanthemum *see* CHRYSANTHEMUM LEAVES

garlic Garlic has long been credited with providing and prolonging physical strength and was fed to Egyptian slaves building the giant pyramids. Throughout the centuries, its medicinal claims have included cures for toothaches, consumption, open wounds and evil demons. A member of the lily family, garlic is a cousin to leeks, chives, onions and shallots. The edible bulb or "head" grows beneath the ground. This bulb is made up of sections called cloves, each encased in its own parchmentlike membrane. Today's major garlic suppliers include the United States (mainly California, Texas and Louisiana), France, Spain, Italy and Mexico. There are three major types of garlic available in the United States: the white-skinned, strongly flavored **American garlic;** the **Mexican** and **Italian garlic**, both of which have mauve-colored skins and a somewhat milder flavor; and the Paul Bunyanesque, white-skinned **elephant garlic** (which is not a *true* garlic, but a relative of the LEEK), the most mildly flavored of the three. Depending on the variety, cloves of American, Mexican and Italian garlic can range from ¹/₂ to 1¹/₂ inches in length. Elephant garlic (grown mainly in California) has bulbs the size of a small grapefruit, with huge cloves averaging 1 ounce each. It can be purchased through mail order and in some gourmet markets. **Green garlic**, typically available only in specialty produce markets and farmer's markets, is young garlic before it begins to form cloves. It resembles a baby LEEK, with a long green top and sometimes just the beginning of a white bulb, sometimes tinged with pink. The flavor of a baby plant is much softer than that of mature garlic. Green garlic is harvested between March and May. Fresh mature garlic is available year-round. Purchase firm, plump bulbs with dry skins.

Avoid heads with soft or shriveled cloves, and those stored in the refrigerated section of the produce department. Store fresh garlic in an open container (away from other foods) in a cool, dark place. Properly stored, unbroken bulbs can be kept up to 8 weeks, though they will begin to dry out toward the end of that time. Once broken from the bulb, individual cloves will keep from 3 to 10 days. Garlic is usually peeled before use in recipes. Among the exceptions are roasted garlic bulbs and the famous dish, "chicken with 40 cloves of garlic," in which unpeeled garlic cloves are baked with chicken in a broth until they become sweet and butter-soft. Crushing, chopping, pressing or puréeing garlic releases more of its essential oils and provides a sharper, more assertive flavor than slicing or leaving it whole. Garlic is readily available in forms other than fresh. Dehydrated **garlic flakes** (sometimes referred to as **instant garlic**) are slices or bits of garlic that must be reconstituted before using (unless added to a liquid-based dish, such as soup or stew). When dehydrated garlic flakes are ground, the result is **garlic powder**. **Garlic salt** is garlic powder blended with salt and a moisture-absorbing agent. **Garlic extract** and **garlic juice** are derived from pressed garlic cloves. Though all of these products are convenient, they're a poor flavor substitute for the less expensive, readily available and easy-to-store fresh garlic. One unfortunate side effect of garlic is that, because its essential oils permeate the lung tissue, it remains with the body long after it's been consumed, affecting breath and even skin odor. Chewing chlorophyll tablets or fresh parsley is helpful but, unfortunately, modern-day science has yet to find the perfect antidote for residual garlic odor.

garlic bread Said to have been invented during the late 1940s boom of Italian-American restaurants, garlic bread consists of Italian or French bread slices, spread on both sides with GARLIC BUTTER and heated in the oven. There are many variations, including bread brushed with olive oil and sprinkled with minced garlic and herbs. It can also be broiled or grilled.

garlic butter Softened butter blended with crushed or minced garlic. The intensity of the garlic flavor is governed by the amount of garlic used and the length of time the mixture is allowed to stand. Garlic butter is used on a broad range of foods including GARLIC BREAD, ESCARGOTS, meats, poultry, fish and vegetables.

garlic chives Long (up to 10 inches) and dark green, these soft, grasslike leaves have a pungent flavor and aroma that's a mélange of common CHIVES and garlic. Garlic chive leaves have thin, flat stems, whereas the stalks with flowers are round and more closely resemble regular chives. Open flowers, though beautiful, are a signal that the chives were picked from a more mature plant and will not be as tender as those with unopened buds. **Yellow chives** have been grown without sunlight and have a mild flavor more akin to onion than garlic. Garlic chives can be found in Asian markets and many produce markets. Choose those that are bright green; store in a plastic bag in the refrigerator for up to a week. They may be snipped with scissors to the desired length and used in both fresh and cooked dishes. Garlic chives are also called *Chinese chives, gow chai, gow choy, ku chai and nira*.

garlic flakes; garlic powder; garlic salt *see* GARLIC

garlic press A kitchen tool used to press a garlic clove through small holes, thereby extracting both pulp and juice. Leaving the skin on the clove facilitates cleaning, which should be done immediately after pressing, before any garlic left in the press dries. The press can also be set in a cup of warm water until cleaning time. Some presses contain teeth that push garlic fragments back out through the holes, making cleaning much easier. Garlic presses can be made of aluminum, stainless steel and strong plastics.

Garnacha; Garnacha Tinta; Garnacho Tinto [gar-NAH-chah TEEN-tah (toh)] *see* GRENACHE

garnacha *see* SOPE

garni [gahr-NEE] French for "garnish," when used as a culinary descriptor. For example, "steak garni" typically means it's accompanied by vegetables and potatoes.

garnish *n.* A decorative, edible accompaniment to finished dishes, from appetizers to desserts. Garnishes can be placed under, around or on food, depending on the dish. They vary from simple sprigs of parsley or exotically carved vegetables on plated food, to CROUTONS in soup, to chocolate leaves on top of chocolate mousse. Garnishes should not only be appealing to the eye, but should also echo or complement the flavor of the dish. **garnish** *v.* To decorate or accompany a dish with a garnish.

garniture [gahr-nih-TEUR] French for "GARNISH."

Garrotxa [gahr-ROH-chah] Rustic SEMISOFT FARMSTEAD cheese that's been made for centuries in Spain's Catalonia region. The 2-pound rounds are briefly immersed in BRINE and then RIPENED in caves for a minimum of 20 days; this process produces a light golden rind with pale gray mold. The interior of this goat's-milk cheese is a chalky white; the texture is firm, smooth and velvety. The flavor is mild and tangy with hints of grass, flowers and nuts. It has a FAT CONTENT of about 50 percent.

garum [GAR-uhm] The ancient Romans used garum as a flavoring much like salt. This extremely pungent sauce was made by fermenting fish in a brine solution for several days in the sun. The resulting liquid was combined with various other flavorings such as oil, pepper, wine and spices. Also called *liquamen*. *See also* FISH SAUCE.

gaspacho *see* GAZPACHO

gaspergoo; gaspergou [gas-per-GOO] A freshwater DRUM that inhabits deep rivers and lakes throughout the United States. Also known as *goo* or *gou,* this fish has a white, lean flesh with a succulently sweet flavor. Gaspergoo is most commonly available in the spring and summer months. It's suitable for frying, grilling, or steaming. *See also* FISH.

gastrique [gah-STREEK] French for "gastric," referring culinarily to a syrupy reduction of caramelized sugar and vinegar, sometimes with the addition of wine. Gastriques are typically used in savory dishes that include fruit, such as oranges or tomatoes.

gastronome [GAS-truh-nohm] A connoisseur of good food—someone with a refined palate. *See also* EPICURE; GLUTTON; GOURMAND; GOURMET.

gastronomy [gas-TRON-uh-mee] The art of fine dining; the science of gourmet food and drink.

gastropod [GAS-truh-pod] Often referred to as a *univalve,* a gastropod can be any of several MOLLUSKS with a single (univalve) shell and single muscle. Among the more common gastropods are the ABALONE, LIMPET, PERIWINKLE, SNAIL and WHELK. With a few exceptions (such as the abalone), gastropods are not as highly regarded culinarily as BIVALVE mollusks such as the CLAM and OYSTER.

gastropub Loosely defined term for a restaurant or bar that serves upscale food and libations in a pub-like atmosphere. The term was invented in 1991 when the owners of the Eagle pub in Clerkenwell, London, decided to go beyond traditional English pub fare and add high-end but still unpretentious dishes. The introduction of fresh, local and high-quality ingredients was a big part of the transition, as was a shift from serving a high percentage of cold dishes to a majority of hot dishes. The owners of gastropubs like the Spotted Pig in New York City and the Hand and Flowers in Buckinghamshire, England, elevated the craft high enough to win coveted Michelin stars for their establishments.

gâteau [ga-TOH] French for "cake."

gâteau Saint-Honoré *see* SAINT-HONORÉ

gatha *see* PACIFIC THREADFIN

gaufrette [goh-FREHT] Thin, lightly sweet, fan-shaped wafers usually served with ice cream, mousse and other such desserts. When baked on a special gaufrette iron (similar to a waffle iron), the wafer's surface is waffled. Before cooling and crisping, gaufrettes are sometimes curled to form an ice cream cone.

gaufrettes pommes de terre [goh-FREHTS pom duh TEHR] Crisp, thin, latticed potato wafers.

gazpacho [gahz-PAH-choh] A refreshingly cold, summertime soup hailing from the Andalusia region in southern Spain. This uncooked soup is usually made from a puréed mixture of fresh tomatoes, sweet bell peppers, onions, celery, cucumber, breadcrumbs, garlic, olive oil, vinegar and sometimes lemon juice. Alternatively, the vegetables may simply be minced and stirred into the puréed tomato base. Gazpacho can be a meal in itself, particularly when extra fresh vegetables such as sliced celery, green onion, cucumber and green pepper are added. Popular garnishes include croutons and diced hard-cooked eggs. An alternative spelling for this soup is *gaspacho*.

G

gefilte fish [geh-FIHL-teh] This popular Jewish dish consists of ground fish (usually CARP, PIKE or WHITEFISH) mixed with eggs, MATZO MEAL and seasonings. The mixture is formed into balls or patties that are then simmered in vegetable or fish stock. After chilling, the gefilte fish is served in its own jellied stock and often garnished with grated horseradish, vegetable relishes or dill pickles. The name comes from the Yiddish term for "stuffed (gefüllte) fish;" in the past the mixture was stuffed back into the fish skin before cooking.

gelatin [JEHL-uh-tihn] An odorless, tasteless and colorless thickening agent, which when dissolved in hot water and then cooled, forms a jelly. It's useful for many purposes such as jelling molded desserts and salads, thickening cold soups and glazing CHAUD-FROID preparations. Gelatin is pure protein derived from bones, cartilage, tendons and other connective tissue of animals. Much of the commercial gelatin today is a by-product of pig skin. Until the advent of commercial gelatin in the late 19th century, jelled dishes were not very popular because housewives had to make their own jelling agent by laboriously boiling calves' feet or knuckles. Their only alternative was to use either the hard-to-obtain ISINGLASS (gelatin from fish air bladders) or CARRAGEEN (a dried seaweed product). **Granulated gelatin** is the most common form of unsweetened commercial gelatin on the market. It's packaged in boxes of $^1/_4$-ounce envelopes and is also available in bulk. Generally, 1 envelope of gelatin will jell 2 cups of liquid. It's important to soak gelatin in cold liquid (whatever the recipe directs) for 3 to 5 minutes before dissolving it. This softens and swells the gelatin granules so they will dissolve smoothly when heated. Not as readily available as granulated gelatin is **leaf** (or **sheet**) **gelatin**, which comes in packages of paper-thin sheets. Four sheets of leaf gelatin equal one package of powdered gelatin. Leaf gelatin must be soaked longer than granulated gelatin and is therefore not as popular. This product is often called for in jelled European dessert recipes. It can be found in some gourmet and bakery supply shops. Sweetened gelatin dessert mix is also available in various artificial fruit flavors.

gelato [jeh-LAH-toh]; *pl.* **gelati** [jeh-LAH-tee] Italian for "ice cream." Gelato doesn't contain as much air as its American counterpart and therefore has a denser texture. An Italian ice cream parlor is called a *gelateria*. *See also* ICE CREAM.

gemelli *see* Pasta Glossary, page 883

gem pan; mini muffin pan A miniature muffin pan designed (depending on the pan) to make 12 to 24 tiny muffins about 1½ inches in diameter. "Gem" is an old-fashioned reference to a small (nonyeast) bread or cake.

genetically modified food *see* BIOTECHNOLOGY; BIOENGINEERED FOODS

genevoise sauce MIREPOIX and ESPAGNOLE with red wine and fish FUMET. The mixture is cooked, reduced and strained, after which ANCHOVY PASTE, butter and minced mushrooms are added. *See also* SAUCE.

genip *see* MAMONCILLO

Genoese, alla; Genovese, alla [ah-lah jehn-oh-EEZ; ah-lah jehn-oh-VEEZ] Italian for "as prepared in the style of Genoa," a seaport city in northwest Italy. Specifically, it means a dish made or accompanied with PESTO, which originated in Genoa.

génoise [zhayn-WAHZ; zhehn-WAHZ] This rich, light cake is made with flour, sugar, eggs, butter and vanilla. It's similar in texture to a moist SPONGE CAKE. It was developed in Genoa, Italy, adapted by the French and is now baked by gourmet cooks throughout Europe and the United States. Génoise is an extremely versatile cake and is used for many elegant presentations such as PETITS FOURS, cake rolls and BAKED ALASKA.

genshu [GIHN-shoo] *see* SAKE

geoduck; gweduck [GOO-ee duhk] This huge, funny-looking SOFT-SHELL CLAM hails from the Pacific Northwest. It averages 3 pounds in weight and is distinguished by a long (up to 18-inch) neck (siphon) that extends from its 6-inch shell. The neck can be cut or ground and used in chowders. The body meat, when sliced, pounded and sautéed, resembles ABALONE. *See also* CLAMS; SHELLFISH.

germ In the food world, the word "germ" refers to a grain (like WHEAT) kernel's nucleus or embryo. Wheat germ is one of the more commercially popular types on the market. The nutritiously endowed germ furnishes thiamine, vitamin E, iron and riboflavin.

German chocolate cake A cake recipe submitted by a Dallas homemaker to a local newspaper in 1957. The name comes from the fact that one of the ingredients is Baker's German's Sweet Chocolate, a chocolate bar similar to milk chocolate developed in the mid-1800s by Sam German for Baker's Chocolate Company. Over the years the apostrophe and the "s" were dropped and this dessert simply became German chocolate cake. The layers are based on chocolate and buttermilk, and the vanilla-flavored cooked frosting and filling contain pecans and coconut. Pundits suggest the cake was probably created prior to 1957, as there were numerous cakes in the South that used buttermilk, sweet chocolate and pecans. However, when this particular recipe was published it became an instant success and caused an immediate spike in sales of the eponymous chocolate bar. The dessert is still popular today and cake mixes are available in supermarkets, as is Baker's German's Sweet Chocolate.

G

German potato salad A bacon-studded potato salad made with a dressing of bacon fat, vinegar, seasonings and sometimes sugar. German potato salad can be served hot, cold or at room temperature. Favorite additions include minced onion, celery and green pepper.

Gewürztraminer [guh-VURTS-trah-mee-ner] The German word *Gewürz* means "spicy," and this white wine is known for its crisp, spicy characteristics. It's a specialty of the French region Alsace—the area that buffers Germany and France—and is also produced in Germany and California. Gewürztraminer has a distinctively pungent, perfumy, yet clean flavor. It's available in varying degrees of sweetness; the drier versions complement fish and poultry, the slightly sweeter styles are perfect for summer SPRITZERS, and the sweet LATE-HARVEST versions make excellent DESSERT WINES. Gewürztraminer is best when drunk fairly young because even the vintage versions won't usually age well over 5 years.

ghee [GEE] Butter that has been slowly melted, thereby separating the milk solids (which sink to the bottom of the pan) from the golden liquid on the surface. This form of CLARIFIED BUTTER is taken a step further by simmering it until all of the moisture evaporates and the milk solids begin to brown, giving the resulting butter a nutty, caramellike flavor and aroma. This extra step also gives ghee a longer life and much higher SMOKE POINT than regular clarified butter. Because the smoke point is raised to almost 375°F, ghee is practical for a variety of sautéing and frying uses. Although it originated in India, the best commercially available ghee comes from

Holland, followed closely by products from Scandinavia and Australia. It's quite expensive, but can be purchased in Middle Eastern, Indian and some gourmet markets. Whereas ghee was once made only with butter derived from water buffalo milk, today it can be made with any unsalted butter. Making it at home is not a difficult task, and flavored ghees are created by simply adding ingredients such as ginger, peppercorns or cumin at the beginning of the clarifying process. Tightly wrapped ghee can be refrigerated for up to 6 months and frozen up to a year.

gheimeh *see* QAYMEH

gherkin [GER-kihn] The young fruit of a variety of small, dark green cucumbers especially grown to make pickles. Gherkins are usually sold in jars, packed in pickling brine. CORNICHONS are the French version of this pickle.

ghoriba; ghriba; ghryba [goh-REE-bah] HAND-FORMED COOKIES of various types made from the Middle East to Morocco. Ghoriba range from crisp SHORTBREAD cookies to chewy MACAROONS and use a large assortment of ingredients including almonds, cinnamon, coconut, sesame seeds and walnuts. Moroccan versions favor using SEMOLINA.

gianduja [zhahn-DOO-yah] Hailing from Switzerland, gianduja is a silky-smooth, hazelnut-flavored chocolate that comes in several styles including milk chocolate and bittersweet chocolate. It's available in gourmet markets and through mail order.

giant garlic *see* ROCAMBOLE

giant hogweed *see* GOLPAR

giant sea bass *see* BASS

giardiniera, alla [ah-lah jahr-dee-NYAY-rah] From the Italian *giardiniere* ("gardener"), culinarily this term refers to dishes served with mixed sliced vegetables.

giblets [JIHB-lihts] Generally, the term "giblets" refers to the heart, liver and gizzard of domesticated fowl and game birds. Sometimes the neck is also included in this grouping. All but the liver are used for flavoring stocks and soups. The liver is usually cooked separately and, in the case of ducks and geese, is considered a delicacy. *See also* VARIETY MEATS.

Gibson [GIHB-suhn] Named for the famous American "Gibson Girl" illustrator, Charles Dana Gibson, this COCKTAIL is identical to the MARTINI (gin and dry VERMOUTH), differing only in that it is served garnished with a tiny white onion instead of an olive.

gigantoni *see* Pasta Glossary, page 883

gigli *see* Pasta Glossary, page 883

gigot [zhee-GOH] French for "leg of mutton." *Gigot d'agneau* is a "leg of lamb."

Gillett method A method by which the heat level of a chile is measured using *high performance liquid chromatography* (HPLC). This technique directly measures the amount of CAPSAICIN rather than using human sensory methods such as those employed when the SCOVILLE SCALE was originally developed. The Gillett method measures the chile's heat level in ASTA pungency units (named for the American Spice Trade Association). Such units are typically converted to the better-known Scoville scale at about 1 ASTA pungency unit to 15 Scoville heat units.

gimlet [GIHM-liht] A COCKTAIL made with SUGAR SYRUP, lime juice, vodka or gin and sometimes soda water. According to the British, the secret of a good gimlet is thorough stirring.

G

gin [JIHN] Made from grain (such as barley, corn or rye), gin is first distilled (*see* DISTILLATION) to a desired alcohol level, then re-distilled with juniper berries and other botanicals (such as angelica, anise, caraway seed, cardamom, cassia bark, citrus peel, coriander seeds, ginger, licorice and orris root) to extract the desired flavors. Distilled water is then added to adjust the alcohol concentration to somewhere between 80 and 95 PROOF. The two primary styles of gin are Dutch and dry. **Dutch gin**, also known as *Hollands, Genever, Jenever* and *Schiedam* gin, is typically made from equal parts of malted (*see* MALT) barley, corn and rye. It has a slightly sweet, malty character and is generally fuller flavored than dry gin. There are two styles of Dutch gin: *Oude* ("old") has a stronger flavor from a higher proportion of barley than the *Jonge* ("young") style, which is lighter in both flavor and texture. **Dry gin**—the preferred choice for most gin drinkers—is made primarily from corn with a small percentage of malted barley and other grains. It's typically DRY (not sweet), aromatic and moderately light in flavor and body. Dry gins made in England (where this style originated) commonly have a slightly higher alcohol content and are more flavorful than American-made gins. Labels indicating "English Dry Gin," "London Dry Gin" or "London Extra Dry Gin" allude to the gin's style, not where it was produced. **Plymouth gin** (also called *Plym*), a dry gin made only in Plymouth, England, is fuller bodied, smoother and stronger flavored than London styles. **Golden gin** has been AGED briefly in wood (although aging is not standard practice for most gin), which contributes a light golden color to the normally colorless spirit. **Old Tom Gin**, a sweetened English-made gin is hard to find outside of Britain. SLOE GIN isn't actually gin, but a LIQUEUR.

gin and bitters *see* PINK GIN

gin fizz A COCKTAIL made with gin, lemon juice, sugar and soda, served in a tall glass over ice. Add an egg yolk for a **Golden Fizz**, an egg white for a **Silver Fizz** and a whole egg for a **Royal Gin Fizz**. Adding ORANGE-FLOWER WATER and cream or milk to a silver fizz transforms it into a **Ramos gin fizz**, a New Orleans original created in the late 1800s by bar owner Henry Ramos.

ginger; gingerroot A plant from tropical and subtropical regions that's grown for its gnarled and bumpy root. Most ginger comes from Jamaica, followed by India, Africa and China. Gingerroot's name comes from the Sanskrit word for "horn root," undoubtedly referring to its knobby appearance. It has a tan skin and a flesh that ranges in color from pale greenish yellow to ivory. The flavor is peppery and slightly sweet, while the aroma is pungent and spicy. This extremely versatile root has long been a mainstay in Asian and Indian cooking and found its way early on into European foods as well. The Chinese, Japanese and East Indians use fresh gingerroot in a variety of forms—grated, ground and slivered—in many savory dishes. Europeans and most Americans, however, are more likely to use the dried ground form of ginger, usually in baked goods. **Fresh ginger** is available in two forms—young and mature. **Young ginger**, sometimes called *spring ginger,* has a pale, thin skin that requires no peeling. It's very tender and has a milder flavor than its mature form. Young ginger can be found in most Asian markets in the springtime. **Mature ginger** has a tough skin that must be carefully peeled away to preserve the delicate, most desirable flesh just under the surface. Look for mature ginger with smooth skin (wrinkled skin indicates that the root is dry and past its prime). It should have a fresh, spicy fragrance. Fresh unpeeled gingerroot, tightly wrapped, can be refrigerated for up to 3 weeks and frozen for up to 6 months. To use frozen ginger, slice off a piece of the unthawed root and return the rest to the freezer. Place peeled gingerroot in a screw-top glass jar, cover with dry SHERRY or MADEIRA and refrigerate up to 3 months. The wine will impart some of its flavor to the ginger—a minor disadvantage to weigh against having peeled ginger ready and waiting. On the plus side, the delicious, ginger-flavored wine can be reused for cooking. The flavor of **dried ground ginger** is very different from that of its fresh form and is not an appropriate substitute for dishes specifying fresh ginger. It is, however, delicious in many savory dishes such as soups, curries and meats, a sprightly addition to fruit compotes, and indispensable in sweets like GINGERBREAD, GINGERSNAPS and many spice cookies. Ginger is the flavor that has long given the popular beverages GINGER ALE and GINGER BEER their claim to fame. In addition to its fresh and dried ground forms, ginger comes in several other guises. **Ginger juice** is simply the juice extracted from the root. It's available in some specialty markets and natural food stores. **Crystallized** or **candied**

G

ginger has been cooked in a sugar syrup and coated with coarse sugar. Another form called **preserved ginger** has been preserved in a sugar-salt mixture. These types of ginger can be found in Asian markets and many supermarkets. They are generally used as a confection or added to desserts. Melon and preserved ginger are a classic combination. **Pickled ginger**, available in Asian markets and many supermarkets, has been preserved in sweet vinegar. It's most often used as a garnish for Asian dishes. The sweet **red candied ginger** is packed in a red sugar syrup. It's used to flavor dishes both sweet and savory. *See also* AROMATIC GINGER; Seasoning Suggestions, page 891.

ginger ale A carbonated, ginger-flavored SOFT DRINK.

ginger beer Made in both nonalcoholic and alcoholic forms, this carbonated beverage tastes like GINGER ALE with a stronger ginger flavor. It's an integral ingredient in the mixed drink, MOSCOW MULE.

G

gingerbread This sweet dates back to the Middle Ages, when fair ladies presented the rather hard, honey-spice bread as a favor to dashing knights going into tournament battle. In those days, gingerbread was intricately shaped and decorated, sometimes with gold leaf. Today, gingerbread generally refers to one of two desserts. It can be a dense, ginger-spiced cookie flavored with molasses or honey and cut into fanciful shapes (such as the popular gingerbread man). Or, particularly in the United States, it can describe a dark, moist cake flavored with molasses, ginger and other spices. This gingerbread "cake" is usually baked in a square pan and often topped with lemon sauce or whipped cream.

gingerroot *see* GINGER

gingersnap A small, very crisp ginger cookie flavored with molasses.

ginjo [JEEN-joh] *see* SAKE

ginkgo nut [GING-koh; JING-koh] This buff-colored, delicately sweet nut comes from the center of the inedible fruit of the maidenhair tree, a native of China. Fresh ginkgo nuts are available during fall and winter and can be found in many Asian and gourmet markets. Their hard shells must be removed with a nutcracker and the nutmeats soaked in hot water to loosen their skins. Ginkgo nuts are also available dried or canned in brine. The canned nuts must be rinsed of brine before using. Ginkgo nuts, which turn bright green when cooked, are particularly popular in Japanese cooking. *See also* NUTS.

ginseng [JIHN-sing] The Chinese name for this sweet licorice-flavored root is "human-shaped root" and indeed some have extraordinarily human shapes. This rather amazing plant has been credited for centuries with being everything from an aphrodisiac to a restorative. Recent scientific discoveries have linked ginseng to the treatment of high blood pressure. It's referred to as **white ginseng** when simply sun-dried. When steamed and dried over a fire or with other heat, it takes on a reddish tinge and is called **red ginseng**. Ginseng is used in soups, for tea and as a medicinal. It's available in Asian markets and natural food stores.

giorno, del *see* DEL GIORNO.

girasole articiocco *see* SUNCHOKE

Girolle; girolle [zhee-ROHL] 1. Invented in the 1980s by Swiss precision engineer Nicolas Crevoisier, a girolle is a cutting instrument specifically designed to shave thin slices of TÊTE DE MOINE cheese. This tool is a downward-facing blade and handle mounted on a stainless steel rod. The rod is inserted into the center of the cheese and the handle turned, which slowly lowers the blade, thereby shaving the cheese into rosettes. 2. The French name for CHANTERELLE.

gizzard Found in the lower stomach of fowl, this muscular pouch grinds the bird's food, often with the aid of stones or grit swallowed for this purpose. The portion that actually does the work is in the center of the pouch and is usually removed before the gizzard reaches the market. Gizzards can be very tough unless cooked slowly with moist heat, such as braising.

Gjetost [YAYT-oost; YEHT-oost] Though Gjetost (or *geitost*) is Norwegian for "goat cheese," this cheese is usually made with a blend of goat's milk, cow's milk, and WHEY. Pure goat's-milk cheeses are labeled *Ekte Gjetost* (or *Geitost*), which means "authentic goat cheese." This Norwegian specialty has a flavor that's faintly sweet and caramellike yet somewhat tangy and salty. The color varies from light to deep-golden brown, and the texture can range from semihard like fudge to the consistency of stiff peanut butter. The brown color and sweetness are the result of an ancient process for making spreadable cheese (called *prim* or *primost)* which involves slowly cooking the milk until the moisture evaporates and the sugars caramelize. Other names that apply to this style of cheese include *brunost* ("brown cheese") and *mysost* (a version made only with cow's milk). Although the FAT CONTENT of Gjetost is generally 30 to 35 percent, there are lower-fat versions, which are identified by the word *lett* ("light") on the label. *See also* CHEESE.

glace [GLAHS] 1. French for "ICE CREAM." 2. The word *glace* is also used in reference to a reduced stock, as in GLACE DE VIANDE.

glacé [glah-SAY] French for "glazed" or "frozen," such as MARRONS GLACÉS (candied chestnuts). It can also refer to the frosting on a cake or frozen desserts or drinks.

glace de viande [glahs duh vee-AHND] French for "meat glaze," *glace de viande* is made by boiling meat juices until they are reduced to a thick syrup. It's used to add flavor and color to sauces.

glacé fruit [glah-SAY] *see* CANDIED FRUIT

Glarnerkäse *see* SAPSAGO

glass noodles *see* CELLOPHANE NOODLES

glasswort *see* SAMPHIRE

Glayva [gla-VAH] This Scottish LIQUEUR is made with scotch whisky, honey and a well-guarded herbal formula.

glaze *n.* A thin, glossy coating for both hot and cold foods. A savory glaze might be a reduced meat stock or ASPIC, whereas a sweet glaze could be anything from melted jelly to a chocolate coating. An EGG WASH brushed on pastry before baking to add color and shine is also called a glaze. glaze *v.* To coat food with a thin, liquid, sweet or savory mixture that will be smooth and shiny after setting.

glögg [GLUHG; GLOEG] Especially popular during Advent, this Swedish spiced-wine punch gets its *punch* from the addition of AQUAVIT or BRANDY. To take the chill off cold winter nights, it's served hot in cups with several almonds and raisins added to each serving.

Gloucester [GLOSS-ter] There are two styles of this cheese—Single Gloucester and Double Gloucester—both of which hail from southwest England's city of Gloucester. **Single Gloucester**, which has been granted a PROTECTED DESIGNATION OF ORIGIN (PDO), is produced with traditional FARMSTEAD methods and only from the milk of Gloucester cows (which may be and typically are skimmed); it may not be artificially colored. It's generally RIPENED anywhere from 10 weeks to 9 months and has a lighter, more crumbly texture than its whole-milk kin. The flavor is milky and slightly sweet with hints of vanilla and caramel. **Double Gloucester** is made with whole milk and is typically ripened for 6 months. It has a firmer, denser texture and fairly mellow flavor, sometimes with nutty traits. At this writing, Double Gloucester doesn't have PDO status and most of this cheese is factory-made. **Cotswald**, also known simply as **pub cheese**, is a Double Gloucester flavored with chive and onion. Gloucester has a FAT CONTENT of about 48 percent. *See also* CHEESE.

Gloucester Old Spot pork [GLOSS-tuhr] *see* HERITAGE PORK

glucose [GLOO-kohs] The most common form of this sugar is **dextroglucose**, a naturally occurring form generally referred to as DEXTROSE (also called *corn sugar* and *grape sugar*). This form of glucose has many sources including grape juice, certain vegetables and honey. It has about half the sweetening power of regular sugar. Because it doesn't crystallize easily, it's used to make commercial candies and frostings, as well as in baked goods, soft drinks and other processed foods. Corn syrup is a form of glucose made from cornstarch.

Glühwein [GLEW-vine] A popular German MULLED WINE, *Glühwein* ("glow wine") is so named not only because it's hot, but because it gives those who drink more than one or two a definite glow. It's typically made with red wine, cloves, cinnamon, sugar or honey and orange or lemon peel.

gluten [GLOO-tihn] Wheat and other cereals that are made into flour contain proteins, one of which is glutenin, commonly known as *gluten*. Viewed alone, gluten is a tough, elastic, grayish substance resembling chewing gum. It's the gluten in flour that, when a dough is kneaded, helps hold in the gas bubbles formed by the leavening agent (*see* LEAVENER). Gas contained within a dough or batter helps a bread or other baked good rise, creating a light structure. Most (but not all) flours contain gluten in varying amounts. Bread (or hard wheat) flour has a high gluten content and is therefore good for yeast breads, which require an elastic framework. On the other hand, low-protein (and therefore low-gluten) cake flour has a softer, less elastic quality and is better suited for cakes. *See also* BREAD; FLOUR; SEITAN.

glutton A person with a gargantuan appetite for both food and drink, often without regard to quality. *See also* EPICURE; GASTRONOME; GOURMAND; GOURMET.

glycerin; glycerine [GLIH-ser-ihn] The commercial name for *glycerol,* a colorless, odorless, syrupy liquid—chemically, an alcohol—obtained from fats and oils and used to retain moisture and add sweetness to foods. It also helps prevent sugar crystallization in foods like candy. Outside the world of food, glycerin is used in cosmetics, inks and certain glues.

gnocchi [NYOH-kee; NOH-kee] 1. Italian for "dumplings," gnocchi can be made from potatoes, flour or FARINA. Eggs or cheese can be added to the dough, and finely chopped spinach is also a popular addition. Gnocchi are generally shaped into little balls, cooked in boiling water and served with butter and Parmesan or a savory sauce. The dough can also be chilled, sliced and either baked or fried. Gnocchi are usually served as a side dish and make excellent accompaniments for meat or poultry. 2. *See also* Pasta Glossary, page 883.

goa bean [GOH-uh] *see* WINGED BEAN

goat Though goat meat has been enjoyed in southern Europe, Latin America and many Mediterranean countries for centuries, it has never really caught on in the United States. The meat of mature goats is extremely tough and strong-flavored. Most goat meat consumed comes from a kid, a baby goat that is usually not more than 6 months old. Kid meat is as tender and delicate as that of young lamb, and it can be prepared in any manner suitable for lamb. It can sometimes be found in specialty meat markets. Goats also provide milk, which is usually made into goat cheese, better known as CHÈVRE. Fresh goat's milk can sometimes be purchased in natural food stores; canned goat's milk is carried in many supermarkets.

goat cheese *see* CHÈVRE

goatfish Found in temperate to tropical seas, the goatfish is so named because of its two long chin barbels, which resemble a goat's whiskers. Probably the most famous member of this fish family is the superior RED MULLET, which is not a mullet at all. Depending on the species, goatfish can range in color from brilliant yellow to rose red. The meat is firm and lean and can be cooked in almost any manner including broiling, frying and baking. In the United States, goatfish is usually only available on the East Coast and throughout the Florida Keys. *See also* FISH.

goat's milk *see* GOAT

gobo; gobo root *see* BURDOCK

gochugaru; gochu garu [GOH-choo-gah-roo] Korean red chili pepper flakes.

gochujang; gochu jang *see* CHILE BEAN PASTE

gohan [goh-HAHN] Japanese cooked white rice that has undergone a precooking process of washing, rinsing and soaking to remove as much starch as possible. This lengthy process can take up to an hour and reduces stickiness in the finished rice.

goi du du *see* SOM TAM

goji berry [GOH-jee] *see* WOLFBERRY

golden Cadillac Named for its luxurious creamy texture and golden color, this COCKTAIL is made with GALLIANO, white CRÈME DE CACAO and heavy cream.

goldencrab *see* CRAB

Golden Delicious apple An all-purpose apple with a yellow to yellow-green skin and a sweet, crisp, juicy flesh that resists browning. Fruit grown in the western United States can be quite bland and doesn't have the flavor complexity of that grown in the eastern portion. *See also* APPLE.

goldeneye *see* ROCKFISH

golden mushroom *see* ENOKI

golden needles *see* TIGER LILY BUDS

golden nugget squash A small (3 to 4 inches in diameter), pumpkin-shaped winter squash with a bright orange skin. The flesh, which is also orange, is sweet and slightly bland. Golden nugget squash is available from late summer through winter. Choose a squash that's heavy for its size. The skin should be colorful but have a dull finish (the latter indicates maturity). If the surface is shiny, the flesh will be flavorless. Golden nugget squash can be stored at room temperature for up to a month. It can be baked or steamed, either whole or halved. *See also* SQUASH.

golden oak *see* SHIITAKE

golden oyster mushroom One of the OYSTER MUSHROOM variants, the golden oyster mushroom has an intense yellow or golden color, a funnel-shaped cap and a short stem. The flesh is white and slightly sour and bitter when raw but develops a nutty, slightly spicy flavor when cooked. *See also* MUSHROOMS.

golden syrup Particularly popular in England (where it's also known as *light* TREACLE), this liquid sweetener has the consistency of CORN SYRUP and a clear golden color. It's made from evaporated sugar cane juice and has a rich, toasty flavor unmatched by any other sweetener. Golden syrup, the most readily available brand being *Lyle's,* can be found in some supermarkets and many gourmet markets. It can be used as a substitute for corn syrup in cooking and baking, and for everything from pancake syrup to ice cream topping.

gold leaf *see* VARAK

Goldwasser [GOLT-vahs-sehr] Also called *Danziger Goldwasser,* this full-bodied LIQUEUR is variously flavored with caraway seed, orange peel and spices. The name, which translates from German as "gold water," comes from the fact that all Goldwassers have minuscule flecks of gold leaf suspended in them. The gold leaf is harmless to drink.

golpar A flowering plant, also known as *giant hogweed, Persian hogweed* or *Russian hogweed,* native to Iran. Its seeds are used in numerous

Persian dishes. The yellowish green seeds, which are usually ground, are sometimes referred to as *angelica seeds* or *angelica powder* but they are unrelated to the herb known as ANGELICA. The seeds have a pleasant, herbaceous aroma and a similar flavor with a slight bitterness. They are used in dishes featuring LEGUMES and in various rice dishes, soups and stews. Golpar powder can be purchased in Middle Eastern markets or through the Internet. The plant is banned in the United States because it produces a noxious sap that's painful to the skin and should not be ingested.

goma [GOH-mah] Japanese for "sesame seed." *Shiro goma* is unhulled white SESAME SEED, *muki goma* is hulled white seed and *kuro goma* is black sesame seed. *Goma abura* is sesame seed oil. All four products are available in Asian markets.

gomashio [goh-MAH-shee-oh] Available in natural food stores and some Asian markets, gomashio is a seasoning composed of sea salt and toasted sesame seeds. *See also* GOMA.

gomme syrup *see* SUGAR SYRUP

goo; gou *see* GASPERGOO

goober A derivative of the African word *nguba,* "goober" is a southern U.S. name for peanut. It's also referred to as a "goober pea."

goongoo bean *see* PIGEON PEA

goose Any of many species of large, web-footed, wild or domestic birds. Geese are much larger than ducks, weighing from 5 to 18 pounds, compared to 3 to 5½ pounds for a duck. The female of the species is simply known as a *goose,* a male as a *gander,* and a young goose—of whichever sex—as a *gosling.* Geese were bred in ancient Egypt, China and India. The Romans revered them because it was a noisy gaggle of geese that alerted 4th-century B.C. Romans that the enemy Gauls were about to attack. Geese are immensely popular in Europe, where they're traditional Christmas holiday fare in many countries. They're also renowned for two French specialties—FOIE GRAS, the creamy-rich enlarged liver from force-fed geese, and CONFIT, goose cooked and preserved in its own fat. Because geese are so fatty, they have not achieved the same popularity in America and therefore, though they're domesticated, have never been mass-marketed. The U.S. government grades the quality of geese with USDA classifications A, B and C. The highest grade is A, and is generally what is found in markets. Grade B geese are less meaty and well finished; those that are grade C are not usually available to the consumer. The grade stamp can usually be found within a shield on the package wrapping. Most geese marketed in the United States are frozen and can be purchased throughout the year. A frozen bird's packaging should be tight and unbroken. The goose should be thawed in the refrigerator and can take up to 2 days to defrost, depending on the size of the bird. Do not refreeze goose once it's been thawed. Fresh geese can be found in some specialty markets and are available from early summer through December. When available, buy goslings (the smaller the better) because they are the most tender. One way to determine age is to check the goose's bill; if it's pliable, the bird is still young. Choose a goose that is plump, with a good fatty layer and skin that is clean and unblemished. Store loosely covered in the coldest section of the refrigerator 2 to 3 days. Remove and store separately any giblets in the body cavity. Because geese have so much fat, they are best roasted. Larger, older birds are tougher and therefore should be cooked using a moist-heat method, such as braising. The fat derived from roasting a goose is prized by many cooks as a cooking fat. Goose benefits from being served with a tart fruit sauce, which helps offset any fatty taste. Geese are high in calories but are a good source of protein and iron. *See also* GAME BIRDS.

gooseberry These large, tart berries grow on bushes and come in many varieties including green, white, yellow and red; their skins can be smooth or fuzzy. Though they're comparatively rare in the United States, they flourish in northern Europe. Gooseberries are in season March through June, depending on the region. If you can find them fresh, choose those that are fairly firm and evenly colored. Canned gooseberries (usually the green variety) are available year-round. Gooseberries make excellent jams, jellies, pies and the dessert for which they're duly famous, FOOL.

goosefish *see* ANGLER

goose liver *see* FOIE GRAS

gordal olive *see* SEVILLANO OLIVE

gordita [gohr-DEE-tah] Spanish for "little fat one," a gordita is a thick (about 1/4 inch) tortilla made of MASA, lard and water or stock and sometimes mashed potatoes. These flat cakes are first partially baked on both sides on a dry COMAL (griddle) just until the masa is set. When cool enough to handle, the edges of the gordita are pinched slightly so that about a 1/4-inch ridge is formed all around the perimeter. The cake is then fried in about 1/2 inch of oil. The fried gordita is then filled with ground pork or CHORIZO and topped variously with cheese, shredded lettuce, onion, etc.

Gorgonzola [gohr-gan-ZOH-lah] Named for a town outside Milan where it was originally made, Gorgonzola is one of Italy's great cheeses. It has an ivory-colored interior that can be lightly or thickly streaked with bluish-green veins. This cow's-milk cheese is rich and creamy with a savory, slightly pungent flavor. Gorgonzola is aged for 2 to 3 months and sometimes up to 6 months. When aged over 6 months, the flavor and aroma can be quite strong—sometimes downright stinky. Younger cheeses are sold as *Gorgonzola dolce*, while longer-aged cheeses are sold as *Gorgonzola naturale* or *Gorgonzola piccante*. Though the only true Gorgonzola comes from Italy's Lombardy and Piedmont regions, there are numerous pretenders (including American and Danish), which for the most part are simply not as good. The FAT CONTENT of Gorgonzola ranges from 39 to 49 percent. *See also* CHEESE.

gorp *see* TRAIL MIX

Gouda [GOO-dah; *Du.* KHOW-dah] Made since the 6th century and Holland's most famous cheese, Gouda represents 60 to 65 percent of the cheese production in that country. It can be made from raw or PASTEURIZED cow's milk, though most of today's product is factory-made with pasteurized milk. Gouda comes in WHEELS that can range from less than 1 pound to 88 pounds. The rind may or may not be covered with wax of various colors. Gouda is RIPENED for 1 to 6 months but a black wax coating indicates an aged Gouda, which has been ripened for at least 12 months and some for up to 5 or 6 years. Depending on the age, a Gouda's interior can range from pale yellow to deep gold with a scattering of EYES. Young versions have a supple, smooth texture; ripened cheeses become hard and flaky and have crunchy white flecks of crystallized protein. The flavor of Gouda can range from delicate and mild for young cheeses to full, rich, fruity and nutty for aged versions. Long-aged cheeses are rich, intense and have notes of butterscotch and toffee. Because Gouda isn't a protected name, it's made in other countries including Ireland, Wales and the United States. The FAT CONTENT for standard Gouda is approximately 48 percent; **double-cream Gouda** (or **Roomkaas**) has cream added, which hikes it up to 60 percent, and the partially skimmed-milk **light Gouda** has 30 to 40 percent fat. Some Goudas are flavored with CUMIN or herbs. *See also* CHEESE.

gougère [goo-ZHEHR] GRUYÈRE-flavored CHOUX PASTRY that is piped into a ring shape before being baked. A gougère can be served hot or cold as an HORS D'OEUVRE or snack.

goulash [GOO-lahsh] Known as *gulyás* in its native Hungary, goulash is a soup/stew made with beef or other meat, onions, potatoes and vegetables, and flavored with Hungarian PAPRIKA. Sometimes, small fingernail-sized egg noodles called **csipetke** are added. Gulyás, which takes its name from the Hungarian cattle stockmen who originated it, is soupier than similar Hungarian dishes like pörkölt or paprikás. **Pörkölt** is drier—more stew-like—and unlike goulash, traditionally does not have potatoes or meat with bones in it. The word *pörkölt* stems from pörkölni, meaning "to roast." Sour cream isn't traditionally used in a pörkölt; if it is, the dish is called a **paprikás**. Paprikás Csirke (made with chicken) is probably the best known. Whereas goulash and pörkölt dishes are made with just about any kind of meat, a **paprikás** utilizes lighter meats like chicken, pork or veal.

gourd [GOHRD] The inedible fruit of various plants with an extremely hard, tough shell. When all the flesh is removed, the shell can be dried and used as a container, utensil or for decorative purposes.

gourmand [goor-MAHND] A gourmand is one who appreciates fine food . . . often to indiscriminate excess. *See also* EPICURE; GASTRONOME; GLUTTON; GOURMET.

gourmet [goor-MAY] 1. One of discriminating palate; a connoisseur of fine food and drink. *See also* EPICURE; GASTRONOME; GLUTTON; GOURMAND. 2. Gourmet food is that which is of the highest quality, perfectly prepared and artfully presented. 3. A gourmet restaurant is one that serves well-prepared, high-quality food.

gow chai; gow choy [gow CHI; gow CHOY] *see* GARLIC CHIVES

gowdie *see* GURNARD

gra-chai *see* FINGERROOT

graham cracker This popular snack was touted as a health food in the 1830s by its creator, Rev. Sylvester Graham, a United States dietary reformer. It's a rectangular-shaped, whole-wheat cracker that has been sweetened, usually with honey. **Graham-cracker crust** is made from a mixture of finely crushed graham crackers, sugar and butter that is pressed into a pie pan. It's usually baked, but can simply be chilled before being filled.

graham flour Whole-wheat flour that is slightly coarser than regular grind. It was developed by Rev. Sylvester Graham, a Connecticut cleric, who was one of the early leaders in health food advocacy. *See also* FLOUR.

grain *see* CEREAL GRAINS

grains of paradise Small, brown, round seeds indigenous to the west coast of Africa and used as a spice. This member of the GINGER and CARDAMOM family is also called *alligator pepper, Guinea pepper* and *Melegueta pepper.* Though hot and pungent, this spice has an exotic spicy quality that hints of ginger, cardamom, CORIANDER, citrus and NUTMEG. Grains of paradise was a popular spice in Europe during the 13th and 14th centuries but lost favor in the 15th and 16th centuries when less expensive spices such as black pepper, cloves, mace and nutmeg became available. Outside of North Africa and the west coast of Africa, this spice is not widely used in everyday cooking. It can occasionally be found in gourmet markets and is usually available through mail order.

grain spirits *see* NEUTRAL SPIRITS

gram flour *see* BESAN

grana; grana cheese [GRAH-nuh] Italian for "grain," referring to any of various very hard cheeses with a granular texture, like Parmigiano-Reggiano (*see* PARMESAN), which are particularly suited for grating. This special texture is the result of long aging, which is usually anywhere from 2 to 7 years, though some (rare) cheeses are ripened up to 20 years. *See also* CHEESE.

granadilla [gran-ah-DEE-yuh] *see* PASSION FRUIT

grandine *see* Pasta Glossary, page 883

Grand Marnier [GRAN mahr-NYAY] A rich, amber-colored, COGNAC-based liqueur flavored with the peels of Haitian bitter oranges, exotic spices and vanilla. **Grand Marnier Cuvée du Centenaire** is a special edition liqueur with a darker amber color and a deeper, more complex flavor. **Grand Marnier Cuvée Spéciale Cent Cinquantenaire** is blended with XO Cognac and packaged in a hand-painted bottle.

Grand-Veneur Sauce *see* POIVRADE

granité (*Fr.*)**; granita** (*It.*) [grah-nee-TAY; grah-nee-TAH] *see* ICE

Granny Smith apple A large, freckled green all-purpose apple with a hard, crisp, moderately juicy flesh that's fairly tart. *See also* APPLE.

granola [gruh-NOH-luh] A breakfast food consisting of various combinations of grains (mainly oats), nuts and dried fruits. Some manufacturers toast their granola with oil and honey, giving it a crisp texture, sweet glaze and more calories. *See also* MUESLI.

grape This edible berry grows in clusters on small shrubs or climbing vines in temperate zones throughout the world including Africa, Asia, Australia, Europe and North and South America. California is the largest U.S. producer of grapes—both for wine and for the table. There are thousands of grape varieties, each with its own particular use and charm. In general, grapes are smooth-skinned and juicy; they may have several seeds in the center or they may be seedless. There are "slip-skin" varieties, which have skins that slip easily off the berry—like a mitten being pulled off a hand—and those with skins that cling stubbornly to the flesh. Grapes are divided into color categories of white or black (also referred to as "red"). White grape varieties range in color from pale yellow-green to light green, and black grapes from light red to purple-black. They're also classified by the way they're used—whether for wine (such as CABERNET or RIESLING), table (like THOMPSON SEEDLESS or RIBIER) or commercial food production, such as MUSCAT grapes for raisins, ZANTE grapes for CURRANTS and CONCORD grapes for grape juice, jams and jellies. Wine grapes, for instance, have high acidity and are therefore too tart for general eating. Table grapes, with their low acid, would make dull, bland-tasting wines. The availability of table grapes depends on the variety. Buy grapes that are plump, full-colored and firmly attached to their stems. White (or green) grapes should have a slight pale yellow hue, a sign of ripeness. Dark grapes should be deeply colored, with no sign of green. In general, grapes should be stored, unwashed and in a plastic bag, in the refrigerator. They will keep for up to a week, though quality will diminish with time. Because most supermarket grapes have been sprayed with insecticide, they should be thoroughly washed and blotted dry with a paper towel just before eating or using. Ideally, grapes should be served at about 60°F, so it's best to remove them from the refrigerator about 30 minutes before serving. Table grapes can be used in salads, for pies and other desserts and of course for out-of-hand eating. Whole grapes are also available canned. Grape juice comes in cans or bottles; grape jelly, jam and preserves in jars. Fresh grapes contain small amounts of vitamin A and a variety of minerals. *See also* CATAWBA; CHAMPAGNE GRAPES; CHARDONNAY; CHENIN BLANC; DELAWARE; EMPEROR; FRENCH COLOMBARD; MERLOT; MUSCADINE; NIAGARA; PETITE SIRAH; PINOT BLANC; PINOT NOIR; SAUVIGNON; SÉMILLON; SULTANA; SYLVANER; TOKAY; ZINFANDEL.

grapefruit This tropical citrus fruit grows in great abundance in Arizona, California, Florida and Texas. Its name comes from the fact that the grapefruit grows in grapelike clusters. There are two main categories of grapefruit—seeded and seedless. They're also broken into color classifications—white, which has a yellowish-white flesh, and pink, the flesh of which can range from pale yellow-pink to brilliant ruby red. Pink grapefruit has a higher amount of vitamin A than does the white. The skins of all varieties of grapefruit are yellow, some with a pink blush. Fresh grapefruit is available year-round—those from Arizona and California are in the market from about January through August; Florida and Texas grapefruits usually arrive around October and last through June. Choose grapefruit that have thin, fine-textured, brightly colored skin. They should be firm yet springy when held in the palm and pressed. The heavier they are for their size, the juicier they'll be. Do not store grapefruit at room temperature for more than a day or two. They keep best (up to 2 weeks) when wrapped in a plastic bag and placed in the vegetable drawer of the refrigerator. Grapefruit is usually eaten fresh, either halved or segmented and used in salads. It can also be sprinkled with brown sugar and broiled.

Canned and frozen forms of grapefruit are available in segments or juice. Grapefruit is a good source of vitamin C. *See also* MELOGOLD; ORO BLANCO.

grapefruit knife A small knife with a curved, flexible blade that is serrated on both sides. It is used to free grapefruit flesh from both rind and membrane.

grape hyacinth *see* CIPOLLINI

grape leaves The large green leaves of the grapevine are often used by Greek and Middle Eastern cooks to wrap foods for cooking, as with DOLMAS. Grape leaves are not usually commercially available fresh so, unless you have a grapevine in your backyard, you'll probably have to buy canned grape leaves packed in brine. They should be rinsed before using to remove some of the salty flavor. Fresh grape leaves must be simmered in water for about 10 minutes to soften them enough to be pliable. In addition to wrapping foods, grape leaves can be used as decorations or garnishes, or in salads. Also called *vine leaves*.

grapeseed oil Extracted from grape seeds, most of this oil comes from France, Italy or Switzerland, with a few sources now in the United States. Some grapeseed oils have a light "grapey" flavor and fragrance but most imported into the United States are on the bland side. Grapeseed oil can be used for salad dressings and, because it has a relatively high SMOKE POINT, it's also good for sautéing. It may be stored at room temperature (70°F or under) or in the refrigerator. Grapeseed oil is available in gourmet food stores and some supermarkets. *See also* FATS AND OILS.

grape sugar *see* DEXTROSE

grappa [GRAHP-pah] A colorless, high alcohol Italian EAU DE VIE distilled from the residue (grape skins and seeds) left in the wine press after the juice is removed for wine. Grappa has been made commercially since the 18th century. There are hundreds of highly individual, markedly different styles of this fiery distillation, which can also have great depth and character. There are also aged grappas, some so complex that they're aged in a series of different woods (such as oak, birch and juniper).

GRAS An acronym for "Generally Recognized as Safe," a term used by the U.S. Food and Drug Administration to describe any substance added to food that is not subject to a full premarket review and FDA approval. For an FDA-approved food additive, the sponsor submits privately held data about the use of the substance to the FDA, which evaluates the data to determine whether the substance is safe for its intended use. On the other hand, to be granted GRAS status, the substance must be accepted widely by qualified experts to be safe under the conditions of its intended use, based on generally available information. There are two ways a substance can be classified as GRAS: by being sanctioned through scientific procedures, or through experience based on common usage in food before 1958.

grasshopper; grasshopper pie A COCKTAIL made with cream, crème de MENTHE and white CRÈME DE CACAO. Because it's very sweet, a grasshopper is usually served after dinner. **Grasshopper pie** is flavored with CRÈME DE MENTHE and white CRÈME DE CACAO, enriched by whipped cream and lightened with beaten egg whites. It typically has a graham-cracker or cookie-crumb crust.

grass mushroom *see* STRAW MUSHROOM

grate To reduce a large piece of food to small particles or thin shreds by rubbing it against a coarse, serrated surface, usually on a kitchen utensil called a GRATER. A FOOD PROCESSOR fitted with the metal blade can also be used to reduce food to small bits or, fitted with the shredding disc, to long, thin strips. The food to be grated should be firm, which in the case of cheese can usually be accomplished by refrigeration. Grating food makes it easier to incorporate with other foods.

grater Graters come in several shapes—the most popular styles are flat, cylindrical and box-shape. They're used to reduce hard foods to small particles or long, thin strips. Most graters are made of metal or plastic that has been perforated with sharp-edged, small- or medium-size holes or slits. Many have handles at the top for a sure grip. Graters made of stainless steel will not rust, whereas those of tinned steel will. *See also* MOULI GRATER; NUTMEG GRATER; RASP GRATER.

gratin; gratinée; alla gratinata [GRAH-tn (*Fr.* gra-TAN); grah-tee-NAY; (*It.* AH-lah grah-tee-NAH-tah)] A *gratin* is any dish that is topped with cheese or breadcrumbs mixed with bits of butter, then heated in the oven or under the broiler until brown and crispy. The terms *au gratin* or *gratinée* refer to any dish prepared in such a manner. Special round or oval **gratin pans** and **dishes** are ovenproof and shallow, which increases a dish's surface area, thereby insuring a larger crispy portion for each serving.

Gravenstein apple All-purpose apple with green skin streaked with red and yellow. The fine-textured, highly aromatic flesh is crisp, juicy and sweetly tart. *See also* APPLE.

Graves [GRAHV] Any of several notable wines from the region of Graves, an important wine-producing area in France's BORDEAUX region. Although the name *Graves* is generally associated with several fine, dry white wines, the reds are also quite distinctive. They are, however, generally bottled under the name of their château of origin, though the Graves designation is usually in fine print somewhere on the label.

graviola [gra-vee-OH-lah] *see* SOURSOP

gravlax; Br. gravlaks [GRAHV-lahks] This Swedish specialty of raw salmon cured in a salt-sugar-dill mixture is prized around the world. It's sliced paper-thin and served on dark bread as an appetizer, on an open-faced sandwich or as part of a smorgasbord, often accompanied by a dill-mustard sauce. Gravlax can usually be found in gourmet markets or specialty fish markets. It can be stored, tightly wrapped, in the refrigerator for up to a week.

gravy A sauce made from meat juices, usually combined with a liquid such as chicken or beef broth, wine or milk and thickened with flour, cornstarch or the like. A gravy may also be the simple juices left in the pan after meat, poultry or fish has been cooked. *See also* SAUCE.

gravy boat An elongated, boat-shaped pitcher used to serve gravy. A gravy boat usually sits on a matching plate, which is used to catch gravy drips. Sometimes the plate is permanently attached to the pitcher. A matching ladle often accompanies a gravy boat. Also called *sauce boat*.

gray trout *see* WEAKFISH

grease *v.* To rub the surface of a pan—such as a griddle, muffin pan or cake pan—with grease or SHORTENING in order to prevent the food prepared in it from sticking. **Grease and flour** refers to rubbing the pan with grease or shortening before lightly dusting it with flour. The flour coating is applied by sprinkling the pan with flour, then inverting it and tapping the bottom of the pan to remove any excess flour. grease *n.* Any RENDERED animal fat, such as bacon, beef or chicken fat.

grease mop An inexpensive kitchen tool that looks like a miniature rag mop made with absorbent white strips. When a grease mop is brushed over the surface of a soup or stock, the strips absorb floating grease. Grease mops (also called *fat mops*) are available in specialty gourmet shops and the cookware section of some department stores. They may be washed with hot, soapy water or placed in a dishwasher.

Greater Indian cardamom *see* BLACK CARDAMOM

Great Lakes lettuce *see* CRISPHEAD LETTUCE

great Northern bean A large white bean that resembles the LIMA BEAN in shape but that has a delicate, distinctive flavor. Great Northern beans are grown in the Midwest and are generally available dried. As with other dried beans, they must be soaked before cooking. They're particularly popular in baked bean dishes and can be substituted for any white beans in most recipes. *See also* BEANS.

grecque, à la [ah lah GREHK] French for "in the Greek style," usually referring to vegetables (such as mushrooms and artichokes) and herbs cooked in olive oil and lemon juice and served cold as an appetizer.

Greek black olive *see* AMFISSA OLIVE

Greek coffee A rich, intensely strong brew made by boiling finely ground coffee and water together in a long-handled, open, brass or copper pot called an *ibrik*. Sugar and spices are sometimes added to the grounds before brewing begins. Greek coffee is often brought to a boil three times before it's considered ready. It's poured directly into tiny DEMITASSE cups, which means that each cup gets its share of fine coffee grounds. Let the coffee sit for a few moments to allow the sediment to settle. *See also* COFFEE.

Greek yogurt Yogurt that's been strained through a filter to remove liquid whey, lactose and sugar, resulting in a thicker, creamier texture. Compared to regular yogurt, Greek yogurt has up to two times the protein, almost half the carbohydrates and about half the sodium content but only about two-thirds of the calcium. Full-fat Greek yogurt has more fat than its full-fat counterpart, so sticking to lowfat or nonfat versions is recommended for those concerned with fat intake.

green bean A long, slender green pod with small seeds inside. The entire pod is edible. It's also called **string bean** (because of the fibrous string—now bred out of the species—that used to run down the pod's seam) and *snap bean* (for the sound the bean makes when broken in half). The **wax bean** is a pale yellow variety of green bean. Green beans are available year-round, with a peak season of May to October. Choose slender beans that are crisp, bright-colored and free of blemishes. Store in the refrigerator, tightly wrapped in a plastic bag, for up to 5 days. Cook gently by steaming or simmering just until tender-crisp. Green beans have a fair amount of vitamins A and C. *See also* BEANS.

green goddess dressing This dressing was created in the 1920s by the chef at San Francisco's Palace Hotel in honor of actor George Arliss, who was appearing locally in a play called "Green Goddess." The classic green goddess dressing is a blend of mayonnaise, tarragon vinegar, anchovies, parsley, chives, tarragon, scallions and garlic. In addition to dressing salads, it's often used as a sauce for fish and shellfish.

green head *see* STRIPED BASS

greenling Found along the Pacific coast of the United States, this rather ugly fish has a huge mouth and sharp teeth. There are nine greenling species but only one, the LINGCOD (*see listing*), is generally sold commercially. *See also* FISH.

green onion *see* SCALLION; WELSH ONION

green pea *see* ENGLISH PEA

green pepper *see* SWEET PEPPERS

green peppercorn *see* PEPPERCORN

greens Edible leaves of certain plants such as the BEET, COLLARD, DAN-DELION and TURNIP. Greens are usually steamed or quickly cooked in some other manner. *See also* AMARANTH; BROCCOLI RAAB; CALLALOO; CHARD; CHICORY; ITALIAN DANDELION; KOHLRABI; MUSTARD GREENS.

green soybeans *see* SOYBEAN

green tea *see* TEA

gremolata; gremolada [greh-moh-LAH-tah] A garnish made of minced parsley, lemon peel and garlic. It's sprinkled over OSSO BUCO and other dishes to add a fresh, sprightly flavor.

Grenache [gruh-NAHSH] This grape comes in both red and white varieties. When used by itself, the word "Grenache" refers to the red version **Grenache Noir**, one of the world's most widely cultivated red grapes. The Grenache grape does well in hot, dry regions. It ripens with very high sugar levels and can produce wines with 15 to 16 percent ALCO-HOL. Grenache wines are sweet, fruity and very low in TANNINS. They're usually lacking in color, except in growing areas where yields are low. The vine originated in Spain where it's called *Garnacha, Garnacha Tinta* (or *Garnacho Tinto*), and is the most widely cultivated red-wine grape in that country. In CHÂTEAUNEUF-DU-PAPE it's used as the primary grape, although it is blended with as many as twelve other VARIETIES. In ROSÉ wines (particularly those from CÔTES-DU-RHÔNE, Côtes du Ventoux, Lirac and Tavel) Grenache is often the dominant grape used. **Grenache Blanc** (or *Garnacha Blanca*) is the white variety of this grape. Although not as popular as the red, it's still widely planted in both Spain and France.

grenadine [grehn-uh-DEEN; GREHN-uh-deen] A sweet, deep red, pomegranate-flavored syrup used to color and flavor drinks and desserts. At one time, grenadine was made exclusively from pomegranates grown on the island of Grenada in the Caribbean. Now other fruit-juice concentrates are also used to make the syrup. Grenadine sometimes contains alcohol, so be sure and check the label.

gribiche sauce [gree-beesh] Cold MAYONNAISE-style sauce with CAPERS, CORNICHONS, CHERVIL, PARSLEY, TARRAGON and JULIENNE of egg whites. Sauce gribiche is traditionally served with cold fish but works well with hot fish, chicken and even french fries.

griddle A special flat, customarily rimless pan designed to cook food (such as pancakes) with a minimal amount of fat or oil. Griddles are usually made of thick, heavy metals that are good heat conductors, such as cast aluminum or cast iron. Some griddles have a nonstick coating. Like a frying pan, they usually have a long handle; some have handgrips on opposite sides.

griddle cake Another name for PANCAKE.

griglia [GREE-lyah] Italian for "grill."

grill *n.* 1. A heavy metal grate that is set over hot coals or other heat source and used to cook foods such as steak or hamburgers. 2. A dish of food (usually meat, such as MIXED GRILL) cooked on a grill. **grill** *v.* To prepare food on a grill over hot coals or other heat source. The term *barbecue* is often used synonymously with grill. *See also* Hand Test for Grilling Temperatures, page 862.

grillade [gruh-LAHD; gree-YAHD] 1. French for "grilled (or broiled) food," usually meat. 2. A CREOLE dish of pieces of pounded round steak seared in hot fat, then braised in a rich sauce with vegetables and tomatoes. Grillade is customarily served with GRITS.

grillardin [gree-yar-dan] *see* BRIGADE SYSTEM

grillettes [gree-YEHT] Morsels of fatty meat (usually pork or duck) that are grilled or fried until very crisp.

grill pan A heavy-weight pan that can range in shape from round to square to rectangular. The common denominators of all grill pans are that they have shallow sides and a ridged cooking surface. The low sides allow for ease in lifting and turning food; the ridges allow fat to drain off and also provide the grill marks many find so appealing. Today most grill pans have non-stick surfaces, making clean-up a snap.

grind To reduce food to small particles. Coffee beans can be ground in a coffee GRINDER, while meats such as beef must be run through a meat grinder. A FOOD PROCESSOR fitted with a metal blade can also grind some foods. Food can be ground to various degrees—fine, medium and coarse.

grinder 1. Any of various hand-driven or electric devices used to reduce food to small particles of varying degrees. **Coffee grinders** are electric and usually have an exposed, disk-style blade inside the unit's container. The grind can be adjusted from *fine* to *coarse*. Some nuts and spices can also be ground in a coffee grinder. **Meat grinders** can be either manual (operated by a hand crank) or electric; the housing can be made of cast iron or tough plastic. Hand-operated meat grinders are attached to a countertop by a clamp-and-screw mechanism, whereas electric models are freestanding. They both work on the same principle, by forcing chunks of meat through a rotating blade, then through a perforated cutting disk. *See also* NUT MILL. 2. In some regions, "grinder" also refers to a huge sandwich; see HERO SANDWICH.

grissini [gruh-SEE-nee] Italian for "breadsticks" (the singular form is *grissino*), referring to thin, crisp breadsticks that originated in Turin, Italy. They're available commercially in many supermarkets.

grits Though now commonly used to mean "HOMINY grits," the term "grits" actually refers to any coarsely ground grain such as corn, oats or rice. Most grits come in a choice of grinds—coarse, medium and fine. Grits can be cooked with water or milk—usually by boiling or baking—and eaten as cereal or served as a side dish. *See also* GROATS.

groats Hulled crushed grain, such as barley, buckwheat or oats. The most widely used are BUCKWHEAT groats (also known as KASHA), which are usually cooked in a manner similar to rice. Though groats are generally thought to be more coarsely ground than GRITS, they come in a variety of grinds including coarse, medium and fine. The two names—grits and groats—are often used synonymously. Groats are widely used in cereals, as a side dish with vegetables or as a thickener and enricher for soup.

grog A hot drink made with rum, a sweetener such as sugar or honey and boiling water. Grog is served in a ceramic or glass mug and often garnished with a slice of lemon and a few whole cloves. It has long been considered a curative for colds but is generally consumed simply for its pleasure- and warmth-giving properties.

gros sel [groh SEHL] *see* SEL

ground beef Beef that has been ground or finely chopped. The price of ground beef (also called *hamburger*) is determined by the cut of meat from which it was made and the amount of fat incorporated into the mix. High-fat mixtures are less costly but will shrink more when cooked. The least expensive product is sold as **regular ground beef** or **regular hamburger**. It's usually made with trimmings of the less expensive cuts such as BRISKET and SHANK, and can contain up to 30 percent fat. The moderately priced **ground chuck** is the next level of ground beef. Because it contains enough fat (about 15 to 20 percent) to give it flavor and make it juicy, yet not enough to cause excess shrinkage, ground chuck is the best meat for hamburgers. The leanest (around 11 percent fat) and most expensive of the ground meats are **ground round** and **ground sirloin**. Though they're great for calorie watchers, they become quite dry when cooked beyond medium-rare. Ground beef is sold fresh and frozen, prepackaged in bulk (usually 1 to 5 pounds) or in preformed patties. It may also be ground to order. The way it is used determines how the beef should be ground. In general, the finer the beef is ground, the more compact it will be when cooked. For instance, firm-textured combinations such as MEATLOAF or MEATBALLS should be made with beef that has been ground at least 2 or 3 times. For hamburgers, however, where a light, juicy texture is preferable, the beef should be coarsely ground. Ground beef should be lightly wrapped before storing in the coldest section of the refrigerator for up to 2 days. To freeze, shape into individual patties or a large, flat disk and wrap with freezer-proof packaging. It can be frozen up to 6 months. *See also* BEEF; HAMBURGER.

ground cherry *see* CAPE GOOSEBERRY

groundnut *see* PEANUT

grouper [GROO-per] Although some weigh ⅓ ton, the average size of this fish is from 5 to 15 pounds. Groupers are found in the waters of the Gulf of Mexico and the North and South Atlantic. They're marketed whole as well as in fillets and steaks. They have a lean, firm flesh that is suitable for baking, broiling, frying, poaching or steaming. The grouper's skin, which is very strongly flavored, should always be removed before cooking. The most popular members of this sea bass family are the **black grouper**, **Nassau grouper**, **red grouper** and **yellowmouth** (or *yellowfin*) grouper. *See also* FISH.

grouse *see* GAME BIRDS

Grown, Produced, and Bottled By *see* WINE LABEL TERMS

gruel [GROO-uhl] A cereal (usually oatmeal) cooked with water or milk and generally of a very thin consistency.

Grünerkäse *see* SAPSAGO

grunion [GRUHN-yuhn] Tiny (3- to 6-ounce) fish found along the Southern California coast, known for their spawning habits. The "running of the grunion" occurs by the light of the full moon as these silvery fish wriggle their way above high tide to spawn in the wet sand. Legally, grunion can only be caught by hand, though many people snare them with nets or scoops. The moderately fat grunion are best broiled, deep-fried or sautéed. *See also* FISH.

grunt 1. Named after the grunting noise it makes, this rich, sweet-flavored fish can be found in the United States mainly in Florida's coastal waters. Anatomically related to the SNAPPER, grunt is generally available only in its region, and is best either broiled or sautéed. *See also* FISH. 2.

An old-fashioned dessert of fruit topped with biscuit dough and stewed. Also called *slump*.

Gruyère [groo-YEHR; gree-YEHR] Swiss Gruyère is named for the valley of the same name in the canton of Fribourg. Though Switzerland now has AOC APPELLATION status for the name *Gruyère*, the word also is used for cheeses made in other nations including Austria, Denmark, Germany and the United States. However, if and when the Swiss obtain the European Union's PROTECTED DESIGNATION OF ORIGIN status, other European countries will have to stop using the name. Gruyère has a semihard to hard texture that's very dense, compact and supple. The hard rind is golden brown, the interior ranges from ivory to medium yellow with occasional EYES. It has a complex flavor that's creamy, fruity, nutty, earthy and mushroomy. With the exception of French Gruyère, most Gruyère-style cheeses are not considered on a par with the Swiss original (though there are FARM-STEAD-produced exceptions). That's because most non-Swiss versions are factory-produced with pasteurized milk, whereas AOC standards for Swiss Gruyères say they can only be made from the raw milk of two milkings of cows fed only grass or hay (no silage) and must be prepared in copper pots. There are three types of Gruyère AOC: *Classic* (ripened for a minimum of 5 months), *Réserve* (10 to 16 months) and *d'Alpage*, which is made only from April through October from milk produced by cows grazing in high Alpine pastures. Gruyère has a FAT CONTENT of between 49 and 53 percent. *See also* CHEESE.

guacamole [gwah-kah-MOH-lee; gwah-kah-MOH-leh] A popular Mexican specialty of mashed avocado mixed with lemon or lime juice and various seasonings (usually chili powder and red pepper). Sometimes finely chopped tomato, green onion and CILANTRO are added. Guacamole can be used as a dip, sauce, topping or side dish. It must be covered closely and tightly to prevent discoloration.

guaje; guaje seed [GWAH-hee] Long, flat, green pods filled with seeds about the size of a small LIMA BEAN and used in Latin American cooking. The pod and seeds have a garlicky quality, and fresh pods are often chopped up and used to flavor various dishes. When the pods dry and turn brown, the seeds are scraped out and can be eaten raw or added to salads or cooked dishes. Roasting the seeds lends a nutty quality, which makes them delicious as a snack. They're also often ground and used as a thickening for cooked sauces. Fresh or dried guaje (also spelled *cuaje* and *huaje*) can be purchased at Latin American markets. In Southeast Asia, guaje pods are known as *wild tamarind*.

guajillo chile [gwah-HEE-yoh] The skin of this dried CHILE is shiny-smooth and a deep, burnished red. The chile is very tough and must be soaked longer than most dried chiles. The flavorful guajillo is pointed, long and narrow (about 4 inches by 1 inch). Because it can be quite hot, the guajillo is also sometimes called the *travieso* ("mischievous") *chile* in reference to its not-so-playful sting. It's used in both sauces and cooked dishes. In its fresh state, the guajillo is called a MIRASOL CHILE. Guajillos are mildly hot, with a SCOVILLE SCALE rating of 2,500 to 5,000.

guanabana; guanábana [gwah-nah-BAH-nah] *see* SOURSOP

guanciale [gwahn-CHAY-lay] Though *guanciale* is Italian for "pillow," this cured meat takes its name from *guancia* ("cheek") because the meat comes from pork jowl. It's cured for a month in salt, pepper, chili powder and sometimes sugar, then hung and aged for another month before being ready for market. Guanciale can be used as a substitute for PANCETTA in sauces or as a flavoring for other dishes.

guar gum A gummy substance obtained from legume-family plants, used as a thickener and STABILIZER in commercial food processing. *See also* GUM ARABIC; GUM TRAGANCANTH; XANTHAN GUM.

guava [GWAH-vah] This sweet, fragrant tropical fruit grows in its native South America as well as in California, Florida and Hawaii. There are many guava varieties, ranging in size from a small egg to a medium apple. Typically, the fruit is slightly oval in shape and about 2 inches in diameter. The color of the guava's thin skin can range from yellow to red to purple-black, the flesh from pale yellow to bright red. Guavas are available from June to March, depending on the region. Choose those that give to gentle palm pressure but that have not yet begun to show spots. To be eaten raw, guavas should be very ripe. Store green guavas at room temperature, ripe ones in the refrigerator's vegetable drawer for up to 4 days. Guavas make excellent jams, preserves and sauces. Canned whole guavas as well as juice, jams, jellies, preserves and sauce are available in many supermarkets. Fresh guavas are a good source of vitamins A and C. *See also* GUAVA PASTE.

guava paste A combination of guava pulp, sugar, pectin and citric acid, which is cooked slowly until exceedingly thick and rich. It comes in individually wrapped bars that are firm enough to slice. Guava paste can be found in Latin markets and some specialty gourmet stores. Slice and serve this low-fat, low-cholesterol sweet as a snack or with cheese or ice cream for dessert.

güero chile [GWEH-roh] The generic term for yellow chiles such as HUNGARIAN WAX or SANTA FE GRANDE. *See also* CHILE.

gugelhopf *see* KUGELHOPF

guindilla chile [GIHN-deel-la] Spanish chile long associated with the Basque country. It measures $1^{1}/_{2}$ to 5 inches long and $^{1}/_{4}$ to $^{1}/_{2}$ inches wide, with a slight curve. When young and green, it is mild and has a green bell pepper and green bean flavor. As it ripens it turns red, then brick red, and develops some piquancy. The SCOVILLE SCALE rating ranges from 100 to 2,500. In Spain, young, small chiles are often pickled in white wine vinegar. The mature red chiles are frequently dried and used as a flavoring ingredient. In between, both green and red guindillas are eaten fresh. Dried whole chiles and jars of pickled green guindillas are available on the Internet.

guinea fowl [GIHN-ee] Thought to have originated in Guinea, West Africa, this small bird is a relative of the chicken and partridge. The meat of the guinea fowl is dark, somewhat dry and has a pleasantly gamey flavor. Guinea hens are more tender than the male of the species. The hens range in size from $^{3}/_{4}$ pound (called *guinea squab*) to about 4 pounds. Guinea fowl are available fresh and frozen. If fresh, loosen package wrapping slightly and remove any giblets from the body cavity before storing in the refrigerator for up to 2 days. Frozen guinea fowl should be thawed overnight in the refrigerator and used within 2 days. Never refreeze fowl once it's thawed. Guinea fowl may be prepared in any way suitable for chicken, keeping in mind that because the meat is drier, moist cooking methods will produce a more satisfactory end result. Any fowl over $2^{1}/_{2}$ pounds should probably be BARDED with fat before cooking to ensure moistness.

Guinea pepper [GIHN-ee] *see* GRAINS OF PARADISE

guinep *see* MAMONCILLO

guk [gook] In Korea, guk and *tang* are soup-like dishes. Tang is slightly thicker, often like a thin stew.

gulab jamun [goo-LAHB JA-muhn] A favorite dessert in India and Pakistan consisting of fried milk balls (typically a mixture of dried milk, flour and cream) soaked in a sugar syrup flavored with rosewater and sometimes CARDAMOM and/or SAFFRON. The dough is formed into small balls and deep-fried to a deep golden brown before being immersed in the flavored syrup for several hours. In Hindi, *gulab* means "rosé," and *jamun* is a dark crimson berry from an evergreen tree native to India. Gulab jamun mixes are available in Indian groceries and some gourmet markets.

gulyás *see* GOULASH

gum arabic A natural additive from the bark of certain varieties of acacia tree. Gum arabic is colorless, tasteless and odorless and is used in commercial food processing to thicken, emulsify and stabilize foods such as candy, ice cream and sweet syrups. *See also* Food Additives Directory, page 900; GUM TRAGACANTH; GUAR GUM; XANTHAM GUM.

gumbo [GUHM-boh] This CREOLE specialty is a mainstay of New Orleans cuisine. It's a thick, stewlike dish that can have any of many ingredients, including vegetables such as okra, tomatoes and onions, and one or several meats or shellfish such as chicken, sausage, ham, shrimp, crab or oysters. The one thing all good gumbos begin with is a dark ROUX, which adds an unmistakable, incomparably rich flavor. Okra serves to thicken the mixture, as does FILÉ POWDER, which must be stirred in just before serving after the pot's off the fire. The famous *gumbo z'herbes* ("with herbs") was once traditionally served on Good Friday and contains at least seven greens (for good luck) such as spinach, mustard greens, collard greens and so on. The name gumbo is a derivation of the African word for "okra."

gum tragacanth [TRAG-uh-kanth] A substance obtained from an Asian shrub, *Astragalus gummifer,* and used in the same way as GUM ARABIC. *See also* Food Additives Directory, page 900; GUAR GUM; XANTHAN GUM.

gunpowder tea This fine Chinese tea is considered the highest grade of green tea and is noted for both its form and its flavor. The small, young tea leaves are rolled into minuscule balls, giving the tea a granular appearance. Gunpowder tea is light in color, with a distinctively sharp flavor. *See also* TEA.

gur [GOOR] *see* JAGGERY

gurnard [GER-nuhrd] The common English name for fish belonging to the family *Triglidae*. These marine fish, which sometimes swim near the surface and make a grunting or croaking noise, are also called *crooner, croonack, gowdie,* and in North America *sea robin*. Their fins allow them to crawl around on the ocean bottom. Most of the species used for food are found in warmer waters in the Atlantic and Mediterranean, although there are a few gurnard species in the Pacific. The gunard's flesh is white, firm and lowfat, which makes it appropriate for frying, baking or poaching. *See also* FISH.

gurnet *see* GURNARD

gusano *see* MEZCAL

gvinas Yisroel *see* KOSHER CHEESE

gway tio *see* RICE NOODLES

gweduck *see* GEODUCK

Gyeta olive *see* GAETA OLIVE

gyoza [gee-OH-zah] Japanese equivalent of a POT STICKER. *See also* WON TON SKINS.

gyro [JEER-oh; ZHEER-oh; *Gk.* YEE-roh] A Greek specialty consisting of meat that is molded around a spit and vertically roasted. The hot roasted meat is shaved off as the spit turns, then tucked into a PITA and topped with grilled onions, sweet peppers and TZATZIKI (cucumber-yogurt sauce). The meats used vary from region to region and can include lamb, pork, chicken and beef. The Middle Eastern version of the gyro is SHAWARMA.

gyuto *see* KNIFE

habanero chile [ah-bah-NYEH-roh] This distinctively flavored, extremely hot CHILE is small and lantern-shaped. It's native to the Caribbean, the Yucatan and the north coast of South America. The habanero ranges from light green to bright orange when ripe. It's generally used for sauces in both its fresh and dried form. The SCOVILLE SCALE rating ranges from 100,000 to 350,000, although special versions are even hotter.

habas [HAH-bahs] *see* FAVA BEAN

haddock [HAD-uhk] A saltwater fish that is closely related to but smaller than COD. The lowfat haddock has a firm texture and mild flavor. It can weigh anywhere from 2 to 6 pounds and is available fresh either whole or in fillets and steaks, and frozen in fillets and steaks. Haddock is suitable for any style of preparation including baking, poaching, sautéing and grilling. Smoked haddock is called FINNAN HADDIE. *See also* FISH.

haemultang [HAM-uhl-tahng] A seafood stew from Korea that's similar to the French BOUILLABAISSE except much spicier. The fresh seafood can include blue crabs, clams, lobster tail, octopus, scallops, shrimp and squid, along with a variety of vegetables. The spicy heat comes from gochujang (*see* CHILE BEAN PASTE).

haggis [HAG-ihs] A Scottish specialty made by stuffing a sheep's (or other animal's) stomach lining with a minced mixture of the animal's organs (heart, liver, lungs, and so on), onion, SUET, oatmeal and seasonings, then simmering the sausage in water for about 4 hours. **Haggamuggie** is a simplified version of haggis made with fish liver.

hairy cucumber; hairy melon *see* FUZZY MELON

hake [HAYK] Related to the COD, hake is a saltwater fish that makes its home in the Atlantic and northern Pacific Oceans. It's low in fat and has white, delicately flavored meat. Ranging in size from 1 to 8 pounds, hake is marketed whole or in fillets and steaks. It comes in fresh, frozen, smoked and salted forms. Hake may be prepared in any way suitable for cod. *See also* FISH.

hakurei *see* SALAD TURNIP

hakusai [HAH-koo-si] *see* CHINESE CABBAGE

half-and-half; half & half *see* CREAM

half bottle *see* WINE BOTTLES

half shell *see* ON THE HALF SHELL

halibut [HAL-uh-buht] Abundant in northern Pacific and Atlantic waters, this large member of the FLATFISH family can weigh up to half a ton. The norm, however, ranges between 50 and 100 pounds. Considered the finest are the young **chicken halibut**, which can weigh anywhere from 2 to 10 pounds. Halibut meat is lowfat, white, firm and mild flavored. Fresh halibut is available year-round but most abundant from March to September. Both fresh and frozen halibut is usually marketed in fillets and steaks. It's suitable for almost any manner of preparation. Halibut cheeks can sometimes be found in specialty fish markets. *See also* FISH.

hallabong *see* DEKOPON

hallacas [ay-YAH-kahs] Hailing from Colombia and Venezuela, hallacas are South America's version of TAMALES. They consist of ground beef, pork or chicken mixed with other foods such as cheese, olives or raisins, surrounded by a ground-corn dough, wrapped in banana leaves and gently boiled. Hallacas are served as both an appetizer and main dish.

hallah *see* CHALLAH

Halloumi; Haloumi; Hallumi [hah-LOO-mee] Popular in Greece, Turkey and the Middle East, Halloumi traces its origins back to Cyprus. This SEMISOFT cheese has been produced for centuries, traditionally from sheep's milk but today goat's milk and occasionally cow's milk are used. The firm but soft and springy cheese can be found in 8- to 12-ounce half-moon shapes or bars. The flavor of this white, moist cheese is mild, tangy, salty, and sometimes minty since mint is often added during cheesemaking. It has a FAT CONTENT of about 47 percent.

halvah; halva [hahl-VAH; HAHL-vah] 1. Hailing from the Middle East, this confection is made from ground SESAME SEED and honey, sometimes with the addition of chopped dried fruit and pistachio nuts. It's available in most supermarkets in wrapped bars, and in Jewish delicatessens in long slabs from which individual slices can be cut. 2. Various sweet Indian puddings made with fruit, grain, legumes, nuts, seeds and/or vegetables. Some are the consistency of fudge, others are fluffier and some are like purées. Halva is also spelled *halwa*.

halwa *see* HALVA

ham The cut of meat from a hog's hind leg, generally from the middle of the shank bone to the aitch (hip) bone. The actual length of the cut varies according to the producer. The unprocessed meat is referred to as **fresh ham**, but most ham goes through a curing process after which it's referred to as **cured ham**. The final flavor of a ham can be attributed to a combination of many factors. Before the animal is slaughtered, those factors include its breed, the type of feed on which it was raised and the age at which it was slaughtered. Most hogs are fed corn, but animals headed for the gourmet market may have treats such as acorns, beechnuts, chestnuts or peanuts added to their diets. After the hog is slaughtered, the meat is usually cured in one of three ways—dry curing, sweet-pickle curing or injection curing. **Dry curing** involves salting the surface of the ham thoroughly, then storing it until the salt saturates the meat. This procedure may be repeated several times. **Sweet-pickle curing** involves immersing the ham in a sweet BRINE with added seasonings (usually a secret recipe of the producer). If sugar is added to the curing mix the ham may be labeled *sugar-cured*. Most mass producers of ham use the **injection-curing** method whereby the ham is injected with brine. This method is sometimes combined with one of the other curing methods. The length of time a ham is cured will affect the final flavor. Most hams for American consumers have a light or mild cure. After curing, a ham may go through a smoking process that adds both flavor and aging capability. The length of time a ham is smoked varies widely depending on the desired result. Those being prepared for the mass market are usually smoked lightly or not at all. Hams for the gourmet palate are more heavily smoked, the process lasting a month or more. The smoked flavor will vary depending on the substance used. Hickory and maple are the woods of preference, and some producers add exotic ingredients such as JUNIPER BERRIES, sage or peat. Once curing and smoking are completed, gourmet hams are usually aged to further develop flavors; most mass-produced hams are not. In some cases, aging can take up to 2 years. Hams are sold in several forms including **boneless** (with the hip, thigh and shank bones removed), **partially boned** (with the hip and/or shank bones removed) and **bone-in**. Since bone contributes flavor to the meat during cooking, most gourmet-ham producers leave some bone in. Hams are marketed in several sizes, the most popular being whole, halves (shank or butt ends only), shank, butt and center-cut slices or steaks ranging in thickness from $1/2$ to $3/4$ inch. Whole hams usually weigh from 8 to 18 pounds. **Canned hams** may either be a whole piece of boneless meat or they may be "formed" from bits and pieces of meat held together with a gelatin mixture. Hams are available fully cooked, partially cooked or uncooked. Those that are **fully cooked** are heated to an internal temperature of 148°F or above, **partially cooked** hams to at least 137°F (which kills the trichina parasite). **Uncooked and partially cooked** hams must be cooked prior to serving. Fully cooked hams, sometimes labled "heat-and-serve" or "ready-to-eat," do not require additional cooking and may be eaten cold or heated until warm. Carefully check the label for instructions. Most hams sold today are of the mass-produced variety sometimes referred to as "city" or "urban" hams. Higher-quality American hams are generally labeled "COUNTRY-CURED" (or "country-style"). The majority of these "country" hams come from Georgia, Kentucky, Tennessee and

Virginia; each region adds its own distinctive style to the ham it produces. Probably the most famous country-cured ham is the SMITHFIELD HAM from the Virginia town of the same name. A wide selection of specially cured hams are also imported from many European countries. The most well known are PROSCIUTTO from Italy, Germany's WESTPHALIAN, France's BAYONNE and the York ham from England. Prosciutto and Westphalian are generally sold in paper-thin slices. *When buying a fresh ham,* look for one with a firm white layer of fat, with a well-marbled lean portion. In younger animals, the meat should be a grayish-pink color; older pork should be a delicate shade of rose. Loosen any packaging material and store the fresh ham in the coldest part of the refrigerator for up to 5 days. *When purchasing a cured ham,* choose one that's firm and plump. The meat should be finely grained and rosy pink. Refrigerate in the ham's original wrapping or container for up to 1 week. Some country-style hams can be stored in a cool place for 1 to 2 months. Longer storage is possible, but moisture evaporation causes the ham to shrink and toughen. Canned hams should be stored according to label directions. Some require refrigeration; others have been sterilized and do not need to be refrigerated until after they've been opened. Ham slices should be wrapped airtight and refrigerated up to 3 days. Ham can be baked, grilled, sautéed, broiled or simmered. Precooked hams can be eaten without additional cooking. Heavily cured country-style hams, depending on how salty they are, may require scrubbing, then soaking up to 24 hours before cooking. *See also* CULATELLO; PARMA HAM; PICNIC HAM.

hamachi [hah-MAH-chee] Japanese name for young YELLOWTAIL.

Haman's hats *see* HAMANTASCHEN

hamantaschen [HAH-mahn-tah-shuhn] These small triangular pastries hold a sweet filling, either of honey-poppy seed, prune or apricot. They're one of the traditional sweets of Purim, a festive Jewish holiday. Also called *Haman's hats* after Haman, the wicked prime minister of Persia who plotted the extermination of Persian Jews. Haman's plot was foiled at the last minute and the joyous festival of Purim was proclaimed in celebration.

hamburger 1. Said to have made its first appearance at the St. Louis Louisiana Purchase Exposition in 1904, the hamburger is one of America's favorite foods. It consists of a cooked patty of ground beef sandwiched between two bread halves, usually in the form of a HAMBURGER BUN. The meat can be mixed with various flavorings including finely chopped onions and herbs, and is sometimes topped with a slice of cheese, in which case it becomes a **cheeseburger**. It's also commonly referred to as a *burger* and *hamburger steak*. The name "hamburger" comes from the seaport town of Hamburg, Germany, where it is thought that 19th-century sailors brought back the idea of raw shredded beef (known today as BEEF TARTARE) after trading with the Baltic provinces of Russia. Some anonymous German chef decided to cook the beef . . . and the rest is history. 2. Ground, shredded or finely chopped beef. *See also* GROUND BEEF.

hamburger bun A soft, round yeast roll 3$\frac{1}{2}$ to 4 inches in diameter, made to fit the size of a HAMBURGER. It may be made with regular or whole-wheat flour and variously topped with flavorings such as sesame seed, poppy seed or toasted chopped onion.

hamburger press A plastic or cast-aluminum utensil that forms perfectly round, flat hamburger patties. It comes in two separate round pieces, the top part having a plunger. The hamburger meat is placed in the bottom half, which is shaped like a disc with $\frac{1}{2}$- to 1-inch sides. The top of the utensil is set over the base and, by pushing the plunger, the hamburger meat inside is pressed into a perfect disk.

Hamburg parsley *see* PARSLEY ROOT

ham hock The hock is the lower portion of a hog's hind leg, made up of meat, fat, bone, gristle and connective tissue. In the market, ham hocks are often cut into 2- to 3-inch lengths. Most have been cured, smoked or both, but fresh hocks can sometimes also be found. Ham hocks are generally used to flavor dishes such as soups, beans and stews that require lengthy, slow cooking. *See also* HAM.

hand cheese *see* HANDKÄSE

hand-formed cookie; hand-shaped cookie Also called *molded* cookie, this style is made by shaping dough by hand into small balls, logs, crescents and other shapes. *See also* COOKIE.

handkäse [HAHND-kay-zeh] The name of this German specialty means "hand cheese," referring to the fact that it's hand-shaped into irregular rounds, cylinders or other forms. It's made from skimmed, sour cow's milk, which gives the cheese a sharp, pungent flavor and very strong (some say overpowering) smell. The rind is gray and the interior off-white and soft. *See also* CHEESE.

hanger steak A thick boneless beef cut weighing 1 to 2 pounds that hangs between the RIB and the SHORT LOIN and connects to and supports the diaphragm. It's flavorful like SKIRT STEAK and, though a bit more tender, still requires careful preparation. Typically, hanger steaks are marinated before being cooked at a high, dry heat to a temperature of rare to medium rare. In the United States this cut is also known as *butcher's steak* (because butchers would save this tasty, unknown cut for themselves) and *hanging tender*; in France it's known as *onglet*.

hanging tender *see* HANGER STEAK

Hangtown Fry This dish is said to have been created during the California Gold Rush in a rowdy burg called Hangtown (now Placerville) because of the town's frequent hangings. It consists of fried breaded oysters cooked together with eggs and fried bacon, rather like an omelet or scramble.

hard-ball stage A test for SUGAR SYRUP desribing the point at which a drop of boiling syrup immersed in cold water forms a rigid ball. Though the ball is hard, it will still be somewhat pliable. On a CANDY THERMOMETER, the hard-ball stage is between 250° and 265°F. *See* Candymaking Cold-Water Tests, page 866.

hard-crack stage A test for SUGAR SYRUP describing the point at which a drop of boiling syrup immersed in cold water separates into hard, brittle threads. On a CANDY THERMOMETER, the hard-crack stage is between 300° and 310°F. *See* Candymaking Cold-Water Tests, page 866.

hardhead *see* DRUM

hard sauce The traditional accompaniment for PLUM PUDDING, hard sauce is made by beating butter, sugar and flavoring together until smooth and creamy. The sugar can be powdered, granulated or brown. The flavoring is generally brandy, rum or whiskey, though vanilla or other extracts may also be used. This mixture is refrigerated until "hard" (the texture of butter). It's often spooned into a decorative mold before chilling and unmolded before serving. Hard sauce is known in England as *brandy butter*.

hard-shell clam One of the two varieties of clam, the other being SOFT-SHELL CLAM. On the East Coast, hard-shell clams, also called by their Indian name, *quahog*, come in three sizes. The smallest are LITTLENECK CLAMS, which have a shell diameter less than 2 inches. Next comes the medium-size CHERRYSTONE CLAM, about 2½ inches across. The largest of this trio is the CHOWDER CLAM (also simply called *large clam*) with a shell diameter of at least 3 inches. Among the West Coast hard-shell varieties are the Pacific LITTLENECK CLAM, the PISMO and the small, sweet BUTTER CLAMS from the Puget Sound. *See also* CLAM.

hardtack Also called *ship biscuit* and *sea bread,* this large, hard biscuit is made with an unsalted, UNLEAVENED flour-and-water dough. After it's baked, hardtack is dried to lengthen shelf life. It's been used at least since the 1800s as a staple for sailors on long voyages.

hare A larger relative of the RABBIT, the hare can weigh as much as 12 to 14 pounds, compared to a rabbit at about 5 pounds. Whether wild or domesticated, hares have a darker flesh and earthier flavor than rabbits. Wild hare, also called *jackrabbit* and *snowshoe rabbit,* generally needs marinating to tenderize it before cooking. Younger animals (1 year or less) can usually be roasted, whereas older animals are best cooked with moist-heat methods such as stewing or braising. One of the most famous dishes made with this animal is JUGGED HARE. Although plentiful in the United States, hare isn't as popular here as in European countries.

haricot beans [AH-ree-koh] A general term for any of various dried seeds that come from several varieties of the green bean. Among the more popular haricot beans are CANNELLINI BEAN, GREAT NORTHERN BEAN and NAVY BEAN. *See also* BEANS.

haricot vert [ah-ree-koh VEHR] French for "green string bean," *haricot* meaning "bean" and *vert* translating as "green."

harina de chuño [ah-REE-nah day CHOO-nyoh] *see* CHUÑO

harira [hah-RIH-rah] A thick, spicy Moroccan soup traditionally served on special occasions, particularly during the holy month of Ramadan at sundown after a day of fasting. Harira typically consists of lamb or chicken, celery, chickpeas, garlic, lentils, onions, rice, tomatoes, noodles (such as vermicelli) and water. It's flavored variously with seasonings including cinnamon, coriander, ginger, paprika, pepper, saffron, turmeric and salt. Harira is usually thickened with a mixture of flour and water or lemon and egg. It's often served as a meal on its own accompanied by dates or figs, hard-boiled eggs and lemon juice or lemon wedges.

harissa [hah-REE-suh] From Tunisia, this fiery-hot sauce is usually made with hot chiles, garlic, cumin, coriander, caraway and olive oil. It's the traditional accompaniment for COUSCOUS but is also used to flavor soups, stews and other dishes. Harissa can be found in cans and jars in Middle Eastern markets. *See also* SAUCE.

haroset [hah-ROH-seht; khah-ROH-seht] A sweet, pasty condiment made of chopped fruit, nuts and sweet red kosher wine traditionally served at the Passover Seder. Haroset, also spelled *charoset* or *charoses,* represents the clay and mortar used by Jewish slaves to construct buildings in Egypt. Apples and raisins are commonly used but dates and figs are frequently utilized as well.

hartshorn *see* AMMONIUM BICARBONATE

harusame [hah-roo-SAH-meh] Translating as "spring rain," harusame are Japanese noodles made from mung bean, soybean, rice or potato flour.

They're available in Asian markets and many supermarkets. Harusame are also called CELLOPHANE NOODLES and Japanese vermicelli.

Harvard beets Sliced beets cooked in a thickened sweet-and-sour sauce composed of vinegar, sugar, water, butter, cornstarch and seasonings. Harvard beets are served hot as a side dish.

Harvey Wallbanger A SCREWDRIVER (VODKA and orange juice) with a FLOAT of GALLIANO, a drink that became wildly popular in the 1970s.

hasenpfeffer [HAH-zuhn-fehf-uhr] Literally translated from German as "hare pepper," this dish is a thick, highly seasoned stew of rabbit meat. Before stewing, the meat is soaked in a wine-vinegar marinade for 1 to 3 days. Hasenpfeffer is often served garnished with sour cream and accompanied by noodles or dumplings.

hash *n.* A dish of finely chopped meat (roast beef and corned beef are the most common), potatoes and seasonings, usually fried together until lightly browned. Other chopped vegetables, such as green pepper, celery and onion, can also be added. Hash is sometimes served with gravy or sauce. hash *v.* To chop food into small pieces.

hash browns; hash-brown potatoes Finely chopped or shredded, cooked potatoes that are fried (often in bacon fat) until well browned. The mixture is usually pressed down into a flat cake in the pan and browned on one side, then turned and browned on the other. It's sometimes only browned on one side. Other flavorings such as chopped onion and green pepper are often added.

hashi [HAH-shee] Japanese CHOPSTICKS, either wood or bamboo, sometimes lacquered and decorated. Also called *o-hashi*. Long chopsticks used for cooking are called **sai-hashi**.

hasty pudding This easy, versatile dish was enjoyed by Colonial Americans both for breakfast and for dessert. It's a simple cornmeal mush made with water or milk and sometimes sweetened with molasses, maple syrup or honey. If the dish isn't sweetened during cooking, a syrup or sweet sauce usually accompanies a hasty pudding. It's served hot, sometimes with milk or cream.

hasu [hah-soo] *see* LOTUS

hatcho miso [HAHT-choh MEE-soh] *see* MISO

haupia [hah-OO-pee-ah] A traditional coconut-flavored Hawaiian dessert frequently served at luaus. For haupia, a mixture of coconut milk, sugar, arrowroot or corn starch and salt is heated until thickened, then poured into a rectangular pan. After being chilled, the haupia—sometimes described as a "stiff pudding"—sets up like a gelatin mixture. Variations include adding crushed pineapple or mango slices.

Haut-Doubs *see* VACHERIN

haute cuisine [OHT kwih-ZEEN (kwee-ZEEN)] Food that is prepared in an elegant or elaborate manner; the very finest food, prepared perfectly. The French word *haute* translates as "high" or "superior," *cuisine* as "cooking" (in general).

Havarti [hah-VAHR-tee] Named after *Havartigaard*, the Danish experimental farm where it was developed, Havarti is often referred to as the Danish TILSIT because of their similarities, though Havarti has a milder aroma and flavor. This cow's-milk cheese has a supple, elastic texture that can range from semisoft to semihard. The thin rind is reddish-yellow to reddish brown, though some are rindless. Havarti has a pale yellow interior with small, irregular EYES. The flavor of young Havarti is mild yet tangy. As the cheese ages, its flavor intensifies and sharpens. Havarti comes in loaves or blocks and is often wrapped in foil. It can be plain or flavored with any of a variety of seasonings including dill, caraway seeds, chives, jalapeño peppers and various herbs and spices. This cheese is also produced in other countries including Australia and the United States. Regular Havarti has a FAT CONTENT of approximately 45 percent; the lowfat version contains 30 percent and the creamy version (enriched with added cream) contains 60 percent fat. *See also* CHEESE.

Havarti Tilsit *see* TILSIT

Hawaiian blue prawn A freshwater prawn that's now being AQUA-CULTURED in Hawaii. It's name comes from the brilliant blue color of its tail. The moderately fat flesh of the Hawaiian blue prawn is sweet and succulent. This CRUSTACEAN can be prepared in any manner suitable for SHRIMP. *See also* PRAWN.

Hawaiian sun fish *see* TILAPIA

haw fun *see* RICE NOODLES

hazelnut These wild nuts grow in clusters on the hazel tree in temperate zones around the world. The fuzzy outer husk opens as the nut ripens, revealing a hard, smooth shell. Italy, Spain, France and Turkey lead the way in hazelnut production. Until the 1940s, the United States imported most hazelnuts; however, they're now grown in Oregon and Washington. Also called *filberts* and *cobnuts,* particularly when cultivated, these sweet, rich, grape-size nuts are used chopped, ground and whole in all manner of sweets, as well as in savory foods such as salads and main dishes. Hazelnuts are usually packaged whole, though some producers are now also offering them chopped—a real timesaver. Hazelnuts have a bitter brown skin that is best removed, usually by heating them at 350°F for 10 to 15 minutes, until the skins begin to flake. By placing a handful of nuts at a time in a dish towel, then folding the towel over the warm nuts and rubbing vigorously, most of the skin will be removed. *See also* HAZELNUT OIL; NUTS.

hazelnut oil A fragrant, full-flavored oil pressed from hazelnuts and tasting like the roasted nut. Most hazelnut oil is imported from France and is therefore expensive. It can be purchased in cans or bottles in gourmet markets and many supermarkets. Hazelnut oil can be stored in a cool (under 65°F) place for up to 3 months. To prevent rancidity, it's safer to store it in the refrigerator. Because it's so strong-flavored, hazelnut oil is generally combined with lighter oils. It can be used in dressings, to flavor sauces and main dishes and in baked goods. *See also* FATS AND OILS.

head cheese; headcheese Not a cheese at all, but a SAUSAGE made from the meaty bits of the head of a calf or pig (sometimes a sheep or cow) that are seasoned, combined with a gelatinous meat broth and cooked in a mold. When cool, the sausage is unmolded and thinly sliced. It's usually eaten at room temperature. Head cheese can be purchased in delicatessens and many supermarkets. In England this sausage is referred to as *brawn,* and in France it's called *fromage de tête*—"cheese of head."

head lettuce Generally, the term *head lettuce* describes those varieties on which the leaves grow in a dense rosette. There are two subcategories—CRISPHEAD (commonly known as *iceberg*) and BUTTERHEAD (the *Bibb* and *Boston* varieties). *See also* LETTUCE.

heart Since heart consists almost entirely of muscle, it tends to be quite tough. In general, the younger the animal, the more tender the heart. Beef heart is the largest of those commonly available, followed by those of calves, lambs and chickens. Choose hearts that are fresh-smelling, plump and red, avoiding those with a brown or gray hue. Refrigerate, loosely wrapped, for no more than a day or two. Before using, remove any excess fat and wash thoroughly. Heart can be braised, stewed or chopped and added to cooked dishes such as stews. Small hearts, such as those from young lambs and pigs, are often stuffed and sautéed or roasted and served one per person. Chicken hearts from a young bird can also be sautéed. *See also* VARIETY MEATS.

hearts of palm The edible inner portion of the stem of the cabbage palm tree, which grows in many tropical climates and is Florida's official state tree. Hearts of palm are slender, ivory-colored, delicately flavored and expensive. They resemble white asparagus, sans tips. Their texture is firm and smooth and the flavor is reminiscent of an artichoke. Each stalk is about 4 inches long and can range in diameter from pencil-thin to 1 to 1½ inches. The hearts of palm we get in the United States are either from Florida or imported from Brazil. When found fresh, they are typically sealed in plastic wrap and should look white with no signs of bruising or browning. Refrigerate and use within 2 to 3 days. Canned hearts of palm are packed in water, and can be found in gourmet markets and many large supermarkets. Once opened, they should be transferred to a nonmetal container with an airtight cover and can be refrigerated in their own liquid for up to a week. Hearts of palm can be used in salads and in main dishes, deep-fried or added to STIR-FRYS.

heirloom seeds The advent of megaagriculture in America has seen the gradual depletion of ancient varieties of native nonhybrid plants. Unfortunately for those who appreciate full-flavored fruits and vegetables, produce-seed conglomerates focus only on those strains that have mass-market appeal—which means they're beautiful and hardy, but not necessarily the best-tasting. Fortunately, about 25 years ago some dedicated individuals began saving what they could of the remaining open-pollinated (without human intervention) seed varieties, which have become known as "heirloom seeds." Among the many heirloom fruits and vegetables grown today are beets, carrots, corn, dried beans, lettuce, potatoes and tomatoes. As the public becomes more aware of these wonderful alternatives, farmers are also becoming more interested. Heirloom produce can be found in some specialty produce markets and farmer's markets.

Hélène [ay-LEHN] *see* POIRE HÉLÈNE

hen *see* FOWL

hen of the woods A dark brownish gray cultivated mushroom that resembles a tightly ruffled puff edged in white. The name of this rich-flavored mushroom is said to come from the fact that its shape vaguely resembles the body of a hen. Also called *maitake* and *kumotake. See also* MUSHROOM.

herbes de Provence [EHRB duh proh-VAWNS] An assortment of dried herbs said to reflect those most commonly used in southern France. The blend can be found packed in tiny clay crocks in the spice section of large supermarkets. The mixture commonly contains BASIL, FENNEL seed, LAVENDER, MARJORAM, ROSEMARY, SAGE, summer SAVORY and THYME. The blend can be used to season dishes of meat, poultry and vegetables. *See also* HERBS.

herb patience dock *see* SORREL

herbs [ERB; Brit. HERB] The fragrant leaves of any of various annual or perennial plants that grow in temperate zones and do not have woody stems. Herbs can be purchased in dried or fresh forms. Some, like CHIVES, are also sold frozen. Some of the more commonly available **fresh herbs** are BASIL, BAY LEAF, CHERVIL, CORIANDER, MARJORAM, MINT, OREGANO, PARSLEY, ROSEMARY, SAGE, SAVORY, TARRAGON and THYME. They can be found at various times of year, depending on the herb—many are available year-round. Choose herbs that have a clean, fresh fragrance and a bright color without any sign of wilting or browning. They can be stored in the refrigerator, wrapped in a barely damp paper towel and sealed airtight in a plastic bag for up to 5 days. For storage up to 10 days (depending on the herb), place the bouquet of herbs, stem end down, in a tall glass and fill with cold water until the ends are covered by 1 inch. Cover the top of the bouquet with a plastic bag, securing it to the glass with a rubber band. Alternatively, the herb bouquet may be placed in a screw-top jar in the same manner and sealed tightly. Either way, the water should be changed every 2 days. Just before using, wash the herbs and blot dry with a paper towel. **Dried herbs** are available year-round in metal or cardboard boxes, bottles, cellophane packages and unglazed ceramic pots. They have a stronger, more concentrated flavor than fresh herbs, but quickly lose their pungency. Crushed or ground herbs become lackluster more quickly than whole herbs. The more airtight the storage container, the longer the herbs will last. Transfer those in cardboard, tin, unglazed ceramic or cellophane to small glass bottles or jars with screw-top lids. Each time you use the herb, make sure the lid is tightly resealed. Store dried herbs in a cool, dark place for a maximum of 6 months. After 3 months, it is best to refrigerate them. Herbs are used to flavor all manner of food and drink. Most should be used judiciously because many of them can be quite pungent. *See also* Seasoning Suggestions, page 891; ANGELICA; BORAGE; BUCKWHEAT; BURNET; CHIVE; COSTMARY; CURRY LEAF; DILL; EPAZOTE; GARLIC CHIVES; HORSERADISH; HYSSOP; LEMON BALM; LEMON GRASS; LEMON VERBENA; SORREL; SPICES; WORMWOOD; YARROW.

Herbsaint Developed and made primarily in New Orleans, Herbsaint is an anise-flavored LIQUEUR that is used in such specialties as OYSTERS ROCKEFELLER.

herb tea *see* TISANE

heritage pork Though once considered unsuitable for mass production techniques, heritage pork breeds are now being raised in answer to consumer demand for higher-quality pork products. Farmers are now using ARTISANAL methods to produce these traditional breeds in humane and healthy ways. The overall result is darker meat streaked with flavorful fat for which leading chefs are clamoring. Following are some of the better-known breeds of heritage pork. The **Berkshire/Kurobuta** breed can be traced back over 300 years. The Berkshire's positive traits were mentioned in historical notes made during the 17th-century stay of Oliver Cromwell's army in Berkshire. In 1823, the first Berkshire hogs were imported into the United States. In the nineteenth century, they were given as a gift to Japan and have since attained a status that rivals that of Japanese KOBE BEEF. In Japan the Berkshire is known as Kurobuta, meaning "black hog." This fatty breed is recognized for its dark and tender flesh with fine marbling and rich flavor. **Duroc** hogs were developed in the United States in the 1830s by breeding two strains of hogs—one from New York, the other from New Jersey. The red Duroc was named after a famous thoroughbred stallion of that time. This breed is known for its excellent marbling, which results in juicy, flavorful meat. **Gloucester Old Spot** is a large, fatty breed that originated in England's Berkeley Valley region. Although not raised in great numbers either in England or the United States, this breed is valued for the high quality of its meat for chops and roasts. **Large Black** is a breed that was developed in the Devon and Cornwall areas of England. As the name implies, this hog is very large and black. Though quite popular at one time, the Large Black is now only raised in limited numbers. It produces juicy, savory meats and lean, full-flavored hams. **Red Wattle** is a breed brought to New Orleans in the 1700s by the French from the South Pacific island of New Caledonia. It has lean, dark, tender, flavorful meat and gets special recognition for its hams. **Tamworth** is a red heritage breed that originated in Ireland. In 1812, it was brought to Sir Robert Peel's estate in Tamworth, England, and subsequently to the United States in 1882. The Tamworth is a lean hog that's considered by many to produce the best bacon in the United States.

Herman; Herman starter *see* YEAST STARTER

hermit An old-fashioned favorite said to have originated in Colonial New England, this spicy, chewy cookie is full of chopped fruits and nuts. It's usually sweetened with molasses or brown sugar. It's said that hermits were named for their long keeping qualities—they're better when hidden away like a hermit for several days.

hero sandwich This huge sandwich goes by many names, depending on where it's made. Among its aliases are *submarine, grinder, hoagie* and *poor boy* (or *po' boy*). Generally, the hero sandwich consists of a small loaf of Italian or French bread (or a large oblong roll), the bottom half of which is heaped with layers of any of various thinly sliced meats, cheeses, tomatoes, pickles, lettuce, peppers—anything for which the cook is in the mood.

herring This huge family of saltwater fish has over a hundred varieties. The popular herring swims in gigantic schools and can be found in the cold waters of the North Atlantic and Pacific oceans. In the United States, two of the most popular members of this family are the American **shad**, (see listing) and the **alewife**, both of which are anadromous, meaning that they migrate from their saltwater habitat to spawn in fresh water. Herring are generally small (ranging between $1/4$ and 1 pound) and silvery. The major exception to that rule is the American shad, which averages 3 to 6 pounds and is prized for its eggs—the delicacy known as SHAD ROE. Young herring are frequently labeled and sold as SARDINES. Fresh herring are available during the spring on both the Pacific and Atlantic coasts. When fresh, the high-fat herring has a fine, soft texture that is suited for baking, sautéing and grilling. The herring's flesh becomes firm when cured by either pickling, salting, smoking or a combination of those techniques. There are many variations of cured herring. **Bismarck herring** are unskinned fillets that have been cured in a mixture of vinegar, sugar, salt and onions. **Rollmops** are Bismarck herring fillets wrapped around a piece of pickle or onion and preserved in spiced vinegar. **Pickled herring** (also called **marinated herring**) have been marinated in vinegar and spices before being bottled in either a sour-cream sauce or a wine sauce. The term can also refer to herring that have been dry-salted before being cured in brine. **Kippered herring** (also called **kippers**) are split, then cured by salting, drying and cold-smoking. **Bloaters** are larger than kippers but treated in a similar manner. They have a slightly milder flavor due to a lighter salting and shorter smoking period. Their name comes from their swollen appearance. **Schmaltz herring** are mature, higher-fat herring that are filleted and preserved in brine. The reddish **Matjes herring** are skinned and filleted before being cured in a spiced sugar-vinegar brine. *See also* FISH.

Herve [ehr-VAY] Made since the 15th century and hailing from the Belgian town of the same name, this cheese may be made from raw or PASTEURIZED COW's milk. The complete PROTECTED DEGINATION OF ORIGIN name is *Fromage de Herve.* Herve comes in cubes or rectangles ranging from $1^3/4$ to 14 ounces. It has a sticky rind that can range in color from pinkish-orange to reddish brown; the interior varies from off-white to pale yellow. Herve has a firm, supple texture that becomes creamy with age. It has a complex, rich flavor profile of sweet, spicy, savory and tangy characteristics. This cheese is RIPENED a minimum of 5 weeks, though 2 to 3 months of aging is not uncommon. During that time the rind is washed every couple of days, typically with beer. The minimum FAT CONTENT for Fromage de Herve is 45 percent. *See also* CHEESE.

hibachi [hih-BAH-chee] Japanese for "fire bowl," a hibachi is just that—a small (generally cast-iron) container made for holding fuel (usually charcoal). A grill that sits on top of the bowl is used to cook various foods. Hibachis come in square, oblong and round models. Because of their compact size, they're completely portable.

hichimi togarashi [hee-CHEE-mee toh-gah-RAH-shee] *see* SHICHIMI TOGARASHI

hickory nut There are 17 varieties of hickory trees, 13 of which are native to the United States. The extremely hard hickory wood is widely used to smoke American hams. All varieties of the hickory tree bear nuts, the most popular being the PECAN, partially due to its thin shell. The common "hickory nut" has an extraordinarily hard shell, the cracking of which usually requires a hammer swung with a great deal of muscle. Hickory nuts have an excellent, rich flavor with a buttery quality due to their high fat content. They're available only in certain parts of the country and are generally sold unshelled. Hickory nuts can be used in a variety of baked goods and in almost any recipe as a substitute for pecans. *See also* NUTS.

high-altitude cooking and baking Simply put, the weight of air on any surface it comes in contact with is called *air* (or *atmospheric*) *pressure*. There's less air pressure at high altitudes because the blanket of air above is thinner than it would be at sea level. As a result, at sea level water boils at 212°F; at an altitude of 7,500 feet, however, it boils at about 198°F because there's not as much air pressure to inhibit the boiling action. This also means that because at high altitudes boiling water is 14° cooler than at sea level, foods will take longer to cook because they're heating at a lower temperature. Lower air pressure also causes boiling water to evaporate more quickly in a high altitude. Therefore boiled foods like dried beans and peas take longer to cook at high altitudes and may require more liquid than at sea level. Meat, poultry and fish usually also require longer cooking times. For deep-fat frying, decrease the fat temperature by 3 degrees for each 1,000 feet above sea level; fry foods for a longer time. Foods stored at high altitudes dry out more quickly than those at low altitudes. That means that an ingredient such as flour is drier and will absorb more liquid. Therefore, slightly more liquid or less flour may be required for cake batters or bread and cookie doughs to reach the proper consistency. Decreased air pressure means that adjustments in some ingredients and cooking time and temperature will have to be made for high-altitude baking, as well as some cooking techniques such as candymaking, deep-fat frying and canning. In general, no recipe adjustment is necessary for YEAST-risen baked goods, although allowing the dough or batter to rise twice before the final pan rising develops a better flavor. Increasing the baking temperature by 25°F will help set the crust faster so bread will not over-rise during the OVEN-SPRING that takes place the first 10 to 15 minutes of baking. For baked goods leavened by BAKING POWDER and BAKING SODA, *see* High-Altitude Baking Adjustments, page 861; Boiling Point of Water at Various Altitudes, page 861.

highball A COCKTAIL served in a tall glass over ice. Usually a simple concoction of whiskey mixed with SODA WATER or plain water.

high performance liquid chromatography *see* GILLETT METHOD

high tea This British tradition is a late-afternoon or early evening meal, usually quite substantial. It originated in the 19th century as a simple, early workingman's supper. High tea can be served buffet-style or set on a table. It includes a variety of dishes such as CORNISH PASTIES, WELSH RABBIT, SCOTCH WOODCOCK and various other meat and fish dishes. There are also plenty of buns, CRUMPETS, biscuits, CLOTTED CREAM and jams, as well as an elaborate array of cakes and pastries and, of course, steaming pots of hot tea. *See also* CREAM TEA.

hijiki [hee-JEE-kee] A Japanese SEAWEED that comes in narrow black ribbons several inches long. After harvesting, it's sun dried, then boiled and dried again. Hijiki (also called *hiziki*) is the most mineral-rich of its genre and has a salty, slightly ANISE character. It's reconstituted in water and used as a vegetable in soups and other dishes.

H

hiki-cha [hee-kee CHAH] *see* MATCHA

Himalayan salt *see* PINK SALT

hime lemon *see* RANGPUR LIME

himepon *see* DEKOPON

hiropon *see* DEKOPON

hiyamugi [hee-yah-MOO-gee] Thin wheat-flour noodles generally served cold either as part of various Japanese dishes or by themselves with a soy-based dipping sauce. Hiyamugi comes in various colors and can be found dried in Asian markets.

hiziki *see* HIJIKI

hoagie [HOH-gee] *see* HERO SANDWICH

hochepot *see* HOTCHPOTCH

hock 1. The lower portion of an animal's leg, generally corresponding to the ankle in a human. *See also* HAM HOCK. 2. A term used in England for any Rhine wine.

hoddeok; hodduk; hotteok [HOH-duhk] Korean pancake that's usually filled with brown sugar, cinnamon and nuts, then baked or deep-fried. Many variations now exist including some savory versions. It's a popular street vendor food, particularly in the winter months.

hoe cake; hoecake *see* JOHNNYCAKE

ho fun *see* RICE NOODLES

hogfish *see* CATFISH

hog jowl The cheek of a hog, which is usually cut into squares before being cured and smoked. Hog jowl is generally only available in the South. Tightly wrapped, it can be refrigerated for up to a week. It's fattier than bacon but can be cut into strips and fried in the same manner. It's also used to flavor stews, bean dishes and the like.

hog maw A pig's stomach, commonly stuffed with a SAUSAGE mixture, simmered until done, then baked until brown. It's usually available only by special order and should be stored in the refrigerator for no more than 2 days. Before using, the stomach should be cleaned of all membrane, rinsed thoroughly, then patted dry.

hogweed *see* GOLPAR

hoisin [HOY-sihn; hoy-SIHN] Also called *Peking sauce,* this thick, reddish-brown sauce is sweet and spicy, and widely used in Chinese cooking. It's a mixture of SOYBEANS, garlic, chile peppers and various spices. Hoisin is mainly used as a table condiment and as a flavoring agent for many meat, poultry and shellfish dishes. It can be found in Asian markets and many large supermarkets. Once opened, canned hoisin should be transferred to a nonmetal container, tightly sealed and refrigerated. Bottled hoisin can be refrigerated as is. Both will keep indefinitely when stored in this manner.

hoja santa [OH-hah SAHN-tah] *see* PEPPER LEAF

holishkes [hoh-LIHSH-kuhs] Originating in eastern Europe, this Jewish dish consists of cabbage leaves stuffed with a mixture of ground beef, onion, eggs and seasonings. The cabbage rolls are baked and served with a SWEET-AND-SOUR sauce. Holishkes are traditional at Sukkot, the fall harvest festival, where they're considered a symbol of plenty. They're also called *praches.*

hollandaise [HOL-uhn-dayz] This smooth, rich, creamy sauce is used to embellish vegetables, fish and egg dishes, such as the classic EGGS BENEDICT. It's made with butter, egg yolks and lemon juice, usually in a DOUBLE BOILER to prevent overheating. *See also* SAUCE.

Holsteiner Katenrauchschinken (PGI) [HOHL-sti-nehr KAT-en-shink-en] Ham from the Schleswig-Holstein region in northern Germany. It has PGI status, requiring that a raw, bone-in ham be salted by hand and cured for 3 to 8 weeks, then cold smoked using beech wood in traditional smokehouses (or modern smoking chambers) for several weeks. The resulting ham has bright-red flesh with slight marbling and a mild, sweet, nutty flavor. Ham products from members of the Schutzgemeinschaft Schleswig-Holsteinischer Schinkenhersteller e.V. (Association for the Protection of Ham-Producers in Schleswig-Holstein) may bear an emblem on them. Non-members may also produce and market Holsteiner Katenrauchschinken hams as long as they follow the specifications during production. *See also* HAM.

homard [oh-MAHR] French for "lobster."

home-fried potatoes; home fries Potatoes that are sliced and fried, often with finely chopped onions or green peppers. The potatoes can either be raw or boiled before slicing. Also called *cottage-fried potatoes*.

hom ha *see* SHRIMP SAUCE

hominy One of the first food gifts the American Indians gave to the colonists, hominy is dried white or yellow corn kernels from which the hull and germ have been removed. This process is done either mechanically or chemically by soaking the corn in slaked lime or lye. Hominy is sold canned, ready-to-eat or dried (which must be reconstituted before using). It's commonly served as a side dish or as part of a casserole. When dried hominy is broken or very coarsely ground it's called **samp**. When ground, it's called **hominy grits**—or simply *grits*—and usually comes in three grinds—fine, medium and coarse. Hominy grits are generally simmered with water or milk until very thick. The mixture can be served in this mushlike form or chilled, cut into squares and fried. In the South, grits are served as a side dish for breakfast or dinner.

homogenize [huh-MAHJ-uh-nize] To create an EMULSION by reducing all the particles to the same size. In homogenized milk, for instance, the fat globules are broken down mechanically until they are evenly and imperceptibly distributed throughout the liquid. Commercial salad dressings are also often homogenized.

hondroelia olive [HOHN-dray-lee-ah] Very large, oval-shaped, brine-cured olive from the town of Astros in southern Greece's Arcadian region. The name translates to "fat olives"—hondroelias can grow up to 2 inches in length and are very meaty with a mild, slightly bitter taste. They range in color from pale tan to greenish-brown. Hondroelias are rare and difficult to find, although some specialty markets do carry them and they're available on the Internet. *See also* OLIVE.

honey A thick, sweet liquid made by bees from flower nectar. Contrary to what many people think, a honey's color and flavor does not derive from the bee, but from the nectar's source. In general, the darker the color the stronger the flavor. There are hundreds of different honeys throughout the world, most of them named for the flower from which they originate. The flowers that produce some of America's most popular honeys are clover, orange blossom and sage. Other honeys, some of which are only available in limited quantities in the region from which they originate, come from the following blossoms: alfalfa, buckwheat, dandelion, heather, linden, raspberry, spearmint and thyme, just to name a few. When using honey in cooking, it's important to know its source—buckwheat honey, for example, has far too strong a flavor to be used in a recipe that calls for orange blossom honey, which has a light, delicate fragrance and flavor. Honey comes in three basic forms: **comb honey**, with the liquid still in the chewy comb, both of which are edible; **chunk-style honey**, which is honey with pieces of the honeycomb included in the jar; and regular **liquid honey** that has been extracted from the comb, much of which has been PASTEURIZED to help prevent crystallization. Other honey products such as **honey butters**, **honey spreads** and **whipped honey** are available at most supermarkets. Store tightly sealed liquid honey in a cool, dry place for up to a year; store comb and chunk honey for 6 months. When refrigerated, honey crystallizes, forming a gooey, grainy mass. It can easily be reliquefied by placing the opened jar either in a microwave oven at 100 percent power for about 30 seconds (depending on the amount), or in a pan of hot water over low heat for 10 to 15 minutes. Honey is widely used as a bread spread and as a sweetener and flavoring agent for baked goods, liquids (such as tea), desserts and in some cases savory dishes like honey-glazed ham or carrots.

honeyberry *see* MAMONCILLO

Honeycrisp apple Considered an all-purpose apple, the Honeycrisp is especially good for out-of-hand eating. It was created at the University of Minnesota in the 1960s by crossing the MACOUN APPLE and the Honey Gold apple. It's a large apple with a mottled red and yellow skin with a bit of green around the stem and a creamy white flesh. The Honeycrisp is quite crisp and juicy with well-balanced flavors. *See also* APPLE.

honeydew melon This sweet, succulent member of the muskmelon family (*see* MELON) was prized by ancient Egyptians thousands of years ago, and ages before that in Persia, where the muskmelon is thought to have originated. Luckily for American honeydew enthusiasts, the melons are now grown in California and parts of the Southwest. The slightly oval honeydew is distinguished by a smooth, creamy-yellow rind and flesh that's extraordinarily juicy and sweet. The common green honeydew has a pastel green flesh, the gold and orange varieties have flesh in those colors respectively. Honeydews range in weight from 4 to 8 pounds and are available May through September from Arizona, California and Texas, and the remainder of the year from Mexico. The gold and orange varieties are not as readily available and can sometimes only be found at specialty produce markets and farmers markets. Perfectly ripe honeydews will have an almost indistinguishable wrinkling on the skin's surface, often detectable only by touch. Choose one that's very heavy for its size. Underripe melons can be matured at room temperature. Wrap ripe melons in a plastic bag and refrigerate up to 5 days. Honeydew melons can be used in salads, desserts, as a garnish and in FRUIT SOUPS. They are a good source of vitamin C.

honeyware *see* ALARIA

Hong Kong milk tea A beverage made with black tea and SWEET-ENED CONDENSED MILK, EVAPORATED MILK and/or sugar. It originated in Hong Kong as a holdover of British colonial rule and the British practice of adding milk and sugar to tea during HIGH TEA. Its popularity has spread outside Hong Kong to other areas, especially in restaurants that serve Hong Kong-style cuisine. The key to good Hong Kong tea is said to be a strong black tea, achieved by simmering black tea leaves (sometimes a mix of various types) in hot water and then pouring this through a sackcloth bag. The tea is reheated and poured through the sackcloth several times to strengthen it. It is then combined with evaporated milk and sugar or sweetened condensed milk. The result is a flavorful, creamy beverage. There is even an annual international milk tea competition held in Hong Kong where competitors vie for the title "Milk Tea King."

honjozo [hohn-JOH-zoh] *see* SAKE

honshimeji; hon-shimeji mushroom [hohn-shee-MEH-jee] One of the members of the SHIMEJI family of mushrooms, considered by the Japanese to be the "true shimeji" and therefore highly prized and expensive. Other mushrooms such as the BEECH MUSHROOM and the PIOPPINI have been referred to as honshimeji in the past but analysis has indicated they are different species. Honshimeji's scientific classification is *Lyophyllum shimeji*. The honshimeji mushroom grows in clusters of dense, thick, off-white stems with tan caps. The texture is crisp and crunchy with juicy flesh that delivers nutty UMAMI flavors. *See also* MUSHROOM.

hooch; hootch Liquor that's either illegally produced (*bootleg*) or just plain cheap. The word hooch is generally associated with whiskey produced during Prohibition (1920–1933); however, the name originated in the late 1800s with a tribe of Alaskan Indians. It comes from *Hoochinoo* (*Hootchinoo*), a Tlingit Indian village on Admiralty Island, Alaska, the inhabitants of which made and sold alcoholic spirits illegally.

Hopfenkäse [HOH-pfern-ke*r*-zer] A HOP-flavored CHEESE made from sour cow's milk. It comes from northwest Germany in the same area famous for WESTPHALIAN HAM. The texture of Hopfenkäse ranges from soft to medium firm. It gains its pleasantly bitter flavor as it dries between layers of hops; it's sometimes flavored with caraway seeds or cumin. Hopfenkäse is a natural companion to full-bodied beer. *Nieheimer* is a German cheese made in a fashion similar to Hopfenkäse, and has a comparable flavor.

hoppin' John; hopping John Said to have originated with African slaves on Southern plantations, hoppin' John is a dish of BLACK-EYED PEAS cooked with SALT PORK and seasonings and served with cooked rice. Tradition says that if hoppin' John is eaten on New Year's day, it will bring good luck.

hops A hardy, vining plant that produces conelike flowers. The dried flowers are used to impart a pleasantly bitter flavor to BEER and ALE. This same plant produces **hop shoots**, which are available commercially in Europe and can be cooked like asparagus.

hop shoots *see* HOPS

horchata [hor-CHAH-tah] Extremely popular in Spain and Mexico, horchatas are drinks made by steeping nuts, grains or CHUFA in water. They're usually lightly sweetened with sugar and sometimes spiced with cinnamon. Horchatas are generally served cold or at room temperature. They come in a wide variety of flavors. *Horchata de arroz* is made with rice, *horchata de almendras* with almonds, and the famous *horchata de chufa* is, of course, made with chufa. Horchatas may be purchased in Latin markets.

horehound A member of the mint family, this downy-leaved plant yields a juice that, culinarily, is generally only used to make horehound candy—a brittle, sugar-drop confection with a slightly bitter undertaste. Extract of horehound is also used to make cough syrup and lozenges.

horned melon *see* KIWANO

horn of plenty mushroom *see* TROMPETTE DE LA MORT

hors d'oeuvre [or DERV] Small savory appetizers served before the meal, customarily with APÉRITIFS or COCKTAILS. They are usually one- or two-bite size and can be cold or hot. Hors d'oeuvre may be in the form of a fancy CANAPÉ or as simple as a selection of CRUDITÉS. The word "hors d'oeuvre" is properly used for both the singular and plural forms. The reason is that the term translates literally as (dishes) "outside the work (meal)" and no matter how many dishes there are, there is only one "work." In today's modern parlance, however, the plural is often spoken and written as *hors d'oeuvres*.

horse bean *see* FAVA BEAN

horse mackerel *see* JACK

horsemint *see* BEE BALM

horseradish This ancient herb (one of the five bitter herbs of the Jewish Passover festival) is a native of eastern Europe but now grows in other parts of Europe as well as the United States. Though it has spiky green leaves that can be used in salads, horseradish is grown mainly for its large, white, pungently spicy roots. Fresh horseradish is available in many supermarkets. Choose roots that are firm with no sign of blemishes or withering. Horseradish should be refrigerated, wrapped in a plastic bag, and peeled before using. It's most often grated and used in sauces or as a condiment with fish or meat. Bottled horseradish is available white (preserved in vinegar), and red (in beet juice). Also available is dried horseradish, which must be reconstituted before using. *See also* WASABI.

hosomaki [hoh-soh-MAH-kee] *see* SUSHI

hot-and-sour A Chinese term for dishes served with a spicy sauce made with CHILES, CHILI OIL, SESAME OIL, garlic, scallions and ginger.

hotatagai *see* SUSHI

hot black bean sauce *see* BEAN SAUCES; BEAN PASTES

hotcake *see* PANCAKE

hotchpotch [HAHCH-pahch] Each country has its own version of this rich, layered, vegetable-and-meat stew. Scots usually add barley and the meat is mutton or beef or sometimes grouse and rabbit. The English call it **hot pot** and their famous **Lancashire hot pot** contains mutton, sheep's kidneys and, when available, oysters, all covered with a layer of potatoes. The Dutch **hutspot** uses beef, whereas in France and Belgium the dish is referred to as **hochepot** and the ingredients include pig's ears and feet.

hot cross buns Traditionally served on Good Friday, these small, lightly sweet yeast buns contain raisins or currants and sometimes chopped candied fruit. A cross is slashed in the top of the unbaked bun; after baking, the cross is filled with powdered sugar icing.

hot dog The term for one of America's favorite sandwiches (the other being the HAMBURGER), which consists of a FRANKFURTER in an oblong-shaped bun with any of various toppings including mustard, ketchup, pickle relish, cheese, sauerkraut and beans. Regular hot dogs are about 6 inches long, while they are also available in foot-long versions. Among the many aliases for hot dogs are *wiener dog, frankfurter, frank* and *tube steak*. *See also* CORN DOG; PIGS IN BLANKETS.

hot mint *see* VIETNAMESE MINT

hot pepper *see* CHILE

hot pot *see* HOTCHPOTCH

hotteok *see* HODDEOK

house In the world of food and drink, the word "house" refers to the restaurant or establishment at hand. For example: 1. **House wine** is one featured by a restaurant or bar and often served in a CARAFE or by the glass. Sometimes, a winery does a special bottling and labels the wines for an establishment. House wines are usually inexpensive wines that offer the diner an economical option to the more pricey, better-known selections on the wine list. Ask the server what the house wine is—he or she should be able to tell you the variety (CHARDONNAY, MERLOT, and so on), brand name and VINTAGE (if any). 2. **House dressing** is generally a salad dressing created by that restaurant's chef. 3. **House brand** typically refers to a liquor (usually inexpensive) that a bar uses for drinks unless a specific brand is requested. 4. **On the house** refers to an item given to the customer for free.

HPLC *see* GILLETT METHOD

huaje [WAH-hee] *see* GUAJE

huarache [WAHR-ah-chee] Because of its similar oblong shape, the huarache is named after the famous woven-leather sandal. This traditional Mexican dish is composed of a thick tortilla-like base made from fried masa, which is topped with FRIJOLES REFRITOS or black beans and variously with bacon, beef, cheese, chicken, CHORIZO, onion, pork, SALSA, and shredded lettuce. The huarache is similar to a SOPE except the huarache is oblong in shape and usually larger.

hubbard squash A very large winter squash with a thick, bumpy, hard shell ranging in color from dark green to bright orange. Hubbards are available from early September to March, either whole or, if extraordinarily large, cut into pieces. Look for those with clean-colored rinds free from blemishes. Store unwrapped in a cool (under 50°F) place (or in the refrigerator) up to 6 months. Hubbard squash is best boiled or baked. Because of its rather grainy texture, the yellow-orange flesh is often mashed or puréed with butter and seasonings before serving. Hubbard squash is an excellent source of vitamin A and contains a fair amount of iron and riboflavin. *See also* SQUASH.

huckleberry A wild, blue-black berry that closely resembles (and is often mistaken for) the BLUEBERRY. The huckleberry, however, has 10 small, hard seeds in the center, whereas the blueberry has many seeds, so tiny and soft that they're barely noticeable. Additionally, the huckleberry has a thicker skin and a flavor that is slightly less sweet and more astringent. Unless you pick them yourself, or have a friend who does, it's unlikely that you'll find fresh huckleberries because they're not cultivated. They're in season from June through August and are good eaten plain or in baked goods such as muffins or pies.

huckleberry potatoes *see* ROUND WHITE POTATOES

huevo [WAY-voh; *Sp*. WEH-voh] Spanish for "egg." *Huevos duros* are "hard-boiled eggs," *huevos pasados por agua* are "soft-boiled eggs," *huevos escalfados* are "poached eggs," *huevos fritos* are "fried eggs" and *huevos revueltos* are "scrambled eggs."

huevos rancheros [WAY-vohs rahn-CHEH-rohs] Spanish for "rancher's eggs," although the more common translation is "country" or "country-style" eggs. Huevos rancheros consists of fried corn TORTILLAS topped with fried eggs and then a layer of SALSA.

huile [WEEL] French for "oil," generally referring to cooking oil. *Huile d'olive* is "olive oil," *huile de noix* is "walnut oil."

huitlacoche [wheet-lah-KOH-chay] *see* CUITLACOCHE

hull *n*. 1. The outer (usually fibrous) covering of a fruit or seed—also called *husk* or *shell*. 2. The attached, leafy calyx of some fruits, such as the strawberry. **hull** *v*. To prepare a food for eating by removing the outer covering or, as in the case of strawberries, the leafy portion at the top. *See also* SCHUCK.

humble pie A 17th century English dish, in which the heart, liver, kidney and other innards of a deer were combined with apples, currants, sugar and spices and baked as a pie. The servants ate this inexpensive but filling repast while the gentry dined on the VENISON. The name comes from the old-English word *numble*, meaning a deer's innards. "A numble pie" became "an umble pie," which eventually worked its way to "a humble pie."

hummus [HOOM-uhs] This thick Middle Eastern sauce is made from mashed CHICKPEAS seasoned with lemon juice, garlic and olive or sesame oil. It's usually served as a dip with pieces of PITA, or as a sauce. When TAHINI (sesame-seed paste) is added, it becomes hummus bi tahina. Middle Eastern markets carry both forms in cans or jars or sometimes fresh.

Hunan cuisine [HOO-nahn] *see* CHINESE CUISINE

hundred-year egg Also called *century egg, thousand-year egg* and *Ming Dynasty egg*, all of which are eggs that have been preserved by being covered with a coating of lime, ashes and salt before being shallowly buried for 100 days. The lime "petrifies" the egg, making it look like it's been buried for at least a century. The black outer coating and shell are removed to reveal a firm, amber-colored white and creamy, dark green yolk. The flavor is pungent and cheeselike. Eggs from chickens are generally used, though duck and goose eggs are also preserved in this manner. Hundred-year eggs are sold individually and can be found in Chinese markets. They will keep at room temperature (under 70°F) for up to 2 weeks or in the refrigerator up to a month. These preserved eggs are usually eaten uncooked, either for breakfast or served as an appetizer, often with accompaniments such as SOY SAUCE or minced ginger.

Hungarian cherry pepper *see* CHERRY PEPPER

Hungarian wax chile A large (3 to 5 inches long and up to 1½ inches in diameter) yellow CHILE that ranges in flavor from mild to hot. Its SCOVILLE SCALE rating ranges from 5,000 to 15,000. Hungarian wax chiles, which have a distinctly waxy flavor, are also called *banana chiles*.

hushpuppy; hush puppy This Southern specialty is a small cornmeal bread, flavored with chopped scallions, deep-fried and served hot. Hushpuppies are a traditional accompaniment for fried catfish. Their name is said to have come from the fact that, to keep hungry dogs from begging for food while the rest of the dinner was being prepared, cooks used to toss scraps of the fried batter to the pets with the admonition, "Hush, puppy!"

husk *see* HULL

hu tieu [hoo TYOO] *see* RICE NOODLES

hutspot *see* HOTCHPOTCH

hydrated lime *see* PICKLING LIME

hydrogenated oil *see* FATS AND OILS; TRANS FATTY ACIDS

hydrolyzed plant protein; hydrolyzed vegetable protein A protein obtained from various foods (like SOYBEANS, corn or wheat), then broken down into amino acids by a chemical process called acid hydrolysis. Hydrolyzed plant or vegetable protein is used as a flavor enhancer in numerous processed foods like soups, chilis, sauces, stews and some meat products like frankfurters. *See also* VEGETABLE PROTEIN.

hydromel [HI-druh-mehl] *see* MEAD

hydroponics [hi-druh-PON-iks] Dating back to the 1930s, hydroponics is the science of growing plants in a liquid nutrient solution rather than in soil. The plants are supported in a sterile, inert medium, such as gravel or peat, and regularly flooded with a nutrient-rich solution, which is drained off and reused until it is no longer beneficial. The air and light in a hydroponic enclosure is strictly controlled to insure optimal production. Increased yields are further insured because hydroponically grown vegetables can be planted much closer together than those in the field. Yet another bonus is that hydroponic farmers are not besieged by weeds and pests, which means their crops are pesticide free. With the science of hydroponics, plants can be grown in areas where the climate is inhospitable or the soil is unsuitable. This means that perfect tomatoes can be grown in the desert or in the middle of winter. *See also* AQUACULTURE.

Hypsizygus tessellatus *see* BEECH MUSHROOM

hyssop [HIHS-up] Any of various herbs belonging to the mint family with aromatic, dark green leaves that have a slightly bitter, minty flavor. Hyssop adds intrigue to salads, fruit dishes (it particularly complements cranberries), soups and stews. It's also used to flavor certain LIQUEURS, such as CHARTREUSE.

i'ausi *see* PACIFIC THREADFIN

Ibérico cheese [ee-BHAY-ree-koh] This Spanish cheese is made with a blend of cow's, goat's, and sheep's milk with not less than 25 percent or more than 40 percent of any one milk. It comes in 2½- to 7-pound wheels with hard, dark yellow-brown rinds that show the imprint of the crosshatch molds used to drain the cheeses. The molds, though typically made of plastic today, are patterned to replicate the fiber (*esparto*) molds of old. Ibérico cheese may be RIPENED anywhere from 2 weeks to 6 months. Of course, the younger the cheese, the softer the texture. Its flavor is rich, buttery, nutty and slightly tangy. This cheese is also called *Queso Ibérico.* Ibérico contains a minimum of 54 percent fat.

Ibérico ham; Iberian ham [ee-BHAY-ree-koh] The highest quality dry-cured ham produced in Spain, where it's known as *Jamón Ibérico.* It's taken from the hind leg of Spanish Ibérico pigs. These pigs, which are raised solely in the southwest of the Iberian Peninsula, are considered to be of higher quality than the white pigs used to produce Spain's SERRANO HAM. **Ibérico ham** comes in three grades that relate to how the pigs are fed. The highest quality hams are called *Jamón Ibérico de Bellota* or *Jamón Ibérico de Montanera,* and are produced from free-range pigs that feed for 6 months (a period called the *montanera*) on whatever's in the pastures, particularly acorns. During the last few months before slaughter the pig's diet consists solely of acorns. The middle quality level is *Jamón Ibérico de Recebo*—pigs that spend time in the pasture and then are fed a mixed diet of grains and acorns. The final quality level is called simply *Jamón Ibérico* or *Jamón de Pata Negra*, the latter meaning "black leg" and referring to the fact that most of the Ibérico pigs are black. The pigs of this last grade are fed with an authorized diet of grains but no acorns. Aging for Ibérico ham varies from 1 to 3 years or more. Production is very limited, which means these hams are some of the most expensive in the world.

Ibores [ee-BOHR-ays] *see* QUESO IBORES

ibrik *see* TURKISH COFFEE

ice *n.* Called *granité* in France and *granita* in Italy, an ice is a frozen mixture of water, sugar and liquid flavoring such as fruit juice, wine or coffee. The proportion is usually 4 parts liquid to 1 part sugar. During the freezing process, ices are generally stirred frequently to produce a slightly granular final texture. **ice** *v.* 1. To chill a food, glass or serving dish in order to get it icy cold and sometimes coated with frost. 2. To spread frosting over the surface of a cake.

ice, dry *see* DRY ICE

ice beer *see* BEER

iceberg lettuce *see* CRISPHEAD LETTUCE

icebox cookie *see* REFRIGERATOR COOKIE

ice cream America's favorite dessert is thought to have originated in the mountains of ancient China, with snow probably used as the base. Today's ice cream is made with a combination of milk products (usually cream combined with fresh, condensed or dry milk), a sweetening agent (sugar, honey, corn syrup or artificial sweetener) and sometimes solid additions such as pieces of chocolate, nuts, fruit and so on. According to FDA regulations, ice creams with solid additions must contain a minimum of 8 percent milk fat, while plain ice creams must have at least 10 percent milk fat. **French ice cream** has a cooked egg-custard base. **Ice milk** is made in much the same way as ice cream, except for the fact that it contains less milk fat and milk solids. The result, other than a lowered calorie count, is a lighter, less creamy texture. Commercial ice creams usually contain stabilizers to improve both texture and body, and to help make them melt resistant. Many also contain artificial coloring. Those made with natural flavorings (for instance, chocolate) will be labeled simply "Chocolate Ice Cream." If the majority of the flavoring is natural with a boost from an artificial-flavor source, the label will read "Chocolate-Flavored Ice Cream"; if over 50 percent of the flavoring is artificial it will read "Artificial Chocolate Ice Cream." All commercial ice creams have "overrun," a term applied to the amount of air they contain. The percentage of overrun ranges from 0 (no air) to 200, a theoretical figure that would be all air. The legal overrun limit for ice cream is 100 percent, which would amount to half air. Ice cream needs some air or it would be rock-hard. But one with 100 percent overrun would have so little body that it would feel mushy in the mouth; it would also melt extremely fast. An ice cream with the more desirable proportion of 20 to 50 percent overrun (10 to 25 percent air) would be denser, creamier and eminently more satisfying. Since the overrun is not listed on the package, the only way to be absolutely sure is to weigh the carton. Ice cream with a 50 percent overrun (25 percent air) will weigh about 18 ounces per pint (subtract about $1\frac{1}{2}$ ounces for the weight of the container). The weight of the ice cream will be proportionately higher with a lower percentage of overrun. During storage, ice cream has a tendency to absorb other food odors and to form ice crystals. For that reason, it's best not to freeze it for more than 2 to 3 days. Sealing the carton airtight in a plastic bag will extend storage life up to a week. Ice cream is used for a plethora of delicious treats including BAKED ALASKAS, BANANA SPLITS and ice-cream bars, sandwiches and cakes (cake layered with ice cream and frozen). *See also* GELATO; GRANITA; ICE; PHILADELPHIA-STYLE ICE CREAM; SHERBET; SORBET.

ice-cream makers (freezers) Generally speaking, there are two basic styles of ice-cream maker—manual and electric. They can be simple or fancy and can cost from $25 to almost $1,000. In addition to ice cream, they can be used to make ice milk, frozen yogurt and frozen drinks. All of them work on the same principle—a canister with a central, vertical paddle (called a dasher) is placed inside a container that holds the freezing agent—either ice and salt, a chemical coolant or an electric refrigeration unit. The inner canister is filled with an ice-cream mixture that the dasher stirs (gently scraping the sides of the canister) when rotated. This stirring action aerates the mixture and keeps it smooth by preventing ice crystals from forming while it freezes. There are several different kinds of ice-cream freezers. Among the **manual-style ice-cream makers** are the old-fashioned, wooden buckets with a metal inner container for the ice-cream mixture. They require ice, rock SALT (which lowers the temperature of the ice) and plenty of physical stamina to turn the crank that rotates the dasher. They usually take 30 to 40 minutes to make 4 to 6 quarts of ice cream. Some of these wooden bucket-style makers have an electric motor that sits on top of the unit, saving manpower. A newer form of manual ice-cream maker is the *prechilled chamber freezer,* which ranges in size from 1 pint to 1½ quarts. The container is placed in the freezer for 24 to 48 hours to freeze the coolant sealed between the walls lining this unit. The ice-cream mixture is poured into the center cavity; a crank-and-dasher assembly and lid covers the entire unit. The hand-rotated crank is turned once every 2 to 3 minutes for 15 to 30 minutes, depending on the amount of ice cream being made. **Electric ice-cream machines** are all equipped with electric motors that rotate either the ice-cream canister or the dasher. There are several different styles and sizes of electric ice-cream machines. The most common is the *self-contained countertop unit* that uses refrigerator ice cubes and table salt, and in which the motor turns the canister. This type can make up to 2 quarts of ice cream. There is also a *small freezer unit* (averaging 1 quart) that doesn't require salt or ice but instead is placed in the freezer compartment of the refrigerator with the electric cord exiting between the freezer's seal and the closed door. In this type, the dasher is motor-turned, while the canister is stationary. The Rolls-Royce of electric ice-cream freezers is the large, *self-contained countertop machine* that has the freezing unit built into it. All that's required for this expensive pleaser is to pour the ice-cream mixture into the canister and flick a button.

ice-cream scoop A utensil used to remove ice cream from a carton or other container while forming the ice cream into a ball or oval shape. Ice-cream scoops come in several styles and sizes. The simplest is a plain metal scoop- or spade-shaped utensil. Next comes one shaped like a half-globe or oval with a spring-action lever in the handle. When squeezed, the lever moves an arc-shaped blade across the scoop's interior and ejects the ice-cream ball. The nonstick-style scoop has antifreeze sealed inside. This model is especially helpful for extremely hard ice cream. Scoops come in many sizes, from tiny to large (about 1 to almost 3 inches in diameter).

ice milk *see* ICE CREAM

ice wine A rich, flavorful DESSERT WINE, which is made by picking grapes that are frozen on the vine, then pressing them before they thaw. Because much of the water in the grapes is frozen, the resulting juice is concentrated—rich in flavor and high in sugar and acid. Ice wines are renowned in Germany, where they're called *Eiswein* (pronounced ICE-vine).

ichimi [ee-CHEE-mee] *see* TOGARASHI

icing *see* FROSTING

icing sugar British for POWDERED SUGAR.

Ida Red An all-purpose apple that's a cross between the Jonathan and the Wagener. Somewhat larger than the Jonathan, the Ida Red, also spelled **Idared**, displays a bright red skin with a firm, creamy-white flesh and exhibits a crisp, tart flavor. It's good as a snack and very popular for baking. The Ida Red was developed in the 1940s the by University of Idaho Agricultural Experiment Station. *See also* APPLE.

iddenlu *see* IDLI

iddly *see* IDLI

idli *pl.* **idlis** [IHD-lee] Small, savory disc, 2 to 3 inches in diameter, made with a fermented batter of rice and black lentils placed in a special idli steamer and then steamed. The **idli steamer** consists of a series of platters with perforated indentations that sit on a center pole one on top of another. The pole and the platters are placed inside a pot with a small amount of boiling water and allowed to steam. Also known as *idly, iddly* and *iddenlu,* these soft, fluffy cakes or dumplings are popular in southern India and served at breakfast and as a snack. They're served with SAMBAR and various accompaniments such as CHUTNEY or sesame oil and ground spices.

IGP *see* PROTECTED GEOGRAPHICAL INDICATION

ika [ee-kah] Japanese for "squid."

ikura [EE-koo-rah] Salmon roe. Ikura is used as a topping for SUSHI.

île flottante [eel floh-TAHNT] *see* FLOATING ISLANDS

imitation cheese Essentially a PROCESSED CHEESE with the butterfat replaced by nonfat milk, vegetable oil or WHEY solids mixed with water. Such products typically have a rubbery texture and lackluster flavor. Looking for a plus side? They have a long shelf life and often require no refrigeration. *See also* SUBSTITUTE CHEESE.

immersion blender This handheld BLENDER is tall, narrow and has a rotary blade at one end. It has variable speeds, is entirely portable and may be immersed right into a pot of soup (or other mixture) to purée or chop the contents. Many immersion blenders come with a whisk attachment (good for whipping cream), and other accoutrements such as strainers or beakers for mixing individual drinks. Some also come with wall mounts.

impératrice, à l' *see* RIZ À L'IMPÉRATRICE

Imperial *see* WINE BOTTLES

incomplete protein *see* COMPLETE PROTEIN

Indian bay leaf Leaf from the plant *Cinnamomum tamam* (or *Indian cinnamon tree*)that's quite different from the BAY LEAF of the bay laurel tree common in Mediterranean countries and California. Indian bay leaves, also known as *cassia leaves, cinnamon leaves, Malabathrum, Malobathrum, Malabar leaf tejpat* and *tej patta*, are longer and wider and have the aroma of CINNAMON and CLOVES, whereas the bay laurel leaves are herbal in nature. The Indian bay leaves are extremely popular in northern India, southern Nepal and Bhutan, particularly for making the spicy, aromatic MOGHUL CUISINE. They can be found in Indian markets. *See also* HERBS; Seasoning Suggestions, page 891.

Indian bread *see* BANNOCK

Indian date *see* TAMARIND

Indian lettuce *see* MINERS' LETTUCE

Indian nut *see* PINE NUT

Indian pudding This hearty, old-fashioned dessert originated in New England. It's a spicy, cornmeal-molasses baked pudding that can sometimes include sliced apples. Indian pudding is usually served with whipped cream, HARD SAUCE or ice cream.

Indian rice Another name for WILD RICE.

Indian River oyster *see* ATLANTIC OYSTER

India pale ale *see* ALE

indienne, à l' [ah lahn-DYEHN] A French term describing Indian-style dishes flavored with curry and served with rice.

Indonesian bay leaf Leaf from the plant *Syzygium polyanthum* that's quite different from the BAY LEAF of the bay laurel tree common in Mediterranean countries and California. The Indonesian bay leaf is also known as *salam leaf* and *daun salam leaf*. This small leaf is sometimes mistakenly called INDIAN BAY LEAF, which is longer and wider and has a different aroma and flavor profile. The Indonesian bay leaf is lightly aromatic and slightly sour. It's not readily available and can only be found in markets serving Indonesian populations. *See also* HERBS; Seasoning Suggestions, page 891.

induction cooking A technology whereby cookware is heated using magnetic energy. It requires a special smooth ceramic cooktop with induction energy coils directly beneath the surface. These coils produce high-frequency alternating current from regular low-voltage direct current. When cookware made of a magnetic-based material is placed on this special stovetop, the molecules in the vessel begin to move so rapidly that the pan (not the stovetop) becomes hot. Removing the pan from the cooking surface produces an immediate slowdown of the gyrating molecules, which means the pan begins to cool. This gives a cook immense control over what's being heated. Although most steel- and cast-iron-based vessels work well, those made of aluminum, copper and some stainless steel can't be used on an induction cooktop because they aren't magnetic. Special pans designed for induction cooking are available but, before making a purchase, first try a simple test on your cookware: if a magnet sticks to its surface, the pan is suitable. In addition to an induction stovetop's obvious advantages of heat control, safety, and energy efficiency, its smooth surface makes it a snap to clean.

Infinity chilli *see* SCOVILLE SCALE

infuser *see* TEA INFUSER

infusion [ihn-FYOO-zhuhn] An infusion is the flavor that's extracted from an ingredient such as tea leaves, herbs or fruit by STEEPING them in a liquid (usually hot), such as water, for tea. In today's culinary parlance, sauces that have been variously flavored (as with herbs) are also called infusions.

injera [ihn-JEER-ah] Soft, spongy Ethiopian flatbread similar to PITA. It's traditionally made with the local grain staple, TEFF, and yeast and is allowed to ferment like a SOURDOUGH STARTER, giving it a slightly sour taste. Only one side is cooked on a griddle, allowing the other side to remain porous. Injera are used to line plates upon which stew is served. The exposed pieces of injera are broken off and used to eat the stew while the porous pieces at the bottom soak up the flavors of the stew and are eaten at the end.

insalata [ihn-sah-LAH-tah; een-sah-LAH-tah] Italian for "salad." *Insalata mista* is a "mixed salad," *insalata verde* is a salad of tossed greens and *insalata della casa* is a "house salad."

insalata caprese [ihn-(een-)sah-LAH-tah kah-PRAY-say] *see* CAPRESE SALAD

instant cocoa *see* COCOA MIX

instant flour *see* FLOUR

instant-read thermometer *see* MEAT THERMOMETER

invert sugar Invert sugar is created by combining a SUGAR SYRUP with a small amount of acid (such as CREAM OF TARTAR or lemon juice) and heating. This inverts, or breaks down, the SUCROSE into its two components, GLUCOSE and FRUCTOSE, thereby reducing the size of the sugar crystals. Because of its fine crystal structure, invert sugar produces a smoother product and is used in making candies such as fondant, and some syrups. The process of making jams and jellies automatically produces invert sugar by combining the natural acid in the fruit with granulated sugar and heating the mixture. Invert sugar can usually be found in jars in cake-decorating supply shops.

involtino; pl. involtini [een-vohl-TEE-noh (nee)] A thin slice of meat, fish or vegetable wrapped around a filling, then typically sautéed before being braised. It's the Italian ROULADE. *See also* BRACIOLA.

Ipswich clam East Coast soft-shell clam named after the town of Ipswich located north of Boston. Although Ipswich-style clams are found from Nova Scotia to Maryland, many think the best ones still come from the mudflats in the area around Ipswich and that they should be the only ones to use the name. The clams range from almost black to light gray and have a sweet, briny flavor. They're delicious steamed but also suitable for batter-dipping and frying. *See also* CLAM.

iriko [ee-REE-koh] *see* SEA CUCUMBER

Irish breakfast tea A strong, robust black-tea blend that includes the superior CEYLON TEA. *See also* TEA.

Irish coffee Guaranteed to warm the cockles of anyone's heart, this hot beverage blends strong coffee, IRISH WHISKEY and a small amount of sugar. It's usually served in a glass mug and topped by a dollop of whipped cream. *See also* COFFEE.

Irish cream liqueurs A genre of LIQUEURS that can range in texture from creamy to milky, in color from beige to pale brown, and in flavor from spiced toffee to honeyed chocolate. Among the more popular Irish cream liqueurs are Bailey's (the original), Carolans, O'Casey's, and St. Brendan's. There are also some "light" Irish creams, all with about 2 percent less alcohol, slightly fewer calories and a lighter texture than the regular version.

Irish mist A LIQUEUR made from a blend of IRISH WHISKEY and heather honey.

Irish moss *see* CARRAGEEN

Irish oatmeal *see* OATS

Irish potato A round, white, thin-skinned potato whose origin is actually South America. It's good for boiling, frying and pan-roasting. *See also* POTATO.

Irish soda bread This classic Irish QUICK BREAD uses baking soda (as the name implies) as its LEAVENER. It's usually made with buttermilk and is speckled with currants and sometimes caraway seed. Before baking, a cross is slashed in the top of the loaf. The purpose of the cross, legend says, is to scare away the devil.

I

Irish stew A traditional layered dish of equal parts seasoned lamb or mutton chops, potatoes and onions. Water or stock is poured over all, the pot is covered tightly and the stew is cooked slowly for 2 to 3 hours. It's best made the day before to allow the flavors to blend.

Irish whiskey A distilled (*see* DISTILLATION) liquor made primarily from barley (malted or unmalted) as well as corn, rye, wheat and oats. Irish whiskeys are triple-distilled for extra smoothness and are AGED in casks for a minimum of 4 (usually 7 to 8) years. The aging casks have typically been used previously for aging bourbon, sherry or rum, the flavors of which contribute unique nuances to the whiskey.

ironing cheese A method used by some cheesemakers to examine the aroma, flavor and texture of a RIPENING cheese. A small metal corer known as a cheese iron is inserted into the interior to obtain a plug of cheese. After the cheese is examined, the plug is replaced and the hole covered with a bit of cheese. Mold occasionally grows around the hole but often the rind just grows over it, hiding the slight imperfection. Nonetheless, many cheesemakers consider this technique a desecration of the cheese.

ironware *see* COOKWARE AND BAKEWARE MATERIALS

irradiation An FDA-approved process by which food is bombarded with low doses of high-frequency energy from gamma rays, X–rays or accelerated electrons. The purpose for this radiation is to extend shelf life by inhibiting maturation and decay through the elimination of micro-organisms and insect invasion. Most foods processed with irradiation will last weeks instead of days. All irradiated foods must bear an international symbol—a plant within a broken circle. Exceptions to this rule are irradiated foods—such as spices and herbs—that are used as an ingredient in other food products. The jury is still out on the safety of irradiated foods. Of concern are potentially toxic elements that irradiation may produce in foods, as well as the possible long-term side effects of eating these treated products. Proponents suggest that irradiation serves as a substitute for many questionable chemicals and preservatives now used in food processing. Those foods currently approved by the FDA for irradiation treatment are: fruits, vegetables, dried spices, herbs, seasonings and teas, pork, white potatoes, wheat and wheat flours. Most food producers, however, have not taken advantage of that approval.

isinglass [I-zuhn-glas; I-zing-glas] Transparent and pure, this form of GELATIN comes from the air bladders of certain fish, especially the STURGEON. It was popular 100 years ago, particularly for making jellies and to CLARIFY wine. With the convenience of today's modern gelatin, isinglass is rarely used.

isomalt [I-soh-mahlt] A sugar substitute that's a sugar alcohol derived from beet sugar. Isomalt is about 40 percent as sweet as sucrose and has half the calories. It's often combined with non-sugar sweeteners like SUCRALOSE to boost its sweetness level. Because of its resistance to crystallization and humidity, pure isomalt is welcomed by confectioners, pastry chefs and others who make sugar sculptures. Thanks to its resistance to humidity, isomalt is good for making hard candies that are less sticky and may have a better shelf life. It's used as a sugar substitute in some foods.

ita-kamaboko [EE-tah kah-mah-BOH-koh] *see* KAMABOKO

Italian bread Almost identical to FRENCH BREAD, with the exception of its shape, which is shorter and plumper than the French BAGUETTE. The top of Italian bread is sometimes sprinkled with sesame seed.

Italian broccoli *see* BROCCOLI RABE

Italian dandelion Although not a true DANDELION, this green looks almost identical to its namesake. The main difference is that the jagged-edged leaves are a deeper green and slightly larger. The Italian dandelion has a tangy, slightly bitter flavor. It can be cooked as well as used in salads. Refrigerate, tightly wrapped in a plastic bag, up to 5 days. Wash thoroughly just before using.

Italian dressing A salad dressing consisting of olive oil and wine vinegar or lemon juice, seasoned variously with ingredients including garlic, oregano, basil, dill and fennel.

Italian meringue A creamy MERINGUE made by slowly beating hot SUGAR SYRUP into stiffly beaten egg whites. Because the sugar syrup is cooked to the SOFT-BALL STAGE, the resulting meringue becomes very dense, glossy and smooth. The same method is used to make BOILED ICING. Italian meringue is used in soufflés, to frost cakes and pastries and to top pies (in the last case it's usually lightly browned in the oven before serving).

Italian parsley *see* PARSLEY

Italian sausage This favorite pizza topping is a coarse pork SAUSAGE, generally sold in plump links. Italian sausage is usually flavored with garlic and fennel seed or anise seed. It comes in two styles—**hot** (flavored with hot, red peppers) and **sweet** (without the added heat). It must be well cooked before serving.

iwashi [ee-WAH-shee] Japanese for "sardine." The Japanese use them in DANGO, TEMPURA and SHIOYAKI dishes and, more recently in SASHIMI and SUSHI dishes.

izakaya [ee-ZAH-kaI-ah] Japanese bar that also serves food. It's similar in nature to an English tavern except that izakaya quite often serve small plates of food in what many consider a TAPAS style.

Izarra [ih-ZAHR-ruh] An herb-flavored LIQUEUR based on ARMAGNAC, Izarra is available in yellow and green varieties, the latter being the stronger of the two.

jack A fish family of over 200 species, including POMPANO, AMBERJACK, *bar jack*, *blue runner*, *crevalle jack*, *green jack*, *horse mackerel* (not a true MACKEREL), *rainbow runner*, *rudderfish*, *trevally*, *yellow jack* and YELLOWTAIL. Although some jack species aren't particularly good to eat, many—particularly pompano—are considered excellent and have a rich, firm, delicately flavored flesh. Jacks are found around the world in the Atlantic, Mediterranean and Pacific. *See also* FISH.

Jack cheese The origin of Jack cheese is most often attributed to David Jacks, a Monterey, California, businessman in the late 1800s. However, historical evidence shows that it actually was based on a recipe for *queso del país* ("country cheese"), brought to California by Franciscan monks in the 1700s. Nevertheless, we do know that David Jacks increased the popularity and demand for this cheese when he began shipping it to San Francisco and points beyond in the United States. The name **Monterey Jack** came about because production was initially centered in Monterey County, California. Eventually, other areas named the cheese for their region, as with **Sonoma Jack** (Sonoma County, California), and now this cheese is made in other parts of the United States. Jack can be made from raw or PASTEURIZED cow's milk. It comes in several styles—semisoft, semihard, hard and GRANA. Jacks typically have a thin rind, though some are rindless. The interior can range from pale yellow to deep golden, depending on the age. While the flavor of young Jacks is delicate, mild and fresh, aged versions (called **dry Jack**) are full-flavored, rich and almost sweet, with hints of fruit and caramel. Young Jack cheese is only RIPENED for a few weeks, while dry Jack is aged for 7 to 10 months or longer. The high-moisture regular Jack cheese comes plain or with added flavorings such as chiles, garlic, herbs, horseradish, chili peppers and onion. The FAT CONTENT for Jack cheese ranges from about 32 percent to more than 50 percent. *See also* CHEESE.

jackfruit This huge relative of the BREADFRUIT and fig can weigh up to 100 pounds, which is how it earned its reputation as the world's largest fruit. The tropical jackfruit grows in parts of Africa, Brazil and Southeast Asia. It has a pebbly skin and misshapen oblong shape. When green, jackfruit is used more like a vegetable and typically cooked—both its flesh and edible seeds are included in curried dishes. The skin of a ripe jackfruit takes on a yellow-brown color, and the yellow flesh is juicy and subtly sweet. The ripe fruit is typically consumed raw, either in salads, desserts or out of hand. In the United States, jackfruit is only available canned or dried.

jackrabbit *see* HARE

Jacob's cattle bean *see* ANASAZI BEAN

Jägermeister [YAH-ger-my-ster] A 70-PROOF, reddish-brown German LIQUEUR with an intensely bitter herb character, edged with cola and a touch of chocolate in the aftertaste. It's a complex blend of 56 different herbs plus fruits, spices, barks, resins and seeds. Serve Jägermeister (German for "hunt master") icy cold to help tame its assertive flavor.

jaggery [JAG-uh-ree] This dark, coarse, unrefined sugar (sometimes referred to as *palm sugar*) can be made either from the sap of various palm trees or from sugar-cane juice. It is primarily used in India, where many categorize sugar made from sugar cane as **jaggery** and that processed from palm trees as **gur**. It comes in several forms, the two most popular being a soft, honeybutter texture and a solid cakelike form. The former is used to spread on breads and confections, while the solid version serves to make candies, and when crushed, to sprinkle on cereal, and so on. Jaggery has a sweet, winey fragrance and flavor that lends distinction to whatever food it embellishes. It can be purchased in East Indian markets. *See also* SUGAR.

jagging wheel *see* PASTRY WHEEL

jalapeño chile [hah-lah-PEH-nyoh] Named after Jalapa, the capital of Veracruz, Mexico, these smooth, dark green (scarlet red when ripe) CHILES are hot, with a SCOVILLE SCALE rating ranging from 2,500 to 8,000. They have a rounded tip and are about 2 inches long and $3/4$ to 1 inch in diameter. Besides their flavor, jalapeños are quite popular because they're so easily seeded (the seeds and veins are extremely hot). They're available fresh and canned and are used in a variety of sauces, sometimes stuffed with cheese, fish or meat, and in a multitude of dishes. In their dried form, jalapeños are known as CHIPOTLES.

jalfrezi [jahl-FRAY-zee; JAHL-frah-zee] A curry dish developed during the time when the British ruled India, as a means of using up leftovers. The genesis of the name is unclear but one theory suggests that *jal* or *jahl* means "spicy hot" and *frezi* means "fry." Regardless, jalfrezi can certainly be a spicy hot STIR-FRY. It originally used leftover pieces of beef or fowl marinated in Indian spices and stir-fried with green peppers, onions, tomatoes and green chiles (which provide the heat). Today the dish is sometimes made using fresh ingredients (not leftovers) and some versions are meatless.

jalousie [JAL-uh-see; ZHAH-loo-zee; zhah-loo-ZEE] A small "cake" made with flaky pastry, filled with a layer of ALMOND PASTE topped with jam. A latticed pastry topping allows the colorful jam filling to show.

jam A thick mixture of fruit, sugar (and sometimes PECTIN) that is cooked until the pieces of fruit are very soft and almost formless. It is used as a bread spread, a filling for pastries and cookies and an ingredient for various desserts. *See also* CONSERVE; JELLY; PRESERVES.

Jamaica flower [juh-MAY-kuh] This member of the hibiscus family isn't officially a flower at all, but the flower's calyx, the portion that covers and protects the bloom before it opens. Dried Jamaica flowers are used to make beverages and produce a sour-sweet flavor and shimmering crimson color. One such drink is the Spanish favorite *agua de Jamaica*—a TISANE made with the flowers, water and sugar. The petals can be found in natural food stores (labeled "Jamaica flowers," "hibiscus flowers" or "Roselle") and in Latin markets (as *flores de Jamaica* or simply *Jamaica*). When selecting flowers, look for those that are brightly colored—dull or dark flowers indicate age and less flavor. Store airtight in a cool, dry place for up to 1 year. Because the flowers have a high acid content, it's necessary to use a non-reactive container, such as glass or stainless steel, when adding them to a recipe.

Jamaican hot chile As the name indicates, this bright red CHILE is extremely hot. Its SCOVILLE SCALE rating ranges from 100,000 to 200,000. It's small (1 to 2 inches in diameter) and has a distorted, irregular shape. Jamaican hots are often used in curried dishes and condiments.

Jamaican jerk seasoning A dry seasoning blend that originated on the Caribbean island after which it's named, and which is used primarily in the preparation of grilled meat. The ingredients can vary, depending on the cook, but Jamaican jerk blend is generally a combination of chiles, thyme, spices (such as cinnamon, ginger, allspice and cloves), garlic and onions. Jerk seasoning can be either rubbed directly onto meat, or blended with a liquid to create a MARINADE. In the Caribbean, the most common meats seasoned in this fashion are pork and chicken. Such preparations are referred to as "jerk pork" and "jerk chicken."

Jamaica pepper *see* ALLSPICE

jambalaya [juhm-buh-LI-yah; jam-buh-LI-yah] One of CREOLE cookery's hallmarks, jambalaya is a versatile dish that combines cooked rice with a variety of ingredients including tomatoes, onion, green peppers and almost any kind of meat, poultry or shellfish. The dish varies widely from cook to cook. It's thought that the name derives from the French *jambon*, meaning "ham," the main ingredient in many of the first jambalayas.

jamberry *see* TOMATILLO

jambon [zhan-BAW*N*] French for "ham." *Jambon fumé* is smoked ham; *jambon cru* is raw ham.

jambon persillé [zham-BAWN pehr-see-YAY] A molded dish of strips or cubes of cooked ham and chopped parsley held together with a meat-wine gelatin. It is served chilled and, when cut into slices, resembles a colorful red-and-green mosaic.

jamón [jah-MOHN; khah-MOHN] Spanish for "ham." *Jamón Serrano* (*see* SERRANO HAM) and *Jamón Ibérico* (*see* IBERICO HAM) are the two most well-known Spanish hams.

jantaboon *see* RICE NOODLES

Japanese amberjack *see* YELLOWTAIL

Japanese artichoke *see* CROSNES

Japanese basil *see* SHISO

Japanese bunching onions *see* WELSH ONION

Japanese citron *see* YUZU

Japanese cucumber Resembling an English (hothouse) CUCUMBER, this vegetable is long and slender with a prickly skin distinguished by tiny white spines on a green background. Unlike the English cucumber, the Japanese variety has some seeds, though not as many as the common cucumber. Its flavor is mild and sweet. The Japanese cucumber, also called *kyuri,* is available in Asian markets and some specialty produce markets. Refrigerate, tightly wrapped, for up to 1 week. Use as you would the common cucumber.

Japanese gelatin *see* AGAR

Japanese horseradish *see* WASABI

Japanese king crab *see* CRAB

Japanese leek *see* WELSH ONION

Japanese medlar *see* LOQUAT

Japanese oyster *see* PACIFIC OYSTER

Japanese pear *see* ASIAN PEAR

Japanese plum *see* LOQUAT

Japanese radish *see* DAIKON

Japanese squash *see* RED KURI

Japanese turnip *see* SALAD TURNIP

Japanese vermicelli *see* HARUSAME

japchae [HAHP-chay] Korean STIR-FRY combing *dangmyeon,* which are VERMICELLI-style noodles made with white sweet potato starch (*see* CELLO-PHANE NOODLES), with vegetables such as carrots, green onion, green peppers, mushrooms and spinach. Thin slices of beef are sometimes added. It's served hot or cold.

jardinière, à la [jahr-duh-NIHR; zhahr-dee-NYEHR] The French term referring to a dish garnished with vegetables, which are served in individual groups arranged around the main dish.

Jarlsberg [YAHRLZ-berg] Hailing from Norway, Jarlsberg originated in the 1830s when Swiss cheesemakers taught some Norwegians how to make an EMMENTAL-style cheese. Though production dwindled over the years, this flavorful cheese was resurrected in the 1960s and today the immensely popular Jarlsberg is exported worldwide. This semihard PASTEURIZED cow's-milk cheese has a thin, hard rind that's pale yellow to yellow-brown in color; some Jarlsbergs are rindless. The ivory to yellow interior has a scattering of large, irregular EYES. It has a smooth, supple texture and a flavor that's buttery and slightly sweet and nutty. Regular Jarlsberg is generally RIPENED for about 6 months, though some are aged for 12 or more months. Jarlsberg has a FAT CONTENT of about 45 percent. There are also low-fat and smoked versions, the latter flavored with LIQUID SMOKE. *See also* CHEESE.

jasmine rice; jasmin rice An AROMATIC RICE from Thailand that has a flavor and fragrance comparable to the expensive BASMATI RICE from India, at a fraction of the cost. *See also* RICE.

javaher polow [jav-a-HEHRR po-LOW] Persian rice dish served at special occasions, especially weddings. The name means "jeweled rice" and refers to browning the rice until a golden crust is formed and incorporating gem-colored fruits and vegetables. Recipes usually call for BASMATI RICE, almonds, pistachios, orange peel, carrot and chopped dried fruit—especially BARBERRIES—but cherries, apricots, golden raisins, or cranberries may be used. SAFFRON and a Persian spice mixture called ADVIEH flavor the dish.

Java pepper *see* CUBEB

jee choy *see* LAVER

jell To congeal a food substance, often with the aid of GELATIN.

jelly 1. A clear, bright mixture made from fruit juice, sugar and sometimes PECTIN. The texture is tender but will be firm enough to hold its shape when turned out of its container. Jelly is used as a bread spread and as a filling for some cakes and cookies. 2. In Britain, jelly is the term used for gelatin dessert. *See also* CONSERVE; JAM; PRESERVES.

jelly bag Used to strain and CLARIFY the juice from fruit in order to prepare jelly. A jelly bag is made from a porous yet closely woven fabric like unbleached muslin. Jelly bags are hung over a bowl with the aid of loops at the top. The crushed fruit is placed in the bowl and left to drain for several hours, preferably overnight. Before use, the jelly bag is rinsed in water and wrung dry. This prevents too much juice from being absorbed into the fabric.

jelly bean This small, brightly colored, egg-shaped candy has a chewy, gelatinous texture and a hard candy coating. Jelly beans come in many flavors including lime, orange, licorice, cherry, chocolate, banana, etc. **Jelly Bellies** is a brand name that is now used generically to describe a miniature (about $1/2$-inch-long) jelly bean. They come in many more exotic flavors such as piña colada, pink lemonade, chocolate fudge-mint, etc.

jellyfish An invertebrate marine animal with a soft, gelatinous, umbrella-like anatomy and long, thin tentacles. Jellyfish is popular in CHINESE CUISINES. Asian markets sell it in a dried, salted form, which must be reconstituted by soaking overnight in warm water. The red matter must then be cut away. Jellyfish toughens if excessively cooked, so it's generally quickly blanched in boiling water for only about 15 seconds. It's customarily shredded and served cold in salads for a crunchy texture.

jelly melon *see* KIWANO

jelly roll Known since the mid-1800s, jelly rolls are cakes made of a thin sheet of SPONGE CAKE, spread with jam or jelly (and sometimes whipped cream or frosting) and rolled up. This type of cake is traditionally sprinkled with powdered sugar, rather than being frosted. When cut, jelly rolls have an attractive pinwheel design. The British term for jelly roll is *Swiss roll*.

jelly roll pan Also known as a *sheet pan,* this rectangular baking pan has about 1-inch-deep sides and is used to make SHEET CAKES or SPONGE CAKES used for JELLY ROLLS. Such pans are usually $15^{1}/2 \times 10^{1}/2 \times 1$ inch; however there is a smaller pan measuring $12 \times 7 \times 3/4$ inch and a larger one measuring $17 \times 11 \times 1$ inch.

jeon [jeon] Korean dishes with ingredients like meat, fish and vegetables that are thinly sliced, coated with flour, dipped in egg and pan-fried or coated with batter and fried like pancakes. They are served in a variety of ways—as appetizers, side dishes and main courses. **Pajeon** is a green onion pancake. **Saengseonjeon** are pan-fried fish fillets.

jeongol [jehn-gohl] Korean equivalent of Western "stew" that's similar to JJIGAE except jeongol is traditionally cooked and served at the table. **Soegogi-jeongol** is beef stew with vegetables.

jerk; jerk seasoning *see* JAMAICAN JERK SEASONING

jerky Also called *jerked meat*, jerky is meat (usually beef) that is cut into long, thin strips and dried (traditionally by the sun). Jerky was a popular staple with early trappers, just as it is with today's backpackers because it keeps almost indefinitely and is light and easy to transport. It's quite tough and salty but is very flavorful and high in protein. *See also* BILTONG.

Jeroboam [jehr-uh-BOH-uhm] *see* WINE BOTTLES

Jerusalem artichoke *see* SUNCHOKE

jeweled rice *see* JAVAHER POLOW

jewfish Found off the coast of Florida and in the Gulf of Mexico, the true jewfish is a member of the GROUPER family and can weigh up to 750 pounds. (Giant SEA BASS are also sometimes referred to as jewfish.) Its firm, white meat is usually sold in steaks and fillets. Jewfish can be cooked in any manner suitable for GROUPER. *See also* FISH.

Jezebel jelly; Jezebel sauce Spicy fruit sauce that became a favorite during the 1950s and 1960s. Its origins and the name Jezebel are a mystery, although most references link the name to the biblical figure. The spicy sauce or jelly has many variations; apple jelly, pineapple preserves, mustard and horseradish are usually the main ingredients, although other fruit jellies or preserves are sometimes used. A popular appetizer option is to pour Jezebel jelly over a block of cream cheese and serve with crackers. Jezebel sauce is also paired with meat dishes like ham, pork roast, pork chops, meatloaf and even turkey sandwiches.

jicama; jícama [HEE-kah-mah] Hailing from Mexico and South America, jicama is a large, bulbous root vegetable with a thin brown skin and white crunchy flesh. Its sweet, nutty flavor is good both raw and cooked. Jicama ranges in size from about 4 ounces up to 6 pounds. It's available year-round and can be purchased in Latin American markets and most supermarkets. It should be stored in the refrigerator in a plastic bag and will last for about 2 weeks. The thin skin should be peeled just before using. Jicama can be steamed, baked, boiled or fried. When cooked briefly, it retains its crisp, WATER CHESTNUT–type texture. Jicama is a fair source of vitamin C and potassium. It's also called *Mexican potato* and *yam bean root*.

jigae *see* JJIGAE

jigger 1. Also called a *shot* or *shot glass*, a jigger is a small drinking glass-shaped container that usually holds about 1½ ounces, but can also be a 1- or 2-ounce size. It's generally used to measure liquor. 2. The term is also used to describe the quantity of liquid such a measure holds, as in "a jigger of whiskey."*See also* PONY; SHOT.

jimbu [jihm-boo] Dried herb used in Tibetan and Nepalese cooking. The plant is a member of the onion family and its flavor is reminiscent of CHIVES with an UMAMI character. Jimbu, which looks like dry brownish-green grass, is used to flavor a variety of dishes including DAL, pickles, meat, salads and vegetables. A technique for bringing out its flavor is to brown jimbu in GHEE or hot oil before adding it to a dish. Jimbu is also known as *aromatic leaf garlic*.

jjigae; jigae [jee-GAY] Korean equivalent of "stew." KIMCHI JJIGAE, made with KIMCHI, and DUBU JJIGAE, made with tofu, are popular versions. *See also* GUK. Jjigae is sometimes spelled *chigae*.

jjim [jeem] Korean braised or steamed dishes. **Galbijjim** is a dish of braised short ribs and other ingredients such as carrots and potatoes. A dish of braised oxtail is called **soekkorijjim**.

Johannisberg Riesling [yoh-HAH-nihs-boerg REEZ-ling (REES-ling); joh-HAN-ihs-burg] *see* RIESLING

John Dory Found in European waters, this incredibly odd-looking fish has an oval, flat body and a large, spiny head. It has a large, dark spot midway on its body. One legend indicates that these spots are St. Peter's thumbprints. Because of this, John Dory is also called *Saint Peter's fish* and *Saint Pierre* by the French. The John Dory's flesh is delicate and mild and can be cooked in a variety of ways including grilling, sautéing and poaching. It's rarely exported to the United States, but PORGY may be substituted for any recipe calling for John Dory. *See also* FISH.

johnnycake; johnny cake, jonnycake Said to be the pancake's precursor, the johnnycake dates back to the early 1700s. It's a rather flat griddlecake made of cornmeal, salt and either boiling water or cold milk; there are strong advocates of both versions. Eggs, oil or melted butter and leavening (such as baking powder) are also often added. Some renditions are oven-baked, more like traditional cornbread. Also called *hoe cake* or *hoecake*.

Jonagold apple Considered to be one of the best culinary apples, the Jonagold is a cross between the GOLDEN DELICIOUS and JONATHAN apples. It has a moderately crisp, very juicy, sweet-tart flesh. The color of this all-purpose apple can depend on the climate in which it's grown and ranges from a mottled red and yellow skin, to red striping, to more predominantly red. *See also* APPLE.

Jonathan apple An all-purpose apple with a bright red skin freckled with gold. Jonathans have a spicy fragrance and the flesh is juicy, sweet-tart and quintessentially appley. Though this apple may be used for cooking, it's not good for baking whole. *See also* APPLE.

jook *see* CONGEE

Jordan almond This large, plump almond is imported from Spain and sold plain as well as encased in hard pastel candy coatings of various colors. *See also* ALMOND; NUTS.

journeyman cook *see* BRIGADE SYSTEM

jugged hare A classic English preparation that begins with cut pieces of HARE that are soaked in a red wine–juniper berry marinade for at least a day. The marinated meat is well browned, then combined in a casserole (traditionally a heatproof crock or jug) with vegetables, seasonings and stock, and baked. When the meat and vegetables are done, the juices are poured off and combined with cream and the reserved hare blood and pulverized liver. The strained sauce is served over the "jugged" hare and vegetables.

jugo [KHOO-goh] A Latin American drink made with water, fresh fruit pulp, ice and sometimes sugar. *See also* BATIDO; MERENGADA.

juicer A manual or electric kitchen device used to extract the juice from fruit, and with some models, vegetables. Most of those used strictly for juicing citrus fruits have a ridged cone onto which a halved fruit is pressed. An old-fashioned form of this tool is the *reamer*, a ridged, teardrop-shaped tool with a handle. A reamer is used primarily for citrus fruits.

jujube 1. [JOO-joob] Also called *Chinese red date* and simply *red date*, this venerable fruit has been prized in China for 4,000 years. The varieties of jujube are myriad—the fruit can be round or ovoid, can range from 1 to 2 inches in diameter and can vary in color from yellowish to yellow-green to red, all with colorful blotching. Jujubes have a crunchy-crisp skin and a flesh akin to that of a spongy apple. The flavor is mildly sweet and not very acidic. The jujube is generally imported from China, though some are being grown on America's West Coast. Some fresh fruit is available (mainly in the western United States) in August and September, usually only in specialty produce markets or through mail order. Dried jujubes—available in Chinese markets—have a leathery skin that, depending on the variety, can be red (most common), off-white or almost black. The flavor of the rather dry, yellowish flesh is prunelike. The dried fruit must be soaked in water before using. Chinese cooks use this fruit in both savory and sweet dishes. 2. [JOO-joo-bee] A tiny fruit-flavored candy with a hard, gummy texture.

juk *see* CONGEE

julep A sweet drink made with any of various LIQUORS, water (still or sparkling), sugar and, sometimes, mint (as with MINT JULEP). The origin of the word *julep* is the Persian word *julâb*, which means "rosewater." In 15th-century England, the word "julep" was used to describe a sugar syrup variously flavored and often mixed with medication.

julienne [joo-lee-EHN; zhoo-LYEHN] *n*. Foods that have been cut into thin, matchstick strips. The food (such as a potato) is first cut into $1/8$-inch-thick slices. The slices are stacked, then cut into $1/8$-inch-thick strips. The strips may then be cut into whatever length is desired. If the object is round, cut a thin slice from the bottom so it will sit firmly and not roll on the work surface. Julienne is most often used as a garnish. **julienne** *v*. To cut food into very thin strips.

jumble; jumbal Dating back to early America, this delicate, crisp, ring-shaped cookie was particularly popular in the 1800s. It's like a thin, rich sugar cookie, often made with sour cream and, formerly, scented with ROSE WATER. Jumbles can also be made with other flavorings such as orange zest or grated coconut.

Junami [joon-ah-MEE] An all-purpose variety of apple developed in Switzerland. The Junami is a cross between the ELSTAR, IDA RED and Maigold apples. A large, slightly irregularly shaped apple, it has a streaky red blush with a few traces of green over a yellow background. The flavor is sweetly tart with floral overtones. It has a crisp, succulent texture. *See also* APPLE.

juniper berry These astringent blue-black berries are native to both Europe and America. Juniper berries are too bitter to eat raw and are usually sold dried and used to flavor meats, sauces, stuffings, etc. They're generally crushed before use to release their flavor. These pungent berries are the hallmark flavoring of GIN. In fact, the name is derived from the French word for juniper berry—*genièvre*, which is the name for gin in France.

junket [JUHNG-kiht] This sweet, mild-flavored dessert is made with milk, sugar, various flavorings and rennin (see rennet), the latter of which coagulates the mixture into a soft puddinglike texture. Junket is served chilled, sometimes accompanied by fruit.

junmai [joon-MI] *see* SAKE

jus [ZHOO] French for "juice," which can refer to both fruit and vegetable juices, as well as the natural juices exuded from meat. *Jus de citron* is "lemon juice," while *jus de viande* means "juices from meat." A dish (usually meat) that is served *au jus* is presented with its own natural juices.

jus lié [zhoo lee-YAY] A sauce made by slightly thickening meat stock or juices with a SLURRY based on CORNSTARCH or ARROWROOT. *See also* SAUCE.

J

kaas [KAHSS] Dutch for "cheese."

kaasdoop [KAHS-doop] A Dutch specialty that's a GOUDA-cheese FONDUE, served with roasted or boiled potatoes and chunks of rye bread.

kabob *see* KEBAB

kabocha squash [kah-BOH-chah] New to the United States market, this winter squash has a beautiful jade green rind with celadon green streaks. When cooked, its pale orange flesh is tender-smooth and sweet. An average kabocha ranges from 2 to 3 pounds, though they have been known to weigh as much as 8 pounds. Choose squash that are heavy for their size. The rind should be dull and firm; avoid any with soft spots. Kabochas can be cooked in any way suitable for ACORN SQUASH, such as baking or steaming. Before cooking, they must be halved and seeded. *See also* SQUASH.

kabu *see* SALAD TURNIP

kaffeekuchen [KAHF-fee- koh-kehn] *see* KUCHEN

kaffir lime *see* MAKRUT LIME

Kahlúa [kah-LOO-ah] Also called *Kahlúa Licor de Café,* this mahogany-colored LIQUEUR has been produced in Mexico for more than a half century. It has a rich and complex roasted coffee flavor layered with vanilla and semisweet chocolate.

kai lan *see* CHINESE KALE

kaki [kah-kee] 1. Japanese for "PERSIMMON," kaki is the name Europeans use for this fruit. 2. **kaki** [KAH-kee] The Japanese use the same word for "oyster," but put a slight vocal accent on the first syllable.

kala *see* PACIFIC THREADFIN

kalács *see* TSOUREKI

kala jeera; kala zeera [KAH-lah JEE-rah] A member of the parsley family grown in northern India and parts of Afghanistan, Bangladesh, Iran and Pakistan. The dark brown, crescent-shaped fruit is popularly known as *black cumin*, although there is some confusion about this since black cumin is sometimes used to refer to another spice, NIGELLA. Kala jeera is very popular in the MOGHUL CUISINE of northern India, where it replaces regular CUMIN, also a member of the parsley family, in many dishes. Uncooked, the spice has a harsh, unpleasant, earthiness that dissipates and becomes nutty and slightly grassy and flowery when cooked. In Kashmir the root is sometimes eaten as a vegetable. Kala jeera, also known by a variety of names such as *kala jira, Kashmiri jira, shahi jira and shahi zeera*, is available in seed and ground forms. As with all seeds, herbs and spices, it should be stored in a cool, dark place for no more than 6 months. *See also* SPICES; Seasoning Suggestions, page 891.

kala loon *see* BLACK SALT

kalamansi [kah-lah-MAHN-see] *see* CALAMONDIN

Kalamata olive (PDO) [kahl-uh-MAH-tuh] An almond-shaped Greek olive (also spelled *calamata*) that ranges in length from about ½ to 1 inch. Kalamatas are a dark eggplant color and have a flavor that can be rich and fruity. They're often slit to allow the wine vinegar MARINADE in which they're soaked to penetrate the flesh. Kalamatas are marketed packed in either olive oil or vinegar. Kalamata olives enjoy PDO status. *See also* OLIVE.

kala namak *see* BLACK SALT

kalbi [KAHL-bee] *see* GALBI

kalbitang *see* GALBITANG

kaldereta *see* CALDERETA

kale This attractive, nonheading member of the cabbage family has been cultivated for over 2,000 years. Though it grows in warm climates, it's happiest in colder climes where for centuries its high vitamin content has made it particularly popular with northern Europeans. Kale has a mild, cabbagey flavor and comes in many varieties and colors. Most kale is easily identified by its frilly leaves arranged in a loose bouquet formation. The color of the leaves of the varieties most commonly available in the United States is deep green variously tinged with shades of blue or purple. There are ornamental varieties in gorgeous shades of lavender, purple and celadon green. Kale's best during the winter months, though it's available year-round in most parts of the country. Choose richly colored, relatively small bunches of kale, avoiding any with limp or yellowing leaves. Store in the coldest section of the refrigerator no longer than 2 or 3 days. After that, the flavor of kale becomes quite strong and the leaves limp. Because the center stalk is tough, it should be removed before the kale is used. Kale may be prepared in any way suitable for spinach and small amounts make a nice addition to salads. Kale, a CRUCIFEROUS vegetable, provides ample amounts of vitamins A and C, folic acid, calcium and iron. *See also* CAVOLO NERO; FLOWERING KALE.

kalimotxo; kalimutxo; kalimocho [ka-lee-MOH-choh] A popular Spanish COCKTAIL made with equal parts of red wine and a cola-based soft drink (usually Coca-Cola) and served over ice, sometimes with a squeeze of lemon. It's also sometimes spelled *calimocho*.

kaljira rice [kahl-jee-rah] Tiny, non-glutinous AROMATIC RICE from Bangladesh that's also known as *small basmati* and *kalo nunia*. Like regular BASMATI, kaljira has a delicate, perfumy, nutlike flavor and aroma. Considered one of the best rice types, it's gained the moniker "prince of rice." It can be found in Indian and Middle Eastern markets, in some supermarkets and on the Internet. *See also* RICE.

kalo nunia *see* KALJIRA RICE

kalsone *see* CALSONE

kamaboko [kah-mah-BOH-koh] A loaf or cake of ground or puréed, steamed fish. Kamaboko is available fresh in Asian markets and is generally white but occasionally has food coloring (usually pink or red, sometimes brown, green or yellow) brushed on the surface. It's used in numerous Japanese preparations including soups, noodles and simmered dishes. **Chikuwa** is kamaboko shaped into rolls formed around bamboo stick. **Ita-kamaboko** is shaped into squares or rectangles on wood planks that are usually made of cypress. *See also* AGEKAMABOKO; SURIMI.

kamote [kah-MOH-tay] *see* BONIATO

kampyo [KAHM-pyoh] Long, beige, ribbonlike strips of gourd that are dried and used as edible ties for various Japanese food packets. Kampyo can also be used as an ingredient in SUSHI and in simmered dishes. It can be found packaged in cellophane in Asian markets. Kampyo strips must be softened in water several hours before using.

K

kamut [kah-MOOT] The name "kamut" comes from the ancient Egyptian word for "wheat." Considered by some to be the great-great grandfather of grains, kamut is a variety of high-protein wheat that has never been hybridized. Kamut's kernels are two to three times the size of most wheat. Not only does this grain have a deliciously nutty flavor, but it also has a higher nutritional value than its modern-day counterparts. It can be found as a whole grain and as flour in natural food stores. It's used commercially mainly for pastas, puffed cereal and crackers. *See also* WHEAT.

kanahena *see* SOFKI

kangaroo Although Australian aborigines have eaten kangaroos for centuries and 19th-century European settlers hunted them for food, it wasn't until the end of the twentieth century that Australians began using kangaroos for anything other than dog food. Recently, Russians, Europeans (particularly Germans) and South Africans have been driving up demand for kangaroo meat, as has the Australian home market where it's now becoming commonplace in supermarkets. Kangaroos are wild and are not currently farm-raised so they fall in the category of GAME ANIMALS. Because of their free-range environment, the foods they eat and their low fat content, kangaroo is deemed one of the healthier meats. It has a flavor somewhere between that of wild rabbit and VENISON. The Australian kangaroo industry produces a wide variety of cuts that are similar to domestic animal cuts. Even with its low fat content, kangaroo is considered one of the more tender game animals, though it's suggested that prime cuts be cooked to no more than medium-rare to prevent drying. Other cuts should be BRAISED with moist heat or roasted with ample BASTING, LARDING or BARDING. Partly because kangaroos are viewed as cute, and in keeping with the theme of calling the meat of deer venison, of cows beef and of pigs pork, the Kangaroo Industry Association of Australia ran a contest in 2005 to name kangaroo meat. The winning moniker was **australus**, though there's been no commercial push to use the name. Kangaroo meat has limited availability in the United States, though a number of mail-order outlets are providing it through the Internet.

kani *see* SUSHI

Kansas City strip steak *see* NEW YORK STEAK

kanten [kan-TEHN] *see* AGAR

kao [KOW] Thai for "rice." *Kao hohm mali* is "JASMINE RICE." *Kao niow* or *kao nieo* is "sticky rice." *Kao tome* means "boiled rice."

kape alamid see KOPI LUWAK

kappamaki [kahp-pah-MAH-kee] Type of SUSHI roll filled with cucumber and SUSHI MESHI and wrapped in NORI. *Kappa*, the word for "cucumber" used in Japanese sushi preparation, refers to a mythical imp that lives near the water. The creatures are said to love cucumbers, which the Japanese throw into the water so the kappa will leave them alone.

kara age [kah-rah AH-geh] Japanese deep-frying technique whereby the food (meat, fish or vegetables) is lightly dusted with flour, cornstarch or KUZU before frying.

karakuchi [kah-RAH-koo-chee] *see* SAKE

karasumi [kah-rah-SOO-mee] see BOTTARGA

karibeck kapi see KOPI LUWAK

kari leaf [KAH-ree] *see* CURRY LEAF

Käse [KI-zer; KAH-zeh] German for "cheese."

Kaseri [Kuh-SEHR-ee] *see* KASSERI

kasha [KAH-shuh] 1. In America, this term refers to roasted BUCKWHEAT groats, which have a toasty, nutty flavor. 2. In Russia, the word *kasha* is used in a broader sense for various cooked grains such as buckwheat, MILLET and oats.

kashi [KAH-shee] *see* OKASHI

kasseri [kuh-SEHR-ee] Made in Greece since the nineteenth century, Kasseri (or *Kaseri*) is a PROTECTED DESIGNATION OF ORIGIN (PDO) cheese and can only be produced in Macedonia, Thessaly and the prefectures of Xanthi and Lesbos. This PASTA FILATA cheese can be made from raw or PASTEURIZED, whole or partially skimmed milk. Though Greek Kasseri is traditionally made with sheep's and goat's milk, there are non-Greek versions made with cow's milk, particularly in the United States. PDO regulations require Kasseri to be RIPENED at least 3 months, though cheeses are aged for 6 months to a year. This cheese has a pale yellow rind that's thin, smooth and glossy. The off-white to pale yellow interior is smooth and elastic and can range from semisoft to semihard, depending on age. Younger versions of Kasseri have a flavor that's delicate, sweet and tangy, while aged cheeses become salty and piquant. The FAT CONTENT ranges from 32 to 52 percent, depending on whether the milk is partially skimmed or not. Kasseri is the cheese used in the famous Greek dish SAGANAKI. *See also* CHEESE.

Katahdin potatoes *see* ROUND WHITE POTATOES

katakuriko [kah-tak-koo-ree-koh] A starch from the katakuri plant (*Erythronium japonicum*). Today there is such limited supply that it's extremely expensive and used only in the best Japanese restaurants. It has largely been replaced with POTATO FLOUR, which is labeled katakuriko and used in most situations.

K

katayef *see* ATAYEF

Katenschinken *see* HOLSTEINER KATENRAUCHSCHINKEN (PGI)

katsamaki [KAHT-sah-mah-kee] A MUSH made from cornmeal that's similar to POLENTA. Katsamaki is the name used in central Greece, whereas *poulenta* and *bazina* are used in other parts of the country. FETA cheese is often used to enrich the Greek versions of polenta.

katsudon [KAH-tsoo-dohn] *see* DONBURI

katsuobushi; katsuo-bushi [KAH-tsuh-oh-boo-shee] Pink flakes of dried bonito (TUNA), which are used in Japanese cooking as a garnish and in some cooked preparations, principally DASHI. The tuna is boiled, smoked, then sun-dried. A special tool is used to flake the extremely hard chunks. Katsuobushi can be purchased in Asian markets and the specialty section of some large supermarkets. Depending on how fresh it is when purchased, it can be stored in a cool, dry place up to a year.

kaymak; kaimaki [KI-mak] The Middle Eastern equivalent of CLOTTED CREAM, kaymak is made by gently heating milk (usually from water buffaloes or goats) until a rich, semisolid layer of cream forms on the surface. After it's cooled, the kaymak is typically used as a spread for bread.

kazunoko [kah-zoo-NOH-koh] Japanese for the yellow, crunchy ROE from HERRING. Because of its high price, kazunoko is often referred to as "yellow diamonds." It's traditionally eaten at the New Year or on other festive occasions. Kazunoko can be found in Asian markets, generally frozen in small containers.

kebab; kabob [kuh-BOB] Small chunks of meat, fish or shellfish that are usually marinated before being threaded on a skewer and grilled over coals. Pieces of vegetables can also accompany the meat on the skewer. Also called *shish kebab* and *shashlik*.

kecap; kecap manis; ketjap manis [KEH-chuhp MAH-nees] Made from SOYBEANS, this intensely dark brown, syrupy-thick Indonesian sauce is similar to, but has a sweeter, more complex flavor than, SOY SAUCE. Kecap is sweetened with palm sugar (*see* JAGGERY) and seasoned with various ingredients, which generally include garlic and STAR ANISE. It's used in MARINADES, as a flavoring in various Indonesian dishes and as a condiment. Kecap can be found in Asian markets. Store indefinitely in a cool, dry place.

K

kedgeree; kegeree [kehj-uh-REE; KEHJ-uh-ree] A spiced East Indian dish of rice, lentils and onions, Anglicized in the 18th century when the English added flaked smoked fish, hard-cooked eggs and a rich cream sauce. Kedgeree is a popular English breakfast dish.

Keemun tea [KEE-muhn] Considered by many to be China's most famous black tea, Keemun comes from the Anhui province in eastern China. It's celebrated for being a mellow, balanced tea with a sweet, fruity flavor and hints of chocolate, pine, smokiness and toastiness. It has a reddish-brown color when brewed. *See also* TEA.

kefir [keh-FEER] Originally made from camel's milk, kefir comes from high in the Caucasus—a 750-mile-long mountain range between the Caspian and Black seas. Today, however, it's more commonly produced from cow's milk. It's a slightly sour brew of fermented milk, most of which contains about $2^1/_2$ percent alcohol. Kefir is reminiscent in both taste and texture of a liquid YOGURT. It's available in cartons or bottles in natural food stores. *See also* KUMISS.

kelp A generic name for any of the edible, brown SEAWEEDS of the family *Laminariaceae. See also* KOMBU.

kencur *see* AROMATIC GINGER, ZEDOARY

Kent Island oyster *see* ATLANTIC OYSTER

Kentucky burgoo *see* BURGOO

Kentucky wonder bean The American name for RUNNER BEAN.

kerisik [kah-REE-seek] Grated coconut pulp that's toasted and then ground into a pulp or paste depending on the desired consistency. Although fresh coconut's the best, DESSICATED COCONUT can be used. Kerisik is a popular ingredient in Indonesian and Malaysian cooking.

kesar [KAY-sar] Indian term for "SAFFRON."

ketchup [KEHCH-uhp; KACH-uhp] *Ke-tsiap*—a spicy pickled-fish condiment popular in 17th-century China—is said to be the origin of the name "ketchup." British seamen brought the *ke-tsiap* home and throughout the years the formula was changed to contain anything from nuts to mushrooms. It wasn't until the late 1700s that canny New Englanders added tomatoes to the blend and it became what we know today as ketchup. Also called *catsup* and *catchup,* this thick, spicy sauce is a traditional American accompaniment for French-fried potatoes, hamburgers and many other foods. Ketchup usually has a tomato foundation, though gourmet markets often carry condiments with similar appellations that might have a base of anything from walnuts to mangoes to mushrooms. Vinegar gives ketchup its tang, while sugar, salt and spices contribute to the blend. In addition to being used as a condiment, ketchup is used as an ingredient in many dishes.

K

ketjap manis *see* KECAP MANIS

kewra *see* SCREWPINE LEAVES

Key lime *see* LIME

Key lime pie A custard pie very similar to a lemon meringue pie, except that it's made with the yellowish, very tart Key lime (*see* LIME) from Florida.

khachapuri [khah-chah-POOR-ee] Similar to the Italian CALZONE, khachapuri is a yeast-dough "package" filled with cheese and baked until the bread is golden and the cheese is melted and bubbly. This specialty hails from Georgia (formerly of the USSR) and comes in various forms, from round to football-shaped, and from a simple and flat to that of a pleated-turban design. It's generally served hot or at room temperature.

khao pun [KAH-oh puhn] *see* RICE NOODLES

khao tom gung *see* CONGEE

khawa [KAH-wah] see KHOA

khoa; khoya [KOH-ah; KOY-ah] Also called khawa, mava and mawa, this East Indian dairy product is created by heating and condensing cow's or water buffalo's milk. The milk can be condensed until it reaches a semi-solid state or stopped at a point where the moisture content is higher—each style has different uses. Khoa powder is also available and can be reconstituted with water. Khoa is used in many desserts that call for condensed milk, such as BARFI and KULFI. Khoa and khoa powder are available in Indian markets.

khoresh; khoresht; khorisht [ko-REHSH] In Persian cuisine, a generic term for stew, generally served with a white rice dish known as CHELO. There are numerous khoreshs, both with meat and meatless.

khoresh ghormeh sabzi [ko-REHSH gor-meh sab-ZEE] Herb stew that's been made for centuries and is often referred to as the Iranian national dish. Along with lamb or beef seasoned with TURMERIC, it contains numerous sautéed herbs and greens and either black-eyed peas or kidney beans. Bits of dried limes (*see* LIMES, DRIED, PERSIAN) and shambalileh (dried FENUGREEK leaves) are added for additional flavor. It's also seen as *khoresh-e gormeh sabzi.*

K

kibbeh; kibbi [KIH-beh; KIH-bee] Particularly popular in Lebanon and Syria, this Middle Eastern dish has myriad variations but basically combines ground meat (usually lamb), BULGHUR WHEAT and various flavorings. The meat may be raw or cooked.

kidney One of the VARIETY MEATS, the kidney is a glandular organ. The most popular kidneys for cooking are beef, veal, lamb and pork. They're easily distinguishable because beef and veal kidneys are multi-lobed while lamb and pork are single-lobed. In general, the texture is more tender and the flavor more delicate in younger animals. The kidneys from younger animals are pale while those from older animals become deep reddish-brown; they're also tougher and stronger-flavored. Look for kidneys that are firm, with a rich, even color. Avoid those with dry spots or a dull surface. Kidneys should be used the day they're purchased, or store loosely wrapped in the refrigerator for up to 1 day. Before cooking, remove skin and any excess fat. Soaking helps reduce the strong odor in kidneys from more mature animals. See a general cookbook for details pertaining to the particular type of kidney you wish to cook. Kidneys may be braised, broiled, simmered or cooked in casseroles, stews and dishes like the famous STEAK AND KIDNEY PIE. All kidneys are a good source of protein, iron, phosphorus, vitamin A, thiamine and riboflavin.

kidney bean A firm, medium-size bean with a dark red skin and cream-colored flesh. Its full-bodied flavor makes it particularly popular for dishes like CHILI CON CARNE and RED BEANS AND RICE. On the downside, it's an enthusiastic producer of flatulence. Unless you live in an area that grows kidney beans, you won't find them fresh but will have to settle for the dried or canned forms. **White kidney beans**—referred to as CANNELLINI BEANS—lack the robust flavor of their red cousins, and are only available dried or canned. The tiny, tender French kidney beans are called FLAGEOLETS and may be purchased dried, canned and, sometimes, frozen. *See also* BEANS.

kieffer lime *see* MAKRUT LIME

kielbasa [kihl-BAH-sah; keel-BAH-sah] Also called *kielbasy* or *Polish sausage,* this smoked SAUSAGE is usually made of pork, though beef can be added. It comes in chunky (about 2 inches in diameter) links and is usually sold precooked and, sometimes, fresh. Kielbasa can be served separately or cut into pieces as part of a dish. Even the precooked kielbasa tastes better when heated.

kijoshu [kee-JOH-shoo] *see* SAKE

kikurage [kee-koo-RAH-geh] *see* WOOD EAR

kimchi; kimchee; kim chee [KIHM-chee] The Korean-born kimchi dates back to the 7th century, when it was a way of pickling and preserving mild-tasting vegetables. It wasn't until the 16th century when CHILES were introduced into Korea that kimchi changed its mild profile to one that was spicy. Today's extraordinarily pungent spicy-hot CONDIMENT is served at almost every Korean meal, though kimchi is fast becoming popular in many upscale restaurants as well as with health-food enthusiasts. Kimchi is comprised of a combination of vegetables (such as cabbage, carrots, radishes or turnips) and flavorings such as garlic, ginger and green onions. Sometimes small pieces of fish (such as baby shrimp or anchovies) are added to the mix. The ingredients are pickled together before being fermented. There are hundreds of kimchi recipes, which vary from region to region and change seasonally, depending on what fresh ingredients are available. In Korea, for example, wintertime kimchi is based primarily on CHINESE CABBAGE and has very hearty characteristics that Koreans savor during the long, cold months. On the other hand, summer foods such as radishes and cucumbers create lighter, fresher kimchi flavors for hotter weather. Kimchi is also used as a component for soup, rice and other dishes. Commercial kimchi can be purchased in Korean markets and natural food stores. It's usually in glass jars in the refrigerated section, and it will keep indefinitely in the fridge. Koreans use **kimchi paste** (also called *gochujang*) as a seasoning when making kimchi and as a table condiment to flavor dishes. It's a mixture of garlic, red chili peppers, fermented soybean paste (*see* MISO), glutinous RICE FLOUR and other flavorings. It's also available in Korean markets.

kimchi jjigae [KIHM-chee jee-GAY] A popular Korean stew consisting of KIMCHI, green onion, garlic, TOFU and various seasonings added to pork browned in sesame oil.

kinako [KEE-nah-koh] *see* SOY FLOUR

king Thai for "GINGER."

kingfish There are two distinct types of fish known as kingfish. The first is actually the regional name for a king MACKEREL. The name of the second type, found along the Atlantic coast, applies to any of several species of DRUM.

king orange This large Florida-grown orange has a rather flattened shape and loose rough skin. It has a juicy, sweetly tart flesh and is in season from December to April. *See also* ORANGE.

kinome [kih-noh-MEH] These young leaves of the prickly ash tree have a fresh, subtle mint flavor and a tender texture. They're occasionally available fresh in Japanese markets during the spring. Kinome is used as a garnish for many Japanese dishes. Store the fresh leaves in a plastic bag in your refrigerator's vegetable drawer. They should be used within 3 to 4 days. Though watercress or mint can be used as a substitute for color, nothing can duplicate the flavor of kinome.

kipfel; kipferln [KIHP-fuhl; KIHP-ferln] 1. A small, crescent-shaped yeast pastry with a filling of chopped nuts and brown sugar. Also known as RUGALACH. 2. A crescent-shaped, butter-rich cookie with either a jam filling or a filling similar to that of the pastry.

kippered herring; kippers *see* HERRING

kir [KEER] White wine that is flavored with a soupçon of CRÈME DE CASSIS, usually served as an APÉRITIF. When made with CHAMPAGNE, it's referred to as a **kir royale**.

Kirsch; Kirschwasser [KEERSH; KEERSH-vah-ser] From the German *Kirsch* ("cherry") and *Wasser* ("water"), this clear BRANDY is distilled from cherry juice and pits. In cookery, it's most prominently known as a flavorful addition to FONDUE and CHERRIES JUBILEE.

Kirschtorte [KEERSH-tort] *see* BLACK FOREST TORTE

kishimen [KEE-shee-mehn] A broad, flat Japanese wheat noodle, which is slightly thicker and wider than the UDON noodle. Kishimen noodles are prepared and used in a similar fashion to udon noodles. *See also* ASIAN NOODLES.

kishke; kishka [KIHSH-keh] A Jewish-American SAUSAGE made with flour, MATZO MEAL, fat, onions and ground meat. The mixture is stuffed into a beef CASING before being steamed, then roasted.

kiss 1. A small, mound-shape, baked MERINGUE, which often contains chopped nuts, cherries or coconut. The texture of a kiss is light and chewy. 2. The term also applies to small one-bite candies, usually commercially produced.

kissel [kee-SUHL] Next to ice cream, Russians claim kissel as their favorite dessert. It's a sweetened fruit purée thickened with either CORN-STARCH or POTATO FLOUR, which gives it a soft-custard texture. Kissel can be served hot or cold, usually topped with cream or a custard sauce.

kiwano [kee-WAH-noh] Hailing from New Zealand and also grown in California, this oval fruit ranges in length from 3 to 5 inches. It has a bright yellow skin studded with stubby "horns," which is why it's also called a *horned melon*. The kiwano's pulp is a pale yellow-green color and jelly-like in texture with a sweet-tart flavor evocative of bananas and cucumbers. Kiwanos are available year-round in specialty produce markets and occasionally in some supermarkets. Choose brightly colored fruit with firm spikes and no sign of soft spots. Store at a cool room temperature for up to a month. To use, cut the fruit in half lengthwise and scoop out the pulp, which can be eaten, seeds and all. Use in drinks, salads and sauces or as a topping for ice cream. Other names for the kiwano are *African horned cucumber, English tomato* and *jelly melon*.

kiwi; kiwifruit; kiwi fruit [KEE-wee] Native to China, this fruit is also known as the *Chinese gooseberry*. The odd-looking kiwi received its moniker from New Zealand's national (and flightless) bird of the same name. It looks like a large brown egg with a covering of fine downy hair. But this rather unusual exterior hides a beautiful brilliant green flesh, spattered with tiny edible black seeds. The kiwi's flavor is elusive. Some say it's reminiscent of pineapple . . . others say strawberry . . . but all agree that it has a sweet-tart flavor unlike any other fruit. The **gold kiwi** is not as hairy as its green kin and has a bright gold flesh with a honey-eyed flavor. The fuzz-free **baby kiwi** has green flesh and is eaten whole and unpeeled, as one would a grape. The kiwi is cultivated in both New Zealand and California. Since New Zealand's seasons are the opposite of ours, this delectable fruit is pretty much available year-round. Ripe kiwis will give slightly to gentle pressure and can be stored in the refrigerator up to 3 weeks. They can be halved and scooped out like a melon or peeled, sliced and used in salads, desserts or as a garnish. In New Zealand, the popular PAVLOVA dessert is a favorite way to feature this fruit's beauty and flavor. Kiwis are a good source of vitamins C and K.

kleftiko [KLEHF-tee-koh] Greek dish based on lamb that's marinated with garlic and lemon juice, then slowly cooked in a sealed container. It's called "stolen meat" or "thieves' meat" after the Klephts, a group of bandits who would steal a lamb and cook it in a covered hole so the smoke, steam and cooking smells would be concealed from the lamb's owner. Today, the covered hole has evolved into an enclosed packet of parchment paper in which the lamb is cooked.

Knackwurst; Knockwurst [NAK-wurst; NAHK-vursht] Short, thick links of precooked beef and/or pork SAUSAGE that is well flavored with garlic. Knackwurst is usually boiled or grilled before serving, often with sauerkraut. The name comes from the German *knack* ("crack") and *wurst* ("sausage"), named for the crackling sound the sausage makes when bitten into.

knaidel, *pl.* **knaidlach** [KNAYD-l; KNAYD-luhkh] *see* MATZO BALL

knead [NEED] A technique used to mix and work a dough in order to form it into a cohesive, pliable mass. During kneading, the network of GLUTEN strands stretches and expands, thereby enabling a dough to hold in the gas bubbles formed by a LEAVENER (which allows it to rise). Kneading is accomplished either manually or by machine—usually a large mixer equipped with a dough hook (some machines have two dough hooks) or a FOOD PROCESSOR with a plastic blade. By hand, kneading is done with a pressing-folding-turning action performed by pressing down into the dough with the heels of both hands, then pushing away from the body. The dough is folded in half and given a quarter turn, and the process is repeated. Depending on the dough, the manual kneading time can range anywhere from 5 to 15 minutes (or more). Well-kneaded dough is smooth and elastic.

knife A sharp-edged instrument used for cutting, peeling, slicing, spreading and so on. Most knife blades are made of steel. **Carbon steel knives** are thought to be sharper and to hold their sharpness longer than stainless steel knives. But carbon steel knives rust and discolor much easier than stainless steel ones. **Stainless steel knives**, also called **stain-resistant**, **stain free** or **rust free**, are not totally resistant to staining or corrosion but the chromium that's added to the steel improves resistance to the elements causing these issues. Some Japanese knife makers produce **steel-clad knives** using a technique that's been around for centuries. A layer of carbon steel is positioned between layers of stainless steel with only the carbon cutting edge exposed. The exposed carbon edge provides the benefits of increased sharpness and the stainless steel jacket provides protection from rust and discoloration. There are two primary techniques for manufacturing knife blades—**forging** and **stamping**. Forged knives have long been considered superior but today high-quality stamped knives are just as good. **Ceramic knives** made from a material called *ceramic zirconia* have been available for several decades. They won't rust, corrode or interact with food and are reputed to be second only to the diamond in hardness. Ceramic knives are very sharp and stay sharp longer than steel knives but they're brittle so there's a risk of breaking a tip or small piece off the cutting edge if handled improperly. Parts of a knife include the handle, heel, bolster, tang and cutting edge. **Knife handles** can be one of many materials including wood, plastic-impregnated wood, plastic, rubber, horn and metal. The section at the widest end of the blade is called the **heel**, which can be very sharp or slightly rounded (dulled) to protect the hand from cuts. The section of metal or ceramic that leads to the handle is called the **bolster**. On many European knives the bolster is large and extends down to the heel protecting fingers (but making sharpening more difficult). Most Japanese-style knives use a bolster that's a straightforward metal collar, providing less protection but making the knife easier to sharpen. The **tang** is the strip of metal or ceramic that extends into the handle so it can be attached to the blade. The tang also helps provide balance to the knife and comes in various forms to help achieve this. **Full tangs** extend all the way to the end of the handle and are found in many European knives. **Partial** or **half tangs** only go part way. **Rat-tail tangs** or **hidden tangs** are long rods that extend into the handle. Full tangs don't necessarily indicate a higher-quality knife. The other tangs allow for lighter, and in many cases better-balanced, knives, as evidenced by many high-quality Japanese versions. Knives come in a variety of different sizes and shapes, each with its own specific use. A **French knife** (also called a *chef's knife*), with its broad, tapered shape and fine edge, is perfect for chopping vegetables. The Japanese version of this knife, called a **gyuto**, is thinner and lighter, resulting in a knife that's sharper than but not as sturdy as most European types. A **slicing knife** cuts cleanly through cooked meat with its long, thin, narrow blade. Knives with **serrated** or **scalloped** edges make neat work of slicing softer foods such as bread, tomatoes and cake. The pointed, short-bladed **paring knife** is easy to handle and makes quick work of peeling, removing cores, and so on. A **boning knife** is a limited-purpose knife that's thin with a tapered tip ideal for boning fowl, beef, lamb, and the like. In Japan an all-purpose knife, called a **santoku**, was created. It looks like a small chef's knife but has a rounded tip. Knives used for table service are usually named after their use, such as dinner, luncheon, fish, butter and steak knives.

knish [kuh-NISH] A pastry of Jewish origin that consists of a piece of dough (baking powder or yeast) that encloses a filling of mashed potatoes, cheese, ground meat and BUCKWHEAT groats. These pastries can be served as a side dish or appetizer.

knob celery *see* CELERY ROOT

knotroot *see* CROSNES

Kobe beef [KOH-beh] An exclusive grade of beef from cattle raised in Kobe, Japan. These pampered cattle are massaged with SAKE and fed a special diet that includes plentiful amounts of beer. The breed of cattle used for Kobe beef is called WAGYU. It develops a higher percentage of intense marbling that improves tenderness and flavor. Kobe beef cannot currently be imported into the United States but wagyu cattle have been brought in. In the U.S. they are often bred with Black Angus cattle so the animals generally are not 100 percent wagyu. This beef is often labeled American-Style Kobe beef, Kobe-style beef or wagyu beef. Wagyu beef is considerably more expensive than other types of beef. *See also* BEEF.

kochu chang; kochujang [koh-choo CHANG] *see* CHILE BEAN PASTE

kofta [KOF-tah] Popular in India, Pakistan and countries in Central Asia, the Middle East, North Africa and the Balkans, koftas are generally described as meatballs, although some are made entirely with vegetables. Throughout these countries there are many variations, and some look more like CROQUETTES or DUMPLINGS or even TURNOVERS. They are usually made of ground or minced meat such as beef or lamb, but the main ingredient could be chicken, fish or potatoes or other vegetables. This is combined with bread crumbs, bulgur wheat, rice, eggs, vegetables and any of various other ingredients (such as green bananas or cabbage) along with favorite local spices, then kneaded until well mixed. Kofta are shaped into balls or other forms and cooked in a variety of different ways—baked, fried, grilled, poached or steamed.

kohana fu [koh-hah-nah FOO] *see* FU

kohlrabi [kohl-RAH-bee] This vegetable is a member of the turnip family and, for that reason, is also called *cabbage turnip*. Like the turnip, both the bulblike stem and greens are edible. There are two varieties of kohlrabi—the green type has a pale green bulb and green leaves with light green veining; purple kohlrabi has a purple root, stems and veining on green leaves. The flesh on both varieties has a creamy white color and a flavor reminiscent of a sassy-sweet blend of mild broccoli and celery root. The leaves have a flavor akin to that of COLLARD GREENS. Kohlrabi is available year-round and ranges from golf-ball to tennis-ball size. The smaller the root, the younger and more tender the kohlrabi. Choose a kohlrabi that is heavy for its size with firm, deeply colored green leaves. Avoid any with soft spots on the bulb or signs of yellowing on leaf tips. Separate the leaves from the bulbs; the former can be refrigerated in a plastic bag for up to 4 days, the bulbs for up to 10 days. Just before using, peel the bulbs; wash the greens in several changes of cold water, blotting dry on paper towels. Kohlrabi can be eaten raw or added to soups, stews and STIR-FRY dishes. It's rich in potassium and vitamin C.

koji [koh-gee] A fermenting catalyst known as Japanese "yeast," used in making myriad products including AMASAKE, MISO, SAKE, SOY SAUCE and TAMARI. Koji is made from either beans or grains that have been inoculated with the mold *Aspergillus*. It's available in Asian markets and many natural food stores. Store in the refrigerator for up to 1 year.

kokam [KOH-kahm] Dark purple, KIWI-sized fruit from a slender ever-green tree known as *Garcinia indica* or **kokum**. The trees are native to the tropical rain forests in an area in western India known as the Western Ghats. Kokam is also known as *aamsul or amsul*. It's related to the MANGO-STEEN and, because of its dark color is sometimes referred to as *black mangosteen*. Either the whole fruit or just the separated rind is sun-dried. The flavor is somewhat fruity with a sour, astringent character. It's used in some parts of India as a replacement for TAMARIND, which is a bit stronger than kokam. In addition to its use in CURRY blends, the dried fruit is often soaked in water, which is then used to flavor savory dishes and in sweetened drinks called CHARBET. The kokam seeds contain edible oil that is used as a replacement for GHEE and in various cosmetics. Dried rind and occasionally a paste made from it can be found in Indian markets. *see* SHERBET

K

kolacky; kolachke [koh-LAH-chee; koh-LAH-kee] Claimed by both Poles and Czechs, these sweet yeast buns are filled with poppy seeds, nuts, jam or a mashed fruit mixture.

kombu; konbu [KOHM-boo] Particularly popular in Japanese cookery, kombu is one of the two basic ingredients used for DASHI (soup stock). It's a long dark brown to grayish-black SEAWEED, which, after harvesting, is sun-dried and folded into sheets. Kombu is sold in Japanese and natural food markets and when stored unopened in a dry place it will keep indefinitely. After opening, store in a cool, dry place for up to 6 months. Kombu has a natural white-powder covering that delivers considerable flavor. For that reason, the surface should be lightly wiped off, not washed. Kombu is used to flavor cooked foods as well as for SUSHI. It's sometimes pickled and used as a CONDIMENT. Kombu is also called simply *kelp*.

kongguksu; konggooksoo [KOHNG-gook-soo] A chilled Korean soup with thin wheat noodles called SOMEN in a savory broth of SOY MILK flavored with sesame seed or nuts and served with cucumbers, tomatoes or watermelon.

konnyaku [kohn-NYAH-koo] A translucent, gelatinous cake made from the starch of a yamlike tuber known as *devil's tongue*. Although konnyaku has no noticeable flavor, it readily absorbs the flavors of the simmered dishes to which it's added. There are two types—*shiru konnyaku,* a refined pearly-white version, and *kuro konnyaku,* an unrefined cake with dark specks in it. Konnyaku is available in the refrigerated section of Asian markets. *See also* SHIRATAKI.

kopi luwak; luwak [KOH-pee LOO-wak] This exceedingly exotic coffee commands the highest prices on the planet. The coffee plants grow on the Indonesian islands of Java, Sulawesi and Sumatra. Kopi is Indonesian for "coffee" and luwak is the local name for a marsupial (the common palm civet or paradoxurus); therefore, "civet coffee." What makes this coffee so unique is that the civet eats only the ripest of coffee berries, which are deposited relatively whole in the animal's feces, forming a log of berries. This might only be a colorful curiosity except for the fact that the enzymes in the animal's digestive tract ostensibly impact the coffee berry by eliminating bitterness and enriching the flavor. Why the natives ever thought to collect and wash the marsupial's droppings is still a mystery. Nevertheless, kopi luwak is produced by lightly roasting the cleaned beans. The resulting coffee is described by some as smooth, rich, heavy and full bodied with flavors of caramel and chocolate. Naturally, naysayers assert that the coffee's reputation is simply hype and there are myriad coffees just as good or better. There's a similar coffee produced in the Philippines called **kape alamid** and a small quantity from south India called **karibeck kapi**. Vietnam produces a version called **weasel coffee** (the product, as you may have guessed, of weasels), however today a synthetically processed imitation is more likely to be found. Kopi Luwak is available on a very limited basis at specialty coffee retailers.

Korean barbecued beef *see* BULGOGI

Korean mint A member of the *agastache* species of the mint family and similar to ANISE HYSSOP. Korean mint is also known as *blue licorice* or *purple giant hyssop*. The plant produces tall, purplish-blue flower-spikes in late spring and early summer. Its leaves are heart-shaped with serrated edges and have a grayish-green color. Their aroma has a bit of a eucalyptus smell but the flavor is sweet and ANISE-like. The leaves are used to flavor teas and in MARINADES and salads, with vegetables and as a GARNISH.

korma [KOR-mah] Popular in India and Pakistan, korma is a spicy curried dish of mutton, lamb or chicken, usually with the addition of onions and sometimes other vegetables.

kosher cheese A product that is strictly controlled and produced under Kosher law (*see* KOSHER FOOD), which means that the animal-derived RENNET typically used for COAGULATION in the beginning stages of cheese-making cannot be used because it conflicts with milk. Most kosher cheese producers use biotech microbial rennet, produced with kosher techniques and ingredients. Today there's a wide selection of kosher cheeses, which are clearly marked as such and can be found in supermarkets as well as specialty cheese stores. Kosher cheese is also known as *gvinas Yisroel* ("cheese made by a Jew").

kosher food [KOH-sher] Food that conforms to strict Jewish Biblical laws pertaining not only to the type of food that may be eaten, but to the kinds of food that can be combined at one meal (for example, meat and dairy products may not be mixed). In order to meet kosher standards and receive the kosher seal, food must be prepared under a rabbi's supervision. In addition to the kinds of animals considered kosher (pigs and rabbits are among the nonkosher group), the laws also decree that animals be fed organically grown food and killed in the most humane manner possible. The word "kosher" is a derivation of the Hebrew *kasher,* meaning "proper" or "pure." Because kosher foods bear an inherent hallmark of wholesomeness and quality, they are rapidly becoming popular with a new market of health-conscious consumers. Kosher foods can be purchased in most supermarkets throughout the United States.

koshi-an *see* AZUKI-AN

Koshihikari rice [koh-shee-hee-KAH-ree] High-quality short-grain rice very popular in Japan. It's highly regarded for its aroma, consistency, natural sweetness and ability to retain firmness once cooked, making it suitable for both SUSHI and general cooking. Koshihikari translates to "light of Koshi," referring to an ancient region located on the west coast of central Japan, an area where much of this rice is now grown. Koshihikari is also grown in California.

koshu [KOH-shoo] *see* SAKE

kourabiedes [koo-rah-bee-YAY-dehs] These popular melt-in-the-mouth Greek cookies are served on festive occasions such as christenings, weddings and holiday celebrations. They're buttery-rich and can contain nuts or not, but are always rolled in powdered sugar after baking. Kourabiedes come in various forms from balls to ovals to S-shapes. At Christmastime, a clove inserted in the top symbolizes the rare spices brought to Christ by the Magi.

kozunak *see* TSOUREKI

krachai *see* FINGERROOT

Krauterkäse *see* SAPSAGO

kreplach [KREHP-luhkh; KREHP-lahk] Of Jewish origin, these small raviolilike (*see* RAVIOLI) noodle dumplings are filled with chopped meat or cheese. They're simmered in broth or included in soup.

kuay taew *see* RICE NOODLES

ku chai [koo CHI] *see* GARLIC CHIVES

Kuchen [KOH -khehn] A fruit- or cheese-filled yeast-raised cake, usually served for breakfast but also enjoyed as a dessert. It originated in Germany but is now enjoyed in many variations throughout much of Europe and the United States. The word *Kaffeekuchen* is German for "coffee cake."

kudzu [KOOD-zoo] It wasn't until 1876 that this fast-growing legume-family plant was introduced to the United States, where it's used primarily as pasturage and for erosion control. Kudzu, however, has been a popular food in Japan and China for thousands of years. Most of the plant can be eaten—the tender leaves and stems can be cooked as with other GREENS. However, it's the tuberous roots (which have been known to weigh up to 450 pounds and reach 7 feet in length) that offer this plant's real premium. These roots are dehydrated and pulverized, and it is this starchy *kudzu powder* that is used culinarily in myriad ways—from thickening soups and sauces to DREDGING foods to be deep-fried. Kudzu powder can be found in Asian markets and some natural food stores. It's high in fiber, protein and vitamins A and D.

kugel [KOO-guhl] Traditionally served on the Jewish Sabbath, kugel is a baked pudding usually made with potatoes or noodles, though meat, vegetables and other ingredients are sometimes included. It's generally served as a side dish, though a sweet version with raisins and spices is equally delicious as dessert.

kugelhopf; kugelhupf [KOO-guhl-hopf] Though generally thought of as Austrian, bakers from Alsace, Germany and Poland also claim credit for this light yeast cake. Kugelhopf is filled with raisins, candied fruits and nuts, and generally embellished with a simple dusting of powdered sugar. It's traditionally baked in a **kugelhopf pan**, a turban-shaped tube mold with swirled sides, which can be found in gourmet kitchenware shops. Also called *gugelhopf.*

kui teow *see* RICE NOODLES

kuku [koo-KOO] Baked Persian egg dish somewhat akin to a FRITTATA. There are several versions—all vegetarian. The herb version (**kuku-ye sabzi**) is standard fare on New Year's Day in Iran. It usually contains green onion, parsley, cilantro, dill and FENUGREEK and is seasoned with the Persian spice blend ADVIEH, salt and pepper. The dish is topped with a garnish featuring BARBERRIES and grape molasses (*see* FRUIT MOLASSES). Other versions include **kuku-ye sibzamini**, made with potatoes, and **kuku-ye bademjun**, using eggplant.

kukui nut *see* CANDLENUT

kulebiaka; koulibiaka [koo-lee-BYAH-kah] *see* COULIBIAC

kulfi [kuhl-fee] Ice cream made in India, Pakistan and neighboring countries that's similar to but denser and creamier than most ice creams found in the United States because it's not whipped. Traditional kulfi is made from KHOA or RABRI and comes in flavors such as cardamom, cream (called *malai*), kewra (SCREWPINE essence), mango, pistachio, raspberry, rose and saffron, but new flavors are being introduced all the time. Kulfi appears in different forms but the traditional one is to freeze the ice cream in conical metal molds. Another tradition is to serve kulfi topped with FALOODA noodles.

kulich [KOO-lihch] A tall cylindrical Russian Easter cake traditionally served with PASHKA (a creamy cheese mold). Kulich is yeast-raised and flavored with raisins, candied fruit and saffron. It's usually crowned with a white powdered sugar icing, sprinkled with chopped candied fruits and almonds and sometimes topped with a rose.

Kumamoto oyster This oyster species is native to Ariake Bay, Kumamoto Prefecture, on the Japanese island of Kyushu. The Kumamoto is small, ranging from $1^3/_4$ to $2^1/_4$ inches across, but has a deep cup and ridges on the shell. The oyster is plump and succulent with a mild brininess and sweet flavor. It's considered superior, especially for eating ON THE HALF SHELL. *See also* OYSTER.

kuminost [KOO-mihn-ohst] *see* NÖKKELOST

kumiss; koumiss [KOO-mihs] Thought to have originated with the Mongols, this acrid, slightly alcoholic beverage is made from fermented mare's or camel's milk. Like KEFIR, today's kumiss is more likely produced from cow's milk. It's often used as a digestive aid.

kümmel [KIHM-uhl; KOO-muhl] Created in Holland and now also produced in Germany, kümmel is a colorless LIQUEUR flavored with a panoply of herbs and seeds including caraway, cumin and fennel. Its name comes from the middle-high German *Kümmel,* which denotes both "cumin" and "caraway."

kumotake *see* HEN OF THE WOODS

kumquat [KUHM-kwaht] This pigmy of the citrus family looks like a tiny oval or round orange. It's cultivated in China, Japan and the United States. The edible golden orange rind is sweet, while the rather dry flesh is very tart. The entire fruit—skin and flesh—is eaten, and very ripe fruit can be sliced and served raw in salads or as a garnish. The kumquat is more likely to be found cooked, however, either candied or pickled whole or in preserves or marmalades. Fresh kumquats are available from November to June. Look for firm fruit without blemishes. Refrigerate wrapped in a plastic bag for up to a month. Kumquats contain good amounts of potassium and vitamins A and C. *See also* LIMEQUAT.

kung pao [gong BAH-oh] A spicy sour-sweet Chinese STIR-FRY dish of chunks or strips of chicken, shrimp or vegetables with sweet peppers, dried CHILES, peanuts, garlic, ginger, wine and soy sauce.

Kurobuta pork [koo-roh-BOO-tah] see HERITAGE PORK

kuro goma [koo-roh goh-mah] *see* GOMA

kushi [koo-SHEE] Japanese for "skewer."

kushiage [koo-shee-AH-geh] A combination of KUSHI and AGEMONO, referring to foods that are coated with egg and bread crumbs, skewered and then deep-fried.

kushiyaki [koo-shee-YAH-kee] A combination of KUSHI and YAKITORI, meaning "skewer grilling" and referring to food put on bamboo skewers and then grilled.

kuzhambu *see* SAMBAR

kuzu *see* KUDZU

kway teow *see* RICE NOODLES

kyuri *see* JAPANESE CUCUMBER

laab; laap; labb [LAHB; LAHP] *see* LARB

label terms *see* Food Label Terms, page 876; A Guide to Food Labels, page 880; WINE LABEL TERMS

Lacinato kale *see* CAVOLO NERO

lactic; lactic acid [LAK-tihk] 1. The word "lactic" is an adjective for things relating to or derived from milk. 2. Lactic acid is a bitter-tasting acid that forms when certain bacteria combine with LACTOSE (milk sugar). It's used to impart a tart flavor, as well as in the preservation of some foods. Lactic acid occurs naturally in the souring of milk and can be found in foods such as cheese and yogurt. It's also used in the production of acid-fermented foods such as pickles and SAUERKRAUT.

lactose; lactose intolerance [LAK-tohs] This sugar occurs naturally in milk and is also called *milk sugar*. It's the least sweet of all the natural sugars and is used commercially in foods such as baby formulas and candies. **Lactose intolerance** or sensitivity is the inability to digest lactose because the small intestine doesn't produce enough lactase, the enzyme needed for lactose digestion. The degree of the intolerance is individual, with some people able to ingest more milk-based products than others. Cheese contains less lactose than milk, with hard, aged cheeses containing only a trace amount.

Lady Alice apple An all-purpose apple with variegated peach and red coloring on a creamy yellow background and a dense, sweet, crisp, juicy flesh that resists browning. The flavor is sweetly tart with a hint of honey. The Lady Alice is not an engineered CROSS but an accidental one created in 1978 by a grower who gouged a Red Delicious apple tree with a disc from his plow. The tree proceeded to send out an entirely different-looking branch and to produce completely unique fruit. *See also* APPLE.

Lady apple Tiny apples that are only about 1½ inches across with a shape that's slightly flattened on the top and bottom. The skin color ranges from brilliant red to yellow with red blushing. Lady apples have a crisp flesh and a mildly sweet-tart flavor. *See also* APPLE.

Lady Baltimore cake A moist, three-layered white cake with a filling of raisins, nuts and sometimes other fruit such as figs. The cake is covered with a fluffy white frosting such as BOILED ICING. It was first mentioned by novelist Owen Wister in his 1906 novel, *Lady Baltimore*. Legend has it that a young woman gave Wister such a cake, which he later chronicled in his novel. *See also* LORD BALTIMORE CAKE.

ladyfinger A light, delicate sponge cake roughly shaped like a rather large, fat finger. It's used as an accompaniment to ice cream, puddings and other desserts, and employed as an integral part of some desserts, such as CHARLOTTES. Ladyfingers can be purchased in bakeries or supermarkets or made at home. They can either be piped onto a baking sheet with a pastry bag or the batter can be spooned into a **ladyfinger pan**, which is a tinned steel tray with 10 oblong indentations. The pan is commonly found in gourmet kitchenware shops.

lager [LAH-guhr] A general style of beer that was originally stored and AGED (lagered) in its cask or vat for 1 to 3 months until free of sediment and crystal clear, after which carbonation was added and the beer was bottled. Modern production techniques now complete this process much more quickly. Lager is a light, bubbly, golden brew that ranks as America's most popular. *See also* BEER.

lagniappe; lagnappe [lan-YAP; LAN-yap] Used primarily in southern Louisiana and southeast Texas, the word *lagniappe* refers to an "unexpected something extra." It could be an additional doughnut (as in "baker's dozen"), a free "one for the road" drink, an unanticipated tip for someone who provides a special service or possibly a complimentary dessert for a regular customer.

la han qua *see* LUO HAN GUO

lahvosh *see* LAVASH

lai fen [li FEHN] *see* RICE NOODLES

lait [LAY] French for "milk," such as in CAFÉ AU LAIT ("coffee with milk") or *lait cru* ("raw milk").

lake trout *see* CHAR

laksa [LAHK-sah] There are two main types of laksa popular in Southeast Asia; both are soup-based dishes made with thick rice noodles. **Curry laksa** or *curry mee* is made with coconut milk, and its creamy texture is enlivened with SAMBAL and other spices such as CORIANDER and LEMON GRASS. Hundreds of variations exist and the additions run the gamut from chicken and bean curd to COCKLES and cooked pork blood. **Asam laksa**, also known as *Penang laksa,* is a thick, sour soup using minced fish, chiles, cucumbers, mint leaves, onion and pineapple and flavored with lemon grass, basil and GALANGAL. The sourness comes from TAMARIND juice, known as *asam* in Malaysia. Penang is a state in Malaysia famous for its asam laksa.

lamb A sheep less than 1 year old, known for its tender meat. Baby lamb and spring lamb are both milk fed. **Baby lamb** is customarily slaughtered at between 6 and 8 weeks old. **Spring lamb** is usually 3 to 5 months old; **regular lamb** is slaughtered under a year of age. Lamb between 12 and

24 months is called **yearling;** when over 2 years, it's referred to as **mutton** and has a much stronger flavor and less tender flesh. There are five USDA grades for lamb based on proportion of fat to lean. Beginning with the best, they are *Prime, Choice, Good, Utility* and *Cull.* When purchasing lamb, let color be the guide. In general, the darker the color, the older the animal. Baby lamb will be pale pink, while regular lamb is pinkish-red. Lamb can be purchased ground and in STEAKS, CHOPS and ROASTS. Lamb VARIETY MEATS can also be purchased. Refrigerate ground and small lamb cuts loosely wrapped for up to 3 days. Roasts can be stored up to 5 days. Ground lamb can be freezer-wrapped and frozen up to 3 months, solid cuts up to 6 months. *See also* Lamb Chart, page 897; BREAST, LAMB; LEG, LAMB; LOIN, LAMB; RIB, LAMB; SHOULDER, LAMB; VARIETY MEATS.

Lambert cherry A sweet cherry variety that's large, round and a deep ruby red. The flesh is sweet, firm and meaty. A superior cherry for out-of-hand eating as well as cooking. *See also* CHERRY.

lambic beer A WHEAT BEER produced, in a small area southwest of Brussels, from 60 to 70 percent malted barley and 30 to 40 percent wheat. The MASH is traditionally made in the winter when conditions are just right for a wild yeast called *Brettanomyces* to start spontaneous FERMENTATION. Lambics are aged in casks anywhere from several months to several years. Younger lambic beers can be sour and slightly cloudy; older versions mellow and lose much of their sour character. A light fruity essence is sometimes infused into lambics when fruit (such as cherries or raspberries) are added to the beer during aging. *See also* BEER.

lambrusco [lam-BROOS-koh] An Italian wine that comes in three versions—red, white and rosé. The style best known by Americans is the pale red, semisweet, slightly effervescent Lambrusco. All three variations are made in both semisweet and DRY styles, the latter being preferred in Italy. Lambrusco wines are not known for their aging capabilities and should be drunk young.

lamb's lettuce *see* CORN SALAD

lampasconi *see* CIPOLLINI

lampone [lahm-POH-neh] Italian for "RASPBERRY."

lamprey [LAM-pree] Varieties of this long (about 21 inches), EEL-shaped fish are found in both fresh and marine waters. It has a delicately flavored but extremely fatty flesh, which makes it indigestible for many people. Lamprey can be cooked whole (if small to medium) or in pieces. It's usually braised in wine, but is suitable for other manners of cooking such as baking or sautéing. *See also* FISH.

Lancashire cheese [LANG-kah-shur; LANG-kuh-sheer] Made in Lancashire, England, this pale-yellow cow's-milk cheese can range from semihard to hard depending on how long it's aged. When young, the flavor is mild yet tangy. It becomes stronger and richer in flavor as it matures. Lancashire, with its delicate, soft and crumbly texture, melts beautifully and is a favorite cheese for WELSH RABBIT (also called *Welsh rarebit*). Lancashire's FAT CONTENT is about 48 percent. *See also* CHEESE.

Lancashire hot pot *see* HOTCHPOTCH

Lane cake Particularly popular throughout the South, this white or yellow cake is layered with a mixture of coconut, nuts and dried fruits and covered with a fluffy white frosting. Lane cake is said to have originated in Clayton, Alabama, when its creator, Emma Rylander Lane, won a prize for it in the state fair.

langostino [lahn-goh-STEEN-oh] Spanish for "PRAWN."

langouste [lahn-GOOST] French for "spiny LOBSTER."

langoustine [lahn-goo-STEEN] French for "PRAWN."

langues-de-chat [lawng-duh-CHAH] *see* CATS' TONGUES

Laos; Laos ginger *see* GALANGAL

lapin [la-PAH/V] French for "RABBIT."

Lapsang Souchong [LAP-sang SOO-shawng] This famous black tea hails from China's Fukian province and is noted for its distinctive smoky essence. *See also* TEA.

larb [LARB] A spicy meat salad popular in Laos and Thailand. Larb is made with minced or ground meat and seasoned with various flavorings including fish sauce, lime juice, chiles, mint and green onion. A variety of meats can be used including beef, chicken, duck, pork and turkey; fish is also an option for larb. The meat and flavorings are typically stir-fried together, then served warm or at room temperature over lettuce, cabbage or an assortment of vegetables. Larb is often served with sticky rice (*see* RICE) to create a fuller meal. It's also spelled *laab, laap, labb* or *larp*.

lard *n.* RENDERED and CLARIFIED pork fat, the quality of which depends on the area the fat came from and the method of rendering. The very best is **leaf lard**, which comes from the fat around the animal's kidneys. Unprocessed lard has quite a strong flavor and a soft texture. Lard can be processed in many ways including filtering, bleaching, hydrogenation and emulsification. In general, processed lard is firmer (about the consistency of VEGETABLE SHORTENING), has a milder, more nutlike flavor and a longer shelf life. Lard is richer than many other fats and therefore makes extremely tender, flaky biscuits and pastries. It's a flavorful fat for frying and is widely used throughout South America and many European countries. When substituting lard for butter in baking, reduce the amount by 20 to 25 percent. All lard should be tightly wrapped to prevent absorption of other flavors. It may be stored at room temperature or in the refrigerator, depending on how it has been processed. Always check the label for storage directions. **lard** *v.* To insert long, thin strips of fat (usually pork) or bacon into a dry cut of meat. The purpose of larding is to make the cooked meat more succulent, tender and flavorful. These strips are commonly referred to as LARDONS and are inserted with a special tool called a LARDING NEEDLE. *See also* BARD.

larding needle A special tool used to LARD meats. There are many styles, but the most common is one that has a sharp, pointed tip and a hollow body. A long, thin strip of the larding agent (usually pork fat or bacon) is inserted into the tool's hollow cavity and the needle is then used to thread the fat through the meat. *See also* LARD *v.*

lardo 1. Italian for "FATBACK." 2. An Italian specialty of pig's-rump fat flavored with herbs and spices and CURED in a salt brine.

lardons; lardoons [LAHR-don; lahr-DOON] 1. Narrow strips of fat used to LARD meats. 2. The French also use the term *lardon* to refer to bacon that has been diced, blanched and fried.

Large Black pork *see* HERITAGE PORK

large clam *see* CHOWDER CLAM

larp [LARP] *see* LARB

lasagna; *pl.* **lasagne** [luh-ZAHN-yah] 1. A wide flat noodle, sometimes with ruffled edges (*see also* Pasta Glossary, page 883). 2. A dish made by layering boiled lasagna noodles with various cheeses (usually including mozzarella) with the cook's choice of sauce, the most common being tomato, meat or BÉCHAMEL. This dish is then baked until bubbly and golden brown. *See also* PASTA.

lassi [LAH-see] A popular chilled yogurt drink in India, which can also be made with buttermilk or extra-rich milk. Lassi is like a healthy MILK SHAKE, the thickness of which depends on the ratio of yogurt to water. Thick *lassi* is made with four parts yogurt to one part water and/or crushed ice. Lassi can be flavored variously with salt, mint, CUMIN, sugar, fruit or fruit juices—even spicy additions such as ground chiles, fresh ginger or garlic. The ingredients are all placed in a blender and processed until the mixture is light and frothy.

late harvest An American wine term referring to wines made from grapes picked toward the end of the harvest (usually late fall), preferably those with BOTRYTIS CINEREA, a fungus that shrivels the grape thereby concentrating its sugar. Late-harvest wines are very sweet and usually have a high alcohol content. The most popular grapes used for these DESSERT WINES are RIESLING, GEWÜRZTRAMINER and SAUVIGNON BLANC.

latke [LAHT-kuh] Traditionally served at Hanukkah, the latke is a pancake usually made from grated potatoes mixed with eggs, onions, MATZO MEAL and seasonings. It's fried and served hot as a side dish.

latte *see* CAFÉ LATTE

laurel leaf; bay laurel *see* BAY LEAF

lavash; lavosh; lahvosh [LAH-vohsh] A round, thin, crisp bread that's also known as *Armenian cracker bread.* It comes in a soft version, as well as in various sizes, ranging from about 6 to 14 inches in diameter. Lavash is available in Middle Eastern markets and most supermarkets. It's the bread used to make the popular ARAM SANDWICH.

lavender Historically known as the "herb of love," lavender is a relative of mint. This aromatic plant has violet flowers and green or pale gray leaves, both of which lend a pleasantly bitter pungency to salad, rubs for poultry and fish and in spice blends, such as HERBS DE PROVENCE. The leaves may also be used to make herb tea or, more accurately, TISANE. You can typically find culinary lavender in natural food stores and some produce markets.

lavender gem This citrus fruit is a white grapefruit-TANGELO cross with a pale pink skin and flesh and a sweet flavor. It's usually available only in specialty produce stores and can be used in any manner appropriate for grapefruit. Lavender gems are also called *wekiwas.*

laver [LAY-vuhr] This highly nutritious dried SEAWEED comes in tissue-thin sheets about 7½ inches square. It has a fresh, tangy-sweet flavor and a dark purple color, which is why it's also called *purple laver.* The Chinese name for this seaweed is *jee choy,* which means "purple vegetable." Before using, laver must be soaked in cold water. After an hour of soaking, it doubles in size. Laver is often used in soups. Strips of it can also be deep-fried and served as an appetizer.

laverbread Old-fashioned Welsh dish made from LAVER that's boiled, pureed and, then usually rolled in oats to form small cakes before fried. It's traditionally served as part of a Welsh breakfast that includes eggs, bacon and COCKLES.

lavosh *see* LAVASH

leaf gelatin *see* GELATIN

leaf lard *see* LARD

leaf lettuce Any of several varieties of lettuce with leaves that branch from a single stalk in a loose bunch rather than forming a tight head. The leaves are crisper and more full-flavored than those of the HEAD LETTUCE varieties. Depending on the variety, leaf lettuce (also called *loose-leaf* and *Simpson lettuce*) can range in color from medium to dark green; some have red-tipped leaves. Among the more popular leaf lettuces are **oak leaf**, **salad bowl**, frilly **red leaf** and crinkly **green leaf**. In general, leaf lettuce is more perishable than head lettuce. Choose bunches with crisp, evenly colored leaves with no sign of wilting or yellowing. As with all greens, leaf lettuce should be washed and either drained completely or blotted with a paper towel to remove any excess moisture before being refrigerated in a plastic bag. It will keep this way up to about 3 days. *See also* LETTUCE.

Leanesse *see* FAT SUBSTITUTES

lean, finely textured beef *see* PINK SLIME

lear oil *see* CANOLA OIL

leather *see* FRUIT LEATHER

leaven To add a leavening agent to a mixture such as a batter or dough in order to make it rise. *See also* AMMONIUM BICARBONATE; BAKING POWDER; BAKING SODA; EGGS; YEAST.

leavener; leavening agent [LEHV-uhn-er] Agents that are used to lighten the texture and increase the volume of baked goods such as breads, cakes and cookies. Baking powder, baking soda and yeast are the most common leaveners used today. When mixed with a liquid they form carbon dioxide gas bubbles, which cause a batter or dough to rise during (and sometimes before) the baking process. Some foods, such as ANGEL FOOD CAKE and SPONGE CAKE, are leavened by the air beaten into egg whites. When heated, the egg whites cook and set, trapping the air inside and creating a light, airy cake.

Leberkäse [LAY-buhr-kah-suh] A smooth, delicate pork PÂTÉ made with onion, garlic and eggs. The tubular SAUSAGE is cut into thick slices and either steamed or gently sautéed. *Leberkäse* (German for "liver cheese") is served warm or at room temperature.

Lebkuchen [LAYB-koo-kuhn] This thick, cakelike cookie is a specialty of Nuremberg and one of the most popular in Germany. It's honey-sweetened, full of spices, CITRON and almonds and often topped with a hard powdered sugar glaze. Lebkuchen has been made for centuries and is often baked in decorative molds to shape the cookie into intricate designs. *See also* COOKIE.

leche [LAY-chay; LEH-cheh] Spanish for "milk."

lecithin [LEHS-uh-thihn] A fatty substance obtained from egg yolks and LEGUMES, used to preserve, emulsify and moisturize food.

leckerle; leckerli [LEH-kehr-lee] This popular Swiss cookie comes in two versions—one made with honey, one with ground almonds. Both are chewy and delicious. The dough is traditionally pressed into special wooden molds, which imprint designs on the surface of the cookies.

leek Native to the Mediterranean countries, the leek has been prized by gourmets for thousands of years. Nero believed leeks would improve his singing voice and is said to have eaten prodigious quantities to that end. In the sixth century A.D., the Welsh made leeks their national symbol because they were convinced that the leeks they wore on their helmets to distinguish them from their enemies strengthened them and helped them win wars. Leeks still hold a flavorful spotlight in today's cuisine. Looking like a giant SCALLION, the leek is related to both the garlic and the onion, though its flavor and fragrance are milder and more subtle. It has a thick, white stalk that's cylindrical in shape and has a slightly bulbous root end. The broad, flat, dark green leaves wrap tightly around each other like a rolled newspaper. Leeks are available year-round in most regions. Choose those with crisp, brightly colored leaves and an unblemished white portion. Avoid any with withered or yellow-spotted leaves. The smaller the leek, the more tender it will be. Refrigerate leeks in a plastic bag up to 5 days. Before using, trim rootlets and leaf ends. Slit the leeks from top to bottom and wash thoroughly to remove all the dirt trapped between the leaf layers. Leeks can be cooked whole as a vegetable or chopped and used in salads, soups and a multitude of other dishes.

lees [LEEZ] The sediment (dregs) of wine or liquor that occurs during fermentation and aging.

leg, lamb Popular, flavorful back leg that's often divided into two sections: the *sirloin half*, which comes from the upper part, has more bone but is more tender and the *shank half* which is the lower shin, is leaner and less tender but quite flavorful. An *American leg* has the bone at the end cut off, while a *French leg* has the meat at the end trimmed away, leaving the bone exposed. The front leg of the lamb is also called *shank*.

legume [lehg-YOOM] Any of thousands of plant species that have seed pods that split along both sides when ripe. Some of the more common legumes used for human consumption are BEANS, LENTILS, PEANUTS, PEAS and

SOYBEANS. Others, such as clover and alfalfa, are used as animal fodder. When the seeds of a legume are dried, they're referred to as PULSES. The high-protein legumes are a staple throughout the world. They contain some vitamin B, carbohydrates, fats and minerals. *See also* BLACK-EYED PEA; CHICKPEA; ENGLISH PEA; FIELD PEA; WINGED BEAN; YARD-LONG BEAN.

legumi [leh-GOO-mee] Italian for "LEGUME."

Leicester; Red Leicester [LESS-ter] This orangy-red cow's-milk cheese was once colored with beet or carrot juice, then with ANNATTO, but coloration was discontinued during World War II and Leicester cheese took on a naturally pale color. When the use of annatto was reinstated after the war, the word "red" was appended to "Leicester" to differentiate the pale style from the dyed version. The name "Red Leicester" stuck, though to distinguish it as such isn't necessary today because all Leicester is the same color—a deep reddish orange. This cheese resembles CHEDDAR but has a higher moisture content. It has a crumbly texture that makes slicing difficult but facilitates grating. The flavor is mellow with a tangy aftertaste. FARMSTEAD versions develop complex flavors of caramel, nuts and citrus. Leicester's FAT CONTENT is about 48 percent. *See also* CHEESE.

Leiden *see* LEYDEN

lekvar [LEHK-vahr] A thick, soft spread made of fruit (usually prunes or apricots) cooked with sugar. This Hungarian specialty is used to fill a variety of pastries and cookies. Lekvar can be purchased in cans or jars in most supermarkets.

lemanderin *see* RANGPUR LIME

lemon Throughout the eons, lemons have been used for a multitude of nonculinary purposes—as an epilepsy remedy, a toothpaste, an invisible ink and a bleaching agent as well as in witchcraft. Though it originated in Southeast Asia, the lemon is now cultivated in tropical and temperate climates around the world, with California leading production in the United States. This bright yellow citrus fruit is oval in shape, with a pronounced bulge on the blossom end. The flesh is juicy and acidic. The lemon can range in size from that of a large egg to that of a small grapefruit. Some have thin skins while others have very thick rinds, which are used to make candied lemon peel. Lemons are available year-round with a peak during the summer months. Choose fruit with smooth, brightly colored skin with no tinge of green (which signals underripeness). Lemons should be firm, plump and heavy for their size. Depending on their condition when purchased, they can be refrigerated in a plastic bag for 2 to 3 weeks. The lemon has a multitude of culinary uses for dishes sweet to savory, as well as a flavoring in many drinks. Few foods add such flavor magic as the simple lemon. **Bottled** and **frozen lemon juice** are also available in most supermarkets. The frozen juice is a passable substitute but the bottled product bears little resemblance to the real thing. Though the lemon is an excellent source of vitamin C (one provides 40 to 70 percent of the minimum daily requirement), it begins to lose its vitamin power soon after it's squeezed. There's a 20 percent loss of vitamin C after only 8 hours at room temperature or 24 hours in the refrigerator. *See also* MEYER LEMON.

lemonade *see* ADE

lemon aspen Pale, lemon-colored fruit that grows on rain forest trees native to Queensland, Australia. The lemon aspen fruit (referred to as a berry) is about the size of a large grape. It has a thin skin, spongy flesh and small dark seeds in a tough, x-shaped core. The acidic lemon aspen has a spicy aroma and flavor that's like a citrus blend with a hint of eucalyptus. The juice is used like that of lemons in Australian cuisine. Availability is limited, typically only through Internet ordering.

lemon balm Widely available in Europe, this herb has lemon-scented, mintlike leaves that are often used to brew an aromatic tea (TISANE). Its slightly tart flavor is used to flavor salads as well as meats and poultry. Also called simply *balm*.

lemon curd *see* CURD

lemon grass One of the most important flavorings in Thai and Vietnamese cooking, this herb has long, thin, gray-green leaves and a woody scallionlike base. Citral, an essential oil also found in lemon peel, gives lemon grass its sour-lemon flavor and fragrance. It is available fresh or dried in Asian (particularly Thai) markets, produce markets and some supermarkets. Choose blemish-free green stalks with white roots. Store fresh lemon grass in the refrigerator, tightly wrapped in a plastic bag, for up to 2 weeks. Use the white base up to where the leaves begin to branch to flavor tea, sauces, soups and curry dishes; discard lemon grass before serving. Lemon grass is also called *citronella root* and *sereh*.

lemon myrtle The leaves of this evergreen plant have a strong smell of lemon and are used to impart their lively, citrusy flavor to baked and cooked items and tea. Native to Queensland and the surrounding coastal areas in Australia, it's also known as **lemon-scented myrtle** and **lemon-scented verbena**. The dark green leaves, which are 2 to 5 inches long, are used fresh or in dried form. Because they are not acidic, the leaves are useful in dairy-based recipes that might curdle from real lemons. Availability is limited, typically only through Internet ordering.

lemon-scented myrtle *see* LEMON MYRTLE

lemon-scented verbena *see* LEMON MYRTLE

lemon sole *see* ENGLISH SOLE

lemon verbena [ver-BEE-nuh] Native to South America, the long, slender leaves of this potent herb have an overpowering lemonlike flavor. For that reason, a light touch is necessary when adding lemon verbena (also called simply *verbena*) to food. It's available dried and sometimes fresh in specialty produce markets. It's used to flavor fruit salads and some sweet dishes, and for tea (TISANE).

lemper ayam [lihm-PER ah-YAM] Indonesian snack of minced chicken coated in sticky rice and wrapped in a banana leaf.

lentil Popular in parts of Europe and a staple throughout much of the Middle East and India, this tiny, lens-shaped PULSE has long been used as a meat substitute. There are three main varieties of lentils. The **French** or **European lentil**, sold with the seed coat on, has a grayish-brown exterior and a creamy yellow interior. The reddish orange **Egyptian** or **red lentil** is smaller, rounder and sans seed coat. There's also a **yellow lentil**. None of these varieties are used fresh but are dried as soon as they're ripe. The regular brown lentils are commonly found in supermarkets whereas the red and yellow lentils, though available in some supermarkets, must usually be purchased in Middle Eastern or East Indian markets. Lentils should be stored airtight at room temperature and will keep up to a year. They can be used as a side dish (puréed, whole and combined with vegetables), in salads, soups and stews. One of the most notable showcases for the lentil is the spicy East Indian DAL. Lentils have a fair amount of calcium and vitamins A and B, and are a good source of iron and phosphorus.

Leopoldia comosa *see* CIPOLLINI

lettuce There are hundreds of lettuce varieties grown throughout the world and, because they peak at different times of year, there's always a plenitude of this universal salad favorite. There are four general lettuce classifications—BUTTERHEAD, CRISPHEAD, LEAF and ROMAINE (*see individual listings*), most of which comprise many varieties. When shopping for any kind of lettuce a general rule of thumb is to choose those that are crisp and free of blemishes. As with all greens, lettuce should be washed and either drained completely or blotted with a paper towel to remove any excess moisture. A SALAD SPINNER, which uses centrifugal force to remove water from leafy greens, is a real time-saver for this process. Never allow lettuce to soak, as the water tends to soften some leaves. Refrigerate washed-and-dried greens airtight in a plastic bag for 3 to 5 days, depending on the variety. All lettuce is low calorie and most of it is rich in calcium, iron and vitamins A and C. Keep in mind that the darker green leaves contain the most nutrients.

levain [loo-VAHN] A YEAST STARTER derived from wild yeast; synonymous with "sourdough starter." Both "sourdough" and "leaven" translate to the French *levain*. Many bakers use levain as a starter for their baked goods instead of commercially available yeast. *Pain au levain* translates to "sourdough bread."

levant [leh-VAHNT] *see* ARAM SANDWICH

le vinaigre de Banyuls [leh vee-NAY-gruh day bah-NYUHLS] *see* VINEGAR

levulose [LEHV-yuh-lohs] *see* FRUCTOSE

Leyden [LAY-den; LI-den] Also known as *Leiden,* this cow's-milk cheese is made on two dozen farms around the town of Leiden in the Zuid-Holland province of the Netherlands. The official (PROTECTED DESIGNATION OF ORIGIN) name of this Dutch cheese is *Boeren Leidse met sleutels*, which translates to "Farmers' Leiden cheese with keys," the last word referring to the imprint of crossed keys on the rind, which represents Leiden's coat of arms. This cheese is semihard to hard with a firm, elastic texture. Leyden has a nutty and creamy flavor with spiciness coming from the embedded cumin seeds. It has an orangish-red rind or is covered in red plastic. Leyden's FAT CONTENT is between 30 and 40 percent. *See also* CHEESE.

LFTB *see* PINK SLIME

liaison [lee-ay-ZON; lee-AY-zon] *see* BINDER

lichee; lichi *see* LYCHEE

Licor 43 *see* CUARENTA Y TRES

licorice; licorice root [LIHK-uh-rihsh; LIHK-uh-rihs] 1. This feathery-leaved plant grows wild throughout southern and parts of central Europe. It's favored for the extract taken from its root and has long been used to flavor confections and medicine. The dark-brown dried root can be found in natural food stores in several forms—chips, 3- to 5-inch-long pencil-like strips (sometimes called *licorice sticks*), and powdered and extract. 2. A candy flavored with licorice extract.

licorice basil *see* BASIL

licorice hyssop *see* ANISE HYSSOP

Liebfraumilch [LEEB-frow-mihlk; LEEP-frow-mihlkh] This lightly sweet German white wine is made from a blend that often includes RIESLING, SYLVANER or Müller-Thurgau grapes. Its quality varies greatly depending on the shipper. *Liebfraumilch* is German for "the milk of our Lady," and was so named because it originally came from the vineyards of a church of the same name, Liebfrauenkirche—"Church of our Lady."

Liederkranz [LEE-duhr-krahntz] This American CHEESE was created in 1882 by Emil Frey, a New York cheesemaker. He named it after a New York singing society of the same name, whose members were great fans of the cheese. This cow's-milk cheese was patterned after LIMBURGER, and its semisoft ivory interior, mildly pungent flavor and distinctive aroma made it a popular favorite. Unfortunately this cheese is no longer being produced, though Marin French Cheese Company produces a similar cheese they call SCHLOSS. *See also* CHEESE.

light cream *see* CREAM

lights The lungs of an animal such as a calf or pig, sometimes used in various preparations like PÂTÉS. Lights can also be sliced and sautéed or used in a stew such as CIVET. Though readily available in Europe, lights are rarely seen in U.S. markets. *See also* VARIETY MEATS.

Liguria olives *see* PONENTINE OLIVE; TAGGIASCA OLIVE

lilikoi [lee-LEE-koy] *see* PASSION FRUIT

Lillet [lee-LAY] A French APÉRITIF made from a blend of wine, BRANDY, fruits and herbs. It originated in the French village of Podensac and has been made since the late 1800s. **Lillet Blanc** is made from white wine and is drier than **Lillet Rouge**, its red-wine counterpart. Both are classically served over ice with an orange twist.

lily buds *see* TIGER LILY BUDS

lima bean [LY-muh] This New World bean was named for Lima, Peru, where it was found as early as 1500. There are two distinct varieties of lima—the **baby lima** and the **Fordhook** (which are not adult baby limas). Both are pale green, plump-bodied and have a slight kidney-shape curve. The Fordhook is larger, plumper and fuller flavored than the baby lima. Fresh limas are available from June to September. They're usually sold in their pods, which should be plump, firm and dark green. The pods can be refrigerated in a plastic bag for up to a week. They should be shelled just before using. Frozen lima beans are available year-round and are labeled according to variety (Fordhook or baby). Canned and dried limas are usually labeled "jumbo," "large" or "small," a designation that relates to size and not variety. In the South, dried limas are frequently referred to as *butter beans.* When mottled with purple they're called *calico* or *speckled butter beans.* A traditional way to serve limas is with corn in SUCCOTASH. They're also used alone as a side dish, in soups and sometimes in salads.

Lima beans contain a good amount of protein, phosphorus, potassium and iron. The lima is also called the *Madagascar bean. See also* BEAN.

limão cravo *see* RANGPUR LIME

Limburger [LIHM-ber-ger] Undoubtedly one of the stinkiest of the strong-smelling cheeses, Limburger has a rind that ranges in color from pinkish orange to reddish brown and a yellow, pasty interior. This strong, pungently flavored cheese is made from cow's milk and is soft-ripened for at least 3 to 4 weeks but often longer. Though it originated in Belgium and is now also made in the United States, most Limburger comes from Germany. The imports continue to ripen during transit, however, and often arrive devastatingly odorous. Though it's definitely an acquired taste, the odor is much stronger than the taste and Limburger has legions of fans. It's made from whole milk and has a FAT CONTENT of at least 50 percent. *See also* CHEESE.

lime This small, lemon-shaped citrus fruit has a thin green skin and a juicy, pale green pulp. Limes grow in tropical and subtropical climes such as Mexico, California, Florida and the Caribbean. Because they're an excellent source of vitamin C, limes were fed to British sailors as a scurvy preventative (the fact that was the springboard for the pejorative nickname "limey"). The two main varieties are the **Persian lime** (the most widely available in the United States) and the **Key lime** from Florida. The latter is smaller, rounder and has a color more yellow than green. Outside of Florida, the Key lime is usually found only in specialty produce markets and some supermarkets that carry gourmet produce. Though Persian limes, also known as *Tahiti limes* or *Bearss limes*, are available year-round, their peak season is from May through August. Look for brightly colored, smooth-skinned limes that are heavy for their size. Small brown areas (SCALD) on the skin won't affect flavor or succulence but a hard or shriveled skin will. Refrigerate uncut limes in a plastic bag for up to 10 days. Cut limes can be stored in the same way up to 5 days. Sweetened or unsweetened **bottled lime juice**, as well as **frozen lime juice** and LIMEADE, are some of the more popular lime products and are available in most supermarkets. The versatile lime has a multitude of uses, from a sprightly addition to mixed drinks (like MARGARITAS), to a marinade for raw fish dishes (such as SEVICHE), to the famous KEY LIME PIE.

limeade *see* ADE

lime pickle 1. Condiment made by cooking chopped limes and various ingredients such as sesame oil or mustard seed oil, chili powder, coriander, cumin, fenugreek, garlic, ginger, salt, sugar and turmeric, then allowing the mixture to age. Lime pickle, which is very popular in India and the rest of South Asia, is made in sweet and sour versions. It's sometimes referred to as *lime relish*. Lime pickle is available in Indian stores and via the Internet. 2. A cucumber soaked in pickling lime instead of BRINE, usually for 24 hours. After soaking, the pickle is thoroughly rinsed and then stored in a mix of PICKLING SPICES, sugar and vinegar. The lime soak produces a crisper, crunchier pickle.

limequat [LIME-kwaht] A tiny (about 2 inches long), round citrus fruit that's a cross between the KUMQUAT and LIME. Limequats have a thin, greenish-yellow rind and pale yellow flesh that has a tart lime flavor. As with kumquats, they may be eaten whole, rind and all. Limequats are available from July to November—look for firm fruit without blemishes. Refrigerate in a plastic bag for up to a month. Use as you would limes, such as in drinks, as a garnish and for MARMALADE.

lime relish *see* LIME PICKLE

limes, dried Persian Limes that are cooked in salty water, then dried. Also known as *limu amani*, they become very hard and almost hollow. Dried Persian limes are frequently used in Indian and Persian cooking to add a flavorful, sour taste. They are sold whole or in powdered form in Middle Eastern groceries; either can be stored in an airtight container for up to 2 years.

limestone lettuce *see* BUTTERHEAD LETTUCE

limoncillo *see* MAMONCILLO

limone [lee-MOH-neh] Italian for "LEMON."

limpa bread [LIHM-puh] Also called *Swedish limpa,* this moist rye bread is flavored with FENNEL or ANISE, CUMIN and orange peel. The result is an immensely flavorful, fragrant loaf of bread.

limpet [LIHM-piht] Easily identified by its coolie hat-shaped shell, this GASTROPOD can be seen clinging to rocks along the seashore. Its meat, which is flavorful but tough, can be consumed raw—either plain or tossed with a VINAIGRETTE dressing. More often, it's tenderized by pounding before being sautéed for a few seconds on each side. Lengthy cooking will toughen the meat. Limpets are usually only available in coastal areas and then only from specialty fish markets. *See also* SHELLFISH.

limu [LEE-moo] Hawaiian for "SEAWEED," of which there are over two dozen varieties included in the native Hawaiian diet. Among the more popular types are the deep green *limu ele'ele,* the reddish-brown *limu kohu,* the pale brown *limu lipoa* and *limu manauea,* which ranges in color from yellow ocher to magenta.

line, to A pan is lined for many reasons—to prevent the mixture in it from sticking, to provide structure to a soft mixture or to add texture and/

or flavor. The lining can be a nonedible material such as PARCHMENT PAPER, thin slices of cake (for structure, as in a CHARLOTTE), slices of bacon (as with a PÂTÉ) or a simple coating of bread or cookie crumbs.

lingcod; ling cod Found on the North American Pacific coast, lingcod is not really a cod but a GREENLING. This fish won't win any beauty contests, but its mildly sweet flavor and firm, lowfat texture makes up for its appearance. Lingcod ranges from 3 to 20 pounds and is available whole or as steaks or fillets. It can be prepared in almost any manner including baking, broiling, frying or grilling. Lingcod also does nicely in soups and stews. *See also* FISH.

lingonberry This tiny COWBERRY (a member of the CRANBERRY family) grows wild in the mountainous regions of Scandinavia, Russia, Canada and—in the United States—Maine. The tart red berries are available fresh only in the regions where they're grown. They can be purchased as sweet sauces or preserves, however, and make excellent accompaniments for pancakes, crêpes, puddings, etc.

lingue di gatto *see* CAT'S TONGUES

linguiça [lihng-GWEE-suh] A slim (about ½ inch in diameter), garlicky Portuguese SAUSAGE that can be found in Latin American markets and many supermarkets. It's used in many Latin dishes such as Brazil's FEIJOADA and Portugal's CALDO VERDE.

linguine *see* Pasta Glossary, page 883

linzertorte [LIHN-zuhr-tort] Though it's now famous around the world, the motherland of this elegant, rich tart is Linz, Austria. Ground almonds, grated lemon rind and spices add their magic to the buttery crust, which is spread with jam (usually raspberry) before being topped with a lattice of crust. After baking, the tart is served at room temperature.

Liptauer [LIP-tow-er] Hailing from and named after a province in Hungary, Liptauer contains about 45 percent fat and is usually made from sheep's milk, although cow's milk is sometimes mixed in. This soft, fresh CHEESE has a mild flavor that is commonly seasoned with herbs, onions, garlic and paprika (which, if used, turns it orangish red—those without can be stark white). There are numerous recipes, with some using as many as 20 ingredients. It's a delicious snack cheese, which, depending on the flavoring, can go nicely with anything from beer to white wine. Liptauer is sold in various sized pots, boxes or other containers. Though in Hungary the cheese itself is referred to as "Liptauer," those in German-speaking countries use the same word to describe the cheese when mixed with flavorings. Liptauer has a FAT CONTENT of about 45 percent. *See also* CHEESE.

liquamen [LIH-kwah-men] *see* GARUM

liqueur [lih-KYOOR; lih-KER] A sweetened spirit flavored with ingredients like seeds, fruits, herbs, flowers, nuts, spices, roots, leaves and barks. The base can be BRANDY, RUM, WHISKEY or other SPIRIT and may be flavored in four ways: *distillation*—alcohol and flavoring agents are blended before being distilled (*see* DISTILLATION); *infusion*— flavorings are steeped in hot water, which is then mixed with the alcohol base; *maceration*—flavoring agents are steeped directly in the alcohol base; *percolation*—alcohol is dripped through the flavoring agents to extract their essences. **Proprietary liqueurs** (such as BÉNÉDICTINE, GALLIANO AND SOUTHERN COMFORT) are made exclusively by specific liqueur houses with secret formulas, some of which have been closely guarded for centuries. **Generic liqueurs** (like AMARETTO and CRÈME DE CACAO) are made by various producers using fairly standard recipes. Quality brands are typically flavored with the finest ingredients, essential oils and extracts; less expensive examples often use artificial flavorings. **Cream liqueurs** are flavored mixtures that have been homogenized with cream. They have a rich mixture that's velvety smooth and creamy, and they require no refrigeration. **Crème liqueurs** (such as CRÈME DE MENTHE) are distinguished by being sweet and syrupy. Liqueurs range widely in alcohol content, generally from about 15 percent (for some IRISH CREAM LIQUEURS) to 55 percent (green CHARTREUSE), although a few "baby liqueurs" like Kahlúa Mudslide contain only 6.5 percent alcohol. Although the word "liqueur" is common usage today, such potables are also called *cordials* and, less frequently, *ratafias*. Liqueurs were originally used (and some still are) as a digestive. They are now usually served after dinner but also play an important role in many cocktails. Liqueurs can also be used in cooking, particularly for desserts. *See also* ABSINTHE; ADVOCAAT; ALIZE DE FRANCE; ANESONE; ANISETTE; CHÉRI-SUISSE; COINTREAU; CRÈME D'ABRICOTS; CRÈME D'AMANDE; CRÈME D'ANANAS; CRÈME DE BANANE; CRÈME DE CASSIS; CRÈME DE CERISE; CRÈME DE NOYAUX; CRÈME DE ROSE; CRÈME DE VIOLETTE; CURAÇAO; DRAMBUIE; EAU DE VIE; FRANGELICO; GLAYVA; GOLDWASSER; GRAND MARNIER; HERBSAINT; IRISH MIST; IZARRA; KAHLÚA; KÜMMEL; MANDARINE LIQUEUR; MARASCHINO; MIDORI; OUZO; PERNOD; PRUNELLE; ROCK AND RYE; SABRA LIQUEUR; SAMBUCA; SLOE GIN; STREGA; TÍA MARÍA; TRIPLE SEC; TUACA.

liquid smoke A brownish-yellow liquid made by capturing and condensing the vapors from burning wet wood chips (usually hickory). Liquid smoke is used to add a smoky quality to foods in an attempt to capture the flavor of wood-fire grilling. It's typically found adjacent to barbecue sauces in the supermarket.

liquor [LIH-kuhr] 1. A distilled, alcoholic beverage made from a fermented MASH of various ingredients including grains or other plants. WHISKEY, GIN, VODKA and RUM are among the most popular. *See also* AQUAVIT;

ARRACK; BOURBON; BRANDY; IRISH WHISKEY; MALT LIQUOR; MESCAL; OKOLEHAO; SCOTCH WHISKY; TEQUILA. 2. An oyster's natural juices are referred to as its "liquor." 3. POT LIQUOR or pot likker refers to the liquid resulting from cooking meats or vegetables.

liquore [lee-KOH-reh] Italian for "LIQUOR."

litchi; litchi nut   *see* LYCHEE

lite   *see* LABEL TERMS

little hogweed   *see* PURSLANE

littleneck clam   Called *littlenecks* on the East Coast and *Pacific littlenecks* on the West Coast, these small, hard-shell clams have a shell diameter of less than 2 inches. They're usually reserved for eating ON THE HALF SHELL. *See also* CLAM.

liver   The largest and one of the most important organs, liver has immense nutritional value . . . providing, that is, that it comes from a fairly young animal. Because liver acts as a clearinghouse for substances that enter the body, it tends to store and absorb unwanted chemicals, medicines and hormones that an animal might be fed. Naturally, the older the animal the greater the accumulation of these unwanted substances, which, according to some, offset liver's nutritional value. For this very reason, many people choose the more expensive calf's liver over beef liver. There are several ways to distinguish between the two. The color of beef liver is reddish-brown, compared to the paler pinkish-brown of calf's liver. Liver from a mature animal also has a stronger odor and flavor than that from a youngster. Additionally, it will be less tender. Besides beef and calf's, the most common animal livers used in cookery are lamb, pork, poultry and goose, the latter used mainly to produce FOIE GRAS. The strongest-flavored and least tender of the livers is pork, while poultry livers are the most mild and tender of the lot. All livers are usually available fresh—beef and chicken livers may also be purchased frozen (though the quality of frozen liver is considerably lower than that of fresh). While chicken livers are sold whole, most of those from other animals are marketed sliced. Look for liver that has a bright color and moist (not slick) surface. It should have a fresh, clean smell. Refrigerate loosely wrapped for no more than a day. Liver can be prepared in a variety of ways though quick sautéing is the most popular. It toughens quickly with overcooking. Liver is rich in iron, protein and vitamin A. *See also* VARIETY MEATS.

liverwurst [LIHV-uhr-wurst; LIHV-uhr-vursht] A broad term for "liver sausage" referring to well-seasoned, ready-to-eat SAUSAGE made from at least 30 percent pork liver mixed with pork or other meat. The texture of liverwurst can range from firm enough to slice to creamy-smooth and spreadable. Liverwurst (the most popular of which is BRAUNSCHWEIGER) can be smoked or plain and comes in large links, loaves and slices. It's typically served for snacks and sandwiches and is especially suited to rye breads.

loaf pan Used for everything from bread to meatloaf to pound cake, the rectangular loaf pan comes in a variety of sizes. The most commonly used size is 9 by 5 inches (3 inches deep), and the $8^1/_2$ by $4^1/_2$ by $2^1/_2$ is a close second. Mini loaf pans are about 2 inches wide and can range in length from 3 to 5 inches. Loaf pans typically have straight sides, though there is a style with pleated ends. There's also a long, narrow, covered loaf pan called a PULLMAN PAN. *See also* COOKWARE AND BAKEWARE MATERIALS.

lo bok *see* DAIKON

lobster Up until the end of the 19th century lobster was so plentiful that it was used for fish bait. Alas, with lobster's ever-increasing popularity (and price), those days are gone forever. This king of the CRUSTACEAN family has a jointed body and limbs covered with a hard shell. The most popular variety in the United States is the **Maine lobster**, also called *American lobster*. It has 5 pairs of legs, the first of which is in the form of large, heavy claws (which contain a good amount of meat). Maine lobsters are found off the Atlantic coast of the northern United States and Canada. They have a closely related European cousin that lives in Mediterranean and South African waters and along Europe's Atlantic coast. **Spiny lobsters** (commonly called *rock lobsters*) are found in waters off Florida, Southern California, Mexico, Australia, New Zealand and South Africa. They're easily distinguished from the Maine lobster by the fact that all 10 of their legs are about the same size. Almost all of the meat is in the tail because the spiny lobster has no claws. That meat is firmer, stringier and not quite as sweet as that of the Maine lobster. Outside California and Florida, most of the spiny lobster meat sold in this country is in the form of frozen tails, usually labeled "rock lobster tails." Live lobsters have a mottled shell splotched with various colors, generally greenish blue and reddish brown. Their shell turns vivid red only after the lobster is cooked. Fresh lobsters are available year-round and are most economical during spring and summer. Female lobsters are prized by many for their delectable CORAL (eggs). Also considered a delicacy is a lobster's TOMALLEY (liver). Because bacteria form quickly in a dead lobster, it's important that it be alive when you buy it. To make sure, pick up the lobster—if the tail curls under the body it's alive. This test is especially important with lobsters that have been stored on ice because they're so sluggish that it's sometimes hard to see movement. Lobsters come in various sizes and are categorized as follows: **jumbo**, over $2^1/_2$ pounds; **large** (or *select*), from $1^1/_2$ to $2^1/_2$ pounds; **quarters**, from $1^1/_4$ to $1^1/_2$ pounds; **eighths**, from $1^1/_8$ to $1^1/_4$ pounds; and **chicken lobsters**, which average about a pound. Lobsters must be purchased the day they're to be cooked. They will die in fresh water, so must either be kept in seawater or wrapped in a wet cloth and stored for no more than a few hours on a bed of ice in the refrigerator. All lobsters must either be cooked live or killed immediately prior to cooking. They may be cleaned before or after cooking, depending on the cooking method and the way in which they are to be used. Though whole lobsters are best simply boiled or broiled, lobster meat may be prepared in a variety of ways. Consult a general cookbook for cleaning and cooking instructions. Whole lobsters and chunk lobster meat are also sold precooked. One caveat when buying whole cooked lobster: be sure the tail is curled, a sign that it was alive when cooked. Frozen and canned cooked lobster meat, as well as raw spiny (or rock) lobster tails, are also available. *See also* SHELLFISH.

lobster butter A COMPOUND BUTTER made by heating ground lobster shells together with butter. Sometimes lobster meat and CORAL are also included. The mixture is then strained into ice water, which hardens the butter. Lobster butter has a multitude of uses including flavoring sauces or soups or as a spread.

lobsterette *see* PRAWN

lobster Newburg *see* NEWBURG

lobster pick Generally made of stainless steel, this long, narrow utensil is used to pull every shred of meat from the hard-to-reach cavities (such as the legs) of lobsters and crabs. The tip of a lobster pick can either be pointed or in the shape of a tiny, two-prong fork.

lobster Thermidor [THUHR-mih-dohr] A dish composed of lobster tails from which the cooked meat is removed, chopped and combined with a BÉCHAMEL flavored with white wine, shallots, tarragon and mustard. The sauced lobster is spooned back into the shells, sprinkled with Parmesan cheese and broiled until golden brown. Crab and shrimp are also sometimes prepared in this manner. The dish is thought to have been named by Napoleon after the month in which he first tasted it (the eleventh month, July 19 to August 17, according to the French Revolutionary calendar).

locavore; localvore [LOH-cah-vohr] A person who tries to eat food produced locally. Originally coined in San Francisco in 2005, *locavore* became the *Oxford American Dictionary*'s word of the year in 2007. The group of women who created the term initially set a goal and challenged other people in the San Francisco Bay Area to eat food produced within a 100-mile radius of where they lived.

locoto chile *see* ROCOTO CHILE

locust bean *see* CAROB

loganberry There's disagreement as to the origin of this beautiful ruby red, BLACKBERRY-shaped berry. Some botanists think it's a separate species while others consider it a raspberry-blackberry hybrid. All agree that it was discovered by California Judge J. H. Logan in the late 1800s. Available in June and July, the loganberry is juicy and sweetly tart, and turns purple-red when very ripe. Choose plump, brightly colored berries that are uniform in size. Avoid soft, shriveled or moldy fruit. Do not wash until ready to use, and store (preferably in a single layer) in a moisture-proof container in the refrigerator for 2 to 3 days. Loganberries are delicious both cooked and fresh. They make wonderful jams and preserves.

loh shee fun *see* RICE NOODLES

loin Depending on the animal, the loin comes from the area on both sides of the backbone extending from the shoulder to the leg (for pork) or from the rib to the leg (in beef, lamb and veal). Beef loin is divided into SHORT LOIN and SIRLOIN. In general, the loin is a tender cut that can be butchered into chops, steaks and roasts.

loin, lamb The loin comes between the RIB and LEG sections and contains the tenderest (and most expensive) cuts of the lamb. It's also referred to as the *saddle*, although some differentiate the saddle as the loin area closest to the LEG. This section produces *loin chops* and the *loin roast*. A *double loin chop* or *English chop* is a single cut containing a chop from both sides of the lamb that's often formed into a circle.

lo mein [loh MAYN] A Chinese dish of boiled noodles combined with various stir-fried ingredients, such as chicken, pork and vegetables. The cooked noodles are tossed with the hot, stir-fried ingredients at the last minute, just until they're heated through and coated with the stir-fry sauce.

lomi-lomi [LOH-mee LOH-mee] Popular at luaus, this Hawaiian dish is a mixture of diced CURED salmon, tomatoes, mild white onions, green onions and various seasonings. The salmon is cured by covering it with salt for a minimum of 8 hours (sometimes a couple of days), which removes the moisture; the fish is rinsed before being diced. The word *lomi* means "massage" or "rub," and the preparation of this dish includes thoroughly mixing (mashing or massaging) the ingredients until they are well integrated. Some recipes call for crushed ice to be mixed in right before serving to add moisture. Lomi-lomi is often served in lettuce cups or the shell of the tomatoes used in the dish.

lomo saltado [LOH-moh SAHL-tah-doh] Peruvian dish of tender beef steak, cut into strips and stir-fried with ingredients such as AJÍ AMARILLO (yellow chile), cilantro, garlic, onions, parsley, red pepper, soy sauce, tomatoes and vinegar. This Asian-Peruvian combination is unusual in that it's served with steamed rice and FRENCH FRIES. Its popularity has spread into other parts of South America.

London broil 1. A FLANK STEAK that has been cut into large pieces, tenderized by marinating, broiled or grilled, then thinly sliced across the grain. 2. A term also used for various thick cuts of meat including sirloin tip (*see* SIRLOIN) and top round (*see* ROUND).

longan [LONG-uhn] Also called *dragon's eye,* this native Southeast Asian fruit is small (about 1 inch in diameter) and round and has a thin brown shell. Inside is a translucent white, juicy-soft pulp that surrounds a large black seed, which gives it an eyeball appearance when halved. The perfumy flavor is delicate and sweet. Fresh longans can occasionally be found in Asian markets and some produce markets from October to May. They may be refrigerated in a plastic bag for up to 3 weeks. The easy-to-peel shell must be removed before eating. Dried and canned longans are available year-round. Longans are eaten as a snack (just pop in your mouth and eat around the seed) and used in some Asian soups, SWEET-AND-SOUR dishes and desserts.

long bean *see* YARD-LONG BEAN

long coriander *see* SAW-LEAF HERB

longhorn cheese *see* COLBY

Long Island duck *see* DUCK

Long Island iced tea A potent mixed drink composed of gin, vodka, cola, and lemon. It's served in a tall glass over ice. Sometimes tequila is also added to the mix.

Long John *see* BISMARCK

long melon *see* CUCUZZA

long-neck clam *see* SOFT-SHELL CLAM

long rice *see* CELLOPHANE NOODLES

looseleaf lettuce *see* LEAF LETTUCE

lop chong; lop cheong *see* CHINESE SAUSAGE

loquat [LOH-kwaht] Though it originated in China, the loquat is also called mayapple, Japanese medlar and Japanese plum. This slightly pear-shaped fruit resembles an apricot in size and color. The juicy, crisp flesh is golden and has a delicate, sweetly tart cherrylike flavor. It surrounds 1 to 3 rather large seeds. Besides China, the loquat grows in Japan, India, Central and part of South America, California, Florida and throughout the Mediterranean. They can be found in produce or farmer's markets and some supermarkets. Loquats bruise easily so they're not good travelers. For that reason, fresh loquats are usually found only in the regions in which they're grown. Domestic fruit can be found April to June, imported loquats in November and December. Choose large fruit with no sign of bruising. Store at room temperature or, if very ripe, refrigerate in a plastic bag. Loquats can be eaten as a snack, added to salads or used in chicken or duck dishes. They're also available dried or canned in Asian markets.

Lord Baltimore cake A three-layered yellow cake with a filling of chopped pecans or almonds, MARASCHINO cherries and MACAROON crumbs. The cake is covered with a fluffy white frosting such as BOILED ICING. *See also* LADY BALTIMORE CAKE.

loroco [loh-ROH-koh] Popular vine with edible flowers and buds grown in Central America. Fresh loroco flowers have a pungent yet nutty character and they're frequently used in the cuisines of El Salvador and Guatemala. Fresh flowers are difficult to find, but preserved flowers are sold in jars in Central American markets.

lotte [LOT] *see* ANGLER

lotus; lotus leaves; lotus root; lotus seed A water lily whose leaves, root and seeds are often used in Asian cooking. The huge **lotus leaves** have a diameter of from 11 to 15 inches. They can be found fresh and dried in Asian markets. These leaves are used both as a flavoring and to wrap sweet and savory mixtures (rice, meat, fruit, etc.) for steaming. The underwater **lotus root** can be up to 4 feet long. It looks like a solid-link chain with 8-inch lengths, each about 3 inches in diameter. It has a reddish-brown skin that must be peeled before using. The lotus root's creamy-white flesh has the crisp texture of a raw potato and a flavor akin to fresh coconut. Besides the fresh form, it's also available canned, dried and candied. Lotus root is used as a vegetable as well as in sweet dishes. The oval, delicately flavored **lotus seeds** are eaten out of hand both in their fresh and dried forms. Dried seeds are also candied and used in desserts and pastry fillings. They can be purchased canned or in bulk in Asian markets. The lotus is also called *hasu* and RENKON.

Louis sauce [LOO-ee] A mixture made of mayonnaise, CHILI SAUCE, cream, scallions, green peppers, lemon juice and seasonings. Although its best known use is in CRAB LOUIS, this dressing is wonderful with all manner of cold seafood. *See also* SAUCE.

loukanika [loo-KAH-nih-kah] Seasoned with orange rind, this Greek SAUSAGE is made with both lamb and pork. Loukanika is a fresh sausage and must therefore be cooked before eating. It's usually cut into chunks and sautéed.

loup *see* BASS

lovage [LUHV-ihj] The French call lovage *céleri bâtard,* "false celery," because of its strong resemblance to that plant. Lovage has been used since Greek and Roman times for everything from a seasoning, to a curative for maladies ranging from indigestion to freckles, to a love potion. It grows up to 7 feet high and has large, dark green, celerylike leaves. The flavor of the pale stalks is that of very strong celery. The leaves, seeds and stalks can be used (in small amounts because of their potent flavor) in salads, stews and other dishes such as fowl and game. The stalks can be cooked as a vegetable. Dried lovage leaves and chopped or powdered stalks can be found in natural food stores and gourmet markets. The seeds are commonly called CELERY SEED. Lovage is also called *smallage* and *smellage.*

love apple A tomato moniker that originated in the 16th century when tomatoes from North Africa were known in Italy as *pomo dei Mori,* "apples of the Moors." That was transliterated to the French *pomme d'amour . . .* "love apple."

lox *see* SMOKED SALMON

luau [LOO-ow] A traditional Hawaiian feast, the highlight of which is usually roast pig. This celebration is almost always accompanied by Hawaiian music, singing and dancing.

Lucques olive [loo-EEK] Although this brine-cured olive takes its name from the Lucca area of Italy's Tuscany region, today it's primarily associated with southern France's Languedoc-Roussillon region. Its shape is like an elongated half-moon, its color is pale to bright green, its flesh is firm but buttery and its flavor is sweet and nutty with hints of avocado. *See also* OLIVE.

luganega; luganeghe [loo-gah-NAY-gah] A long, undivided, fresh pork SAUSAGE from northern Italy. It's best broiled or boiled; the cooked sausage can be added to everything from sauces to POLENTA.

lumache *see* Pasta Glossary, page 883

lumpfish Any of various FISH from the *Cyclopterus lumpus* family found in the North Atlantic. The pelvic fins of these large round fish are joined, forming a large lump (which is actually a suction disk). Lumpfish are renowed for their ROE (*see also* CAVIAR). The best cooking method for their oily flesh is poaching.

lumpfish caviar *see* CAVIAR

lumpia; lumpia wrapper   [LOOM-pee-ah] Hailing from the Philippines and Indonesia, the lumpia is a version of the EGG ROLL and consists of a **lumpia wrapper** (a thin "skin" made of flour or cornstarch, eggs and water) wrapped around a filling and fried. Sometimes a lettuce leaf is used to enfold the filling mixture, in which case lumpia is not fried. The filling can be made of chopped raw or cooked vegetables, meat, shrimp or a combination. Lumpia are typically served as a snack or appetizer.

luo han guo   [loooh hahn goooh] Plant native to southern China and grown mainly in Guangxi Province. Thirteenth-century monks were thought to be the first to use its round green fruit, which is why it's also called *monk fruit; luo han* means "monk" and *guo* means "fruit." Other names include *arhat fruit, Buddha fruit* or *la han qua*. The fruit is dried and used for a number of purposes. In China it's been used for centuries to treat sore throats, as a longevity aid and as a sweetener. Because the extract from luo han guo has up to 300 times the sweetness of sugar, it's also gaining recognition in other parts of the world as a natural low-calorie sweetener that may be beneficial for people suffering from hypoglycemia and diabetes. Luo han guo can be purchased at health food stores, Chinese food stores and through the Internet as a supplement. It also appears in a number of products such as juices, teas, protein bars and breakfast cereals.

lupin; lupine; lupini bean   [LOO-pihn] Cultivated for thousands of years, the lupin has long been an important crop for many Mediterranean cultures. Some varieties of this LEGUME-family plant produce bitter, highly toxic seeds (beans) that must be soaked extensively before they can be safely consumed. It wasn't until the 1920s that nontoxic varieties were developed successfully. Such beans were called sweet lupin (as opposed to bitter) and require no soaking to rid them of toxicity. The most widely cultivated is the **white lupin**, a large, white, flat, circular bean reminiscent of the FAVA BEAN. This variety has cultivars that produce both sweet and bitter beans. There's also a white, sweet **Andean lupin**, also called *tarwi* or *tarhui*. Lupins are toasted, salted and eaten as a snack or served as an appetizer. They're also ground and used as flour. Such products are most commonly available through Internet ordering.

lutefisk; lutfisk   [LOO-tuh-FIHSK] A Scandinavian specialty made with unsalted dried COD. The age-old preparation method is to soak the dried cod in regularly changed cold water for a period of eight days. The cod is then soaked for two days in a mixture of water and potash lye, after which it's soaked for two more days in fresh water. (Thankfully, for fans of this dish, ready-to-cook lutefisk is commercially available.) The final step is simmering the fish for 10 to 15 minutes, just until it becomes translucent. Just before serving, lutefisk is sprinkled with ALLSPICE, salt and white pepper. It's accompanied with BÉCHAMEL and, typically, boiled potatoes.

luwak [LOO-wak] *see* KOPI LUWAK

lychee [LEE-chee] One of China's cherished fruits for over 2,000 years, the small (1 to 2 inches in diameter) lychee has a rough, bright red shell. The creamy ivory flesh surrounds a single seed and is juicy, smooth and delicately sweet with nuances of cherry and banana. Native to Southeast Asia, the lychee is cultivated in subtropical regions including California, Florida and Hawaii. Fresh lychees are available from June to September. Choose those with brightly colored skins that are heavy for their size and free of blemishes. Place in a plastic bag and refrigerate unshelled for up to 10 days. Break the shell by pressing on one end, then pinch the center of the shell to pop out the fruit. The seed will have to be cut away. Eat plain or as part of a fruit salad or dessert, or add to a cooked dish just before serving. Canned and dried lychees are available year-round. When dried they're often referred to as *lychee nuts* because they resemble a nut—the shell turns a dark reddish brown and the flesh becomes brown and crisp. They're eaten as a snack, much in the same way as nuts or candy. Also called *lichee, litchi* and *litchi nuts*.

lyonnaise, à la [ly-uh-NAYZ; lee-oh-NEHZ] A French term for "in the manner of Lyons," a city in central France known for its excellent food. It refers to dishes prepared or garnished with onions, such as *pommes lyonnaise,* which are sliced potatoes fried with onions.

Lyonnaise sauce A classic French sauce made with white wine, sautéed onions and DEMI-GLACE. The sauce is strained before being served with meats and sometimes poultry. *See also* SAUCE.

lyophilization [li-ahf-uh-li-ZAY-shuhn] *see* FREEZE DRYING

macadamia nut [mak-uh-DAY-mee-uh] As hard as it is to believe, the macadamia tree was first grown only for ornamental purposes. Thankfully, the buttery-rich, slightly sweet nature of the tree's nut was eventually discovered and has been prized ever since. The macadamia tree is native to Australia and was named for John McAdam, the Scottish-born chemist who cultivated it. In the 1890s the macadamia journeyed from Tasmania to be cultivated in Hawaii (now its largest exporter) and, eventually, California. Because of its extremely hard shell, this marble-size, golden brown nut is usually sold shelled, either roasted or raw. It has a high fat content and should be stored in the refrigerator or freezer to prevent rancidity. Macadamias are widely used in a variety of sweet and savory dishes. *See also* NUTS.

macarones *see* Pasta Glossary, page 883

macaroni [mak-uh-ROH-nee] Legend has it that upon being served a dish of this food, an early Italian sovereign exclaimed "*Ma caroni!*" meaning "how very dear." This semolina-and-water PASTA does not traditionally contain eggs. Most macaronis are tube-shape, but there are other forms including **shells**, **twists** and **ribbons**. Among the best-known tube shapes are: **elbow** (a short, curved tube); **ditalini** (tiny, very short tubes); **mostaccioli** (large, 2-inch-long tubes cut on the diagonal, with a ridged or plain surface); **penne** (large, straight tubes cut on the diagonal); **rigatoni** (short, grooved tubes); and **ziti** (long, thin tubes). Most macaronis almost double in size during cooking. The Italian spelling of the word is *maccheroni. See also* Pasta Glossary, page 883.

macaroon [mak-uh-ROON] A small cookie classically made of almond paste or ground almonds (or both) mixed with sugar and egg whites. Almond macaroons can be chewy, crunchy or a combined texture with the outside crisp and the inside chewy. There is also a **coconut macaroon**, which substitutes coconut for the almonds. Macaroons can be flavored with various ingredients such as chocolate, maraschino cherries or orange peel.

maccheroni [mahk-kay-ROH-nee] The Italian word for all types of MACARONI, from hollow tubes, to shells, to twists. *See also* Pasta Glossary, page 883.

macchiato [mah-kee-YAH-toh] *see* CAFÉ MACCHIATO

mace [MAYS] This spice tastes and smells like a pungent version of NUTMEG, and for a very good reason . . . mace is the bright red membrane that covers the nutmeg seed. After the membrane is removed and dried it becomes a yellow-orange color. It's sold ground and, less frequently, whole (in which case it's called a "blade"). Mace is used to flavor all manner of foods, sweet to savory. *See also* SPICES; Seasoning Suggestions, page 891.

macédoine [mas-eh-DWAHN] A dish of colorful, attractively cut fresh fruits or, less commonly, vegetables, either of which may be raw or cooked. The fruits are customarily either briefly soaked or drizzled with a mixture of SUGAR SYRUP and LIQUEUR. A fruit macédoine is served for dessert, either cold or FLAMBÉED. For a savory macédoine, each vegetable is cooked separately, then artfully arranged together on a plate and dressed with seasoned melted butter. It can be served as a side dish or a first course.

macerate [MAS-uh-rayt] To soak a food (usually fruit) in a liquid in order to infuse it with the liquid's flavor. A spirit such as brandy, rum or a LIQUEUR is usually the macerating liquid. *See also* MARINATE.

mâche [MAHSH] *see* CORN SALAD

mackerel [MAK-uhr-uhl] Any of several species of fish found in the Atlantic Ocean off both the North American and European coasts. The **king mackerel** (also called *kingfish*) is probably the most well known of this family of fish. The mackerel has a firm, high-fat flesh with a pleasant savory flavor. When small (about 1 pound), it's sold whole. Larger fish are cut into fillets and steaks. Mackerel is also available smoked or salted. The latter must be soaked overnight before using to leach excess salt. Mackerel can be cooked in almost any manner including broiling, baking and sautéing. *See also* FISH.

Mackinaw trout *see* CHAR

Macoun apple [muh-KOON] An all-purpose apple that's a cross between a MCINTOSH and a Jersey Black. The color is a deep red with some green spots. The flesh is crisp and juicy with a perfumy, sweetly tart flavor. *See also* APPLE.

Madagascar bean [mad-uh-GAS-kahr] *see* LIMA BEAN

mad cow disease *see* BOVINE SPONGIFORM ENCEPHALOPATHY

Maddelena olive *see* ALFONSO OLIVE

Made and Bottled By *see* WINE LABEL TERMS

Madeira [muh-DEER-uh] Named after the Portuguese-owned island where it's made, Madeira is a distinctive FORTIFIED WINE that's subjected to a lengthy heating process during maturation. It can range in color from pale blond to deep tawny and runs the gamut from quite dry to very sweet. The pale golden **Sercial** is the lightest, driest Madeira, while the rich, dark **Malmsey** is the sweetest. **Bual** and **Verdelho** are both medium-sweet wines. The flavor of American-made Madeiras cannot compare with that of the Portuguese originals, but then they're a fraction of the price. The lighter Madeiras are often served as APÉRITIFS, while the richer, darker Malmsey is perfect for after-dinner sipping. Madeira is also an excellent cooking wine and can be used in both sweet and savory preparations.

madeleine [MAD-l-ihn; mad-LEHN] Exalted by Proust in his *Remembrance of Things Past,* the madeleine is a small, buttery sponge cake that's eaten as a cookie, often dipped in coffee or tea. These feather-light cakes are baked in a special madeleine pan (or plaque), which has 12 indentations that resemble an elongated scallop shell. Madeleines are best eaten fresh from the oven, while the inside is moist and warm and the exterior exquisitely crisp.

Madras [MAH-drahs] Curry dish invented by British Indian restaurants but not typically found in India by that name. There is a city in southern India that used to be called Madras but is now known as Chennai. It's thought that one of the spice blends found there made its way to England many years ago. But there are many variations of Madras curry, so it's hard to pinpoint what that original recipe would have been. Madras curry is usually red or reddish-brown, spicy hot and slightly sour.

madrilène [MAD-ruh-lehn; mad-rih-LAYN] 1. A CONSOMMÉ flavored with fresh tomato juice. Madrilène may be served hot or cold; in the latter instance it's usually jellied. A lemon slice or wedge is the traditional accompaniment. Canned madrilène is available in most supermarkets. It should be shaken well before being refrigerated to set. 2. *À la madrilène* is French for "in the manner of Madrid" and refers to many foods that are cooked or flavored with tomatoes or tomato juice.

mafalda; *pl.* **mafalde** *see* Pasta Glossary, page 883

magdalena [mahg-dah-LAY-nah] Thought by some to be Spain's answer to the French MADELEINE, magdalenas are small sponge cakes made with eggs, flour and olive oil—although many modern versions use sunflower oil instead. Although these small cakes have been made for special holidays since the Middle Ages, they are now so popular that they're an everyday pleasure for most Spaniards. Magdalenas have an invitingly tender, moist texture and shiny, golden brown tops. They come in three basic shapes—the classic, high-domed round, a flat-topped round and an oblong shape.

magenbrot [ma-gehn-broht] Gingerbread spice cookie popular in Germany and parts of Switzerland. *Magenbrot* means "stomach bread," and the cookie is presumably called that because it is low in fat and includes spices such as cinnamon, cloves, ginger and nutmeg that aid in digestion. These cookies are a tradition at Christmastime.

magliette *see* Pasta Glossary, page 883

magnum; double magnum [MAG-nuhm] *see* WINE BOTTLES

magret; maigret [mah-GRAY; may-GRAY] Duck breast from a bird that's been force-fed and fattened to produce FOIE GRAS. Magrets were traditionally used for CONFIT. Today the boned breasts (skin and underlying fat attached) are often prepared by grilling, skin-side down, until the skin's very crisp, then flipping and cooking only until very rare. This technique allows the melted fat to permeate the meat. The breast of a duck that has not been force-fed is sometimes called a FILLET.

mah gu gai pin *see* MOO GOO GAI PAN

mahi mahi; mahi-mahi [MAH-hee MAH-hee] Though this is actually a type of dolphin, it shouldn't be confused with the dolphin that is a mammal. To avoid this misunderstanding, the Hawaiian name *mahi mahi* is becoming more widespread. Also called *dolphinfish* and *dorado,* mahi mahi is found in warm waters throughout the world. It's a moderately fat fish with firm, flavorful flesh. It ranges in weight from 3 to 45 pounds and can be purchased in steaks or fillets. Mahi mahi is best prepared simply, as in grilling or broiling. *See also* FISH.

mahleb; mahlab [MAH-lehb] Used in the Middle East as a flavoring in baked goods, mahleb is ground black-cherry pits. It can be purchased in Greek or Middle Eastern markets, either prepackaged or ground to order.

Mahón; Mahón-Menorca (DO; PDO) [mah-OWN; mah-HONE] SEMIHARD to HARD cheese from Menorca, the outermost of Spain's Balearic Islands, that is named after the island's capital and port. Mahón, which dates back 4,000 to 5,000 years, is made mainly from cow's milk although up to 5 percent sheep's milk may be included. It comes in 5- to 6-pound squares, which are aged to various maturities; *fresco* (fresh) has 10 days of aging, *semi-curado* (medium-ripe) is aged over 2 months, *curado* (cured) for 5 months, and *viejo* (old) for 10 months. The flavor is somewhat acidic and salty, with buttery, fruity and nutty nuances. As with all cheese, the older the Mahón the more assertive the flavor. The FAT CONTENT of this cheese ranges from 38 to 45 percent.

M

Maibowle [MI-bohl] *see* MAY WINE

maicoba bean [mah-KOH-bah] *see* PERUANO BEAN

maida [MI-dah] White, unbleached all-purpose flour used in East Indian baking. Maida, also called *maitha*, is highly refined, with all the bran and wheat germ removed. It's used for many foods including cakes, breads like NAAN and pastries like SAMOSAS.

mai fun *see* RICE NOODLES

Maillard reaction Also known as the *browning reaction*, the chemical interaction between a reducing sugar and an amino acid ordinarily caused by heating. Explained by Louis-Camille Maillard in 1912 the reaction influences food by browning it, changing the flavor and adding crispiness. It's what happens when steaks brown during cooking, or when toast is made, onions are fried and breads are baked. It's a slightly different chemical process from CARAMELIZING, which only involves sugar and no amino acid, but the results appear very similar.

maïs [*Fr.* mah-EESS]; mais [*It.* MY-ees]; Mais [*Gr.* MIGHSS] French, Italian and German for "CORN" or "corn on the cob."

maison [may-ZOHN] French for "house." On a menu, such a designation—like *pâté maison*—refers to a specialty of the house or to the fact that the dish was made by the house chef.

mai tai [MI-ti] A potent mixed drink made with light and dark rums, ORGEAT SYRUP, CURAÇAO, orange and lime juices and any other touches the bartender might add. It's served over ice and garnished with a skewer of fresh fruit. The mai tai is said to have been created by Victor Bergeron, the original owner of Trader Vic's restaurant, who said he created it for a couple of Tahitian friends. On tasting it, they reportedly exclaimed, "Mai Tai!" meaning "out of this world."

maitake [mi-ih-TAH-kay (-kee)] *see* HEN OF THE WOODS

maitha [MAY-thah] *see* MAIDA

maître d' butter; maître d'hôtel butter [MAY-truh (MAY-tehr) doh-TELL] A COMPOUND BUTTER made by blending together softened butter, lemon juice or vinegar, chopped parsley and seasonings. It is served as an accompaniment to fish, poultry and meat.

maître d'hôtel; maître d' [MAY-truh (MAY-tehr) doh-TELL; may-truh Dee] *see* BRIGADE SYSTEM

maiz [mah-EES; *Sp.* mah-EETH] Spanish for CORN.

maize [MAYZ] British for CORN.

maize mushroom *see* CUITLACOCHE

makovník *see* MAKOWIEC

makový závin *see* MAKOWIEC

makowiec [mah-KOH-vihts] Traditional Polish pastry made by spreading a rich, poppy seed filling on a sheet of sweetened yeast dough, rolling it up like a JELLY ROLL and then baking it. Recipes for the filling vary and sometimes include almonds or walnuts in addition to the poppy seeds. The filling can also be purchased in cans at most supermarkets. Makowiec is customarily served around the Christmas and Easter holidays. Neighboring countries make similar pastries that go by various names such as *bejgli, bulochki s makom, makovník, makový závin* and *Mohnstriezel*.

makrut lime; lime leaf Grown in Southeast Asia and Hawaii, the makrut lime tree produces small, pear-shaped citrus fruit with a skin that's bright yellow-green, bumpy and wrinkled. The glossy, dark green **makrut lime leaves**, which are used in cooking (particularly in Thai cuisine), have a unique double shape and look like two leaves that are joined end to end. Dried makrut lime rind and leaves, which have a mysterious floral-citrus aroma, can be found in Asian markets. Fresh leaves, which have a more intense, fragrant aroma, are sometimes available as well. The makrut lime is also known as the *kaffir lime* and *kieffer lime.*

Malabar leaf *see* INDIAN BAY LEAF

Malabathrum; Malobathrum *see* INDIAN BAY LEAF

malanga; málanga [mah-LAHN-gah] A large, dense and starchy potatolike tuber belonging to the same family as the TARO ROOT. There are several varieties of malanga, which is also known as *new cocoyam, tannia* and *yautia.* All have a long, tapered, uneven shape with skins that can range in color from reddish to yellowish brown. The flesh color varies from cream to pale yellow, though some varieties are a pale grayish purple. Because raw malanga can irritate the throat, this tuber should be peeled and cooked. The resulting flavor is earthy and somewhat nutlike. Handled properly, malanga is extremely easy to digest and touted as being very hypoallergenic. It's also dried and processed into flour, which is used as a substitute for wheat flour. Like taro root leaves, those of the malanga are called *callaloo* in the Caribbean. They're prepared and eaten like mustard or turnip greens or used in callaloo soup. Malanga can be found in Latin American markets and some specialty produce stores. Choose firm, smooth roots; refrigerate for up to 4 days. Much like the potato, the malanga may be prepared in a variety of ways including boiling, frying and baking.

Maldon salt *see* FLEUR DE SEL

malic acid [MAL-ihk; MAH-lihk] A natural acid found in sour apples and other fruits. In winemaking, when certain bacteria convert malic acid to LACTIC ACID (which is much less strong and sour), a process called "malolactic fermentation" occurs. This reduces the wine's tartness, adds complexity to the flavor and sometimes contributes a slight sparkle. Malic acid is used as an acidulant as well as a flavoring agent in the processing of some foods.

malinalco chile *see* ROCOTO CHILE

malloreddus *see* Pasta Glossary, page 883

Malmsey *see* MADEIRA

malossol caviar [MAHL-oh-sahl] *see* CAVIAR

Malpeque oyster *see* ATLANTIC OYSTER

malsouka; malsouqa [mal-SOO-kah] *see* WARKA

malt [MAWLT] 1. A grain (typically barley) that is sprouted, kiln-dried and ground into a mellow, slightly sweet-flavored powder. This powdered malt has many uses including making vinegar, brewing beer, distilling liquor and as a nutritious additive to many foods. **Malted-milk powder** and **malt vinegar** are two of the most popular malt products available today. *See also* MALT SYRUP. 2. A soda-fountain drink, also called *malted*, that is a thick, rich mixture of malted-milk powder, milk, ice cream and a flavoring such as chocolate or vanilla. *See also* MILK SHAKE.

maltagliati *see* Pasta Glossary, page 883

Maltaise sauce; Maltese [mahl-TEHZ; mahl-TEEZ] HOLLANDAISE blended with orange juice and grated orange rind, used to top cooked vegetables, particularly asparagus and green beans. *See also* SAUCE.

malted milk A delicious, nourishing and distinctively flavored beverage made by mixing milk with either plain or chocolate-flavored malted milk powder (*see* MALT).

malted milk powder *see* MALT

malt extract *see* MALT SYRUP

malt liquor A beer that has a relatively high alcohol content by weight—usually from 5 to 8 percent. Several varieties reach as high as 9 percent alcohol, which makes such brews ineligible to be labeled "BEER" or "LAGER." *See also* BEER.

M

maltose [MAHL-tohs] Also called *malt sugar,* this disaccharide plays an important role in the fermentation of alcohol by converting starch to sugar. It also occurs when enzymes react with starches (such as wheat flour) to produce carbon dioxide gas (which is what makes most bread doughs rise).

malt sugar *see* MALTOSE

malt syrup A natural sweetener made from a filtered, evaporated mash of ground corn and sprouted BARLEY. Found in natural food stores, malt syrup has an earthy, full-bodied flavor and is 75 to 80 percent as sweet as honey. Plain malt syrup is sweeter than the hop-flavored style, which has a bitter edge. Malt syrup may be substituted for other syrupy sweeteners. It's also referred to as *malt extract*.

malt vinegar *see* MALT; VINEGAR

malt whisk(e)y A WHISK(E)Y made from not less than 51 percent malted barley. *See also* SCOTCH WHISKY; SINGLE MALT WHISK(E)Y.

mame [mah-meh] Japanese for "bean."

mamey sapote; mamee; mamey apple [mah-MAY sah-POH-tay] Popular in the Caribbean Islands, Central America and Florida, the mamey sapote (*Pouteria sapota*) is unrelated to the BLACK SAPOTE and the WHITE SAPOTE. It's shaped like a large, pointed peach and covered with a russet-brown rind that's thick, rough and woody. The flesh, which ranges in color from salmon-pink to golden-red, is firm and smooth with a sweet flavor reminiscent of a honeyed blend of apricots and almonds. Mamey sapotes are typically available from July through October. Select fruit that has a reddish cast to the skin; store at room temperature for up to a week. Mamey sapotes are good in drinks (smoothies and cocktails), desserts and for out-of-hand eating.

mamoncillo; mamon [MAH-mohn-see-yoh] Edible fruit from trees native to South America that are eaten both sweet and sour. The fruit has leathery green skin, ranges in size from 2 to 5 inches long and 1 to 1$^1/_2$ inches wide and has yellowish-orange pulp. When eaten sour, mamoncillo—also called *ackee*, *genip*, *honeyberry*, *limoncillo*, *guinep*, *quenepa*, and *Spanish lime*—is generally accompanied by chili powder, lime, and/or salt. Sweet versions are eaten out of hand without additions. The fruit is also made into jam and jelly. Mamoncillo is typically in season from June through October. Availability is limited, but mamoncillo can be found in some ethnic markets.

M

mamoul, maamoul; ma'amoul [MAH-muhl] A SHORT Middle Eastern cookie or pastry traditionally filled either with dates, pistachios or walnuts but sometimes with almonds or figs. Each type of filled cookie is shaped differently to distinguish them from one another. The date-filled cookie is dome-shaped with a flattened top, the pistachio-filled cookie has an elongated oval shape and the walnut-filled one is dome-shaped with a rounded top. They can be hand-formed or made using special wooden molds. Mamoul come in three sizes—bite-size, medium and large. Most versions are made with SEMOLINA. *Mamoul-mad* are made in baking pans with bottom and top layers of dough and the selected filling. Once baked, they are cut into rectangles.

manao [mah-NOW] Thai for "lime."

Manchego [mahn-CHAY-goh] Spain's most famous CHEESE, so named because it originally was made only from the milk of Manchego sheep that grazed the famous plains of La Mancha. It's sometimes called the cheese of Don Quixote because Cervantes mentioned it in his novel, *Don Quixote of La Mancha*. Manchego, also know as *Queso Manchego,* is a rich, golden, semihard to hard cheese that has a full, buttery flavor that's still somewhat piquant. The two versions that are most commonly exported are *curado*, aged between 3 and 4 months, and *viejo*, aged 9 to 12 months. Another variation, *Manchego en aceite* ("in oil"), has been ripened for 1 year, during which time it's bathed in olive oil. Manchego has a FAT CONTENT of about 50 percent. *See also* CHEESE.

Mandarin cuisine [MAN-duh-rihn] *see* CHINESE CUISINE

Mandarine Napoléon [MAN-duh-rihn nuh-POH-lee-uhn] Made in Belgium from tangerines, this perfumy, BRANDY-based LIQUEUR has a silky texture and candied orange flavor.

Mandarin orange [MAN-duh-rihn] A loose-skinned orange category that includes several varieties that can be sweet or tart, seedless or not and can range in size from as small as an egg to as large as a medium grapefruit. They all, however, have skins that slip easily off the fruit. Among the more well-known mandarin-orange family members are clementine, dancy, satsuma and tangerine. The tiny **clementine** has a thin peel and a tangy-sweet red-orange flesh that's usually seedless. It's cultivated in Spain and North Africa and can usually be found only in specialty produce markets. **Dancy oranges** are similar in size and color (and equally rich-flavored) to clementines but have a plenitude of seeds. The small Japanese **satsuma oranges** are almost seedless. Most of the canned mandarin oranges on the market are satsumas. The most common mandarin found in the United States is the **tangerine**, which has a thick, rough skin and sweet flesh. It was named for the city of Tangier, Morocco. Mandarin oranges can, depending on the variety, be found in the market from November through June. *See also* ORANGE; TANGELO.

M

Mandarin pancakes Chinese CRÊPES, usually made with wheat flour and used to wrap foods such as PEKING DUCK.

mandarinquat As its name suggests, cross between a MANDARIN ORANGE and a KUMQUAT. It's somewhat bulbous, with a petite neck at its stem, and slightly larger than a kumquat. Like a kumquat, it can be eaten skin and all. The rind is mildly floral and sweet; the flesh is sweeter than a kumquat's but still has some tartness. Mandarinquats can be sliced and served raw in salads, with cheese or as a garnish, or they can be cooked, either candied or pickled whole or in preserves or marmalades; they do have lots of tiny seeds. Fresh mandarinquats are available in the winter months. Look for firm fruit without blemishes. Refrigerate in a plastic bag for up to 2 weeks.

mandelbrot [MAHN-duhl-broht] From the German words *mandel* ("almond") and *brot* ("bread"), this Jewish favorite is a crisp almond bread that is eaten as a cookie.

mandoline [MAHN-duh-lihn; mahn-duh-LEEN] A compact, hand-operated machine with various adjustable blades for thin to thick slicing and for JULIENNE and FRENCH-FRY cutting. Mandolines have folding legs and come in both wood- or stainless steel-frame models. They're used to cut firm vegetables and fruits (such as potatoes and apples) with uniformity and precision. On most machines, the food is held in a metal carriage on guides so that fingers aren't in danger.

manger [mahn-ZHAY] French for "eat."

mange-tout [mawnzh-TOO] French for "eat everything," referring to a bean or pea, such as the SUGAR SNAP PEA, where everything—pod to seed—is edible.

mangiare [mahn-JAH-ray] Italian for "eat."

mangiatutto [mahn-jah-TOO-toh] Italian for "eat it all" (*see* MANGE-TOUT).

maguro *see* SUSHI

mango [MANG-goh] The mango tree is considered sacred in India, the land of the fruit's origin. Now this delectable fruit is cultivated in temperate climates around the world, including California and Florida. There are many species of mango, which come in a wide variety of shapes (oblong, kidney and round) and sizes (from about 6 ounces to 4 pounds). Depending on the variety, their skin color can range from yellow-orange to yellow-green to yellow with brilliant red blushing. The fragrant flesh is a brilliant golden orange, exceedingly juicy and exotically sweet and tart. Perhaps the only negative to the mango is the huge, flat seed that traverses its length. Mangoes are in season from May to September, though imported fruit can be found throughout the remainder of the year. Look for fruit with an unblemished, yellow skin blushed with red. Because the seed is so oversized, the larger the mango the higher the fruit-to-seed ratio. Underripe fruit can be placed in a paper bag at room temperature. Ripe mangoes can be placed in a plastic bag and held refrigerated for up to 5 days. Mangoes must be peeled and the fruit carefully carved away from the large seed. To do this, stand the fruit on its wide end and use a sharp knife to vertically cut away the fruit, sliding the knife along the seed on one side, then repeating on the other. You'll have to guess about

M

where the seed is. This will give you two large pieces. Then cut away the remaining flesh and use as desired. *Or,* you can peel the mango and use a gadget called a "mango pitter," which handles the job in one stroke. Mangoes need no embellishment and are delicious simply peeled and eaten plain. They're also wonderful in fruit salads, smoothies, salsas, desserts and chutneys. Mango can also be chopped and added to cooked foods such as rice or STIR-FRY dishes just before serving. Fresh mangoes are rich in vitamins A and C. **Canned mangoes** and **mango nectar** are available in many supermarkets. **Mango purée** or **pulp** can be found fresh in some natural food stores as well as Indian and Latin markets, and frozen in some supermarkets. Packaged **dried mango** comes in chunks and strips and is available in natural food stores and many gourmet markets. It must be rehydrated in warm water for about 4 hours before being used in baked goods, PRESERVES, etc. **Green mango** is the unripe fruit, which has many uses in the cuisines of India, Malaysia and Thailand. This tart fruit is used fresh in various vegetable and lentil dishes, as well as to tenderize meat (just like PAPAYA, green mango contains enzymes that will break down connective tissue). Fresh green mango is pickled and sold as a condiment for Indian dishes. Dried green mango has many uses, one of the most popular being to make AMCHOOR, an Indian seasoning used to flavor many dishes. Green mango may be purchased in various forms in Asian and Indian markets.

mango powder *see* AMCHOOR

mangosteen [MANG-uh-steen] Widely cultivated in the Asian tropics, the mangosteen is no relation to the mango. In size and structure, it's much like a tangerine, having 5 to 8 fruit segments. The segmented flesh is soft, cream-colored and juicy. It has a tantalizingly sweet-tart flavor that is extremely refreshing. The hard skin of the mangosteen is a dark purple-brown. Unfortunately, the mangosteen is rarely imported to the United States.

M

Manhattan One of the true classic cocktails, said to have been created in 1874 by a bartender at New York's Manhattan Club for a fête given by Lady Randolph Churchill (Winston's American mum) in honor of the newly elected governor Samuel J. Tilden. The Manhattan is made with RYE WHISKEY (or other blended whiskey) or BOURBON, sweet VERMOUTH and BITTERS, and is served either STRAIGHT UP or ON THE ROCKS, and garnished with a MARASCHINO CHERRY. A **perfect Manhattan** uses equal parts sweet and dry vermouth, while a **dry Manhattan** employs only dry vermouth.

manicotti *see* Pasta Glossary, page 883

manioc [MAN-ee-ok] *see* CASSAVA

manjar; manjur [MAN-jar] *see* DULCE DE LECHE

mannitol [MAN-ih-tahl] A white, crystalline sweetener added to processed foods for thickening, stabilizing and sweetening.

manteca [mahn-TAY-kah] Word used for "butter" in parts of Spain and in some Latin American countries such as Chile and Argentina. In other parts of Spain and countries such as Mexico and Guatemala, *manteca* means "lard." The countries that use *manteca* to mean butter refer to lard as **manteca de cerdo**. *See also* BURRINO; MANTEQUILLA.

mantequilla [MAHN-teh-KEE-yah] Used in much of Latin America as the word for "butter." *See also* MANTECA.

manti [MAHN-tee] A dumpling that dates back many centuries in Central Asia and the surrounding regions. Manti remains popular today in a variety of cuisines. A spicy meat mixture is placed inside basic pasta-like dough, boiled, steamed or fried and customarily covered with a garlicky yogurt sauce. The meat mixture traditionally consisted of lamb, onions and spices but beef has become popular as well. As with any dish that's been around for centuries, variations abound, both with the filling and the sauces used to top the dish. Depending on the culture, the filling might include chicken, CHICKPEAS, pumpkin, potato or squash and a variety of spices. Tomato- and vinegar-based sauces are also used.

manzana chile *see* ROCOTO CHILE

manzanilla [mahn-zuh-NEE-yuh; mahn-suh-NEEL-yuh] *see* CHAMOMILE; SHERRY

Manzanilla; Manzanillo olive [mahn-zuh-NEE-yuh; mahn-suh-NEEL-yuh; -yoh] Small- to medium-size, oval-shaped Spanish olive that's brine-cured. It ranges from greenish-brown to bluish-black depending on maturity. Manzanillas have firm texture and flavors ranging from nutty to smoky to slightly bitter. They're found pitted and unpitted with various stuffings like garlic or pimento. *See also* SPANISH OLIVES; OLIVE.

M

maple syrup; maple sugar The American Indians taught the Colonists how to tap the maple tree for its sap and boil it down to what the Indians called "sweetwater." Canada, New York and Vermont are all known for their superior maple products. The maple-tapping season (called "sugar season") usually begins sometime around mid-February and can last anywhere from 4 to 6 weeks. The "sugarmakers" insert spouts into the maple trees (a grove of which is called a "sugarbush") and hang buckets from them to catch the sap. Some companies connect plastic tubing to the spout, running it from tree to tree and eventually directly to a large holding tank where it's stored until ready to be processed. The sap is then taken to the "sugarhouse," where it's boiled until evaporated to the desired degree. Quite simply, **maple syrup** is sap that has been boiled until much of the water has evaporated and the sap is thick and syrupy. At the beginning of the sugar season, when the sap is concentrated, it only takes about 20 gallons of it to make a gallon of syrup, whereas toward the end of the season it may take up to 50 gallons of sap. **Maple sugar**, which is about twice as sweet as granulated white sugar, is the result of continuing to boil the sap until the liquid has almost entirely evaporated. In between those two stages at least two other products are made: **maple honey** (thicker than syrup) and **maple cream** or **butter** (thick and spreadable). Maple syrup is graded according to color and flavor. Generally, U.S. grades are: **Fancy** or **Grade AA**, a light amber colored syrup with a mild flavor; **Grade A** is medium amber and mellow-flavored; **Grade B** is dark amber and hearty flavored; and **Grade C** is very dark with a robust, molasseslike flavor. Since the processing of maple syrup is labor-intensive, pure maple syrup is quite expensive. A less costly product labeled **maple-flavored syrup** is a combination of less expensive syrup (such as CORN SYRUP) and a small amount of pure maple syrup. **Pancake syrups** are usually nothing more than corn syrup flavored with artificial maple extract. Pure maple syrup should be refrigerated after opening. Warm to room temperature before serving.

maraschino cherry [mar-uh-SKEE-noh; mar-uh-SHEE-noh] This specially treated fruit can be made from any variety of cherry, though the ROYAL ANN is most often used. The cherries are pitted and then MACERATED in a flavored SUGAR SYRUP (usually almond flavor for red cherries, mint for green). At one time they were traditionally flavored with MARASCHINO LIQUEUR, though such an extravagance is now rare. The cherries are then dyed red or green. The federal government has now banned the use of the harmful dyes that were used until recently. Maraschino cherries can be purchased with or without stems. They're used as a garnish for desserts and cocktails, as well as in baked goods and fruit salads.

maraschino liqueur [mar-uh-SKEE-noh; mar-uh-SHEE-noh] A bittersweet, cherry-flavored Italian LIQUEUR made from wild *marasca* cherries (and their crushed pits) grown in the area of Trieste.

marble potatoes *see* POTATO

marbling Flecks or thin streaks of fat that run throughout a piece of meat, enhancing its flavor, tenderness and juiciness. Very lean cuts of meat are sometimes artificially marbled (*see* LARD *v.*).

marc [MARK; *Fr.* MAHR] 1. The residue (skins, pits, seeds, etc.) remaining after the juice has been pressed from a fruit, usually grapes. 2. A potent EAU DE VIE distilled from this mixture. It's the French counterpart to GRAPPA.

marchands de vin [mar-SHAW*N* duh VA*N*] A French sauce (the name of which means "wine merchants") made from a heavily reduced mixture of full-bodied red wine, chopped SHALLOTS, cracked pepper and GLACE DE VIANDE. At the last minute, butter, lemon juice and minced parsley are whisked into the REDUCTION. Marchands de vin, which is sometimes chilled until firm, is a popular accompaniment for grilled or roasted meats. *See also* SAUCE.

Marcona almond [mahr-KOH-nah] This large, wide, flat almond is imported from Spain, where it's primarily grown in the Catalonia region. Though ubiquitous in Spain, Marcona almonds didn't become popular in the United States until the late 1990s. Sometimes referred to as "the queen of almonds," the Marcona has a higher fat content than California-grown almonds and is known for its soft crunch and rich, sweet flavor. Marcona almonds are available either fried in olive or sunflower oil and salted or raw and blanched. *See also* ALMOND; NUTS.

Marengo, à la; alla [muh-RENG-goh] A veal or chicken dish in which the meat is sautéed in olive oil, then braised with tomatoes, onions, olives, garlic, white wine or brandy and seasonings. Sometimes scrambled eggs accompany the dish. It's said to have been created by Napoleon's chef after the 1800 Battle of Marengo.

margarine [MAHR-juh-rihn; MAHRJ-rihn] A butter substitute developed and patented by French chemist Hippolyte Mège-Mouriés in 1869. His creation was the result of a contest promoted by the Emperor Napoleon III to find an inexpensive alternative for the then scarce and expensive butter. Although the original version included beef fat renderings, today's margarines are based on vegetable oils (*see* FATS AND OILS). In order for margarine to become solid, the oil must undergo a chemical transformation known as hydrogenation—indicated as "hydrogenated" (or "partially hydrogenated") oils on a label. During hydrogenation, extra hydrogen atoms are pumped into unsaturated fat, a process that creates TRANS FATTY ACIDS and converts the mixture into a saturated fat, thereby obliterating any benefits it had as a polyunsaturate. Some researchers believe that hydrogenated oils may actually be more damaging than regular saturated fats for those limiting cholesterol in their diets, but the jury's still out on that debate. Those margarines lowest in cholesterol are made from a high percentage of polyunsaturated canola, safflower or corn oil. To make this butter substitute taste and look more like the real thing, cream or milk is often added. Food coloring, preservatives, emulsifiers and vitamins A and D are also common additives. Careful label scrutiny is advised because the ingredients affect everything from flavor to texture to nutritive value. **Regular margarine** must contain 80 percent fat. The remaining 20 percent consists of liquid, coloring, flavoring and other additives. Margarine is available salted and unsalted. So are **butter-margarine blends**, which are usually proportioned 40 to 60 percent respectively. **Cholesterol-lowering margarines** hit the market in 1999. These "miracle margarines" contain no hydrogenated trans fatty acids and are typically made from a blend of oils such as PALM OIL, SOYBEAN OIL, CANOLA OIL and OLIVE OIL. They can lower cholesterol levels in the blood by as much as 10 percent, with each percentage point creating a 3 percent drop in the risk of heart disease. They're made with plant-derived compounds (sterol and stanol esters) that obstruct cholesterol absorption. **Soft margarine** is made with all vegetable oils (no animal fats) and remains soft and spreadable when cold. **Whipped margarine** has had air (which sometimes can equal half the volume) beaten into it, making it fluffy and easy to spread. Because of the added air, it cannot be substituted for regular margarine in baked goods. So-called **liquid margarine** is soft enough to be squeezable when cold and comes in pliable bottles made specifically for that purpose. It's convenient for basting and for foods such as corn on the cob and waffles. There are also many **reduced-fat margarines** on the market today. These products range from about 25 percent to 65 percent less fat than regular margarine. There's even **fat-free margarine**, the ingredients of which include gelatin, rice starch and lactose. The first ingredient listed on reduced-fat margarine labels is *water,* which means they can't be substituted for regular margarine for baking and frying, and which also means they can make toast soggy. Margarine comes in 1-pound packages—either in 4 (4-ounce) sticks or in 2 (8-ounce) tubs. It's also available in 1-pound tubs. All margarine readily absorbs flavors and therefore should be wrapped airtight for storage. Refrigerate margarine for up to 2 months; freeze for up to 6 months. In its early days, margarine was also known as *oleomargarine. See also* BUTTER; FATS AND OILS; Food Label Terms, page 876.

margarita [mahr-gah-REE-tah] A COCKTAIL made with tequila, an orange-flavored LIQUEUR (usually TRIPLE SEC) and lime juice. The rim of the glass is traditionally dipped in lime juice, then coarse salt. A margarita may be served STRAIGHT UP or ON THE ROCKS. It can also be blended with ice into a slushy consistency.

margherite *see* Pasta Glossary, page 883

marguery sauce [mahr-guh-*R*AY] A sauce made from a reduced mixture of white wine and fish stock blended with egg yolks and butter. The sauce, which was developed by French chef Nicolas Marguery in the late 1800s, is most often served with mild fish, such as SOLE. *See also* SAUCE.

marigold A bright yellow flower used culinarily to flavor and add color to salads, soups and other dishes. The petals are sometimes dried, powdered and used as a coloring agent. *See also* FLOWERS, EDIBLE.

marinade [MEHR-ih-nayd] A seasoned liquid in which foods such as meat, fish and vegetables are soaked (marinated) in order to absorb flavor and, in some instances, to be tenderized. Most marinades contain an acid (lemon juice, vinegar or wine) and herbs or spices. The acid ingredient is especially important for tough cuts of meat because it serves as a tenderizer. Because most marinades contain acid ingredients, the marinating should be done in a glass, ceramic or stainless-steel container—never in aluminum. *See also* MARINATE.

marinara sauce; alla marinara [mah-ree-NAHR-uh] A highly seasoned Italian tomato sauce made with onions, garlic, and oregano, and used on pasta, meats, and pizza. The term "alla marinara" refers to a dish served with this kind of sauce. Outside the U.S., it is often referred to as *Neopolitan Sauce* or *Napoli Sauce*. In Italy, marinara sauce may sometimes contain seafood. *See also* SAUCE.

marinate [MEHR-ih-nayt] To soak a food such as meat, fish or vegetables in a seasoned liquid mixture called a MARINADE. The purpose of marinating is for the food to absorb the flavors of the marinade or, as in the case of a tough cut of meat, to tenderize. Because most marinades contain acid ingredients, the marinating should be done in a glass, ceramic or stainless-steel container—never in aluminum. Foods should be covered and refrigerated while they're marinating. When fruits are similarly soaked, the term used is MACERATE.

marinière [mah-reen-YEHR] 1. *À la marinière* is a French phrase meaning "mariner's style." It refers to the preparation of SHELLFISH with white wine and herbs. It can also refer to a fish dish garnished with mussels. 2. *Marinière sauce* is a mussel stock–based BERCY SAUCE enriched with butter or egg yolks.

maritozzi [mahr-ee-TOH-tsee] Sweet, BRIOCHE-like Italian bun made with bread dough, pine nuts, raisins, sugar and sometimes orange ZEST. It's often slit and filled with whipped cream and is known as *maritozzi con panna*. Originally it was the custom for a groom to give his future bride these buns as a sign of his affection. (*Marito* is Italian for "husband.") It's also customarily served during Lent, but in much of Italy maritozzi is available year-round.

marjolaine [mahr-zhoh-LAYN; mahr-zhoh-LEHN] 1. A long, rectangular DACQUOISE made with ground almonds and hazelnuts and layered with chocolate BUTTERCREAM. 2. French for "MARJORAM."

marjoram [MAHR-juhr-uhm] Early Greeks wove marjoram into funeral wreaths and planted it on graves to symbolize their loved ones' happiness both in life and beyond. There are many species of this ancient herb, which is a member of the mint family. The most widely available is **sweet marjoram**, usually simply called "marjoram." It has oval, inch-long, pale green leaves and a mild, sweet, oreganolike flavor (**wild marjoram** is another name for OREGANO). Marjoram is available fresh in some produce markets and supermarkets with large fresh-herb sections. More often, it is found dried in small bottles or cans. There's also a very hardy species called **pot marjoram**, which has a stronger, slightly bitter flavor. It's found throughout Mediterranean countries but rarely seen in the United States. Marjoram can be used to flavor a variety of foods, particularly meats (especially lamb and veal) and vegetables. Because marjoram's flavor is so delicate, it's best added toward the end of the cooking time so its essence doesn't dissipate. *See also* HERBS; Seasoning Suggestions, page 891.

markook *see* SAJ

Marlborough pie [MAHRL-bur-oh] This Massachusetts specialty is a single-crust pie with a custardlike filling of applesauce, eggs, cream and sometimes SHERRY. Many Massachusetts families serve it as a traditional Thanksgiving dessert.

marmalade [MAHR-muh-layd] A preserve containing pieces of fruit rind, especially CITRUS FRUIT. The original marmalades were made from quince—the Portuguese word *marmelada* means "quince jam." Now, however, Seville oranges are the most popular fruit for making marmalades.

marmite [mahr-MEET] A tall, covered, straight-sided cooking pot from France, used for long-cooking stews and dishes such as CASSOULET and POT-AU-FEU. It's usually made of EARTHENWARE. *Petites marmites* are identically shaped miniature covered pots used as soup bowls.

Marmite [MAHR-mite] The brand name of a British YEAST EXTRACT product created in 1902, the same year as the coronation of Edward VII. Now owned by CPC (United Kingdom), Marmite is a dark brown, concentrated paste with a flavor that's assertively salty (though less so than its Australian cousin VEGEMITE) with a slightly sweet undertaste. It's one of the UK's most popular spreads (indeed, much of Britain has been raised on it) and is used for everything from morning toast to sandwiches to flavoring soups and stews. There are also Marmite cubes. Marmite can be found in some specialty gourmet stores and is available through mail order.

Marmora *see* DANABLU

Maroilles; Marolles (AOC; PDO) [mah-RWAHL] SEMISOFT cheese first made 1,000 years ago at the monastery at Maroilles, a town in northern France's Nord-Pas-de-Calais region. It's made from both pasteurized and unpasteurized cow's milk and comes in $4^1/_2$-ounce to $1^1/_2$-pound squares with rinds that are yellow to dark gold with tinges of red. This is an exceedingly smelly cheese, which is why its nickname is *vieux puant* ("old stinker"). The flavor, which is savory, meaty, pungent and slightly tangy, is strong but milder than the aroma. The smallest size is aged a minimum of 3 weeks and the larger sizes for at least 5 weeks, although 2 to 4 months is more common. Maroilles, also spelled *Marolles*, has a minimum FAT CONTENT of 45 percent.

Marolles *see* MAROILLES

marqooq *see* SAJ

marron; marron glacé [ma-ROHN glah-SAY] Marron is French for "CHESTNUT." Marrons glacés are chestnuts that have been preserved in a sweet syrup. They can be found in jars or cans in most supermarkets and are quite expensive. They're eaten as a confection, chopped and used to top desserts such as ice cream and mixed fruit or used to make desserts such as the rich MONT BLANC.

marrow A soft, fatty tissue found in the hollow center of an animal's leg bones and, though not as plentiful, in the spinal bones. It isn't widely consumed in the United States, but marrow is considered a delicacy by many Europeans and is the highlight of the famous Milanese specialty OSSO BUCO. Marrowbones (those that contain marrow) can be purchased at meat markets and most supermarkets (though special ordering may be necessary). They should be wrapped, refrigerated and used within a day or two of purchase. Marrow is extremely light and digestible. It can be cooked in the bone (and removed afterwards) or it may be removed first and cooked separately. The common methods of preparation are baking or poaching, after which the marrow is often spread on toast and served as an appetizer. A special long, narrow utensil called a *marrow spoon* or *scoop* can be used to extract the marrow from the bone. Marrow is also added to soups for body and flavor. It has the same calorie count as beef fat and contains a small amount of protein. *See also* MARROWBONE.

marrow bean Grown chiefly in the East, this is the largest and roundest of the WHITE BEAN category. Marrow beans are typically found fresh only in the region where they're grown, but are available dried year-round in most supermarkets. They're customarily served sauced as a side dish, in the manner of a pasta. *See also* BEANS.

marrowbone A bone, usually from the thigh and upper legs of beef, containing MARROW. The long bones are usually cut into 2- to 3-inch lengths. *See also* VARIETY MEATS.

marrow spoon *see* MARROW

marrow squash *see* VEGETABLE MARROW

Marsala [mahr-SAH-lah] Imported from Sicily and made from local grapes, Marsala is Italy's most famous FORTIFIED WINE. Marsalas have a rich, smoky flavor, much of which comes from oxidation during AGING, as with SHERRY and MADEIRA. Marsala wines are made in various styles—*secco* (dry), *semisecco* (semisweet) and *dolce* (sweet). The quality levels are **Fine** (the lowest level)—at least 17 percent alcohol and 1 year wood aging; **Superiore**—at least 18 percent alcohol and 2 years wood aging; **Superiore Riserva** (also labeled *Giaribaldi Dolce (GD)*, *London Particular (LP)* or *Superior Old Marsala (SOM)*—at least 4 years wood aging; and **Vergine** (the highest quality)—at least 5 years wood aging (Vergine stravecchio or riserva must be aged a minimum of 10 years). Dry Marsalas are typically served as APERITIFS, whereas many of the semisweet and sweet styles make better DESSERT WINES. The label terms **ambra** and **oro** indicate wines made from white grapes; **rubino** wines are made from red grapes. **Cremevo** (*Cremevo Zabaione Vino Aromatizzato*)—once called **Marsala Speciali**—is a flavored wine made with 80 percent Marsala plus various other ingredients like eggs or coffee.

marshmallow [MAHRSH-mehl-oh] Once created from the sweetened extract of the roots of the marshmallow plant, this sweet is now commercially made from corn syrup, gelatin, GUM ARABIC, sugar and flavorings. Light, fluffy marshmallows come packaged in regular size (about 1½ inches in diameter) and miniature (½ inch in diameter). They may be white or pastel colors. Marshmallows are used variously to top hot chocolate and dishes such as sweet potatoes. They can be stored at room temperature, tightly sealed, for at least 6 months and can be frozen for up to a year.

marshmallow crème (fluff) A thick, fluffy, marshmallow-flavor mixture available in jars or plastic tubs in supermarkets. The original version was Marshmallow Fluff, started in 1920 by two young entrepreneurs H. Allen Durkee and Fred L. Mower. Over the years, Durkee-Mower, Inc. created a Fluff empire, complete with a popular weekly "Flufferettes" radio show and cookbook. Marshmallow crème (fluff) is used in fudge and other candies, as an ice-cream topping and cake filling and for the ever popular FLUFFERNUTTER sandwich.

martini [mahr-TEE-nee] Perhaps the most fashionable cocktail of all time, and certainly the favorite of numerous characters in novels and motion pictures, the martini is striking in its simplicity, containing only GIN and dry VERMOUTH. Stories abound regarding the martini's origin; according to the most popular (and logical) one, it's a descendant of the

Martinez, which is claimed to have been created in Martinez, California, in 1849 and is, in turn, an offspring of the MANHATTAN. Over the years, that early four-component Martinez recipe has transitioned into a two-ingredient, much drier (see DRY) martini, which replaces its predecessor's slight sweetness with an icy austerity. At the beginning of the 19th century, when popular usage of the word "martini" took hold, the drink's proportions were equal parts gin and dry vermouth. By about 1915, the ratio was two parts gin to one part vermouth, with four-to-one being the norm by World War II. Today it's not uncommon to see ratios of six, eight, twelve or fifteen parts gin to one part vermouth. Bottom line: The less vermouth, the drier the martini. Martinis are garnished with either a green olive or a lemon twist. A martini may be served STRAIGHT UP or ON THE ROCKS. It may also be made with vodka, in which case it's called a **vodka martini**. A GIBSON is a martini garnished with a tiny white onion.

maruzze *see* Pasta Glossary, page 883

marzipan [MAHR-zih-pan] A sweet, pliable mixture of ALMOND PASTE, sugar and sometimes unbeaten egg whites. It's often tinted with FOOD COLORING and molded into a variety of forms including fruits, animals and holiday shapes. Some fancy commercial marzipan fruit is colored so convincingly that it can almost be mistaken for the real thing. Marzipan is also rolled into thin sheets and used either to cover cakes or to cut into strips to form ribbons, bows and a variety of other shapes. Marzipan is available in most supermarkets, packaged in cans or plastic-wrapped logs.

masa; masa harina [MAH-sah ah-REE-nah] Spanish for "dough," *masa* is the traditional dough used to make corn TORTILLAS. It's made with sun- or fire-dried corn kernels that have been cooked in limewater (water mixed with calcium oxide). After having been cooked, then soaked in the limewater overnight, the wet corn is ground into masa. **Masa harina** (literally "dough flour") is flour made from dried masa.

masago [mah-SAH-goh] Japanese for the ROE of SMELT, masago's tiny eggs and mild flavor make it a popular topping for SASHIMI and SUSHI. It's available in Asian markets, usually in the frozen food section.

masala [mah-SAH-lah] A word used throughout India for a spice blend with myriad variations. It can refer to a simple combination of two or three spices (such as CARDAMOM, CORIANDER and MACE) or a complex blend of 10 or more ingredients. The principal masala blend used in India is GARAM MASALA, the variations of which are countless, depending on the cook and the dish being seasoned.

masala chai [mah-SAH-lah chai] *see* CHAI

masala dosa [mah-SAH-lah DOH-sha] A very thin, crisp pancake, called a DOSA, filled with a spicy onion and potato filling. The filling is often flavored with GARAM MASALA and CHAAT MASALA. Masala dosa, which is very popular in southern India and the surrounding regions, is often eaten at breakfast and usually served with CHUTNEY.

mascarpone [mah-skar-POH-nay] Hailing from Italy's Lombardy region, mascarpone is a buttery-rich DOUBLE-CREAM to triple-cream cow's-milk cheese. (Technically it's not cheese but rather CURDLED cream because citric or tartaric acid is used rather than RENNET.). It's ivory-colored, soft and delicate, and ranges in texture from that of a light CLOTTED CREAM to that of room-temperature butter. It's versatile enough to be blended with other flavors and is sometimes sold sweetened with fruit. In Italy's Friuli region a favorite blend is mascarpone mixed with anchovies, mustard and spices. But in truth, this delicately flavored cheese needs little embellishment other than being topped with fruit.

mash *n.* Grain or malt that is ground or crushed before being steeped in hot water. Mash is used in brewing beer and in the fermentation of whiskey. **Sour mash** is made by adding a portion of the old mash to help ferment each new batch in the same way as a portion of SOURDOUGH STARTER is the genesis of each new batch of sourdough bread. **mash** *v.* To crush a food (such as cooked potatoes) into a smooth, evenly textured mixture.

Massaman curry [mahd-SA-man] A curry dish that's associated with southern Thailand, though its origins seem to be in India. It's often served at special occasions, especially weddings. Massaman curry is traditionally made with beef but chicken, duck, pork and tofu versions are also cooked. It may contain bay leaves, CARDAMOM, chili, cinnamon, COCONUT MILK, FISH SAUCE, PALM SUGAR, potatoes, roasted peanuts or cashews, STAR ANISE and TAMARIND sauce. Some recipes call for MASSAMAN CURRY PASTE (homemade or purchased) for added flavor. The name is also spelled *Masaman, Matsaman, Massamun, Mussamun, Mutsaman* and *Mutsamun*.

Massaman curry paste A paste used in many Thai curries for flavor and a key ingredient in MASSAMAN CURRY. It typically contains some, if not all, of the following ingredients: cloves, CUMIN, CARDAMOM, chiles, cinnamon, coriander, COCONUT MILK, FISH SAUCE, GALANGAL, garlic, KAFFIR LIME LEAVES, LEMONGRASS, MACE, nutmeg, onion, PALM SUGAR, peppercorns, shallot and SHRIMP PASTE. The paste can be made at home and stored for up to 2 weeks in the refrigerator, or frozen. It's also available in Asian markets.

massa pevide *see* CANJA

mastic The eponymous resin of the mastic tree, which grows throughout the Mediterranean and is cultivated specifically for its resin. Mastic has a sweet, aromatic, licoricelike flavor that's highly prized throughout the Middle East as a flavoring for a variety of edibles including desserts, breads, chewing gum, and some savory dishes like COUSCOUS and TAGINES. It's also used to flavor LIQUEURS, including the Greek *Masticha,* a popular APÉRITIF similar to OUZO. Mastic is available in Greek and other Middle Eastern markets. It comes in packets of crystals, which must be crushed into a powder before using.

Mataro [mah-TAH-roh] *see* MOURVÈDRE

mat beans *see* MOTH BEANS

matcha [MAH-tchah] A brilliant green powdered tea served in the Japanese tea ceremony. Matcha, also called *hiki-cha*, is made from very high quality tea, which is too bitter for most western palates.

matjes herring *see* HERRING

matsutake mushroom [maht-soo-TAH-kay; maht-soo-TAH-kee] This dark brown Japanese wild mushroom has a dense, meaty texture and nutty, fragrant flavor. It's available fresh from late fall to midwinter, usually only in Japanese markets or specialty produce stores. Canned *matsutake* are also marketed. These mushrooms can be cooked by a variety of methods including braising, grilling, steaming and frying. *See also* MUSHROOM.

matzo; matzoh [MAHT-suh] A thin, brittle, UNLEAVENED bread traditionally eaten during the Jewish Passover holiday. Tradition states that matzo is made only with water and flour but some modern-day versions include flavorings like onion. Matzo can be found in Jewish markets as well as most supermarkets. *See also* MATZO MEAL.

matzo ball Also called a *knaidel (pl. knaidlach)*, this small, round dumpling is made with MATZO MEAL, eggs, chicken fat and seasonings. Matzo balls are usually cooked and served in chicken soup.

matzo brei [MAHT-suh bri] A Jewish dish made with pieces of MATZO that have been soaked in hot water, squeezed dry, then dipped in beaten egg and fried like FRENCH TOAST. Matzo brei is typically served with cinnamon-sugar, maple syrup or honey.

matzo meal Ground MATZO, generally available in two textures—fine and medium. Matzo meal is used in a variety of foods including GEFILTE FISH, MATZO BALLS and pancakes. It's also used to thicken soups and for breading foods to be fried. Matzo meal is available in Jewish markets and most supermarkets.

Maultaschen [MOWL-tah-shihn] NOODLE dough stuffed with various fillings, similar to large ravioli. The filling is traditionally made with ground meat, leftover roast meat, or bits of BRATWURST combined with breadcrumbs, eggs and parsley plus salt, pepper and nutmeg for seasoning. Onions and spinach are commonly used as well. Some versions are meatless. Maultaschen are originally from the historical region of Swabia, which is similar to the modern-day Baden-Württemberg state in southwestern Germany. Maultaschen were considered a meal for poorer people, as the filling was often made from leftovers and old bread; today they're standard fare. Once cooked in broth or salted water, they are served several different ways—in broth, browned in butter or baked with cheese on top. They're a traditional food during the Easter season.

mava; mawa [MAH-vah; MAH-wah] *see* KHOA

May apple Though poisonous when green, the yellow, egg-shaped May apple can be safely eaten after ripening. This member of the barberry family is about the size of a large cherry. It's lightly sweet and acidic and makes very good preserves. The May apple is found in the East but is rarely available in markets.

mayi moulin *see* FUNCHE

mayo coba (mayocoba) bean [mah-yoh KOH-bah] *see* PERUANO BEAN

mayonnaise [MAY-uh-nayz; may-uh-NAYZ] A thick, creamy dressing that's an EMULSION of vegetable oil, egg yolks, lemon juice or vinegar and seasonings. If egg yolks aren't used, the product is called salad dressing, which is also sweeter than mayonnaise. Commercial mayonnaise (which must contain at least 65 percent oil by weight) sometimes contains other additions including emulsifiers and sweeteners. There are many **reduced-fat mayonnaises**—ranging from about 25 percent to 50 percent less fat than regular margarine—as well as **fat-free mayonnaise**. Besides less oil (or none, as the case with fat-free spreads), these mayonnaises contain ingredients like modified food starch, cellulose gel and other thickeners and emulsifiers, all of which help contribute to the proper consistency. Electric mixers, blenders and food processors make homemade mayonnaise a cinch. All mayonnaise should be refrigerated once made or opened. Unfortunately, the homemade style—which is far superior in taste and texture—lasts only 3 to 4 days. The commercial product can be stored up to 6 months. Mayonnaise is widely used as a spread, a dressing and a sauce. It's also used as the base for a plethora of other mixtures including TARTAR SAUCE, THOUSAND ISLAND DRESSING, AÏOLI and RÉMOULADE.

May wine A German white-wine punch flavored with WOODRUFF. Also called *Maibowle,* May wine is sold bottled and can be found in some gourmet liquor and wine stores.

McIntosh apple [MAK-ihn-tahsh] This all-purpose apple has a bright red skin sometimes tinged with green. Its flesh is medium-crisp and juicy, and its flavor is tartly sweet and perfumy. The McIntosh doesn't hold up to lengthy cooking. *See also* APPLE.

mead [MEED] Dating back to Biblical times, mead is a beverage made by fermenting honey, water and yeast with flavorings such as herbs, spices or flowers. Mead was popular in early England and, though not widely distributed today, is still bottled. The word **hydromel** (an Old French word for mead) describes the lowest level of alcoholic strength for this potable; *standard* and *sack* are stronger versions. It comes from the Greek *hydro* ("water") and *meli* ("honey").

meal 1. The coarsely ground seeds of any edible grain such as oats or corn. 2. Any dry, ground substance such as bone or dried fish meal. 3. Finely ground nuts.

mealy 1. Having a dry or powdery texture that resembles MEAL. 2. A term used to describe the texture of a baked potato as slightly dry and almost crumbly.

measurements *see* U.S. Measurement Equivalents, page 869

measuring cups Containers that come in graduated sizes, used to measure amounts of food. **Dry measuring cups** come in nested sets that can include 2-cup, 1-cup, $1/2$-cup, $1/3$-cup, $1/4$-cup and $1/8$-cup (2-tablespoon) sizes. The dry ingredient can either be stirred first (as with flour and powdered sugar) or simply spooned lightly into the cup, then leveled off with the straight edge of a knife. Brown sugar and shortening should be packed tightly into the cup before being leveled off. For foods such as coconut, nuts and chocolate chips, the cups should be filled, then leveled off with your fingers. **Liquid measuring cups** range in size from 1 to 4 cups. To use, simply pour in liquid and read measurement at eye level. *See also* METRIC SYSTEM; U.S. Measurement Equivalents, page 869.

meat analogs; meat substitutes A category of meatlike products created from various SOYBEAN byproducts including TEXTURED VEGETABLE PROTEIN, soy protein concentrate and sometimes TEMPEH or TOFU. Meat analogs come in myriad forms including fat-free soy bacon (bits and strips); low-fat soy sausage (links and patties); "hamburgers," which come in patties and may contain grains and vegetables; and "hot dogs," which can sometimes contain tofu. Meat analog products must be refrigerated and should be used within a week of purchase. They can be prepared as one would meat (grilled, sautéed, broiled) but cook more quickly than meat. Pans should be sprayed with vegetable spray to prevent sticking. Meat substitutes can be found in natural food stores and most supermarkets.

meat glue *see* TRANSGLUTAMINASE

meat grinder *see* GRINDER

meatloaf; meat loaf Ground meat (such as beef, turkey, lamb or pork) mixed with various seasonings (like onions, bell peppers, herbs, ketchup, and so on) and bound (*see* BIND) with eggs or bread-crumbs. The mixture can be either spooned into a loaf pan or hand-formed into a loaf shape and placed in a baking pan before being baked. Meatloaves can be topped with various ingredients such as cheese or sauce, and served both hot and cold.

meat tenderizers Hanging and aging is how many meat processors tenderize meat, but the home cook can easily do so by simple mechanical or chemical methods. **Tenderizing meat mechanically** is accomplished by breaking down the meat's tough fibers through pounding. *Meat pounders* (also called *meat bats, mallets* and *tenderizers*) come in metal or wood and in a plethora of sizes and shapes. They can be large or small, have horizontal or vertical handles and be round-, square- or mallet-shaped. Some have smooth surfaces while others are ridged. **Tenderizing meat chemically** refers to softening the meat fibers by long, slow cooking, by MARINATING it in an acid-based MARINADE, or by using a commercial meat tenderizer. Most forms of the latter are a white powder, composed mostly of a papaya extract called **papain**, an enzyme that breaks down tough meat fibers. The use of this enzyme is nothing new— South American cooks have been using papaya juice to tenderize meat for ages. Powdered meat tenderizer is available at most supermarkets. Most brands contain salt, sugar (in the form of DEXTROSE) and the anticaking agent calcium stearate.

meat thermometer Cooks use this tool to read the temperature of meat in order to ascertain when it has reached the desired degree of doneness. The dials on meat thermometers not only indicate the temperature, but some also have a scale indicating at what degree each type of meat (beef, lamb, pork, etc.) is done. A thermometer can be inserted at the beginning of the cooking time and left in throughout the duration. There are also **instant-read thermometers** that take the reading in just a few seconds; these are inserted into the meat toward the end of the cooking time. Meat thermometers come with 1- or 2-inch dials, usually measuring from 0° (sometimes 100°) to 220°F. Look for those with thin probes, which make smaller holes in the meat and therefore allow less juices to escape. Always insert a meat thermometer as near to the center of the meat as possible, avoiding bone or gristle areas. *See also* CANDY THERMOMETER; FREEZER/REFRIGERATOR THERMOMETER; OVEN THERMOMETER.

medallion [meh-DAL-yuhn] A small coin-shaped piece of meat, usually beef, veal or pork.

Mediterranean caviar *see* BOTTARGA

mee fun *see* RICE NOODLES

mee krob [MEE krob] Also called *mi krob,* the name of this Thai dish literally translates to "crispy noodles," and mee krob is based on deep-fried rice noodles that crisp and puff up when fried. In Thai these noodles are called *sen mee* (*see* RICE NOODLES). The noodles are tossed with a SWEET-AND-SOUR-flavored STIR-FRY, which has many variations but typically contains ingredients such as fish, shrimp and/or pork, vegetables and/or fresh bean sprouts, lemon or lime juice, green onions, chiles, shredded KAFFIR LIME leaves or peel and garlic.

mee tye bak *see* RICE NOODLES

mela [MEH-lah] Italian for "APPLE."

melanzana [meh-lahn-ZAH-nah] Italian for "EGGPLANT."

Melba sauce Created by the famous French chef Auguste Escoffier for Australian opera singer Dame Nellie Melba, this sauce is a combination of puréed and strained fresh raspberries, red currant jelly, sugar and cornstarch. It's classically used to adorn the dessert PEACH MELBA but can also top ice cream, fruit, pound cakes and puddings. *See also* SAUCE.

Melba toast Also created by Auguste Escoffier for opera singer Dame Nellie Melba (*see* MELBA SAUCE), this toast is exceedingly thin and dry. It's sold packaged in most supermarkets and is used to accompany soups, salads and the like.

Melegueta pepper [meh-leh-GAY-tah] *see* GRAINS OF PARADISE

mellowfruit *see* PEPINO

melogold A cross between a POMELO and a white grapefruit developed in 1958 at the University of California Riverside. The melogold slightly bigger than a medium-size grapefruit. The rind is thicker and changes from green to golden yellow as it matures. The flesh is pale yellow and very sweet with minor tartness and contains few seeds. Avoid fruit that is overly soft; choose fruit that's heavy for its size. Store at room temperature for up to 2 weeks, or in the refrigerator for up to a month. The melogold is available in the winter months through early spring.

melon Hieroglyphics dating back to 2400 B.C. show that Egyptians knew the pleasures of these sweet, perfumy fruits even then. Today there are hundreds of melon varieties, all of which belong to the gourd family, as do squash and pumpkin. In general, melons are relatively large, tough-skinned fruits with juicy flesh and plentiful seeds, either clustered in the fibrous center or, as with watermelon, more broadly scattered. The skins can range in color from creamy white to celadon green to jade green, with many variations and shades in between. Flesh colors vary similarly and include shades of salmon, cream, golden, lime-green, pink and orange. These fruits grow on one of two species of vines, one of which bears WATERMELON, the other of which bears three different types of melon—the European cantaloupe, the muskmelon and the winter melon (not to be confused with WINTER MELON squash). Varieties in the category of **European cantaloupe** (named after Catalupo, Italy) include the CHARENTAIS and the GALIA. Such melons are notable for their dark-green grooves—segmented markings from stem to blossom end, which make them easy to spot in the produce section. **Muskmelons** are also known as *netted melons* because of their skin, which looks like it's covered with a rough, thick netting. Melons in this category include the American CANTALOUPE and PERSIAN MELON. They're exceedingly aromatic but, if picked before mature, never really reach their sweet and flavorful potential. Although muskmelons of one variety or another are available throughout most of the year, they're most abundant from late summer to early fall. **Winter melons** are so named because they mature later than the other two categories, reaching their prime in late autumn. In general, such melons (which include CASABA and HONEYDEW) have harder rinds and are not as aromatic as those in the previous two categories. Unlike other types of melon, winter melons will continue to ripen nicely off the vine if left at room temperature. Of course, to further complicate matters, there are also hybrids of more than one category, such as the CRENSHAW, which is a cross between the cantaloupe and the casaba. **To choose a melon**, use your thumb to gently press the blossom end (opposite the stem)—if it gives noticeably the melon is ripe. Melons should be heavy for their size and have a sweet aroma. Refer to each melon listing for specifics on choosing that variety. Store melons at room temperature until ready to use. Cut melon should be wrapped in plastic wrap and refrigerated for up to 5 days. To prepare melon, cut in half and scoop out the seeds with a large spoon. Depending on how the melon will be used, the rind can be removed and the melon cut or scooped into balls (*see* MELON BALLER). As with most fruit, the flavor of melon will be better at room temperature. Besides being used in fruit bowls and salads, melon can be made into a cold soup, added at the last minute to STIR-FRY dishes or added to fresh salsas. *See also* CAMOUFLAGE MELON; CHARENTAIS MELON; GALIA MELON; SANTA CLAUS MELON; SHARLYN MELON; SPANISH MELON; WATERMELON.

melon baller A small, bowl-shaped tool used to cut round- or oval-shaped pieces of melon. The best melon ballers are rigidly constructed with wood or metal handles and sharp-edged, stainless-steel bowls, which come in a range of sizes, from about $1/4$ inch to 1 inch.

melone *see* Pasta Glossary, page 883

melt *n.* 1. This VARIETY MEAT is the spleen of an animal (typically calf or pig), which can be cooked for human consumption, but is typically used for pet food. Melt, an elongated organ with a dark reddish brown color and a spongy texture, can sometimes be special ordered from meat markets. 2. A name for a sandwich (usually open-faced) topped with melted cheese, as in a "tuna melt." **melt** *v.* Using heat to convert food (such as butter or chocolate) from a solid to a liquid or semiliquid.

Melton Mowbray pork pie Pork pie named after Melton Mowbray, a town in Leicestershire, England, about 90 miles northwest of London. The pie is unique because it's baked without a pie pan, resulting in an irregular shape with bowed sides. It became a favorite of fox hunters in the 19th century and, because the recipe's not overly complicated, producers outside the area began to make pork pies using the Melton Mowbray name. In 1999 producers in Melton Mowbray applied to the European Union to recognize their pie as a PROTECTED GEOGRAPHICAL INDICATION (PGI); they were granted PGI status in 2008. To be a true Melton Mowbray pork pie, the pie must be made within a specific geographic area around the town, baked free-standing (no pie pan) and made with at least 30 percent fresh (not cured) pork, which is chopped not minced. Additionally, pork gelatin or pork stock, LARD or SHORTENING, wheat flour, water, salt and spices (particularly pepper) may be used. Preservatives and artificial colors and flavors may not. Some pork pies include a whole boiled egg in the middle; this is not traditional and not allowed for a true Melton Mowbray pork pie.

membrillo [mem-BREE-yoh] *see* QUINCE

memela *see* SOPE

mentaiko [mehn-tah-EE-koh] POLLOCK ROE that's been marinated. One of the most popular versions in Japan is the very spicy KARASHI MENTAIKO, which is seasoned with TOGARASHI (hot Japanese chiles).

menudo [meh-NOO-doh; meh-NOO-thoh] A hearty, spicy soup made with TRIPE, CALF'S FEET, green CHILES, HOMINY and seasonings. It's usually garnished with lime wedges, bowls of chopped chiles and onion and served with hot TORTILLAS. Menudo has long been touted as a hangover cure and is particularly popular in Mexico on New Year's morning.

mer [MEHR] French for "sea." *Fruits de mer* means "fruits of the sea," referring to a seafood combination.

mère de vinaigre *see* MOTHER OF VINEGAR

merengada [may-rayn-GAH-dah] A Latin American "milk shake" made with milk, fresh fruit pulp, ice and, sometimes, sugar. *See also* BATIDO; JUGO.

meringue [muh-RANG] Very simply, a meringue is a mixture of stiffly beaten egg whites and granulated sugar. In order for the sugar to dissolve completely (and therefore produce an absolutely smooth meringue), it must be beaten into the whites a tablespoon at a time. **Soft meringue** is used as a swirled topping for pies, puddings and other desserts such as BAKED ALASKA. It's baked only until the peaks are nicely browned and the valleys golden. **Hard meringues** begin by being piped onto a PARCHMENT-lined baking sheet. They're usually round and may be large or small. They're then baked at a very low temperature (about 200°F) for as long as 2 hours and left in the turned-off oven until completely dry. Hard meringues often have a center depression that is filled with ice cream, custard, whipped cream and fruit, etc. Tiny, one- or two-bite size, mound-shape meringues are called KISSES and are eaten as a confection. Kisses often contain chopped nuts, cherries or coconut. They may be baked until completely dry or just until crisp on the outside and chewy inside. An **Italian meringue** is made by gradually pouring hot SUGAR SYRUP over stiffly beaten egg whites, then beating constantly until the mixture is smooth and satiny. This versatile mixture may be used to create either soft or hard meringues.

Meritage [MEHR-ih-tihj] A wine term (a compound of the words "merit" and "heritage") instituted in 1989 as a certification mark registered with the U.S. Department of Trademarks and Patents. It was coined by a group of vintners who sought to establish standards of identification for a category of American blended wines made with traditional BORDEAUX grape varieties. The Meritage Association was formed to help identify quality American wine blends that, because they're not made with at least 75 percent of a single variety, can't use the variety name on the label. This forced many producers of excellent wines to either use generic names (like CLARET or Red Table Wine) or proprietary names (like the Joseph Phelps Vineyards *Insignia*)—practices that caused great confusion in the marketplace. To be designated as Meritage, a wine must meet the following standards: 1. It must be a blend of two or more Bordeaux grape varieties—for red wines these are Cabernet Franc, CABERNET SAUVIGNON, Carmenere, Gros Verdot, Malbec, MERLOT, PETITE VERDOT and St. Macaire, and for whites they're SAUVIGNON BLANC, MUSCADET and SÉMILLON (no more than 90 percent of any single variety may go into a Meritage wine); 2. It must be the winery's best wine of its type; 3. It must be produced and bottled by a U.S. winery from grapes that carry a U.S. APPELLATION; and 4. Its production is limited to a maximum 25,000 cases per VINTAGE. Wineries that are approved for the Meritage designation may use it in various ways on the label. They may simply use the word Meritage alone, or Meritage in conjunction with their own proprietary name (as with *Cardinale* from Kendall-Jackson Vineyards) or use only their proprietary name.

Merlot [mer-LOH] A red-wine grape widely grown in France's Pomerol and Saint-Émilion districts of BORDEAUX and, to a lesser extent, in California and the Pacific Northwest. The wine it produces is similar in flavor to CABERNET SAUVIGNON, but tends to be softer and more mellow. It also matures sooner than Cabernet. Though the Merlot grape has been principally used for blending in the United States, it's now beginning to be appreciated on its own. The French have long known its value as is indicated by the great Château Petrus of Pomerol, which is often 100 percent Merlot.

mescal *see* MEZCAL

mesclun [MEHS-kluhn; *Fr.* KLAH/V] Found in specialty produce markets and many supermarkets, mesclun (also called *salad mix* and *gourmet salad mix*) is simply a potpourri of young, small salad greens. The mix varies depending on the source, but among those greens commonly included are ARUGULA, DANDELION, FRISÉE, MIZUNA, OAK LEAF, MÂCHE, RADICCHIO and SORREL. Choose mesclun with crisp leaves and no sign of wilting. Refrigerate in a plastic bag for up to 5 days. Wash and blot dry just before using.

mesophilic cultures *see* STARTER

mesquite [meh-SKEET] A low-slung hardwood tree that grows wild throughout the southwestern United States and northern Mexico. Used in barbecuing and smoking foods, mesquite wood gives off a slightly sweet smoke.

Metaxa [muh-TAHK-suh] An amber-colored, sweetened Greek BRANDY based on red grapes and flavored with herbs and spices. Metaxas have a winelike flavor reminiscent of MUSCAT GRAPES. The **Seven-Star Amphora Metaxa** has a caramelized, nutty flavor, and the finest rendition—**Metaxa Grande Fine**—is full and rich and resembles SHERRY.

methi *see* FENUGREEK

méthode champenoise [may-TOHD (may-TOD) shahm-peh-NWAHZ] Developed in France's CHAMPAGNE region, this traditional method of making sparkling wine consists of blending various still WINES to make a CUVÉE representative of the winery's style. After the wines are blended, a bottling DOSAGE and special yeasts are added, and the cuvée is immediately bottled and corked. The yeast and sugar in the dosage create a secondary FERMENTATION in the bottle, producing additional alcohol and carbon dioxide gas, which gives the wine its effervescence. Sediment produced during the second fermentation is removed through riddling (or *rémuage*), a process by which the bottles are positioned downward at a 45° angle in specially built racks called *pupitres*. Every 3 or 4 days, a trained workman gives the bottles a shake and a slight turn, gradually increases the angle of tilt, and drops the bottle back in the rack with a slight whack. In 6 to 8 weeks, all the bottles are positioned straight downward and the sediment has collected in the neck. Although riddling was once done entirely by hand, today many wineries employ machines that dramatically shorten this lengthy procedure. After riddling comes disgorging (or *dégorgement*), whereby the sediment is removed. Just before final bottling, a "shipping dosage" (*dosage d'expedition*) containing sugar and some of the same cuvée (reserved for this purpose) is added—the percentage of sugar determines the degree of the wine's sweetness. The term "méthode champenoise" can be used only on labels of wines made by this method.

Methuselah [meh-THOO-zuh-luh] *see* WINE BOTTLES

metric system A system of weights and measures that's used throughout much of the world. The basic units are the *gram* for weight and the *meter* for length. When calculating conversions, the same figure (0.236) is used whether converting *to* or *from* metric. The only difference is that, when converting to metric (as from cups to liters), you *multiply* the number of cups by 0.236 to get the equivalent in liters. When converting from metric (as from liters to cups), you *divide* the liters by 0.236 to get the cup equivalency. *See also* Metric Conversion Formulas, page 873.

Mettwurst [MEHT-wurst; MEHT-vursht] Also called *Schmierwurst* because it's soft enough to smear or spread, this German pork SAUSAGE is bright red, fatty and seasoned with coriander and white pepper. Though it's uncooked, mettwurst is cured, smoked and ready to eat. It's usually spread on bread or crackers.

meunière [muhn-YEHR] French for "miller's wife," referring to a style of cooking whereby a food (usually fish) is seasoned, lightly dusted with flour and sautéed simply in butter. Such a preparation is served with **beurre meunière**, which is BEURRE NOISETTE flavored with lemon juice and parsley.

Mexican breadfruit *see* MONSTERA

Mexican chocolate Flavored with cinnamon, almonds and vanilla, this sweet chocolate is available in Latin markets and some supermarkets. Mexican chocolate has a much grainier texture than other chocolates.

It's used in the preparation of a Mexican hot chocolate drink and certain Mexican specialties such as *mole poblano* (*see* MOLE), a CHILE-almond sauce usually served with fowl. One ounce semisweet chocolate, $^1/_2$ teaspoon ground cinnamon and 1 drop almond extract can be substituted for 1 ounce Mexican chocolate.

Mexican coriander see SAW-LEAF HERB

Mexican green tomato see TOMATILLO

Mexican potato *see* JICAMA

Mexican tea *see* EPAZOTE

Mexican wedding cake A buttery, melt-in-your-mouth cookie that's usually ball-shaped and generally contains finely chopped almonds, pecans or hazelnuts. It's usually rolled in powdered sugar while still hot, then again after the cookie has cooled. Many countries have their own rendition of this rich cookie. Two versions are **Russian tea cakes** and Spain's **polvorones**.

Mexican yellow bean *see* PERUANO BEAN

Meyer lemon Botanists believe this relatively new LEMON-family member is a cross between a lemon and an orange. It's named after F. N. Meyer who in 1908 imported it into the United States from China where it's been grown for centuries. Meyer lemons have a rounder shape and smoother skin than common commercial lemons; their color ranges from deep yellow to yellow-orange. The aromatic juice is sweeter and less acidic than that of regular lemons. Meyer lemons are available from October through May in specialty produce markets and many supermarkets. Choose firm fruit that's heavy for its size. Refrigerate in a plastic bag for up to 2 weeks.

mezcal [mehs-KAL] Called "the nectar of the (Aztec) gods" by Cortez, mezcal is a potent, clear liquor that originated in Oaxaca, a state in southeastern Mexico. The word "mezcal," sometimes spelled *mescal,* comes from the Náhuatl *mexcalmetl* ("agave species"). Like TEQUILA, mezcal is produced from the AGAVE plant but, whereas tequila must be made from the blue agave and produced from plants grown only in a specified area, mezcal may be produced from any of several species and can be made anywhere in Mexico. Bottles of mezcal labeled *Mezcal de Gusanitos* contain a small worm (the *gusano*), said to give strength to anyone who swallows it. Most mezcal, which has a smoky, peppery character, is quite crude and is often flavored and sweetened, presumably to mask its rough flavor. Although mezcal is enjoyed all over Mexico, it's just beginning to catch on elsewhere. *See also* PULQUE; TEQUILA.

meze [MEH-zay] Greek for "HORS D'OEUVRE" or "appetizer."

mezzaluna [mehz-zuh-LOO-nuh] Also called a *crescent cutter,* the mezzaluna ("half-moon") is a curved steel chopping blade with a vertical wooden handle at each end. It's used to mince or chop food by rocking the blade from side to side on a cutting board.

mezzani *see* Pasta Glossary, page 883

miche [MEESH] *see* BOULE

Microplane® *see* RASP GRATER

microwave oven A microwave oven cooks with high-frequency radio waves that cause food molecules to vibrate, creating friction that heats and cooks the food. Microwaves travel so fast (and therefore cook food quickly) because they're extremely short. Nonmetal containers are used in these special ovens because microwaves pass through them (unlike metal), thereby cooking the food from all angles (top, bottom and sides) at once. The fact that the waves pass through glass and ceramics means that the containers stay relatively cool while the food they contain becomes quite hot. The exception is when, during long cooking periods, the food can make the container very hot. Ideally, containers and products like paper towels and paper plates suitable for microwave cooking should be labeled "microwave safe." Because microwaves only penetrate about 1 inch into food, the center of most foods is cooked by heat conduction. This also means that thin pieces of food cook faster than those that are thick. Some microwave ovens have turntables for even microwave distribution. Others have revolving antennae for the same purpose. Microwave ovens use relatively little energy and do not heat up the kitchen. Microwave ovens range in power from about 500 watts to about 1650 watts. Knowing the wattage of your oven is vital to following microwave-oven recipes, most of which are written for 700-watt models. Factors that affect how quickly food cooks in a microwave oven include: the temperature of the food when cooking begins; the volume of food being cooked at one time; the size and shape of the food; the amount of fat, sugar and moisture in the food (fat and sugar speed the cooking; moisture impedes it); bone distribution; and food density (carrots, for example, are much more dense than eggplant). *See also* Microwave Oven Conversion Chart, page 863.

Midori [mih-DOOR-ee] A bright green Japanese LIQUEUR that tastes like HONEYDEW MELON.

mi fen *see* RICE NOODLES

migliaccio *see* CASTAGNACCIO

mignonette; mignonnette [meen-yawn-NEHT] 1. A small, coin-shaped piece of meat, usually lamb. Also called *noisette* or *medallion*. 2. The term *poivre mignonnette* more commonly refers to coarsely ground white PEPPERCORNS. 3. Historically, a mignonnette was a small cloth sachet filled with peppercorns and cloves, used to flavor soups and stews much in the way a BOUQUET GARNI is used today.

mi krob *see* MEE KROB

milanaise, à la [mee-lah-NEHZ] A French cookery term for PASTA tossed with butter and grated cheese and topped with a tomato sauce made with shredded ham, pickled tongue, mushrooms and truffles.

milanese, alla [mee-lah-NEH-zeh] Italian for "in the style of Milan," referring to food (usually meat) dipped in beaten egg, then into a bread-crumb-Parmesan mixture and fried in butter.

Milano salami *see* SALAMI

milfoil [MIHL-foyl] *see* YARROW

milk Milk has been used for human consumption for thousands and thousands of years, as proven by cave drawings showing cows being milked. Today cow's milk is still one of the most popular (especially in the United States) animal milks consumed by humans. Around the world, people drink the milk from many other animals including camels, goats, llamas, reindeer, sheep and water buffalo. Most milk packs a nutritional punch and contains protein, calcium, phosphorus, vitamins A and D, LAC-TOSE (milk sugar) and riboflavin. On the minus side, milk's natural sodium content is quite high. Most milk sold in the United States today is PAS-TEURIZED, which means the microorganisms that cause diseases (such as salmonella and hepatitis) and spoilage have been destroyed by heating, then quick-cooling, the milk. Pasteurization eliminates the possibility of disease and gives milk a longer shelf life. Most commercial milk products have also been HOMOGENIZED, meaning that the milk fat globules have been broken down mechanically until they are evenly and imperceptibly distributed throughout the milk. The end result is that the cream does not separate from the milk and the liquid is uniformly smooth. In 1993, the Federal Drug Administration approved supplementing dairy cows with a genetically produced hormone protein known as bovine somato-tropin (BST). BST is a naturally occurring growth hormone that's found in all cows. When bioengineered BST is injected into dairy cows, their milk production increases by up to 25 percent. Scientists assert that the composition of milk from BST-injected cows is not altered in any way and has no biological effect on humans, although many opponents are not convinced. There is no mandatory labeling for milk from BST-supplemented cows. However, in some smaller market areas, you may find dairy products voluntarily labeled as "farmer certified to not come from BST-supplemented cows." Milk is available in many varieties. **Raw** (or *unpasteurized*) **milk**, usually only commercially available in natural food stores, has not been pasteurized. Advocates say it's better nutritionally because vitamins and natural enzymes have not been destroyed by heat. The dairies that are certified to sell raw milk have rigid hygiene standards and their herds are inspected regularly. But the milk is still not pasteurized and therefore carries some potential risk of disease. Almost all other pasteurized and homogenized milks are fortified with vitamins A and D. **Whole milk** is the milk just as it came from the cow and contains about 3½ percent milk fat. **Lowfat milk** comes in two basic types: *2 percent,* meaning 98 percent of the fat has been removed; and *1 percent,* which is 99 percent fat-free. A few lowfat milks contain only ½ percent milk fat but they're not widely available. **Nonfat** or **skim milk** must by law contain less than ½ percent milk fat. Both lowfat and nonfat milk are available with milk solids added, in which case the label states "Protein-fortified." Not only does this boost the protein to 10 grams per cup, but it also adds body and richness. Federal law requires that both lowfat and nonfat milk be fortified with 2,000 International Units (IU) of vitamin A per quart. Though vitamin D fortification is optional, 400 IU per quart is usually also added. **Buttermilk** of times past was the liquid left after butter was churned. Today it is made commercially by adding special bacteria to nonfat or lowfat milk, giving it a slightly thickened texture and tangy flavor. Some manufacturers add flecks of butter to give it an authentic look. **Creamline milk** is unhomogenized (and may be pasteurized or not) so the cream naturally rises to the top of the milk. **Dry** or **powdered buttermilk** is also available (*see* DRY MILK). **Sweet acidophilus milk** (whole, lowfat or nonfat) has had friendly and healthful lactobacillus acidophilus bacteria added to it. It tastes and looks just like regular milk but many scientists believe it has an advantage because the acidophilus culture restores nature's balance to the digestive tract. **Low-sodium milk**, in which 90 percent of the sodium is replaced by potassium, is a special product available in limited supply for those on sodium-restricted diets. **Lactose-reduced lowfat milk** is for people suffering from lactose intolerance. The lactose content in this special lowfat milk has been reduced to only 30 percent. **Ultrapasteurized milk** has been quickly heated to about 300°F, then vacuum-packed. It may be stored without refrigeration for up to 6 months until opened, after which it must be refrigerated. Though the high heat destroys spoilage-causing microorganisms, it also gives a "cooked" flavor to the milk. **Chocolate milk** is whole milk with sugar and chocolate added to it. **Chocolate dairy drink** (sometimes labeled simply **chocolate drink**) is skim milk with the same flavorings added. In either case, if cocoa is used instead of chocolate, the product is labeled "chocolate-flavored drink." There are a variety of **dry milk** and **canned milk** products on the market. (*See* DRY MILK, EVAPORATED MILK *and* SWEETENED CONDENSED MILK). **Buying milk:** Always check the date on the carton to make sure the milk you're buying is the freshest available. Pull dates (*see* OPEN DATING) are intentionally conservative, and most milk in a market with rapid turnover will keep at least a week after purchase. **Storing milk:** Refrigerate milk as soon as you get it home from the store. Milk readily absorbs flavors so always close milk cartons or other containers tightly. The storage life of milk is reduced greatly when allowed to sit out at room temperature for 30 minutes or more, as it would if put in a pitcher for serving. Rather than returning such milk to its original carton, cover the pitcher with plastic wrap, refrigerate and use that milk within 2 days. *See also* SOY MILK, *as well as listings for milk's most widely distributed by-products:* BUTTER; CHEESE; CREAM; SOUR CREAM; YOGURT.

milk fat; milkfat The fatty particles in milk that are separated out to make cream and subsequently butter. The higher the milk fat content in milk, cream, ice cream, etc., the richer and more caloric the product.

milk powder *see* DRY MILK

milk punch An alcoholic drink made with liquor (typically rum, whiskey or brandy), milk, sugar and sometimes vanilla. The mixture is usually blended with crushed ice and strained into a tall glass.

milk shake This American original consists of a blended combination of milk, ice cream and flavored syrup, fruit or other flavorings. The drink is quickly made with the aid of a BLENDER and is sometimes enriched with an added egg. *See also* MALTED MILK.

milk sugar *see* LACTOSE

milk tea *see* HONG KONG MILK TEA

milk toast Buttered toast, sometimes sprinkled with cinnamon and sugar, over which hot milk is poured. It was once popular fare for children and the ailing.

mille-feuille [meel-FWEE] French for "a thousand leaves," this classic dessert is made with two large oblong pieces of crisp PUFF PASTRY spread with whipped cream, custard, jam or fruit purée. The pastries are stacked and topped with another pastry layer, which is generally dusted with powdered sugar. A serrated knife is used to cut the dessert into individual servings. Savory mille-feuille can be filled with cheese and served as an appetizer.

millet [MIHL-leht] Though America cultivates this cereal grass almost exclusively for fodder and bird seed, millet is a staple for almost $1/3$ of the world's population, particularly in disadvantaged regions of Asia and Africa. There are many varieties of millet, most of which are rich in protein. Millet has a bland flavor that lends itself well as a background to other seasonings. It's prepared like rice by boiling it in water and is used to make hot cereal and dishes like PILAF. Ground millet is used as a flour to make puddings, breads and cakes. Millet can be found in Asian markets and natural food stores.

Mimolette; Mimolette Française [mee-moh-LEHT (frahn-SAY)] Bright orange, ball-shaped cheese that originated in Flanders during the Middle Ages. At that time, Flanders included parts of northern France, Belgium and the Netherlands, which is why Mimolette is still produced in some of these areas. It's also known as *Mimolette Française*, *Boule de Lille* and *Vieux Lille* (many of the cheeses were originally RIPENED in Lille, a city in northern France near the Belgian border). The bright orange color of Mimolette comes from ANNATTO, a natural dye derived from the achiote tree. Mimolette has a progression of RIPENING stages: *jeune* ("young") is aged 3 months, *demi-étuvée* or *demi-vieille* ("half old") for 6 months, *vieille en étuvée* ("old") for 12 months and *très vieille* ("very old") for 2 years. Younger versions have a mild flavor with fruity, nutty nuances; older cheeses have a fuller, tangier flavor. Young cheeses are firm and compact, while older ones become hard and brittle. It has a FAT CONTENT of about 40 to 45 percent. *See also* CHEESE.

mimosa [mih-MOH-suh] 1. A garnish so named because it resembles the yellow mimosa flower. Consisting of finely chopped, hard-cooked egg yolk, it is sprinkled over salads and vegetables. 2. A COCKTAIL of equal parts CHAMPAGNE and orange juice, served icy cold but not over ice. It's a favorite with brunch.

mince [MIHNS] To cut food into very small pieces. Minced food is in smaller pieces than chopped food. *See also* CHOP.

mincemeat A rich, spicy preserve made of fruit (usually chopped cherries, dried apricots, apples or pears, raisins and candied citrus peel), nuts, beef SUET, various spices and brandy or rum. Old-time mincemeats included minced, cooked lean meat (usually beef)—hence the name. Most modern versions do not use meat. The ingredients are combined, then covered and allowed to mature for a month for the flavors to mingle and mellow. Commercially prepared mincemeat is available in jars in most supermarkets—particularly around Thanksgiving and Christmas. Mincemeat can be used in many dishes including pies, tarts, puddings and cookies.

mineral water Water containing various minerals and sometimes gases, taken from wells or natural springs. Mineral water is often effervescent and was once drunk almost exclusively for medicinal purposes. It's now commonly used as a refreshing beverage, either alone or mixed with flavoring.

miners' lettuce A plant that grows abundantly in northern California and is high in vitamins A and C. In the 1800s gold rush miners ate it frequently in order to avoid getting scurvy. This plant with its mild flavor and heart-shaped leaves is also called *claytonia, Indian lettuce, spring beauty* and *winter purslane*. It's great in salads and can be steamed or lightly boiled. Miners' lettuce doesn't mind cool weather and grows late into the fall season and, in milder climates, clear through the winter months. *See also* PURSLANE.

minestra [mih-NAYS-truh] Italian for "soup," *minestra* most often describes a soup of medium thickness, frequently containing meat and vegetables. **Minestrina** ("little soup") is a thin broth, while **minestrone** ("big soup") refers to a thick vegetable soup that generally contains pasta and sometimes peas or beans. It's usually topped liberally with grated Parmesan cheese and is hearty enough to be considered a complete meal.

minestrone *see* MINESTRA

Ming Dynasty egg *see* HUNDRED-YEAR EGG

mini-burger *see* SLIDER

mini muffin pan *see* GEM PAN

Minneola *see* TANGELO

mint Long a symbol of hospitality, Greek mythology claims that mint was once the nymph Mentha. She angered Pluto's wife Persephone, who turned her into this aromatic herb. There are over 30 species of mint, the two most popular and widely available being peppermint and spearmint. **Peppermint** is the more pungent of the two. It has bright green leaves, purple-tinged stems and a peppery flavor. **Spearmint** leaves are gray-green or true green and have a milder flavor and fragrance. Mint grows wild throughout the world and is cultivated in Europe, the United States and Asia. It's most plentiful during summer months but many markets carry it year-round. Choose leaves that are evenly colored with no sign of wilting. Store a bunch of mint, stems down, in a glass of water with a plastic bag over the leaves. Refrigerate in this manner for up to a week, changing the water every 2 days. Mint is used in both sweet and savory dishes and in drinks such as the famous MINT JULEP. Mint is available fresh, dried, as an EXTRACT, and in the form of **oil of spearmint** or **oil of peppermint**, both highly concentrated flavorings. Most forms can usually be found in supermarkets. *See also* HERBS; Seasoning Suggestions, page 891.

mint geranium *see* COSTMARY

mint julep One of Kentucky's claims to fame, the mint julep is an alcoholic drink made with fresh mint (sometimes MUDDLED with sugar), bourbon and plenty of crushed ice. It's traditionally served in an iced silver or pewter mug at the running of the famous Kentucky Derby. *See also* JULEP.

minute steak A very thin, boneless beefsteak sometimes scored for tenderizing. It's small (6 to 9 ounces) and therefore usually cooked briefly—1 minute per side—over very high heat.

mirabelle [mihr-uh-BEHL; MIHR-uh-behl] 1. Grown in Great Britain (where it's called *cherry plum*) and parts of Europe, the small, round mirabelle plum ranges in color from golden yellow to red. It's sweet, but not acidic enough to make it very interesting when eaten raw. It does, however, make delicious tarts and preserves. *See also* PLUM. 2. A fine EAU DE VIE of the same name made from the mirabelle plum.

mirasol chile [mih-RAH-sohl] These 4- to 5-inch-long, 1- to 2-inch-wide CHILES are erect and grow toward the sun—hence their name, which means "looking at the sun." They are green to orange-red to reddish-brown in color depending on ripeness. Their flavor is full bodied, spicy, berry-like and mildly hot, with a SCOVILLE SCALE rating of 2,500 to 5,000. Fresh mirasol chiles are used in a variety of meat and vegetable dishes. When dried, they are called GUAJILLO CHILES.

mirepoix; mirepois [mihr-PWAH] A mixture of diced carrots, onions, celery and herbs sautéed in butter. Sometimes ham or bacon is added. Mirepoix is used to season sauces, soups and stews, as well as for a bed on which to braise foods, usually meats or fish. A **white mirepoix** omits the carrots and often incorporates mushrooms and/or parsnips.

mirin [MIHR-ihn] A low-alcohol, sweet, golden wine made from glutinous rice. Essential to the Japanese cook, mirin adds sweetness and flavor to a variety of dishes, sauces and glazes. It's available in all Japanese markets and the gourmet section of some supermarkets. Mirin is also referred to simply as *rice wine*. *See also* RICE WINE; SAKE.

mirliton [MIHR-lih-ton] *see* CHAYOTE

mise en place [MEEZ ahn plahs] A French term referring to having all the ingredients necessary for a dish prepared and ready to combine up to the point of cooking.

miso [MEE-soh] Also called *bean paste,* this Japanese culinary mainstay has the consistency of peanut butter and comes in a wide variety of flavors and colors. This fermented SOYBEAN paste has three basic categories—

barley miso, rice miso and soybean miso—all of which are developed by injecting cooked soybeans with a mold (*koji*) cultivated in either a barley, rice or soybean base. Additionally, the miso's color, flavor and texture are affected by the amounts of soybeans, *koji* and salt used. It's further influenced by the length of time it is aged, which can range from 6 months to 3 years. Miso is a basic flavoring in much of Japanese cooking. The lighter-colored versions are used in more delicate soups and sauces, and the darker colored in heavier dishes. There are also low-salt varieties available. **Shinshu miso** is a golden yellow, all-purpose variety with a mellow flavor and rather high salt content. There are regional favorites such as **sendai miso**, a fragrant, reddish-brown variety found in northern Japan, and the dark brown **hatcho miso**, popular in central Japan. **Akamiso**, or **red miso**, is reddish brown and Japan's most popular salty rice miso. **Shiromiso**, or **white miso**, is light colored and sweet. It's widely used throughout Japan. Miso is used in sauces, soups, marinades, dips, main dishes, salad dressings and as a table condiment. It's easily digested and extremely nutritious, having rich amounts of B vitamins and protein. Miso can be found in Japanese markets and natural food stores. It should be refrigerated in an airtight container.

Mission olive The Mission olive, also known as the common *black olive,* is actually a ripe green olive that obtains its characteristic color and flavor from lye curing and oxygenation. Some green versions are available in the marketplace. Both the black and the green types have a mild taste. The Mission olive was introduced to California during the late 1700s as the Franciscan missions were established. *See also* OLIVE.

mist Any drink in which undiluted spirits are poured into a glass (typically short) filled with crushed ice. For example, if SCOTCH were used, the drink would be called a "Scotch Mist."

misto [MEES-toh] Italian for "mixed" or "mixture." For example, FRITO MISTO ("mixed fry") refers to fried foods, BOLLITO MISTO ("mixed boil") refers to boiled meats and INSALATA misto is a "mixed salad."

mitmita [miht-miht-AH] An Ethiopian spice blend containing chile peppers, cardamom, cloves, salt and various other spices such as cinnamon, cumin and ginger. It's used as a seasoning or condiment.

mixed grill A dish of grilled or broiled meats, which can include lamb chops, beefsteak, liver, kidneys, bacon and sausages and is usually accompanied by grilled or broiled mushrooms, tomatoes and potatoes.

mixer 1. Any of various electric kitchen machines used to beat, mix or whip foods. There are two basic kinds—stationary (or stand) and portable (or hand-held). **Stationary mixers** have more powerful motors and therefore can handle heavier mixing jobs. They also take up more counter space. In addition to the standard beaters, stationary mixers are usually equipped with an assortment of attachments that can include dough hooks, wire whisks and flat, paddle-style beaters. Many have attachments such as citrus juicers, ice crushers, pasta makers, sausage stuffers and meat grinders. **Portable mixers**, as the name implies, can be used anywhere. Their small size is due in part to a small motor, which also limits these machines to smaller tasks. But size also makes the portable mixer easy to store. *See also* ROTARY BEATER. 2. Beverages such as soda water, cola or fruit juice that are combined with liquor to make a COCKTAIL.

mizuna [mih-ZOO-nuh] Hailing from Japan, this feathery, delicate salad green can be found in farmer's markets and specialty produce markets from spring through summer. It's often found in MESCLUN, a special salad-green mix. Choose mizuna (also called *siu cai*) by its crisp, green leaves, avoiding any wilted or browning specimens. Refrigerate in a plastic bag for up to 5 days. Wash and thoroughly dry just before using.

mizutaki [mee-zoo-TAH-kee] Japanese for "water-simmered," referring to a Japanese dish made in a single pot consisting of chicken and vegetables simmered in water and other seasonings. The dish is served from the pot at the table along with various condiments such as PONZU, radishes, green onions, ginger and lemon. *See also* CHIRINABE; NABEMONO.

mocha [MOH-kah] 1. Originally the word "mocha" referred only to a very fine coffee grown in Arabia and shipped from Yemen's port of Mocha. Today, this strong, slightly bitter coffee is still available but not as popular as it was in the 16th and 17th centuries. 2. A hot coffee-and-chocolate beverage. This flavor combination is also used in desserts, icings, candies and sweet sauces. *See also* CAFÉ MOCHA.

mochi; mochigome; mochiko [MOH-chee; MOH-chee-goh-meh; MOH-chee-koh] A sweet, short-grained, very glutinous rice with a high starch content. Mochigome or mochi is commonly used to make rice cakes (also called mochi), for which it is pounded in large tubs until it becomes extremely sticky. It is then formed into balls or squares, which can be found in Japanese markets. Mochi is also used in confections and rice dishes. **Mochiko** is a rice flour made from mochi. *See also* RICE; RICE FLOUR.

mock turtle soup This soup has nothing to do with turtles but is made instead from a calf's head cooked in water. After cooking, most recipes call for the head to be taken out of the broth and cooled, after which the meat is removed and cut into small pieces. Just before serving, the meat is returned to the clear, brownish broth, which is often flavored with wine and various spices, and usually thickened. Mock turtle soup is sometimes garnished with calves' BRAINS.

Moghul cuisine Highly evolved cuisine popular in northern India and the surrounding area. It developed during the Moghul rule of India, which started in 1527 and lasted for more than 200 years. The cuisines of Persia, the Hindus and the Arabs merged during this period, when lavish palaces including the Taj Mahal were built. Popular dishes in Moghul cuisine include BIRYANI, KEBABS, KOFTAS, KORMAS, SAMOSAS, and TANDOORI dishes. Lamb is the meat of choice although some chicken is used. Aromatic spices such as CARDAMOM, cinnamon, cloves, CORIANDER, CUMIN, ginger, INDIAN BAY LEAVES, mint, SAFFRON and TURMERIC are used, especially in the biryani rice dishes. Nuts like pistachios and almonds also play an important role.

mo gwa *see* FUZZY MELON

Mohnstriezel *see* MAKOWIEC

moi *see* PACIFIC THREADFIN

moisten This term is often used in baking recipes to instruct that only enough liquid be added to flour and other dry ingredients to make them damp or moist, but not wet.

mojama [moh-HAH-mah; moh-KHAH-mah] Salt-cured (*see* CURE) TUNA loins produced mainly in Spain's southern provinces of Huelva, Cádiz and Almeria. The Moors, who inhabited this area centuries ago, introduced this tuna preservation technique that's still used today. The word "mojama" is derived from *musama*, Moorish for "dry." The tuna loins are packed in salt for several days, rinsed and then dried for about 3 weeks. During this process the tuna loses about 50 percent of its weight and turns dark red to reddish brown. The flesh becomes firm, succulent and mildly sweet with a concentrated tuna flavor. Mojama is traditionally sliced very, very thin, drizzled with olive oil and served as TAPAS. It's exceedingly versatile and can be used in a variety of other dishes, such as with pasta or rice or as part of a salad.

Mojito [moh-HEE-toh] A COCKTAIL made by combining lime juice, sugar and mint leaves in a tall glass, then crushing the mint slightly with the back of a spoon. The glass is then filled with crushed ice, a JIGGER of rum and, sometimes, a SPRITZ of soda. Mojitos are garnished with a mint sprig.

mojo; mojo sauce [MOH-hoh] A sauce that comes in many variations (most of which are spicy-hot) and is ubiquitous in the Canary Islands, Cuba and other parts of the Caribbean. In the Canary Islands mojo comes in several forms—red (based on red peppers), green (green peppers) and orange (carrot), all flavored with garlic, oil, vinegar and various other ingredients. The red is often paired with potatoes, the green with fish and the orange with beef. Cuba has a proliferation of bitter oranges (*see* ORANGE), so much of the mojo in that country is flavored with orange juice. Although mojo recipes abound, most include the basics of garlic, oil, onions, various seasonings (such as CUMIN and CILANTRO), red peppers, chiles and the juice from limes and/or sour oranges. *See also* SAUCE.

mojo de ajo [MOH-hoh day AH-hoh] A Mexican garlic sauce created by slowly simmering diced or slivered peeled garlic cloves in oil and/or butter until pale golden brown. Slowly cooked this way, the garlic sweetens and flavors the oil. At this point, other ingredients (such as chiles, lime juice and CILANTRO or parsley) may be added. Sometimes the garlic-flavored oil is strained and served separately with the garlic-chile mixture. **Camarones al mojo de ajo** (shrimp with this sauce) is a popular favorite. *See also* SAUCE.

molasses [muh-LAS-sihz] During the refining of sugar cane and sugar beets, the juice squeezed from these plants is boiled to a syrupy mixture from which sugar crystals are extracted. The remaining brownish-black liquid is molasses. **Light molasses** comes from the first boiling of the sugar syrup and is lighter in both flavor and color. It's often used as a pancake and waffle syrup. **Dark molasses** comes from a second boiling and is darker, thicker and less sweet than light molasses. It's generally used as a flavoring in American classics such as GINGERBREAD, SHOOFLY PIE, INDIAN PUDDING and BOSTON BAKED BEANS. **Blackstrap molasses** comes from the third boiling and is what amounts to the dregs of the barrel. It's very thick, dark and somewhat bitter. Though it's popular with health-food followers, it's more commonly used as a cattle food. Contrary to what many believe, blackstrap is not a nutritional panacea. In truth, it's only fractionally richer than the other types of molasses in iron, calcium and phosphorus and many of its minerals are not assimilable. **Sorghum molasses** is the syrup produced from the cereal grain SORGHUM. Whether or not molasses is **sulphured** or **unsulphured** depends on whether sulphur was used in the processing. In general, unsulphured molasses is lighter and has a cleaner sugar-cane flavor. *See also* TREACLE.

molcajete y tejolete [mohl-kah-HEH-teh ee teh-hoh-LOH-teh] The Mexican term for "MORTAR AND PESTLE"—*molcajete* being the mortar, *tejolete* the pestle. The black, rough texture of both pieces is a result of the fact that they're made of basalt (volcanic rock). They are used in the traditional manner for grinding spices and herbs and other mixtures. They're also used as serving dishes for preparations such as GUACAMOLE in Mexican restaurants.

mold *n.* 1. A container, usually distinctively shaped, into which a food is placed in order to take on the shape of that container. Molds can range in size from tiny, individual candy-size molds to large pudding molds. The food (such as butter, chocolate, ice cream, ASPIC, PÂTÉ or a gelatin-based dessert) is poured or packed into the mold and then customarily refrigerated until it becomes firm enough to hold its shape. 2. The finished dish made in such a container. 3. Any of thousands of varieties of fungi that grow on food items such as bread, cheese, fruit and jam. Molds grow best when the food is acidic and the environment is warm, damp and dark, with some air circulation. Mold reproduces from its spores, which are carried through the air until they find the right food and environment to germinate. Most molds are simply nuisances that spoil food but are not harmful. Among the beneficial molds are those purposely nurtured to create wonderful blue cheeses like ROQUEFORT and STILTON, and that which grows on the rind of CAMEMBERT, providing its distinctive flavor. **mold** *v.* To form food into a distinctive shape either by hand-forming (as with a bread dough) or by pouring (as with ASPIC) into a decorative mold and chilling or freezing until firm.

molded cookie *see* HAND-FORMED COOKIES

mole [MOH-lay] From the Nahuatl *molli,* meaning "concoction," mole is a rich, dark, reddish-brown sauce usually served with poultry. There are many variations of this spicy Mexican specialty, usually depending on what's in the cook's kitchen. Generally, mole is a smooth, cooked blend of onion, garlic, several varieties of CHILES, ground seeds (such as sesame seeds or pumpkin seeds—known as *pepitas*) and a small amount of MEXICAN CHOCOLATE, its best-known ingredient. (Some Americanized mole recipes use bitter chocolate.) The chocolate contributes richness to the sauce without adding overt sweetness. *See also* SAUCE.

molecular gastronomy The application of chemistry and physics to the culinary world by using experimental lab techniques in the kitchen. Those on this culinary quest for answers include everyone from professionals to home chefs. The myriad issues explored in the molecular gastronomy field include: devising new cooking methods to improve the eventual outcome; testing various production methods to see how they affect the final flavor and texture of food; and determining how food enjoyment is affected by mood, environment, company and so on. The scientific techniques and equipment used by some are often cutting edge and can include everything from lasers to enzymes to liquid nitrogen. *See also* SODIUM ALGINATE.

mollusk [MAHL-uhsk] One of the two main classifications of SHELLFISH (the other being CRUSTACEAN), mollusks are invertebrates with soft bodies covered by a shell of one or more pieces. Mollusks are further divided into

GASTROPODS (also called *univalves*), such as the ABALONE and SNAIL; BIVALVES, like the CLAM and OYSTER; and CEPHALOPODS, such as the OCTOPUS and SQUID. *See also* CONCH; CUTTLEFISH; MUSSEL; PERIWINKLE; SCALLOP; WHELK.

momi; momi milk tea [MOH-mee] *see* BUBBLE TEA

momiji oroshi [moh-MIH-jee OH-rah-shee] Japanese condiment made from grated DAIKON and red chiles. The traditional way to make it is to poke holes in the daikon with a chopstick, insert the red chile peppers and then grate the daikon and peppers.

momo [moh-moh] Small sautéed or steamed dumpling popular in Nepal, Tibet and surrounding Himalayan areas. Momos can be filled with cheese, meat, vegetables or even sweet ingredients. The wrapper is simply dough made from flour and water; sometimes a little oil, salt and/or baking powder is added. Momos are usually served with a tomato sauce or tomato-based CHUTNEY. *See also* PEPPER LEAF.

monastery cheeses A style of SEMISOFT cow's-milk cheese that originated in Christian religious orders, primarily in Belgium, France and Switzerland. Some monasteries still produce these cheeses but the bulk of the production comes from nonsectarian factories. Monastery cheeses, also called *monk's cheeses* and *Trappist cheeses,* are recognized as having pronounced flavor and aroma. Among the better-known examples are MUNSTER and PONT L'EVEQUE.

Monastrell [maw-nahs-TRRELL] see MOURVÈDRE

Mongolian grill This audience-participation cooking is said to have originated during the time of Genghis Khan when his warriors in the field would sit around grills and enjoy cooking their own food. The basic approach is for each diner to dip thin slices of lamb (or other meat) into a ginger-soy sauce MARINADE before placing them on a hot grill (usually a large HIBACHI) set on the center of the table. Each individual cooks his or her meat (the Mongolian grill) according to personal preference. The grill is sometimes garnished with chopped scallions, mushrooms or watercress and eaten on plain buns.

Mongolian hot pot; Mongolian firepot This is a kind of Chinese FONDUE, also known as *Chinese firepot* or *boiling firepot*. A giant communal pot of slowly simmering stock is placed in the center of the table and the participants are provided with a variety of raw, thinly sliced meats (lamb, beef, fish, poultry, etc.) and vegetables. Diners immerse pieces of their food into the simmering stock, cook it to their liking and, if desired, dip the food into one of a selection of CONDIMENTS. After the food is cooked, the rich broth is consumed by any who have room for it.

monkey bread 1. A sweet yeast bread formed by arranging small clumps of dough (which are usually dipped in melted butter) in 3 or 4 overlapping layers in a pan. The pan can be round, oblong or tube-shape. After baking, the clumps cling together to form a solid loaf. Monkey bread can be sweet (flavored with raisins, nuts, cinnamon and sugar) or savory (often made with grated cheese). 2. A gourdlike fruit of the baobab, a thick-trunked tree native to Africa. The extremely high-starch fruit is generally only eaten by monkeys.

monkeyface eel These 14- to 30-inch-long eel-like fish, which are not eels at all but rather members of the prickleback family, are found in tide pools and rocky reefs along the Pacific coast, from southern Oregon to Baja California. They are becoming popular because of their delicate, mild flavor and meaty flesh, which lend themselves to a variety of culinary preparations. Unfortunately, they are not caught commercially in any significant numbers. Because of their habitat, they are often caught using a technique called "pole poking," which involves a long pole and tiny piece of wire with a baited hook. The pole is poked into the nooks and crannies where the monkeyface eel dwells in hopes of snaring one.

monkfish *see* ANGLER FISH

monk fruit *see* LUO HAN GUO

monosodium glutamate; MSG [mon-uh-SOH-dee-uhm GLOO-tuh-mayt] Commonly known as *MSG,* this white crystalline powder is derived from glutamic acid, one of the 22 amino acids. This natural amino acid is found in SEAWEED, vegetables, cereal gluten and the residue of sugar beets. It was first discovered by Japanese scientists in the 1920s. Japan, where MSG is known as *aji-no-moto,* is still today's largest producer of MSG, a popular flavor enhancer in Japanese and Chinese cooking. Even though it has no pronounced flavor of its own, monosodium glutamate has the ability to intensify the flavor of savory foods. Some people have reactions to MSG that cause them to suffer from a variety of maladies including dizziness, headache, flushing and burning sensations. MSG is found in the spice section of supermarkets either as monosodium glutamate, MSG or under brand names such as *Ac'cent.* Many seasoning mixes also contain MSG. Additionally, it's present in many processed foods such as snack foods, frozen entrées, salad dressings and soups. Be aware that many ingredients naturally contain MSG, but are not required by the Food and Drug Administration to be labeled as such. These ingredients include HYDROLYZED PLANT PROTEIN, *hydrolyzed vegetable protein,* KOMBU *extract* and *natural flavoring* or *seasoning.*

monounsaturated oils; monounsaturates [mon-oh-uhn-SACH-uh-ray-tihd] *see* FATS AND OILS

monstera [mon-STEH-ruh] Also called *ceriman* and *Mexican bread-fruit,* this unique tropical-American fruit looks like a narrow, foot-long pine cone. The thick, green skin has hexagonal scales that individually separate and pop off as the fruit begins to ripen. Inside, the ripe, off-white flesh is formed in segments correlating to the skin's pattern. It's creamy-smooth and resembles a very firm custard. The flavor is sweet-tart and reminiscent of pineapple with touches of banana and mango. If underripe, however, the monstera has an off-taste and an irritant that will inflame both mouth and throat. In the United States, the monstera can be found in California, Florida and a few other locales that have produce markets specializing in exotic fruit. The monstera should be ripened at room temperature until the scales pop off and expose the luscious fruit, which is best plucked out and eaten plain with a spoon or fork.

Montasio [mohn-TAH-zyoh] Hailing from Italy's Friuli-Venezia Giulia region, Montasio is a cow's-milk CHEESE with a flavor that can range from extremely mild (almost nondescript) when young to full-flavored, nutty and sharp when aged. Depending on RIPENING time, Montasio can range in texture from semisoft to hard. It's produced in three different styles: "fresh" is aged for about 2 months, "medium" for 5 to 10 months and the "aged" version for 1 to 4 years. Montasio's FAT CONTENT ranges from 32 to 34 percent. *See also* CHEESE.

mont blanc [mawh*n* BLAH*N*] A classic dessert of sweetened, puréed chestnuts subtly flavored with vanilla. The mixture is RICED and mounded into a high, fluffy mountain on a platter. This sweet alp is capped with whipped cream or crème CHANTILLY. Mont Blanc ("white mountain") is a peak in the French Alps near the Italian border.

Mont d'Or *see* VACHERIN

monté au beurre; monter au beurre [mawn-TAY oh BURR] *see* MOUNT, TO

Monte Cristo sandwich [MON-tee KRIHS-toh] A sandwich consisting of slices of cooked chicken or turkey, cheese (usually Swiss) and sometimes baked ham. The sandwich is dipped into beaten egg and sautéed in butter until golden brown.

Monterey Jack *see* JACK CHEESE

Montmorency, à la [mont-muh-REHN-see; mawn-moh-rahn-SEE] A term meaning "made or served with cherries," applying to various desserts and entrées such as *caneton à la Montmorency*—roast duckling with cherry sauce.

Montmorency cherry [mont-muh-REHN-see] An extremely popular sour cherry and the primary cherry grown to be sold fresh (most sour cherries are used for canning purposes). The skin is a medium red and the extremely juicy flesh a creamy beige. As with most sour cherries, cooking brings out the fresh, tart flavor of the Montmorency. It can be used in cold soups, in entrée sauces or in desserts. *See also* CHERRY.

Montpellier butter *see* BEURRE DE MONTPELLIER

Montrachet [mawn-ruh-SHAY] A white, unaged (*see* RIPEN) goat's-milk cheese (*see* CHÈVRE) from France's Burgundy region. Montrachet has a soft, moist and creamy texture and a mildly tangy flavor. It's usually sold in logs covered in a gray, salted ASH. Montrachet is best when quite young and fresh. *See also* CHEESE.

moo goo gai pan [moo goo gi-PAN] Chinese-American stir-fried dish of sliced or cubed chicken with ingredients such as mushrooms, BAMBOO SHOOTS, CHINESE CABBAGE, SNOW PEAS and WATER CHESTNUTS. It's typically seasoned with garlic, ginger, SOY SAUCE, rice wine and sesame oil. Moo goo gai pan is served in a light sauce of chicken broth, OYSTER SAUCE, sugar and cornstarch. Also called *mah gu gai pin*.

moonfish *see* OPAH

moonshine *see* CORN WHISKEY

moo shu *see* MU SHU

mop A barbecue or other thick sauce brushed over meat during grilling for flavor and moisture retention.

Moravian Christmas cookies [moh-RAY-vee-uhn] A spicy ginger-molasses cookie traditionally served at Christmastime in Moravia, a historic region of the Czech Republic. The Moravian settlements in the United States—particularly in Old Salem, North Carolina—continue this tradition by making these cookies ultrathin and cutting them into various festive shapes.

moraya [moh-RAH-yah] *see* CHUÑO

Morbier (AOC; PDO) [mohr-bee-AY] A SEMISOFT cow's-milk cheese created in the 19th century as a way of using up surplus CURD from making large 100-pound wheels of COMTÉ. Excess Comté curd from the morning milking was covered with a layer of ASH for two purposes—to prevent a rind from forming and keep pests away. Later the ash would be overlaid with the surplus curd from the evening milking, and then the curds would be pressed and RIPENED. Today, Morbier, which is named after a small village in eastern France's Franche-Comté region, is made on its own from a single milking. To replicate the original look, cheesemakers cut the cheese in half horizontally and sprinkle ash or vegetable coloring over the bottom portion. Morbier is ripened for at least 30 days and more commonly for 2 to 4 months. The flat 11- to 20-pound wheels have a rind that's thick, leathery and golden brown with white and gray splotches. The cheese's interior is ivory with a scattering of irregular EYES, with that thin layer of ash or vegetable coloring in the middle. The texture of the cheese is supple, smooth and firm. The flavor is slightly piquant with hints of fruit, grass, nuts and yeast. It has a minimum FAT CONTENT of 45 percent.

morel [muh-REHL] Belonging to the same fungus species as the truffle, the morel is an edible wild mushroom. Its spongy, honeycombed, cone-shape cap ranges in size from 2 to 4 inches high and in color from a rich tan to an extremely dark brown. The morel is widely applauded by gourmets, who savor its smoky, earthy, nutty flavor. In general, the darker the mushroom the stronger the flavor. Wild morels usually appear in specialty produce markets in April and the season can last through June. Cultivated morels may appear sporadically throughout the year. Choose fresh specimens that have a firm yet spongy texture. Imported canned morels can be found in gourmet markets year-round. Dried morels have a more intense, smokier flavor than fresh ones and have the advantage of being available year-round. The marvelous flavor of the morel needs little embellishment and this mushroom is best when simply sautéed in butter. *See also* MUSHROOM.

morello cherry; English morello cherry [muh-REHL-oh] Seldom found fresh, this sour CHERRY has a dark red skin and flesh and is used in a variety of processed products. The morello cherry is actually a group of sour cherries that have red-pigmented skin and flesh. In the past there were numerous morello cultivars, but today only the generic morello is easily found. The blood-red juice is used in liqueurs and brandies, and the cherries can be found canned, packed in syrup, dried and in preserves. The sharp, sour taste makes the Morello unsuitable for eating raw but perfect for cooking.

morita chile [moh-REE-tah] A variety of CHIPOTLE CHILE (a dried, smoked JALAPEÑO) grown in the northern Mexican state of Chihuahua. They are not smoked as long as other types of chipotles leaving them with slightly fruitier flavors. Most chipotle chiles in the U.S. are of the morita variety. They have A SCOVILLE SCALE RATING OF 2,500 TO 8,000.

Mornay sauce [mohr-NAY] A BÉCHAMEL to which cheese, usually PARMESAN and SWISS, has been added. It's sometimes varied by the addition of fish or chicken stock or, for added richness, cream or egg yolks. Mornay sauce is served with eggs, fish, shellfish, vegetables and chicken. *See also* SAUCE.

Moroccan olive There are several different varieties of Moroccan olives such as the GAETA OLIVE or the PICHOLINE OLIVE. There's a medium-size black version that's dry-cured, resulting in a wrinkled flesh, soft meat and slightly bitter flavor. There's also a larger greenish version that's cured in vinegary brine that usually contains various herbs and spices. The result is a soft-textured olive with salty, spicy flavor. *See also* OLIVE.

mortadella [mohr-tuh-DEHL-uh] This smoked SAUSAGE originated in Bologna, Italy, and is the original from which the slang name "baloney" came. It's made with ground beef and pork, cubes of pork fat and seasonings. The Italian version, which is not imported because it requires additional cooking steps before the U.S. government will approve it, is air-dried and has a smooth, delicate flavor. Canned, cooked versions are imported from Italy but don't taste like the original. The American mortadella is basically bologna with cubes of pork fat and garlic flavoring. The Germans produce an excellent mortadella that contains pistachio nuts.

mortar and pestle [MOR-tuhr and PEHS-tl] A mortar is a bowl-shaped container and a pestle is a rounded, batlike instrument. As a pair, the mortar and pestle are used for grinding and pulverizing spices, herbs and other foods. The pestle is pressed against the mortar and rotated, grinding the ingredient between them until the desired consistency is obtained. The mortar and pestle are usually made from the same material, generally marble, hardwood, porcelain or stoneware. The Mexican term for mortar and pestle is "MOLCAJETE Y TEJOLETE."

morue [moh-*R*EW] The French term for dried salt cod (*see* COD). *See also* SALTFISH.

Moscovite Sauce *see* POIVRADE

Moscow mule Said to have the kick of a mule, this COCKTAIL is made by filling a copper mug (the traditional container) or glass with ice cubes and adding a generous amount of vodka (2 to 3 ounces), a squeeze of lemon or lime juice and topping with GINGER BEER. A Moscow mule is garnished with a lime wedge and a cucumber stick. The drink was developed in the late 1940s as part of a Smirnoff vodka promotion and has been popular ever since.

mostaccioli *see* Pasta Glossary, page 883

mostarda; mostarda di frutta [moh-STAHR-dah; dee FROO-tah] A condiment of various fruits (such as apricots, cherries, figs, oranges, peaches, pears and quince) preserved in a spicy-sweet mustard-flavored syrup. The fruit, which may be either whole or cut into large pieces, is simmered in sweetened water or grape MUST. Once cooked, the fruit is removed from the liquid and set aside. Ground mustard seed or mustard oil and vinegar are added to the sweet liquid and the mixture is further reduced before being recombined with the fruit. The resulting spicy sweet-and-sour condiment can pack a heady punch, although most commercially produced mostarda (the best known of which is the mixed-fruit Mostarda di Cremona) is fairly moderately flavored. Mostarda is traditionally eaten with boiled or roasted meats, cheese and bread. The word *mostarda* does not mean "mustard" but actually is derived from the Latin word *mustum* ("must"), referring to the original and classic use of grape must for the base. The Italian word for mustard is actually *senape*.

moth beans [MOHT] Oblong, light tan to reddish brown beans with a yellow interior, moth beans are *tiny*—generally less than 3/16 of an inch long. Also known as *dew, mat, mot, muth, papillon* and *Turkish gram* beans, they have a slightly sweet, nutty flavor. Moth beans are widely used in Indian and Asian cooking as well as for sprouting (*see* SPROUTS). *See also* BEANS.

mother of vinegar A slimy, gummy substance made up of various bacteria—specifically *Mycoderma aceti*—that cause fermentation in wine and cider and turn them into vinegar. Known as *mère de vinaigre* in French and sometimes simply as "mother" in English, its growth is best fostered in a medium-warm environment (60°–85°F). The mother should be transferred to a new mixture or discarded once the liquid has turned to vinegar.

moule [MOOL] French for "MUSSEL."

Mouli grater [MOO-lee] A French rotary grater that is perfect for grating small amounts of foods like cheese, chocolate and nuts. The hand-held unit consists of two sections with hinged handles. The end of one handle contains a food hopper with a grating cylinder and a crank for rotating the cylinder. The other section has a rounded surface that acts as a clamp, pressing the food to be grated into the grating cylinder. The hinged handles are held in one hand and squeezed so that the food presses against the grating cylinder. Meanwhile, the other hand turns the crank, causing the cylinder to rotate and the food to be grated.

mount, to A cooking technique whereby small chunks of cold, unsalted butter are whisked into a sauce just before serving to add flavor, texture and a glossy appearance. The French term for this technique is *monté* (or *monter*) *au beurre,* or "lifted with butter."

mountain berry *see* CLOUDBERRY

mountain cranberry *see* COWBERRY

mountain oysters *see* FRIES

mountain pepper Term that refers both to the leaves and berries that grow on native shrubs and small trees in the cool highlands of southeastern Australia, especially Tasmania, Victoria and New South Wales. Both leaves and berries are used fresh and in dried form in Australia, but the dried form is what reaches the United States. The flavor is mildly hot, somewhat like that of the SZECHUAN PEPPER. Though not related to the PEPPERCORN family, the dried berries resemble black peppercorns and can be used in a PEPPERMILL; the mountain pepper berries are decidedly stronger, however, and less of the spice is required. The leaves are a bit milder and have a hint of BAY LEAF to them, though they are still spicy. The plant was introduced to Cornwall, United Kingdom, where it is widely used in local dishes and known as *Cornish pepperleaf.* The leaves and berries of a similar, related plant known as *Dorrigo pepper* or *northern pepperbush* are also harvested and used similarly.

mountain spinach *see* ORACHE

Mourvèdre [moor-VEH-druh] Though best known today for its presence in southern France, this red-wine grape is Spain's second most widely planted red variety after GRENACHE, and is called *Monastrell* in that country. Mourvèdre produces good-quality, garnet-colored wines with spicy, peppery characteristics. They can, however, be a bit TANNIC and hard and are at their best when blended with other grape varieties. In red wines—such as those from CÔTES DU RHÔNE and CHÂTEAUNEUF-DE-PAPE—Mourvèdre is used to improve color and structure. Although there's recently been renewed interest in California, only small amounts of this variety are currently grown in California and Australia, where it's also known as *Mataro.*

moussaka; mousaka [MOO-sah-kah] Originally from Greece, moussaka is a popular dish throughout most of the Near East. Its basic form consists of sliced eggplant and ground lamb or beef that are layered, then baked. The variations, however, are endless and the dish is often covered with a BÉCHAMEL enriched with eggs and/or cheese. Other variations include the addition of onions, artichokes, tomatoes or potatoes.

mousse [MOOS] 1. A French term meaning "froth" or "foam," mousse is a rich, airy dish that can be either sweet or savory and hot or cold. Cold dessert mousses are usually made with fruit purée or a flavoring such as chocolate. Their fluffiness is due to the addition of whipped cream or beaten egg whites and they're often fortified with gelatin. Savory mousses can be made from meat, fish, shellfish, FOIE GRAS, cheese or even vegetables. Hot mousses usually get their light texture from the addition of beaten egg whites. They're generally baked in a WATER BATH to prevent the mixture from curdling. 2. When applied to wine, the word *mousse* describes the foam that forms on the surface of CHAMPAGNE or other sparkling wine when it's first poured. Mousse is analogous to the term "head," which is the foam on a freshly poured glass of beer.

mousse de foie gras *see* FOIE GRAS

mousseline [moos-LEEN] 1. Any sauce to which whipped cream or beaten egg whites have been added just prior to serving to give it a light, airy consistency. **Mousseline sauce** is HOLLANDAISE blended with whipped cream. 2. Various dishes based on meat, fish, shellfish or FOIE GRAS (usually puréed) to which whipped cream or, less frequently, beaten egg whites are added to lighten the texture. 3. A term applied to any of various dishes or baked goods that have a light and delicate texture.

moutarde [moo-TARD] French for "mustard."

mouthfeel; mouth feel Used by professional tasters as well as foodies, the term "mouthfeel" describes just that—how a food (such as cheese) or potable (wine or beer) feels in the mouth. Depending on what's being tasted, the descriptors may include everything from "full-bodied" to "light" to "dense." The permutations are endless.

mozzarella [maht-suh-REHL-lah; moht-suh-REHL-lah] Hailing from southern Italy, mozzarella is a mild, white fresh cheese that's made by the special PASTA FILATA process, whereby the CURD is dipped into hot WHEY, then stretched and kneaded to the desired consistency. At one time, mozzarella was made only from the milk of water buffaloes. Today, however, it's typically made with cow's milk. Mozzarella comes in two basic styles. Most **regular mozzarella**, which can be found in lowfat and nonfat forms in supermarkets, is factory produced. It has a semisoft, elastic texture and is drier and not as delicately flavored as its fresher counterpart. This style of mozzarella is best used for cooking and is popular for pizza because of its excellent melting qualities. **Fresh mozzarella**, which is usually packaged in whey or water, is often labeled "Italian style." It's generally made from whole milk and has a much softer texture and a sweet, delicate flavor. **Mozzarella di bufala** (also called simply **buffalo mozzarella**) is the most prized of the fresh mozzarellas. Most buffalo mozzarella available in the United States is made from a combination of water buffalo milk and cow's milk. Two popular forms of fresh mozzarella are **boconccini**, which are little (about 1 inch in diameter) balls that are commonly marinated in olive oil and sometimes herbs, and the even smaller cherry-sized **ciliegini**. There's also a smoked version called **mozzarella affumicata** and the unique **manteca**, in which the mozzarella is molded around a lump of butter. Fresh mozzarella can be found in Italian markets, cheese shops and some supermarkets. It's excellent simply spread on bread with salt, pepper and a little olive oil. *See also* CHEESE.

MSG *see* MONOSODIUM GLUTAMATE

muddle To mash or crush ingredients with a spoon or a muddler (a rod with a flattened end). Usually identified with the preparation of mixed drinks, such as when mint leaves and sugar are muddled together for a MINT JULEP.

Muenster [MUHN-stuhr; MOON-ster] *see* MUNSTER

muesli [MYOOS-lee] Developed as a health food by Swiss nutritionist Dr. Bircher-Benner near the end of the 19th century, muesli has since become a popular breakfast cereal. The German word *muesli* means "mixture," and this one can include raw or toasted cereals (oats, wheat, millet, barley, etc.), dried fruits (such as raisins, apricots and apples), nuts, bran, wheat germ, sugar and dried-milk solids. It is usually eaten with milk, yogurt or fruit juice. There are myriad commercial variations available in supermarkets, usually labeled GRANOLA.

muffin A small, cakelike bread that can be made with a variety of flours and often contains fruits and nuts. Most American-style muffins fall into the QUICK BREAD category and are LEAVENED with either baking powder or baking soda. The yeast-raised type, such as the ENGLISH MUFFIN, is generally finer in texture. These small breads are made in a MUFFIN PAN. Muffins can be sweet or savory and, though they were once considered breakfast or tea fare, are now also served with lunch and dinner.

muffin pan; muffin tin A special baking pan with 6 or 12 cup-shaped depressions that hold the muffin batter. Each standard muffin cup is about $2^{1}/_{2}$ inches in diameter. There are also giant muffin pans with $3^{1}/_{4}$-inch cups, miniature muffin pans (GEM PANS) in which the diameter of each indentation is $1^{1}/_{4}$ to 2 inches and muffin top pans, which are about 4 inches in diameter and only $^{1}/_{2}$ inch deep.

muffuletta; muffaletta [moof-fuh-LEHT-tuh] A specialty of New Orleans, this HERO-style sandwich originated in 1906 at the Central Grocery, which many think still makes the best muffuletta in Louisiana. The sandwich consists of a round loaf of crusty Italian bread, split and filled with layers of sliced PROVOLONE, Genoa SALAMI and ham topped with "olive salad," a chopped mixture of green, unstuffed olives, PIMIENTOS, celery, garlic, cocktail onions, CAPERS, oregano, parsley, olive oil, red-wine vinegar, salt and pepper. The olive salad is what sets the muffuletta apart from any other sandwich of its ilk.

muhammara [moo-hahm-MRAH] A traditional Mediterranean dip made from hot and sweet red peppers, walnuts, POMEGRANATE MOLASSES and spices.

muki goma [moo-kee goh-mah] *see* GOMA

mulato chile [moo-LAH-toh] This long (4- to 5-inch) dark brown CHILE is a type of dried POBLANO. It has a light fruity nuance and a much more pronounced smoky character than its relative, the ANCHO. The mulato is essential for making MOLE. It's mildly hot, with a SCOVILLE SCALE rating ranging from 2,500 to 3,000.

mulberry There are three principal varieties of the mulberry—black, red and white. The black (really purplish-black) variety is commonly found in Europe, the red in the eastern and southern United States and the white in Asia. Mulberries look somewhat like blackberries in size and shape. When fully ripe, their flavor is sweet-sour but somewhat bland. Unripe berries are inedibly sour. Mulberries are not commercially grown in the United States but grow wild from Massachusetts to the Gulf states and as far west as Nebraska. They can be eaten raw or used for jams, jellies, desserts and mulberry wine.

mulet barbe *see* PACIFIC THREADFIN

mulet tikus *see* PACIFIC THREADFIN

mull To flavor a beverage by heating it with various ingredients such as herbs, spices, fruit and sugar. The beverages most often infused in this fashion are wine, cider and beer. *See also* MULLED WINE.

mulled wine Red or white wine that is heated with various citrus fruits and spices such as cinnamon, cloves, allspice or nutmeg. Mulled wine is generally sweetened with sugar and often fortified with a spirit, usually BRANDY. Some recipes call for stirring the hot wine mixture into beaten eggs, which adds flavor and body to the beverage.

mullet [MUHL-iht] The appellation "mullet" is used to identify many fish that are not mullets at all—such as the highly prized RED MULLET, which actually belongs to the GOATFISH family. True mullets belong to the gray mullet family and are commercially available in the United States as *striped mullet* and *silver mullet*. These silver-gray, moderate- to high-fat fish range in size from ½ to 4 pounds. They have firm white flesh with a mild, nutlike flavor. Mullet can be found year-round in most South Atlantic and Gulf states, less frequently elsewhere. They may be fried, baked, broiled or poached. *See also* FISH.

mulligan stew Said to have originated in hobo camps during the early 1900s, mulligan stew is a sort of catch-all dish of whatever is available. It usually contains meat, potatoes and vegetables in just about any combination. The name indicates that its origins might come from IRISH STEW, but it's also often compared to Kentucky BURGOO. The cook at a hobo camp responsible for putting this tasty concoction together was called a "mulligan-mixer."

mulligatawny soup [muhl-ih-guh-TAW-nee] The name derives from the Tamil, a people inhabiting southern India and the surrounding area, and means "pepper water." This soup is based on a rich meat or vegetable broth highly seasoned with curry and other spices. It usually contains bits of chicken (sometimes other meats), and can also include rice, eggs, coconut shreds and even cream.

mul naengmyeon *see* NAENGMYEON

Münchener [mewn-chner] A dark, MALT-flavored, LAGER-style BEER. In Europe, the term *Münchener* is used primarily to distinguish dark from light lagers.

mung bean A small dried bean with yellow flesh and a skin that is normally green but sometimes yellow or black. It's most commonly used to grow bean SPROUTS. Mung beans are widely used in both China and India. They need no presoaking and when cooked have a tender texture and slightly sweet flavor. Dried mung beans are ground into flour, which is used to make noodles in China and a variety of dishes in India. *See also* BEANS.

Munster [MUHN-stuhr; MOON-ster] This widely imitated cheese varies greatly, from that of the French original produced in Alsace's Vosges Mountains around the village of Munster to versions made in the United States. The highly prized European Munsters have pinkish-orange to reddish-brown rinds and a smooth, pale yellow interior with small holes. The texture is semisoft and the flavor ranges from mild when young to quite complex and assertive when aged. Raw-milk Munsters are more highly regarded, but those with less than 60 days of RIPENING cannot be imported to the United States at this time. The minimum FAT CONTENT for Munster is 45 percent. The American versions, often spelled *Muenster*, have an orange rind, a lighter yellow interior and a decidedly bland flavor that in no way resembles the more robust European originals. *See also* CHEESE.

Muscadet [meuhs-kah-DAY] The French produce this light, dry white wine from Muscadet grapes grown in the Loire Valley. Although not as great as other French whites (like BURGUNDY and CHABLIS), Muscadet is quite good, particularly in light of its reasonable price. It should be served chilled and goes nicely with fish and poultry.

Muscadine grape [MUHS-kuh-dihn] Found in the southeastern United States, this thick-skinned purple grape has a strong, musky flavor.

It's a native American grape grown mainly to be eaten although it's also used to make a limited amount of wine. In fact, the muscadine was one of the first varieties from which wine was made in America. One of its varieties—the *scuppernong*—is used to make a sweet wine that is still popular in the South. *See also* GRAPE.

Muscari comosum *see* CIPOLLINI

muscatel wine [muhs-kuh-TEHL] A rich, sweet dessert wine created from the MUSCAT GRAPE. It's made from both the black and white varieties, so its color can range from golden to amber to pale amber-red. Muscatel's flavor typifies the characteristically musty flavor of the muscat grape.

Muscat grape [MUHS-kat; MUHS-kuht] Any of several varieties of white or black grapes. The characteristic trait of the muscat is its sweet, musky flavor. Muscat grapes are grown around the world in temperate climates such as Italy, France, Greece, Spain and California. In addition to being eaten out of hand and made into raisins, the Muscat grape is used to make a variety of fragrant wines.

muscovy duck *see* DUCK

mush A thick, cooked mixture made by cooking cornmeal with milk or water. It's served as a breakfast dish by adding melted butter, milk or maple syrup. Mush can also be cooked, poured into a pan and cooled, at which point it becomes solid. It's then cut into squares, sautéed until golden brown (much like POLENTA) and served hot, sometimes with gravy, as a side dish.

mushimono [moo-shee-MOH-noh] Japanese term referring to steamed foods.

mushroom Early Greeks and Romans are thought to be among the first cultivators of mushrooms, using them in a wide array of dishes. Today there are literally thousands of varieties of this fleshy fungus. Sizes and shapes vary tremendously and colors can range from white to black with a full gamut of colors in between. The cap's texture can be smooth, pitted, honeycombed or ruffled and flavors range from bland to rich, nutty and earthy. The cultivated mushroom is what's commonly found in most U.S. supermarkets today. However, those that more readily excite the palate are the more exotic **wild mushrooms** such as CÈPE, CHANTERELLE, ENOKI, MOREL, PUFFBALL, SHIITAKE and WOOD EAR. Because so many wild mushrooms are poisonous, it's vitally important to know which species are edible and which are not. Extreme caution should be taken when picking them yourself. The readily available **cultivated white mushroom** has a mild, earthy flavor. The cap ranges in size from $1/2$ to 3 inches in diameter and in color from white to pale tan. Those labeled "button mushrooms" are simply the small youngsters of the cultivated variety. These common mushrooms are available year-round but are at their peak in fall and winter. They're sold in bulk and in 8-ounce packages. Look for those that are firm and evenly colored with tightly closed caps. If all the gills are showing, the mushrooms are past their prime. Avoid specimens that are broken, damaged or have soft spots or a dark-tinged surface. If the mushrooms are to be cooked whole, select those of equal size so they will cook evenly. Fresh mushrooms should be stored with cool air circulating around them. Therefore, they should be placed on a tray in a single layer, covered with a damp paper towel and refrigerated for up to 3 days. Before use, they should be wiped with a damp paper towel or, if necessary, rinsed with cold water and dried thoroughly. Mushrooms should never be soaked because they absorb water and will become mushy. Trim the stem ends and prepare according to directions. **Canned mushrooms** are available in several forms including whole, chopped, sliced and caps only. **Frozen** or **freeze-dried mushrooms** are also available. **Dried mushrooms** are available either whole or in slices, bits or pieces. They should be stored in a cool, dry place for up to 6 months. Mushrooms are one of nature's most versatile foods and can be used in hundreds of ways and cooked in almost any way imaginable. *See also* BEECH; BLACK TRUMPET; BLEWIT; CREMINO; HEN OF THE WOODS; HONSHIMEJI; MATSUTAKE; NAMEKO; OYSTER MUSHROOM; PIOPPINI; POM POM; PORTOBELLO; STRAW MUSHROOM; TROMPETTE DE LA MORT.

mu shu [MOO shoo] A stir-fried Chinese dish containing shredded pork, scallions, TIGER LILY BUDS, WOOD EARS and various seasonings. This mixture is scrambled with eggs, rolled in small thin pancakes (called *mu shu pancakes* or *Peking doilies*) and served hot. Also called *moo shu*.

muskellunge; muskie [MUHS-kuh-luhnj] *see* PIKE

musk lime *see* CALAMONDIN

muskmelon *see* MELON

mussel [MUHS-uhl] Archaeological findings indicate that this BIVALVE MOLLUSK (*see both listings*) has been used as food for over 20,000 years. Europeans love mussels, which are cultivated on special farms to meet the high demand. Americans, however, have never been as enamored of mussels as they have of oysters and clams, and huge quantities along U.S. coasts go unharvested. There are dozens of mussel species, all of which have an extremely thin, oblong shell that can range in color from indigo blue to bright green to yellowish-brown. Depending on the species, the shell can be from $1\frac{1}{2}$ to 6 inches in length. The creamy-tan meat is tougher than that of either the oyster or clam but it has a delicious, slightly sweet flavor. The most abundant mussel is the **blue** (or

common) **mussel** found along the Mediterranean, Atlantic and Pacific coasts. Its shell is dark blue and 2 to 3 inches in length. The **green-lipped mussel** is imported from New Zealand (which is why it's also called *New Zealand green mussel*) and has a large (3 to 4 inches long), bright green shell. Live, fresh mussels are generally available year-round. On the West Coast, however, the mussel season is November through April. This is because microscopic organisms (of "red tide" notoriety) make mussels unsafe to eat during the spring and summer months. Buy mussels with tightly closed shells or those that snap shut when tapped—otherwise they're not alive and fresh. Avoid those with broken shells, that feel heavy (meaning they're full of sand) or that feel light and loose when shaken (signalling that the mussel is dead). Shucked mussels should be plump, their liquid clear. Smaller mussels will be more tender than large ones. Fresh mussels, live or shucked, should be stored in the refrigerator and used within a day or two. Plain and smoked mussels packed in oil are also available. Mussels may be steamed, fried, baked or used as an ingredient in dishes like BOUILLABAISSE or PAELLA. *See also* SHELLFISH.

must The freshly pressed juice of grapes or other fruit before fermentation occurs. Must can include pulp, skins and seeds.

mustard; mustard seed; powdered mustard Any of several species of plant grown for its acrid seeds and leaves, which are called MUSTARD GREENS. The mustard plant belongs to the same family as broccoli, Brussels sprouts, collards, kale and kohlrabi. Down through the centuries it has been used for culinary as well as medicinal purposes; the most notable example of the latter is mustard's purported efficacy as a curative for the common cold. The name is said to come from a Roman mixture of crushed mustard seed and MUST (unfermented grape juice), which was called *mustum ardens* ("burning wine"). Likewise, the French word *moutarde* ("mustard") comes from a contraction of their *moust* ("must") and a form of *ardent* ("hot" or "fiery"). There are two major types of **mustard seed**—white (or *yellow*) and brown (or *Asian*). A third species, the black mustard seed, has been replaced for most purposes by the brown species because the latter can be grown and harvested more economically. White mustard seeds are much larger than the brown variety but a lot less pungent. They're the main ingredient in American-style mustards. White and brown seeds are blended to make ENGLISH MUSTARD. Brown mustard seeds are used for pickling and as a seasoning, and are the main ingredient in European and Chinese mustards. Mustard seeds are sold whole, ground into powder or processed further into prepared mustard. **Powdered mustard** is simply finely ground mustard seed. Mustard seeds can be stored for up to a year in a dry, dark place and powdered mustard for about 6 months. Whole seeds are used for pickling, flavoring cooked meats and vegetables and as a source for freshly ground mustard.

Powdered mustards and freshly ground seeds are used in sauces, as a seasoning in main dishes and as an ingredient in salad dressings. *See also* MUSTARD OIL; MUSTARD, PREPARED; Seasoning Suggestions, page 891.

mustard, prepared Prepared mustard is generally made from powdered mustard combined with seasonings and a liquid such as water, vinegar, wine, beer or MUST. *American-style prepared mustard* is a mild mixture made from the less-pungent white seed flavored with vinegar and turmeric (which makes it yellow) and sometimes sugar. *European* and *Chinese prepared mustards* are made from brown seeds and are much zestier and more flavorful. The French are famous for their tangy DIJON MUSTARD, made with brown or black seeds. The German prepared mustards can range from very hot to sweet and mild. Chinese mustards are usually the hottest and most pungent of the prepared mustards. A multitude of domestic and imported prepared mustards are readily available in supermarkets. Unopened, prepared mustard can be stored in a cool, dark place for about 2 years; once opened, it should be refrigerated. *See also* CREOLE MUSTARD; ENGLISH MUSTARD; MUSTARD; MUSTARD GREENS; MUSTARD OIL.

mustard greens The peppery leaves of the mustard plant are a popular SOUL FOOD ingredient, ranking second only to COLLARD GREENS. The leaves are a rich, dark green and have a pungent mustard flavor. Though they can be found year-round in some locales, fresh mustard greens are most abundant from December through April. They're also available frozen and canned. When choosing fresh greens, look for crisp young leaves with a rich green color. Reject those with yellow, flabby or pitted leaves or thick, fibrous stems. Refrigerate greens, tightly sealed in a plastic bag, for up to a week. Wash them just before using. Mustard greens can be steamed, sautéed or simmered. They are usually served as a side dish, often flavored with onion, garlic, ham, salt pork or bacon. Mustard greens, a CRUCIFEROUS vegetable, are an excellent source of vitamins A and C, thiamine and riboflavin. *See also* MUSTARD; MUSTARD OIL; MUSTARD, PREPARED.

mustard oil An extremely hot, pungent oil expressed from mustard seeds (*see* MUSTARD). Mustard oil should be stored in the refrigerator and will keep for up to about 6 months. It can be used (sparingly because of the heat) in STIR-FRYS, salad dressings and MARINADES. *See also* FATS AND OILS.

mustard seed *see* MUSTARD

musubi *see* ONIGIRI

muth beans *see* MOTH BEANS

mutton *see* LAMB

muttonfish *see* ABALONE

mysost [MY-sohst] *see* GJETOST

naan; nan [NAHN] An East Indian, white-flour FLAT-BREAD that is lightly leavened by a natural YEAST STARTER developed from airborne yeasts. Naan is traditionally baked in a TANDOOR OVEN. A flattened round of dough is placed on a cloth puff that is used to slap the bread directly onto the side of the special high-heat oven. In less than 60 seconds, the bread puffs slightly, browns on the side touching the oven wall and takes on a light smoky flavor. The bread is speared with a skewer and removed from the oven wall to be served hot.

nabemono [nah-beh-MOH-noh] This Japanese term translates to "things-in-a-pot" and refers to a category of communal one-pot meals that are popular in Japan, particularly during cold weather. Ingredients are prepared in bite-size portions in advance, then cooked at the table in broth or oil. With some dishes, ingredients are added one at a time and when the dish is ready it's served family style. With other dishes, participants actually cook their own food in the hot liquid or oil, much like a FONDUE Bourguignonne. Various condiments and sauces are served to flavor the just-cooked foods. *See also* CHIRINABE; MIZUTAKI.

nacho [NAH-choh] A crisp TORTILLA chip topped with melted cheese (usually CHEDDAR) and chopped CHILES, usually served as an appetizer or snack. Nachos sometimes appear on menus as "Mexican pizza," in which case they generally have additional toppings such as cooked, ground CHORIZO, onions and sometimes olives.

naengmyeon [NAYN-myeon] Korean dishes based on cold buckwheat noodles. *Mul naengmyeon* is a popular Korean dish consisting of long, thin buckwheat noodles served in a cold beef broth along with slices of beef, cucumber, Korean pear and boiled egg. In *bibim naengmyeon*, the broth is replaced with spicy gochujang (*see* CHILE BEAN PASTE), which is blended with the other ingredients and served more like a salad. Often the broth is served on the side. Although buckwheat is the traditional noodle, on rare occasions other noodle types like arrowroot are used. Naengmyeon is also spelled *naengmyun*.

Nafplion; Naphlion olive [NAHF-plee-ohn] Small to medium-size olive ranging in color from pale green to dark green to brown. Nafplion olives are cracked (*see* OLIVE) and brine-cured, resulting in a strong salty flavor with traces of smoke and nuts. They're produced around the town of Nafplio in southern Greece's Peloponnese.

Naga Jolokia pepper *see* SCOVILLE SCALE

naganegi [nah-gah] A longer, thicker version of NEGI (WELSH ONION), grown by heaping soil around the stem while it is growing. The Japanese value naganegi because it has more white stem, which can be used in cooking.

Naga Viper chile *see* SCOVILLE SCALE

nama [NAH-mah] *see* SAKE

nameko [NAH-meh-koh] A small Japanese mushroom that ranges in color from orange to amber to gold. The nameko has a soft almost gelatinous texture and a rich, earthy aroma and flavor. It's highly regarded and used primarily in Japanese soups and one-pot dishes. Though nameko mushrooms are seldom found fresh in the United States, they're available canned in Asian markets. The nameko is sometimes also called *cinnamon cap. See also* MUSHROOM.

nam pla [nahm PLAH] Popular in Thailand, nam pla is a salty, fermented FISH SAUCE with an extremely pungent odor. It's used as a condiment, sauce and seasoning ingredient. Nam pla is popular throughout Southeast Asia and is known as *nuoc nam* in Vietnam and as *shottsuru* in Japan. Ancient Romans used a nam pla counterpart called GARUM.

nam prik [nahm PRIHK] Thailand's counterpart to SAMBAL, nam prik is a general term for various condiments and sauces used to accompany a variety of foods including fish, rice and vegetables. The ingredients used vary from region to region and can include CHILES, garlic, dried fish, trasi, TAMARIND concentrate, fruit (such as green MANGO) and nuts.

Nam prik pao [nahm PRIHK PAH-oh] Often referred to as *roasted chili paste* or *roasted chili jam*, nam prik pao is one of Thailand's most popular condiments and is found in many Thai recipes. Pan-roasted chiles, garlic and shallots form the base but FISH SAUCE, PALM SUGAR, TAMARIND paste, dried shrimp (*see* SHRIMP, DRIED) and/or SHRIMP PASTE are usually added for more flavor. The ingredients are all ground and cooked in a little oil until they resemble a loose jam.

nan *see* NAAN

Nantua sauce [nan-TOO-uh] A BÉCHAMEL-based sauce made with cream and CRAYFISH butter and garnished with crayfish tails. Nantua sauce is served with seafood or egg dishes. *See also* SAUCE.

nan'you-agonashi *see* PACIFIC THREADFIN

nap To coat food lightly with a sauce so that it completely covers the food with a thin, even layer. From the French word for "tablecloth," *nappe*.

napa cabbage *see* CHINESE CABBAGE

Napoleon [nuh-POH-lee-uhn] A delectable dessert made with crisp layers of PUFF PASTRY spread with CRÈME PÂTISSIÈRE and either glazed with a thin icing or dusted with powdered sugar. Napoleons are usually made in small rectangular shapes just large enough for an individual serving.

Napoleon cherry Another name for the ROYAL ANN CHERRY.

napoletana, alla [AH-lah nah-poh-leh-TAH-nah] Italian for "Neopolitan style," referring culinarily to dishes reflective of Naples, usually those including tomatoes, onion, garlic, herbs and olive oil.

Napoli salami *see* SALAMI

Napoli sauce *see* MARINARA SAUCE

nappage [na-PAHZH] French for "topping," referring to a GLAZE brushed on desserts and pastries. Nappage provides gloss and protects dessert or pastry fruit from drying out. It can be made by thinning jam with water or purchased in bulk. Specialty producers make a variety of flavors including apricot, cherry, lemon, passion fruit and strawberry.

Nashi pear *see* ASIAN PEAR

nasi goreng [nahg-SEE goh-REHNG] The Indonesian term for "fried rice," of which there are hundreds of versions throughout Indonesia, Malaysia and the surrounding areas. The rice is cooked with various ingredients including shrimp or other shellfish, meat, chicken, eggs, onions, chiles, garlic, cucumber, peanuts and a wide array of seasonings. If noodles are substituted for rice, the dish is called *bahmi goreng.*

nasi lemak [NAH-see leh-MAHK] An aromatic rice dish considered by many to be the national dish of Malaysia. The name means "fat rice" and refers to the creamy richness attained by cooking the rice in coconut milk. The aromatics come from SCREWPINE LEAVES (also known as pandan or pandanus leaves), which provide a highly fragrant floral aroma. Sometimes LEMON GRASS, ginger or both are added. Nasi lemak is eaten throughout the day and is traditionally served with fried ANCHOVIES, cucumber slices, hardboiled egg, SAMBAL, and often roasted peanuts. Some of the favorite variations include the addition of fried chicken or stewed beef. Nasi lemak is also eaten in many of the surrounding countries in Southeast Asia, each putting a local twist on the dish.

nasturtium [nuh-STER-shuhm] All parts of this beautiful plant are eaten except the roots. Young leaves and stems add a peppery accent to salads and sandwiches, or be can used in dishes as a WATERCRESS substitute. The flower blossoms may be minced and used to flavor butter, cream cheese or vinegar, and the whole flowers are colorful and delicious in salads or as a garnish. Nasturtium seeds and immature flower buds can be pickled and used like capers. *See also* FLOWERS, EDIBLE.

natto [NAH-toh] Steamed, fermented and mashed SOYBEANS with a glutinous texture and strong cheeselike flavor. Natto is particularly popular in Japan, where it's used as a flavoring and table CONDIMENT and is greatly favored served over rice for breakfast. It's often mixed with other ingredients such as mustard, SOY SAUCE and chives.

navel orange Grown in California, Arizona and Florida, the navel is an excellent eating orange. Its name originates from the fact that the blossom end resembles the human navel. This large fruit has a bright-orange skin that's thick and easy to peel. The pulp is sweet, flavorful and seedless. One variety of the navel orange is the **Cara Cara**, which has a reddish pink flesh and a flavor evoking strawberries and raspberries. Available from late fall through late spring, the navel orange is sometimes called *Washington, Riverside* or *Bahia navel. See also* ORANGE.

navy bean This small white LEGUME, also known as *Yankee bean,* gets its name from the fact that the U.S. Navy has served it as a staple since the mid-1800s. The navy bean is widely used for commercially canned pork and beans. It also makes wonderful soups and is often used in the preparation of BOSTON BAKED BEANS (though New Englanders prefer using the smaller PEA BEAN for this purpose). Navy beans require lengthy, slow cooking. *See also* BEANS; FRENCH NAVY BEANS.

naw mai [nahw MI] Thai for "BAMBOO SHOOT."

Neapolitan ice cream [nee-uh-PAHL-uh-tuhn] Brick-shaped ice cream made up of three differently flavored ice creams (usually vanilla, chocolate and strawberry). It's normally served in slices, each of which displays the tricolored ice cream. Other desserts (or gelatin salads) made in three distinct layers are also labeled "neapolitan."

neat 1. A term referring to liquor that is drunk undiluted by ice, water or MIXERS. 2. An old term used mainly in England for a member of the bovine family such as the ox or cow. Neat's foot jelly was what today is called CALF'S FOOT JELLY.

Nebbiolo [neh-b'YOH-loh] The fog (*nebbia* in Italian) that rolls over the hills of northern Piedmont and the regions nearby helps the Nebbiolo grape ripen properly, thereby creating some of Italy's finest red wines. Wines made from Nebbiolo grapes are associated with highly regarded wines from the regions of BAROLO, BARBARESCO, Gattinara, Ghemme and Spanna. These dark-colored wines are rich and full bodied with aromas and flavors that are suggestive of chocolate, licorice, raspberries, truffles and violets. Nebbiolo wines are typically long-lived and require significant aging to develop and soften. Nebbiolo has not been planted in significant amounts outside of northwest Italy.

N

Nebuchadnezzar [nehb-uh-kuhd-NEHZ-uhr] *see* WINE BOTTLES

nectarine [nehk-tah-REEN] The nectarine's flesh is sweet, succulent and firmer than that of its relative, the peach. When ripe, its smooth skin is a brilliant golden yellow with generous blushes of red. Nectarines are available from midspring to late September with a peak during July and August. Look for fragrant, brightly colored fruit that gives slightly to the touch. Avoid those with bruises or other blemishes as well as those that are hard or overly green. Slightly underripe nectarines can be left to ripen at room temperature for a couple of days. Ripe fruit should be refrigerated and used within 5 days. They're wonderful eaten out of hand and can be used in salads, a variety of fresh and cooked desserts and as a garnish for many hot and cold dishes. Nectarines contain a fair amount of vitamins A and C.

needling A technique used in BLUE-VEINED CHEESE production whereby cheese that has been inoculated with mold spores is punctured with metal skewers. The holes let oxygen feed the bacteria, creating the characteristic blue veining throughout the cheese's interior. Also sometimes called *spiking*.

negi [neh-gee] Japanese for "WELSH ONION." Because of their similarity, LEEKS and SCALLIONS are sometimes also referred to as negi. *See also* NAGANEGI; RAKKYO; TAMANEGI.

Negroni [neh-GROH-nee] A COCKTAIL made with equal parts GIN, CAMPARI and sweet or dry VERMOUTH (classically sweet), stirred together with ice, then strained into a cocktail glass, topped with a splash of soda and garnished with a lemon twist. Legend has it that it was created in 1919 when Italian Count Camillo Negroni asked a Florence bartender to add gin to his AMERICANO.

nen dzem fen *see* RICE NOODLES

neole *see* PIZZELLA

Neopolitan sauce *see* MARINARA SAUCE

Neotame [NEE-oh-taym] An ARTIFICIAL SWEETENER invented in 1990 and FDA approved in 2002, Neotame is 8,000 times sweeter than sugar. It's an analog of ASPARTAME and can be used in both hot and cold mixtures, as well as for baking. *See also* ACESULFAME-K; ALITAME; ASPARTAME; SACCHARIN; SUCRALOSE.

Nepal cardamom *see* BLACK CARDAMOM

Nepalese bell chile *see* BISHOP'S CROWN CHILE

Nesselrode [NEHS-uhl-rohd] Count Nesselrode, the 19th-century Russian diplomat, lived and ate lavishly and had a number of rich dishes dedicated to him. The most famous is Nesselrode pudding, developed by his head chef Mouy. It consists of cream-enriched CUSTARD mixed with CHESTNUT purée, candied fruits, currants, raisins and MARASCHINO LIQUEUR. This elegant mixture is often frozen, or made into a pie or dessert sauce. Other dishes named after the Count include a game soup and a braised sweetbread dish, but none gained the same fame as the Nesselrode pudding.

nettles; stinging nettles Any of several plants of the genus *Urtica,* which have long, toothed leaves and myriad hairlike fibers that contain formic acid, which irritates the skin on contact. *Urtica dioica* is the nettle most commonly used culinarily. Nettles must be cooked to destroy their stinging effect, and only the young shoots and leaf tops are used.

Neufchâtel [NEUF-sha-tell] 1. The French original, hailing from the town of Neufchâtel in the region of Normandy, is a soft, white, unripened cheese made from raw or pasteurized cow's milk. It undergoes RIPENING for a minimum of 10 days, but often for 4 weeks or more. When young, the flavor of Neufchâtel is slightly salty but delicate and mild. It becomes more pungent with age. The cheese has a minimum FAT CONTENT of 45 percent. Neufchâtel is available in a variety of shapes—square, rectangular, cylindrical and the special heart-shape variety called *Coeur de Bray*. 2. For information on the American version of Neufchatel, *see* CREAM CHEESE.

neutral spirits Colorless, flavorless 95 percent (190 PROOF) ALCOHOLS used for blending with straight whiskeys and as a base for potables such as GIN and VODKA. **Grain spirits** are WOOD-AGED neutral spirits that have been aged in wood, which contributes mellow flavor nuances. *See also* DISTILLATION.

nevole *see* PIZZELLA

Newburg An extraordinarily rich dish of chopped cooked shellfish (usually lobster, crab and shrimp) in an elegant sauce composed of butter, cream, egg yolks, SHERRY and seasonings. It's usually served over buttered toast points. The sauce can be used with other foods, in which case the dish is usually given the appellation "newburg."

new cocoyam *see* MALANGA

New England boiled dinner Originally made with salted beef, today this East Coast classic more commonly contains corned beef, ham or SALT PORK. Additional items such as chicken, cabbage, potatoes, parsnips, onions, carrots and seasonings are added at various times and slowly simmered together to create this hearty one-pot meal. New England boiled dinner is traditionally accompanied by horseradish and mustard.

New England clam chowder *see* CHOWDER

New Guinea bean *see* CUCUZZA

new potato *see* POTATO

Newtown Pippin apple Taking its name from the village of Newtown on Long Island, where it was first grown in the 1700s, this all-purpose apple is also referred to simply as *Pippin*. Its skin ranges from bright green at harvest time to a mellow yellow-green to yellow. The flesh is crisp and juicy with a slightly tart flavor. Newtown Pippins brown quickly when cut. *See also* APPLE.

New York steak Also known as *New York strip steak* and *shell steak,* this cut of meat comes from the most tender section of beef, the SHORT LOIN. It's the boneless top loin muscle and is equivalent to a PORTERHOUSE steak minus tenderloin and bone. Depending on the region, it's also marketed as *Delmonico steak, Kansas City (strip) steak, shell steak, sirloin club steak* and *strip steak.* This tender cut may be broiled, grilled or sautéed.

New Zealand yam *see* OCA

ngo gai [ngaw GUY] *see* SAW-LEAF HERB

ngo om *see* RICE PADDY HERB

Niagara grape A North American table grape grown in the eastern United States and, because it doesn't ship well, found only in the areas where it's grown. The large, juicy Niagara is in season from September through October. It's round to oval in shape, pale greenish-white and has a sweet, foxy flavor. A limited number of Niagara grapes are made into wine. *See also* GRAPE.

niboshi [nee-BOH-shee] Dried sardines, most often used in Japanese cuisine for creating a stronger-flavored soup stock than the more popular DASHI. Niboshi is also eaten as a snack and used as a flavoring ingredient in various dishes.

niçoise, à la [nee-SWAHZ] A French phrase that means "as prepared in Nice," typifying the cuisine found in and around that French Riviera city. This cooking style is identified with hot and cold dishes that include the integral ingredients of tomatoes, black olives, garlic and ANCHOVIES. **Salade niçoise** contains these basic ingredients plus French green beans, onions, tuna, hard-cooked eggs and herbs.

niçoise olive [nee-SWAHZ] Hailing from the Provence region of France (but also grown in Italy and Morocco), this small, oval olive ranges in color from purple-brown to brown-black. Niçoise olives are cured in brine and packed in olive oil. Good specimens have a rich, nutty, mellow flavor. *See also* OLIVE.

niçoise salad *see* NIÇOISE, À LA

Nieheimer [NEE-hi-mer] *see* HOPFENKÄSE

nigella seed [ni-JELL-uh; nee-JELL-uh] Also called *black onion seeds,* these tiny, angular, deep black seeds have a nutty, peppery flavor. They're used in India and the Middle East as a seasoning for vegetables, LEGUMES and breads. Nigella seeds are sometimes erroneously referred to as black CUMIN, an entirely different species. They can be found in Middle Eastern and Indian markets. *See also* SPICES.

nigiri sushi [nee-JEE-ree SOO-shee] *see* SUSHI

nigori [nee-GOH-ree] *see* SAKE

nijisseiki *see* ASIAN PEAR

niku [nee-koo] Japanese for "meat."

nikujaga [nee-koo-jah-gah] Type of NIMONO (simmered dish) featuring thinly sliced meat (usually beef) and potatoes plus various vegetables.

nimono [nee-MOH-noh] Japanese foods such as fish, meat and vegetables that are simmered in a seasoned broth. The broth may be flavored with various seasonings including DASHI, MISO, fresh ginger, red chiles or simply salt.

nira [NEE-rah] *see* GARLIC CHIVES

nixtamal; nixtamalado [neesh-TUH-mahl] Corn kernels that have been covered with a mixture of water and slaked lime (or wood ash), cooked, then removed from the heat and allowed to soak in the alkaline water. The corn is then thoroughly rinsed and rubbed to remove the lime and any remaining attached hulls. The end result is nixtamal or HOMINY which, when dried and ground, becomes MASA. Nixtamalization dates as far back as 1500 B.C.E. and was used by the ancient Mayans and Aztecs. The process makes the corn easier to grind and enhances its protein and vitamin content, particularly that of niacin. Ground nixtamal is used to make TAMALE dough and corn TORTILLAS; the whole kernels are used in POSOLE.

Noah's pudding *see* ASURE

noble rot *see* BOTRYTIS CINEREA

nocciola [noh-chee-OH-lah] Italian for "HAZELNUT."

noce [NOH-cheh] Italian for "NUT."

noce di cocco [NOH-cheh dee KOH-koh] Italian for "COCONUT."

nockerl [NOK-uhrl] There are two basic versions of this Austrian dumpling. The heartier, flour-based, savory rendition is served in soups and stews. The sweet version, known as **Salzburger nockerl**, contains very little flour and is made fluffy by the addition of stiffly beaten egg whites. It's generally used as an addition to fruit soups or served for dessert accompanied by fruit.

no-eyed pea *see* PIGEON PEA

nog 1. A nickname for EGGNOG. 2. Any beverage made with beaten egg, milk and usually liquor. 3. In certain parts of England the term "nog" refers to strong ALE.

noisette [nwah-ZEHT] 1. French for "HAZELNUT." 2. A small, tender, round slice of meat (usually lamb, beef or veal) taken from the rib or loin. *See also* BEURRE NOISETTE; POMMES NOISETTE.

noix [NWAH] French for "nut" or "walnut."

Nökkelost Also called *Kuminost,* this Norwegian cheese can be made from raw or PASTEURIZED cow's milk and is typically ripened 3 months, though sometimes longer. The thin rind is pale to golden yellow and is sometimes covered with red wax. The smooth and supple semihard interior is ivory to pale yellow and studded with seeds and clove buds. Nökkelost has a creamy, tangy, nutty and spicy flavor that intensifies with age. The spiciness of this cheese comes from the addition of cumin seeds, cloves and/or caraway seeds, which is why Nökkelost is sometimes referred to as "clove cheese." Regular Nökkelost has a FAT CONTENT of about 45 percent; lowfat versions are also available. *See also* CHEESE.

nondairy creamer Though called a "creamer," this product neither contains dairy products nor tastes particularly like cream. Its main function is to lighten the color and dilute the flavor of coffee. Nondairy creamers are made from ingredients such as COCONUT OIL, PALM OIL or hydrogenated oil, sweeteners, emulsifiers and preservatives. Because they're so high in saturated fat, these pseudocream products are not recommended for those on low-cholesterol diets. Nondairy creamers are sold in several forms—powdered, liquid and frozen.

nonnutritive sweeteners *see* ARTIFICIAL SWEETENERS

nonpareil [non-puh-REHL] 1. A tiny colored-sugar pellet used to decorate cakes, cookies, candy, etc. 2. A confection consisting of a small chocolate disc covered with these colored candy pellets. 3. A French term meaning "without equal," most often used in reference to small pickled CAPERS from the region of Provence in France.

nonreactive pan (metal) *see* COOKWARE AND BAKEWARE MATERIALS

nonstick finishes *see* COOKWARE AND BAKEWARE MATERIALS

nonstick spray *see* COOKING SPRAY

nonvintage wine *see* VINTAGE; WINE

noodles The main difference between noodles and MACARONI or SPA-GHETTI is that, in addition to flour and water, noodles contain eggs or egg yolks. Noodles can be cut into flat, thick or thin strips of various lengths, as well as into squares. A wide variety of noodles is available in markets, including those enriched with vitamins and minerals, and colored noodles (red tinted with tomato paste or beet juice and green with spinach). Noodles are sold fresh (these should be refrigerated for no more than 3 days) and dried (best stored in a cool, dry place for no more than 6 months). *See also* ASIAN NOODLES; PASTA.

nopales [noh-PAH-lays] Long popular in Mexico, these fleshy oval leaves (also called *pads* or *paddles*) of the *nopal* (PRICKLY PEAR) cactus are gaining popularity in the United States. They range in color from pale to dark green and have a delicate, slightly tart green-bean flavor. Though fresh *nopales* (also called *cactus leaves*) are available year-round in Latin markets and some supermarkets, they're at their most tender and juicy best in the spring. Look for small, firm, pale-green *nopales* with no sign of wrinkling. Refrigerate tightly wrapped for up to a week. Before use, the thorns must be removed; a VEGETABLE PEELER will shave them off quickly. The flesh is generally cut into small pieces or strips, simmered in water until tender and used in a variety of dishes from scrambled eggs to salads. **Nopalitos** (nopales that are diced or cut into strips) are available canned (pickled or packed in water). **Acitrónes** are candied nopales, packed in sugar syrup and available in cans or jars.

nopalitos [noh-pah-LEE-tohs] *see* NOPALES

nori [NOH-ree] Paper-thin sheets of dried SEAWEED that can range in color from dark green to dark purple to black. They have a sweet ocean taste and are popular at Japanese meals. Nori is generally used for wrapping sushi and rice balls. When finely cut it serves as a seasoning or garnish. It can be purchased toasted (labeled *yakinori*); if purchased plain, it is usually lightly toasted before being used. Nori that has been brushed with SOY SAUCE is called *ajisuke-nori.* Japanese markets and some supermarkets carry nori either in plastic packaging or canned. All nori is very rich in protein, vitamins, calcium, iron and other minerals.

normande, à la; normande sauce [nohr-MAHND] A French phrase meaning "in the style of Normandy," referring to dishes based on the cooking of that region. Most commonly, it refers to fish (generally SOLE) garnished with shellfish (such as OYSTERS, SHRIMP and MUSSELS), mushrooms and TRUFFLES. Such a dish is usually served in **normande sauce**, a fish stock–based VELOUTÉ enriched with butter, cream and egg yolks. Other Normandy-style dishes include those made with regional products such as butter, fresh cream, apples, apple cider and CALVADOS.

northern pepperbush *see* MOUNTAIN PEPPER

Northern Spy apple An all-purpose apple with a bright red skin streaked with yellow and darker crimson. The flesh is very crisp and juicy, the flavor sweetly tart. *See also* APPLE.

Northwest Greening apple *see* APPLE

nose In the wine world, the word "nose" refers to the olfactory sense of wine. Some ENOPHILES use the term as a descriptor for wines with an extremely intense BOUQUET, although common usage doesn't generally connote quality.

nougat [NOO-guht] Particularly popular in southern Europe, this confection is made with sugar or honey, roasted nuts (such as almonds, walnuts, pistachios or hazelnuts) and sometimes chopped candied fruit or bits of chocolate. It can be chewy or hard and variously colored. *White nougat* is made with beaten egg white and is therefore softer. *Brown nougat* is made with caramelized sugar and, in addition to being a darker color, is normally firmer in texture. Italy is known for its *torrone*, an egg-white based nougat typically flavored with almonds and pistachios, though some versions are exotically flavored, as with STREGA liqueur. In Spain such nougats are known as *turrón*.

nouvelle cuisine [noo-vehl kwee-ZEEN] A French term meaning "new cooking," referring to a culinary style, begun in the early 1970s, that moved away from the rich, heavy style of classic French cuisine toward fresher, lighter food served in smaller portions. The sauces are lighter because they're REDUCED instead of being thickened with flour. Nouvelle cuisine vegetables are quickly cooked and therefore are tender yet slightly crisp.

Nova Scotia salmon *see* SMOKED SALMON

noyaux [nwah-YOH] *see* CRÈME DE NOYAUX

nuoc cham [noo-ahk CHAHM] A Vietnamese CONDIMENT that's based on NUOC NAM (fish sauce) combined with various seasonings that can include red chiles, garlic, lime juice, ginger and sugar.

nuoc nam [noo-AHK NAHM] Vietnamese for FISH SAUCE. *See also* NAM PLA.

nursehound *see* DOGFISH

nutmeg When Columbus sailed from Spain looking for the East Indies, nutmeg was one of the spices for which he was searching. Native to the Spice Islands, this seed from the nutmeg tree (a tropical evergreen) was extremely popular throughout much of the world from the 15th to the 19th century. When the fruit of the tree is picked, it is split to reveal the nutmeg seed surrounded by a lacy membrane that, when dried and ground, becomes the spice MACE. The hard, egg-shaped nutmeg seed is grayish-brown and about 1 inch long. The flavor and aroma are delicately warm, spicy and sweet. Nutmeg is sold ground or whole. Whole nutmeg freshly ground with a NUTMEG GRATER or GRINDER is superior to that which is commercially ground and packaged. Nutmeg is excellent when used in baked goods, milk- or cream-based preparations like custards, white sauces or eggnog and on fruits and vegetables—particularly potatoes, spinach and squash. *See also* SPICES; Seasoning Suggestions, page 891.

nutmeg grater; nutmeg grinder Small tools used to turn the whole NUTMEG seed into a coarse powder. A **nutmeg grater** has a fine-rasp, slightly curved surface. The grating is accomplished by rubbing the nutmeg across the grater's surface. Many graters store the whole nutmegs in containers attached to the bottom or back of the unit. A **nutmeg grinder** resembles a pepper grinder, except the cavity is designed specifically to hold a whole nutmeg with a small 4-pronged plate at the end of a central, spring-mounted post. The spring serves to keep downward pressure on the nutmeg, forcing it into a sharp blade that, when the crank is rotated, grates the nutmeg.

nut mill A utensil that attaches to the top of a countertop by means of a clamp-and-screw housing. Shelled nuts are placed in a top opening. When a hand crank is rotated, the nuts are pressed against a grating drum, which pulverizes them without releasing their natural oil. Nut mills are usually made of enameled cast iron.

nuts Any of various dry fruits that generally consist of an edible kernel enclosed in a shell that can range from medium-hard, thin and brittle to woody and tough. Botanically speaking, some foods we know as nuts are actually seeds (such as the BRAZIL NUT) or LEGUMES (like the PEANUT). Among the more popular of the other "nuts" are ALMONDS, CASHEWS, CHESTNUTS, MACADAMIAS, PECANS, PISTACHIOS, PINE NUTS and WALNUTS. Most nuts are sold both shelled and unshelled. Shelled nuts come in many forms including blanched or not, whole, halved, chopped, sliced or minced. Additionally, shelled nuts come raw, dry-roasted, oil-roasted, with or without salt,

N

smoked, candied and with various flavorings such as jalapeño and garlic. They're sold in plastic bags and boxes, and vacuum-packed in cans and jars. When buying unshelled nuts in bulk, choose those that are heavy for their size, with solid shells sans cracks or holes. The nut's kernel should not be loose enough to rattle when shaken. Shelled nuts should be plump, crisp and uniform in color and size. In general, nuts should be purchased as fresh as possible. Rancid nutmeats will ruin whatever food they flavor. To be sure that nuts are fresh—whether shelled or unshelled—buy them from a supplier with rapid turnover. Because of their high fat content, rancidity is always a hazard with nuts. For that reason they should be stored airtight in a cool place. Shelled nuts can be refrigerated in this manner up to 4 months, frozen up to 6 months. As a general rule (and depending on their freshness at the time of storage), unshelled nuts will keep about twice as long as shelled. Popular nut by-products include meal or flour (usually found in natural food stores) and nut butter and oils (the most popular being almond, hazelnut, peanut and walnut oils). Nuts are high in calcium, folic acid, magnesium, potassium, vitamin E and fiber. Some scientific studies have concluded that a daily portion of just 1 ounce of nuts rich in monounsaturated fat (*see* FATS AND OILS) can reduce the risk of heart disease by up to 10 percent. The nuts highest in monounsaturated fat are almonds, Brazil nuts, hazelnuts, macadamia nuts, pecans, pistachios and walnuts. And, although 1 ounce of nuts delivers about 180 calories and 17 fat grams, 50 to 80 percent of that fat is monounsaturated (the "good" fat that helps reduce the level of LDL—the "bad" cholesterol). Nuts are wonderful simply eaten out of hand as well as used in a wide variety of sweet and savory dishes for meals from breakfast to dinner. The flavor of most nuts benefits from a light toasting, either on stovetop or in the oven. Some people develop allergies to nuts that can be quite serious. Residue from processing nuts on equipment used to process other foods can be enough to contaminate these other foods and cause serious and even fatal reactions. Although allergies to PEANUTS (actually a LEGUME) are most common, some people are allergic to other nuts as well. Those allergic to peanuts may not be allergic to other nuts and vice versa. The term **tree nuts** is used to differentiate nuts from peanuts and is used on product labels. *See also* BLACK WALNUT; BUTTERNUT; CANDLENUT; ENGLISH WALNUT; GINKGO NUT; HAZELNUT; HICKORY NUT.

Nyons olive [nee-yohn] Small to medium-size olive from the commune of Nyons in southeastern France. The olives, which are violet black, are all from the Tanche cultivar, which is also known as *le perle noire* or "the black pearl." The olives can be found brine-cured or dry-cured (*see* OLIVES); they have wrinkled skins and a slightly salty, slightly bitter flavor with a fruity, nutty quality. The olive oil from Nyons olives achieved AOC status in 1994. *See also* OLIVE.

oakleaf lettuce *see* LEAF LETTUCE

oat bran *see* OATS

oat flour *see* OATS

oatmeal *see* OATS

oats According to a definition in Samuel Johnson's 1755 *Dictionary of the English Language,* oats were "a grain which in England is generally given to horses, but which in Scotland supports the people." Since oats are by far the most nutritious of the cereal grasses, it would appear that the Scots were ahead of the rest of us. Today, whole oats are still used as animal fodder. Humans don't usually consume them until after the oats have been cleaned, toasted, hulled and cleaned again, after which time they become **oat groats** (which still contain most of the original nutrients). Oat groats can be cooked and served as cereal, or prepared in the same manner as rice and used as a side dish or in a dish such as a salad or stuffing. When steamed and flattened with huge rollers, oat groats become regular **rolled oats** (also called *old-fashioned oats*). They take about 15 minutes to cook. **Quick-cooking rolled oats** are groats that have been cut into several pieces before being steamed and rolled into thinner flakes. Though they cook in about 5 minutes, many think the flavor and texture are never quite as satisfying as with regular rolled oats. Old-fashioned oats and quick-cooking oats can usually be interchanged in recipes. **Instant oats**, however, are not interchangeable because they're made with cut groats that have been precooked and dried before being rolled. This precooking process so softens the oat pieces that, after being combined with a liquid, the mixture can turn baked goods such as muffins or cookies into gooey lumps. Most instant oatmeal is packaged with salt, sugar and other flavorings. **Scotch oats** or **steel-cut oats** or **Irish oatmeal** are all names for groats that have been cut into 2 to 3 pieces and not rolled. They take considerably longer to cook than rolled oats and have a decidedly chewy texture. **Oat flour** is made from groats that have been ground into powder. It contains no gluten, however, so—for baked goods that need to rise, like yeast breads—must be combined with a flour that does. **Oat bran** is the outer casing of the oat and is particularly high in soluble fiber, thought to be a leading contender in the fight against high cholesterol. Oat bran, groats, flour and Scotch oats are more likely to be found in natural food stores than supermarkets. Oats are high in vitamin B1 and contain a good amount of vitamins B2 and E.

Oaxaca cheese [wuh-HAH-kuh] *see* ASADERO

O'Brien potatoes Although the origin of the name is vague, it seems to come from the longtime association between the Irish and potatoes. The dish consists of diced potatoes (sometimes precooked) that are fried with chopped onions and PIMIENTOS until the potatoes are crisp and brown. Some variations use sweet red or green peppers instead of pimientos.

oca [OH-kah] 1. Small, knobby tubers native to South America and used widely in the cookery of the Inca and Mayan civilizations. Ocas may be white, pink or red and have a firm potatolike flesh that can range in flavor from intensely sweet to slightly acidic. Choose firm, unblemished specimens; store in a cool, dark place for up to 1 month. Cook ocas in any manner suitable for potatoes. Also called *New Zealand yam* and *papa roja.* 2. Italian for "GOOSE."

oceanic bonito *see* TUNA

ocean perch *see* PERCH

octopus [AHK-tuh-puhs] Though there are some 50-foot specimens—and despite the fact that it's also called *devilfish*—this monster of the deep is not particularly fearful and seldom reaches the size seen in the movies. In fact, the majority reach only 1 to 2 feet (tentacles extended) and weigh about 3 pounds. As a member of the CEPHALOPOD class in the MOLLUSK family, the octopus is related to the SQUID and CUTTLEFISH. Its rich diet of clams and scallops gives it a highly flavorful meat that, though rubbery, is extremely popular in Japan and the Mediterranean countries. Predressed fresh and frozen octopus is available in many supermarkets and specialty fish markets. As with most species, those that are younger and smaller are more tender. The 8 tentacles and the body to which they're attached are edible, but the eyes, mouth area and viscera are discarded. The ink sac contains a black liquid that can be used to color and flavor foods such as pasta, soups and stews. Smoked and canned octopus are also available. Octopus can be eaten in a variety of ways including raw, boiled and pickled, sautéed, deep-fried or for more mature specimens, simmered or boiled for several hours. *See also* SHELLFISH.

oenology [ee-NAHL-uh-jee] *see* ENOLOGY

oenophile [EE-nuh-file] *see* ENOPHILE

oeuf(s) [UHF(S)] French for "EGG." *Oeuf à la coque* [ah lah KOK] is a soft-cooked egg in the shell; *oeuf au plat* [oh PLAH], an egg fried or baked in butter; *oeuf brouillés* [brwee-YAY], scrambled eggs; *oeuf dur* [DEWR], a hard-cooked egg; *oeuf en cocotte* [awn koh-KOT], egg baked in an individual cup; *oeuf farci* [FAR-see], STUFFED EGG; *oeuf frit* [FREE], fried egg; *oeuf mollet* [moh-LAY], soft-cooked and shelled; *oeuf poché* [poh-SHAY], poached egg. *See also* OEUF EN GELÉE; OEUFS À LA NEIGE.

oeuf en gelée [uhf awn jheh-LAY] An egg that's poached and chilled in ASPIC. A small oval, tin "oeuf en gelée" mold (found in kitchenware shops) is typically used for this dish.

oeufs à la neige [OUFS ah lah nehzh] *see* FLOATING ISLANDS

offal [OH-fuhl; OFF-uhl] *see* VARIETY MEATS

o-hashi [oh-HAH-shee] *see* HASHI

oignon [uhn-YOH*N*] French for "onion."

oignon brûlé *see* ONION BRÛLÉ

oignon piqué *see* ONION PIQUÉ

oil of peppermint; oil of spearmint *see* MINT

oils Oils have been used for cooking since prehistoric times. In general, oils come from vegetable sources—plants, nuts, seeds, etc. An oil is extracted from its source by one of two methods. In the **solvent-extraction method**, the ground ingredient is soaked in a chemical solvent that is later removed by boiling. The second method produces **cold pressed oils**, which is somewhat a misnomer because the mixture is heated to temperatures up to 160°F before being pressed to extract the oil. After the oil is extracted, it's either left in its crude state or refined. **Refined oils**—those found on most supermarket shelves—have been treated until they're transparent. They have a delicate, somewhat neutral, flavor, an increased SMOKE POINT and a longer shelf life. **Unrefined (or crude) oils** are usually cloudy and have an intense flavor and odor that clearly signals their origin. Most oils can be stored, sealed airtight, on the kitchen shelf for up to 2 months. Oils with a high proportion of monounsaturates—such as olive oil and peanut oil—are more perishable. Once opened, they should be refrigerated if kept longer than a month. Because they turn rancid quickly, unrefined oils should always be refrigerated. *See* FATS AND OILS *listing for detailed information on hydrogenated, monounsaturated and polyunsaturated oils. See also* ALMOND OIL; CANOLA OIL; CHILI OIL; COCONUT OIL; CORN OIL; GRAPESEED OIL; HAZELNUT OIL; MUSTARD OIL; OLIVE OIL; PALM OIL; PEANUT OIL; SAFFLOWER OIL; SESAME OIL; SUNFLOWER SEEDS; SOYBEAN OIL; TRANS FATTY ACIDS; VEGETABLE OIL; WALNUT OIL.

oilstone *see* WHETSTONE

okara [oh-KAH-rah] The residue that is left after the liquid is drained off when making soybean curd (TOFU). This white by-product resembles wet sawdust. Okara, which is high in protein and fiber, is used in Japanese cooking for soups, vegetable dishes and even salads. Commercially, it's used in some baked goods and MEAT ANALOGS. It can be found in Asian markets that sell fresh tofu.

okashi [oh-KAH-shee] Japanese for confections, pastries and sweets. Sometimes spelled simply *kashi*.

oke [OH-kee] *see* OKOLEHAO

okolehao [oh-koh-leh-HAH-oh] An 80 PROOF Hawaiian liquor made from a mash of the TI plant. It's often substituted for rum and, like rum, comes in white (colorless) and golden versions. Okolehao is known on the islands as *oke*.

okra [OH-kruh] Ethiopian slaves brought the okra plant to America's South, where it's still popular today. The green okra pods have a ridged skin and a tapered, oblong shape. Although available fresh year-round in the South, the season for the rest of the country is from about May through October. When buying fresh okra look for firm, brightly colored pods under 4 inches long. Larger pods may be tough and fibrous. Avoid those that are dull in color, limp or blemished. Refrigerate okra in a plastic bag for up to 3 days. Canned and frozen okra is also available. These green pods can be prepared in a variety of ways including braising, baking and frying. When cooked, okra gives off a rather viscous substance that serves to thicken any liquid in which it is cooked. Throughout the South, it's a favorite ingredient in many dishes, the best known being GUMBO, where it's used both for thickening and for flavor. Fresh okra contains fair amounts of vitamins A and C.

oladi [oh-LAH-dee] Russian pancake similar to a small buttermilk pancake made with KEFIR instead of buttermilk.

olallieberry; olallie berry [AHL-uh-lee] Grown mainly on the West Coast, this cross between a YOUNGBERRY and a LOGANBERRY has a distinctive, sweet flavor and resembles a large, elongated BLACKBERRY. It's delicious both fresh and cooked and makes excellent jams and jellies.

old fashioned cocktail Said to have been made initially with a brand of Kentucky bourbon called "Old 1776" in the late 1800s, this drink is made by combining WHISKEY (usually BOURBON or RYE), a small amount of water, a dash of BITTERS and a sugar cube (or the equivalent amount of sugar syrup). It's served over ice in a squat, eponymous old-fashioned glass—and garnished with an orange slice and a MARASCHINO CHERRY.

oleomargarine *see* MARGARINE

Olestra *see* FAT SUBSTITUTES

olio [OH-lyoh] Italian for "OIL."

oliva [oh-LEE-vah] Italian for "OLIVE."

olivada [oh-lee-VAH-dah] An Italian olive spread, which is generally a simple combination of puréed Italian black olives, olive oil and black pepper.

olive The olive branch has long been a symbol of peace, and the silvery-leaved olive tree has been considered sacred at least as far back as the 17th century B.C. Native to the Mediterranean area, the olive is a small, oily fruit that contains a pit. It's grown both for its fruit and its oil in sub-tropical zones including the United States (Arizona, California and New Mexico), Latin America and throughout the Mediterranean. Olive varieties number in the dozens and vary in size and flavor. All fresh olives are bitter and the final flavor of the fruit greatly depends on how ripe it is when picked and the processing it receives. Underripe olives are always green, whereas ripe olives may be either green or black. SPANISH OLIVES are normally picked young. The common **black olive** or MISSION OLIVE is a ripe green olive that obtains its characteristic color and flavor from lye curing and oxygenation. Olives that are tree ripened turn dark brown or black naturally. The majority of these olives are used for oil but the rest are brine or salt-cured and are usually packed in olive oil or a vinegar solution. The Greek KALAMATA and the French NIÇOISE OLIVES are two of the more popular imported ripe olives. **Dry-cured olives** have been packed in salt, which removes most of their moisture and creates dry, wrinkled fruit. These olives are sometimes rubbed with olive oil or packed with herbs. **Cracked olives** have the flesh split open either by hand or machine so that the flavor of BRINES OR MARINADES can permeate the meat quicker. Cracked olives are also called **slit olives** and **split olives**. Both domestic and imported olives are available bottled, canned and in bulk year-round in a variety of forms including whole (pitted, unpitted and stuffed), sliced and chopped. Unopened olives can be stored at room temperature for up to 2 years. Once opened they can be refrigerated in their own liquid (in a nonmetal container) for several weeks. *See also* OLIVE OIL; ALFONSO OLIVE; AMFISSA OLIVE; ARBEQUINA OLIVE; ATALANTA OLIVE; BELLA DI CERIGNOLA OLIVE; ELITSES OLIVE; FARGA ARAGON OLIVE; GAETA OLIVE; HONDROELIA OLIVE; LUCQUES OLIVE; MANZANILLA OLIVE; NAFPLION OLIVE; NYONS OLIVE; PICHOLINE OLIVE; PONENTINE OLIVE; SEVILLANO OLIVE; TAGGIASCA OLIVE.

olive oil Pressing tree-ripened olives extracts a flavorful, monounsaturated oil that is prized throughout the world both for cooking (particularly in Mediterranean countries) and for salads. Today's marketplace provides a wide selection of domestic olive oil (most of which comes from California) and imported oils from France, Greece, Italy and Spain. The flavor, color and fragrance of olive oils can vary dramatically depending on distinctions such as growing region and the crop's condition. All olive oils are graded in accordance with the degree of acidity they contain. The best are **cold-pressed**, a chemical-free process that involves only pressure, which produces a natural level of low acidity. **Extra virgin olive oil**, the cold-pressed result of the first pressing of the olives, is only 1 percent acid. It's considered the finest and fruitiest of the olive oils and is therefore also the most expensive. Extra virgin olive oil can range from a crystalline champagne color to greenish-golden to bright green. In general, the deeper the color, the more intense the olive flavor. After extra virgin, olive oils are classified in order of ascending acidity. **Virgin olive oil** is also a first-press oil, with a slightly higher level of acidity of between 1 and 3 percent. **Fino olive oil** is a blend of extra virgin and virgin oils (*fino* is Italian for "fine"). Products labeled simply **olive oil** (once called *pure olive oil*) contain a combination of refined olive oil and virgin or extra virgin oil. The new **light olive oil** (an American marketing term) contains the same amount of beneficial monounsaturated fat as regular olive oil and it also has exactly the same number of calories. What the term "light" refers to is that—because of an extremely fine filtration process—this olive oil is lighter in both color and fragrance, and has little of the classic olive-oil flavor. It's this rather nondescript flavor that makes "light" olive oil perfect for baking and cooking where regular olive oil's obvious essence might be undesirable. The filtration process for this light-style oil also gives it a higher SMOKE POINT than regular olive oil. Light olive oils can therefore be used for high-heat frying, whereas regular olive oil is better suited for low- to medium-heat cooking, as well as for many uncooked foods such as salad dressings and MARINADES. The International Olive Oil Institute recommends using pure olive oil for frying, since the flavor of extra virgin olive oil tends to break down at frying temperatures, making the added expense a waste. Olive oil should be stored in a cool, dark place for up to 6 months. It can be refrigerated, in which case it will last up to a year. Chilled olive oil becomes cloudy and too thick to pour. However, it will clear and become liquid again when brought to room temperature. *See also* FATS AND OILS.

oloroso [oh-loh-ROH-soh] *see* SHERRY

Olympia oyster [oh-LIHM-pee-uh] Native to the Pacific Coast, the Olympia oyster is found primarily in the Pacific Northwest around Washington's Puget Sound. It's very small, seldom exceeding 1 1/2 inches. The Olympia has an excellent flavor and is a favorite for eating ON THE HALF SHELL. Because they are so small, it takes a fair number to satisfy most oyster aficionados. *See also* OYSTER.

O

omakase [OH-mah-KAH-say] Japanese for "entrusting," the word *omakase* is often associated with SUSHI restaurants. In this venue it indicates "chef's choice" or "putting your trust in the chef." Omakase is essentially a tasting menu left up to the sushi chef, which sometimes requires an adventuresome spirit from the diner, and perhaps a fat wallet.

Omega-3 oils *see* FATS AND OILS

omelet; omelette [AHM-leht] A mixture of eggs, seasonings and sometimes water or milk, cooked in butter until firm and filled or topped with various fillings such as cheese, ham, mushrooms, onions, peppers, sausage and herbs. Sweet omelets can be filled with jelly, custard or fruit, sprinkled with powdered sugar or flamed with various LIQUORS or LIQUEURS. For fluffy omelets, the whites and yolks can be beaten separately and folded together. They can also be served flat or folded. *See also* FRITTATA; OMELET PAN.

omelet pan A pan with shallow sloping sides, a flat bottom and a long handle. It's designed for easy movement, turning and removal of an OMELET or other egg mixtures. Omelet pans range from 6 to 10 inches in diameter and can be made of aluminum, plain or enameled cast iron or stainless steel. Many of today's omelet pans have NONSTICK FINISHES.

omusubi *see* ONIGIRI

onglet [awn-LAY] *see* HANGER STEAK

onigiri [oh-NEE-gee-ree] Rice formed in balls or triangles with a filling of something strong and savory. The fillings are quite varied and can include UMEBOSHI (pickled plums), KATSUOBUSHI (dried BONITO flakes), KOMBU (sun-dried seaweed) or SHIOZAKE (salted salmon). They are often wrapped with a strip of NORI. Onigiri are a popular snack food in Japan and are carried in stores throughout the country. They are sometimes referred to as *musubi* or *omusubi*. In Hawaii SPAM musubi is quite popular.

onion Related to the lily, this underground bulb is prized around the world for the magic it makes in a multitude of dishes with its pungent flavor and odor. There are two main classifications of onion—**green onions** (also called SCALLIONS) and **dry onions**, which are simply mature onions with a juicy flesh covered with dry, papery skin. Dry onions come in a wide range of sizes, shapes and flavors. Among those that are mild flavored are the white or yellow **Bermuda onion**, available March through June; the larger, more spherical **Spanish onion**, which is usually yellow skinned (but can be white) and typically in season from August to May; and the **red** or **Italian onion**, which is available year-round. The stronger-flavored **globe onions** can have yellow, red or white skins. They can range from 1 to 4 inches in diameter and in flavor from mildly pungent to quite sharp. Among the special onion varieties are three exceedingly juicy specimens. The **Maui onion**, hailing—as its name implies—from the Hawaiian island of the same name, is sweet, mild and crisply moist. It can range in color from white to pale yellow and is usually shaped like a slightly flattened sphere. The Maui onion's season is from April to July. **Vidalia onions** are the namesake of Vidalia, Georgia, where they thrive. At their best, these large, pale yellow onions are exceedingly sweet and juicy. They're usually available much of the year in the regions where grown and from May through July elsewhere. The state of Washington is the source of **Walla Walla onions**, named after the city of the same name. Large, round and golden, they're in season from June to September but are often available outside their growing area only by mail order. **Oso Sweet onions** hail from South America and, as their name suggests, are extremely succulent and sweet and, in fact, contain almost 50 percent more sugar than Vidalias. They're available in specialty produce markets from January through March. Another import is the **Rio Sweet onion**, which is predictably sweet and available from October through December. Tiny **pearl onions** are mild-flavored and about the size of a small marble. They can be cooked (and are often creamed) and served as a side dish or pickled and used as a CONDIMENT or garnish (as in the GIBSON cocktail). **Boiling onions** are about 1 inch in diameter and mildly flavored. They're cooked as a side dish, used in stews and pickled. When buying onions, choose those that are heavy for their size with dry, papery skins with no signs of spotting or moisture. Avoid onions with soft spots. Store in a cool, dry place with good air circulation for up to 2 months (depending on their condition when purchased). Humidity breeds spoilage in dry onions. Once cut, an onion should be tightly wrapped, refrigerated and used within 4 days. Most onions cause tearing (caused by sulfuric compounds) to some extent—some just watery eyes, others giant crocodile tears. Freezing the onion for 20 minutes before chopping helps, but then so does wearing safety goggles. Dried or freeze-dried onion by-products include **onion powder** (ground dehydrated onion), **onion salt** (onion powder and salt), **onion flakes** and **onion flavoring cubes**. Onions are also sold canned or pickled (usually pearl onions) and frozen (whole or chopped). Onions contain a fair amount of vitamin C with traces of other vitamins and minerals. *See also* CHIVE; CIPOLLINI; LEEK; SCALLION; SHALLOT; WELSH ONION.

onion brûlé; *Fr.* **oignon brûlé** [broo-LAY; uhn-YOHN broo-LAY] *Brûlé* is French for "burned," and onion brûlé is a charred onion used to impart flavor and color to STOCKS, especially vegetable stocks. Make it by cutting an onion in half, laying the cut side down on a hot pan or griddle and charring the onion until it's almost black.

onion piqué; onion piquet; *Fr.* **oignon piqué** [pee-KAY; uhn-YOH*N* pee-KAY] A raw, peeled onion with cloves and bay leaves inserted into it. The word *piqué* is taken from the French *piquer*, meaning "prick," which refers to the clove stem sticking through the bay leaf and pricking the onion to remain in place. Onion piqué is usually steeped in milk as a means of adding flavor when making a BÉCHAMEL sauce. It's sometimes referred to as a *stuck onion* or *pricked onion*.

onion powder *see* ONION

onion salt *see* ONION

onion seed, black *see* NIGELLA SEEDS

onion squash *see* RED KURI

ono [OH-noh] *see* WAHOO

on the half shell A phrase commonly used to describe raw oysters served on the bottom shell only, usually on a plate of crushed ice or, in the case of cooked dishes such as OYSTERS ROCKEFELLER, on a bed of rock salt. Some oyster lovers eat these fresh oysters without any CONDIMENTS, sipping the oyster liquor from its bottom shell. Others adorn theirs with lemon juice, horseradish, TABASCO SAUCE, COCKTAIL SAUCE, ketchup or vinegar.

on the house *see* HOUSE

on the rocks A term for a beverage (usually LIQUOR) served over ice without added water or other MIXER.

oolong tea [OO-long] *see* TEA

opah [OH-pah] Also called *moonfish,* the opah is a marine fish that can reach up to 200 pounds. It's found in warm waters throughout the world but that which is available in the United States usually comes from Hawaii. The pinkish flesh of this fish is rich, full flavored and fine textured. It's suitable for baking, poaching and steaming. *See also* FISH.

opakapaka; opaka-paka [oh-pah-kah-PAH-kah] A deep water marine fish found in the waters surrounding the Hawaiian Islands. Its sweet, delicate flesh ranges from white to pink in color; however, cooked opakapaka is always white. It can run from lean to fat, depending on the season (they're fatter in the winter). Opakapaka is suitable for almost any cooking method. In Hawaii, it's also referred to as *pink snapper. See also* FISH.

open dating *see* PRODUCT DATING

open-faced A descriptor used culinarily for a "sandwich" consisting of one slice of bread topped with various ingredients such as sliced meat, cheese, pickles, etc. Open-faced sandwiches are very popular in Scandinavia, where they've become an art form with elaborately arranged and decorated combinations. For the most part, open-faced sandwiches are cold, but there are also hot ones, which usually consist of bread topped with meat slices and gravy.

oplet *see* SEA ANEMONE

opo *see* CUCUZZA

orache; orach [OHR-ihch] Although there are numerous species of orache, and many of them edible, it's the **garden orache** (*Atriplex. hortensis*) that's most popular and cultivated by gardeners. Also known as *red orach*e, *mountain spinach* or *French spinach*, this upright annual with leaves that can vary from yellow to green to red to grayish purple has a spinach-like flavor. The other common name for orache is *saltbush*, as many of these plants endure salty environments and retain some of that saltiness in their leaves. When picked young, orache may be used raw in salads. Orache can also be cooked (usually by boiling or sautéing) and used as a vegetable or as part of a dish.

orange Contrary to what most of us think, this fruit was not named for its color. Instead, the word *orange* comes from a transliteration of the sanskrit *naranga* . . . which comes from the Tamil *naru* . . . which means "fragrant." It's thought that the reason oranges have long been associated with fertility (and therefore, weddings) is because this lush evergreen tree can simultaneously produce flowers, fruit and foliage. Though oranges originated in Southeast Asia, they now also thrive around the world in warm-climate areas including Portugal, Spain, North Africa and, in the United States (the world's largest producer), Arizona, California, Florida and Texas. There are three basic types of orange—sweet, loose-skinned and bitter. **Sweet oranges** are prized both for eating and for their juice. They're generally large and have skins that are more difficult to remove than their loose-skinned relatives. They may have seeds or be seedless. Among the more popular sweet oranges are the seedless NAVEL, the juicy, coarse-grained VALENCIA and the thin-skinned, red-fleshed BLOOD ORANGE. Sweet oranges are better eaten fresh than cooked. **Loose-skinned oranges** are so named because their skins easily slip off the fruit. Their segments are also loose and divide with ease. Members of the MANDARIN ORANGE family are all loose skinned; they vary in flavor from sweet to tart-sweet. **Bitter oranges**, the most well-known of which are the SEVILLE and the BERGAMOT, are—as their name implies—too sour and astringent to eat raw. Instead, they're cooked in preparations such as MARMALADE and BIGA-

RADE SAUCE. Bitter oranges are also greatly valued for their peel, which is candied, and their essential oils, which are used to flavor foods as well as some LIQUEURS, such as CURAÇAO. Most of the bitter orange supply comes from Spain. USDA grading of oranges is voluntary and not considered necessary by most growers. The two grades used are **U.S**. **Fancy** (best) and **U.S**. **No**. **1**. Fresh oranges are available year-round at different times, depending on the variety. Choose fruit that is firm and heavy for its size, with no mold or spongy spots. Unfortunately, because oranges are sometimes dyed with food coloring, a bright color isn't necessarily an indicator of quality. Regreening sometimes occurs in fully ripe oranges, particularly with Valencias. A rough, brownish area (russeting) on the skin doesn't affect flavor or quality either. Oranges can be stored at cool room temperature for a day or so, but should then be refrigerated and can be kept there for up to 2 weeks. Oranges are an excellent source of vitamin C and contain some vitamin A. Once cut or squeezed, however, the vitamin C quickly begins to dissipate. After only 8 hours at room temperature or 24 hours in the refrigerator, there's a 20 percent vitamin C loss. Canned, bottled and frozen-concentrate orange juices have a greatly decreased vitamin C content. *See also* KING ORANGE; TEMPLE ORANGE.

orange-flower water A perfumy distillation of bitter-orange blossoms. Orange-flower water is used as a flavoring in baked goods, various sweet and savory dishes and a variety of drinks, such as the Ramos GIN FIZZ cocktail.

orange Hokkaido squash *see* RED KURI

orange pekoe tea *see* PEKOE

orange roughy [RUHF-ee] This New Zealand fish (also known as *slimehead*) is fast becoming popular in the United States. It's low in fat, has firm white flesh and a mild flavor. Orange roughy is available in specialty fish markets and some supermarkets. It can be poached, baked, broiled or fried. *See also* FISH.

orca bean *see* CALYPSO BEAN

orchid chile *see* BISHOP'S CROWN CHILE

orecchiette *see* Pasta Glossary, page 883

oregano [oh-rehg-uh-noh] Greek for "joy of the mountain," oregano was almost unheard of in the United States until soldiers came back from Italian World War II assignments raving about it. This herb, sometimes called *wild marjoram,* belongs to the mint family and is related to both marjoram and THYME. Oregano is similar to marjoram but is not as sweet and has a stronger, more pungent flavor and aroma. Because of its pungency, it requires a bit more caution in its use. Mediterranean oregano is milder than the Mexican variety, which is generally used in highly spiced dishes. Fresh Mediterranean or European oregano is sometimes available in gourmet produce sections of supermarkets and in Italian or Greek markets. Choose bright-green, fresh-looking bunches with no sign of wilting or yellowing. Refrigerate in a plastic bag for up to 3 days. Dried Mediterranean oregano is readily available in any supermarket in both crumbled and powdered forms. The stronger-flavored Mexican oregano can generally be found in its dried form in Latin markets. As with all dried herbs, oregano should be stored in a cool, dark place for no more than 6 months. Oregano goes extremely well with tomato-based dishes and is a familiar pizza herb. *See also* HERBS; Seasoning Suggestions, page 891.

organic foods The term "organic" loosely describes food that has been cultivated and/or processed without the use of chemicals of any sort including fertilizers, insecticides, artificial coloring or flavoring and additives. But it took on a more rigorous meaning in 2002, when the federal government created the National Organic Program (NOP), administered by the United States Department of Agriculture (USDA). The NOP develops, implements, and administers national production, handling and labeling standards for organic agricultural products. It also accredits the certifying agents (foreign and domestic) who inspect organic production and handling operations to certify that they meet USDA standards. These accredited certifying agents are audited annually. Standards for the NOP are spelled out in a more than 550-page document that's continually being updated. A 15-member National Organic Standards Board (NOSB) assists the Secretary of Agriculture with standards and implementation of the program. The NOSB is comprised of farmers/growers, handlers/processors, retailers, scientists, consumer/public interest advocates, environmentalists, and USDA-accredited certifying agents. The standards indicate that any agricultural product that is sold, labeled or represented as "100 percent organic," "organic," or "made with organic specified ingredients or food group(s))" must be produced and handled in accordance with the requirements specified in various parts of the standards. The standards cover all phases of food production, processing, delivery and retail sale. Farmers and food processors that use the word "organic" in reference to their businesses and products must be certified organic by one of accredited certifying agents. Producers whose gross agricultural income from organic sales does not surpass $5,000 but still follow NOP standards can use the term "organic" but not "certified organic." In summary, "organic" pertains to food and how it is produced and processed. Genetically modified organisms and irradiation are not used. The following table indicates labeling that can appear on organic products and what it means.

Label says:	Ingredients	USDA Seal	Certifi- cation Agent	Example
100% Organic	100% organic ingredients	Allowed	Must be listed	100% Organic Cereal
Organic	At least 95% organic ingredients plus up to 5% non-organic ingredients that are approved	Allowed	Must be listed	Organic Cereal
Made with Organic Ingredients	At least 70% organic plus up to 30% non-organic ingredients that are approved or non-organic agricultural ingredients	Not allowed	Must be listed	Cereal made with organic oats, raisins, and dates
nothing (non-organic products)	Products with more than 30% non-organic ingredients	Not allowed	None	(Ingredients may only be mentioned in the ingre- dient list.) Ingredients: organic oats, organic raisins

orgeat syrup [ohr-zhay] The original version of this sweet syrup was made with a barley-almond blend. Today, however, it's made with almonds, sugar and ROSE WATER or ORANGE-FLOWER WATER. Orgeat syrup has a pronounced almond taste and is used to flavor many cocktails including the MAI TAI and SCORPION.

oriental radish *see* DAIKON

ormer [OHR-muhr] *see* ABALONE

oro blanco [OH-roh BLAHN-koh] Spanish for "white gold," the oro blanco is a POMELO hybrid developed in 1958. This bright yellow fruit is grapefruit-size and has a thick pomelolike rind and a sweet, almost seedless flesh. Choose fruit that's heavy for its size. Store at room temperature for up to 2 weeks, in the refrigerator for up to a month.

orzo [OHR-zoh] Italian for "BARLEY." *See also* Pasta Glossary, page 883.

osafki *see* SOFKI

osetra *see* CAVIAR

osso buco; ossobuco [AW-soh BOO-koh; OH-soh BOO-koh] An Italian dish made of veal shanks braised with olive oil, white wine, stock, onions, tomatoes, garlic, anchovies, carrots, celery and lemon peel. Traditionally, osso buco is garnished with GREMOLATA and served accompanied by RISOTTO. In Italian, OSSO BUCO means "pierced bone."

ostrica [oh-STREE-kah] Italian for "OYSTER."

ostrich [AWS-trihch] Hailing from Africa and parts of southwest Asia, the ostrich is a huge flightless bird that can weigh up to 250 pounds and reach up to 7 feet in height. Ostriches have long been raised for their skin, feathers and meat, the latter of which is compared to very lean beef. Ostrich meat is showing up more and more on menus, a direct correlation to the fact that the United States now boasts hundreds of ostrich ranches. Though some specialty meat markets may carry (or will special order) ostrich meat, it is still uncommon.

ostrich fern *see* FIDDLEHEAD FERN

Oswego tea *see* BEE BALM

ouzo [OO-zoh] From Greece, this clear, sweet anise–flavored LIQUEUR is usually served as an APÉRITIF. It's generally mixed with water, which turns it whitish and opaque.

oven-spring A baking term that describes the rapid rising action of yeast doughs during the first 10 to 20 minutes after being placed in a hot oven. The heat reacts with the yeast by increasing and expanding the carbon dioxide gas, which plumps the dough. During this crucial ovenspring period, it's important not to open the oven door, which will create a draft and reduce the heat. This rising will continue until the interior temperature of the dough reaches 140°F, killing the yeast.

oven thermometer A thermometer designed to read oven temperatures, which are often inaccurately indicated by the oven dial. Erroneous oven temperatures can create all kinds of culinary havoc, from gooey centers in baked goods to burning or drying of a wide range of foods. Oven thermometers can vary in quality and, consequently, price. The springstyle thermometer available in most supermarkets can become unreliable with a small jolt or with continual use. Mercury oven thermometers, available in gourmet supply shops, are more accurate and reliable. *See also* CANDY THERMOMETER; FREEZER/ REFRIGERATOR THERMOMETER; MEAT THERMOMETER; Oven Temperatures—Fahrenheit, Celsius, British, French, page 863.

oxalic acid [ahk-SAL-ihk] This acid occurs in many plants and is poisonous in excessive amounts. Some of the plants that contain a measurable amount of oxalic acid are SORREL, SPINACH and RHUBARB. Because it forms insoluble compounds with calcium and iron, inhibiting their absorption by the human body, oxalic acid greatly diminishes the purported nutritional punch of spinach.

oxtail The oxtail was once really from an ox but nowadays the term generally refers to beef or veal tail. Though it's quite bony, this cut of meat is very flavorful. Because it can be extremely tough (depending on the age of the animal), oxtail requires long, slow braising. It's often used for stews or soups such as the hearty English classic oxtail soup, which includes vegetables, barley and herbs and is often flavored with SHERRY or MADEIRA. *See also* VARIETY MEATS.

oyakodon [oh-YAH-koh-dohn] DONBURI dish with chicken and egg. *Oyako* is Japanese for "parent and child," indicating that the chicken is the parent and the egg is the child.

oyster Though 18th-century satirist Jonathan Swift once wrote, "He was a bold man that first ate an oyster," this BIVALVE has been a culinary favorite for thousands of years. The hard, rough, gray shell contains a meat that can vary in color from creamy beige to pale gray, in flavor from salty to bland and in texture from tender to firm. There are both natural and cultivated oyster beds throughout the world. In the United States, there are three primary species of oysters that are commercially harvested—Pacific (or Japanese), Eastern (or Atlantic) and the Olympia. Each species is sold under different names depending on where they're harvested. OLYMPIA OYSTERS are rarely larger than $1\frac{1}{2}$ inches and hail from Washington's Puget Sound. The PACIFIC OYSTER (or *Japanese oyster*) is found along the Pacific seaboard and can reach up to a foot long. Considered culinarily superior to the Pacific oysters are ATLANTIC OYSTERS (or *Eastern oysters*), the most well known of which is the BLUEPOINT. Others from the Atlantic seaboard—named for their place of origin—include Apalachicola, Cape Cod, Chincoteague, Indian River, Kent Island, Malpeque and Wellfleet. In Europe, the French are famous for their BELON OYSTERS (which are now also being farmed in the United States) and their green-tinged Marennes oysters; the English have their Colchester, Helford and Whitstable oysters; and the Irish have Galway oysters. Fresh oysters are available year-round. Today's widespread refrigeration keeps them cool during hot weather, debunking the old myth of not eating them during months spelled without an "r." However, oysters are at their best—particularly for serving raw ON THE HALF SHELL—during fall and winter because they spawn during the summer months and become soft and fatty. Shipping costs generally prohibit movement of oysters far from their beds, limiting the abundant supply to local varieties. Live oysters are best as fresh as possible and therefore should be purchased from a store with good turnover. Reject those that do not have tightly closed shells or that don't snap shut when tapped. The smaller the oyster is (for its species) the younger and more tender it will be. Fresh, SHUCKED oysters are also available and should be plump, uniform in size, have good color, smell fresh and be packaged in clear, not cloudy oyster LIQUOR. Live oysters should be covered with a damp towel and refrigerated (larger shell down) up to 3 days. The sooner they're used the better they'll taste. Refrigerate shucked oysters in their liquor and use within 2 days. Oysters are also available canned in water or their own liquor, frozen and smoked. Oysters in the shell can be served raw, baked, steamed, grilled or in specialty dishes such as OYSTERS ROCKEFELLER. Shucked oysters can be batter-fried, sautéed, grilled, used in soups or stews or in special preparations such as dressings, poultry stuffings or appetizers like ANGELS ON HORSEBACK. Oysters are high in calcium, niacin and iron, as well as a good source of protein. *See also* KUMAMOTO OYSTER; SHELLFISH.

oyster cap *see* OYSTER MUSHROOM

oyster crab A diminutive (less than 1 inch wide) soft-shell crab that makes its home inside an oyster and lives off the food its host eats. Oyster crabs are certainly not found in all oysters, and most oyster processing plants don't bother to collect them during shucking so the supply is very limited. They're best prepared simply sautéed in butter. Gourmets consider these pale-pink CRUSTACEANS a delicacy. *See also* CRAB.

oyster mushroom A fan-shaped mushroom that grows both wild and cultivated in close clusters, often on rotting tree trunks. They're also called *oyster caps, tree mushrooms, tree oyster mushrooms, summer oyster mushrooms* and *pleurotte*. The cap varies in color from pale gray to dark brownish-gray. The stems are grayish-white. The flavor of raw oyster mushrooms is fairly robust and slightly peppery but becomes much milder when cooked. There are many variants including the ABALONE OYSTER MUSHROOM, BLUE OYSTER MUSHROOM and GOLDEN OYSTER MUSHROOM. They're available in some areas year-round, particularly in specialty produce and Asian markets. Young oyster mushrooms ($1\frac{1}{2}$ inches in diameter and under) are considered the best. Also available are canned oyster mushrooms, which should be rinsed before using. *See also* MUSHROOM.

oyster plant *see* SALSIFY

oyster sauce A dark-brown sauce consisting of oysters, brine and SOY SAUCE cooked until thick and concentrated. It's a popular Asian seasoning used to prepare myriad dishes (particularly STIR-FRY dishes) and as a table CONDIMENT. Oyster sauce imparts a richness to dishes without overpowering their natural flavor. It's available in many supermarkets and all Asian markets. *See also* SAUCE.

oysters Bienville A dish named in honor of Jean Baptiste Le Moyne, Sieur de Bienville, the founder of New Orleans. Oysters Bienville was created in the late 1930s at one of New Orleans's most famous restaurants, Antoine's. It consists of oysters ON THE HALF SHELL topped with a BÉCHAMEL flavored with SHERRY and CAYENNE and mixed with sautéed garlic, shallots, mushrooms and minced shrimp. A bread-crumb–grated cheese mixture is sprinkled over the top and the oysters are baked on a bed of rock salt until bubbly and browned.

oysters on the half shell *see* ON THE HALF SHELL

oysters Rockefeller Created at Antoine's restaurant in New Orleans in the late 1890s, this popular dish was reportedly named for John D. Rockefeller because it's so rich. Today there are many versions of this classic, the most common being oysters ON THE HALF SHELL topped with a mixture of chopped spinach, butter, breadcrumbs and seasonings and either baked or broiled. The shells are usually placed on a bed of rock salt, which keeps them from toppling and spilling the ingredients. The original oysters Rockefeller is said to have been made with watercress, not spinach.

ozoni [oh-ZOH-nee] A Japanese soup that's traditionally served at New Year's festivities, although it's popular at other times of the year as well. Also called simply *zoni,* this soup contains pieces of chicken and various other ingredients (depending on the cook) including DASHI, DAIKON and other vegetables. Ozoni is served in deep bowls over rice cakes.

pabellón A meal consisting of shredded meat (sometimes fish), black beans and rice that some refer to as the national dish of Venezuela. Variations proliferate; the most popular include fried plantains and/or a fried egg on top.

pacaya [pah-KAH-yah] The cluster of flowers of the pacaya palm is used in dishes in Central America and Mexico. The flowers are blanched in boiling water briefly before being eaten. They can be used as a vegetable or in salad. For a favorite dish found in El Salvador, Guatemala and Honduras, the pacaya is prepared much like Mexican CHILES RELLENOS. The flower fronds are dipped in a batter of whipped egg whites, salt, chile powder and sometimes corn flour and then quickly fried until the batter is crisp and the flower cooked al dente. The flavor has been variously compared to baby corn, HEARTS OF PALM and asparagus. Jars of preserved pacaya can be found in Central American and Mexican markets.

paccheri *see* Pasta Glossary, page 883

Pacific littleneck clam *see* LITTLENECK CLAM

Pacific oyster Also called the *Japanese oyster,* this species has an elongated fragile shell that can reach up to a foot across. It's found along the Pacific seaboard and is too large and tough to be eaten ON THE HALF SHELL. Because of its size, the Pacific oyster is generally cut up and used in soups, stews and other cooked dishes. *See also* OYSTER.

Pacific pompano *see* BUTTERFISH

Pacific Rim Cuisine *see* FUSION FOOD

Pacific threadfin Medium-sized, silver-gray fish of the group *Polydactylus sexfilis*, found in subtropical and tropical waters in various parts of the world. Also known as *sixfingered threadfin* and *moi* in Hawaii and other parts of Polynesia, these fish are prized for their sweet, delicate flavor. In Hawaii they were called the "fish of kings" and saved for Hawaiian royalty; commoners could be sentenced to death if found eating them. Pacific threadfin is also called *atkaru, becadulce, bou na pana, dagi, gatha, i'ausi, kala, mulet barbe, mulut tikus, nan'you-agonashi* and *umi'umia* in various parts of the world. They are commercially available as aquafarmed (*see* AQUACULTURE) fish, as quantities are extremely limited from the wild. They may be baked, pan-fried or sautéed but many chefs prefer them just poached or steamed. *See also* FISH.

pack date *see* PRODUCT DATING

paddy straw mushrooms *see* STRAW MUSHROOMS

pad thai Thailand's most well known noodle dish, pad thai combines cooked rice noodles, TOFU, shrimp, crushed peanuts, NAM PLA, bean SPROUTS, garlic, chiles and eggs, all stir-fried together.

P

paella; paella pan [pi-AY-yuh; pi-AYL-yuh] A Spanish dish of SAFFRON-flavored rice combined with a variety of meats and shellfish (such as shrimp, lobster, clams, chicken, pork, ham and CHORIZO), garlic, onions, peas, artichoke hearts and tomatoes. It's named after the special two-handled **paella pan** in which it's prepared and served. The pan is wide, shallow and 13 to 14 inches in diameter. A well-made paella will have a caramelized crust of rice, called **socarrat**, at the bottom of the paella pan. It's highly prized.

paglia e fieno [PAH-lyah ay FYAY-noh] Italian for "straw and hay," paglia e fieno is a mixture of yellow pasta (made with egg) and green pasta (based on spinach). The combined pastas (usually a style like TAGLIATELLE or FETTUCCINE) are often served with a cream sauce, with additional color added with bits of ham or RADICCHIO. Dried paglia e fieno can be found in Italian markets and some supermarkets.

paiche [PIE-sheh] This large (200-pound-plus), freshwater fish, also known as *arapaima* and *pirarucu*, is found wild in South America in the Amazon River. Today you're likely to find them only in upscale restaurants, as availability is limited. In Brazil, commercial fishing of paiche is not allowed because of overfishing. Paiche found in restaurants is farm-raised. Part of paiche's appeal is the large steaks derived from it with few or no bones. It has a texture similar to COD or CHILEAN SEA BASS and a rich, elegant flavor.

paillard [PI-yahrd] A SCALLOP of veal (also beef or chicken) that is quickly grilled or sautéed.

pain [PA*N*] 1. French for "bread" or "loaf of bread." Various types of bread in France include: **pain aux noix** (nut bread), **pain complet** (whole wheat bread), **pain d'épices** (spiced or gingerbread), **pain grillé** (toasted bread), **pain de mie** (sliced, packaged white bread), **pain ordinaire** (peasant bread), **pain perdu** (FRENCH TOAST) and **pain petit** (roll). 2. The word *pain* is also used in France to describe a baked, molded loaf of FORCEMEAT bound with a PANADE. Such a meat, poultry, fish or vegetable *pain* can be served hot, cold or at room temperature.

pain perdu [pah*n* pehr-DOO] *see* FRENCH TOAST

pajeon *see* JEON

pakora [pah-KOOR-ah] A deep-fried FRITTER popular in India. The batter is generally based on BESAN flour (ground CHICKPEAS) and can contain most anything including vegetables, fruit, rice, fish or meat. Usually small, the crisply fried pakoras are most often served as appetizers or snacks.

palabok *see* RICE NOODLES

palacsinta [pah-lah-SHIHN-tuh] A thin Hungarian pancake or CRÊPE, referred to by the Austrians as *palatchinken*. They are usually assembled in a stack of 6 or 7, layered with a filling. The savory rendition is often filled with chopped ham, lobster, pork, veal, mushrooms or other vegetables combined with a cream sauce or sour cream. The dessert version is made with slightly sweeter batter and spread with a sweet filling such as jam. Before serving, the stack is cut into wedges.

palak paneer; palak panir [PAH-lehk pah-NEER] In India, *palak* means "spinach"; PANEER is a type of fresh, unripened CHEESE. It's logical, therefore, that palak paneer dishes contain spinach and cheese. Such dishes can include various other ingredients and be prepared in many ways. For example, *palak paneer pulau* is a rice dish with spinach, paneer, lemon juice and various seasonings like CORIANDER, CAYENNE PEPPER, CUMIN and MUSTARD. *Palak paneer sak* contains finely chopped (sometimes puréed) spinach and chiles along with various seasonings and fried cubes of paneer.

pale ale *see* ALE

paleron [pa-leh-ROHN] Term for a French cut of beef that's essentially equivalent to a TOP BLADE STEAK—a cut from the CHUCK section near the shoulder blade.

palm heart *see* HEARTS OF PALM

palmier [pahlm-YAY] Also called *palm leaves,* this crispy delicacy is PUFF PASTRY dough that is sprinkled with granulated sugar, folded and rolled several times, then cut into thin strips. After baking, these golden brown, caramelized pastries are served with coffee or tea or as a dessert accompaniment.

palm oil; palm-kernel oil The reddish-orange oil extracted from the pulp of the fruit of the African palm. It's extremely high in saturated fat (78 percent) and has a distinctive flavor that is popular in West African and Brazilian cooking. **Palm-kernel oil**, though also extremely high in saturated fat, is a different oil extracted from the nut or kernel of palms. It's a yellowish-white color and has a pleasantly mild flavor. Palm-kernel oil is used in the manufacture of margarine and cosmetics. It's usually listed on labels simply as "palm oil." Palm oil is also known as *dendê oil*. *See also* FATS AND OILS.

palm sugar *see* JAGGERY

pamplemousse [pah*n*-pler-MOOSS] French for "GRAPEFRUIT."

palm tree cabbage *see* CAVOLO NERO

pan [PAHN] Spanish for "bread." **Pan integral** is whole wheat bread, **pan tostado** is toasted bread. A **panadería** is a bakery.

panada; panade [*It.*, *Sp.* pah-NAH-dah; *Fr.* pah-NAHD] 1. A thick paste made by mixing breadcrumbs, flour, rice, etc. with water, milk, stock, butter or sometimes egg yolks. It's used to bind meatballs, fish cakes, FORCEMEATS and QUENELLES. 2. A sweet or savory soup made with breadcrumbs and various other ingredients. It may be strained before serving.

Panama orange *see* CALAMONDIN

panarët *see* TSOUREKI

pan bagnat [pan ban-YAH] Popular in Southern France, both in cafés and for picnics, *pan bagnat* is a sandwich composed of a large, split loaf or bun, the inside of which is brushed with olive oil, then filled with green pepper slices, black olives, onion slices, anchovies, tomato slices and hard-cooked egg slices—all drizzled with VINAIGRETTE.

pan-broil; panbroil To cook meats or fish quickly in a heavy, ungreased (or lightly greased) frying pan over high heat. Drippings are poured off as they form.

Panca chile *see* AJÍ PANCA

pancake As one of humankind's oldest forms of bread, the versatile pancake has hundreds of variations and is served for breakfast, lunch and dinner and as appetizers, entrées and desserts. Pancakes begin as a batter that is poured into rounds, either on a griddle or in a skillet, and cooked over high heat. These round cakes vary in thickness from the wafer-thin French CRÊPE to the much thicker American breakfast pancake (also called *hotcake, griddlecake* and *flapjack*). Many countries have specialty pancakes such as Hungarian PALACSINTA and Russian BLINI; SWEDISH PANCAKE.

pancake syrup *see* MAPLE SYRUP

pancake turner *see* TURNERS

pancetta [pan-CHEH-tuh] Called "Italian bacon," pancetta is cured with salt and spices but not traditionally smoked (though there are now a few beechwood- and oak-smoked versions). Flavorful, slightly salty pancetta comes in a sausagelike roll of pink meat and white fat from the hog's belly portion. It's used in Italian cooking to flavor sauces, pasta dishes,

FORCEMEATS, vegetables and meats. Pancetta can be tightly wrapped and refrigerated for up to 3 weeks, or frozen up to 6 months.

pancit bihon *see* RICE NOODLES

pandanus leaves *see* SCREWPINE LEAVES

pan di Spagna [pahn dee SPAH-nyah] Italian for "Spanish bread," referring to SPONGECAKE.

pandowdy Also called *apple pandowdy,* this DEEP-DISH dessert is made of sliced apples, butter, spices, brown sugar or molasses, all topped with a biscuit batter that becomes crisp and crumbly after baking. It can be served hot or at room temperature and is often accompanied by cream or ice cream. The origin of the name is unclear, although some seem to think it comes from the dessert's dowdy (plain and old-fashioned) appearance.

pan drippings *see* DRIPPINGS

pane [PAH-nay] Italian for "bread." **Pane francese** [frahn-CHEH-zeh] is FRENCH BREAD, **pane integrale** [een-the-GRAH-leh] is whole wheat bread and **pane nero** [NEH-roh] is BLACK BREAD. A PANETTERIA is a bread bakery, as opposed to PASTICCERIA, a bakery that sells pastries.

paneer A fresh, unripened cheese, similar to FARMER CHEESE or POT CHEESE. Paneer, also spelled *panir,* is made from whole cow's or buffalo's milk and CURDLED with lemon or lime juice or with WHEY from a previous batch. It's essentially the same cheese as CHENNA, but paneer has been pressed until its texture is firm—comparable to that of TOFU. Paneer, which is customarily diced and sautéed, is used throughout India in a variety of dishes including DAL, salads and vegetables; it's an essential protein source in many vegetarian diets.

paneer saag *see* SAAG

panela *see* PILONCILLO; QUESO BLANCO

panetteria [pah-nayt-tay-REE-ah] Italian for a bakery that sells bread. *See also* PANE; PASTICCERIA.

panettone [pan-uh-TOH-nee] A sweet yeast bread made with raisins, CITRON, PINE NUTS and ANISE. It's baked in a tall, cylindrical, straight-sided mold called a **panettone pan**. Panettone originated in Milan, Italy, and is traditionally served at Christmastime, but also for celebrations such as weddings and christenings. It can be served as a bread, coffeecake or dessert.

panforte [pan-FOHR-teh] Because this confection is a specialty of Siena, Italy, it's also called *Siena cake*. This dense, flat cake is rich with honey, hazelnuts, almonds, candied CITRON, citrus peel, cocoa and spices. It contains only a tiny amount of flour—just enough to hold the fruits and nuts together. After baking, *panforte* becomes hard and chewy.

pan-fry *see* FRY

panino; pl. panini [pah-NEE-noh; pah-NEE-nee] Italian for "small bread," referring to a sandwich or roll.

panir [pah-NEER] *see* PANEER

panko [PAHN-koh] Hailing from Japan, panko is a type of crisp, light, large breadcrumb. The crumbs are used to coat foods for frying or sautéing, as well as in recipes. Because it's coarser than most breadcrumbs, panko creates a deliciously crunchy crust. It can be found in Asian markets and the ethnic section of many supermarkets.

panna [PAH-nah] Italian for "cream."

panna cotta [PAH-nah KOH-tah] Italian for "cooked cream" *panna cotta* is a light, silky eggless custard, which is often flavored with caramel. It's served cold, accompanied with fruit or chocolate sauce.

panocha *see* PILONCILLO

pans, baking *see* BAKEWARE

pans, cooking *see* COOKWARE

pans, materials for *see* COOKWARE AND BAKEWARE MATERIALS

pan sizes *see* Pan Substitution Chart, page 859

pansotti *see* Pasta Glossary, page 883

panucho [PAH-noh-choh] From Mexico's Yucatán peninsula, this popular dish consists of a thick, tortilla-like cake that's cooked on a COMAL (griddle) or skillet without oil, slit, then stuffed with FRIJOLES REFRITOS or black beans. It's then lightly fried and topped with chicken or turkey, avocado, lettuce, tomato and possibly pickled red onion and HABANERO chiles.

panzanella [pahn-zah-NEHL-lah] An Italian bread salad made with onions, tomatoes, basil, olive oil, vinegar and seasonings and chunks of bread. Some versions also include cucumbers, anchovies and/or peppers. More traditional recipes call for soaking the bread in water and then squeezing the water out. Others suggest browning the bread in olive oil before adding it to the salad.

panzarotti; panzerotti [pahn-zah-RAHT-tee] 1. This Italian dish (usually spelled *panzarotti*) consists of a square RAVIOLI-style pouch of dough filled with cheese, tomato sauce and various additions such as spinach, sausage or PEPPERONI. Panzarotti are most often deep-fried, though they can be baked. They can be served plain or with a sauce. 2. A preparation (typically spelled *panzerotti*) that's similar to the first except that it's made with circles of pizza-like dough folded over a filling and sealed, creating a half-moon or crescent shape very much like a CALZONE. These vary in size from bite-sized to a full individual serving. The half-moon panzerotti are often dipped in egg and then fried but can also be baked. Fillings vary from cheese, to a combination of cheese and meat, to savory mixtures such as anchovies, black olives, capers, onions and tomatoes.

papain [puh-PAY-ihn] An enzyme extracted from PAPAYA and employed as a meat tenderizer, and as an agent used to CLARIFY liquids (especially beer). *See also* MEAT TENDERIZERS.

papa roja [pah-pah ROH-hah] Spanish for "red potato" (*see* OCA).

papaw [PA-paw] Both the PAPAYA and the papaw are sometimes referred to as *pawpaw,* which is thoroughly confusing because they're entirely different fruits. The papaw is a North American native that's a member of the CHERIMOYA family. It can range from 2 to 6 inches long and looks like a fat, dark-brown banana. The aromatic flesh is pale yellow and peppered with a profusion of seeds. It has a custardlike texture and a sweet flavor reminiscent of bananas and pears. Papaws are seldom cultivated and are rarely found in markets.

papaya [puh-PI-yuh; puh-PAH-yuh] Like the PAPAW, the papaya is native to the Americas (and in some regions, it's also called *pawpaw*). But with those two comparisons the similarities end. The papaya tree is a horticultural wonder, growing from seed to a 20-foot, fruit-bearing tree in less than 18 months. Papayas are cultivated in semitropical zones around the world and can range in size from 1 to 20 pounds. The papaya variety found most often in the United States is the **Solo**, grown in Hawaii and Florida; it's also called the *Hawaiian papaya*. It's large (about 6 inches long and 1 to 2 pounds in weight) and pear shaped; when ripe, it has a vivid golden-orange skin. The similarly colored flesh is juicy and silky smooth, with an exotic sweet-tart flavor. The rather large center cavity is packed with shiny, grayish-black seeds. Though the peppery seeds are edible (and make a delicious salad dressing), they're generally discarded. The **Mexican papaya** has a green skin and a salmon-red flesh. Look for richly colored papayas that give slightly to palm pressure. Slightly green papayas will ripen quickly at room temperature, especially if placed in a paper bag. Refrigerate completely ripe fruit and use as soon as possible. Ripe papaya is best eaten raw, whereas slightly green fruit can be cooked as a vegetable. Papaya juice (or nectar) is available in many supermarkets and natural food stores. The fruit contains PAPAIN, a digestive enzyme that is used chiefly in MEAT TENDERIZERS. Papaya is a very good source of vitamins A and C. *See also* BABÁCO.

papaya salad *see* SOM TAM

papillon beans *see* MOTH BEANS

papillote [pah-pee-YOHT; PAH-peh-loht] 1. The French word for a paper frill used to decorate the tips of rib bones, such as those on CROWN ROASTS. 2. *En papillote* refers to food baked inside a wrapping of greased PARCHMENT PAPER. As the food bakes and lets off steam, the parchment puffs up into a dome shape. At the table, the paper is slit and peeled back to reveal the food.

pappadam; poppadum [PAH-pah-duhm] A wafer-thin East Indian bread made with LENTIL flour. This TORTILLAlike bread can be unseasoned (as preferred in southern India) or variously flavored with red or black pepper, garlic or other seasonings, as in northern India. *Pappadams* are available in Indian markets in various sizes and flavors. Deep-fried *pappadams* puff up to almost double their original size. Grilling them over an open flame will give them a smoky flavor.

pappardelle *see* Pasta Glossary, page 883

paprika [pa-PREE-kuh; PAP-ree-kuh] Used as a seasoning and garnish for a plethora of savory dishes, paprika is a powder made by grinding aromatic sweet red pepper pods. The pods are quite tough, so several grindings are necessary to produce the proper texture. The flavor of paprika can range from mild to pungent and hot, the color from bright orange-red to deep blood-red. Most commercial paprika comes from Spain, South America, California and Hungary, with the Hungarian variety considered by many to be superior. Indeed, Hungarian cuisine has long used paprika as a mainstay flavoring rather than simply as a garnish. **Pimenton** is a special Spanish paprika made from peppers that have been slowly smoked and dried over oak fires. The process gives the peppers a rich, smoky quality. There are three versions of pimenton—sweet and mild (*dulce*), bittersweet medium-hot (*agridulce*) and hot (*picante*). *Pimentón de Murcia* and *Pimentón de la Vera* have both been awarded PROTECTED DESIGNATION OF ORIGIN status by the European Union. This coveted standing means products labeled as such must be produced using traditional techniques and only in specific areas of Spain. All supermarkets carry mild paprikas, while ethnic markets must be searched out for the more pungent varieties; gourmet markets carry exotic styles such as pimenton. As with all herbs and spices, paprika should be stored in a cool, dark place for no more than 6 months. *See also* SPICES; Seasoning Suggestions, page 891.

paprikás *see* GOULASH

paprikás csirke [PAH-pree-kash CHEER-kah] *see* GOULASH

paratha [pah-RAH-tah] This flaky East Indian bread is made with whole-wheat flour and fried on a griddle. Parathas range from the simple to the exotic. The basic version simply has GHEE (clarified butter) brushed between multiple layers of dough that are then folded and rolled out again. This technique creates a flaky bread resembling puff pastry. More exotic paratha versions are stuffed with various chopped vegetables, fruits, herbs or spices, and named for those ingredients. For example, **aloo paratha** (stuffed with potatoes and onions), **gobi paratha** (cauliflower), PANEER **paratha** (cheese) and **pudina paratha** (mint).

P

parboil To partially cook food by boiling it briefly in water. This time-saving technique is used in particular for dense foods such as carrots. If parboiled, they can be added at the last minute with quick-cooking ingredients (such as bean sprouts and celery) in preparations such as STIR-FRY dishes. The parboiling insures that all the ingredients will complete cooking at the same time. *See also* BLANCH; PARCOOK.

parboiled rice *see* RICE

parch, to To dry grains or starchy vegetables like corn, peas and beans by roasting slightly without burning.

parchment paper A heavy, grease- and moisture-resistant paper with a number of culinary uses including lining baking pans, wrapping foods that are to be baked en PAPILLOTE and to make disposable PASTRY BAGS. Parchment paper is available in gourmet kitchenware stores and many supermarkets, either in rolls or in packages of 8- or 9-inch rounds.

parcook To partially cook a food that will be finished later.

pare To remove the thin outer layer of foods like fruits and vegetables with a small, short-bladed knife (called a paring knife) or with a vegetable peeler.

pareve; parve [PAHR-uh-vuh; PAHR-vuh] A Jewish term describing food made without animal or dairy ingredients. According to KOSHER dietary laws, animal food cannot be consumed at the same meal with dairy food, but a pareve food may be combined or eaten with either. In order to be pareve, breads and cakes must be made with vegetable oils and not with butter or other animal fat.

parfait [pahr-FAY] 1. In the United States, this dessert consists of ice cream layered with flavored syrup or fruit and whipped cream. It's often topped with whipped cream, nuts and sometimes a MARASCHINO CHERRY. 2. A French parfait is a frozen custard dessert made with egg yolks, sugar, whipped cream and a flavoring such as fruit purée. In French, *parfait* means "perfect," which is how many view this dessert. Both American and French parfaits are served in tall, narrow, footed "parfait glasses."

paring knife *see* KNIFE

Paris-Brest [pa-ree-BREHST] A delightful French dessert said to have been created by a pastry chef in honor of a bicycle race between Paris and Brest. It consists of a baked almond-topped CHOUX PASTRY ring (patterned after a bicycle tire) that is split and filled with a praline-flavored BUTTERCREAM.

parisienne sauce [puh-ree-zee-EHN] A creamy sauce, classically used to top cold asparagus, made by blending cream cheese, oil, lemon juice, CHERVIL and sometimes PAPRIKA. *See also* SAUCE.

Parker House roll; Parkerhouse A yeast roll that became famous during the late 19th century at the Parker House, a Boston hotel. It gets its special shape when an off-center crease is made in a round piece of dough before it's folded in half. The result after baking is a light, puffy bun.

Parma ham [PAHR-muh] The true PROSCIUTTO, this superior Italian ham hails from northern Italy's province of Parma, the same area famous for Parmesan cheese. The special diet of chestnuts and WHEY (from the cheese-making process) that Parma pigs enjoy results in an excellent quality of meat. Parma hams are seasoned, salt-cured and air-dried but not smoked. They have a rosy-brown flesh that is firm and dense. The best of these special hams come from the little village of Langhirano, just south of the city of Parma. Parma hams are usually thinly sliced and eaten raw as an appetizer (often with melon) but they can be used in cooking as well. Italians use the rind to flavor soups. *See also* HAM.

Parmentier [par-mawn-TYAY] A culinary term referring to dishes garnished or made with potatoes. This designator honors Frenchman Antoine-Augustin Parmentier, an 18th-century French botanist who devoted his lifetime to promoting the potato's attributes and who persuaded Louis XVI to encourage the cultivation of potatoes.

Parmesan [PAHR-muh-zahn] This hard, dry cheese is made from skimmed or partially skimmed cow's milk. It has a hard, pale-golden rind and a straw-colored interior with a rich, sharp flavor. There are Parmesan cheeses made in Argentina, Australia and the United States, but none compares with Italy's preeminent **Parmigiano-Reggiano**, with its granular texture that melts in the mouth. Whereas most U.S. renditions are typically aged a minimum of 10 months, Parmigiano-Reggianos are more often aged at least 2 years. Those labeled *stravecchio* have been aged 3 years, while *stravecchiones* are 4 or more years old. Their complex flavor and extremely granular texture are a result of the long aging. The words Parmigiano-Reggiano stenciled on the rind mean that the cheese was produced in the areas of Bologna, Mantua, Modena or Parma (from which the name of this cheese originated). The name *Parmigiano* is used in parts of Italy for GRANA CHEESES that don't meet PROTECTED DESIGNATION OF ORIGIN requirements for Parmigiano-Reggiano, such as specific areas of production, what the cattle eat, lengthy aging and so on. Parmesan cheeses in other countries have comparatively lax regulations. Parmesans are primarily used for grating and in Italy are termed *grana*, meaning "grain" and referring to their granular textures. Pregrated Parmesan is available but in no way compares with the freshly grated cheese—save your money. Both domestic and imported Parmesans are available in specialty cheese stores, Italian markets and many supermarkets. Parmigiano-Reggiano and most other Parmesans are made from partially skimmed or skimmed cow's milk, which delivers a cheese with a FAT CONTENT of around 32 percent. *See also* CHEESE.

parmigiana, alla [pahr-muh-ZHAH-nuh] A term describing food that is made or cooked with PARMESAN CHEESE. For instance, veal parmigiana is a pounded veal cutlet dipped in an egg-milk solution and then into a mixture of breadcrumbs, grated Parmesan cheese and seasonings. The cutlet is then sautéed and covered with a tomato sauce. **Eggplant parmigiana** consists of eggplant slices prepared in the same manner. Slices of MOZZARELLA CHEESE are sometimes melted on top of the food prior to adding the tomato sauce.

Parmigiano-Reggiano [pahr-muh-ZHAH-noh reh-zhee-AH-noh] *see* PARMESAN CHEESE

parsley In ancient times parsley wreaths were used to ward off drunkenness—though proof of their efficacy in that capacity is scarce. Today, this slightly peppery, fresh-flavored herb is more commonly used as a flavoring and garnish. Though there are more than 30 varieties of this herb, the most popular are **curly-leaf parsley** and the more strongly flavored **Italian** or **flat-leaf parsley**. Fresh curly leaf parsley is widely available year-round, while Italian parsley must sometimes be searched out in gourmet produce markets. Parsley is sold in bunches and should be chosen for its bright-green leaves that show no sign of wilting. Wash fresh parsley, shaking off excess moisture, and wrap first in paper towels, then in a plastic bag. Refrigerate for up to a week. **Dried parsley** is available in the spice section of most supermarkets but bears little resemblance to the flavor of fresh. Parsley is an excellent source of vitamins A and C. *See also* HERBS; Seasoning Suggestions, page 891.

P

parsley root Also called *Hamburg parsley* and *turnip-rooted parsley,* this parsley subspecies is grown for its beige, carrotlike root, which tastes like a carrot-celery cross with a touch of CELERY ROOT. It's used in soups, stews and simply as a vegetable. Parsley root is in season from about August to May. Choose firm roots without soft spots; the leaves should be feathery and bright green. Refrigerate in a plastic bag for up to a week. Remove leaves just before using roots, which may be peeled or not. The leaves may be used in the same manner as regular parsley.

parsnip Europeans brought the parsnip to the United States in the early 1600s but this creamy-white root has never become an American favorite. The first frost of the year converts the parsnip's starch to sugar and gives it a pleasantly sweet flavor. Fresh parsnips are available year-round with the peak period during fall and winter. Look for small to medium, well-shaped roots; avoid limp, shriveled or spotted parsnips. They can be refrigerated in a plastic bag for up to 2 weeks. Parsnips are suitable for almost any method of cooking including baking, boiling, sautéing and steaming. They're often boiled, then mashed like potatoes. Parsnips contain small amounts of iron and vitamin C.

parson's nose *see* POPE'S NOSE

partridge Strictly speaking, there are two main varieties of this GAME BIRD—the **gray partridge** and the **red-legged partridge**—neither of which is a North American native. In various regions of the United States, the name "partridge" is erroneously applied to other birds including the ruffed grouse, QUAIL and bobwhite. All of these birds are plump and have white, tender, slightly gamey flesh. Frozen partridges are available at some specialty meat and poultry markets. They usually weigh 12 to 14 ounces. Partridges can be cooked in a variety of ways including roasting, broiling and braising. The meat also makes a tasty addition to soups and stews.

partridge sole *see* SOLE

pasanda [puh-SAHN-duh] Indian/Pakistani curry dish that dates back to the Moghul rulers of India (*see* MOGHUL CUISINE). Although it's usually associated with a mild curry containing almonds, cream or yogurt and mild spices, the name actually pertains to preparing the meat, which is pounded, cut into strips and marinated. Traditionally, lamb or boneless chicken is used.

pasilla chile [pah-SEE-yah] In its fresh form this CHILE is called a CHILACA. It's generally 6 to 8 inches long and 1 to 1½ inches in diameter. The rich-flavored, medium-hot pasilla is a blackish-brown color, which is why it's also called *chile negro*. Its SCOVILLE SCALE rating ranges from 1,000 to 4,000. This chile is sold whole, and powdered. It's particularly good for use in sauces.

paskha; pashka [PAHS-kah; PAHSH-kah] A Russian sweet cheese mold traditionally served at Easter. It consists of a combination of sweetened POT CHEESE (or cottage cheese), nuts (usually almonds) and candied or dried fruit. Classically, this mixture is molded into the shape of a four-sided pyramid. The paskha is decorated with nuts or candy to form the letters *XB*, which stands for "Christ is risen." Paskha is the traditional accompaniment for the sweet yeast cake KULICH.

passion fruit; passionfruit This tropical fruit is said to be named not for the passionate propensity it promotes but because particular parts of the plant's flowers resemble different symbols of Christ's crucifixion, such as the crown of thorns. Though native to Brazil, passion fruit (also called *granadilla*) is now also grown in Australia, California, Florida, Hawaii (where it's called *lilikoi*) and New Zealand. The most common variety marketed in the United States is egg-shaped and about 3 inches long. When ripe, it has a dimpled, deep purple-brown skin and a golden, jellylike pulp surrounding tiny, edible black seeds. The flavor is seductively sweet-tart and the fragrance tropical and perfumy. **Vanilla passion fruit** is elongated (rather like a straight banana) and yellow. This variety—also sometimes dubbed *yellow* or *banana passion fruit*—has a pale green flesh and a flavor akin to vanilla. Depending on the locale, fresh passion fruit is available year-round in Latin and produce markets and many supermarkets. Passion fruit will be shriveled looking when fully ripe. Ripen fruit at room temperature until it reaches that stage. Store ripe passion fruit in the refrigerator for up to a week. It can be served plain as a dessert or used to flavor a variety of foods like sauces, ice creams and beverages. Canned passion-fruit nectar is available in many supermarkets. Passion fruit contains a small amount of vitamins A and C.

pasta [PAH-stuh] Though many pundits claim that Marco Polo brought the idea of noodles back with him to Italy from China, the truth is that this food form existed in both places independently long before Polo's expeditions. In fact, archaeological documentation now points to the fact that noodles probably originated in central Asia, possibly dating back to at least 1000 B.C. Almost every country has a form of pasta. The Germans enjoy SPAETZLE, Poles have their PIEROGI and throughout the Orient there are dozens of noodles, usually made with rice or soy flour rather than wheat flour (see ASIAN NOODLES). In Italian, the word *pasta* means "paste," and refers to the dough made by combining durum wheat flour called SEMOLINA with a liquid, usually water or milk. The term "pasta" is used broadly and generically to describe a wide variety of noodles made from this type of dough. Some doughs have a little egg added, though doughs made with only flour and eggs are generally referred to as NOODLES. There are hundreds of shapes, sizes, thicknesses and colors of pasta.

MACARONI and SPAGHETTI are probably the most popular, though each of those categories has many size and shape varieties. Additionally, there are dozens of fancy shapes such as conchiglie (shells), farfalle (bows) and rotelle (little corkscrews). Other pastas, such as ravioli and tortellini, have fillings. Some pastas are colored, often with spinach (green), beet juice or tomato paste (red) and squid ink (charcoal gray). Pasta also comes in both dried and fresh forms. As a general rule, imported **dried pasta** is superior to American factory-made products, mainly because the imported pasta is only made with semolina, which doesn't absorb too much water and is pleasantly firm when cooked AL DENTE. A good selection of dried pastas can be found in most supermarkets, and an even broader variety is available in Italian markets. It should be stored airtight in a cool, dry place and can be kept almost indefinitely. **Fresh pasta** is often made with eggs instead of water; it can increasingly be found in many supermarkets and is always available in Italian markets. Because it's highly perishable, it must be refrigerated airtight and can be stored in this manner for about 4 days. It can also be frozen for up to a month. Fresh pastas cook in a fraction of the time necessary for dried pastas. When it comes to saucing pasta, a general rule is to use light sauces for delicate pastas like capelli d'angelo and chunky, heavy sauces for sturdy pastas such as fusilli. *See also* Pasta Glossary, page 883.

pasta e fagioli [PAH-stah eh fah-JYOH-lee] Italian for "pasta and beans." This dish is actually a hearty soup of pasta, beans, vegetables and pork, flavored with garlic and olive oil.

pasta filata [PAH-stuh fee-(fih)-LAH-tuh] Italian for "spun paste," *pasta filata* refers to the stretched-curd CHEESES made famous in Italy, such as MOZZARELLA, PROVOLONE and CACIOCAVALLO. Such cheeses are made using a special technique whereby the curd is given a hot WHEY bath, then kneaded and stretched to the desired pliable consistency. At this point, the cheese can be formed into the desired shape, which can range from a simple ball to a braid. Such cheeses are also called *plastic-curd, pulled-curd, spun curd* and *stretched-curd.*

pasta machines There are two basic types of machines that can be used to make homemade pasta—the roller type and the extruder type. **Roller-type pasta machines** come in hand-cranked and electric versions. Both come with several attachments—usually one pair of smooth rollers for rolling out the sheets of dough, and two notched pairs (one narrow and one wide) used to cut noodles. With this type of machine, the dough is run between the smooth rollers at increasingly thinner settings until it reaches the desired thickness. The sheets of dough are then fed through either pair of the notched rollers, which cut them into noodles. Some machines have additional attachments, such as crinkle-edge cutters for making lasagne noodles. **Extruder pasta machines** mix the dough inside the unit, then force it out through special plates with variously shaped perforations. Depending on the perforations, solid or hollow-shaped pastas can be produced. Both types of pasta machines are generally available in gourmet kitchenware stores and the small-appliance section of many department stores.

pasta primavera *see* PRIMAVERA

pastel de tres leches [pahss-TAYL day trays LAY-chays] A popular special-occasion dessert throughout Latin America, *pastel de tres leches* means "cake of three milks" (or "three milks cake"). Though thought to have originated in Nicaragua, it's also found in other countries including Costa Rica, Cuba, Guatemala, Mexico, Venezuela and now the United States. The name *tres leches* ("three milks") refers to an integral part of the cake—a sauce made with EVAPORATED MILK, SWEETENED CONDENSED MILK and fresh milk or cream. Once the baked cake has cooled, the top is perforated and the sauce drizzled over it so it can saturate the cake. The resulting cake, which is dense and moist but not overly wet, is usually finished with a topping of whipped cream or meringue.

pastelle *see* FUNCHE

pasteurize; pasteurization [PAS-chuh-rize; PAS-tuh-rize] To kill bacteria by heating milk or other liquids to moderately high temperatures for a short period of time. Milk must be heated to at least 145°F for not less than 30 minutes or at least 161°F for 15 seconds, and then rapidly cooled to between 45° and 55°F. The process was discovered by the famous French scientist Louis Pasteur while he was researching the cause of beer and wine spoilage. Although pasteurization is used in beer processing and for some wines and fruit juices, the major beneficiary is milk. Pasteurization kills the bacteria in milk that were once responsible for transmitting diseases such as typhoid fever, tuberculosis, scarlet fever, polio and dysentery. LACTIC ACID bacteria, which cause milk to sour, are not destroyed by pasteurization. Neither is the food value of milk greatly diminished by the process. *See also* HOMOGENIZE.

pasticceria [pah-steet-cheh-REE-ah] Italian for "pastry shop." *See also* PANE for *panetteria*.

pastilla [pah-STEE-yuh] *see* B'STEEYA

pastille [pas-TEEL] A small, round, hard confection made of sugar, water and various flavorings. In the United States pastilles are usually referred to as drops, as in lemon drops.

pastina *see* Pasta Glossary, page 883

pastis [pas-TEES] 1. Similar to PERNOD, this clear, strong (90 PROOF), licorice-flavored APÉRITIF is very popular in the south of France. It's usually mixed with water, which turns it whitish and cloudy. 2. Any of various yeast-leavened pastries of southwestern France such as *pastis Beranais,* which is flavored with brandy and ORANGE-FLOWER WATER.

pastitsio [pah-STEET-see-oh] A baked Greek casserole dish consisting of pasta (SPAGHETTI or MACARONI), ground beef or lamb, grated cheese, tomatoes, seasonings (including cinnamon) and BÉCHAMEL.

pasticho [pas-TEE-choh] Venezuela's answer to LASAGNA and very similar to Greece's PASTITSIO, this oven-baked casserole layers pasta (usually MACARONI), ground beef, ham, mozzarella and Parmesan, all topped with a rich BÉCHAMEL.

pasto [PAHS-toh] Italian for "meal."

pastrami [puh-STRAH-mee] A highly seasoned beef made from a cut of plate, BRISKET or ROUND. After the fat is trimmed, the meat's surface is rubbed with salt and a seasoning paste that can include garlic, ground peppercorns, cinnamon, red pepper, cloves, allspice and coriander seeds. The meat is dry-cured, smoked and cooked. Pastrami can be served hot or cold, usually as a sandwich on rye bread. It's widely available in chunks or presliced in most supermarkets.

pastry 1. Any of various UNLEAVENED doughs, the basics of which include butter (or other fat), flour and water. Examples include PUFF PASTRY, PÂTE BRISÉE (pie pastry) and PÂTE SUCRÉE (sweet short pastry). 2. A general term for sweet baked goods such as DANISH PASTRIES and NAPOLEONS.

pastry bag A cone-shaped bag with two open ends. The small end is pointed and can be fitted with decorative tips of different sizes and designs, while doughs, whipped cream, fillings, etc. are spooned into the large end. When the bag is squeezed, the contents are forced through the tip. Pastry bags have a multitude of uses including decorating cakes, forming pastries or cookies and piping decorative borders. They come in various sizes and can be made of a variety of materials, including nylon and plastic-lined cotton or canvas, polyester and plastic. Pastry bags can be found in gourmet shops, some supermarkets and the kitchenware section of most department stores.

pastry blender A kitchen implement consisting of 5 or 6 parallel U-shaped, sturdy steel wires, both ends of which are attached to a wooden handle. It's used in making pastry dough to cut cold fat (usually butter) into a flour mixture, evenly distributing the tiny pieces of fat without warming them.

pastry brush A small brush used for applying glazes to breads, pastries, cookies, etc. either before or after baking. The best all-purpose size has a width of 1 to $1^1/_2$ inches. Pastry brushes can be made of nylon bristles, sterilized natural bristles or goose feathers. Natural-bristle brushes are considered best because they're softer and hold more liquid. Goose feathers are excellent for egg glazes because they leave a thin, even coating. The harder nylon bristles will last longer but may melt if accidentally touched to a hot surface. Softer bristles are especially desirable for delicate unbaked pastries where harder bristles might leave unwanted marks.

pastry cloth A large, lightweight canvas cloth on which pastry dough can be rolled out. Rubbing flour down into the fibers makes the pastry cloth an excellent nonstick surface. After use, the cloth must be thoroughly cleaned before storing. Otherwise, any fat residue in the cloth will turn rancid and affect the flavor of future doughs.

pastry comb *see* CAKE COMB

pastry cream *see* CRÈME PATISSIÈRE

pastry flour *see* FLOUR

pastry jagger *see* PASTRY WHEEL

pastry scraper *see* DOUGH SCRAPER

pastry wheel A small utensil consisting of a sharp cutting wheel attached to a handle. Small pastry wheels with plain cutting edges are used to mark and cut rolled-out pastry or cookie dough. Larger, plain-edged wheels are used to cut pizza. **Jagging wheels** or **pastry jaggers** have fluted edges that cut a decorative design in pastry doughs.

pasty [PAS-tee] *see* CORNISH PASTY

Patagonian toothfish Marketed as *Chilean sea bass*, this popular fish has silky, snow-white flesh with a rich, mild flavor. It's very versatile and lends itself to baking, broiling, grilling or sautéing. Patagonian toothfish live in the cold coastal seas of the southern Atlantic, southern Pacific, Indian and Southern oceans. Because of its popularity, the toothfish population is in severe decline from overfishing. In addition, concern about high mercury levels has elicited warnings to limit the amount of toothfish in the diet (currently one to two times per month). The Antarctic toothfish is a close relative and very similar.

patata [pah-TAH-tah] Italian for "potato."

pâte [PAHT] This word (without an accent over the "e") is French for "dough," "paste," "batter" or "pastry." PÂTE BRISÉE is pie dough or short pastry; PÂTE SUCRÉE is sweet pastry. PASTA is translated as *pâte alimentaire,* ALMOND PASTE as *pâte d'amandes* and TOMATO PASTE as *pâte de tomates.*

pâté [pah-TAY; pa-TAY] French for "pie," this word—with accent over the "e"—generally refers to various elegant, well-seasoned ground-meat preparations. A pâté can be satiny-smooth and spreadable or, like country pâté, coarsely textured. It can be made from a finely ground or chunky mixture of meats (such as pork, veal, liver or ham), fish, poultry, game, vegetables, etc. Seasonings and fat are typically also included in the mixture. Pâtés may be cooked in a crust, in which case they're referred to as **pâté en croûte**. They may also be cooked in a pork fat–lined container called a terrine (or any other similar-size mold), in which case they're called **pâté en terrine**. Traditional parlance says that when such a mixture is cooked and served in a terrine, the dish is also called a terrine, and when unmolded it becomes a pâté. Today, however, the two terms are often used interchangeably. Pâtés may be hot or cold and are usually served as a first course or appetizer.

patea *see* PATHIA

pâte à choux [paht ah SHOO] *see* CHOUX PASTRY

pâte brisée [paht bree-ZAY] A French term for "SHORT PASTRY," a rich flaky dough used for sweet and savory crusts for dishes such as pies, tarts, QUICHES and BARQUETTES.

pâte de coings *see* QUINCE

pâté de foie gras *see* FOIE GRAS

pâte fermentée *see* YEAST STARTER

pâte feuilletée [paht fuh-yuh-TAY] The French term for "PUFF PASTRY." *See also* FEUILLETAGE.

pâte sablée [PAHT sah-BLAY] A very rich, sweetened, SHORT pastry used for FLANS, pies and tarts. Sablé is French for "sand" and this pastry dough is rich and crumbly, more so than even PÂTE SUCRÉE.

pâte sucrée [paht soo-KRAY] A French term for a rich, sweetened SHORT pastry used for desserts such as pies, tarts and filled cookies.

pathia; patia; patea [pah-TEE-uh] Spicy, sweet-and-sour curry dish particularly popular with the Parsi community in western India. Dried red chiles and fresh green chiles provide the heat; sugar, sweet chutney and/or sweet fruit create the sweetness; and lemon or lime juice, vinegar or TAMARIND add the sour. Chicken, lamb or prawns are common ingredients.

patia *see* PATHIA

patis [pah-TEES] A pungent-flavored sauce made from salted, fermented fish. Patis is used both as a flavoring sauce and condiment. *See also* BAGOONG; FISH SAUCE; SAUCE; SHRIMP SAUCE.

pâtisserie [puh-TIHS-uh-ree; pah-tees-REE] This French word has three different meanings: 1. The general category of sweet baked goods including cakes, cookies, cream puffs, etc. 2. The art of pastrymaking. 3. A shop where pastries are made and sold.

pâtissier [pah-tees-SYAY] *see* BRIGADE SYSTEM

pattona *see* CASTAGNACCIO

patty 1. A small, thin round of ground or finely chopped food such as meat (as with a hamburger patty), fish or vegetables. 2. A round, flat piece of candy, such as the peppermint patty.

pattypan squash A round, flattish summer squash with a scalloped edge, which is why it's also called *scalloped squash.* Tender young pattypans can be identified by their pale-green skin (which turns white as the squash matures) and small size (3 to 4 inches in diameter). The thin, smooth to slightly bumpy skin, is usually not removed. Pattypan squash can be cooked the same as other summer squash. *See also* SQUASH.

patty shell Usually made of PUFF PASTRY, this small cup-shaped shell is used to hold creamed dishes of meat, poultry, fish or vegetables. Fresh patty shells are available in bakeries, while frozen unbaked shells can usually be found in supermarkets.

paua [pah-OO-ah] *see* ABALONE

paupiette [poh-PYEHT] A thin slice of meat—usually veal or beef—rolled around a filling of finely ground meat or vegetables. The paupiette can be fried, baked or braised in wine or stock. Paupiettes, also called ROULADES, are sometimes wrapped in bacon before being cooked.

pavé [pah-VAY] French for a square or rectangular "paving stone" or "cobblestone." In culinary usage the word refers to: 1. A square or rectangular dessert consisting of several layers of sponge cake filled with BUTTERCREAM or other filling and coated with FROSTING; 2. a square-shaped, aspic-coated mousse made of meat, fish or poultry, usually served cold. It can also be made with a sweet mousse.

Pavlova [pav-LOH-vuh] Hailing from Australia, this famous dessert is named after the Russian ballerina Anna Pavlova. It consists of a crisp MERINGUE base topped with whipped cream and fruit such as strawberries, PASSION FRUIT and KIWI. A pavlova is usually served with fruit sauce or additional whipped cream.

pawpaw [PAW-paw] Another name for both PAPAYA and PAPAW.

PDO *see* PROTECTED DESIGNATION OF ORIGIN (PDO)

pea There are many varieties of pea, all members of the LEGUME family. Some—like the ENGLISH PEA (the common garden pea)—are grown to be eaten fresh, removed from their pods. Others, like the FIELD PEA, are grown specifically to be used dried. POD PEAS are those that are eaten pod and all, namely, the SNOW PEA and SUGAR SNAP PEA. *See also* BLACK-EYED PEA; CHICKPEA; PEA SHOOTS.

pea bean The smallest of the dried white beans, the others being NAVY BEAN, GREAT NORTHERN BEAN and MARROW BEAN (in order of ascending size). Pea beans are very popular in the Northeast and are the first choice for BOSTON BAKED BEANS. Some producers and packagers do not differentiate between pea beans and navy beans, so packages identified as white beans may contain both. Pea beans are also used in soups. They require long, slow cooking. *See also* BEANS.

peach Native to China, this fruit came to Europe (and subsequently to the New World) via Persia, hence its ancient appellation *Persian apple*. Throughout its evolution, the peach has propagated hundreds of varieties that vary greatly in color and flavor. In general, a peach falls into one of two classifications—**freestone**, in which case the stone or pit falls easily away from the flesh, and **clingstone**, where the fruit adheres stubbornly to the pit. It's the freestones that are more commonly found in markets, while the firmer-textured clingstones are widely used for commercial purposes. The peach's velvety skin can range from pink-blushed creamy-white to red-blushed yellow and its flesh from pinkish-white to yellow-gold. Peaches are available from May to October in most regions of the United States. Southern hemisphere imports are frequently found in coastal cities during the winter. Look for intensely fragrant fruit that gives slightly to palm pressure. Because peaches bruise easily they should be thoroughly perused for soft spots. Avoid those with signs of greening. To ripen underripe peaches, place them in a paper bag, pierce the bag in several places, and set it aside at room temperature for a couple of days. Adding an apple to the bag will speed ripening because apples exude ethylene gas, which speeds the ripening process. Refrigerate ripe peaches in a plastic bag for up to 5 days. Bring to room temperature before eating. Because of their fuzzy skins, peaches are often peeled before eating. This can be done easily by BLANCHING the peach in boiling water for about 30 seconds, then plunging it into icy-cold water. Canned peaches are available, sliced or in halves, packed either in sugar syrup or water. Frozen peach slices are also available, as are dried peach halves. Peaches contain both vitamins A and C.

peach Melba A dessert created in the late 1800s by the famous French chef Escoffier for Dame Nellie Melba, a popular Australian opera singer. It's made with two peach halves that have been poached in syrup and cooled. Each peach half is placed hollow side down on top of a scoop of vanilla ice cream, then topped with MELBA (raspberry) SAUCE and sometimes with whipped cream and sliced almonds.

peanut Though today peanuts are considered a rather common nut, ancient Peruvians held them in such high esteem that they buried pots of peanuts with their mummified dead to nourish them during their long journey to the hereafter. Peanuts are widely grown throughout the southern United States and about half the national crop is used to make PEANUT BUTTER. At one stage of its growth, the peanut plant looks very much like the common garden pea plant . . . which is not at all illogical, since the peanut is actually a LEGUME, not a NUT. The nuts (or seeds) have a papery brown skin and are contained in a thin, netted, tan-colored pod. Peanuts are also called *groundnuts* (as well as *earthnuts* and, in the South, GOO-BERS or *goober peas*) because, after flowering, the plant bends down to the earth and buries its pods in the ground. Though there are several varieties of peanut, the two most popular are the Virginia and the Spanish peanut. The **Virginia peanut** is larger and more oval in shape than the smaller, rounder **Spanish peanut**. Peanuts are sold unshelled and shelled. The former should have clean, unbroken shells and should not rattle when shaken. Shelled peanuts, often available in vacuum-sealed jars or cans, are usually roasted and sometimes salted. Refrigerate unshelled peanuts tightly wrapped for up to 6 months. Vacuum-packed shelled peanuts can be stored unopened at room temperature for up to a year. Once opened, shelled peanuts should be refrigerated airtight and used within 3 months. Peanuts are high in fat and rich in protein. The two most popular peanut by-products are PEANUT BUTTER and PEANUT OIL.

peanut butter Developed in 1890 and promoted as a health food at the 1904 St. Louis World's Fair, peanut butter is a blend of ground shelled peanuts, vegetable oil (often hydrogenated) and usually a small amount of salt. Some contain sugar and additives to improve creaminess and prevent the oil from separating. It takes around 850 peanuts to produce an 18-ounce jar of peanut butter. **Reduced-fat peanut butter** only contains about 60 percent of the peanuts of the regular version, replacing them with maltodextrin (a type of cornstarch) and soy protein. Both versions contain the same number of calories per serving (about 190), but reduced-fat peanut butter has 12 grams of fat, compared to 16 grams for the regular. **Natural peanut butter** uses only peanuts and oil, usually PEANUT OIL. Peanut butter is sold in two forms—smooth or chunky, which contains bits of peanut. It can be easily made at home in a blender or food processor. Natural peanut butter must be refrigerated after opening and can be stored in this manner up to 6 months. Most other commercial peanut butters can be stored at room temperature for up to 6 months. Peanut butter is high in fat and contains fair amounts of iron, niacin and protein. *See also* PEANUT.

peanut oil A clear oil pressed from peanuts; it is used for salads and, because it has a high SMOKE POINT, especially prized for frying. Most American peanut oils are mild-flavored, whereas Chinese peanut oils have a distinctive peanut flavor. Peanut oil is about 50 percent monounsaturated and 30 percent polyunsaturated. If stored in a cool, dark place it will keep indefinitely. *See also* FATS AND OILS.

pea pods *see* POD PEAS

pear There are over 5,000 varieties of pears grown throughout the world in temperate climates. France is known for its superior pears and in the United States most of the crop comes from California, Oregon and Washington. Mother Nature protected the easily bruised pear by making it better when picked while still hard. Unlike most fruit, it improves in both texture and flavor after it's picked. Pears range in shape from spherical to bell-shaped and in color from celadon green to golden yellow to tawny red. Ripe pears are juicy and, depending on the variety, can range in flavor from spicy to sweet to tart-sweet. Pears are in season from late July to early spring, depending on the variety and the region. Choose those that are fragrant and free of blemishes. Store at room temperature until ripe; refrigerate ripe fruit. It's not necessary to peel pears before using, but, if they are peeled, they should be dipped in ACIDULATED WATER to prevent the flesh from browning. For cooking, choose fruit that is still quite firm. Pears are also available dried as well as canned in either water, SUGAR SYRUP or their natural juice. They contain small amounts of phosphorus and vitamin A. *See also* ANJOU; ASIAN; BARTLETT; BOSC; COMICE; SECKEL.

pearl barley *see* BARLEY

pearl onion *see* ONION

pearl sago *see* SAGO

pearl tea *see* BUBBLE TEA

pear pepper *see* ROCOTO CHILE

pea shoots The thin tendrils and uppermost leaves of pea plants, typically SNOW PEAS, but also ENGLISH PEAS. The fragile pea shoots are tender yet crisp with a subtle pea flavor. They can be found in farmer's markets, some specialty produce stores and Chinese markets (where they're called *dau miu*). Pea shoots are available year-round, depending on the locale, but are best in the spring. Choose those that are bright green and fresh looking with no sign of yellowing. Refrigerate shoots (wrapped in a paper towel, then in a plastic bag) for no more than 2 days. Wash and remove excess moisture in a salad spinner or by blotting with a paper towel. Snip off any thick stems and chop tendrils and leaves as desired. Pea shoots may be used raw in salads or stirred into hot dishes (such as soups or STIR-FRYS) at the last minute.

pecan [pih-KAHN; pih-KAN; PEE-kan] This native American nut, a member of the HICKORY family, has a fat content of over 70 percent. Pecan trees prefer temperate climates and are widely grown in Georgia, Oklahoma and Texas, and as far north as Virginia. The nut's smooth, tan shell averages about 1 inch in length and, though hard, is relatively thin. The buttery-rich kernel is golden-brown on the outside and beige inside. Chopped or halved shelled pecans are available year-round in cellophane packages, cans and jars. Though unshelled pecans are also available throughout the year, their peak season is during the autumn months. Choose unshelled pecans by their clean, unblemished, uncracked shells. When shaken, the kernel should not rattle. Store tightly wrapped in a cool, dry place for up to 6 months. Refrigerate shelled pecans in an airtight container for up to 3 months, or freeze up to 6 months. Care must be taken when storing pecans because their high fat content invites rancidity. Pecans are favorites for eating out of hand, as well as for using in a variety of sweet and savory dishes. Probably the most well-known pecan dessert is the deliciously rich Southern pecan pie, usually dolloped generously with whipped cream. *See also* NUTS.

pecan rice *see* WILD PECAN RICE

pecora [PEH-koh-rah] Italian for "sheep," seen on the labels of some cheese made with that milk.

pecorino [peh-kuh-REE-noh] In Italy, cheese made from sheep's milk is known as *pecorino*. The most widely known is *Pecorino Romano*, followed by *Pecorino Sardo, Pecorino Siciliano* and *Pecorino Toscano*, all of which have DENOMINAZIONE DI ORIGINE CONTROLLATA (DOC) status. There are myriad non-DOC pecorinos, most of which are aged and classified as GRANA (hard, granular and sharply flavored); however, the young, unaged *Ricotta pecorino* is soft, white and mild in flavor. Aged pecorinos range in color from off-white to pale yellow and have a sharp, pungent flavor. These hard, dry cheeses are good for grating and are used mainly in cooking. They can be used in any recipe that calls for PARMESAN CHEESE, especially if a sharper flavor is desired. *See also* CHEESE.

pectin [PEHK-tihn] Present in various ripe fruits and vegetables, this natural, water-soluble substance is used for its thickening properties in the preparation of jams, jellies and preserves. The gelatinlike pectin is added to fruits that don't have enough natural pectin to JELL by themselves. If pectin isn't used, the alternative is to continue cooking the mixture until it's reduced to the desired consistency. Pectin only works properly when mixed with the correct balance of sugar and acid. It's available in two forms—liquid (usually made from apples) and dry (from citrus fruits or apples).

peel *n.* 1. The rind or skin of a fruit or vegetable, such as a tomato or potato peel. 2. A flat, smooth, shovellike tool used to slide pizzas and yeast breads onto a BAKING STONE or BAKING SHEET in an oven. Also called a *pizza peel* and *baker's peel,* this implement is made of hardwood and can usually be found in gourmet specialty shops. **peel** *v.* To use a knife or VEGETABLE PEELER to remove the rind or skin from a fruit or vegetable, as to peel a potato.

Peking cabbage *see* CHINESE CABBAGE

Peking duck [PEE-king; PAY-king] 1. An elaborately prepared Chinese dish that starts with air being pumped between a duck's skin and flesh. The duck is then coated with a honey mixture and hung until the skin is dry and hard. After the duck is roasted the skin becomes golden and intensely crisp. While hot, it's cut into small squares and served with thin pancakes (called Peking doilies) or steamed buns, accompanied by scallions and HOISIN. The meat is considered a secondary attraction and is usually served after the skin. This specialty is also sometimes called *Beijing* [BAY-jeeng] *duck.* 2. A variety of mallard (*see* DUCK).

Peking sauce *see* HOISIN

Peking-Shantung cuisine [PEE-king shan-TUNG] *see* CHINESE CUISINE

pekmez *see* FRUIT MOLASSES

pekoe tea [PEE-koh] Because similar-size tea leaves brew at the same speed (larger, coarser leaves take longer), tea leaves are graded and sorted by size. **Orange pekoe** is the grade for the smallest leaves, which are picked from the top of the plant. "Pekoe" describes medium-size, slightly coarser tea leaves. *See also* TEA.

pemmican [PEHM-ih-kuhn] Pulverized dried meat or fish mixed with hot fat and dried berries and/or other dried fruit into a thick paste, and then formed into loafs or small cakes. Some regional variations of pemmican use parched corn instead of dried meat. This food originated with North American Indians as a nutritious, spoilage-resistant food good for traveling. Pemmican, which can be eaten out of hand or added to hot water to make a soup, was adopted by early American pioneers, hunters and others on the move.

Penang laksa *see* LAKSA

penicillium [pen-ih-SIHL-ee-uhm] Fungi that are members of the genus *Penicillium*. These typically blue to green fungi are used in the production of penicillin and grow as MOLDS on RIPENING cheese, decaying fruit, old bread, and so on. Several *penicilliums* are used in cheesemaking, the most popular being **Penicillium camemberti** and **Penicillium candidum**, used for SOFT-RIPENED CHEESES like CAMEMBERT and BRIE; **Penicillium glaucum**, used for BLUE-VEINED CHEESES such as BLEU D'AUVERGNE and Bleu de Bresse; **Penicillium gorgonzola**, used for GORGONZOLA; and **Penicillium roqueforti**, used for ROQUEFORT.

penne *see* Pasta Glossary, page 883

penuche; panocha; penuchi [puh-NOO-chee] A creamy, fudgelike candy made with brown sugar, butter, milk or cream and vanilla. Chopped nuts are sometimes added. The mixture is heated to the SOFT-BALL STAGE, whipped until thick and either dropped onto a cookie sheet or poured into a pan and allowed to set. The name is derived from the Mexican word for "raw sugar" or "brown sugar."

pepe [PAY-pay] Italian for "pepper," black or white.

peperonata [pehp-uh-roh-NAH-tah] An Italian mixture of sweet peppers, tomatoes, onions and garlic cooked in olive oil. It's served hot as a CONDIMENT with meats or cold as an ANTIPASTO.

pepino; pepino melon [puh-PEE-noh] 1. A fragrant fruit that originated in Peru, though it's now grown in New Zealand, California and other subtropical and temperate climates. Though sometimes referred to as a *pepino melon,* the pepino isn't a melon at all, but rather a member of the nightshade family, as are eggplants and tomatoes. The exotic-looking pepino has a smooth, glossy, golden skin streaked with violet. It can range in size anywhere from that of a plum to that of a large papaya. The skin, seeds and flesh are all edible. The perfumy yellow-gold flesh is juicy and lightly sweet, with a mild cantaloupe flavor. Pepinos are available from late fall to midspring in specialty produce markets and some supermarkets that carry exotic produce. Choose those that are fragrant and give slightly to palm pressure. They can be ripened at room temperature, if necessary. Judge the ripeness by the deep-golden background color. Pepinos should be peeled before using for out-of-hand eating, in fruit salads or as an accompaniment or garnish to meats or vegetables. They're also called *mellowfruit* and *treemelon*. 2. Spanish and Portuguese for "cucumber."

pepitas [puh-PEE-tahs] These edible *pumpkin seeds* are a popular ingredient in Mexican cooking. With their white hull removed, they are a medium-dark green and have a deliciously delicate flavor, which is even better when the seeds are roasted and salted. Pepitas are sold salted, roasted and raw, and with or without hulls.

Peppadew pepper [PEP-pah-doo] The trademarked name of a CAPSICUM-family pepper that's purported to be the first new fruit introduced to the world market since the KIWI's debut some thirty years ago. Though thought to be a native of Central America, this pepper was discovered by Johan Steenkamp in 1994, growing wild in South Africa. He experimented with them, trademarked the name and patented a secret preparation technique. Also called *piquanté* or *sweet piquanté pepper*, the tiny Peppadew resembles a cross between a cherry TOMATO and a very small red pepper. The flavor is a unique blend of sweet and spicy. Though these peppers come in mild and hot versions, the difference is simply the result of the pickling solution used during processing. Peppadew ketchup and other products are available in most supermarkets.

pepper, black and white *see* PEPPERCORN

pepper, chile *see* CHILE

pepper, hot *see* CHILE

pepper, sweet green or red *see* SWEET PEPPER

peppercorn Most cooks today don't appreciate the plentiful and inexpensive supply of a spice that was once so valuable and rare it was sometimes used as currency. Its merit was so high that many of the European sailing expeditions during the 15th century were undertaken with the main purpose of finding alternate trade routes to the Far East, the primary source of the prized peppercorn and other spices. Pepper in one form or other is used around the world to enhance the flavor of both savory and sweet dishes. Because it stimulates gastric juices, it delivers a digestive bonus as well. The world's most popular spice is a berry that grows in grapelike clusters on the pepper plant (*Piper nigrum*), a climbing vine native to India and Indonesia. The berry is processed to produce three basic types of peppercorn—black, white and green. The most common is the black peppercorn, which is picked when the berry is not quite ripe, then dried until it shrivels and the skin turns dark brown to black. It's the strongest flavored of the three—slightly hot with a hint of sweetness. Among the best black peppers are the Tellicherry and the Lampong. The less pungent white peppercorn has been allowed to ripen, after which the skin is removed and the berry is dried. The result is a smaller, smoother-skinned, light-tan berry with a milder flavor. White pepper is used to a great extent for appearance, usually in light-colored sauces or foods where dark specks of black pepper would stand out. The green peppercorn is the soft, underripe berry that's usually preserved in brine. It has a fresh flavor that's less pungent than the berry in its other forms. Black and white peppercorns are available whole, cracked and coarsely or finely ground. Whole peppercorns freshly ground with a pepper mill deliver more flavor than does preground pepper, which loses its flavor fairly quickly. Whole dried peppercorns can be stored in a cool, dark place for about a year; ground pepper will keep its flavor for about 4 months. Green peppercorns packed in brine are available in jars and cans. They should be refrigerated once opened and can be kept for 1 month. Water-packed green peppercorns must also be refrigerated but will only keep for about a week. Freeze-dried green peppercorns are also available and can be stored in a cool, dark place for up to 6 months. *See also* CAYENNE PEPPER; PINK PEPPERCORN; SZECHUAN PEPPER; Seasoning Suggestions, page 891.

pepper leaf; pepperleaf A bright to dark green leaf from a pepper-family plant grown from southern Mexico down through northern South America. The pepper leaf is oval shaped with a tapered point. It has an aromatic flavor somewhat similar to that of SASSAFRAS with notes of anise, black pepper and nutmeg. Younger leaves have more forceful characteristics; older ones are milder. In locales where they're grown, fresh pepper leaves are commonly used to wrap foods like fish, poultry, beef and shrimp so the flavor is imparted during cooking. The leaves are also added to soups and stews and used for herbal tea. Dried leaves can be found in Latin American markets, but they're not as flavorful as fresh leaves, which can usually only be found in farmer's markets. Also known as *eared pepper, hoja santa, momo, root beer plant, sacred pepper* and *yerba santa.*

pepper hash A favorite in the Philadelphia area, where it's served with seafood dishes such as fried oysters, soft-shell crabs and grilled catfish. The basic recipe for pepper hash includes coarsely chopped cabbage, diced green bell peppers, sugar or honey, cider or white vinegar, salt and pepper. Quite often red bell peppers are included as well. There are myriad variations that include ingredients such as carrots, celery seed or mustard seed, garlic and so on.

pepper mill A hand-held grinder designed for crushing dry peppercorns. Pepper mills are made from a variety of materials including plastic, wood and ceramic. The internal grinding mechanism is generally made of stainless steel. Good pepper mills can be adjusted to produce fine or coarse grinds. Freshly ground pepper has a sharper, more lively flavor than the preground variety.

peppermint *see* MINT

peppermint schnapps *see* SCHNAPPS

pepperoncini; peperoncini [pep-per-awn-CHEE-nee] Also called *Tuscan peppers,* these thin, 2- to 3-inch-long CHILES have a bright red, wrinkled skin. They have a slightly sweet flavor and are mild, with a SCOVILLE SCALE rating of 100 to 500. *Pepperoncini* are most often sold pickled and used as part of an ANTIPASTO.

pepperoni; peperoni [pehp-puh-ROH-nee] An Italian SALAMI made of pork and beef highly seasoned with black and red pepper. This slender, firm, air-dried SAUSAGE is ready to eat, often sliced very thin and used as an appetizer. It can also be used to add flavor to many cooked dishes, as those who love pepperoni pizza will attest.

pepper pot; pepperpot 1. A thick soup of TRIPE, meat, vegetables, pepper and other seasonings. It's also called *Philadelphia pepper pot.* The soup is said to have been created during the desperate winter of 1777–1778, when Washington's army was down to tripe, peppercorns and various scraps of other food. The cook devised this tasty dish and named it in honor of his hometown, Philadelphia. 2. A West Indian soup or stew containing meat or seafood, vegetables, chiles, cayenne pepper, a variety of other seasonings and usually CASSAREEP.

pepper steak 1. A beefsteak generously sprinkled with coarsely ground black pepper, sautéed in butter and served with a sauce made from pan drippings, stock, wine and cream. Pepper steak is sometimes flamed with BRANDY or COGNAC. In French it's called *steak au poivre.* 2. A Chinese STIR-FRY dish consisting of strips of steak, green pepper and onion cooked with SOY SAUCE and other seasonings.

pequín chile A tiny (½-inch-long), oval, red-orange dried CHILE. With a SCOVILLE SCALE rating of 30,000 to 60,000, pequíns are fiery hot and have a slightly sweet, smoky flavor. They're also called *chile pequeño;* in their wild form they're known as *tepín* or *chiltepín.*

pera [PAY-rah] Italian for "pear."

perch Any of various spiny-finned freshwater fish found in North America and Europe. In the United States the best known is the **yellow perch**, found mainly in the East and Midwest. In France, the **common** or **river perch** is highly favored. These similar-looking fish have olive-green backs blending to yellow on the sides, dark vertical bands and reddish-orange fins. They have a mild, delicate flavor and firm flesh with a low fat content. Related to the true perch are the **pike perch** (so called because their bodies resemble the PIKE), the best known of which are the **wall-**

eyed pike and the **sauger** or **sand pike**. There are several saltwater fish that are incorrectly called perch including the **white perch** (really a member of the BASS family) and the **ocean perch** (a member of the ROCK-FISH family). Perch range in size from ½ to 3 pounds. They're available fresh and frozen, whole and filleted. Small perch are usually best broiled or sautéed. Larger ones can be prepared in a variety of ways including poaching, steaming, baking and in soups and stews. *See also* FISH.

perciatelli *see* Pasta Glossary, page 883

perfect A COCKTAIL term for drinks made with half sweet and half dry VERMOUTH. For instance, a MANHATTAN, which is made with sweet vermouth, becomes a "perfect Manhattan" when made with equal parts sweet and dry vermouth.

périgourdine, à la [pay-ree-goor-DEEN] French for "as prepared in the style of Périgord," referring to dishes garnished or flavored with TRUFFLES as well as those served with PÉRIGUEUX SAUCE. The term is derived from France's Périgord region, which is famous for its black truffles.

Périgueux sauce [pay-ree-GOUH] A rich brown sauce flavored with MADEIRA and TRUFFLES. The sauce, which goes with a variety of dishes including meat, game, poultry and eggs, is named after Périgueux, a city in the Périgord region of Southwest France that is noted for its truffles. Dishes using the sauce are often labeled *à la* PÉRIGOURDINE or simply *Périgueux*. *See also* SAUCE.

perilla *see* SHISO

peri peri chile *see* BISHOP'S CROWN CHILE

periwinkle [PEHR-ih-wing-kuhl] There are over 300 species of this conical, spiral-shelled GASTROPOD MOLLUSK (*see both listings*), but few are edible. Periwinkles, also called *bigaros, sea snails* or *winkles,* are found attached to rocks, wharves, pilings, etc. in both fresh and sea water. The most common edible periwinkle is found along the Atlantic coasts of Europe and North America. It grows to about 1 inch in size and is gray to dark olive with reddish-brown bands. Periwinkles are popular in Europe but rarely found in the United States. They're usually boiled in their shells, then extracted with a small pick.

Pernod [pehr-NOH] A yellowish, licorice-flavored LIQUEUR similar to ABSINTHE. Pernod is very popular in France and is usually mixed with water, which turns it whitish and cloudy.

perón chile *see* ROCOTO CHILE

perry A pear CIDER made similarly to apple cider, except pears require more delicate handling than apples. Perry is also slightly sweeter than apple cider because pears contain SORBITOL, a natural sweetener that doesn't convert to alcohol during FERMENTATION. This potable has been made for centuries in England, Sweden and France (where it's called *poiré*).

Persian apple *see* PEACH

Persian dried limes *see* LIMES, DRIED, PERSIAN

Persian hogweed *see* GOLPAR

Persian melon A large green muskmelon (*see* MELON) with a delicate netting on the rind and a rich salmon-colored flesh. Persian melons weigh around 5 pounds (larger than a CANTALOUPE) and have a delectably sweet flavor. They're available from July through October, with a peak in the late summer. Choose Persian melons that are heavy for their size; the rind should be pale green with a delicate netting. Avoid melons with soft spots. Store unripe Persian melons at room temperature, ripe melons in the refrigerator for up to 5 days.

Persian walnut *see* ENGLISH WALNUT

persillade [pehr-see-YAHD] *Persil* is French for "parsley" and persillade is a mixture of chopped parsley and garlic. It's usually added as a flavoring or garnish to dishes just before cooking is complete. A dish finished in this fashion is often described as a *persillé*. For example, lamb *persillé* is a lamb dish topped with persillade mixed with breadcrumbs.

persimmon [puhr-SIHM-muhn] The most widely available persimmon in the United States is the **Hachiya**, also called *Japanese persimmon* and *kaki*. It's large (up to 3 inches in diameter) and round, with a slightly elongated, pointed base. The **Fuyu** persimmon is smaller and more tomato-shaped. When ripe, both have a red-orange skin and flesh. The Hachiya is quite soft when completely ripe and has a smooth, creamy texture and a tangy-sweet flavor. If eaten even slightly underripe, the Hachiya will pucker the mouth with an incredible astringency. The Fuyu, however, is still firm when ripe and is not at all astringent. **Cinnamon persimmon**, a subvariety of the Hachiya, has a brilliant golden-orange skin and flesh, the latter of which is speckled with cinnamon-colored flecks. It can be eaten when firm or slightly soft, as one would a Fuyu. **Sharon fruit** is a sweet, round Israeli persimmon that can be eaten slightly underripe. It's found in Europe and the Middle East. Persimmons are available from October to February. Choose fruit that is plump and soft but not mushy (the Fuyu should be quite firm). The skin should be smooth, glossy and brightly colored. Persimmons that are not quite ripe can be ripened at room temperature. Store ripe fruit in the refrigerator for up to 3 days. Persimmons can be used in baked goods, puddings and other desserts, as well as eaten out of hand. They contain a good amount of vitamin A and some vitamin C.

peruano bean [peh-roo-AH-noh] A small, oval, ivory to pale yellow dried bean common in Latin American cooking and a staple of northern Mexico's cuisine. Peruanos have a light, buttery flavor and a soft, creamy texture. They're also called *azufrado beans, canaria beans, canario beans, maicoba beans, mayo coba beans, mayocoba beans, Mexican yellow beans* and *Peruvian beans. See also* BEANS.

Peruvian bean *see* PERUANO BEAN

Peruvian carrot *see* ARRACACHA

pesca [PEH-skah] Italian for "peach."

pescatora, alla [AH-lah pehs-kah-TOH-rah] Italian for "fisherman's style" (*pesce* means "fish"), which can refer to any seafood dish.

pesce [PAYSH-shay] Italian for "fish."

pestle [PEHS-tl; PEHS-tuhl] *see* MORTAR AND PESTLE

pesto [PEH-stoh] Italian for "pounded," pesto is an uncooked sauce made with fresh basil, garlic, PINE NUTS, PARMESAN or PECORINO CHEESE and olive oil. The ingredients can either be crushed with MORTAR AND PESTLE or finely chopped with a food processor. This classic, fresh-tasting sauce originated in Genoa, Italy, and although used on a variety of dishes, it is a favorite with pasta. Now there are "pestos" made from myriad other ingredients from CILANTRO to MINT. *See also* SAUCE.

Peter Heering A Danish LIQUEUR invented in the 1830s by Peter Heering. It's ruby red and has a complex black cherry flavor that's not overly sweet. Also called *Cherry Heering.*

petit déjeuner [puh-TEE day-zhoo-NAY] French for "breakfast."

petite marmite [peh-TEET mahr-MEET] A type of POT-AU-FEU served in its own cooking vessel. Petite marmite is usually made from beef, chicken, MARROW bones and various vegetables including cabbage. This mélange is slowly cooked in water, producing a rich broth that's served with grated cheese as the first course accompanied by the bone marrow, which is spread on toast. The meat and vegetables are then served as the main course.

Petite Sirah; Petite Syrah [peh-TEET sih-RAH] Grown mainly in California, this red wine grape produces a big, robust and peppery wine.

Although not as popular as California's CABERNET SAUVIGNON, PINOT NOIR or ZINFANDEL, Petite Sirah has a following among those who like big, full-bodied wines. The Petite Sirah grape is also used as a blending grape to give a little more zest and complexity to other red wines. In California, the Petite Sirah grape was long thought to be SYRAH, a theory now discounted by enologists (*see* ENOLOGY). During the 1990s, DNA analysis proved there is a relationship between the two grapes: Most of California's Petite Sirah is the same as Durif, a lesser-known variety in the RHONE and one of Durif's parents, as shown by DNA evidence. This variety is also spelled *Petit Syrah* and *Petit Sirah*.

petit four [PEH-tee fohr; puh-tee FOOR] 1. Any of various bite-size iced and elaborately decorated cakes. *Petits fours* can be made with any flavor cake, though white and chocolate are the most common. 2. The French also use this term to describe small, fancy cookies.

petit-gris [peh-tee-GREE] *see* SNAIL

petit pain [puh-tee PAN] French for a bread roll. *See also* PAIN.

petits pois [peh-tee PWAH] The French term for "small young green peas." *See also* ENGLISH PEA.

Petit Suisse [peh-TEE SWEES] A rich, soft French cheese that, because it contains a minimum 60 percent milk fat, ranks as a DOUBLE-CREAM cheese. It's the consistency of very soft CREAM CHEESE and has a delicate, sweetly tangy flavor. Petit Suisse is usually sold in small cylinders or flat squares. The most popular brand of Petit Suisse is GERVAIS, named after Charles Gervais at Les Halles in Paris, who received the original version from a Normandy farmer's wife to sell. She'd produced the cheese at the suggestion of one of the Swiss farmhands, hence the Swiss connection. It was through Gervais' deft production and marketing methods that Petit Suisse became so widely popular. *See also* CHEESE.

petrale sole [peh-TRAH-lee SOHL] Not a true SOLE, but rather a FLOUNDER that is found in the Pacific Ocean from Alaska to Mexico. It's highly prized for its excellent flavor and fine-textured, lowfat flesh. Those found in the market generally weigh from 1 to 5 pounds. They can be purchased fresh and frozen, whole or in fillets. Petrale sole can be prepared in almost any manner including sautéing, broiling, grilling and poaching. *See also* FISH; FLATFISH.

pezzoccheri *see* Pasta Glossary, page 883

Pfeffernüsse; Pfeffernuesse [FEHF-fuhr-noos] Traditionally served at Christmastime, *Pfeffernüsse* (German for "peppernuts") are very popular in many European countries. Scandinavians call them *pepperka-*

ker in Norway, *pepparnotter* in Sweden and *pebernodder* in Denmark. These tiny ball-shaped cookies are full of spices such as cinnamon, cardamom, ginger and the ingredient for which they're named—black pepper.

Pfifferling *see* CHANTERELLE

Pflaume [PFLOW-meh] German for "plum."

phaal *see* PHALL

phak khayang *see* RICE PADDY HERB

phall; phaal; phal [fal] Exceedingly hot curry dish created by Indian restaurants in England. It contains numerous different very hot chiles such as HABANERO, scotch bonnet and Bhut Naga Jolokia (*see* SCOVILLE SCALE). It usually contains beef, chicken or lamb, tomatoes and tomato puree, along with various seasonings such as chili powder, CORIANDER, CUMIN, FENUGREEK and GARAM MASALA.

pheasant [FEH-suhnt] A medium-size GAME BIRD, originally from Asia but now found in Europe and North America. As with many birds, the male has a more brilliant plumage than the female and is larger, weighing $2\frac{1}{2}$ to 5 pounds compared to the female's 3-pound average. The female's flesh is plumper, juicier and more tender. Very young cocks and hens may be roasted as is but older pheasants should be BARDED or cooked with moist heat because their flesh is lean and dry. Farm-raised pheasants do not have the same flavor as the wild birds. Pheasants are sometimes found dressed and frozen in specialty meat markets, usually by special order.

Philadelphia cheese steak *see* CHEESE STEAK

Philadelphia pepper pot *see* PEPPER POT

Philadelphia snapper soup *see* SNAPPER SOUP

Philadelphia-style ice cream Ice Cream whose ingredients include cream, sugar and flavorings but no eggs or egg-based custard, which are found in French ice cream (*see* ICE CREAM).

pho [fuh] A traditional Vietnamese noodle dish, pho consists of meat and *banh pho*, a medium-wide rice stick noodle (*see* RICE NOODLES) served in a bowl of clear broth flavored with seasonings such as STAR ANISE and blackened ginger and onion. Accompaniments served with pho to be added by the diner include Thai basil, bean sprouts, chili peppers, green or white onions, wedges of lemon or lime, mint, *ngo gai* (see SAW-LEAF HERB) and cilantro. Accompanying sauces can include BEAN SAUCE, chili sauce, FISH SAUCE and HOISIN. Pho is most commonly made with beef broth and served with thin slices of rare to medium-rare beef, in which case it's called *bo pho*. Variations include chicken, fish, pork or meatballs.

phyllo [FEE-loh] Literally translated, the Greek word *phyllo* means "leaf." Culinarily, it refers to tissue-thin layers of pastry dough used in various Greek and Near Eastern sweet and savory preparations, the best known being BAKLAVA and SPANAKOPITA. Phyllo (also spelled *filo*) is very similar to STRUDEL dough. Packaged fresh and frozen phyllo dough is readily available—the former in Greek markets, the latter in supermarkets. Unopened, phyllo can be stored in the refrigerator for up to a month. Once opened, use within 2 to 3 days. Frozen phyllo can be stored for up to 1 year. Thaw overnight in the refrigerator. Refreezing phyllo will make it brittle.

physalis [fih-ZAL-ihs] *see* CAPE GOOSEBERRY

Piave [PYAH-vay] Cow's-milk cheese created in the 1960s by the *Cooperativa Latte Brusche*, a dairy cooperative located in the Veneto region in northeastern Italy. Piave is named for the Piave River that runs from the Alps to the plains north and east of Venice. It ranges from SEMI-SOFT TO HARD and is RIPENED to produce different styles: *fresco* is aged 20 to 60 days, *mezzano* for 60 to 180 days, *vecchio* for over 180 days, and *stravecchio* (or *vecchio Oro del Tempo*) is aged for more than a year. Younger versions have a delicate, slightly sweet, fruity flavor; aged versions are full-flavored, nutty and piquant with hints of caramel. Piave comes in 11- to 15-pound flat wheels with a rind that's pale yellow to yellowish brown; its interior is pale yellow without EYES. The FAT CONTENT of this cheese ranges from 35 to 40 percent.

pibimbap [pee-BIHM-bahp] *see* BIBIMBAP

picada *see* SOPE

picadillo [pee-kah-DEE-yoh] This dish, a favorite in many Spanish-speaking countries, consists of ground pork and beef or veal plus tomatoes, garlic, onions and whatever else the regional version dictates. In Cuba it's served with rice and black beans. In Mexico, picadillo is used as a stuffing for various dishes.

picante [pee-KAHN-tay] Spanish for "spicy."

piccalilli [PIHK-uh-lih-lee] A highly seasoned pickled vegetable relish. The ingredients vary from recipe to recipe and can include tomatoes, sweet peppers, onions, zucchini, cucumber, cauliflower, beans, etc.

piccante [pee-KAHN-teh] Italian for "spicy."

piccata [pih-KAH-tuh] 1. The Italian word for a veal ESCALOPE. 2. A classic dish of a seasoned and floured veal escalope that's quickly sautéed and served with a sauce made from the pan drippings, lemon juice and chopped parsley. Chicken is also sometimes prepared in this manner.

Picholine olive [pee-shoh-LEEN] Medium-size, almond-shaped French olive that's cured in a salty brine that often contains herbs and spices. Its color ranges from green to purplish-black depending on maturity. Picholine olives have a firm texture and a delicate, lightly salty flavor with herbal and nutty nuances. A California version is normally marinated in citric acid. Picholines are also grown in Morocco. *See also* OLIVE.

pickerel [PIHK-uh-ruhl] *see* PIKE

pickle *n.* Food that has been preserved in a seasoned brine or vinegar mixture. Among the more popular foods used for pickling are cucumbers, pearl onions, cauliflower, baby corn, watermelon rind, pig's feet and herring. Pickles can be sour, sweet, hot or variously flavored, such as with DILL for the popular dill pickle. **pickle** *v.* To preserve food in a vinegar mixture or brine. *See also* CURE.

pickled cheese *see* FETA

pickled cucumber *see* TEA MELON

pickled herring *see* HERRING

pickling lime Calcium hydroxide. Pickling lime has numerous uses including pickling cucumbers and other foods (*see* LIME PICKLES.) It is also known as *builders lime*, *hydrated lime* and *slack lime*.

pickling spices A spice blend used in mixtures to PICKLE various foods, as well as to season certain dishes. The blend can differ greatly according to the manufacturer, and the ingredients (usually whole or in coarse pieces) can include allspice, bay leaves, cardamom, cinnamon, cloves, coriander, ginger, mustard seeds and peppercorns. Prepackaged pickling spice mixes are sold in most supermarkets.

picnic ham Not really a true ham (which comes from the pig's back leg), the picnic ham is taken from the upper part of the foreleg and includes a portion of the shoulder. This cut is also more accurately referred to as the *picnic shoulder* or *pork shoulder*. The picnic ham is smoked, which gives it a very hamlike flavor. It often has the bone removed. Though it's slightly tougher (requiring longer cooking) and has more waste because of the bone structure, picnic ham is a good, inexpensive substitute for regular ham. *See also* HAM.

picnic shoulder *see* PICNIC HAM

pico de gallo [PEE-koh day GI-yoh] Spanish for "rooster's beak," *pico de gallo* is a relish made of finely chopped ingredients like JICAMA, oranges, onions, bell peppers, jalapeño peppers and cucumbers, along with various seasonings. This condiment was so named because it was once purportedly eaten with the thumb and finger, an action that resembles a rooster's pecking beak.

pie A sweet or savory dish made with a crust and filling (such as fruit, pudding, meat or vegetable). Pies can have bottom crusts only, or top and bottom crusts or, as with DEEP-DISH pies, only a top crust. Sweet pies are generally served as dessert and savory pies as the main course or appetizer. Crusts can be made of a variety of mixtures including short crust pastry, PUFF PASTRY, cookie crumbs, MERINGUE and even, as with SHEPHERD'S PIE, mashed potatoes. *See also* TART.

pie crust *see* CRUST

pied bleu mushroom *see* BLEWIT MUSHROOM

pie pans (tins, plates) Any of various size round containers used for baking pies. Pie pans come in a variety of materials including aluminum, glass, steel (black and tinned) and stoneware. For crisp crusts, dark metal pans are the best. Pie pans have gently sloping sides, whereas tart tins have straight sides. Standard pie pans come in 8, 9 and 10 inches in diameter and range from 1 to 1^1/$_2$ inches deep. Deep-dish pie plates typically range from 9 to 11 inches in diameter, and from 1^1/$_2$ to 2 inches deep. *See also* COOKWARE AND BAKEWARE MATERIALS; Pan Substitution Chart, page 859.

pie plant; pieplant *see* RHUBARB

pierogi A Polish specialty of half-moon-shape noodle DUMPLINGS filled with a savory or sweet minced mixture. Classic fillings include various mixtures of cabbage, SAUERKRAUT, onions, potatoes and FARMER'S CHEESE. Minced meat and other vegetables may also be used. Sweet fillings typically include fruit such as prunes or blueberries. After the pierogi are cooked in boiling water, they're sometimes sautéed in butter and can be topped with toasted breadcrumbs, sauce or sour cream. They can be served as a first course or side dish. *See also* PIROZHKI.

pie weights Small pelletlike metal or ceramic weights used when baking an unfilled pie or tart crust to keep it from shrinking. The weights (from 1 to 2 cups) are poured into a foil-lined unbaked pie crust. The shell is then partially baked, the foil and weights lifted out, and then the baking is finished. Pie weights can be found in gourmet shops. *See also* BAKE BLIND.

pigeonneau [pee-zhaw*n*-NOH] French for "SQUAB."

pigeon pea Native to Africa, this tiny LEGUME is also called *gandule, goongoo bean, Congo bean* and *no-eyed pea*. In the United States it's particularly popular in southern states where it grows in long, twisted fuzzy pods. The peas are about the size of the standard garden pea and are usually a grayish-yellow color. Pigeon peas can be eaten raw but are most often dried and split. They're available dried in many supermarkets and can often be found fresh, frozen and canned in the regions where they're grown, as well as Latin American and Indian markets. Pigeon peas are cooked like dried beans. *See also* BEANS.

pignoli; pignon [peen-YOH-lee; peen-YAWN] The Italian and French words, respectively, for "PINE NUT."

pig's feet Called *trotters* by the British, these are the feet and ankles of pigs. Because they're bony and sinewy, pig's feet require long, slow cooking. They're quite flavorful and full of natural gelatin. Pig's feet are available pickled, fresh and smoked—the latter two are particularly good in soups, stews and sauces. *See also* PORK; VARIETY MEATS.

pigs in blankets A term that is generally used to describe a SAU-SAGE with an outside covering (blanket). The most common example is a small cocktail sausage wrapped in pie dough and baked, then served as an appetizer. Pigs in blankets can also refer to breakfast sausages wrapped in pancakes or any other similar style of food. *See also* CORN DOG; HOT DOG; FRANKFURTER.

pigweed *see* PURSLANE

pike A family of freshwater fish that includes the pike, pickerel and muskellunge. They all have long bodies, large mouths and ferocious-look-ing teeth. Pickerel are the smallest—generally weighing 2 to 3 pounds. Pike range from 4 to 10 pounds and the muskellunge (or *muskie*) aver-ages from 10 to 30 pounds but can reach up to 60 pounds and 6 feet in length. The walleyed pike is not a pike but rather a PERCH. The pike family of fish is known for its lean, firm, lowfat (but bony) flesh. Although fished mainly for sport in the United States, they are imported from Canada and available fresh and frozen, either whole, filleted or in steaks. Pike can be cooked in almost any manner available. It's the fish traditionally used in France's fish QUENELLES, as well as the Jewish GEFILTE FISH. *See also* FISH.

pilaf [PEE-lahf; PIH-lahf] This rice- or BULGHUR-based dish (also called *pilau*) originated in the Near East and always begins by first browning the rice in butter or oil before cooking it in stock. Pilafs can be variously seasoned and usually contain other ingredients such as chopped cooked vegetables, meats, seafood or poultry. In India they're highly spiced with CURRY. Pilaf can be served as a side dish or main dish.

pilau [pih-LOW] *see* PILAF

pilchard [PIHL-chuhrd] A small, high-fat saltwater fish found in abundance off the European Atlantic coast from Scandinavia to Portugal. Though Europeans can buy fresh pilchard from July to December, it's usually canned in oil or tomato sauce like SARDINES. *See also* FISH.

piloncillo [pee-lawn-SEE-yoh] Popular in Mexican cooking, piloncillo is unrefined cane sugar shaped into truncated cones that can range in size from about 1 ounce to about 7 ounces. Piloncillo can range in color from light to mahogany brown—the darker the color, the stronger the molasses flavor. The same sugar formed into a rounded loaf is called **panela**, and rounds or squares of coarser, darker sugar are called **panocha**. All forms are very hard and should either be chopped by hand (a food processor might break) or dissolved in the liquid called for in the recipe. Piloncillo can be found in Latin markets and some supermarkets.

Pilsner; Pilsener [PIHLZ-nuhr] Originally this term referred to a very fine beer brewed in Pilsen, in the Czech Republic. Today, however, it more commonly refers to any pale, light LAGER. Pilsners generally have a mild (some say bland) flavor, although a few reflect a pronounced HOPS characteristic. *See also* BEER.

Pilsner glass A footed, tall glass that tapers from the mouth to the base. It's generally used to serve beer.

pimenta Cambuci chile *see* BISHOP'S CROWN CHILE

Piment d'Espelette (AOC; PDO) [PEE-moh*n* DEHS-puhl-eht] Although not native to the Basque region—it was brought to the area from Mexico in the 16th century—the Espelette pepper has become a specialty of the region. This CHILI PEPPER is bright red, with a long tapered body and a flavor that's slightly sweet and rich with spicy heat similar to a JALAPEÑO. The Basques use this pepper much like black PEPPERCORNS are used in the United States—on just about everything. Piment d'Espelette received AOC approval in 2000 and it's still the only spice in France to achieve that status. To carry the name Piment d'Esplette AOC, the peppers must be grown within the village of Espelette or one of the other nine named villages in the Nive Valley and left to sun dry for at least 15 days, although 2½ to 3 months produces the best results. The peppers are usually sold dried and can be purchased whole or in powdered form, but they're sometimes available fresh and as a PURÉE. *See also* SPICES.

pimenton; pimentón [pee-MEN-tohn] *see* PAPRIKA

pimiento; pimento [pih-MYEHN-toh; pih-MEN-toh] 1. A large, red, heart-shaped SWEET PEPPER that measures 3 to 4 inches long and 2 to 3 inches wide. The flesh of the pimiento (Spanish for "pepper") is sweet, succulent and more aromatic than that of the red bell pepper.

Fresh pimientos may be found from late summer to early fall in specialty produce markets and some supermakets. Canned and bottled pimientos (halves, strips or pieces) are available year-round. Pimientos are the familiar red stuffing found in green olives. Much of the pimiento crop is used for PAPRIKA. 2. *Pimento* is the name of the tree from which ALLSPICE comes.

piña colada [PEEN-yuh koh-LAH-duh] Literally translated, this Spanish phrase means "strained pineapple." A piña colada is a tropically flavored drink made with coconut cream, pineapple juice and rum served over ice and usually garnished with a pineapple chunk.

Piñata; Piñata apple [pee-NYAH-tah] All-purpose apple developed in Germany and introduced in 1986 as *Pinova*. It's also known as *Sonata* and *Corail*. Stemit Growers in Washington state acquired the exclusive rights for the U.S. market and named it **Piñata** (a combination of Pinova and Sonata). It's a medium-large apple with a mottled pink and yellow-orange skin and a creamy white flesh. The Piñata is quite crisp and juicy with sweet apple flavors along with hints of banana and pineapple. The coloring and flavors are a result of its parentage, which includes Cox's Orange Pippin, Duchess of Oldenburg and GOLDEN DELICIOUS varieties. *See also* APPLE.

pinbone *see* SIRLOIN

pinch A measuring term referring to the amount of a dry ingredient (such as salt or pepper) that can be held between the tips of the thumb and forefinger. It's equivalent to approximately $1/16$ teaspoon. *See also* DASH.

pineapple This tropical beauty received its appellation from the English because of its resemblance to the pine cone. Most other Europeans call it *ananas* derived from the Paraguayan *nana* meaning "excellent (or exquisite) fruit." The pineapple is native to Central and South America, where symbolic representations of its form were found in pre-Incan ruins. Hawaii, now this fruit's leading producer, didn't see its first pineapple until the late 1700s. For centuries the pineapple (in the form of carved wood, stone sculptures and the like) has been used to symbolize hospitality. The two major varieties found commercially in the United States are the Cayenne (from Hawaii) and the Red Spanish (mainly from Florida and Puerto Rico). The **Cayenne pineapple**, the longer and more cylindrical of the two, has a golden-yellow skin and long, swordlike leaves sprouting from a single tuft. The **Red Spanish pineapple** is squatter in shape, has a reddish golden-brown skin and leaves that radiate from several tufts. Mexico grows a third variety called the **Sugar Loaf**, a large, exquisitely flavored specimen whose skin is still green when ripe. Because it doesn't ship well, the Sugar Loaf is rarely imported into the United States. Pineapples can weigh up to 20 pounds, though the average size marketed ranges between 2 and 5 pounds. All varieties have bumpy diamond-patterned skins. Though there are slight flavor variations depending on the variety, all ripe pineapple is exceedingly juicy and has a tangy sweet-tart flavor. Fresh pineapple is available year-round with a peak season from March to July. This is one fruit that must be picked ripe because the starch will not convert to sugar once it's off the plant. Choose pineapples that are slightly soft to the touch with a full, strong color (depending on the variety) and no sign of greening. The leaves should be crisp and green with no yellow or brown tips. Overripe pineapples show their advanced state with soft or dark areas on the skin. Refrigerate fresh pineapple tightly wrapped for up to 3 days. If it's slightly underripe, keeping it at room temperature for several days will reduce its acidity (though it won't increase its sweetness). Pineapple is available canned (in its own juice or in sugar syrup), crushed or in chunks, slices or tidbits. It can also be found frozen and candied. Pineapple can be used in a variety of dishes including fresh fruit desserts and salads, and as a garnish for vegetables and meats. It's also delicious cooked—either simply sautéed or broiled, or in a dish like the famous pineapple UPSIDE-DOWN CAKE. Fresh and frozen pineapple cannot be used in gelatin mixtures because of a natural enzyme that prevents them from setting (canned pineapple doesn't cause a problem). Pineapples are a fair source of vitamins A and C.

pineapple guava *see* FEIJOA

Pineau des Charentes [pee-noh day shahr-ohnt] A sweet, fortified APÉRITIF made by combining lightly fermented grape MUST with COGNAC, then aging it. There are white, ROSÉ, and red versions. The white Pineau des Charentes is aged for a minimum of 18 months, with 12 months of that time in oak barrels. The red and rosé Pineau des Charentes are aged for a minimum of 14 months, with 8 months in oak barrels. *Vieux* ("old") versions for all three are aged for a minimum of 5 years in oak barrels. A minimum of 10 years oak aging is required for those labeled *trés vieux* ("very old").

pine nut Also called *Indian nut, piñon, pignoli* and *pignolia* this high-fat nut comes from several varieties of pine trees. The nuts are actually inside the pine cone, which generally must be heated to facilitate their removal. This labor-intensive process is what makes these nuts so expensive. Pine nuts grow in China, Italy, Mexico, North Africa and the southwestern United States. There are two main varieties. Both have a thin shell with an ivory-colored nutmeat that averages about $1/2$ inch in length. The **Mediterranean** or **Italian pine nut** is from the stone pine. It's torpedo-shaped, has a light, delicate flavor and is the more expensive of the two. The stronger-flavored **Chinese pine nut** is shaped like a squat triangle.

Its pungent pine flavor can easily overpower some foods. Pine nuts can be found in bulk in natural food stores, and packaged in many supermarkets. The Chinese variety will more likely be available in Asian markets. Because of their high fat content, pine nuts turn rancid quickly. They should be stored airtight in the refrigerator for up to 3 months, frozen for up to 9 months. Pine nuts can be used in a variety of sweet and savory dishes and are well known for their flavorful addition to the classic Italian PESTO. *See also* NUTS.

pinga [peen-gah] *see* CACHAÇA

pink bean A smooth, reddish-brown dried bean that is very popular in the western United States. It's interchangeable with the PINTO BEAN in any dish. Pink beans are used to make REFRIED BEANS and CHILI CON CARNE. They're available in dried form year-round in most supermarkets. *See also* BEANS.

pink gin A British favorite that's also referred to simply as *gin and bitters*. This mix of gin and ANGOSTURA BITTERS, which provides the pink color, is usually served without ice, but sometimes it comes with a splash of cold water.

pink lady A COCKTAIL consisting of gin, lemon or lime juice, GRENADINE, egg white and cream. It's shaken with ice, then strained into a shallow, stemmed cocktail glass. *See also* WHITE LADY.

Pink Lady apple This all-purpose apple is a cross between the GOLDEN DELICIOUS and Lady Williams varieties. Its skin color can range from pinkish red to pale red; its crisp, juicy flesh is perfumy and sweetly tart with a hint of champagne. *See also* APPLE.

Pink Pearl apple Medium-sized all-purpose apple with pale yellow-green skin and occasional slight red blush. Its name comes from the crisp, juicy flesh that ranges from fuchsia to streaky pink. It's very aromatic and delivers a slightly tart taste. *See also* APPLE.

pink peppercorn Pink peppercorns are not true peppercorns but actually the dried berries from the *Baies* rose plant. They're cultivated in Madagascar and imported via France, hence their exorbitant price. These rose-hued berries are pungent and slightly sweet. Pink peppercorns can be found in gourmet stores either freeze-dried or packed in brine or water. Once opened, refrigerate water-packed berries for about a week, those packed in brine for 3 to 4 weeks. Freeze-dried pink peppercorns can be stored in a cool, dark place for about 6 months. Pink peppercorns are used as colorful, flavorful additions to a variety of sauces and meat and fish dishes. Though there was once widespread controversy regarding their safety, pink peppercorns have now been approved by the Food and Drug Administration. They should not, however, be confused with pink berries (also referred to as peppercorns) from an ornamental plant in Florida and California that can cause severe allergic reactions if eaten. *See also* PEPPERCORN.

pink salmon *see* SALMON

pink salt 1. A pinkish rock salt (*see* SALT), often marketed as **Himalayan salt**, mined in Pakistan (although salt mined in other parts of the world now use these same names). Iron oxide causes the pinkish tint. 2. *See also* SODIUM NITRATE.

pink slime Pejorative name given to **boneless lean beef trimmings** (BLBT) or **lean, finely textured beef** (LFTB) processed from high-fat beef trimmings and connective tissue. During the process, meat fat, which is about 50 percent of the trimmings, is separated out by use of heat and centrifugal force. This results in a meat byproduct that's between 5 and 10 percent fat. The meat byproduct is then treated with ammonia gas to kill bacteria such as *E. coli and Salmonella* and then frozen. It's used as an additive to ground beef products. The resulting product, which is approved by the USDA, has come under attack by various opponents.

pink snapper *see* OPAKAPAKA

pinoli [pee-NOH-lee] Italian for "PINE NUT."

piñon [PIHN-yuhn] Spanish for "PINE NUT."

Pinot Blanc [PEE-noh BLAHN; PEE-noh BLAHNGK] A variety of white grape that is used in some white ALSATIAN WINES and bottled as a varietal wine by a few California wineries. Pinot Blanc wine is crisp and dry but has less intensity and flavor than CHARDONNAY. Its price is also considerably lower. Pinot Blanc goes well with chicken and seafood.

Pinot Chardonnay [PEE-noh shar-dn-AY] *see* CHARDONNAY

Pinot Noir [PEE-noh NWAHR] The red grape that produces the spicy, rich, complex French red BURGUNDIES as well as Pinot Noirs from California, Oregon and Washington. It's also important in making French CHAMPAGNES and American sparkling wines. French Burgundy wines like Romanée-Conti and Chambertin are world renowned for being elegant, soft and smooth. They also command tremendous prices. The American Pinot Noirs are less expensive and some—particularly those from California and Oregon—are rapidly gaining in excellence and popularity. Pinot Noirs go well with almost any food.

Pinova *see* PIÑATA; PINATA APPLE

pinto bean A small, flavorful bean with reddish-brown streaks on a pale pink background (pinto is Spanish for "painted"). Pinto beans are popular throughout the United States and most Spanish-speaking countries. They're often served with rice or used in soups and stews. The pinto can be used interchangeably with the PINK BEAN, which is lighter in color prior to cooking but looks the same afterwards. Both the pinto and pink bean are commonly used in the preparation of REFRIED BEANS and CHILI CON CARNE. Pintos are available canned and dried year-round. They are also called *red Mexican beans*. *See also* BEANS.

pinzimonio [peen-zee-mohn-yoh] Raw seasonal vegetables served with olive oil and salt seasoned with fresh herbs and pepper. The vegetables are dipped in the olive oil and then into the seasoned salt prior to eating. Pinzimonio is the Italian version of CRUDITÉS.

pioppini mushroom [PYOHP-pee-nee] One of the members of the SHIMEJI family of mushrooms, also called *black poplar, velvet pippini, velvet piopparello* and *Agrocybe aegerita* (its scientific). It's cultivated in Japan and other parts of the world, including Australia and the United States, and grows wild on trees and stumps including black poplar trees. The pioppini has a thin, light tan stem with a dark brown cap and meaty flesh. The flavor is rich, peppery and nutty. Look for solid examples, avoiding any with broken or shriveled caps. *See also* MUSHROOM.

pipérade [pee-pay-RAHD] This dish from the Basque region of France has many versions but is always based on tomatoes and sweet green peppers cooked in olive oil. Additions can include onions, garlic, ham, bacon or other vegetables and quite often lightly beaten egg. Depending on how hearty it is, pipérade can be served as a side dish or main dish.

pipikaula [pee-pee-kow-lah] A Hawaiian specialty of dried, spiced beef that's akin to beef JERKY.

pippin apple *see* NEWTOWN PIPPIN

pips Another term for the small seeds found in fruits such as grapes, oranges and apples.

piquant [pee-KAHN] French for a flavor that can be spicy, tart or pungent.

piquanté pepper [pee-KAHN-tay] *see* PEPPADEW PEPPER

piquante sauce [pee-KAHNT] A spicy brown sauce made with shallots, white wine, vinegar, GHERKINS, parsley and various herbs and seasonings. It's served with sliced meats such as pork, tongue and beef. *See also* SAUCE.

piqué *see* ONION PIQUÉ

pique-nique; pique-niquer [peek-NEEK; peek-nee-KAY] French for the noun and verb form (respectively) of "picnic."

pirarucu *see* PAICHE

pirog [peh-ROHG]; *pl.* **pirogi (piroghi)** [peh-ROH-gee; *Ru.* peh-roh-GEE] Russian for "pie," from the word *pir,* meaning "feast." *See also* PIROZHKI.

pirogi *see* PIROZHKI

pirozhki [peh-RAWSH-kee; *Ru.* peh-rawzh-KEE] Small Russian TURN-OVERS with a pastry wrapper enclosing various savory (meat, seafood, cheese or vegetables) or sweet (usually fruit) fillings. The shape can vary from rectangular to half moon to triangular. Pirozhki can be baked or fried. They're served as an HORS D'OEUVRES or as accompaniments to soups or salads. **Pirogi** are larger versions of pirozhki, and are served as the entrée.

pisco [PEE-skoh] A clear to pale straw-colored, potent South American BRANDY that dates back to the Incas. Piscos are produced primarily in Peru and Chile and most are made from a 100 percent MUSCAT-based wine, although some are produced from a blend of grapes. They're briefly aged in clay jars and have a spicy, exotic flavor (often compared to that of beeswax) with orange blossom overtones.

piselli [pee-SHE-lee] Italian for "peas."

pismo clam [PIHS-moh] This Pacific hard-shell clam is considered one of the choicest of its genre. it's also becoming one of the scarcest. Pismos are tender, sweet and large—usually with a minimum shell diameter of 5 inches. The adductor muscle (which hinges the two shells) is so tender that it can be served ON THE HALF SHELL. The body meat can be steamed, fried or used in chowder. *See also* CLAM.

pissaladeira [pee-sah-lah-DAY-rah] A speciality of the Italian Riviera, this is Italy's counterpart of France's PISSALADIÈRE.

pissaladière [pee-sah-lah-DYEHR] A flaky pizzalike tart topped with onions, anchovies, black olives and sometimes tomatoes. Pissaladière is a specialty of Nice, in southern France.

pissenlit *see* DANDELION GREENS

pistachio [pih-STASH-ee-oh; pih-STAH-shee-oh] Cultivated in California, Italy, Turkey and Iran, the pistachio nut has a hard, tan shell that encloses a pale green nut. The shells of some pistachios are colored

red (with vegetable dye), while others have been blanched until white. The California Pistachio Commission states that these nuts are dyed for two reasons: because many people find that form familiar; and so they're easier to spot in a bowl of mixed nuts. Pistachios are available year-round shelled and unshelled, either raw or roasted and salted or not. When buying unshelled pistachios make sure the shells are partially open—not only because it's a great help in getting the nutmeat out, but because closed shells mean the nutmeat is immature. Pistachio nuts have a delicate, subtle flavor that is wonderful either for eating out of hand or for flavoring both sweet and savory dishes. Pistachio nuts are rich in calcium, thiamine, phosphorus, iron and Vitamin A. *See also* NUTS.

pisto [PEES-toh] A Spanish vegetable dish originally from La Mancha, south of Madrid. Pisto can include chopped tomatoes, sweet red or green peppers, onions, garlic, mushrooms, eggplant and sundry other vegetables all cooked together. Sometimes ham or other meat is added. This Spanish favorite can be eaten hot or cold, served as a main course, side dish or appetizer.

pistou [pees-TOO] A mixture of crushed basil, garlic and olive oil used as a CONDIMENT or sauce. It's the French version of Italy's PESTO. *See also* SOUPE AU PISTOU.

pit *v.* To remove the stone or seed of a fruit. This is most often done by using a sharp knife to cut it loose or a specialized utensil (known as a PITTER) to push it out. **pit** *n.* The stone or seed of a fruit such as a cherry, peach, apricot or plum.

pita [PEE-tah] Also called *pocket bread,* this Middle Eastern FLATBREAD can be made of white or whole-wheat flour. Each pita round splits horizontally to form a pocket into which a wide variety of ingredients can be stuffed to make a sandwich. Throughout the Middle East, pitas are served with meals or cut into wedges and used as dippers for dishes such as BABA GHANOUSH and HUMMUS. Pita bread is available in Middle Eastern markets and in most supermarkets.

pitaya [pee-TAY-ah] *see* DRAGON FRUIT

pith The soft, white, somewhat bitter, spongy layer that lies between the outer peel and the flesh of a CITRUS FRUIT.

pithaya *see* DRAGON FRUIT

pithiviers [pee-tee-VYAY] Taking its name from the French town of Pithiviers, this classic French "cake" is composed of an almond cream (FRANGIPANE) encased between two PUFF PASTRY rounds.

piticelle *see* BURRINO

pitter, olive or cherry A fairly simple tool consisting of two attached hinged handles, one with a ring at the end, the other with a blunt prong. The olive or cherry is placed in the ring and the handles are squeezed together, forcing the prong through the fruit and pushing the pit out through the hole in the ring. Pitters (also called *stoners*) come in various designs and sizes. They can be found in gourmet shops and in the kitchenware section of many department stores.

pizza [PEET-suh] Made popular in the United States by soldiers who brought the idea back from Italy at the end of World War II, pizza is thought to have evolved from early Egyptian FLATBREAD. Literally translated, the word means "pie," but it has come to represent a round savory tart made with a crisp yeast dough covered with tomato sauce, MOZZARELLA CHEESE and other ingredients such as peppers, onions, Italian sausage, mushrooms, anchovies and PEPPERONI. Variations such as deep-dish pizza, with its thick breadlike crust, have been popular over the years. Many menus now feature pizzas sans tomato sauce and mozzarella cheese. They're topped instead with ingredients such as sun-dried tomatoes, duck sausage, fresh basil, smoked salmon, goat cheese or wild mushrooms. *See also* PIZZA PAN.

pizza pan A round metal sheet used to bake pizza. The typical pizza pan ranges in diameter from 12 to 15 inches and has a shallow, rounded raised rim. For aficionados of thick crusts, there are deep-dish pizza pans with 2-inch sides. Perforated pizza pans have dozens of small holes, which allow moisture to escape and promote even browning. Pizza pans can be found in gourmet kitchen shops.

pizza peel *see* PEEL

pizza stone *see* BAKING STONE

pizza wheel A tool containing a sharp, 2- to 4-inch stainless steel rotating wheel attached to a handle made of rubber, plastic or wood. A pizza wheel can be used to cut items other than a pizza, such as a TART.

pizzella [peet-TSEHL-lah]; *pl.* **pizzelle** [peet-TSEHL-leh] Originating in Italy's Abruzzo region, these small, thin, waffle-like cookies get their distinctive look from being cooked on a special patterned PIZZELLE IRON. Pizzelle (sometimes spelled **pizzele**) are made with butter (or margarine, shortening or vegetable oil), eggs, flour, sugar and usually vanilla and anise flavorings; other ingredients such as lemon or orange peel, almond extract, and rum are sometimes used. They can be very thin, firm and crisp or thicker, soft and chewy depending on the recipe. In and around Abruzzo, the variations have different names, like **cancellate**, **ferratele**, **neole** or **nevole** (the latter two are usually the thicker, softer style). When warm, the softer versions can be formed into a tube or cone and then stuffed with cream, chocolate or other sweet filling. Fillings are sometimes placed between two pizzelle, forming a sandwich.

pizzelle iron [peet-TSEHL-leh] Special iron used to make PIZZELLE. Similar to a WAFFLE IRON, pizzelle irons may be fan-shaped, round, or square and produce different patterns such as diamonds, snowflakes, squares or stripes. Pizzelle irons can be electric or designed for stovetop cooking. Electric pizzelle irons have heating elements in both sides, thereby cooking the two sides of the cookie at once. Irons heated on top of a stove must be turned over once during cooking to finish the second side. Irons vary and produce pizzelle of different sizes; some are designed with multiple forms so that more than one pizzella can be produced at a time. Some irons come with multiple, changeable plates, allowing different sizes and designs.

plaice [PLAYC] The **American plaice**, also called *Canadian plaice* and *dab*, is a member of the FLOUNDER family, which is found on both sides of the Atlantic. The fish can be various shades of reddish- to gray-brown and has a lowfat, fine-textured flesh with a mild, sweet flavor. The American plaice can get as large as 12 pounds but is usually marketed in the 2- to 3-pound range. It's available fresh and frozen, either whole or filleted. The **European plaice**, a similar fish but with different coloring, is found in the North Sea and is widely popular in Europe. Both the American and European plaice are suitable for almost any cooking method. *See also* FISH; FLATFISH.

plancha [PLAN-chah] A flattop grill made of thin metal originated by the Spaniards, who got the idea from the flat clay surfaces the Aztecs used for cooking corn dough. Menu items listed as *a la plancha* are grilled items.

plank; planking A cooking method handed down by American Indians whereby meat or fish is cooked—usually by baking or broiling—on a wooden board. Planking imparts a soupçon of the wood's flavor to the food. Food referred to as "planked" has been cooked in this manner.

plantain [PLAN-tihn] *see* BANANA

plastic curd cheese *see* PASTA FILATA

plastic wrap The ability of this versatile food wrap to cling to both food and containers makes it superior for forming an airtight seal. There are many varieties of plastic wrap, some of which are thicker, cling better and have better moisture-vapor retention than others. Most plastic wraps are made of *polyethylene,* whose components are not absorbed by foods to any degree. The wrap that is considered to have the best cling and moisture retention is made of *polyvinylidene chloride,* another leading brand is made of *polyvinyl chloride* (*PVC*). For added flexibility, both require the addition of plasticizers that, if in direct extended contact with food, can be absorbed. However, the USDA has approved their use with food and, though little is known of the effects of human ingestion of plasticizers over a prolonged period of time, there is no current evidence that they are harmful. There is some concern, however, that wraps containing plasticizers can transfer their components to food during lengthy heating in a microwave oven.

plate scrappers *see* FREEGAN

plett pan Used to make SWEDISH PANCAKES, a plett is a cast iron (*see* CAST IRON COOKWARE) griddle with 7 round (3 inches in diameter) shallow indentations.

pleurotte [pluhr-AHT] The French name for the OYSTER MUSHROOM.

plonk [PLONGK] British slang for low-quality wine.

plover [PLUH-vuhr; PLOH-vuhr] A small GAME BIRD that's farm-raised in the United States (where it can't be hunted legally) and also imported from Europe. It's available on a limited basis in specialty poultry markets. The **golden plover** is considered superior and has a delicate and delicious meat. Plover is usually roasted.

plum There are hundreds of plum varieties cultivated throughout the world. All grow in clusters, have smooth, deeply colored skin and a center pit. Plums can range in shape from oval to round and in size from 1 to 3 inches in diameter. Their color can be yellow, green, red, purple, indigo blue and almost anything in between. The pale silvery-gray, filmy-looking coating on a plum's skin is natural and doesn't affect quality. In general, plums can be divided into two categories: Japanese and European. Japanese plums (which actually originated in China) are the larger of the two and have a juicier, softer flesh. European plums are good eaten fresh, but are particularly well suited to drying and cooking. The Japanese varieties include **Coe's Golden Drop**—yellow skin and rich, sweet flesh; **greengage**—small and round with a greenish-yellow skin and tangy-sweet flesh; **Santa Rosa**—large and dark purple with yellow flesh; and **Satsuma**—dark red skin and sweet red flesh; European varieties include **D'Agen**—used to make PRUNES; **damson**—small and oval-shaped with an indigo skin and tart yellow-green flesh; and **Robe de Sergeant**—dark bluish-purple with a sweet flesh. Fresh plums are available from May to late October; those from South America can be found January through March in some regions. Choose firm plums that give slightly to palm pressure. Avoid those with skin blemishes such as cracks, soft spots or brown discolorations, the latter indicating sunburn. Very firm plums may be stored at room temperature until slightly soft. Refrigerate ripe plums in a plastic bag for up to 4 days. Some plums are grown specifically to be dried as prunes. The majority, however, are enjoyed fresh for out-of-hand eating or for use in a wide variety of sweet and savory preparations. Also available are canned plums, packed in either water or sugar syrup. Plums contain a fair amount of vitamin A and potassium. *See also* BEACH PLUM; MIRABELLE; PLUMCOT; QUETSCH; SLOE.

plumcot The original cross between a PLUM and an APRICOT, created by renowned American horticulturist Luther Burbank. There are now several varieties of this fruit, all of which are a cross of these two fruits. All types of this cross, particularly the plumcot, have an intensely sweet and fruit flavor that, though akin to that of its parents, is likened to an incomparable blend of fruit juices. The true plumcot, with its generally equal heritage of plum and apricot, has a plumlike shape, smooth, dark red skin and an almost spicy flesh. The other two most notable apricot-plum crosses are the **aprium** (which has a predominantly apricot parentage and closely resembles the apricot in shape, flavor and skin fuzz) and the **pluot** (which has a predominantly plum parentage resulting in the plum's shape and generally smooth skin). Plumcots are more readily available than apriums and pluots, and can be found from May to October in produce markets and some supermarkets. Besides the United States, plum and apricot hybrids are also being produced throughout the world in Chile, Europe, South America and South Africa.

plum-duff *see* SPOTTED DICK

plump, to To soak dried fruit (such as raisins) in liquid until the fruit softens and swells slightly from absorbing some of the liquid.

plum pudding The name of this specialty comes from the fact that it originally contained plums, which it no longer does. Instead, this traditional Christmas dessert is made with SUET, dried currants, raisins, almonds and spices. It's either steamed or boiled and is often served warm, flamed with brandy or rum, and accompanied by HARD SAUCE.

plum sauce Also called *duck sauce,* this thick, sweet-and-sour condiment is made with plums, apricots, sugar and seasonings. Plum sauce is most often served with duck, pork or spareribs. *See also* SAUCE.

plum tomato *see* TOMATO

pluot *see* PLUMCOT

poach To cook food gently in liquid just below the boiling point when the liquid's surface is beginning to show some quivering movement. The amount and temperature of the liquid used depends on the food being poached. Meats and poultry are usually simmered in stock, fish in COURT-BOUILLON and eggs in lightly salted water, often with a little vinegar added. Fruit is often poached in a light SUGAR SYRUP. Poaching produces a delicate flavor in foods, while imparting some of the liquid's flavor to the ingredient being poached.

poblano chile [poh-BLAH-noh] A dark (sometimes almost black) green CHILE with a rich flavor that varies from mild to snappy; it has a SCOVILLE SCALE rating of 1,000 to 2,000. The darkest poblanos have the richest flavor. This chile is about 2½ to 3 inches wide and 4 to 5 inches long, tapering from top to bottom in a triangular shape. The very best poblanos are found in central Mexico, though they are now also grown in the U.S. Southwest. Fresh poblanos can be found in Latin markets and in many supermarkets. Their peak season is summer and early fall. They're also available canned. Ripe poblanos turn a reddish-brown color and are sweeter than the green. In their dried state they're known as ANCHO or MULATO chiles. Poblanos can be used in a variety of dishes, but are perhaps best known as the chile of choice for CHILES RELLENOS.

pocket bread *see* PITA

pod The natural outer covering that houses the seeds of legumes like BEANS, LENTILS, PEAS and SOYBEANS. The pods of many legumes are too tough to be eaten and must be removed (SHELLED), whereas some—like the SNOW PEA—have very tender pods that are deliciously edible.

pod pea A pea that's completely edible, including the pod. Examples include the SNOW PEA and SUGAR SNAP PEA. *See also* PEA.

poha [POH-hah] The Hawaiian name for CAPE GOOSEBERRY.

pohole [poh-HOH-lay] *see* FIDDLEHEAD FERN

poi [POY; POH-ee] This native Hawaiian dish is definitely an acquired taste. It's made from cooked TARO ROOT that is pounded to a smooth paste, then mixed with water, the amount depending on how the poi is to be served. Since poi is eaten with the fingers, its consistency is measured accordingly and ranges from "one-finger" (the thickest) to "three-finger" (the thinnest). Poi is generally fermented for several days, which gives it a sour, acidic taste. It can be eaten by itself, mixed with milk to make a porridge or served as a CONDIMENT for meat and fish. Poi is available in cans in Hawaii and in some specialty stores on the mainland.

point, à *see* À POINT

poire [PWAHR]; **poiré** [pwah-RAY] French for "pear," *poiré* is a pear CIDER (*see* PERRY).

poire Hélène [pwahr ay-LEHN] A dessert consisting of a pear that has been poached in a vanilla-flavored SUGAR SYRUP, chilled, then placed on a scoop of vanilla ice cream and topped with warm chocolate sauce. This dessert is also called *belle Hélène.*

Poire Williams [pwahr WEEL-yahms (VEEL-yahms)] A crystal clear, pear-flavored EAU DE VIE made in Switzerland and France. Premier brands are distinguished by a whole pear inside the bottle, a feat accomplished by placing a bottle over the budding fruit and allowing it to grow inside. After the pear is picked and the bottle removed from the branch, the bottle is filled with a BRANDY made from the Williams pear.

pois [PWAH] French for "pea" or "peas." *Petits pois* are small green peas.

poisson [pwah-SOH*N*] French for "fish." *Poisson d'eau douce* is "freshwater fish," *poisson de mer* is "seawater fish."

poissonier [pwah-soh-nyay] *see* BRIGADE SYSTEM

poivrade [pwah-VRAHD] 1. A family of French sauces with pepper (*poivre*) as a key ingredient. The best known of these is **poivrade sauce**, a mixture of caramelized MIREPOIX, white wine, vinegar, brown stock and crushed peppercorns; it's generally served with beef or GAME ANIMALS. **Chevreuil Sauce** is similar except red wine is used instead of white. **Grand-Veneur Sauce** is another close variation with the addition of red CURRANT jelly and cream. **Moscovite Sauce** is a poivrade flavored with juniper berries and Málaga, a sweet FORTIFIED wine from southern Spain. 2. The French name for a small violet-colored ARTICHOKE grown in Italy, Spain and southern France, particularly in Provence where the local variety is known as "Violet of Provence." The poivrade, with hints of grassiness and hazelnut, is much more flavorful than the more widely grown globe artichoke. Picked young, it can be eaten raw with a sprinkling of salt or vinaigrette. It can also be cooked in a variety of ways including steaming, sautéing and braising. *See also* SAUCE.

poivre [PWAHV-r] French for "pepper." *Poivre blanc* is white pepper and *poivre gris* or *poivre noir* is black pepper.

poivre mignonnette *see* MIGNONNETTE

poke [POH-keh] Hawaiian version of tuna TARTARE consisting of cubed raw fish, usually yellowfin TUNA (AHI), along with seaweed, CANDLENUTS and various seasonings.

polenta [poh-LEHN-tah] A staple of northern Italy, polenta is a MUSH made from cornmeal. It can be eaten hot with a little butter or cooled until firm, cut into squares and fried. Polenta is sometimes mixed with cheese such as PARMESAN or GORGONZOLA. It can be served as a first course or side dish and makes hearty breakfast fare.

Polish sausage *see* KIELBASA

pollo [*It.* POH-loh; *Sp.* POH-yoh] Italian and Spanish for "chicken."

pollock; pollack [POL-uhk] This member of the COD family is found in the North Atlantic. The low- to moderate-fat flesh is white, firm and has a delicate, slightly sweet flavor. The pollock can reach about 35 pounds but is normally found in markets between 4 and 10 pounds. It's available fresh, frozen and smoked, either whole or in fillets or steaks. Pollock may be prepared in any way suitable for cod. It's often used to make SURIMI. *See also* FISH.

polo; polow [PO-lo] In Persian cuisine, an elaborate version of CHELO (BASMATI RICE that's boiled and then steamed) that's layered with meat, fruit and/or vegetables and various herbs.

polonaise, à la [poh-loh-NEHZ] French for "in the manner of Poland," generally referring to cooked vegetables (most often cauliflower or asparagus) that are sprinkled with chopped hard-cooked egg, bread-crumbs, parsley and melted butter.

polvorone [pohl-voh-ROHN-ay] *see* MEXICAN WEDDING CAKE

polyunsaturated oil; polyunsaturates [pol-ee-uhn-SATCH-uh-ray-tehd] *see* FATS AND OILS

pomace [PUH-muss] The residue (skins, pits, seeds and pulp) that remains after a wine or juice has been pressed. Pomace is sometimes processed to make a BRANDY variously known as pomace brandy, EAU DE VIE, MARC (in France) and GRAPPA (in Italy and California).

pomegranate; pomegranate molasses [POM-uh-gran-uht] Nature's most labor-intensive fruit is about the size of a large orange and has a thin, leathery skin that can range in color from red to pink-blushed yellow. Inside are hundreds of seeds packed in compartments that are separated by bitter, cream-colored membranes. Each tiny, edible seed is surrounded by a translucent, brilliant-red pulp that has a sparkling sweet-tart flavor. This seed covering is called an **aril** (or **arillus**). Pomegranates are grown throughout Asia, the Mediterranean countries, Africa, India and in California. In the United States they're available from August through December. Choose those that are heavy for their size and have a bright, fresh color and blemish-free skin. Refrigerate for up to 2 months or store in a cool, dark place for up to a month. To use, cut the pomegranate in half and pry out the pulp-encased seeds, removing any of the light-colored membrane that may adhere. Be sure to wear an apron and gloves, as pomegranate stains are almost indelible. An easy way around the staining is to seed this fruit under water. Fill a sink with cold water, hold the pomegranate submerged in one hand and use a knife to cut it in half with the other. Use your fingers to pull apart the pomegranate, removing the membrane and seeds. The seeds will float to the water's surface. Pomegranate seeds can be eaten as fruit, used as a garnish on sweet and savory dishes or pressed to extract the juice. They're rich in potassium and contain a fair amount of vitamin C. **Pomegranate juice** has become immensely popular and can be found in supermarkets in a variety of permutations including plain or mixed with other juices such as cherry, tangerine or blueberry. **Pomegranate molasses** is a thick, syrupy pomegranate juice reduction that has a rich, tart flavor with a slightly sweet edge. It can be found in Middle Eastern markets and some gourmet markets and is used in Mediterranean dishes (such as in Turkey's MUHAMMARA) or as a marinade for grilled meats. ANARDANA are dried pomegranate seeds.

pomelo; pommelo; pummelo [pom-EH-loh] This giant citrus fruit is native to Malaysia (where it still grows abundantly) and thought to be ancestor to the GRAPEFRUIT. Like grapefruits, pomelos vary greatly in color, size and shape. They range from cantaloupe-size to as large as a 25-pound watermelon and have very thick, soft rind that can vary in color from yellow to pale yellowish-brown to pink. The light yellow to coral-pink flesh can vary from juicy to slightly dry and from seductively spicy-sweet to tangy and tart. The pomelo is also called *shaddock* after an English sea captain who introduced the seed to the West Indies. The French name for this fruit is *chadec.* It's also called *Chinese grapefruit*; the Chinese word for pomelo is a homophone for "blessing," which is why many consider this fruit auspicious. Pomelos are available in the winter from produce markets and some farmer's markets. Choose fruit that is heavy for its size, blemish-free and sweetly fragrant. Store in the refrigerator for up to a week. Pomelos may be used in any way suitable for GRAPEFRUIT. They're high in vitamin C and potassium. *See also* ORO BLANCO.

pomfret [POM-friht] *see* BUTTERFISH

pomme [POM] French for "apple."

pomme de terre [pom duh TEHR] A French phrase that literally means "apple of the earth," but which refers to the potato. The phrase is usually shortened to simply *pommes,* as in *pommes frites* (FRENCH FRIES).

pommelo *see* POMELO

pommes Anna [pom ANNA] Translated as "Anna potatoes," this classic French dish is a simple preparation of thinly sliced potatoes baked in a shallow dish or pie plate. Layers of potatoes are buttered and sprinkled with salt and pepper. The dish is then tightly covered with foil and the top weighted. After baking, the dish is inverted onto a serving plate and the potatoes turned out. The resulting potato "pie" is brown and crisp on the outside and soft and buttery on the inside. It's cut into wedges to serve.

pommes dauphine *see* DAUPHINE

pommes frites [pom FREET] French for "FRENCH FRIES."

pommes lyonnaise [pom ly-uh-NAYZ] Thinly sliced potatoes sautéed with onions.

pommes noisette [POM nwah-ZEHT] *Noisette* is French for "hazelnut," and this term refers to potatoes that have been cut into tiny, hazelnut-shape balls before being sautéed in butter until well browned.

pommes soufflées [pom soo-FLAY] Also known as *soufflé potatoes,* these crisp potato puffs are the result of deep-frying thinly sliced potatoes twice. The first time the potatoes are fried in 300°F oil. After cooling, they're fried in 375°F oil until they inflate and turn golden brown.

pomodoro [poh-moh-DAW-roh] Literally translating to "golden apple," pomodoro is Italian for "tomato" (the first tomatoes in Italy were a yellowish color). Dishes described as *al pomodoro* are served with a tomato sauce.

pompano [PAHM-puh-noh] 1. A member of the JACK family, this saltwater fish is found in waters off South Atlantic and Gulf states. Its succulent, fine-textured, moderately fat flesh has a mild, delicate flavor. Pompano is considered by many to be America's finest fish—one reason, no doubt, that it's so expensive. It's marketed whole and in fillets, both fresh and frozen. Pompano may be prepared by almost any cooking method. The most famous dish made from this fish is **pompano en papillote**, where it's baked in PARCHMENT PAPER with mushrooms and VELOUTÉ. 2. **Pacific pompano** is a variety of BUTTERFISH. *See also* FISH.

pompelmo [pohm-pehl-moh] Italian for "grapefruit."

pom pom mushroom A beautiful white mushroom named for its resemblance to a cheerleader's pompoms. This firm yet feathery specimen ranges from 4 to 10 inches in diameter. It can be found in some produce markets throughout the year. Select those with a bright white color and no signs of yellowing. *See also* MUSHROOM.

Ponentine olive [POH-ehn-tihn-ee] Small, brine-cured olive from northwestern Italy's Liguria region. It's purplish-black and oval-shaped with a point on the end and sometimes has an attached stem. Ponentines are often packed in vinegar and oil. Their flesh is firm and crisp, with a mild, nutty flavor. *See also* OLIVE.

Pont l'Évêque [PAW*N*-lay-VEHK] This uncooked, ripened cheese was well known as far back as the 13th century. It's name comes from the village of Pont-l'Evêque near Le Havre in northern Normandy. It's made from whole or partially skimmed cow's milk and has a milk fat content of at least 45 percent. The square-shape cheese has a golden or golden-orange rind. The interior is ivory to pale yellow with a creamy, softly oozing texture and a fresh, sweet-tart flavor. A well-ripened Pont l'Évêque will smell strong but not stinky. Avoid those that are gummy or bitter tasting. Pont l'Évêque has a minimum FAT CONTENT of 45 percent. *See also* CHEESE.

pony 1. A small (about 1 ounce) bar measure, which is sometimes also used to serve LIQUEURS. 2. The term also refers to the amount of liquid such a glass holds (usually 1 ounce), as in a pony of whiskey. *See also* SHOT; JIGGER.

ponzu [PON-zoo] A Japanese sauce made with lemon juice or RICE VINEGAR, SOY SAUCE, MIRIN and/or SAKE, KOMBU (SEAWEED) and dried bonito flakes (KATSUOBUSHI). Ponzu is used as a dipping sauce with dishes like SASHIMI and with one-pot dishes like CHIRINABE. *See also* SAUCE.

poolish *see* YEAST STARTER

poorboy; po' boy *see* HERO SANDWICH

poori; puri [POOR-ee] This deep-fried bread is round, flat and UNLEAVENED. It's made with whole-wheat flour, water and GHEE or other fat—the dough is almost identical to that for CHAPATI. Poori is very popular in northern India as well as in neighboring Pakistan.

poor knights of Windsor English version of FRENCH TOAST named after a 14th century military organization set up to help knights who had financial difficulty after fighting for Edward III. It's usually made with stale bread dipped into a mixture of SHERRY, milk and sugar, and then into egg yolks, before being fried.

popadam; poppadum *see* PAPPADOM

popcorn; popped corn Said to date back at least 6,000 years, popcorn is a special variety of dried corn that pops open and puffs up when heated. This transformation occurs because of a high amount of natural moisture trapped inside the hull. Heating the corn creates immense pressure, which bursts open the hull, turning the kernel inside-out. Popcorn comes in many styles, from white to yellow to red to blue, from plain to flavored, and from oil-popped to air-popped. There's also special popcorn formulated for use in the MICROWAVE OVEN, as well as ears of popcorn, the kernels of which pop right on the cob. For regular (sans oil) packaged popcorn, 1 tablespoon of oil plus $1/2$ cup corn kernels yields about 4 cups of popped corn. Unpopped popcorn can be stored at room temperature for about a year, but retains its natural moisture (which means it will produce larger popped kernels) better if stored *airtight* in the refrigerator or freezer. Popcorn packaged with oil in its own "pan" should be stored no longer than about 3 months at room temperature. One cup of plain popcorn equals about 30 calories; 1 cup buttered popcorn equals 90 to 120 calories, depending on the amount of butter.

popcorn shrimp Typically served as an appetizer, popcorn shrimp are breaded, deep-fried, bite-sized pieces of SHRIMP that can be eaten like popcorn. This creation originally used only the sweet, firm ROCK SHRIMP, but today other small shrimp or pieces of large shrimp are also often used.

pope's nose Also known as a *parson's nose,* this is the stubby tail protuberance of a dressed fowl. It seems to have originated as a derogatory term meant to demean Catholics in England during the late 17th century.

popover A puffy, muffin-size bread with a crisp brown crust and a somewhat hollow, moist interior. Basic popovers begin with a simple batter of eggs, milk, butter and flour. The high proportion of liquid in the batter creates steam that LEAVENS the bread. Popovers *may be* baked in muffin tins or special **popover pans**, which have six extra-deep cups. The name is said to come from the fact that as the batter bakes and expands, it "pops over" the sides of the cup-shaped indentations. Popovers can be plain or variously flavored with items such as cheese, spices or herbs.

poppy seed; poppyseed These small, dried, bluish-gray seeds of the poppy plant measure less than $1/16$ inch in diameter—it takes about 900,000 of them to equal a pound. Poppy seeds have a crunchy texture and a nutty flavor. They're used as a filling in various cakes, pastries and coffee cakes, as a topping for myriad baked goods, in salad dressings and in a variety of cooked dishes—particularly those originating in central Europe, the Middle East and India. Poppy seeds can be purchased whole or ground in most supermarkets. There are also beige and brown poppy seeds, which are more commonly available in Asian or Middle Eastern markets. Because of their high oil content, all poppy seeds are prone to rancidity. They should therefore be stored, airtight, in the refrigerator for up to 6 months. The flavor of poppy seed is augmented by toasting. *See also* SPICES; Seasoning Suggestions, page 891.

porchetta [pohr-KAYT-tah] An Italian dish of slow-roasted boneless suckling pig. Sometimes larger pigs or parts such as pork bellies, pork shoulders or pork loins are used. Prior to roasting, the meat is seasoned with a mixture of flavorings including fennel, garlic, pepper, rosemary and salt; sometimes it's stuffed with onions, garlic and herbs. During roasting, the meat is basted with olive oil and/or wine. Porchetta is sometimes spelled *porquetta,* and American versions are sometimes referred to as *porkcetta, porkchetta* or *porketta.*

porcino; *pl.* **porcini** [pohr-CHEE-nee] Also called *cèpes,* these delicious, earthy treasures are members of the *Boletus edulis* species of wild mushroom. They're pale brown in color and can weigh from an ounce or two up to a pound. Their caps can range from 1 to 10 inches in diameter. Porcini have a smooth, meaty texture and pungent, woodsy flavor that is much regaled. You'll seldom find them fresh in the United States but you might try looking for them in specialty produce markets in late spring or in the autumn. If you get lucky, choose those with firm, large (about 6-inch) caps and pale undersides. The dried form of this mushroom is more readily available. Choose those that are a tan to pale brown in color; avoid those that are crumbly. Dried porcini must be softened in hot water for about 20 minutes before using. They can be substituted for cultivated mushrooms in most recipes. One ounce of dried mushrooms will serve about 4 people in soups, stuffings, stews and the like. Porcini are also known as *Boletes* and *Steinpilze. See also* MUSHROOM.

porgy [POHR-gee] Widely known as *sea bream,* there are many different varieties of this fish family in the United States and around the world. The most popular United States porgy is the **scup,** which is found in Atlantic waters. Porgies have a firm, low-fat flesh with a delicate, mild flavor. Although some grow to 20 pounds, most fall into the $1/2$- to 3-pound range. They're available fresh and frozen, and are generally sold whole. The porgy is suitable for almost any method of cooking, including baking, grilling and frying. *See also* FISH.

pork The tried-but-true saying that everything but the pig's squeal can be used is accurate indeed. Though pigs are bred primarily for their meat (commonly referred to as pork) and fat, the trimmings and lesser cuts (feet, jowl, tail, etc.) are used for SAUSAGE, the bristles for brushes, the hair for furniture and the skin for leather. The majority of pork in the marketplace today is CURED—like BACON and HAM—while the remainder is termed "fresh." Slaughterhouses can (but usually don't) request and pay for their pork to be graded by the U.S. Department of Agriculture (USDA). The grades are USDA 1, 2, 3, 4 and utility—from the best downwards—based on the proportion of lean to fat. Whether graded or not, all pork used for intrastate commerce is subjected to state or federal inspection for wholesomeness, insuring that the slaughter and processing of the animal was done under sanitary conditions. Pork shipped interstate must be federally inspected. Today's pork is leaner (about $1/3$ fewer calories) and higher in protein than that consumed just 10 years ago. (*See* HERITAGE PORK for the flipside of that coin: traditionally bred hogs with generous fat marbling.) Thanks to improved feeding techniques, trichinosis in pork is now also rarely an issue. Normal precautions should still be taken, however, such as washing anything (hands, knives, cutting boards, etc.) that comes in contact with raw pork and never tasting uncooked pork. Cooking it to an internal temperature of 137°F will kill any trichinae. However, allowing for a safety margin for thermometer inaccuracy, most experts recommend an internal temperature of from 150° to 165°F, which will still produce a juicy, tender result. The 170° to 185°F temperature recommended in many cookbooks produces overcooked meat. Though pork generally refers to young swine under a year old, most pork today is slaughtered at between 6 to 9 months, producing a leaner, more tender meat. Look for pork that is pale pink with a small amount of marbling and white (not yellow) fat. The darker pink the flesh, the older the animal. Fresh pork that will be used within 6 hours of purchase may be refrigerated in its store packaging. Otherwise, remove the packaging and store loosely wrapped with waxed paper in the coldest part of the refrigerator for up to 2 days. Wrapped airtight, pork can be frozen from 3 to 6 months, with the larger cuts having longer storage capabilities than chops or ground meat. Some of the more popular fresh pork cuts are **pork chops**, **pork loin** and **pork ribs**. The most popular cured pork products include ham, bacon, CANADIAN BACON and SALT PORK. *See also* Pork Chart, page 898; CHOP; CROWN ROAST; CUTLET; FATBACK; HERITAGE PORK; KIDNEY; PICNIC HAM; PIG'S FEET; SHANK; SPARERIBS; SWEETBREADS; TONGUE; TRIPE; VARIETY MEATS.

porkcetta; porkchetta; porketta [pohr-KAYT-tah] *see* POR-CHETTA

pörkölt *see* GOULASH

pork pie *see* MELTON MOWBRAY PORK PIE

pork sausage, fresh A general category for uncooked SAUSAGE made with fresh ground pork and pork fat, usually mildly seasoned with pepper and sage. Under U.S. law, fresh pork sausage cannot contain more than 50 percent fat or 3 percent added moisture. It comes in link, patty and bulk form.

pork shoulder *see* PICNIC HAM

porquetta [pohr-KAYT-tah] *see* PORCHETTA

porra *see* SALMOREJO

porridge [POR-ihj] A thick, puddinglike dish made of cereal or grain (usually oatmeal) cooked in water or milk. Porridge is usually eaten hot for breakfast with sugar and milk or cream.

port; Porto A sweet FORTIFIED WINE whose name derives from the fact that such wines are shipped out of the Portugese city of Oporto. Today, there's a specific region in northern Portugal's Douro Valley that has exacting regulations for producing quality port wines. There are four basic categories of port—Vintage, Tawny, Ruby and White. **Vintage Ports**, the best and most expensive, must be made from grapes of a single VINTAGE and only from the best "declared" (those considered superior) vintages. A port producer won't make a traditional vintage port in undeclared years but will make other types of port wine. Vintage ports must be bottled within 2 years; the very best can age 50 years or more. **Tawny Ports**, tawny in color and ready to drink when bottled, are made from a blend of grapes from several different years and can be aged in wood for as long as 40 years (labels typically indicate the number of years); low-priced versions are blends of white and ruby ports. **Ruby Ports**, generally the least expensive, are made from lower-quality wine, wood-aged for about 2 years and bottled while still youthful, fruity and bright red in color. **White Ports** are those made from white grapes (the DRY versions undergo a longer FERMENTATION). Within the four basic port categories are many types. **Single quinta Ports** are essentially vintage ports made in nondeclared years—they are still considered excellent. **Second label vintage Ports** are produced when the vintage is quite good, but not quite good enough to be declared. **Late Bottled Vintage Ports (LBV)** and **Colheita Ports** (also called *Single Vintage Ports* or *Dated Ports*) are made from single-vintage grapes that aren't as high quality as those for vintage ports. LBVs are aged in wood from 4 to 6 years and are considered high-quality ruby ports; Colheita ports have been wood-aged at least 7 years and fall into the tawny port category. Both are ready to drink when bottled and don't have the aging potential of Vintage Ports. **Crusted Ports**—a blend of two or three wines from different vintages—are aged for 3 or 4 years before being bottled and, like vintage port, improve with bottle aging. **Vintage Character Ports**—the lightest and fruitiest and ready to drink when bottled—are essentially high-quality ruby ports, blended from several vintages and wood-aged. In countries other than Portugal, port is a generic name for wines created in the image of the Portuguese originals. Inexpensive "ports" will generally label their wines simply Ruby or Tawny port. There are some non-Portuguese vintage ports that are made either from native Portuguese varieties or often ZINFANDEL or CABERNET SAUVIGNON.

porter A heavy, dark-brown, strongly flavored beer. The dark color and strong flavor come from the addition of roasted MALT. Originally brewed in a bitter style, some of today's porters are slightly sweet. Porters are usually higher in alcohol than regular LAGER beers. *See also* BEER.

porterhouse steak A steak cut from the large end of the SHORT LOIN containing meat from both the tenderloin (the most tender cut of meat) and the top loin muscle. This is one of the best and most expensive steaks. *See also* BEEF; Beef Chart, page 896.

portobello mushroom; portabello; portobella [por-toh-BEHL-loh] An extremely large, dark brown mushroom that is simply the fully mature form of the CREMINO, which in turn is a variation of the common cultivated white mushroom. The name "portobello" began to be used in the 1980s as a brilliant marketing ploy to popularize an unglamorous mushroom that, more often than not, had to be disposed of because growers couldn't sell them. The portobello mushroom, which can easily measure 6 inches in diameter, has an open, flat cap. Because it's the elder of the species, the portobello's gills are fully exposed, which means that some of the mushroom's moisture has evaporated. The reduced moisture concentrates and enriches the flavor and creates a dense, meaty texture. Portobellos can be found in gourmet produce markets as well as many supermarkets. Their stems are very woody and should be removed (but saved for soups, stocks, etc.). The caps can be used chopped, as with most mushrooms, but the portobello is much more dramatic used whole. It's particularly popular grilled and used in a sandwich, or cut into thick slices for a salad or entrée. *See also* MUSHROOM.

Port-Salut [POHR sah-LOO] A semisoft cheese first made by 19th-century Trappist monks at the Monastery of Port-du-Salut in the Brittany region of France. It's made from cow's milk and comes in thick 5-pound cylinders (about 9 inches in diameter) with an orange rind and ivory interior. It has a mild, savory flavor, a smooth, satiny texture and a FAT CONTENT of 45 percent. SAFR, a giant dairy company in Lorraine, produces most Port-Salut. A FARMSTEAD version, called Entrammes, is produced by the monks. *See also* CHEESE.

posole; pozole [poh-SOH-leh] A thick, hearty soup usually eaten as a main course. It consists of pork (sometimes chicken) meat and broth, HOMINY, onion, garlic, dried CHILES and CILANTRO. It's usually served with chopped lettuce, radishes, onions, cheese and cilantro, which diners can add to the soup as they please. Posole originated in Jalisco, in the middle of Mexico's Pacific Coast region, and is traditionally served at Christmastime.

posset [POS-iht] In the Middle Ages this hearty hot drink was considered a remedy for colds. It consists of hot milk, wine or ale, sugar and spices. Some versions add beaten egg, making it even richer.

postre [POHS-tray] Spanish for "dessert."

pot *n.* A round, deep cooking container that usually has two handles and a lid. Pots can range from small to large. Except for SKILLETS, most cooking containers can be called pots. **pot** *v.* An older method of preserving food by cooking it in plenty of fat and a small amount of water. After cooking, the food is placed in small pots or jars and covered with a layer of fat. As the fat cools and hardens it forms an airtight seal, protecting the food from airborne bacteria. Refrigeration and other modern food-packaging methods have limited the necessity for potting foods, but some traditional dishes like French CONFITS are still potted and enjoyed today.

potable *adj.* [POH-tuh-bl] A word used to describe a liquid suitable for drinking, such as *potable* water. **potable** *n.* Any beverage, particularly those containing alcohol.

potage [poh-TAHZH] The French have three separate words for soup. CONSOMMÉ is a clear, thin broth. *Soupe* refers to a thick, hearty mélange with chunks of food. Potage falls somewhere between the first two in texture and thickness. A potage is usually puréed and is often thickened slightly with cream or egg yolks. Today, the words *soupe* and *potage* are often used interchangeably.

potassium nitrate *see* SALTPETER

potato; potatoes The ancient Incas were cultivating this humble tuber thousands of years ago. The potato was not readily accepted in Europe, however, because it was known to be a member of the nightshade family (as are the tomato and eggplant) and therefore thought to be poisonous. In the 16th century, Sir Walter Raleigh was instrumental in debunking the poisonous potato superstition when he planted them on property he owned in Ireland. The Irish knew a good thing when they saw it and a hundred years later were growing and consuming the potato in great quantities. Today, hundreds of varieties of this popular vegetable are grown around the world. In America, the potato can be divided into four basic categories: russet, long white, round white and round red. **Russet potatoes** (also called *old potatoes, baking potatoes* and, sometimes, *Idaho potatoes*—after the state leading in production) have an elliptical shape with a rough, brown skin and numerous eyes. The russet's white flesh is somewhat dry and mealy after cooking. This potato's low moisture and high starch content make it excellent for baking, mashing and frying. Varieties include *Russet Burbank, Russet Arcadia, Russet Norkotah* and *Butte.* **Long white potatoes** have a similar shape as the russet but they have thin, pale gray-brown skins with almost imperceptible eyes. They're sometimes called *white rose* or *California long whites,* after the state in which they were developed. Long whites can be baked, boiled or fried. The thumb-size baby long whites are called **fingerling potatoes**. The medium-size **round white** and **round red potatoes** are also commonly referred to as *boiling potatoes*. They're almost identical except that the round white has a freckled brown skin and the round red a reddish-brown coat. They both have a waxy flesh that contains less starch and more moisture than the russet and long white. This makes them better suited for boiling (they're both commonly used to make mashed potatoes) than for baking. They're also good for roasting and frying. The round white is grown mainly in the Northeast where it's sometimes referred to by one of its variety names, *Katahdin*. The round red is cultivated mainly in the Northwest. **Yukon gold potatoes** have a skin and flesh that ranges from buttery yellow to golden. These boiling potatoes have a moist, almost succulent texture and make excellent mashed potatoes. There are a variety of relatively new potatoes in the marketplace, most of which aren't new at all but rather heritage vegetables that date back centuries. Among the more distinctive examples are the **All Blue potatoes**, which range in color from bluish purple to purple-black. These small potatoes have a dense texture and are good for boiling. Other purple potatoes have skin colors that range from lavender to dark blue and flesh that can be from white to beige with purple streaking. Among the **red-fleshed potatoes** are the *huckleberry* (red skin and flesh) and the *blossom* (pinkish-red skin and flesh). **New potatoes** are simply young potatoes (any variety). They haven't had time to convert their sugar fully into starch and consequently have a crisp, waxy texture and thin, undeveloped wispy skins. New potatoes are small enough to cook whole and are excellent boiled or pan-roasted. Because they retain their shape after being cooked and cut, new potatoes are particularly suited for use in potato salad. The season for new potatoes is spring to early summer. **Marble potatoes** are smaller, younger versions of new potatoes. They can be from any variety and are young, tender and bite-sized, with very thin skins and buttery flesh. Because they are marble-sized, they are very easy to prepare (no cutting involved) and cook (skins and all). Potatoes of one variety or another are available year-round. Choose potatoes that are suitable for the desired method of cooking. All potatoes should be firm, well-shaped (for their type) and blemish-free. New potatoes may be missing some of their feathery skin but other types should not have any bald spots. Avoid potatoes that are wrinkled, sprouted or cracked. A green tinge—indicative of prolonged light exposure—is caused by the alkaloid solanine, which can be toxic if eaten in quantity. This bitter green portion can be cut or scraped off and the potato used in the normal fashion. Store potatoes in a cool, dark, well-ventilated place for up to 2 weeks. New potatoes should be used within 3 days of purchase. Refrigerating potatoes causes them to become quite sweet and to turn dark when cooked. Warm temperatures encourage sprouting and shriveling. Potatoes are probably the most versatile vegetable in the world and can be cooked in any way imaginable. They're available in a wide selection of commercial products including POTATO CHIPS, instant mashed potatoes (dehydrated cooked potatoes), canned new potatoes and a plethora of frozen products including HASH BROWNS, FRENCH FRIES and stuffed baked potatoes. Potatoes are not at all hard on the waistline (a 6-ounce potato contains only about 120 calories) and pack a nutritional punch. They're low in sodium, high in potassium and an important source of complex carbohydrates and vitamins C and B-6, as well as a storehouse of minerals. Neither SWEET POTATOES nor YAMS are botanically related to the potato. *See also* ALLUMETTES; CHIPS; DELMONICO POTATOES; DUCHESS POTATOES; FORESTIÈRE; FRENCH FRIES; GAUFRETTES POMMES DE TERRE; GERMAN POTATO SALAD; HASH BROWNS; HOME-FRIED POTATOES; IRISH POTATO; O'BRIEN POTATOES; PARMENTIER; POMMES ANNA; POMMES DAUPHINE; POMME DE TERRE; POMMES FRITES; POMMES LYONNAISE; POMMES NOISETTE; POMMES SOUFFLÉES; POTATO FLOUR; POTATO SALAD; RÖSTI; STRAW POTATOES.

potato chips Because these deep-fried, thinly sliced potatoes were invented by the chef of a Saratoga Springs, New York, hotel in the mid-19th-century, they're also called *Saratoga chips*. These all-American favorites come commercially in a wide selection of sizes, cuts (ripple and flat), thicknesses, and flavors such as chive, barbecue and NACHO. Most commercial potato chips contain preservatives; those labeled "natural" usually do not. Some are salted while others are labeled "low-salt"; though most potato chips are skinless, others do include the flavorful skin. There are even chips made from mashed potatoes formed into perfect rounds and packed into crushproof cardboard cylinders. All potato chips should be stored in an air-tight container in a cool, dark place. The storage time depends on whether or not they contain preservatives and how old they were when purchased. Some chips have a freshness date stamped on the package.

potato flour Also called *potato starch,* this gluten-free flour is made from cooked, dried and ground potatoes. It's used as a thickener and, because it produces a moist crumb, in some baked goods.

potato ricer *see* RICER

potato salad A salad of cooked, diced or cubed potatoes mixed with other ingredients such as chopped onion, green peppers, celery, hard-cooked eggs, seasonings and a mayonnaise- or sour cream–based dressing. German potato salad, often served hot, is bound with a vinegar-bacon fat dressing.

potato starch *see* POTATO FLOUR

pot-au-feu [poh-toh-FEUH] "Pot on fire" is the literal translation of this French phrase. Culinarily it refers to a French dish of meat and vegetables slowly cooked in water. The resulting rich broth is served with croutons as a first course, followed by an entrée of the meat and vegetables. Any combination of meat and vegetables can be used and the mix varies according to the region. If the meat has MARROW-filled bones, the marrow can be served on toast as another course preceding the entrée.

pot beans; pot of beans *see* FRIJOLES DE LA OLLA

pot cheese A soft, fresh CHEESE that is basically COTTAGE CHEESE that is drained longer and therefore has a drier, slightly grainy texture, which is why it's also called *dry-curd cottage cheese*.

pot de crème; pot-au-crème [poh duh KREHM; poht-oh-KREHM] French for "pot of cream," this dessert consists of a creamy-rich custard prepared and served in tiny (about 3-ounce) pot-shaped cups. Though the classic flavoring is vanilla, *pot de crème* comes in many variations including chocolate and coffee.

potimarron *see* RED KURI

potlikker; pot liquor The vitamin-rich liquid left after cooking greens, vegetables, meat, etc. This broth is particularly popular in the southern United States and is traditionally served separately with cornbread or CORN PONE.

potluck 1. A meal at which each guest brings a prepared dish (salad, entrée, vegetable, dessert, etc.) that is shared by everyone else. 2. Whatever food is available in the house for a meal.

pot marjoram *see* MARJORAM

pot pie; potpie A dish of chunks of meat or poultry, chopped vegetables and rich sauce, combined in a deep bowl or casserole, topped with a pastry crust and baked.

pot roast *n.* Usually an inexpensive, less tender cut of beef that is first browned, then braised very slowly in a covered pot with a little liquid. The result is a flavorful, tender piece of meat. CHUCK or ROUND cuts are the most popular for this dish. The dish is called **Yankee pot roast** when vegetables are added to the pot partway through the cooking process. **pot roast** *v.* To cook meat by browning, then braising in a covered pot either on top of the stove or in the oven.

pots and pans *see* COOKWARE AND BAKEWARE MATERIALS

pot stickers Small dumplings made of WON TON SKINS filled with ground meat or shellfish, chopped water chestnuts, scallions and seasonings. The pot stickers are browned on one side, then turned and simmered in broth. Pot stickers are usually served as appetizers, accompanied with various dipping sauces.

potted shrimp Finely diced or puréed cooked shrimp mixed with seasoned butter, then placed in small pots covered with additional melted butter and refrigerated. Potted shrimp is usually spread on toast and served as an HORS D'OEUVRE. *See also* POT *v.*

poularde [poo-LAHRD] The French term referring to a fat chicken or hen suitable for roasting.

poulenta *see* KATSAMAKI

poulet [poo-LAY] The French word for a young, tender spring chicken.

poultry Any domesticated bird used as food. Centuries ago the Chinese began raising a variety of birds that were gradually brought to the West via Asia, Greece and Rome. Today there are many domesticated varieties of poultry including CHICKEN, TURKEY, DUCK, GOOSE, Rock Cornish hen (*see* CHICKEN), GUINEA FOWL and PHEASANT. All poultry ranks high nutritionally. It's classified as a complete protein, is a good source of calcium, phosphorus and iron and contains riboflavin, thiamine and niacin. *See* CHICKEN *for information regarding purchasing, storing and preparing poultry.*

poultry shears A scissorlike implement designed to cut up poultry. A good pair of poultry shears has slip-proof handles and slightly curved blades, one with a serrated and notched edge for gripping the flesh and cutting bones. Poultry shears make easy work of cutting up a duck, snipping out the backbone of a chicken or cutting up a stewing hen to be used for stock. They also perform additional useful tasks such as trimming artichokes and other vegetables.

pound cake Originally this fine-textured loaf cake was made with one pound each of flour, butter, sugar and eggs, plus a flavoring like vanilla or lemon. A myriad of variations have evolved throughout the years, with additions such as leavening (baking powder or baking soda) and flavorings such as coconut, nuts, raisins and dried fruit. With reduced cholesterol and calories in mind, there are now pound cakes made with vegetable oil, as well as nonfat versions.

pourriture noble [poo-ree-tyoor NAW-bluh] *see* BOTRYTIS CINEREA

pousse-café; Pousse-Café [poos ka-FAY] 1. This French term literally means "push the coffee," and in France refers in general to cordials, brandies, etc. that might be served after dinner with coffee. 2. In the United States, it refers to a very elaborate, multicolored after-dinner drink made by layering 2 to 7 or more various LIQUEURS on top of one another without disturbing the layer below. A slender, straight-sided liqueur glass is used and the heaviest (usually the sweetest) liqueurs are poured in first. The pousse-Café debuted in New Orleans in the mid-19th century and was all the rage by the early 1900s.

poussin [poo-SAHN] French for a very young, small CHICKEN. Also called *petit poussin* and *squat chicken.*

poutine [poo-TEEN] The ultimate in French-Canadian junk food, poutine is a mélange of warm french fries, topped with fresh cheese curds, then smothered with gravy. The subject of the gravy is widely debated—some say it should be beef, others declare chicken gravy is the only way to go, and still others proclaim a spicy barbecue sauce is the answer. This Québécois favorite is consumed while hot with a fork.

powdered milk *see* DRY MILK

powdered sugar *see* SUGAR

pozole *see* POSOLE

praches *see* HOLISHKES

Prague powder #1; Prague powder #2 *see* SODIUM NITRATE

prairie oyster *see* FRIES

praline [PRAH-leen; prah-LEEN; PRAY-leen] 1. A brittle confection made of almonds and CARAMELIZED sugar. It may be eaten as candy, ground and used as a filling or dessert ingredient, or sprinkled atop desserts as a garnish. 2. A special patty-shaped candy from Louisiana made with pecans and brown sugar.

praliné [pra-lee-NAY] A food that is garnished, coated or made with PRALINE or almonds.

prawn There is a great deal of confusion about this term because it's used to describe several different SHELLFISH. 1. The first definition refers to a species that's part of the lobster family and includes those CRUSTACEANS variously called *Dublin Bay prawn, Danish lobster, Italian scampi, langoustine* (French), *langostino* (Spanish), *Caribbean lobsterette* and *Florida lobsterette*. These "prawns" have bodies shaped like tiny Maine LOBSTERS including minuscule claws. The meat has a sweet, delicate flavor that some claim is better than either lobster or shrimp. These "prawns" are 6 to 8 inches in length and have pale-red bodies deepening to dark-red tails. 2. A second definition applies to the freshwater prawn (identified by the Latin name *Macrobrachium*); the term distinguishes SHRIMP as living in salt water and prawns as freshwater creatures. In truth, these prawns migrate (much like salmon) from salt water to fresh water to spawn. They look like a cross between a shrimp and a lobster, with their bodies having narrower abdomens and longer legs than shrimp. *See also* HAWAIIAN BLUE PRAWN. 3. The term "prawn" is also loosely used to describe any large shrimp, especially those that come 15 (or fewer) to the pound (also called "jumbo shrimp").

pre-ferement *see* YEAST STARTER

prepared mustard *see* MUSTARD, PREPARED

preserve; preserves 1. Fruit cooked with sugar and usually PEC-TIN, used as a spread for bread. Preserves differ from JAM in that the fruit is left in medium to large chunks rather than being puréed. *See also* CON-SERVE; JELLY. 2. To prepare foods so that they can be kept for long periods of time without spoiling or deteriorating. Depending on the food and the length of time it's to be stored, preserving can be accomplished in a number of different ways including refrigeration, freezing, canning, salt-ing, smoking, freeze-drying, dehydrating and pickling.

preserved lemons Lemons that have been MACERATED in a salt–lemon juice brine (sometimes with spices such as cinnamon, cloves and coriander) for about 30 days. Preserved lemons have a silken texture and a distinctive flavor. They're an indispensable ingredient and flavoring in Moroccan cooking and used as a flavoring by many of today's leading chefs.

preserved sweet melon *see* TEA MELON

pressed cookie Fancy cookies that are formed by pressing dough through a COOKIE PRESS or PASTRY BAG fitted with a decorative tip. *See also* COOKIE.

pressed duck 1. A French specialty in which the breast and legs are removed from a cooked duck. The remainder of the bird is compressed in a special implement called a DUCK PRESS, which extracts all the juices. The extracted juice is mixed with reduced red wine, cognac and butter to produce a delicious sauce that is served with the sliced breast and legs. 2. A Chinese dish in which the duck is steamed, boned and flattened, then steamed and flattened again. The duck is then cut into quarters and deep-fried to a golden brown. Before serving, it's cut into squares and served on a bed of shredded lettuce, garnished with toasted almonds and accompanied with a pungent sauce.

pressing A process in cheesemaking by which WHEY is removed from the CURDS, which helps join the curds together and produces a uniform consistency in the final cheese. Once cheese is placed in a mold, it can be pressed in different ways—by hand, mechanically (with hydraulic presses) or by stacking the molds so the weight of the cheeses does the pressing. Cheeses aren't always pressed. For example, soft cheeses like CHÈVRE are placed in a perforated mold and gravity drains the whey. *See also* CHEDDARING.

pressure cooker A special cooking pot with a locking, airtight lid and a valve system to regulate internal pressure. Pressure cookers operate on a principle whereby the steam that builds up inside the pressurized pot cooks food at a very high temperature. This reduces the cooking time by as much as two-thirds without destroying the food's nutritional value. Newer pressure cooker designs feature built-in valves and indicator rods that indicate the pressure. Traditional models are equipped with detachable pressure regulators that can adjust the pressure for low (5 pounds), medium (10 pounds) or high (15 pounds). The more pounds of pressure, the higher the internal temperature and the quicker the food cooks. Pressure cookers have a safety valve, which will automatically vent the steam should there be a malfunction. There are many styles of pressure cookers on the market today, most of which are made for stovetop cooking. But there are also small pressure cookers that can be used in a microwave oven. Some of the newer pressure cookers have built-in pressure regulators. Pressure cookers are useful for foods that would normally be cooked with moist heat such as soups, stews, steamed puddings, tough cuts of meat, artichokes, etc. They can also be used for canning, and there are special **pressure canners** made specifically for this purpose.

pretzel [PREHT-zuhl] The pretzel can be traced back to the Romans, although the twisted loose knot shape is thought to have been introduced in the early part of the 7th century. The first U.S. commercial pretzel factory was established in 1861 in Lititz, Pennsylvania. There are two main types of pretzel—hard and crisp or soft and chewy (the older of the two forms). The latter is often sold hot with mustard by street vendors from their pretzel carts. Pretzels can be sprinkled with coarse salt or not, and shaped in the form of knots, sticks or rings. Crisp pretzels are available in many sizes, shapes and even flavors (such as rye) in supermarkets.

prezzo fisso [PREHT-zoh FEE-soh] Italian for "fixed price," referring to a complete meal served by a restaurant or hotel for a preset price. The French counterpart is PRIX FIXE.

prick To make small holes in the surface of food. The best example is an unfilled pie dough that is pricked all over with the tines of a fork so it bakes without blistering or rising (*see* BAKE BLIND).

pricked onion *see* ONION PIQUÉ

prickly pear *see* CACTUS PEAR

Prima Donna [pree-mah DAH-nah] SEMIHARD COW's-milk cheese from the Netherlands that resembles a GOUDA. However, because it's made with partially skimmed milk and has a FAT CONTENT below the minimum 48 percent required for Gouda it can't be called that. The 25- to 30-pound wheels come with a dark blue or a red wax coating. Those with a dark blue covering are younger cheeses that have been aged for a minimum of 6 months. Their texture is smooth and supple and the flavor is rich, fruity and nutty. Those cheeses with red wax are called Prima Donna *Maturo* and are RIPENED for 16 months or more. These are similar to aged Goudas such as Beemster, Rembrandt and Saenkanter. The red wax versions are harder, flaky and brittle, and full of crunchy bits of sweet, crystallized protein; they have rich caramel and butterscotch flavors.

primavera, alla [pree-muh-VEHR-uh] This Italian phrase means "spring style" and culinarily refers to the use of fresh vegetables (raw or blanched) as a garnish to various dishes. One of the most popular dishes prepared in this manner is **pasta primavera**, pasta tossed or topped with diced or JULIENNED cooked vegetables.

prime rib The term "prime rib" is often incorrectly used as a label for what is actually a RIB ROAST. Culinarily, the term "prime" actually refers to the highest USDA beef grade. It's only given to the finest beef, hallmarked by even marbling and a creamy layer of fat. Very little prime beef makes it past the better hotels and restaurants or prestige butchers. The best grade of beef generally found in supermarkets is USDA Choice. Therefore, although "prime rib" is how rib roast is often labeled, chances are that it's USDA Choice beef. *See* BEEF; Beef Chart, page 896.

primost *see* GJETOST

prince of rice *see* KAIJIRA RICE

printanière, à la [ah lah prah*n*-tah-NYEHR] Taken from *printemps* ("spring"), this French term means "in the style of spring" and describes a dish garnished with tiny (or small-cut) spring vegetables, such as peas, asparagus tips and baby carrots.

prix fixe [PREE FIHKS; PREE FEEKS] A French phrase meaning "fixed price," referring to a complete meal served by a restaurant or hotel for a preset price. Sometimes a menu offers several choices for each course for this set price. *See also* À LA CARTE; TABLE D'HÔTE.

processed cheese Mass-marketed cheese products known for their long shelf life, average flavor and a texture that's often chewy. On the plus side, such products melt smoothly and without separating, thanks only to added EMULSIFIERS. Processed cheese is also known as *pasteurized process(ed) cheese* and *American cheese,* though the latter tag also can be used to refer to mild CHEDDARS. It was invented by Swiss citizens Walter Gerber and Fritz Stettler in 1911, and American James L. Kraft was granted a patent for it in 1916. Kraft introduced the pre-sliced form in 1950. Today processed cheeses are made by blending and heating shredded or ground pasteurized cheeses (one or more of a similar variety) with ingredients such as salt and other seasonings, water, coloring, emulsifiers and preservatives. Defective cheeses (with minor faults in rind, texture and flavor) may be used in the mix. The mixture is cooked until the cheese becomes homogenous, smooth and glossy, then molded and sometimes cut into slices or bite-size pieces. Processed cheeses don't undergo further aging, so both flavor and texture are static. By law, most processed cheeses must contain no more than 43 percent moisture and at least 47 percent fat content. **Processed cheese food** may have added water, WHEY solids, dry milk or dehydrated milkfat, which means it contains less real cheese (at least 51 percent); it must have a minimum fat content of 23 percent and maximum moisture content of 44 percent. **Processed cheese spread** has less milkfat (minimum of 20 percent), a higher moisture content (between 44 and 60 percent) and must be spreadable at 70°F. **Processed cheese product** is simply a processed cheese with lower moisture and milkfat percentages. *See also* CHEESE; COLD PACK CHEESE; IMITATION CHEESE; SUBSTITUTE CHEESE.

Produced and Bottled By *see* WINE LABEL TERMS

product dating There are several types of dates found on today's food packaging. Such dates are not typically safety dates, but are used primarily to assist purchasers in determining when a product is at its best quality and to help retailers determine display life. The term **open dating** refers to the use of a calendar date as opposed to a code. **Closed (coded) dates** are packing numbers used by the manufacturer to assist in rotating stock and tracking products. **Pack date** refers to when the product was packaged. **Sell-by date** advises the purveyor how long to display a product; shoppers should buy the product by that date or choose another one. The **use by date**, or **best if used by** (or **before**) **date**, is determined by the manufacturer and is the date after which the food is no longer considered to be at peak quality, though it certainly still should be safe to consume if handled properly. At this writing, the United States has no uniform food dating system, and the use of such dates can vary from state to state.

profiterole [*Fr.* proh-FIH-ter-ohl; *It.* pro-fee-the-ROH-leh] A miniature CREAM PUFF filled with either a sweet or savory mixture. Savory profiteroles are usually served as appetizers. One of the most famous desserts made with these tiny pastries is the elaborate CROQUEMBOUCHE.

pro hom *see* AROMATIC GINGER

proof *n.* A term used to indicate the amount of alcohol in LIQUOR or other spirits. In the United States, proof is exactly twice the percentage of alcohol. Therefore, a bottle of liquor labeled "86 Proof" contains 43 percent alcohol. **proof** *v.* To dissolve YEAST in a warm liquid (sometimes with a small amount of sugar) and set it aside in a warm place for 5 to 10 minutes until it swells and becomes bubbly. This technique proves that the yeast is alive and active and therefore capable of LEAVENING a bread or other baked good.

prosciutto [proh-SHOO-toh] Italian for "ham," prosciutto is a term broadly used to describe a ham that has been seasoned, salt-cured (but not smoked) and air-dried. The meat is pressed, which produces a firm, dense texture. Italy's PARMA HAM is the true prosciutto, although others are also now made in the United States. Italian prosciuttos are designated **prosciutto cotto**, which is cooked, and **prosciutto crudo**, which is raw (though, because of its curing, ready to eat). This type of Italian ham is also labeled according to its city or region of origin, for example **prosciutto di Parma** and **prosciutto di San Daniele**. Prosciutto is available in gourmet and Italian markets and some supermarkets. It's usually sold in transparently thin slices. Prosciutto is best eaten as is and is a classic first course when served with melon or figs. It can also be added at the last minute to cooked foods such as pastas or vegetables. Prolonged cooking will toughen it.

Protected Designation of Origin (PDO) In 1992, the European Union (EU) approved two categories of protected names— PROTECTED GEOGRAPHICAL INDICATION (PGI) and Protected Designation of Origin (PDO), the latter having more restrictions on its use. The PDO is designed to protect and recognize indigenous agricultural products, foodstuffs, wine and spirits of member countries. Before applying for a PDO, a product must first be approved by its country's national system of standards, which include rigorous quality and production regulations. To use a particular name in the product, the item's quality or traits must be attributable to the particular geographical environment where it's produced, such as local traditions, soil attributes, water and climate—factors that cannot be duplicated elsewhere. All production must occur in this geographical area, and there must be a very close connection between the environment and the product's prominent characteristics. Though the PDO acronym is most commonly used in Europe, this designation goes by other names in some countries: **DOP** (Denominazione di Origine Protetta in Italy and Denominação de Origem in Portugal) and **AOP** (Appellation d'Origine Protégé) in France. See also APPELLATION; PROTECTED GEOGRAPHICAL INDICATION.

Protected Geographical Indication (PGI) A protected-name category created in 1992 by the European Union for the agricultural products, foodstuffs, wine and spirits of member countries. The PGI category is not as restrictive as the PROTECTED DESIGNATION OF ORIGIN (PDO) category. Like those with PDO designations, PGI products must be produced in the geographic area used in the name, but all the production steps do not need to occur in that area. All that's required is that the item's characteristics are either a result of the geographical area, or that it benefits from a good reputation because of the area. Though PGI is the most common acronym for this designation, it's also known as IGP. *See also* APPELLATION.

proteins Composed of amino acids, proteins perform myriad essential functions for the body including supplying energy and building and repairing tissues. Proteins are obtained from both animal and vegetable sources including eggs, fish and meat.

Provençal, à la [proh-vahn-SAHL] A term referring to dishes prepared in the style of Provence, a region in southeastern France. Garlic, tomatoes and olive oil are the major trademark of Provençal cooking. Onions, olives, mushrooms, anchovies and eggplant also play a prominent part in many of these dishes.

provole *see* BURRINO

provolone; Provolone Valpadana [proh-voh-LOH-nee vahl-pah-DAH-nah] Although originally from southern Italy's Basilicata region, this cow's-milk cheese is now also made in the Valpadana (the Po Valley) of northern Italy and labeled *Provolone Valpadana*. Provolone has a firm texture and a mild, tangy flavor. It has a pale- to golden-yellow rind and comes in various forms, though the squat pear shape is most recognizable. Most provolone, called *dolce* (mild), is aged for 2 to 3 months and has a pale-yellow color and delicate flavor. However, some, called *piccante* (strong), are aged 6 months to a year or more. As the cheese ripens, the color becomes a richer yellow and the flavor more pronounced. Both styles are sometimes smoked, which produces brownish-golden rinds and smoky flavors. The FAT CONTENT for Provolone Valpadana is about 45 percent. Provolone is an excellent cooking cheese and aged versions can be used for grating. Provolone is also now manufactured in the United States. *See also* CHEESE.

prune 1. A prune is simply a dried plum, the word coming from the Latin *prunum* for "plum." The French, however, call a fresh plum *prune*, while their word for prune is *pruneau*. To further complicate matters, after this dried fruit had been known as a prune for centuries, in 2001 American prune growers got Food and Drug Administration approval to call prunes "dried plums." Which, of course, they always have been, so why change a good thing? Because growers were hoping that consumers who saw prunes as medicinal food, to be eaten only when necessary, would now see "dried plums" not only as healthful and nutritional but also more appealing. Today U.S. labels list both names, while exported fruit is still sold as "prunes." This venerable dried fruit can be traced back to Roman times and has long been a popular northern European winter favorite because it can be stored without problem. Although any plum can become a prune, those with the greatest flavor, sweetness and firmness are best suited for that use. Commercial dehydration has replaced sun-drying as the primary production method. Though the best prunes are found in the fall, they're available year-round and come in various sizes (small, medium, large, extra large and jumbo). When purchasing prunes look for those that are slightly soft and somewhat flexible. They should have a bluish-black skin and be blemish-free. Store them airtight in a cool, dry place (or refrigerate) for up to six months. Prunes can be eaten out of hand or used in a variety of sweet and savory dishes. **Prune purée**, which can be found in jars in most supermarkets, is broadly touted (primarily by the California Prune Board) as a fat substitute. In baked goods, substituting prune purée for butter or other fat can reduce cholesterol to zero and calories by up to 30 percent. The purée contributes moisture, a slightly chewy texture and a pruny flavor that can range from mild to moderately aggressive, depending on the other flavors in the food. 2. A variety of Italian plum.

prunelle [proo-NEHL] A sweet, pale-green, BRANDY-based LIQUEUR flavored with SLOES (wild plums).

pub cheese *see* GLOUCESTER

pudding 1. A dessert that's typically thick and soft, and which may be served cold or hot. Whereas CUSTARDS are characteristically light and always set with eggs, puddings can be thickened variously with anything from eggs to CORNSTARCH to flour. They can be light in texture (such as BLANCMANGE) or more dense (as with BREAD PUDDING). 2. The term "pudding" can also refer to non-sweet mixtures, such as a savory bread pudding flavored with cheese and studded with vegetables. 3. A British term used generically for "dessert." 4. The label "pudding" is also applied to foods that aren't puddings at all, such as blood pudding (*see* BLOOD SAUSAGE) and YORKSHIRE PUDDING.

pueblo bread; pueblo adobe bread A Native American bread made by the pueblo-dwelling Indians of the Southwest and baked in the adobe ovens common to their dwellings. The bread's made from unbleached flour, salt, yeast, water, lard or shortening and sometimes sugar and/or eggs. A hot fire is started in the adobe oven and allowed to burn out. The ashes are immediately removed and the bread is then baked.

Puerto Rican cherry *see* ACEROLA

puffball mushroom A firm, round, white mushroom that can range in size from 4 ounces to a giant 50-pounder. It has a mild, nutty flavor that complements many foods. Puffball mushrooms are available sporadically in specialty produce markets. They can be cut into thick or thin slices, breaded and sautéed, or chopped and used in a variety of dishes. *See also* MUSHROOM.

puff pastry The French call this rich, delicate, multilayered pastry PÂTE FEUILLETÉE. It's made by placing pats of chilled fat (usually butter) between layers of pastry dough, then rolling it out, folding it in thirds and letting it rest. This process, which is repeated 6 to 8 times, produces a pastry comprising hundreds of layers of dough and butter. When baked, the moisture in the butter creates steam, causing the dough to puff and separate into hundreds of flaky layers. Puff pastry is used to make a variety of crisp creations including CROISSANTS, NAPOLEONS, PALMIERS and ALLUMETTES. It's also used as a wrapping for various foods such as meats, cheese and fruit.

pugliese [poo-LYEH-seh] Hailing from Italy's Apulia region, this large, oblong bread has a soft white interior and crunchy crust.

pulgogi *see* BULGOGI

pulla chile *see* PUYA CHILE

pulled curd cheese *see* PASTA FILATA

pullet [POOL-iht] A young hen, less than 1 year old. *See also* CHICKEN.

Pullman pan; Pullman loaf A long and narrow (about 13 by 4 by 4 inches) LOAF PAN with a cover that slides on. It's used specifically for baking bread (called a *pullman loaf* or *pain de mie*). Because the bread bakes in a confined space, the texture is firm and fine and the crust soft, both of which make it perfect for CANAPÉS, MELBA TOAST and the like. The word "pullman" describes something long and narrow in design (as in the railroad Pullman car, or the luggage called the Pullman case), and is so named after George Mortimer Pullman, 19th century American industrialist and inventor. *See also* COOKWARE AND BAKEWARE MATERIALS.

pulque [POOL-keh] The unofficial national drink of Mexico, where it's made, and hailing back to the Aztecs, pulque is a thick, milky-white, mildly alcoholic beverage fermented (*see* FERMENTATION) from the juice of various species of AGAVE. To make it more palatable, pulque is often flavored with any of various ingredients including CHILES, fruits, herbs, nuts, spices and sugar. *See also* MEZCAL; TEQUILA.

pulse The dried seed of any of several LEGUMES including BEANS, PEAS and LENTILS.

pulverize To reduce to powder or dust, usually by crushing, pounding or grinding.

pummelo *see* POMELO

pumpernickel [PUHM-puhr-nihk-uhl] A coarse dark bread with a slightly sour taste. Pumpernickel is usually made of a high proportion of rye flour and a small amount of wheat flour. Molasses is often used to add both color and flavor.

pumpkin When the Colonists landed in North America they found the Indians growing and using pumpkins. This large, ungainly fruit was enthusiastically embraced by the new Americans and subsequently pumpkin pie became a national Thanksgiving tradition. It was so loved that one early Connecticut colony delayed Thanksgiving because the molasses needed to make this popular pie wasn't readily available. Large, round and orange, the pumpkin is a member of the gourd family, which also includes all varieties of MELON, WATERMELON and SQUASH. Its orange flesh has a mild, sweet flavor and the seeds—husked and roasted—are delicately nutty. Pumpkin seeds are commonly known as PEPITAS. Fresh pumpkins are available in the fall and winter and some specimens have weighed in at well over 100 pounds. In general, however, the flesh from smaller sizes will be more tender and succulent. Choose pumpkins that are free from blemishes and heavy for their size. Store whole pumpkins at room temperature up to a month or refrigerate up to 3 months. Puréed pumpkin is also available canned. Pumpkin may be prepared in almost any way suitable for winter squash. It's a good source of vitamin A.

pumpkin seed oil A robustly flavored oil made from roasted pumpkin seeds (*see* PEPITAS). The color of this fairly thick oil is a khaki-green. Because of its strong flavor, pumpkin seed oil is best combined with other oils in cooking, salad dressings and other preparations. *See also* FATS AND OILS.

pumpkin seeds *see* PEPITAS

punch A beverage that mixes various ingredients (such as LIQUOR, LIQUEUR, WINE, fruit juices and carbonated beverages). Punch may be cold or hot and is typically made in large quantities and served from a large "punch bowl." It's often garnished with fresh fruit. Some punches add milk or cream (as in EGGNOG). "Cups" are punches made in a pitcher and poured into glasses or cups.

punt The indentation in the bottom of a wine or champagne bottle, designed for two basic purposes—catching sediment and reinforcing the bottle. It also makes a convenient handhold when pouring wine.

pupu; pu pu [POO-poo] The Hawaiian term for any hot or cold appetizer, which can include a wide range of items such as macadamia nuts, WON TONS, chunks of fresh pineapple or coconut and barbecued meats.

pupusa [poo-POO-suh] Thick hand-made corn cakes filled with ingredients that can include cheese, a finely ground pork mixture called CHICHARRÓN, FRIJOLES REFRITOS and flowers called LOROCO. Pupusas are very popular in Central America, especially El Salvador, where they are considered a national dish and the second Sunday in November is celebrated as National Pupusa Day. Pupusas are generally served with a fermented or pickled cabbage slaw called CURTIDO.

purée; puree [pyuh-RAY] *n.* Any food (usually a fruit or vegetable) that is finely mashed to a smooth, thick consistency. Purées can be used as a garnish, served as a side dish or added as a thickener to sauces or soups. **purée** *v.* To grind or mash food until it's completely smooth. This can be accomplished by one of several methods including using a food processor or blender or by forcing the food through a STRAINER or FOOD MILL.

purée de foie gras *see* FOIE GRAS

puri *see* POORI

purple giant hyssop *see* KOREAN MINT

purple laver *see* LAVER

purslane [PERS-lin (layn)] This succulent is a native of India and the Middle East and now grows readily elsewhere, including Europe and Asia, where it's enthusiastically consumed. In America's recent history, purslane has more often than not been viewed as a weed, though this was not always the case. Its reputation is now changing, however, because of purslane's nutritional content. Not only is it a good source of calcium, copper, iron, magnesium, manganese, niacin, phosphorus, potassium, riboflavin and vitamins A, B6 and C, but contains more of the essential fatty acid Omega-3 than most other plants. Purslane has round, smooth, reddish stems and small, oblong, green leaves. The stems and leaves can be eaten raw in salads, cooked briefly and used as a green, or added to soups. Purslane has a mild, fresh flavor with a slightly tart, citrusy character. Cultivated purslane is available primarily in the summer, typically at produce markets and farmer's markets. Purslane is also called *little hogweed*, *pigweed*, *pusley*, *verdolaga* and *vertolaga*. *Winter purslane* (*see* MINERS' LETTUCE) is different.

pusley *see* PURSLANE

puttanesca sauce; alla puttanesca [poot-tah-NEHS-kah] Generally served with pasta, this sauce is a spicy mélange of tomatoes, onions, capers, black olives, anchovies, oregano and garlic, all cooked together in olive oil. A dish on a menu described as *alla puttanesca* signals that it's served with this sauce. The name *puttanesca* is a derivation of *puttana*, which in Italian means "whore." According to one story, the name purportedly comes from the fact that the intense fragrance of this sauce was like a siren's call to the men who visited such "ladies of pleasure." *See also* SAUCE.

puya chile [POO-yuh] This narrow, 3- to 4-inch-long pepper starts out green, becomes bright red then transitions to a purplish red as it matures. The puya CHILE, sometimes spelled *pulla,* has a rich, slightly fruity flavor similar to that of a GUAJILLO but, with a SCOVILLE SCALE rating of 5,000 to 10,000, it packs a bit more heat.

pyramide cheese [pih-rah-MEED] A truncated pyramid is the shape of this small French CHÈVRE that's often coated with an edible darkgray vegetable ash. This CHEESE is produced around the central Loire valley area of France. Pyramide can range in texture from soft to slightly crumbly and, depending on age, in flavor from mild to sharp. It's wonderful served with crackers or bread and fruit.

qamar el deen; qamar el din *see* AMARDINE

qatayef *see* ATAYEF

qaymeh [GAY-meh] Popular Persian lamb stew with tomatoes and split peas seasoned with dried limes (*see* LIMES, DRIED, PERSIAN), TURMERIC and ADVIEH. Qaymeh is also seen as *gheimeh*.

quadrettini *see* Pasta Glossary, page 883

quadrucci *see* Pasta Glossary, page 883

quahog [KWAH-hog] The American Indian name for the East Coast hard-shell clam. The term "quahog" is also sometimes used to describe the largest of these hard-shell clams. Also known as CHOWDER (or *large*) CLAM.

quail [KWAYL] The American quail is not related to the European quail, a migratory GAME BIRD belonging to the partridge family. But when colonists discovered birds that resembled the European version they called them by the same name. American quail are known by various names depending on the region—*bobwhite* in the East, *partridge* in the South, *quail* in the North and *blue quail* in the Southwest. Other notable members of this family are **California quail**, **mountain quail** and **Montezuma quail**. American quail nest on the ground and are not migratory—in fact, they'd rather walk than fly. They're very social and travel in small groups called coveys. The meat of the American quail is white and delicately flavored. In general, they should be cooked like other game birds—young birds can be roasted, broiled or fried and older fowl should be cooked with moist heat. Most of the quail marketed today are raised on game bird farms. Fresh quail can be ordered through specialty butchers, who might also carry frozen quail.

quark [kwark, kvark] German for "CURD," quark is a soft, unripened cow's-milk cheese that can be made from PASTEURIZED whole, partially skimmed or fat-free milk. Depending on the milk's FAT CONTENT and how much WHEY is removed, it can range in texture from that of SOUR CREAM to that of RICOTTA. Quark has a fresh, faintly tangy flavor similar to sour cream and comes in two versions—low-fat and nonfat. Though the calories are the same in low-fat Quark and low-fat sour cream (about 35 per ounce), Quark's texture is richer. Quark can be found plain or flavored with anything from herbs to fruit to garlic. It's used to top baked potatoes and as an ingredient in a variety of dishes including cheesecakes, dips, salads and sauces. In Austria, it's referred to as *Topfen;* in Central Europe it's spelled *Quarg* and *Kvarg. See also* CHEESE.

quatre épices [KAH-tr ay-PEES] A French phrase meaning "four spices," referring to any of several finely ground spice mixtures. Though there's no standard mixture for quatre épices, the blend is usually mixed from the following selection: pepper (usually white), nutmeg, ginger, cinnamon or cloves. Quatre épices is used to flavor soups, stews and vegetables. *See also* SPICES.

quattro formaggi [KWAH-troh fohr-MAHJ-jee] Italian for "four cheeses," referring to a sauce made with four cheeses; it's typically served with pasta.

queen olive *see* SEVILLANO OLIVE

queijo [KAY-zhoo] Portuguese for "cheese."

quenelle [kuh-NEHL] 1. Traditionally, a light, delicate dumpling made of seasoned minced or ground fish, meat or vegetables bound with eggs or PANADA. This mixture is formed into small ovals (usually by pressing a spoonful of ingredients lightly against the bowl of second spoon) and gently poached in stock. Quenelles are typically served with a rich sauce and can be used as a first course, main course or garnish. 2. Sweet items such as ice cream, chocolate mousse and sorbet that are shaped in the same manner.

quenepa *see* MAMONCILLO

quesadilla [keh-sah-DEE-yah] A flour TORTILLA filled with a savory mixture, then folded in half to form a half–moon shape. The filling can include shredded cheese, cooked meat, REFRIED BEANS or a combination of items. After the tortilla is filled and folded, it's toasted under a broiler or fried. Quesadillas are usually cut into wedges before being served, often as an appetizer.

queso; quesuco [KAY-soh; kay-SOO-koh] Spanish for "cheese" and "small cheese," respectively.

queso añejo; queso añejado [KAY-soh ah-NYAY-hoh (ah-nyay-hah-doh)] *see* COJITA

queso blanco [KAY-soh BLAHN-koh] A family of cheeses that exists all over Latin America in various renditions. These cheeses were probably introduced by the Spaniards and particularly the cheesemaking monks that settled in the New World. Some are made like COTTAGE CHEESE from skim milk, like **queso fresco**. **Panela** is a fresh white cheese made from either whole or partly skimmed milk; if drained in a basket it's called **queso de canasta** in Mexico. Fresh, pressed, uncooked cheese made from whole or partly skimmed milk is called **queso de prensa** ("pressed cheese") in several Latin American countries. Most queso blanco cheeses are not aged but rather are eaten within a few days of being produced and fall into the **queso blanco fresco** ("fresh") category. Others, like **queso de bagaces** and **queso de crema**, are pressed and RIPENED anywhere from 2 weeks to 2 months. Some queso blanco cheeses are smoked for a few days, which produces a darker color and a smoky flavor; others have added flavorings such as green chiles. An interesting trait of all these cheeses is that they don't really melt when heated; they get soft but hold their basic shape. They're used in dishes like enchiladas, burritos and quesadillas and also make good frying cheeses, which are called **queso para freír**. *See also* CHEESE.

queso de bagaces *see* QUESO BLANCO

queso de canasta *see* QUESO BLANCO

queso de crema *see* QUESO BLANCO

Queso de la Serena (DO; PDO) [KAY-soh day lah she-RAY-nah] SOFT to SEMISOFT sheep's-milk cheese from La Serena, an area located in southwestern Spain's Extremadura region. Queso de la Serena (also simply called *Serena* or *La Serena*) is RIPENED in molds and turned daily for a minimum of 2 months. This results in 2- to 4-pound flattened wheels with slightly bulging sides and uneven tops. Both pasteurized and unpasteurized milk are used; they're curdled with an extract of a dried wild thistle (*Yerbacuajo*), which gives the cheese a subtle hint of bitterness. This combines with the buttery rich, nutty and tangy flavor for an interesting taste experience. Younger, chilled Serena can be sliced, but fully ripe versions are creamy and supple and can be eaten with a spoon. Serena has a FAT CONTENT of 45 to 50 percent.

Queso de los Ibores *see* QUESO IBORES

Queso del Valle del Roncal *see* RONCAL

queso de prensa *see* QUESO BLANCO

queso fresco *see* QUESO BLANCO

queso fundido [KAY-soh fuhn-DEE-doh] Spanish for "melted cheese," queso fundido is a south-of-the-border rendition of FONDUE. The base is usually JACK cheese, and additions may include chopped CHORIZO or beef, tomatoes, onions, garlic and JALAPEÑOS. Queso fundido is usually served as an appetizer, accompanied by tortilla chips for dipping. *See also* FONDUTA.

Queso Ibérico *see* IBÉRICO CHEESE

Queso Ibores (DO) [KAY-soh ee-BOHR-ays] SEMISOFT to SEMIHARD goat's-milk cheese from the Extremadura region of southwestern Spain. The 1- to 2-pound wheels are ripened for a minimum of 2 months. Queso

Ibores has a smooth, creamy texture and a rich, aromatic flavor that becomes sharper with age. The rind ranges in color from yellow to deep orange (the latter due to being hand-rubbed with smoked paprika instead of olive oil during RIPENING). The cheese's FAT CONTENT ranges from 45 to 50 percent. This cheese is also called *Queso de los Ibores* or simply *Ibores*.

Queso Manchego *see* MANCHEGO

queso para freír *see* QUESO BLANCO

quetsch [KETCH] A variety of PLUM used primarily to make an Alsatian EAU DE VIE of the same name. This plum is also used in desserts and LIQUEURS.

quiche [KEESH] This dish originated in northeastern France in the region of Alsace-Lorraine. It consists of a pastry shell filled with a savory custard made of eggs, cream, seasonings and various other ingredients such as onions, mushrooms, ham, shellfish or herbs. The most notable of these savory pies is the **quiche Lorraine**, which has crisp bacon bits (and sometimes GRUYÈRE cheese) added to the custard filling. Quiche is classically baked in a **quiche pan**, which has fluted, straight sides and ranges in diameter from 8 to 12 inches (individual-size pans are 4 inches), and is about $1^1/_2$ inches deep. Metal quiche pans have removable bottoms, glass and porcelain "dishes" have solid bottoms. Quiche can be served as a lunch or dinner entrée, or as a first course or HORS D'OEUVRE.

quick bread Bread that is quick to make because it doesn't require kneading or rising time. That's because the LEAVENER in such a bread is usually baking powder or baking soda, which, when combined with moisture, starts the rising process immediately. In the case of double-acting baking powder, oven heat causes a second burst of rising power. Eggs can also be used to leaven quick breads. This genre includes most BISCUITS, MUFFINS, POPOVERS and a wide variety of sweet and savory loaf breads.

quince [KWIHNC] Ancient Romans used the flowers and fruit of the quince tree for everything from perfume to honey. It was also considered a symbol of love and given to one's intended as a sign of commitment. Though the quince has been around for over 4,000 years throughout Asia and the Mediterranean countries, it's never been particularly popular with Americans. This yellow-skinned fruit looks and tastes like a cross between an apple and a pear. The hard, yellow-white flesh is quite dry and has an astringent, tart flavor, which makes it better cooked than raw. Quinces are available in supermarkets from September through December. Select those that are large, firm and yellow with little or no sign of green. Wrap in a plastic bag and refrigerate for up to 2 months; peel before using in cooked dishes. Because the quince has such an astringently tart flavor and high pectin content, Europeans have traditionally used it to make jams, jellies and preserves. **Quince paste** has a very firm texture akin to that of a gumdrop. The Spanish call it membrillo (also *crema de membrillo* and *dulce de membrillo*), and in France it's known as **pâte de coings** (or *cotignac*). Quince paste is a classic accompaniment for cheese, with a very thin slice of it served atop a slice of cheese. Quince paste is sometimes referred to as *quince cheese* or *quince jelly,* although those mixtures are typically softer and spreadable.

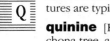

quinine [KWI-nine] An alkaloid that comes from the bark of the cinchona tree, an evergreen native to the mountainous areas of Central and South America. Quinine is the base flavor in most BITTERS and contributes the bitter essence to TONIC WATER.

quinine water [KWI-nine] *see* TONIC WATER

quinoa [KEEN-wah] Although quinoa is new to the American market, it was a staple of the ancient Incas, who called it "the mother grain." To this day it's an important food in South American cuisine. Hailed as the "supergrain of the future," quinoa contains more protein than any other grain. It's considered a *complete protein* because it contains all eight essential amino acids. Quinoa is also higher in unsaturated fats and lower in carbohydrates than most grains, and it provides a rich and balanced source of vital nutrients. Tiny and bead-shaped, the ivory-colored quinoa cooks like rice (taking half the time of regular rice) and expands to four times its original volume. Its flavor is delicate, almost bland, and has been compared to that of COUSCOUS. Quinoa is lighter than but can be used in any way suitable for rice—as part of a main dish, a side dish, in soups, in salads and even in puddings. It's available packaged as a grain, ground into flour and in several forms of pasta. Quinoa can be found in natural food stores and some supermarkets.

quinquinelle [kween-kwee-NEH-leh] Italian for "QUENELLES."

rabe Another name for BROCCOLI RABE.

rabbit The domesticated members of the rabbit family (a rodent relation) have fine-textured flesh that is almost totally white meat. They're plumper and less strongly flavored than their wild counterparts. A mature rabbit averages between 3 and 5 pounds, much smaller than its relative the HARE (typically between 6 and 12 pounds). Fresh and frozen rabbit is available dressed either whole or cut into pieces. The best will be young and weigh between 2 and 2½ pounds, and should have light-colored flesh. These are the most tender and mild-flavored and can be prepared in any manner suitable for young chicken (such as frying, grilling or roasting). Older or wild rabbits benefit from moist-heat cooking such as braising. *See also* GAME ANIMALS.

rabdi *see* RABRI

rabri [RAHB-ree] Sweetened milk slowly reduced over low heat until quite thick. It's often flavored with ROSEWATER and/or CARDAMOM and topped with almond or pistachio nuts. Rabri is served as a dessert by itself, used as a part of other desserts, mixed with fruit or used as a topping. It's sometimes spelled *rabdi*. *See also* KHOA.

rack of lamb A portion of the rib section of a lamb, usually containing eight ribs. A rack of lamb can be cut into chops or served in one piece—either as a rack or formed into a CROWN ROAST. *See also* Lamb Chart, page 897; LAMB.

Raclette; raclette [rah-KLEHT, ra-KLEHT] 1. A cow's-milk cheese from Switzerland's Valais canton that was made as far back as the Middle Ages. Although smaller in size, it's similar to GRUYÈRE in both texture (semifirm and dotted with small holes) and flavor (mellow and nutty). It's ripened for a minimum of 2 months but more typically for 4 to 6 months. It can be found in specialty cheese stores and many supermarkets. The minimum FAT CONTENT of Raclette is 45 percent. *See also* CHEESE. 2. A dish by the same name consisting of a chunk of Raclette cheese that is exposed to heat (traditionally an open fire) and scraped off as it melts. (Electric raclette machines are also available.) The word *raclette* comes from *racler,* French for "to scrape." It's served as a meal with boiled potatoes, dark bread and CORNICHONS or other pickled vegetables.

radiatore *see* Pasta Glossary, page 883

radicchio [rah-DEE-kee-oh] This red-leafed Italian CHICORY is most often used as a salad green. There are several varieties of radicchio, but the two most widely available in the United States are *Verona* and *Treviso*. The **radicchio di Verona** has burgundy-red leaves with white ribs. It grows in a small, loose head similar to BUTTERHEAD LETTUCE. The leaves of **radicchio di Treviso** (commonly referred to simply as *Treviso*) are narrow and pointed and form tighter, more tapered heads. They also have white ribs but can range in color from pink to dark red. Other radicchio varieties have variegated or speckled leaves in beautiful shades of pink, red and green. All radicchios have tender but firm leaves with a slightly bitter flavor. Radicchio is available year-round, with a peak season from midwinter to early spring. Choose heads that have crisp, full-colored leaves with no sign of browning. Store in a plastic bag in the refrigerator for up to a week. Besides being used in salads, radicchio may also be cooked by grilling, sautéing or baking.

radish From the Latin *radix,* meaning "root," the radish is in fact the root of a plant in the mustard family. Its skin can vary in color from white to red to purple to black (and many shades in between). In shape and size, the radish can be round, oval or elongated and can run the gamut from globes $1/2$ inch in diameter to carrotlike giants (such as the DAIKON) $1^{1}/_{2}$ eet in length. The most common variety found in American markets is the globular or oval-shaped red-skinned radish, which ranges in size from that of a small cherry to that of a tiny orange. The flavor can be mild to peppery, depending on factors such as variety and age. Available year-round, radishes are sold both trimmed (in plastic bags) and with their greens and roots attached. Choose those that feel firm when gently squeezed. If the radish gives to pressure, the interior will likely be pithy instead of crisp. Any attached leaves should be green and crisp. Remove and discard leaves and refrigerate radishes in a plastic bag for up to 5 days. Wash and trim root ends just before using. For added crispness, soak radishes in icewater for a couple of hours. Though radishes are most often used raw in salads, as garnishes and for CRUDITÉS, they can also be cooked. **Radish sprouts** can be used as a peppery accent to salads and as a garnish for a variety of cold and hot dishes. They can be found in specialty produce markets, natural food stores and some supermarkets. *See also* BLACK RADISH.

ragoût [ra-GOO] A derivative of the French verb *ragoûter,* meaning "to stimulate the appetite," ragoût is a thick, rich, well-seasoned stew of meat, poultry or fish and sometimes vegetables.

ragu; ragu Bolognese; ragu alla Bolognese; Bolognese sauce [rah-GOO boh-loh-NYEH-zeh] A thick, full-bodied meat sauce that's a staple of northern Italy's Bologna region. Ragu usually contains ground beef (and sometimes pork), PANCETTA, tomatoes, onions, celery, carrots and garlic, enhanced with wine, milk or cream and seasonings. The term *alla Bolognese* (in French, *à la Bolognese*) on a menu designates a pasta or other dish sauced with ragu. The words for Italian ragu and French RAGOÛT (though for entirely different dishes) are both derived from the verb *ragoûter,* which means "to stimulate the appetite." *See also* SAUCE.

rainbow runner *see* JACK

rainbow trout *see* TROUT

raisin [RAY-zihn] In the most basic terms, a raisin is simply a dried grape. About half of the world's raisin supply comes from California. The most common grapes used for raisins are THOMPSON SEEDLESS, Zante (*see* CHAMPAGNE GRAPES) and MUSCAT. Grapes are either sun-dried or dehydrated mechanically. Both dark and golden seedless raisins can be made from Thompson seedless grapes. The difference is that the dark raisins are sun-dried for several weeks, thereby producing their shriveled appearance and dark color. Golden raisins have been treated with sulphur dioxide (to prevent their color from darkening) and dried with artificial heat, thereby producing a moister, plumper product. The tiny seedless Zante grapes produce dried currants, and muscat grapes (which usually have their seeds removed before processing) create a dark, perfumy and intensely sweet raisin. All raisins can be stored tightly wrapped at room temperature for several months. For prolonged storage (up to a year), they should be refrigerated in a tightly sealed plastic bag. Raisins can be eaten out of hand, as well as used in a variety of baked goods and in cooked and raw dishes. They have a high natural sugar content, contain a variety of vitamins and minerals and are especially rich in iron. *See also* CURRANTS.

raita [RI-tah] YOGURT salads popular in India, raitas are a combination of thick, whole-milk yogurt and various chopped vegetables like cucumbers, eggplant, potatoes or spinach, or fruits such as bananas or tomatoes. Typically used as condiments, raitas are variously seasoned with black mustard seeds, GARAM MASALA and herbs such as chervil, coriander, cumin, dill, mint, parsley or tarragon. Raitas are designed to be a cooling counterbalance for many spicy Indian dishes.

raki; rakee [RAH-kee] An anise-flavored BRANDY made in Turkey and the Balkans and distilled from grains, grapes, or plums.

rakkyo; rakyo [RAH-kyoh] A type of Japanese shallot, which is usually uncooked and pickled in light vinegar. It's typically used as a garnish with grilled fish and meat and can be found in Asian markets.

rambutan [ram-BOOT-n] Indigenous to the Malay Archipelago, this remarkable looking fruit has a rind that's covered in dark, soft, flexible "bristles." The rambutan is small (1 to 2 inches in diameter) and, depending on the variety, the rind color can be crimson, orange, yellow or green. Inside, a single seed is surrounded by a translucent, grapelike flesh that has a sweet, delicate flavor, which is much like but slightly more acidic than that of the LITCHI (to which it's related). Rambutans are available from about August to May, though typically only in specialty produce markets and some Asian markets. The shells should be intact and the bristles flexible and not dry. Refrigerate in a plastic bag for up to a week. The thin rind is easy to peel off; after which the whole rambutan can be popped into the mouth, the flesh eaten and the seed discarded. Or, the seed can be removed and the flesh used in salads, jellies or ice cream.

ramekin [RAM-ih-kihn] 1. An individual baking dish (3 to 4 inches in diameter) that resembles a miniature soufflé dish. Ramekins are usually made of porcelain or earthenware and can be used for both sweet and savory dishes—either baked or chilled. 2. A tiny baked pastry filled with a creamy cheese custard.

ramen [RAH-mehn] 1. Asian instant-style deep-fried noodles that are usually sold in cellophane packages, sometimes with bits of dehydrated vegetables and broth mix. 2. A Japanese dish of noodles, small pieces of meat and vegetables and broth.

Ramos gin fizz; Ramos fizz [RAY-mohs] *see* GIN FIZZ

ramp This wild onion grows from Canada to the Carolinas and resembles a SCALLION with broad leaves. Also known as *wild leek,* ramp has an assertive, garlicky-onion flavor. It can be found—usually only in specialty produce markets—from March to July. Choose those that are firm with bright-colored greenery. Wrap tightly in a plastic bag and refrigerate for up to a week. Trim the root ends just before using. Though the flavor of a ramp is slightly stronger than the LEEK, SCALLION or ONION, it can be used—raw or cooked—in many dishes as a substitute for any of those three.

ram's horn *see* RATTE

ranchero sauce [ran-CHEH-roh; rahn-CHEH-roh] A picant tomato-based sauce that includes onions, green chiles such as SERRANOS or JALAPEÑOS and seasonings. This Mexican SALSA is most often associated with the dish, HUEVOS RANCHEROS. *See also* SAUCE.

range chicken *see* CHICKEN

rangpur lime [ruhng-poor] Actually not a lime but rather a CROSS between a LEMON and a MANDARIN ORANGE. Although its bright-orange peel and flesh would seem to suggest it might be sweet, it's quite sour and acidic; there is a floral character to the flavor, however. It has some characteristics of a Mandarin orange in that the skin is easy to peel and the flesh easily segmented. The rangpur lime, which is named after the city of Rangpur, Bangladesh, makes great MARMALADE and can be used as a substitute for real lemons and limes where its tartness can be enjoyed. It's also known as *Canton lemon, hime lemon, lemandarin* and *limão cravo*.

rape 1. Another name for BROCCOLI RABE. 2. The residue of grape stalks, stems and skins after the juice has been extracted for winemaking.

rapeseed oil Rapeseed oil, expressed from rape seeds, is commonly marketed under the name CANOLA OIL. Once used only in parts of Europe and the Middle East, rapeseed oil has been discovered to have more cho-lesterol-balancing MONOUNSATURATED FAT than any other oil except OLIVE OIL. *See also* CANOLA OIL.

rapini [rah-PEE-nee] Another name for BROCCOLI RABE.

rarebit *see* WELSH RAREBIT

rascasse [rahs-KAHSS] This firm, white-fleshed member of the scorpion fish family is abundant in the Mediterranean. The French red rascasse has been made famous as an indispensable ingredient in BOUIL-LABAISSE. *See also* FISH.

ras el hanout An exotic and complex Moroccan spice blend that, depending on the preparer, can contain up to 50 ingredients. *Ras el hanout* means "head of the shop," purportedly because shop owners cre-ate their own unique blend, which can include ginger, anise, cinnamon, nutmeg, peppercorns, cloves, cardamom, dried flowers (such as lavender and rose), NIGELLA, mace, GALANGAL and turmeric. Traditionally, this spice blend also includes APHRODISIACS like the Spanish fly beetle.

rasher 1. A strip or slice of meat such as bacon or ham. 2. A serving of two to three thin pieces of such meat.

raspberry [RAZ-behr-ee] Considered by many the most intensely fla-vored member of the berry family, the raspberry is composed of many connecting drupelets (individual sections of fruit, each with its own seed) surrounding a central core. There are three main varieties—black, golden and red, the latter being the most widely available. Depending on the region, red raspberries are available pretty much year-round, with the peak season from May through September. Golden raspberries have a limited availability from June through September, and black raspberries can typically only be found from mid-June to mid-August. Golden and black berries are more likely to be carried at produce markets and farm-er's markets. Choose brightly colored, plump berries sans hull. If the hulls are still attached, the berries were picked too early and will undoubtedly be tart. Avoid soft, shriveled or moldy berries. Store (preferably in a single layer) in a moistureproof container in the refrigerator for 2 to 3 days. If necessary, rinse lightly just before serving. Raspberries are very fragile and are at their best served fresh with just a kiss of cream. They also make excellent jam. Seedless raspberry jam is available commercially. The berries contain a fair amount of iron, potassium and vitamins A and C.

rasp grater Handheld tool with razor-sharp edges used to zest citrus; grate hard cheeses, garlic, ginger or nutmeg; or shave chocolate. Microplane originated the rasp grater, which the company adapted from wood-working rasps used to contour and smooth wood.

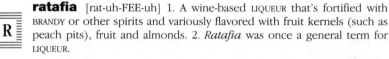

ratafia [rat-uh-FEE-uh] 1. A wine-based LIQUEUR that's fortified with BRANDY or other spirits and variously flavored with fruit kernels (such as peach pits), fruit and almonds. 2. *Ratafia* was once a general term for LIQUEUR.

ratatouille [ra-tuh-TOO-ee; ra-tuh-TWEE] A popular dish from the French region of Provence that combines eggplant, tomatoes, onions, bell peppers, zucchini, garlic and herbs—all simmered in olive oil. The vegetables can vary according to the cook. They can be cooked together, or cooked separately and then combined and heated briefly together. Ratatouille can be served hot, cold or at room temperature, either as a side dish or as an appetizer with bread or crackers.

rat's tail chile *see* CHILE DE ÁRBOL

rat's tails *see* RICE NOODLES

ratte; ratte, la [raht] Small- to medium-size creamy potato variety considered to be native to both Denmark and France. Also known as *asparges, ram's horn* and *Ratte de Touget,* its name translates to "the rat," apparently because its shape, which is like a FINGERLING potato, resembles a small rat. Rattes range in size from 3 to 8 inches, with yellow flesh and a subtle nutty flavor. *See also* POTATO.

Ratte de Touget *see* RATTE

rattlesnake bean A medium-size, oblong dried bean with a light brown skin streaked with mahogany. Rattlesnake beans have a strong, tangy flavor that stands up to fiery spices. *See also* BEANS.

rau ram *see* VIETNAMESE MINT

ravioli [rav-ee-OH-lee; ra-VYOH-lee] An Italian specialty of little square or round pillows of noodle dough filled with any of various mixtures such as cheese, meat or vegetables. Ravioli are boiled, then sometimes baked with a cream, cheese or tomato sauce. Chinese-style ravioli are called WON TONS; Jewish-style are KREPLACH. *See also* PASTA; Pasta Glossary, page 883.

raw milk *see* MILK

raw sugar *see* SUGAR

ray *see* SKATE

razor clam The most famous West Coast SOFT-SHELL CLAM, the razor clam is so-named because its shell resembles a folded, old-fashioned straight razor. It's best when steamed. *See also* CLAM.

rbGH; rbST The commonly used acronyms for the genetically engineered *recombinant bovine growth hormone*, which is also called *recombinant bovine somatotropin*. Scientists created it to replicate the naturally occurring protein hormone bovine somatotropin (BST), which is secreted by the pituitary glands of cattle, as well as human beings, dogs and other animals. The natural bST is also known as a growth hormone because it influences the metabolism of proteins, carbohydrates and lipids. The artificially produced rbGH is injected into cattle to stimulate milk production, increasing it anywhere from 10 to 40 percent. It's allowed in the United States and the European Union countries but banned in Canada. To date, there are no long-term studies to prove whether or not rbGH milk is harmful to humans, though it can produce health problems in cows. Health advocates are endeavoring to have this artificial hormone banned in the United States but those concerned about health issues should look for milk products labeled "rbGH-free" or "rbST-free."

RDA An acronym for "Recommended Dietary Allowance," the U.S. government-recommended daily amounts for protein, vitamins and minerals for healthy adults. Such amounts are ballpark figures and may vary slightly according to gender and conditions such as pregnancy, and so forth. *See also* Food Label Terms, page 876.

reamer [REE-muhr] *see* JUICER

Reblochon; Reblochon de Savoie [reh-bluh-SHOH*N* deuh SAH-vwah] This uncooked, washed rind French cows'-milk CHEESE has a couple of explanations for the derivation of its name. One relates to *reblocher*, a word meaning "to milk again," and the other to *reblessa*, which means "to steal" in a local dialect. Both point to the late Middle Ages, when farmers used milk to pay rent and/or taxes. When tax collectors or landlords arrived, the farmer would pretend to milk the cows until they were dry and pay up. After the officials had left, the farmer would remilk the supposedly dry cows. This second milking had a higher butterfat content, which produced rich, creamy cheeses. Reblochon has a creamy-soft texture that becomes oozy as the cheese ripens. The flavor is rich, complex and savory. Reblochon has a beige to reddish-orange rind with velvety white mold and an ivory interior. It's sold in 8$\frac{1}{2}$-ounce to 1$\frac{1}{4}$-pound wheels. Its minimum FAT CONTENT is 45 percent. Reblochon is made from raw milk, and if it's ripened for less than 60 days it is not currently allowed into the United States. The imported version, **Fromage de Savoie**, is made with pasteurized milk and not considered as good. *See also* CHEESE.

recao *see* SAW-LEAF HERB

recombinant bovine growth hormone; recombinant bovine somatotropin *see* RBGH

reconstitute [ree-KON-stih-toot;   ree-KON-stih-tyoot] Culinarily, the term means to return a dehydrated food (such as dried milk) to its original consistency by adding a liquid, usually water.

red bean Popular in Mexico and the southwestern United States, this dark red, medium-size bean is a favorite for making CHILI CON CARNE and REFRIED BEANS (*refritos*). Red beans are available dried in most supermarkets. *See also* BEANS; RED BEANS AND RICE.

red beans and rice One of Louisiana's best-known contributions to American regional cuisine, this dish combines red KIDNEY BEANS, water, ham (or bacon or SALT PORK), onions and seasonings (usually including CAYENNE). This mélange is slowly simmered until tender and flavorful. The beans, which create a thick natural gravy, are served with bits of ham over white rice. This dish was purportedly so loved by famous trumpeter Louis Armstrong that he used to sign his personal letters "Red beans and ricely yours."

red bell pepper *see* SWEET PEPPERS

red cabbage *see* CABBAGE

red caviar *see* CAVIAR

red cooking A Chinese cooking method whereby food (such as chicken) is BRAISED in SOY SAUCE, thereby changing the color to a deep, dark reddish brown.

red date *see* CHINESE DATE

Red Delicious apple This distinctive-looking apple is brilliant red in color, with an elongated shape and five knobs at its base. It's juicy and sweet but lacks any distinguishing tartness, which makes it good for eating out of hand but not for cooking. *See also* APPLE.

red drum *see* DRUM

redeye gravy A traditional southern gravy made by combining the drippings from fried ham (purists insist on COUNTRY-CURED HAM *only*) with water and hot coffee—the latter being optional. The mixture is cooked until slightly REDUCED. It's served with the ham and spooned atop biscuits, cornbread, and the like.

redfish *see* DRUM

red flannel hash A New England specialty made by frying chopped cooked beets, potatoes, onions and crisp bacon together until crusty and brown. Traditionally about 85 percent of the volume should be beets. Red flannel hash is usually served with cornbread.

red kuri [KOO-ree] This winter squash is the shape, size and color of a small pumpkin, without the creases. The firm yellow flesh is sweet and nutty. Red kuri squash can be baked, steamed or simmered. Its peak season is from late summer through mid-winter. Choose squash that are heavy for their size; avoid those with soft spots. Red kuri squash can be kept up to 6 weeks in cool, dry storage. It's very popular in Japan and is known as *Japanese squash orange Hokkaido squash* and *uchiki kuri squash*. Other names include *baby red hubbard squash, onion squash* and *potimarron. See also* SQUASH.

red leaf lettuce *see* LEAF LETTUCE

Red Leicester *see* LEICESTER

red Mexican bean *see* PINTO BEAN

red mullet This reddish-pink marine fish is not really a true MULLET but a Mediterranean member of the GOATFISH family. The red mullet ranges in size from $1/2$ to 2 pounds and has very firm, lean flesh. It's found on menus all over Europe but is rarely available in the United States. *See also* FISH.

red orache *see* ORACHE

red pepper; red pepper flakes A generic term applied to any of several varieties of hot, red CHILES. The most commonly available forms are ground red pepper and red pepper flakes.

red savina *see* SCOVILLE SCALE

red shiso *see* SHISO

red smear *see* WASH RIND

red snapper *see* SNAPPER

red snapper soup *see* SNAPPER SOUP

reduce Culinarily, to boil a liquid (usually stock, wine or a sauce mixture) rapidly until the volume is reduced by evaporation, thereby thickening the consistency and intensifying the flavor. Such a mixture is sometimes referred to as a *reduction*.

reduction *see* REDUCE

red velvet cake Ask ten experts about the origins of this bright red chocolate cake with creamy white icing, and you'll get at least six different answers. One legend is that it was first served at New York's Waldorf Astoria Hotel in the 1920s (some say it was the 1950s). Others swear that red velvet cake has its roots in southern cooking. The flavor isn't strongly chocolate; the ratio is typically 2 tablespoons cocoa powder per $2\frac{1}{2}$ cups flour. And, though some believe the color comes from the chemical reaction between the cocoa and baking soda, the truth is that it's due to a healthy dose ($1\frac{1}{2}$ to 2 ounces) of red food coloring. Some recipes call for boiled beets as a color enhancer. This novelty cake got a boost in popularity in the late 1980s from the film *Steel Magnolias,* where it was served as an armadillo-shaped groom's cake.

Red Wattle pork *see* HERITAGE PORK

refresh In cooking, to immerse a hot food in cold water to cool it quickly and stop the cooking process.

refried beans *see* FRIJOLES REFRITOS

refrigerator cookie Also called *icebox cookie,* this style of cookie is made by forming the dough into a log, wrapping in plastic wrap or waxed paper and chilling until firm. The dough is then sliced into rounds and baked. *See also* COOKIE.

refrigerator thermometer *see* FREEZER/REFRIGERATOR THERMOMETER

refritos [reh-FREE-tohs] *see* FRIJOLES REFRITOS

Reggiano Parmigiano [reh-JYAH-noh pahr-muh-ZHAH-noh] *see* PARMESAN

Rehoboam [ree-uh-BOH-uhm] *see* WINE BOTTLES

reindeer [RAYN-deer] *see* GAME ANIMALS

rémoulade [ray-muh-LAHD] This classic French sauce is made by combining MAYONNAISE (usually homemade) with mustard, CAPERS and chopped GHERKINS, herbs and ANCHOVIES. It's served chilled as an accompaniment to cold meat, fish and shellfish. *See also* SAUCE.

rendang [rihn-DANG] A spicy braised meat dish popular in Indonesia, Malaysia, Thailand and nearby areas. Rendang is cooked with coconut milk and/or KERISIK, GALANGAL, LEMONGRASS, KAFFIR LIME LEAVES and other ingredients such as CANDLENUT, cardamom, chiles, cinnamon, cloves, garlic, ginger, INDONESIAN BAY LEAF, shallots, STAR ANISE, TAMARIND and TURMERIC, depending on the regional variation. The key is to slowly cook rendang for hours until all the liquid is gone, leaving a caramelized coating of spices on very tender pieces of meat. All types of meats are used; beef (*rendang daging*) is the most popular. Chicken is *rendang ayam* and duck is either *rendang itiak* or *rendag bebek*. Rendang is usually served with steamed rice.

render To melt animal fat over low heat so that it separates from any connective pieces of tissue, which, during rendering, turn brown and crisp and are generally referred to as CRACKLINGS. The resulting clear fat is then strained through a paper filter or fine CHEESECLOTH to remove any residue. *Try out* is synonymous to *render*.

renkon *see* LOTUS

rennet [RIHN-niht] For centuries cheesemakers have used animal rennet, which is comprised primarily of the enzyme **rennin** (also called *chymosin* and *rennet*) and obtained from the gastric juice found in the fourth stomach (*abomasum*) of young ruminants. This coagulating enzyme is used to curdle milk in foods such as cheese and JUNKET. But today there are other "rennet" choices, in part due to the widely fluctuating price of animal rennet and also because animal products are a problem for some Jews and VEGETARIANS. **Vegetable-based** coagulants are substances organically extracted from a variety of plants including thistles, nettles, fig leaves and safflowers. They have a coagulating effect almost as powerful as their animal-derived counterparts. **Bio-engineered rennets** are produced by introducing the animal's rennin-encoding DNA into a yeast or bacteria micro-organism, which can then be cultured to create rennin. Alternatively, bio-synthesis can be used to do the same thing without the use of animal cells. **Microbial enzyme** coagulants are made from the fermentation of fungi or bacteria. They act like rennet and are relatively inexpensive. Rennin is available in most supermarkets in tablet or powdered form. Other types of coagulants can often be found through suppliers of cheesemaking paraphernalia.

rennin [REN-ihn] *see* RENNET

reshteh *see* CALSONE

restaurant staff *see* BRIGADE SYSTEM

restaurateur [rehs-tuhr-uh-TOOR; rehs-tuhr-uh-TUHR] A restaurant owner or manager. A popular misconception is that the word is pronounced the same as "restaurant," whereas in actuality, there is no "n" in *restaurateur*.

resurrection lily *see* AROMATIC GINGER

retsina [reht-SEE-nah] Made for more than 3,000 years, this traditional Greek wine has been resinated—treated with pine-tree resin. The resin gives the wine a distinctively sappy, turpentinelike flavor that, according to most non-Greeks, is an acquired taste. Retsinas are either white or rosé and should be served very cold.

Reuben sandwich [ROO-behn] Reportedly originally named for its creator, Arthur Reuben (owner of New York's once-famous and now-defunct Reuben's delicatessen), this sandwich is made with generous layers of corned beef, Swiss cheese and sauerkraut on sourdough rye bread. Reuben is said to have created the original version (which was reportedly made with ham) for Annette Seelos, the leading lady in a Charlie Chaplin film being shot in 1914. Another version of this famous sandwich's origin is that an Omaha wholesale grocer (Reuben Kay) invented it during a poker game in 1955. It gained national prominence when one of his poker partner's employees entered the recipe in a national sandwich contest the following year and won. The Reuben can be served either cold or sautéed.

Rhode Island Greening apple A large, green to yellow-green fruit renowned as a cooking apple. It has a sweet-tart flesh that seems to intensify in flavor when cooked, which is why most of the crop is sold for commercial processing (applesauce, pies and so forth). *See also* APPLE.

Rhône wines [ROHN] Wines from France's Rhône region, which follows the Rhône river for approximately 125 miles in southeastern France. The northern part of the region contains many great individual APPELLATIONS including Côte Rôtie, Condrieu, Château Grillet, Saint-Joseph and Hermitage. The dominant grapes here are SYRAH for red wines and Marsanne, Roussanne and Viognier for whites. The most famous appellation in the south is CHÂTEAUNEUF-DU-PAPE. Most of the southern Rhône vineyards produce wines with the CÔTES DU RHÔNE appellation. In the southern Rhône the principal red grape is Grenache. The white grapes used include Bourboulenc, Clairette, Marsanne, Muscardine, Picardan, Roussanne and Piquepoul (or *Picpoule*).

rhubarb [ROO-bahrb] The thick, celerylike stalks of this buckwheat-family member can reach up to 2 feet long. They're the only edible portion of the plant—the leaves contain OXALIC ACID and can therefore be toxic. Though rhubarb is generally eaten as a fruit, it's botanically a vegetable. There are many varieties of this extremely tart food, most of which fall into two basic types—hothouse and field grown. Hothouse rhubarb is distinguished by its pink to pale red stalks and yellow-green leaves, whereas field-grown plants (which are more pronounced in flavor) have cherry red stalks and green leaves. Hothouse rhubarb is available from around December to March, while the field-grown plant can usually be found from March to October, with a peak from April to June. Choose crisp stalks that are brightly hued. The leaves should be fresh-looking and blemish-free. Highly perishable, fresh rhubarb should be refrigerated, tightly wrapped in a plastic bag, for up to 3 days. Wash and remove leaves just before using. Because of its intense tartness, rhubarb is usually combined with a considerable amount of sugar. It makes delicious sauces, jams and desserts and in some regions is also known as *pieplant* because of its popularity for that purpose. In America, a traditional flavor combination is rhubarb and strawberries; in Britain, rhubarb and ginger. Rhubarb contains a fair amount of vitamin A.

rhubarb chard *see* CHARD

rib 1. The meat cut (beef, lamb or veal) from between the SHORT LOIN and the CHUCK. Chops, steaks and roasts (depending on the animal) are cut from the rib section, which is very tender. *See also* RIB ROAST; RIB STEAK. 2. A single stalk of a celery bunch, though some cooks refer to the entire bunch as a rib. In general, the words *rib* and *stalk* describe the same thing.

rib, lamb The tender rib section features eight ribs that can be cut into *rib chops* (or *double rib chops* if two ribs are used) or left whole to create a *rack of lamb* (also called *rib roast* or *rack roast*). If the rack's formed into a circle, it's called a CROWN ROAST. If the meat is trimed away from the tips of the bones, it's called a *French* or *Frenched rack* or, in the case of a chop, a *French* or *Frenched chop*. *See also* LEG, LAMB.

ribbon A cooking term describing the texture of an egg-and-sugar mixture that has been beaten until pale and extremely thick. When the beater or whisk is lifted, the batter falls slowly back onto the surface of the mixture, forming a ribbonlike pattern that, after a few seconds, sinks back into the batter.

rib-eye steak *see* RIB STEAK

Ribier grape [RIHB-yuhr] One of America's best-selling grapes, the Ribier is large, round and has a tough blue-black skin. The flesh is juicy, sweet and contains a few seeds. *See also* GRAPE.

riblets *see* BREAST, LAMB

ribollita [ree-boh-LEE-tah] The word *ribollita* means "twice boiled," referring to the fact that this Tuscan soup was originally simply leftover MINESTRONE, reheated the next day and mixed with chunks of bread. But today this rich, thick soup is much more than "leftovers." Slices or chunks of garlic-rubbed bread can be layered either with minestrone, but also simply with chicken broth, PARMESAN cheese and cooked vegetables and white beans. The entire mixture is baked until bubbly hot, then served with a drizzle of olive oil.

rib roast A beef roast from the rib section between the SHORT LOIN and the CHUCK. The three most popular styles are standing rib roast, rolled rib roast and rib-eye roast. The **standing rib roast** usually includes at least three ribs (less than that is really just a very thick steak). It's roasted standing upright, resting on its rack of ribs, thereby allowing the top layer of fat to melt and self-baste the meat. A **rolled rib roast** has had the bones removed before being rolled and tied into a cylinder. Removing the bones also slightly diminishes the flavor of this roast. The boneless **rib-eye roast** is the center, most desirable and tender portion of the rib section. Therefore, it's also the most expensive. Many rib roasts are often inappropriately labeled PRIME RIB. In fact, they can't be called prime rib unless the cut actually comes from USDA Prime beef—rarely found in meat markets today. *See also* BEEF; Beef Chart, page 896.

rib steak This tender, flavorful beef steak is a boneless cut from the rib section (between the SHORT LOIN and the CHUCK). If the bones are removed the result is the extremely tender *rib-eye steak*. Both should be quickly cooked by grilling, broiling or frying. *See also* BEEF; RIB ROAST; Beef Chart, page 896.

ricciolini *see* Pasta Glossary, page 883

rice *n.* This ancient and venerable grain has been cultivated since at least 5000 B.C., and archaeological explorations in China have uncovered sealed pots of rice that are almost 8,000 years old. Today, rice is a staple for almost half the world's population—particularly in parts of China, India, Indonesia, Japan and Southeast Asia. The 7,000-plus varieties of rice are grown in one of two ways. *Aquatic rice* (paddy-grown) is cultivated in flooded fields. The lower-yielding, lower-quality *hill-grown rice* can be grown on almost any tropical or subtropical terrain. The major rice-growing states in the United States are Arkansas, California, Louisiana, Mississippi, Missouri and Texas. Rice is commercially classified by its size—long-, medium- or short-grain. The length of **long-grain rice** is four to five times that of its width. There are both white and brown varieties of long-grain rice, which, when cooked, produce light, dry grains that separate easily. One of the more exotic varieties in the long-grain category is the perfumy East Indian BASMATI RICE. **Short-grain rice** has fat, almost round grains that have a higher starch content than either the long- or medium-grain varieties. When cooked, it tends to be quite moist and viscous, causing the grains to stick together. This variety (also called *pearl rice, sticky rice* and *glutinous rice,* though it's gluten-free) is preferred in the Orient because it's easy to handle with chopsticks. Italian

ARBORIO RICE—used to make creamy RISOTTOS—and the Japanese MOCHI are also varieties of short-grain rice. **Medium-grain rice**, as could be expected from its name, has a size and character between the other two. It's shorter and moister than long-grain and generally not as starchy as short-grain. Though fairly fluffy right after being cooked, medium-grain rice begins to clump once it starts to cool. Rice can be further divided into two other broad categories—brown and white. Long-grain rice belongs to *indica,* one of the two main varieties of rice; medium-grain and short-grain rice belong to the other main variety, *japonica.* **Brown rice** is the entire grain with only the inedible outer husk removed. The nutritious, high-fiber bran coating gives it a light tan color, nutlike flavor and chewy texture. The presence of the bran means that brown rice is subject to rancidity, which limits its shelf life to only about 6 months. It also takes slightly longer to cook (about 30 minutes total) than regular white long-grain rice. There is a *quick brown rice* (which has been partially cooked, then dehydrated) that cooks in only about 15 minutes, and an *instant brown rice* that takes only 10 minutes. **White rice** has had the husk, bran and germ removed. Regular white rice is sometimes referred to as *polished rice.* For *converted* or *parboiled white rice,* the unhulled grain has been soaked, pressure-steamed and dried before milling. This treatment gelatinizes the starch in the grain (for fluffy, separated cooked rice) and infuses some of the nutrients of the bran and germ into the kernel's heart. Converted rice has a pale beige cast and takes slightly longer to cook than regular white rice. *Talc-coated rice* is white rice that has a coating of talc and glucose, which gives it a glossy appearance. The coating acts as a preservative and the practice was once widely used to protect exported rice during long sea voyages. Today coated rice (which is clearly labeled as such) is available only in a few ethnic markets, usually those specializing in South American foods. It must be thoroughly rinsed before being cooked, as there is a chance that the talc can be contaminated with asbestos. **Instant** or **quick white rice** has been fully or partially cooked before being dehydrated and packaged. It takes only a few minutes to prepare but delivers lackluster results in both flavor and texture. **Rice bran**, the grain's outer layer, is high in soluble fiber and research indicates that, like oat bran, it's effective in lowering cholesterol. Rice should be stored in an airtight container in a cool, dark, dry place. White rice can be stored this way almost indefinitely, brown rice up to 6 months. The life of the latter can be extended considerably by refrigeration. Rice can be prepared in a multitude of ways, the method greatly depending on the type of rice. Consult a general cookbook for cooking directions. Rice, which is cholesterol- and gluten-free, is low in sodium, contains only a trace of fat and is an excellent source of complex carbohydrates. Enriched or converted rice contains calcium, iron and many B-complex vitamins, with brown rice being slightly richer in all the nutrients. *See also* AROMATIC RICE; BALDO RICE;

CARNAROLI RICE; JASMINE RICE; RICE FLOUR; RIZCOUS; SHINMA; TEXMATI RICE; VIALONE NANO RICE; WEHANI RICE; WILD RICE; WILD PECAN RICE. **rice** *v.* To push cooked food through a perforated kitchen utensil called a RICER. The result is food that looks vaguely ricelike.

rice bran *see* RICE

rice fettuccine *see* RICE NOODLES

rice flour
Regular rice flour is a fine, powdery flour made from regular white rice. It's used mainly for baked goods. **Glutinous** or **sweet rice flour** (such as the Japanese MOCHI) is made from high-starch short-grain rice. It's widely used in Asian cooking to thicken sauces and for some desserts.

rice-flour noodles *see* RICE NOODLES

rice noodles
Any of several varieties of noodles made from rice, rice flour or rice powder, which are typically used in many Cambodian, Chinese, Laotian, Japanese, Malaysian, Thai and Vietnamese dishes. **Rice vermicelli** (also known as *banh hoi, bee hoon, bihoon mai fun, mee fun, mi fen, pancit bihon* and *sen mee*) are extremely thin noodles made from rice powder. They resemble long, translucent white hairs and, when deep-fried, explode dramatically into a tangle of airy, crunchy strands that are a traditional ingredient in Chinese chicken salad and Thai MEE KROB. Rice vermicelli can also be presoaked and used in soups and STIR-FRY dishes. **Rice stick noodles** (or simply **rice sticks**) are made from rice powder and come in thin, medium and wide widths. The thin noodles (known as *bun, palabok* and *sen yai*) are used in STIR-FRYS and soups and deep-fried as a proxy for rice vermicelli. Medium-wide noodles (known as *rice fettuccine, ban pho, ho fun, haw fun, gway tio, kway teow, kui teow, lai fen* and *sen lek*) are considered an all-purpose noodle. They're used in a wide variety of dishes (stir-frys, soups and salads) and as an accompaniment to meat dishes. The widest rice stick noodles are known as *chantaboon, jantaboon, sen chan, sha ha fun* and *shan shui ho fun.* They're used primarily in stir-frys and soups. When used in stir-frys their edges often become crispy while the inner portion remains soft. Rice stick noodles should be presoaked and briefly boiled before using. **Rice river noodles** are made from rice flour and wheat starch and are also called *chow fun guo tiao, fen noodles, hu tieu, khao pun, kuay taew, rice ribbon noodles, sha he fen* and *sha ho fen.* They're sold in sheets or in various widths cut from large sheets. As sheets they can be used to wrap meats and vegetables as in some DIM SUM dishes. When cut into thinner strips they're used like rice stick noodles. Rice river noodles are available fresh, usually with a light coating of oil to prevent them from sticking together or drying. **Silver pin noodles** are thick, round noodles about 2

inches long made from cooked rice that's pressed and rolled. They're also known as *rat's tails, loh shee fun, mee tye bak* and *nen dzem fen*. Silver pin noodles are used in stir-frys and can be added directly without pre-soaking. Rice noodles can be found in Asian markets, natural food stores and some supermarkets. Dry noodles are typically sold in coiled nests packaged in cellophane; fresh noodles are in plastic-wrapped trays in the refrigerated section. *See also* ASIAN NOODLES.

rice paddy herb A pale green, small-leafed herb native to Southeast Asia where it grows in hot, high-humidity environments, such as rice paddies. Rice paddy herb goes by various names including *ngo om, phak khayang, seui fa* and *shui fu rong*. It has a flavor suggesting citrus and CUMIN and an undertaste some describe as soapy. Rice paddy herb is primarily found in Vietnamese dishes such as *canh chua ca* (a hot and sour fish soup), as an accompaniment to PHO and in curries. Its growing environment makes it hard to find outside of Southeast Asia, though some Vietnamese markets carry it.

rice paper An edible, translucent paper made from a dough of water combined with the pith of an Asian shrub called, appropriately enough, the rice-paper plant (or rice-paper tree). RICE FLOUR is sometimes also used. The paper comes in various sizes—small to large, round or square. Rice paper can be used to wrap foods to be eaten as is or deep-fried. It's also useful as a baking-sheet liner on which delicate cookies are baked. After baking, the cookies may be removed from the sheet without damage and the flavorless rice paper (which sticks to the cookies' bottoms) eaten along with the confection. Rice paper can be found in Asian markets and some supermarkets.

ricer Also called a *potato ricer,* this kitchen utensil resembles a large garlic press. Cooked food such as potatoes, carrots or turnips is placed in the container. A lever-operated plunger is pushed down into the food, forcing it out through numerous tiny holes in the bottom of the container. The result is food that (vaguely) resembles grains of rice. Ricers come in a variety of shapes, the most common being a 3- to 4-inch round basket or a V-shaped bucket. They're generally made of chromed steel or cast aluminum and can be found in specialty cookware shops.

rice ribbon noodles *see* RICE NOODLES

rice ring *see* RING MOLD

rice sticks *see* RICE NOODLES

rice vermicelli *see* RICE NOODLES

rice vinegar There are Japanese as well as Chinese rice vinegars, both made from fermented rice, and both slightly milder than most Western vinegars. Chinese rice vinegar comes in three types: white (clear or pale amber), used mainly in SWEET-AND-SOUR dishes; red, a popular accompaniment for boiled or steamed crab; and black, used mainly as a table CONDIMENT. The almost colorless Japanese rice vinegar is used in a variety of Japanese preparations, including SUSHI rice and SUNOMONO (vinegared salads). Rice vinegar can be found in Asian markets and some supermarkets.

rice wine A sweet, golden wine made from fermenting freshly steamed glutinous rice. Most rice wines are low in alcohol. The most well-known Japanese rice wines are SAKE and MIRIN; those from China include SHAOXING, Chia Fan, Shan Niang and Yen Hung.

rickey [RIHK-ee] A drink made with lime (sometimes lemon) juice, soda water and liquor, usually gin or whiskey. If sugar is added, the drink becomes a TOM COLLINS. A nonalcoholic rickey always has sugar or sugar syrup added to it.

ricotta [rih-KAHT-tuh; ree-KOH-tah] It's thought that ricotta came about in order to use the huge amounts of WHEY produced by Italy's cheesemaking industry—a dilemma causing environmental problems. *Ricotta* comes from the Latin *recocta,* meaning "recooked," which refers to the most common types of ricotta that use reheated whey. During reheating, protein particles rise to the surface, are skimmed off, strained and placed in perforated molds or baskets to drain further. The resulting rich, fresh cheese is slightly grainy but smoother than cottage cheese. It's white, moist and has a slightly sweet flavor. Of course, ricotta technically isn't a cheese at all but a "dairy product" because neither STARTER nor RENNET is used in the process. **Ricotta Romana**, also called *ricotta gentile*, is made in this way using sheep's whey left over from making Pecorino Romano (*see* PECORINO). Some ricottas are made with partially skimmed milk in lieu of whey or with milk added to the whey, resulting in a higher FAT CONTENT. There are many approaches to making ricotta and myriad variations in both texture and flavor, though all versions are generally fresh, soft and moist. There are exceptions. **Ricotta salata** is quite different. It's produced in Sicily, Sardinia and several regions of mainland Italy. *Salata* means "salty," and this cheese is made by salting and pressing fresh ricotta before aging it for about 3 months. The result is a firm, snow-white cheese that's smooth, pliable and somewhat similar to FETA, though not as salty. It has a sweet, milky, slightly nutty flavor. Some ricotta salatas are aged for a year or more until they are hard enough to be grating cheeses. If the word **affumicata** is used it means the ricotta has been smoked; its exterior will be grayish white to reddish gold to brown. There are myriad smoked versions. For example, **ricotta fumo di ginepro**, produced in

Abruzzo and Molise, is distinctively smoked with juniper wood. **Ricotta forte** is made by taking leftover fresh ricotta and kneading it periodically for several months before placing it in small clay pots to age for about a year. This results in soft, creamy-brown paste that's exceedingly pungent and piquant. **Ricotta infornata** is made by baking drained ricotta in a greased pan or clay pot for about a half hour or until the surface begins to brown. The cheese's interior turns pale golden and the exterior a deep golden brown. Ricotta infornata is traditionally eaten fresh, but it's also allowed to age and become hard enough to be used as a grating cheese. **American ricottas** are typically made with a combination of whey and whole or skim milk, which usually produces a wetter, creamier style of ricotta than Italian versions. *See also* CHEESE.

Riesling [REEZ-ling; REES-ling] Riesling is considered one of the world's great white wine grapes and produces some of the very best white wines. It's a native of Germany, where it's believed to have been cultivated for at least 500—and possibly as long as 2,000—years. Riesling wines are delicate but complex, and characterized by a spicy, fruity flavor, flower-scented BOUQUET and long finish. Riesling is vinified in a variety of styles ranging from DRY to very sweet. In Germany, these sweet wines—which are usually affected by BOTRYTIS CINEREA—are graded in ascending order of sweetness as AUSLESE, BEERENAUSLESE and TROCKENBEERENAUSLESE. California winemakers now produce high-quality, German-style Rieslings, which are lighter, more delicate, and slightly to medium-sweet. Because the name "Riesling" is used in many ways, it's sometimes difficult to find wines truly made from this variety. In California, for instance, **Johannisberg Riesling** is the true Riesling, whereas Gray Riesling and Emerald Riesling are actually other varieties. A bottle of California wine labeled simply "Riesling" usually means that the wine's made from one of the lesser varieties, not Johannisberg Riesling.

rigatoni *see* Pasta Glossary, page 883

rijsttafel [RRI-stah-fuhl; RIHS-tah-fuhl] Dutch for "rice table," rijst-tafel is the Dutch version of an Indonesian meal consisting of hot rice accompanied by a profusion of small, well-seasoned side dishes such as steamed or fried seafoods and meats, vegetables, fruits, sauces, CONDI-MENTS, etc. The Dutch adopted this style of dining during their occupation of Indonesia in the 18th and 19th centuries.

rillettes [ree-YEHTS] Meat, usually pork but also rabbit, goose, poultry, fish, etc., that is slowly cooked in seasoned fat and then pounded or pulverized (along with some of the fat) into a paste. This mixture is then packed in small pots, RAMEKINS or other containers and covered with a thin layer of fat. Rillettes can be stored for several weeks in the refrigerator providing the fatty seal is not broken. This mixture, resembling a smooth PÂTÉ, is served cold, usually as an appetizer spread on toast or bread.

ring mold Used for everything from cakes to breads to gelatin dishes, ring molds range in diameter from 2 to 7 inches and are 2 to 2½ inches deep. These molds are typically made of aluminum or glass; their center hole is larger than that of a BUNDT or TUBE PAN. The ring mold is also known as a *rice ring,* in which case it's used to mold hot rice. After being inverted on a serving plate, the rice ring is typically filled with a creamed chicken or seafood mixture.

ripening; ripen, to In the cheese world, the term *ripening* (also called *aging, curing* or *finishing*) refers to the final and, for most cheeses, most important step of cheesemaking—when the cheese is brought to its optimal maturity of flavor, texture and aroma. During this time, the cheese is kept at carefully controlled levels of humidity and temperature, sometimes in cool, moist natural caves, such as France's Cambalou caverns for ROQUEFORT. But cheese is aged more commonly in ripening rooms where temperature, humidity and air circulation can be closely monitored. Part of the art of ripening is balancing the perfect environment with the precise number of days each style of cheese needs to ripen. For example, soft cheeses such as CAMEMBERT ripen quickly, and therefore require relatively low temperatures and high humidity (around 95 percent). Conversely, most hard cheeses take longer to ripen and therefore typically age best at a lower humidity level of no more than about 80 percent. The style of a cheese dictates the length of time it's allowed to ripen, which ranges from a few days, to several weeks, to up to 2 years or more. During lengthy periods of ripening, the cheese loses moisture, which intensifies its flavors and aromas. The time and labor costs, added to a cheese's weight loss during long-term aging, contribute to the higher price of such cheeses compared to mass-produced examples. In the United States ripened cheese must either be made from PASTEURIZED milk or must be aged for a minimum of 60 days at a temperature of not less than 35°F. *See also* AFFINAGE; AFFINÉ.

ripe olive *see* OLIVE

ripieno; *pl.* **ripieni;** [ree-PYAY-nee] The Italian term for foods that are "stuffed," such as *carciofi ripieni*—"stuffed artichokes."

ris [REE] French for "SWEETBREADS." *Ris de veau* are from a calf, *ris d'agneau* from a lamb.

riserva [ree-ZEHR-vah] Italian for "reserve," which in the wine world can only be applied to APPELLATION wines that have been AGED longer than regular wines. The better wines are usually chosen to become riservas. The total aging time varies from wine to wine.

rishta *see* CALSONE

riso [REE-soh] Italian for "rice." Also a rice-shaped PASTA (*see* Pasta Glossary, page 883).

risotto [rih-SAW-toh; ree-ZAW-toh] An Italian rice specialty made by stirring hot stock into a mixture of rice (and often chopped onions) that has been sautéed in butter. The stock is added 1⁄2 cup at a time and the mixture is stirred continually while it cooks until all the liquid is absorbed before more stock is added. This labor-intensive technique results in rice that is delectably creamy while the grains remain separate and firm. Risottos can be flavored variously with ingredients such as chicken, shellfish, sausage, vegetables, cheese, white wine and herbs. The famous **risotto Milanese** is scented with SAFFRON. The use of Italian ARBORIO RICE is traditional in the preparation of risotto. BALDO, CARNAROLI and VIALONE NANO, which are other types of Italian rice that are used.

rissole [rih-SOHL; ree-SOHL] 1. Sweet- or savory-filled pastry (often shaped like a TURNOVER) that is fried or baked and served as an appetizer, side dish or dessert. 2. Small, partially cooked potato balls that are browned in butter until crisp.

rissolé [RIHS-uh-lee; rihs-uh-LAY; ree-saw-LAY] Food that has been fried until crisp and brown.

ristorante [ree-stoh-RAHN-the] Italian for "restaurant." *See also* TRATTORIA.

ristra [REE-strah] A Spanish term referring to a handstrung rope of foods, primarily CHILES or heads of garlic. Though ristras are used for decoration, many people let the chiles dry and use them in cooking, pulling them off one-by-one from the bottom. Dried garlic ristras are used strictly for decoration.

riz [REE] French for "rice."

Rizcous [REEZ-koos] Produced in California, Rizcous is a product composed of broken brown rice grains. In its cooked form, it resembles its namesake, COUSCOUS.

riz à l'impératrice [REE ahl-ahn-pehr-ah-TREES] 1. French for "rice as the empress likes it," *riz à l'impératrice* is a very rich rice pudding made with vanilla custard, whipped cream and crystallized fruit (which is often soaked in KIRSCH). 2. The term *à l'impératrice* is used to describe a variety of rich sweet or savory dishes.

roast *n.* 1. A piece of meat—such as a RIB ROAST—that's large enough to serve more than one person. Such a meat cut is usually cooked by the roasting method. 2. Food, usually meat, that has been prepared by roasting. **roast** *v.* To oven-cook food (from meats to vegetables) in a shallow uncovered pan, a method that ideally produces a well-browned exterior and moist interior. The temperatures for roasting are typically higher than for BAKING, and the pan must be uncovered so the food doesn't stew in its own juices. Another common denominator for roasting is that it requires fat, either as part of the food (as with duck), or added (as one would to roasted potatoes). Cuts of meat or poultry to be roasted must be reasonably tender—tougher pieces are better served with moist cooking methods such as BRAISING.

roaster *see* CHICKEN

roasting rack A slightly raised rack—usually made of stainless steel—that elevates meat above the pan in which it's roasting. This prevents the meat from cooking in any drippings and allows adequate air circulation for even cooking and browning. Roasting racks can be flat, V-shaped or adjustable so they can be used either way.

Robert sauce [roh-BAYR] Classic French brown sauce with a reduction of lightly cooked onions and white wine plus DEMI-GLACE and mustard (traditionally DIJON). Usually served with meats, especially pork.

Robiola [roh-bee-OH-lah] A soft, fresh cheese made throughout northern Italy in a variety of styles, Robiola can be made from cow's, goat's and/or sheep's milk. These cheeses are usually small (from 6 to 14 ounces) and wheel- or square-shaped. Their rinds are either bloomy or washed and range in color from white to pale golden to pinkish. Interiors range from snowy white to ivory. Robiolas are typically aged for 3 weeks or less and at that point are very creamy. However, some are aged up to 3 months and have a much drier texture. Flavors range from delicate, mild and tangy when young to more pungent with longer RIPENING. Occasionally Robiolas are wrapped in pine boughs or leaves (such as rosemary, cabbage, fig, grape or walnut). **Robiola Piedmont** is a generic name for Robiola cheeses made throughout Piedmont. **Robiola Lombardia** is a generic name for TALEGGIO-style washed-rind cheeses made throughout the Lombardy region. Smaller versions of Robiola are sometimes called *Robiolina*. *See also* CHEESE.

Rob Roy A COCKTAIL made with SCOTCH, sweet VERMOUTH and BITTERS. It's sometimes called a *Scotch Manhattan* because it substitutes scotch for the bourbon used in the standard MANHATTAN recipe.

rocambole [ROK-uhm-bohl] Also called *sand leek* and *giant garlic,* rocambole has LEEKlike bulbs that taste like mild garlic. It grows wild (and is sometimes cultivated) throughout Europe and may be used in any

way suitable for garlic. Rocambole is rarely commercially available in the United States but might be spotted at farmer's markets.

rock and rye An American rye whiskey–based LIQUEUR flavored with lemon or orange essence and distinguished by a chunk of ROCK CANDY in the bottom of each bottle.

rock bass *see* SUNFISH

rock bun Also called *rock cake*, this spicy British cross between a cookie and a small cake is full of coarsely chopped dried fruit. It's baked in small mounds, which take on a rocklike appearance.

rock candy A simple hard candy made by allowing a concentrated SUGAR SYRUP to evaporate slowly (sometimes for up to a week), during which time it crystallizes into chunks. The crystals can be formed around strings or small sticks (the latter can be used as stir sticks for sweet drinks). Small rock-candy crystals can be used as a fancy sweetener for tea or coffee. ROCK AND RYE liqueur has a large chunk of rock candy in the bottom of the bottle. Rock candy can be made at home or purchased in candy shops.

Rock Cornish hen; Rock Cornish game hen *see* CHICKEN

rock crab *see* CRAB

rocket *see* ARUGULA

rockfish 1. With over 50 varieties, this is the largest of the Pacific Coast fish families. The lowfat rockfish can be broken down into two broad categories—deep-bodied and elongated. The flesh of the deep-bodied varieties (such as **yellowtail**, **blue rockfish** and **goldeneye**) is firmer and more full-flavored than the softer, milder flesh of the elongated species (like **bocaccio**, **chilipepper** and **shortbelly**). Rockfish range widely in color from reddish-pink with black-tipped fins to orange-mottled brown to dark olive green with bright yellow fins. They average from 5 to 15 pounds and are sold whole or in fillets. The firm-fleshed rockfish is suitable for virtually any cooking method, whereas the softer flesh of the elongated varieties must be handled gently—preferably baked or poached. Some rockfish are marketed as "Pacific snapper" or "Pacific red snapper," but they are not related to the true Atlantic RED SNAPPER. 2. STRIPED BASS is also referred to as "rockfish."

rock lobster *see* LOBSTER

rock salt *see* SALT

rock shrimp This SHRIMP-family member resembles a miniature lobster and is wild-caught from Virginia to the Gulf of Mexico, along the coast of California and in the Caribbean. The name comes from the thick, rock-hard shells that are immensely difficult to remove by hand. Today the shrimp shells (and heads) are more typically removed by machines, the advent of which greatly increased the popularity of rock shrimp. Recognition became even broader after the shrimp were promoted as POPCORN SHRIMP. The texture of rock shrimp is firm and slightly chewy, the flavor sweet and similar to that of lobster. Rock shrimp range in size from 25 to 110 per pound and most are sold sans shell (both fresh and frozen). They're available frozen year-round and are generally available fresh from July through November, peaking in September.

rock sugar Not as sweet as regular granulated sugar, rock sugar comes in the form of amber-colored crystals, the result of sugar cooked until it begins to color. It's used to sweeten certain Chinese teas and meat glazes. *See also* SUGAR.

Rocky Mountain Oyster *see* FRIES

rocky road A bumpy-textured candy that's a mixture of miniature marshmallows, nuts and sometimes small chunks of dark, white or milk chocolate. The candy is so named because it resembles a "rocky road" in appearance. This favorite flavor combination is also used for a number of desserts from ice cream to pies.

rocoto chile [roh-COH-toh] This CHILE grows throughout Central and South America and Mexico and goes by many names including *caballo* ("horse"), *cera, cirhuleo, ciruelo, locoto, malinalco, manzana* (or *apple pepper*), and *perón* (or *pear pepper*). The chiles are pear- or apple-shaped and can grow from 2 to 3 inches in length. The color ranges from green to yellow to orange to red. They are hot, with a SCOVILLE SCALE rating of 30,000 to 100,000. Due to the thickness of their skin, they are hard to dry and are usually eaten fresh.

roe [ROH] This delicacy falls into two categories—hard roe and soft roe. **Hard roe** is female fish eggs, while **soft roe** (also called *white roe*) is the milt of male fish. The eggs of some CRUSTACEANS (such as lobster) are referred to as CORAL. Roe can range in size from 1 to 2 ounces to over 3 pounds. If the fish is small, the roe is cooked inside the whole fish. The roe of medium and large fish is usually removed and cooked separately. Most fish roe is edible but others (including that of the great BARRACUDA and some members of the puffer (*see* FUGU) and trunkfish families) are toxic. The choicest roe comes from CARP, HERRING, MACKEREL and SHAD, but those from COD, FLOUNDER, HADDOCK, LUMPFISH, MULLET, PERCH, PIKE, SALMON, STURGEON and WHITEFISH also have their fans. Salting roe transforms it into CAVIAR. Roe is marketed fresh, frozen and canned. Fresh roe is available in the spring. It should have a clean smell and look moist and firm. The extremely fragile membrane that holds the eggs or milt must be gently washed before preparation. Roe can be sautéed, poached or, providing it's medium-size or larger, broiled. It can also be used in sauces. *See also* BOTTARGA; KAZUNOKO; MASAGO; TOBIKO; UNI.

rogan josh; roghan josh [ROH-gahn johsh] A curry dish from the Kashmir region introduced to that area during the Moghul rule of India. There are several interpretations of the name. One indicates that in Persian *rogan* means "oil" and *josh* means "hot." The dish is prepared by cooking the meat (usually lamb) in oil or clarified butter at a very high temperature, then blending in various seasonings such as ANISE, BLACK CARDAMOM, cinnamon, cloves, CUMIN, CORIANDER, ginger and paprika. There are numerous variations, many of which use onion, tomatoes and yogurt. Others use ASAFETIDA, fennel and nutmeg. This medium-hot dish is usually served with rice.

rolled cookie A cookie made by rolling a rather firm dough into an even (thick to thin) layer, then cutting the dough into various shapes with a COOKIE CUTTER before baking. *See also* COOKIE.

rolled oats *see* OATS

rolled roast *see* RIB ROAST

rolling boil *see* BOIL

rolling cookie cutter *see* COOKIE CUTTER

rolling pin A kitchen tool used primarily to roll out dough, but also handy for a number of other culinary tasks including crushing crackers, shaping cookies like TUILES and flattening meats such as chicken breasts. Rolling pins can be made of almost any material including brass, ceramic, copper, glass, marble, plastic and porcelain. The favored material, however, is hardwood. The heavier pins deliver the best results because their weight and balance produce smoother doughs with less effort. There are many rolling pin styles but by far the most popular and easiest for most people to use are the **American or bakers' rolling pins**. Those of higher quality are characterized by sturdy handles anchored with a steel rod running through the center of the pin and fitted with ball bearings. Many professional cooks prefer the **straight French rolling pin** (a solid piece of hardwood sans handles) because they get the "feel" of the dough under their palms. The **tapered rolling pin** is larger in the center and tapers to both ends, which allows it to be rotated during the rolling process—a feature particularly useful for rolling circles of dough. There are also "cool" rolling pins made of ceramic, marble, glass or plastic, some of which are hollow and can be filled with ice or iced water. These special-purpose pins are designed to work with delicate pastry doughs that become difficult as they warm.

rollmops *see* HERRING

roll out A baking term that describes the technique of using a ROLLING PIN to flatten a dough (such as for a pie crust or cookies) into a thin, even layer.

romaine lettuce [roh-MAYN] Because it's said to have originated on the Aegean island of Cos, romaine is also called *Cos lettuce*. Romaine's elongated head has dark green outer leaves that lighten to pale celadon in the center. The leaves are crisp and slightly bitter and the crunchy midrib is particularly succulent. Romaine adds crunch and flavor to mixed green salads and is the lettuce of choice for CAESAR SALADS. *See also* LETTUCE.

Romanesca cauliflower; Romanesco [roh-mah-NEHS-kah (koh)] Though classified as (and also called) a *summer cauliflower,* this vegetable's appearance is so uniquely striking that it deserves its own listing. Like regular cauliflower, Romanesca has a tightly compact head of florets attached by clusters of stalks—but there the similarity in appearance ends. Romanesca, which hails from northern Italy, is a beautiful pale lime green color; its florets, rather than being rounded, rise in a pyramid of pointed, spiraling cones. Its flavor is somewhat more delicate than that of regular cauliflower. Romanesca is available only briefly—from September through November. Choose a firm head with crisp leaves. Store in a plastic bag in the refrigerator for up to 1 week. Romanesca can be cooked in any fashion suitable for regular cauliflower. It makes beautiful CRUDITÉS, and is stunning cooked whole. *See also* BROCCOFLOWER; CAULIFLOWER.

Roman mushroom *see* CREMINO

Romano [roh-MAH-noh] There are several different styles of Romano, all of which take their name from the city of Rome. Probably the best known is the sharp, tangy **Pecorino Romano**, made with sheep's milk. **Caprino Romano** is an extremely sharp goat's-milk version, **Vacchino Romano** a very mild cow's-milk CHEESE. Most U.S. Romanos are made of cow's milk or a combination of cow's milk and goat's or sheep's milk. Cheese lovers normally favor the sheep's- and goat's-milk versions, which have sharper, tangier, more pronounced flavors than the milder cow's-milk versions. In general, the pale yellow Romano is very firm and mostly used for grating. It has a FAT CONTENT of approximately 27 to 29 percent. *See also* CHEESE; PECORINO CHEESE.

Rome Beauty apple This large apple has a deep red skin with some yellow speckling and a firm, mildly sweet flesh. It's the fruit of choice for whole baked apples. *See also* APPLE.

romesco [roh-MEHS-koh] A classic sauce from Catalonia, Spain, *romesco* is a finely ground mixture of tomatoes, red bell peppers, onion, garlic, almonds and olive oil. It's typically served with grilled fish or poultry. *See also* SAUCE.

Roncal (DO; PDO) [ROHNG-kahl] HARD sheep's-milk cheese from Spain's Roncal Valley in the Navarre region at the foot of the Pyrénées. Roncal is produced by a cooperative of shepherds from the seven villages of the Roncal Valley. The cooperative was formed in the Middle Ages; today it still manages the region's natural resources and oversees cheese production. Both FARMSTEAD and factory versions of the cheese are produced, and both follow cheesemaking traditions passed on for centuries. The 4- to 7-pound wheels are immersed in BRINE for 36 hours and then RIPENED for a minimum of 4 months. This results in rinds ranging from straw-colored to reddish brown to dark gray. The interior is beige to amber-colored with a scattering of small EYES. Roncal is herbaceous and nutty, and its sweetness becomes increasingly piquant with age. It has a FAT CONTENT of 45 to 50 percent. This cheese is also called *Queso del Valle del Roncal.*

rondeau [rawn-DOH] *see* BRAZIER

rooibos [ROY-bos] Plant grown in South Africa's Western Cape region that's used to make a popular herbal tea. Rooibos tea is also referred to as *bush tea, redbush tea* and *red tea*. It's become quite popular outside of South Africa and many tea companies now package rooibos teas. In addition, Starbucks produces a rooibos tea latte. The tea is caffeine-free and high in antioxidants; its flavor is described in terms like *smoky, honey, woody, spicy* and *caramel*. A red version in which the rooibos leaves are oxidized is the most popular, but a green version that's not oxidized is also produced.

Roomkaas [ROOM-kahss] *see* GOUDA

root beer Created in the mid-1800s by Philadelphia pharmacist Charles Hires, the original root beer was a (very) low-alcohol, naturally effervescent beverage made by fermenting a blend of sugar and yeast with various roots, herbs and barks such as SARSAPARILLA, SASSAFRAS, wild cherry, WINTERGREEN and GINGER. Today's commercial root beer is completely nonalcoholic and generally contains sugar, caramel coloring, a combination of artificial and natural flavorings (including some of those originally used) and carbonated water for sparkle.

root beer plant *see* PEPPER LEAF

ropa vieja [ROH-pah VYAY-hah] Spanish for "old clothes," *ropa vieja* is a classic Cuban dish of shredded cooked beef (such as leftover pot roast) in a spicy tomato sauce.

Roquefort [rohk-FOR] If not the "king of cheeses" as many proclaim, Roquefort is at least one of the oldest and best known in the world. This blue cheese has been enjoyed since Roman times (Caesar was a fan) and was a favorite of Charlemagne. It is made from sheep's milk that is exposed to a mold known as *Penicillium roqueforti* and aged for 3 months or more in the limestone caverns of Mount Combalou near the village of Roquefort in southwestern France. Although production of this cheese can be started in other specified regions of France, this is the only place true Roquefort can be aged. It is RIPENED for a minimum of 3 months, usually 4 months, and often for 9 months or more. Roquefort has a creamy-rich texture and pungent, piquant, somewhat salty flavor. It has a creamy white interior with blue veins and an ivory rind. It's sold in squat foil-wrapped cylinders. True Roquefort can be authenticated by a red sheep on the wrapper's emblem. The name "Roquefort" is protected by law from imitators of this remarkable cheese. For example, salad dressings made from blue cheese other than Roquefort cannot be labeled "Roquefort dressing." In addition to salad dressings, Roquefort can be used in a wide variety of preparations from savory breads to CANAPE spreads. Aficionados love Roquefort at the end of a meal served only with a fine SAUTERNES, PORT or other DESSERT WINE. The minimum FAT CONTENT for Roquefort is 52 percent. *See also* CHEESE.

roquette *see* ARUGULA

rosamarina *see* Pasta Glossary, page 883

rosato [roh-SAH-toh] Italian for "ROSE WINE."

rosé; rosé wine [roh-ZAY] Rosé wine is usually made from red grapes but—contrary to the normal process of making red wine—the skins and stems are typically removed within 2 to 3 days. This brief contact with the skins and stems gives the wine its light pink (or rose) color. It also, however, is the reason that rosés lack the body and (some would say) the character of most red or white wines. In general, rosés are very light-bodied and slightly sweet. They should be served chilled and can accompany a variety of lightly flavored foods.

rose hips Though too tart to eat raw, the ripe reddish-orange fruit of the rose (especially the wild or dog rose) is often used to make jellies and jams, syrup, tea and wine. Because they're an excellent source of vitamin C, rose hips are also dried and ground into powder (and sometimes made into tablets) and sold in natural food stores.

rosemary Used since 500 B.C., rosemary is native to the Mediterranean area (where it grows wild) but is now cultivated throughout Europe and the United States. Early on, this mint-family member was used to cure ailments of the nervous system. Rosemary's silver-green, needle-shaped leaves are highly aromatic and their flavor hints of both lemon and pine. This herb is available in whole-leaf form (fresh and dried) as well as powdered. Rosemary ESSENCE is used both to flavor food and to scent cosmetics. Rosemary can be used as a seasoning in a variety of dishes including fruit salads, soups, vegetables, meat (particularly lamb), fish and egg dishes, stuffings and dressings. *See also* HERBS; Seasoning Suggestions, page 891.

rosette; rosette iron [roh-ZEHT] A small fried pastry made by dipping a rosette iron first into a thin, sweet batter, then into hot deep fat. When the mixture turns crisp and golden brown, the rosette is removed from the iron and drained on paper towels. While warm, these pastries are usually sprinkled with cinnamon-sugar. A nonsweetened batter may be used to make savory rosettes, which can be sprinkled with salt and served as an appetizer. A **rosette iron** has a long metal rod with a heat-proof handle at one end and various decorative shapes (such as a butterfly, heart, star or flower) that can be attached to the other end.

rose syrup Syrup made from sugar and ROSE WATER. It's very popular on the Indian subcontinent, in the Middle East and China but is also used in the West.

rose water A distillation of rose petals that has the intensely perfumy flavor and fragrance of its source. Rose water has been a popular flavoring for centuries in the cuisines of the Middle East, India and China. In addition to culinary uses, rose water is also used in religious ceremonies and as a fragrance in some cosmetics.

Rossini [roh-SEE-nee] Dishes that include FOIE GRAS, TRUFFLES and a rich, DEMI-GLACE-based sauce—either as an integral part or as a garnish. TOURNEDOS Rossini and eggs Rossini are two popular examples. Such dishes were named after 19th-century Italian composer Gioacchino Rossini because of his intense love of food.

rösti [RAW-stee; ROOSH-tee] In Switzerland *rösti* means "crisp and golden." The term refers to foods (today, usually shredded potatoes) sautéed on both sides until crisp and browned. **Rösti potatoes** are pressed into a flattened pancake shape while browning.

rotary beater A hand-powered kitchen utensil with two beaters connected to a gear-driven wheel with a handle—all of which is attached to a housing topped with a handle-grip. The rotary beater requires two hands to operate—one to hold the unit, the other to turn the wheel. As the gear-driven wheel is turned, the two beaters rotate, providing aeration that can whip cream, eggs, batters, etc. The best rotary beaters have rounded, stainless-steel hoops and nylon gears. Others are made of cast aluminum, chromed steel or plastic.

rotelle *see* Pasta Glossary, page 883

roti [ROH-tee] 1. An UNLEAVENED griddle-baked bread from India, usually made with whole wheat flour. The roti is finished over an open flame for 10 to 15 seconds, a technique that causes it to fill with steam and puff up like a balloon. *See also* CHAPATI and PARATHA. 2. In Caribbean cookery, a *roti* is a CREPElike wheat wrapper filled with curried vegetables, fish or meat.

rôti [roh-TEE] French for "roast" or "roasted."

rôtie [roh-TEE] 1. A CANAPÉ consisting of a slice of toast spread with PÂTÉ or FORCEMEAT. 2. Also simply a toasted slice of bread.

rotini *see* Pasta Glossary, page 883

rotisserie [roh-TIHS-uh-ree] 1. A unit that cooks food while it slowly rotates. A rotisserie contains a spit fitted with a pair of prongs that slide along its length. Food (usually meat) is impaled on the spit and the prongs (which are inserted on each side of the food) are screwed tightly into place to hold the food securely. Modern rotisseries have a motor that automatically turns the shaft, while their predecessors relied on humanpower. Many ovens and outdoor barbecue units have built-in electric rotisseries. This type of cooking allows heat to circulate evenly around the food while it self-bastes with its own juices. 2. A restaurant or meat shop that specializes in roasted meats. 3. The area where roasting is done (usually in a large restaurant kitchen), often by specially trained chefs (*rôtisseurs*).

rotisseur [raw-tee-see-YAY] *see* BRIGADE SYSTEM

roughage *see* FIBER, DIETARY

rouille [roo-EE; roo-YUH] Literally French for "rust." Culinarily, rouille is a fiery-flavored, rust-colored sauce of hot chiles, garlic, fresh breadcrumbs and olive oil pounded into a paste and often mixed with fish stock. It's served as a garnish with fish and fish stews such as BOUILLABAISSE. *See also* SAUCE.

roulade [roo-LAHD] 1. The French term for a thin slice of meat rolled around a filling such as mushrooms, breadcrumbs, cheese or a mixture of vegetables and cheese or meat. The rolled package is usually secured with string or a wooden pick. A roulade is browned before being baked or braised in wine or stock. Also referred to as *paupiette, bird* and, in Italy, *braciola*. 2. The term *roulade* also refers to a SOUFFLÉ-type mixture that's spread on a JELLY ROLL PAN, baked until firm but still moist, then spread with a savory or sweet filling and rolled up in jelly-roll fashion.

Rouladen [roo-LAH-dn] Germany's version of the French ROULADE. Rouladen comes in many variations, such as *Rindsrouladen*—slices of beef rolled around a pickle, onion and bacon mixture, and *Kohlrouladen*—cabbage leaves rolled around a ground beef mixture.

round, beef This section of the hind leg of beef extends from the rump to the ankle. Since the leg has been toughened by exercise, the round is less tender than some cuts. There are six major sections into which the round can be divided: the rump; the four main muscles (top round, sirloin tip, bottom round and eye of round); and the heel. The **rump** is a flavorful triangular cut taken from the upper part of the round. It's generally cut into *rump steaks* or two or three roasts that, when boned and rolled, are referred to as *rump roasts*. Those with the bone in are called *standing rump roasts*. Pieces from the rump section are best cooked by moist-heat methods. The **top round**, which lies on the inside of the leg, is the most tender of the four muscles in the round. Thick top-round cuts are often called *butterball steak* or *London broil,* whereas thin cuts are referred to simply as *top round steak*. The boneless **sirloin tip** is also called *top sirloin, triangle* and *loin tip*. The better grades can be oven-roasted; otherwise moist-heat methods should be used. The **bottom round** can vary greatly in tenderness from one end of the cut to the other. It's usually cut into steaks (which are often CUBED) or the *bottom round roast*. The well-flavored **eye of the round** is the least tender muscle, although many mistakenly think otherwise because it looks like the TENDERLOIN. Both steaks and roasts from this cut require slow, moist-heat cooking. A cut that includes all four of these muscles is usually called *round steak* and those cut from the top (and which are of the best grades) can be cooked with dry heat. Near the bottom of the round is the toughest cut, the **heel of the round**. It's generally used for ground meat but can sometimes be found as a roast. *See also* BEEF; Beef Chart, page 896.

round bone *see* SIRLOIN

roundfish *see* FISH

roux [ROO] A mixture of flour and fat that, after being slowly cooked over low heat, is used to thicken mixtures such as soups and sauces. There are three classic roux—white, blond and brown. The color and flavor is determined by the length of time the mixture is cooked. Both **white roux** and **blond roux** are made with butter. The former is cooked just until it begins to turn beige and the latter until pale golden. Both are used to thicken cream and white sauces and light soups. The fuller-flavored **brown roux** can be made with butter, drippings or pork or beef fat. It's cooked to a deep golden brown and used for rich, dark soups and sauces. CAJUN and CREOLE dishes use a lard-based roux, which is cooked (sometimes for almost an hour) until a beautiful mahogany brown. This dark nutty-flavored base is indispensable for specialties like GUMBO.

Royal Ann cherry Big and heart-shaped, this firm and juicy sweet cherry has a golden-pink skin and flesh. The Royal Ann (also called *Napoleon*) is used mainly for commercial canning and to make MARASCHINO CHERRIES. It's delicious for out-of-hand eating as well. *See also* CHERRY.

royal icing An icing made of powdered sugar, egg whites and a few drops of lemon juice. It hardens when dry, making it a favorite for durable decorations (such as flowers and leaves) and ornamental writing. Royal icing is often tinted with FOOD COLORING.

royal olive *see* SEVILLANO OLIVE

Royalp; Royalp Tilsiter *see* TILSIT

rub Also called *dry rub,* a rub is typically a mixture of herbs and spices (and usually salt) that is spread over the outside of meat, fish and sometimes even vegetables a few hours before cooking. This blend may be completely dry or mixed with a small amount of liquid to achieve a pastelike texture. Rubs infuse foods with flavor, which intensifies during cooking (usually barbecuing, grilling or roasting). Sugar added to the rub carmelizes with heat, adding a deep rich color and flavor. *See also* MOP.

rubber spatula *see* SPATULA

ruby port; ruby Porto *see* PORT

rucola [ROO-koh-lah] Italian for "ARUGULA."

rudderfish *see* JACK

rugalach; rugelach [RUHG-uh-luhkh] A Hanukkah tradition, rugalach are bite-size, often crescent-shaped cookies that can have any of several fillings including raisins (or other fruit) and nuts, poppy-seed paste or jam. They're generally made with a rich cream-cheese dough.

rum A LIQUOR distilled from fermented sugarcane juice. Most of the world's rum comes from the Caribbean, though it's also made in Argentina, Australia, Brazil, Hawaii, Indonesia, Madagascar, Peru, the Philippines and the continental United States. Rum's production begins by extracting the juice from sugarcane, then boiling it until it's reduced to a thick syrup, which is clarified before being separated into crystallized sugar and molasses. The molasses is mixed with water and yeast, fermented (*see* FERMENTATION), then distilled (*see* DISTILLATION). Rum is oak-aged for 1 to 10 years, depending on the style, then bottled at anywhere from 80 to 151 proof. There are four basic styles of rum: light-bodied, medium-bodied, dark and spiced or aromatic. **Light-bodied rums** (also called *white, light* or *silver*) are typically aged for 6 to 12 months in uncharred oak barrels, a process that produces DRY, colorless, faintly sweet potables. **Medium-bodied rums** (also called *gold* or *amber*) are richer flavored, deeper colored (from the addition of caramel and, sometimes, through longer aging) and mellower than light rums. They're also aged about 3 years; **añejo rums** are aged for 4 to 10 years. **Dark rums** are typically aged for 5 to 7 years (some for decades) and are produced in pot STILLS. They have a full body and rich flavors, aromas and textures, and are often compared to fine COGNACS. **Jamaican rum** is the eponymous term for dark rums from that country. **Demerara rum** is a dark, medium-bodied, very aromatic style produced in Guyana. It's typically bottled at extremely high (151) proofs. **Spiced or aromatic rums** have an exotic, aromatic quality from the addition of spices or other tropical flavorings. **Flavored rums**, typically made from light-bodied rums, are infused with the essence of ingredients, such as fruit or coconut. They're often bottled at less than 80 proof.

rumaki [ruh-MAH-kee] A hot HORS D'OEUVRE consisting of a strip of bacon wrapped around a slice of WATER CHESTNUT and a bite-size piece of chicken liver that has been marinated overnight in a soy sauce–ginger–garlic mixture. Sometimes the water chestnut slice is inserted into a slit made in the chicken liver. This combination is skewered with a toothpick before being grilled or broiled until the bacon is crisp.

rump roast; rump steak *see* ROUND

runner bean This climbing plant—one of Britain's favorite green beans—was brought to the British Isles in the 17th century for decorative use because of its beautiful flowers. The scarlet runner bean has a long, thick GREEN BEAN-type pod that's meaty, tender and stringless when young. Inside are distinctively flavored, red-streaked beige, medium-size seeds. Young runners may be prepared in any way suitable for green beans. In U.S. markets fresh runner beans are often called *Kentucky wonder beans.* The shelled dried beans can be cooked like PINTO or PINK BEANS.

ruote; ruote de carro *see* Pasta Glossary, page 883

rusk [RUHSK] Known in France as *biscotte* and in Germany as ZWIE-BACK, a rusk is a slice of yeast bread (thick or thin) that is baked until dry, crisp and golden brown. Rusks, plain, sweetened or flavored, are available in most supermarkets.

russet potato *see* POTATO

Russian dressing Actually American in origin, this salad dressing includes mayonnaise, pimiento, chili sauce (or ketchup), chives and various herbs. Some think that the "Russian" title comes from the fact that earlier versions of this dressing contained CAVIAR, for which Russia has long been famous.

Russian hogweed *see* GOLPAR

Russian tea cake *see* MEXICAN WEDDING CAKE

rusty nail A COCKTAIL made with equal parts of SCOTCH and DRAMBUIE and served over ice.

rutabaga [ROO-tuh-bay-guh] This cabbage-family root vegetable resembles a large (3 to 5 inches in diameter) TURNIP and, in fact, is thought to be a cross between cabbage and turnip. The name comes from the Swedish *rotabagge,* which is why this vegetable is also called a *Swede* or *Swedish turnip*. Rutabagas have a thin, pale yellow skin and a slightly sweet, firm flesh of the same color. There is also a white variety but it is not generally commercially available. This root vegetable is available year-round with a peak season of September through June. Choose those that are smooth, firm and heavy for their size. Rutabagas can be refrigerated in a plastic bag for up to 2 weeks. They may be prepared in any way suitable for turnips. Rutabagas, which are a CRUCIFEROUS vegetable, contain small amounts of vitamins A and C.

rye; rye flour Rye is a CEREAL GRAIN that's related to BARLEY and WHEAT and has a faintly sour trait. Milled from this hardy cereal grass, **rye flour** contains less GLUTEN (protein) than all-purpose or whole-wheat flour. For that reason, it won't produce a well-risen loaf of bread without the addition of some higher-protein flour. Rye flour is also heavier and darker in color than most other flours, which is why it produces dark, dense loaves. There are several different types of rye flour, the most common of which is **medium rye flour**, available in most supermarkets. **Light** or **dark rye flours**, as well as **pumpernickel flour** (which is dark and coarsely ground), are available in natural food stores and some supermarkets. *See also* FLOUR.

rye whiskey Though wheat and barley are often used in the MASH, U.S. law requires that this American WHISKEY be made with a minimum of 51 percent rye. Rye has a flavor that is similar to a smooth, rich BOURBON with assertively spicy undertones. **Straight ryes** are those from a single distiller, while **blended ryes** are a combination of several straight ryes. *See also* LIQUOR.

saag; sag; sak [sahg] In Indian cooking, the term *saag* can refer to different greens such as COLLARD GREENS, FENU-GREEK leaves, KALE, MUSTARD GREENS and particularly spinach, although multiple varieties of greens are often used. **Paneer saag**, a vegetarian dish with greens and Indian cheese, is quite popular.

saba [sah-BAH] Japanese for "MACKEREL." *Gomosaba*, *bonsaba*, *masaba* and *sekisaba* refer to various mackerel varieties.

sabayon [sah-bah-YAW*N*] French for "ZABAGLIONE."

sablé [SAH-blay] This classic French cookie is said to hail from Caen, in the province of Normandy. The French word *sable* means "sand," and the cookies are so named because of their delicate, crumbly texture. Sablés can be variously flavored with additions such as almonds or lemon or orange zest. They can also be dipped in chocolate or two cookies may be sandwiched together with jam.

sablefish [SAY-bl-fihsh] Also known as *Alaska cod, black cod* and *butterfish*, the sablefish is actually neither a COD nor a BUTTERFISH. It ranges in size from 1 to 10 pounds and is found in deep waters off the Pacific Northwest coast. The white flesh of the sablefish is soft-textured and mild-flavored. Its high fat content makes it an excellent fish for smoking and it's commonly marketed as *smoked black cod*. Sablefish is available year-round whole, as well as in fillets and steaks. It can be prepared in a variety of ways including baking, broiling or frying. *See also* FISH.

Sabra liqueur [SAH-bruh] A chocolate-orange-flavored LIQUEUR made in Israel.

sac *see* SAJ

saccharin [SAK-uh-rihn] Containing only 1/8 calorie per teaspoon, this ARTIFICIAL SWEETENER is said to be 300 times sweeter than sugar. Saccharin was discovered by accident in the late 1800s by scientists at Johns Hopkins University. Though it's widely used to sweeten a multitude of commercial foods and beverages—as well as in the home—some find that it has a decidedly bitter aftertaste. This unpleasant effect is particularly noticeable when a food sweetened with saccharin is heated. Saccharin is available in both powdered and liquid forms in supermarkets. It has been the center of controversy during the last few decades because of its reported possible carcinogenic effects. Because the issue is still being researched, the FDA requires that saccharin products carry a warning label to that effect. *See also* ACESULFAME-K; ALITAME; ASPARTAME, SUCRALOSE.

Sachertorte; Sacher torte [SAH-kuhr-tohrt] An extremely rich Viennese classic made with layers (usually three) of chocolate cake filled with apricot jam and enrobed in a creamy-rich chocolate glaze. Sachertorte is traditionally served with billows of whipped cream. It was created in 1832 by Franz Sacher, of the famous family of Viennese hoteliers and restaurateurs.

sacred pepper *see* PEPPER LEAF

saddle A cut of meat (most often lamb, mutton, veal or venison) that is the unseparated LOIN (from rib to leg) from both sides of the animal. The saddle is a very tender cut and makes an elegant (but expensive) roast.

saengseonjeon *see* JEON

safflower oil This flavorless, colorless oil is expressed from the seeds of the safflower, also called *saffron thistle* or *bastard saffron*. It contains more polyunsaturates than any other oil, has a high SMOKE POINT (which makes it good for deep-frying) and is favored for salad dressings because it doesn't solidify when chilled. *See also* FATS AND OILS.

saffron [SAF-ruhn] It's no wonder that saffron—the yellow-orange stigmas from a small purple crocus (*Crocus sativus*)—is the world's most expensive spice. Each flower provides only three stigmas, which must be carefully hand-picked and then dried—an extremely labor-intensive process. It takes over 14,000 of these tiny stigmas for each ounce of saffron. Thousands of years ago saffron was used not only to flavor food and beverages but to make medicines and to dye cloth and body oils a deep yellow. Today this pungent, aromatic spice is primarily used to flavor and tint food. Fortunately (because it's so pricey), a little saffron goes a long way. It's integral to hundreds of dishes like BOUILLABAISSE, RISOTTO Milanese and PAELLA, and flavors many European baked goods. Saffron is marketed in both powdered form and in threads (the whole stigmas). Powdered saffron loses its flavor more readily and can be easily adulterated with imitations. The threads should be crushed just before using. Store saffron airtight in a cool, dark place for up to 6 months. *See also* SPICES; Seasoning Suggestions, page 891.

sag *see* SAAG

Saga blue Hailing from Denmark, this soft, DOUBLE-CREAM CHEESE can sometimes reach almost triple-cream status in richness. It has delicate blue veins and an elegant, mellow flavor. Saga blue has a tender, white, edible rind. *See also* CHEESE.

saganaki [sah-gah-NAH-kee] A popular Greek appetizer in which ½-inch-thick slices of KASSERI CHEESE are fried in butter or olive oil. Saganaki is sprinkled with lemon juice (and sometimes fresh oregano) and served with PITA BREAD. Some Greek restaurants have a dramatic form of presentation: the cheese is first soaked in alcohol (such as BRANDY), then flambéed before being doused with lemon juice. Saganaki is generally served as an appetizer or first course.

sage [SAYJ] This native Mediterranean herb has been enjoyed for centuries for both its culinary and medicinal uses. The name comes from a derivative of the Latin *salvus,* meaning "safe," a reference to the herb's believed healing powers. The narrow, oval, gray-green leaves of this pungent herb are slightly bitter and have a musty mint taste and aroma. There's also a variety called **pineapple sage**, which has an intensely sweet pineapple scent. Small bunches of fresh sage are available year-round in many supermarkets. Choose sage by its fresh color and aroma. Refrigerate wrapped in a paper towel and sealed in a plastic bag for up to 4 days. Dried sage comes whole, rubbed (crumbled) and ground. It should be stored in a cool, dark place for no more than 6 months. Sage is commonly used in dishes containing pork, cheese and beans, and in poultry and game stuffings. Sausage makers also frequently use it to flavor their products. *See also* HERBS; Seasoning Suggestions, page 891.

sago [SAY-goh] A starch extracted from the sago (and other tropical) palms that is processed into flour, meal and pearl sago, which is similar to tapioca. South Pacific cooks frequently use sago for baking and for thickening soups, puddings and other desserts. In the Orient and in India it's used as a flour and in the United States it's occasionally used as a thickener.

sai-hashi *see* HASHI

Saint-Germain [san-zhehr-MAHN] A French term describing various dishes garnished or made with fresh green peas or pea purée. **Potage Saint-Germain** is a thick pea soup enriched with butter.

Saint-Honoré; gâteau Saint-Honoré [ga-TOH san-toh-naw-RAY] A traditional French cake named for Saint Honoré, the patron saint of pastry bakers. It consists of a base of PÂTE BRISÉE topped with a ring of CREAM PUFFS that are dipped in caramel prior to being positioned on the base. This caramel coating "glues" the puffs together. The center of the ring is then filled with Saint-Honoré cream (also known as crème Chiboust)—CRÈME PÂTISSIÈRE lightened with ITALIAN MERINGUE. Though not classic, sometimes sweetened whipped cream is used as a filling.

Saint John's bread *see* CAROB

Saint Joseph's Day Cake *see* ZEPPOLA

Saint-Malo sauce [san-ma-loh] Classic white-wine fish sauce that includes mustard, shallot butter and anchovy paste. Saint-Malo sauce, named after the port city in northwestern France's Brittany region, is a favorite with grilled fish, especially BRILL, SKATE and TURBOT. *See also* SAUCE.

Saint-Nectaire (AOC; PDO) [san NEHK-tehr] SEMISOFT COW'S-milk cheese from the mountainous Auvergne region in central France. Saint-Nectaire has been produced there for centuries and took its name in the 17th century from a prominent local family headed by Henri de Sennecterre. He presented Louis XIV with the cheese, which became one of the king's favorites. Cattle graze in high mountain pastures in the summer and fall, and the best cheeses are produced during this time. Cheeses with an oval green label imprinted with *"fermier"* are farmstead versions and are considered the most flavorful. Regrettably, these **unpasteurized** cheeses currently cannot be exported to the United States because they are not aged over 60 days (*see* UNPASTEURIZED MILK/IMPORTED CHEESE DILEMMA). Fortunately, small artisanal cheesemakers produce outstanding pasteurized versions. Those with a square green label are factory-produced and aren't generally as good. Saint-Nectaire cheeses come in 3½- to 4-pound wheels with tough, gray rinds that are covered with red, yellow and white molds. The cheese's interior is ivory to pale yellow with a scattering of small EYES. Saint-Nectaire's texture is creamy and supple, and the complex flavor is earthy and mushroomy with a slight sharpness and hints of grass and nuts. The minimum FAT CONTENT for this cheese is 45 percent.

Saint Peter's fish *see* TILAPIA; JOHN DORY

Saint Pierre French name for JOHN DORY.

saj; saj bread [SAHG] 1. A large, flat or domed griddle. The domed or convex version looks somewhat like an inverted WOK. It's used to quickly bake very thin FLATBREADS and to cook meat and other foods. Similar griddles are found in various parts of Asia and known as *sac, tava, tavah, tawa* and *tawah*. 2. A very thin flatbread made in various Middle Eastern countries on a domed griddle, called saj. Saj bread, also called *makook* or *maqooq*, is similar to CHAPATI made in India.

sak *see* SAAG

sake [SAH-kay; SAH-kee] 1. Although it's often called *Japanese rice wine*, many don't think of sake as wine because it's not made from fruit. In fact, some people consider it a beer because it's produced from grain. However, the United States Tax and Trade Bureau (previously the Bureau of Alcohol, Tobacco and Firearms) has settled any dispute by categorizing sake in Class 6—"wine from other agricultural products." Sake is made up of rice, water, KOJI, yeast and sometimes a small amount of distilled alcohol. It's produced in several steps, during which time specially selected rice undergoes FERMENTATION, which converts the starch to sugar and then to ALCOHOL and carbon dioxide. After fermentation, the liquid is drawn off, filtered, heated and transferred to casks for maturing. None of the carbon dioxide is retained so there's no effervescence. The alcohol content of sake ranges from 15 to 19 percent, which is high for beer and low for most grain-based spirits, but in the range of some wines. Though there are myriad types of rice used for brewing sake, what differentiates the various types of sake is how much of each grain of rice is milled or polished away and whether or not distilled alcohol is added to the mix. **Seimaibuai**, or **seimai buai**, is the Japanese term for milling, describing how much of the rice grain is polished away or milled, which influences the sake's flavor. Some sake labels list a percentage number, referring to how much of the rice grain is left. Generally, the lower the percentage, the more the rice has been polished away, and the more elegant, refined and high-quality the sake. There are six main styles of sake: **junmai** has 70 percent remaining rice grain and no added distilled alcohol—the flavor is full, clean and well structured; **honjozo** has 70 percent residual rice grain and a small amount of added alcohol—it's light and mildly fragrant; **junmai ginjo** has 60 percent remaining rice grain and no distilled alcohol—the flavor is light, fruity and refined; **ginjo** has 60 percent residual rice grain plus added alcohol—the flavor is light, fruity, aromatic and refined; **junmai dai ginjo** or **junmai daiginjo** has 50 percent of the rice hull and no distilled alcohol—the flavor is complex, yet light and fragrant; and **dai ginjo** or **daiginjo** has 50 percent of the rice hull plus alcohol—a fragrantly light flavor with good complexity. When the word *junmai* appears alone or in combination with other descriptors, it means the sake has not been supplemented with distilled alcohol. The addition of alcohol is neither good or bad—it simply produces a slightly different sake, both in texture and in flavor. Because **seishu** is the legal name for sake, the word **shu** is officially added to sake terms, as in *junami-shu* or *ginjo-shu*. **Futsuu-shu** is sake that doesn't fit into one of the six previously listed sake categories. Most sake is filtered and clear, but the word **nigori** denotes sake that is unfiltered and slightly cloudy. **Amakuchi** describes sake that has a sweet flavor whereas **karakuchi** refers to one that's DRY. Most sake is diluted with a small amount of water so that the alcohol level is 16 percent or less. The term **genshu** indicates the sake is undiluted and has an alcohol range of 17 to 19 percent. Sake typically is PASTEURIZED twice; unpasteurized versions are labeled **nama**. Freshly brewed sake that has been stored in cedar tanks is called **taru** (cedar sake). If sake instead of water is added during the brewing process, the result is **kijoshu** (dessert sake). Though most sake is not aged longer than the fermentation cycle, **koshu** is a style specially produced to mature for years, and the sake yellows as it grows older. At one time it was traditional to serve sake warm, but today most premium sake is served either at room temperature or slightly chilled. Lower-end versions are often still warmed to obscure the flavor. Besides being a popular potable, sake is used in Japanese cooking, particularly in sauces and marinades. As with wine, sake begins to degrade as soon as it's opened. Tightly seal, store in the refrigerator and consume as soon as possible. 2. In some parts of Japan, *sake* may refer to the general category of alcoholic beverages, not just the beverage made from rice. *See also* MIRIN; SHOCHU; SUSHI.

salad bowl lettuce *see* LEAF LETTUCE

salad burnet *see* BURNET

salad dressing *see* MAYONNAISE

salade composé [suh-LAHD com-poh-ZAY] *see* COMPOSED SALAD

salade de taupe *see* DANDELION GREENS

salad spinner A kitchen utensil that uses centrifugal force to dry freshly washed salad greens, herbs, etc. Wet ingredients are placed in an inner basket. The basket is set into an outer container fitted with a lid with a gear-operated handle or pull-cord. As the handle is turned (or cord pulled), the perforated inner container spins rapidly, forcing moisture off the food out through the perforations and into the outer container.

salad turnip Comparable to a radish, the salad turnip is crisp, sweet and peppery. It's also called *Japanese turnip, kabu* or *hakurei* (the actual TURNIP variety). Fast becoming a favorite in raw form in salads, these smooth, white, roundish roots are also sautéed or roasted, offering a bit more flavor and zest than regular turnips. The smooth, dark-green tops are also edible and can be used in salads or cooked. To reduce moisture loss in the roots, it's best to detach the green tops and refrigerate them separately.

salamander [SAL-uh-man-duhr] 1. A kitchen tool used to brown the top of foods. It consists of a long iron rod with a cast-iron disk at one end and a wooden handle at the other. The disk is heated over a burner until red-hot before being passed closely over food. In addition to quickly browning foods, salamanders are used for dishes (such as CRÈME BRÛLÉE) that require that a surface layer of sugar be caramelized quickly so that the custard below remains cold. They can be purchased in cookware shops and the kitchenware section of most department stores. 2. A small broiler unit in a professional oven that quickly browns the tops of dishes.

salambo; salammbo [SAHL-amh-boh] Small, round or oval pastry made of CHOUX PASTRY filled with pastry cream and topped with caramel, chocolate or colored FONDANT. Salambos, which are like small ÉCLAIRS, can have different flavored fillings and are sometimes topped with chocolate sprinkles or a candied violet.

salami *It.* **salame** [sah-LAH-mee] The name applied to a family of SAUSAGES similar to CERVELATS. Both styles are uncooked but safe to eat without cooking because they've been cured (*see* CURE). Salamis, however, tend to be more boldly seasoned (particularly with garlic), coarser, drier and, unlike cervelats, rarely smoked. They're usually air-dried and, vary in size, shape, seasoning and curing process. Though they're usually made from a mixture of beef and pork, the KOSHER versions are strictly beef. Among the best-known Italian salamis are **Genoa** (pork and veal, seasoned with pepper, garlic and red wine), **cotto** (pork and beef, flavored with garlic and studded with peppercorns), **Milano** (pork, beef and pork fat, seasoned with garlic, pepper and white wine) and **Napoli** (pork and beef, spiced with both red and black pepper). Other salamis include **Danish** (finely ground pork and veal, lightly spiced), **French** (beef and pork, variously seasoned with pepper and/or herbs) and **German** (a smoked combination of finely ground pork and beef). The nonpork **kosher salamis** are cooked and semisoft. Italian-American favorites include Alesandri and Alpino. FRIZZES and PEPPERONI are also salami-type sausages. With the CASING uncut, whole dry salamis will keep for several years. Once cut, they should be tightly wrapped and refrigerated for up to two weeks. Salami is best served at room temperature and can be eaten as a snack or as part of an ANTIPASTO platter, or chopped and used in dishes such as soups and salads.

Salatrim *see* FAT SUBSTITUTES

salbute [SAHL-boo-tay] This small, thick, tortilla-like cake, found on Mexico's Yucatan Peninsula, is similar to the SOPE found in other parts of Mexico. Salbutes are usually topped with avocado, lettuce, tomato, turkey and possibly pickled red onion and HABANERO chiles.

sale [sah-leh] Italian for "salt."

salicornia *see* SAMPHIRE

Salisbury steak [SAWLZ-beh-ree] Essentially a ground-beef patty that has been flavored with minced onion and seasonings before being fried or broiled. It was named after a 19th-century English physician, Dr. J. H. Salisbury, who recommended that his patients eat plenty of beef for all manner of ailments. Salisbury steak is often served with gravy made from pan drippings.

Sally Lunn This rich, slightly sweet yeast bread was brought to the Colonies from England and subsequently became a favorite in the South. There are several tales as to its origin, the most popular being that Sally

Lunn, an 18th-century woman from Bath, England, created this delicate cakelike bread in her tiny bakery for her prominent patrons' tea parties. Those original Sally Lunns were baked as large buns, split horizontally and slathered with thick CLOTTED CREAM.

salmagundi [sal-muh-GUHN-dee] 1. A COMPOSED SALAD including greens, chopped cooked meats and vegetables (the latter sometimes pickled), anchovies, hard-cooked eggs and pickles. The ingredients are artfully arranged on a platter and drizzled with dressing. 2. A general term for a stew or other multi-ingredient dish.

Salmanazar [sal-muh-NAZ-uhr] *see* WINE BOTTLES

salmi; *Fr.* **salmis** [SAHL-mee]; *It.* **salmì** [saHl-mee] A highly seasoned, wine-based RAGOÛT made with minced, partially roasted game birds, mushrooms and, sometimes, truffles. Other game, such as rabbit, may be used.

salmon [SAM-uhn] Salmon was an important food to many early American Indians whose superstitions prevented certain tribe members from handling or eating the fish lest they anger its spirit and cause it to leave their waters forever. Salmon are anadromous, meaning that they migrate from their saltwater habitat to spawn in fresh water. Over the years, some salmon have become landlocked in freshwater lakes. In general, the flesh of those salmon is less flavorful than that of their sea-running relatives. There is an increasing volume of AQUACULTURED salmon being imported into the United States today—most of it from Norway, although Chile's salmon farming industry is now giving the Norwegians some competition. Although farmed salmon are raised in salt water, their flesh doesn't have the same rich nuances in flavor and texture as that of their wild relations. There are several varieties of North American salmon. All but one are found off the Pacific coast, and about 90 percent come from Alaskan waters. Among the best Pacific salmon is the superior **Chinook** or **king salmon**, which can reach up to 120 pounds. The color of its high-fat, soft-textured flesh ranges from off-white to bright red. Other high-fat salmon include the **coho** or **silver salmon**, with its firm-textured, pink to red-orange flesh, and the **sockeye** or **red salmon** (highly prized for canning) with its firm, deep red flesh. Not as fatty as the preceding species are the **pink** or **humpback salmon**—the smallest, most delicately flavored of the Pacific varieties—and the **chum** or **dog salmon**, which is distinguished by having the lightest color and lowest fat content. Pacific salmon are in season from spring through fall. The population of the once-abundant **Atlantic salmon** has diminished greatly over the years because of industrial pollution of both North American and European tributaries. The Atlantic salmon has a high-fat flesh that's pink and succulent. Canada provides most of the Atlantic salmon, which is in season from summer to early winter. Depending on the variety, salmon is sold whole or in fillets or steaks. It's also available canned and as SMOKED SALMON, which comes in a variety of styles. The increasingly popular bright red salmon roe (*see* CAVIAR) is readily available in most supermarkets. Fresh salmon is integral to some of the world's most famous dishes, including GRAVLAX and COU-LIBIAC. It can be served as a main course, in salads, as a spread or dip . . . its uses are myriad. All salmon are high in protein as well as a rich source of vitamin A, the B-group vitamins and Omega-3 oils. *See also* FISH.

salmone [sahl-moH-neh] Italian for "salmon."

salmonella [sal-muh-NEHL-uh] A strain of bacteria that can enter the human system through contaminated water or food such as meat or poultry, and eggs with cracked shells. Other foods can be contaminated by touching salmonella-carrying foods or unwashed surfaces (like cutting boards) that have had contact with them. The presence of salmonella is difficult to detect because it gives no obvious warnings (such as an off smell or taste). The bacteria can cause stomach pain, nausea, vomiting, diarrhea, headache, fever and chills. It can attack in as little time as 6 to 7 hours or take as long as 3 days. It seldom causes death and can be cured with antibiotics.

salmorejo [sahl-moh-REH-hoh] A cold soup similar to GAZPACHO but much thicker—thick enough that it's sometimes used as a dipping sauce. Salmorejo is associated with the southern Spanish region Andalusia, but its roots may date back to Mesopotamia. It's uncooked and is usually made from a puréed mixture of fresh tomatoes, breadcrumbs, garlic, olive oil and vinegar. Variations sometimes add lemon, onion and red pepper. Popular garnishes include diced SERRANO HAM or IBÉRICO HAM and diced hard-cooked eggs. Salmorejo is also called *ardoria* or *porra*.

salpicon; salpicón [sal-pee-KO*N*] 1. A French term describing cooked, diced ingredients bound with a sauce (for savory ingredients), or syrup or cream (for fruit mixtures), and used for fillings or garnishes. Fish, meat, poultry, mushrooms, truffles and vegetables are often included in savory salpicons, which are used to make CANAPÉS, to fill BARQUETTES or CROUSTADES, to make CROQUETTES and as a garnish. 2. A dish found in various styles throughout Latin America. It often consists of shredded meat such as beef, chicken, crab, fish, or venison mixed with various vegetables. Salpicón is usually served cold or at room temperature as an entrée salad, as a filling for soft TACOS, or as a topping for TOSTADAS. 3. In some Latin American cuisines, salpicón is a spicy salsa, often made with HABANERO chiles and orange or lime juice, that's used to marinate or dress the ingredients in the dish described above.

salsa [SAHL-sah] The Mexican and Spanish word for "sauce," which can signify cooked or fresh mixtures. *Salsa cruda* is "uncooked salsa"; *salsa verde* is "green salsa," which is typically based on TOMATILLOS, green CHILES and CILANTRO. Salsas can range in spiciness from mild to mouth-searing. Fresh salsas are located in a market's refrigerated section. At home, they should be tightly covered and refrigerated for up to 5 days. Unopened cooked salsas can be stored at room temperature for 6 months; once opened, refrigerate them for up to 1 month.

salsiccia; *pl.* **salsicce** [sahl-SEET-chyah; sahl-SEET-chay] Italian for "SAUSAGE(S)."

salsify [SAL-sih-fee] This root vegetable is also known as *oyster plant* because its taste resembles a delicately flavored oyster with nuances of artichoke hearts. The parsnip-shaped vegetable can reach up to 12 inches in length and 2½ inches in diameter. Salsify (also called *white salsify*) has a tan-colored skin and off-white flesh. It's forked and has myriad tiny rootlets. The so-called black salsify is actually a root relative called *scorzonera*. It's long, relatively straight, and has a dark brown and cream-colored flesh. Though salsify is more popular in Europe than in the United States, it can be found here from fall through spring in some Spanish, Italian, Greek and produce markets. Choose well-formed roots that are firm, heavy for their size and fairly smooth. Refrigerate, wrapped in a plastic bag, up to 2 weeks; peel before using. Salsify is generally eaten plain as a vegetable (raw or cooked), or used in savory pies and soups.

salt Today salt is inexpensive and universally available, but that wasn't always the case. Because of its importance in food preservation and the fact that the human body requires it (for the regulation of fluid balance), salt has been an extremely valuable commodity throughout the ages. It was even once used as a method of exchange—Roman soldiers received a salt allowance as part of their pay. Salt was valued by the ancient Hebrews and Greeks throughout the Middle Ages and well into the 19th century when it began to become more plentiful and therefore reasonable in price. Salt (sodium chloride) comes either from salt mines or from the sea. Most of today's salt is mined and comes from large deposits left by dried salt lakes throughout the world. **Table salt**, a fine-grained refined salt with additives that make it free-flowing, is mainly used in cooking and as a table condiment. **Iodized salt** is table salt with added iodine (sodium iodide)—particularly important in areas that lack natural iodine, an important preventative for hypothyroidism. **Kosher salt** is an additive-free coarse-grained salt. It's used by some Jews in the preparation of meat, as well as by gourmet cooks who prefer its texture and flavor. **Sea salt** is the type used down through the ages and is the result of the evaporation of sea water—the more costly of the two processes. It comes in fine-grained or larger crystals. FLEUR DE SEL and SEL GRIS are natural, solar-evaporated sea salts that are hand-harvested, from the Atlantic marshes in Brittany, France, using a 2,000-year-old tradition. They have a mellow, sweet-salty flavor. **Rock salt** has an off-white cast because it's not as refined as other salts, which means it retains more minerals and harmless impurities. It comes in chunky crystals and is used predominantly as a bed on which to serve baked oysters and clams and to combine with ice to make ice cream in crank-style ice-cream makers. (*See also* PINK SALT.) **Pickling salt** is a fine-grained salt used to make brines for pickles, sauerkraut, etc. It contains no additives, which would cloud the brine. **Sour salt** (*see* CITRIC ACID), also called *citric salt,* is extracted from acidic fruits, such as lemons and limes. It's used to add tartness to traditional dishes like BORSCHT. **Seasoned salt** is regular salt combined with other flavoring ingredients, examples being onion salt, garlic salt and celery salt. **Salt substitutes**, frequently used by those on low-salt diets, are products containing little or no sodium. *See also* BLACK SALT; PINK SALT.

saltbush *see* ORACHE

salt cod *see* COD

salt-cured *see* CURE

salteña [sahl-TAY-nyah] A type of EMPANADA found in Bolivia. Although flat on the bottom, it's somewhat football-shaped, with a braid-like fold running across the top to seal in the filling. Besides their distinctive shape, the savory meat-and-vegetable filling, which is juicy and somewhat sweet and spicy, sets them apart as well. Vegetarian and cheese versions are also prepared.

saltfish A popular ingredient in Caribbean cuisine, saltfish is simply that—salted, dried fish, usually COD, though other fish (such as MACKEREL) can be used. Saltfish is an integral ingredient in Jamaica's national dish, "saltfish and ACKEE." It's available in pieces in Caribbean, Italian and Asian markets. Choose segments with white flesh, rather than yellow; the skin should be attached. Store, wrapped airtight, in a cool, dark place indefinitely. Before using, soak for 12 to 24 hours, changing the water every 4 to 5 hours. The soaking softens the flesh and each water change reduces the salt. Drain the last batch of soaking water and pour boiling water over the saltfish; cover and allow to soak for about 15 minutes, or until the flesh is soft. The word for saltfish in Spanish is *bacalao,* in French it's *morue* and in Italian it's *baccalà.*

saltimbocca [sahl-tihm-BOH-kuh] Literally translated, this Italian term means "jump mouth." It refers to a Roman specialty made of finely sliced veal sprinkled with sage and topped with a thin slice of PROSCIUTTO.

It's sautéed in butter, then braised in white wine. Sometimes the meat layers are rolled and secured with picks before being cooked.

saltpeter; saltpetre 1. The common name used for potassium nitrate, a naturally occurring chemical compound that has a variety of uses, both for food and otherwise. It's used for food preservation and color retention, particularly in cured meats such as bacon, bologna, corned beef, ham, hot dogs and pepperoni, though potassium nitrate has been replaced in most cases by SODIUM NITRATE/nitrite. It was also used in the production of ice cream; when mixed with ice it freezes foods faster than ice alone. In the non-food world, it's utilized for fireworks, gunpowder, as a component in fertilizer and so on. Though it's rumored to be used in prisons, the military and all-male colleges to blunt the male sex drive, there's no evidence to suggest that's true. 2. Another chemical compound referred to as saltpeter is SODIUM NITRATE.

S

salt pork So named because it is salt-cured, this is a layer of fat (usually with some streaks of lean) that is cut from the pig's belly and sides. Salt pork is often confused with FATBACK, which is unsalted. It varies in degree of saltiness and often must be BLANCHED to extract excess salt before being used. It's similar to bacon but much fattier and unsmoked. Salt pork can be refrigerated tightly wrapped for up to a month. It's used primarily as a flavoring and is an important ingredient in many dishes throughout New England and the South.

salt-rising bread A bread popular in the 1800s, before yeast LEAVENING was readily available. It relies on a FERMENTED mixture of warm milk or water, flour, cornmeal, sugar and salt to give it rising power. Salt-rising bread has a very smooth texture with a tangy flavor and aroma.

salty black beans *see* FERMENTED BLACK BEANS

salumi [sah-LOO-mee] A family of Italian-style cured or preserved meats (typically pork). Included in the hundreds of salumi are CAPOCOLLO, COPPA, CULATELLO, GUANCIALE, PANCETTA, PROSCIUTTO and SPECK. The word may refer to meat that has been salt-cured, smoked or preserved in fat, as well as to PÂTÉS and cooked sausages. Some salumi have CASINGS, while others don't.

Salzburger nockerl *see* NOCKERL

samaki [sah-MAH-kee] Swahili word for "fish." **Samaki wa nazi** is a fish curry made with coconut milk that's popular in Tanzania and Zanzibar. Also popular in East African countries is **samaki wa kupaka**, which is fish grilled and basted with a coconut milk and tamarind sauce.

sambahr *see* SAMBAR

sambal [SAHM-bahl] Popular throughout Indonesia, Malaysia and southern India, a sambal is a multipurpose CONDIMENT. Its most basic form is *sambal oelek,* a simple mixture of CHILES, brown sugar and salt. Another popular blend is *sambal bajak* (or *badjak*), which adds CANDLENUTS, garlic, KAFFIR LIME LEAVES, onion, TRASSI, GALANGAL, TAMARIND concentrate and COCONUT MILK. Sambals have a multitude of variations, however, depending on the ingredients added, which can include coconut, meat, seafood or vegetables. Sambals are usually served as an accompaniment to rice and curried dishes, either as a condiment or as a side dish. Sambal oelek and bajak, as well as some variations, can be found in Indonesian and some Chinese markets.

sambar; sambaar [SAAM-bahr] A vegetable stew made with PIGEON PEAS, TAMARIND, various vegetables and seasonings that's popular in southern India as well as surrounding areas. There are endless variations for sambar, also known as *sambahr* and *kuzhambu*. It's eaten on a daily basis and usually served with rice, but it may be accompanied by IDLI, DOSA and VADA.

samboosa; sambosa *see* SAMBUSAK

sambuca [sam-BOO-kuh] A colorless, anise-flavored LIQUEUR made in Italy, sambuca is based on the elderberry. The fruit of the elder, of the genus Sambucus, is the origin of the name. It's drier (see DRY) than most potables of its kind and is frequently served with 3 to 4 coffee beans floating on the surface. The liqueur is ignited, which "roasts" the beans and infuses the liqueur with flavor. **Sambuca negra** is a dark brown, coffee-flavored version.

sambusak; sanbusak; sambusa [sahm-BOO-zahk; sahn-BOO-zahk] Small, flaky pastries, stuffed with meat fillings, meatless fillings and/or cheese, popular throughout the Middle East. They are baked or fried and come in various shapes—triangles, crescents, rounds and rectangles. Sambusaks are similar to Indian SAMOSAS. Both *sambusak* and *samosa* come from the Persian word *sanbosag*. Other spellings for this food include *sambosa, samboosa, samsa* and *sambusa*.

samgytetang [tahm-GEHT-tahng] Samgytetang is a Korean dish whose name means "ginseng chicken soup." As the name suggests, the main ingredients are ginseng and a young chicken. The chicken is stuffed with rice, then cooked in a broth that includes garlic, GINSENG, ginger and JUJUBES.

samn; samna; samneh *see* SMEN

samosa [sah-MOH-sah] In India, street pushcarts and roadside vendors sell their delicious samosas to passersby who enjoy immediate gratification from these satisfying snacks. Samosas are fried, triangular pastries that may be filled with vegetables or meat or a combination of both. In the United States, these delicious packages are most often served as appetizers in East Indian restaurants.

samp Broken or coarsely ground HOMINY.

samphire [SAM-fy-uhr] There are two edible, very similar plants known as samphire. The first is *Crithmum maritimum* (commonly referred to as *rock samphire*), which grows along the coasts of Great Britain and northwestern Europe and is available in the United States only through costly import. What we have in the United States is the second type of samphire known as *salicornia* (also called *glasswort, marsh samphire, sea bean* and *sea pickle*). It's abundant along both the Pacific and Atlantic coasts and has spiky green leaves that are so arranged as to make the plant look somewhat like a spindly, miniature cactus, sans needles. Both the leaves and stem are crisp, aromatic and taste of a salty sea breeze. They're often pickled and can sometimes be found in jars in gourmet markets. Fresh salicornia can be found from summer through fall, though it's at its most tender during summer months. Choose crisp, brightly colored sprigs with no sign of softness. Refrigerate tightly wrapped for up to 2 weeks—though the sooner salicornia is used the better the flavor. It's best used fresh, either in salads or as a garnish. When cooked, salicornia tends to taste quite salty and fishy.

samsa *see* SAMBUSAK

Samsoe; Samsø [SAM-soh] Named for the island where it originated, this national cheese of Denmark was created in the 19th century when the Danish king brought in a Swiss cheesemaker to assist in diversifying Denmark's cheesemaking. Samsoe's a semihard, Swiss-style cow's-milk cheese modeled after EMMENTAL. It has a glossy, amber to dark reddish-brown rind, a pale yellow interior accented with small irregular holes and a distinctive, mild, nutlike flavor. The minimum FAT CONTENT for standard Samsoe is 45 percent; the lower-fat version has at least 30 percent fat. *See also* CHEESE.

sanchal *see* BLACK SALT

sand dab A small FLATFISH found in Pacific waters from Southern California to Alaska. It has a sweet, delicately moist flesh that's quite low in fat. Sand dabs are marketed whole and usually range from 4 to 12 ounces. They can be prepared by almost any cooking method including baking, broiling, poaching and sautéing. *See also* DAB; FISH.

sancocho [SAN-coh-choh] A traditional Latin American stew or soup consisting of chunks of meat or fish and vegetables. Variations abound and may include rice, beans, plantains (*see* BANANA), potatoes, YUCA, wine and rum.

sand leek *see* ROCAMBOLE

sand pike *see* PERCH

sand shark *see* DOGFISH

sand sole *see* SOLE

Sangiovese [san-joh-VAY-zeh; san-jaw-VAY-zeh] One of the top two red grapes (the other being Nebbiolo) in Italy, believed to have originated in Tuscany, where it dominates today. Sangiovese wines are typically high in ACID, have moderate to high TANNINS and a flavor that's lightly fruity with a hint of earthiness. Most are not long-lived and will last for less than 10 years. One strain of Sangiovese is Brunello ("little dark one"), the grape responsible for the potent and long-lived BRUNELLO DI MONTALCINO. Sangiovese is the dominant grape in Italy's CHIANTI wines.

sangría [san-GREE-uh] The blood-red color of this beverage inspired its name, which is derived from the Spanish word for "blood." Sangría is made with red wine, fruit juices, soda water, fruit and sometimes LIQUEURS and BRANDY or COGNAC. Sangría *blanco* (white sangría) is made with white wine. Both are served cold over ice and make a refreshing cooler on a hot summer day.

sangrita Although sometimes confused with SANGRÍA, this Spanish/Mexican drink is not the same at all. There are many variations, but sangrita is typically a blended mixture of tomatoes (or tomato juice), orange juice and lemon or lime juice, with a fiery element added through CHILES, chile powder or TABASCO SAUCE. Sangrita is served chilled, usually with a shot of TEQUILA.

sansho [SAHN-show] A mildly hot Japanese seasoning made from the aromatic berries of the prickly ash tree, which are dried and ground into a powder. It's the same spice that the Chinese call SZECHUAN PEPPER.

Santa Claus melon From the outside a Santa Claus melon, with its long oval shape and splotchy green-and-yellow skin, looks like a small WATERMELON. Inside, however, its yellowish-green flesh looks and tastes more like HONEYDEW MELON. This member of the muskmelon family (*see* MELON) grows to about a foot in length, with some specimens weighing as much as 10 pounds. Santa Claus melon, also called *Christmas melon,* was so named because its peak season is in December. Choose a melon that is slightly soft at the blossom end, heavy for its size and has a yellowish cast to the rind. Avoid those with soft spots or with damaged skin.

Santa Fe Grande chile These small, tapered, conical CHILES are generally marketed when yellow, though if allowed to mature longer, they turn orange or red. Santa Fe Grandes have a slightly sweet taste and are mildly hot, with a SCOVILLE SCALE rating of 500 to 700. They may be used in both cooked and raw dishes.

santoku *see* KNIFE

saoto *see* SOTO

sapa *see* FRUIT MOLASSES

sapodilla [sap-oh-DEE-yuh] The fruit of a native Central American tree that also yields chicle, from which chewing gum is made. The sapodilla ranges from 2 to 6 inches in diameter and has a rough, russet-brown skin. The flesh is soft, juicy and transluscent, ranges in color from yellowish to pinkish brown, and has a flavor that's akin to that of maple syrup. Choose fruit that's slightly soft and reveals a yellow color when scratched. Sapodillas will ripen at room temperature; refrigerate ripe fruit for up to 1 week. Enjoy alone or add to salads or fruit compotes.

sapote [sah-POH-tay] *see* BLACK SAPOTE; MAMEY SAPOTE; WHITE SAPOTE

Sapsago; Sap Sago [sap-SAY-goh] Also known as *Grünerkäse* ("green cheese"), *Glarnerkäse*, *Krauterkäse* and *Schbzieger*, Sapsago is a hard, truncated-cone-shaped cheese from Switzerland. It's made from non-fat milk, WHEY or buttermilk (or sometimes a combination of the three) and contains less than 10 percent fat. Its light grayish-green color and pungent herbal flavor come from the addition of blue melilot, a special variety of clover and/or FENUGREEK, a plant known for its pleasantly bitter, slightly sweet seeds. Sapsago is used primarily for grating and adds interest to everything from salads to pasta. *See also* CHEESE.

Saratoga chips *see* POTATO CHIPS

sardine [sahr-DEEN] A generic term applied broadly to any of various small, soft-boned, saltwater fish such as SPRAT and young PILCHARD and HERRING. These tiny fish are iridescent and silvery and swim in huge schools, usually near the water's surface. Fresh sardines are available on a limited basis during the summer months, usually only along the coast where they're caught. In general, their fatty flesh is best when grilled, broiled or fried. In the United States, sardines are more commonly found salted, smoked or canned, either in oil, tomato sauce or mustard sauce. Some are packed as is, while others are skinned, boned and sold as fillets. The name is thought to have come from the young pilchards caught off the coast of Sardinia, which were one of the first fish packed in oil. *See also* FISH.

sarsaparilla [sas-puh-RIHL-uh] Originally derived from the dried roots of tropical smilax vines, this flavor is usually associated with a carbonated drink popular in the mid-1800s. Today's sarsaparilla products—including the soft drink—use artificial flavorings.

sarume [sah-ROO-meh] *see* CUTTLEFISH

sashimi [sah-SHEE-mee] Sliced raw fish that is served with CONDIMENTS such as shredded DAIKON radish or GINGERROOT, WASABI and SOY SAUCE. Because it's served raw, only the freshest and highest-quality fish should be used for sashimi. Some Japanese restaurants keep the fish alive in water until just before preparing it. Special sashimi chefs are trained in slicing the fish in a particular way—depending on the variety—for the best presentation and eating enjoyment. Sashimi is usually the first course in the Japanese meal and sashimi bars abound in the United States for Westerners with Eastern tastes. *See also* SUSHI.

sassafras [SAS-uh-fras] The leaves of the native North American sassafras (*albidum* or *variifolium*) tree, which are dried and used to make FILÉ POWDER and sassafras tea. The root bark is used as a flavoring agent in ROOT BEER.

saté; satay [sah-TAY] An Indonesian favorite consisting of small marinated cubes of meat, fish or poultry threaded on skewers and grilled or broiled. Saté is usually served with a spicy peanut sauce. It's a favorite snack food but is also often served for an appetizer and sometimes as a main dish.

satsumaage *see* AGEKAMABOKO

satsuma orange [sat-SOO-muh] *see* MANDARIN ORANGE

saturated fat [SATCH-uh-ray-tihd] *see* FATS AND OILS

sauce *v.* To cover or mix a food with a sauce. **sauce** *n.* In the most basic terms, a sauce is a flavored liquid designed to accompany food in order to enhance or bring out its flavor. In the days before refrigeration, however, sauces were more often used to smother the taste of foods that had begun to go bad. The French are credited with refining the sophisticated art of saucemaking. It was the 19th-century French chef Antonin Carême who evolved an intricate methodology by which hundreds of derivative sauces were classified under one of four "mother sauces": Those are: ESPAGNOLE (brown stock-based), VELOUTÉ (white stock-based), BÉCHAMEL (milk-based), and ALLEMANDE (egg-enriched velouté). Add to these a fifth group—EMULSIFIED sauces, such as HOLLANDAISE and MAYONNAISE. Myriad variations may be created from these five basic sauces by adding ingredients such as cheese, cream, garlic, herbs, shallots, spices and so on. *See also* ADOBO SAUCE; ALBERT SAUCE; ALBUFÉRA SAUCE; ALFREDO SAUCE; AURORE SAUCE; BAGNA CAUDA; BARBECUE SAUCE; BÉARNAISE; BERCY SAUCE; BEURRE BLANC; BIGARADE SAUCE; BOLOGNESE; BORDELAISE SAUCE; BREAD SAUCE; BROWN SAUCE; BROWN STOCK; CHASSEUR SAUCE; CHILI SAUCE; CHIMICHURRI; CHORON SAUCE; COCKTAIL SAUCE; COLBERT SAUCE; COULIS; CREAM SAUCE; CRÈME ANGLAISE; CUMBERLAND SAUCE; DEMI-GLACE; DIABLE SAUCE; DIPLOMAT SAUCE; FIGARO SAUCE; GARUM; GENEVOISE SAUCE; GRIBICHE SAUCE; HARD SAUCE; HARISSA; HOISIN; HUMMUS; KECAP MANIS; KETCHUP; LOUIS SAUCE; LYONNAISE SAUCE; MALTAISE SAUCE; MARCH-ANDS DE VIN; MARGUERY SAUCE; MARINARA SAUCE; MELBA SAUCE; MOLE; MORNAY SAUCE; MOUSSELINE; NAM PLA; NANTUA SAUCE; NEWBURG SAUCE; NORMANDE SAUCE; NUOC CHAM; OYSTER SAUCE; PARISIENNE SAUCE; PERIGUEUX SAUCE; PESTO; PIQUANTE SAUCE; PISTOU; PLUM SAUCE; PONZU; PUTTANESCA SAUCE; RAGÙ; RANCHERO SAUCE; RÉMOULADE; ROBERT SAUCE; ROMESCO; ROUILLE; SHRIMP SAUCE; SKORDALIA; SOFRITO; SOUBISE; SOY SAUCE; SUPREME SAUCE; TABASCO; TAMARI; TARTAR SAUCE; TENTSUYU; TOMATO SAUCE; TONNATO SAUCE; VERTE SAUCE; VINAIGRETTE; WHITE STOCK; WORCES-TERSHIRE SAUCE.

sauce Albuféra *see* ALBUFÉRA SAUCE

sauce boat; sauceboat *see* GRAVY BOAT

sauce foyot *see* VALOIS SAUCE

sauce gribiche *see* GRIBICHE SAUCE

saucepan A round cooking utensil with a relatively long handle and (usually) a tight-fitting cover. The sides can be straight or flared and deep (the standard shape) or as shallow as 3 inches. Depending on the style, the versatile saucepan has a multitude of uses including making soups and sauces, boiling vegetables and other foods, braising and even sauté-ing (in the low-sided models). Saucepans come in sizes ranging from 1 pint to 4 quarts. They are made from various materials including alumi-num, anodized aluminum, ceramic, copper, enameled (cast iron or steel), glass and stainless steel. Choose saucepans that are well balanced, with handles that allow the pan to be easily lifted.

sauce piquante *see* PIQUANTE SAUCE

sauce Robert *see* ROBERT SAUCE

sauce Saint-Malo *see* SAINT-MALO SAUCE

sauce valois *see* VALOIS SAUCE

saucier [saw-see-YAY] *see* BRIGADE SYSTEM

saucisse [soh-SEES] French for "small SAUSAGE."

saucisson [soh-see-SAWN] A large, smoke-cured SAUSAGE.

sauerbraten [SOW-uhr-brah-tihn; ZOW-uhr-brah-tihn] German for "sour roast," sauerbraten is a German specialty made by marinating a beef roast in a sour-sweet MARINADE for 2 to 3 days before browning it, then simmering the meat in the marinade for several hours. The result is an extremely tender roast and a delicious sauce. Sauerbraten is traditionally served with dumplings, boiled potatoes or noodles.

sauerkraut [SOW-uhr-krowt] Although sauerkraut—German for "sour cabbage"—is thought of as a German invention, Chinese laborers building the Great Wall of China over 2,000 years ago ate it as standard fare. Chinese sauerkraut, made from shredded cabbage fermented in RICE WINE, eventually found its way to Europe, where the Germans and Alsatians adopted it as a favorite. Today's sauerkraut is made by combining shredded cabbage, salt and sometimes spices, and allowing the mixture to ferment. It can be purchased in jars and cans in supermarkets. Fresh sauerkraut is sold in delicatessens and in plastic bags in a supermarket's refrigerated section. It should be rinsed before being used in casseroles, as a side dish and even on sandwiches like the famous REUBEN SANDWICH. Sauerkraut is an excellent source of vitamin C as well as of some of the B vitamins.

sauger *see* PERCH

sausage [SAW-sihj] What started out simply as a means of using and preserving all of the animal trimmings has turned into the art of sausage-making. Simply put, sausage is ground meat mixed with fat, salt and other seasonings, preservatives and sometimes fillers. Such a mixture is usually packed into a CASING. Sausages can differ dramatically depending on their ingredients, additives, shape, curing technique, level of dryness and whether fresh or cooked. Most sausages are made with pork or pork combined with other meat, but there are also those made almost entirely from beef, veal, lamb, chicken or game animals. All contain varying amounts of fat. Seasonings can run the gamut from garlic to nutmeg. Some sausages are hot and spicy and others so mild they border on bland. Many sausages today contain additives to help preserve, thicken or color the mixture. Some sausages use fillers (such as various cereals, soybean flour and dried-milk solids) to stretch the meat. The most common shape for sausage is link, which varies in size and shape depending on the type of sausage. Other sausage (fresh) is sold in bulk, which can then be used to mix with other meats or made into patties or balls. Sausage can be fresh or CURED with salt or smoke (or both). Curing extends storage life. Some sausages are also dried; the drying times can vary from a few days to as much as 6 months. The sausage becomes firmer the longer it's dried. Sausage can be fully cooked (ready to eat), partially cooked (enough to kill any trichinae) and uncooked, which may or may not require cooking depending on how or whether it's been cured. All these factors produce an almost endless number of sausages that can be used in a variety of ways and which appeal to a multitude of tastes. *See also* ANDOUILLE; ANDOUILLETTE; BANGER; BAUERWURST; BIERWURST; BLOOD SAUSAGE; BOCKWURST; BOLOGNA; BOUDIN BLANC; BRATWURST; BRAUNSCHWEIGER; CASING; CERVELAT; CHAURICE; CHINESE SAUSAGE; CHIPOLATA; CHORIZO; COTECHINO; COTTO; CREPINETTE; FRANKFURTER; FRIZZES; HAGGIS; HEAD CHEESE; ITALIAN SAUSAGE; KIELBASA; KISHKE; KNACKWURST; LEBERKÄSE; LINGUIÇA; LIVERWURST; LOP CHONG; LOUKANIKA; LUGANEGA; METTWURST; MORTADELLA; PEPPERONI; PORK SAUSAGE; SALAMI; SALSICCIA; SAUCISSE; SAUCISSON; SUMMER SAUSAGE; THURINGER; TONGUE SAUSAGE; TOULOUSE; WEISSWURST; WURST; ZAMPONE; ZUNGENWURST.

sauté; sautéed; sautéing [saw-TAY; soh-TAY] To cook food quickly in a small amount of oil or other fat in a skillet or sauté pan over direct heat. *See also* FRY.

sauté pan A wide pan with straight or slightly curved sides that are generally a little higher than those of a frying pan. It has a long handle on one side; heavy sauté pans usually have a loop handle on the other side so the pan can be easily lifted. Sauté pans are most often made of stainless steel, enameled cast iron, aluminum, anodized aluminum or copper. As the name suggests, a sauté pan efficiently browns and cooks meats and a variety of other foods.

Sauternes; Sauterne [soh-TERN] 1. An elegant sweet wine from the Sauternes region of western France. It's made from SAUVIGNON BLANC or SÉMILLON grapes that have been infected by a beneficial mold called BOTRYTIS CINEREA, which causes the grapes to shrivel, leaving a sugary fruit with concentrated flavors. The best Sauternes come from vines that have been hand-picked (as many as 12 separate times) to ensure that the grapes are not removed from the vines before reaching the perfect degree of ripeness required for these wines. French winemakers only produce sweet Sauternes in years when the grapes are perfectly ripened and botrytis infected—otherwise they turn their grapes into DRY wines. The eminent Château d'Yquem, the most famous of the châteaux in Sauternes, undisputedly makes the best wines in the area. Sauternes are most notable as DESSERT WINES but, because of their high acidity, they also make excellent partners for rich dishes like PÂTÉ, CAVIAR and FOIE GRAS. 2. **Sauterne** is a generic name used in the United States for some inexpensive, DRY to semisweet white wines made from various mediocre grapes.

Sauvignon   Blanc [SOH-vihn-yoh*n* BLAH*N*; SOH-vee-nyaw*n* BLAH*N*GK] Widely cultivated in France and California (and also grown in Italy, Australia, New Zealand and Chile), the Sauvignon Blanc grape imparts a grassy, herbaceous flavor to wine. It's one of the main grapes used to produce the elegant dry wines from Bordeaux (**Graves**) and the Loire Valley (**Pouilly-Fumé**), as well as the seductively sweet SAUTERNES. Many wineries—particularly in California—use this grape to produce wonderful wines that are bottled under the variety name Sauvignon Blanc (sometimes labeled *Fumé Blanc*).

savarin [SAV-uh-rihn; sa-va-RAN] This variation on the BABA is made without raisins and baked in a large RING MOLD. Named after Brillat-Savarin, a famous 18th-century food writer, this rich yeast cake is soaked with rum-flavored syrup and filled with PASTRY CREAM, crème CHANTILLY or fresh fruit.

savory [SAY-vuh-ree] *n.* An herb of which there are two types, summer and winter, both closely related to the mint family. Savory has an aroma and flavor reminiscent of a cross between thyme and mint. Summer savory is slightly milder than the winter variety but both are strongly flavored and should be used with discretion. Dried savory is available year-round; fresh savory can be found in specialty produce markets. Savory adds a piquant flavor to many foods including PÂTÉS, soups, meat, fish and bean dishes. *See also* HERBS; Seasoning Suggestions, page 891. **savory** *adj.* A term describing food that is not sweet but rather piquant and full-flavored.

savoury [SAY-vuh-ree] A British term initially used to describe dishes that were served after dessert to cleanse and refresh the palate. Today it more often refers to tidbits served as appetizers, as well as to more substantial dishes that can be served for lunch, HIGH TEA or light supper.

savoy cabbage This mellow-flavored cabbage is considered by many to be one of the best of its genre for cooking. Savoy has a loose, full head of crinkled leaves varying from dark to pale green. Choose a head that's heavy for its size. The leaves should be crisp, not limp, and there should be no sign of browning. Refrigerate, tightly wrapped, in a plastic bag for up to 1 week. *See also* CABBAGE.

saw-leaf herb; saw-tooth herb A variety of CORIANDER native to Central America but now grown and very popular in other parts of Latin America and Southeast Asia. Saw-leaf herb goes by many other names including *chandon benit, culantro, fitweed, long coriander, Mexican coriander, ngo gai, recao, shadon beni, shadow beni, spiritweed, Tabasco parsley, thorny coriander* and *wild coriander.* It has 4- to 5-inch-long, thick green leaves with jagged edges and a flavor similar to but earthier and stronger than CILANTRO. Like cilantro, saw-leaf herb has a distinctive flavor that lends itself to highly spiced foods, and it's widely used in Asian and Latin American cooking. It's harder to grow and not as readily available as cilantro but can be found in some Latin American and Asian markets, usually in plastic bags or plastic-wrapped Styrofoam trays. Choose leaves with a bright, even color and no sign of wilting—black leaves indicate rot. Saw-leaf may be stored for up to 1 week in a plastic bag in the refrigerator. Just before using, wash and blot dry with paper towels.

Sazerac [SAZ-uh-rak] A COCKTAIL consisting of whiskey, SUGAR SYRUP and a dash each of BITTERS and PERNOD. Its name comes from the fact that it was originally served at the Sazerac Coffee House in New Orleans. The first of these potent drinks is said to have been made with Sazerac-du-Forge, a French brandy.

sbityen [ZBEET-yen] Hailing from Russia, sbityen is a hot potable made with water, honey, vodka or brandy, and flavored with lemon, ginger, cinnamon, cloves and peppercorns.

sbriciolona [sbree-chyoh-LOH-nah] *see* FINOCCHIONA

Sbrinz [ZBRIHNZ] Hailing from the central mountains of Switzerland, Sbrinz is this country's oldest cheese and thought to be the one that Roman scholar and naturalist Pliny the Elder referred to in the 1st century A.D. as *caseus helveticus* ("Swiss cheese"). There's some speculation that the Italians modeled their hard cheeses Grana Padano and Parmigiano-Reggiano (*see* PARMESAN)after Sbrinz. It's made from whole cow's milk and aged from $1\frac{1}{2}$ to 4 years. If aged less than this, it is called *Spalen*. Sbrinz has a yellowish-gold interior with a golden-brown rind. The mellow flavor is fruity, nutty, spicy and toffeelike, intensifying as the cheese ages. It has a FAT CONTENT of at least 45 percent. *See also* CHEESE.

scald [SKAWLD] *n.* A dry, tan- or brown-colored area on the skin of a fruit, such as an apple. It's usually caused by overexposure to sunlight and rarely affects the fruit quality. **scald** *v.* 1. A cooking technique—often used to retard the souring of milk—whereby a liquid is heated to just below the boiling point. 2. To plunge food such as tomatoes or peaches into boiling water (or to pour boiling water over them), in order to loosen their skin and facilitate peeling. Also referred to as BLANCH.

scale, to; scaler A technique by which the scales are removed from the skin of a fish, generally with a dull knife or a special kitchen tool called a fish scaler. Working from the tail to the head, the scales are scraped in the opposite direction from which they lie.

scale, kitchen A kitchen device used to accurately record the weight of ingredients. Kitchen scales are particularly important for consistent baking results and for weighing meats in order to estimate cooking time. Though there are many styles of kitchen scales, there are two basic types—spring and balance scales. **Spring scales** register weight when an item is placed in the weighing pan, which then depresses a spring attached to a recording dial. A *bowl scale* is a type of spring scale which uses a bowl container rather than a shallow-sided pan. As spring scales get older the spring may weaken, thereby reducing the scale's accuracy. The more accurate **balance scales** usually have a pan for ingredients on one side and a platform for weights on the other. The ingredient's weight is determined when it balances with the weights on the other side. The main disadvantage of a balance scale is that it usually takes up more room than a spring scale. The less popular **beam balance scales** use weights that slide along two bars. The correct weight registers when the bars balance.

scallion [SKAL-yuhn] The name "scallion" is applied to several members of the onion family including a distinct variety called scallion, immature onions (commonly called *green onions*), young leeks, WELSH ONIONS and sometimes the tops of young shallots. In each case the vegetable has a white base that has not fully developed into a bulb and green leaves that are long and straight. Both parts are edible. True scallions are generally identified by the fact that the sides of the base are straight, whereas the others are usually slightly curved, showing the beginnings of a bulb. All can be used interchangeably although true scallions have a milder flavor than immature onions. Scallions are available year-round but are at their peak during spring and summer. Choose those with crisp, bright green tops and a firm white base. Store, wrapped in a plastic bag, in the vegetable crisper section of the refrigerator for up to 5 days. Scallions can be cooked whole as a vegetable much as you would a LEEK. They can also be chopped and used in salads, soups and a multitude of other dishes for flavor.

scallop [SKAHL-uhp; SKAL-uhp] *n.* 1. This popular BIVALVE MOLLUSK (*see both listings*) has two beautiful fan-shaped shells that are often used as containers in which to serve dishes such as COQUILLES ST. JACQUES. Though the entire scallop including the ROE is edible (and relished by many Europeans), the portion most commonly found in U.S. markets is the adductor muscle that hinges the two shells. There are many scallop species but in general they're classified into two broad groups—bay scallops and sea scallops. **Bay scallops**, generally found only on the East Coast, are very tiny (the muscle is about ½ inch in diameter). They average about 100 per pound and their meat is sweeter and more succulent than that of the sea scallop. They're also more expensive because they're less plentiful. The small *calico scallops*—though they're deep-sea creatures—are often sold as bay scallops on the West Coast. They're found in the Gulf of Mexico and along the east coast of Florida. The muscle of the larger, more widely available **sea scallop** averages 1½ inches in diameter (about 30 to the pound) and is not as tender as the smaller varieties. Though slightly chewier, the meat is still sweet and moist. **Diver scallops** is a term used for those that are hand-picked by divers, whereas traditionally scallops are harvested by trawling boats using chains and nets. The shells of hand-harvested scallops aren't damaged as they might be with trawling, and the scallops don't contain as much grit. Naturally, this relatively labor-intensive harvest method means diver scallops command higher prices. One caveat: Many fishing industry experts say that regular trawled scallops are being sold as diver scallops. Bottom line: Find a fishmonger you can trust. The color of scallops ranges from pale beige to creamy pink. If scallops are stark white, it's a sign that they've been soaked in water—a marketing ploy to increase the weight. Fresh bay scallops are available on the East Coast in the fall, whereas the peak season for fresh sea scallops is midfall to midspring. Because scallops perish quickly out of water, they're usually sold shucked. All fresh scallops should have a sweet smell and a fresh, moist sheen. They should be refrigerated immediately after purchase and used within a day or two. Frozen scallops are generally available year-round, either breaded or plain. Scallops benefit from brief cooking and are suitable for a variety of preparation methods including sautéing, grilling, broiling and poaching. They're also used in soups, stews and salads. *See also* MOLLUSK; SHELLFISH. 2. A thin, boneless, round- or oval-shaped slice of meat or fish that is usually lightly breaded and quickly sautéed. Known as *escalope* in French. **scallop** *v.* 1. To prepare a food (most notably potatoes) by layering slices of it with cream or a creamy sauce in a casserole. Scalloped foods are often topped with bread or cracker crumbs before being baked. 2. To form a decorative edge in the raised rim of pie dough. Also referred to as CRIMP and FLUTE. *See also* SCALLOPS, DRIED.

scalloped squash *see* PATTYPAN SQUASH

scaloppine; scaloppina [skah-loh-PEE-nee; skah-loh-PEE-nah] An Italian term for a thin SCALLOP of meat, typically veal, in which case it's *scallopine di vitello.* The meat is DREDGED in flour, then sautéed and served variously. For instance, *scaloppine al marsala* is flavored with MARSALA, *scaloppine al limone* is accented with lemon juice, and *scaloppine alla milanese* is dipped in egg, then in a breadcrumb-PARMESAN mixture before being fried in butter.

scallops, dried Also called *conpoy*, the dried adductor muscles of scallops. Dried scallops, which have a strong, clean ocean smell and deliver rich UMAMI flavor, are used in numerous Chinese and Japanese dishes and are a valued ingredient in Hong Kong Cantonese cooking. Use whole, chopped in small pieces or shredded, as an addition to soups, stuffing, STIR-FRY and noodle dishes, and salads. For most dishes, the scallops need to be reconstituted in warm water before use. The water in which they're soaked is sometimes added to the dish for flavor. Dried scallops, especially whole ones, are expensive; unless a recipe calls for whole ones for presentation, just buy pieces. Most people believe the Japanese variety is superior.

Scamorza [skah-MOHR-tsah] Today this Italian CHEESE is usually made from whole cow's milk (sometimes mixed with sheep's or goat's milk), though it was originally made only from buffalo milk. It's a PASTA FILATA type of cheese that is basically a very firm, slightly salty MOZZARELLA. Scamorza, which contains about 44 percent milk fat, has a creamy white color and a mild, nutty flavor. It's sold in small ovals or gourd shapes and can sometimes be found smoked. Scamorza can be used in much the same way as mozzarella, generally as a table cheese or in cooking. *See also* CHEESE.

scampi [SKAM-pee] 1. The Italian name for the tail portion of any of several varieties of lobsterettes, the most well known being the Dublin Bay PRAWN. *Scampo* is the singular form of the word. 2. On U.S. restaurant menus, the term is often used to describe large SHRIMP that are split, brushed with garlic oil or butter and broiled.

schaum torte; schaumtorten [SHOWM tohrt] This classic dessert from Austria consists of baked MERINGUE layers filled with fruit and topped with whipped cream.

Schbzieger [SHB-zee-guhr] *see* SAPSAGO

schkembe chorba *see* CHORBA

schlag [SHLAHG] A German word (used mainly in Austria) for "whipped cream." *Mit schlag* means "with whipped cream," which is how Austrians love to top many foods and beverages including fruit, desserts and coffee.

Schloss; Schlosskäse; Schlosskaese [SHLOSS; SHLOSS-kai-zer (-kah-zeh)] Though also produced in Germany, Switzerland and the United States, Schloss originated in Austria and was inspired by the more famous LIMBURGER. It's made from either whole or partially skimmed pasteurized cow's milk and is RIPENED for 3 to 4 weeks. Though not as odoriferous as Limburger, Schloss is smooth, creamy and supple with a savory, spicy and pungent flavor. Also called *Schlosskäse* or *Schlosskaese* ("castle cheese").

schmaltz [SHMAHLTZ; SHMOHLTZ] A rendered chicken fat (sometimes flavored with onions, apples and seasonings) that is strained and used in many dishes of Middle European Jewish origin much like butter—both in cooking and as a spread for bread.

schmaltz herring [SHMAHLTZ] *see* HERRING

schmear [SHMEER] Thought to have come from the Yiddish word *shmirn* ("to smear or grease"), the word schmear is used in the culinary world to describe a dab of something like mayonnaise or cream cheese that's spread on a roll, bagel, etc. More recently, cream cheese is combined with flavorings such as onions, garlic and bell peppers to create a spread that's commercially packaged as a "schmear."

Schmierwurst [SHMEER-wurst(-vurst)] *see* METTWURST

Schnapps; Schnaps [SHNAHPS; SHNAPS] Any of several strong, colorless alcoholic beverages made from grains or potatoes. The word comes from the German *Schnaps,* meaning "mouthful." Although sweet **peppermint Schnapps** is undoubtedly the most widely known version, this potable may be flavored variously with herbs and seeds (including aniseed, caraway seed, dill and fennel) and can range from sweet to DRY.

schnitzel [SHNIHT-suhl] German for "CUTLET," usually describing meat that is dipped in egg, breaded and fried. **Wiener Schnitzel** is a veal cutlet prepared in this manner.

schnitz un knepp [SHNIHTS uhn NEHP] A Pennsylvania Dutch dish of dried apples that are soaked in water before being cooked in that liquid with ham. Spoonfuls of batter are added to the cooking liquid to make dumplings.

Schwarzwälder Kirschtorte [SHVAHRTS-vahlt-uhr KEERSH-tort] German for BLACK FOREST TORTE.

scone [SKOHN; *Br.* SKON] This Scottish QUICK BREAD is said to have taken its name from the Stone of Destiny (or Scone), the place where Scottish kings were once crowned. The original triangular-shaped scone was made with oats and griddle-baked. Today's versions are more often flour-based and baked in the oven. They come in various shapes including triangles, rounds, squares and diamonds. Scones can be savory or sweet and are usually eaten for breakfast or tea.

score To make shallow cuts (usually in a diamond pattern) in the surface of certain foods, such as meat or fish. This is done for several reasons: as a decoration on some foods (breads and meats); as a means of assisting flavor absorption (as with MARINATED foods); to tenderize less tender cuts of meat; and to allow excess fat to drain during cooking.

scorpion [SKOR-pee-uhn] A potent COCKTAIL consisting of light rum, brandy, orange juice, lemon juice and ORGEAT SYRUP, served over ice.

scorzonera [skor-tsoh-NEH-rah] *see* SALSIFY

Scotch; Scotch whisky Made only in Scotland, this distinctive liquor uses barley for flavoring instead of the corn that's used for most American whiskies. The characteristic smoky flavor of Scotch comes from the fact that the sprouted malted barley is dried over peat fires. Although

Scotch must be distilled and AGED for 3 years (the majority for 5 to 10 years) in Scotland, it may be bottled in other countries. There are two main types of Scotch—malt and grain. **Malt whisky** is produced in an old-fashioned pot still (*see* DISTILLATION) and aged for up to 15 years. It's made from malted barley—grain that's been germinated or sprouted, which converts its starch to sugar. **Grain whisky** is distilled in a continuous still and made with malted barley mixed with various unmalted grains—primarily corn, but also barley and wheat. It's aged for 6 to 8 years and used primarily for blending. **Blended Scotch** is a combination of up to 50 different malt whiskies plus grain whisky. Such Scotches are blended for consistency and have a more uniform aroma and flavor than single-malts. **Single-malt (unblended) Scotch** is malt Scotch that's produced and bottled by a single distillery without being blended with other Scotch whiskys. It varies significantly from distiller to distiller because of distillation techniques, AGING practices, differences in the local water and myriad other environmental factors. **Highlands Scotch** and **Lowlands Scotch** are single-malt Scotch descriptors referring simply to geographical locations but not necessarily describing particular flavor characteristics. To determine the boundary between highlands and lowlands, draw a line across Scotland from Greenrock to Dundee, which would be the border between the Highlands (north of the line) and the Lowlands (south of the line). Traditionally, whiskies made in Scotland are spelled without the "e." *See also* LIQUOR; WHISKEY.

Scotch ale *see* ALE

Scotch barley *see* BARLEY

Scotch bonnet chile This small (1 to 1½ inches in diameter), irregularly shaped CHILE ranges in color from yellow to orange to red. The Scotch bonnet is one of the hottest of the chiles, with a SCOVILLE SCALE rating of 100,00 to 350,000, and is closely related to the equally fiery JAMAICAN HOT and the HABANERO.

Scotch broth A Scottish soup made with lamb or mutton, barley and various vegetables. Also known as *barley broth*.

Scotch egg A hard-cooked egg that is coated with sausage, dipped into beaten egg, rolled in breadcrumbs and deep-fried. Scotch eggs are halved or quartered lengthwise and may be served hot or cold, usually as an appetizer.

Scotch woodcock A British specialty consisting of toast spread with anchovy paste and topped with a softly scrambled mixture of eggs and cream. It can be served as a first course or entrée.

Scoville scale A measure of a chili pepper's heat level, developed in 1912 by Wilbur Scoville. The test itself, called the *Scoville Organoleptic Test*, involved progressive dilutions of a pepper's extract with sugar water until a group of tasters could not detect a burning sensation. A number was assigned to a chile based on the amount of dilution required to reach this point. Though the test relied on the subjective nature of the human tasters, the scale is still in use today although the GILLETT METHOD, which does not use human testers, is primarily relied on, with results calculated back to the Scoville scale. At one end, pure CAPSSAICIN registers 15,000,000 to 16,000,000 Scoville heat units, and at the other, sweet bell peppers have a 0 rating. In 1994 the RED SAVINA, a selectively bred HABANERO CHILE, was certified (and recognized by Guinness World Records) as the world's hottest pepper, with a range of 350,000 to 577,000. In 2000 India reported that the Bhut Naga Jolokia pepper was tested at 855,000, and in 2004 a second test showed a rating of 1,041,427. Also battling for top spot is the Dorset Naga pepper, developed in Dorset, England, which tested from 661,000 to over 1,000,000 on the Scoville scale. These were followed by the Naga Viper, the Infinity Chilli and the Trinidad Scorpion Butch T, all of which registered over 1,000,000. In 2012 the Trinidad Moruga Scorpion was proclaimed the hottest after it was measured at over 2,000,000. However, according to New Mexico State University's Chile Pepper Institute, which does some of the testing, the Bhut Naga Jolokia is still the hottest commercially cultivated chile. To put these results in perspective, a regular JALAPEÑO CHILE tests at a range of between 2,500 to 8,000, and the extremely hot HABANERO CHILE in the range of 100,000 to 300,000.

scrapple The name of this Pennsylvania Dutch dish is derived from the finely chopped "scraps" of cooked pork that are mixed with fine-ground cornmeal, pork broth and seasonings before being cooked into a MUSH. The mush is packed into loaf pans and cooled. Slices of the scrapple are then cut from the loaves, fried in butter and served hot, usually for breakfast or brunch.

screwdriver A mixed drink of orange juice and vodka served over ice. Its origins are unknown but the most popular tale is that it was named in the 1950s by American oil-rig workers stationed in the Middle East who opened and stirred cans of this mixture with their screwdrivers.

screwpine leaves; screw pine Popular in the cooking of Southeast Asia (particularly Indonesian, Malasian and Thai), screwpine leaves have a floral flavor and are used most often to flavor rice dishes and puddings. Their intense green hue also makes them useful as a natural food coloring. Screwpine leaves are available in Asian markets—sometimes fresh and always dried. They're also called *daun pandan, pandanus* and *kewra.*

scrod [SKRAHD] *see* COD

scroggin [SKRAH-gihn] *see* TRAIL MIX

scungilli [skuhn-GEE-lee] *see* WHELK

scup [SKUHP] *see* PORGY

scuppernong grape [SKUHP-uhr-nawng] *see* MUSCADINE GRAPE

sea anemone [uh-NIHM-uh-nee] Any of many varieties of flowerlike marine animals of which two—the **oplet** and the **beadlet**—are used as food in France. The body cavity is cut into pieces and usually either batter-fried or used in soups.

sea bass A term used to describe any of various saltwater fish, most of which aren't members of the BASS family. BLACK SEA BASS is a true bass (as is STRIPED BASS), but **white sea bass**, which is generally marketed simply as "sea bass," is actually a member of the DRUM family. The **giant sea bass** is related to the GROUPER family and can weigh as much as 550 pounds. It's sometimes mistakenly called both *black sea bass* and *jewfish*. Sea bass can be found whole and in steaks or fillets. In general, the flesh is lean to moderately fat and is suitable for almost any method of cooking including baking, broiling, poaching and sautéing. *See also* FISH.

sea bean *see* SAMPHIRE

sea bread *see* HARDTACK

sea bream *see* BREAM; PORGY

sea cucumber A marine animal whose name comes from its cucumberlike shape. It has short tentacles at one end. It's also known as *sea slug*. Though it is seldom found fresh in the United States, it's sold dried (usually marketed as *trepang, iriko* or *bêche-de-mer*) in Asian markets. It must be soaked in water for at least 24 hours, during which time it doubles in size and takes on a gelatinous quality. Its texture is rather rubbery and it's therefore most often used in soups.

sea devil *see* ANGLER

seafoam *see* DIVINITY

seafood Any edible FISH or SHELLFISH that comes from the sea.

sea pickle *see* SAMPHIRE

sear To brown meat quickly by subjecting it to very high heat either in a skillet, under a broiler or in a very hot oven. The object of searing is to seal in the meat's juices, which is why British cooks often use the word "seal" to mean the same thing.

sea robin *see* GURNARD

sea salt *see* SALT

seashell pasta *see* Pasta Glossary, page 883

sea slug *see* SEA CUCUMBER

sea snail *see* PERIWINKLE

season 1. To flavor foods in order to improve their taste. *See also* SEA-SONING. 2. To age meat, which helps both to tenderize it and to improve its flavor. 3. To smooth out the microscopic roughness of new pots and pans, particularly cast iron, which might cause foods to stick to the cooking surface. This is normally done by coating the cooking surface with vegetable oil, then heating the pan in a 350°F oven for about an hour. Continued use and gentle cleaning will improve the seasoning. Pans may occasionally need reseasoning.

seasoned salt *see* SALT

seasoning Ingredients added to food to intensify or improve its flavor. Some of the most commonly used seasonings include herbs (such as oregano, rosemary and basil), spices (like cinnamon, nutmeg, cloves and allspice), condiments (such as Worcestershire sauce, soy sauce and mustard), a variety of vinegars and—the most common of all—salt and pepper. *See also* Seasoning Suggestions, page 891.

seatrout *see* WEAKFISH

sea urchin Rarely found on U.S. menus, this marine animal is considered a delicacy throughout Japan and many Mediterranean countries. There are many varieties (ranging in diameter from 1 to 10 inches) but all have a hard shell covered by prickly spines that make it look like a pincushion. Though it can be briefly cooked, sea urchin ROE is more often scooped out of the shell with a spoon and consumed raw. A popular method of serving sea urchin roe is to heap it atop a slice of French bread and sprinkle it with lemon juice.

sea vegetables Another name for a wide variety of ocean plants commonly known as SEAWEED.

seaweed An important food source in many Asian cultures, seaweed is a primitive sea plant belonging to the algae family with origins dating back millions of years. Japanese cuisine employs different varieties (such as KOMBU, LAVER and NORI) for many uses including soups, vegetables, tea, SUSHI and as a general seasoning. The Irish are partial to the seaweed known as CARRAGEEN, and AGAR is widely used throughout Asia. Seaweed is a rich source of iodine, an important nutrient. Many seaweeds also provide ALGINIC ACID, a jellylike substance that's used as a stabilizer and thickener in a wide variety of commercially processed foods such as ice creams, puddings, flavored milk drinks, pie fillings, soups and syrups. *See also* DULSE; HIJIKI; KELP; LIMU; WAKAME.

sec [SEHK] This French word literally means "dry" and when used to describe still (nonbubbly) wines, indicates that the wine has little if any residual sugar left after fermentation, meaning the wine is dry (not sweet). In sparkling wines such as CHAMPAGNE, however, the word takes on quite another meaning: "sec" indicates a relatively sweet wine (DEMI-SEC even sweeter), while the driest sparkling wines are referred to as BRUT.

Seckel pear [SEHK-uhl] An 18th-century Pennsylvania farmer (for whom it was named) is credited with introducing the Seckel pear. It's a small, russet-colored fruit with a sweet, spicy flavor. The Seckel's firm flesh makes it excellent for both cooking and canning but some people find it too crisp for out-of-hand eating. It's available late August through December. *See also* PEAR.

sediment The grainy deposit sometimes found in wine bottles, most often with older wines. Sediment is not a bad sign but in fact may indicate a superior wine. It should be allowed to settle completely before the wine is DECANTED into another container so that when the wine is served no sediment transfers to the glass.

seed *v.* To remove the seeds from foods, such as fruits or vegetables. **seed(s)** *n. see* ACHIOTE SEED; ANISE SEED; CARAWAY SEED; CELERY SEED; CORIANDER SEED; DILL SEED; FLAX SEED; GUAJE SEED; HEIRLOOM SEEDS; LOTUS SEED; MUSTARD SEED; NIGELLA SEED; PEPITAS; POPPY SEED; SESAME SEED; SUNFLOWER SEED.

seed sprouts *see* SPROUTS

seimaibuai [say-my-BOO-i-ee] *see* SAKE

seishu [SAY-shoo] *see* SAKE

seitan [SAY-tan] A protein-rich food made from wheat GLUTEN and used in many VEGETARIAN dishes. Seitan's firm texture is definitively chewy and meatlike (which is why it's also called *wheat meat*), its flavor rather neutral. That mildness, however, allows seitan to be a kitchen chameleon that easily picks up the flavors of the foods with which it is cooked. Available in the refrigerator section of natural food stores and Asian markets, seitan typically comes in foil- or plastic-wrapped cakes that may be square or rectangular and that average about $1/2$-inch thick. It also comes in 8-ounce plastic tubs. Check the expiration date on fresh seitan. Seitan is also sold as *wheat gluten,* a powdered form that can be mixed with water. The wheat gluten–water mixture, however, doesn't have the same chewy texture as commercially packaged seitan. For the best texture and flavor add seitan to cooked dishes at the last minute, heating just until it is warmed through.

seize A word applied culinarily to melted chocolate that becomes a thick, lumpy mass. Seizing occurs when a minute amount of liquid or steam comes in contact with melted chocolate, in which case the chocolate clumps and hardens. To correct seized chocolate, add a small amount (no more than 1 tablespoon per 6 ounces of chocolate) of clarified butter, cocoa butter or vegetable oil into the chocolate, stirring until once again smooth. Be aware that the added fat may affect the texture of the final product. *See also* CHOCOLATE.

Sekt [ZEHKT] A German term for "sparkling wine." *See also* CHAMPAGNE.

sel [SEHL] French for "salt." *Sel marin* is "sea salt," *gros sel* is "rock (or coarse) salt."

sel fin *see* SEL GRIS

self-rising flour *see* FLOUR

sel gris [SEHL GREE] French for "gray salt," referring to sea salt harvested from sea pans in the manner described under FLEUR DE SEL. Sel gris is not as fine and delicate as fleur de sel; it has coarser grains and is denser. If the coarse grains are refined into smaller crystals, it's often sold as *sel fin* ("fine salt.") Sel gris is used both as a condiment to be sprinkled on food and as a seasoning agent like normal salt. Avoid those that are too gray or dirty looking.

sell by date *see* PRODUCT DATING

sell date *see* OPEN DATING

Selles-sur-Cher (AOC; PDO) [sehl-soor-SHEHR] SEMISOFT TO SEMI-HARD goat's-milk cheese from an area around Selles-sur-Cher, a small town in France's southern Loire Valley. The 5- to 7-ounce wheels have rinds that are thin and coated with black ash. The cheeses must be aged a minimum of 10 days, though they're often RIPENED for 3 to 4 weeks. The result is a soft and creamy texture, which becomes drier and firmer with age, and a sweet, slightly tangy flavor, which becomes fuller and stronger as the cheeses ripen. Selles-sur-Cher cheeses have a FAT CONTENT of about 45 percent.

seltzer water [SELT-suhr] A flavorless, naturally effervescent water that takes its name from the town of Nieder Selters in the Weisbaden region of Germany. Human-made "seltzer," also referred to as *soda water,* was introduced in the latter half of the 18th century when carbon dioxide was injected into water. The original seltzer was the forerunner to soda pops, which came into being in the 1840s when flavors were added to seltzer water. *See also* SODA WATER.

semicooked cheese *see* COOKING CHEESE

semi de melone *see* Pasta Glossary, page 883

semifreddo; *Sp.* **semifrío** [say-mee-FRAYD-doh; *Sp.* say-mee-FREE-oh] Italian for "half cold," *semifreddo* culinarily refers to any of various chilled or partially frozen desserts including cake, ice cream, fruit and custard or whipped cream. Such a dessert's Spanish counterpart is called *semifrío*.

semihard cheese One way of classifying cheese is by texture and the moisture content that impacts that texture. Semihard cheese ranges between 40 and 50 percent moisture and has been pressed (*see* PRESSING) but may or may not have been cooked (*see* COOKING). Semihard cheeses include EDAM, EMMENTAL and GOUDA. *See also* SOFT CHEESE; SEMISOFT CHEESE; HARD CHEESE; VERY HARD CHEESE.

Sémillon [say-mee-YOHN; seh-mee-YOHN] A white grape grown in France and, to a lesser extent, in California, Australia, Chile and Argentina. Sémillon is bottled on a limited basis as both a DRY and semisweet VARIETAL WINE. It's also sometimes blended with SAUVIGNON BLANC. Its greatest claim to fame, however, is its susceptibility to BOTRYTIS CINEREA, making it one of the grapes most often used for DESSERT WINES such as the French SAUTERNES and some U.S. LATE-HARVEST wines.

semisoft cheese One way of classifying cheese is by texture and the moisture content that impacts that texture. Semisoft cheese has a moisture content of between 50 and 75 percent. It may or may not be pressed (*see* PRESSING) and cooked (*see* COOKING), depending on the cheese. Examples include FONTINA, HAVARTI and TELEME. *See also* SOFT CHEESE; SEMIHARD CHEESE; HARD CHEESE; VERY HARD CHEESE.

semneh *see* SMEN

semolina [seh-muh-LEE-nuh] 1. Durum wheat that is more coarsely ground than normal wheat flours, a result that is often obtained by sifting out the finer flour. Most good PASTA is made from semolina. It is also used to make GNOCCHI, puddings and soups and in various confections. *See also* WHEAT. 2. Similarly ground grains are sometimes referred to as "semolina" but with the grain's name attached—corn semolina, rice semolina, etc.

senape [SAI-nah-pay] Italian for "MUSTARD."

sen chan; sen lek; sen mee; sen yai *see* RICE NOODLES

sendai miso *see* MISO

seolleongtang [teol-LUHN-tahng] A Korean soup that's anglicized as "ox bone soup." It's made by simmering ox bones, along with meat cuts like BRISKET and seasonings such as onions and garlic, for many hours to fully extract the flavors. It's served with rice and other accompaniments.

Serena *see* QUESO DE LA SERENA

Serpent of Sicily *see* CUCUZZA

Serrano ham Hailing from Spain, this ham comes from the hind leg of white Spanish pigs and is dry-cured for 7 to 13 months. In Spain it's known as *Jamón Serrano* ("mountain ham")—*jamón* means "ham," and *serrano* refers to the *sierra*, or mountains. The name comes from the traditional practice of curing these hams in mountain drying sheds, though today this primarily is done in modern plants that duplicate the atmospheric conditions of the old sheds. Produced throughout Spain, a country in which ham is highly regarded, the high-quality Serrano ham is similar to PROSCIUTTO. Spaniards, however, feel their highest quality ham comes from Iberian or Ibérico pigs (*see* IBERICO HAM). Serrano ham is sometimes labeled as *Jamón Reserva, Jamón Curado* and *Jamón Extra,* but such names don't seem to have any official significance regarding handling or aging.

Sercial *see* MADEIRA

sereh *see* LEMON GRASS

serrano chile [seh-RRAH-noh] A small (about 1½ inches long), slightly pointed CHILE that has a very hot, savory flavor. It has a SCOVILLE SCALE rating ranging from 10,000 to 23,000. As it matures, its smooth, bright green skin turns scarlet red, then yellow. Fresh serranos can be found in Latin markets and some supermarkets. They are also available canned, pickled or packed in oil, sometimes with carrots, onions or other vegetables. Serranos can be used fresh or cooked in various dishes and sauces such as GUACAMOLE and SALSA. The dried serrano chile, also known as *chile seco,* comes whole and powdered and is generally used in sauces.

servelat *see* CERVELAT

serviette [ser-vee-EHT] The British and Australian term for "table napkin."

sesame leaf *see* SHISO

sesame oil [SEHS-uh-mee] Expressed from SESAME SEED, sesame oil comes in two basic types. One is light in color and flavor and has a deliciously nutty nuance. It's excellent for everything from salad dressings to sautéing. The darker, Asian sesame oil has a much stronger flavor and fragrance and is used as a flavor accent for some Asian dishes. Sesame oil is high in polyunsaturated fats ranking fourth behind safflower, soybean and corn oil. Its average SMOKE POINT is 420°F, making it excellent for frying. Sesame oil is particularly popular in India as well as in the Orient. *See also* FATS AND OILS.

sesame seed [SEHS-uh-mee] History tells us that sesame seed is the first recorded seasoning, dating back to 3000 B.C. Assyria. It grows widely in India and throughout the Orient. The seeds were brought to America by African slaves, who called it *benné* (BEHN-nee) *seed,* and it subsequently became very popular in Southern cooking. These tiny, flat seeds come in shades of brown, red and black, but those most commonly found are a pale grayish-ivory. Sesame seed has a nutty, slightly sweet flavor that makes it versatile enough for use in baked goods such as breads, cakes and cookies, in confections like the Middle Eastern HALVAH and in salads and other savory dishes. The seed is available packaged in supermarkets and can be found in bulk in Middle Eastern markets and natural food stores. Because of a high oil content, sesame seed turns rancid quickly. It can be stored airtight in a cool, dark place for up to 3 months, refrigerated up to 6 months or frozen up to a year. *See also* Seasoning Suggestions, page 891.

sesame seed paste A creamy paste made of roasted ground sesame seeds and used in Chinese cooking.

set, to To allow food to become firm, as with a gelatin-based dish.

seui fa *see* RICE PADDY HERB

sev; sev press [SAYV] An East Indian snack of crispy, deep-fried chickpea noodles that are about the thickness of spaghetti, some slightly thicker than others. Sev comes plain or flavored with various seasonings such as AJOWAN, chili powder, CUMIN, garlic, spinach and TURMERIC. This spicy mix can range from slightly hot to scorching. Some versions include other items like nuts and fried or roasted lentils. Sev, which can be found in specialty Indian markets, is also sometimes sprinkled on top of Indian dishes. A **sev press** is a mechanical device for extruding batter or dough in noodle form for dishes such as SEV or FALOODA NOODLES. The presses usually come with an assortment of plates for making noodles of different sizes.

seven-minute frosting A fluffy, meringue-type frosting consisting of egg whites, sugar, cream of tartar, water and vanilla. The mixture is beaten constantly in the top of a double boiler over hot water. When stiff peaks form (a process which, as the name suggests, takes about 7 minutes), the frosting is done.

seven spice seasoning *see* SHICHIMI TOGARASHI

seviche [seh-VEE-chee; seh-VEE-cheh; seh-VEESH] An appetizer popular in Latin America consisting of raw fish marinated in citrus (usually lime) juice. The action of the acid in the lime juice "cooks" the fish, thereby firming the flesh and turning it opaque. Onions, tomatoes and green peppers are often added to the marinade. Only very fresh fish should be used for this dish. POMPANO, red SNAPPER and SOLE are the fish most often selected for seviche (which is also spelled *ceviche* and *cebiche*).

Sevillano olive [SEH-vee-yahn-noh) Originally from the area around Seville, the capital city of Spain's Andalusia region, this olive is now grown worldwide. It's large and meaty, ranges in color from green to greenish-purple and has a large pit. When the pit's removed the olive can be stuffed with any number of items. The flavor is fresh and mellow but not very notable, so the Sevillano is often packed with seasoning blends to provide additional flavor. The Sevillano is also known as *gordal, queen* and *royal.* *See also* OLIVE.

Seville orange [seh-VIHL] A popular bitter orange grown in the Mediterranean region. It has a thick, rough skin and an extremely tart, bitter flesh full of seeds. Because of its high acid content, the Seville is not an eating orange but (because of that same acidity) is extremely popular for making marmalades as well as LIQUEURS such as COINTREAU, CURAÇAO, GRAND MARNIER and TRIPLE SEC. The Seville orange also finds its way into sauces and relishes, and is a particular favorite with duck because its acidity helps counteract the fatty flavor. The dried peel is often used for seasoning. *See also* ORANGE.

sev press *see* SEV

sevruga caviar [sehv-ROO-guh] *see* CAVIAR

shabu-shabu [SHAH-boo SHAH-boo] A Japanese dish consisting of raw meat (usually paper-thin slices of beef) and raw vegetables cooked by each diner at the table in a pot of hot broth. The freshly cooked ingredients can be dipped into a variety of sauces provided for additional flavor. Once the meat and vegetables have been cooked and eaten, the broth, sometimes with noodles added, is then served. The name is said to come from the sound that's made as the meat is gently swished through the broth.

shad Ranging from 3 to 6 pounds, shad is the largest member of the American HERRING family (*Alosa sapidissima*). Shad are anadromous, meaning that they migrate from their saltwater habitat to spawn in fresh water. They have a moderately firm, beige-colored flesh that's distinctively rich but replete with bones. Shad lends itself to baking and grilling.

Shad roe is a much sought-after springtime delicacy. The roe is encased in two delicately transparent oval-shaped membranes. These roe-filled sacs can be sautéed, poached or broiled and should be cooked just until the center is slightly pink. Shad roe has a rich, slightly sweet nutty flavor.

shaddock [SHAD-uhk] *see* POMELO

shadon beni; shadow beni *see* SAW-LEAF HERB

shad roe *see* ROE; SHAD

sha ha fun; sha he fen; sha ho fen *see* RICE NOODLES

shakshuka; shakshouka [shahk-SHOO-kah] Popular in North Africa (especially in Tunisia) and the Middle East (particularly in Israel), shakshuka is a dish consisting of eggs cooked in a thick, spicy sauce of tomatoes, peppers, onions, garlic and seasonings. This dish has many variations, but most cook the eggs in indentations made in the thick sauce. Shakshuka is also spelled *chachouka*, *chouchouka*, and *chackchouka*.

shallot [SHAL-uht; shuh-LOT] The name of this onion-family member (*Allium ascalonicum*) comes from Ascalon, an ancient Palestinian city where the shallot is thought to have originated. Shallots are formed more like garlic than onions, with a head composed of multiple cloves, each covered with a thin, papery skin. The skin color can vary from pale brown to pale gray to rose, and the off-white flesh is usually barely tinged with green or purple. The two main types of shallots are the **Jersey** or **"false" shallot** (the larger of the two) and the more subtly flavored **"true" shallot**. *Fresh green shallots* are available in the spring, but as with garlic and onions, *dry shallots* (i.e., with dry skins and moist flesh) are available year-round. Choose dry-skinned shallots that are plump and firm; there should be no sign of wrinkling or sprouting. Refrigerate fresh shallots for up to a week. Store dry shallots in a cool, dry, well-ventilated place for up to a month. Freeze-dried and dehydrated forms are also available. Shallots are favored for their mild onion flavor and can be used in the same manner as onions.

shambalileh; shanbalile *see* FENUGREEK

shamogi; shamoji [shah-MOH-gee] A round Japanese spoon or paddle made from wood or bamboo, traditionally used only to toss and serve rice.

shandy; shandygaff A popular drink in the Caribbean, shandy was introduced by the British and dates back to at least the late 19th century. It's an icy cold mixture of equal parts BEER or ALE and GINGER BEER (sometimes GINGER ALE). *Shandygaff,* the original form of the word, is thought to come from the London vernacular for a pint of beer ("shant of gatter")—*shanty* being a public house, *gatter* being an idiom for "water."

Shanghai cooking [SHANG-hi] *see* CHINESE CUISINE

shank The front leg of beef, veal, lamb or pork. Though very flavorful, it's full of connective tissue and is some of the toughest meat on the animal. It therefore requires a long, slow cooking method such as braising. Beef shank is used for ground beef; a popular veal shank preparation is OSSO BUCO. *See also* LEG, LAMB.

shan shui ho fun *see* RICE NOODLES

shaomai *see* SIU MAI

Shaoshing wine; Shao hsing wine *see* SHAOXING WINE

Shaoxing wine [shaow-SHEEN] A Chinese RICE WINE that takes its name from an area in northern China. Premium Shaoxing wine, which can be AGED for many years, is highly regarded as a potable while lesser grades are typically used for cooking. Shaoxing wine is frequently called for in recipes because of its good quality. However, note that bottles labeled "Shaoxing *Cooking* Wine" have added salt (*see* COOKING WINE). Shaoxing wine is available in Asian markets and in some supermarkets. Dry SHERRY is considered a good substitute. Also called *Shaoshing wine, Shao hsing wine, Chinese rice wine* and *yellow wine.*

sharbat [SHAHR-baht] Popular throughout India, the Middle East and Pakistan, sharbat is a cold, sweet nonalcoholic drink flavored variously with ingredients that can range from fruit juice to nuts to flower petals. The texture of sharbat can range from thin to so thick it can be eaten with a spoon. The word *sharbat* is the foundation of present-day SHERBET.

shari [shah-REE] *see* SUSHI MESHI

shark Though the United States has only recently begun to appreciate the merits of this fish, other cultures have eaten shark for eons. Some of the more popular shark species are *leopard, mako, soupfin* and *thresher.* Sharks marketed for food range in size from 15 to 120 pounds. Though some of the smaller ones are sold whole, fillets, steaks or chunks are the more common market forms. The shark's flavorful, lowfat flesh is dense and meatlike. Because of its metabolism, however, it has a tendency to smell of ammonia. This off-putting odor can easily be eliminated by soaking the fish in milk or ACIDULATED WATER. Shark can be prepared in a variety of ways including broiling, grilling, baking, poaching and frying. It's also delicious in soups, and cold, cooked shark can be used in salads. *See also* DOGFISH; FISH; SHARK'S FIN.

shark's fin Reputed to be an aphrodisiac, this expensive delicacy is actually the cartilage of the shark's dorsal fin, pectoral fin and the lower portion of the tail fin. Though the fins of many shark species can be used, the soupfin shark is the one most broadly utilized for this purpose. Dried shark's fin can be found in Asian markets and is sold either whole or in shreds (sans skin and bones). The latter is more expensive because the labor-intensive work of removing the cartilage from the fin's framework is already done. Shark's fin cartilage provides a protein-rich gelatin that is used in Chinese cooking mainly to thicken soups—most notably, shark's fin soup.

Sharlyn melon A large melon averaging about 9 pounds, the Sharlyn has a netted rind that ranges in color from beigy gold to tan. Its shape is like that of an elongated CANTALOUPE, and the pale green flesh is perfumy, sweet and creamy—something like a cross between a cantaloupe and a HONEYDEW MELON. The Sharlyn is available from about late June through September. It should be heavy for its size and have a sweet fragrance. *See also* MELON.

sharmoola; sharmoula [shar-MOO-lah] *see* CHERMOULA

Sharon fruit *see* PERSIMMON

sharpening steel A long, pointed, thin round rod (also called a *butcher's steel*) made of extremely hard, high-carbon steel (some of diamond steel or ceramic) and used to keep a fine edge on sharp knives. The rod is attached to a handle, which usually has a guard to protect the user's hand from the knife blade. Sharpening steels come in a variety of sizes, the ideal being about 12 inches long. Knives are sharpened by drawing them (while applying slight pressure) across the steel at a 20- to 30-degree angle 5 to 6 times on both sides of the blade prior to each use. Dull blades will not be helped by a sharpening steel; they need to be resharpened on a WHETSTONE and then fine-honed on a steel. For maximum efficiency, choose a sharpening steel that is longer than the knife to be sharpened. To prevent metal filings from building up, occasionally clean the steel according to manufacturer's directions.

shashlik [shahsh-LIHK; SHAHSH-lihk] *see* SHISH KEBAB

shawarma; shawerma; shawirma [shuh-WAHR-mah; sh-WAHR-mah] A Middle Eastern version of the GYRO, shawarma consists of spiced, marinated lamb (sometimes chicken or veal) that has been molded around a vertical, rotating spit and slowly roasted. Thin slices of the meat are shaved off as the spit keeps turning. The hot meat is wrapped in LAVASH or PITA bread, spread with HUMMUS or TAHINI and topped with shredded vegetables. In Turkey the shawarma is known as *doner kebab*.

she-crab soup This creamy South Carolina specialty is made with crab meat and ROE and flavored with sherry and WORCESTERSHIRE SAUCE. Since fresh crab roe is available only in the spring, she-crab soup is seasonal.

sheet cake A thin cake (such as a GENOISE) that's baked in a JELLY ROLL PAN (also known as a *sheet pan*) and used for rolled cakes such as BÛCHE DE NOËL and JELLY ROLLS.

sheet pan *see* JELLY ROLL PAN

shell *n. see* HULL. **shell** *v.* To remove the shell or tough outer covering of a food such as nuts, eggs, garden peas, etc. *See also* SHUCK.

shell bean *see* CRANBERRY BEAN

shellfish A broad term for all aquatic animals that have a shell of some kind. Shellfish are separated into two basic categories—CRUSTACEANS and MOLLUSKS. **Crustaceans** include CRABS, CRAYFISH, LOBSTER and SHRIMP. **Mollusks** are divided into three groups—GASTROPODS (also called *univalves*) such as the ABALONE and SNAIL; BIVALVES like the CLAM and OYSTER; and CEPHALOPODS like OCTOPUS and SQUID. *See also* FISH.

shell steak Depending on the locale, shell steak is another name for either a boneless CLUB STEAK or a NEW YORK STEAK. In either case a shell steak should be tender, since both the club and the New York are cut from the SHORT LOIN, the most tender section of BEEF. *See also* BEEF; Beef Chart, page 896.

shepherd's pie A dish of cooked ground or diced meat (traditionally lamb or mutton) mixed with gravy (and sometimes vegetables) and topped with mashed potatoes. The pie is then baked until the mixture is hot and the potato "crust" browns. Shepherd's pie was originally created as an economical way to use leftovers from the ubiquitous "Sunday roast."

sherbet [SHER-biht] The origins of sherbet can be traced to a popular Middle Eastern drink (*charbet*) made of sweetened fruit juice and water. Today the term *sherbet* commonly refers to a frozen mixture of sweetened fruit juice (or other liquid such as wine) and water. It can also contain milk, egg whites and/or gelatin. Sherbet is lighter than ICE CREAM but richer than an ICE. *See also* SORBET.

sherry A FORTIFIED WINE originally made in and around the town of Jerez in the Andalusia region of southern Spain. It's now also made in the United States and other parts of the world such as Australia and South Africa. As with many wines, sherries range from connoisseur quality to inexpensive mass-produced versions. The Spanish are the acknowledged experts, using the *solera* system of topping off older wines with the more recently made sherry. Thus there are no vintage sherries and the quality is consistent year after year. Sherries range in color, flavor and sweetness. **Fino**, considered by many to be the world's finest sherry, is pale, delicate and very DRY. Finos are excellent when young but should not be aged because they don't improve and may lose some of their vitality. They're often served chilled as an APÉRITIF. **Manzanilla** sherries are very dry, delicate finos with a hint of saltiness, a character derived from the seaside town, Sanlúcar de Barrameda, in which they're made. Manzanillas are served cold, often to accompany seafood. **Amontillado**, considered a medium sherry, has a distinctly nutty flavor. Sometimes labeled *milk sherry,* amontillados are aged longer than finos and are typically sweeter, softer and darker in color. **Oloroso** sherries are sweet, fuller flavored and darker in color than dry or medium sherries. They are usually aged longer and are also more expensive. Olorosos are often labeled *cream* or *golden* sherries. Sherries can be drunk as an APÉRITIF or after dinner. Dry sherries are usually drunk chilled, sweet sherries at room temperature.

shichimi togarashi; shichimi [shee-CHEE-mee toh-gah-RAH-shee] A peppery Japanese condiment made of seven different seasonings including red chile flakes (TOGARASHI), SANSHO, white sesame seeds, NORI (seaweed) flakes, bits of dried mandarin orange peel, black hemp seeds and white poppy seeds. Shichimi togarashi is available in hot, medium and mild strengths in most Asian markets. It's also called *hichimi togarashi* and *seven spice seasoning.*

shiitake [shee-TAH-kay] Though originally from Japan and Korea, the delicious shiitake mushroom is now being cultivated in the United States (where it's often called *golden oak*) in a number of states including California, Pennsylvania, Vermont, Washington and Virginia. The cap of the shiitake is dark brown, sometimes with tan striations, and can be as large as 8 to 10 inches across. The average size, however, is 3 to 6 inches in diameter. The meaty flesh has a full-bodied (some say steak-like), bosky flavor. Shiitake stems are extremely tough and are therefore usually removed. Don't throw them out, however—they add wonderful flavor to stocks and sauces. Discard the stems after they've been used for flavoring. Though both fresh and dried shiitakes are now available almost year-round in many supermarkets, they're very expensive. Spring and autumn are the seasons when fresh shiitakes are most plentiful. Choose plump mushrooms with edges that curl under. Avoid any with broken or shriveled caps. The versatile shiitake is suitable for almost any cooking method including sautéing, broiling and baking. Shiitake mushrooms are also called *Chinese black mushrooms* and *forest mushrooms. See also* MUSHROOM.

shimeji [shee-MEH-jee] The Japanese name for a group of mushroom varieties, both farmed and wild. Wild versions grow on trees including oak, pine and beech. They grow in clumps with stems of 1 to 3 inches and caps no larger than a quarter. Colors range from white to brown. Some varieties that are considered shimeji are BEECH or clamshell mushrooms,

PIOPPINI and HONSHIMEJI. *Shimeji* has been a bit of a catchall term in the past and confusion still exists regarding what falls in this category and what doesn't. *See also* MUSHROOM.

shinma; shinmai [SHEEN-mah] Japanese "new rice" that's harvested in the early fall. It's sweeter and more tender than regular rice and therefore requires less water and a shorter cooking time. This highly regarded rice is also spelled *shinmei*.

shinshu miso *see* MISO

shio koji [shee-oh koh-gee] A fermented mixture of water, *shio* (sea salt) and rice-based KOJI. *Koji* has been in use for centuries in Japan as a basis for SOY SAUCE and SAKE, but this combination of salt and koji as a seasoning agent is a recent phenomenon, not only in Japan but in the United States. The taste of shio koji is like a light MISO that's slightly salty and provides that fifth element of taste, UMAMI. Chefs are using shio koji in place of salt in myriad recipes to add an extra dimension to the flavor. At this writing shio koji is hard to get in the United States but is available at some Japanese markets and on the Internet. As popular as it's becoming, it will likely be more widely available soon. There are also numerous recipes for making your own shio koji.

shioyaki [shee-oh-YAH-kee] Japanese for "salt-grilled," referring to a traditional method of grilling beef, poultry or fish in particular. Instead of coating food with sauce, generous amounts of salt are rubbed over the surface. The meat or fish is often set aside for 30 minutes or more before being broiled or cooked over very hot coals.

shiozake [shee-oh-zah-keh] Salted chum salmon (*see* SALMON).

ship biscuit *see* HARDTACK

shipkas chile *see* BULGARIAN CARROT PEPPER

shiranuhi; shiranui *see* DEKOPON

shirataki [shee-rah-TAH-kee] Thin, translucent, gelatinous noodles made from the starch of a yamlike tuber known as *Devil's Tongue*. Shirataki, which are the shredded form of KONNYAKU, have no discernable taste but absorb the dominant flavors of the soup or dish to which they're added. They can be found both in dry and soft forms in Asian markets and some supermarkets. The word *shirataki* means "white waterfall," alluding to the appearance of these noodles.

Shiraz *see* SYRAH

shrikhand [shree-KAND] Popular Indian dessert consisting of strained yogurt (*see* CHAKKA), that is sweetened, infused with cardamom, saffron and sometimes other flavorings like nutmeg and mixed with diced fruit, nuts and/or CHAROLI SEEDS.

Shirley Temple A nonalcoholic drink made with GRENADINE syrup and ginger ale and garnished with a MARASCHINO CHERRY. It's popular with children who want to have a "cocktail" with the adults and was named after the 1930s child star.

shiro goma [shee-roh GOH-mah] *see* GOMA

shiromiso *see* MISO

shirred eggs [SHERD] Eggs baked in a small cup or bowl with a covering of cream or milk and often topped with buttered breadcrumbs. The whites of the cooked eggs are typically firm, the yolks soft.

shirumono [shi-roo-MOH-noh] The Japanese term for all soups, with *suimono* specifically referring to clear soups or broths.

shish kebab [SHIHSH kuh-bob] Chunks of marinated meat (sometimes fish) and vegetables that are threaded on a skewer and grilled or broiled. Also called *shashlik*.

shiso [SHEE-soh] Aromatic green, jagged-edged leaf from the perilla (or *beefsteak*) plant, which is part of the mint and basil family. The versatile green shiso is used in salads, SUSHI and SASHIMI, cooked dishes like TEMPURA and as a garnish. Green shiso is available fresh from summer to fall in Asian markets. It's also called *perilla* and *Japanese basil*. The less common and less aromatic **red shiso** is from a different plant species and is more likely to be found pickled than fresh. In Korea, references to *sesame leaf* are likely to mean shiso.

shkembe chorba *see* CHORBA

shochu [show-CHOO] A traditional distilled (*see* DISTILLATION) liquor popular in Japan, especially the far western and southern regions where it's sometimes also called SAKE. Shochu is made from a variety of ingredients such as barley (mug), brown sugar (kokutou), buckwheat (soba), sweet potatoes (imo) and rice. There are two basic distillation methods. **Honkaku** or **otsu-rui** refers to shochus that are distilled only once, resulting in stronger flavors that reflect their basic ingredients. **Kou-rui** indicates the shochu has been through multiple distillations, leading to a smoother liquor with less pronounced flavors. The honkaku shochus are considered the premium versions, much the way single-malt SCOTCH or small-batch BOURBON is viewed as higher quality. **Awamori** is a special single-distilled shochu that's been produced in Okinawa for over 500 years and uses its own unique mold during fermentation. It's considered in the very top category of shochus. Many shochus have an ALCOHOL BY VOLUME of only 25 percent, which is low compared to liquors like bourbon, gin, scotch and vodka, but some have up to 45 percent, which is similar to the other liquors. Shochu is drunk like most other liquor—in COCKTAILS, NEAT, ON THE ROCKS and, particularly popular, mixed with a small amount of hot water, which releases the aromatics and increases the flavor.

shoepeg corn; shoe peg corn *see* CORN

shoga [SHOW-gah] Japanese for "GINGER." *See also* AMAZU SHOGA; BENI SHOGA.

shoofly pie Thought to be of Pennsylvania Dutch origin, the extremely sweet filling of a shoofly pie is a mixture of molasses, brown sugar, water and butter. There are several different stories concerning the origin of the pie's name. One is that it's so sweet that one must shoo away the flies; another declares that the pie was originally made to attract flies away from other foods.

shooter 1. A one-gulp libation that, until the late 1970s, referred to a simple SHOT of straight spirits (whiskey, vodka and so on) served in a SHOT GLASS. Today's shooters—with names like B-52 and Kamikaze—are no longer simple but have metamorphosed into concoctions of two or more spirits, sometimes layered, sometimes shaken. All shooters are served NEAT. Those who actually like the taste of a good cocktail tend to shake their heads in disbelief at the current shooter craze, for knocking the drink back in one gulp leaves little impression in the mouth. 2. Raw OYSTERS served ON THE HALF SHELL are sometimes called oyster shooters.

short A term used culinarily to describe a nonyeast pastry or cookie dough with a high proportion of fat to flour. The baked goods made from short doughs are tender, rich, crumbly and crisp.

short belly *see* ROCKFISH

shortbread Though it's now a year-round favorite, this tender-crisp, butter-rich cookie was once associated mainly with Christmas and Hogmanay (Scottish New Year's Eve). The traditional round shape comes from the ancient Yule BANNOCK, which was notched around the edges to signify the sun's rays. The classic way of making shortbread is to press the dough into a shallow earthenware mold that is decoratively carved. After baking, the large round cookie is turned out of the mold and cut into wedges. Today, more often than not, shortbread cookies are formed into simple squares or rounds.

shortcake Though it's most commonly a rich biscuit, shortcake can also refer simply to cake. The classic American shortcake is a large, sweet biscuit that is split in half, then filled and topped with sliced or chopped fruit (traditionally strawberries) and softly whipped cream. Shortcake is most often thought of as a dessert but savory versions can be made by filling and topping the biscuit with creamed chicken or other food.

shortening *see* VEGETABLE SHORTENING

short loin Of the major wholesale cuts of beef, this is the most tender. It lies in the middle of the back between the sirloin and the rib, and the muscles in this section do little that could toughen them. The two main muscles in the short loin are the tenderloin and the top loin. The elongated **tenderloin** muscle (when separated from the bone and the rest of the short loin) can be sold as *tenderloin roasts* (often labeled *chateaubriands*), or cut into *tournedos* or *filet mignon* steaks. The **top loin** muscle with the bone attached is called a *club steak*. When removed from the bone, the same muscle is marketed as *New York* (or *Kansas City*) *strip steak* or *Delmonico steak*. When the bone is left in and portions of both the tenderloin and top loin muscles are included, the short loin is the source of *porterhouse steaks* and *T-bone steaks*. *See also* BEEF; Beef Chart, page 896. *For information on specific meat cuts, see individual listings.*

short plate A section of beef that lies below the primary rib (*see* RIB ROAST). It contains some of the SHORT RIB and SKIRT STEAK sections.

short ribs Rectangles of beef about 2 inches by 3 inches, usually taken from the CHUCK and SHORT PLATE cuts. Short ribs consist of layers of fat and meat and contain pieces of the rib bone. They're very tough and require long, slow, moist-heat cooking. *See also* BEEF; Beef Chart, page 896.

shot; shot glass A small amount of alcohol, generally ranging from 1 to 2 ounces. A **shot glass** is the tiny drinking glass–shaped container in which such an amount is measured and/or served. An order for "a shot of whiskey" in a bar will produce a shot glass filled with spirits. The word *jigger* is synonymous with shot.

shottsuru [shoht-TSOO-roo] A Japanese FISH SAUCE.

shoulder, lamb This large, flavorful cut yields *shoulder chops* (also called *arm chops*) and *blade chops* that can be braised, broiled or grilled, as well as *shoulder roasts* (either square-cut or boned and rolled).

shoyu [SHOH-yoo] Japanese for SOY SAUCE.

shred To cut food into narrow strips, either by hand or by using a grater or a food processor fitted with a shredding disk. Cooked meat can be shredded by pulling it apart with two forks.

shrimp This delicious CRUSTACEAN is America's favorite SHELLFISH. Most of the shrimp in the United States comes from bordering waters, notably the Atlantic and Pacific Oceans and the Gulf Coast. There are hundreds of shrimp species, most of which can be divided into two broad classifications—warm-water shrimp and cold-water shrimp. As a broad and general rule, the colder the water, the smaller and more succulent the shrimp. Shrimp come in all manner of colors including reddish- to light brown, pink, deep red, grayish-white, yellow, gray-green and dark green. Some have color striations or mottling on their shells. Because of a heat-caused chemical change, most shrimp shells change color (such as from pale pink to bright red or from red to black) when cooked. Shrimp are marketed according to size (number per pound), but market terms vary greatly from region to region and from fish market to fish market. Keeping that variance in mind, the general size categories into which shrimp fall are: **colossal** (10 or less per pound), **jumbo** (11–15), **extra-large** (16–20), **large** (21–30), **medium** (31–35), **small** (36–45) and **miniature** (about 100). In the United States, jumbo and colossal shrimp are commonly called "prawns," though the PRAWN is, in fact, a different species. Though there are slight differences in texture and flavor, the different sizes (except the miniatures) can usually be substituted for each other. As a rule, the larger the shrimp, the larger the price. In general, 1 pound of whole, raw shrimp yields 1/2 to 3/4 pound of cooked meat. Shrimp are available year-round and are usually sold sans head and sometimes legs. When raw and unshelled, they're referred to as "green shrimp." Many forms of shrimp are found in the marketplace—shelled or unshelled, raw or cooked and fresh or frozen. There are also processed shrimp products such as breaded or stuffed, frozen shrimp, shrimp spread, dried shrimp (*see* SHRIMP, DRIED), SHRIMP PASTE, and SHRIMP SAUCE (the last two found in Asian markets). Raw shrimp should smell of the sea with no hint of ammonia. Cooked, shelled shrimp should look plump and succulent. Before storing fresh, uncooked shrimp, rinse them under cold, running water and drain thoroughly. Tightly cover and refrigerate for up to 2 days. Cooked shrimp can be refrigerated for up to 3 days. Freeze shrimp for up to 3 months. Thaw in its freezer wrapping overnight in the refrigerator, or place package in cold water until defrosted. Whether or not to DEVEIN shrimp is a matter of personal preference. In general, small and medium shrimp do not need deveining except for cosmetic purposes. However, because the intestinal vein of larger shrimp contains grit, it should be removed. Shrimp can be prepared in a variety of ways including boiling, frying and grilling. *See also* POPCORN SHRIMP; ROCK SHRIMP.

shrimp boil *see* CRAB BOIL

shrimp, dried Small, orangish-pink, dried shellfish are used in Asia and Latin America as a flavoring in many dishes. Dried shrimp, which have a strong fishy taste, are used whole, chopped or ground as an addition to soups, stuffings, STIR-FRY and noodle dishes, and salads. For most dishes, the shrimp need to be reconstituted in warm water before being used. This water in which they're soaked is sometimes added to the dish for flavor. Dried shrimp can be found in small cellophane bags in Asian markets.

shrimp paste A southeast Asian shrimp paste, known variously as *terasi, trasi* and *trassi*. It comes in cakes that can range from soft and grayish-pink to firm and brownish in color. Shrimp paste is made by grinding up salted, fermented shrimp and has a strong, salty, fishy flavor. It's used sparingly in myriad Asian preparations, particularly soups, sauces and rice dishes. The pungent odor dissipates somewhat during cooking. *See also* SHRIMP SAUCE.

shrimp sauce A moist version of SHRIMP PASTE, with the same strong, salty shrimp flavor. Shrimp sauce is pink in color when fresh but will begin to gray as it ages. It's used both as a condiment and flavoring. Shrimp sauce is also known as *bagoong, hom ha* and *patis. See also* FISH SAUCE; SAUCE.

shrub Colonial-day shrubs were spiked with liquor (usually brandy or rum) but today these fruit juice, sugar and vinegar drinks are usually non-alcoholic. Shrubs are served over ice, with or without soda water.

shu [SHOO] *see* SAKE

shuck To remove the shell from SHELLFISH such as oysters or clams. Also, to peel the husk from an ear of corn.

shui fu rong *see* RICE PADDY HERB

shumai; **shuumai** *see* SIU MAI

shungiku *see* CHRYSANTHEMUM LEAVES

Siamese ginger *see* GALANGAL

sichuan peppercorn *see* SZECHUAN PEPPER

sidecar The appellation of this COCKTAIL is said to have come from its originator, who always traveled in a motorcycle sidecar. It consists of BRANDY, orange-flavored LIQUEUR (such as COINTREAU or TRIPLE SEC) and lemon juice, shaken with ice and strained into a cocktail glass.

Siena cake [see-EH-nuh] *see* PANFORTE

sieve [SIHV] *n. see* STRAINER. **sieve** *v.* To strain liquid or particles of food through the mesh or perforated holes of a sieve or STRAINER.

sift To pass dry ingredients through a fine-mesh SIFTER so any large pieces can be removed. Sifting also incorporates air to make ingredients (such as powdered sugar or flour) lighter.

sifter A mesh-bottomed kitchen utensil used to SIFT ingredients such as flour or powdered sugar. Sifters are usually made of stainless steel or heavy-weight plastic. There are versions with rotary cranks as well as those that are battery operated.

silk gourd *see* ASIAN OKRA

Silpat The brand name of an FDA-approved nonstick baking and countertop sheet produced by several manufacturers. It's made of silicone with a reinforced glass weave, does not require greasing and provides even heat transfer. Silpat is effective at temperatures ranging from –40°F to 480°F. It comes in several sizes, the most popular being $16 \times 11^7/_8$ inches (fits in a JELLY ROLL PAN), $24^1/_2 \times 16^1/_2$ inches (for countertop use in rolling out doughs and such) and a $10^1/_4$-inch octagonal shape for microwave ovens. Silpat mats can be found at gourmet shops and many department store kitchenware sections.

silver ear *see* WOOD EAR

silver fizz *see* GIN FIZZ

silver leaf *see* VARAK

silver skin; silverskin Term for the thin, pearlescent membrane found on certain cuts of meat, such as a tenderloin. Silver skin is very tough and must be removed (with a sharp knife) in order to prevent the meat from curling during cooking.

simmer To cook food gently in liquid at a temperature (about 185°F) low enough that tiny bubbles just begin to break the surface.

Simplesse *see* FAT SUBSTITUTES

simple syrup *see* SUGAR SYRUP

Simpson lettuce *see* LEAF LETTUCE

Singapore sling Said to have originated at Singapore's Raffles Hotel, this COCKTAIL consists of gin, cherry brandy and lemon juice shaken with ice and strained into a tall glass. The drink is finished by topping it off with soda water.

single-malt whiskey *see* WHISKEY

siomai; siomay *see* SIU MAI

sirloin This cut of beef lies between the very tender SHORT LOIN and the much tougher ROUND. As would be expected, the meat cuts from the portion near the short loin are more tender than those closer to the round. Sirloin is usually cut into steaks or roasts. Bone removed, the cuts are referred to by the names of the three main muscles. **Top sirloin** is a continuation of the tender top loin muscle of the short loin. The **tenderloin** is part of the tenderest muscle (which also continues from the short loin) and the **bottom sirloin**, which is part of the same (less tender) **sirloin tip** muscle found in the ROUND. The best-known bone-in sirloin steaks (in order of tenderness) are **pinbone**, **flat bone**, **round bone** and **wedge bone**. *See also* BEEF; Beef Chart, page 896.

sirloin club steak *see* NEW YORK STEAK

sirniki *see* SYRNIKI

sirop de gomme *see* SUGAR SYRUP

sirsak [SIR-sak] *see* SOURSOP

siu mai; siu maai [soo MI] A Cantonese steamed dumpling frequently found on DIM SUM menus. Siu mai, also spelled *shaomai*, is made with circular gyoza (*see* WON TON SKINS) stuffed with a DICED filling that usually includes black mushrooms, fresh ginger, green onions or scallions, pork and/or prawns and water chestnuts. There are variations of siu mai that use chicken or beef instead of pork or prawns. The top of the dumplings is often garnished with items like grated carrots, peas or diced mushrooms. The Japanese have also adopted this dumpling, calling it *shumai* or *shuumai*; it's often found as part of a BENTO BOX. Similar dumplings are made in Indonesia (*siomay*) and the Philippines (*siomai*).

sixfingered threadfin *see* PACIFIC THREADFIN

sizzling rice soup A Chinese specialty consisting of broth combined with chicken or pork (and sometimes shrimp) and various vegetables. Deep-fried rice squares are placed in each soup bowl; when the soup is ladled over the squares, the rice sizzles and pops.

skate This odd-looking kite-shaped fish is closely related to **rays** and SHARKS. Although the names *skate* and *ray* are often used interchangeably, they are somewhat different creatures. Both have winglike pectoral fins that undulate as the fish meanders in the water. Rays are generally larger and have a long, slender barbed spine; skates do not. The fins are the most edible part of both skates and rays (although the meat from the back of very large rays is sometimes eaten). The **skate**'s delicious flesh is firm, white and sweet, not unlike that of the SCALLOP; it's high in fat and cooks and eats like fish. Like TUNA, the **ray**'s meat is dense, deep red in color, low in fat and cooks and eats like a tender beef steak. Depending on the region, both are available year-round. Occasionally the cheeks of the fish, called **skate knobs**, are found on menus. Unless skate is dressed within minutes of being caught it must, like shark meat, be soaked in ACIDULATED WATER to remove its natural ammonia odor. Skate and ray can be prepared in a variety of ways including poaching, baking and frying. *See also* FISH.

skate knobs *see* SKATE

skewer [SKYOO-uhr] *n.* A long, thin, pointed rod that comes in various sizes. Skewers are made of metal or wood; the former often has a ring at one end. They're most often used to hold meat in place during cooking, as well as to skewer meat and vegetables to be grilled for SHISH KEBAB. The best skewers are square or flat—shapes that hold food securely when moved. **skewer** *v.* To impale small pieces of food on skewers.

skillet *see* FRYING PAN

skim To remove the top layer from a liquid, such as cream from milk or foam and fat from stock, soups, sauces, etc.

skimmer A metal kitchen utensil consisting of a handle attached to either a perforated disk or a shallow bowl-shaped wire mesh. Skimmers are used to lift foods out of hot liquids or to remove unwanted surface fat and foamy residue from soups, etc.

skim milk *see* MILK

skin *v.* To remove the skin of food before or after cooking. Skinning is done for a variety of reasons including appearance, taste and diet. Foods that are often skinned include poultry, fish and game.

skirt steak Cut from the beef SHORT PLATE, the skirt steak is the diaphragm muscle (which lies between the abdomen and chest cavity). It's a long, flat piece of meat that's flavorful but rather tough. Properly cooked, skirt steak can be quite tender and delicious. It can either be quickly grilled, or stuffed, rolled and braised. Recently, skirt steak has become quite fashionable because of the delicious Southwestern dish, FAJITAS. *See also* BEEF; Beef Chart, page 896.

skordalia [skor-dahl-YAH] A Greek sauce or dip made with puréed baked potatoes, garlic, lemon juice, olive oil, vinegar, parsley and sometimes breadcrumbs or ground nuts. Skordalia is served with various dishes including grilled meats, poultry and fish, soups and as a dip for raw vegetables and/or bread. *See also* SAUCE.

slack lime *see* PICKLING LIME

slider Small sandwich served on a bun roughly $2^1/_2$ to 3 inches across. It usually denotes a small hamburger and is often referred to as a mini-burger. The name was coined by White Castle, a fast food chain based in Columbus, Ohio. The chain originally used the name *slyder* for the small sandwich but now uses the trademarked name Original Slider. Sliders have evolved from their hamburger base to include delicious adaptations with ingredients such as tuna, crab cakes, pulled pork or eggplant. They can be served as appetizers or HORS D'OEUVRES and, several at once, as an entrée.

slimehead *see* ORANGE ROUGHY

sling An alcoholic drink made with lemon juice, powdered sugar and a LIQUOR such as BRANDY, GIN, VODKA or WHISKEY. Slings are usually served in an old-fashioned glass, but occasionally they're served in a tall glass and topped off with soda water as in the SINGAPORE SLING.

sliver *n.* A long, thin piece of food such as meat or cheese, or a thin wedge of pie. **sliver** *v.* To cut food into thin strips.

slivovitz [SLIHV-uh-vihts; SLIHV-uh-wihts; SCHLIHV-uh-vihts] A dry, colorless, slightly bitter plum BRANDY.

sloe [SLOH] This wild European PLUM is the fruit of the blackthorn (*Prunus spinosa*), which also bears showy white flowers. The purple-skinned sloe has an extremely tart yellow flesh. Though too sour for out-of-hand eating, sloes are used for jams, jellies and to flavor LIQUEURS such as PRUNELLE and SLOE GIN. They're not generally available fresh in the United States.

sloe gin [sloh JIHN] A LIQUEUR made by steeping pricked or crushed SLOES in gin.

Sloppy Joe A sandwich composed of a split hamburger bun topped with a mixture of cooked ground beef, onions, green peppers and spicy tomato sauce. The name seems to be related to its appearance and the fact that it's messy to eat.

slow cooker Also called a *crockpot,* the slow cooker is an electric "casserole" that cooks food with low, steady, moist heat. It's designed to cook food over a period of 8 to 12 hours. These appliances range in size from 1 to 6 quarts. Slow cookers can cook a dish while you're at work, and they don't heat up the kitchen. On the minus side is that some vegetables (like celery) can become mushy before the other ingredients are done.

slumgullion [sluhm-GUHL-yuhn] This slang term originated during the California Gold Rush and described dishes (usually stews) made from leftovers.

slump An old-fashioned New England dessert of fruit, usually berries, topped with biscuit dough and stewed until the biscuit topping is cooked through. Also called *grunt*.

slurry A thin paste of water and starch (flour, CORNSTARCH or ARROWROOT), which is added to hot preparations (such as soups, stews and sauces) as a thickener. After the slurry has been added, the mixture is typically stirred and cooked for a few minutes in order to thicken and lose any raw taste.

slyder *see* SLIDER

smallage; smellage [SMAW-lihj] *see* LOVAGE

small basmati rice *see* KALJIRA RICE

sman *see* SMEN

smash Said to have been named after the finely crushed ice over which this sweet alcoholic drink is served, a smash is basically a short JULEP.

smear-ripened *see* WASH RIND

smelly tofu *see* STINKY TOFU

smelt The smelt is anadromous, meaning that it migrates from its North American saltwater habitat to spawn in fresh water. It's a small (average 4 to 7 inches long) fish with a translucent silver-green back shading into shimmering silver sides and belly. Its delicate flesh is rich, oily and mild-flavored. There are many varieties of this fish, the most widely distributed being the **rainbow smelt**, found along the Atlantic coast. Two popular Pacific Coast varieties are **whitebait** and **eulachon**. The latter is also called **candlefish**, a nickname that came about because Indians would dry these high-fat fish, run a wick through the flesh and use them for candles. Fresh smelts are best from September through May. Because they're very perishable, many are now flash-frozen immediately after being caught. They are also available canned. Smelts are marketed whole and are usually eaten that way—head, viscera and bones. Though they can be cooked in a variety of ways, they're generally simply coated with flour and fried. *See also* FISH.

smen In North African and Middle Eastern cooking, smen usually made from sheep's and/or goat's milk, that's been processed to preserve it. One technique is similar to the way GHEE is made, which is to slowly melt butter so the milk solids separate, and then to simmer until the milk solids turn light brown. The solids are then separated out, leaving a form of CLARIFIED BUTTER that has a nutty, caramel-like flavor and aroma. Salt is usually stirred in and the mixture stored in sealed containers until it's used. The other technique for making smen is to knead flavored water into cut-up pieces of butter and then drain the excess water out. The ball of flavored butter is then stored in a sealed container. Some smen is stored so long that it takes on characteristics of old, smelly cheeses, becoming very strong and, some think, rancid-like; this old smen is highly valued. Throughout North Africa and the Middle East, smen has various names including *samn, samna, samneh, semneh, sman* and *sminn*.

sminn *see* SMEN

Smithfield ham Considered by many to be the premier COUNTRY-CURED HAM, the Smithfield is said to have been so loved by Queen Victoria that she had six sent to her household every week. Although these special hams were once produced from hogs raised on a privileged diet of acorns, hickory nuts and peanuts, today's Smithfield hams come from grain-fed hogs. To be accorded the appellation of "Smithfield," the hams must be cured and processed in the area of Smithfield, Virginia. The elaborate processing includes dry-curing, seasoning, lengthy hickory smoking and aging of 6 to 12 months (sometimes up to 2 years). The result is a lean, dark-colored ham with a flavor that's rich, salty and dry. Smithfield ham can be purchased through mail order or from gourmet butcher shops or food stores. It may be served raw like PROSCIUTTO, but it's usually baked or boiled. Before being cooked, Smithfields must be soaked 12 to 24 hours to remove excess saltiness. *See also* HAM.

smoke curing; smoked *see* CURE

smoked salmon Fresh salmon that has undergone a smoking process, usually by one of two methods—hot-smoking or cold-smoking. **Hot-smoking** is a process by which the fish is smoked from 6 to 12 hours at temperatures ranging from 120° to 180°F. The time and temperature depend on the size of the fish, how close it is to the source of smoke and the degree of flavor desired. In **cold-smoking**, a temperature of 70° to 90°F is maintained and the fish might remain in the smokehouse for anywhere from 1 day to 3 weeks. There are many types of smoked salmon. **Indian-cure salmon** is brined fish that has been cold-smoked for up to 2 weeks, which results in a form of salmon JERKY. **Kippered salmon**—U.S. style—is a chunk, steak or fillet that has been soaked in a mild brine and hot-smoked. It's usually made from chinook salmon that has been dyed red. European kippered salmon differs in that it's a whole salmon that has been split before being brined and cold-smoked. Traditionally, **lox** is brine-cured salmon that's not smoked and typically saltier than regular smoked salmon. Some lox, however, has had sugar added to the brine, which produces a less salty product. Today the lines are blurred, since much of what is sold as lox is cold-smoked. Lox is a favorite in American-Jewish cuisine, particularly when served with BAGELS and cream cheese. **Belly lox** is more expensive than regular lox because it's made from the more desirable flesh on the sides of the stomach. **Nova** or **Nova Scotia salmon** (sometimes called **Nova Lox**) is an idiom used in the eastern United States that broadly describes cold-smoked salmon. **Scotch-smoked**, **Danish-smoked** and **Irish-smoked salmon** are all geographical references to cold-smoked *Atlantic* salmon (whereas the Pacific species—usually coho or chinook—treated in this manner is generally simply labeled *smoked salmon*). **Squaw candy** consists of thin strips of salmon that has been cured in a salt-sugar brine before being hot-smoked. Other fish such as trout and haddock can also be smoked. *See also* SALMON.

smoke point The stage at which heated fat begins to emit smoke and acrid odors, and impart an unpleasant flavor to foods. The higher the smoke point, the better suited a fat is for frying. Because both reusing fat and exposing it to air reduces its smoke point, it should be discarded after being used three times. Though processing affects an individual fat's smoke point slightly, the ranges for some of the more common fats are: butter (350°F); lard (361° to 401°F); vegetable shortenings (356° to 370°F); vegetable oils (441° to 450°F)—corn, grapeseed, peanut and safflower oils all have high smoke points, while that of olive oil is relatively low (about 375°F). *See also* FATS AND OILS; Smoke Points of Popular Oils Chart, page 867.

smooth hound *see* DOGFISH

smoothie; smoothee A beverage made by blending fruit with yogurt, milk or ice cream until it's thick and smooth.

s'more A gooey–sweet dessert made by toasting a marshmallow over a fire (or gas burner, if need be), then sandwiching the hot marshmallow and a thin square of chocolate between two graham crackers and slightly squeezing this union together so that the marshmallow squishes out on the graham crackers. S'mores can also be made by making these "sandwiches" and heating them in an oven. The name comes from the notion that they're so good one always wants "some more." S'mores have long been a well-known campfire treat.

smorgasbord; *Sw.* **smörgåsbord** [SMOHR-guhs-bohrd; SCHMOHR-guhs-bohrd] Swedish for "bread and butter table," smorgasbord has come to refer to a buffet consisting of a variety of foods such as various HORS D'OEUVRE, OPEN-FACED SANDWICHES, salads, cooked vegetables (which may be served hot or cold), pickled or marinated fish, sliced meats, cheeses and desserts. A smorgasbord may be simple or elaborate and can consist entirely of appetizers or make up the entire meal.

smørrebrød [SMUHR-uh-bruth] Danish OPEN-FACED SANDWICHES.

smothered steak *see* SWISS STEAK

snail Prehistoric sites have uncovered piles of this GASTROPOD MOLLUSK'S spiral shell, indicating that snails were popular early on. They were greatly favored by ancient Romans, who cultivated special vineyards on which the snails could feed and fatten. The best-known varieties today are the vineyard or Burgundy snail and the *petit-gris*. The **vineyard snail** has a diet of grape leaves and, though it grows slowly and is somewhat difficult to raise, is considered the best eating. It grows to about 1³/₄ inches, has a streaked, dull, yellowish brown shell and mottled flesh. The smaller (about 1 inch) French **petit-gris** is now being cultivated in the United States and has a brownish-gray shell and flesh. Other varieties are cultivated in Algeria, Turkey, China, Indonesia and Africa but are not as highly esteemed as the vineyard snail and petit-gris. Fresh snails are available year-round and can be found in specialty markets. Fresh American-cultivated snails do not require the purification period that European snails do but should be used the same day they're purchased. Snails are usually boiled before being baked or broiled in the shell with a seasoned butter. Canned snails and packaged snail shells are available in gourmet markets and many supermarkets. *See also* SNAIL PLATE; SNAIL TONGS; SHELLFISH.

snail plate Special ovenproof plates with six small indentations, designed to hold snails served in their shell in place so they don't roll around while being cooked or eaten.

snail tongs Small, spring-operated tongs used to hold hot snail shells while extracting the snail. Unlike most tongs, these open by squeezing the handles. When the pressure is released, the tongs snap securely around the snail shell.

snake gourd *see* CUCUZZA

snap bean *see* GREEN BEAN

snapper There are about 250 species of this saltwater fish, 15 of which can be found in United States waters from the Gulf of Mexico to the coastal waters of North Carolina. Some of the better-known species include the **gray snapper**, **mutton snapper**, **schoolmaster snapper** and **yellowtail snapper**. By far the best known and most popular, however, is the **red snapper**, so named because of its reddish-pink skin and red eyes. Its flesh is firm textured and contains very little fat. Red snapper grows to 35 pounds but is most commonly marketed in the 2- to 8-pound range. The smaller sizes are often sold whole, while larger snappers can be purchased in steaks and fillets. Snapper is available fresh all year with the peak season in the summer months. It's suitable for virtually any cooking method. Though some varieties of ROCKFISH are marketed under the names "Pacific snapper" and "red snapper," and a variety of TILEFISH is called "yellow snapper," none of these are true snapper. *See also* FISH.

snapper soup A dense, heavy brown soup popular in the Philadelphia area and commonly referred to as *Philadelphia snapper soup*. It's also called *snapping turtle soup*, since it's traditionally made with meat from snapping turtles (or snappers). It usually includes beef and/or veal stock, carrots, celery, onions and various herbs and is flavored with sherry. A different soup, called **red snapper soup**, comes in various styles and uses the popular RED SNAPPER fish.

snickerdoodle [SNIHK-uhr-doo-dl] Originating in 19th-century New England, this whimsically named cookie has a characteristically crackly surface and can be either crisp or soft. The dough sometimes contains nutmeg and cinnamon as well as raisins and nuts. Traditionally, snickerdoodles are sprinkled with cinnamon sugar before being baked. The name appears to have no particular meaning or purpose . . . other than fun.

snifter A short-stemmed, pear-shape glass that's larger at the bottom than it is at the top. Snifters are recommended for drinking fine BRANDY. When the brandy-filled snifter is cradled in the hands, the liquid—warmed by body heat—releases its delightful aroma.

snow A light, frothy dessert made by chilling a mixture of stiffly beaten egg whites, sugar, gelatin and various flavorings. Adding lemon juice, for example, creates lemon snow.

snow crab *see* CRAB

snow eggs *see* FLOATING ISLANDS

snow pea The fact that this LEGUME is entirely edible—including the pod—accounts for its French name, *mange-tout* (or *mangetout*), for "eat it all." Its almost translucent, bright green pod is thin and crisp. The tiny seeds inside are tender and sweet. Snow peas are available year-round with peak seasons in the spring and fall. Choose crisp, brightly colored pods with small seeds. Refrigerate in a plastic bag for up to 3 days. Both tips of a snow pea should be pinched off just before using. They're an essential vegetable in Chinese cooking and may also be used raw in salads. Snow peas are also called *Chinese snow peas*. *See also* PEA; PEA SHOOTS.

snow puff mushroom *see* ENOKI

snowshoe rabbit *see* HARE

soba [SOH-buh] A Japanese noodle made from buckwheat and wheat flour, which gives it a dark brownish-gray color. **Chasoba** is a variation of the noodle made with green tea. *See also* ASIAN NOODLES.

socarrat *see* PAELLA

sockeye salmon *see* SALMON

soda 1. Another name for BAKING SODA. 2. A generic term for any flavored SOFT DRINK. 3. Any of many SODA WATERS. 4. A concoction of one or more scoops of ice cream topped with a flavored SOFT DRINK or SODA WATER and flavored syrup.

soda bread A QUICK BREAD that is LEAVENED with baking soda combined with an acid ingredient, usually buttermilk. IRISH SODA BREAD is the best known of this genre.

soda water Water that has been highly charged with carbon dioxide, which gives it effervescence. Soda water, also called *club soda* or just plain *carbonated water,* contains a small amount of sodium bicarbonate, which, because it's alkaline, can help neutralize an acidic stomach. Soda water is combined with sweeteners and flavorings to produce a variety of SOFT DRINKS. Many COCKTAILS also use soda water as an ingredient. *See also* SELTZER WATER.

sodium alginate Sodium salt of *alginic acid* (also known as *algin)*, a substance extracted from brown algae. Sodium alginate is used in MOLECULAR GASTRONOMY by some of the world's top restaurants. Combining it with calcium lactate, chefs like Ferran Adrià (head chef at the famous, now-closed, Michelin 3-star restaurant elBulli) are able to create encapsulated spheres of liquid that act like caviar and explode in the mouth when eaten.

sodium nitrate; sodium nitrite Sodium nitrate is a chemical compound, sometimes referred to as SALTPETER (which is usually really potassium nitrate). It appears naturally in leafy green vegetables and, like potassium nitrate, is used to cure and retain color in meat products. **Sodium nitrite** is a similar compound used in much the same way. Over time sodium nitrate breaks down and becomes sodium nitrite. Nitrate/nitrite compounds inhibit botulism, but generations of improved refrigeration and freezing techniques have allowed the food processing industry to reduce the use of such additives. Sodium nitrate and sodium nitrite also have a number of non-food uses. **Pink salt**, sometimes called **curing salt**, or **DQ curing salt**, is a mixture of 93.75 percent table salt (*see* SALT) and 6.25 percent sodium nitrite and is commonly called for in recipes for homemade cured meats and sausages. **Prague powder #2** is similar, with a small amount of sodium nitrate added.

Soegogi-jeongol *see* JEONGOL

soekkorijjim *see* JJIM

sofki; sofkey [zhee-OHFF-gay; zaw-OHFF-key] A soup or gruel, traditionally made with ground corn meal, wood ash and water, popular with American Indians in the southeast United States, particularly the Creek. To make sofki, corn meal is soaked and then boiled in water. Meanwhile, water is poured through clean wood ash to create lye water, which is added to the cooking corn meal to soften the corn. As the corn meal continues to cook, water is added until the dish is thick but still a bit watery. The cooked corn meal is then cooled and allowed to sour over several days. Modern preparations sometimes use baking soda instead of wood ash. Pounded hickory nuts are often added for flavor. Sofki is also known as *kanahena*, *osafki* and *tsoshi*. Tradtionally, the Creek make large batches of sofki, which are always available to serve visitors when they come—its way of showing their hospitality.

sofrito (*Sp.*); **soffrito** (*It.*) [soh-FREE-toh] 1. The Spanish *sofrito* is a sauce made by sautéing ANNATTO SEEDS in rendered pork fat. The seeds are removed before chopped onions, green peppers, garlic, pork and various herbs are cooked in the flavored, now-red oil until the ingredients are tender and the mixture is thick. The sauce is used in recipes as needed. 2. The Italian *soffrito* is a similar mixture (usually chopped celery, green peppers, onions, garlic and herbs) sautéed in olive oil and used to flavor soups, sauces and meat dishes. *See also* SAUCE.

soft-ball stage A test for SUGAR SYRUP describing the point at which a drop of boiling syrup immersed in cold water forms a soft ball that flattens of its own accord when removed. On a CANDY THERMOMETER, the soft-ball stage is between 234° and 240°F. *See also* Candymaking Cold-Water Tests, page 866.

soft cheese One way of classifying cheese is by texture and the moisture content that impacts that texture. Soft cheese is uncooked cheese that has not been pressed (*see* PRESSING), which provides a high moisture content of around 80 percent. Most soft cheeses (such as BRIE, CRESCENZA and REBLOCHON) undergo RIPENING for a relatively short period of time. *See also* SEMISOFT CHEESE; SEMIHARD CHEESE; HARD CHEESE; VERY HARD CHEESE.

soft-crack stage A test for SUGAR SYRUP describing the point at which a drop of boiling syrup immersed in cold water separates into hard though pliable threads. On a CANDY THERMOMETER, the soft-crack stage is between 270° and 290°F. *See also* Candymaking Cold-Water Tests, page 866.

soft drinks A generic term applied to beverages that do not contain alcohol. Soft drinks are most often thought of as carbonated, though effervescence is not a requisite.

soft-ripened cheeses This type of cheese ripens (*see* RIPENING) from the outside in. When cheese is exposed to MOLD naturally, or when the surface is brushed or sprayed with a harmless bacteria (such as PENICIL-LIUM CAMEMBERTI), surface ripening occurs. Soft-ripened cheeses are also known as *bacterial-ripened, surface-ripened* or *bloomy-rind cheeses*. They normally have a unique flavor, an edible rind, and a soft or semisoft texture. Examples include BRIE, CAMEMBERT and LIMBURGER.

soft-shell clam; soft clam This variety of clam actually has a thin, brittle shell. The soft-shell clam can't completely close its shell because of a long neck (or siphon) that extends beyond its edge. This long extension is why the soft-shell is also referred to as a *long-neck clam*. There are several types of soft-shells but the most prevalent are the IPS-WICH, STEAMER, RAZOR and GEODUCK CLAM. *See also* CLAM.

soft-shell crab *see* CRAB; OYSTER CRAB

soft wheat *see* WHEAT

soja *see* SOYBEAN

sole The popularity of sole dates back at least to the ancient Romans, who called it *solea Jovi* (Jupiter's sandal), undoubtedly because of the elongated-oval shape of this FLATFISH. Though a number of FLOUNDER family members (such as Petrale sole, lemon sole, rex sole and butter sole) are incorrectly called sole in the United States, the highly prized **true sole** is found only in European waters. The best-known of these is the **Dover sole** (also called *Channel sole*), which is found in coastal waters from Denmark to the Mediterranean Sea. The body of the Dover sole averages about a foot long and ranges in color from pale gray to dark brown on the top side, with the underside a pale beige. Its delicately flavored flesh has a fine, firm texture. True Dover sole is imported frozen to the United States from several of the northern European countries and is available in better fish markets. Other true sole include the **thickback** and the **sand** (or **partridge**) **sole**, both smaller and less flavorful than the Dover. Much of what is sold as Dover sole in the United States is actually flounder. Sole can be prepared in a variety of ways including poaching, steaming, baking, broiling and sautéing. It's ideally suited for combining with other foods and sauces. *See also* FISH.

sole Véronique *see* VÉRONIQUE

somen [SOH-mehn] A thin, white Japanese noodle made from wheat flour. A yellowish version, called *tamago somen,* is made with egg yolk. Somen, which is similar to VERMICELLI, is often served cold during the summer months, but is also frequently served in soups. Somen is also spelled *somyeon. See also* ASIAN NOODLES.

sommelier [saw-muh-LLAY] The French term for a steward or waiter in charge of wine. For hundreds of years, sommeliers were responsible for the cellaring and serving of wines for royalty. Eventually the tradition of the sommelier spread to restaurants, where such an individual is expected to have extensive knowledge of wines and their suitability with various dishes. *See also* BRIGADE SYSTEM.

som tam; som tum [sohm tahm; toom] Thailand's most popular and most famous salad. *Som* means "sour" and denotes the taste created by the chiles, FISH SAUCE, garlic, lime and SHALLOT used in the salad. *Tam* means "to pound" and refers to the MORTAR AND PESTLE used to pound and grind the various ingredients, including palm sugar and tomatoes, as they are added to the dish. The chief ingredient is usually a jumble of shredded, unripe papaya; it provides an almost flavorless yet crunchy background for the contrast of dynamic flavors—hot, salty, sour and sweet. A version with dried shrimp and peanuts is called *som tam thai,* and when salted crab is added it's called *som tam phooh;* both are very popular adaptations. Variations also include many other ingredients such as carrots, cucumbers, green beans, unripe bananas and unripe mango. This type of salad originated in Laos, where it's called *tam mak hoong* or *dtam mak huhng* and where it veers toward being hotter and saltier. Similar salads are called *bok l'hong* in Cambodia and *goi du du* in Vietnam. Sticky rice is often served as a side with these salads.

somyeon *see* SOMEN

Sonata *see* PIÑATA; PIÑATA APPLE

Sonoma Jack cheese *see* JACK CHEESE

soondubu jjigae; soondooboo chigae [SOON-doo-boo jee-GAY] A popular Korean stew featuring soft TOFU that may also include beef, pork, seafood and vegetables. The spicy heat level is controlled by the amount of GOCHUGARU (red chili pepper flakes) that's added. A simpler tofu stew is called DUBU JJIGAE.

sopa [SOH-pah] Spanish for "soup."

sopa de albóndigas *see* ALBÓNDIGA

sopaipilla [soh-pi-PEE-yuh] This crisp, puffy, deep-fried pastry resembles an air-filled pillow. The sopaipilla is thought to have originated in Albuquerque, New Mexico, more than 200 years ago. It's a favorite Southwestern U.S. dessert, usually served with honey or syrup flavored with anise or cinnamon. Sopaipillas are also sometimes filled with savory ingredients like REFRIED BEANS.

sopa seca [SOH-pah SEH-kuh] Literally translated as "dry soup," sopa seca is really not a soup at all. It is, in fact, a dish usually based on rice, VERMICELLI or dry TORTILLA strips combined with tomatoes, onions and garlic and cooked in a broth. It's assumed that the name comes from the fact that, although the mixture begins "soupy," it is cooked until the liquid is entirely absorbed—thereby becoming a "dry soup." The Mexicans usually serve sopa seca as a luncheon dish or as a separate course, much as Italians serve a pasta course.

sope [SOH-pay] Traditional Mexican dish with a thick, round tortilla-like base made from fried masa, which is topped with FRIJOLES REFRITOS or black beans and variously with meats, cheese, shredded lettuce, onion, SALSA and the like. Sopes can vary in size depending on their use. Small ones, sometimes referred to as *sopecitos*, can be used as appetizers and larger ones for an entrée. *Garnachas* and *memelas*, from the Mexican state of Oaxaca, and *picadas* are similar dishes.

sorbet [sor-BAY] French for "SHERBET," which Italians call *sorbetto*. Sorbet is sometimes distinguished from sherbet by the fact that it never contains milk. It's also often a softer consistency than sherbet. Savory or lightly sweetened sorbets are often served either as a palate refresher between courses or as dessert. They're sometimes also called ICES or GRANITAS, though both of these mixtures are generally more granular in texture than a sorbet. *See also* SHERBET.

sorbitol [SOR-bih-tawl] A sweetener found naturally in some fruits and SEAWEEDS. Besides being used as an ARTIFICIAL SWEETENER, sorbitol is employed as a thickener and stabilizer in candies, gums and numerous other food products.

sorghum [SOR-guhm] This cereal grass has broad, cornlike leaves and huge clusters of cereal grain at the end of tall, pithy stalks. Sorghum is a powerhouse of nutrition but, though it's the third leading cereal crop in the United States, almost all of it is used for animal fodder. Around the world, however, it's the third largest food grain. A few U.S. mills do sell it by mail order. One sorghum by-product the United States does use for human consumption is the sweet juice extracted from the stalks, which, like that from the sugarcane, is boiled down to produce a thick syrup called **sorghum molasses** (also *sorghum syrup* or simply *sorghum*). It's often used as a table syrup and to sweeten and flavor baked goods.

sorrel [SOR-uhl] Any of several varieties of a hardy perennial herb belonging to the buckwheat family, all with some degree of acidity and sourness resulting from the presence of OXALIC ACID. Sorrel has grown wild for centuries throughout Asia, Europe and North America. The most strongly flavored of the sorrels is the **garden** or **belleville sorrel**, also called *sour dock* and *sour grass*. The mildest variety is **dock sorrel**, also called *spinach dock* and *herb patience dock*. As all sorrel matures it becomes more acidic. Sorrel leaves are shaped much like those of spinach and range from pale to dark green in color and from 2 to 12 inches in length. Fresh sorrel is available in limited supply year-round with a peak season in the spring. It should be chosen for its bright green, crisp leaves. Sorrel with woody-looking stems or leaves that are yellow or wilted should be avoided. Refrigerate fresh sorrel in a plastic bag for up to 3 days. Gourmet food stores sometimes carry cooked sorrel in jars and cans. The more acidic sorrels are used to flavor cream soups, puréed as accompaniments for meats and vegetables or used in omelets and breads. In the spring, when at its youngest and mildest, sorrel is used in salads or cooked as a vegetable. It's high in vitamin A and contains some calcium, phosphorus, potassium, magnesium and vitamin C.

sotanghon *see* CELLOPHANE NOODLES

soto [SOH-toh] Also spelled *saoto*, a traditional soup served throughout most of Indonesia and in surrounding areas. It's prepared myriad ways, but generally contains broth, meat and vegetables along with regional variations of seasonings and accompanying condiments. Beef, chicken, mutton, offal (*see* VARIETY MEATS) and water buffalo are generally used. Soto with a yellowish-orange cast usually indicates the presence of TURMERIC. Broths are often clear but coconut milk appears in some versions. CANDLENUT, cloves, coriander, GALANGAL, garlic, ginger, lemongrass and star anise are some of the seasonings used. Soto is often served with rice, rice cakes, noodles or potato cakes. Other accompaniments range from fried SHALLOTS to boiled eggs, SAMBAL, fried TOFU and grilled TRIPE.

soubise [soo-BEEZ] 1. A rich, velvety sauce made by combining BÉCHAMEL with puréed cooked onions and sometimes a small amount of cream. 2. A meat accompaniment of puréed cooked onions and rice. 3. A term applied to dishes (such as **eggs à la soubise**) topped with or accompanied by a creamy onion sauce. *See also* SAUCE.

soufflé [soo-FLAY] A light, airy mixture that usually begins with a thick egg yolk–based sauce or purée that is lightened by stiffly beaten egg whites. Soufflés may be savory or sweet, hot or cold. Baked soufflés are much more fragile than those that are chilled or frozen because the hot air entrapped in the soufflé begins to escape (causing the mixture to deflate) as soon as the dish is removed from the oven. Savory soufflés are usually served as a main dish, are almost always hot and can be made with a variety of ingredients including cheese, meat, fish or vegetables. Dessert soufflés may be baked, chilled or frozen and are most often flavored with fruit purées, chocolate, lemon or LIQUEURS. Both sweet and savory soufflés are often accompanied by a complementary sauce. Soufflés are customarily baked in a classic **soufflé dish**, which is round and has straight sides to facilitate the soufflé's rising. These special dishes are ovenproof and come in a variety of sizes ranging from $3^{1}/_{2}$-ounce (individual) to 2-quart. They're available in kitchenware shops and the housewares section of most department stores. Foil or parchment "collars" are sometimes wrapped around the outside of a soufflé dish so that the top of the foil or paper rises about 2 inches above the rim of the dish. Such collars are used for cold dessert soufflés so that the sides of the frozen or molded mixture are supported until they set. Once the collar is removed, the soufflé stands tall and appears to "rise" out of the dish.

soufflé dish *see* SOUFFLÉ

soufflé potatoes *see* POMMES SOUFFLÉES

soul food Though this traditional African-American fare has long been popular in the South, the term itself is relatively new (circa 1960). The expression "soul food" is thought to have derived from the cultural spirit and soul-satisfying flavors of black-American food. Some of the dishes commonly thought of as soul food include HAM HOCKS, GRITS, CHITTERLINGS, BLACK-EYED PEAS and COLLARD GREENS.

soun *see* CELLOPHANE NOODLES

soup Theoretically, a soup can be any combination of vegetables, meat or fish cooked in a liquid. It may be thick (like GUMBO), thin (such as a CONSOMMÉ), smooth (like a BISQUE) or chunky (CHOWDER or BOUILLABAISSE). Though most soups are hot, some like VICHYSSOISE and many FRUIT SOUPS are served cold. Soups are often garnished with flavor enhancers such as CROUTONS, grated or cubed cheese or sour cream. They can be served as a first course or as a meal, in which case they're often accompanied by a sandwich or salad. *See also* AVGO-LEMONO; BILLY BI; BIRD'S NEST; BORSCHT; BOURRIDE; CALDO VERDE; CALLALOO; CAUDIÈRE; CHLODNIK; COCK-A-LEEKIE; COTRIADE; COULIS; CUSH; DASHI; DUBARRY; FRUIT SOUP; GARBURE; GAZPACHO; MENUDO; MINESTRA; MOCK TURTLE; MULLIGATAWNY; OZONI; PANADA; PEPPER POT; PISTOU; POSOLE; RIBOLLITA; SCOTCH BROTH; SHE-CRAB SOUP; SIZZLING RICE SOUP; WON TON SOUP.

soupe [SOOP] The French term for a hearty soup. *See also* POTAGE.

soup dumpling *see* XIAO LONG BAO

soupe au pistou [soop oh pees-TOO] A French vegetable soup (similiar to an Italian MINESTRONE) made with green beans, white beans, onions, potatoes, tomatoes and VERMICELLI. It's seasoned with PISTOU, a mixture of crushed basil, garlic and olive oil.

sour *n.* A COCKTAIL made by combining liquor with lemon juice and a little sugar. It's usually shaken with crushed ice and can be strained and served ON THE ROCKS or STRAIGHT UP. Sours are often garnished with an orange slice and a MARASCHINO CHERRY. Though the **whiskey sour** is probably the most famous of these cocktails, they can be made with many other liquors including bourbon, gin and rum. **sour** *adj.* Having a sharp, tart taste, usually from an acidic ingredient such as lemon juice or vinegar.

sour cream Commercial sour cream contains from 18 to 20 percent fat, and has been treated with a lactic acid culture to add its characteristic tang. Sour cream often contains additional ingredients such as GELATIN, rennin (*see* RENNET) or vegetable enzymes. **Light sour cream** contains about 40 percent less fat than regular sour cream because it's made from half-and-half. There's also a **nonfat sour cream**, which is thickened with stabilizers. Refrigerate sour cream in its carton for up to a week after the date stamped on the bottom of the container. If any mold forms on the cream's surface, discard all of the sour cream. *See also* SOY SOUR CREAM.

sour dock *see* SORREL

sourdough; sourdough bread A bread with a slightly sour, tangy flavor created by using a special YEAST STARTER as the LEAVENER. San Francisco is known for its superior sourdough bread and many food stores in the area sell packages of dry sourdough starter for home bread bakers. Though most sourdoughs are made from all-purpose flour, there are many delicious variations including those made from whole-wheat or rye flour.

sourdough starter *see* YEAST STARTER

sour grass *see* SORREL

sour mash *see* BOURBON

sour salt *see* CITRIC ACID; SALT

soursop [SOW-er-sahp] Also called *corossol, graviola, guanabana, guanábana* and *sirsak,* the soursop is native to the tropical regions of the Caribbean and Central and South America. It's also grown in tropical areas in Africa, Southeast Asia and Australia, and to a limited extent in southern Florida. Belonging to the genus *Annona,* the soursop (*A. muricata*) is one of several members of the Annona family, which also includes the CHERIMOYA and SWEETSOP. This large tropical fruit can weigh 6 pounds or more and be up to 12 inches long and 6 inches wide. The soursop has a green, leathery skin that's covered with prickly spines. Its flesh is creamy white, peppered with brownish-black seeds and has a tropical fruit flavor that's slightly more acidic than other members of its family. Depending on the region, fresh soursop can be available year-round, typically found in Latin and specialty produce markets. Purchase fruit that's firm, heavy for its size and without skin blemishes; avoid those with brown splotching. Store at room temperature until ripe (they'll give slightly with soft pressure), then refrigerate, well wrapped, for up to a week. Soursop pulp is processed into juice, ice cream, sorbet and candy. Pulp in syrup is sometimes available in ethnic markets. Soursops contain a fair amount of niacin, iron, potassium and vitamins B1, B2 and C.

souse *n.* 1. Food that's been pickled (*see* PICKLE). 2. The BRINE used in pickling. 3. A pork luncheon meat bound (*see* BIND) with a brine-based gelatin mixture. 4. A drunkard. **souse** *v.* To pickle food.

sous chef [SOO shef] *see* BRIGADE SYSTEM

sous vide [soo VEED] French for "under vacuum," sous vide is a food-packaging technique pioneered in Europe whereby fresh ingredients are combined into various dishes, vacuum-packed in individual-portion pouches, cooked under a vacuum, then chilled. *Sous vide* food is used most often by hotels, restaurants and caterers, though it's expected to become increasingly available in supermarkets.

Southern Comfort Produced in St. Louis, Missouri, this traditional American LIQUEUR is made from bourbon and peaches. Southern Comfort is potent at 100 PROOF (50 percent alcohol).

souvlaki; souvlakia [soo-VLAH-kee; soo-VLAH-kee-uh] This Greek specialty consists of lamb chunks that have been MARINATED in a mixture of oil, lemon juice, oregano and seasonings before being skewered and grilled. Some souvlakia skewers also include chunks of vegetables such as green pepper or onion.

soybean; soya bean It's thought that the first written record of soybeans is dated 2838 B.C., and the Chinese have been cultivating them for thousands of years. So important are soybeans to the Chinese that they're considered one of the five sacred grains ("Wu Ku") along with rice, wheat, barley and millet. Soybeans didn't find their way to Japan until the 6th century and to Europe until the 17th century. Their extraordinary nutritive value was not scientifically confirmed until the 20th century. Although the United States didn't really become interested in soybeans until the 1920s, it now supplies about 75 percent of the world's total production. There are over 1,000 varieties of this nutritious LEGUME, ranging in size from as small as a pea to as large as a cherry. Soybean pods, which are covered with a fine tawny to gray fuzz, range in color from tan to black. The beans themselves come in various combinations of red, yellow, green, brown and black. **Dried soybeans** are mature beans that have been shelled and dried. Their flavor is generally quite bland, which may explain why they weren't embraced by Western cultures until their nutritive value was discovered. Unlike other legumes, the soybean is low in carbohydrates and high in protein—in fact, soy protein is the most economical source of protein in the world. Soy products are also a good source of iron and contain vitamins B1 and B2 and an essential oil—linoleic acid, one of the Omega-3 fatty acids. Because they're inexpensive and nutrition-packed, soybeans are used to produce a wide variety of products including KECAP; MEAT ANALOGS; MISO; NATTO; OKARA; SOYBEAN OIL; SOY CHEESE; SOY FLOUR; SOY ICE CREAM; SOY MARGARINE; SOY MAYONNAISE; SOY MILK; SOY NUTS; SOY SAUCE; SOY SOUR CREAM; SOY YOGURT; TAMARI; TEMPEH; TOFU; and YUBA. Soybeans can be cooked (after being presoaked) like any other dried bean to be used in soups, stews, casseroles, etc. They can also be sprouted (*see* SPROUTS) and used in salads or as a cooked vegetable. **Green soybeans**—commonly called by their Japanese name, *edamame*—are fresh soybeans—picked when they're fully grown but before they're completely mature. They're generally left in their pods, which are a bright green color with characteristic fuzz. Edamame are easy to digest and extremely high in protein and fiber. They're available pretty much year-round, with a peak from spring through fall. You'll find them in natural food stores, specialty produce markets, Asian markets and some supermarkets. They can also be found frozen, typically in 1-pound bags. Edamame are sold raw or ready-to-eat. If you buy the raw form, steam them for 20 minutes in the pod, then refrigerate until chilled. Serve edamame in their pods as a snack or appetizer. Pop the pods and shell them as you would peanuts. Soybean by-products are used in making margarines, as emulsifiers in many processed foods and in nonfood items such as soaps and plastics. Dried soybeans, beans for sprouting and a huge variety of soybean products are available in supermarkets, Asian markets and natural food stores. The soybean is also called *soya bean* and *soja*. *See also* BEANS; TEXTURED VEGETABLE PROTEIN.

soybean curd *see* TOFU

soybean oil Extracted from soybeans, this light yellowish oil is high in both polyunsaturated fats (58 percent) and monounsaturated fats (23 percent), and low in saturated fats (15 percent). It's used extensively in the United States in the manufacture of MARGARINE and SHORTENING. Soybean oil has long been a popular cooking oil in Chinese cuisine and is gaining favor in the United States because it is inexpensive, healthful and has a high SMOKE POINT. *See also* FATS AND OILS.

soybeans, roasted *see* SOY NUTS

soy cheese A cheeselike product made from SOY MILK that comes in full-, low- and nonfat versions and in a variety of types including cheddar, mozzarella and Parmesan. There's also a soy cream cheese, sold in plain and seasoned versions. Most soy cheeses contain casein, a milk protein, so dairy-sensitive individuals should read labels carefully. Cheese lovers find the flavor and texture of soy cheeses inferior, largely because they have a significantly lower fat content than their dairy counterparts. Most soy versions are best enjoyed chilled or at room temperature; many separate when heated. Soy cheeses can be found in natural food stores and most supermarkets.

soy flour This finely ground flour is made from soybeans and, unlike many flours, is very high in protein (twice that of wheat flour) and low in carbohydrates. Soy flour is ordinarily mixed with other flours rather than being used alone. It has a wide variety of uses such as for baking and to bind sauces. In Japan, it's very popular for making confections. Soy flour is sold in natural food stores—sometimes under the name *kinako*—and in some supermarkets.

soy ice cream A nondairy frozen dessert based on SOY MILK. This "ice cream" comes in a variety of styles (including high-fat premium, low-fat and sugar-free) and flavors ranging from various fruits to chocolate. The fat in soy ice cream is typically partially hydrogenated (see FATS AND OILS) SOYBEAN OIL, although other oils such as PALM-KERNEL OIL are also used. Soy ice cream can be found in supermarkets as well as in natural food stores.

soy margarine Any MARGARINE made from SOYBEAN OIL, which means it contains no SATURATED FAT.

soy mayonnaise Although all commercial mayonnaise products are made from SOYBEAN OIL, there are TOFU-based styles that are free of eggs as well as SATURATED FAT. These can commonly be found in natural food stores.

soy milk Higher in protein than cow's milk, this milky, iron-rich liquid is a nondairy product made by pressing ground, cooked SOYBEANS. Soy milk is cholesterol-free and low in calcium, fat and sodium. It makes an excellent milk substitute for anyone with a milk allergy; such milk substitutes are often fortified with calcium. There are also soy-based formulas for infants with milk allergies. Soy milk has a tendency to curdle when mixed with acidic ingredients such as lemon juice and wine; it's intentionally curdled in the making of TOFU.

soy nuts; roasted soybeans Resembling miniature dry-roasted peanuts, soy nuts are made by roasting whole, water-soaked dried SOY-

BEANS. They're extremely crunchy and have a nutlike flavor. Packages of soy nuts (lightly salted or salt free) can be found in natural food stores and some supermarkets. They can be stored at room temperature for up to a month. Eat soy nuts as a snack, add to salads or sprinkle over dishes as a garnish.

soy pea *see* SOYBEAN

soy sauce This extremely important ingredient in Asian cooking is a dark, salty sauce made by fermenting boiled SOYBEANS and roasted wheat or barley. Although there is essentially one main type of soy sauce widely made in the United States, China and Japan produce a number of varieties ranging in color from light to dark and in texture from thin to very thick. In general, **light soy sauce** is thinner and saltier than its dark counterpart. Its flavor and color is also lighter and it may be used in dishes without darkening them. **Dark soy sauce** is slightly thicker than light soy sauce but generally not as salty. It has a richer flavor and color (which is usually darkened with CARAMEL). **Chinese black soy** is extremely dark and thick, a result obtained from the addition of MOLASSES. The Japanese **tamari** is very similiar—thick, rich and extremely dark. Unless otherwise indicated on the label, soy sauce may be kept for many months in a cool, dark place. There are also many low-sodium or "lite" soy sauces available on the market. Soy sauce is used to flavor soups, sauces, marinades, meat, fish and vegetables, as well as for a table condiment. *See also* SAUCE.

soy sour cream A lactose-free product made from SOY MILK treated with a souring agent. It has a consistency and cooking properties similar to that of dairy SOUR CREAM and may be substituted in equal quantities for it. Soy sour cream can be found in natural food stores as well as some supermarkets (look in the kosher or gourmet cheese areas). It must be refrigerated and should be used within a week of purchase.

soy sprouts *see* SPROUTS

soy yogurt; soygurt A product made by treating SOY MILK with live (friendly) bacteria, just as YOGURT is produced. Soy yogurt has a flavor and consistency that simulates that of dairy yogurt. It's available plain or fruit flavored and can be found in natural food stores. It must be refrigerated and should be used within a week of purchase. Use it in any way suitable for regular yogurt.

spaetzle [SHPEHT-sluh; SHPEHT-sehl; SHPEHT-slee] Literally translated from German as "little sparrow," spaetzle is a dish of tiny noodles or dumplings made with flour, eggs, water or milk, salt and sometimes nutmeg. The spaetzle dough can be firm enough to be rolled and cut into slivers or soft enough to be forced through a SIEVE or COLANDER with large holes. The small pieces of dough are usually boiled before being tossed with butter or added to soups or other dishes. In Germany, spaetzle is served as a side dish much like potatoes or rice, and is often accompanied by a sauce or gravy.

spaghetti [spuh-GEHT-ee] Like its cousin MACARONI, spaghetti is made from SEMOLINA and water. Sometimes eggs are added. The name of this PASTA comes from the Italian word for "strings" and in general spaghetti is in the form of long, thin strands that are round and solid. **Spaghettini** is very thin spaghetti (but thicker than vermicelli). Some spaghettis—like fettuccine and linguine—are flat rather than round. On the other hand, fusilli is a spiral shape, rather than being straight. *See also* Pasta Glossary, page 883.

spaghettini *see* SPAGHETTI

spaghetti squash Also called *vegetable spaghetti,* this creamy-yellow, watermelon-shaped winter squash was so named because of its flesh, which, when cooked, separates into yellow-gold spaghettilike strands. Averaging from 4 to 8 pounds, spaghetti squash are available year-round with a peak season from early fall through winter. Choose squash that are hard and smooth with an even pale yellow color. Avoid greenish squash (a sign of immaturity) and those with bruised or damaged spots. Store uncut spaghetti squash at room temperature for up to 3 weeks. After the whole squash is baked, the rather bland-tasting strands can be removed from the shell and served with sauce, like pasta. They can also be served as part of a casserole or cold as a salad ingredient. *See also* SQUASH.

Spalen *see* SBRINZ

Spam Brand name of a canned seasoned pork product, created in the United States by the Hormel Company in 1926. This product was originally called "Spiced Ham," but got a name change in the 1930s via a contest with a grand prize of $100. And so the name "Spam" was born. Because it wasn't rationed like beef, Spam became an all-American staple during World War II. Several styles are now available including regular, low-sodium and smoked.

spanakopita [span-uh-KOH-pih-tuh] Of Greek origin, this savory pie consists of top and bottom PHYLLO-dough crusts with a filling of sautéed spinach and onions mixed with FETA CHEESE, eggs and seasonings.

Spanish lime *see* MAMONCILLO

Spanish melon A large and egg-shaped melon with a ribbed green skin and a pale green flesh. Its flavor is succulent and sweet, much like that of a CRENSHAW MELON. Spanish melons are available from early July to November. *See also* MELON.

Spanish olives Olives that are picked young, soaked in lye and then fermented in brine for 6 to 12 months. When bottled, they're packed in a weak brine and sold in a variety of forms including pitted, unpitted or stuffed with items such as PIMIENTOS, almonds, onions and JALAPEÑOS. Olives picked in a riper state contain more oil and are a deeper green color. *See also* MANZANILLA OLIVE; OLIVE.

Spanish onion *see* ONION

spareribs A long, narrow cut of meat taken from the lower portion of the ribs and breastbone of a hog. Spareribs are quite fatty, which contributes to their delicious flavor. Barbecuing spareribs (usually after they've been MARINATED) is the most popular method of preparation. *See also* PORK; Pork Chart, page 898; BREAST, LAMB.

sparkling wine *see* WINE

spatchcock [SPACH-kahk] *v.* An older cooking term that's recently come back into vogue and describes splitting a small bird down the back, then opening out and flattening the two sides like a book. It's similar to the term BUTTERFLY, though spatchcock refers only to fowl, whereas butterflying typically applies to boneless cuts (meat, poultry, fish and so on). *n.* A bird that's split and spread in preparation for roasting or broiling.

Spätlese [SHPAYT-lay-zuh] German for "late picking," this wine term refers to grapes that are picked after the regular harvest. Because such fruit is riper, it contains more sugar and produces wines that are rich and sweet. The selective picking process also makes them quite expensive. *See also* AUSLESE; BEERENAUSLESE; TROCKENBEERENAUSLESE.

spatula [SPACH-oo-luh] A flattish, rather narrow kitchen utensil that comes in a variety of shapes and sizes. Depending on the material from which it's made (which includes wood, metal, rubber and plastic), spatulas can be used for a plethora of kitchen tasks. Rigid wood spatulas are good for scraping the sides of pots and turning foods, whereas softer plastic or rubber spatulas are better for stirring ingredients in a curved bowl and folding mixtures together. Flexible metal spatulas—both long and short—are perfect for spreading frosting on cakes. *See also* TURNER.

spätzle *see* SPAETZLE

spearmint *see* MINT

Speck; speck [SHPECK; spehk] Respectively, German and Italian for "bacon." In Germany, *Speck* is essentially LARD, while in Italy it more closely resembles American bacon. Unlike the U.S. version, however, Italy's speck comes from hog legs, rather than the belly portion. It hails from Italy's Alto Adige region and has PROTECTED GEOGRAPHICAL INDICATION designation. Speck is salted and seasoned with black pepper, pimento, garlic and juniper berries before being cured for about a month. It then undergoes 10 days of cold smoking with ash, beechwood or juniper, and further aging that can last for several months. Speck can be served thinly sliced as an ANTIPASTO, or diced and used in cooking in place of bacon or PANCETTA.

speckled butter bean *see* LIMA BEAN

spelt Native to southern Europe, where it's been used for millenniums, spelt is an ancient CEREAL GRAIN that has a mellow nutty flavor. The easily digestible, highly nutritious spelt has a slightly higher protein content than WHEAT. Spelt flour, available in natural food stores, can be substituted for wheat flour in baked goods. Whereas spelt was once thought to be safe for those sensitive to wheat, studies now show that some wheat-allergic people may also react as readily to spelt.

Spencer steak Also called a *boneless rib-eye steak* (*see* RIB STEAK), this flavorful, tender cut of beef comes from the rib section. In some parts of the United States this is called a DELMONICO STEAK.

Spice Parisienne [pa-ree-ZYEHN] The market name for a complex spice and herb blend, also called EPICES FINES. French cooks usually make their own blends, which can vary greatly depending on the individual. In general, Spice Parisienne includes WHITE PEPPER, ALLSPICE, MACE, NUTMEG, CLOVES, CINNAMON, BAY LEAVES, SAGE, MARJORAM and ROSEMARY. As with all spices, this blend should be stored in a cool, dark place for no more than 6 months. *See also* SPICES.

spices Pungent or aromatic seasonings obtained from the bark, buds, fruit, roots, seeds or stems of various plants and trees (whereas HERBS usually come from the leafy part of a plant). Spices were prized long before recorded history. Though they've always been used to flavor food and drink, throughout the eons spices have also been favored for a plethora of other uses including crowning emperors, making medicines and perfumes, religious ceremonies and as burial accoutrements for the wealthy. Over 3,000 years ago the Arabs monopolized the spice trade, bringing their rare cargo back from India and the Orient by arduous camel caravans. During the Middle Ages the demand for spices was so high that they became rich commodities—a pound of mace could buy three sheep and the same amount of peppercorns could buy freedom for a serf. By that time Venice had a tight hold on Western commerce and controlled the incredibly lucrative European spice trade. That Venetian monopoly was an important catalyst for the expeditions that resulted in the discovery of the New World. Today, the United States is the world's major spice buyer. Among the more popular spices are ALLSPICE, CARDAMOM, CINNAMON, CLOVES,

GINGER, MACE, NUTMEG, PAPRIKA, PEPPER, SAFFRON and TURMERIC. Spices are also sold in blends, such as CURRY POWDER and SPICE PARISIENNE. Many spices are available in both whole and ground forms. Ground spices quickly lose their aroma and flavor, so it's wise to buy them in small quantities. Whole spices can be ground as needed. Store spices in airtight containers in a cool, dark place for no more than 6 months. To refresh spices that have been on the shelf too long, heat them in a dry skillet over medium heat or in a 375°F oven for 3 to 5 minutes. Spices are used to enhance a wide variety of food, both sweet and savory. They should be used sparingly so they don't overpower the foods being seasoned. *See also* ANISE; CARAWAY SEED; CAYENNE PEPPER; CELERY SEED; CHILI POWDER; CORIANDER; CUMIN; DUKKA; FENNEL; GRAINS OF PARADISE; MASTIC; MUSTARD; RAS EL HANOUT; RED PEPPER; SANSHO; SESAME SEED; SZECHUAN PEPPER; ZA'ATAR; Seasoning Suggestions, page 891.

spider Portable handheld strainer with a metal wire basket, which looks like a spider web, attached to a long, flat handle usually made out of bamboo. The spider allows quick draining of various foods without getting out a big strainer. It handles food in boiling water or broth and hot oil.

spigola [spee-GOH-lah] *see* BRANZINO

spiking *see* NEEDLING

spinach [SPIHN-ihch] Originating in the Middle East, spinach was being grown in Spain during the 8th century, and the Spaniards are the ones who eventually brought it to the United States. Popeye's addiction to this "power-packed" vegetable comes from the fact that it's a rich source of iron as well as of vitamins A and C. But because spinach contains OXALIC ACID—which inhibits the body's absorption of calcium and iron—the truth is that its nutritional value is somewhat diminished. It's this same oxalic acid that gives spinach its slightly bitter taste, which is prized by some while others find it off-putting. Spinach has dark green leaves that, depending on the variety, may be either curled or smooth. The smaller **New Zealand spinach** has flat, spade-shape leaves that are often covered with a fine fuzz. Fresh spinach is available year-round. Choose leaves that are crisp and dark green with a nice fresh fragrance. Avoid those that are limp, damaged or discolored. Refrigerate in a plastic bag for up to 3 days. Spinach, which is usually very gritty, must be thoroughly rinsed. Frozen and canned spinach is also available. Spinach may be used raw in salads, or cooked (usually by boiling or sautéing) and used as a vegetable or as part of a dish. Many dishes that use spinach as an integral ingredient are appended with the phrase À LA FLORENTINE. *See also* WATER SPINACH.

spinach dock *see* SORREL

spinaci [spee-NAH-chee] Italian for "spinach."

spiny dogfish *see* DOGFISH

spiny lobster *see* LOBSTER

spirit(s) A general term for alcoholic beverages. *See also* ALCOHOL; LIQUOR.

spiritweed *see* SAW-LEAF HERB

spit; spit roast A spit is simply a metal rod, used culinarily to skewer food (typically meat) to be cooked as the spit is turned. Spit roasting is commonly done over an open fire or barbecue grill, though some ovens are equipped with spits. The spit is turned either by hand or mechanically, thereby cooking the food evenly. If a meat cut is fatty, it bastes itself as it turns on the spit.

spleen *see* MELT

split *see* WINE BOTTLES

split pea *see* FIELD PEA

sponge [SPUHNJ] 1. A frothy, GELATIN-based dessert that has been lightened by the addition of beaten egg whites. Sometimes whipped cream is added, though it makes the dessert richer and not as airy. Sponges may be variously flavored, usually with fruit purées. 2. A mixture made by combining the yeast with some of the flour and liquid called for in a bread recipe. The thick, batterlike mixture is covered and set aside until it bubbles and becomes foamy, which, depending on the combination of ingredients, can take up to 8 hours. During this time, the sponge develops a tangy flavor. The remaining ingredients are added to this sponge and the bread is kneaded and baked as usual. Using a sponge also makes the final loaf slightly denser.

sponge cake; spongecake This light, airy cake gets its ethereal texture from beaten egg whites, which are folded into a fluffy mixture of beaten egg yolks and sugar. They get their leavening power entirely from eggs. Sponge cakes are further characterized by the fact that they do not contain shortening of any kind. The cakes can be variously flavored with anything from lemon ZEST to ground almonds.

spoom A frothy type of SHERBET made with a light SUGAR SYRUP mixed with a liquid such as fruit juice, CHAMPAGNE or SAUTERNES. Halfway through the freezing process, the mixture is combined with uncooked MERINGUE, which gives spoom its airy texture. The Italians call this frozen specialty *spuma,* which means "foam" or "froth."

spoon bread; spoonbread A puddinglike bread usually based on cornmeal and baked in a casserole dish. Spoon bread is generally served as a side dish and, in fact, is soft enough that it must be eaten with a spoon or fork.

spoon cabbage; spoon mustard *see* TATSOI

spot *see* DRUM

spotted dick; spotted dog Popular British boiled (sometimes steamed or baked) puddings made with SUET (usually beef), breadcrumbs and flour, and "spotted" with raisins. The pudding mixture is wrapped in a cloth and cooked until done. Spotted dick has raisins throughout the pudding, spotted dog has them scattered over the outside of the pudding. This pudding is sometimes called *plum-duff.*

spotted sea trout *see* WEAKFISH

sprat A close relative of the HERRING, the sprat is a small (about 6 inches in length) fish that can be found off the European Atlantic coast. Because of its high fat content, sprats are perfect for broiling or grilling. They're also available either salted or smoked. The smallest sprats are packed in oil, in which case they're usually called **brisling** or **brisling sardines**. *See also* FISH.

spring beauty *see* MINERS' LETTUCE

springerle [SPRING-uhr-lee; SHPRING-uhr-luh] One of Germany's most famous Christmas sweets, the anise-flavored springerle are beautiful embossed cookies that originated centuries ago in the German duchy of Swabia. The embossed designs on the cookie's surface are formed with a special carved wooden rolling pin, which, when rolled over the dough, imprints it decoratively. Alternatively, the dough can be pressed into a carved cookie mold. Once the dough is imprinted with the design, the cookies are allowed to sit out at room temperature overnight. This allows the dough's surface to dry so the design will remain as the cookie bakes.

springform pan A round pan with high, straight sides (2½ to 3 inches) that expand with the aid of a spring or clamp. The separate bottom of the pan can be removed from the sides when the clamp is released. This allows cakes, tortes or cheesecakes that might otherwise be difficult to remove from the pan to be extricated easily by simply removing the pan's sides. Springform pans range in diameter from 6 to 12 inches.

spring roll *see* EGG ROLL

spritz [SPRIHTS; SHPRIHTS] *n.* 1. Rich, buttery Scandinavian cookies formed into a variety of fanciful shapes when the dough is forced through a COOKIE PRESS. 2. A small amount of liquid, as in a "spritz" of lemon juice. The name comes from *spritzen,* which is German for "to squirt or spray." **spritz** *v.* To quickly spray or squirt, as in adding a "spritz" of soda to a mixed drink.

spritzer [SPRIHT-suhr] A tall, chilled drink, customarily made with wine and SODA WATER.

sprouts The crisp, tender sprouts of various germinated beans and seeds. **Mung bean sprouts**, used often in Chinese cooking, are the most popular. However, other seeds and beans—such as **alfalfa** and **radish** seeds, **lentils**, **soybeans** and **wheat berries**—may also be sprouted. For optimum crispness, sprouts are best eaten raw. They may also be stir-fried or sautéed, but should only be cooked for 30 seconds or less; longer cooking will wilt the sprouts. Though you may grow your own fresh sprouts (refer to a general cookbook), they're available year-round in most large supermarkets. Choose crisp-looking sprouts with the buds attached; avoid musty-smelling, dark or slimy-looking sprouts. Mung-bean sprouts should be refrigerated in a plastic bag for no more than 3 days. More delicate sprouts—like alfalfa sprouts—should be refrigerated in the ventilated plastic container in which they're usually sold and kept for no more than 2 days. Canned mung-bean sprouts—available in most supermarkets—do not have either the texture or flavor of fresh.

spuma [SPOO-muh] *see* SPOOM

spumante; *pl.* **spumanti** [spoo-MAHN-tay; spoo-MAHN-tee] Italian for "sparkling," as in wine. *See also* ASTI SPUMANTE; FRIZZANTE.

spumone; spumoni [spoo-MOH-nee (neh)] This frozen molded Italian dessert consists of two layers of ice cream (such as chocolate and vanilla) between which is sandwiched a layer of sweetened whipped cream that has been flavored with rum and mixed with toasted nuts and candied fruit. Sometimes the ice cream is lightened with whipped cream or beaten egg whites before being spooned into the mold. Spumoni is cut into slices and sometimes served with a sweet sauce that complements the ice cream flavors.

spun curd *see* PASTA FILATA

spun sugar Fine strands of hardened boiled sugar that are used to decorate various desserts. Spun sugar begins by cooking sugar, water and CREAM OF TARTAR to the HARD-CRACK STAGE. A fork or whisk is then used to dip into the sugar syrup and draw out fine threads. These hairlike strands can be placed directly on a dessert or on a waxed paper–lined surface, then transferred later to the dish. Once the spun sugar hardens, it may also be gathered and sprinkled or arranged on top of a dessert. COTTON CANDY is a popular form of spun sugar.

spur dog *see* DOGFISH

squab [SKWAHB] A young (about 4 weeks old) domesticated pigeon that has never flown and is therefore extremely tender. It was a popular special-occasion dish in Victorian England. Squabs usually weigh 1 pound or less and have delicately flavored dark meat. Fresh squab is available throughout the summer months (year-round in some regions) in gourmet markets. Frozen squab is marketed year-round. Choose fresh birds by their plump, firm appearance. Store as for CHICKEN. Likewise, squab can be prepared in any manner suitable for chicken. A classic method is to stuff and roast it.

squab chicken *see* CHICKEN; POUSSIN

squash [SKWAHSH] 1. The fruit of various members of the gourd family native to the Western Hemisphere. There is evidence of squash being eaten in Mexico as far back as 5500 B.C., and in South America over 2,000 years ago. Squash varies widely in size, shape and color. Generally, they're divided into two categories—*summer squash* and *winter squash*. **Summer squash** have thin, edible skins and soft seeds. The tender flesh has a high water content, a mild flavor and doesn't require long cooking. The most widely available varieties of summer squash are CROOKNECK, PAT-TYPAN and ZUCCHINI. Summer squash is best from early through late summer, although some varieties are available year-round in certain regions. Select the smaller specimens with bright-colored skin free of spots and bruises. Summer squash is very perishable and should be refrigerated in a plastic bag for no more than 5 days. It can be prepared by a variety of methods including steaming, baking, sautéing and deep-frying. Summer squash are high in vitamins A and C as well as niacin. **Winter squash** have hard, thick skins and seeds. The deep yellow to orange flesh is firmer than that of summer squash and therefore requires longer cooking. Winter squash varieties include ACORN, BUTTERCUP, BUTTERNUT, HUBBARD, SPAGHETTI and TURBAN. Though most varieties are available year-round, winter squash is best from early fall through the winter. Choose squash that are heavy for their size and have a hard, deep-colored rind free of blemishes or moldy spots. The hard skin of a winter squash protects the flesh and allows it to be stored longer than summer squash. It does not require refrigeration and can be kept in a cool, dark place for a month or more, depending on the variety. Once the seeds are removed, winter squash can be baked, steamed or simmered. They're a good source of iron, riboflavin and vitamins A (more than summer squash) and C. *See also* CALABAZA; CUSHAW;

DELICATA; GOLDEN NUGGET; KABOCHA; PUMPKIN; VEGETABLE MARROW; SQUASH BLOS-SOMS. 2. In Britain, squash is also a citrus-based soft drink.

squash blossoms The flowers from either summer or winter squash are edible and delicious. Squash blossoms come in varying shades of yellow and orange, with flavors that hint of the squash itself. They can be found from late spring through early fall in specialty produce markets as well as Italian, Latin and Filipino markets. Squash blossoms are naturally soft and somewhat limp, but choose those that look fresh, with closed buds. They're extremely perishable and should be stored in the refrigerator for no more than a day. Squash blossoms may be used as a garnish (whole or slivered) for almost everything from soups to main dishes. They also add color and flavor to salads. The most common method of cooking them is sautéing, often after coating the blossoms with a light batter. Squash blossoms are sometimes stuffed with ingredients such as soft cheese before being baked or batter-dipped and fried. They contain vitamins A and C, as well as iron and calcium. *See also* FLOWERS, EDIBLE.

squaw candy see SMOKED SALMON

squeakers Freshly made CURDS of CHEDDAR that are packaged and sold on the day they're made. Bite-sized, mild-flavored and randomly-shaped, squeakers were invented by Wisconsin cheesemakers and get their name from the fact that they squeak audibly when eaten. *See also* CHEESE.

squeteague [skwee-TEEG] *see* WEAKFISH

squid [SKWIHD] As a ten-armed member of the CEPHALOPOD class in the MOLLUSK family, squid is related to both the OCTOPUS and CUTTLEFISH. Squid meat has a firm, chewy texture and mild, somewhat sweet flavor. Also called *calamari,* squid can range in size from 1 inch to the seldom seen 80-foot behemoth of the deep. Smaller squid are marketed in fresh, frozen, canned, sun-dried and pickled forms. They are very popular in Asian and Mediterranean cuisines and can be found in ethnic markets and some supermarkets. When buying fresh squid choose those that are small and whole with clear eyes and an ocean-fresh fragrance. They should be refrigerated, airtight, for no more than a day or two. Squid can be pan-fried, baked, boiled, stir-fried or coated with batter and deep-fried. The cooking time should always be short, since the texture becomes rubbery when overcooked. Squid is used raw by the Japanese in SUSHI dishes. The ink can be extracted from the ink sacs and used to color preparations like PASTA or to flavor dishes such as *calamares en su tinta* ("squid in their ink"), a popular Spanish dish. Squid are rich in protein and phosphorus. *See also* SHELLFISH.

squidhound *see* STRIPED BASS

Sriracha sauce Thai hot sauce named after the seaside town of Si Racha, which is located along the Gulf of Thailand. The town's well known for its seafood, which is usually served with Sriracha sauce. The bright red sauce, a mixture of sun-ripened chiles, garlic, sugar, salt and vinegar, has the consistency of American KETCHUP. Sriracha sauce has become so popular that it's as ubiquitous on the Southeast Asian table as ketchup is on the American, and it's gaining popularity in a variety of other cuisines. Sriracha sauce found in most U.S. food outlets is made by an Ameican company, Huy Fong Foods, and differs from the traditional version found around Si Racha. The Thai version is thinner, sweeter and spicier. It contains no preservatives and must be refrigerated after opening. *See also* SAUCE.

stabilizers Additives used to help maintain emulsions or prevent degeneration in foods. Dextrin and gums like GUM ARABIC, GUM TRAGACANTH, GUAR GUM and XANTHAN GUM are commonly used stabilizers.

stagiaire [stah-zhee-EHR] A French term that essentially means "apprentice." Stagiaires are typically not paid; if they receive a salary, it's usually nominal.

stainless steel cookware *see* COOKWARE AND BAKEWARE MATERIALS

Stamp and Go A Caribbean mainstay of fried, battered codfish cakes, which can be variously flavored with ANNATTO, CHILES and onions.

standing rib roast *see* RIB ROAST

standing rump roast *see* ROUND

star anise A star-shaped, dark brown pod that contains a pea-size seed in each of its eight segments. Native to China, star anise comes from a small evergreen tree. Although the flavor of its seeds is derived from anethol (the same oil that gives ANISE seed its pronounced flavor), star anise has a different heritage—the magnolia family. Its flavor is slightly more bitter than that of regular anise seed. In Asian cuisines, star anise is a commonly used spice and tea flavoring. It's also widely used to flavor LIQUEURS and baked goods in Western cultures. It can be found whole in Asian markets and some supermarkets, and as a ground ingredient in Chinese FIVE-SPICE POWDER.

star fruit When cut crosswise, this showy fruit has a striking star shape, which gives it its name. Also called *carambola,* this fruit favors tropical climates and thrives in Caribbean countries, Hawaii, Central and South America and parts of Asia. The star fruit ranges from 3 to 5 inches long and is easy to identify by the five definitive ribs that traverse its length. Its thin skin is a glossy golden yellow, its matching flesh beautifully translucent and dotted occasionally with a dark seed. When ripe, the star fruit is exceedingly juicy and fragrant. Its flavor, depending on the variety, can range from exotically sweet to refreshingly tart. In general, the broader set the ribs, the sweeter the fruit. Star fruit is available year-round in some locales but is at its prime from summer's end to late winter. Choose firm fruit that has a bright, even color. Those with greening on the ribs may be ripened at room temperature. Use ripe star fruit within a few days or store, wrapped tightly in a plastic bag, in the refrigerator for up to a week. Star fruit, which do not require peeling, are delicious eaten out of hand, or used in salads, desserts or as a garnish.

starter; starter culture In the world of cheese, a starter, also known as a *bacterial culture* or *starter culture,* typically consists of enzymes or other microorganisms, bacterial or mold spores, LACTIC ACID (sometimes from the previous day's milk or WHEY) and natural elements. Two types of cultures are used: thermophilic cultures work best at temperatures over 100°F and mesophilic cultures function at temperatures between 70° and 100°F. Starters work by converting the milk's LACTOSE (milk sugar) into lactic acid. This is done to balance the milk's acidity (pH level) so the CASEIN (milk protein) will more readily COAGULATE into a CURD when RENNET is added. The type of starter contributes to a cheese's flavor, texture and other characteristics, depending on the style of cheese. For instance, *Penicillium roqueforti* in a ROQUEFORT starter produces this cheese's distinctive blue veins; *Propionibacter shermanii* is added to the starter for EMMENTAL to create its characteristic EYES; and *Penicillium candidum* or *Penicillium camemberti* in the starter of BRIE and CAMEMBERT is what makes such cheeses ripen from the outside in, rather than vice versa. *See also* YEAST STARTER.

station chef *see* BRIGADE SYSTEM

Stayman Winesap apple This all-purpose apple is a cross between the RED DELICIOUS and WINESAP varieties. Its yellow skin is almost covered with red stripes. The juicy, crisp flesh is aromatic and slightly tart. *See also* APPLE.

steak and kidney pie A traditional British dish consisting of a cooked mixture of chopped beef, kidneys, mushrooms, onions and beef stock. This mixture is placed in a pie or casserole dish, covered with a pastry crust and baked until crisp and brown. Sometimes potatoes, hard-cooked eggs or oysters are also added to the dish.

steak au poivre [oh PWAHV-rh] Steak that is covered with coarsely ground pepper before being sautéed or broiled. Steak au poivre is usually finished either by topping it with a chunk of sweet butter or by making a simple sauce from the pan drippings. Elaborate presentations often call for flaming (*see* FLAMBÉ) the steak with BRANDY. Also called *pepper steak*.

steak fries *see* FRENCH FRIES

steak tartare *see* BEEF TARTARE

steam, to Cooking method whereby food is placed on a rack or in a special steamer basket over boiling or simmering water in a covered pan. Steaming does a better job than boiling or poaching of retaining a food's flavor, shape, texture and many of the nutrients.

steamed bread BOSTON BROWN BREAD is probably the most famous steamed bread in the United States. This type of bread is made by placing a batter in a covered container on a rack set over gently boiling water in a large pot. The pot is covered and the bread steamed for about 3 hours. It can also be made in a pressure cooker in about half the time. The bread doesn't require a special container in which to be steamed—a 12-ounce coffee can covered with aluminum foil works nicely. The characteristic texture of steamed breads is moist and tender.

steamed buns A slightly sweet Chinese yeast bun that's baked in a bamboo steamer. The result is a soft, puffy, white bun with a slightly shiny surface. Steamed buns are served with many Chinese dishes and are a staple of the DIM SUM repertoire.

steamed pudding A sweet or savory pudding that is cooked (usually in a special STEAMED-PUDDING MOLD) on a rack over boiling water in a covered pot. The pudding mold is usually decorative so that when the finished pudding (which is firm) is unmolded it retains its decorative shape. Steamed puddings can take up to 3 hours to cook on stovetop, half that time in a pressure cooker. They're customarily served with a sauce. The traditional Christmas PLUM PUDDING, for instance, is customarily accompanied with HARD SAUCE.

steamed-pudding mold Although STEAMED PUDDING can be cooked in a variety of containers, there are special steamed-pudding molds with decorative sides and bottom, as well as a lid that clamps tightly shut. Many molds also have a central tube (like an angel-food cake pan) that provides more even heat distribution, thereby cooking the pudding more evenly.

steamer clam East Coast soft-shell clam with a thin, brittle shell that doesn't close entirely due to the long, rubbery neck (siphon) extending from the body. Steamers are the smallest of the Atlantic soft-shell variety. They are, as their name indicates, delicious steamed. They're also suitable for batter-dipping and frying. *See also* CLAM.

steaming; steamer Cooking method whereby food is placed on a rack or in a special steamer basket over simmering water in a covered pan. Steaming does a better job than boiling or poaching of retaining a food's flavor, shape, texture and many of the nutrients. Special **steamer** inserts can be purchased for almost any saucepan. There are also asparagus steamers, which are about 8 inches tall and specifically designed for this vegetable. However you steam food, make sure the pan has a tight-fitting lid to retain the moisture.

steel *see* SHARPENING STEEL; STAINLESS STEEL COOKWARE

steel-clad *see* KNIFE

steelground *see* FLOUR

steep To soak dry ingredients such as tea leaves, ground coffee, herbs, spices, etc. in liquid (usually hot) until the flavor is infused into the liquid. *See also* INFUSION.

Steinpilze *see* PORCINO

stelline *see* Pasta Glossary, page 883

sterlet caviar *see* CAVIAR

stevia [STEE-vee-ah] Also known as *sweetleaf* or *sugarleaf*, this plant is native to Central and South America and now cultivated in other parts of the world as a natural sweetener. The extract from stevia has up to 400 times the sweetness of sugar (depending on the quality of the plant) and contains no calories. Proponents feel it's ideal for people suffering from hypoglycemia and diabetes. Inhabitants of Central and South America have used it for centuries, and Japan has used it commercially as a sweetener for almost 30 years without issue. Nevertheless, it's banned as a food ADDITIVE in a number of countries, including the United States, because of safety concerns. It can, however, be purchased at health food stores as a supplement and is available in liquid extract and powdered form and as fresh or dried leaves.

stew *n.* Any dish that is prepared by stewing. The term is most often applied to dishes that contain meat, vegetables and a thick soup-like broth resulting from a combination of the stewing liquid and the natural juices of the food being stewed. **stew** *v.* A method of cooking by which food is barely covered with liquid and simmered slowly for a long period of time in a tightly covered pot. Stewing not only tenderizes tough pieces of meat but also allows the flavors of the ingredients to blend deliciously.

stewing chicken *see* CHICKEN

sticky rice *see* RICE

stifado [stee-FAH-doh] A casserole-baked Greek stew made with meat (beef or lamb), tomatoes, pearl onions, white wine, garlic, cinnamon and oregano.

still *see* DISTILLATION

still wine *see* WINE

Stilton [STIHL-tn] This marvelous BLUE CHEESE is the English contender for "King of Cheeses." It ranks as one of the top three blues in the world, along with GORGONZOLA and ROQUEFORT. Although it is made in parts of Leicestershire, Derbyshire and Nottinghamshire, it received its name in the 18th century because it was first sold in the small village of Stilton in Huntingdonshire. Intriguingly, no Stilton is made in Stilton. It never has been, and now legally cannot be, because the village is not in one of the approved shires. Stilton is made from whole cow's milk and allowed to ripen for 2 to 4 months, during which time it is skewered numerous times to encourage the growth of *Pencillium roqueforti* mold (also present in ROQUEFORT CHEESE). This process creates a pale yellow interior with blue-green veins. The texture is rich and creamy (45 percent fat) but slightly crumbly. The flavor is rich, creamy and savory with the pungency of blue cheese. Stilton is sold in tall cylinders with a crusty brownish-gray rind. In addition to this better-known blue version, there is also a **white Stilton** that isn't exposed to *Pencillium roqueforti* and therefore doesn't develop the blue veining. It has a mild and slightly sour flavor. Stilton is at its best eaten by itself with a glass of PORT or a full-bodied dry red wine. Stilton has a FAT CONTENT of about 48 percent. *See also* CHEESE.

stinger A COCKTAIL classically made with equal parts BRANDY or COGNAC and white CRÈME DE MENTHE. Other stinger versions can be made substituting another spirit or LIQUEUR for the brandy or cognac, but the white crème de menthe is intrinsic to the drink.

stinging nettles *see* NETTLES

stinky tofu A dish of fermented tofu that's popular in a number of Asian countries. The name comes from the overwhelming smell, which has been compared to an intense LIMBURGER cheese, rotting garbage, manure or another Asian favorite, fresh DURIAN. Stinky tofu is prepared by fermenting it in a brine of any number of fermented ingredients including AMARANTH greens, BAMBOO SHOOTS, garlic, meat, mustard greens, onions, shrimp, soy milk and various other vegetables. The brine can take several months or more to reach the correct stage. Enthusiasts claim that, once you get past the smell, stinky tofu has a mild taste and a velvety, custard-like texture. Of course the longer it's fermented in the brine the stronger the smell and taste, like a strong-smelling cheese such as ÉPOISSES DE

BOURGOGNE—the longer it ages the stronger smelling and more pungently flavored it becomes. Stinky tofu is usually fried or deep-fried but can be steamed or stewed and is usually served with a spicy chili sauce. Stinky tofu is also known as *smelly tofu* or by its Chinese name, *chou dofu* or *chou doufu*.

stir-fry *n.* Any dish of food that has been prepared by the stir-fry method. **stir-fry** *v.* To quickly fry small pieces of food in a large pan over very high heat while constantly and briskly stirring the food. This cooking technique, which is associated with Asian cooking and the WOK, requires a minimum amount of fat and results in food that is crisply tender.

stock In the most basic terms, stock is the strained liquid that is the result of cooking vegetables, meat or fish and other seasoning ingredients in water. A **brown stock** is made by browning bones, vegetables and other ingredients before they're cooked in the liquid. Most soups begin with a stock of some kind, and many sauces are based on REDUCED stocks.

stollen [STOH-luhn; SHTOH-luhn] Germany's traditional Christmas yeast bread, stollen is a rich, dried fruit–filled loaf that's often topped with a powdered sugar icing and decorated with candied cherries. It's shaped like a folded oval and somewhat resembles a giant PARKER HOUSE ROLL.

stone crab *see* CRAB

stone fruit *see* DRUPE

stone-ground flour *see* FLOUR

stoneware *see* COOKWARE AND BAKEWARE MATERIALS

stout [STOWT] A strong, dark beer that originated in the British Isles. **Dry stout or Irish stout** has a hoppier (*see* HOPS) character and is less malty (*see* MALT). American versions are often made with a combination of pale malt and dark-roasted *unmalted* barley, while European stouts are generally made totally with malted barley. **Guinness** is the most famous of the dry stouts. **Sweet stout**, an English version, is less bitter and often lower in alcohol. Some are referred to as **milk stouts** because of their slightly lactic flavor. **Oatmeal stout** is a style of sweet stout that uses oatmeal, which adds a silky-smooth mouth feel. **Russian** (or **Imperial**) **stout** was originally a very strong-flavored, high-alcohol brew produced in Britain from the late 1700s until the early 1900s for export to Russia. Modern versions—also strongly flavored and high in alcohol—are unpasteurized, cask-aged for 2 months and bottle-aged for a year. *See also* BEER.

stovetop smoker Clever cookware that allows food to be smoked indoors without setting off the smoke alarm. This low-fat style of cooking delivers succulent, smoky food even on rainy days. The stovetop smoker is 15 × 11 × 3½ inches, made of heavy-gauge stainless steel and features storage-friendly retractable handles, drip tray, rack and slide-on cover. Included with the set are several types of finely cut wood chips, ranging in flavor from mesquite to hickory. A spoonful of the wood chips is placed in the center of the pan, topped by the drip tray and rack, on which the food is placed. The cover slides on and the pan is placed over high heat. As soon as a puff of smoke sneaks out between pan and cover, the heat is reduced and the food cooks according to the manufacturer's instructions. This cooking method delivers smoky flavors to everything from meat to fish to tofu to vegetables—corn on the cob is never better. The stovetop smoker can accommodate whole chickens and hams simply by tightly tenting the pan with heavy-duty foil.

stracchino [straht-CHEE-noh] A large family of typically soft, square-shaped cheeses made throughout Italy's Lombardy region since at least the 10th century. The term comes from the word *stracch*, which is Lombardian dialect for "tired" or "exhausted," referring to the weary cows after their lengthy trek down from the alpine meadows to the valleys where they could be milked. That long journey concentrated the milk, making it more acidic and richer than that of cows that had grazed only on the plains. Numerous cheeses start or end their names with stracchino, but others that fit into this category don't. Well-known cheeses in this family include CRESCENZA, TALEGGIO and ROBIOLA. *See also* CHEESE.

stracciatella [STRAHT-chah-TEHL-lah] 1. Italy's answer to EGG DROP soup, popular in Rome and other parts of central Italy. Eggs mixed with grated PARMESAN, pepper, salt and sometimes SEMOLINA and nutmeg are stirred into boiling broth. The swirled, cooked eggs form raglike strands in the broth (*straccio* is Italian for "rag"). 2. Plain or vanilla ice cream or GELATO with chocolate bits or shavings dispersed throughout.

straight up; straight A term used to describe COCKTAILS that are served without ice.

strain 1. To pour a liquid or dry ingredient through a SIEVE, STRAINER or CHEESECLOTH to remove undesirable particles. 2. To press soft food through the holes of a sieve, which results in a puréed texture. Food for infants or those on special diets is sometimes processed this way.

strained yogurt *see* GREEK YOGURT

strainer A kitchen utensil with a perforated or mesh bottom used to strain liquids or semiliquids, or to sift dry ingredients such as flour or powdered sugar. Strainers, also called *sieves,* come in a variety of sizes, shapes and mesh densities. There are flat-bottomed, drum-shaped strainers with interchangeable meshes of different coarseness, as well as those that are bowl-shaped or conical. Strainers are made of various materials including stainless steel, tinned steel and aluminum. The better ones have strong handles and frames and contain hooks for resting the strainer on top of pots or bowls.

strawberries Romanoff This deliciously decadent dessert is made by soaking strawberries in orange juice and CURAÇAO or COINTREAU, then serving them topped with whipped cream. It's one of many dishes named after the Russian royal family by French chefs.

strawberry Sixteenth-century author William Butler wrote this tribute to the strawberry: "Doubtless God could have made a better berry, but doubtless God never did." Red, juicy and conically shaped, the strawberry is a member of the rose family and has grown wild for centuries in both the Americas and Europe. The Romans valued the fruit for its reputed therapeutic powers for everything from loose teeth to gastritis. However, it wasn't until the late 13th century that the plant was first cultivated. The most common American variety is the result of several centuries of crossbreeding of the wild Virginia strawberry (North America's main native strawberry) and a Chilean variety. It's probably today's most hardy berry and is able to withstand both shipping and storage. More flavorful, however, are European Alpine strawberries—the tiny, exquisitely sweet wild strawberries of France known as *fraises des bois* ("strawberries of the woods"). They're considered by many to be the "queen of strawberries." Strawberries vary in size, shape and color (some are off-white or yellowish). In general, the flavor of the smaller berries is better than that of the larger varieties since the latter are often watery. Fresh strawberries are available year-round in many regions of the country, with the peak season from April to September, again depending on the locale. Choose brightly colored, plump berries that still have their green caps attached and which are uniform in size. Avoid soft, shriveled or moldy berries. Do not wash until ready to use, and store (preferably in a single layer on a paper towel) in a moistureproof container in the refrigerator for 2 to 3 days. Fresh strawberries are wonderful eaten with cream, macerated in wine or LIQUEUR or used in various desserts. Canned and frozen strawberries are also available. Commercial strawberry products include preserves, jams, jellies, syrups and various desserts. Strawberries are an excellent source of vitamin C and also provide some potassium and iron.

strawberry huller An oversized tweezer-like device used for removing the green stems from strawberries. Its tweezer-like capabilities can be used for other kitchen tasks as well.

strawberry shortcake *see* SHORTCAKE

straw mushroom Popular in Asian cooking, straw mushrooms are so named because they're grown on straw that's been used in a paddy. This musty, earthy growing medium contributes its distinct nuances to this mushroom's flavor. Tiny (about 1 to 1½ inches in diameter) and coolie-shaped, straw mushrooms range in color from pale tan when young to dark charcoal gray when mature. Fresh specimens of this cultivated mushroom can sometimes be found in specialty produce markets. More readily available are canned straw mushrooms, which are found in Asian markets. Also known as paddy straw mushrooms and grass mushrooms. *See also* MUSHROOMS.

straw potatoes Potatoes cut into very thin, long sticks and then deep-fried.

Strega [STRAY-guh] Italian for "witch." This LIQUEUR has a refreshing floral-herb flavor, a brilliant, shimmering yellow-green color, and is made from over 70 herbs. It's also called *Liquore Strega*.

stretched curd cheese *see* PASTA FILATA

streusel [STROO-zuhl; SHTROY-zuhl] A crumbly topping consisting of flour, sugar, butter and various spices that is sprinkled on coffeecakes, breads, muffins and cakes. The word *streusel* is German for "sprinkle" or "strew."

string bean *see* GREEN BEAN

string cheese A PASTA FILATA cheese (such as MOZZARELLA) that has been stretched into a long, thin strand, then stacked in switchback fashion before being packaged. Also called *Syrian* or *Armenian string cheese*, this popular edible is mild flavored and chewy. Kids young and old love to pull off the strings and eat it out of hand. *See also* CHEESE.

strip steak *see* NEW YORK STEAK

striped bass From the Atlantic coast, this true BASS is also called *striper, greenhead, squidhound* and, in the Chesapeake Bay region, *rockfish* (not to be confused with the species ROCKFISH). The striped bass is anadromous, meaning that it migrates from a saltwater habitat to spawn in fresh water. It can range in size from 2 to 70 pounds, though market weight is usually between 2 and 15 pounds. The striped bass is olive green fading to silver, and has 6 to 8 longitudinal black stripes. It has a moderately fat, firm-textured flesh with a mild, sweet flavor. Striped bass can be prepared in a variety of ways including broiling, grilling, poaching and steaming. Both **white bass** and **yellow bass** are freshwater members of the striped bass family. *See also* FISH.

stroganoff [STRAW-guh-noff; STROH-guh-noff] Named after 19th-century Russian diplomat Count Paul Stroganov, this dish consists of thin slices of tender beef (usually TENDERLOIN or TOP LOIN), onions and mushrooms, all sautéed in butter and combined with a sour-cream sauce. Stroganoff is usually accompanied by RICE PILAF.

stromboli [strahm-BOH-lee] A specialty of Philadelphia, a stromboli is a CALZONElike enclosed sandwich of cheese (usually MOZZARELLA) and PEPPERONI (or other meat) wrapped in pizza dough.

strudel [STROOD-l; SHTROO-duhl] German for "whirlpool" or "eddy," *strudel* is a type of pastry made up of many layers of very thin dough spread with a filling, then rolled and baked until crisp and golden brown. It's particularly popular in Germany, Austria and much of central Europe. The paper-thin *strudel* dough resembles PHYLLO and is equally difficult to handle. Apple strudel is probably the most famous of this genre, but the filling variations are limitless and can be savory or sweet.

stuck onion *see* ONION PIQUÉ

stud *v.* Culinarily, "stud" means to insert flavor-enhancing or decorative edible items (such as whole cloves, slivered almonds or garlic slivers) partway into the surface of a food so that they protrude slightly. For example, hams are often studded with cloves.

stuffed egg A hard-cooked egg that has been cut in half lengthwise and the yolk removed, mashed and mixed with any of various flavorings, such as minced fresh herbs, WORCESTERSHIRE SAUCE, mustard, CURRY POWDER, and so on. Other finely chopped ingredients including chives, toasted nuts, bell peppers, chutney, and so forth, may be added. Enough mayonnaise or sour cream is blended into the mixture to make it soft and moist. This mixture is spooned back into the egg-white halves, the top garnished with a sprinkle of paprika. Adding CAYENNE PEPPER or a hot sauce like TABASCO PEPPER makes it a **deviled egg**.

stuffing A mixture used to stuff poultry, fish, meat and some vegetables. It can be cooked separately or in the food in which it is stuffed. Stuffings (also called *dressings*) are usually well seasoned and based on breadcrumbs or cubes, though rice, potatoes, herb mixtures or other foods may also be used.

sturgeon [STER-juhn] A large migratory fish known for its delicious flesh, excellent ROE (the true CAVIAR) and ISINGLASS. This prized fish was so favored by England's King Edward II that he gave it royal status, which meant that all sturgeon caught had to be offered to the king. Sturgeon are anadromous, meaning that they migrate from their saltwater habitat to spawn in fresh water. Their average weight is 60 pounds but gargantuan specimens can reach over 3,000 pounds. The sturgeon's long, thin body is pale gray and has large scales. Its rich, high-fat flesh has a fresh, delicate flavor and is so firm that it's almost meatlike. Sturgeon are fished in the Black and Caspian Seas and in the United States, mainly in the Pacific Northwest and along the Southern Atlantic. The best U.S. variety is the **white sturgeon**, and the smaller specimens are considered the best eating. Fresh sturgeon comes whole (up to about 8 pounds), in steaks or in chunks. It can be braised, grilled, broiled, sautéed or baked. The supply of this fish in its fresh form, however, is limited and most of that caught in U.S. waters is smoked. Frozen and canned (pickled or smoked) forms are also available. *See also* FISH.

su [SOO] Japanese rice vinegar. The mild and slightly sweet su may be used variously, such as a dressing for SUNOMONO (vinegared food) and other foods, for seasoning, in ACIDULATED WATER to retain color in vegetables and in SUSHI MESHI, the rice used for SUSHI dishes. It's available in Asian markets and most larger supermakets.

sub gum A general Chinese-cookery descriptor for dishes (such as WON TON or noodles) that are cooked or garnished with a medley of poultry, meat and fish, or with a mélange of vegetables.

submarine sandwich *see* HERO SANDWICH

substitute cheese A product produced with imitation milks or other nondairy components (such as SOY MILK) and vegetable oil replacing the butterfat. Also called *analog cheeses*, such substitutes are LACTOSE-free and lower in fat but lack any likeness to the flavor and texture of real cheese. *See also* IMITATION CHEESE; PROCESSED CHEESE.

substitutions *see* Substituting Ingredients, page 854; Pan Substitution Chart, page 859.

succory *see* CHICORY

succotash [SUHK-uh-tash] This southern United States favorite is a cooked dish of lima beans, corn kernels and sometimes chopped red and green sweet peppers. The name is taken from the Naragansett Indian word *msickquatash*, "boiled whole kernels of corn."

Sucralose An ARTIFICIAL SWEETENER that's about 600 times sweeter than sugar. Its trade name is *Splenda*. This crystalline, free-flowing sweetener is both water soluble and stable, making it appropriate for a broad range of foods and beverages. *See also* ACESULFAME-K; ALITAME; ASPARTAME; SACCHARIN.

sucrose [SOO-krohs] A crystalline, water-soluble sugar obtained from sugarcane, sugar beets and SORGHUM. Sucrose also forms the greater part of MAPLE SUGAR. It's sweeter than GLUCOSE but not as sweet as FRUCTOSE. *See also* SUGAR.

suet [SOO-iht] Found in beef, sheep and other animals, suet is the solid white fat found around the kidneys and loins. Many British recipes call for it to lend richness to pastries, puddings, stuffings and MINCEMEATS. Suet was once widely used to make tallow candles.

sugar Once a luxury only the extremely affluent could afford, sugar was called "white gold" because it was so scarce and expensive. Although Persia and ancient Arabia were cultivating sugar in the 4th century B.C., the Western World didn't know of it until the 8th century when the Moors conquered the Iberian peninsula. Early sugar wasn't the granulated, alabaster substance most of us know today. Instead, it came in the form of large, solid loaves or blocks ranging in color from off-white to light brown. Chunks of this rock-hard substance had to be chiseled off and ground to a powder with a MORTAR AND PESTLE. Modern-day sugar is no longer scarce or expensive and comes in myriad forms from many origins. Sugarcane and sugar beets are the sources of most of today's sugar, also known as SUCROSE (which also comes from maple sap—*see* MAPLE SUGAR— and SORGHUM). Other common forms of sugar are DEXTROSE (grape or corn sugar), FRUCTOSE (levulose), LACTOSE (milk sugar) and MALTOSE (malt sugar). The uses for sugar are countless. Besides its sweetening value, sugar adds tenderness to doughs, stability to mixtures such as beaten egg whites for MERINGUE, golden-brown surfaces to baked goods and, in sufficient quantity, it contributes to the preservation of some foods. **Granulated** or **white sugar** is highly refined cane or beet sugar. This free-flowing sweetener is the most common form both for table use and for cooking. Granulated sugar is also available in cubes or tablets of various sizes, as well as a variety of textures. **Superfine sugar**, known in Britain as **castor** (or *caster*) **sugar**, is more finely granulated. Because it dissolves almost instantly, superfine sugar is perfect for making meringues and sweetening cold liquids. It can be substituted for regular granulated sugar cup for cup. **Powdered** or **confectioners' sugar** is granulated sugar that has been crushed into a fine powder. To prevent clumping, a small amount (about 3 percent) of CORNSTARCH is added. Powdered sugar must generally be sifted before using. Because it dissolves so readily, it's often used to make icings and candy. It's also used decoratively, as a fine dusting on desserts. One and three-quarters (packed) cups powdered sugar equals 1 cup granulated sugar. Powdered sugar is called *icing sugar* in Britain and *sucre glace* in France. **Decorating** or **coarse sugar** (also called *sugar crystals* or *crystal sugar*) has granules about four times larger than those of regular granulated sugar. It's used for decorating baked goods and can be found in cake-decorating supply shops and gourmet markets. ROCK CANDY is an even larger form of sugar crystals. **Colored sugar**, also used for decorating, is tinted granulated sugar and can be found in several crystal sizes. **Flavored sugar** is granulated sugar that's been combined or scented with various ingredients such as cinnamon or vanilla (*see* VANILLA SUGAR). *All granulated sugar can be stored indefinitely if tightly sealed and kept in a cool, dry place.* Today's **brown sugar** is white sugar combined with MOLASSES, which gives it a soft texture. The two most commonly marketed styles of brown sugar are *light* and *dark,* with some manufacturers providing variations in between. In general, the lighter the brown sugar, the more delicate the flavor. The very dark or "old-fashioned" style has a more intense molasses flavor. Brown sugar is usually sold in 1-pound boxes or plastic bags—the latter help the sugar retain its moisture and keep it soft. Hardened brown sugar can be resoftened by placing it with an apple wedge in a plastic bag and sealing tightly for 1 to 2 days. A firmly packed cup of brown sugar may be substituted for 1 cup granulated sugar. Both free-pouring and liquid brown sugar are also now available. Neither of these forms should be substituted for regular brown sugar in recipes. Though similar in color, brown sugar should not be confused with **raw sugar**, the residue left after sugarcane has been processed to remove the molasses and refine the sugar crystals. The flavor of raw sugar is akin to that of brown sugar. In this raw state, however, sugar may contain contaminants such as molds and fibers. The so-called raw sugar marketed in the United States has been purified, negating much of what is thought to be its superior nutritive value. Two popular types of raw sugar are the coarse-textured dry **Demerara sugar** from the Demerara area of Guyana, and the moist, fine-textured **Barbados sugar**. **Turbinado sugar** is raw sugar that has been steam-cleaned. The coarse turbinado crystals are blond colored and have a delicate molasses flavor. Other sources of sugar include maple sap, palm sap and sorghum. Almost 100 percent of sugar is carbohydrate. Granulated white sugar contains about 770 calories per cup, as does the same weight (which equals about 2 cups) of powdered sugar. A cup of brown sugar is slightly higher at 820 calories. It also contains 187 milligrams of calcium, 56 of phosphorous, 4.8 of iron, 757 of potassium and 97 of sodium, compared to only scant traces of those nutrients found in granulated sugar. ARTIFICIAL SWEETENERS such as ASPARTAME and SACCHARIN are essentially calorie-free and are used as a sugar substitute both commercially and by the home cook. Sugar also comes in syrup form, the most common being CANE SYRUP, CORN SYRUP, GOLDEN SYRUP, HONEY, MAPLE SYRUP, MOLASSES, SORGHUM and TREACLE. *See also* GLUCOSE; INVERT SUGAR; JAGGERY; PULLED SUGAR; ROCK SUGAR; SPUN SUGAR.

sugar apple *see* SWEETSOP

sugarcane stalks Hailing from Hawaii, packaged sugarcane stalks are now sold in some specialty produce markets. Also called sugarcane *batons* and *sticks,* these stalks have been boiled to make them edible.

They should be stored, tightly wrapped, in the refrigerator. Though sweet, sugarcane contains only about one-fifth the amount of sugar found in most candies. It's generally used as a snack or garnish. To use, strip the light brown skin away from the white flesh, then cut into chunks or strips.

sugarleaf *see* STEVIA

sugar loaf A type of DELICATA SQUASH that's slightly smaller in size, generally 4 to 8 inches in length, with cream- to tan-colored skin. The flesh is mild, nutty and sweet. Its peak season is from late summer through late fall. Choose squash that are heavy for their size; avoid those with soft spots. Sugar loaf squash can be stored up to 3 weeks at an average room temperature. As with other winter squash, the sugar loaf is best baked or steamed. It's a good source of potassium, iron and vitamins A and C. *See also* SQUASH.

sugar pea *see* SUGAR SNAP PEA

sugarplum A small confection, often consisting of fruit such as a candied cherry or dried apricot surrounded by FONDANT.

sugar snap pea Also called *sugar pea,* this sweet pea is a cross between the ENGLISH PEA and the SNOW PEA. It's entirely edible—pod and all. Sugar snap peas are available year-round. Choose plump, crisp pods with a bright green color. Refrigerate in a plastic bag for up to 3 days. Sugar snap peas should be served raw or only briefly cooked in order to retain their crisp texture. *See also* PEA.

sugar substitutes *see* ARTIFICIAL SWEETENERS; XYLITOL

sugar syrup Also called *simple syrup*, *gomme syrup* and *sirop de gomme,* sugar syrup is a solution of sugar and water that is cooked over low heat until clear, then boiled for a minute or so. Sugar syrup can be made in various densities—thin (3 parts water to 1 part sugar), medium (2 parts water to 1 part sugar) and heavy (equal parts water and sugar). Depending on the thickness, sugar syrups have various uses including soaking cakes (such as BABAS), glazing baked goods, poaching or preserving fruit, adding to frostings, etc. Sugar syrups are the basis for most candies and can be flavored with a variety of EXTRACTS, juices, LIQUEURS, etc. *See also* CARAMEL; CANDY.

suimono [soo-ee-MOH-noh] *see* SHIRUMONO

sukgat *see* CHRYSANTHEMUM LEAVES

sukiyaki [soo-kee-YAH-kee; skee-YAH-kee] Known in Japan as the "friendship dish" because it appeals to foreigners, sukiyaki consists of STIR-FRIED bite-size pieces of meat, vegetables and sometimes noodles and TOFU. It's flavored with SOY SAUCE, DASHI (or other broth) and MIRIN and is usually prepared at the table. Before eating each bite, diners dip their cooked food into beaten raw egg.

sulemani namak *see* BLACK SALT

sulfites [SUHL-fites] The salts of sulfurous acid, which may be used in food processing for any of various reasons, including the deterrence of insects and diseases, inhibiting bacterial growth and preventing spoilage or oxidation. Sulfites, which may be added as a preservative to packaged and processed foods, can cause severe allergic reactions (such as hives, shortness of breath and even anaphylactic shock) in certain individuals. For that reason, in 1986 the Food and Drug Administration prohibited their use on "fresh fruits and vegetables intended to be sold or served raw to consumers." In the United States, the words "Contains Sulfites" (or similar verbiage) are mandatory on labels of foods that include sulfites.

sultana [suhl-TAN-uh] Originating in Smyrna, Turkey, this small, pale golden-green grape was once used to make wine. Today, however, it's cultivated primarily for raisins. Its offspring in the United States is known as the Thompson seedless grape. *See also* RAISIN.

sumac; sumaq [SOO-mak] The brick- to dark purple–red berries of a decorative bush that grows wild throughout the Middle East and in parts of Italy. Sumac, which is sold ground or in its dried-berry form, has a pleasantly fruity, astringent taste that complements everything from fish to meat to vegetables. Sumac can be found in Middle Eastern markets. *See also* SPICES.

summer cauliflower *see* ROMANESCA

summer coating *see* CONFECTIONERY COATING

summer oyster mushroom *see* OYSTER MUSHROOM

summer pudding This classic English dessert consists of sweetened fresh berries and often red CURRANTS that are briefly cooked, then cooled before being placed in a bread-lined casserole dish. The fruit is topped with additional slices of bread, covered with a plate and weighted overnight in the refrigerator. The cold dessert is unmolded and served with whipped cream.

summer sausage Any dried or smoked SAUSAGE that can be kept without benefit of refrigeration.

summer squash *see* SQUASH

Sumo *see* DEKOPON

sunchoke Though also called a *Jerusalem artichoke,* this vegetable is not truly an artichoke but a variety of sunflower with a lumpy, brown-skinned tuber that often resembles a gingerroot. It also has nothing to do with Jerusalem—that moniker actually comes from the Italian word for sunflower, *girasole.* The white flesh of this vegetable is nutty, sweet and crunchy. Sunchokes are available year-round but best from about October to March. Select those that are firm and fresh-looking and not soft or wrinkled. Handle carefully, as sunchokes easily bruise. Store in a plastic bag in the refrigerator for up to a week. After that, they will begin to wither because of moisture loss. They may be peeled or, because the skin is very thin and quite nutritious, simply washed well before being used. Sunchokes can be eaten raw in salads or cooked by boiling or steaming and served as a side dish. They also make a delicious soup. Aluminum or iron pans will cause this tuber to turn an unappetizing pale gray. In France, the sunchoke is known as *topinambou,* and in Italy as *girasole articiocco.*

sundae One to three scoops of ice cream, topped with one or more sweet sauces and various other ingredients including fruit, nuts and whipped cream. The sundae is said to have originated in the late 19th century because moralists decried the consumption of carbonated soda on Sunday . . . even in the popular weekend treat, ice-cream sodas. The noncorruptive "dry" version of that treat was ice cream topped with syrup and named after the day on which soda was banned. The spelling of this frozen confection was changed to "sundae" so as not to be sacrilegious.

sun-dried tomatoes *see* TOMATO

sunfish Any of a large variety of North American freshwater fish noted for their interesting shapes and bright colors. Members of this family include largemouth, smallmouth, redeye, rock and spotted BASS, and both the white and black CRAPPIE. *See also* FISH.

sunflower seed The showy sunflower, with its bright yellow petals radiating from a dark hub of seeds, can reach up to 12 inches in diameter. This tall, rangy plant is thought to be so named because its flowers resemble the sun, and because they twist on their stems to follow the sun throughout the day. Sunflowers were cultivated by the Indians of the Americas long before Europeans discovered them. Today, the Russians are one of the largest sunflower seed producers in the world. Though it's the state flower of Kansas, the largest United States sunflower producers are California, Minnesota and North Dakota. The seeds have a hard black-and-white striped shell that must be removed. Sunflower seeds can be dried or roasted (either in or out of the shell), and are sold either plain or salted. They can be eaten as a snack, used in salads or sandwiches or added to a variety of cooked dishes or baked goods. The iron-rich sunflower seeds are, by weight, 47 percent fat and 24 percent protein.

sunflower-seed oil Extracted from sunflower seeds, this pale yellow, delicately flavored oil is very high in polyunsaturated fat and low in saturated fat. Though it has a relatively low SMOKE POINT, sunflower-seed oil is used in cooking as well as for salad dressings. *See also* FATS AND OILS.

sunomono [SOO-noh-moh-noh] Japanese for "vinegared things," with a meaning similar to a salad. Sunomono ingredients may be raw or cooked and include items like broccoli, cabbage, carrots, cauliflower, celery, cucumber, daikon, lettuce, mushrooms, onions, pea pods, spinach, string beans, seaweed and sometimes seafood, meat or poultry. The saladlike ingredients are coated with vinegar that's usually sweetened with sugar and flavored with various seasonings. *See also* AEMONO.

superfine sugar *see* SUGAR

suppli [SOO-plee] An Italian-style CROQUETTE made with RISOTTO (or other cooked rice) that has been bound with beaten egg, then shaped around a filling of cheese (though meat or various vegetables may be used). The croquette is then dipped in beaten egg, rolled in breadcrumbs and fried until crisp and heated through.

suprême; supreme *n.* Term used to describe food that's been processed so only the flesh is left. With a chicken or fish, this would require removal of the skin and bones, leaving only the flesh. With an orange the resulting separated orange segments would have the skin, pith, membrane and seeds all removed. *Suprême de volaille* is a dish using a boneless, skinless chicken breast. **supreme** *v.* To prepare food in such a way, leaving only the flesh.

supreme sauce; sauce suprême An extraordinarily rich mélange made by combining equal parts VELOUTÉ and chicken or veal stock with mushroom-cooking liquid and heavy cream, and REDUCING the mixture by two-thirds. The sauce is finished by whisking in butter and cream. *See also* SAUCE.

surface-ripened cheeses *see* SOFT-RIPENED CHEESES

surf n' turf; surf and turf An American slang menu term for an entrée that includes both seafood and meat, such as a lobster tail and a beef filet.

surimi [soo-REE-mee] A term meaning "formed fish" and referring to fish pulp that's formed into various shapes. Surimi and the similar KAMABOKO have been made for centuries by the Japanese and are thought to date as far back as 1100 A.D. Most surimi found in North America is made from Alaska POLLOCK, a fish with a lean, firm flesh that has a delicate, slightly sweet flavor. Pacific WHITING is also beginning to be used for surimi but its flesh is so soft that it requires the addition of egg whites and potatoes to be firm enough for processing. To become surimi, fish is skinned, boned, repeatedly rinsed to eliminate any fishiness and pigment and ground into a paste. This odorless white paste is then mixed with a flavor concentrate made from real shellfish, the solution from boiled shells or artificial flavorings. The paste is then formed, cooked and cut into the various shapes of the seafood it's imitating, which in the United States is usually crab legs, lobster chunks, shrimp and scallops. Lastly, surimi is colored to complete its transformation from fish to shellfish look-alike. Surimi is available in the refrigerator or freezer section of most supermarkets. It can be kept unopened in the refrigerator for up to 2 months, in the freezer for up to 6 months. Once opened, use surimi within 3 days. Surimi (which is sometimes simply labeled "imitation crabmeat," "imitation lobster," etc.) is best when used as an ingredient in salads, casseroles and soups.

sushi [SOO-shee] A Japanese specialty based on boiled rice flavored with a sweetened RICE VINEGAR, a mixture called SUSHI MESHI. Once cooled, the rice has a glossy sheen and separates easily. There is a wide variety of sushi including **nigiri sushi** (thin slices of raw fish seasoned with WASABI and wrapped around or layered with this rice), **hosomaki** (thin sushi rolls) and **futomaki** (thick sushi rolls). To make these rolls, various chopped vegetables, raw fish, pickles, TOFU, etc. are enclosed in sushi rice and wrapped in thin sheets of NORI (seaweed). The rolls are then cut into slices. Sushi are designed to be finger food and can be served as appetizers, snacks or a full meal. SOY SAUCE is often served with sushi for dipping. Some popular sushi toppings are **amaebi** (sweet tasting prawn), **anago** (sea eel), **ebi** (prawn or shrimp), **hamachi** (yellowfin tuna), **hotatagai** (scallops), **ika** (squid), **ikura** (salmon roe), **kani** (crabmeat), **maguro** (tuna), **sake** (salmon), **suzuki** (striped bass), **tai** (red snapper), **tako** (octopus), **tomago** (sweetened egg omelet), **toro** (fatty, tuna belly), **unagi** (freshwater eel) and **uni** (sea urchin roe). *See also* SASHIMI.

sushi meshi [SOO-shee MEH-shee] The rice used in SUSHI dishes, made by tossing freshly cooked rice with a dressing made of vinegar, sugar and salt (Asian markets carry a packaged mix of this dressing). The rice-dressing mixture is fanned during tossing to help cool the rice quickly. Sushi meshi is also called *shari.*

sustainable agriculture Although the term has different meanings to various groups, the 1990 Farm Bill delineated the U.S. government's definition as "an integrated system of plant and animal production practices having a site-specific application that will, over the long term, satisfy human food and fiber needs; enhance environmental quality and the natural resource base upon which the agricultural economy depends; make the most efficient use of nonrenewable resources and on-farm resources and integrate, where appropriate, natural biological cycles and controls; sustain the economic viability of farm operations; and enhance the quality of life for farmers and society as a whole." The advocacy organization Sustainable Table has a simpler definition: "Sustainable agriculture is a way of raising food that is healthy for consumers and animals, does not harm the environment, is humane for workers, respects animals, provides a fair wage to the farmer, and supports and enhances rural communities."

suun *see* CELLOPHANE NOODLES

suze [SEUZ] A bright-yellow, extremely bitter and astringent French APÉRITIF based on gentian root.

suzuki *see* SUSHI

suzza melon *see* CUCUZZA

swamp potato *see* ARROWHEAD

sweat, to A technique by which ingredients, particularly vegetables, are cooked in a small amount of fat over low heat. The ingredients are covered directly with a piece of foil or parchment paper, then the pot is tightly covered. With this method, the ingredients soften without browning, and cook in their own juices.

swede *see* RUTABAGA

Swedish limpa bread *see* LIMPA BREAD

Swedish meatballs A blend of ground meat (often a combination of beef, pork or veal), sautéed onions, milk-soaked breadcrumbs, beaten egg and seasonings. This mixture is formed into small ($1/2$-inch) balls before being sautéed until brown. Swedish meatballs are served in a pale brown cream sauce made by combining the pan drippings with cream or milk. They're a popular buffet item or hot appetizer and are seen on most Swedish SMORGASBORDS.

Swedish pancake Small (about 3 inches in diameter) delicately moist, rich pancake traditionally served with butter and LINGONBERRIES. Swedish pancakes (plättar) are classically made in a PLETT PAN, which has 7 round, shallow indentations. In Sweden, these pancakes are served for dessert.

Swedish turnip *see* RUTABAGA

sweet acidophilus milk [ass-ih-DOFF-uh-luhs] *see* MILK

sweet-and-sour This term is used to describe dishes that have a flavor balanced between sweet and pungent, usually accomplished by combining sugar and vinegar. The flavor is often incorporated into a sauce or dressing that can be served with meat, fish or vegetables. The Chinese are famous for their sweet-and-sour specialties and the Germans are noted for their delicious sweet-and-sour cabbage dishes.

sweet basil *see* BASIL

sweetbreads Prized by gourmets throughout the world, sweetbreads are the thymus glands (called neck or throat sweetbreads) and pancreas (called heart, chest or stomach sweetbreads) of young animals, usually calf or lamb, sometimes pig. The former is elongated, the latter rounder and larger. The heart sweetbread is considered the more delectable (and is therefore more expensive) of the two because of its delicate flavor and firmer, creamy-smooth texture. Sweetbreads from milk-fed veal or young calves are considered the best. Those from young lamb are quite good, but beef sweetbreads are tougher and pork sweetbreads (unless from a piglet) have a rather strong flavor. Veal, young calf and beef sweetbreads are available year-round in specialty meat markets, whereas those from lamb and pork must usually be special-ordered. Choose sweetbreads that are white (they become redder as the animal ages), plump and firm. They're very perishable and should be prepared within 24 hours of purchase. Before being cooked, sweetbreads must be soaked in several changes of ACIDULATED WATER and their outer membrane removed. Some recipes call for the glands to be blanched to firm them, and refrigerated until ready for use. Sweetbreads can be prepared in a variety of ways including poaching, sautéing and braising. They are also sometimes used in PÂTÉS and SOUFFLÉS. *See also* VARIETY MEATS.

sweet bean paste *see* BEAN SAUCES; BEAN PASTES

sweet cicely [SIHS-uh-lee] *see* CHERVIL

sweet cider *see* CIDER

sweet cucumber *see* TEA MELON

sweet dumpling squash A small winter squash that's 4 to 5 inches in diameter and weighs 6 to 8 ounces. Its skin is pale tan to light yellow with stripes ranging from green to orange. The flesh is pale yellow to light orange with a sweet flavor. They're available from September through December.

sweetened condensed milk A mixture of whole milk and sugar, 40 to 45 percent of which is sugar. This mixture is heated until about 60 percent of the water evaporates. The resulting condensed mixture is extremely sticky and sweet. Unsweetened condensed milk is referred to as EVAPORATED MILK. Store unopened sweetened condensed milk at room temperature for up to 6 months. Once opened, transfer the unused milk to an airtight container, refrigerate and use within 5 days. Sweetened condensed milk is used in baked goods and desserts such as candies, puddings, pies, etc.

sweetleaf *see* STEVIA

sweet marjoram *see* MARJORAM

sweetmeat A small piece of something sweet such as a PETIT FOUR, candied fruit, nut or candy.

sweet peppers In the United States, the term "sweet pepper" encompasses a wide variety of mild peppers that, like the CHILE, belong to the *Capsicum* family. Both sweet and hot peppers are native to tropical areas of the Western Hemisphere and were brought back by Christopher Columbus to his homeland where they quickly found their way into Spanish cuisine. Sweet peppers can range in color from pale to dark green, from yellow to orange to red, and from purple to brown to black. Their color can be solid or variegated. Their usually juicy flesh can be thick or thin and the flavors can range from bland to sweet to bittersweet. The best known sweet peppers are the **bell peppers**, so-named for their rather bell-like shape. They have a mild, sweet flavor and crisp, exceedingly juicy flesh. When young, the majority of bell peppers are a rich, bright green, but there are also yellow, orange, purple, red and brown bell peppers. The red bells are simply vine-ripened green bell peppers that, because they've ripened longer, are very sweet. Bell peppers vary from $3\frac{1}{2}$ to $5\frac{1}{2}$ inches long and from $2\frac{1}{2}$ to 4 inches wide. Green bell peppers are available all year long, while the red, orange, yellow, purple and brown varieties are found sporadically throughout the year. With their tops cut off and seeds removed, bell peppers are excellent for stuffing with a variety of fillings. The large, red, heart-shaped PIMIENTO is another popular sweet pepper. Fresh pimientos are available in some specialty produce markets from late summer to fall. Canned or bottled pimientos are marketed year-round in halves, strips and small pieces. Pimientos are the familiar red stuffing found in green olives. Other sweet pepper varieties include the thin, curved, green **bull's horn;** the long, tapered **Cubanelle**, which can range in color from yellow to red; and the **sweet banana pepper**, which is long, yellow and banana-shaped. Most sweet peppers are available year-round with a peak from July through September. Choose peppers that are firm, have a richly colored, shiny skin and that are heavy for their size. Avoid those that are limp, shriveled or that have soft or bruised spots. Store peppers in a plastic bag in the refrigerator for up to a week. Sweet peppers are used raw in salads and as part of a vegetable platter served with various dips. In cooking, they find their way into a variety of dishes and can be sautéed, baked, grilled, braised and steamed. Sweet peppers are an excellent source of vitamin C and contain fair amounts of vitamin

A and small amounts of calcium, phosphorus, iron, thiamine, riboflavin and niacin.

sweet piquanté pepper [pee-KAHN-tay] *see* PEPPADEW PEPPER

sweet potato This large edible tuber belongs to the morning-glory family and is native to tropical areas of the Americas. There are many varieties of sweet potato but the two that are widely grown commercially are a pale sweet potato and the darker-skinned variety Americans tagged "yam" to distinguish it from its lighter-fleshed kin. In actuality, the true YAM (*see* listing) is not related to the sweet potato at all. The pale sweet potato has a thin, light yellow skin and a light yellow flesh. Its flavor is not sweet and after being cooked, it has a dry and crumbly texture, much like that of a white baking potato. The darker sweet potato (the most common varieties being Beauregard and Garnet) has a thicker skin which can range in color from dark orange to pale red. The flesh, which is sweeter and moister than the pale variety, can vary in color from vivid to deep orange. Fresh sweet potatoes are available year-round, with a peak season in the winter months. When buying fresh sweet potatoes choose those that are relatively small to medium in size with smooth, unbruised skins. Sweet potatoes don't store well unless the environment is just right, which is dry, dark and around 55°F. Under perfect conditions they can be stored for 3 to 4 weeks. Otherwise, store in a cool, dark place and use within a week of purchase. Do not refrigerate. Sweet potatoes—particularly the pale variety—can be substituted for regular potatoes in most recipes. They can be prepared in a variety of ways including baking, boiling and sautéing. Sweet-potato chips can now be found on some restaurant menus. Canned and frozen sweet potatoes are available year-round and are often labeled as yams. Sweet potatoes are high in vitamins A and C. *See also* BONIATO; POTATO.

sweet potato squash *see* DELICATA SQUASH

sweetsop Also called *sugar apple,* the sweetsop is the egg-shaped fruit of a small tropical-American tree belonging to the genus *Annona.* The sweetsop (*A. squamosa*) is one of several members of the Annona family, including CHERIMOYA and SOURSOP. It has a thick, coarse yellow-green (sometimes purple-tinged) skin and yellow flesh with dark seeds. Often mistaken for its cousin, the cherimoya, the sweetsop has a very sweet, custardlike flesh that's divided into segments like a citrus fruit. It's grown in Florida and California and is usually available from midsummer to midwinter only in the locales where it's grown. After the skin and seeds are removed, sweetsops are usually eaten raw and often used in desserts.

sweet tea pickle *see* TEA MELON

sweet woodruff *see* WOODRUFF

Swiss chard *see* CHARD

Swiss cheese; Swiss-style cheese A generic term for cheeses patterned after Switzerland's EMMENTAL, and made throughout the world in myriad countries including Argentina, Austria, Denmark, Finland, France, Germany, Italy, Russia and the United States. Made with partially skimmed cow's milk, Swiss cheese in general has a pale yellow color, a nutty, slightly sweet flavor and large EYES. The eyes form during a RIPENING period of about 30 days in warm rooms where heat-loving bacteria begin to ferment and throw off carbon dioxide bubbles, creating holes in the cheese that can range in size from that of a cherry to that of a walnut. Total RIPENING time for Swiss cheese can take anywhere from 2 to 12 months. Regular Swiss cheese can come in wheels of 185 to 210 pounds, and rectangles weighing 25 to 28 pounds. The minimum FAT CONTENT for most Swiss cheeses is 43 percent. A smaller format (2- to 5-pound wheels) is known as **Baby Swiss**, a version typically made with whole milk. Baby Swiss also isn't aged as long as the regular version, has smaller and fewer eyes, a softer texture and a milder, sweeter flavor. Many producers make a smoked rendition of Baby Swiss. *See also* CHEESE.

Swiss fondue *see* FONDUE

Swiss roll *see* JELLY ROLL

Swiss steak Called *smothered steak* in England, this dish begins with a thick cut of beef—usually ROUND or CHUCK—that has been tenderized by pounding, coated with flour and browned on both sides. The meat is then smothered with chopped tomatoes, onions, carrots, celery, beef broth and various seasonings before being covered and braised, baked or simmered for about 2 hours.

swordfish This large food and sport fish is found in temperate waters throughout the world. Swordfish average between 200 to 600 pounds, though some specimens caught weigh over 1,000 pounds. They have a distinctive saillike dorsal fin and a striking swordlike projection extending from the upper jaw. Their mild-flavored, moderately fat flesh is firm, dense and meatlike, making swordfish one of the most popular fish in the United States. Fresh swordfish is available from late spring to early fall, whereas it's available frozen year-round. Both forms are sold in steaks and chunks. Because it's so firm, swordfish can be prepared in almost any manner including sautéing, grilling, broiling, baking and poaching. *See also* FISH.

syllabub [SIHL-uh-buhb] This thick, frothy drink or dessert originated in old England. It's traditionally made by beating milk with wine or ale, sugar, spices and sometimes beaten egg whites. A richer version made with cream can be used as a topping for cakes, cookies, fruit, etc. It's thought that the name of this concoction originated during Elizabethan times and is a combination of the words *Sille* (a French wine that was used in the mixture) and *bub* (Old-English slang for "bubbling drink").

Sylvaner; Silvaner [sihl-VAN-uhr; sihl-VAH-ner; *Ger.* zihl-vah-nehr] Long popular in Germany and surrounding areas of Europe, this white wine grape is now being grown in other parts of the world such as the United States and Chile. Though the wine produced from Sylvaner grapes is light and pleasant, it's not as flavorful or fruity as Germany's Johannisberg RIESLING.

syr [sihr] Russian for "cheese."

Syrah [see-RAH] A high-quality red wine grape that gained its reputation in France's RHÔNE region. In the northern Rhône, Syrah is the principal grape of the esteemed wines from Cornas, Côte-Rôtie, Crozes-Hermitage, Hermitage and Saint-Joseph. In the southern Rhône, Syrah is used to contribute flavor and structure to the multi-variety wines from CHÂTEAUNEUF-DU-PAPE and CÔTES-DU-RHÔNE. When young, Syrah wines are deep-colored and tannic (*see* TANNIN), with spicy and peppery qualities. Mature Syrahs show characteristics of sweet blackberries, blackcurrants and plums. In Australia Syrah is called *Shiraz* and is that country's most widely planted red grape. *See also* PETITE SIRAH.

Syrian marjoram *see* ZA'ATAR

syrniki; sirniki [sihr-NEE-kee] Russian in origin, syrniki is a dish of fried cheese cakes that can be served sweet—sprinkled with powdered sugar and sour cream—or savory, topped with sour cream and herbs such as dill. Syrniki are made with a mixture of POT CHEESE or FARMER'S CHEESE, flour and beaten eggs, which is formed into cakes before being sautéed on both sides until brown.

Szechuan cuisine [SEHCH-wahn] *see* CHINESE CUISINE

Szechuan pepper; Szechwan [SEHCH-wahn; SEHCH-oo-ahn] Native to the Szechuan province of China, this mildly hot spice comes from the prickly ash tree. Though not related to the PEPPERCORN family, Szechuan berries resemble black peppercorns but contain a tiny seed. Szechuan pepper has a distinctive flavor and fragrance. It can be found in Asian markets and specialty stores in whole or powdered form. Whole berries are often heated before being ground to bring out their tantalizing flavor and aroma. Szechuan pepper is also known as *anise pepper, Chinese pepper, fagara, flower pepper, sansho, Sichuan pepper* and *timur.*

tabasco parsley *see* SAW-LEAF HERB

Tabasco Sauce [tuh-BAS-koh] A trademarked name held by the McIlhenny family since the mid-1800s, describing a fiery sauce made from tabasco peppers (barrel-fermented for 3 years), vinegar and salt. The tabasco pepper is a very hot, small red CHILE that originated in the Mexican state of Tabasco. The word *tabasco* means "damp earth." Tabasco Sauce adds zest to numerous dishes as well as being integral to the famous BLOODY MARY cocktail. In addition to its original Tabasco Sauce, the McIlhenny Company now produces several Tabasco–brand sauces including green pepper sauce, garlic pepper sauce and habanero pepper sauce. *See also* SAUCE.

tabbouleh [tuh-BOO-luh] A Middle Eastern dish of BULGHUR WHEAT mixed with chopped tomatoes, onions, parsley, mint, olive oil and lemon juice. It's served cold, often with a crisp bread such as LAVOSH.

table d'hôte [tah-buhl DOHT] This French term literally means "the table of the host." On restaurant menus, however, *table d'hôte* refers to a complete meal of several courses for the price of the entrée. *See also* À LA CARTE; PRIX FIXE.

table divers *see* FREEGAN

tacchino [tah-KEE-noh] Italian for "turkey."

taco [tah-KOH] A Mexican-style "sandwich" consisting of a folded corn TORTILLA filled with various ingredients such as beef, pork, chicken, CHORIZO sausage, tomatoes, lettuce, cheese, onion, GUACAMOLE, REFRIED BEANS and SALSA. Most tacos in the United States are made with crisp (fried) tortilla shells, but there are also "soft" (pliable) versions. The latter are more likely to be found in the Southwest and California. Tacos may be eaten as an entrée or snack.

tacos al pastor [tah-KOHS ahl pahs-TOHR] *see* AL PASTOR

tadig; tahdig [ta-DEEG] In Persian cuisine a number of rice dishes are cooked so that a crusty, golden layer of rice forms at the bottom and on the sides of the cooking pot. This tasty crust is called tadig. When cooking's complete, the pot holding the rice dish is often cooled in water, tipped upside down on a plate and tapped so the rice slides out easily with the golden layer of crust on top. Tadig is prized and often served to guests first to honor them.

taffy [TAF-fee] Soft and chewy, taffy is a candy made with sugar, butter and various flavorings. Its supple consistency is achieved by twisting and pulling the candy as it cools into long, pliable strands, which are then usually cut into bite-size chunks. The famous **saltwater taffy**, made popular in the late 1800s in Atlantic City, was so named because it used a small amount of salt water in the mixture. Today's saltwater taffy doesn't necessarily follow tradition. *See also* TOFFEE.

Taggiasca olive [TAHG-gee-ahs-kah; TAG-gee-ahs-kah] Small, brine-cured olive from northwestern Italy's Liguria region. The brownish-black, egg-shaped olives aren't too meaty but the flesh is firm and crisp and the flavor is mild, fruity and nutty. *See also* OLIVE.

tagine [tay-jeen] 1. A cooking container used in North African countries such as Algeria, Morocco and Tunisia. The tagine, also spelled **tajine** or **tajin**, is comprised of a flat, circular plate-like bottom and a cone-shaped lid. Much like the familiar casserole dish, the tagine can be used for cooking and serving food. Traditionally tagines have been made from clay that's often glazed or decorated. But modern versions are being manufactured with cast-iron bottoms, allowing for higher temperatures that can brown ingredients at the beginning of the cooking process. 2. The name given to any of various Moroccan stews featuring meat or poultry gently simmered with vegetables, olives, preserved lemons, garlic and spices like CINNAMON, CUMIN, GINGER, PEPPER, SAFFRON and TURMERIC. Tagines are often served with COUSCOUS. The dish is named after the tagine container in which it's cooked.

tagliarini *see* Pasta Glossary, page 883

tagliatelle *see* Pasta Glossary, page 883

tagliolini *see* Pasta Glossary, page 883

tah chin; tahcheen [ta-CHEEN] Persian dish that combines partially cooked rice with egg yolks, SAFFRON and yogurt; the rice is then layered in a pot with chicken, lamb or vegetables such as eggplant. As the dish is baked a crispy, golden crust (*see* TADIG; TAHDIG) forms on the bottom and sides of the pot. When cooking's complete, the pot holding the rice dish is tipped upside down and emptied on a plate with the golden layer of crust on top.

tahdig *see* TADIG

tahini [tah-HEE-nee] Used in Middle Eastern cooking, tahini is a thick paste made of ground SESAME SEED. It's used to flavor various dishes such as HUMMUS and BABA GHANOUSH.

tai *see* SUSHI

tail *see* OXTAIL

tailed pepper *see* CUBEB

tajine *see* TAGINE

tako *see* SUSHI

Taleggio [tahl-EH-zhee-oh] Hailing from Italy's Lombardy region where it's been made since at least the 10th century, this rich, semisoft cheese is made from whole cow's milk. Its flavor can range from mild, sweet and nutty to rich and mushroomy, depending on its age. The rind is thin and soft and varies in color from yellow to orange to pink with spots of gray mold. When young, Taleggio's interior is pale yellow and its texture creamy and pliable. As it ages it darkens to deep yellow and becomes rather runny. Taleggio, which is made in 4- to 5-pound squares, belongs to a category of cheeses know as STRACCHINO. It has a FAT CONTENT of about 48 percent. *See also* CHEESE.

tamago [tah-mah-goh] Japanese for "egg."

tamago somen [tah-MAH-goh SOH-mehn] *see* SOMEN

tamagoyaki [tah-mah-goh-YAH-kee] An "omelet" cooked Japanese style. DASHI, MIRIN or sugar and soy sauce are added to the eggs, which are lightly beaten. It's then cooked in a square or rectangular pan (**tamagoyaki pan**) and folded or rolled. The slightly sweet egg mixture appears regularly in BENTO BOXES, as a SUSHI topping and often stuffed with various fillings and eaten separately. Tamagoyaki is sometimes shortened to tamago.

tamale; *Sp.* **tamal** [tuh-MAH-lee; tuh-MAHL] From the *Nahuatl* word (*tamalii*), the tamale is a popular Mexican dish that consists of various fillings (such as finely chopped meat and vegetables) coated with a MASA dough and wrapped in a softened CORN HUSK. This package is then tied and steamed until the dough is cooked through. The corn husk is peeled back before the tamale is eaten. Although savory tamales are the most popular in the United States, many cooks in Mexico also serve sweet tamales, usually filled with fruit.

tamale pie A dish made with the ingredients of a regular TAMALE (cornmeal batter, ground meat, cheese and seasonings), except the ingredients are layered and baked in a dish instead of wrapped in a CORN HUSK.

tamanegi [tah-mah-neh-gee] Japanese for "onion," referring to the type we know in the United States. *See also* NEGI; NAGANEGI; RAKKYO.

tamari [tuh-MAH-ree] A style of SOY SAUCE made with SOYBEANS and little or no wheat. Tamari is a thicker, slightly darker sauce that has a distinctively rich, mellow flavor. It's used primarily as a table CONDIMENT, as a dipping sauce or for basting. People with gluten sensitivity can use the wheat-free versions.

tamarillo [tam-uh-RIHL-oh; tam-uh-REE-oh] Native to South America, this egg-shaped fruit is also known as a *tree tomato*. Although not yet widely accepted in the United States, the tamarillo is very popular in South and Central America, the Caribbean, and parts of Asia, New Zealand (from where most of the fruit in the United States is imported) and Australia. The tamarillo has a tough, bitter skin that can be various glossy shades of red, purple, amber or yellow. The tart but very flavorful golden pink flesh is purple-tinged around the seeds. Tamarillos are available from May through October in specialty produce stores and some supermarkets. Choose firm, blemish-free fruit that's heavy for its size. When ripe, tamarillos should be fragrant and should yield slightly to palm pressure. They can be ripened at room temperature. Once ripe, they should be refrigerated, tightly wrapped in a plastic bag, up to 10 days. Tamarillos can be eaten fresh or cooked, and are used for both sweet and savory dishes. One requisite, however, is sugar, which reduces the fruit's natural tartness and enhances its flavor. Tamarillos are a good source of vitamins A and C.

tamarind; tamarindo [TAM-uh-rihnd] Also known as *Indian date,* the tamarind is the fruit pod of a tall shade tree native to Asia and northern Africa and widely grown in India. The large (5- to 8-inch-long) pods grow in clusters and contain up to 10 seeds and a dark brown sour-sweet pulp with a flavor reminiscent of lemons, apricots and dates. Tamarind pulp concentrate is popular as a flavoring in East Indian and Middle Eastern cuisines much like lemon juice is in Western culture. It's used to season full-flavored foods such as CHUTNEYS, CURRY dishes and pickled fish. Additionally, tamarind is used to make a sweet syrup flavoring soft drinks. It's also an integral ingredient in Worcestershire sauce. Fresh tamarind pods are available in the spring and summer in Asian, Caribbean and Indian markets, specialty produce markets, natural food stores and some supermarkets. Choose pods that are plump and relatively unbroken. Store in a plastic bag at a cool room temperature for up to 2 months. To use pods, crack open and peel off the brittle shell. Pull off the fibrous strings and cut the pulp away from the seeds. Put the pulp in a bowl or pan and cover with boiling water; let stand for several hours or overnight. Use a slotted spoon to scoop the pulp out of the water; press the pulp through a sieve. Cover and refrigerate strained pulp for up to a month, or freeze for up to a year. Tamarind can be found in ethnic markets in various forms including jars of concentrated pulp with seeds, canned paste, whole pods dried into "bricks," syrup or powder.

tambaqui [tahm-BAH-kee] A large vegetarian member of the piranha family, the tambaqui is native to the Amazon River. It has a firm, white flesh that tastes more like veal or pork than fish. Outside of Brazil, tambaqui is obtainable solely in frozen form. In the United States, it's typically available only in upscale restaurants.

tamis [TAM-ee; tam-EE; TAM-ihs] Also called *tammycloth,* a tamis is a worsted-cloth STRAINER used to strain liquid mixtures such as sauces.

tam mak hoong *see* SOM TAM

tammycloth *see* TAMIS

Tamworth pork *see* HERITAGE PORK

Tanche olive *see* NYONS OLIVE

tandoori coloring; tandoori paste [tahn-DOOR-ee] Available in Indian markets, this coloring is used to give foods the traditional red-orange tint of TANDOOR OVEN cooking. Tandoori paste can be rubbed directly onto the surface of meats; the powder is generally stirred into a MARINADE.

tandoor oven; tandoori [tahn-DOOR; tahn-DOOR-ee] Used throughout India (and found in Indian restaurants throughout the world), the traditional rounded-top tandoor oven is made of brick and clay. It's used to bake foods over direct heat produced from a smoky fire. The dough for the delicious Indian bread NAAN is slapped directly onto the oven's clay walls and left to bake until puffy and lightly browned. Meats cooked in the tall, rather cylindrical tandoor are usually skewered and thrust into the oven's heat, which is so intense (usually over 500°F) that it cooks a chicken half in less than 5 minutes. Chicken and other meats cooked with this method are identified as *tandoori chicken,* etc.

tang [tahng] 1. Chinese for "soup." In Korea, *guk* and tang are soup-like dishes. Tang is slightly thicker, often like a thin stew. 2. *See* KNIFE

tangelo [tan-JEHL-oh] A juicy, sweetly tart citrus fruit with few seeds that takes its name from the fact that it's a cross between the TANGERINE and the POMELO. There are many hybrids of this loose-skinned fruit, ranging in size from that of a tiny orange to that of a small grapefruit. The skins, which can be rough to smooth, range in color from yellow-orange to deep orange. The most common variety of tangelo available in the United States is the **Minneola,** which is easily recognized by its nipple-shaped stem end. Tangelos are in season from November through March. *See also* ORANGE.

tangerine [tan-juh-REEN] *see* MANDARIN ORANGE

tangho *see* CHRYSANTHEMUM LEAVES

tangor [tan-JOHR] This loose-skinned, easy-to-peel orange is some-what oval in shape and has a rough, thick, deep-orange skin. It's a cross between a TANGERINE and a sweet orange, and its name is a combination of "tang" and "or" from these two species. The tangor has a sweetly tart flesh and a goodly number of seeds. It's in season from December to March. The *temple orange* is one of the most widely available tangors. *See also* ORANGE.

tannia *see* MALANGA

tannin [TAN-ihn] An astringent substance found in the seeds and stems of grapes, the bark of some trees and in tea. Tannin is important in the making of good red wines, aiding them in long and graceful aging. When such wines are young, the tannin often gives them a noticeable astringency—a quality that diminishes as the wine ages, mellows and develops character.

tan o *see* CHRYSANTHEMUM LEAVES

tapas [TAH-pahs] Popular throughout Spain in bars and restaurants, *tapas* are appetizers that usually accompany SHERRY or other APÉRITIFS or COCKTAILS. They can also form an entire meal and can range from simple items such as olives or cubes of ham and cheese to more elaborate preparations like cold omelets, snails in a spicy sauce, stuffed peppers and miniature sandwiches.

tapenade [TA-puh-nahd; ta-pen-AHD] Hailing from France's Provence region, tapenade is a thick paste made from capers, anchovies, ripe olives, olive oil, lemon juice, seasonings and sometimes small pieces of tuna. It's used as a CONDIMENT and served with CRUDITÉS, fish, meat, etc.

tapioca; tapioca flour [tap-ee-OH-kuh] A starchy substance extracted from the root of the YUCA plant. It's available in several forms including granules, flakes, pellets (called *pearl tapioca*) and flour or starch. The most widely available forms are **tapioca flour** (also called *cassava flour*) and **pearl tapioca**. The flour is used as a thickening agent for soups, fruit fillings, glazes, etc., much like CORNSTARCH. Pearl tapioca is used mainly to make pudding and comes in several sizes, regular or instant forms and in a variety of prepackaged flavors. Pearl tapioca is available in most supermarkets, whereas the other forms are more commonly found in natural food stores and Asian markets. If stored in a cool, dark place, all types of tapioca will keep indefinitely.

tapioca ball drink; tapioca milk tea *see* BUBBLE TEA

taramasalata [tah-rah-mah-sah-LAH-tah] This Greek specialty is a thick, creamy mixture made with *tarama* (pale orange carp ROE), lemon juice, milk-soaked breadcrumbs, olive oil and seasonings. *Taramasalata* is usually served with bread or crackers as an HORS D'OEUVRE. It may also be used as a dip for CRUDITÉS.

taro root [TAHR-oh; TEHR-oh] A starchy, potatolike tuber with a brown, fibrous skin and gray-white (sometimes purple-tinged) flesh. Taro is grown in tropical areas and is an important starchy food in West Africa, the Caribbean and Polynesian islands. A variety of taro grown in the southern United States since the early 1900s is called **dasheen**. Taro roots range in length from about 5 inches to a foot or more, and can be several inches wide. Though acrid-tasting in its raw state, the root has a somewhat nutlike flavor when cooked. It's also extremely easy to digest. It should be noted, however, that some varieties are highly toxic unless thoroughly cooked. The taro root has large edible leaves (called *callaloo* in the Caribbean) which can be prepared and eaten like mustard or turnip greens. Taro root can be found in ethnic markets and some specialty produce stores. Choose roots that are firm and smooth and refrigerate up to 4 days. Much like the potato, the taro root may be prepared in a variety of ways including boiling, frying and baking. In Hawaii, it's used to make the famous (or infamous) POI. *See also* MALANGA.

tarragon [TEHR-uh-gon; TEHR-uh-guhn] Narrow, pointed, dark green leaves distinguish this perennial aromatic herb known for its distinctive aniselike flavor. Tarragon is widely used in classic French cooking for a variety of dishes including chicken, fish and vegetables, as well as many sauces, the best known being BÉARNAISE. It's also an integral ingredient in various herbal combinations such as FINES HERBES. Tarragon is available year-round in fresh, dried and powdered forms. Care should be taken when using tarragon since its assertiveness can easily dominate other flavors. Tarragon vinegar is a popular item in gourmet markets. *See also* HERBS; Seasoning Suggestions, page 891.

tart *n.* Very simply, a tart is a pastry crust with shallow sides, a filling and no top crust. It's typically made in a TART PAN. The filling can be sweet (such as fruit or sweet custard) or savory (like meat, cheese or savory custard). Depending on the type of tart, the pastry shell can be baked and then filled, or filled and then baked. Tarts can be bite-size (often served as HORS D'OEUVRE), individual-size (sometimes called *tartlets*) or full-size. They can be used as appetizers, entrées or desserts. *See also* TARTE TATIN. **tart** *adj.* Sharp, acidic or sour.

tartare [tar-TAR] A dish of coarsely ground or finely chopped high-quality, raw lean meat or fish that has been seasoned with salt, pepper, herbs and other ingredients such as onion, shallots or capers. The best know is **beef tartare**, which is thought to have originated in the Baltic provinces of Russia where, in medieval times, the Tartars shredded red meat with a knife and ate it raw. Today the seasoned raw meat is usually shaped into a mound with an indentation in the top, into which is placed a raw egg yolk. Beef tartare (also referred to as *steak tartare*) is usually served with capers, chopped parsley and onions. Seafood variations include TUNA tartare and SALMON tartare.

Tartarian cherry; black Tartarian cherry [tar-TAIR-ee-uhn] Large and heart-shaped, the Tartarian cherry has a dark purple, almost black, skin and flesh. Inside the thin skin the flesh is sweet, juicy and extremely flavorful. The Tartarian cherry is available from May to September. *See also* CHERRY.

tartaric acid [tahr-TAR-ihk; tahr-TAHR-ihk] A natural crystalline compound found in plants, especially those with tart characteristics such as TAMARIND and unripe grapes. The principal acid in wine, tartaric acid is the component that promotes graceful aging and crispness of flavor. One of the by-products of tartaric acid is CREAM OF TARTAR, which is used in baking and candy-making.

tartar sauce; tartare sauce [TAHR-tuhr] Based on MAYONNAISE, tartar sauce is a mixture of minced capers, dill pickles, onions or shallots, olives, lemon juice or vinegar and seasonings. It's traditionally served with fried fish, but can also be used with vegetables. *See also* SAUCE.

tarte Tatin [tart tah-TAN] A famous French upside-down apple TART made by covering the bottom of a shallow baking dish with butter and sugar, then apples and finally a pastry crust. While baking, the sugar and butter create a delicious CARAMEL that becomes the topping when the tart is inverted onto a serving plate. The tart was created by two French sisters who lived in the Loire Valley and earned their living making it. The French call this dessert *tarte des demoiselles Tatin*, "the tart of two unmarried women named Tatin."

tartine [tar-TEEN] French for a slice of buttered bread, which can be topped with any of various other spreads from jam to cheese.

tart pan Used to bake everything from tarts to QUICHES, the tart pan has fluted, straight sides (as opposed to the sloped sides of a PIE PAN). It can range in diameter from 8 to 12 inches (individual-size pans are 4 inches), and is typically $1\frac{1}{2}$ inches deep. Metal tart pans have removable bottoms, glass and porcelain have solid bottoms.

tartufo [tahr-TOO-foh] Italian for "TRUFFLE."

taru [TAH-roo] *see* SAKE

Tasmania bean *see* CUCUZZA

tassel hyacinth *see* CIPOLLINI

tasso [TAH-soh; TA-soh] Much to the disappointment of many, this Cajun specialty is generally hard to find outside Louisiana. Tasso is a lean chunk of cured pork (usually shoulder) or beef that's been richly seasoned with ingredients such as red pepper, garlic, FILÉ POWDER and any of several other herbs or spices, depending on the manufacturer. It's then smoked for about (again, depending on the cook) 2 days. The result is a firm, smoky and flavorfully tangy meat that is principally used for seasoning. Outside of Cajun country, tasso is available in some specialty gourmet shops and by mail order. It can be refrigerated, tightly wrapped, for up to a week. Though it's sometimes referred to as *tasso ham* and is most often finely chopped and used (like ham, PROSCIUTTO, PANCETTA or SALT PORK) to flavor foods such as beans, eggs and pastas, the spicy-hot tasso most definitely isn't ham.

tastevin [taht-VAHN; tahst-VAHN] A wine-tasting cup, usually worn on a chain or ribbon around the neck of a SOMMELIER.

tatsoi; tat soi [taht-SOY] Also known as *spoon cabbage and Chinese flat cabbage,* tatsoi has small, dark green spoon-shaped leaves with a pale stem. Its flavor is sweet and earthy with a mild mustard tang. The leaves make a flavorful addition to salads and can also be added at the last minute to STIR-FRY and other cooked dishes. The crunchy stalks of mature tatsoi can be used as one would use celery.

tatsuta-age [tah-tsoo-tah-ah-geh] Japanese AGEMONO (deep-frying) technique. Chicken or seafood pieces are marinated in MIRIN, SAKE and/or SOY SAUCE, coated with KUDZU POWDER or KATAKURIKO and then deep-fried.

tava; tavah *see* SAJ

tawa; tawah *see* SAJ

tawny port [TAW-nee] *see* PORT

T-bone steak Cut from the center of the SHORT LOIN, this steak has a T-shaped bone that separates the small tenderloin section from the larger top loin. The porterhouse steak differs from the T-bone in that it contains a larger portion of the tenderloin. *See also* BEEF; Beef Chart, page 896.

tchorba [CHOR-bah] *see* CHORBA

te (Sp. tay); tè (It. teh) Spanish and Italian for "tea."

tea Tea is native to China, where it grew wild until the Chinese determined that the leaves helped flavor the flat taste of the water they boiled to prevent getting sick. Tea plant cultivation in China began about

4,000 years ago but it wasn't until the 8th century A.D. that outsiders (the Japanese) discovered it. Europeans were finally introduced to tea during the 17th century and the British (who were the true tea lovers) spread its use by implementing new growing areas such as India. In fact, the English so enjoy their tea that they developed a meal around it, HIGH TEA. Tea also played an important role in the development of the United States—its taxation led to the Boston Tea Party, one of the issues that triggered the War of Independence. Americans further influenced tea use both by inventing tea bags and by starting the practice of drinking iced tea at the St. Louis World's Fair in 1904. The word "tea" can refer to the beverage, the leaves used to make the beverage and the magnolia-related evergreen shrub from which the leaves come. All tea plants belong to the same species but varying climates, soils, etc. combine in different ways to create a plethora of distinctive leaves. The processing of those leaves is responsible for the individual characteristics of each tea. Leaves are sorted by size—those that are young and tender are superior to older, coarser leaves. Black, green and oolong tea are the main types produced during processing. Black tea comes from leaves that have been fermented before being heated and dried. Such leaves produce a dark reddish-brown brew. Black teas are graded according to the size of the leaf; *orange pekoe* describes leaves that are smaller than the medium-size coarser PEKOE leaves. Although black tea flavors vary, most are more assertive than those of green or oolong teas. Among the more well-known black teas are DARJEELING, ENGLISH BREAKFAST and LAPSANG SOUCHONG. Green tea, favored among Asians, is produced from leaves that are steamed and dried but *not* fermented. Such leaves produce a greenish-yellow tea and a flavor that's slightly bitter and closer to the taste of the fresh leaf. Two of the more well-known green teas are TENCHA and GUNPOWDER. Scientific studies have shown that both black and green teas increase the body's ANTIOXIDANT activity by up to about 45 percent. They are also said to have antibacterial powers against cavities and gum disease. Oolong tea is produced from leaves that are partially fermented, a process that creates teas with a flavor, color and aroma that falls between black tea and green tea. The best known oolong is FORMOSA OOLONG, from Taiwan. In addition to these three main types of tea there are specialty teas. Such teas are flavored with various floral or spice additions such as jasmine or chrysanthemum blossoms, or orange or lemon peel. Instant tea, which dissolves quickly in cold or hot water, consists of brewed tea that is dehydrated and granulated. It often contains sugar or sugar substitutes and other flavorings such as cinnamon or lemon. Herb tea (*see* TISANE) is not a true tea based on tea-shrub leaves, but rather an infusion of various herbs, flowers and spices. Both black teas (in leaf and tea-bag form) and instant teas are readily available in most supermarkets. Other teas can be found in great variety in natural food stores, Asian markets and stores specializing in tea and coffee. *See also* ASSAM; CAMOMILE; CEYLON; CHAI; CREAM TEA; EARL GREY; FORMOSA OOLONG; HIGH TEA; IRISH BREAKFAST TEA; LAPSANG SOUCHONG; MATCHA; SASSAFRAS; TEA INFUSER; TENCHA.

tea egg A Chinese specialty prepared by hard-cooking eggs, crushing (but not peeling) the shells, then simmering the eggs in strong tea for about an hour. The tea seeps through the cracked shell, thereby flavoring the egg and giving it a marbleized appearance. Tea eggs are usually served as an appetizer.

tea infuser A small, perforated, basketlike container with a hinged opening. Loose tea is placed inside the infuser, which is then closed and lowered into a teapot, whereupon boiling water is added (*see* INFUSION). The tiny holes in the infuser allow the water to interact with the tea leaves. A tiny chain with a hook at one end is attached to the top of the infuser— the hook slips over the rim of the teapot so the infuser can easily be retrieved, thereby straining the tea leaves. There are also single-cup infusers, which are shaped like two perforated teaspoons that fasten together. Tea infusers are usually made of stainless or chromed steel, although there are also porcelain and silver models. *See also* HIGH TEA; TEA.

tea melon Also called *sweet cucumber*, the yellow-colored tea melon is tiny (2 inches long) and shaped like a cucumber. It has a sweet, mild flavor and a delightfully crisp texture. This mini vegetable is most often preserved, usually in honey and spices but sometimes in SOY SAUCE. Tea melon is not sold fresh in the United States but can be found in preserved form in Asian markets. Once preserved, it goes by many names including *Chinese pickle, preserved sweet melon, sweet tea pickle* and *pickled cucumber*. Tea melon is usually served as a CONDIMENT or pickle and is also used to flavor various Asian dishes.

Tee [TAY] German for "tea."

teff; tef A minuscule (about $1/32$ inch in diameter) CEREAL GRAIN native to northern Africa. It's been a staple of Ethiopia for eons and is now being grown in the United States in Idaho. The mildly nutty-flavored teff is high in protein and carbohydrates and a good source of calcium and iron. It can be found in natural food stores.

tejolete [teh-hoh-LOH-teh] *see* MOLCAJETE Y TEJOLETE

tejpat; tej patta *see* INDIAN BAY LEAF

tekkamaki [tehk-kah-MAH-kee] Type of SUSHI roll filled with raw tuna and SUSHI MESHI and wrapped in NORI. Sometimes WASABI and scallions are added.

Teleme [TEHL-uh-may] Available mainly in northern California, Teleme CHEESE is similar in texture to domestic BRIE. It contains about 50 percent milk fat and has a pronounced tangy flavor. When young, Teleme's texture is soft and creamy. As it ages, it becomes runnier and stronger in flavor.

telera *see* BOLILLO

tempeh; tempe [TEHM-pay] A SOYBEAN cake made by fermenting cooked soybeans, which are formed into a firm, dense, chewy cake with a yeasty, nutty flavor. The high-protein tempeh is cholesterol free and extremely low in fat. It's often used as a meat substitute to make foods like vegetarian burgers because it readily absorbs flavors and holds its shape when cooked. It can also be crumbled and added to sauces and casseroles. Tempeh cakes are available fresh and frozen in natural food stores and some supermarkets. Store tempeh in the refrigerator for up to 2 weeks; freeze for up to 3 months.

temperatures *see* General Temperature Equivalents, page 862; Microwave Oven Conversion Chart, page 863; Oven Temperatures, page 863

tempering A technique by which chocolate is stabilized through a melting-and-cooling process, thereby making it more malleable and glossy. Commerically available chocolate is already tempered, but this condition changes when chocolate is melted. Tempering chocolate isn't necessary for most recipes, but is often done when the chocolate will be used for candymaking or decorations. Chocolate must be tempered because it contains COCOA BUTTER, a fat that may form crystals after chocolate is melted and cooled. If these crystals aren't stabilized through tempering, they can form dull gray streaks called BLOOM. The *classic tempering method* is to melt chocolate until it reaches a temperature of 115°F. Two-thirds of the melted chocolate is then spread on a marble slab and worked back and forth with a metal spatula until it becomes thick and reaches a temperature of about 80°F. This thickened chocolate is then transferred back into the remaining one-third melted chocolate and reheated to about 89°F for semisweet chocolate, about 85°F for milk or white chocolate. The *quick tempering method* is to melt two-thirds of the chocolate to be tempered to a temperature of 115°F then add the remaining one-third (finely chopped) chocolate to the melted mixture, stirring until the mixture has reached 89°F and is smooth. *See also* CHOCOLATE.

temple orange *see* TANGOR

tempura [tehm-POOR-uh; TEHM-poor-uh] A Japanese specialty of batter-dipped, deep-fried pieces of fish or vegetables. Tempura, which is usually accompanied by SOY SAUCE, can be served as an HORS D'OEUVRE, first course or entrée.

temu kunci *see* FINGERROOT

Tencha tea Considered one of the finest of the green teas, Tencha hails from Japan and is commonly used for tea ceremonies. *See also* TEA.

tenderizer *see* MEAT TENDERIZERS

tenderloin *see* SHORT LOIN

tendon [tehn-DOHN] A type of DONBURI dish consisting of TEMPURA-fried shrimp and a DASHI-based broth served over boiled rice.

Tennessee whiskey A straight WHISKEY that is, for the most part, very similar to BOURBON, which is why it's sometimes called "Tennessee bourbon." It must be made from a MASH of at least 51 percent of a single grain (usually, but not always, corn), must not exceed 160 PROOF (80 percent alcohol), must be aged in oak barrels for 2 years and may only be diluted with water to no less than 80 proof. The biggest difference between bourbon and Tennessee whiskey is that the latter is slowly filtered through large vats of sugar-maple charcoal, which gives it a definitively sweet characteristic.

tentsuyu [TENT-soo-yoo] Japanese dipping sauce for TEMPURA, made of DASHI, MIRIN and SOY SAUCE. Tentsuyu is available in bottles or cans in Asian markets. *See also* SAUCE.

tepache [tay-PAH-chay] A type of low-alcohol hard CIDER made primarily from the flesh and rind of pineapple. Sometimes other fruits such as apples and oranges are added to the blend. Spices such as allspice, cinnamon and clove add flavor, and PILONCILLO or regular brown sugar is added for sweetness. The drink is popular in Mexico and has been made there for centuries. Tepache is fermented for just a few days so it has only a slight fizziness. Beer is often added to augment the beverage.

tepín *see* PEQUÍN CHILE

tequila [teh-KEE-luh] A colorless or pale straw-colored liquor made by fermenting and distilling the sweet sap of the AGAVE plant. Tequila is made in and around the small town of Tequila, in Mexico's Jalisco province. In order to be classified as tequila, distilled spirits must be produced from blue agave plants grown in a precisely delineated area in the five Mexican states of Guanajuato, Jalisco, Michoacan, Mayarit and Tamaulipas. Tequilas labeled "100% Blue Agave" are considered the best. Mexican law states that tequila must be made with *at least* 51 percent blue agave; the remaining 49 percent is most commonly sugarcane, although other raw products may be used. Tequila is generally bottled at 80 proof although some of the AGED versions are bottled at higher alcohol levels. There are four categories of tequila: *blanco, joven abocado, reposado* and *añejo.* Tequila **blanco** (also known as *white, silver* or *plata*) is bottled soon after distillation. Its smooth, fresh flavor has an herbaceous, peppery quality. Tequila **joven abocado** (also called *gold*) is a tequila blanco with flavoring and coloring added; it doesn't have to be aged. Tequila **reposado** may also contain added flavoring and coloring and must be aged at least 2 months but can be aged for up to a year. The wood aging (usually in oak) endows reposados with hints of vanilla and spice and produces character more mellow than that of tequila blanco. Some reposados also use the word "gold" on their label, which gives the impression that golds have been aged, although there's no such legal requirement. Tequila **añejo** is aged for at least 1 year (and often 2 to 3 years). The smooth, elegant and complex flavor of the best añejos is often compared to that of fine COGNACS. *See also* MEZCAL; PULQUE.

terasi [teh-RAH-see] *see* SHRIMP PASTE

teriyaki [tehr-uh-YAH-kee; tehr-ee-YAK-kee] *n.* 1. A Japanese dish of food, such as beef or chicken, that has been marinated in a mixture of SOY SAUCE, SAKE (or SHERRY), sugar, ginger and seasonings before being grilled, broiled or fried. The sugar in the marinade gives the cooked food a slight glaze. 2. A homemade or commercially prepared sauce made with the above ingredients.

terrapin [TEHR-uh-pihn] *see* TURTLE

terrine A cooking container made of glazed earthenware, ceramic or enameled cast iron with vertical sides and a lid. Terrines come in various sizes and shapes including round and rectangular. PÂTÉ cooked in them is called *pâté en terrine (see* PÂTÉ*). See also* TUREEN.

terroir [teh-RWAAR] French for "soil," though in the culinary world *terroir* has an expanded meaning referring to a sense of place—the contribution of environmental factors that affect the final product, such as wine or cheese. With wine, this can include reference to the type of soil (chalky, claylike, gravelly, sandy), as well as other, such as altitude, vineyard position relative to the sun, angle of incline and water drainage. With cheese, both pasturage and water are affected by the environment; milk from an animal that grazed in a salt-air climate will be different from that of an animal that's grazed in the mountains. Likewise, cheeses aged in a natural cave will be differently nuanced than those that have matured in man-made aging rooms. The word *terroir* is now also associated with other ARTISANAL foods.

testicles *see* FRIES

Tête de Moine [teht deuh MWAHN] Originally known as *Bellelay, Tête de Moine* ("monk's head") hails from Switzerland and was created by the monks at the Abbey of Bellelay, which was founded in 1136. It's made from raw cow's milk, RIPENED for 3 to 6 months and has a compact, supple texture that ranges from semihard to hard. The flavor is a tangy, earthy mélange of fruit and nuts. Tête de Moine has a FAT CONTENT of at least 51 percent. The traditional way to serve this cheese is to remove the top of the rind and then to shave or scrape off paper-thin "petals" of cheese. Tête de Moine owes much of its current success to the GIROLLE, a specially designed tool for shaving this cheese into thin layers. *See also* CHEESE.

Tetrazzini [teh-trah-ZEE-nee] *see* CHICKEN TETRAZZINI

Texmati rice An AROMATIC RICE that's a cross between American long-grain rice and BASMATI. It has more flavor and fragrance than its American parent and less than basmati. Texmati comes in both white and brown versions, with the brown having a nuttier nuance than the white. *See also* RICE.

Tex-Mex A term given to food (music, etc.) based on the combined cultures of Texas and Mexico. Tex-Mex food encompasses a wide variety of dishes such as BURRITOS, NACHOS and TACOS.

textured vegetable protein; TVP A bland-tasting, dried, granular product produced from highly refined defatted SOYBEAN meal. It's used in countless MEAT ANALOG products, from soy burgers to hot dogs, and also as an extender in myriad processed foods from breakfast cereal to frozen desserts. TVP can be found in bulk and 1-pound bags in natural food stores. It should be noted that TVP can cause gastric distress because it contains gas-producing oligosaccharides (*see* BEANS).

TG; TGase *see* TRANSGLUTAMINASE

Thai basil *see* BASIL

Thai chile [TI] Only about 1 to 1½ inches long and ¼ inch in diameter, this diminutive CHILE packs a fiery punch that doesn't dissipate with cooking. It has a SCOVILLE SCALE rating ranging from 50,000 to 100,000. The thin-fleshed Thai chile ranges in color from green to red when fully ripe. It's a popular addition in many Southeast Asian dishes. The **bird chile** is the dried form. It's so named because drying causes the chile to hook into a bird's-beak shape.

Thai coffee [TI] Coffee mixed with SWEETENED CONDENSED MILK.

Thai eggplant A tiny (1 to 2 inches in diameter) eggplant that ranges in color from green to white to green with white stripes. Thai eggplant has a crunchy, slightly bitter flesh that lends itself to pickled condiments, such as NAM PRIK. It can be found in Thai markets and should be refrigerated, tightly wrapped in a plastic bag, for up to 1 week.

Thai ginger [TI] *see* GALANGAL

the [teh] Italian for "tea." Also "tea."

Thermidor [THER-mih-dohr] *see* LOBSTER THERMIDOR

thermometer *see* CANDY THERMOMETER; FREEZER/REFRIGERATOR THERMOMETER; MEAT THERMOMETER; OVEN THERMOMETER

thermophilic cultures *see* STARTER

thickback *see* SOLE

thimbleberry [THIHM-buhl-bair-ee] Any of several thimble-shaped American raspberries, especially the black raspberry. *See also* RASPBERRY.

thin To dilute mixtures such as soups, sauces, batters, etc., by adding more liquid.

Thompson seedless grape The best-selling grape in the United States, the Thompson seedless is medium-size with a thin, pale green skin. It contains no seeds and has a sweet, rather bland flavor. Its peak season is from June to November. *See also* GRAPE.

thorny coriander *see* SAW-LEAF HERB

thosai *see* DOSA

Thousand Island dressing A MAYONNAISE-based salad dressing made with CHILI SAUCE and finely chopped ingredients such as stuffed green olives, green peppers, pickles, onions and hard-cooked egg. It's also sometimes used as a sandwich spread.

thousand-year egg *see* HUNDRED-YEAR EGG

threadfin *see* PACIFIC THREADFIN

thread stage A test for SUGAR SYRUP in which a drop of boiling syrup forms a soft 2-inch thread when immersed in cold water. On a CANDY THERMOMETER, the thread stage is between 230° and 234°F. *See also* Candymaking Cold-Water Tests, page 866.

three bird roast *see* TURDUCKEN

three milks cake *see* PASTEL DE TRES LECHES

thuck *see* TTEOK

Thuringer [THOOR-ihn-juhr; TOOR-ihn-juhr] Any of several fresh and smoked sausages named for the former German region of Thuringia. Thuringers include some CERVELATS and BLOOD SAUSAGES. The spices CORIANDER and CARAWAY SEED are integral to many of these sausages.

thyme [TIME] There are several varieties of this mint-family member, a perennial herb native to southern Europe and the Mediterranean. **Garden thyme**, the most often used variety, is a bush with gray-green leaves giving off a pungent minty, light-lemon aroma. Subvarieties include the narrow-leafed *French thyme* and broad-leafed *English thyme*. The most well-known subvariety of **wild thyme**—a thick ground cover—is *lemon thyme,* an herb with a more pronounced lemon aroma than garden thyme. Whatever the variety, thyme is widely used in cooking to add flavor to vegetables, meat, poultry and fish dishes, soups and cream sauces. It's a basic herb of French cuisine and integral to BOUQUET GARNI. Fresh thyme is available in some specialty produce shops and supermarkets. Dried thyme—both leaf and powder form—is commonly available in supermarkets. As with all herbs, thyme should be stored in a cool, dark place for no more than 6 months. *See also* HERBS; Seasoning Suggestions, page 891.

Tia Maria [tee-uh muh-REE-uh] A rum-based, coffee-flavored Jamaican LIQUEUR made from Blue Mountain coffee. It's drier (*see* DRY) and lighter than KAHLÚA.

tian [TYAH/V] A French word from the Provençal language describing a shallow, EARTHENWARE casserole, as well as the food that it contains. A typical tian consists of layered, sliced vegetables (such as eggplant, bell peppers and tomatoes) baked until tender. A tian is usually topped by breadcrumbs and sometimes grated cheese. The vegetables may also be chopped, and sometimes bits of meat are included.

Tibetan goji berry [tih-BEH-tan GOH-jee] *see* WOLFBERRY

tiger lily buds Also called *golden needles* and simply *lily buds,* the dried golden buds of the tiger lily are 2 to 3 inches long and have a delicate, musky-sweet flavor. They're used both as vegetable and garnish in various STIR-FRIED dishes. The delicate tiger lily buds are available in 4- to 8-ounce cellophane bags in Asian markets. They must be soaked in water prior to using.

tiger nuts *see* CHUFA

tikka [TEE-kah] Hindi for chunks of meat cooked on skewers; similar to KEBAB.

tilapia [tuh-LAH-pee-uh] An important food fish in Africa for eons, tilapia are AQUACULTURED around the world from Asia, to South America, to the United States and Canada. The lowfat flesh is white (sometimes tinged with pink), sweet and fine-textured. It's suitable for baking, broiling, grilling and steaming. The tilapia is also called *St. Peter's fish* and, in Hawaii, *Hawaiian sun fish*. *See also* FISH.

ti leaves [TEE] The leaves of a member of the AGAVE family, used in Polynesia to wrap foods to be cooked. The leaves are removed before the food is eaten. Dried ti leaves, which can be found in some ethnic markets, must be soaked to soften before using. A Hawaiian liquor called OKOLEHAO is made from a mash of the ti plant.

tilefish A diet of crab and other CRUSTACEANS gives the tilefish a marvelously delicate flavor. This Atlantic-based fish is multicolored and dotted with distinctive yellow spots. Its lowfat flesh is very firm yet tender. The tilefish ranges from 2 to over 50 pounds. Atlantic tilefish is available fresh and frozen in whole (smaller ones), steak and fillet forms. It's suitable for almost any method of cooking. *See also* FISH.

Tillamook [TIHL-uh-mook] A yellow CHEDDAR produced in and around Tillamook, Oregon. It is made from raw milk and ranges in flavor from mild to sharp. Aged Tillamook is highly prized but seldom seen anywhere but the West Coast. *See also* CHEESE.

Tilsit; Tilsiter [TIHL-ziht; TIHL-zih-ter] A CHEESE that originated in Tilsit, East Prussia (Tilsit is now part of Russia and known as Sovetsk), when Dutch immigrants accidentally created it while attempting to make GOUDA. It's now made in a variety of forms in various other countries including Denmark, where it's sometimes called *Havarti Tilsit*; Germany, where it's *Tilsiter;* or *Tollenser;* and Switzerland, where it was called *Royalp* or *Royalp Tilsiter* but today is generally referred to as *Tilsiter* or *Tilsit*. Tilsit has a semisoft to semihard texture with irregular eyes or cracks. Commercially produced Tilsit is made from PASTEURIZED milk and has a pale yellow interior surrounded by a dark reddish-yellow rind. Its flavor is mild, spicy and tangy but becomes stronger and more pungent with age. A very strong version, called **Farmhouse Tilsit**, is made from raw milk and is aged for about 5 months, which creates a cheese approaching LIMBURGER in aroma. *See also* CHEESE.

timbale [TIHM-buhl; tihm-BAHL] 1. A mold, generally high-sided, drum-shaped and slightly tapered at the bottom and closed end, used to bake various dishes. 2. A dish—usually based on custard, FORCEMEAT or RISOTTO combined with meat, fish, vegetables, cheese, etc.—baked in such a mold. The dish is unmolded and often served as an entrée (and sometimes as a first course) with a sauce such as BÉCHAMEL. 3. A pastry shell made by dipping a timbale iron first into a batter, then into deep, hot fat. When the crisp pastry is pushed off the iron and cooled, it can be filled with a sweet or savory mixture. **Timbale irons** come in various sizes and shapes such as hearts, stars and butterflies. They're available in specialty cookware stores.

timballo [teem-BAH-loh] Italian for "TIMBALE."

timur *see* SZECHUAN PEPPER

tips An acronym for "to insure prompt service," tips are gratuities given to a server, bellhop, etc. for providing a service.

tipsy parson; tipsy pudding Similar to TRIFLE, this old-fashioned English dessert consists of several layers of SPONGE CAKE soaked with wine or BRANDY, sprinkled with almonds and layered with whipped cream or custard. It was thought that too much of this would make one tipsy.

tiramisù; tirami sù [tih-ruh-mee-SOO; tih-ruh-MEE-soo] 1. The translation for *tiramisu* is "carry me up" (or "pick me up"), and many assume the unspoken continuation must surely be "to heaven." *Tiramisu* is an airy mélange of sponge cake or ladyfingers dipped in a coffee-MARSALA mixture, then layered with MASCARPONE and grated chocolate. Although *tiramisu* is sometimes referred to as an Italian TRIFLE, its texture is much lighter than that dessert. 2. A dark brown Italian LIQUEUR with a pronounced coffee-almond flavor.

tisane [tih-ZAN; tih-ZAHN] A tealike drink (commonly called *herb tea*) made by steeping any of various herbs, flowers, spices, etc. in boiling water. Such brews have long been used for their calming and rejuvenating qualities. Some of the herbs more commonly used for tisane blends are balm, chamomile, hyssop, mint and tansy.

tlacoyo [tihl-ah-KOHY-oh] Traditional Mexican dish consisting of a very thick, torpedo-shaped cake made from fried or toasted masa that is filled with black beans, cheese, FAVA BEANS, FRIJOLES REFRITOS and a finely ground pork mixture called CHICHARRÓN, topped with salsa. It's similar to the Mexican GORDITA, which is round, and the PUPUSA from El Salvador.

tlayudas *see* CLAYUDAS

toad-in-the-hole This comically named British dish consists of a YORKSHIRE PUDDING batter to which small cooked link sausages are added. The dish is baked until the batter puffs up around the sausages (making them the "toads in the hole") and becomes golden brown. It's most often served for lunch or dinner.

tobiko [toh-BEE-koh] The bright orange-red ROE of the FLYING FISH. With its crunchy texture and mildly sweet flavor, tobiko is widely used in Hawaiian and Japanese cuisine. **Wasabi tobiko** is a brilliant lime green color and hot on the palate, both effects resulting from mixing tobiko with the Japanese horseradish, WASABI. Both are available in Asian markets, usually frozen.

toddy; *pl.* **toddies** [TOD-ee] Although toddy has different meanings around the world, in the United States and Britain, it refers to a hot water-based drink, generally spiced and liberally laced with alcohol. The word comes from *tari,* the Hindu word used for the sap or juice of a palm tree. In Asia, this sap was often fermented to create an alcoholic beverage. British sailors picked up on the idea, which eventually evolved into the toddy.

toffee; toffy [TAWF-ee] A candy made by cooking sugar, water (or cream) and usually butter to anywhere from 260° to 310°F on a CANDY THERMOMETER, depending on whether a chewy or crunchy toffee is preferred. Other ingredients such as nuts may be added. *See also* TAFFY.

tofu [TOH-foo] Also known as *soybean curd* and *bean curd,* custardlike white tofu is made from curdled SOY MILK, an iron-rich liquid extracted from ground, cooked SOYBEANS. The resulting curds are drained and pressed in a fashion similar to cheesemaking. The firmness of the resulting tofu depends on how much WHEY has been extracted. Tofu has a bland, slightly nutty flavor that gives it a chameleonlike capability to take on the flavor of the food with which it's cooked. It's texture is smooth and creamy yet it's firm enough to slice. Tofu comes in regular, low-fat and nonfat varieties, and in extra-firm, firm and soft styles. There's also a **silken tofu** (named for its silky-smooth texture) that comes in soft, regular and firm styles. Tofu is available in natural food stores, Asian markets and most supermarkets. The cakes are sold in a variety of forms including the following: packed in water in sealed plastic containers; vacuumpacked in plastic without water; aseptically sealed in packaging that may be kept unopened at room temperature for up to 8 months; in bulk in large, open crocks of water; and freeze-dried, a product that must be reconstituted with boiling water. Tofu, which is sometimes fortified with calcium, is very perishable and should be refrigerated for no more than a week. If it's packaged in water, drain it and cover with fresh water. All tofu should be stored covered with water, which should be changed daily. Tofu can be frozen up to 3 months. Freezing will change its texture, making it slightly chewier. The versatile tofu can be sliced, diced or mashed and used in a variety of dishes including soups, STIR-FRY dishes, casseroles, salads, sandwiches, salad dressings and sauces. It's easy to digest, low in calories, calcium and sodium, high in protein and cholesterol-free—all of which makes it one of today's most healthful foods.

togarashi [toh-gah-RAH-shee] Small, hot, red Japanese CHILE available fresh and in various dried forms—rounds, flakes and powder. Togarashi is also known as *ichimi.*

Tokay grape; Tokay wine [toh-KAY] 1. A large, oval California table grape (also called *Flame Tokay*) with a thick red skin and bland-tasting flesh with seeds. Tokays are available from August through December. They're also sometimes used to make wine of the same name. 2. Tokay is also a sweet white wine from Hungary's Tokay region, which is made primarily from the Furmint grape. BOTRYTIS CINEREA–infected grapes from the better vintages produce marvelous DESSERT WINES that rival the best from France and Germany.

Tollenser *see* TILSIT

Toll House cookie This—the original chocolate-chip cookie—was created in the 1930s by Ruth Wakefield, who ran the Toll House Restaurant outside of Whitman, Massachusetts. Mrs. Wakefield, in a moment of brilliant inspiration, cut up bars of chocolate to add to a basic butter-cookie dough. History was made. Today, the chocolate-chip cookie is the most popular in the United States.

toma [TOH-mah] *see* TOMME

tomalley [TOM-al-ee; toh-MAL-ee] Considered a delicacy, tomalley is the green-colored liver of a LOBSTER. It may be eaten alone but is often also added to sauces.

Tom and Jerry Favored by skiers and cold-weather captives, the Tom and Jerry is a hot drink made with beaten eggs, hot milk or water, liquor (such as brandy, bourbon or rum), sugar and spices. It's served in a large mug and usually sprinkled with grated nutmeg. The drink takes its name from the principal characters in the early 19th-century novel, *Life in London.*

tomatillo [tohm-ah-TEE-oh] This fruit, which is also called *Mexican green tomato,* belongs to the same nightshade family as the tomato. In fact, it resembles a small green tomato in size, shape and appearance except for the fact that it has a thin parchmentlike covering. The papery husk is a clue to the fact that the tomatillo is also related to the CAPE GOOSE-BERRY. Although tomatillos can ripen to yellow, they are generally used while still green and quite firm. Their flavor has hints of lemon, apple and herbs. Tomatillos are available sporadically year-round in specialty produce stores, Latin American markets and some supermarkets. Choose firm fruit with dry, tight-fitting husks. Store in a paper bag in the refrigerator for up to a month. Remove husk and wash fruit before using. Cooking enhances the tomatillo's flavor and softens its thick skin. Tomatillos are popular in Mexican and Southwest cooking for use in a variety of dishes including GUACAMOLE and many sauces. They can be used raw in salads and SALSAS for a more acidic taste. Canned tomatillos are available in ethnic markets. Tomatillos are rich in vitamin A and contain a good amount of vitamin C. The tomatillo is also called *jamberry*.

tomato; tomatoes [tuh-MAY-toh; tuh-MAH-toh] Like the potato and eggplant, the tomato is a member of the nightshade family. It's the fruit of a vine native to South America. By the time European explorers arrived in the New World, the tomato had made its way up into Central America and Mexico. The Spanish carried plants back home from Mexico, but it took some time for tomatoes to be accepted in Spain because it was thought that—like various other members of the nightshade family—they were poisonous. Some tomato advocates, however, claimed the fruit had aphrodisiac powers and, in fact, the French called them *pommes d'amour,* "love apples." It wasn't until the 1900s that the tomato gained some measure of popularity in the United States. Today this fruit is one of America's favorite "vegetables," a classification the government gave the tomato for trade purposes in 1893. Dozens of tomato varieties are available today—ranging widely in size, shape and color. Among the most commonly marketed is the **beefsteak tomato**, which is delicious both raw and cooked. It's large, bright red and slightly elliptical in shape. **Globe tomatoes** are medium-size, firm and juicy. Like the beefsteak, they're good both raw and cooked. Another variety is the **plum tomato** (also called *Italian plum* and *Roma*), a flavorful egg-shaped tomato that comes in red and yellow versions. **Grape tomatoes** are baby romas. The medium-size **green tomato** has a piquant flavor, which makes it excellent for frying, broiling and adding to relishes. The small **cherry tomato** is about 1 inch in diameter and can be red or yellow-gold in color. It's very popular—both for eating and as a garnish—because of its bright color and excellent flavor. The yellow cherry tomato is slightly less acidic than the red and therefore somewhat blander in flavor. Though it's long been popular raw in salads, the cherry tomato is gaining favor as a cooked side dish, quickly sautéed with herbs. The **yellow pear tomato** is slightly smaller than the cherry tomato and resembles a tiny pear. It's used in the same manner as the cherry tomato. **Currant tomatoes** are the tiniest of the species, measuring only about 0.7 inches in diameter and weighing about $1/8$ ounce. They come in both red and yellow varieties and have a sweet, crisp flesh. Finding a niche in some produce markets are several unique looking and extremely flavorful **heirloom tomatoes** (*see* HEIRLOOM SEEDS). Among the many popular varieties are the **purple tomatoes**

(such as *Purple Calabash, Brandywine* and *Cherokee Purple*), the skins of which can range in color from a dusky pink with purple shoulders to a dusky rose-purple. Depending on the variety, the flesh color can vary from crimson to a brownish purple-pink. **Bicolored and striped tomatoes** (such as *Marvel Striped, Big White Pink Stripe* and *Hillbilly*) have an orangey skin with faint red striations. This fruit's bicolor flesh is a brilliant yellow with a red center. Fresh tomatoes are available year-round, with the peak season from June through September. The most succulent, flavorful tomatoes are those that are "vine-ripened," usually only available in specialty produce markets. Unfortunately, such tomatoes are very perishable, which is why supermarkets almost always carry tomatoes that have been picked green and ripened with ethylene gas or in special warming rooms. Such tomatoes will never have the texture, aroma and taste of the vine-ripened fruit. Choose firm, well-shaped tomatoes that are noticeably fragrant and richly colored (for their variety). They should be free from blemishes, heavy for their size and give slightly to palm pressure. Ripe tomatoes should be stored at room temperature and used within a few days. They should never be refrigerated—cold temperatures make the flesh pulpy and kill the flavor. Unripe fruit can be ripened by placing it in a pierced paper bag with an apple for several days at room temperature (65° to 75°F). Do not refrigerate or set in the sun. Tomato skins can be removed by BLANCHING. **Sun-dried tomatoes** are, as the name indicates, dried in the sun (or by other, artificial methods). The result is a chewy, intensely flavored, sweet, dark red tomato. Sun-dried tomatoes are usually either packed in oil or dry-packed in cellophane. The dry-pack type benefits from soaking in oil or other liquid before use. Sun-dried tomatoes add their rich flavor to sauces, soups, sandwiches, salads and myriad other dishes. **Canned tomatoes** are available in various forms including peeled, whole, crushed, and those with herbs such as oregano and/or basil added. **Tomato paste**, which is available in cans and tubes, consists of tomatoes that have been cooked for several hours, strained and reduced to a deep red, richly flavored concentrate. Canned **tomato purée** consists of tomatoes that have been cooked briefly and strained, resulting in a thick liquid. **Tomato sauce** is a slightly thinner tomato purée, often with seasonings and other flavorings added so that it is ready to use in various dishes or as a base for other sauces. Tomatoes are rich in vitamin C and contain appreciable amounts of vitamins A and B, potassium, iron and phosphorus. A medium tomato has about as much fiber as a slice of whole-wheat bread and only about 35 calories. *See also* TOMATILLO.

tomato aspic *see* ASPIC

tomato paste *see* TOMATO

tomato purée *see* TOMATO

tomato sauce *see* TOMATO

tombo [TOHM-boh] The Hawaiian name for albacore TUNA.

Tom Collins *see* COLLINS

tom kha; tome kha [tohm kah] A creamy, spicy soup popular in Laos, Thailand and nearby countries. Its main ingredients are COCONUT MILK, GALANGAL and LEMON GRASS. The most popular version, *tom kha kai* or *tom kha gai,* has chicken added; *kha* is Thai for "galangal" and *kai* or *gai* is "chicken." Other variations have beef, shrimp, mushrooms, pork or tofu in them. Additional ingredients typically included are chili peppers or NAM PRIK PAO, CILANTRO or CORIANDER, FISH SAUCE, KAFFIR LIME LEAVES and STRAW MUSHROOMS. The result is creamy, hot, sour and salty, with a hint of sweetness.

tomme; tome; tommette [TOM] A French term (presumably from the Greek *tomos*) for a section, or part of the whole. Throughout the ages of cheese terminology, the term has evolved to describe various cheeses: small cheeses made from partial milkings, those produced from small-yield winter milkings, and cheeses made from the milk of more than one herd—in general, small cheeses produced when there wasn't enough milk to make large ones. Today the words *tomme* and *tome* typically refer to a range of small- to medium-size cheeses with a rounded WHEEL shape. Such cheeses can be made from a single milk (cow's, goat's or sheep's) or a mixture of milks. The smallest version is a *tommette*, which typically weighs under a pound. In Italy such cheeses are called *toma. See also* CHEESE.

Tomme d'Abondance *see* ABONDANCE

Tomme de Savoie (AOC; PGI) [TOM deuh sah-VWAH] SEMI-SOFT TO SEMIHARD COW's-milk cheese made in the Savoie and Haut-Savoie départements in the mountains of eastern France. These $3^{1}/_{2}$- to 12-pound wheels are made from milk that's left over from making the 40- to 150-pound wheels of BEAUFORT, one of the area's top cheeses. These smaller Tomme de Savoie wheels are RIPENED for 2 to 3 months, producing thick, brownish-gray rinds with patches of red and yellow mold and interiors that are white to pale yellow with a few small EYES. The younger cheeses are soft and supple; those with more age slightly firmer. The flavor of Tomme de Savoie is mild, delicate and somewhat milky, nutty and savory. There's a wide range for FAT CONTENT (from 20 to 45 percent or more) depending on whether whole milk or partially skimmed milk is used. Look for the label term *fabriqué en Savoie* ("made in Savoie") to ensure that you're purchasing an authentic Tomme de Savoie cheese.

tom yum; tom yam; tome yum [tohm yoom; tohm yahm] A clear hot-and-sour soup popular in Laos, Thailand and nearby countries.

The hot is provided by crushed chili peppers or NAM PRIK PAO; the sour comes from the LEMON GRASS and fresh lime juice. Recipes vary but usually contain FISH SAUCE, GALANGAL, KAFFIR LIME LEAVES and STRAW MUSHROOMS. Chicken broth or shrimp broth are often used as a base. When prawns or shrimp are added it's called *tom yum goong* or *tom yam kung*, and it's *tom yum gai* or *tom yam kai* when chicken is added. Numerous other variations abound including some with a small amount of COCONUT MILK. Thai soups with a lot of coconut milk in them are usually called TOM KHA, not tom yum.

tongho *see* CHRYSANTHEMUM LEAVES

tongue [TUHNG] Tongues of beef, veal, lamb and pork are nutritious and appetizing VARIETY MEATS. They can be found fresh, pickled, smoked and CORNED and can be prepared in a variety of ways to be served hot or cold. All tongue is tough and requires long, slow cooking to make it tender. Beef tongues weigh from 2 to 5 pounds, veal tongues from $\frac{1}{2}$ to 2 pounds, pork tongues about 1 pound and lamb tongues around $\frac{1}{4}$ pound. Fresh tongue should be refrigerated for no more than a day before cooking. Scrub thoroughly before using.

tongue sausage A SAUSAGE made from TONGUE plus various other meats and often pistachios. It's available in large or small links.

tonic water [TAHN-ik] Also called *quinine water,* tonic is water charged with carbon dioxide and flavored with fruit EXTRACTS, sugar and usually a soupçon of QUININE. It's popular as a mixer, such as with gin to create "gin and tonic."

tonka bean Taken from the pod of a tropical South American tree, this dark wrinkled seed is known for its amazing aroma, which is reminiscent of vanilla with hints of almonds, caramel, cherries, cinnamon and cloves. The thumb-sized, egg-shaped pods each contain one seed slightly bigger than an almond. Although they've been used as a vanilla substitute, in perfume, soft drinks, candies and tobacco products, tonka beans have been banned in the United States since 1954 because they contain coumarin. Although tonka beans don't seem to have any anti-coagulant characteristics themselves, the beans can be processed to make anti-coagulant drugs from coumarin. Therefore, the FDA deems them illegal. Nonetheless, enterprising chefs are using tonka beans in some of their creative dishes. In most cases, tonka beans are used sparingly, in the form of shavings, so a single bean can be used in multiple dishes. But, as of this writing, they're still illegal.

tonkatsu [tohn-KAHT-soo] A favorite Japanese comfort food consisting of a pork cutlet that's DREDGED in flour, dipped in beaten egg and PANKO and deep-fried. *Ton* is Japanese for "pork" and *katsu* is the shortened version of *katsuretsu*, meaning "cutlet." Tonkatsu is served in myriad ways—from a simple sandwich to elaborate haute cuisine. It's so popular that some Japanese restaurants specialize in tonkatsu. It was introduced to Japan by Europeans but has been Japanized over the years. One traditionally popular plate is the pork cutlet, a bowl of rice and thinly sliced cabbage. There are other *katsu* dishes featuring other meats, but tonkatsu is the most popular. *See also* DONBURI.

tonnato [tohn-NAH-toh] From the Italian *tonno* ("tuna"), the word *tonnato* refers culinarily to dishes that are somehow prepared with or accompanied by tuna. The most well-known preparation is *vitello tonnato*, which consists of cold, sliced, roasted veal accompanied with a sauce of puréed tuna, anchovy filets, capers, lemon juice and olive oil.

tonno [TOH-noh] Italian for "tuna."

topfen [TOP-fuhn] Austrian for "QUARK."

topinambour *see* SUNCHOKE

top blade steak Flavorful cut of beef from the CHUCK section near the shoulder blade. It can be tender enough for grilling, broiling or sautéing if the connective tissue is removed or it's marinated first, but it's definitely more tender if braised. The top blade steak is also known as top boneless chuck steak and flat iron steak, although the flat iron steak, differs slightly in that the connective tissue is already removed.

top boneless chuck steak *see* TOP BLADE STEAK

top loin *see* SHORT LOIN

top round *see* ROUND

top sirloin *see* SIRLOIN

toque [TOHK] Although toque describes at least three different hat styles, in the culinary world it refers to the tall white hat worn by a chef. Toques range from pouffy and relaxed to stiff and pleated. They were first worn by chefs in the 1820s.

torchon *see* FOIE GRAS

toro *see* SUSHI

torrone [tohr-ROH-nay] *see* NOUGAT

torta [TOHR-tuh] 1. Italian for "tart," "pie" or "cake." 2. Spanish for "cake," "loaf" or "sandwich."

torte [TOHRT] A rich cake, often made with little or no flour but instead with ground nuts or breadcrumbs, eggs, sugar and flavorings. Tortes are often multilayered and filled with BUTTERCREAM, jams, etc.

tortellini; tortelloni *see* Pasta Glossary, page 883

tortiglioni *see* Pasta Glossary, page 883

tortilla [tohr-TEE-yuh] 1. Mexico's everyday bread, the UNLEAVENED tortilla is round and flat—it resembles a very thin pancake. The hand-shaped tortilla can be made from corn flour (MASA) or wheat flour, but is always baked on a griddle (COMAL). It can be eaten plain or wrapped around various fillings. Tortillas are the base for BURRITOS, TACOS and a multitude of other dishes. Both corn and flour tortillas are sold prepackaged in the refrigerator section of most supermarkets. 2. In Spain, the word *tortilla* refers to a thin OMELET, the traditional version of which contains potatoes and Spanish onions. Other ingredients that may be used include ham, CHORIZO and peppers.

tortoise [TOHR-tuhs] *see* TURTLE

tortoni [tohr-TOH-nee] Hailing from Italy, this rich frozen dessert consists of sweetened whipped cream (sometimes ice cream) flavored with spirits such as SHERRY or RUM and combined or topped with chopped almonds or MACAROON crumbs. This dessert is often called *biscuit tortoni,* especially when served in small paper cups.

toshay *see* DOSA

Tostilocos; Tosti locos A Mexican fast-food dish consisting of a base usually made of Tostitos corn chips covered with a variety of toppings including CHAMOY, cucumber, CUERITOS, hot sauce, jicama, lime juice and peanuts. In Tijuana, where this chip dish is thought to have originated, Tostilocos vendors are everywhere—at sporting events, in city parks and even outside bars. A popular serving method is to simply split open a bag of Tostitos (although Cheetos and other snack foods are sometimes used) and pile the toppings on the chips in the bag.

toss, to To turn pieces of food over multiple times, thereby mixing the ingredients together. The term is most often applied to salad, where various ingredients and the salad dressing are tossed together, mixing the ingredients and coating them with the dressing.

tostada [toh-STAH-duh] A crisp-fried TORTILLA (corn or flour) topped with various ingredients such as REFRIED BEANS, shredded chicken or beef, shredded lettuce, diced tomatoes, grated cheese, sour cream or GUACAMOLE. Tostadas can be large or small and served as an appetizer or entrée.

tostones [tohs-TOH-nays] Green ½-inch-thick plantain slices (*see* BANANA) that have been soaked in cold ADOBO-flavored water before being deep-fried. After cooling, the slices are flattened slightly and fried again until crisp. Popular in Puerto Rico and the Dominican Republic, tostones are served as a side dish.

Toulouse [too-LOOZ] A small French SAUSAGE made of coarsely diced pork flavored with wine, garlic and seasonings. Toulouse is usually braised or fried and is good in dishes such as CASSOULET.

tourage [too-RAHJ] A French term for the technique of making PUFF PASTRY whereby the dough is repeatedly folded into thirds, rolled out and folded into thirds again. This process creates hundreds of flaky pastry layers.

tournant [toor-NAH*N*] *see* BRIGADE SYSTEM

tournedo [TOOR-nih-doh; toor-nih-DOH] A beef steak cut from the TENDERLOIN, measuring ¾ to 1 inch thick and 2 to 2½ inches in diameter. Since tournedos are very lean, they're sometimes wrapped in pork fat or bacon prior to cooking. They're classically served on fried bread rounds and topped with a sauce.

trail mix A dry snack food that typically consists of a combination of ingredients such as nuts, seeds, dried fruit (like cranberries or raisins), GRANOLA clusters, coconut and sometimes chocolate or carob, in the form of chips or M&Ms. Trail mix began as a convenient energy booster for hikers and campers, but is just as often found today computer-side. It was once popularly referred to as *gorp*, which urban legend suggests is an acronym for "good old raisins and peanuts" or "granola, oats, raisins and peanuts," but which may just as readily date back to the early 1900s, when gorp referred to "eating greedily." In Australia, New Zealand and the U.K., trail mix is referred to as *scroggin*.

trans fatty acids A type of fat created when oils are hydrogenated, which chemically transforms them from their normal liquid state (at room temperature) into solids. During the hydrogenation procedure extra hydrogen atoms are pumped into unsaturated fat, thereby creating trans fatty acids. This process converts the mixture into a saturated fat, which obliterates its polyunsaturate benefits. Trans fatty acids can be found in a wide array of processed foods including cookies and MARGARINES. Any food with "hydrogenated oils" or "partially hydrogenated oils" on the label contains trans fatty acids. Some researchers believe such foods may actually be more damaging than regular saturated fats to those watching their cholesterol, saying trans fatty acids decrease the good (HDL) cholesterol and increase the bad LDLs. Other scientists argue that the evidence is inconclusive and that trans fatty acids are no worse than butter. In either case, it would seem that "moderation" is the watchword when consuming foods containing trans fatty acids. *See also* FATS AND OILS.

transglutaminase; TG; TGase [trans-GLOO-tah-mee-neez] Naturally occurring enzyme that binds protein molecules together. It's known as *meat glue* because it's used to bind chunks of meat together and allows them to be formed into a single piece. Since it can bind any protein to another, it can be used to bind things like chicken and seafood together or many small pieces of various items into a "sausage" without a CASING. Some imitation crab meat (*see* SURIMI) is now made with transglutaminase. Even proponents acknowledge that some uses are not wise since some foods have different cooking rates and, if combined, would not be done at the same time. They also acknowledge that combining many small pieces of beef would result in a very funny-looking "steak." They say, though, that it allows uniform portions, reduces waste and allows creativity in the kitchen that wasn't possible in the past. In addition, proponents point to the fact that enzymes from papaya are used as meat tenderizers and the animal enzyme rennet is used in cheesemaking. Opponents say there are safety concerns. Even though the FDA recognizes transglutaminase as a GRAS product (generally recognized as safe) when used properly, the concern is for improper use. For example, it's considered safe if bound food is cooked to at least 165 degrees, but what if it isn't? Some are also concerned that meat from different animals glued together could have bacteria issues that aren't a concern with a single piece of muscle meat, and that tracking any problems back to a sick animal would be more difficult because of this. Opponents want more transparency, pointing out that food processers don't currently have to disclose use of transglutaminase and that consumers ought to know if it's being used.

Trapani salt *see* FLEUR DE SEL

Trappist beer Dating back to the Middle Ages, Trappist beers are any of the ALES produced by the six brewing abbeys still in existence (Schaapskooi in the Netherlands; Chimay, Orval, Rochefort, St. Sixtus and Westmalle in Belgium). They're generally dark amber to brown in color, strongly flavored and range in alcohol from about 6 to 12 percent. *See also* BEER.

trash fish A term for fish that fishermen generally throw away because there's little or no commercial value. Trash fish that aren't discarded are generally used for the manufacture of chicken feed. Occasionally, trash fish make the transition from being detritus to being in demand, as in the case of lobster (long ago) and, more recently, MONKFISH.

trasi; trassi *see* SHRIMP PASTE

trassi *see* BALACHAN

trattoria [trah-toh-REE-ah] The Italian term for a casual café. *See also* RISTORANTE.

treacle [TREE-kuhl] A term used mainly in Great Britain for the syrupy by-product created during sugar refining. There are two types: **dark treacle**—which is very much like MOLASSES and which has a somewhat bitter taste, and **light treacle**, which contains fewer impurities than the dark variety, has a lighter flavor and is also called GOLDEN SYRUP.

tree ear *see* WOOD EAR

treemelon *see* PEPINO

tree mushroom; tree oyster *see* OYSTER MUSHROOM

tree nuts *see* NUTS

tree spinach *see* CHAYA LEAF

tree tomato *see* TAMARILLO

treif [trayf] Term derived from the Hebrew word for "torn," referring to foods that are non-KOSHER. Treif is also spelled *trayf*, *treyf* and *tref*.

trenette *see* Pasta Glossary, page 878

trenne *see* Pasta Glossary, page 878

trepang *see* SEA CUCUMBER

tres leches, pastel de [trays LAY-chays, pahss-TAYL day] *see* PASTEL DE TRES LECHES

trevally *see* JACK

Treviso [tray-VEE-soh] *see* RADICCHIO

triangle tip *see* ROUND, BEEF

trifle [TRI-fuhl] Originally from England, this dessert consists of SPONGE CAKE or LADYFINGERS doused with spirits (usually SHERRY), covered with jam and custard, topped with whipped cream and garnished with candied or fresh fruit, nuts or grated chocolate. Trifle is refrigerated for several hours before serving.

Trinidad Moruga Scorpion chile *see* SCOVILLE SCALE

Trinidad Scorpion Butch T chile *see* SCOVILLE SCALE

tripe The tripe found in most markets today is the lining of beef stomach, though that from pork and sheep also fall under the definition. There are two beef stomach chambers and three kinds of tripe, all of which are tough and require long cooking. The best tripe, from the second stomach chamber, is called **honeycomb tripe** because the inner side has a pattern similiar to a honeycomb. It's the most tender and subtly flavored. **Pocket tripe** is cut from the end of the second stomach chamber. It's shaped like a pocket with the inside also being honeycombed. The least desirable **plain or smooth tripe** (with a smooth texture on both sides) comes from the first stomach. Tripe is available fresh (which is actually partially cooked by the packer) in most supermarkets. Choose tripe with a pale off-white color and store for up to a day in the refrigerator. Tripe is also available pickled and canned. The most famous French dish using this VARIETY MEAT is the Norman dish called *tripes à la mode de Caen*— tripe braised with carrots, onions and cider. In Spanish-speaking countries, *menudo* (tripe soup) is a well-known favorite. *See also* VARIETY MEATS.

triple-cream (crème) cheese *see* DOUBLE-CREAM CHEESE

Triple Sec [TRIH-pl-sehk] A clear LIQUEUR flavored with the peels of both sweet and bitter oranges. It's one of the most elegant of the CURAÇAOS. Although the name means "triple DRY," this smooth, fruity potable is sweet, though not cloying. *See also* COINTREAU; CURAÇAO.

tripolini *see* Pasta Glossary, page 883

trippa [TREE-pah] Italian for "TRIPE."

triticale [triht-ih-KAY-lee] This extremely nutritious hybrid of wheat (*Triticum*) and rye (*Secale*) contains more protein and less gluten than wheat and has a nutty-sweet flavor. It comes in several forms including whole berry, flakes and flour and can be found in natural food stores. Triticale flour is also available in some supermarkets. Whole triticale can be cooked and used in a variety of dishes including cereals, casseroles, PILAF-style dishes, etc. Because triticale flour is low in gluten, bread made from it alone is quite heavy. For that reason, it's usually combined half-and-half with wheat flour.

trivet [TRIHV-iht] A short-legged (or otherwise raised) stand used to support hot dishes and protect the surface of a table.

Trockenbeerenauslese [trawk-uhn-bay-ruhn-OWS-lay-zuh] Germany's highest classification for very sweet wines made from grapes left on the vine until nearly dry. Because these grapes, picked one by one at fullest maturity, are very concentrated in flavor and sugar, they produce extremely rich, nectarous wines. *Trockenbeerenauslese* wines are very rare and therefore even more expensive than BEERENAUSLESE wines. *See also* AUSLESE; SPÄTLESE.

trompette de la mort mushroom [trawn-PEHT deh lah MAWR] French for "trumpet of death," this wild mushroom is, in fact, trumpet-shaped. Its cap is thin and gently ruffled, its color ranges from dark gray to black. The flavor of this mushroom is rich, deep and somewhat nutty. Also called *black chanterelle, horn of plenty* and *trumpet of death,* this mushroom can be found fresh from about August to November. The dried form is often available in specialty produce markets and some supermarkets. *See also* MUSHROOM.

trotters *see* PIG'S FEET

trout [TROWT] A large group of fishes belonging to the same family as SALMON and WHITEFISH. Though most trout are freshwater fish, some live in marine waters. When the first European settlers arrived in North America, trout were very abundant. By the late 1860s, however, a number of factors including overfishing and pollution caused the trout population to diminish drastically. By the end of the 19th century trout hatcheries—along with other prevention and regenerative measures taken to forestall the extinction of this delicious fish—were in existence. Today trout are plentiful and vary widely in appearance and size. In general, their flesh is firm-textured with medium to high fat content. Probably the best known of the freshwater species is the **rainbow trout**, which, though native to California, has been transplanted to many different countries and is now one of the most popular varieties in the world. Rainbow trout can grow to up to 50 pounds, but most commercially raised fish average around 8 ounces. **Brook** or **speckled trout** are small (6 to 8 inches long) but considered by many as the best eating. Other popular species include **steelhead** or **salmon trout** (a large—up to 35 pounds—subspecies of the rainbow trout), **cutthroat trout** and **brown trout**. Saltwater trout or sea trout species, which are generally available only on the East Coast, include **gray trout**, **silver trout**, **spotted trout** and **white trout**. Trout are available whole—fresh and frozen—and in fillets. They're most often fried but can also be poached, baked, steamed, grilled and broiled. Whole trout is often stuffed before being cooked. In addition to fresh and frozen, trout can also be found canned, smoked and kippered. *See also* FISH; BLACKFISH; CHAR; WEAKFISH.

truffle [TRUHF-uhl; TROO-fuhl] It's hard to believe that one of the rarest and most expensive foods in the world is located by pigs and dogs. This exceptional fungus grows 3 to 12 inches underground near the roots of trees (usually oak but also chestnut, hazel and beech), never beyond the range of the branches. The difficult-to-find truffle is routed out by animals that have been specially trained for several years. Pigs have keener noses, but dogs are less inclined to gobble up the prize. Once the truffle is found, the farmer (*trufficulteur*) scrapes back the earth, being careful not to touch the truffle with his hands (which will cause the fungus to rot). If the truffle isn't ripe, it's carefully reburied for future harvesting. This methodically slow and labor-intensive harvesting method is what makes truffles so extremely expensive. Truffles have been prized by gourmets for centuries and were credited by the ancient Greeks and Romans with both therapeutic and aphrodisiac powers. A truffle has a rather unappealing appearance—round and irregularly shaped with a thick, rough, wrinkled skin that varies in color from almost black to off-white. Of the almost 70 known varieties, the most desirable is the **black truffle**, also known as *black diamond,* of France's Périgord and Quercy regions and the Umbria region of Italy. Its extremely pungent flesh is black (really very dark brown) with white striations. The next most popular is the **white truffle** (actually off-white or beige) of Italy's Piedmont region, with its earthy, garlicky aroma and flavor. Fresh imported truffles are available from late fall to midwinter in specialty markets. Choose firm, well-shaped truffles with no sign of blemishes. Truffles should be used as soon as possible after purchase but can be stored up to 3 days in the refrigerator. To take full advantage of their perfumy fragrance, bury them in a container of rice or whole eggs and cover tightly before refrigerating. The scent will permeate whatever truffles are stored with, giving the cook a flavor bonus. Brush any surface dust off the truffle and peel the dark species (saving the peelings for soups). White truffles need not be peeled. Canned truffles, truffle paste in a tube and, to a limited extent, frozen truffles are also found in specialty stores. Dark truffles are generally used to flavor foods such as omelets, POLENTAS, RISOTTOS and sauces, like the famous PÉRIGUEUX. The more mildly flavored white truffles are usually served raw by grating them over foods such as pasta or cheese dishes. They're also added at the last minute to cooked dishes. A special implement called a TRUFFLE SLICER can be used to shave off paper-thin slivers and slices of truffle. Dishes flavored or garnished with truffles are often referred to as À LA PÉRIGOURDINE. *See also* TRUFFLE, CHOCOLATE.

truffle, chocolate [TRUHF-uhl; TROO-fuhl] A rich confection made with a mélange of melted chocolate, butter or cream, sugar and various flavorings such as liquors, liqueurs, spices, vanilla, coffee and nuts. After the mixture is cooled, it's rolled into balls and coated with various coverings such as unsweetened cocoa powder (the classic coating), chocolate sprinkles, shaved chocolate or sugar. Some truffles are dipped in melted white or dark chocolate, which, after cooling, becomes a hard coating. These confections were so named because the original, cocoa-coated and rather misshapen truffle resembled the famous and rare fungus of the same name.

truffle slicer A small kitchen device consisting of an adjustable blade mounted on a stainless-steel frame. The slicer's blade is held at a

45-degree angle and the TRUFFLE is pressed down and across it, allowing the blade to shave off small slivers and slices.

truite [TRWEET] French for "trout."

trumpet of death *see* TROMPETTE DE LA MORT

truss To secure poultry or other food (usually meat) with string, pins or skewers so the food maintains a compact shape during cooking.

trussing needle Long stainless-steel needles threaded with twine and used to TRUSS food. They vary in size, usually somewhere from 4 to 10 inches in length.

try out *see* RENDER

tsoshi *see* SOFKI

tsoureki [soo-REH-kee] A sweet, egg-enriched, BRIOCHE-like bread made in Greece, Turkey and various western Asian and eastern European countries. It's known by a variety of names including *choreg, chorek, corek, çörek, cozonac, kalács, kozunak* and *panarët*. These breads contain butter, eggs, flour, milk, sugar, yeast and various flavorings and fillings depending on the region. Often baked in braided form, they are prominent on Christian holidays, especially Easter.

tsubu-an *see* AZUKI-AN

tsukemono [tsoo-keh-MOH-noh] The general name for Japanese-style pickled vegetables, which are served with practically every Japanese meal, breakfast included. There are numerous pickling techniques and a wide variety of vegetables that are pickled.

tsukune [tsoo-KOO-neh] Savory meatball made from minced fish, meat or poultry that's kneaded with egg to form a paste, then molded into balls. They can be cooked in various ways such as AGEMONO (deep-fried), NIMONO (simmered in broth), YAKIMONO (grilled, broiled or pan-fried) or YAKITORI (skewered then grilled).

tteok [TEOK] Korean rice cakes made with glutinous RICE FLOUR. They're similar to Japanese MOCHI. Tteok is also spelled *ddeock, ddeog, duk, dduk* and *thuck.*

tteokbokki [TEOK-boo-kee] Streets of large Korean cities are filled with vendors selling this popular snack food. Tteokbokki, also spelled *ddukbookie* or *ddukbooki*, is a spicy rice cakes stew. It contains TTEOK (Korean rice cakes) and fish cakes, along with garlic, onion, soy sauce and gochujang (*see* CHILE BEAN PASTE) and GOCHUGARU (red chili pepper flakes) for spicy heat. Variations abound; they can include beef, carrots, mung bean sprouts, noodles and SHIITAKE mushrooms.

tua lisong [too-a lee-SONG] Thai for "peanut." *Tua lisong kua* means "roasted peanuts."

Tuaca [too-AH-kah] A BRANDY-based LIQUEUR from the Tuscan region of Italy. The color of pale honey, Tuaca is flavored with citrus fruits and spices and has a taste that hints of butterscotch.

tube pan A round pan with deep sides and a hollow center tube used for baking cake, especially ANGEL FOOD or SPONGE CAKE. The tube promotes even baking for the center of the cake. *See also* BUNDT PAN.

tube steak Another name for a HOT DOG.

tubetti *see* Pasta Glossary, page 883

tuile [TWEEL] French for "tile," this thin, crisp cookie is placed over a rounded object (like a rolling pin) while still hot from the oven. (There is also a special tuile mold, over which the hot cookies may be placed.) Once cooled and stiff, the cookie resembles a curved roof tile. The classic tuile is made with crushed almonds but the cookie can also be flavored with orange, lemon, vanilla or other nuts.

tukbaegi [TOOK-bay-gee] Korean earthenware bowl used for cooking soups and stews and sometimes for serving them. Occasionally, its name is attached to the dish being prepared in it, such as tukbaegi BULGOGI.

tulipe [too-LEEP] French for "tulip," culinarily referring to a thin cookie that is gathered into a ruffled-flower shape while still warm and placed into a cup mold (such as a muffin tin) to cool. It can also be draped over an inverted water glass. The crisp cookie cup is used as an edible container for berries, MOUSSE or ice cream.

tuna [TOO-nuh] Found in temperate marine waters throughout the world, tuna is a member of the MACKEREL family. It's probably the most popular fish used for canning today. There are numerous varieties of tuna, the best known being albacore, bluefin, yellowfin and bonito. All tunas have a distinctively rich-flavored flesh that is moderate to high in fat, firmly textured, flaky and tender. The high-fat **albacore** weighs in the 10- to 60-pound range, has the lightest flesh (white with a hint of pink) and is the only tuna that can be called "white." Its mild flavor and prized white flesh make it the most expensive canned tuna. **Yellowfin tunas** (also called *ahi*) are usually larger than albacores, reaching up to 300 pounds. Their flesh is pale pink (it must be called "light"), with a flavor slightly stronger than that of the albacore. Among the largest tunas are the **bluefin**, which can weigh over 1,000 pounds. Young bluefins have a lighter flesh and are less strongly flavored, but as they grow into adulthood, their flesh turns dark red and their flavor becomes more pronounced. The small **bonitos** rarely exceed 25 pounds. They range from moderate- to high-fat and are the most strongly flavored of the tunas. Many Japanese dishes use dried bonito, called KATSUOBUSHI. **Skipjack tunas** (also known as *Arctic bonito, oceanic bonito, watermelon* and, in Hawaii, *aku*) get their name because they seem to "skip" out of the water. They can weigh up to 40 pounds, but are more typically ranged from 6 to 8 pounds. Skipjack flesh is similar to that of yellowfin tuna. Depending on the variety, fresh tuna is available seasonally—generally starting in late spring and continuing into early fall. Frozen tuna is available year-round and is sold in both steaks and fillets. It may be cooked by almost any method including baking, broiling, grilling and frying. **Canned tuna** is precooked and is sold as albacore (or white meat) and light meat. It comes in three grades, the best being *solid* or *fancy* (large pieces), followed by *chunk* (smaller pieces) and *flaked* or *grated* (bits and pieces). Canned tuna is packed in either water or oil. *See also* FISH.

tun cornmeal *see* FUNCHE

tunta [TOON-tah] *see* CHUÑO

turban squash A family of winter squashes with hard bumpy shells and turbanlike formations at the blossom end. BUTTERCUP SQUASH is one of the more popular varieties. Turban squashes come in various sizes ranging from 2 to 15 inches in diameter at the base. Because they're quite colorful, with varying bright hues of orange, green and yellow, turban squashes are often used for decoration rather than eating. They can be baked, steamed or simmered. *See also* SQUASH.

turbinado sugar [tur-bih-NAH-doh] *see* SUGAR

turbot [TER-boh; TER-buht] 1. Found in European waters from Iceland to the Mediterranean, this highly prized FLATFISH has firm, lean, white flesh with a mild flavor. Many Europeans rate turbot in the same category as the highly regarded Dover SOLE. Turbot can reach 30 pounds but are generally marketed at weights closer to 3 to 6 pounds. They're usually imported frozen to the United States. They may be poached, steamed, baked, broiled or fried. 2. The market name used for several types of FLOUNDER found in the Pacific. *See also* FISH.

turducken [ter-DUHK-ehn] A dish consisting of a small de-boned chicken stuffed inside a de-boned duck stuffed inside a turkey that's de-boned except for legs and wings. The chicken's cavity and spaces between each of the birds are filled with STUFFING. This can vary from recipe to recipe, with some recipes including a different stuffing for each bird and others having a single type. The name is a combination of the birds used—TURkey-DUCk-chicKEN. The dish, which has become quite popular at Thanksgiving, has more complex flavors than just turkey and is easier to slice since the bones have been removed. Though Paul Prudhomme is often credited with creating the turducken, there is some dispute about its origin; he has, however, certainly promoted it and helped make it popular. It's also gained great fame from football announcer John Madden, who was certain to mention turducken during games occurring around Thanksgiving time. Turducken isn't totally unique; the English have their **three bird roast**, which generally consists of a goose, stuffed with chicken, stuffed with pheasant.

tureen [too-REEN; tyoo-REEN] Any of various deep, lidded dishes used for the table service of soups, stews and the like.

turkey For most families, Thanksgiving dinner would be unthinkable without this large native-American bird on the table. Long before the arrival of European settlers, wild turkeys populated the United States, Mexico and Central America and the Aztecs were busily domesticating them. The *conquistadores* took some of these domesticated birds back to Spain, and before long Europeans were breeding them into a much plumper version. Interestingly enough, European settlers brought some of these domesticated birds back to the New World in the 1600s and eventually began crossing them with America's wild turkeys. Most U.S. turkeys raised today are from the White Holland variety, which has been bred to produce a maximum of white meat (a U.S. favorite). In fact, the breasts of today's turkeys are so massive that they must rely on artificial insemination because they can't get close enough to mate. Although male (*tom*) turkeys can reach 70 pounds, those over 20 pounds are becoming less and less available. The female (*hen*) turkey usually weighs from 8 to 16 pounds. Gaining in popularity is a smaller version of both sexes (sometimes called a *fryer-roaster*), which weighs in at between 5 and 8 pounds. The trend toward these compact turkeys is the result of both smaller families and the desire of turkey producers to make turkey everyday rather than exclusively holiday fare. **Heritage turkeys**—the bird Benjamin Franklin favored over the eagle for America's national bird—were nearly extinct by the 1990s. Their popularity is now on the rise; by 2004, about 20,000 were being raised, and that number is climbing. There's no clear definition of exactly what constitutes a heritage turkey, although the term generally refers to varieties officially recognized by the American Poultry Association beginning in the 1870s. Eight varieties of heritage turkey are currently of particular interest: Beltsville Small White, Bourbon Red, Jersey Buff, Narragansett, Royal Palm, Slate, Standard Bronze and White Holland. What heritage turkeys have in common is that they are usually FREE-RANGE and have smaller breasts and larger thighs and legs, which provides a better balance between light meat and dark meat. Heritage turkeys are immensely more flavorful and the color of the meat (both dark and white) is darker than that of a standard turkey. The texture is firmer but not tough and certainly not mushy like some standard turkeys. Heritage breeds can be found in specialty meat markets and some supermarkets. Turkeys are available fresh and frozen year-round. They're sold both whole and as parts—such as breasts or drumsticks. Some whole turkeys have had a built-in plastic thermometer implanted that pops up when the turkey is done. **Self-basting turkeys** have been injected with butter or vegetable oil. Smoked turkey—whole or breast—is also available, as is canned boned turkey. Turkey is very similar to chicken in many regards, including USDA grading. *See* CHICKEN *for information on purchasing, storing and preparing turkey.*

Turkish coffee Very strong coffee made by bringing finely ground (almost to a powder) coffee, sugar and water to a boil three times, allowing it to cool very briefly between boilings. Sometimes spices like CARDAMOM, CINNAMON or NUTMEG are added to the brew. Turkish coffee is made in a special long-handled, open, brass or copper pot called a *cezve* or *ibrik* and served in tiny cups immediately after the third boil. The creamy foam that forms on the coffee's surface is said to be a sign of good fortune for anyone who gets some in their cup. Allow a few minutes after Turkish coffee is poured to let the grounds settle. *See also* COFFEE.

Turkish delight Called *rahat loukoum* ("rest for the throat") in Turkey, this rubbery-textured candy is extremely popular throughout the Middle East. It's made from CORNSTARCH or GELATIN, sugar, honey and fruit juice or jelly, and is often tinted pink or green. Chopped almonds, pistachio nuts, pine nuts or hazelnuts are frequently added. Once the candy becomes firm, it is cut into small squares and coated with powdered sugar. Turkish delight is available commercially in candy shops and some supermarkets.

Turkish gram *see* MOTH BEANS

turmeric [TER-muh-rihk] Used in cooking since 600 B.C., turmeric is the root of a tropical plant related to GINGER. Though native to the Orient, this spice is now also cultivated in India and the Caribbean. It has a bitter, pungent flavor and an intense yellow-orange color. In Biblical times, turmeric was often used to make perfume, a comment on its rather exotic fragrance. Today it's used mainly to add both flavor and color to food. Turmeric is very popular in East Indian cooking and is almost always used in CURRY preparations. It's also a primary ingredient in MUSTARD and is what gives American-style prepared mustard its bright yellow color. Powdered turmeric is widely available in supermarkets. As with all spices, it should be stored in a cool, dark place for no more than 6 months. *See also* SPICES; Seasoning Suggestions, page 891.

turner A utensil for lifting or removing food such as pancakes, hamburgers, eggs and cookies from a pan or baking sheet, or for turning food that's being cooked so the second side can brown. Turners come in a variety of shapes and designs in order to meet different cooking tasks. Some have holes or slots to allow liquids or fats to drain off the item being lifted. Others are shaped for special uses—like the Chinese turner, which has curved edges to fit WOK contours. Turners are usually made of nylon (so as not to scratch NONSTICK FINISHES) or stainless steel. *See also* SPATULA.

turnip Not only is this root vegetable easy to grow, but it keeps well, too. Because of this, turnips have long been popular in Great Britain and northern Europe. The white-fleshed turnip has a white skin with a purple-tinged top. The so-called **yellow turnip** is actually a turnip relative, the RUTABAGA. Small, young turnips have a delicate, slightly sweet taste. As they age, however, their taste becomes stronger and their texture coarser, sometimes almost woody. Fresh turnips are available year-round, with the peak season from October through March. Choose heavy-for-their-size small turnips, as they are the youngsters and will be more delicately flavored and textured. The roots should be firm and the greens (if attached) bright-colored and fresh-looking. Though turnips can be refrigerated, tightly wrapped, for 2 weeks, they do best in a cool (55°F), well-ventilated area such as a root cellar. Before using, they should be washed, trimmed and peeled. Turnips may be boiled or steamed, then mashed or puréed. They can also be stir-fried, cubed and tossed with butter, or used raw in salads. Turnips, a CRUCIFEROUS vegetable, are a fair source of vitamin C. *See also* TURNIP GREENS.

turnip greens Long a popular SOUL FOOD, turnip greens are slightly sweet when young but, as with aging TURNIPS, can become quite tough and strong-tasting as they age. Fresh greens are available year-round, with the peak season from October through March. Choose those that are crisp-looking with a good even color. Avoid greens that are wilted or off-colored. Refrigerate in a plastic bag for up to 3 days. Thoroughly wash and remove any thick ribs before preparing. Turnip greens may be cooked in a variety of ways including boiling, sautéing, steaming and stir-frying. They can be served alone as a vegetable or cooked and served with other greens. Canned and frozen turnip greens are also available in some regions. Turnip greens are an excellent source of vitamins A and C and a good source of riboflavin, calcium and iron.

turnip-rooted celery *see* CELERY ROOT

turnip-rooted parsley *see* PARSLEY ROOT

turnovers Pastry-dough circles or squares that are covered with a sweet or savory filling, then folded in half to create a pastry in the shape of a triangle or semicircle. The edges are usually pinched or crimped to prevent the filling from leaking. Turnovers may be baked or deep-fried. They can range from bite-size to about 6 inches across and can be served as appetizers, luncheon entrées or desserts.

turophile [TOOR-uh-file] A person who loves cheese, taken from the Greek words for cheese (*turos*) and loving (*philos*).

turrón [too-RROHN] *see* NOUGAT

turtle Any of several varieties of reptiles that can live in fresh water, salt water or on land and have a hard shell covering their bodies. Some turtles can grow quite large, weighing over 1,000 pounds. For culinary purposes the **sea** or **green turtle**—found in temperate marine waters—is best known. It has a smooth olive green shell and green to whitish flesh; the green flesh is considered superior. These turtles are often made into a thick turtle soup that usually includes MADEIRA or SHERRY as an ingredient. **Terrapin**, a small (7- to 8-inch) turtle species that inhabits fresh or brackish water, is considered by many to have the best meat. Terrapin meat is sometimes pounded and served like steak. **Tortoises** live on land and are considered less desirable than terrapin or sea turtles. Regardless of the species, the meat of the female is much more tender than that of the male. Conservation measures have limited the availability of this reptile, but some turtle meat can be found in East Coast markets, along the Gulf Coast and in Chinese markets in various regions. Canned and frozen turtle meat can sometimes be found in specialty food stores. *See also* MOCK TURTLE SOUP.

turtle bean *see* BLACK BEAN

Tuscan cabbage; Tuscan kale *see* CAVOLO NERO

Tuscan peppers *see* PEPPERONCINI

tutti-frutti [TOO-tee FROO-tee] 1. An Italian term meaning "all fruits" that refers to a preserve made with various diced fruits mixed with sugar and brandy. It's since been used to describe ice cream or other desserts that contain a variety of minced, candied fruits. 2. A synthetic, fruity flavoring used in various gums and candies.

TVP *see* TEXTURED VEGETABLE PROTEIN

Tybo [TI-boh] Similar to a mild-flavored SAMSOE, this Danish, loaf-shaped CHEESE is made from cows' milk. Its yellow rind encloses a cream-colored interior dotted with holes. Its mild taste makes it good for sandwiches, salads, sauces and a variety of cooked dishes. Some tybos are flavored with caraway seeds.

tyramine *see* CHEESE

tzatziki [dzah-DZEE-kee] A Greek sauce made with drained plain YOGURT, grated or chopped cucumber, minced garlic, olive oil, vinegar and minced fresh dill or mint. Tzatziki may be served as a dip, cracker spread (if made with *thick* yogurt), or CONDIMENT for fried foods or sandwiches such as a GYRO. *See also* SAUCE.

tzimmes [TSIHM-ihs] Traditionally served on Rosh Hashana, this sweet Jewish dish consists of various combinations of fruits, meat and vegetables. Tzimmes may include brisket of beef, sweet potatoes, potatoes, FARFEL, prunes and other dried fruit, carrots or apples—all flavored with honey and often cinnamon. This casserole-style dish is cooked at very low heat so the flavors have a chance to blend.

Ubatatuba Cambuci chile *see* BISHOP'S CROWN CHILE

uchiki kuri squash *see* RED KURI

udo [OO-doh] A Japanese vegetable that belongs to the GINSENG family. Its tender stalks resemble ASPARAGUS but have a light FENNEL flavor. Udo is used raw in salads or lightly cooked in soups and other dishes.

udon [oo-DOHN] A thick Japanese noodle similiar to spaghetti. It can be round or squared and can be made from wheat or corn flour. Fresh and dried udon are available in Asian markets.

ugli fruit [UHG-lee] Its origins are vague, but the native Jamaican ugli fruit (also called *uniq fruit*) is believed to be a TANGERINE-GRAPEFRUIT hybrid (though the POMELO may also have been involved). It ranges in size between that of a NAVEL ORANGE and a giant grapefruit. Its acid-sweet flavor suggests grapefruit with hints of orange. The extremely thick, yellow-green skin fits rather loosely over the large, juicy, yellow-orange pulp sections. Ugli fruit is available on a limited basis from winter to spring. Choose fruit that's heavy for its size and that gives slightly to palm pressure. Store at room temperature and use within 5 days or refrigerate up to 3 weeks. Ugli fruit may be prepared and eaten in any way suitable for grapefruit. It's an excellent source of vitamin C.

umami [oo-MAH-mee] It's long been accepted in the Western world that there are four elements of taste: sweet, salty, sour and bitter. In 1908, Tokyo Imperial University researcher Kikunae Ikeda identified a fifth taste that he called "umami," a word that has no exact English translation, but which may be loosely interpreted as "delicious" or "savory"—that is, the essence of flavor, another dimension. Ikeda determined that glutamic acid (glutamate) was the ingredient that produced this unique fifth taste and developed the seasoning MONOSODIUM GLUTAMATE (MSG) to provide the umami flavor. Ikeda concluded that, of the five tastes, umami and sweetness were the only two the palate perceives as singularly pleasant. Compared to the other four tastes, umami is exceedingly subtle, manifesting more as an overall distinctive palate sensation than a taste.

umeboshi; ume [oo-meh-BOH-she] Pickled Japanese plums that are picked before they're ripe, then soaked in brine and red SHISO leaves, the latter of which adds flavor and a pink coloring. This Japanese condiment is very salty and tart and is a popular adjunct to most Japanese meals, including breakfast. Puréed umeboshi, called *bainiku,* is used as a seasoning. Umeboshi can be found in jars and cans in Asian markets and in some gourmet markets.

umi'umia *see* PACIFIC THREADFIN

unagi *see* SUSHI

uni [oo-nee] The ROE of SEA URCHIN, the red version of which is more expensive than the yellow, though they taste very similar.

uniq fruit *see* UGLI FRUIT

univalve [YOO-nuh-valv] *see* GASTROPOD

unleavened [uhn-LEHV-uhnd] A word describing baked goods (breads, cakes, etc.) that contain no LEAVENER, such as BAKING POWDER, BAKING SODA or YEAST. Among the most popular unleavened breads are LAH-VOSH. *See also* BREAD.

unmold To remove molded food from the container (usually a decorative MOLD) in which it was made. The process generally requires inverting the container over a serving plate.

unpasteurized milk/imported cheese dilemma According to the U.S. Food and Drug Administration, cheese made with unpasteurized milk must be ripened for 60 days or more. Cheeses with less aging cannot be legally imported into the United States. Also banned are all RAW-MILK "soft cheeses" (including SEMISOFT and SOFT-RIPENED) even if aged for more than 60 days. In order to export their cheese, many countries are creating pasteurized-milk versions of raw-milk cheeses that age under 2 months. Regrettably, flash PASTEURIZATION (heating at 161°F for 15 seconds) is most often used. It typically produces a telltale "cooked" flavor and slows down the RIPENING process of cheese, which affects its complexity, character, flavor and texture. Fortunately, a technique called heat treatment pasteurization is used by ARTISAN cheesemakers around the world (including those in the United States). This method involves gently warming the milk at 145°F for 30 minutes. This practice produces a cheese that's closer to the versions made with unpasteurized milk and with more natural flavor. Nevertheless, informed cheese lovers view the FDA's ban on raw-milk cheeses—all in the name of food safety—as unrealistic. Raw-milk cheeses have been consumed on a daily basis for centuries without any major issues. What's true is that most food-borne illness from cheese is caused by post-production contamination, whether or not the cheese has been made with pasteurized milk.

unsalted butter *see* BUTTER

unsaturated fat *see* FATS AND OILS

uovo [oo-OH-voh] Italian for "egg."

uovo di tonno [WAH-voh dee TOH-noh] *see* BOTTARGA

up *see* STRAIGHT UP

upside-down cake Of this genre, the most popular is undoubtedly the traditional pineapple upside-down cake. Any fruit can be used, however, and this dessert is made by covering the bottom of a cake pan with butter and sugar topped with decoratively arranged fruit, then cake batter. During the baking process, the sugar, butter and fruit juices combine to create a CARAMELIZED glaze. Before serving, the cake is inverted onto a serving plate so the glazed fruit becomes the top of the cake.

use by date *see* PRODUCT DATING

usuzukuri [oo-soo-zoo-KOO-ree] SASHIMI technique whereby firm-fleshed fish are sliced very thin, then carefully arranged on a plate.

vacherin [vash-RAN] A dessert consisting of several crisp MERINGUE rings stacked on top of each other and placed on a meringue or pastry base. Alternatively, the rings may be made with almond paste. This "container" may be filled with ice cream or crème CHANTILLY and/or various fruits.

Vacherin [vash-RAN] Any of several rich and creamy cow's-milk cheeses from France or Switzerland. The names are a bit confusing because France and Switzerland both called their cheese **Vacherin Mont d'Or** until the Swiss gained lawful use of the name in 1973. The French later determined their cheese could be called either **Vacherin du Haut-Doubs** or simply **Mont d'Or**. The Swiss and French cheeses, which are made right across the border from each other, are very similar except that the Swiss versions can use either raw or pasteurized milk, whereas the French cheeses are made only with unpasteurized cow's milk. Both the French and Swiss versions are made in wheels weighing 6½ pounds or less and encircled by a band of wood. Their rinds are light to dark gold with patches of white mold, their interiors ivory colored and their semisoft texture is smooth and creamy, almost becoming runny with RIPENING. Their complex flavors have earthy and mushroomy traits. Vacherin du Haut-Doubs has a minimum FAT CONTENT of 45 percent. The Swiss make another cheese, called **Vacherin Fribourgeois**, in the canton of Fribourg in western Switzerland. It's produced in 15- to 20-pound wheels that have golden to reddish-brown rinds and pale yellow interiors with small irregular EYES. It's semihard with a smooth, supple texture and flavors exhibiting nuts, spices and caramel. *See also* CHEESE.

vada [VAH-dah] A deep-fried FRITTER popular in southern India. The batter is generally based on one of the many varieties of DAL or potatoes. If dal is used, it's soaked, then ground into a paste and often whipped. Almost anything can be added for flavoring and variation. Usually 2 to 4 inches across and sometimes with a hole like a doughnut, they are often eaten as an appetizer or snack, or as an accompaniment to a main dish. A CHUTNEY or SAMBAR is often served with vadas.

vadouvan; vaudouvan [va-doo-VAHN] This mixture of ingredients has been described as a French version of an Indian spice blend. And like India's popular spice blend GARAM MASALA, there are many variations of vadouvan. It can include BLACK PEPPER, CARDAMOM, CLOVES, CORIANDER, CUMIN, DRIED CHILES, FENUGREEK, MUSTARD SEEDS, NUTMEG, TURMERIC and other spices, as well as sautéed and roasted garlic, onions and shallots. It adds a mellow and sophisticated curry flavor to a variety of dishes. Vadouvan can be found on the Internet and in specialty food stores. If you make your own, store in an airtight container in a refrigerator for up to a month or freeze for up to 6 months.

Valencia orange [vuh-LEHN-she-uh; vuh-LEHN-shuh; vuh-LEHN-see-uh] Grown in Arizona, California, Florida and Texas, the Valencia orange has a thin, deep golden skin that's difficult to peel. Its flesh is sweet, juicy and contains few seeds. The Valencia is good both as a juice fruit and for eating out of hand. *See also* ORANGE.

valois sauce [val-wah] Also known as *foyot sauce*, a BÉARNAISE SAUCE with GLACE DE VIANDE (meat glaze) added to give it a fuller, meatier flavor. It's great as an accompaniment to grilled or sautéed meats. *See also* SAUCE.

Valpolicella [vahl-paw-lee-CHEHL-lah] Produced in northern Italy, this dry red wine is light-bodied and has a fragrant bouquet and fruity flavor. It's best served young and is sometimes viewed as Italy's version of a French BEAUJOLAIS.

vanilla [vuh-NIHL-uh; vuh-NEHL-uh] Dictionaries describe the term "plain-vanilla" as something "simple, plain or ordinary." Few statements could be further from the truth—for there is definitely nothing ordinary about the seductively aromatic vanilla bean. This long, thin pod is the fruit of a luminous celadon-colored orchid (*vanilla planifolia*), which, of over 20,000 orchid varieties, is the only one that bears anything edible. Native to tropical America, the vanilla bean was cultivated and processed by the Aztecs, who used it to flavor their cocoa-based drink, *xocolatl,* later transliterated to *chocolatl.* That basic flavoring wisdom is still true today . . . vanilla deliciously heightens chocolate's flavor. The vanilla bean was once considered an aphrodisiac, and was so rare that it was reserved for royalty. Because of the extremely labor-intensive, time-consuming process by which it's obtained, pure vanilla is still relatively expensive today. The saga begins with the orchid blossoms, which open only one day a year (and then only for a few hours). Because this particular orchid has only one natural pollinator (the Melipona bee), which cannot possibly handle the task in such a small period of time, the flower must be hand-pollinated—otherwise, no vanilla bean. After pollination, pods take 6 weeks to reach full size (6 to 10 inches long), and 8 to 9 months after that to mature. The mature pods, which must be hand-picked, are green and have none of the familiar vanilla flavor or fragrance. For that they need curing, a 3- to 6-month process that begins with a 20-second boiling-water bath followed by sun heating. Once the beans are hot, they're wrapped in blankets and allowed to sweat. Over a period of months of drying in the sun by day and sweating in blankets at night, the beans ferment, shrinking by 400 percent and turning their characteristic dark brown. The better grades of beans become thinly coated with a white, powdery coating called *vanillin* (which is also produced synthetically). Today, the three most common types of **vanilla beans** are Bourbon-Madagascar, Mexican and Tahitian. **Bourbon-Madagascar vanilla beans** come from Madagascar,

V

off the southeast coast of Africa, and its neighbor 420 miles away—the West Indian island of Réunion. They're rich and sweet and the thinnest of the three types of beans. About 75 percent of the world's vanilla-bean supply comes from the Madagascar area. The thick **Mexican vanilla beans** come from environs surrounding Veracruz. They have a smooth, rich flavor but are scarcer than the Bourbon-Madascar beans because most areas where the orchid once thrived are now dedicated to oil fields and orange groves. Additionally, some Mexican vanilla products—though considerably cheaper than their U.S. supermarket counterparts—are suspect because they contain coumarin (banned by the FDA), a potentially toxic substance that can cause liver and kidney damage. Unfortunately, there's no way for the consumer to tell which Mexican vanilla products contain this toxin so the best safeguard is to buy Mexican vanilla beans from a reliable source. **Tahitian vanilla beans** are the thickest and the darkest (a blackish brown) of the three types. It's intensely aromatic, though not as flavorful as the other two types of beans. **Vanilla powder** is the whole, dried bean ground until powdery. Its flavor doesn't evaporate when heated as readily as that of vanilla extract, which makes it better suited for baked goods, custards, etc. Vanilla powder is available in specialty cake decorating supply shops, some gourmet markets and through mail order. **Vanilla extract** is the most common form of vanilla used today. It's made by MACERATING chopped beans in an alcohol-water solution in order to extract the flavor; the mixture is then aged for several months. To meet FDA standards, **pure vanilla extract** must contain 13.35 ounces of vanilla beans per gallon during extraction and 35 percent alcohol. The resulting brown liquid is clear and richly fragrant. (There are double- and triple-strength vanilla extracts, as well as a **vanilla essence**—so strong that only a drop or two is needed—available through special suppliers by mail order.) You can count on products labeled "natural vanilla flavor" containing only pure vanilla extract. **Imitation vanilla** is composed entirely of artificial flavorings (most of which are paper-industry by-products treated with chemicals). It often has a harsh quality that leaves a bitter aftertaste. Pure vanilla extract is about twice as expensive as its imitation counterpart, but there's no real comparison in flavor intensity and quality, and only about half the amount is needed. Vanilla descriptions on labels can be confusing. *Natural vanillin* is a substance intrinsic to the vanilla bean, whereas *artificial vanillin* is made from wood-pulp by-products. *Vanilla flavoring* describes a blend of pure and imitation vanilla. In the United States, a label that reads *vanilla ice cream* may only be made with pure vanilla extract and/or vanilla beans, whereas *vanilla-flavored ice cream* may contain up to 42 percent artificial flavorings and *artificial-flavored ice cream* contains *only* imitation flavorings. Vanilla extracts are readily available and vanilla beans can be found in supermarkets and most specialty food stores. Most commercial vanilla beans are Bourbon-Madagascar; Tahitian and Mexican beans (as well as better grades of Bourbon-Madagascar) are more readily available through mail order. Extracts can be stored indefinitely if sealed airtight and kept in a cool, dark place. Vanilla beans should be wrapped tightly in plastic wrap, placed in an airtight jar and refrigerated. They can be stored in this manner for about 6 months. In order for its flavor not to dissipate, vanilla extract should be added to cooked mixtures after they've been briefly cooled. To use vanilla beans, slit them lengthwise down the center and scrape out the thousands of diminutive seeds. These seeds can be added directly to foods such as ice-cream mixtures, shortening to be used for pastry dough, sauces, etc. Homemade vanilla extract can be made by placing a split bean in a jar containing 3/4 cup vodka, sealing and letting it stand for 6 months. Vanilla beans may also be used to make deliciously fragrant VANILLA SUGAR. Whole beans that have been used to flavor sauces or other mixtures may be rinsed, dried and stored for reuse. Vanilla adds flavor magic to a multitude of sweet and some savory dishes.

vanilla sugar Wonderfully fragrant and flavorful sugar made by burying vanilla beans in granulated or powdered sugar—usually in the proportion of two beans for each pound of sugar. The mixture is stored in an airtight container for about a week before the vanilla bean is removed. The result is a delicious and perfumy sugar that can be used as an ingredient or decoration for baked goods, fruit and other desserts. Vanilla beans may be reused in this fashion for up to 6 months.

vanillin *see* VANILLA

varak; varaq [VAH-ruhk] Edible, gossamer-thin sheets of pure silver or gold that for centuries have been popular decorations in India for special-occasion desserts, confections, nuts and rice dishes. Varak sheets, which are flavorless and odorless, can be found in Indian markets and cake decorating supply shops. The gold- and silver-leaf sheets usually come in packages of twenty-four, each section sandwiched between two sheets of paper. Varak sheets are so fragile that they dissolve easily with human touch and can be torn by the barest breath of air. For that reason, it's best to remove the top piece of paper from a sheet of varak and then invert the varak on top of the food to be decorated. The varak will stick to the food, and the paper can be peeled off. Varak will keep indefinitely if stored in an airtight container (to prevent tarnishing) in a cool, dry place. Also called *vark*.

varietal wine [vuh-RI-ih-tuhl] A term describing wines made chiefly from one variety of grape. Such wines portray the dominant characteristics of the primary grape used. Among the more popular varietal wines are CABERNET SAUVIGNON, CHARDONNAY, CHENIN BLANC, GEWÜRZTRAMINER, PETITE SIRAH, PINOT NOIR, SAUVIGNON BLANC and ZINFANDEL.

variety meats Called *offal* in Great Britain, variety meats are animal innards and extremities that can be used in cooking or in the production of foods such as sausage. The category includes BRAINS, cheeks (*see* BATH CHAPS), intestines (CHITTERLINGS), feet and ankles (PIG'S FEET), HEART, KIDNEYS, lungs (LIGHTS), LIVER, MARROWBONE, spleen (MELT), stomach (TRIPE; HOG MAW), tail (*see* OXTAIL), testicles (FRIES), thymus and pancreas (SWEETBREADS) and TONGUE.

vark *see* VARAK

vatapá [vah-tah-PAH] A paste made in Brazil that contains coconut milk, ground nuts, shrimp and other seasonings. It's used as an accompaniment for various dishes, especially as a filling for ACARAJÉ.

veal Though there are no precise age standards for veal, the term is generally used to describe a young calf from 1 to 3 months old. **Milk-fed veal** comes from calves up to 12 weeks old who have not been weaned from their mother's milk. Their delicately textured flesh is firm and creamy white with a pale grayish-pink tinge. **Formula-fed veal** can come from calves up to about 4 months old, fed a special diet of milk solids, fats, various nutrients and water. The meat from formula-fed veal is not as rich or delicate as milk-fed veal because of the diet's missing milk fat. The term **Bob veal** applies to calves younger than 1 month old. Their pale, shell-pink flesh is quite bland and the texture is soft. In all true veal, the animals haven't been allowed to eat grains or grasses, either of which would cause the flesh to darken. Calves between 6 and 12 months old are called **baby beef**, and have flesh that's coarser, stronger-flavored and from pink to light red in color. True veal is usually plentiful in the spring and late winter. At other times of the year, calves over 3 months old are often sold as veal. The USDA grades veal in six different categories; from highest to lowest they are Prime, Choice, Good, Standard, Utility and Cull. The last three grades are rarely sold in retail outlets. When choosing veal, let color be your guide. The flesh should be creamy white—barely tinged with grayish-pink—and the fat white. Meat that's pink turning red means the so-called "veal" is older than it should be. Veal's texture should be firm, finely grained and smooth. *For storage information, see listing for* BEEF. Veal is often cooked by moist-heat methods to compensate for its lack of natural fat. It is easy to overcook and dry out, so careful attention must be paid during preparation. The delicate flavor and fine texture of veal have appealed to diners for centuries. Among the numerous dishes created to highlight this meat are veal CORDON BLEU, veal MARENGO, VEAL ORL-

OFF, VEAL OSCAR, OSSO BUCO, veal PARMIGIANA, VEAL PICCATA and veal SCALOPPINE. *See also* Veal Chart, page 899.

veal cordon bleu *see* CORDON BLEU

veal Marengo *see* MARENGO

veal Orloff [OR-lawf] This classic presentation begins with a braised loin of veal carved into even horizontal slices. Each slice is spread with a thin layer of puréed sautéed mushrooms and onions. The coated slices are stacked back in place and tied together to reform the loin. Then the layered loin is smothered with additional mushroom-onion purée, topped with BÉCHAMEL and grated Parmesan cheese and oven-browned for about 10 minutes.

veal Oscar; veal Oskar [OS-kuhr] Said to have been named in honor of Sweden's King Oscar II, who was especially partial to its ingredients, this dish consists of sautéed veal cutlets topped with crab or CRAYFISH meat and BÉARNAISE. Veal Oscar is finished with a garnish of asparagus spears.

veal parmigiana; veal Parmesan *see* PARMIGIANA, À LA

veal piccata *see* PICCATA

veau [VOH] French for "veal."

vedura [vay-DOO-rah] Italian for "vegetable."

vegan [VEE-guhn] *see* VEGETARIAN

Vegemite [VEJ-uh-mite] The brand name of a Kraft Foods YEAST EXTRACT product, which is wildly popular in Australia. Vegemite was the brainchild of a young Australian named Fred Walker that was created in 1922 by his company's chief scientist, Dr. Cyril Callister. This thick, dark brown, intensely salty paste is flavored with a variety of ingredients including celery and onions. It's used as a bread spread and is a favorite on breakfast toast. Australians are weaned on it but, for all but the initiated, it's definitely an acquired taste. Vegemite can be found in some specialty gourmet stores and is available through mail order. *See also* MARMITE.

vegetable amaranth *see* AMARANTH

vegetable cooking spray *see* COOKING SPRAY

vegetable marrow Cultivated in England, this green, oval summer squash can grow to the size of a watermelon. It's closely related to the ZUCCHINI and can be cooked in any manner suitable for that vegetable. Because of its bland flavor, vegetable marrow (also called *marrow squash*) is often stuffed with a meat mixture. It's available in limited supplies in some specialty produce markets during the summer months. *See also* SQUASH.

vegetable oils Any of various edible oils made from a plant source, such as vegetables, nuts or seeds. *See also* ALMOND OIL; CANOLA OIL; CORN OIL; COTTONSEED OIL; FATS AND OILS; GRAPESEED OIL; HAZELNUT OIL; OLIVE OIL; PEANUT OIL; PUMPKIN SEED OIL; SAFFLOWER OIL; SESAME OIL; SOYBEAN OIL; SUNFLOWER SEED OIL; WALNUT OIL.

vegetable peeler A kitchen utensil designed to peel away the outer skin of vegetables. Vegetable peelers come in many designs and are made from a variety of materials. The better ones have a swivel-action blade that conforms to the contour of the vegetable being peeled, thereby cutting away a minimum of skin.

vegetable protein Also called *plant protein* or *textured vegetable protein*, this product is obtained from protein-rich SOYBEANS. The beans are ground and processed through a spinning/extrusion technique until they become strands of almost pure PROTEIN. Vegetable protein is used in commercial meat and poultry products as a binder and extender. It can be found in foods such as meat substitutes, luncheon meats and sausages, as well as in packaged sauces, soups and other processed foods. Although nutritiously rich, vegetable protein can't match the flavor and aroma of the meat products. *See also* HYDROLYZED PLANT PROTEIN.

vegetable shortening A solid fat made from vegetable oils, such as SOYBEAN and COTTONSEED OIL. Although made from oil, shortening has been chemically transformed into a solid state through hydrogenation (*see* FATS AND OILS), a process that creates TRANS FATTY ACIDS and converts the mixture into a saturated fat, thereby destroying any polyunsaturate benefits. Vegetable shortening is virtually flavorless and may be substituted for other fats in baking and cooking. It can be stored at room temperature for up to a year.

vegetable spaghetti *see* SPAGHETTI SQUASH

vegetable sponge *see* ASIAN OKRA

vegetarian [veh-juh-TEHR-ee-uhn] Very simply, a vegetarian is one who eschews the consumption of meat or other animal foods. However, vegetarianism, which has been practiced since ancient times, is certainly not one-faceted. The wide-ranging custom of vegetarianism may be based on a variety of personal principles including religious (certain Hindu and Buddhist sects), ethical (cruelty to animals and more efficient use of world food resources), nutritional (the healthy benefits of reducing fat and cholesterol) and economic (nonmeat products are, on the average, less expensive). There are several types of vegetarians today. **Vegans,**

who are the purists of the vegetarian world and who have the most limited diet, refuse to eat all animal-derivative foods including butter, cheese, eggs and milk. **Ovo-lacto vegetarians** consider such animal-related foods acceptable but, of course, do not eat meat. Then there are those vegetarians who will eat fish and/or poultry, but not other animal meat. Across the board, most vegetarians prefer their food organically grown and (if they eat fish and fowl) organically fed. Vegetarians get their PROTEIN from a variety of sources, such as foods from the large family of LEGUMES. *See also* FLEXITARIAN; FRUITARIAN.

vegetarian cheese Any cheese produced with non-animal coagulants (*see* RENNET). Labels will identify such cheeses as "suitable for vegetarians." The ingredients list may include terms such as "microbial enzyme" or "vegetable rennet," pointing to animal-free production. Vegetarian cheeses are widely available in natural food stores and most supermarkets. *See also* CHEESE.

velouté [veh-loo-TAY] One of the four original "mother sauces" (*see* SAUCE), velouté is, in the most basic terms, a WHITE STOCK thickened with white ROUX. It is the foundation for myriad sauces and can be flavored in infinite ways. For example, ALLEMANDE SAUCE is an egg-enriched velouté. *See also* SAUCE.

velvet hammer A rich, creamy COCKTAIL made with COINTREAU or TRIPLE SEC, TÍA MARÍA, heavy cream and sometimes BRANDY. The mixture is shaken with ice and strained into a cocktail glass. The result is smooth but potent.

velvet piopparello mushroom *see* PIOPPINI MUSHROOM

velvet pippini mushroom *see* PIOPPINI MUSHROOM

velvet stem mushroom *see* ENOKI

venison [VEHN-ih-suhn; VEHN-ih-zuhn] *see* GAME ANIMALS

verbena [ver-BEE-nuh] *see* LEMON VERBENA

Verdelho *see* MADEIRA

verdolaga *see* PURSLANE

verdure [vehr-DOO-reh] Italian for "vegetables."

verjuice; *Fr.* **verjus** [VER-joos; *Fr.* vehr-ZHOO] An acidic, slightly sour liquid made from unripe fruit, primarily grapes and sometimes apples. The word derives from *vert jus,* French for "green juice," referring to the fact that the juice comes from high-acid, low-sugar semiripe grapes that were thinned from the vines. Verjuice is used in preparations like sauces and mustards to heighten flavor, much as lemon juice or vinegar would be employed, though it's a more gentle acidulant. Not widely used since medieval and Renaissance times, verjuice is now enjoying a comeback in many dishes. It can be found in gourmet shops, natural food stores and by mail-order. Refrigerate opened verjuice for up to 3 months.

vermicelli *see* Pasta Glossary, page 883

vermouth [ver-mooth] A FORTIFIED WINE that some historians date back to the time of Hippocrates, when it was used as a medicinal. The word "vermouth" comes from the German *wermut* or *vermut* ("wormwood") which, before it was declared poisonous, was the principal flavoring ingredient. Today's vermouths are flavored with a complex formula of myriad botanicals including herbs, spices, flowers and seeds, the exact recipe depending on the producer. There are two primary styles of vermouth—sweet (red) and DRY (white). All vermouths are derived from white wines. **Sweet vermouth** was introduced in 1786 by Italian Antonio Benedetto Carpano. It has a slightly sweet flavor and a reddish-brown color from the addition of caramel. This Italian-style vermouth is served as an APÉRITIF and used in slightly sweet cocktails like the AMERICANO. **Dry vermouth**, created by Frenchman Joseph Noilly in 1800, is also called *French vermouth,* although today it's also produced in other countries including Italy and the United States. Dry vermouth is served as an apéritif and used in dry cocktails like MARTINIS. Drinks made with half sweet and half dry vermouth are referred to as "perfect," as in a perfect MANHATTAN. A vermouth's flavor begins to dissipate as soon as it's opened so it should be stored in the refrigerator for no more than 3 months.

Véronique [vay-roh-NEEK] A term describing dishes garnished with seedless white grapes. One of the most popular of these dishes is **sole Véronique**—fillet of SOLE poached in white wine, covered with a white sauce and garnished with white grapes.

verte, sauce [VEHRT] French for "green sauce," describing a green-colored MAYONNAISE. To obtain the color, a green ingredient (such as parsley, spinach or watercress) is BLANCHED, puréed, then placed in the middle of a kitchen towel and squeezed tightly. The extracted juice is mixed with mayonnaise, resulting in a green-colored mixture that simply tastes like mayonnaise. Sauce verte is typically served with cold fish dishes. *See also* SAUCE.

vertolaga *see* PURSLANE

very hard cheeses One way of classifying cheese is by texture and the moisture content that impacts that texture. Very hard cheeses, such as dry JACK and PARMESAN, have the lowest moisture (in the low 30 percentile) and are particularly good for grating. *See also* SOFT CHEESE; SEMISOFT CHEESE; SEMIHARD CHEESE; HARD CHEESE.

vialone nano rice [vee-ah-LOH-nay nah-noh] A round short-grain rice that's smaller than the more famous ARBORIO RICE, similarly starchy. Vialone nano is favored by chefs in the Veneto region of Italy for making RISOTTO; others think it's almost as good as CARNAROLI RICE. Vialone nano is more difficult to find than Arborio but is available in Italian markets and through the Internet. *See also* RICE.

viande [vee-YAWND] French for "meat."

Vichy carrots [VIH-shee] A dish of thinly sliced carrots that are combined with a small amount of water (to be authentic it must be VICHY WATER), butter and sugar, then covered and cooked over low heat until tender. Vichy carrots (also called *carrots à la Vichy*) are garnished with minced parsley.

vichyssoise [vihsh-ee-SWAHZ; VEE-she-swahz] A rich, creamy potato-and-leek soup that's served cold, garnished with chopped chives. In this country it's often mispronouced "vinsch-ee-SWAH."

Vichy water [VIH-shee] 1. A naturally sparkling mineral water from the springs located in and around central France's well-known spa city of Vichy. This famous potable is the water that is supposed to be used to prepare VICHY CARROTS. 2. This term is sometimes also used to describe sparkling mineral water that resembles the true Vichy water.

viejo cheese *see* MANCHEGO CHEESE

Vienna beer An amber red, lager-style (*see* LAGER) beer originally produced in Vienna, Austria. The color is derived from kilned MALT, which has a reddish color. Vienna beers have a malty, lightly hopped (*see* HOPS) flavor. *See also* BEER.

Viennese coffee [vee-uh-NEEZ] Strong, sweetened hot coffee, served in a tall glass and crowned with whipped cream. *See also* COFFEE.

Vietnamese mint; Vietnamese cilantro; Vietnamese coriander This pungent herb is not really part of the mint family—in fact, its characteristics are closer to that of its other popular name, *Vietnamese coriander*. It has a peppery spiciness with hints of CILANTRO, citrus and mint. The fresh leaves, which are dark green with tan spots on the top and purplish red on the bottom, are frequently used in Vietnamese cooking. Look for it in Vietnamese markets; it may be under its Vietnamese name, *rau ram*. Choose leaves with no sign of wilting and refrigerate for up to 1 week in a plastic bag. Or place the bunch, stems down, in a glass of water and cover with a plastic bag, securing the bag to the glass with a rubber band. Refrigerate, changing water every 2 or 3 days. Just before using Vietnamese mint, wash and pat dry with paper towels. Both the leaves and relatively tender stems can be used in fresh or cooked dishes. This herb is also called *Cambodian mint, daun keson, hot mint* and *Vietnamese cilantro*.

Vieux Lille *see* MIMOLETTE

vin [VAN] French for "wine." *Vin maison* is "house wine," *vin ordinaire* is "ordinary (or table) wine," *vin de table* is "table wine," *vin rouge* is "red wine" and *vin blanc* is "white wine."

vinaigre [vee-NAY-gruh] French for "vinegar."

vinaigrette [vihn-uh-GREHT] A basic oil-and-vinegar combination, generally used to dress salad greens and other cold vegetable, meat or fish dishes. In its simplest form, vinaigrette consists of oil, vinegar (usually 3 parts oil to 1 part vinegar), salt and pepper. More elaborate variations can include any of various ingredients such as spices, herbs, shallots, onions, mustard, etc. *See also* SAUCE.

vindaloo [VIHN-dah-loo] Specialties of central and southwestern coastal India, vindaloos are the most mouth-searing of the CURRY dishes. The complicated roasted spice blend on which they're based can contain any of various ingredients including mustard seeds, cumin seeds, ginger, peppercorns, fenugreek seeds, cloves and coriander seeds. Red chiles are a must and TAMARIND concentrate is favored. Vindaloo sauce is typically combined with meat and served with rice. Premade vindaloo pastes and dried spice blends are available in Indian markets.

vinegar [VIHN-ih-ger] Derived from the French *vin aigre,* "sour wine," vinegar is made by bacterial activity that converts fermented liquids such as wine, beer or cider into a weak solution of ACETIC ACID (the constituent that makes it sour). Vinegar has been used for centuries for everything from beverages (like SHRUBS), to an odor-diminisher for strong foods such as cabbage and onions, to a hair rinse and softener. There are myriad vinegar varieties found in markets today, and the following are among the most commonly available. **Apple cider vinegar** (also called *cider vinegar)* is made from fermented apple cider and has a faintly sweet apple flavor. **Cane vinegar** is based on the juice of sugarcane; it has a rich and mellow, slightly sweet flavor and golden color. **Distilled white vinegar** (or simply *distilled vinegar*) is exceedingly high in acetic acid and is very sour and rather harsh-tasting. It's often made from a grain-alcohol base. **Fruit vinegars** come in a bevy of flavors made from the juice of various fruits including raspberries, mangos and oranges. **Herb vinegars** are made by steeping fresh herbs in warm vinegar for a period of time until the vinegar is completely infused with the ingredient's flavor. Such vinegars may be based on a single herb (such as tarragon) or a combination of herbs and other flavorings (such as oregano and garlic). **Malt vinegar** is a mellow-flavored favorite in Britain, particularly with FISH AND CHIPS. It's based on malted BARLEY and sometimes colored with CARAMEL. **Rice vinegar**, made from fermented rice, is mild, slightly sweet and used widely in Japanese and Chinese cooking. It's a key element in dishes such as SUSHI. **Wine vinegars** can be made from either red or white wine and can range in flavor from pleasantly pungent to rather ordinary. Two of the most highly regarded vinegar styles come from Italy and France. From Italy comes the exquisite Italian **balsamic vinegar**, made in and around the areas of Modena and Reggio Emilia. It's produced from white Trebbiano grapes, the MUST of which is cooked and concentrated until deep, dark and rich. The vinegar continues to gain its dark color and pungent sweetness from a lengthy period of aging in barrels of various woods (such as chestnut, juniper and mulberry) and in graduating sizes, from larger to smaller as the vinegar ages over a period of years. It should be noted that many balsamic vinegars contain SULFITES, which are primarily added to inhibit the growth of unfavorable, flavor-detracting bacteria. Balsamic vinegars range in age from young (3 to 5 years), to middle-aged (6 to 12 years) to the noble older versions, which can range from 12 to over 100 years old. By law, a vinegar labeled *aceto balsamico tradizionale di Modena* must have been wood-aged for a minimum of 12 years. The word *stravecchio* on the label tells you the balsamic's been aged at least 25 years. Older, high-quality balsamics are sometimes used as an APERITIF or DIGESTIF after a meal. **White balsamic vinegar** also comes from Modena, Italy, but is made by an entirely different process than classic balsamic vinegar. The grape undergoes pressurized cooking, which prevents the caramelization of both flavor and color. White balsamic vinegar is only aged 1 year in uncharred barrels, further assuring both color and flavor will remain light. It's used in food preparations where additional color is not desired. France gives us **Banyuls vinegar** (*le vinaigre de Banyuls*), which hails from the area around the seaside town of Banyuls-sur-Mer, a region wine lovers know for its unusual fortified wines. Comparing favorably with Italian balsamic vinegars and aged Spanish sherry vinegars, Banyuls begins life as one of the local wines (typically GRENACHE) and spends 5 years or more maturing in oak barrels. During the final year of aging, vinegar from an older batch is added to trigger the ultimate conversion from wine to vinegar. The result is a tart blend replete with complex aromas of allspice, anise, nuts and vanilla. From the area of southern Spain around Jerez de la Frontera comes not only SHERRY but aged **sherry vinegar** as well. Like balsamic vinegar, some sherry vinegars are aged for years—30, 50 or even 75. And though not as well known as balsamic vinegars, these aged Spanish vinegars rival many of their Italian counterparts in quality, flavor and character. Vinegar is essential in making pickles, mustards and VINAIGRETTES. It adds a jolt of flavor to numerous sauces, MARINADES and dressings, and to preparations such as SAUERBRATEN, SWEET-AND-SOUR dishes and marinated HERRING. It's also widely used as a table CONDIMENT in many cultures. Vinegar should be stored airtight in a cool, dark place. Unopened, it will keep indefinitely; once opened it can be stored for about 6 months. *See also* MOTHER OF VINEGAR; SU.

vine leaves *see* GRAPE LEAVES

vino [VEE-noh] Italian and Spanish for "WINE."

vintage [VIHN-tihj] A term in the wine world that describes both the year of the actual grape harvest and the wine made from those grapes. In the United States, the label may list the **vintage year** if 95 percent of the wine comes from grapes harvested that year. If a blend of grapes from 2 or more years is used, the wine is **nonvintage** (*NV*), but that doesn't mean it's not as good as a vintage wine. Consumers should consider a vintage year only as a general guideline. An excellent year for a growing region translates to a generally superior quality—which means there are more choices for fine wines of that vintage. In the end, however, each wine must be judged on its own merit.

vintage wine *see* VINTAGE; WINE

Viognier; Vionnier [vee-oh-NYAY] An esteemed white-wine grape that was once very rare because of the limited acreage planted throughout the world. Its low yield and susceptibility to vineyard diseases made Viognier wines extremely difficult to find. This has all changed in the last decade as Viognier has became very popular and growers around the world have been adding it to their vineyards. California has gone from less than 100 acres in the early 1990s to several thousand acres. Similar interest in this variety has taken place in the Languedoc-Roussillon region of France and in parts of Australia, Italy, Spain, South Africa and South America. Viognier wines are known for their vibrant floral qualities and an intriguing BOUQUET reminiscent of apricots, peaches and pears.

violet, crystallized *see* CRYSTALLIZED FLOWERS

Virginia ham *see* SMITHFIELD HAM

Virgin Mary *see* BLOODY MARY

vitello [vee-TEHL-loh] Italian for "veal."

vitello tonnato [vee-TEHL-loh toh-NAH-toh] A classic Italian dish of braised veal tenderloin that's cut into thin slices and topped with a creamy, velvety smooth sauce made by puréeing the cooking liquid with canned tuna, CAPERS, ANCHOVIES, hard-cooked egg yolk and cream or mayonnaise. Vitello tonnato is served at room temperature or slightly chilled.

viticulture [VIHT-ih-kuhl-cher] The science or study of growing grapes for wine.

vodka [VOD-kuh] A clear, colorless, unaged liquor, the name of which comes from the Russian *zhiznennaia voda,* "water of life." Vodkas can be made from everything from potatoes to beets, although those made from grain (primarily barley and wheat, sometimes rye or corn) are considered the best. Vodka's purity is the result of DISTILLATION at high proof levels, then filtration through activated charcoal to remove most remaining impurities that would contribute distinctive characteristics. Some vodkas are triple-filtered for ultimate purity. Even so, vodka connoisseurs note distinct flavor differences when vodkas are tasted at room temperature sans mixers. In general, however, vodka served STRAIGHT should be served icy cold. **Flavored vodkas**, long common in Russia and Poland, may be flavored with anything from fruits to hot peppers. Some flavored vodkas are sweetened slightly.

vol-au-vent [vawl-oh-VAHN] Said to have been created by the famous French chef Carême, a *vol-au-vent* is a PUFF PASTRY shell that resembles a pot with a lid. It can be small (individual-size) or large (6 to 8 inches in diameter). The pastry is classically filled with a cream sauce–based mixture, usually of chicken, fish, meat or vegetables. The puff-pastry lid is set on top of the filling. This dish may be served as an appetizer or an entrée. The term *vol-au-vent,* "flying in the wind," refers to the pastry's incredible lightness.

Vouvray [voo-VRAY; voo-vreh] Any of various white wines made in and around the French village of Vouvray in the Loire Valley, usually from CHENIN BLANC grapes. These wines can vary greatly, with a broad range including dry, semisweet, sweet, slightly sparkling or fully sparkling. Vouvrays can range from average to excellent, depending on the vintner.

V.S.; V.S.O.P.; V.V.S.O.P. *see* COGNAC

waffle [WAHF-fuhl] The honeycombed surface of this crisp, light bread is perfect for holding pockets of syrup. Waffles are made by pouring a light batter onto one side of a waffle iron, a special hinged cooking utensil with two honeycomb patterned griddles. The second side is closed over the batter and the waffle is cooked until browned and crisp. **Waffle irons** can be electric or designed for stovetop cooking. Electric waffle irons have heating elements in both sides, thereby cooking the two sides of the bread at once. Irons heated on top of a stove must be turned over once during cooking to finish the second side. There are a number of waffle-iron shapes available including square, rectangular, round and even heart-shape. **Belgian waffles**, which are often heaped with fresh strawberries and whipped cream, are made on special waffle makers with particularly large, deep grids. Most modern waffle irons have nonstick surfaces. Waffles are popular not only for breakfast, but for desserts as well. Savory waffles can be topped with creamed meat or vegetable mixtures.

waffle iron *see* WAFFLE

wagyu [WAH-joo] Breed of cattle used to produce the famous KOBE BEEF. In fact, it's several breeds of cattle with similar characteristics. Key to them all is the ability to develop a higher percentage of intense marbling, which improves tenderness and flavor. And the fat has a higher proportion of unsaturated fat than in other breeds. There are four major breeds—Black Wagyu, Brown Wagyu, Poll Wagyu and Shorthorn Wagyu—and numerous sub-breeds. In addition to Kobe, other well-known Japanese wagyu brands are Mishima, Matsusaka and Ōmi. Other countries including Australia and the United States are raising wagyu cattle. In the U.S. they are often bred with Black Angus cattle so the animals are generally not 100 percent wagyu. The beef is often labeled American-style Kobe beef, Kobe-style beef or wagyu beef. Wagyu beef is considerably more expensive than other types of beef.

wahoo [wah-HOO; WAH-hoo] With a flavor often compared to that of ALBACORE, the wahoo's moderate- to high-fat flesh is fine, white (with a little red) and slightly sweet. In fact, Hawaiians call this fish *ono,* which means "sweet." Wahoo are normally caught in the 20- to 40-pound range although they can get much larger. Those that reach the market are usually in the form of chunks or in fillet pieces. Wahoo may be baked, broiled or grilled. *See also* FISH.

waitron Though not commonly used today, this unisex term was coined in the 1980s for waitresses and waiters.

wakame [wah-KAH-meh] A deep green, edible SEAWEED popular in Japan and other Asian countries. It's used like a vegetable in soups and simmered dishes, as well as occasionally in salads. The browner versions are more strongly flavored. Wakame is available both in fresh and dried forms in Asian markets, specialty markets and natural food stores.

Waldorf salad [WAWL-dorf] Created at New York's Waldorf-Astoria Hotel in the 1890s, the original version of this salad contained only apples, celery and mayonnaise. Chopped walnuts later became an integral part of the dish. Waldorf salad is usually served on top of a bed of lettuce.

walleyed pike *see* PERCH

walnut The fruit of the walnut tree, which grows in temperate zones throughout the world. The two most popular varieties of walnut are the ENGLISH (also called *Persian*) WALNUT and the BLACK WALNUT. A close relative is the BUTTERNUT, also referred to as *white walnut*. English walnuts are the most widely available and come in many varieties—some with moderately thick shells, others with shells so thin a tiny bird can crack them open. They're available year-round and come in three main sizes: large, medium and babies. When buying walnuts in the shell, choose those free of cracks or holes. Shelled walnuts should be plump, meaty and crisp; shriveled nutmeats are past their prime. Walnuts in the shell can be stored in a cool, dry place up to 3 months. Shelled nutmeats should be refrigerated, tightly covered, up to 6 months. They can be frozen up to a year. Walnuts are delicious in a variety of sweet and savory dishes and baked goods. They're also used to make a fragrant, flavorful oil (*see* WALNUT OIL). *See also* NUTS.

walnut oil A distinctively nutty-flavored oil extracted from walnut meats. Walnut oil is expensive and can be found in supermarkets, gourmet food stores and natural food stores. Store in a cool, dark place for up to 3 months; refrigerate to prevent rancidity. The French term for walnut oil is *huile de noix*. *See also* FATS AND OILS.

warka; warqa [WAHR-kah] Thin sheets of pastry used in North African cooking for dishes such as BREK (or brik) or B'STEEYA (or bistilla). Warka, also spelled *ouarka*, are the Moroccan versions; in Tunisia they are called *malsouka* or *malsouqa* and in Algeria *dioul*. They are somewhat like PHYLLO or EGG ROLL SKINS but not exactly like either of them— warka are sturdier than phyllo. They can be made at home but are difficult and require high-gluten flour. Warka can be found in some ethnic groceries and on the Internet. Sometimes they are referred to as *brick dough, brik dough* or *feuilles de brick*.

wasabi; wasabe [WAH-sah-bee] This Japanese version of HORSERAD- ISH comes from the root of an Asian plant. It's used to make a green- colored CONDIMENT that has a sharp, pungent, fiery flavor. Wasabi, which is also called *Japanese horseradish,* is available in both paste and powder form in specialty and Asian markets as well as supermarkets. Some specialty produce markets carry fresh wasabi, which may be grated like horseradish. Unfortunately, true wasabi is difficult to grow and is not frequently cultivated outside of Japan. What's found in the United States is often a blend of horseradish, mustard and food coloring. True wasabi aficionados refer to these substitutes as "western wasabi" or "faux wasabi."

wash rind; washed-rind cheeses A method of periodically washing (brushing, rubbing) the rinds of certain cheeses with a liquid in order to keep the surface moist and supple. Although BRINE is most frequently used for this RIPENING technique, other liquids employed include beer, brandy, cider, oil, WHEY and wine. This technique can be performed by hand or by machine. Maintaining a moist rind stimulates the growth of *brevibacterium linens*, a friendly BACTERIA that ripens the cheese from the outside in (*see* SOFT-RIPENED CHEESES) and creates a rind with various shades of pink, orange or red. The final product usually has a moist rind with a uniquely earthy, mushroomy flavor. Notable washed-rind cheeses include ÉPOISSES DE BOURGOGNE, PONT-L'ÉVÊQUE and TALEGGIO. The terms *red smear* and *smear-ripened* are sometimes used synonymously for washed rind.

wassail [WAHS-uhl; WAHS-ayl] *Ves heill,* Norse for "be in good health," is an old toast and the origin of this word. Wassail is a drink consisting of ALE or wine sweetened with sugar and flavored with spices. This brew is traditionally served in a large "wassail bowl," garnished with small roasted apples and ladled into serving cups.

water bath The French call this cooking technique *bain marie*. It consists of placing a container (pan, bowl, soufflé dish, etc.) of food in a large, shallow pan of warm water, which surrounds the food with gentle heat. The food may be cooked in this manner either in an oven or on top of a range. This technique is designed to cook delicate dishes such as custards, sauces and savory mousses without breaking or curdling them. It can also be used to keep cooked foods warm.

water biscuit A bland, crisp cracker that's often served with cheese and wine. The fact that the cracker is almost flavorless makes it a perfect foil for most foods because it allows their natural flavor to be appreciated.

water chestnut The edible corm of a water plant indigenous to Southeast Asia. The water chestnut's brownish-black skin resembles that of a true chestnut, but its flesh is white, crunchy and juicy. The flavor is bland with a hint of sweetness. Water chestnuts are very popular in Asian cooking, especially in STIR-FRIED dishes where their crunchy texture is a standout. Water chestnuts are available fresh in most Chinese markets. Choose firm chestnuts with no sign of soft spots or shriveling. Refrigerate unwashed chesnuts in a plastic bag for up to 2 weeks. Wash well and peel before using raw or in cooked dishes. Water chestnuts are also available canned—either whole or sliced—in most supermarkets, but the fresh are superior. *See also* WATER CHESTNUT POWDER.

water chestnut powder (flour) A powdered starch ground from dried water chestnuts. It's used as a thickener in Asian cooking. Like CORNSTARCH, it's mixed with a small amount of water before being added to the hot mixture to be thickened. It can also be used to DREDGE foods before frying. Water chestnut powder is available in Asian markets and in some natural food stores.

watercress Cool running water is the growing ground for this member of the mustard family, which can often be found in the wild in and around streams and brooks. Watercress has small, crisp, dark green leaves. Its pungent flavor is slightly bitter and has a peppery snap. Watercress is available year-round and is customarily sold in small bouquets. Choose crisp leaves with deep, vibrant color. There should be no sign of yellowing or wilting. Refrigerate in a plastic bag (or stems-down in a glass of water covered with a plastic bag) for up to 5 days. Wash and shake dry just before using. Watercress may be used in salads, sandwiches, soups and a variety of cooked dishes. It's also a popular garnish, fast replacing the ubiquitous parsley.

watermelon Native to Africa, the watermelon is considered less sophisticated than other categories of MELON because it lacks flavor complexity and has a watery texture. But there are those who wouldn't trade a slice of watermelon on a hot summer day for anything. Though there are myriad watermelon varieties, they all share the characteristic sweet, juicy, crisp flesh. Watermelons come in a variety of shapes (from huge and ovoid to small and round) and colors, with rinds ranging from solid-colored to striped, and flesh that can be red, pink, ivory, orange or yellow. The seeds may be speckled or solid and variously colored—black, brown, green, red or white. America's most popular watermelon is the large, elongated-oval shape with a variegated or striped, two-tone green or gray-green rind. It averages 15 to 35 pounds but may be much smaller or larger, depending on the variety. (According to the Guinness Book of World Records, the largest watermelon ever grown was 262 pounds.) There are even relatively tiny varieties about the size of a medium cantaloupe. An abundance of shiny, black seeds dot the sweet, red, refreshingly moist flesh. **Seedless watermelons** actually do, more often than not, have a few scattered seeds. What seeds there are, however, are small, soft and edible. All parts of the watermelon can be used. Asians love the roasted seeds, and the pickled rind is a favorite in many parts of the world. Watermelons are available May to September, though they're at their peak from mid-June to late August. They're sold whole as well as in halves, quarters or by the slice. Look for symmetrical melons without any flat sides. Depending on the variety, the shape can be round or an oblong oval. Slap the side of the watermelon—if it resounds with a hollow thump, it's a good indicator that the melon is ripe. The rind should be dull (not shiny) and just barely yield to pressure. Never take home a melon with soft spots, gashes or other blemishes on the rind. Cut watermelons should display a brightly colored flesh. An abundance of small, white seeds means the melon is immature. Avoid cut melons with a grainy or dry-looking flesh. Store whole watermelon in the refrigerator if at all possible and keep no more than a week. If it's too large for your unit, keep in a cool, dark place. Cut watermelon should always be tightly wrapped, refrigerated and used within a day or so. It should be served cold, either in wedges or made into balls and served as part of a fruit cup or salad. Watermelon contains a fair amount of vitamins A and C. *See also* MELON.

water spinach Also known as *swamp spinach,* this vegetable is native to tropical India and gets its name because it's cultivated both on water-bogged and dry land. Water spinach has slender, graceful medium to dark green leaves that can be up to 18 inches long. Although not related to common SPINACH, its flavor and fragrance resemble it. Also called *pahk boong* or *ong choy* it's available in Asian markets and can be refrigerated in a plastic bag for up to 4 days. All but the bottom half of the stems can be eaten. Water spinach is typically used in STIR-FRY dishes.

waterzooi [VAH-tuhr-zoh-ee] This classic Belgian dish is a creamy-rich fish stew that can be made with either fresh- or saltwater fish. A chicken rendition is also popular. All versions include a variety of vegetables and herbs, and are enriched with egg yolks, cream and butter.

wax bean *see* GREEN BEAN

wax paper; waxed paper Semitransparent paper with a thin coating of wax on both sides. Because of its moistureproof and nonstick characteristics, wax paper used to play a major role in the kitchen for duties such as covering food and lining baking pans. In recent years, however, wax paper has been replaced in many of its roles by aluminum foil or plastic wrap.

weakfish A member of the DRUM fish family but different from the croaker and black and red drums. Its name comes from the weak flesh around the mouth that tears easily when hooked. It has white, lean, finely textured flesh and is considered an excellent food fish. This species, which is found in the Atlantic and parts of the Pacific along both North and South America, is also called *seatrout, spotted sea trout, squeteague, gray trout* and *corvina* (or *corbina*). *See also* FISH.

weasel coffee *see* KOPI LUWAK

wedge bone *see* SIRLOIN

Wehani rice [weh-HAH-nee] Considered an AROMATIC RICE, Wehani is a light clay-colored brown rice (*see* RICE) that splits slightly when cooked. It resembles cooked WILD RICE and has a fragrance akin to popcorn. Wehani, which is related to BASMATI RICE, was developed at the famous rice-growing Lundberg Family Farms in Richvale, California.

weisswurst [VICE-voorst; VICE-vurscht] German for "white sausage," weisswurst is a delicate SAUSAGE made with veal, cream and eggs. It's traditionally served during Oktoberfest with sweet mustard, rye bread and beer.

wekiwa *see* LAVENDER GEM

well-and-tree platter A platter with troughs formed into the bottom to resemble bare tree branches attached to a central trunk, at one end of which is a shallow well. Such a configuration allows the juices of meats being cut on the platter to drain.

Wellfleet oyster *see* ATLANTIC OYSTER

Wellington, beef *see* BEEF WELLINGTON

welsh onion Despite the misleading name, welsh onions originated in China or Siberia, not Wales. They are also called *bunching onions, Japanese bunching onions* and *Japanese leeks* along with broadly used names like *green onion,* SCALLION and *spring onion.* This onion variety is more popular in Asia than the onions commonly grown in the United States. They have a light onion flavor and, although they have a slightly different taste, can be used interchangeably with true scallions. They also differ from true scallions in that welsh onions have a slight bulge at the base and hollow leaves, whereas scallions have a straight-sided base and flat leaves. Choose those with crisp, bright-green tops and a firm white base. Store, wrapped in a plastic bag, in the vegetable crisper section of the refrigerator for up to 5 days. Welsh onions can be cooked whole as a vegetable much as you would a LEEK. They can also be chopped and used in salads, soups and a multitude of other dishes for flavor.

Welsh rabbit; Welsh rarebit This popular British dish consists of a melted mixture of CHEDDAR CHEESE, beer (sometimes ALE or milk) and seasonings served over toast. The cheese mixture can also be toasted on the bread. Welsh rabbit is usually served as a main course or for HIGH TEA, often accompanied with tomatoes. Welsh rabbit becomes a *golden buck* when topped with a poached egg.

Western sandwich *see* DENVER SANDWICH

West Indian pumpkin *see* CALABAZA

West Indies cherry *see* ACEROLA

Westphalian ham [wehst-FAYL-yuhn] Extremely fine ham produced from pigs raised on acorns in Germany's Westphalia forest. Westphalian ham is cured before being slowly smoked over beechwood mixed with juniper branches. The combination of the gourmet diet, curing and smoking results in a dark brown, very dense ham with a distinctive, light smoky flavor. Connoisseurs consider these hams among the best. *See also* HAM.

wheat Thought to have been growing since Paleolithic times and cultivated for at least 6,000 years, wheat is the world's largest CEREAL-grass crop. Its status as a staple is second only to rice. One reason for its popularity is that—unlike other cereals—wheat contains a relatively high amount of GLUTEN, the protein that provides the elasticity necessary for excellent breadmaking. Though there are over 30,000 varieties of wheat, the three major types are hard wheat, soft wheat and durum wheat. **Hard wheat** is high in protein (10 to 14 percent) and yields a flour rich in gluten, making it particularly suitable for YEAST BREADS. The low-protein (6 to 10 percent) **soft wheat** yields a flour lower in gluten and therefore better suited for tender baked goods such as biscuits and cakes. **Durum wheat**, although high in gluten, is not good for baking. Instead, it's most often ground into SEMOLINA, the basis for excellent pasta. In the United States, wheat is also classified according to the time of year it is sown—namely, **spring wheat** and **winter wheat** (which is actually sown in the fall). The unprocessed wheat kernel, commonly known as a *wheat berry,* is made up of three major portions—BRAN, germ and endosperm. **Wheat bran**, the rough outer covering, has very little nutritional value but plenty of fiber. During milling, the bran is removed from the kernel. It's sold separately and used to add flavor and fiber to baked goods. **Wheat germ**, essentially the embryo of the berry, is a concentrated source of vitamins, minerals and protein. It has a nutty flavor and is very oily, which causes it to turn rancid quickly. Wheat germ is sold in both toasted and natural forms and is used to add nutrition to a variety of foods. *Wheat germ oil,* an extraction of the germ, is strongly flavored and expensive. The **wheat endosperm**, which makes up the majority of the kernel, is full of starch, protein, niacin and iron. It's the primary source of many wheat flours. In addition to flour, wheat is available in several other forms including wheat berries, cracked wheat and BULGHUR WHEAT. **Wheat berries** are whole, unprocessed kernels, whereas **cracked wheat** is the whole berry broken into coarse, medium and fine fragments. Both are sold in natural food stores and may be cooked as cereal, or in PILAFS, breads or other dishes. *See also* KAMUT.

wheat beer A beer made from malted wheat, characterized by its pale color and subtle, LAGERlike flavor. Technically, it should be classified as an ALE since it's a top-fermented brew. *See also* BEER.

wheat berries *see* WHEAT

wheat bran *see* BRAN; WHEAT

wheat germ *see* WHEAT

wheat gluten *see* SEITAN

wheat meat *see* SEITAN

wheel A cheese shape that's cylindrical and relatively flat, with a diameter about three to four times its height. *See also* CHEESE.

whelk [HWEHLK; wehlk] This member of the GASTROPOD branch of the MOLLUSK family is a large marine snail. It has a beautiful spiraled shell and a rather tough but flavorful footlike muscle. Although the **waved whelk** is found along America's northern Atlantic coast, it has never gained wide popularity in the United States. **Knobbed whelks** and **channeled whelks** are also marketed in the States. Fresh whelks are generally available in the spring and fall. They're also available cooked, preserved in vinegar and canned. Because of their lack of popularity, whelks may be difficult to find except in Chinese or Italian markets or specialty food stores. Whelk is naturally tough and must usually be tenderized by pounding. It benefits from brief, gentle cooking. The Italians refer to whelk as *scungilli,* and the famous *scungilli marinara* is a garlicky dish of whelk cooked in a tomato sauce flavored with basil, oregano and hot pepper seeds.

whetstone [HWEHT-stohn; WEHT-stohn] Whetstones, also called *oilstones,* are rectangular blocks made of the extremely hard carborundum (a composition of silicon carbide). They are fine grained, often with one side slightly coarser than the other. Knives should periodically be honed on whetstones to keep them really sharp. This is done by first lubricating the stone with oil or water, then drawing the knife blade with slight pressure across the whetstone at about a 20-degree angle. Doing this 5 to 6 times on each side of the knife is adequate. If the whetstone's two sides are of differing textures, this activity should be performed first on the coarser side and finished on the finer-grained side. This will give the knife an even sharper edge. The sharpness of a knife's blade can be maintained by using a SHARPENING STEEL prior to each use.

whey [HWAY; way] The watery liquid that separates from the solids (CURDS) in cheesemaking. Whey is sometimes further processed into **whey cheese** (*see* CHEESE). It can be separated another step, with butter being made from the fattier share. Whey is also used in processed foods such as crackers. Primarily, however, whey is more often used as livestock feed than it is in the human diet.

whip *n.* 1. A gelatin-based dessert that's airy and light because of the addition of either whipped cream or stiffly beaten egg whites. Such desserts are usually made with fruit purée but can also be flavored with other ingredients such as chocolate or coffee. 2. Another name for a WHISK. **whip** *v.* To beat ingredients, such as egg whites, cream, etc., thereby incorporating air into them and increasing their volume until they are light and fluffy.

whipping cream *see* CREAM

whisk [HWIHSK; WIHSK] Also called a *whip,* this kitchen utensil consists of a series of looped wires forming a three-dimensional teardrop shape. The wires are joined and held together with a long handle. Whisks are used for whipping ingredients (such as cream, eggs, sauces, etc.), thereby incorporating air into them. They come in different sizes for different tasks and are most often made of stainless steel or tinned steel.

whiskey; whisky [HWIHSK-ee; WIHSK-ee] An alcoholic DISTILLATE obtained from a fermented mash of grains such as barley, rye or corn. The name comes from the Celtic (Gaelic) *uisqebaugh* (pronounced oos-kee-BAW or whis-kee-BAW), which means "water of life." Many factors influence a whiskey's quality and flavor including the type of grain and yeast used, the method of DISTILLATION, how it's AGED and the water source. **Straight whiskey** must be made from at least 51 percent of a grain, must not exceed 160 PROOF (80 percent alcohol), must be aged in oak barrels for 2 years and may only be diluted with water to no less than 80 proof. BOURBON, TENNESSEE WHISKEY and RYE WHISKEY are all straight whiskeys. **Blended whiskey** is a combination of two or more 100-proof straight whiskeys blended with NEUTRAL SPIRITS, grain spirits or light whiskeys. **Light whiskey** has been distilled to a higher-than-normal alcohol level (typically more than 160 proof) then diluted with water to a greater extent than usual. It gets its distinctive character from being stored in charred oak containers. Such whiskies are generally used for blending. **Single-malt whiskey** is made only from malted barley and from a single distillery. Such whiskeys are typically richer in flavor and usually more expensive than blended whiskey. There are myriad single-malt SCOTCH whiskeys as well as some single-malt IRISH WHISKEYS available. The countries with the highest whiskey production are Canada, Ireland, Great

Britain (Scotland) and the United States. Traditionally, whiskies made in Scotland and Canada are spelled *whisky,* sans the "e." *See also* CANADIAN WHISKY; CORN WHISKEY; HOOCH.

whiskey sour *see* SOUR

whitebait *see* SMELT

white bass *see* STRIPED BASS

white bean A generic term applied to any of several dried beans falling into the four categories of MARROW BEANS, GREAT NORTHERN BEANS, NAVY BEANS and PEA BEANS.

white carrot *see* ARRACACHA

white chocolate Not really *chocolate* at all, white chocolate contains no chocolate liquor (*see* CHOCOLATE), which means it has little, if any, chocolate flavor. The FDA has established a standard of identity for white chocolate as a product that contains cocoa butter, milk solids, nutritive carbohydrate sweeteners and other suitable ingredients, such as LECITHIN and VANILLA. Melt white chocolate very slowly over low heat to keep it from scorching and clumping.

whitefish Found in lakes and streams throughout North America, the whitefish is a member of the SALMON family. Its high-fat, mild-flavored flesh is firm and white. Fresh whitefish can be found year-round and are generally marketed whole (from 2 to 6 pounds) or in fillets. They're also available frozen and smoked. Whitefish can be poached, baked, broiled or grilled. The ROE can be cooked or used for CAVIAR. *See also* FISH.

white lady A COCKTAIL made with white CRÈME DE MENTHE, COINTREAU and lemon juice shaken with ice, then strained into a stemmed cocktail glass. *See also* PINK LADY.

white lightning *see* CORN WHISKEY

white mustard cabbage *see* BOK CHOY

white pepper; white peppercorn *see* PEPPERCORN

white pine mushroom *see* MATSUTAKE MUSHROOM

white pudding A British SAUSAGE made of white meat (such as chicken or pork), fat, some type of grain (such as OATMEAL) and seasonings. Its counterpart is black pudding (*see* BLOOD SAUSAGE). *See also* BOUDIN BLANC.

White Riesling *see* RIESLING

White Russian *see* BLACK RUSSIAN

white sapote [sah-POH-tay] A tropical fruit native to Mexico and Central America, though it's also grown in California and Florida. The white sapote comes from a tropical tree in the family *Rutaceae,* and the fruit is said to induce sleep and have a calming effect on the nervous system. This fruit is plum-shaped and about the size of a small orange. The thin skin ranges in color from chartreuse to yellow. The ivory-colored flesh has a creamy, custardlike texture and a sweet flavor that is reminiscent of a peach-avocado-vanilla blend. The flesh contains from 3 to 5 medium-size seeds, which should be removed. White sapotes are available from October to February in some specialty produce markets and farmer's markets. Ripen at room temperature as you would an avocado. Store ripe fruit in the refrigerator for up to 3 days. The white sapote is also called *zapote blanco* and—like the CHERIMOYA—is sometimes referred to as *custard apple. See also* BLACK SAPOTE; MAMEY SAPOTE.

white sauce *see* BÉCHAMEL

white seabass *see* DRUM

white stock Any STOCK made from beef, veal, chicken, fish or vegetables, simmered in water with aromatic vegetables (typically onions, carrots and celery). Because the ingredients haven't been browned (as in a BROWN STOCK), the stock is pale in color. *See also* SAUCE.

white turmeric *see* ZEDOARY

white walnut *see* BUTTERNUT

whiting Small gray and silver fish related to both COD and HAKE. They're sometimes called *silver hake.* The whiting's lowfat flesh is white, firm textured and delicately flavored. The fish weighs between 1 and 5 pounds and is marketed (fresh and frozen) both whole and in fillets. Whiting is also available salted and smoked. It can be poached, steamed, broiled, panfried or baked. *See also* FISH.

whole-wheat flour *see* FLOUR

whortleberry [HWUHR-tl-behr-ee] *see* BILBERRY

wiener [WEE-nuhr] *see* FRANKFURTER

wiener dog Another name for a HOT DOG.

Wiener Schnitzel; Wienerschnitzel [VEE-nuhr SHNIHT-suhl] German for "Viennese cutlet," this famous Viennese dish actually originated in France. It's a veal SCALLOP that is dipped in flour, beaten egg and breadcrumbs before being sautéed. *Wiener schnitzel* is usually garnished with lemon slices and sometimes hard-cooked egg, anchovies or capers.

wild coriander *see* SAW-LEAF HERB

wild leek *see* RAMP

wild marjoram *see* OREGANO

wild pecan rice Hailing from Louisiana, this AROMATIC RICE is a hybrid (its parents have no relation to either wild rice or pecans) with a rich, nutty flavor and a cooked fragrance akin to popcorn. It's also called simply *pecan rice,* and is available in gourmet markets and some supermarkets. *See also* RICE.

wild rice Known for its luxurious nutty flavor and chewy texture, wild rice isn't really rice at all. Instead, it's a long-grain marsh grass native to the northern Great Lakes area, where it's harvested by the local Indians. There's also now commercial wild rice production in California, as well as several Midwest states. It's important to clean wild rice thoroughly before cooking it. The best method is to place the rice in a medium bowl and fill it with cold water. Give it a couple of stirs and set aside for a few minutes. Any debris will float to the surface and the water can then be poured off. Depending on the method used, wild rice can take up to an hour to cook; overcooking will produce starchy results. Admittedly, wild rice is expensive, but both pleasure and budget are extended by combining it with brown rice or BULGHUR WHEAT. Wild rice is also called *Indian rice*. *See also* RICE.

wild tamarind *see* GUAJE

wine Unless otherwise specified, wine refers to the naturally fermented juice of grapes. More broadly, the term can include alcoholic beverages created from other fruits and even vegetables. Wine has a rich history that has evolved along with that of humankind. Its historical roots reach back almost 12,000 years. As various cultures spread out into new parts of the world, so did the grapevine and the art of winemaking. Today there are vineyards throughout the world with good wine being produced in far-ranging locations from the United States to South Africa to Australia to South America to Europe. Wine is broadly classified in the following categories: 1. **still** (nonsparkling) **wines**—including red, white and rosé—which can be DRY (nonsweet), semisweet and sweet; 2. **sparkling wines**, including French CHAMPAGNES as well as effervescent wines from other parts of the world; 3. **fortified wines**, such as SHERRY and PORT, which have been augmented with a dose of BRANDY or other spirit; and 4. **aromatic** (or **aromatized**) **wines**, such as VERMOUTH, which have been flavored with ingredients like herbs or spices. **Vintage wine** is that which is made with 95 percent of the grapes harvested in a specific year; the year or "vintage" is indicated on the wine label. **Nonvintage wine** is made from the juice of grapes harvested from several years; there's no year noted on the label of such wine. BLUSH WINES are made with red grapes, but the juice has had a very brief contact with the grape skins, which produces pale pink wines. **Alcohol-free wines** are those produced by one of several special processes to remove the alcohol. Such wines are also called *dealcoholized wines* and *nonalcoholic wine.* Legally nonalcoholic products, such potables contain less than 0.5 percent alcohol (oddly enough, about the same amount in most freshly squeezed orange juice). That in itself makes this product appealing to many, but weight watchers love the fact that dealcoholized wine has less than half the calories of regular wine. And to top it all off, according to The American Journal of Clinical Nutrition, nonalcoholic red wine is also good for the heart. But don't expect these nonalcoholic alternatives to have the subtlety, body and mouthfeel of real wine. They don't, primarily because alcohol contributes to all of those characteristics. Still, there are some good dealcoholized wines on the market in a variety of styles including reds, whites, rosés and sparkling wines. You can even find some varietal wines like Chardonnay, Cabernet Sauvignon, Merlot and Johannisberg Riesling. Alcohol-free wines can be found at liquor stores and some supermarkets and are typically grouped together. **Wine storage** locations should be dark, vibration free and at an even temperature. The ideal temperature is 55°F, however, anywhere from 45° to 70°F is acceptable, providing the temperature is consistent. The higher the temperature, the faster a wine will age. Wine bottles should be stored on their sides to prevent the cork from drying and shrinking, which would allow air to enter the bottle and disrupt the wine's flavor. **Serving temperatures:** White wine should be served at a range of between 50° and 55°F; red wine at around 65°F. Refrigerating white wine for more than 2 hours before serving can dull its flavor and aroma. Avoid drips when pouring wine by giving the bottle a slight twist just as you finish pouring. *See also* ACETIC ACID; ALSATIAN WINES; AMERICAN VITICULTURAL AREA; APPELLATION; ASTI SPUMANTE; AUSLESE; BARBARESCO; BARBERA; BARDOLINO; BAROLO; BAROSSA VALLEY; BEAUJOLAIS; BEERENAUSLESE; BLANC DE BLANCS; BLANC DE NOIRS; BOTRYTIS CINEREA; BOUQUET; BRUNELLO DI MONTALCINO; BURGUNDY; BYRRH; CABERNET FRANC; CABERNET SAUVIGNON; CARIGNAN; CAVA; CHABLIS; CHARACTER; CHARDONNAY; CHÂTEAU-BOTTLED; CHÂTEAUNEUF-DU-PAPE; CHENIN BLANC; CHIANTI; CINSAUT; CLARET; CLASSICO; COGNAC; COLD DUCK; COOKING WINE; CORKAGE; CORKSCREW; CÔTES DU RHÔNE; CUVÉE; DECANT; DECANTER; DELAWARE GRAPE; DEMI-SEC; DESSERT WINE; DOSAGE; DUBONNET; ENOLOGY; FINING; FINO; FORTIFIED WINE; FRENCH COLOMBARD; GEWÜRZTRAMINER; GLÜHWEIN; GRAVES; GRENACHE; KIR; LAMBRUSCO; LATE HARVEST; LEES; LIEBFRAUMILCH; LILLET; MADEIRA; MALIC ACID; MANZANILLA; MARC; MARSALA; MAY WINE; MERLOT; MÉTHODE CHAMPENOISE; MIRIN; MOURVÈDRE; MULLED WINE; MUSCADET; MUSCADINE GRAPE; MUSCAT GRAPE; MUSCATEL WINE; MUST; NEBBIOLO; NIAGARA GRAPE; NOSE; OLOROSO; PASTEURIZATION; PETITE SIRAH; PINOT BLANC; PINOT CHARDONNAY; PINOT NOIR; POMACE; RAPE; RETSINA; RHÔNE WINES;

RICE WINE; RIESLING; RISERVA; ROSATO; ROSÉ WINES; SAKE; SANGIOVESE; SANGRÍA; SAUTERNES; SAUVIGNON BLANC; SEC; SEDIMENT; SEMILLON; SHAOXING; SOMMELIER; SPÄTLESE; SPRITZER; SPUMANTE; SYLVANER; SYRAH; TANNIN; TARTARIC ACID; TOKAY GRAPE; TROCKENBEERENAUSLESE; VALPOLICELLA; VARIETAL WINE; VIN; VINTAGE; VIOGNIER; VITICULTURE; VOUVRAY; WINE BOTTLES; WINE LABEL TERMS; YEAST; ZINFANDEL. For complete and detailed wine-related information, see *Wine Lover's Companion*, published by Barron's Educational Series, Inc.

wine bottles Since 1979, metric standards have been in use in the United States and the *standard wine bottle* size was set at 750 milliliters (ml) or approximately 25.4 ounces, which is almost exactly equivalent to an American fifth ($4/5$ of a quart or 25.6 ounces). In answer to the stricter driving/alcohol limits in many U.S. states, the wine industry recently introduced a new 500-ml bottle size, which is $2/3$ of a standard bottle. In France's BEAUJOLAIS area a 500-ml bottle (which they call a POT) has long been used. In the United States, other legal bottle sizes include 50 ml, 100 ml, 187 ml, 375 ml, 1 liter, 1.5 liter and 3 liter. Wine may also be bottled in sizes larger than 3 liters if the capacity is in even liter sizes—4 liters, 5 liters, 6 liters, etc. Other bottle terminology, although not legally defined in the United States, is still sometimes used in wine circles. These terms, which include French bottle descriptions and approximate bottle sizes, are: **split**—equivalent to 187 ml or $1/4$ of a standard wine bottle; **half bottle**—375 ml; **magnum**—1.5 liters/2 standard bottles; **double magnum**—3 liters/4 standard bottles (in BORDEAUX); **Jeroboam**—3 liters/4 standard bottles (in CHAMPAGNE) or 4.5 liters/6 standard bottles (in Bordeaux); **Rehoboam**—4.5 liters/6 standard bottles (in Champagne); **Methuselah**—6 liters/8 standard bottles (in Champagne); **Imperial**—6 liters/8 standard bottles (in Bordeaux); **Salmanazar**—9 liters/12 standard bottles; **Balthazar**—12 liters/16 standard bottles; and **Nebuchadnezzar**—15 liters/20 standard bottles.

wine label terms Confused by American wine label terms? Here's an explanation: **Estate Bottled**—100 percent of the grapes used were grown in the winery's own vineyards or came from vineyards controlled by the winery in the same APPELLATION. Furthermore, such wines must be vinified and bottled at that winery. The term **château bottled** has a comparable meaning. Both refer to a wines considered superior in quality and CHARACTER. European phrases comparable to "estate bottled" are as follows: in France—*Mis En Bouteille au Domaine, Mis au Domaine, Mis en Bouteille a la Propriete* and *Mis en Bouteille du Chateau;* in Italy—*Imbottigliato All'origine;* and in Germany—*Erzeugerabfullung.* **Grown, Produced and Bottled By** is comparable to "Estate Bottled" and indicates that the grapes were grown at the winery's vineyards (or vineyards controlled by the winery) and that the wine was vinified and bottled at the winery. **Produced and Bottled By** means that the winery crushed, fermented and bottled at least 75 percent of the wine in that particular bottling, but not that the winery grew the grapes. **Made and Bottled By** means that a minimum of 10 percent of the wine was fermented (*see* FERMENTATION) at the winery—the other 90 percent could be from other sources. This designation does not generally indicate the quality implied by the phrase "Produced and Bottled By." **Bottled by** alone on a label indicates that the only role the winery most likely played in the wine's production was to purchase and bottle wine made somewhere else.

Winesap apple An all-purpose apple with a glossy, deep, multicolored red skin. Its flesh is juicy and crisp and sweet without much acid. *See also* APPLE.

winged bean Also called *goa bean,* this tropical LEGUME is rapidly becoming a staple throughout the poorer regions of the world where it grows. The reasons are basic: it grows quickly, is disease resistant and is high in protein. The winged bean is also valued because it's entirely edible, including the shoots, flowers, roots, leaves, pods and seeds. The pods, which can be green, purple or various shades of red, are four-sided and flare from the center into ruffled ridges or "wings." These beans have a flavor similar to that of a CRANBERRY BEAN with a hint of GREEN BEAN. The texture is like that of a starchy green bean. Winged beans may be found in specialty produce markets and some supermarkets. Choose small beans with no sign of discoloration. Refrigerate, tightly wrapped in a plastic bag, for up to 3 days. Wash and trim before using. Winged beans may be prepared in any way suitable for green beans. *See also* BEANS.

winkle *see* PERIWINKLE

wintergreen The name of this evergreen plant, which is native to eastern North America, comes from the fact that it retains foliage all winter long. In addition to its rich green leaves, wintergreen bears white flowers and bright red berries. The leaves produce a pungent oil that's used to flavor a variety of products including candy, gum, medicine, etc. Wintergreen is also known as *checkerberry*.

winter gourd *see* WINTER MELON

winter melon A double misnomer because the tropical winter melon is harvested in the summer and is a squash, rather than a melon. The name "winter" comes from the snowlike blotching that occurs on mature squashes. Winter melons can range in color from pale to dark green, are shaped somewhat like a watermelon and can weigh up to 100 pounds. The porous flesh is white and has a flavor reminiscent of ZUCCHINI. Winter melon is available year-round in Chinese markets and sometimes in specialty produce stores. It's typically sold in large slices wrapped in plastic. Store in the refrigerator for up to 5 days. Before using, peel off the skin and scoop out the seeds. It should be cooked briefly and is popular in STIR-FRY dishes as well as various Asian soups, especially winter melon soup, which is classically served in a scooped-out winter-melon shell. Winter melon is also called *ash pumpkin* (or *ash gourd*), *dong qua* (or *dung gwa*), *Chinese preserving melon* (because this squash is a popular candy preserve) and *winter gourd* (or *winter squash*).

Winter Nellis Pear A small, almost neckless pear with yellowish-green skin covered with light, brownish dots. The firm flesh is sweet and succulent with a rich, spicy flavor. It's good for out-of-hand eating and for cooking and canning. It's a late ripener that's available from November through April.

winter purslane *see* MINERS' LETTUCE

winter squash *see* SQUASH; WINTER MELON

witloof [WIHT-lohf] *see* ENDIVE

wok [WAHK] A round-bottomed cooking utensil popular in Asian cooking, where its uses include stir-frying, steaming, braising, stewing and even deep-frying. Woks are usually made of carbon steel or cast iron but they can also be made of anodized aluminum and stainless steel. They come in various sizes and can have two small handles, one long handle or one long handle and one small handle. They are generally accompanied by a ring-shaped stand for use on a Western gas stovetop. Special flat-bottom woks are also available for use on electric stoves. Electric woks (usually with a NONSTICK FINISH) are also available.

wolfberry A fruit popular in China and other areas of Eastern Asia, where it's been an important part of traditional medicine for several millennia. Wolfberries are exceedingly rich in nutrients including amino acids, antioxidants, carotenoids, vitamins and minerals. Because of this, they've gained a reputation in Western cultures as a superfood. In the United States the wolfberry often goes by the name *goji berry* or *Tibetan goji berry*. This bright red berry is between $3/8$ and $3/4$ inch long and shaped like a plump almond. It belongs to the nightshade family, which includes eggplants, potatoes and tomatoes. Dried wolfberries taste like a combination of raisins and dried cranberries with a slight nutty quality. This berry is most often found as juice, typically blended with other fruit juices; sometimes dried berry bits are embedded in energy bars. Natural food stores also carry wolfberry juice concentrate, powder and capsules. Though Tibet is often associated with the goji berry, most of these berries are imported from China.

wong bok *see* CHINESE CABBAGE

won tons; wonton [WAHN-tahn] A Chinese specialty similar to an Italian RAVIOLI. These bite-size dumplings consist of paper-thin dough pillows filled with a minced mixture of meat, seafood and/or vegetables. The dough comes prepackaged as WON TON SKINS. Won tons may be boiled, steamed or deep-fried and served as an appetizer, snack or side dish, usually with several sauces. They are, of course, intrinsic to WON TON SOUP.

won ton skins Paper-thin squares of dough made from flour, water, eggs and salt, and used to make WON TONS, EGG ROLLS and similar preparations. Won ton skins can be purchased prepackaged in some supermarkets and in most Chinese markets. The wrappers usually come in both squares and circles and are available in various thicknesses. **Gyoza won ton skins** are round instead of square and are used primarily to make POT STICKERS.

won ton soup A Chinese dish of WON TONS cooked in and served in a clear broth flavored variously with ingredients like scallions, celery and SOY SAUCE. The soup is often garnished with JULIENNED strips of chicken, pork, vegetables, etc. The broth's flavor as well as the garnishes are prepared to correspond to the won ton filling.

woodcock A small, plump GAME BIRD with a rich, dark flesh. The American woodcock is smaller than the Eurasian species. Woodcocks are typically roasted without being eviscerated, as the entrails are considered a delicacy.

wood ear A variety of mushroom also known as *cloud ear, tree ear* (the larger, thicker specimens) or *silver ear* (albinos). They have a slightly crunchy texture and delicate, almost bland flavor that more often than not absorbs the taste of the more strongly flavored ingredients with which they are cooked. Asian markets sell fresh and dried wood ears, the latter of which, except for the albino varieties, look like brownish-black, dried chips. Upon reconstituting they increase 5 to 6 times in size and resemble the shape of an ear. Wood ears are popular in STIR-FRY dishes and soups and are often combined with TIGER LILY BUDS. *See also* MUSHROOM.

woodruff Often described as having the smell of freshly cut hay, woodruff is the leaf of a ground cover native to Europe. Its most famous use is as a flavoring in MAY WINE, a white-wine punch popular in Germany. In Germany and Austria, woodruff is also used to season sausages, candies and many cooked dishes. Live plants are available through many nurseries, and the dried herb is available in gourmet stores and through mail order. Also called *sweet woodruff*.

wood sugar *see* XYLITOL

Worcestershire sauce [WOOS-tuhr-shuhr; WOOS-tuhr-sheer] Though this CONDIMENT was originally developed in India by the English, it takes its name from the fact that it was first bottled in Worcester, England. It's a thin, dark, rather piquant sauce used to season meats, gravies, soups and vegetable juices, and as a table condiment. It's also an essential ingredient in the popular BLOODY MARY cocktail. Worcestershire's formula usually includes garlic, soy sauce, tamarind, onions, molasses, lime, anchovies, vinegar and various seasonings. It's widely available in supermarkets.

wormseed *see* EPAZOTE

wormwood A bitter, aromatic herb used in flavoring ABSINTHE, some wines such as VERMOUTH, and occasionally (but not in the United States) in cooking. In the past, wormwood was popular as a medicinal herb for colds, stomach problems and rheumatism. Because the flavoring oil extracted from this herb is potentially poisonous, the United States has banned preparations (such as absinthe) made with an excessive amount of it. *See also* HERBS.

wurst [WURST; vursht] German for "SAUSAGE."

xanthan gum [ZAN-thuhn] Produced from the fermentation of corn sugar, xanthan gum is used as a thickener, EMULSIFIER and STABILIZER in foods such as dairy products and salad dressings. *See also* Food Additives Directory, page 900; GUAR GUM; GUM ARABIC; GUM TRAGACANTH.

xiao long bao [sheeow long bahow] A type of STEAMED BUN that's usually filled with pork but is also made with other fillings such as chicken, crab, shrimp and vegetables. It's often called a *soup dumpling* because the filling of the enclosed bun contains gelatin-based ASPIC along with the meat or vegetables. As the bun is steamed the aspic melts, becoming a rich soup, which a properly made bun will keep enclosed and not let leak out. Xiao long bao should be made small enough to eat in a single bite so the combination of bun, filling and rich soup is easily consumed at one time.

XO sauce [ihx-oh] Rich, spicy, chunky seafood sauce made from various ingredients, some of which are quite expensive such as DRIED SCALLOPS and high-end Chinese cured hams. Other ingredients might include DRIED SHRIMP, garlic, ginger and red chiles. Created in Hong Kong in the 1980s, it takes its name from the XO, or "extra old," designation used on some high-end French COGNACS. There is no Cognac in the sauce, but Cognac is highly regarded in Hong Kong so the XO name was chosen to denote the sauce's esteemed status. An article in *Vogue China* proclaimed it "CAVIAR of the East." XO sauce is used to enrich the flavor of a variety of foods including most fish, meat and vegetable dishes plus those made with noodles, rice and tofu. XO suace is available in Chinese markets and on the Internet.

 xuxu *see* CHAYOTE

Xylitol [ZI-lih-tahl] A white crystalline sweetener that was discovered almost simultaneously by French and German scientists in the late 19th century. Xylitol occurs naturally in fruit (such as berries and plums) and vegetables (such as corn and mushrooms). However, most of it is extracted from birch trees, which is why it's also known as *birch sugar* or *wood sugar*. Xylitol looks and tastes like regular sugar, though it has a slight (and harmless) cooling effect on the tongue. Gram for gram, xylitol is about as sweet as SUCROSE but contains roughly 40 percent fewer calories. It may be used measure for measure in cooking and baking and, unlike ARTIFICIAL SWEETENERS, does not leave a bitter aftertaste. Because it's a low-glycemic sweetener, xylitol has become popular with diabetics.

yabby; yabbie Australian for "CRAYFISH."

yaki fu [yah-kee FOO] *see* FU

yakimono [yah-kee-MOH-noh] The Japanese term for foods (usually meat) that are grilled, broiled or pan-fried. The ingredients are generally either marinated in sauce or salted (*see* SHIOYAKI). They're then skewered so they retain their shape and grilled over a hot fire so the skin (if any) is very crisp while the meat stays tender and juicy. YAKITORI is a specific type of yakimono dish using chicken.

yakinori [yah-kee-NOH-ree] *see* NORI

yakitori [yah-kee-TOH-ree] A Japanese term meaning "grilled" (*yaki*) "fowl" (*tori*), usually referring to small pieces of marinated chicken that are skewered and grilled.

yam This thick, tropical-vine tuber is popular in South and Central America, the West Indies and parts of Asia and Africa. Although SWEET POTATOES and yams are similar in many ways and therefore often confused with one another, they are from different plant species. In the southern United States, sweet potatoes are often called yams and to add to the confusion, canned sweet potatoes are frequently labeled yams. True yams, however, are not widely marketed and are seldom grown in the United States. Though they can be similar in size and shape to sweet potatoes, yams contain more natural sugar and have a higher moisture content. On the downside, they're not as rich in vitamins A and C as sweet potatoes. There are over 150 species of yam grown throughout the world. They can range in size from that of a small potato to behemoths over 7½ feet long and 120 pounds. Depending on the variety, a yam's flesh may be various shades of off-white, yellow, purple or pink, and the skin from off-white to dark brown. The texture of this vegetable can range from moist and tender to coarse, dry and mealy. Yams can be found in most Latin American markets, often in chunks, sold by weight. When buying yams, select unblemished specimens with tight, unwrinkled skins. Store in a place that's cool, dark and dry for up to 2 weeks. Do not refrigerate. Yams may be substituted for sweet potatoes in most recipes.

yang nyum jang [yahng nyom jahng] A spicy Korean sauce composed of garlic, gochujang (*see* CHILE BEAN PASTE), GOCHUGARU (red chili pepper flakes), pepper, sesame oil, soy sauce and sugar.

Yankee bean *see* NAVY BEAN

Yankee pot roast *see* POT ROAST

yard-long bean A pencil-thin LEGUME that resembles a GREEN BEAN except that it can grow up to about 3 feet long (though it's usually picked at 18 inches or less). Yard-long beans belong to the same plant family as the BLACK-EYED PEA. In fact, in parts of China the bean is allowed to mature until full-fledged peas are produced in the pod. Yard-longs have a flavor similar to but not as sweet as that of a green bean, with hints of its black-eyed-pea lineage. The texture of the pod is more pliable and not as crisp as that of a green bean. This LEGUME, also called *Chinese long bean*, *long bean* or *asparagus bean*, can be found year-round (with peak season in the fall) in most Asian markets and some supermarkets with specialty produce sections. Select those that are small (which equates to younger) and very flexible; the peas should not have matured. Refrigerate in a plastic bag for up to 5 days. Yard-long beans are most often cut into 2-inch lengths and sautéed or STIR-FRIED. Overcooking will make them mushy. These beans are rich in vitamin A and contain a fair amount of vitamin C.

Yarg *see* CORNISH YARG

yarrow [YAR-oh; YEHR-oh] Any of several very pungent, aromatic herbs found in Europe and North America. Known as milfoil in Europe, yarrow has a very strong aroma and flavor and is therefore used sparingly to flavor salads, soups and occasionally egg dishes. It may also be used to brew a TISANE (herb tea).

yautia *see* MALANGA

yeast [YEEST] Yeast is a living, microscopic, single-cell organism that, as it grows, converts its food (through a process known as fermentation) into alcohol and carbon dioxide. This trait is what endears yeast to wine-makers, brewmasters and breadbakers. In the making of wine and beer, the yeast's manufacture of alcohol is desired and necessary for the final product; and carbon dioxide is what makes BEER and CHAMPAGNE effervescent. The art of breadmaking needs the carbon dioxide produced by yeast in order for certain doughs to rise. To multiply and grow, all yeast needs is the right environment, which includes moisture, food (in the form of sugar or starch) and a warm, nurturing temperature (70° to 85°F is best). Wild yeast spores are constantly floating in the air and landing on uncovered foods and liquids. No one's sure when these wild spores first interacted with foods but it's known that the Egyptians used yeast as a LEAVENING agent more than 5,000 years ago. Wine and other fermented beverages were made for millennia before that. Today, scientists have been able to isolate and identify the various yeasts that are best for wine-making, beermaking and baking. The two types commercially available are baker's yeast and brewer's yeast. **Baker's yeast**, as the name implies, is used as a leavener. It's catagorized into three basic types—active dry

Y

yeast, compressed fresh yeast and YEAST STARTERS. **Active dry yeast** is in the form of tiny, dehydrated granules. The yeast cells are alive but dormant because of the lack of moisture. When mixed with a warm liquid (105° to 115°F), the cells once again become active. Active dry yeast is available in two forms, *regular* and *quick-rising*, of which the latter takes about half as long to leaven bread. They may be used interchangeably (with adjustments in rising time) and both are available in ¼-ounce envelopes. Regular active dry yeast may also be purchased in 4-ounce jars or in bulk in some natural food stores. It should be stored in a cool, dry place, but can also be refrigerated or frozen. It should always be at room temperature before being dissolved in liquid. Properly stored, it's reliable when used by the expiration date, which should be stamped on the envelope or jar label. One package of dry yeast is equal to 1 scant tablespoon dry yeast or 1 cake of compressed fresh yeast. **Compressed fresh yeast**, which comes in tiny (0.06-ounce), square cakes, is moist and extremely perishable. It must be refrigerated and used within a week or two, or by the date indicated on the package. It can be frozen, but should be defrosted at room temperature and used immediately. One cake of fresh yeast can be substituted for one envelope of dry yeast. The use of compressed fresh yeast has been primarily replaced by the more convenient active dry yeast. All baker's yeast should be given a test called proofing to make sure it's still alive. To proof yeast, dissolve it in warm water and add a pinch of sugar. Set the mixture aside in a warm place for 5 to 10 minutes. If it begins to swell and foam, the yeast is alive, active and capable of leavening bread. Brewer's yeasts are special non-leavening yeasts used in beermaking. Because it's a rich source of B vitamins, brewer's yeast is also used as a food supplement. It's available in natural food stores. **Brewer's yeasts** are also marketed in specialty beermaking equipment shops, with different strains used for different beers.

yeast bread Any bread that uses YEAST as the LEAVENING agent. As the yeast ferments, it converts the flour's starchy nutrients into alcohol and carbon dioxide gas. The gas bubbles trapped in the elastic GLUTEN mesh of the dough are what make it rise. Oven heat kills the yeast and evaporates the alcohol. The gas expands in a final burst of energy and causes the bread to rise. Among the more well-known yeast breads are BRIOCHE, CROISSANTS, FRENCH BREAD and SOURDOUGH BREAD.

yeast extract A vitamin-B-rich mixture made by combining vegetable extract and the extracted liquid of fresh yeast. It ranges in texture from liquid to a light paste. Yeast extract is used as a seasoning and as the base for various products like MARMITE and VEGEMITE.

yeast starter Prior to the evolution of commercially available baking powders and yeasts during the 19th century, yeast starters were the

LEAVENERS used in breadmaking. Such starters are a simple mixture of flour, water, sugar and YEAST. (At one time, airborne yeast was the only source used, but today convenient commercially packaged baker's yeast is more common.) This batter is set aside in a warm place until the yeast ferments and the mixture is foamy. A portion of the starter—usually about 2 cups— is removed and used as the base and leavener for some bread recipes. Once fermented, yeast starters—the most famous of which is *sourdough starter*—can be kept going in the right environment for years simply by adding equal parts flour and water. *Herman starter* is a colloquialism (of unknown origin) for a honey- or sugar-sweetened starter used primarily for sweet breads. **Pre-ferment** is a term used to refer to yeast starters made ahead of time, versus adding active dry yeast or compressed fresh yeast during breadmaking. A sourdough starter is considered a pre-ferment, although some apply the term only to yeast starters originating from baker's yeast. There are several names for the pre-ferments including *biga,* an Italian term for a somewhat dry pre-ferment; *poolish*, a French term for a fairly wet version; and *pâte fermentée*, a French term meaning "fermented dough" referring to a pre-ferment created by taking dough set aside from prior breadmaking and adding flour and water to feed the yeast organisms. Starter should be refrigerated and can be stored this way indefinitely as long as it's replenished every 2 weeks. Before using or replenishing, it should be brought to room temperature. If a starter turns orange or pink and develops an unpleasantly acrid odor, undesirable bacteria have invaded it and the mixture must be discarded. Two cups of the foamy starter mixture can be substituted for each package of yeast called for in a recipe.

yellow berry *see* CLOUDBERRY

yellow chile *see* AJÍ AMARILLO

yellow-eyed pea *see* BLACK-EYED PEA

yellowfin tuna *see* TUNA

yellowtail 1. A class of fish with several species that's a member of the JACK family. It's related to POMPANO, with a flavor and texture similar to that of TUNA. The *California yellowtail,* a large game fish that can weigh up to 100 pounds, is found off the coast of Southern California and south into Mexican waters. The waters around Australia and New Zealand are home to the *southern yellowtail* or *yellowtail kingfish*, which can weigh over 100 pounds. In the ocean around Japan there's a slightly smaller yellowtail (60 to 70 pounds), which is called *Japanese amberjack.* The Japanese prize their yellowtail and farm-raise them for use in SUSHI and SASHIMI. These are generally no larger than 20 pounds—the smaller fish are labeled *hamachi,* the larger ones *buri*. In general, yellowtail is prepared in a manner similar to tuna. 2. A variety of SNAPPER. *See also* ROCKFISH; FISH.

yellow wine *see* SHAOXING WINE

yerba maté (mate) [YER-bah MAH-tay] The maté is a South American holly-family tree grown primarily in Argentina, Brazil and Paraguay and widely cultivated to make a tealike drink called yerba maté. The leaves and young twigs of this tree are dried, shredded, then typically aged for 1 year in cedar containers before being marketed as yerba maté loose-leaf tea, tea bags or as a bottled drink. South Americans have been sipping this energy-boosting brew for centuries and its popularity has now spread to points around the globe. The traditional South American way to consume yerba maté is to brew it in a hollow gourd (also called *maté* in Spanish) and share it communally by drinking it through a *bombilla,* a special metal straw that strains out the leaves. Whether brewed in a gourd or not, it's important to use hot, not boiling, water to steep this "tea." Yerba maté has an earthy, herbal flavor that many have to sweeten to make it potable. Most bottled-drink versions are pre-sweetened. Gram for gram, yerba maté has the same amount of caffeine as coffee, though the energy effect is more sustainable than that of coffee. Yerba maté can be found in Latin markets, natural food stores and many supermarkets. It's also known as *Brazilian tea, Paraguay tea* and simply *maté.*

yerba santa [YER-bah SAHN-tah] *see* PEPPER LEAF

yin-yang bean *see* CALYPSO BEAN

yogurt; yoghurt [YOH-gert] A dairy product that's the result of milk that has fermented and coagulated because it's been invaded by friendly bacteria. This can be accomplished naturally by keeping the milk at about 110°F for several hours. The end result is a creamy-textured yogurt with an astringent, slightly tart taste. Yogurt-making is thought to have been originated by nomadic Balkan tribes thousands of years ago, probably first by accident and then as a means of preserving milk. Today, yogurt is made commercially in carefully controlled environments and the requisite bacteria (usually *Lactobacillus bulgaricus* and *Streptococcus thermophilus*) are added to the milk. Though yogurt can be made from the milk of many animals, cow's milk is the most commonly used. There are a variety of commercial yogurts now produced. **Plain yogurt** is made from whole milk, lowfat or nonfat milk without additional flavoring ingredients. **Flavored yogurt** has sugar and either artificial flavorings or natural fruit (or both) added. Some flavored yogurts contain gelatin or stabilizers for a thicker texture. Fruit-flavored yogurts can either have the fruit on the bottom (to be mixed in by the consumer) or be already stirred—in which case they're referred to as *Swiss-style*. **Frozen yogurt**—which resembles soft-serve ice cream in texture—has become very popular and competes head-to-head in some markets with ice cream. The health benefits of yogurt have long been touted. It is certainly a good source of B vitamins, protein and calcium and is much more digestible than fresh milk. It's also said to keep the intestinal system populated with good bacteria and therefore in healthy condition. These benefits, however, are thought to be lost when yogurt is frozen, which destroys most of the beneficial bacteria. *See also* CHAKKA; GREEK YOGURT; SOY YOGURT.

yokan [YOH-kahn] This Japanese confection is made with AGAR (the jelling agent), sugar and AZUKI-BEAN paste. Other flavorings such as persimmons or chestnuts are also sometimes used. Yokan, which is sold in Asian markets, will keep indefinitely in the refrigerator.

York Imperial apple An all-purpose apple that has a red skin streaked with yellow. The firm off-white flesh is juicy and tartly sweet. *See also* APPLE.

Yorkshire pudding [YORK-sheer; YORK-shuhr] British roast beef wouldn't be complete without Yorkshire pudding, which is like a cross between a POPOVER and a SOUFFLÉ and not at all like a pudding. It's made with a batter of eggs, milk and flour, baked in beef drippings until puffy, crisp and golden brown. It may be prepared in a shallow baking dish, muffin tins or other small containers, or in the same pan as the roast. Like a hot soufflé, Yorkshire pudding will deflate shortly after it's removed from the oven. This specialty takes its name from England's northern county of Yorkshire.

yosenabe [yoh-seh-NAH-beh] A type of NABEMONO (one-pot meal) consisting of chicken, seafood and vegetables all combined in a single pot of seasoned broth—kind of a Japanese BOUILLABAISE.

youngberry A hybrid BLACKBERRY variety with dark red color and sweet, juicy flesh. *See also* BERRIES.

yuba [YOO-bah] The "skin" that forms when SOY MILK is heated. The delicate skin is carefully removed and usually dried in sheets or folded and dried in sticks. Yuba sheets are rehydrated by covering with a wet towel; yuba sticks are soaked in water. Yuba, with its creamy, nutlike flavor, is often used in vegetarian dishes as a meat substitute. It can be found in most Asian markets. Sheets of yuba can be used to wrap other foods that can then be braised, deep-fried or steamed. The sticks are sometimes deep-fried to a crispy brown, to be eaten alone or broken into pieces for use in other dishes. Yuba sticks are sometimes called *bamboo* because of their look-alike quality.

yuca; yuca root [YUHK-uh] Though native to South America, the majority of yuca now comes from Africa, where it's an important staple.

Also called *cassava* and *manioc,* the yuca is a tuber that ranges from 6 to 15 inches in length and from 2 to 3 inches in diameter. It has a tough brown skin which, when peeled, reveals a crisp, white flesh that's bland and starchy. There are many varieties of yuca but only two main categories, sweet and bitter. Both contain a poisonous compound, which is why yuca should never be eaten raw. The toxins found in sweet yuca are concentrated in the skin, so peeling is mandatory. The bitter form is specially processed to make CASSAREEP and TAPIOCA. Sweet yuca is available year-round in Asian and Latin American markets. Choose hard specimens that are evenly shaped and don't be surprised by a waxy coating, which is there for the tuber's protection. Store yuca in a cool, dark place for up to a week, refrigerate (wrapped in paper towels and then a plastic bag) for up to 2 weeks. Peel until only the white flesh remains; the inedible fibrous center may be removed before or after cooking. Yuca is typically boiled, roasted or cut into thin slices and fried for chips.

yu choy sum [yoo choy SUM] A relative of BOK CHOY, this vegetable has long, graceful yellow-green stems with dark green leaves and, sometimes, tiny yellow or purple flowers. It has a tangy flavor akin to spinach and is wonderful steamed or stir-fried (*see* STIR-FRY) or added to soups. Yu choy sum is available in Asian markets. Choose unblemished bunches with firm stalks and brightly colored leaves. Refrigerate in a plastic bag for up to 1 week and wash well before using. *See also* CHOY SUM.

yukpo [YOOK-poh] Korean version of beef JERKY. Thin slices of beef are marinated in soy sauce, then dried.

yule log [YOOL] *see* BÛCHE-DE NOËL

yuzu [YOO-zoo] Hailing from Japan, this sour citrus fruit is about the size of a tangerine. The yuzu, which is a cross between a Japanese citrus known as *ichang papeda* and a sour mandarin orange, has a bumpy green skin that turns MEYER-LEMON yellow when fully ripe. The flesh is yellow, heavily seeded and doesn't yield much juice. Also called a *Japanese citron,* the yuzu is explosively fragrant and has a briskly tart flavor reminiscent of limes and oranges. USDA restrictions prevent the import of fresh yuzus from Japan and domestic production is in its infancy. If you happen to find them fresh at a farmer's market, choose fruit that's heavy for its size. Green fruit may be kept at room temperature until the rind turns yellow; fully ripe fruit should be refrigerated for up to 3 weeks. The form of yuzu most readily available in the United States is bottled juice, on the shelf or in the freezer section of Japanese markets. There you also might find *yuzu kosho,* a paste comprised of yuzu rind, chiles and salt. Yuzu juice is used in various ways including in cocktails, CEVICHE, SASHIMI, VINAIGRETTE and to flavor Asian soups.

Y

za'atar [ZAH-tahr] 1. A pungent, strongly aromatic herb with soft, dark green leaves. It's native to the Middle East and tastes like an amalgam of marjoram, oregano and thyme. In Arabic, za'atar means "thyme," and, to confuse matters, this herb is also called *Syrian marjoram*. 2. A popular, pungent Middle Eastern spice blend composed of toasted SESAME SEEDS, dried THYME, dried MARJORAM and SUMAC. It's mixed with olive oil and salt and is drizzled over hot bread or used as a dip for bread. Za'atar (also spelled *zahtar*) is also sprinkled over meats and vegetables as a seasoning. It can be found at most Middle Eastern groceries.

zabaglione; zabaione [zah-bahl-YOH-nay] One of Italy's great gifts to the rest of the world, zabaglione is an ethereal dessert made by whisking together egg yolks, wine (traditionally MARSALA) and sugar. This beating is done over simmering water so that the egg yolks cook as they thicken into a light, foamy custard. Traditional zabaglione must be made just before serving. (There is also a frozen version.) The warm froth can be served either as a dessert by itself or as a sauce over cake, fruit, ice cream or pastry. In France it's called *sabayon* or *sabayon sauce*.

zahtar *see* ZA'ATAR

zakuska; *pl.* **zakuski; zakouski** [zuh-KOOS-kuh; zuh-KOOS-kee] A Russian HORS D'OEUVRE, which could include any of a variety of foods such as ANCHOVIES, BLINIS, CAVIAR, cheeses, fish, oysters and fish- or meat-filled pastries. A zakuska assortment is generally served with bottles of ice-cold vodka.

zampone [tsasm-POH-nay] A specialty of Modena, Italy, zampone is a unique SAUSAGE created by stuffing a mixture of seasoned ground pork into a boned pig's foot rather than a CASING.

Zante grape [ZAN-tee] *see* CHAMPAGNE GRAPES

zapote blanco *see* WHITE SAPOTE

zapote negro *see* BLACK SAPOTE

zensai [zen-SI] Japanese term for APPETIZERS, small items served before a meal.

zeppola [ZEHP-poh-lah]; *pl.* **zeppole** [ZEHP-poh-leh] An Italian doughnut-type pastry that's typically fried but can also be baked. Zeppole can have various fillings such as custard, honey and almonds, jelly or a sweetened RICOTTA mixture. Unfilled styles are typically topped with cinnamon-sugar, powdered sugar or honey. Zeppole are also called **Saint Joseph's Day Cakes** because of their association with the Feast of St. Joseph (*La Festa di San Giuseppe*), which is celebrated on March 19. On this day they're sold by myriad street vendors in the Naples region (where zepolle originated) and in Italian sections of some American cities. Savory zeppole, such as those with anchovies, are also popular.

zhen shou nai cha *see* BUBBLE TEA

zest The perfumy outermost skin layer of citrus fruit (usually oranges or lemons), which is removed with the aid of a CITRUS ZESTER, paring knife or VEGETABLE PEELER. Only the colored portion of the skin (and not the white pith) is considered the zest. The aromatic oils in citrus zest are what add so much flavor to food. Zest can be used to flavor raw or cooked and sweet or savory dishes.

zester *see* CITRUS ZESTER

Zinfandel [ZIHN-fuhn-dehl] A red wine grape originally thought to be indigenous to California. Recently, however, experts have concluded that the Zinfandel grape was brought to the United States from Italy's Puglia region, and is a descendant of the *primitivo grape* grown there. Regardless, the Zinfandel grape—with its spicy, raspberry flavors—makes marvelous, fruity red wines ranging from lighter styles to big, rich bottlings that can rival CABERNET SAUVIGNON. In the 1980s, **white Zinfandel** (a BLUSH WINE) also gained considerable popularity. Occasionally, late-picked grapes full of concentrated sugar are made into **late-harvest Zinfandels** and served as DESSERT WINE or in place of PORT.

zingara, à la [zihn-GAH-rah] This French phrase translates to "gypsy style" and refers to a garnish consisting of chopped ham, tongue, mushrooms and TRUFFLES combined with tomato sauce, tarragon and sometimes MADEIRA. This garnish is served with meat, poultry and sometimes eggs.

ziti; zitoni *see* Pasta Glossary, page 883

zombie [ZAHM-bee] Extraordinarily potent, this COCKTAIL is made with at least two types each of rum and LIQUEUR plus two or three fruit juices such as pineapple, orange and lime. It's usually served in a large goblet over crushed ice, garnished with slices of pineapple and orange and a MARASCHINO CHERRY. The origin of the name is unknown, but it's been said that one or two of these drinks can make one feel numb . . . rather like a zombie.

zoni *see* OZONI

zucchero [ZOO-keh-roh] Italian for "sugar."

zucchini [zoo-KEE-nee] A popular summer squash shaped like a slightly curved cylinder, a bit smaller at the top than the bottom. A zucchini's skin color can vary from dark to light green, sometimes with yellow markings that give it a mottled or striped look. The off-white flesh has a very pale green cast and the flavor is light and delicate. Common market length is 4 to 8 inches long and 2 to 3 inches thick. However, some specimens are as tiny as a finger while others—usually home-grown—can reach a mammoth 2 feet long by 6 inches in diameter (or more). Fresh zucchini is available year-round in most supermarkets, with a peak period during late spring. Select small zucchini, which will be younger and therefore more tender and have thinner skins. The skins should be free of blemishes and have a vibrant color. Zucchini can be cooked by a variety of methods including steaming, grilling, sautéing, deep-frying and baking. *See also* SQUASH.

zuccotto [zoo-KOHT-toh] Thought to have been inspired by the cupola of Florence, Italy's, Duomo (the city's main cathedral), this dome-shaped dessert begins with a bowl lined with LIQUEUR-moistened cake (usually pound cake) slices. The bowl is then filled with a mixture of sweetened whipped cream, chopped or grated chocolate and various chopped nuts before being topped with additional cake slices. The zuccotto is refrigerated at least a day so the filling can set. It's inverted onto a plate before being served.

Zucker [TZOO-ker] German for "sugar."

zungenwurst [TZOON-ghen-wurst (vurst)] A variety of German BLOOD SAUSAGE that contains chunks of pickled TONGUE. This dried sausage can be eaten raw, but is more commonly sliced and browned in butter or bacon fat.

zuppa [ZOO-puh] Italian for "soup."

zuppa inglese [ZOO-puh een-GLAY-zeh] Literally translated as "English soup," this Italian dish is, in fact, a refrigerated dessert similar to the British favorite, TRIFLE. It's made with rum-sprinkled slices of sponge cake layered with a rich custard or whipped cream (or both) and candied fruit or toasted almonds (or both).

zuzza *see* CUCUZZA

zwieback [ZWI-bak; ZWI-bahk; SWI-bak; SWI-bahk] This German word translates to "twice baked" and refers to bread that is baked, cut into slices and then returned to the oven until very crisp and dry. Zwieback, which has a hint of sweetness to it, is popular for its digestibility and is often served to younger children or to people who have digestive problems. It is commercially available in most stores. *See also* RUSK.

APPENDIX

Ingredient Equivalents

Food	Amount	Approximate Equivalent
Almonds	1 lb in shell	1⅓ to 2 cups
	1 lb shelled	3 to 3½ cups whole; 4 cups slivered
	1 cup	4 oz
Anchovies	2-oz can	10 to 12 anchovies
	1 fillet	½ tsp anchovy paste
Anchovy paste	2-oz tube	4 Tbsp
Apples	1 lb fresh	3 medium; 2¾ cups chopped; 3 cups sliced; 1⅓ cups sauce
	1 lb dried	4⅓ cups; 8 cups cooked
Apricots	1 lb fresh	8 to 14; 2½ cups sliced or halved
	1 lb dried	2¾ cups; 5½ cups cooked
Asparagus	1 lb fresh	12 to 20 spears; 3½ cups chopped
	10 oz frozen	2 cups
Avocados	1 lb	2½ cups chopped; 1½ cups puréed
	1 medium	1 cup purée
Bacon	1 lb raw	18 to 22 regular slices; 20 thin; 10 to 14 thick
	1 lb cooked	1½ cups crumbled
	1 slice, cooked	1 Tbsp crumbled
Bamboo shoots	8-oz can	1¼ cups sliced
Bananas	1 lb fresh	3 to 4 medium; 2 cups sliced; 1¾ cups mashed; 1 cup dried slices
	1 medium	½ cup puréed
	1 lb dried	4½ cups slices
Barley	1 cup medium	3½ to 4 cups cooked
	1 cup quick-cooking	3 cups cooked
Bean curd (see Tofu)		

Food	Amount	Approximate Equivalent
Beans, black	1 lb dried	2⅓ cups; 4¾ cups cooked
	1 cup dried	2 cups cooked
	15½-oz can	2 cups
Beans, fava	1 lb dried	2 cups; 4½ cups cooked
	1 cup dried	2¼ cups cooked
Beans, fresh shell	1 lb	1 cup shelled
Beans, garbanzo	1 lb dried	2 cups; 5 cups cooked
	1 cup dried	2½ cups cooked
Beans, green	1 lb fresh	3½ cups whole
	9 oz frozen	1½ cups
	15½-oz can	1¾ cups
Beans, kidney	1 lb dried	2½ cups; 5½ cups cooked
	1 cup dried	2½ cups cooked
Beans, lima	1 lb dried	2⅔ cups; 6 cups cooked
	1 cup dried	2½ cups cooked
Beans, navy	1 lb dried	2⅓ cups; 5½ cups cooked
	1 cup dried	2¼ cups cooked
Beans, pinto	1 lb dried	2 cups; 5 cups cooked
	1 cup dried	2¼ cups cooked
Beans, refried	16-oz can	1¾ cups
Beans, soy	1 lb dried	2 cups; 5 cups cooked
	1 cup dried	2½ cups cooked
Bean sprouts	1 lb	3 to 4 cups; 1½ to 2 cups cooked
Beets	1 lb, trimmed	2 cups, chopped or sliced and cooked
	15-oz can	1¾ cups
Bell peppers (*see* Peppers, bell)		
Berries (*see* individual listings)		
Blackberries	1 pint fresh	2 cups
	10 oz frozen	2 cups
Blueberries	1 pint fresh	2 cups
	10 oz frozen	1½ cups
Brazil nuts	1 lb shelled	3 cups
Bread	1-lb loaf	14 to 18 regular slices; 24 to 28 thin slices; 7 cups crumbs

Food	Amount	Approximate Equivalent
	1 slice	½ cup fresh crumbs; ⅓ cup dried crumbs; 1 scant cup fresh cubes; ¾ cup toasted cubes
Breadcrumbs	8-oz package	2⅓ cups
	7 cups fresh	1 lb bread, crust removed
	½ cup fresh	1 slice bread
	⅓ cup dry	1 slice toast
Broccoli	1 lb fresh	2 cups chopped
	10 oz frozen	1½ cups chopped
Brussels sprouts	1 lb fresh	3 cups; 20 to 24 sprouts
	10 oz frozen	18 to 24 sprouts
Bulgur	1 cup	3¾ cups cooked
Butter/margarine	1 lb regular	2 cups; 4 sticks; 2 small tubs
	¼ lb regular	1 stick; ½ cup; 8 Tbsp; ⅓ cup clarified
	1 lb whipped	3 cups regular
Butter-flavored granules	¾ tsp	1 Tbsp butter
Cabbage	1 lb	3½ to 4½ cups shredded; 2 cups cooked
Cantaloupe	1 medium	2 lbs; 3 cups diced
Carrots	1 lb, trimmed	3 cups chopped; 2½ cups grated; 2 cups cooked
	1 to 2 medium	1 cup shredded
	14 oz frozen	2½ cups sliced
Cashew nuts	1 lb	3⅓ cups
Cauliflower	1 lb fresh	2½ to 3 cups florets; 1½ to 2 cups chopped
	10 oz frozen	2 cups chopped or sliced
Caviar	1 oz	1 heaping Tbsp
Celery	2 medium ribs	½ cup chopped or sliced
Celery root (celeriac)	1½ lbs	4 cups grated; 1¾ cup cooked, puréed
Cheese (blue)	4 oz	1 cup crumbled

Food	Amount	Approximate Equivalent
Cheese (cheddar, Jack)	1 lb	4 cups grated or shredded
Cheese (cottage)	16 oz	2 cups
Cheese (cream)	8 oz	1 cup
	3 oz	6 Tbsp
Cheese (Parmesan, Romano)	¼ lb	1 cup grated
Cheese, ricotta	7½ oz	1 cup
Cherries	1 lb fresh	2½ to 3 cups pitted
	10 oz frozen	1 cup
	16-oz can	1½ cups drained
Chestnut purée	10-oz can	25 whole chestnuts; 1⅓ cups purée
Chestnuts	1½ lb unpeeled	35 to 40 large; 1 lb peeled
	1 lb peeled	2½ cups; 2 cups purée
Chicken	3 to 3½ lbs	3 cups cooked meat
	1 large whole breast	1½ cups cooked, chopped meat
Chickpeas (see Beans, garbanzo)		
Chocolate	6 oz chips	1 cup
	8 oz squares	8 (1-oz) squares
Clams, medium	3 dozen in shell	4 cups shucked
Cocoa powder	8-oz pkg.	2¾ cups
Coconut	1 medium	4 to 5 cups shredded
	7-oz bag shredded or flaked	3 cups
	3½-oz can	1⅓ cups
Cookies		
Chocolate wafers	18 to 20 cookies	1 cup crumbs
Oreos or Hydrox (single cream)	22 cookies	1½ cups crumbs
Vanilla wafers	22 cookies	1 cup crumbs
Corn	2 medium ears	1 to 1¼ cups kernels
	10 oz frozen kernels	1¾ cups
	12-oz can	1½ cups
Cornmeal	1 lb	3 cups uncooked
	1 cup	4 cups cooked

Food	Amount	Approximate Equivalent
Cornstarch	1 lb	3 cups
Corn syrup, light or dark	16 fl oz	2 cups
Cottage cheese (*see* Cheese, cottage)		
Couscous	1 cup	2½ cups cooked
Crab	1 lb in shell	1 to 1½ cups meat
	1 lb meat	3 cups
	7½-oz can	1 cup
Crackers	15 graham squares	1 cup crumbs
	28 soda/saltine crackers	1 cup crumbs
Cranberries	12 oz fresh or frozen	3 cups; 4 cups sauce
Cranberry sauce	1-lb can	1⅔ cups
Cream	½ pint light	1 cup; 8 oz
	½ pint whipping	1 cup; 2 cups whipped
	½ pint sour	1 cup
Cream cheese (*see* Cheese, cream)		
Crenshaw melon	1 medium	3 lb; 4 to 5 cups cubed
Cucumber	1 medium	1½ cups chopped or sliced
Currants	10-oz pkg. dried	2 cups
Dates	1 lb unpitted	2½ cups pitted and chopped
	8-oz pkg. pitted	1¼ cups chopped
Eggplant	1 lb	3½ cups diced raw; 1¾ cup cooked
Egg roll skins (wrappers)	1 lb	14 wrappers
Eggs, whole, large	1 dozen	2⅓ cups
	5 eggs	1 cup
	1 egg	3 Tbsp
Egg whites, large	1 doz	1½ cups
	7 to 8 whites	1 cup
	2 whites	2½ to 3 cups stiffly beaten
	1 white	2 Tbsp

Food	Amount	Approximate Equivalent
Egg yolks, large	1 doz	⅞ cup
	11 to 12 yolks	1 cup
	1 yolk	1 to 1½ Tbsp
Eggs, hard-cooked	1 egg	6 slices; ¼ to ⅓ cup chopped
Egg substitute	¼ cup liquid	1 large egg
	2 Tbsp	1 large yolk
Fennel	1 lb	2 small bulbs
Figs	1 lb fresh	12 medium
	1 lb dried	3 cups chopped
Filberts (see Hazelnuts)		
Flour	1 lb all-purpose, bread, self-rising	3 cups sifted
	1 lb cake, pastry	4½ to 5 cups sifted
	1 lb gluten	3 cups sifted
	1 lb rice	3½ cups sifted
	1 lb rye	3½ cups sifted
	1 lb whole wheat	3½ cups unsifted
Fruit, most kinds	15-oz can	1⅓ cups, drained
	16 oz frozen	1¼ cups
Garlic	1 head	12 to 16 cloves
	1 medium clove	½ tsp minced; ⅛ tsp garlic powder
Gelatin, unflavored	¼-oz pkg	1 Tbsp granulated; 3½ (4″ × 9″) sheets
Ginger	2-inch piece	2 Tbsp minced
Graham crackers (see Crackers)		
Grapefruit	1 lb fresh	1 medium; 1½ cups segments; ¾ to 1 cup juice
Grapes	1 lb	2½ to 3 cups
Green beans (see Beans, green)		
Green onions (see Onions, green)		
Greens (beet, chard, kale, etc.)	1 lb fresh	1⅓ to 2 cups cooked

Food	Amount	Approximate Equivalent
Grits	1 lb	3 cups
	1 cup	3⅓ cups cooked
Half & half (*see* Cream)		
Ham	½ lb boneless	1¼ to 1½ cups chopped
Hazelnuts	1 lb in shell	1½ cups
	1 lb shelled	3½ cups whole
Hearts of palm	14-oz can	6 to 7 pieces
Herbs	1 Tbsp fresh, chopped	1 tsp dried, crumbled
Hominy	1 lb whole	2½ cups
	1 cup whole	6⅔ cups cooked
	1 cup grits	4½ cups cooked
Honey	1 lb	1⅓ cups
Horseradish	1 Tbsp bottled	2 tsp freshly grated
Ice cream/ice milk/ sherbet	1 qt	4 cups
Ice cubes, standard size	3 to 4 cubes	1 cup crushed ice
Kasha	1 cup	2½ to 3 cups cooked
Ketchup	16-oz bottle	1⅔ cups
Kiwifruit	2	¾ cup chopped or sliced
Lard	1 lb	2 cups
Leeks	1 lb	2 cups trimmed, chopped; 1 cup cooked
Lemons	1 lb	4 to 6 medium; 1 cup juice
	1 medium	3 Tbsp juice; 2 to 3 tsp zest
Lentils	1 lb dried	2¼ cups; 5 cups cooked
Lettuce	1 lb	6 cups pieces
Lima Beans (*see* Beans, Lima)		
Limes	1 lb	6 to 8 medium; ¾ cup juice
	1 medium	1 to 2 Tbsp juice; 1 tsp zest
Lobster	1 to 1½ lbs	2½ to 3 cups meat
Macaroni, elbow	8 oz	4 cups cooked
	1 cup	1¾ cups cooked
Mangoes	1 medium	12 oz; ¾ to 1 cup chopped
Maple syrup	16 fl oz	2 cups
Margarine (*see* Butter)		

Food	Amount	Approximate Equivalent
Marshmallow crème	7 to 7½ oz-jar	2½ cups
	16-oz jar	5¼ cups
	1 Tbsp	1 large marshmallow
Marshmallows	1 lb large	60
	1 cup large	6 to 7 marshmallows
	1 cup miniature	85 marshmallows
	10½ oz mini	400 pieces
Meat, ground	1 lb	2 cups uncooked
Melon (see Cantaloupe; Crenshaw; Watermelon)		
Milk, all types	1 qt fresh	4 cups
Milk, evaporated	5-oz can	⅔ cup
	12-oz can	1½ cups
Milk, powdered	1⅓ cups	1 quart reconstituted
	⅓ cup	1 cup reconstituted
Milk, sweet, condensed	14-oz can	1¾ cups
Molasses	12 fl oz	1½ cups
Mushrooms, common	1 lb fresh	5 cups sliced; 6 cups chopped; 3 oz dried, reconstituted
	4 oz	⅔ cup sliced
	3 oz dried	1 lb fresh
Mussels	1 lb medium	9 to 12 mussels; ¾ to 1 cup meat
Mustard	1 tsp dry	1 Tbsp prepared
Nectarines	1 lb	3 to 4 medium; 2 cups chopped; 2½ cups sliced; 1½ cups puréed
Noodles, 1-inch pieces	8 oz	4 cups cooked
	1 cup	1¾ cups cooked
Nuts (see individual listings)		
Oats, rolled	1 lb	5 cups uncooked
	1 cup	1¾ cups cooked
Oil, all types	1 qt	4 cups
	24-oz bottle	3 cups
Okra	1 lb fresh	2¼ cups chopped, cooked

Food	Amount	Approximate Equivalent
	10 oz frozen	1¼ cups chopped
	15½-oz can	1¾ cups chopped
Onions, green	5, bulbs only	½ cup chopped
	5 with tops	1¾ cups chopped
Onions, white or yellow	1 lb fresh	4 medium onions; 3½ to 4 cups chopped or sliced
	1 medium	¾ to 1 cup chopped or sliced
	12 oz frozen	3 cups chopped
Oranges	1 lb	3 medium; 1 to ¼ cups juice
	1 medium	⅓ to ½ cup juice; 1½ Tbsp zest
Oranges, Mandarin	11-oz can	1¼ cups segments, drained
Oysters	1 cup shucked	13 to 19 medium
	3.66-oz can smoked	14 to 16 oysters
Papaya	1 medium	10 to 12 oz; 1½ to 2 cups chopped or sliced
Parsnips	1 lb	4 medium; 2 cups chopped; 2½ cups sliced
Pasta (*see* Macaroni; Noodles; Spaghetti)		
Peaches	1 lb fresh	4 medium; 2½ cups chopped or sliced; 1½ cups purée
	1 medium	½ to ¾ cup chopped or sliced
	10 oz frozen	1½ cups sliced
	15-oz can	6 to 8 halves; 1¾ cups slices
	1 lb dried	2¾ cups; 6 cups cooked
Peanut butter	18-oz jar	1¾ cups
Peanuts	1 lb in shell	3 cups shelled
	1 lb shelled	3½ to 4 cups
	2 cups nuts	1 cup peanut butter
Pears	1 lb fresh	3 medium; 2 cups sliced

Food	Amount	Approximate Equivalent
	1 medium	½ cup sliced
	1 lb dried	2¾ cups; 5½ cups cooked
Peas, black-eyed	1 lb fresh	2⅓ cups
	10 oz frozen	1½ cups
	15½-oz can	1¾ cups
Peas, green	1 lb fresh, in pod	1 cup shelled
	10 oz frozen	2 cups
	15-oz can	2 cups
Peas, split	1 lb dried	2¼ cups; 5 cups cooked
Pecans	1 lb in shell	3 cups shelled
	1 lb shelled	4 cups halves; 3¾ cups chopped
Peppers, bell	1 lb	2 large; 2½ cups chopped; 3 cups sliced
	1 medium	1 cup chopped
Phyllo	1-lb package	25 sheets
Pineapple	1 medium	5 cups cubes
Pine nuts	8 oz	1½ cups
Pistachios	1 lb in shell	3 cups shelled
	1 lb shelled	3½ to 4 cups
Plums	1 lb fresh	2½ cups sliced; 2 cups cooked
	15½-oz can	3 cups sliced or chopped
Pomegranate	1 medium	½ cup seeds
Popcorn	3 Tbsp	6 cups popped
Potatoes, sweet	1 lb fresh	3 medium; 3½ to 4 cups chopped or sliced
	15½-oz can	1½ to 1¾ cups
Potatoes, white, red, russet	1 lb	3½ to 4 cups chopped or sliced; 2 cups mashed
Prunes	1 lb	2½ cups; 4 to 4½ cups cooked
Pumpkin	1 lb fresh	1 cup cooked and mashed
	15-oz can	1¾ cups mashed
	29-oz can	3½ cups mashed
Radishes	½ lb	1½ cups sliced; 10 to 14 radishes
Raisins	15 oz	2½ cups

Food	Amount	Approximate Equivalent
Raspberries	½ pint fresh	1⅓ cups
	10 oz frozen	1¾ cups
Rhubarb	1 lb fresh	2 cups chopped and cooked
	12 oz frozen	1½ cups chopped and sliced
Rice	1 cup regular	3 cups cooked
	1 cup converted	3¾ cups cooked
	1 cup instant	2 cups cooked
	1 cup brown	3½ to 4 cups cooked
	1 cup wild	3½ to 4 cups cooked
Rutabaga	1 lb	2½ cups cubed
Saltines (see Crackers)		
Sauerkraut	1 lb	2 cups
Scallions (see Onions, green)		
Scallops	1 lb medium	2 cups
Shallots	4 oz	½ cup chopped
Shortening, vegetable	1 lb	2½ cups
Shrimp	1 lb in shell	11 to 15 jumbo; 16 to 20 extra large; 21 to 30 large; 31 to 35 medium; 36 to 45 small; 100+ miniature
	1 lb shelled	8 oz meat; 2 cups cooked
Soda crackers (see Crackers)		
Sour Cream (see Cream)		
Spaghetti (12 inches long)	1 lb	7 to 8 cups cooked
Spinach	1 lb fresh	10 cups; 1½ cups cooked
	10 oz frozen	1½ cups; 1 cup cooked and drained
Sprouts (see Bean sprouts)		
Squash	1 lb summer	3 medium; 3 cups sliced
	1 lb winter	1 cup cooked and mashed

Food	Amount	Approximate Equivalent
Strawberries	1 pint fresh	1½ to 2 cups sliced
	10 oz frozen	1½ cups
Sugar	1 lb brown	2¼ cups packed
	1 lb confectioners'	3½ to 4 cups unsifted; 4½ cups sifted
	1 lb granulated	2 cups
	1 lb superfine	2⅓ cups
Sweet potatoes (*see* Potatoes, sweet)		
Tangerines	1 lb	4 medium; 2 cups sections
Tofu	1 lb	2¾ cups cubes; 2 cups crumbled; 1⅔ cups puréed
Tomatoes	1 lb	3 medium; 1½ cups chopped; 2 cups sliced
	14½-oz can	1¾ cups, including juice
Tomato paste	4½-oz tube	5 Tbsp
	6-oz can	¾ cup
Tuna	6-oz can	⅔ to ¾ cup, drained
Turkey	6 lb	7 cups cooked meat
	12 lb	16 cups cooked meat
Turnips	1 lb	3 to 4 medium; 2½ cups cooked, chopped
Walnuts	1 lb in shell	2 cups nuts
	1 lb shelled	3¾ cups halves; 3½ cups chopped
Watermelon	10 lb	20 cups cubed
Wheat germ	12 oz	3 cups
Wine	375 ml	half bottle; 12.7 oz; ample 1½ cups
	750 ml	regular bottle; 25.4 oz; scant 3¼ cups
	1 liter	33.8 oz; 4¼ cups
	magnum	1.5 liters; 50.7 oz; 6⅓ cups
Won ton skins (wrappers)	1 lb	60 wrappers
Yeast, active dry	¼-oz pkg	1 scant Tbsp; 0.6 oz compressed fresh
Yogurt	8 oz	1 cup; ½ pint

Substituting Ingredients

Ever been in the middle of a recipe and found you didn't have an ingredient you needed? The following emergency substitutions can be made with satisfactory results in most recipes.

Ingredient	Amount	Substitute
Anchovy	1 fillet	½ tsp anchovy paste
Arrowroot	1 rounded tsp	1 rounded tsp potato starch; or 1½ tsp cornstarch; or 2½ tsp rice starch; or 1 Tbsp all-purpose flour or quick-cooking tapioca
Baking Powder, double acting	1 tsp	¼ tsp baking soda + ⅝ tsp cream of tartar; or ¼ tsp baking soda + ½ cup buttermilk or sour milk (reduce liquid in recipe by ½ cup); or ¼ tsp baking soda + ⅜ cup molasses (reduce liquid in recipe by ¼ cup, adjust sweetener); or 1½ tsp phosphate or tartrate baking powder
Breadcrumbs, dry	1 cup	¾ cup cracker crumbs
Broth, Chicken or Beef	1 cup	1 bouillon cube or 1 tsp granules dissolved in 1 cup boiling water
Butter	1 cup	1 cup regular margarine; or ⅞ cup vegetable oil, lard or vegetable shortening; or ⅘ cup strained bacon fat; or ¾ cup strained chicken fat
Buttermilk (see Milk)		
Cheese, cottage	1 cup	1 cup ricotta
Chocolate	3 oz milk	2½ oz semisweet

Ingredient	Amount	Substitute
		chocolate + 1 oz whole milk powder + 1½ Tbsp sugar
	1 oz semi-sweet	½ oz unsweetened chocolate + 1 Tbsp granulated sugar
	6 oz semi-sweet chips	rounded ½ cup unsweetened cocoa + ½ cup granulated sugar + 3 Tbsp melted butter or margarine
	1 oz (1 square) unsweetened	3 Tbsp unsweetened cocoa + 1 Tbsp melted butter or margarine
Cornstarch	1 Tbsp	2½ tsp arrowroot or potato starch; 5 tsp rice starch; or 2 Tbsp all-purpose flour or quick-cooking tapioca
Corn Syrup	1 cup dark	¾ light corn syrup + ¼ cup light molasses
	1 cup (light/dark)	1¼ cups granulated or packed brown sugar + ¼ cup liquid*
Cracker Crumbs	1 cup	1¼ cup dried breadcrumbs
Cream (*see also* Sour Cream)	1 cup half-and-half	½ cup light cream + ½ cup whole milk. *For cooking and baking only:* 1½ Tbsp melted butter + enough whole milk to equal 1 cup
	1 cup light	*For cooking and baking only:* 3 Tbsp melted butter + enough whole milk to equal 1 cup
	1 cup whipping	*For whipping:* ¾ cup ice-cold evaporated

Ingredient	Amount	Substitute
		milk; or 4 oz frozen whipped dessert topping; or 1¼-oz package dessert topping mix, prepared. *For cooking and baking, not whipping:* ¾ cup whole milk + ⅓ cup melted butter
Crème Fraîche	1 cup	½ cup *each* sour cream and whipping cream
Egg, large	1 whole	2 egg yolks + 1 Tbsp cold water; or 3½ Tbsp thawed frozen egg or egg substitute; or 2½ Tbsp *each* powdered whole egg and water
	1 white	2 Tbsp thawed frozen egg white; or 1 Tbsp powdered egg white + 2 Tbsp water
	2 yolks	*For thickening sauces:* 1 whole egg
Flour (for thickening)	1 Tbsp all-purpose	1 rounded tsp arrowroot or potato starch; or 1½ tsp cornstarch; or 2½ tsp rice starch; or 1 Tbsp quick-cooking tapioca
Flour	1 cup sifted all-purpose	1 cup minus 2 Tbsp *unsifted* all-purpose flour
	1 cup sifted cake	1 cup minus 2 Tbsp *sifted* all-purpose flour
	1 cup sifted self-rising	1 cup *sifted* all-purpose flour + 1½ tsp baking powder and ⅛ tsp salt
Garlic	1 small clove	⅛ tsp garlic powder
Ginger	1 Tbsp chpd.	⅛ tsp powdered ginger;

Ingredient	Amount	Substitute
		or 1 Tbsp rinsed, chopped candied ginger
Half-and-half (see Cream)		
Herbs	1 Tbsp fresh	1 tsp dried herbs; or ¾ tsp ground herbs
Honey	1 cup	1¼ cups granulated sugar + ⅓ cup liquid*
Ketchup	½ cup	½ cup tomato sauce + 2 Tbsp sugar + 1 Tbsp. vinegar
Lemon juice	1 tsp	½ tsp vinegar
Milk	1 cup nonfat	⅓ cup nonfat dry milk + ¾ cup water
	1 cup sour or buttermilk	1 Tbsp lemon juice or white vinegar + enough milk to equal 1 cup (let stand 5 minutes); or 1 cup plain yogurt; or 1¾ tsp cream of tartar + 1 cup milk
Milk	1 cup whole	1 cup nonfat milk + 2 Tbsp melted butter or margarine; or ½ cup evaporated whole milk + ½ cup water; or ⅞ cup water + ¼ cup powdered whole milk; or ⅞ cup water + ¼ cup powdered skim milk + 2½ tsp melted butter or margarine; or 1 cup soy milk
Mushrooms	½ lb	1 (6-oz) can, drained
Mustard	1 Tbsp prepared	1 tsp powdered mustard
Onion	1 small	1 Tbsp instant minced; ½ Tbsp onion powder

Ingredient	Amount	Substitute
Sour cream	1 cup	1 cup plain yogurt; or ¾ cup buttermilk or plain yogurt + ⅓ cup melted butter; or 1 Tbsp lemon juice + enough evaporated whole milk to equal 1 cup
Sugar	1 cup confectioners'	½ cup + 1 Tbsp granulated sugar
	1 cup light brown	½ cup packed brown sugar + ½ cup granulated sugar
	1 cup granulated	1¾ cups confectioners' sugar; or 1 cup packed brown sugar; or 1 cup superfine sugar
Tomato juice	1 cup	½ cup tomato sauce + ½ cup water
Tomato sauce	1 cup	½ cup tomato paste + ½ cup water
Vanilla extract	1 tsp	1-inch piece vanilla bean
Vinegar	1 tsp	2 tsp lemon juice
Yeast, active dry	¼-oz env.	1 scant Tbsp active dry yeast; or 1 (0.06-oz) cake compressed fresh yeast
Yogurt	1 cup	1 cup buttermilk; or 1 cup milk + 1 Tbsp lemon juice

---

* Use whatever liquid the recipe calls for.

NOTE: Asterisked substitutions for honey and corn syrup are based on how the ingredients interact in the recipe and not on the flavor or sweetness.

Pan Substitution Chart

Although it's best to use the pan size called for in a recipe, it's not always possible. When substituting pans, choose one with the same volume and similar depth. Remember that using a different pan size requires an adjustment in baking time—a cake baked in a deeper pan than called for will need a slightly longer time to bake. To measure a pan's volume, fill it with water, then measure the liquid. A pan's width is measured from inside edge to inside edge, the depth from the inside bottom of the pan to the rim.

Pan Size	Approximate Volume
1¾" × ¾" mini muffin cup	⅛ cup (2 Tbsp)
2¾" × 1⅛" muffin cup	¼ cup
2¾" × 1⅜" muffin cup	scant ½ cup
3" × 1¼" giant muffin cup	⅝ cup
5½" × 3" × 2½" loaf	2 cups
7" × 1¼" pie	2 cups
5" × 2" round cake	2⅔ cups
6" × 4½" × 3" loaf	3 cups
8" × 1¼" pie	3 cups
6¼" × 2½" ring mold	3½ cups
6" × 2" round cake	3¾ cups
1-quart souffle	4 cups
8" × 1½" pie	4 cups
8" × 1½" round cake	4 cups
8" × 4" × 2½" loaf	4 cups
9" × 1¼" pie	4 cups
11¾" × 7½" × ¾" jelly roll	4 cups
8½" × 2½" ring mold	4½ cups
8½" × 4¼" × 3 loaf	5 cups
9" × 1½" pie	5 cups
7" × 2" round cake	5¼ cups
7½" × 3" Bundt	6 cups
8" × 2" round cake	6 cups
8" × 1½" square	6 cups
9" × 1½" round cake	6 cups
10" × 2" pie (deep-dish)	6 cups

Pan Size	Approximate Volume
11" × 7" × 2" rectangular	6 cups
8" × 8" × 2" square	8 cups
9" × 5" × 3" loaf	8 cups
9" × 2" pie (deep-dish)	8 cups
9" × 2" round cake	8 cups
9" × 9" × 1½" square	8 cups
9½" brioche	8 cups
11" × 7" × 2" rectangular	8 cups
9" × 3" Bundt	9 cups
8" × 3" tube	9 cups
9" × 9" × 2" square	10 cups
9½" × 2½" springform	10 cups
9" × 3" tube	10 cups
15½" × 10½" × 1" jelly roll	10 cups
9" × 4" Kugelhopf (tube)	11 cups
10" × 2" round cake	11 cups
10" × 3½" Bundt (tube)	12 cups
9" × 3" tube	12 cups
10" × 2½" springform	12 cups
17¼" × 11½" × 1" jelly roll	13 cups
13" × 9" × 2" rectangular	15 cups
12" × 2" round cake	15½ cups
10" × 4" tube	16 cups

High-Altitude Baking Adjustments

Feet above Sea Level	Baking Powder (reduce each tsp by)	Sugar (reduce each cup by)	Liquid (for each cup add)
3,000	⅛ tsp	½ to 1 Tbsp	1 to 2 Tbsp
5,000	⅛ to ¼ tsp	½ to 2 Tbsp	2 to 4 Tbsp
7,000 and above	¼ tsp	1 to 3 Tbsp	3 to 4 Tbsp

At altitudes over 4,000 feet:

Egg whites should be beaten only to soft-peak stage.
Oven temperature should be increased by 25°F (11°C).
Baking time should be decreased by about 5 minutes.

See also HIGH-ALTITUDE COOKING AND BAKING.

Boiling Point of Water at Various Altitudes

Altitude	Boiling Point of Water	
Sea level	212.0°F	100.0°C
2,000 feet	208.4°F	98.4°C
5,000 feet	203.0°F	95.0°C
7,500 feet	198.4°F	92.4°C
10,000 feet	194.0°F	90.0°C

General Temperature Equivalents

	Fahrenheit	Celsius
Freezer	0°	−18°
Water freezes	32°	0°
Refrigerator	40°	4°
Wine storage	55°	13°
Room temperature	68°	20°
Dough-rising temperature	80° to 95°	27° to 35°
Lukewarm	98.5°	37°
Water simmers	180°	82°
Water boils	212°	100°

Hand Test for Grilling Temperatures

Once coals are covered with a uniform layer of fine gray ash, the fire temperature can be tested by removing the grid and placing your hand, palm down, at grid level. The number of seconds you can comfortably hold your hand there will give you a rule of thumb for how hot the fire is.

Temperature	Seconds
Hot (for searing)	2
Medium-hot (for grilling)	3
Medium (for grilling)	4
Medium-low (covered cooking)	5
Low (covered cooking)	6

Oven Temperatures
(Fahrenheit, Celsius, British, French)

Oven Level	Fahrenheit	Celsius	British (Regulo) Gas Mark	French Gas Setting
Warming Foods	200° to 250°	93° to 121°	0 to ¼	2 to 3
Very Low (or Slow)	250° to 275°	121° to 133°	½ to 1	3
Low (or Slow)	300° to 325°	149° to 163°	2 to 3	4
Moderate	350° to 375°	177° to 190°	4 to 5	4 to 5
Hot	400° to 425°	204° to 218°	6 to 7	5 to 6
Very Hot	450° to 475°	232° to 246°	8 to 9	6
Extremely Hot	500° to 525°	260° to 274°	10	

Fahrenheit/Celsius Conversion Formulas

Celsius to Fahrenheit: multiply Celsius by 1.8, then add 32
Fahrenheit to Celsius: subtract 32 and multiply by 0.5556

Microwave Oven Conversion Chart

The easiest way to use the chart on the next page is to find the row containing the wattage of your microwave oven then go across the row until you find the column containing the wattage of the microwave oven used in the recipe. Once found, this box will contain the amount of time for each minute the recipe calls for. For example, if your oven produced 900 watts and the recipe uses an oven with 700 watts, each minute the recipe calls for will take only 51 seconds. If the recipe calls for 12 minutes, then it will take approximately 10 minutes and 12 seconds in your 900 watt oven. If your oven produces 900 watts and the recipe uses an oven with 1100 watts, then each minute the recipe calls for will take 1 minute and 13 seconds. If the recipe calls for 12 minutes, then it will take approximately 14 minutes and 36 seconds in your 900 watt oven.

Wattage of Microwave in Recipe

	500	600	700	800	900	1000	1100	1200	1300	1400	1500	1650
500	1m	1m 12s	1m 24s	1m 36s	1m 48s	2m	2m 12s	2m 24s	2m 36s	2m 48s	3m	3m 18s
600	50s	1m	1m 10s	1m 20s	1m 30s	1m 40s	1m 50s	2m	2m 10s	2m 20s	2m 30s	2m 45s
700	43s	51s	1m	1m 9s	1m 17s	1m 26s	1m 34s	1m 43s	1m 51s	2m	2m 9s	2m 21s
800	38s	45s	51s	1m	1m 8s	1m 15s	1m 23s	1m 30s	1m 38s	1m 45s	1m 53s	2m 4s
900	33s	40s	47s	53s	1m	1m 7s	1m 13s	1m 20s	1m 27s	1m 33s	1m 40s	1m 50s
1000	30s	36s	42s	48s	54s	1m	1m 6s	1m 12s	1m 18s	1m 24s	1m 30s	1m 39s
1100	27s	33s	38s	44s	49s	55s	1m	1m 5s	1m 11s	1m 16s	1m 22s	1m 30s
1200	25s	30s	35s	40s	45s	50s	55s	1m	1m 5s	1m 10s	1m 15s	1m 23s
1300	23s	28s	32s	37s	42s	46s	51s	55s	1m	1m 5s	1m 9s	1m 16s
1400	21s	26s	30s	34s	39s	43s	47s	51s	56s	1m	1m 4s	1m 11s
1500	20s	24s	28s	32s	36s	40s	44s	48s	52s	56s	1m	1m 6s
1650	18s	22s	25s	29s	33s	37s	40s	44s	47s	51s	55s	1m

m = minutes   s = seconds

Wattage of Your Microwave

Recommended Safe Cooking Temperatures

Heating food to the right temperature destroys harmful microorganisms.

	Fahrenheit	Celsius
Beef/Lamb/Veal		
Rare	140°	60°
Medium	160°	71°
Well Done	170°	77°
Chicken/Duck/Goose	175° to 180°	79° to 82°
Eggs		
Fried, poached, coddled	cook until yolk and white are firm	
Casseroles, sauces, custards	160°	71°
Fish	120° to 137°	49° to 58°
Ground meats		
Beef, lamb, pork	160°	71°
Chicken, turkey	165°	74°
Ostrich/Emu	160°	71°
Pâté	170°	77°
Pork		
Chops, roast	160° to 165°	71° to 74°
Cured	140°	60°
Rabbit	180°	82°
Sausage	160°	71°
Stuffing (inside or outside poultry)	180°	82°
Turkey		
Bone-In	180°	82°
Boneless roast	170°	77°

Candymaking Cold-Water Tests

Stage of Hardness	Temperature	When a small amount of sugar syrup is dropped into very cold water it:
Thread	223° to 234°F (106° to 112°C)	Forms a soft 2-inch thread
Soft ball	234° to 240°F (112° to 116°C)	Forms a soft ball that flattens of its own accord when removed
Firm ball	242° to 248°F (116° to 120°C)	Forms a firm but pliable ball
Hard ball	250° to 265°F (121° to 129°C)	Forms a rigid ball that is still somewhat pliable
Soft crack	270° to 290°F (132° to 143°C)	Separates into hard but pliable threads
Hard crack	300° to 310°F (149° to 154°C)	Separates into hard, brittle threads
Light Caramel	320° to 338°F (160° to 170°C)	Turns a pale golden color and turns transparent
Dark Caramel	350° to 360°F (176° to 182°C)	Turns dark amber to dark reddish brown

Frying Temperatures

If you don't have a CANDY/FAT THERMOMETER, test the temperature of the hot oil by dropping a 2-inch square of bread into it and timing it to see how long it takes to turn golden brown.

Fahrenheit	Celsius	Seconds
345°–355°	174°–179°	65
355°–365°	179°–185°	60
365°–375°	185°–190°	50
375°–385°	190°–196°	40
385°–395°	196°–202°	20

Smoke Points of Popular Oils

Many factors make an oil's exact SMOKE POINT difficult to determine, including how it's been processed and the additives it contains. In general, unrefined oils have extremely low smoke points. The following refined oils are listed in order of highest to lowest approximate smoke points.

Oil	Approximate Smoke Point
Peanut	450°F
Safflower	450°F
Soybean	450°F
Grapeseed	445°F
Canola	435°F
Corn	410°F
Olive	410°F
Sesame Seed	410°F
Sunflower	390°F

Fatty Acid Profiles of Popular Oils

Saturated fats (the nutritional "bad guys") are associated with some cancers and increased cholesterol levels, a contributing factor to heart disease. **Polyunsaturated fats** are relatively healthy, and **monounsaturated fats** are known to help reduce levels of LDL (the bad) cholesterol. The following percentages are approximate and may vary from brand to brand. *See also* FATS AND OILS.

Oils	Saturated %	Polyunsaturated %	Monounsaturated %
Canola	6	32	62
Almond	9	26	65
Safflower	9	76	15
Hazelnut	11	14	75
Sunflower	12	66	22
Corn	13	62	25
Grapeseed	13	70	17
Olive	14	10	76
Soybean	14	61	25
Walnut	16	56	28
Peanut	17	35	48
Sesame Seed	18	41	41
Avocado	20	11	69
Cottonseed	26	53	21
Palm Kernel	83	5	12
Coconut	89	3	8

U.S. Measurement Equivalents

pinch/dash	$\frac{1}{16}$ teaspoon
$\frac{1}{2}$ teaspoon	30 drops
1 teaspoon	$\frac{1}{3}$ tablespoon
3 teaspoons	1 tablespoon
$\frac{1}{2}$ tablespoon	$1\frac{1}{2}$ teaspoons
1 tablespoon	3 teaspoons; $\frac{1}{2}$ fluid ounce
2 tablespoons	$\frac{1}{8}$ cup; 1 fluid ounce
3 tablespoons	$1\frac{1}{2}$ fluid ounces; 1 jigger
jigger	$1\frac{1}{2}$ fluid ounces; 3 tablespoons
4 tablespoons	$\frac{1}{4}$ cup; 2 fluid ounces
$5\frac{1}{3}$ tablespoons	$\frac{1}{3}$ cup; 5 tablespoons + 1 teaspoon
8 tablespoons	$\frac{1}{2}$ cup; 4 fluid ounces
$10\frac{2}{3}$ tablespoons	$\frac{2}{3}$ cup; 10 tablespoons + 2 teaspoons
12 tablespoons	$\frac{3}{4}$ cup; 6 fluid ounces
16 tablespoons	1 cup; 8 fluid ounces; $\frac{1}{2}$ pint
$\frac{1}{8}$ cup	2 tablespoons; 1 fluid ounce
$\frac{1}{4}$ cup	4 tablespoons; 2 fluid ounces
$\frac{1}{3}$ cup	5 tablespoons + 1 teaspoon
$\frac{3}{8}$ cup	$\frac{1}{4}$ cup + 2 tablespoons
$\frac{1}{2}$ cup	8 tablespoons; 4 fluid ounces
$\frac{2}{3}$ cup	10 tablespoons; plus 2 teaspoons
$\frac{5}{8}$ cup	$\frac{1}{2}$ cup + 2 tablespoons
$\frac{3}{4}$ cup	12 tablespoons; 6 fluid ounces
$\frac{7}{8}$ cup	$\frac{3}{4}$ cup + 2 tablespoons
1 cup	16 tablespoons; $\frac{1}{2}$ pint; 8 fluid ounces
2 cups	1 pint; 16 fluid ounces
3 cups	$1\frac{1}{2}$ pints; 24 fluid ounces
4 cups	1 quart; 32 fluid ounces
8 cups	2 quarts; 64 fluid ounces
1 pint	2 cups; 16 fluid ounces
2 pints	1 quart; 32 fluid ounces
1 quart	2 pints; 4 cups; 32 fluid ounces
4 quarts	1 gallon; 8 pints
1 gallon	4 quarts; 8 pints; 16 cups; 128 fluid ounces
8 quarts	1 peck
4 pecks	1 bushel

Wine and Spirit Bottle Sizes

In the United States, the standard wine and spirit bottle size is 750 milliliters (ml), approximately 25.4 ounces—almost exactly equivalent to an American fifth (⅕ of a quart, 25.6 ounces). Other legal U.S. wine bottle sizes range from 100 ml to 3 liters, and various bottle-size terms (including French bottle names) are sometimes used. Older spirit bottle descriptors (such as half-pint, pint, fifth and half-gallon) are no longer accurate for standard bottle sizes, although the fifth is so close in size that the term is still widely used.

WINE BOTTLE SIZES

Common Bottle Terminology	Metric Measure	Fluid Ounces
Miniature	100 ml	3.4 oz
Split	187 ml	6.3 oz
Half-bottle	375 ml	12.7 oz
500-milliliter	500 ml	16.9 oz
Bottle/750-milliliter	750 ml	25.4 oz
One Liter	1 liter	33.8 oz
Magnum	1.5 liter	50.7 oz
Double Magnum;	3 liters	101.5 oz
Jeroboam (in Champagne, France)		
Rehoboam (in Champagne, France);	4.5 liters	152.2 oz
Jeroboam (in Bordeaux, France)		
Methuselah (in Champagne, France)	6 liters	202.9 oz
Imperial (in Bordeaux, France)	6 liters	202.9 oz
Salmanazar	9 liters	304.4 oz
Balthazar	12 liters	405.8 oz
Nebuchadnezzar	15 liters	507.3 oz

SPIRIT BOTTLE SIZES
(Name Corresponds with Bottle Size)

100	ml	3.4 oz
200	ml	6.8 oz
500	ml	16.9 oz
750	ml	25.4 oz
1	liter	33.8 oz
1.75	liter	59.2 oz

Approximate Metric Equivalents

Metrics are rounded to the nearest decimal point in most cases.

VOLUME (ml = milliliter)

U.S.	Metric
¼ teaspoon	1 ml
½ teaspoon	2.5 ml
¾ teaspoon	4 ml
1 teaspoon	5 ml
1¼ teaspoons	6 ml
1½ teaspoons	7.5 ml
1¾ teaspoons	8.5 ml
2 teaspoons	10 ml
1 tablespoon	15 ml
2 tablespoons	30 ml
¼ cup	59 ml
⅓ cup	79 ml
½ cup	118 ml
⅔ cup	158 ml
¾ cup	178 ml
1 cup	237 ml
1½ cups	355 ml
2 cups (1 pint)	473 ml
3 cups	710 ml
4 cups (1 quart)	.95 liter
1.06 quarts	1 liter
4 quarts (1 gallon)	3.8 liters

WEIGHT

U.S.	Metric
.035 ounce	1 gram
¼ ounce	7 grams
½ ounce	14 grams
¾ ounce	21 grams
1 ounce	28 grams
1½ ounces	42.5 grams
2 ounces	57 grams
3 ounces	85 grams
4 ounces	113 grams
5 ounces	142 grams
6 ounces	170 grams
7 ounces	198 grams
8 ounces	227 grams
16 ounces (1 lb)	454 grams
2.2 lbs	1 kilogram

Metric Conversion Formulas

The metric system of weights and measures is used by most of the world's countries, although the United States still primarily uses American Standard measurements. Following are some formulas to help you with conversions.

To convert	Do this
Centimeters to inches	divide centimeters by 2.54
Cups to liters	multiply cups by 0.236
Cups to milliliters	multiply cups by 236.59
Gallons to liters	multiply gallons by 3.785
Grams to ounces	divide grams by 28.35
Inches to centimeters	multiply inches by 2.54
Kilograms to pounds	divide kilograms by 0.454
Liters to cups	divide liters by 0.236
Liters to gallons	divide liters by 3.785
Liters to pints	divide liters by 0.473
Liters to quarts	divide liters by 0.946
Milliliters to cups	divide milliliters by 236.59
Milliliters to fluid ounces	divide milliliters by 29.57
Milliliters to tablespoons	divide milliliters by 14.79
Milliliters to teaspoons	divide milliliters by 4.93
Ounces to grams	multiply ounces by 28.35
Ounces to milliliters	multiply ounces by 29.57
Pints to liters	multiply pints by 0.473
Pounds to kilograms	multiply pounds by 0.454
Quarts to liters	multiply quarts by 0.946
Tablespoons to milliliters	multiply tablespoons by 14.79
Teaspoons to milliliters	multiply teaspoons by 4.93

MyPlate

In 2011, MyPlate replaced the USDA's Food Guide Pyramid (or MyPyramid) as the visual representing dietary guidelines for Americans. Most view the new approach as an improvement over the almost two-decade-old pyramid, which many complained was too confusing. The new graphic shows a main plate with four categories—vegetables, fruits, grains and protein—and a smaller plate with dairy. The USDA established a website, *www.ChooseMyPlate.gov*, that details how the five food groups fit into a healthy diet and lots of information about healthy eating, including the 2010 Dietary Guidelines for Americans.

U. S. Department of Agriculture

MyPlate suggests the following for a 2,000-calorie daily food plan. These recommendations will vary depending on sex, age and physical activity. The website is designed to help personalize these guidelines.

Vegetables Eat 2½ cups every day, with each cup equivalent to 1 cup of raw or cooked vegetables or vegetable juice or 2 cups of leafy salad greens. MyPlate recommends eating more red, orange and dark-green veggies like tomatoes, sweet potatoes and broccoli in main dishes and adding beans or peas to salads (kidney or chickpeas), soups (split peas or lentils) and side dishes (pinto or baked beans), or serving these vegetables as a main dish. Fresh, frozen and canned vegetables all count. Choose "reduced sodium" or "no-salt-added" canned vegetables.

Fruits Eat 2 cups every day, with each cup equivalent to 1 cup of raw or cooked fruit or 100 percent fruit juice or ½ cup dried fruit. MyPlate recommends using fruits as snacks, salads and desserts. At breakfast, top your cereal with bananas or strawberries, or add blueberries to pancakes. You can buy fruits that are dried, frozen and canned (in water or 100% juice), as well as fresh fruits. Select 100 percent fruit juice when choosing juices.

Grains Eat 6 ounces every day, with each ounce equivalent to 1 slice of bread, ½ cup of cooked rice, cereal or pasta, or 1 ounce of ready-to-eat cereal. MyPlate recommends substituting whole-grain choices for refined-grain breads, bagels, rolls, breakfast cereals, crackers, rice and pasta; checking the ingredients list on product labels for the words *whole* or *whole grain* before the grain ingredient name; and choosing products that name a whole grain first on the ingredients list.

Dairy Get 3 cups every day, with each cup equivalent to 1 cup of milk, yogurt or fortified soymilk or 1½ ounces natural or 2 ounces processed cheese. MyPlate recommends choosing skim (fat-free) or 1 percent (lowfat) milk. They have the same amount of calcium and other essential nutrients as whole milk, but less fat and calories. Try topping fruit salads and baked potatoes with lowfat yogurt. If you are lactose intolerant, try lactose-free milk or fortified soymilk (soy beverage).

Protein foods Eat 5½ ounces every day, with each ounce equivalent to 1 ounce of lean meat, poultry or fish; 1 egg; 1 tablespoon of peanut butter; ½ ounce nuts or seeds or ¼ cup beans or peas. MyPlate recommends eating a variety of foods from the protein food group each week, such as seafood, beans and peas, and nuts as well as lean meats, poultry and eggs. Twice a week, make seafood the protein on your plate. Choose meats and ground beef that are at least 90 percent lean. Trim or drain fat from meat and remove skin from poultry to cut fat and calories.

Food Label Terms

In the United States, understanding food labels is easier than ever. Labeling laws now require processed food labels to include specific information as well as to clarify four important areas.

1. Package claims are now federally defined and regulated.
2. Serving sizes must be comparable for similar foods.
3. The percentage of a particular nutrient in the food is easily found in the "% Daily Value" column.
4. How much (or how little) of the major nutrients consumers should eat on a daily basis appears in the "Daily Values" section. (*See* A Guide to Food Labels, page 880.)

When checking a packaged food label, remember that most list ingredients in descending order by *weight,* not by *amount.* For example, a cereal with four ingredients, of which sugar is the third listed, most likely contains a small percentage of sugar. Labels must now include the *total amount of fat, saturated fat* and *unsaturated fat (see* FATS AND OILS), although detailing the various types of the latter is optional. However, be aware that there's currently a major information gap in this labeling scheme. That's because TRANS FATTY ACIDS (essentially unsaturated fat that's been transformed into saturated fat through hydrogenation), which may be part of the total fat listed, aren't classified as "saturated." To check, do this: Add the amount of saturated and unsaturated fat together—if the total doesn't equal the figure for *total fat,* the difference can most likely be attributed to trans fatty acids, which in essence means "saturated fat."

Label terms can help you choose the kind of food you want to eat, whether higher in fiber or lower in fat or sodium. Following are some of the most common food label terms ("serving" refers to the serving size on the product label).

Calorie Terms

Reduced calorie—at least 25 percent fewer calories than in a product's regular form.
Low calorie—40 calories or fewer per serving; less than 0.4 calories per gram of food.
Calorie Free or **No Calories**—less than 5 calories per serving.

Light or Lite—one third fewer calories than in the product's regular form; or less than 50 percent fat per serving. If over half the calories are from fat, the fat content must be reduced by at least 50 percent.

Fat Terms

Reduced Fat—at least 25 percent less fat than found in a product's regular form.

Reduced Saturated Fat—same as "reduced fat," but in reference to saturated fat.

Low Fat—3 grams or less fat per serving.

__% Fat Free—may only be used for "low-fat" products, with the percentage based on the amount (by weight) of fat in 100 grams of food (a 100-gram serving of a food labeled "98% Fat Free" would contain 2 grams of fat).

Low in Saturated Fat—1 gram or less saturated fat per serving, with no more than 15 percent of calories from saturated fat.

Fat Free—less than ½ gram per serving, providing there are no added fat or oil ingredients in a product's recipe.

Saturated Fat Free—similar to "Fat Free," but with less than ½ gram saturated fat and less than ½ gram trans fatty acids per serving.

Trans Fat or **Trans**—*see* TRANS FATTY ACIDS in main section for a description of this saturated fat.

Cholesterol Terms

Reduced Cholesterol—at least 25 percent less cholesterol than found in a product's regular version, and 2 grams or less saturated fat per serving.

Low in Cholesterol—20 milligrams or less cholesterol per serving and 2 grams or less of saturated fat.

Cholesterol Free—less than 2 milligrams of cholesterol per serving and 2 grams or less of saturated fat.

Sugar Terms

Reduced Sugar—at least 25 percent less sugar than found in a product's regular version.

No Added Sugars—no sugars (including ingredients containing sugar like fruit juice or applesauce) added during processing, and that processing doesn't increase the sugar content above the amount naturally present in the ingredients.

Sugar Free—less than 0.5 gram per serving.

Sodium Terms

Reduced Sodium—at least 25 percent less sodium than found in a similar food's original form.

Light in Sodium—50 percent less sodium per serving, referring only to foods with more than 40 calories or 3 grams of fat per serving.

Low Sodium—140 milligrams or less per serving.

Very Low Sodium—35 milligrams or less sodium per serving.

Unsalted or **No Added Salt**—doesn't necessarily mean a food is sodium free, but only that no salt was used during processing. If not salt free, the label will state: "Not a sodium free food" or "Not for control of sodium in the diet."

Sodium Free or **Salt Free**—less than 5 milligrams per serving.

Fiber Terms

High Fiber—5 grams or more per serving. Food must also meet "low fat" definition, or state level of total fat.

Good Source of Fiber—2.5 to 4.9 grams per serving.

More Fiber or **Added Fiber**—at least 2.5 grams more per serving than in reference food.

Other Label Terms

Enriched or **Fortified**—contains 10 percent or more of the per-serving Daily Value for protein, vitamins, minerals, dietary fiber or potassium.

Extra Lean—*see* following definition of *lean.*

Fresh—raw food that has not been processed in any way, either by freezing or with heat.

Fresh frozen—food quickly frozen from its fresh state.

Good source of—contains 10 to 19 percent of the listed ingredient's Daily Value per serving.

Lean—packaged meat, poultry or seafood with less than 10 grams total fat, less than 4 grams saturated fat, and less than 95 milligrams cholesterol per 100 grams. **Extra Lean** has less than 5 grams total fat, less than 2 grams saturated fat, and less than 95 milligrams cholesterol per 100 grams.

Natural—a general term with no legal parameters, typically meaning that the product has no artificial ingredients or *intentional* additives. When the word "natural" is applied to meat or poultry, it generally means the product is minimally processed and free of artificial ingredients.

Natural Flavorings—flavorings derived from a spice, fruit or fruit juice, edible yeast, herb, bark, bud, root, leaf or similar plant material, meat, seafood, poultry, egg, dairy product whose significant function in food is flavoring rather than nutritional. However, these broad parameters include ingredients like hydrolyzed protein and hydrolyzed vegetable protein (HVP), both of which contain monosodium glutamate (MSG).

Rich In, High In or **Excellent Source of**—contains 20 percent or more of the Daily Value per serving.

RDA stands for "Recommended Dietary Allowance," the government-recommended daily amounts of protein, vitamins and minerals for healthy adults. Such amounts are ballpark figures and may vary slightly according to gender, conditions such as pregnancy, and so forth.

More details are available on the Food and Drug Administration website at *www.fda.gov/Food/GuidanceComplianceRegulatory Information/GuidanceDocuments/FoodLabelingNutrition/ FoodLabelingGuide/default.htm.*

See also ADDITIVES; ORGANIC FOODS.

A Guide to Food Labels

Consistent serving sizes in each category

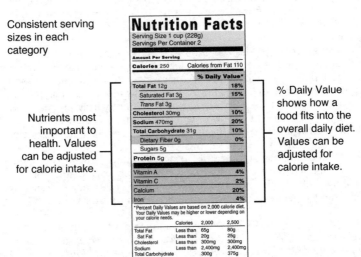

Nutrition Facts
Serving Size 1 cup (228g)
Servings Per Container 2

Amount Per Serving

Calories 250   Calories from Fat 110

                     % Daily Value*

Total Fat 12g	**18%**
Saturated Fat 3g	**15%**
Trans Fat 3g	
Cholesterol 30mg	**10%**
Sodium 470mg	**20%**
Total Carbohydrate 31g	**10%**
Dietary Fiber 0g	**0%**
Sugars 5g	
Protein 5g	
Vitamin A	4%
Vitamin C	2%
Calcium	20%
Iron	4%

*Percent Daily Values are based on 2,000 calorie diet.
Your Daily Values may be higher or lower depending on
your calorie needs.

	Calories	2,000	2,500
Total Fat	Less than	65g	80g
Sat Fat	Less than	20g	25g
Cholesterol	Less than	300mg	300mg
Sodium	Less than	2,400mg	2,400mg
Total Carbohydrate		300g	375g
Dietary Fiber		25g	30g

Nutrients most important to health. Values can be adjusted for calorie intake.

% Daily Value shows how a food fits into the overall daily diet. Values can be adjusted for calorie intake.

Calories per gram: Fat = 9, Carbohydrate = 4, Protein = 4; Alcohol = 7

Daily Values—The "percent" numbers on food labels are a reference for the recommended daily amounts of vitamins, minerals and major nutrients. Here's the breakdown:

Calories	2,000	2,500
Fat	65g or less	80g or less
Total carbohydrate	300g	375g
Dietary fiber	25g	30g
Saturated fat	20g or less	25g or less
Cholesterol	300mg or less	300mg or less
Protein	50g	60g
Sodium	2,400mg or less	2,400mg or less
Potassium	3,500mg	3,500mg
Vitamin A	5,000 Intl. Units (IU)	5,000 IU
Vitamin C	60mg	60mg
Calcium	1,000mg	1,000mg
Iron	18mg	18mg

Apple Varieties and Suggested Uses

In the A to Z section of *The New Food Lover's Companion* there are entries for the most common varieties of apples. The chart below summarizes these entries.

Variety	Eating/ Baking*	Texture	Taste	Harvest**
Baldwin	Both	Very Crisp	Sweet-Tart	Oct
Braeburn	Both	Very Crisp	Sweet	Oct
Caville Blanc d'Hiver	Baking	Crisp	Sweet-Tart	Oct
Chenango	Both	Crisp	Sweet	Aug
Cortland	Both	Crisp	Sweet-Tart	Sept
Empire	Both	Crisp	Sweet-Tart	Oct
Fuji	Both	Crisp	Sweet	Oct
Gala	Both— Eating	Crisp	Sweet	Sept
Golden Delicious	Both— Eating	Crisp	Sweet	Oct
Granny Smith	Both	Very Crisp	Tart	Nov
Gravenstein	Both— Baking	Crisp	Sweet-Tart	Aug
Honey Crisp	Both— Eating	Crisp	Sweet	Sept
Ida Red	Both	Crisp	Tart	Oct
Jonagold	Both	Crisp	Sweet-Tart	Oct
Jonathon	Both— Baking	Crisp	Sweet-Tart	Sept
Lady	Eating	Slightly-Crisp	Sweet-Tart	Nov
Lady Alice	Both	Crisp	Sweet-Tart	Jan

Variety	Eating/ Baking*	Texture	Taste	Harvest**
Macoun	Both— Eating	Crisp	Sweet	Sept
McIntosh	Both— Eating	Crisp	Sweet-Tart	Sept
Newtown Pippin	Both	Crisp	Tart	Oct
Northern Spy	Both	Very Crisp	Sweet-Tart	Oct
Piñata	Both	Crisp	Sweet	Sept
Pink Lady	Both	Crisp	Sweet-Tart	Oct
Pink Pearl	Both— Baking	Crisp	Tart	Aug
Red Delicious	Eating	Crisp	Sweet	Oct
Rhode Island Greening	Both— Baking	Very Crisp	Sweet-Tart	Sept
Rome Beauty	Baking	Very Crisp	Sweet	Oct
Stayman Winesap	Both	Crisp	Tart	Oct
Winesap	Both	Crisp	Sweet	Oct
York Imperial	Both	Crisp	Sweet-Tart	Nov

*Some apples are good for both eating and baking but are mainly used one way. The chief way they are used is also indicated.

**This is only an approximate guide to when each variety is harvested— many factors enter into the actual harvest time.

Pasta Glossary

There are hundreds of different pasta shapes and sizes and the confusion is exacerbated by manufacturers using different names for the same shape (for example, fusilli and rotini). Following are some of the pastas most commonly available in supermarkets and Italian markets. Small caps indicate there is more information in this book's general listings. *See also* listing for PASTA.

acini di pepe [ah-CHEE-nee dee PAY-pay] "Peppercorns." Tiny and rice-shaped.

agnolotti [ah-nyoh-LAH-tee] "Priests' caps." Small, crescent-shaped, stuffed ravioli-style (*see* RAVIOLI) pasta.

anelli; anellini [ah-NEHL-lee; ah-nehl-LEE-nee] "Small rings." Tiny rings; *anellini* being the smallest version.

anellone [ah-nehl-LOH-neh] "Large rings."

angel hair *see* capelli d'angelo

anolini [ah-noh-LEE-nee] Small, crescent-shaped, ruffle-edged RAVIOLI.

bavettine; bavette [bah-veh-TEE-neh; bah-VEH-teh] "Narrow ribbons."

bucatini; bucatoni [boo-kah-TEE-nee] Hollow, long strands, slightly thicker than SPAGHETTI. *Bucatoni* are the thicker of the two.

canestrini [kah-neh-STREE-nee] "Little baskets." Small, ridged and hourglass shaped.

cannaroni [kah-nah-ROH-nee] "Wide tubes"; also call *zitoni*.

cannelloni [kah-neh-LOH-nee] "Large reeds." Large, round tubes (or squares rolled into tubes), typically stuffed then baked with a sauce.

capelli d'angelo [kah-PELL-ee DAN-zheh-low] "Angel hair." Long, extremely fine, delicate strands. Also called *angel hair*.

capellini [kah-pehl-LEE-nee] Thin strands, slightly thicker than capelli d'angelo. Sometimes sold in nests. Also called *fidelini*.

cappelletti [kap-peh-LEHT-tee] "Little hats." Hat-shaped stuffed pasta, similar to RAVIOLI.

cavatappi [kah-vah-TAH-pee] "Corkscrew." Short, thin, ridged MACARONI spirals.

cavatelli [kah-vah-TEHL-lee] Short, narrow, ripple-edged shells.

chifferi [KEE-feh-ree] Small (1-inch), curved MACARONI.

ciciones [chee-chee-YOH-nehs] *see* malloreddus

conchiglie [kohn-KEE-lyeh] "Conch shells." Shell-shaped, typically ridged.

conchiglioni [kohn-kee-LYOH-nee] Larger version of conchiglie.

coralli [koh-RAH-lee] Tiny rings; generally used for soup.

corzetti [kohr-TSEH-tee] Round, relatively flat and about 2 inches in diameter; stamped with various patterns.

creste di galli; creste [KRAY-stay dee GAHL-lee] "Cockscombs." Medium-size and curved with a ruffled crest on the outside edge.

diavolini [dyah-voh- LEE-nee] "Little devils." Small, semicircular tubes.

ditali [dih-TAH-lee] "Thimbles." Small, very short tubes of MACARONI.

ditalini [dih-tah-LEE-nee] Tiny ditali.

elbow pasta Any of a wide variety of short, curved tubular pastas, such as MACARONI.

farfalle [fahr-FAH-lay] "Butterflies." Bow- or butterfly-shape.

farfallini [fahr-fah-LEE-nee] Small farfalle.

farfallone [fahr-fah-LOH-nay] Large farfalle.

fedelini [fay-day-LEE-nee] "Little faithful ones." Very fine SPAGHETTI.

fettucce [fay-TOO-cheh] The widest (about ½ inch) of the fettuccine noodles.

fettuccelle [fay-too-CHEHL-leh] The thinnest (about ⅛ inch) of the fettuccine family.

fettuccine; fettuccini [feht-tuh-CHEE-neh (-nee)] "Little ribbons." Thin, flat egg noodles about ¼ inch wide.

fidelini [fih-deh-LEE-nee] "Little faithful ones." Another name for CAPELLINI.

fideos [fih-DAY-ohs] Thin strands coiled in bunches.

fischietti [fee-SKYEHT-tee] "Small whistle." The smallest of the tube pastas.

fusilli [fyoo-SEE-lee] "Little springs." A spiraled SPAGHETTI. *Fusilli lunghi* is long (10 to 12 inches); cut fusilli is about 1½ inches long.

garganelli [gahr-gah-NEHL-lee] 1¼- to 2¾-inch squares with ridges on one side, rolled obliquely into a thin cylinder.

gemelli [jay-MEHL-lee] "Twins." Short, 1½-inch-long twists that resemble two strands of spaghetti twisted together.

gigantoni [jee-gahn-TOH-nee] "Super giants." Huge MACARONI that's about 1½ inches in diameter and 2 inches long.

gigli [JEE-lyee] Ruffled-edged and shaped like closed lily.

gnocchi [NYOH-kee] Small, ripple-edged shells. *See also* GNOCCHI.

grandine [grahn-DEE-nee] "Hailstones." Tiny little bits of pasta that may resemble hailstones.

lasagna; *pl.* **lasagne** [luh-ZAHN-yah] Long, very broad noodles (2 to 3 inches wide) with straight or rippled edges. *See also* LASAGNA.

linguine [lihn-GWEE-nee; lihn-GWEE-neh] "Little tongues." Very narrow (⅛ inch wide or less), long ribbons.

lumache [loo-MAH-keh] "Snails." Large shells intended for stuffing.

macarones [mah-kah-ROH-nehs] *see* malloreddus

macaroni; *It.* **maccheroni** [mah-kah-ROH-nee ; mahk-kay-ROH-nee] Tube shapes of various lengths. *See also* MACARONI.

maccheroni Italian for MACARONI.

mafalda; *pl.* **mafalde** [mahl-FAHL-dah (-deh)] Broad, flat, ripple-edged noodles.

magliette [mah-LYAY-tah (-tay)] "Links." Short, curved tubes.

malloreddus [mahl-loh-REHD-duhs] "Small bulls." Small, ridged and elongated; often flavored with SAFFRON. Also called *ciciones* and *maca-rones.*

maltagliati [mahl-tah-LYAH-tee] Flat, thin, 2-inch-long triangular-shapes used for soups.

manicotti [man-ee-KOHT-ee; man-nee-KOH-tee] "Little muffs." Very large tubes about 4 inches long and 1 inch in diameter; used for stuffing.

margherite [mahr-geh-REE-teh] "Daisies." Narrow flat noodles with one rippled edge.

maruzze [mah-ROO-tseh] "Seashells." Shell shapes in several sizes from tiny to jumbo.

melone *see* semi di melone

mezzani [meh-TSAH-nee] Very short, curved tubes.

mostaccioli [moh-stah-CHYOH-lee] "Little moustaches." Two-inch-long ridged or smooth tubes.

orecchiette [oh-ray-KYEHT-teh] "Little ears." Tiny disk shapes.

orzo [OHR-zoh] "Barley." Tiny, rice-shaped; used in soups.

paccheri [pah- KAY-ree] Short, wide tubes similar to RIGATONI.

pansotti; pansoti [pan-SOHT-tee] "Pot bellied." Triangular-shaped, stuffed RAVIOLI with pinked edges.

pappardelle [pah-pahr-DEHL-leh] "Gulp down." Flat, long, wide (about ⅝ inch) noodles with rippled edges.

pastina [pah-STEE-nah] "Tiny dough." Any of various tiny shapes (such as acini di pepe); generally used in soups.

penne [PEN-neh; PEN-nay] "Pens" or "quills." Diagonally cut smooth tubes. *Penne rigate* have ridged sides.

perciatelli [payr-chah-TEH-lee] Thin, hollow, about twice as thick as spaghetti; similar to bucatini.

pizzoccheri [peet-tsoh-KAY-ree] Thick buckwheat noodles.

quadrettini [kwah-dray-TEE-nee] Small flat squares used in soup.

quadrucci [kwah-DROO-chee] Tiny flat squares used in soup.

radiatore [rah-dyah-TOH-reh] "Little radiators." Short, chunky shapes (about 1 inch long and ½ inch in diameter) that resemble tiny radiators with rippled edges.

ravioli [rav-ee-OH-lee; ra-VYOH-lee] Square-shape and stuffed. *See also* RAVIOLI.

ricciolini [ree-chee-yoh-LEE-nee] Wide, softly twisted noodles about 2 inches long.

rigatoni [rig-ah-TOH-nee] Large grooved MACARONI about 1½ inches wide.

riso [REE-soh] Rice-shaped, similar to ORZO.

rosamarina [roh-sah-mah-REE-nah] Pumpkin-seed shapes; used for soups.